If you're serious about exam suc
it's time to Concentr

Business Law Concentrate, James Marson

Business law exams and assessments are often quite different to the other assessments you might be faced with on your business course. *Business Law Concentrate* is a high quality revision guide which covers all of the key topics, with a number of features to help you to prepare for exams and suggest ways to improve your marks:

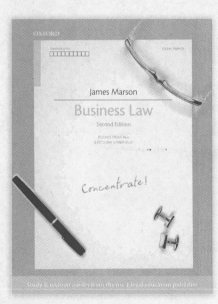

* ❋ Key cases and legal principles are clearly presented for easy reference
* ❋ Common pitfalls are highlighted to ensure you avoid them
* ❋ *Looking for extra marks?* gives you advice on how to impress examiners
* ❋ A glossary of key terms provides useful definitions
* ❋ A key facts list for each chapter enables you to remember the essential points of a topic
* ❋ Links between topics and useful assessment tips are provided
* ❋ Sample questions with outline answers provide guidance on how to structure a good answer.

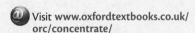 **Visit www.oxfordtextbooks.co.uk/orc/concentrate/**

Additional valuable online resources accompany Business Law Concentrate:

→ Self-marking multiple-choice questions
→ Interactive flashcards of glossary and key cases
→ Outline answers to exam questions
→ Diagnostic test—where do I need to concentrate?

Business Law

Third Edition

James Marson

Principal Lecturer in Law, Sheffield Hallam University

OXFORD

UNIVERSITY PRESS

OXFORD
UNIVERSITY PRESS

Great Clarendon Street, Oxford, OX2 6DP,
United Kingdom

Oxford University Press is a department of the University of Oxford.
It furthers the University's objective of excellence in research, scholarship,
and education by publishing worldwide. Oxford is a registered trade mark of
Oxford University Press in the UK and in certain other countries

© Oxford University Press 2013

The moral rights of the author have been asserted

First edition 2009
Second edition 2011
Impression: 1

British Library Cataloguing in Publication Data

Data available

ISBN 978-0-19-967183-0

Printed in Italy by
L.E.G.O. S.p.A.—Lavis TN

For Katy, Isabelle and Mia—without whom I would have nothing

New to this Edition:

New cases in this edition include:

Autoclenz Ltd v Belcher & Ors [2011] UKSC 41

Barr v Biffa Waste Services [2012] EWCA (Civ) 312

Claramoda Limited v Zoomphase Limited (T/A Jenny Packham) [2009] EWHC 2857 (Comm)

Daventry District Council v Daventry & District Housing Ltd [2011] EWCA Civ 1153

Edwards v Chesterfield Royal Hospital NHS Foundation Trust; Botham v MoD [2011] UKSC 58

Infection Control Enterprises Limited v Virrage Industries Ltd [2009] EWHC 2602 (QB)

Jones v Ruth [2011] EWCA Civ 804, [2012] 1 WLR 1495

Lucasfilm Limited v Ainsworth [2011] UKSC 39

Rabone v Pennine Care NHS Foundation Trust [2012] UKSC 2

Re: Sigma Finance Corporation (in administrative receivership) [2009] UKSC 2

Richard Weddall v Barchester Healthcare [2012] EWCA (Civ) 25

Tekdata Interconnections Limited v Amphenol Ltd [2009] EWCA Civ 1209

Wallbank v Wallbank Fox Designs [2012] EWCA (Civ) 25

Weight Watchers (UK) Ltd v Her Majesty's Revenue & Customs (HMRC) (2011) FTC/57–59/2010

New (and proposed) legislation included:

The Enterprise and Regulatory Reform Bill

The Unfair Dismissal and Statement of Reasons for Dismissal (Variation of Qualifying Period) Order 2012

Preface and Summary of Changes Made Since the Second Edition

I would like to begin by expressing my sincere thanks to my publishers at OUP and in particular John Carroll and Jacqueline Senior for their assistance and support. They have provided innovative suggestions for improvements to the content and presentation of the text, sourced pertinent and helpful reviews of the previous edition, and approached the development of this edition with great enthusiasm and energy.

The third edition of this text has been the most interesting and challenging to write. At the time of completing this preface, the Government has announced significant changes to the structure and operation of employment tribunals, incorporating legislative changes and issuing several consultation documents on issues of cost awards, consultation in relation to reform of redundancy law, and significant reductions in awards following unfair dismissals. Reforms are also proposed to the regulation of intellectual property law. As many of these developments have not been finalized, they are referred to in the text, but full details will be provided in the Online Resource Centre in due course.

The Companies Act 2006 has been subject to procedural changes that are incorporated, along with several case law developments in the other jurisdictions including agency, contract, intellectual property, and tortious liability. Each of these developments, and their impact on businesses, have been incorporated into this edition.

I have continued to develop and use flow charts, diagrams, and business link boxes to aid understanding and demonstrate how the law operates in business relationships. Further, sample documents are now stored on the Online Resource Centre providing a real-world example of incorporating a business, contracts, dismissal notices, and the statutory forms to bring and defend claims of unfair dismissal. A link to these documents is placed in the text where appropriate.

The Online Resource Centre contains several additional chapters that could not be included in this text. The topics of business ethics; The Consumer Protection from Unfair Trading Regulations 2008; corporate manslaughter; and the Legal Services Act 2007 are provided. These will further your understanding, provide a more holistic coverage of business law as it applies to consumers and corporations, and it ensures that the requirements of professional bodies such as the Chartered Institute of Management Accountants and the Association of Chartered Certified Accountants are satisfied. The Online Resource Centre also contains, among others, outline answers to the end of chapter questions, multiple choice and fill-in-the-blank question banks, iPod-compatible downloadable glossaries of key terms and cases that will be a useful revision and self-test aid.

Finally, I wish to express my thanks and unremitting love to Dr Katy Ferris, without whom I would have been unable to write this edition. Katy always encourages my writing, supports my academic efforts, and most of all, she has given me the most wonderful aspect of my life, my beautiful daughters Isabelle and Mia.

Enjoy your studies.

James Marson, Sheffield.
September 2012

Guide to the Online Resource Centre

Business Law is fully supported by an Online Resource Centre, which offers valuable student and lecturer materials to complement your textbook and enhance the learning experience. Go to www.oxfordtextbooks.co.uk/orc/marson3e/ to ensure you're getting the most out of your textbook.

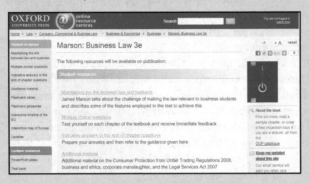

Student resources

The resources explained below offer innovative online tools which support your learning, helping you to fulfil your potential in your business law assessments and exams. Visit www.oxfordtextbooks.co.uk/orc/marson3e/ to try the resources for yourself.

Multiple-choice questions

Use these questions to test your knowledge of the law covered within each chapter of the textbook. Immediate feedback on your answers makes it easy for you to assess your level of understanding.

Indicative answers to the end-of-chapter questions

Each chapter of the book contains end-of-chapter questions. Prepare your own answer, then check here for guidance on what an exemplary answer should include—ideal for exam preparation.

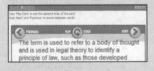

Flashcard cases and glossary

These interactive flashcards will help you to memorize key cases and terms and are ideal for revision.

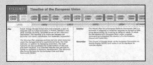

Interactive timeline of the EU

Use this interactive resource to learn more about the key dates in EU law history.

Interactive map of Europe

An interactive map, with hot-spots on all EU member states, provides factual information on each member country. This will give you some extra context for your law studies.

Timeline: implementation of the Companies Act 2006

Company law is a crucial topic in business law and the Companies Act 2006 is the most important piece of recent legislation. Use this timeline to find detailed information on the implementation of the provisions of the Act.

Additional material

For those wanting to expand their knowledge, additional material on the courts and the consumer protection from unfair trading regulations is featured.

Updates

Th e law moves incredibly quickly, so ensure your knowledge is up to date by regularly referring to this summary of key developments.

Lecturer resources

Access to the following resources is limited to lecturers only.

PowerPoint slides

Customizable PowerPoint slides covering key points from each chapter of the text for use in your teaching.

Testbank of multiple-choice questions

Many business law courses require students to be assessed at least in some part, by multiple-choice questions. Downloadable to your VLE, a bank of 200 questions with answers, feedback, and page references which refer students to the relevant coverage within the book enable you to offer you students the ideal exam preparations

Outline Contents

Detailed Contents

http://www.oxfordtextbooks.co.uk/orc/marson3e
Visit the Online Resource Centre for information on business ethics; the Consumer Protection for
Unfair Trading Regulations 2008; corporate manslaughter; and the Legal Services Act 2007

Table of Cases

Table of Legislation

TABLE OF SECONDARY LEGISLATION

Treaties

TABLE OF PRACTICE DIRECTIONS

TABLE OF CODES OF PRACTICE

TABLE OF EUROPEAN LEGISLATION

Directives

Studying Law

Why does it matter?

How would you feel if your company lost a lot of money because you made a mistake negotiating a contract? Or you were prosecuted for failing to meet health and safety standards? Understanding how the law affects business is absolutely essential to ensure those entering the profession can effectively manage the myriad legal implications businesses are subject to. To be successful in a business career, you must thus have knowledge of the laws most commonly affecting undertakings, and the ability to apply these laws in business situations. These skills will ensure you can make decisions correctly, quickly, and with certainty, whilst being able to readily identify when expert advice is required. This chapter begins by identifying why it is important to study law. It identifies strategies and good practice that will help you be successful in your studies, and it concludes by identifying how to use the book and its Online Resource Centre. Business law is a distinct topic from other modules on accountancy, business, and management courses. You need to think about business problems from a legal standpoint and you must know the relevant laws—you cannot bluff knowledge of the law. This approach will ensure you answer legal questions with reference to the law, which is crucial to being successful in your business law module.

Learning outcomes

Following reading this chapter you should be in a position to:

- identify why it is important, and indeed necessary, to study business law for your future business careers (1.2);
- identify strategies and tactics that will assist you in being successful in your studies (1.3–1.3.4.3);
- understand the features contained in this text and how they can assist you in your learning and development (1.4).

⚷ Key terms

These terms will be used in the chapter and it may be helpful to be aware of what they mean or refer back to them when reading through the chapter.

Case law
These are reports of cases that have been decided by the courts. You can 'identify' case law as the report contains the names of each of the parties (for example, *Donoghue v Stevenson*).

Doctrine
This term is used to refer to a body of thought and is used in legal theory to identify a principle of law, such as those developed through the common law.

Law reports
Case law is reported in law reports, which identify the facts of a particular case and the rulings/judgment of the court. Those that are reported have some importance in developing **precedent** or identifying the interpretation of statutes and so on. These reports are published by commercial organizations and as such the case may be produced in any or all of the available reports (including the *Law Reports (Appeal Cases, Chancery Division, Family Division and Queen's Bench Division)*; the *Weekly Law Reports*; the *All England Law Reports*; and, increasingly, specialized reports for specific areas of law such as the *Family Law Reports* and *Butterworths Medico-Legal Reports*.

Precedent
The aspect of case law (the *ratio decidendi*) that becomes binding on all lower courts. The judges in a case will spend time explaining, with reference to previous cases, how and why they have arrived at a decision, and whether the case establishing the precedent should be followed or distinguished.

Statute
A law created through Parliament, and also referred to as legislation.

1.1 Introduction

Online
Resource
Centre

It should be noted that whilst textbooks aim to provide the guidance and information required to pass courses that have business law as a component, it is your *understanding* of the topic that is essential. This means not just reading the textbook and regurgitating the material in an answer to a question, but thinking about how the law affects a business and how the law is applied in practical business scenarios. By reading and understanding the law, and gaining experience from answering questions in your classes, and those examples provided in this text, you will gain confidence in how to use your legal knowledge to tackle real-life business problems. Remember, regurgitating facts you have learned may be an effective short-term measure that assists in passing examinations, but this approach will likely lead to you making costly professional mistakes once in practice. Lack of knowledge is usually found out in business; it will be exploited by the other party, and will generally result in a competitive disadvantage. Your understanding of the law will be demonstrated through the feedback in classes, and it can also be gauged by using the questions included in this text and the Online Resource Centre (where indicative answers are included for your reference).

1.2 Why study law?

This is a question many students raise. Students who study business law are often undertaking courses in Accountancy; Business; Engineering; Information Management; Financial Services; and Management (to name but a few). The topic may thus not readily appear relevant to your chosen careers, and this is especially so when the topic becomes difficult. However, knowledge of the law is absolutely essential when you enter your business career. You will typically be involved in the recruitment of individuals and the termination of contracts of employment (therefore any number of elements of employment law will be applicable); as managers you will often have responsibility for the agreement of contracts that will bind the organization for which you work (contract law is applicable here); you may have responsibility for the health and safety of workers or be involved in situations where the public visit company premises (involving employment law and the law of torts); and for entrepreneurs, the formation of business organizations into sole traders, partnerships, limited liability partnerships, limited companies, and public limited companies requires an awareness of company law and its compliance.

Of course, it is correct to raise at this point that these are roles that may be more suitable to consideration by experts (lawyers). However, whilst legal experts are necessary at various times, there are day-to-day matters where advice from a lawyer may be unnecessary, time-consuming in waiting for a response, and potentially very expensive. It is not uncommon for a solicitor to charge in excess of £200–300 per hour for his/her time (and up to £600 an hour for a partner of the better firms), a barrister can charge several thousand pounds per day for appearances in court, and hence a business requires its management personnel or accountants to have an understanding of the law, in order to deal with more rudimentary issues, and also to be aware of when expert assistance is required.

1.3 How to be successful in your studies

An effective strategy to your studies must be adopted from the outset. Having purchased this text, you are on your way! Ensure that you attend your lectures and make notes wherever appropriate (I think this should be done after the lecture so you can concentrate on what the lecturer is saying, but this is a matter of personal preference). Following the lecture, read the relevant chapter(s) in the textbook. Finally, use the notes and the textbook to prepare for your class questions. The seminars are where your learning can be greatly advanced, as you will be able to discuss the law and engage in legal arguments with your tutor and class colleagues.

1.3.1 How to answer 'law' questions

I am often approached by students who are concerned that, as non-law students, they do not know how to answer a 'law' question. It is a necessary truth that few areas of law are 'black and white' in which an answer is guaranteed to be right or wrong, but by 'grounding' your answer with use of **case law** or statutory materials, you will be ensuring that your answer is based on a legal principle or **doctrine**, and the lecturer can identify how you have arrived at your conclusion. This text includes some of the most important case law and statutory materials that are necessary for your understanding of the topics included. There is a description of the law, and then an attempt to place this into context and explain how the law is used and why it is important to be aware of it. There are references to the actual case law contained in the **law reports**, and interested readers can find these 'primary' materials[1] themselves. However, the value of a textbook is that the case summaries, and commentary regarding its importance and/or the point of law established, will save you the time in finding, reading, and interpreting these primary sources.

Online Resource Centre

1.3.2 Examples of answering law questions

I advise my students to adopt a three-step approach when answering law questions (see **Figure 1.1**). Examples are provided on the Online Resource Centre of the use of this three-step process in answering problem-type and essay questions.

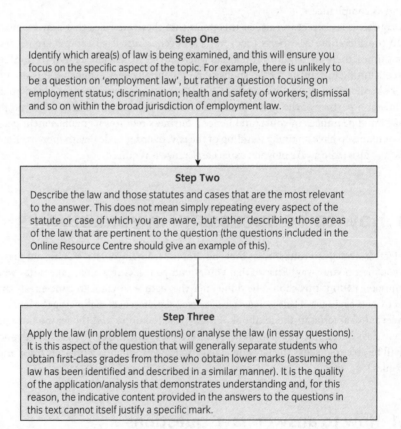

Step One

Identify which area(s) of law is being examined, and this will ensure you focus on the specific aspect of the topic. For example, there is unlikely to be a question on 'employment law', but rather a question focusing on employment status; discrimination; health and safety of workers; dismissal and so on within the broad jurisdiction of employment law.

Step Two

Describe the law and those statutes and cases that are the most relevant to the answer. This does not mean simply repeating every aspect of the statute or case of which you are aware, but rather describing those areas of the law that are pertinent to the question (the questions included in the Online Resource Centre should give an example of this).

Step Three

Apply the law (in problem questions) or analyse the law (in essay questions). It is this aspect of the question that will generally separate students who obtain first-class grades from those who obtain lower marks (assuming the law has been identified and described in a similar manner). It is the quality of the application/analysis that demonstrates understanding and, for this reason, the indicative content provided in the answers to the questions in this text cannot itself justify a specific mark.

Figure 1.1 How to Answer 'Law' Questions

---

[1] Primary materials include sources of law such as cases and statutes before they have undergone some form of analysis or commentary. Textbooks and articles written in journals, for example, are known as 'secondary' materials.

1.3.3 What a lecturer is looking for in assessments

There are certain generic characteristics that will be tested in most learning outcomes. You will need to adopt different styles for problem-based (scenario) questions, where a situation is outlined and you are asked to advise the parties as to their legal position, and essay-type questions, which require an analysis of a legal position or statement, but the following are useful guides for the collection of appropriate materials and their presentation:

- **The quality of research materials:** It is always good practice to demonstrate that you have found the appropriate case law and statutory materials, and incorporate these in a table to identify to the lecturer that the relevant law is included.

- **Use the legal materials: Statutes** and case law are widely available and are identified in this text, with commentary provided. Having identified the area of law being questioned, ensure you use the appropriate materials to assist you in providing a full and complete response. Your assessor will be looking for relevant references to statutes and case law (where appropriate) in your answer, but also the use of these materials—such as citing case law to 'ground' the legal point you are making. Remember, laws do not just appear. They are derived from case law, statutes, customs or treaties and so on, so when a point of law is made (for example, where an individual will be defined as an employee or an independent contractor), cite the law that proves your assertion.

- **Reference to literature:** In an essay-type question, it is important to utilize resources such as books, research reports, and journal articles to identify and analyse authors' comments on legal issues. In order to respond to these you will need to refer to the relevant literature to demonstrate that you have researched and understood the contribution that has already been provided on the topic by others; and this enables you to make a considered and meaningful response.

    In problem questions reference to literature refers to citing and using the correct case law and statutory materials in your answer. An assessor will be looking for evidence that you can identify the area of law that is being examined, the relevant case law and statutory materials, and that you have applied the law to the problem in your advice to the parties. This ensures you demonstrate awareness of the relevant sources of law, and also that you can prioritize the most relevant facts from minor issues.

- **Presentation of sources:** When preparing answers for written assessments, the names of cases (case law) should be presented either as <u>underlined</u> or (as is used in this text) in *italics*. This immediately identifies when a case is being referred to and it is easier for the assessor to detect those cases used in an answer. The cases should also include the full references (year and where reported)—its 'citation'—and citations are included in this text for each case. Books and journal articles that are used (mainly in essay-type answers) should include all the important referencing materials that would assist another reader in finding these resources. This text includes references to books and journal articles to enable you to undertake further research into particular topics and these may be used as a template for presentation in essays or other written work. Remember to include all your sources or you may find yourself accused of plagiarism. In examinations, the case name is usually sufficient (rather than the full citation) and the year of the case (although it is wise to ask your tutor whether he/she expects the date to be included).

- **Answer the question:** Any form of assessment will ask the candidate to do something—analyse a statement, advise parties, and so on. I am unaware of any form of assessment that has asked the candidate to state everything he/she knows about a particular topic/area of law.

Therefore, if you are asked to advise parties, having described the relevant law and discussed its application to the given facts, *advise* the parties. In the same way, if an essay question asks for an analysis of the usefulness of a particular statute, then conclude with this answer.

1.3.4 Presentation of written answers/essays

This author does not presuppose to identify how each module leader for business law will want written work to be presented or the content that is required. However, by practising with the questions included in this book, and by preparing for your classes, you will gain the experience of how to produce answers to 'law' questions. Further, there are common features regarding the presentation of answers that may be indicative of good practice:

- Use formal language and avoid slang unless this is part of a direct quotation.
- Ensure grammar and punctuation is correct, and make use of the spell check facility available in word processing packages.
- The assessed work should begin with an introduction that identifies what is included, and the main conclusions to be drawn.
- It should be presented in the third person (use 'the author' or 'it is contended' rather than 'I think') and the tense used should remain constant.
- Do not repeat the question in either an essay or examination answer. This merely gives the impression that you have nothing else to write, and it will not improve your grade.
- Always include a conclusion to your answer that summarizes your main arguments and answers the question set.

Following such simple guidelines make assessed written work much easier to read and understand. The arguments are more likely to flow when you use a logical structure and this will certainly improve your work. However, as always, content is more important than style—research the topic, be prepared, and do not attend examinations thinking your wit will help you pass. You either know case law and statutes or you do not, and law modules require the law to be used, so a lack of knowledge will severely damage your opportunities for success.

1.3.4.1 *Include a bibliography*

The bibliography contains the full list and references to books, journal articles, research reports, Parliamentary papers and proceedings, government publications, online resources, newspaper articles and so on that have influenced the production of the assessed work (usually an essay or presentation that requires the submission of a paper copy). This is typically presented after the main body of work and, whilst there are various methods on how to present a bibliography or references list,[2] the style adopted in this text is as follows:

- **Books**: Author Name(s); Year of Publication; Title (in quotation marks); Edition (if applicable); Publisher: City.

    Steele, J. (2010) 'Tort Law: Text, Cases, and Materials' 2nd Edition, Oxford University Press: Oxford.

- **Journal articles**: Author Name(s); Year of Publication; Title (in quotation marks); Journal Title (in *italics*); Volume Number; Edition Number/Season; Page Number.

---

[2] Students will generally be required to produce a bibliography for their assessed written work. However, journals (for example) require a references list. This is a specific list of any works that have been directly used or quoted in the written submission.

Craig, P. (2000) 'The Fall and Renewal of the Commission: Accountability, Contract and Administrative Organisation' *European Law Journal*, Vol. 6, No. 2, p. 98.

- **Chapters in edited works**: Author Name(s); Year of Publication; Title (in quotation marks); Author Name of Main Book; Year of Publication; Title (in *italics*); Publisher: City.

  Prechal, S. (1997) 'EC Requirements for an Effective Remedy' in Lonbay, J. and Biondi, A. (Eds.) (1997) *Remedies for Breach of EC Law* John Wiley and Sons: Chichester, New York, Brisbane, Toronto, Singapore.

- **Parliamentary papers** (these may be used to discuss (for example) the meaning given to, or underlying purpose of, legislation when it was in the form of a Bill): The Speaker's Name; Volume of Hansard (since 1909 the House of Lords (HL) or House of Commons (HC); Column Number(s); Date (in parentheses).

  Lord Hailsham LC, 338 HL Debs, Col. 398–9 (29 January 1983).

- **Other materials** (such as government papers): Organization Name; Title (in *Italics*); Date; Reference Number.

  Department of Health and Social Security, *Reform of the Supplementary Benefits Scheme* (1970) Cmnd 7773.

  The bibliography should be structured in alphabetical order, and then in reverse chronological order (the latest publication by the author listed first).

  Where two or more works from the same author(s) are entered for the same year then the prefix of a, b, c and so on should be used next to the year of publication.

  Ellis, E. (1994a) 'The Definition of Discrimination in European Community Sex Equality Law' *European Law Review*, December, p. 563.

- Ellis, E. (1994b) 'Recent Case Law of the ECJ on the Equal Treatment of Women and Men' *Common Market Law Review* Vol. 31, p. 43.

1.3.4.2 *Table of cases*

Following the bibliography, a table with a list of all the cases cited in the assessed work, and their full references, should be included. These are presented in alphabetical order.

Chapelton v Barry UDC [1940] 1 KB 532.

Olley v Marlborough Court Ltd [1949] 1 KB 532.

Thornton v Shoe Lane Parking Ltd [1971] 2 QB 163.

1.3.4.3 *Table of statutes*

The table of statutes identifies each of the statutes that have been cited. These are presented in alphabetical order with the title and year.

The Equality Act 2010

The Unfair Contract Terms Act 1977

The Unfair Terms in Consumer Contract Regulations 1999

1.4 **How to use this textbook**

The textbook includes the following features which are designed to assist you in your understanding of the law:

- **'Why does it matter?' and 'Business Link' boxes**: These are included to provide some focus to the topic that is being presented and to demonstrate the relevance of why you should be interested in reading the section. The aim of this text is to identify that you *need* to have knowledge of the law in order to succeed (survive?) in business. It is not simply to enable you to pass the examination in a business law module.

• **Learning outcomes**: The aim of learning outcomes is to identify what you will be expected to have gained from having read the chapter, and they may act as a checklist to focus your attention on specific aspects of the topic. They are presented with the appropriate section(s) of the chapter identified for ease of navigation.

• **Key terms:** These are listed for each chapter to ensure that non-lawyers are not disadvantaged when reading this book and faced with legal terms and concepts. They are also included in the Online Resource Centre as flashcards to allow you to test your knowledge.

• **Diagrams**: Flow charts and tables are included to aid in your understanding of complex or difficult concepts. They offer an alternative method of learning and help you visualize important features.

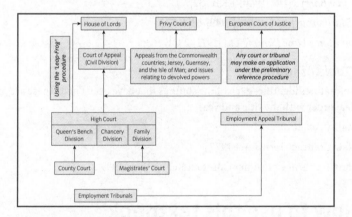

• **Summary of key points**: A summary of the key points is included at the end of each chapter to act as a revision aid and to focus your attention on important concepts raised. They are an effective method of consolidating your learning and are particularly useful in the preparation and revision for examinations.

- **Further reading**: These include further information and sources that are relevant to your studies. Once you have read this text and understood the underlying principles of the law, then use this further reading to expand your knowledge of a particular point of law.

- **Useful websites**: The law moves incredibly quickly and it is imperative that you keep up-to-date with developments. The websites identified contain valuable information from trusted sources where you will be able to obtain further information about topics or information that is focused on businesses and the law.

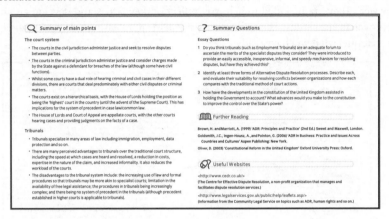

- **Online Resource Centre**: This resource contains the indicative content for the end-of-chapter questions included in the text; multiple choice questions for each chapter; summaries of cases to supplement those in the text; information on areas of law not contained in the text such as enforcement mechanisms of law through the European Union (EU) and ethical considerations of business for those studying CIMA and ACCA accredited courses; and, of course, regular updates on the law and areas of interest. Please ensure you bookmark this website and refer to it regularly. It will ensure your knowledge of the law is up-to-date and will certainly assist you in your assessments.

Online
Resource
Centre

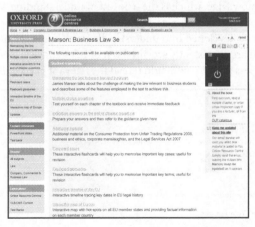

- **QR Code images**: QR Code is a registered trademark of DENSO WAVE INCORPORATED. These matrix, or two- dimensional, barcodes are readable from mobile phones with cameras and smartphones. You can scan the code with your mobile device to launch the relevant webpage from the Online Resource Centre for this section of your study. If your mobile device doesn't have a QR Code reader try this website for advice—<http://www.mobile-barcodes.com/qr-code-software> or simply access via the home page <http://www.oxfordtextbooks.co.uk/orc/marson3e/>.

The text also includes a series of questions that are designed to focus your attention on interesting/contentious areas of law, and will also assist you in the preparation for your assessments.

- **Thinking Point questions:** These are questions that are raised but do not contain any 'answer'. They are included to help you reflect on key issues and develop an analytical approach to your study. This will also assist you in appreciating how you should question (or critique) what you have read.

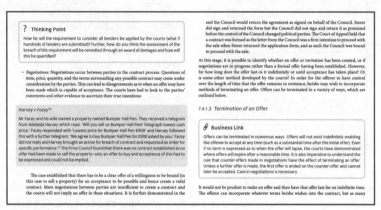

- **Multiple Choice Questions (MCQs)**: These are short questions (presented in the Online Resource Centre) with a list of possible 'answers' and you simply choose the statement or answer that you consider is correct. They are included as many forms of assessment now involve this type of question, but it should be remembered that the summary questions are by far the best way of assessing your understanding. Summary questions involve the *application* of knowledge, which is the true test of understanding, whilst MCQs enable a quick measure of awareness of facts. Use the MCQs as the starting position of awareness, which can then be developed into understanding and application/critique in summary questions. If you are consistently scoring 9 out of 10 or above you are progressing well. If you are scoring less than 7 you should reread the relevant parts of the chapter.

Online Resource Centre

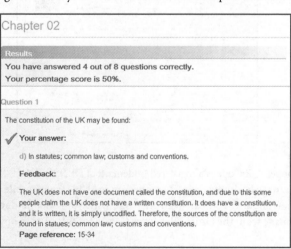

- **Summary questions**: These questions are contained at the conclusion of the chapters and enable you to self-test and reinforce what you will have learnt in the chapter. They are written in the style typical of seminar or exam questions and so will be a useful way to practice your technique for answering law questions. The questions you are presented with in this text and in preparation for your classes are designed to demonstrate problems you may encounter in your business careers, and also to assist in preparation for assessments. Therefore your exam revision begins with your first class and is supplemented through your reading. Once you have prepared an answer you can then compare this to the answer that is provided on the Online Resource Centre.

  Note: This author is neither sufficiently arrogant nor naive to consider that a 'model' answer can be provided! You should refer to these for guidance only and speak to your lecturer before completing an assignment to be clear about the learning outcomes of your assessment. What is included in the Online Resource Centre is the 'indicative content' of the answer. The grade that is actually provided, even with each element of this content included, will be based on the description of the law, its application, the clarity of the argument, and any number of factors that contribute to an overall grade.

Online
Resource
Centre

 Conclusion

This chapter has identified how to effectively study the law and what techniques may be incorporated to prepare for, and present, answers in seminars and assessed work. If you incorporate these elements into your study pattern, you may gain more from your studies and achieve greater success for your efforts. You need to work hard in order to be successful, especially when you are studying so many legal jurisdictions, but spend your time reflecting on what you have read, ask yourself 'Why was it important that I read the case/statute?' and use the seminars and self-test questions in this text to assess your own understanding and develop your skills in responding to legal problems.

I wish you success in your studies and your future business careers.

 Further reading

The following may be useful for reference and expansion on the points raised in this chapter:

Finch, E. and Fafinski, S. (2011) 'Legal Skills' 3rd Edition, Oxford University Press: Oxford.

Penner, J.E. (2008) 'The Law Student's Dictionary' 13th Edition, Oxford University Press: Oxford.

Strong, S.I. (2010) 'How to Write Law Essays and Exams' 3rd Edition, Oxford University Press: Oxford.

Wacks, R. (2008) 'Law: A Very Short Introduction' Oxford University Press: Oxford.

 Online Resource Centre

http://www.oxfordtextbooks.co.uk/orc/marson3e/
Why not visit the Online Resource Centre and try multiple choice questions associated with this chapter to test your understanding of the topic. You will also find relevant updates to the law.

The English Legal System

2 The Law, the Constitution, and Human Rights in the UK

Why does it matter?

Many texts begin with an outline of the constitution of the State for completeness, and readers may feel that a descriptive account of how laws are made and the court structure is academically necessary, but perhaps irrelevant to their study of business- and accountancy-related subjects. In reality, the English legal system and the constitution involve the fundamental 'building blocks' and rules upon which are based the system of creation and administration of law. Businesses are predominantly concerned with civil law (law between private parties), but an awareness of criminal law and the courts governing this jurisdiction is also necessary. By having an appreciation of Parliament's authority to make laws, and the underlying rules that govern the actions of those within Parliament; and by understanding key principles such as the 'separation of powers', 'supremacy of Parliament' and so on, the reader will have a better understanding of English law. This in turn will make understanding the role of judicial decisions and precedent, and its impact in contract and torts, for instance, much more relevant, and will be invaluable when considering the implications for the United Kingdom's (UK) membership of the European Union (EU).

Learning outcomes

Following reading this chapter you should be in a position to:

- identify the sources that establish the constitution of the UK (2.5.1–2.5.1.5)
- identify the essential features of the constitution (2.5.2–2.5.2.4)
- identify the rights protected through the European Convention on Human Rights (2.6.1–2.6.1.2)
- explain the impact on the judiciary and legislature of the incorporation of the Human Rights Act (HRA) 1998 (2.6.2–2.6.2.2).

⚷ Key terms

These terms will be used in the chapter and it may be helpful to be aware of what they mean or refer back to them when reading through the chapter.

Balance of probabilities

The test used to establish liability/guilt in civil cases, which is a lesser test than of 'beyond reasonable doubt' used in criminal cases. The facts of the case and the evidence presented will be assessed to determine whether the court is satisfied that the claim has been proved.

Claimant/appellant

The party who is bringing the action and is named first in the proceedings (e.g. Carlill in *Carlill v Carbolic Smoke Ball Co.* [1893]). Note that older cases refer to this party as the 'plaintiff' but from 26 October 1999 the term 'plaintiff' was replaced with 'claimant' under the Civil Procedure Rules 1999.

Collective ministerial responsibility

Ministers with responsibility for government departments are members of the Cabinet. They have the ability, in Cabinet discussions, to contribute to policy. However, when the Cabinet collectively establishes a policy, each of the Ministers must follow this (or the convention is that if he/she cannot support the Government he/she must resign his/her Ministry).

Constitution

The constitution is a system defining the power of the State and State bodies, and regulating their actions, thereby ensuring accountability.

Executive

It is a broad concept that, whilst generally attributed to the Government (and specifically the Cabinet), can include any organ that administers power.

Individual ministerial responsibility

A government Minister has responsibility for the actions of him/herself, and his/her department.

Inter alia

The Latin phrase meaning 'among other things'.

Judiciary

The body of the judges that interpret and apply the law. The 'judiciary' often refers to the senior judges in the Court of Appeal, the Supreme Court, and the judicial wing of the Privy Council.

Legislature

The body that passes legislation. In terms of the concept of separation of powers, this is generally Parliament.

Parliament

Parliament involves the House of Commons and the House of Lords at Westminster, and also the monarch. All three institutions are involved in the legislative system, and Parliament assists in scrutinizing the work of the Government and holding it to account.

Parliamentary supremacy

Parliament at Westminster is where primary legislation is created. A key element of the constitution is that Parliament has the power to make or repeal any legislation, and it cannot bind successive Parliaments. Therefore, tyranny and abuse of power is avoided, as the public may elect a new Parliament at a general election.

Rule of law

A theory that identifies fundamental principles which provide for a just and fair system of law, and which ensures tyranny and abuse is avoided. For example, everyone is equal before the law.

Separation of powers

To ensure too much power is not vested in one body, and a system of accountability through 'checks and balances' exists, the three elements of the State (the executive, the legislature, and the judiciary) must have clear demarcation between them. This ensures there is sufficient independence in these three branches of government.

Statute

A statute refers to an act of the legislature. It may also be referred to as an 'Act of Parliament' or 'legislation'.

2.1 Introduction

Studies of the English legal system primarily consist of a description, and an evaluation,[1] of the institutions and personnel involved in the practice and administration of justice. Therefore the courts, tribunals, and the judiciary are discussed, their powers and the rationale for such authority are outlined, and the mechanisms of control and accountability identified. The aim of such study is to demonstrate how the mechanisms in the justice system work, and to give confidence in these or to outline aspects that require greater control. The English legal system exists to determine the institutions and bodies that create and administer a just system of law.[2]

A just legal system incorporates principles including equality before the law; laws are accessible to all and are applied by an independent judiciary; a system of review of decisions is available; and a system of 'checks and balances' of State institutions are present. These are fundamental to a fair society. In the first three chapters of substantive law considered in this text, the English legal system is discussed, and each of these features is considered. This chapter begins by outlining what the law is and some important constitutional principles. Remember at this stage, the UK does possess a **constitution** and it is uncodified not unwritten.

2.2 The development of English law

The law consists of a body of rules, created through **Parliament**, the common law[3] and equity,[4] whose jurisdiction extends to private and public bodies. The law provides for remedies and sanctions for transgressions, and establishes a system of rules to regulate behaviour

---

[1] For an excellent evaluative and critical study of the English legal system see Cownie, F. Bradney, A. and Burton, M. (2010) 'English Legal System in Context' (5th Edition), Oxford University Press: Oxford.

[2] Malinowski, a legal scholar, had observed that legal institutions were used to maintain 'law and order' and to resolve conflicts between those in society. (Malinowski, B. (1926) 'Crime and Custom in Savage Society' Routledge: London).

[3] See **3.2.1**.   [4] See **3.2.2**.

at individual and State levels. Legal disputes may be initiated by individuals or an organization of the State, and these are heard in a relevant court or tribunal. Such a system of laws is necessary for the functioning of any society, and for these to be codified and developed in a representative democracy such as the one in the UK, ensures, as far as is possible, transparency and equity. It ensures, *inter alia*, that legislators are accountable to the electorate and have to answer questions on how taxes are raised and where they are spent; it ensures that the State provides a system of public order and safety for its citizens; it enables business relationships to be entered into on the basis that they will be respected and enforced when necessary; and it protects the vulnerable from abuse and provides fundamental rights that cannot be removed.

2.3 The differing sources of law

The common law, equity and Parliament have each helped to develop the English legal system. Whilst these sources are discussed more fully in Chapter 3, it is sufficient at this stage to remark that before Parliament became the supreme law-making body in 1688, the courts in the country had been deciding cases and, in this role, developing rules. Parliament respected the rules established through the common law and would only act to change them where necessary. Therefore these three sources of law must be viewed as a system as a whole, each with a positive and important role to play in defining the laws of the UK.

The law is also separated into public and private jurisdictions. Public law is primarily concerned with the State and its interaction with private bodies in that State.[5] Therefore, constitutional matters and the criminal laws are a concern of the State. It is important to note in such proceedings that the case is brought by the State as the offence is contrary to a law in the UK. This does not seek, necessarily, to compensate the victim (if any) in the matter but rather to punish the offender/protect the public from the offender. Only the State is permitted to take such action. However, this does not prevent the victim who has suffered a loss from seeking to recover any losses sustained through an action in private/civil law.[6] This generally involves an action for damages (the legal term for monetary compensation) and does not allow the injured party to seek punishment of the offender, only to compensate him/her for any losses incurred. The majority of this text concerns itself with the civil law, although an incident may involve both criminal and civil law actions.

2.4 Criminal and civil law

It is important to recognize that, as stated above, whilst the same situation may involve both civil and criminal liability, they are separate branches of the law and have different procedures and purposes. Criminal law seeks to regulate actions that are against established laws, and it outlines actions that are 'against the law' rather than identifying what a person is entitled to do. The law and sanctions imposed can act as a deterrent to others, it may seek to protect the public from danger, and it may also seek to rehabilitate the transgressor and

---

[5] It also includes the State's interaction with other States in international treaties, challenges by private parties against, for example, secondary legislation and so on.

[6] Examples include (but are clearly not restricted to) contract law, torts, employment law, and company law.

re-introduce him/her back into society. Above all, it acts as a punishment for the illegal act committed. The burden of proof in criminal cases is 'beyond reasonable doubt' and the protection afforded the accused in such cases is that it is the responsibility of the prosecution to find the defendant guilty; he/she does not have to prove his/her innocence.

In comparison, civil law regulates actions between parties in agreements they have voluntarily entered or where society has placed an obligation to take reasonable care not to cause damage or injure others. It provides a mechanism to enable appropriate remedies to be available in such instances. There exist several courts and tribunals that consider civil disputes, and have specialist forums to provide a settlement, and the cases are decided on 'the **balance of probabilities**'. The case begins with the **claimant** bringing an action against the defendant, and the claimant outlines the basis of this legal action, and quantifies the remedy he/she is seeking (usually damages, but other remedies may be involved depending on the nature of the claim).

2.5 The constitution of the United Kingdom

 Business Link

A constitution is a system of rules outlining the powers, in this respect, of the State. The State only derives power to act, such as creating laws, imposing fines/imprisoning the guilty and so on, because of a legal right. Awareness of the powers of the State, where these powers are located, and how they developed, will provide a better understanding of the fundamental nature of the English legal system. For example, the changes to the constitution of the UK, following accession to the EU Treaty, can only be understood through an examination of the constitutional principles underpinning our system of law. Reading these chapters, along with those outlining the EU, will enable the significance of EU membership to Parliament, the judiciary, and to citizens, to become more readily apparent.

A constitution is a mechanism that outlines the rights and power of the State in relation to its citizens and indeed the whole system of regulation of the Government (all institutions of the State). As the State has ultimate power to establish laws and imprison its citizens, it is a requirement that specific rules are established to ensure tyranny is avoided. Many countries create a written document called a 'constitution' following a revolution, when they remove an unjust ruling monarchy,[7] when they overthrow an occupier,[8] or when several countries unite to form a new union. It has often been stated that the UK has an 'unwritten' constitution because it does not possess a single document entitled a 'constitution' as do Canada, France, the United States of America (USA) and so on. In fact, the UK's constitution contains several written documents that collectively establish its constitutional underpinnings. In statutory form these include the Magna Carta, the Bill of Rights, the Human Rights Act 1998, and the European Communities Act 1972. There is a contribution from case law that further adds to

---

[7] Such as France removing its monarchy on 10 August 1792 during the French Revolution.

[8] Such as the USA overthrowing the British and in the political vacuum establishing their constitution on 17 September 1787.

the constitution.[9] Therefore it is more accurate to say that the UK has an uncodified constitution rather than it being unwritten.[10]

The significance of the UK having its constitution found in several documents and consisting of general Acts of Parliament (which like any other Act of Parliament can be repealed or altered with no special requirements necessary) is that it is very easy to affect the constitution.[11] Therefore the constitution is continually changing and evolving to reflect society's views and needs, and such a 'flexible' constitution may be viewed as an advantage or disadvantage (depending on your point of view).[12]

2.5.1 Sources of the constitution

The sources of the constitution are relatively complex and a full account cannot be included in a text of this nature.[13] However, the main features of these sources are identified below.

2.5.1.1 *Statutory materials*

The statutory sources of the constitution include a plethora of texts, some of which have greater application than others, but each is entrenched in the legislative make-up of the UK. One of the first documents written on the constitution was the Magna Carta[14] 1215, and supremacy to Parliament from the monarch was established through the Bill of Rights 1689. More recently, the European Communities Act 1972 not only formally led to the UK's membership of the Treaty but, as noted in **Chapter 5**, fundamentally changed the supremacy of Parliament by 'surrendering' parts of it to the EU. The Human Rights Act 1998 (in force in October 2000) gave legislative effect to the European Convention on Human Rights and provided rights for individuals against government/State bodies and the public services more generally. The constitution has been altered through devolving powers to the regions through the Scotland Act 1998, the Government of Wales Act 1998, and the Northern Ireland Act 1998, which established rights for their own Parliaments and Assemblies, and provide for certain changes in primary and secondary legislation to be adopted by these bodies. Further

---

[9] *Entick v Carrington* [1765] 19 St Tr 1030 and *Malone v Commissioner of Police for the Metropolis (No. 2)* [1979] 2 WLR 700.

[10] For an excellent introduction and consideration of constitutional law see Bradley, A. W. and Ewing, K. D. (2010) 'Constitutional and Administrative Law' (15th Edition) Pearson: London.

[11] For example, in 1994 the Criminal Justice and Public Order Act, s. 34 altered the previous position (and cornerstone of most democratic jurisdictions) of an absolute right of silence for suspects, the result being that if a suspect does not disclose information before being charged or under questioning, which they may reasonably have been expected to do, then the courts and jury may 'draw such inferences from the failure as appear proper' (s. 34(2)(d)).

[12] In the USA, which of course has a written constitution, there exists great difficulty with altering the constitution, which has witnessed unfortunate consequences such as 'the right of people to keep and bear arms' (a right codifying existing provisions from the English Bill of Rights). When the right was established amidst the concept of the needs of citizens to protect themselves in the absence of a standing army, its imposition was relevant and necessary (the second Amendment to the constitution ratified on 15 December 1791). In 2013, with the police and armed forces offering 'adequate' public protection, is it necessary to continue with a federal right for a private individual to possess weapons to protect themselves and their property?

[13] See Dicey, A. V. (1885) 'Introduction to the Study of the Law of the Constitution' Liberty Classics: Indianapolis for an historical discussion of the sources of the constitution.

[14] The Magna Carta, granted by King John, established the rights to be enjoyed by the community, in terms of the recognition of a free church; that people were not to be subject to unjust taxation; and it embodied rules of natural justice.

pieces of legislation that may be considered to be part of the constitution include the House of Lords Act 1999 and the Constitutional Reform Act 2005. This section does not intend to be an exhaustive list of the legislation establishing the constitution, but rather to demonstrate Acts that exist which have implications for State powers.

2.5.1.2 *Treaties*

The UK has a dualist constitution, establishing Parliament as the highest legislative authority, and international law as subordinate to this.[15] The UK has held membership, among others, of the International Convention on Human Rights, the European Convention on Human Rights, and the International Labour Organization treaties. Each of these has had an effect on the impact of the State with its citizens and has often existed as an outward sign of a governmental commitment to the important rights detailed in these treaties. However, if a government considered aspects of these treaties to be against the public interest or contrary to its wider agenda, the offending article or provision may have been disregarded or repealed. The major distinction to the general rule of treaties and the effect of international law on domestic law is the EU. The European Communities Act 1972 gave effect to the EU and has led to EU law taking primacy over inconsistent domestic law.[16]

2.5.1.3 *Case law/the common law*

The common law has been a vitally important source in the establishment of constitutional rules. Through the following case example, the judiciary has demonstrated the restriction on the State exercising powers without authority.

Entick v Carrington

Facts:

John Entick had in his possession books and papers that the Secretary of State considered were seditious and sought to seize as evidence. Nathan Carrington and others, acting on the advice of the Secretary, entered Entick's premises relying on a warrant produced by the Secretary. Entick considered this action to be unlawful and brought proceedings against Carrington for the unlawful entry and for seizing property without authority. The Secretary of State insisted that the right to issue the warrant was within the State's power. However, the court held that the action amounted to a trespass and the Secretary of State did not possess the power to issue a warrant. It stated that there was no common law or legislative Act that provided the power for the Secretary to issue a warrant, and hence the action was illegal. If the court had provided the State with the power requested by the Secretary that would have been to elevate its position to legislator, for which, clearly, the court did not have authority.

Authority for:

A State's right to exercise power must derive from some express authority— deriving from legislation or common law. Therefore the State can only act when it has authority to do so. The reverse is true for individuals in the State. They are entitled to do anything, unless it is specifically denied by the State.

---

[15]   Hence, if the international law did not have a corresponding domestic Act of Parliament, the judiciary was largely unable to give to the individual access to enforce that right in the domestic courts.

[16]   See **5.2**.

2.5.1.4 *Conventions/customs*

Constitutional conventions may be referred to as 'soft law' and are not enforceable as is legislation or the common law. However, they establish important principles that are respected and followed by the State. Although mainly unwritten in nature, conventions are more frequently being transposed in written documents (such as codes of conduct) that are then distributed to (for example) Ministers and Members of Parliament to aid transparency and understanding. Conventions were established to make Ministers responsible for their actions and those of the department they lead, through **individual** and **collective ministerial responsibility**; they protect the public from abuse by the monarch by ensuring Royal Assent would be given to all the Bills presented by Parliament; they ensure the monarch will ask the leader of the party with a majority (or largest single minority) at a General Election to form a government; the Queen's speech at the opening of Parliament is prepared by her Ministers (the Government); and the Prime Minister will be selected from the House of Commons and not the House of Lords.

2.5.1.5 *Prerogative powers*

The necessity for constitutional powers (and the basis for Parliament's existence) has been in part because of the existence of prerogative powers. These are often referred to as the Royal Prerogative (as they were exercised by the monarch) but have been provided to the Government for it to exercise. Prerogative powers are so called because of the power of the body that was empowered to wield them. The monarch, before 1688, held the power as the ultimate legislative authority and therefore held the right to sign treaties, declare war, appoint the judiciary and so on. These rights have been provided to the Government, and are exercised by the Prime Minister (in consultation with the monarch). There exist prerogative powers that remain the remit of the monarch (dissolving Parliament, providing Royal Assent to Bills and so on) but these are increasingly ceremonial in nature. As the Government has the authority to take the actions as listed above, without necessarily requiring the consent of Parliament, then abuse is possible, and whilst unlikely to take place as the UK is a democratic country, Parliament must remain vigilant to potential abuse through holding the Government to account. A system of checks and balances exist through the work of the House of Lords, the committee system, Parliamentary question times, debates, and votes of confidence.

2.5.2 Essential features of the constitution

There are underlying principles in which the constitution of the UK operates. These are important to identify and bear in mind, as they have implications for the UK's membership of the EU, and the State's power to legislate and provide a system of justice.

2.5.2.1 *The rule of law*

The theorist Dicey is credited as defining features of what is called the **'rule of law'** and its importance to the constitution to ensure tyranny and abuse were avoided. The rule of law provides for fundamental features of a just and fair society, and whilst when critiqued these may be questioned as to their applicability in the modern era, the broad principles remain as the foundations for a just system of law. Essentially, Dicey identified the rule in three aspects:[17]

1 No one can suffer a penalty except for a clear breach of the law, and there exists the absolute supremacy of regular law as opposed to the influence of arbitrary power. The powers

---

[17] Dicey, A. V. (1885) 'Introduction to the Study of the Law of the Constitution' Liberty Classics: Indianapolis.

of the State to impose sanctions against the population must exclude arbitrariness and wide discretionary power.

2 Everyone should be equal before the law, subject to the ordinary law of the land administered by the ordinary courts.

3 The rights of the individual are to be secured by the ordinary remedies in private law administered by the courts, rather than through a list of rights outlined in a formal (constitutional) document. The common law developed by the judiciary provides citizens with their rights and freedoms from undue interference by the State.[18]

2.5.2.2 *Parliamentary supremacy*

It has been asserted that the first Parliament was assembled in 1265 to provide counsel to Henry III and consisted of various representatives of the shires, cities, and boroughs in England.[19] Parliament provides legitimacy for decisions that affect the country and achieves this through a system of representative democracy. Whilst the judiciary has made (and continues to make) significant contributions to the body of law, they are unaccountable to the public. Parliament is publicly accountable through direct elections, serving the will of the electorate, and therefore, compared with the common law, Parliament's laws are held to be supreme.[20] Parliament has been, since 1688, the supreme law-making body in the country and as such has the power to 'make and unmake'[21] any laws. Laws may be enacted, others may be repealed, but it is an essential feature of Parliament that it is free to legislate in the interests of the country.[22] As such, old legislation may specifically be repealed, and hence removed from the **statute** books, but also, more recent laws may be passed that contradict the old legislation. On this basis, the older legislation is to be considered repealed by implication. Therefore, given two Acts of Parliament, the courts will apply and hold applicable the newer of the two if they are in conflict, even if the older legislation purported to be the definitive Act on the subject. This is the doctrine of 'implied repeal'[23] that ensures that Parliament cannot bind successive governments from legislating in whatever way they see fit. However, if it appears to the judiciary that Parliament could not have intended for newer legislation to

---

[18] Rights such as freedom of expression, freedom of association (freedom to be members of trades unions, for example) had been granted through the courts. English law had respected individual freedom and is one reason why there had been no specific human rights legislation as the courts had always protected rights in this area.

[19] Bradley, A. W. and Ewing, K. D. (2003) 'Constitutional and Administrative Law' (13th Edition) Pearson Education: Harlow, p. 49.

[20] It is this respect for Parliament's law that distinguishes it from many other jurisdictions that have a written constitution, such as the USA. There the Supreme Court has the ability to determine whether an Act of Congress is constitutional (*Marbury v Madison* [1803] 1 Cranch 137).

[21] According to Dicey, A. V. (1885) 'Introduction to the Study of the Law of the Constitution' Liberty Classics: Indianapolis.

[22] This essentially ensures that Parliament cannot bind future Parliaments. However, this is clearly an over-simplification of a very complex constitutional topic and it is beyond the scope of this text to offer an adequate and complete consideration. For example, when Parliament returns power to a former colony country, this is performed through an Act of Parliament and as such the Act states that Parliament can no longer legislate with any effect over that State. However, under the doctrine of supremacy of Parliament, this legislation could be repealed and the State would come back under the control of the UK. Clearly this would be impossible in practical terms. See *Ndlwana v Hofmeyr* [1937] AD 229 and *Blackburn v Attorney General* [1971] 1 WLR 1037 for judicial comment.

[23] Without this doctrine, a government may seek to restrict future governments from repealing legislation by entrenching it. Even legislation such as the European Communities Act 1972 and the Human Rights Act 1998 (which form part of the constitution of the UK) may be repealed in the same way as any other piece of legislation.

repeal previous legislation, the judiciary may have the right not to give effect to the newer legislative provision.[24]

Supremacy of Parliament further has the power of ensuring the judiciary are subservient to Parliament and must apply legislation even if they disagree with it.[25] If primary legislation[26] has been lawfully passed, no court in the UK (even the Supreme Court) can call it unconstitutional,[27] invalid, or refuse to enforce it.[28] There is a mechanism available for the courts to review the decisions of public bodies (a government Minister, local authority planning department and so on). These bodies are provided with powers and are governed as to the execution of these powers. Where an affected individual claims that these powers have not been complied with, or that the decision taken was beyond the powers bestowed on the body that took it, the courts may review the decision and provide a remedy. This system of 'judicial review' enables control of the administration of the power bestowed by Parliament, but this does not extend to reviewing the specific Act passed by Parliament.

> **? Thinking Point**
>
> Do you consider the doctrine of implied repeal to be an example of the supremacy of Parliament or rather a limitation on its powers? Compare *Vauxhall Estates Ltd v Liverpool Corporation* and *Ellen Street Estates Ltd v Ministry of Health* when forming your opinions.

2.5.2.3 *The separation of powers*

Separation of powers is an important facet of the constitution and seeks to establish a system of checks and balances between State institutions and to ensure a degree of separation between their functions. It has been criticized, and has been considered unrealistic and unachievable in reality, but the tenet of the principle is important in the public perception of fairness. The concept of placing too much power in one organ of the State without a means of ensuring accountability is alien to many countries, and those with a written constitution, including Australia, Germany, and the USA, have specific measures included in their constitutions to separate these powers.[29] In the UK, whilst there is no written constitution comparable with the aforementioned countries, the concept of separation of powers is still maintained. This was noted by the French constitutional theorist, Montesquieu, who commented on the UK constitution in the 18th century and remarked, 'When legislative power is united with executive power in

---

[24] See the judgment of Laws LJ in *Thorburn v Sunderland City Council* [2002] 4 All ER 156 in terms of implied repeal and the decision of the judiciary in the *Factortame* [1991] 1 AC 603 case.

[25] However, consider this in light of the *Factortame* case (**5.6.3**).

[26] There is no judicial review available for primary Acts of Parliament. However, secondary legislation (delegated legislation) such as Statutory Instruments, By-Laws, and Orders in Council may be subject to review by the courts as to whether they have been enacted under the rules established in the 'enabling' Act, and to ensure they have not been enacted *ultra vires* (beyond their power).

[27] Although it has been hypothesized that if Parliament 'did the unthinkable' and legislated in a manner that prevented the judiciary from upholding the rule of law, then the judiciary may insist that there be a limit to the supremacy of Parliament (Lord Woolf of Barnes (1995) 'Droit Public—English Style' *Public Law*, p. 57).

[28] However, see **Chapter 5** and the considerations following the *Factortame* series of decisions that also demonstrate the effect on the constitution of the UK's membership of the EU.

[29] For a comparative study of the constitutions of France, Germany, and Russia, and their application to the UK model see Skach, C. (2007) 'The "Newest" Separation of Powers: Semipresidentialism' *International Journal of Constitutional Law*, Vol. 5, No. 1, p. 93.

a single person or in a single body of the magistracy, there is no liberty. Nor is there liberty if the power of judging is not separate from legislative power and from executive power.'[30] There are essentially three organs of the State that hold power: the **executive** (which is responsible for the administration of the country[31] and for initiating legislation); the **legislature** (which is responsible for enacting laws and for holding the executive to account); and the **judiciary** (which has the role of interpreting and applying the law),[32] and it is necessary that they have distinct domains in decision-making and the legal system. In this way, they can check on the decisions being made and ensure reviews are possible. To this end it is essential that the constitution provides for an independent judiciary to ensure the rule of law.[33]

In conclusion of this section, it should be remembered that no system can have a true demarcation of the powers of the State as outlined above, and indeed in many areas the UK has 'transgressed' this constitutional doctrine.[34] However, by enabling interaction between these organs, as long as adequate independent 'checks and balances' exist, better government and administration is often the result.

2.5.2.4 *No retrospective laws*

The general principle is that citizens have a right to know the laws that affect them before any criminal sanctions may be imposed. For this reason, laws are made available through the internet, in public libraries and so on, and this is also the reason why ignorance of the law is no defence. As such, a lawful action today should not, retrospectively, be made unlawful by a subsequent Act criminalizing that action passed tomorrow. However, there are exceptions, such as the War Crimes Act 1991,[35] which covered crimes and illegal acts committed during the Second World War. Obviously, the general rule regarding the distaste for retrospective laws is understandable, and a point expressed through the European Convention on Human Rights,[36] but it can be deviated from if the nature of the legislation necessitates.

2.6 **Human rights**

The protection of human rights encompasses a wide range of liberties (including the social rights of accessible and competent health care; adequate housing; and the regulation of employment relationships through the prevention of abuses of managerial prerogative and

---

[30] Cohler, A.M., Miller, B. C., and Stone, H. (Eds.) (1989) 'Montesquieu The Spirit of the Laws' Cambridge University Press: Cambridge.

[31] This would include, *inter alia*, maintaining law and order, representing the country in negotiations with the EU and foreign States, and providing social and welfare services.

[32] For a discussion of the role of the judiciary in protecting the constitution see Cohn, M. (2007) 'Judicial Activism in the House of Lords: A Composite Constitutionalist Approach' *Public Law*, Spring, p. 95.

[33] A. V. Dicey considered it to be '... the absolute supremacy ... of regular law as opposed to the influence of arbitrary power ...' and that 'a man may be punished for a breach of law, but he cannot be punished for nothing else'. ((1885) 'Introduction to the Study of the Law of the Constitution' Liberty Classics: Indianapolis).

[34] For example, Ministers are part of the Executive, but also play an important role in the legislature (which also includes having the power to create delegated legislation bestowed upon them). The most commonly cited 'breach' of the separation of powers was the role of the Lord Chancellor that involved being a member of the Cabinet (executive), (formerly) the head of the judiciary (judiciary), and a member of the House of Lords (legislative). Several articles and commentaries had criticized this office before changes to the role of the Lord Chancellor were made through the Constitutional Reform Act 2005 (forfeiting the right to sit as a judge).

[35] For a discussion on this aspect of retrospective legislation see Ganz, G. (1992) 'The War Crimes Act 1991—Why No Constitutional Crisis?' *Modern Law Review*, Vol. 55, p. 87.

[36] Article 7 of the Convention expressly prohibits retrospective legislation which would criminalize an act which would otherwise have not constituted an offence when committed.

discrimination). Whilst these are·undeniably vital for the betterment of society, human rights and the subsequent legislative initiatives have focused on social and political rights, and therefore the European Convention and the Human Rights Act (HRA) 1998 have sought to protect freedoms of assembly, religion, life, voting at elections and so on. The UK has been signatory to the European Convention on Human Rights (the Convention) since 1951, and incorporated these provisions through domestic legislation in 1998 (the HRA 1998, in force on 2 October 2000). However, it had been accepted that the UK respected human rights before membership of the ECHR or enactment of the HRA 1998, and these principles were the cornerstone upon which the legal system was based.

2.6.1 **The European Convention on Human Rights**

European Convention on Human Rights

The European Convention was signed in 1950 and ratified by the UK in 1951 (coming into force in 1953). Evidently, this was an international treaty and as such it governed the relations between those States that were signatories to it, ensuring respect for the human rights outlined in the Convention and providing for a system of accountability for abuses. Being an international treaty, the Convention protected individuals[37] against actions by the State (rather than claims against other individuals), and sought to regulate the State in its legislative activities. It thereby restricted the State from enacting legislation that contradicted the Convention (although, as with other international treaties (including the EU Treaty), various derogations of these rights existed in areas such as war and national security). When the derogations were exercised by the State, it was the duty of the State to inform the Secretary-General of the Council of Europe of the measures.[38]

Table 2.1 Convention rights

Article Number	Convention Right
2	The right to life[39]
3	Freedom from torture or to inhumane or degrading treatment or punishment
4	Freedom from slavery or forced or compulsory labour
6	The right to fair trial
8	The right to respect for private and family life, his home and his correspondence
9	Freedom of thought, conscience and religion
10	Freedom of expression
11	Freedom of peaceful assembly and freedom of assembly
12	The right to marry and found a family
14	The enjoyment of the Convention rights without discrimination on any ground
Article 2 of the First Protocol	The right to an education
Article 3 of the First Protocol	The right to take part in free elections by secret ballot
The Sixth Protocol	The abolition of the death penalty

[37]　This included all persons regardless of whether they possessed 'citizen' status.
[38]　Under Article 15 of the Convention.
[39]　Article 2. Note that in *McCann v United Kingdom* [1996] 21 EHRR 97 the use of force by members of the British armed forces in Gibraltar was considered to be a breach of Article 2.

2.6.1.1 *Convention rights*

The Convention, and the subsequent extensions to the provisions through the various protocols agreed by the signatory States, ensured that the most significant civic and political rights were to be respected and protected. The rights included in the Convention are further to be enjoyed without discrimination on any ground including 'sex, race, colour, language, religion, political or other opinion, national or social origin, property, birth or other status' as identified in Article 14.

2.6.1.2 *Enforcement*

Updated measures to deal with enforcement were effected through the Eleventh Protocol, which abolished the Commission and instead provided for a permanent court. The European Court of Human Rights (ECtHR) (based at Strasbourg) was established with judges from each signatory State who are selected by the Parliamentary Assembly of the Council of Europe from a shortlist by the State of three judges,[40] and who remain in office for a six-year tenure (after which this tenure may be reviewed). A significant change from the original Convention is that enforcement of human rights now enables individuals to apply directly to have their case heard by the ECtHR. In order to do so, it is expected that the individual claimant has exhausted all domestic remedies and brought his/her claim within six months of the final decision in the State. The ECtHR then has to ensure that the claim is admissible and involves a point of law that it has not already decided.[41]

The composition of the ECtHR is usually three judges sitting in a chamber who determine the admissibility of the claim. If the claim is determined to be admissible through a unanimous vote, then a chamber consisting of seven judges is convened to decide admissibility and the merits of the case. In the most serious cases involving the provisions of the Convention and Protocols, a Grand Chamber of 17 judges is convened. The decisions of the ECtHR are final[42] and it is empowered to award 'just satisfaction' to the successful claimant.[43]

2.6.2 **The Human Rights Act 1998**

Human
Rights Act
1998

> *◊* **Business Link**
>
> Human rights generally establish a system for the protection and respect of rights between the State and individual, rather than between private parties. However, these rights affect the legislative abilities of the State; they affect the interpretation of Statutes; and, for those working for or with the State (for example, local authorities), the HRA 1998 is vertically directly effective and can be the source of litigation.

The Labour Party[44] and members of the judiciary[45] had considered the impact of the UK's membership of the European Convention and the difficulty in ensuring individuals had

---

[40]   Article 22.

[41]   This is because domestic courts/State authority bodies are under an obligation to take into account previous decisions by the ECtHR in their rulings.

[42]   Article 29.   [43]   Article 41.

[44]   The Labour Party, whilst in opposition in 1996 produced the paper 'Bringing Rights Home' that highlighted that party's intention to ensure human rights were accessible and enforceable in the UK courts.

[45]   Lord Browne-Wilkinson (1992) 'The Infiltration of a Bill of Rights' *Public Law*, p. 397.

access to their human rights.[46] Whilst it was undeniable that in most situations the UK had recognized human rights and built its legal system on ensuring respect for civil and political rights, underpinned through accountability, there were groups of people who were affected by powers or decisions of the State that they considered had breached their rights.[47] This was further compounded by the number of successful cases decided against the UK at the ECtHR. Under the UK's dualist system, alleged transgressions of these international laws did not enable the judiciary to provide any meaningful remedy. In order to seek 'justice', the individual had to travel to Strasbourg and have the case heard before the ECtHR. This gave the impression that individuals may not be able to get justice in the UK, and therefore a change in the legal system was necessary to empower the judiciary to hear claims of abuses of human rights and provide a remedy. Following enactment of the HRA 1998, cases involving European Convention rights can be heard by the UK courts and mechanisms are in place to provide for the application of effective enforcement measures. The HRA 1998 includes Articles 2–12 and 14 of the Convention, Articles 1–3 of the First Protocol, and Articles 1 and 2 of the Sixth Protocol.

When enacting legislation, HRA 1998, s. 19 provides that the relevant Minister responsible for the Bill make a statement regarding its compatibility with the Act, or otherwise to declare to Parliament that he/she is unable to offer such a statement of compatibility, but the Government wishes to proceed with the Bill regardless. This ensures Acts that impact on human rights are considered in light of the HRA 1998 and the Convention, and also offers guidance to the judiciary in applying and interpreting the legislation.

2.6.2.1 *Powers granted to the judiciary*

One concern postulated in the consideration of enacting the HRA 1998 was that courts in the UK would be elevated to 'Supreme Court' status (in the USA model), whereby the court would be able to strike down legislation that transgressed the HRA 1998. This, evidently, would attempt to usurp the power of Parliament to legislate in whichever way it wished, and also would impact upon other constitutional principles such as the separation of powers. Therefore, in order to protect the constitution, the HRA 1998 identified the extent of the powers of the judiciary in matters concerning human rights, and provided for strict rules on the powers of enforcement.

The judiciary has an obligation to interpret primary and secondary legislation, and the common law, consistently with the Convention,[48] to ensure that as far as possible[49] human rights are given complete effect.[50] This generally results in courts providing a consistent interpretation of the law in light of the Convention, but note that in *R v Horncastle et al*,[51] the Supreme Court decided differently from the ECtHR in relation to Article 6. The Supreme Court, naturally, fully respects the ECtHR and accedes to that Court's expertise in the area of interpretation of the Convention, and therefore did not take this action lightly. As this ruling contradicted the ECtHR's decision in *Al-Khawaja and Tahery v United Kingdom*,[52]

---

[46] Points that had been already raised by the judiciary and academic commentators. See Bingham, T. H. (1993) 'The European Convention on Human Rights: Time to Incorporate' Vol. 109 *Law Quarterly Review*, p. 390 and Lord Woolf of Barnes (1995) *ibid*.

[47] However, for a discussion against the necessity of a Human Rights Act see Lyell, Sir N. (1997) 'Whither Strasbourg? Why Britain Should Think Long and Hard before Incorporating the European Convention on Human Rights' *European Human Rights Law Review*, p. 136.

[48] And through s. 2 of the HRA 1998 to take into account previous decisions and opinions of the ECtHR.

[49] This evidently protects Parliamentary sovereignty in that the judiciary may not change the wording of legislation or alter its meaning simply to comply with the Convention. See *Ghaidan v Godin-Mendoza* [2004] UKHL 30.

[50] Section 3(1).   [51] [2009] UKSC 14.   [52] (2009) 49 EHRR 1.

Lords Mance and Hope went into great detail addressing the decisions of the ECtHR and the reasoning behind departing from its decisions.

If a consistent method of statutory interpretation[53] is not possible, then the HRA 1998 enables the judiciary to issue a 'declaration of incompatibility'.[54] The declaration has no legal force to change the legislation or affect its validity, but rather the incompatibility of the legislation with the HRA 1998 informs Parliament that there is a concern and Parliament may then choose to review the incompatible legislation.[55] Following the review, the Government may amend the legislation that transgresses Convention rights through a 'remedial order'.[56]

2.6.2.2 *Vertical effect of the Act*

The HRA 1998, and the Convention that preceded it, places an obligation on the State, including public authorities,[57] to act in accordance with the rights established in those documents. Direct challenges can be made against public authorities, including local and central government, and the common law is also subject to the Act. HRA 1998, s. 7 allows a party with 'sufficient interest' in the matter to claim against an authority for breach of the Act, or to use it as a defence against an action. Following a successful claim, the court or tribunal is empowered to issue a remedy within its jurisdiction as it 'considers just and appropriate',[58] although there must be a civil action to be awarded damages.[59] Therefore the HRA 1998 regulates (in respect of human rights) what legislative action the State may and may not take, and enables a party who feels his/her rights have been adversely affected by legislation or the powers of a public authority to bring a claim (effectively against the State (the 'vertical effect')).

As a consequence, the HRA 1998 affects the State in its enactment, amendment, and interpretation of laws with a human rights element, but it does not provide a clear right to use the provisions of the Act in proceedings between private parties,[60] (called 'horizontal effect').[61] It is worthy of note that whilst a party *may not* rely directly on the HRA 1998 as a cause of action, he/she may use the Act to interpret existing laws to comply with it, or it may be used to extend existing rights provided through the common law.[62] An example of the limitation of the horizontal application of human rights was demonstrated in *Copsey v WWB Devon Clays Ltd*[63] Here, the company (carrying on a business in quarrying) wished to alter the work shift pattern to a rotating seven-day system and required the workforce, especially sand processing operators such as Copsey, to agree to the change. Copsey, a devout Christian, refused to work

---

[53] For a discussion of interpretation see Marshall, G. (1998) 'Interpreting Interpretation in the Human Rights Bill' *Public Law*, p. 167.

[54] Section 4(2).

[55] Lord Irvine of Lairg (1998) 'The Development of Human Rights in Britain under an Incorporated Convention on Human Rights' *Public Law*, p. 221.

[56] Section 10 and Sch. 2 of the Human Rights Act provide for such an order, but it may also be made following a decision by the ECHR.

[57] Section 6.   [58] Section 8(2) and (3).

[59] For a review of the effects of the HRA 1998 see Clayton, R. (2007) 'The Human Rights Act Six Years On: Where Are We Now?' *European Human Rights Law Review*, 1, p. 11.

[60] However, for a reconsideration and discussion of the horizontal effect of the HRA 1998 in the private sphere (in the context of employment disputes) see Collins, H. (2006) 'The Protection of Civil Liberties in the Workplace' *Modern Law Review*, Vol. 69, No. 4, p. 619.

[61] 'Horizontal' because the private parties are on the same level as regards power, authority, and obligation to enact legislation or exercise powers granted through Parliament. See **6.2.2.1** for further discussion of this concept in relation to the law of the EU.

[62] This has most clearly been demonstrated in the case of the dispute between 'OK Magazine' and 'Hello!' regarding the publication of wedding pictures of Michael Douglas and Catherine Zeta-Jones: *Douglas v Hello!* [2001] QB 967.

[63] [2005] EWCA Civ 932.

on Sundays. The employer offered Copsey a number of alternative options such as a different role at the company or a generous redundancy package, but he refused each. Consequently, Copsey was dismissed and part of his claim of unfair dismissal included a breach of Art. 9 of the Convention.[64] The Court of Appeal held that Copsey had not been dismissed due to his religious beliefs, but rather the principal reason was 'some other substantial reason'[65]—essentially that an employer is allowed to reorganize his/her business to reflect changing business requirements. The dismissal was fair and in relation to Copsey's argument regarding a breach of Art. 9 of the Convention, Mummery LJ stated that as a principle of law, where a Christian employee is dismissed for refusing to work Sundays, Art. 9 of the Convention is not engaged.

 Conclusion

This opening chapter of the English legal system has outlined some of the most significant constitutional principles protecting the UK and holding to account those who wield power in State institutions. Human rights are also playing an increasing role not only in establishing restraints on the actions of the State, but also in the relationships between private bodies.[66] Having established these constitutional 'building blocks', the text continues by identifying the various sources of law, and how judicial decisions affect future cases through the doctrine of 'precedent'.

 Summary of main points

- The laws of England and Wales are created through Parliament, the common law and equity.
- The two jurisdictions of law, broadly speaking, are criminal and civil.
- Criminal laws regulate actions that contravene established laws.
- In civil law, the innocent party instigates the claim against the defendant and the case is decided on the 'balance of probabilities'.

The constitution

- A constitution is a mechanism to regulate the powers of the State, and its use of these powers.
- In the UK, the constitution was developed over many centuries and the UK has a written, but uncodified, constitution.

The sources of the constitution

- There are various sources of the UK's constitution.
- Statutory materials include the Magna Carta, the Bill of Rights, the EC treaties, the Human Rights Act 1998, and the Constitutional Reform Act 2005.

---

[64] Note that Copsey was dismissed in 2002. The Employment Equality (Religion or Belief) Regulations 2003 came into effect on 2 December 2003 and would have allowed for the possibility of protection against such a dismissal had Copsey been dismissed following the introduction of the Regulations.

[65] See **18.2.3.5**.

[66] Examples include employment relationships. See *Copsey v WBB Devon Clays* [2005] EWCA Civ 932 and *X v Y* [2004] EWCA Civ 662.

- Case law/the common law has been a mechanism where constitutional rules were developed by the courts. These sought to restrict the powers of personnel of the State from exercising powers that had not been granted.
- Conventions and customs are not enforceable in the way that legislation and the common law is, and as such it is often referred to as a form of 'soft law'. For example, conventions have established codes of practice for the conduct of Members of Parliament and the responsibilities they undertake.
- Prerogative powers empowered the monarch to exercise powers such as dissolving Parliament, declaring war and so on (although most of these powers are now exercised by the Government).

Essential features of the constitution

- These features are important protections in the restriction of the State's exercise of power and the fundamental rights to which individuals are entitled.
- The rule of law established a set of principles to ensure tyranny and abuse of the State's power was avoided, and to establish fundamental rights that citizens were entitled to benefit from.
- Parliamentary supremacy was formed following the removal of James II as monarch and established Parliament as the supreme law-making body in the country (although the monarch still has to provide Royal Assent to legislation before it becomes effective).
- Parliament cannot bind successive Parliaments—therefore the new Parliament is entitled to repeal or change any previous Act regardless of attempts to entrench it.
- Newer Acts are deemed to implicitly repeal inconsistent prior Acts under the doctrine of Implied Repeal, unless Parliament makes an explicit notice to the contrary.
- Parliament's laws are deemed the highest form of law due to the election of members to this body, whilst the judiciary is not publicly elected. Therefore the judiciary has an obligation to follow the laws of Parliament and does not have the right to challenge the enacted law as being 'unconstitutional' (as exists in other jurisdictions).
- Separation of powers instils a system of checks and balances where the three main organs of the State (the executive, the legislature, and the judiciary) are separated in an attempt to avoid abuse of power.
- As a general rule, legislation should not be introduced retrospectively. This ensures that citizens have the ability to be aware of laws that could make their actions unlawful.

Human rights

- The UK became signatory to the European Convention in 1951. This sought to regulate the actions of the State and provide a set of fundamental rights for individuals.
- The rights included freedom from discrimination based on sex, race, and religious and political views; the right to life; freedom from torture and inhumane punishment; the right to a fair trial; and freedom of expression.
- The Convention provided for enforcement through the ECtHR (based in Strasbourg).
- An individual with a claim based on the Convention's rights would exhaust all domestic remedies, and then proceed to the ECtHR. As this is an international treaty and the UK has a dualist constitution, the judges in the UK were limited as to the remedies they could provide for a breach of the Convention.

- This led to the UK enacting the HRA 1998 that came into force on 1 October 2000. This legislation provides, essentially, for the same rights as are contained in the European Convention. It enables the individual to have a remedy provided by a domestic court without having to travel to Strasbourg.

- The HRA 1998 must be interpreted in the spirit of the European Convention (using a purposive approach to interpretation) and the UK courts must also use the case law established by the ECtHR.

- When enacting new legislation that may have an effect on the HRA 1998, the Minister of the government department responsible for the Bill makes a declaration that the Bill either does or does not breach, or intend to breach, the HRA 1998.

- The HRA is used to interpret other rights. It cannot be used horizontally (a private individual against another private individual) but rather is used by an individual where the State (a concept that is broadly interpreted) has infringed his/her human rights.

- Following enactment of the HRA 1998, the judiciary may hear cases involving an alleged breach of the Act, and are empowered to issue a 'declaration of incompatibility' if the law, as interpreted with the HRA 1998, contravenes the claimant's human rights. There is no authority to strike down conflicting legislation.

- Following the declaration, Parliament may choose to change the offending statute to conform to the HRA 1998 through a 'remedial order' by the Government.

- If the individual is unhappy with the decision from the domestic courts, appeals are possible to the ECtHR.

 Summary questions

Essay questions

1. 'The dualist constitution of the UK is a detriment to individuals as it provides the State with the choice of adhering to international agreements or not. Given this deficit of the constitution, international treaties are not worth the paper they are written on.'
   Critically assess the above statement. In your answer, give specific examples of international treaties which the UK has either repealed or disregarded.

2. The UK requires a formal written constitution if fundamental rights, evident in most democratic jurisdictions, are not to be abrogated by governments who rely on the apathy of the general public to remove essential protection against tyranny.
   Discuss.

Problem questions

1. All Bright Consumables (ABC) Ltd operates a business involving the manufacture and sale of various electronic gadgets. The electronics division has seen rapid expansion in the past few months following the successful manufacture and sales of a new tablet computer. As such it wishes to reorganise the business and move to a seven-day production shift pattern.
   Edward was an employee of ABC and is a devout Christian. ABC asked Edward, as part of this expansion, to agree to work some Sundays as part of the shift rotation. He refused. Edward's religious beliefs prevented him from working on Sundays. As a

compromise, ABC had offered Edward a different job within the organization which did not include working on Sundays, but he refused. ABC then offered Edward a generous redundancy package if he was unable to work the required Sundays, which he also refused. In light of this inability to work the required shift pattern, following the necessary dismissal procedures, ABC dismissed Edward.

Edward has lodged an unfair dismissal claim and part of this legal action accuses ABC of breaching European Convention, Art. 9 (concerning freedom of thought, conscience, and religion).

Consider the likelihood of Edward being successful and how human rights legislation impacts on employment relationships.

2. You have recently been appointed as the Human Resources Director of ABC Ltd. The company is aware of the requirements on the board of directors from the Companies Act 2006, s. 172, the Equality Act 2010, and the Human Rights Act 1998.

Write a briefing memo to the members of the board as to the most applicable human rights issues that will affect the company. Consider in your answer the obligations on the company to protect its workers against discrimination from colleagues and third parties. Further, explain the steps the board should take to govern its relationship with suppliers and manufacturers as part of its sourcing of products from the Far East and India.

Further reading

Ewing, K. D. (1999) 'The Human Rights Act and Parliament Democracy' *Modern Law Review*, Vol. 62, No. 1, p. 79.

Hunt, M. (1998) 'The "Horizontal Effect" of the Human Rights Act' *Public Law*, p. 423.

Phillipson, G. (1999) 'The Human Rights Act, 'Horizontal Effect and the Common Law: a Bang or a Whimper?' *Modern Law Review*, Vol. 62, p. 824.

Stevens, R. (1997) 'The Independence of the Judiciary: The View from the Lord Chancellor's Office' Clarendon Press: Oxford.

Young, A. L. (2002) 'Remedial and Substantive Horizontality: the Common Law and *Douglas v Hello! Ltd' Public Law*, p. 232.

Useful websites

http://www.amnesty.org.uk/
(The website of the campaigning organization whose purpose is to protect people wherever justice, fairness, freedom and truth are denied. Many useful resources and links are provided on the website).

http://www.business-humanrights.org/
(A website focusing on the interaction between business and human rights. It has a global, rather than simply a UK perspective. It includes materials on corporate compliance and assessment with human rights, and contains various links to sources such as the United Nations and the International Labour Organization).

http://www.coe.int/
(The website of the Council of Europe with links to the European Convention on Human Rights and other treaties. It also contains information on the work of the Council to protect human rights and fundamental freedoms.)

http://www.echr.coe.int/echr/
(The website for information on the European Court of Human Rights. This provides details of the work and jurisdiction of the Court, and its case law.)

http://www.equalityhumanrights.com/
(The website of the Equality and Human Rights Commission containing advice and publications on all aspects of equality issues).

http://www.liberty-human-rights.org.uk/index.php
(The website of the organization Liberty which seeks to advance rights and freedoms through public campaigning, test case litigation, parliamentary lobbying, policy analysis and the provision of free advice and information).

@ Online Resource Centre

http://www.oxfordtextbooks.co.uk/orc/marson3e/
Why not visit the Online Resource Centre and try multiple choice questions associated with this chapter to test your understanding of the topic. You will also find relevant updates to the law.

3 Sources of Law, Statutory Interpretation, and the Legislative Process

Why does it matter?

An understanding of the sources of law governing individuals and organizations is required if one is to know where to find rules regulating conduct. Laws derive from Parliament, but the judiciary 'make law' through precedent, and laws have also been made through customs and conventions. Understanding the decisions from previous cases will enable disputes between businesses, or between the business and its workforce, to either be avoided due to the confidence of knowing how a case will be handled if it proceeds to court/tribunal (and this information can be relayed to the other party), or to be resolved without expensive legal advice. Government departments such as the Department for Business Innovation & Skills (or BIS) regularly invite opinions on draft Bills, and awareness of the progress of potential laws enables constructive dialogue between the State and businesses to occur. This can only strengthen the links between the two and help to produce legislation in the best interests of all in society.

Learning outcomes

Following reading this chapter you should be in a position to:

- identify where the laws that govern England are located (3.2–3.2.5)
- explain what is meant by the terms 'common law'/'case law'; 'equity'; 'legislation'; 'customs and conventions' (3.2.1–3.2.5)
- identify and explain the use of the various methods available to the judiciary when interpreting statutes (literal; golden; mischief; and purposive approaches) (3.2.1.3–3.2.1.5)
- explain the process of how a Bill becomes an Act of Parliament (3.3.4)
- identify the sources of delegated legislation and explain the uses of each of the three methods (3.4.1–3.4.4)
- understand the work of Standing Committees in ensuring legislation is effectively considered (3.5.1).

🔓 **Key terms**

These terms will be used in the chapter and it may be helpful to be aware of what they mean or refer back to them when reading through the chapter.

Common law
Law created through judicial decisions. It is a body of law that was being developed before a united system of government had been formed in England.

Delegated legislation
Laws that enable an individual/body to pass legislation under the authority and control of Parliament. These include Statutory Instruments; Orders in Council; and by-laws.

Legislation
Law created through, or under the authority of, Parliament. It is the highest form of law and is not subject to challenge by the courts.

Obiter dicta
These are statements made by judges that are not part of the *ratio*, and hence are not part of the judgment of the case. They are not binding on lower courts but they are of persuasive authority and may be followed in future cases where the issue has been raised.

Precedent
This is a system where the decisions of higher courts (through case law/common law) bind lower courts due to the hierarchical system of the court structure. Precedent is established from the *ratio decidendi* of the case.

Ratio decidendi
This is the part of the judicial decision that is binding on all lower courts. The judiciary explain the previous case law and establish the legal principle according to which the case has been decided. The *ratio* is not identified as such, but rather it has to be 'found' through reading the judgment and identifying the salient factors leading to the decision.

Statutory interpretation
The wording of legislation is precisely drafted but this still requires interpretation and application by the judiciary. There are various methods of interpreting these laws.

3.1 Introduction

This chapter introduces elements of the administration of the legal system. The chapter begins by identifying the various sources of law in England and Wales. It continues with an examination of the roles played by the judiciary in interpreting and applying the legislation. It demonstrates the active and important role adopted by the judges in giving the full effect of the law. The law-making process is considered, along with the workings of the parliamentary system and the use of delegated **legislation** when expert knowledge is required or because of the pressures on parliamentary time. Sources of the law are initially considered to identify where laws may derive, and the 'hierarchy' of the laws in England. The law-making system is identified and the passage of a Bill (the intentions of future legislation) to its completion as a piece of legislation is considered, along with the protection afforded through scrutiny of these Bills by Parliament. The chapter concludes by identifying and critiquing the ability of Parliament to delegate the responsibility of passing legislation. It acknowledges the necessity for this method of creating legislation, whilst also highlighting some of the perceived dangers in terms of accountability and scrutiny.

 Business Link

It is important to be aware of the sources of law that affect individuals and businesses. Business law modules examined at Higher Education and through professional bodies require an awareness of these sources. However, of much greater significance is that awareness of the sources of regulation that affect business will provide the tools to enable professionals to continue to keep abreast of developments in the law, and to know where to find existing laws and those that are to be implemented. This knowledge will facilitate proactive and lawful decision-making.

3.2 Sources of law

In order to identify the law governing an area such as contract, employment relations and so on, it is necessary to understand the sources of those laws and how they have impacted on the legal system. As the constitution of the UK has been developing over several hundreds of years, various sources have contributed to it:

3.2.1 Case law/common law

Before an effective and united system of government existed in the UK, laws had been created through judges, on a regional basis, in deciding cases brought before them. These regions therefore established systems of law (Scotland being the most distinct from the others) which were known as the '**common law**'. The laws created from this source were very important to the regulation of activities and were to be respected by Parliament. As a consequence, Parliament did not legislate where the common law had already established a law that did not require any alteration, and Parliament would only legislate against the common law where necessary. The common law has the advantage of being created through reference to practical cases, and so the law has been created in real-life situations, it is flexible and can be adapted to reflect changes in society, and it is created by judges who have extensive experience in practising and applying the law.

The common law is so called where there was a law created by the judiciary and no Statute existed.[1] It is also sometimes known as case law (evidently because it was created through a court case), but this may be more applicable to a court giving an interpretation of a statutory provision. However, these terms are often used interchangeably and unless it is specified, they should be assumed to refer to the same judge-made law.

---

1 As is particularly evident in the law of contract where, due to the principle of freedom of contract, Parliament had no need to regulate an area of law that was capable of self-regulation.

3.2.1.1 *The binding force of precedent*

At this stage it is important to realize that the rationale for the common law to be referred to as a source of law is that, whilst established by judges, it has a binding effect on lower courts. This is known as **precedent** and works on a hierarchical structure,[2] so the highest court will bind those below it, but importantly, precedent does not bind the court that established the rule[3] and that court may reverse the decision in the next case it hears. This element of the law was created through the doctrine of *stare decisis* (which means 'stand by what has been previously decided'). Having established a precedent, judges in lower courts (hearing future cases) will follow the same decision if a similar case with comparable points of law is presented. A judge in a lower court may deviate from a precedent where some material difference between the precedent and the case before him/her exists. This is known as 'distinguishing' a precedent, and as long as the judge explains the distinction, making reference to the precedent and why he/she believes the facts are sufficiently different to allow a deviation from it, this is within his/her powers.

3.2.1.2 *The* ratio decidendi *and* obiter dicta

For a precedent to be established, the rule must have formed the **ratio decidendi** of the decision (this is the reason for the decision). This rule, consequently, must have involved a point of law[4] rather than simply have been an aspect of the facts of the case. The court may also make a pronouncement **obiter dicta** ('something said by the way'), which, as it was not pertinent to the judgment provided in the case, will not form a precedent but may form a persuasive authority if a future case does come before the courts with a similar legal position. This means that the judges are not bound by *obiter dicta* as they are by *ratio decidendi*, but they may refer to the *obiter* and be influenced by it in their rulings in future cases.

3.2.1.3 *Statutory interpretation*

The legislature passes the Acts of Parliament and these are interpreted and applied by the judiciary. The judges therefore look towards the text of the legislation in their rulings, and if its provisions are uncertain or ambiguous, their task is to interpret and give it meaning. Despite the comprehensive drafting of legislation, following the debate and deliberation it receives in its passage through Parliament, there may be errors contained in the text or there may be aspects of the provisions that are challenged by the parties. In the interpretation of the legislation, the judges must follow the principles that are designed to assist them in understanding the meaning Parliament intended to give the legislation.

3.2.1.4 *Aids to assistance in interpretation*

To assist the judiciary in the correct interpretation and application of the legislation as enacted by Parliament, the following mechanisms may be used. Within the legislation, the courts may look to the 'long title' of the Act in instances of ambiguity to identify what the Act was designed to achieve. This is not a particularly useful mechanism in most cases, but it

---

[2] The rationale for this is that the highest courts (the appellate courts) will have heard and have had access to all the relevant facts and arguments involved in the case, and hence can make a more informed decision. They are also the courts considering the legal principles rather than concentrating on the facts of the case, as is the situation with the lower courts.

[3] Although be aware of the distinction with the Court of Appeal.

[4] An example may be seen in the case of *Bolton v Stone* [1951] AC 850 where the legal principle established was that in order to breach a duty to take care, the defendant must have exposed the claimant to unreasonable risk of harm.

exists and has been used in judgments.[5] The courts may also use the punctuation employed in the text where it would help to remove some ambiguity,[6] and many pieces of legislation contain examples of how the legislation should be interpreted.[7] There are also aids that are not within the text of the legislation, but were included in the debates and consideration of its passage through Parliament, and as the rules on the use of these materials have been somewhat relaxed following *Pepper v Hart*,[8] sources such as Hansard can now be used if they would benefit the judges' interpretation of legislation. The judges may refer to dictionaries for definition of the text of a statute in the Literal method of interpretation, and the courts have also been permitted to refer to Reports of the Law Commission and White Papers when using the Mischief Rule.[9] Further, the courts have developed guides for the correct construction of words that are used in legislation to ensure conformity and fairness:

1 *Ejusdem generis*: This guide has been developed to direct the interpretation of 'general' words used in legislation, that follow specific words, to be read in the context of those specific words.

2 *Expressio unius est exclusio alterius*: If one word or specific definition is provided in the legislation, then this is constructed to naturally and implicitly exclude all other things.

3 *Noscitur a sociis*: The interpretation of a word derives from the other words and the context in which they are used.

3.2.1.5 *Methods of statutory interpretation*

- *The Literal Rule:* This has been a method of interpretation traditionally used in the courts and, as its name suggests, involves the judges looking at the text of the legislation and giving it its plain and ordinary meaning. It is the most 'pure' form of interpretation as the intention of Parliament is sought through a direct examination of the text. There are many examples of the courts considering the interpretation of legislation (the most significant being provided by the Court of Appeal and the House of Lords (now Supreme Court)).[10] Assistance has also been provided in this matter through Parliament enacting the Interpretation Act 1978, which enables judges to seek definitions of words beyond just the Oxford English Dictionary and similar materials–that may not provide the meaning Parliament had intended.

- *The Golden Rule:* This method of interpretation provides the court with the option of interpreting ambiguous legislation in a way that would otherwise lead to an absurd result if its literal meaning were given.[11] This, however, is only one use of the method of interpretation, and where the wording of the text is clear, yet its literal application would lead to a result that is against public policy, then the Golden Rule may be used in preference to the Literal Rule. To exemplify the first scenario, *Adler v George*[12] involved the application of the Official Secrets Act 1920, s. 3 that made it an offence to obstruct the actions of

---

[5] Such as where the Lords referred to the Abortion Act 1967 in *Royal College of Nursing v Department of Health and Social Security* [1981] 1 All ER 545.

[6] *Director of Public Prosecution v Schildkamp* [1971] AC 1.

[7] As utilized in the Consumer Credit Act 1974 in Schedule 2.

[8] [1993] AC 593.   [9] *Davis v Johnson* [1978] AC 264.

[10] See *R v Hillingdon London Borough Council ex parte Puhlhofe* [1986] 1 All ER 467, and *Unwin v Hanson* [1891] 2 QB 115.

[11] As defined in *Grey v Pearson* [1857] 6 HL Cas 1.   [12] [1964] 2 QB 7.

the armed forces 'in the vicinity of' a prohibited place.[13] The offence committed by the defendant was obstructing a member of Her Majesty's forces engaged in security detail at a Royal Air Force station. As such, the offence took place 'in' a prohibited place rather than 'in the vicinity' which the literal text of the legislation stated. As a literal interpretation would be absurd (and have led to the discharge of the defendant), the Golden Rule was used to give the true effect to the Act so it read 'in or in the vicinity of'.

In the second example involving public policy, it must be remembered that the Golden Rule is sparingly used so as not to abuse the judges' power and reinterpret what Parliament has already created. One obvious effective use of this rule can be witnessed in *Re Sigsworth*,[14] which involved the beneficiary of a dead person's estate. However, in this case the beneficiary (the son) had murdered his mother (the victim), and under the relevant law,[15] he was entitled to claim from her estate. The strict, literal meaning of the Act clearly gave the murderer the right to claim, but such a result would have been against the public policy of allowing a murderer to profit from his/her crime. Consequently, the court would not interpret the legislation in accordance with its literal meaning, even though it was not unambiguous.

- *The Mischief Rule:* As the name suggests, this rule of interpretation looks to the mischief that the legislation was enacted to avoid, and interprets it accordingly. This rule was established in light of *Heydon's Case*,[16] and has been applied by the courts in modern scenarios. In *Smith v Hughes*,[17] the Street Offences Act 1959 was passed to stop prostitution in the 'street or public place'[18] and obviously to restrict the activities of this action. To circumvent the legislation, a prostitute solicited from inside her house and as such was not in a street or public place in accordance with the literal interpretation of the Act. The courts considered that the legislation had been enacted to stop the mischief of prostitution, whether the soliciting occurred in a street or in the person's own home (by tapping on the balcony rail or window pane to draw the attention of men passing in the street), and therefore it was interpreted that 'street or public place' could include the person's home.

- *The Purposive/Teleological Method:* Particularly following the UK's accession to the European Union (EU), the courts in this jurisdiction have an obligation to follow the Court of Justice of the European Union's decisions (when considering laws either emanating from the EU or with an EU dimension) to use a purposive approach to interpretation. As opposed to the previous rules of interpretation outlined, this approach looks to the spirit or intent of the legislation, and seeks to give effect to it in as wide a means as possible. A similar approach is used with the Human Rights Act 1998 following the European Convention on Human Rights and the case law of the European Court of Human Rights as sources of interpretation.

3.2.2 Equity

Whilst an ordinary interpretation of the word 'equity' means 'fairness', the legal meaning is more complex. Equity was developed along with the common law, where civil actions were based on a document known as a 'writ' that identified the legal grounds for the action. Ever

---

[13] The text of the statute read: 'No person in the vicinity of any prohibited place shall obstruct . . . any member of His Majesty's forces engaged on guard, sentry, patrol, or similar duty in relation to the prohibited place . . .'

[14] [1935] Ch 89.   [15] The Administration of Estates Act 1925.   [16] [1584] 3 Co Rep 7a.

[17] [1960] 1 WLR 830.   [18] Section 1.

more writs were developed to include the increasing number of claims being made, but at sometime in the 13th century the process of new writs was halted. The claimants in these new cases had to use the existing writs and if their particular claim did not fall into one of the existing writs, then they could not proceed with their action through the common law. There was a further problem with the common law, in that it was becoming increasingly prescriptive and the only remedy available was damages. In many cases this is what the injured party wanted, but there were situations where a monetary payment would not adequately compensate the claimant.[19] In order for individuals in these circumstances to pursue their claims, they began petitioning the Chancellor, who could decide the cases following an investigation, but this was a very unsatisfactory method of achieving a settlement.[20] The solutions being provided by the Chancellor were welcomed and appeared to be a fairer means of providing a remedy beyond damages in the common law—equity offered injunctions, specific performance, rectification, and rescission.[21] The Judicature Acts 1873 and 1875 provided that equity, and the common law, could be provided by all courts (at their discretion in the case of equitable remedies), and there would not be different procedures to obtain each of the remedies available.

It must be noted that as equity provides a wider range of remedies than does the common law, it is based on underlying maxims that must be adhered to.[22] The first is that parties to equity must 'come with clean hands'. This essentially means that a claimant who wishes to avail him or herself of an equitable remedy (such as an injunction) must not have acted in a wrongful manner. A second rule is that the claimant who wishes to seek an equitable remedy must act in an equitable manner, and thirdly, the claimant must bring his/her claim in a reasonable time, with no unreasonably long delays.[23]

3.2.3 Legislation

Legislation is created through Parliament, and came to the fore following the supremacy of Parliament through the 'Glorious Revolution' in 1688, where the ultimate authority to create legislation moved from the monarch to Parliament. Legislation is usually initiated by the Government and passed through Parliament in the form of general Public Acts. These laws have the power to apply to everyone in a country (such as England) or may have application to the entire UK. The legislation passed may be in the form of primary legislation (through Parliament) or through secondary legislation whose power has been provided through a government Minister (known as delegated legislation).

3.2.3.1 *Parliamentary supremacy*

Parliament became the supreme law-making body in England following what became known as the 'Glorious Revolution'[24] in 1688. Prior to this, the monarch held the power to

---

[19] See Chapter 12 for a discussion on the available remedies in contractual disputes.

[20] The reasons for the dissatisfaction included the lack of oral testimony accepted as evidence; disclosure of documents was not a requirement, and there were no rules binding the actions of the Chancellor, therefore, a system of precedent was missing from the cases being decided.

[21] The remedy of rectification provides for words in a document to be changed if they do not express the true intentions of the parties.

[22] Note there are other principles than the three listed here, but these are the most relevant in the context of this section of the text.

[23] For an excellent source of further reading on this issue see Watt, G. (2009) 'Todd & Watt's Cases and Materials on Equity and Trusts' 7th Edition, Oxford University Press: Oxford.

[24] Whilst some have questioned whether a revolution occurred at all, it is termed 'glorious' in that, unlike other revolutions, this did not involve widespread bloodshed or civil war.

create laws (and indeed still holds the constitutional role of granting the Royal Assent as the final stage in the legislative process). King James II, a Catholic, succeeded to the throne when his brother, Charles II, died on 6 February 1685. James II attempted to impose his religious views on the rest of the country, to the disquiet of the Anglican clergy and the majority of the population. He also attempted to remove power from Parliament, enabling him to pass laws without reproach. This led James' Protestant son-in-law (William of Orange) to intervene and when he arrived in Devon, England, with his troops on 5 November 1688, James exiled himself to France. This led to the Bill of Rights being established in December 1689, which held that Parliament was to be the supreme law-making body in the country, and a Protestant must occupy the throne.

Unlike the common law, which can be altered quickly by superior courts to reflect changes in society or the needs of the law, legislation can only be changed following a repeal of that law or it being superseded through a newer piece of legislation that contradicts it (implied repeal).

3.2.4 Customs

Custom is used in the law increasingly sparingly in the modern era, but had been used to provide for accepted practice such as the long-established rule that allowed fishermen to dry their nets on private land. In order for the custom to have the force of law, it must satisfy several criteria, including the 'time immemorial' clause where it must be established that the claimed right has existed at least since 1189, and could have been exercised since that date.[25] The custom must have clear boundaries and be sufficiently precise to enable a court to enforce such a right, it must have been specific to a certain region or locality that the court can identify, and it must not conflict with legislation otherwise it will fail to be established as an enforceable law.

3.2.5 Conventions

A convention is an accepted way in which something will be done and may be more coarsely referred to as 'playing by the rules of the game'. These are usually historical ways, derived from established practices, in which individuals will act. However, they do adapt to modern society and are subject to change and/or modification. They are part of the uncodified constitution of the UK, and sometimes are (re)produced in written forms to 'formalize' the rule. Examples include that the Prime Minister must be a member of the House of Commons and not the Lords; the monarch must accept the party with the largest number of seats in Parliament to form the government; and the monarch must give assent to legislation passed through Parliament. Consequently, conventions are more generally applicable to constitutional matters rather than the laws created by Parliament or the common law, but they have a significant impact as a source of law.

---

[25] See *Wyld v Silver* [1963] Ch 243.

3.3 How laws are created: the legislative process

> ## 🔗 Business Link
>
> Legislation is not necessarily the product of the Government and interested MPs' initiatives in isolation. Pressure groups lobby the Government, identifying where legislation is required or expressing their concerns at new legislative proposals. Businesses and bodies that represent them (such as the Confederation of British Industry) can interact with the legislators and have an impact on the nature of the legislation that may impact upon, for example, labour and industrial relations; competition laws; taxation and so on. This allows interested parties to get involved and positively impact on the legislation that will directly affect them.

Parliament exists, along with other functions, to pass legislation that governs individuals, organizations, and institutions in the State. Legislation begins with a Bill that outlines the scope and intentions of the law, and this is debated and voted upon by both Houses of Parliament (the Commons and the Lords).[26] Generally, the Bill begins the process at the Commons, and then, having proceeded through the various stages, it moves to the Lords to be debated in the same way. If both Houses agree, the Bill will be sent for Royal Assent and will become law. As the Lords is a second chamber and unelected, the Parliament Acts 1911 and 1949 impose restrictions on its ability to prevent the passing of legislation.

3.3.1 The House of Commons

The House of Commons is a body that enables citizens to elect individuals as MPs to represent their constituency and who are members of a political party. The party with the largest number of MPs may form a government that dictates the legislative calendar in Parliament and proposes Bills that may become Acts of Parliament.

3.3.2 The House of Lords

The House of Lords functions as a legislative body (to initiate Bills and to review the Bills sent to it by the Commons) although it is an unelected upper chamber.

The monarch selects individuals for membership to the Lords (following recommendation from the Prime Minister and through the Appointments Commission). The Lords fulfil the function of reviewing the legislative proposals sent from the Commons.

3.3.3 Types of Bill

Whilst it is true that the Government is elected to pass legislation and has a mandate to govern the country, this is not the only source of Bills to pass into legislation. It may be the most

---

[26] The upper chamber.

successful, but others exist and demonstrate the nature of the system that allows individual MPs and corporations to advance proposals for legislation.

3.3.3.1 *Government Bills*

The individual Minister for the government department introduces the Bill which, as it is supported by the members of the political party in power, generally ensures its success. The Government is elected to dictate the legislative calendar of the House. However, there are ways in which backbench MPs may seek to initiate legislation that may pass the relevant stages and become an Act. These are through Private Members' Bills and seven were successfully passed (there were 43 Government Bills that received Royal Assent) in the 2010–12 sessions of Parliament.

3.3.3.2 *Private Members' Bills*

An individual MP or private peer in the House of Lords may introduce a Bill that is, usually, of wider public moral/social concern. Without the support of the Government, due to the constraints of parliamentary time, such Bills are unlikely to be passed. However, MPs may also raise the issue in Parliament or the media, and bring the issue to the public's attention for debate and scrutiny.

3.3.3.3 *Private Bills*

Bills may also be presented by organizations from outside of Parliament (companies and local authorities) in areas that they have a specific interest, to obtain powers for themselves to take actions in excess of those provided by the law. Private Bills are not intended to alter the law for the country, but rather are focused on a specific locality or industry/individual, and are most commonly witnessed in additional powers being granted to local authorities.

3.3.3.4 *Public Bills*

These are the Bills that do affect the UK, unless it is specified that they are only to apply to certain regions. Much of the legislation that is discussed in this text refers to laws that began as Public Bills.

3.3.4 From a Bill to an Act: the stages of a Parliamentary Bill

Initial interest

Before a Bill is formulated, the Government may produce documents that set out the nature of the legislation required and may do so in a Green Paper or a White Paper. The Government is increasingly moving towards producing draft and pre-legislative Bills so that interested parties (such as businesses) can comment on the proposals, and this provides an additional level of scrutiny.

The Draft Bill

Having identified the nature and scope of the law the Government wishes to create (perhaps from a commitment made in the Queen's speech at the opening of Parliament), lawyers from the Parliamentary Counsel Office liaise with the relevant government department to draft a Bill that is presented to Parliament.

Figure 3.1 Stages of a Parliament Bill

The First Reading

On the first day of its presentation to Parliament, the Bill is allocated a number and The Stationery Office prints the Bill for the House (such Bills can begin in either the Commons or the Lords, but this section assumes they have begun in the Commons). Explanatory notes accompany the Bill for further detail.

The Second Reading

Having printed the Bill, it can proceed to this second stage where the real process of debating and considering the proposal begins. The House considers the nature and content of the Bill, its implications are discussed in rather broad terms, and these debates are reproduced in Hansard to form a permanent record of the proceedings.

Committee Stage

A Standing Committee is established for each Bill presented to the House,[27] which takes each clause and Schedule of the Bill and examines it, either agreeing with its inclusion, or deleting it from the subsequent document. This may lead to a wider discussion of the Bill and it is possible to include additional clauses and Schedules if the Committee feels this is appropriate.

The Report Stage

Having had the individual clauses and Schedules considered at the Committee stage, the Report Stage may make further amendments to the Bill, but will not consider any aspects of the Bill that were not considered by the Committee. This enables MPs who were not members of the Committee to forward amendments and allows for reflection of the Bill. At this stage the House may accept the amendments made by the Committee or reverse those made.

The Third Reading

The final stage of the Bill in the Commons is the Third Reading, which occurs directly following the Report. The House considers the Bill, which may have been amended by the Committee or at the Report Stage, and is somewhat of a formality with a very quick debate. No amendments are permissible at this Stage.

The House of Lords Stages

Having successfully passed through the Third Reading in the Commons, the Bill is sent to the Lords and follows a similar process to that which is followed in the Commons. However, in the Lords, the Committee Stage is usually held by a Whole House Committee (as opposed to a Standing Committee), and amendments are permissible at the Third Reading.

If the Bill passes the Stages as outlined above, and the Lords make an amendment to it, the amendment(s) is printed and sent to the Commons for consideration. The Commons then has the option to agree with the amendment(s) and accept it; agree with the amendments

---

[27] As there may be several Bills at any one time, each Committee is denoted through Standing Committee A, Standing Committee B and so on.

along with amendments of its own (and ask the Lords to agree); or it may disagree and send the Lords reasons for this, requesting that it considers the matter further. Assuming the Lords has not amended the Bill, it informs the Commons of this fact and the Bill proceeds to Royal Assent.

3.3.4.1 *Royal Assent*

Once a Bill has been through the relevant stages and has been debated in the Houses to a situation where the Commons and the Lords agree on the content, it proceeds to the monarch for Royal Assent. No legislation is valid until it has been given this Assent, and once provided, the Bill becomes an Act of Parliament.

These stages of the progression of a Bill to an Act must be completed within one Session of Parliament and if that does not happen then the Bill is to be presented again at the next Session (completing each stage a second time). However, a possibility exists for the Bill to be 'carried-over' from one Session of Parliament to the next, and since an agreement was concluded by the House on 29 October 2002, a Minister may move a Motion to have a Public Bill not completed in the current Session of Parliament, resumed in the following Session.

? Thinking Point

Who, outside Parliament, may influence legislation being enacted or propose a Bill that may ultimately become legislation? Who protects the interests of businesses in England and what influence do they have in the legislative process?

3.4 Non-Parliament legislation: secondary legislation

𝓰 Business Link

The majority of laws passed are not through Parliament's primary legislation, but rather through secondary, delegated legislation. It is necessary to be aware of the sources and the controls that are available to scrutinize these measures. For example, if legislation is to be made through a by-law by a local authority, it may be wise for businesses affected by the proposal to share their views, or seek clarification on the issue from the Authority, before the legislation is passed. Where a Statutory Instrument is used that affects a business, the local Member of Parliament may be able to raise any questions regarding the measure on behalf of the business. Scrutiny assists in ensuring all points of view have been considered, and that the views of small businesses are valued and respected by Parliament.

It can be seen that passing legislation is a complex, time-consuming, and potentially difficult exercise. Parliament also does not have the necessary time to pass each piece of legislation itself and so may delegate such authority to other bodies.

3.4.1 Delegated legislation

Not all of the legislation that is passed and takes effect in this country is passed in Westminster. **Delegated legislation** refers to legislation that is passed by someone other than Parliament (under Parliament's authority). The authority that is provided is done so through an 'enabling' or 'parent' Act that establishes a framework of the law, and enables the delegated legislation to provide the detail. There are three types of delegated legislation—Statutory Instruments; Orders in Council; and by-laws.

3.4.2 Statutory Instruments

Statutory Instruments are a method of law-making that allows legislation to be subsequently brought into effect or changed without the necessity for Parliament to pass new legislation each time. The Bill is passed through Parliament as described above, but the legislation may omit the technical details of the legislation (such as the date on which different elements of the law will come into effect, or to change the level of fines or awards of compensation and so on).[28] This power is then provided to a Minister to complete the tasks necessary as outlined in the enabling Act. The legislation is drafted by the legal office of the relevant government department, is given a number, and is identified by 'SI' on the legislation to denote it has been passed through a Statutory Instrument.[29] Parliament passes approximately 3,000 SIs a year.[30]

Statutory Instruments are subject to control by Parliament through the method by which they must be laid before Parliament—*negative resolutions* and *positive resolutions*. There is also Parliamentary scrutiny available through the Joint Committees on Statutory Instruments, which is a Select Committee that may take oral and written evidence from the relevant government department. It should be noted, however, that these Committees do not consider the merits of the Statutory Instrument but seek to ensure that the Minister's powers have been exercised in accordance with the provisions of the enabling Act (the procedural rather than substantive aspects of the proposals).

3.4.3 Orders in Council

Orders in Council are issued 'by and with the advice of Her Majesty's Privy Council'. Again, an enabling Act is issued to identify the extent and powers that may be passed through this secondary (and in some situations, primary) form of legislation. Orders in Council may be used for emergency legislation[31] but in their ordinary function they provide legislation where an ordinary Statutory Instrument would be inappropriate. An example is where powers were transferred from Ministers of the UK Government to those in devolved assemblies, including the Scotland Act 1998 (Transfer of Functions to the Scottish Ministers Etc) Order 1999

---

[28] A further specific example is the power for a 'remedial order' to be made where legislation, which has been found to be incompatible with the Human Rights Act 1998, can be altered through a Statutory Instrument (s. 10).

[29] The full text of all Statutory Instruments since 1988 are available at: http://www.opsi.gov.uk/stat.htm.

[30] In 2011 there were 3,133 Statutory Instruments passed (source: http://www.legislation.gov.uk/uksi).

[31] Under the Civil Contingencies Act 2004.

(SI 1999/1750). It is also the mechanism used to give effect to the resolutions of the United Nations Security Council.[32]

3.4.4 By-laws

Local authorities and public corporations are given powers through enabling Acts such as the Local Government Act 1972 and the Public Health Act 1936 to create by-laws.

3.5 Control of delegated legislation

Control exists through scrutiny by Standing Committees, debates in Parliament, and through the courts.[33]

3.5.1 Control through Standing Committees

Statutory Instruments subject to the affirmative/positive procedure are automatically referred to Standing Committee if a Minister puts in a motion to that effect. The Committees are established to consider the specific item of delegated legislation and, having completed their duties, are discharged. The Committee debates the instrument, with a maximum time allowed of between 90 minutes and 2 hours and 30 minutes, and reports to the House on its findings. With Instruments subject to the affirmative resolution procedure, it is normal for formal approval to be provided the next day, without any debate.

3.5.2 Control through debates in Parliament

The precise method of control through Parliament is contained in the Statutory Instruments Act 1946, and is further defined in the enabling Act, but will generally fall into one of two categories: the negative resolution procedure or the positive resolution procedure. Increasingly, Statutory Instruments are debated on the floor of the House, although finding the Parliamentary time to ensure a successful debate can take place is difficult. These generally happen at the end of the day and may only be debated for up to one-and-a-half hours.

3.5.2.1 *Negative resolution procedure*

The function of the negative resolution is that the delegated legislation (Instrument) will become law unless there is an objection from the House.

The procedures under this resolution are:

1 The Instrument is laid before Parliament in draft form and cannot be made if disapproved within 40 days.

2 The Instrument is laid before Parliament after making, and is subject to annulment if such a motion is passed within 40 days.

---

[32] Section 1 of the United Nations Act 1946.

[33] The courts have reviewed Orders in Council in *R v Foreign Secretary, ex parte Bancoult* [2001] QB 1067; and by-laws in *Kruse v Johnson* [1898] 2 QB 91.

The Instrument will become law on the date specified within it, unless there is a motion[34] for annulment by either the Commons or the Lords. The time period for the motion is usually 40 days including the day on which it was laid before Parliament, and no account is taken of time when Parliament is dissolved. Any MP may make this motion.

? Thinking Point

Which MPs do you think would be likely to seek out the delegated legislation and review its content? Do you think that such an MP would necessarily have the skills and insight to identify any problems with the Act or be able to critique its full implications ahead of its enactment?

3.5.2.2 *Positive/affirmative resolution procedure*

The nature of the positive resolution results in the Instrument not becoming law unless approved by the House. This procedure accounts for approximately 10 per cent of such Instruments.

The procedures under this Resolution are:

1 The Instrument is laid before Parliament but cannot be made unless both Houses approve the draft.

2 The Instrument is laid before Parliament after making, but cannot come into force until it has been approved.

3 The Instrument is laid before Parliament after making, and will take effect immediately but cannot continue in force unless it is approved in either 28 or 40 days (as appropriate).

The very nature of this Procedure provides a more thorough control as it actively requires Parliament's approval for the Instrument to progress into law. The period for approval is generally 28 days, but can be 40 days. This time excludes when Parliament is dissolved or adjourned. The approval process does not enable a debate of the Instrument (unless the enabling Act expressly provides for this), but only an acceptance of it or a move to annul (depending on the type of procedure). Procedures exist where the Instrument is only published for information and does not require Parliamentary scrutiny. Further, procedures even exist where the Instrument does not need to be laid before Parliament.

The Instruments have to be identified through notice in the local press one month before publication, and they must be available for minimal cost and for public inspection (the most common form of access is through the internet site as noted at footnote 29, but they are also available from the Stationery Office).

3.5.3 **Control through the courts**

As the legislation is being passed by a body other than Parliament, the Instrument is subject to review by the courts. However, the merits of the Instrument are not subject to challenge but rather the measures taken by the body/Minister are. As such, the provisions in the

---

[34] Such motions are called 'Prayers'.

Instrument may be quashed on the grounds of *ultra vires*,[35] inconsistency with Statutes,[36] uncertainty,[37] or unreasonableness.[38]

 Conclusion

The chapter has demonstrated the various sources of law affecting individuals and organizations in England. It has also outlined the methods of legislating and the distinction between laws passed through Parliament and those passed under delegated legislation. Controls exist to ensure debate and accountability in the passage of these Bills into Acts of Parliament. However, it is open to question whether these mechanisms provide the robust system of scrutiny that would be expected.

The following chapter identifies the court structure in the UK and the increasingly important role played by Alternative Dispute Resolution techniques. Arbitration, conciliation, and mediation are being used by businesses to avoid court actions when disputes occur, in an attempt to reduce costs and to maintain the business relationships that are normally killed when disputes involve lawyers and the courts.

 Summary of main points

Sources of law

- There are various sources of English law that will have an impact on individuals and businesses.

The common law

- The judiciary had created a system of establishing laws before a united system of government was formed, and this is known as the common law.

- Judges spend time preparing a judgment that outlines previous case law authorities, and with reference to these, explain how they have arrived at the decision. From this detailed information the *ratio* may be found.

- The *ratio* is 'the reason for the decision' and requires lower courts to follow the rules established in previous cases. The system of precedent is hierarchical, and it is binding on 'lower' courts.

- The judgment may also include pronouncements that do not form part of the decision (the legal issue under consideration). This part of the judgment is *obiter dicta* and is not binding but rather is of persuasive authority.

Statutory interpretation

- When interpreting legislation, the judiciary is subject to rules in how such an interpretation may be given. Intrinsic and extrinsic sources may be used to assist them.

---

[35] As occurred in *Commissioners of Customs & Excise v Cure & Deeley Ltd* [1962] 1 QB 340.

[36] The Statutory Instrument will be considered void if it is created in conflict with EU laws as provided for under the European Communities Act 1972, s. 2(4).

[37] An example was provided involving Local Authority by-laws in *Percy v Hall* [1996] 4 All ER 523.

[38] See *Strickland v Haynes* [1896] 1 QB 290.

- The methods of interpreting statutes can be summarized in four categories—the literal approach, the golden approach, the mischief approach, and the purposive approach.

Equity

- Equity was developed along with the common law to provide more appropriate remedies beyond damages, available under the common law, which often failed to adequately compensate the injured party.
- Equitable remedies include injunctions, specific performance, rectification, and rescission. Being 'equitable' remedies, they are available at the discretion of the courts and they will not be awarded where the injured party has not acted equitably; he/she must have acted in an equitable manner, and he/she must seek the remedy in a 'reasonable' time.

Legislation

- Parliament's role, among others, is to legislate for the country.
- Parliament's law is supreme (above the common law and equity) because of the 'Glorious Revolution' in 1688, where Parliament superseded the monarch as the supreme law-making body.
- Parliament also has the power to delegate legislative authority to bodies such as Ministers, Local Authorities, and the Privy Council.

Customs

- Whilst little used, they have created laws that are respected if they satisfy the test of 'time immemorial'. They must also be sufficiently precise for the courts to enforce the right, be specific to a locality, region and/or industry, and they must not conflict with statutes.

Conventions

- Conventions are known as 'soft' law and establish principles that are abided by. They are increasingly codified into codes of practice.

The stages of a Parliamentary Bill

- An Act begins life as a Bill.
- The Bill has its First Reading where its title is presented, it is issued with a number, and The Stationery Office prints it for the House.
- At the Second Reading, a debate is possible and the Opposition may defeat the Bill by tabling a 'reasoned amendment'.
- The Bill then proceeds to a Standing Committee, which debates and considers the Bill clause by clause. In the Lords, the Committee Stage is usually held by a Whole House Committee as opposed to a Standing Committee.
- The Report Stage will decide on the issues raised at the Committee Stage and allows for those Members not part of the Committee to forward amendments and reflect on the Bill.
- The Third Reading involves a quick debate on any changes made at the Committee and Report Stages.

- (Where the Bill began in the Commons) the Lords may make amendments as they see fit and these are then sent back to the Commons for agreement or further debate.

- Having passed each of these stages and with agreement from both Houses, the Bill is sent for Royal Assent.

Control over the power of the House of Lords

- The House of Lords is the unelected second-chamber that can stall legislation by making amendments with which the Commons may not agree. There is protection against this chamber stopping the Commons from having a Bill enacted, through the Parliament Acts 1911 and 1949.

Non-parliament legislation: secondary legislation

- Legislation may be delegated from Parliament to another body due to the time constraints on Parliament, the need for expertise, the fact that legislation may be needed in an emergency, or because the changes may be so slight as not to warrant the passage of the Bill in the manner outlined above.

- The three types of delegated legislation are Statutory Instruments, Orders in Council, and by-laws.

Control of delegated legislation

- Standing Committees have been specifically established to review Statutory Instruments and European Union documents.

- Delegated legislation, generally, is subject to either a negative resolution procedure or a positive resolution procedure.

- The courts may also review the power to create the legislation, or to ensure that the requirements as established in the enabling Act were followed, but they are not empowered to consider the merits of the legislation.

 Summary questions

Essay questions

1. Governments in the UK are elected to create legislation, however this power may be abused if accountability is not ensured. The role of the Government in this respect therefore requires a system of checks and balances to be exercised to ensure public scrutiny. Identify how Parliament can maintain accountability of the Government and critically assess its effectiveness in this role.

2. 'Delegated legislation is a necessary requirement for the effective functioning of the legislative process, it is a purposeful use of expertise, and it enables Parliament to concentrate on issues of national significance.'
   Discuss.

Problem questions

1. The planning department of Redmount Borough Council (RBC) has been given the power (through delegated legislation) to build a new road through park land. This legislation

will enable the compulsory purchase of farmland and privately owned park land where necessary to facilitate the build programme. The enabling Act requires RBC to consult with local people regarding the impact of this proposal before a final decision is made. Further, the Council is required to consult with interested pressure groups when reaching its conclusion.

The Council failed to consult with many of the local residents, instead restricting its consultation to three of the most powerful businessmen in the area. Having obtained their agreement (probably in part due to the purchase price of their property and the fact they do not live in the area), RBC sought to proceed with the build.

Advise Francis, a farmer who lives and owns property in an area proposed for the new road, who was not consulted, as to any mechanism available to him to challenge the decision. Further, explain who may be the most powerful groups involved in the decision-making in terms of the Parliamentary process, media campaigning, and gaining the support of other powerful groups.

2. The (fictitious) Police and National Security Act 2005 provides that, in relation to the increased security risks from terrorist activities in recent years, retailers may not offer for sale prohibited items. The list of prohibited items identified in the statute includes radio-based devices which may be used to hear communications between members of the police service. As Ron (an off-duty police officer) was walking past a retail outlet of ABC, he looked in the window he saw a newly developed police scanner displaying a price tag of £85. The information on the display box of the scanner lists as one of its features—'full access to police communications—listen to what they don't want you to hear'.

Ron knew of the Act, having attended a briefing session run by the police service, and reports ABC to the appropriate authorities. Consequently, ABC is charged with a breach of the 2005 Act.

In relation to the methods of statutory interpretation available to the judiciary, assess the potential liability of ABC in the above scenario.

 Further reading

Harden, I. and Lewis, N. (1986) 'The Noble Lie: The British Constitution and the Rule of Law' Hutchinson: London.

Lord Devlin (1976) 'Judges as Lawmakers' *Modern Law Review,* Vol. 39, p. 1.

Page, E. C. (2001) 'Governing by Numbers: Delegated Legislation and Everyday Policy-Making' Hart: Oxford.

Useful Websites

http://www.bis.gov.uk/
(The website of the government Department of Business Innovation and Skills. This website contains a wealth of material and access to various sources of information to achieve the department's goal of building a dynamic and competitive UK economy).

http://www.judiciary.gov.uk/about-the-judiciary/advisory-bodies/cjc/
(The website of the Civil Justice Council–an advisory public body with the responsibility for overseeing and coordinating the modernization of the civil justice system.)

http://www.judiciary.gov.uk/
(The website of the judiciary of England and Wales. It has information including case law and sentencing decisions, and has a very useful interactive learning suite with features such as 'you be the judge'. It is informative and easily navigable).

http://www.legislation.gov.uk/
(The Legislation website provides information on legislation, where and how this has been amended, provisions which are not yet in force, how legislation has been amended for different jurisdictions (such as for England and Wales and for Scotland), and links between affecting and affected legislation.)

http://www.number10.gov.uk/
(The website for the office of the Prime Minister.)

http://www.opsi.gov.uk/legislation/about_legislation.htm/
(Legislation of the UK from 1988 to the present day.)

http://www.parliament.uk/
(Details of the role of Parliament, its members, standards, and business.)

http://www.parliament.uk/about/how.cfm/
(Details of how laws are made, the role and powers of committees, and the workings of the Commons and the Lords.)

 Online Resource Centre

http://www.oxfordtextbooks.co.uk/orc/marson3e/
Why not visit the Online Resource Centre and try multiple choice questions associated with this chapter to test your understanding of the topic. You will also find relevant updates to the law.

4

The Court Structure and Alternative Forms of Dispute Resolution

Why does it matter?

The courts in the English legal system, and the increasing use of Alternative Dispute Resolution mechanisms, are relevant to businesses as they are used either to settle disputes or for dispute avoidance. Businesses will, at least occasionally, become involved in disputes with suppliers, customers, or their workforce, and the following chapter outlines the mechanisms for seeking an outcome to such disputes. Knowing the appropriate court, or the mechanisms for non-legal action that exist to offer a settlement to disputes, may enable a more speedy resolution to business problems. Not all disputes will have a justiciable remedy or perhaps even require recourse to the courts, but the courts' position in the application of legal rules and administration of justice necessitates their discussion.

Learning outcomes

Following reading this chapter you should be in a position to:

- identify the judiciary in the courts in both civil and criminal jurisdictions (4.2.2–4.2.3.1)
- explain the hierarchy of the court structure and its jurisdiction (4.2.4–4.2.10.2)
- critique the creation of tribunals and contrast their role with the courts (4.3–4.3.4)
- identify examples of alternative mechanisms to dispute resolution and where they may be most appropriately used (4.4–4.4.4.3).

Key terms

These terms will be used in the chapter and it may be helpful to be aware of what they mean or refer back to them when reading through the chapter.

ADR
Alternative forms of dispute resolution have been developed in an attempt to settle disputes between parties without recourse to litigation. The term is typically used when referring to mediation, conciliation, and arbitration techniques.

> **Supreme Court**
> The judicial function of the House of Lords became the Supreme Court on 1 October 2009. It more clearly separates the (previous) legislative and judicial functions held by the Lords.

4.1 Introduction

This chapter concludes the section on the English legal system with consideration of the court structure and the hierarchy of the courts. Having described the constitution and the sources of laws in the United Kingdom in the previous chapters, this chapter identifies where these laws are interpreted and utilized in the legal system—courts and tribunals. The jurisdiction of the courts and the personnel within them are described and a comparison is drawn between these forums for the administration of justice. It is important for those in business to be aware of the work of at least one tribunal—the Employment Tribunal, as many employment-related disputes ultimately progress here.

4.2 The court system and appointment process

It should be understood that the term 'court' is rather difficult to accurately define in any practical sense due to the variety of courts that exist in the English legal system, and those administered by the State and other non-State-administered bodies.[1] What is easier to achieve is a description of the work undertaken by the courts (and for the purposes of this text the discussion is limited to the State-administered courts) and the role of the personnel within them.

4.2.1 An overview of the courts

Parliament provides the rules under which the various courts and tribunals in the legal system must work. This identifies the powers and jurisdiction of the court, and the role of judges/arbitrators in this process. Courts are a forum for disputes to be heard and judgments to be provided. They exist for disputes between parties to be considered (in civil law) and determine a defendant's guilt or innocence (in criminal cases).

The passage into law of the Legal Services Act 2007 has had a significant impact on the legal profession and opportunities for greater access to courts through, *inter alia*, increased rights of audience of lawyers. It also aimed to assist individuals in their relationship with providers of legal services (for example consumer legal complaints), through the creation of the Office for Legal Complaints. Given the word constraints of this text, the Online Resource Centre contains additional materials on this topic.

Some courts may hear both civil and criminal cases under their jurisdiction (such as the Court of Appeal and the **Supreme Court,** which both hear criminal and civil cases, but there is a clear demarcation between the two jurisdictions). The courts also exist under a hierarchical system

Online Resource Centre

---

[1] For example, Jewish law has the Beth Din and Muslim law has the UK Islamic Shari'a Council.

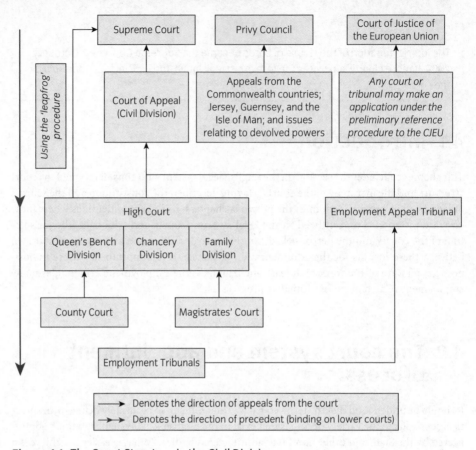

Figure 4.1 The Court Structure in the Civil Division

where a decision of the higher court is binding as a precedent on those courts below it. These decisions are not (always) binding on the court that has provided the judgment (it can reverse the judgment in some later case) or on any court(s) above it. Figure 4.1 demonstrates the structure of the civil court system and the arrows demonstrate how precedents bind lower courts.

As is evident from this diagram, the courts at the top are the superior courts and deal with appeals and/or the most complex and important cases.[2] The courts at the lower end hear the more simple cases or those that are just beginning and may need to be referred higher. As shown in Figure 4.1, tribunals sit at the bottom, yet it should be noted that whilst some are still referred to as tribunals, they are in fact courts and are specialists in that jurisdiction of law. Such an example is the Employment Appeals Tribunal, where appeals from decisions of an Employment Tribunal are heard.

4.2.2 Judiciary

The judiciary refers to the judges who preside over the cases heard in the courts in the civil and criminal jurisdictions. There are a variety of judges, established on a hierarchical

---

[2] Considering the points of law applied in the case rather than the facts.

basis, who sit in the courts in the English legal system. The most senior of these is the Lord Chief Justice (the head of the Court of Appeal (Criminal Division) and the Queen's Bench Division of the High Court), whose responsibilities include representing the judiciary as a body to Parliament; the second most senior judge is the Master of the Rolls (the head of the Court of Appeal (Civil Division)); then there is the President of the Family Division and the Vice-Chancellor[3] (Head of the Chancery Division of the High Court).

Next in the hierarchy are the Lord Justices who, along with the Lord Chief Justice and the Master of the Rolls, sit in the Court of Appeal.

As of 2012 there were 110 High Court Judges in post: 17 assigned to the Chancery Division, 19 to the Queen's Bench Division, and 74 to the Family Division.

The next level of the judiciary involves Circuit Judges and District Judges. In 2012 there were 141 District Judges in the Magistrates' Court who support the lay magistrates in the Court and consider the full range of cases before the Court, either sitting with the lay magistrates or sitting alone.[4]

Justices of the Peace (lay magistrates) are the volunteers who sit in the Magistrates' Court and are appointed by the Lord Chancellor on behalf of the monarch (with the exception of Greater Manchester, Merseyside, and Lancashire, where the appointments are made by the Chancellor to the Duchy of Lancaster). In the Magistrates' Court they sit in a bench of three, and when sitting in the Youth Court or Family Proceedings Court, there must be at least one man and one woman. When in the Crown Court, the Justices sit with a Judge to hear appeals and cases committed from the Magistrates' Court, for sentence.

The historical restriction to the position of a judge to persons previously engaged as a barrister was changed under the Courts and Legal Services Act 1990. The Act provided for solicitors to have the opportunity to become judges if they possessed the 'rights of audience' in the particular court, and it was to broaden the opportunities for those engaged in the legal services to aspire to the highest positions in the 'industry'. The right of audience is identified in s. 71(3) of the Act and includes the Supreme Court; High Court; Crown Court; County Court; Magistrates' Court; and a 'general qualification' covering rights of audience in the Supreme Court, County Court, and Magistrates' Court.

4.2.3 Appointment proceedings

Part of the previous Labour Government's commitment to improving the transparency and openness of government led to the Constitutional Reform Act 2005.[5] This piece of legislation was broad and included the development of the Supreme Court that became the highest court. The function of the Lord Chancellor (the office with responsibility for the judges) was changed,[6] as this office was largely responsible for the appointment of judges that had been viewed with scepticism by commentators as being opaque. Consequently, there was little transparency in the selection of these judges. There was a disproportionately small number of

---

[3] The office has the responsibility for cases involving substantial sums of money and legal financial issues of national significance.

[4] http://www.judiciary.gov.uk/publications-and-reports/statistics/diversity-stats-and-gen-overview.

[5] For an historic account of the development of the Supreme Court and a comparison with the US model of a Supreme Court, see Lord Mance (2006) 'Constitutional Reforms, the Supreme Court and the Law Lords' *Civil Justice Quarterly*, Vol. 25, p. 155.

[6] In the Constitutional Reform Bill the Government's intention was to abolish the position of Lord Chancellor. However, following pressure from the House of Lords regarding the history of the position (it had been in existence for some 1,400 years before this Bill) and its importance, the position was maintained, albeit with significant modifications.

judges representing the various ethic minority groups in the country; few appointments were made of those with disabilities; and judges were frequently ridiculed as being out of touch with society. Therefore, the system of appointments was revised under the Act, with the creation of the Judicial Appointments Commission.

4.2.3.1 *The Judicial Appointments Commission*[7]

The Commission is composed of 15 members, a chairperson, five 'lay' members, five members acting from a judicial capacity, two legal professionals, a tribunal member, and a lay magistrate.[8] The role of the Commission is to select the judges on the basis of the merits of their application, in discussion with the panel, with the need for accountability and transparency to remain a focus of the appointment process. The Commission also has a requirement to consider the current composition of the judiciary and have regard to increasing its diversity.[9]

The judges to the Supreme Court are required to possess sufficient knowledge and practical experience of the law. The initial members of the Court were the 12 Law Lords.[10] When a vacancy arises, the Lord Chancellor formulates a selection panel that includes a member of the Commission to select a person from the candidates and report this to the Lord Chancellor who may accept the decision, reject it, or require the panel to reconsider its decision. The Lord Chancellor then passes this information of the successful candidate to the Prime Minister who makes the recommendation to the monarch for the appointment to the Supreme Court. For judges to the lower courts (High Court Judge, District Judge and so on) the Commission makes the recommendation to the Lord Chancellor, who in turn makes the recommendation to the monarch.

? Thinking Point

Do you consider that the Appointments Commission will make the appointment of senior members of the judiciary more transparent and more reflective of society? What was the problem with the previous system of appointment that necessitated this change?

4.2.4 **The Supreme Court**

The Supreme Court replaced the judicial function of the House of Lords from 1 October 2009. It is located in the old Middlesex Guildhall in Parliament Square which is intended to provide the Justices of the Supreme Court (the new name of the 'Law Lords') with greater space to undertake their functions (than was available in the House of Lords).

The Supreme Court is the final court of appeal in civil cases for the courts of the UK, and is the final court of appeal for criminal cases for the courts of England, Wales and Northern Ireland. The Supreme Court hears cases involving matters of general importance. It uses the case law and precedents developed by the House of Lords, and the Court is required to ensure its independence from the executive is maintained.[11]

---

[7] http://jac.judiciary.gov.uk/   [8] Sch. 12.
[9] Sections 63–64 of the Constitutional Reform Act 2005.   [10] Section 27(8).
[11] Section 3 of the Constitutional Reform Act 2005.

The Law Lords who were present in the judicial branch of the House of Lords became the first Justices of the Supreme Court. There are 12 Justices, the President of the Supreme Court is Lord Neuberger (previously the Master of the Rolls), and there is only one female Justice (Lady Hale). The Justices will, like other judges, retire at 70 (Judicial Pensions and Retirement Act 1992) so that they do not continue in office beyond useful service. Judges may sit part-time until 75 years old, and it was mooted whether the Justices of the Supreme Court should be able to continue full-time until this age (bearing in mind the length of service usually required before being chosen to serve at the Supreme Court). This was not accepted and the retirement age remains.

The qualifications required for appointment to the Supreme Court are governed by the Constitutional Reform Act 2005 ss. 25[12]–31:

1 He/she must have held 'high judicial office' (which includes High Court Judges of England and Wales and Northern Ireland; Court of Appeal Judges of England and Wales and Northern Ireland; and Judges of the Court of Session in Scotland) for two years; or

2 He/she must possess a 15-year Superior Court qualification/or have been a qualifying practitioner for the 15-year duration.

4.2.5 The Court of Appeal

The Court of Appeal hears civil and criminal cases in its two divisions and forms part of the Senior Courts of England and Wales with the High Court and Crown Court.[13] The Court of Appeal is composed of up to 37 'ordinary judges' (known as Lord (or Lady) Justice of Appeal), and judges including those from the Lords, the Lord Chancellor, the president of the Queen's Bench of the High Court and similar qualified judges.[14] To qualify for appointment to the Court of Appeal, he/she must have held a 10-year High Court qualification[15] or have been a High Court Judge.

The Court of Appeal has a president—in the civil division the position is occupied by the Master of the Rolls, and in the criminal division by the Lord Chief Justice. In the civil division, the Court hears appeals from the High Court and the County Courts, although it is possible for the appeal to 'leapfrog' the Court of Appeal and move straight to the Supreme Court.[16] The Court consists, usually, of three judges, or cases may be heard by two judges in cases appealed from the High Court that could have been brought in a County Court. The law prevents a judge in the Court of Appeal from hearing an appeal from his/her own decisions, in the interests of natural justice and to give the public confidence in an appeals process.[17]

4.2.6 The Privy Council

The Privy Council holds two positions in the constitution: a legislative role, and a role as a court of appeal. Its historic roots date back to when the Privy Council would assist the

---

[12] As amended by sections 50–52 of the Tribunals and Enforcement Act 2007.

[13] Under s. 1(1) of the Supreme Court Act 1981 (which, following the Constitutional Reform Act 2005 was renamed the Senior Courts Act 1981).

[14] Section 2 (1) and (2) of the Supreme Court Act 1981.

[15] Section 71 of the Courts and Legal Services Act 1990.

[16] Sections 12–15 of the Administration of Justice Act 1969.

[17] Section 56 of the Senior Courts Act 1981.

monarch in matters of State. However, as with other institutions, it has evolved as the country evolved. The Privy Council consists of the Cabinet Ministers (the Right Honourable Members of Parliament) and a number of junior Ministers, who meet every month. Its role is predominantly concerned with the affairs of chartered bodies (those companies and charities incorporated by Royal Charter).

In its judicial role,[18] the Privy Council (the Judicial Committee) consists of the Lord Chancellor (and previous Lord Chancellors), the Lords of Appeal in Ordinary, other Privy Council members who hold or have held high judicial office, and other judges in superior courts in other Commonwealth countries. It is the final court of appeal for UK overseas territories and the Commonwealth countries that have opted to retain appeals to the UK (Her Majesty in Council).[19] It also has jurisdiction to hear appeals from Jersey, Guernsey, and the Isle of Man; from the Disciplinary Committee of the Royal College of Veterinary Surgeons; from certain Schemes of the Church Commissioners under the Pastoral Measure 1983; and it hears and determines issues relating to the powers and functions of the legislative and executive authorities established under the various devolution Acts for Scotland and Northern Ireland, and the competence and functions of the Assembly for Wales. The Judicial Committee hears 55–65 appeals per year, and sits in chambers of five judges for Commonwealth cases, usually with three judges for other matters. In civil cases, leave to appeal is usually obtained as of right, as it is in cases involving constitutional interpretation.

4.2.7 **The High Court**

The High Court is separated into three jurisdictions with specific areas of expertise: the Queen's Bench Division, the Chancery Division, and the Family Division. The trial will normally take place before a High Court Judge (or Deputy High Court Judge), who will also hear any pre-trial reviews or other interim applications. Generally, cases are heard by one judge, and appeals from the Court (that require permission) are heard by the Court of Appeal, with further appeals to the Supreme Court. Where a Master hears the case, an appeal is first heard by a High Court Judge, and then it may proceed as any other appeal.

The Divisional Court of the Queen's Bench hears the appeals from the County Court, and has jurisdiction to hear appeals from the criminal jurisdiction from cases started in the Magistrates' Court and those appealed from the Crown Court. These criminal issues are relevant in a business scenario due to the criminal liability imposed by legislation, including the Consumer Protection Act 1987 and the Consumer Protection from Unfair Trading Regulations 2008. When handling the criminal cases, the Court sits with two or three High Court Judges[20] and they have the power to uphold the decision, reverse it, amend it, or to send the case back to the referring court. An appeal from the Divisional Court is heard by the House of Lords.

4.2.7.1 *The Queen's Bench*

The Queen's Bench is the division that considers cases involving contract (breach of contract), torts (personal injury, negligence, libel, and slander), non-payment of debts, and possession of land or property. The President of the Queen's Bench is the Lord Chief Justice and a

---

[18] http://www.jcpc.gov.uk/

[19] The countries include Antigua and Barbuda, the Cook Islands, the Falkland Islands, Gibraltar, and St Helena.

[20] One of whom will be the Lord Chief Justice or a Lord Justice of Appeal.

Lord Justice of Appeal has been appointed as the Vice-President, along with the High Court Judges who preside over the cases. A judge is appointed to handle the Jury List, and another is in charge of the Trial List. Masters (junior judges) hear less serious cases.

The Division is further sub-divided into the specialist courts of the Admiralty Court, the Technology and Construction Court, and the Commercial Court. Due to the specialism of each Court, they publish their own Guide or Practice Direction that modifies in certain circumstances the Civil Procedure Rules (CPR) 1999.

4.2.7.2 *Chancery Division*

The Chancery Division is based in the Thomas Moore Building in the Royal Courts of Justice and is sub-divided into the Chancery Chambers and Bankruptcy and Companies Court. The Division considers claims including trusts, probate (when this is contested), companies, company liquidation, land, claims for the dissolution of partnerships, commercial disputes, revenue issues (such as appeals against taxation under VAT or Income Tax), and intellectual property issues in the Patents Court.

4.2.7.3 *Family Division*

The Family Division considers all matrimonial issues under the Children Act 1989, the Child Abduction and Custody Act 1985, and matters arising from Part IV of the Family Law Act 1996. It deals with cases involving family matters of a broad jurisdiction, and can include issues of domestic violence, wardship and adoption, and divorce and annulments. It is, however, of little significance in the study of business law.

4.2.8 **The County Court**

The County Court[21] is the 'lowest' of the courts, but this does not reflect its significance in the English legal system or indeed its contribution to the administration of justice. The Court hears many cases with a business emphasis, and as such, it follows the High Court in possessing unlimited jurisdiction to hear contract and torts claims. The main distinction in whether the case is heard in the County Court or the High Court is the expected value of the claim (the figure that the claimant may reasonably expect to be awarded by the court). In the absence of a claim including personal injury, if the value of the claim is less than £25,000 then it will generally be heard in the County Court. If the claim involves a value of over £50,000 then it will generally be heard in the High Court. The majority of the cases heard in the Court are undertaken by Circuit Judges, Recorders, District Judges, and Deputy District Judges. When reference is made to the 'small claims court' it is in reality the County Court using the 'Small Claims Track'.

The Court hears claims including breach of contract, faulty goods, goods not supplied, claims for bad workmanship, personal injury and so on. It will deal with many of the claims between a consumer and a trader and there exist mechanisms to assist in reaching a speedy resolution to a dispute. Cases in the County Court are heard by a District Judge when the issue is straightforward or the matter is uncontested. Where the issue is more complex, a Circuit Judge will hear the case, and appeals from the County Court will proceed to the High Court.

---

[21] Of which there are approximately 220 in England and Wales but, as of September 2012, 46 have been closed due to the austerity measures introduced by the Government. A further court closure is expected in March 2013 and two more in April 2013.

Judgments of the Court will be entered into the Registry of County Court Judgments, which is a public document and is often used by credit agencies prior to an offer of a loan or where goods are to be paid for over a period of time. Having settled the judgment, the party's name is removed from the Register. If this is completed within one month of the judgment, the name is removed immediately, but if this is after one month, the name will be held on the Registry and removed following a period of six years. This is very important for individuals and businesses who may wish to obtain credit in the future, and for those who would have to make such a declaration to a potential business partner under the duty of 'good faith'. Simply doing nothing when an action is initiated is not wise and seeking advice from legal and non-legal sources is always to be recommended.

4.2.9 The tracking system

Having established that a dispute between businesses or within a business cannot be resolved informally and amicably, the 'last resort' of resolving the dispute may be to have a court determine the issue. When a claim is initiated, the courts will assign it to one of the following claims tracks—the small claims, fast or multi-track, which has implications for costs, the value of the claim, the privacy available to the parties, and the time allowed (or considered necessary) to dispense with the claim.

4.2.9.1 *The Small Claims Track*

The courts and the parties may decide that the case is most appropriately conducted under the Small Claims Track. When a case is initiated, the parties are sent a questionnaire (called an 'allocation questionnaire') that identifies the most cost-effective and just method of dispensing with the case. If the claim involves a dispute with an amount of less than £5,000; if it involves a situation such as consumer claims (faulty goods, poor workmanship, problems with the sale or supply of goods and services and so on), accident claims, disputes between landlords and tenants and so on, and it will involve minimal preparation, then it may be suitable for this track. Such claims will not normally involve many witnesses or any difficult or complex points of law, otherwise a different track may be more appropriate. The major benefit to a claim under this track is that legal costs are not generally awarded against the losing party.

4.2.9.2 *The Fast-Track and Multi-Track*

The court will ask the parties for their views on the most appropriate track to use in the case, but will use the Fast-Track if the claim involves a claim in excess of £5,000 but less than £15,000, and if the case will take no longer than 30 weeks to prepare and take no more than one day in court (assessed at 5 hours). If the case involves either a claim of more than £15,000 or will take longer than 30 weeks then the judge may allocate the case to the Multi-Track, where each case is allocated on the basis of its circumstances. In these cases, the party that wins his/her case will expect to recover some (or all) of the costs involved in their case from the losing party. When this involves the legal fees, and of course the losing party will have to pay his/her own expenses and legal fees, court action is something not to be entered into lightly.[22]

---

[22] See 'Compensation Culture: It's Time to Draw a Line in the Sand' *Sunday Times* 22 August 2010, which comments on employers who adopted a policy of settling *all* employment disputes due to the expense of litigation.

Again, an allocation questionnaire is completed by the parties and it is expected that both parties cooperate and return the questionnaire to the court within 14 days of receiving it. The cooperation will involve the parties agreeing on the most appropriate track to use, the length of time the parties believe the trial will take, the time needed for preparation, and whether experts will be needed.

4.2.10 Criminal Courts

 Business Link

Disputes between private parties will generally be heard in the civil courts. However, it is important to recognize the important role played by the criminal courts in the regulation of business activities. These courts may determine issues surrounding the licensing of public houses, civil debts and so on. The courts will also regulate businesses where there have been transgressions regarding misleading marketing or unfair trading. The criminal courts will determine issues such as these and may impose punishment upon conviction.

As stated above, the Supreme Court, Court of Appeal, Privy Council, and High Court have jurisdiction over criminal law matters in addition to their civil law responsibilities. The remaining courts specific to the criminal law are the Crown Court and the Magistrates' Court. The Magistrates' Court will refer a case to the Crown Court (usually) where the maximum possible sentence for imprisonment it has the power to impose (six months)[23] is likely to be exceeded following conviction of the defendant, or where the maximum fine that may be imposed (£5,000) is insufficient. If, following the trial the defendant is acquitted, insofar as no other offences are pending, he/she is free to leave court.

4.2.10.1 *The Crown Court*

The Crown Court handles the following types of cases:

- the more serious criminal offences, and these are tried before a judge and jury;
- appeals from the Magistrates' Court, and these are tried before a judge and at least two magistrates; and
- defendants who have been convicted in the Magistrates' Court and are referred to the Crown Court for sentencing.

Offences heard by the Crown Court are divided into three categories of seriousness. Class 1 offences are the most serious and as such include murder, genocide, manslaughter, piracy and so on. Class 2 offences include rape, and various other sexual offences. Class 3 includes all other offences not included in the first two classes.[24] A Circuit Judge will generally hear cases at the Crown Court (such as class 3 offences). However, in cases of significance or complexity

---

[23] However, note that the Magistrate's Court can impose two consecutive six-month prison sentences (hence a 12-month sentence) for offences triable 'either way'.

[24] 'The Consolidated Criminal Practice Direction' available from the Ministry of Justice: http://www.justice.gov.uk/criminal/procrules_fin/contents/practice_direction/pd_consolidated.htm#6199416.

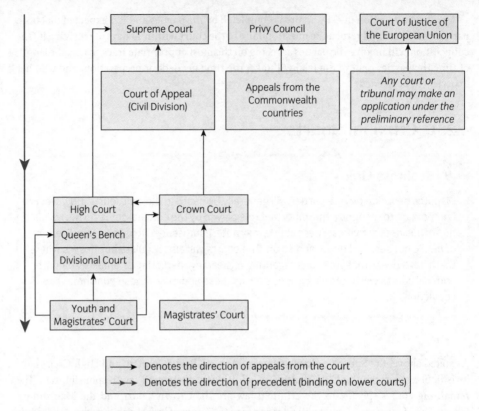

Figure 4.2 The Court Structure in the Criminal Division

(such as in class 1 and 2 offences), the case will be heard by a High Court Judge. The cases involving a jury trial will involve the judge assessing the evidence, the application of the rules of the court and so on, whilst the role of the jury is to consider the facts and the weight to be placed on the evidence heard. The jury will then decide whether they consider the defendant guilty or not-guilty, and having found the defendant guilty, the judge passes sentence. Appeals on the basis of the conviction or sentence are possible from the Crown Court (see Figure 4.2) and these are heard by the Court of Appeal (Criminal Division).

4.2.10.2 *The Magistrates' Court*

The Magistrates' Court plays a key role in the administration of the criminal justice system, as the vast majority of cases begin at the Magistrates' Court and most are concluded there. There is a single head of the Court (the Senior District Judge—the Chief Magistrate) who has responsibility for the administration of the bench.

The Magistrates' Court hears both civil and criminal cases. Examples of the criminal aspects handled by the Court have been identified above, and the civil element includes licensing, betting and gaming, family issues,[25] civil debts,[26] complaints regarding council tax and so on. The Court also has a division called the Youth Court where three specifically trained magistrates hear cases involved with young people between 10 and 17 years of age.

---

[25] This can include matrimonial problems of maintenance and removal of the spouse from the matrimonial home, and welfare issues including adoption proceedings and supervision orders.

[26] Such as issues with National Insurance contributions; arrears of income tax and so on.

If the case involves an allegation of a particularly serious offence (in which an adult would be subject to imprisonment for a term of 14 years or more) then the Magistrates' Court can commit the accused for trial in the Crown Court. Appeals are available from a conviction at the Magistrates' Court,[27] or against the imposition of a sentence, and appeals in criminal law are somewhat 'easier'[28] than those in the civil law, but it must be considered that the Crown Court, upon the appeal (where the case is retried), may increase the sentence issued, although they may not exceed the maximum sentence that is available in the Magistrates' Court.

4.3 Tribunals

4.3.1 Introduction

Tribunals were established as an alternative to the traditional court system, with an emphasis on greater informality. Tribunals were created on a regional basis, with areas of local knowledge and expertise in areas such as welfare, immigration, and employment. Tribunals were so called because of the three members: a legally qualified chairperson,[29] along with two independent wing (lay) members with expertise/experience in the area (in Employment Tribunals these offer expertise from an employer's perspective (for example, from the Confederation of British Industry) and from an employee's perspective (for example, from a trade union or Trades Union Congress)). The tribunal does not provide a judgment but rather makes an award, and as the binding force of precedent moves downwards the tribunal is not bound by decisions made in other cases heard in tribunals, although they frequently look to such decisions when considering a case. If an appeal has to be made, then the case will progress to the High Court (although in employment matters this is to the Employment Appeals Tribunal). Appeals are established on the basis of a point of law, or that the tribunal came to a conclusion which no reasonable tribunal could have reached. This is a particularly difficult test to prove, and it operates on a similar basis to natural justice.

4.3.2 The advantages of the tribunal system

The following elements can be identified as the advantages that tribunals are supposed to have over courts:

- *Speed of cases:* Tribunals enable an effective balance to be established between the legality of the hearings and the formalities to which any 'real' hearing must adhere. To this effect, the chairperson of the tribunal is legally qualified and works within the rules established for each tribunal, and he/she has the ability to assist claimants in presenting their case if they attend unrepresented. The decisions of the tribunals are also provided more quickly than in the courts, with awards frequently being made within the day of the hearing.

- *Reduction in costs:* Tribunals were created to eliminate the necessity for legal representation, removing this very expensive aspect of the legal system. The less formalistic rules and procedures in tribunals removed the necessity for lawyers. Tribunals also do not

---

[27] Therefore, to avail him/herself of this opportunity the defendant must have pleaded not guilty and been tried and found guilty.

[28] Easier in respect of the appeal being allowed on the facts of the case or law. An appeal is allowed on more grounds than the civil law due to the fact that the individual's liberty is at stake.

[29] Note that from 1 December 2007, chairpersons of the Employment Tribunals are referred to as Employment Judges (Tribunals, Courts and Enforcement Act 2007, Sch. 8, para. 36).

always charge fees, unlike courts, and costs are not always awarded against the losing side (although Employment Tribunals have this discretion if they feel it appropriate).[30]

- *Expert knowledge in jurisdiction and locality*: Employment Tribunals were established to hear claims on disputes between employers and employees. They would therefore begin to establish a body of expertise in these specific areas and this would assist in deciding future cases more expeditiously. A further benefit would be that as tribunals were regionally based, they would be able to establish an understanding and expertise of practices in the local region.

- *Informality*: There are various tribunals, and each has its own jurisdiction and methods of work. However, they are generally less formal and therefore, it is hoped, less intimidating than courts.

- *Reducing the workload of courts*: As cases such as disputes in employment are heard by Employment Tribunals, the courts would be free to hear other claims with the perceived result that it would assist in speeding up the judicial system by reducing their workload.

- *Reasoned hearings*: Tribunals are presided by a legally qualified chairperson (e.g. an Employment Judge), and work within the rules established by law. Therefore, when decisions are made, these are based on the rule of law and the parties can have confidence that justice was seen to be done. There is also an appeals procedure.

4.3.3 **The disadvantages of tribunals**

Given the advantages identified for the adoption and justification of the tribunal system, the disadvantages and limitations to the system must be considered.

- *Increased formality*: Tribunals were designed to be informal systems. However, they have increasingly become legalistic and barristers have begun to specialize in certain jurisdictions (such as employment law). The increasing competence of tribunals in legal jurisdictions, and the technical rules governing claims and the formalities of procedure, have lessened this distinct advantage.

- *Limitation in legal assistance*: The term 'legal aid'[31] was replaced following the introduction of the Legal Services Commission, developed after the passing of the Access to Justice Act 1999. However, this assistance is not available for individuals in the presentation of claims at tribunal.

- *The complexity of the tribunal system*: The perception of the system of tribunals as being less formal and legalistic than courts is now increasingly unrealistic. Employment Tribunals are a very good example of this increasingly complexity. When they were first established (and known as industrial tribunals) their jurisdiction was unfair dismissal legislation. However, there are now well over 60 different jurisdictions.

- *No precedent in tribunals*: Tribunals are not bound by the decisions of other tribunals, and with reference to Employment Tribunals, as many of the decisions are determined with a strong emphasis on the facts of the case, then decisions can be made that appear to contradict cases with similar facts. This can be seen most clearly in Part V of this book.

---

[30] However, see the press release by Vince Cable regarding changes in the operation of procedures (including costs and fees) at Employment Tribunals on 14 September 2012 (http://www.bis.gov.uk/newsroom). Updates will be available on the Online Resource Centre.

[31] Now the Community Legal Service Fund.

4.3.4 Employment Tribunals

As Employment Tribunals,[32] above other tribunals, are likely to be of most interest to employers and businesses, they are selected for a brief description. These tribunals hear disputes between employers and employees/workers, and also claims based on EU laws.[33] Cases must be lodged on an approved form available from the Employment Tribunals Service (ETS), and once this has been accepted by the ETS (as being on the correct form, within the correct time limits and so on) the employer to whom the claim relates is provided with a response form that must be completed and returned within 28 days (unless an extension is requested and supported with reasons for the request). The Employment Judge determines whether the extension is to be granted, and also sends copies of the claim to the Advisory, Conciliation and Arbitration Service (ACAS), which will appoint a conciliator to attempt to get the parties to resolve their case without recourse to the tribunal.

The judge will decide whether they wish to convene a pre-hearing review, and this decision may be made if either party requests the hearing. Typically, such reviews are used to determine whether the claim should be struck out at that stage. They may be used to determine entitlements to initiate or defend the claim; and they may be used to consider whether a deposit should be paid where a case is particularly weak. If the case passes this pre-hearing, it continues on to the full hearing. Costs are not normally awarded in tribunal cases, however the judge has the option to award up to £10,000 against a party that was legally represented where his/her claim had no reasonable prospect of success, or he/she behaved unreasonably or was abusive/disruptive in the proceedings. Note that at the time of writing, the Government has announced that it intends to take forward 80 per cent of the proposals from Adrian Beecroft's 2012 report on employment law.[34] The major implications of the changes will mean the ability of Employment Judges to strike claims out at the pre-hearing review, and for an unfair dismissal claim to reach a hearing will require the claimant to deposit £1,200!

Before a case of unfair dismissal or a request to flexible working is heard at an Employment Tribunal, the parties are provided with an option to have the case referred to the ACAS Arbitration Scheme. This scheme is voluntary and increases the focus and advancement of alternative mechanisms of dispute resolution rather than traditional court/tribunal actions to resolve problems between parties.

4.4 Alternative Dispute Resolution

 Business Link

In England, the courts work in an adversarial system where one party brings an action against another party. Applied to business or employment scenarios, this may damage or even 'kill' the relationship with the effect that the business relationship ends (consider the 2012 court cases between Apple and Samsung). It may also lead to a negative

---

[32] Note that as of April 2012, in cases of unfair dismissal, judges may sit alone—without the use of the two wing members. See *McCafferty v Royal Mail Group Ltd* [2012] UKEATS/0002/12/BI and especially the comments by Lady Smith about the potential consequences of this change.

[33] *Impact v Minister for Agriculture and Food (Ireland)* [2008] EUECJ C-268/06.

[34] http://bis.gov.uk/assets/biscore/employment-matters/docs/a/12–830-adrian-beecroft-report-issues-government-is-considering.

view of the parties as being hostile, uncompromising, and litigious. Therefore, dispute resolution techniques may help to resolve differences without ending relationships; they are generally much quicker than court cases, and they may be less expensive than retaining solicitors and barristers.

This chapter has identified the courts and tribunals in the English legal system. The text also discusses the law and its application in jurisdictions including company, competition, contract, employment, and torts laws. This includes a description of the relevant statutes and a discussion of the cases heard before the courts and tribunals. The courts and tribunals are often the forums for disputes to be adjudicated, and they too have been subject to the need for more effective means of resolving disputes.[35] Further, other methods are being introduced that move away from the adversarial system of law that is necessary in the courts, to a more conciliatory means of dispute resolution.

4.4.1 **The need for Alternative Dispute Resolution**

ADR has several benefits for the parties, including some of the following features:

- *Cooperation v adversarial approaches:* Traditional court cases are based on an adversarial system where the parties attempt to 'win' rather than work cooperatively to establish a mutually acceptable resolution. For those in business, when such a system is applied internally (for example, between the directors of a firm, or between management and the staff), the ramifications for a dispute that leads to court action could ultimately result in the firm being dissolved, or its adverse effects may impact on employee relations affecting morale, productivity, sales, and outputs. In all situations it is likely to be discordant between members of the business. It is disruptive and can exacerbate relatively minor issues into much larger, and unnecessary, problems.

- *Speed of resolution:* ADR reduces the congestion of the courts by removing disputes between parties to be heard through mediation or arbitration.

- *Costs:* The rationale for a perception of cost-savings in ADR as opposed to legal action is that many initiatives are being established by the courts, businesses and organizations outside the court structure, that offer cost-effective, or free, services to the parties. Although for businesses a mediator or arbitrator may have to be paid to provide the ADR service, this is typically much cheaper than hiring a solicitor, or retaining legal counsel.

- *Expertise in resolution:* Disputes between businesses may involve a disagreement based on a technical difficulty or a dispute that requires expertise and knowledge of the industry and its practice. The courts do not always have this knowledge, but through ADR the dispute may be heard by an arbitrator with expertise in the industry, or who has specific knowledge of the area, and can facilitate a more speedy resolution.

- *Informality:* Even though lawyers may still be involved in the process, ADR is a more informal and less intimidating forum than the courts, and this encourages effective dispute resolution through a structured mechanism.

---

[35] This can be seen in the CPR introduced in April 1999, as part of the reforms identified by Lord Woolf in his report 'Access to Justice' in 1986. This noted the necessity for fair, speedy, and proportionate mechanisms to resolve disputes.

- *Compliance:* A legal judgment may be provided against the party having 'lost' a case, but actually enforcing the judgment may be more difficult.[36] There is a higher success rate of compliance with orders when ADR is used.

- *Privacy:* Whilst most court cases are available to the public to attend and can lead, in some cases, to high-profile judgments, ADR is more confidential and allows a level of privacy not readily available in court. For parties that would rather have disputes dealt with in a more discreet environment, ADR offers significant improvements over court action.

4.4.2 Disadvantages of ADR

There are several advantages to parties using ADR to resolve their disputes, but these are context-specific, and may not be advantageous in all circumstances. Further, it should not be underestimated that some claimants want 'their day in court' and do not want to mediate a resolution.

- *Legal protection:* The courts are based on specific rules outlined in legislation regarding the choice of judge and the powers of the court. These are general protections that are lost when ADR is chosen, and to ensure that it is a valid means of resolving disputes, the decisions made in ADR may be binding on the parties.

- *Duplication of fees:* It is possible that ADR cannot resolve the dispute between the parties. In this scenario, there will have been costs in the ADR process, and then legal fees will also have to be paid to resolve the dispute in the courts.

- *Legal expertise:* Whilst the mediators and arbitrators in ADR may be available to offer expertise in technical or industrial matters, they are not experts in law or legal procedures. Therefore, in the absence of judges hearing evidence, important points of law or statutory protections may be missed or not considered in the resolution process.

- *Lack of use:* In spite of the numerous advantages of ADR over the courts in resolving disputes, there is a proportionately low take-up rate.

- *Imbalance of power relations:* Mediation and negotiation may be successful if the parties are of even powers and may be able to negotiate on similar terms. However, in reality the parties do not have the same powers. For example, in employment disputes, frequently the employer will not mediate where they feel their position is strong, and individuals will often settle claims with a lesser settlement than may have been provided if the issue had gone to court/tribunal.

The use of ADR has to be carefully considered and its implications understood before it is used as a method for resolving disputes. It should not be viewed as a panacea for all dispute resolutions.

4.4.3 Dispute resolution in the courts

There had been a growing desire from within and outside the judiciary and legal professions to establish a means for disputes to adopt some of the principles of ADR. Following the Woolf

---

[36] For example, research published by the Ministry of Justice in May 2009 identified that 39 per cent of respondents had not received the compensation they had been awarded following successful employment dispute claims. Of those who had been paid, 27 per cent were being paid in instalments (Adams, L., Moore, A., Gore, K., and Browne, J. (2009) 'Research into Enforcement of Employment Tribunal Awards in England and Wales' Ministry of Justice, Research Series 9/09).

Report (1986), the emphasis was on settling disputes before they came before the courts. These are used more by parties involved in civil and family disputes, rather than between businesses, but they are still relevant to individuals' disputes (such as the sole trader and his/ her client, and consumers).

Under the CPR 1999, courts are required to undertake case management including 'encouraging the parties to use an alternative dispute resolution procedure if the court considers it appropriate and facilitating the use of such procedure'.[37] The courts are further empowered to stay (halt) the proceedings when the parties request or if the court identifies this as appropriate to enable a settlement through ADR.[38] The courts may also make an order for costs against a party that has failed to utilize ADR when this would have been appropriate[39] but the parties cannot be compelled to use ADR.[40]

4.4.4 Alternative forms of dispute resolution

There are many approaches to ADR including internal dispute resolution techniques, negotiations, the ombudsman scheme and so on. Internal techniques may not involve third parties, utilize any procedures for the use of arguments or evidence in the dispute, or indeed produce enforceable solutions. However, they are informal and may produce a mutually acceptable resolution. They are also being increasingly used in employment disputes to prevent resort to tribunal. The ombudsman scheme is used in banking, public services, and central and local government. The process for using ADR will begin with some form of negotiation then, unless there is an arbitration agreement in the contract (as often included in construction cases), the parties may attempt some form of mediation, and then possibly move towards conciliation and then arbitration in the event that the dispute cannot be resolved. This is a very broad topic and it is beyond the scope of this text to include all the facets of this form of dispute resolution; however, the most commonly used mechanisms include arbitration, mediation, and conciliation.

4.4.4.1 Arbitration

This is a voluntary system of ADR and involves the parties relying on the services of an arbitrator who is an independent, fair, and impartial third party,[41] and is often legally trained or is an expert in the subject matter of the dispute.[42] The arbitrator and his/her employees or agents, are immune from liability unless he/she can be shown to have acted in bad faith (or had failed to act at all).[43] The process has the benefit of privacy and the arbitrator will decide the case on the basis of the evidence, with the application of the law, and the decision is legally binding upon the parties. The Arbitration Act 1996 provides for the dispute to be resolved according to rules of procedure similar to those used in the High Court, and as such, due to the 'legal' nature of this method of ADR, it may not prove to be less expensive than traditional court action, particularly as 'legal aid' is unavailable in arbitration. Section 1 identifies that

---

[37] Rule 1.4(2)(e).   [38] Rule 26.4.   [39] Rule 44.5.

[40] *Halsey v Milton Keynes General NHS Trust* [2004] EWCA Civ 576, where the Court of Appeal held that to impose ADR could amount to a breach of Article 6 of the European Convention on Human Rights.

[41] Section 33(a) of the Arbitration Act 1996.

[42] A list of appropriate arbitrators is available from the Institute of Arbitration.

[43] Section 29 of the Arbitration Act 1996.

the objective of arbitration is to produce a fair resolution of disputes by an independent tribunal without unnecessary delay or expense; and that the parties should be free to agree how their disputes are resolved.

Arbitration may be selected as a means of dispute resolution by the parties, the parties may be referred to it by the court, or an Act of Parliament may require it. The parties may apply to the court hearing the case to stay the proceedings if the matter involves an aspect of the dispute that they had agreed to be dealt with under arbitration.[44] Arbitration may also involve the entire case, or it may be selected as appropriate for one aspect of the dispute. As such, it has flexibility in approach. When it is selected, the parties should do everything in their power to ensure compliance with procedural and evidential matters, and to limit any delays in the proceedings.[45] The arbitrator provides his/her decision (an award) and this is binding on the parties, although an appeal process exists (to, and with the permission of the High Court) on a point of law, or with the permission of each party. Such appeals are, however, not commonplace. Whilst the hearings under arbitration are conducted in a judicial manner and are subject to the rules of natural justice, they have the benefit of being private and hence in business, a firm's actions, or its contractual dealings, financial records and so on, are not subject to public scrutiny.

4.4.4.2 *Mediation*

Mediation may be 'evaluative' (where an assessment is made of the 'legal' issues of the subject forming the dispute) or it can involve a 'facilitative approach' (where the emphasis is on assisting the parties to resolve their differences in a mutually acceptable way). The parties appoint the mediator (as opposed to an independent body as is the case with arbitration or litigation) and where the process is successful in establishing a resolution, this may form the basis of a legally binding agreement between the parties, unless there is a provision between the parties that such agreements are not to be binding. The mediator will establish a set of 'ground rules' by which the dispute will be assessed, and he/she will gather information from each of the parties. This is where a specific concern of mediation has been identified. The gathering, and sharing, of information may be undertaken not to reach a settlement or compromise, but may rather be used surreptitiously to obtain information regarding the strength or weaknesses of the other party's claim. This form of ADR is a significant mechanism in attempting to resolve disputes and indeed is a feature considered by the European Union in a Directive transposed into domestic legislation on 20 May 2011.[46]

4.4.4.3 *Conciliation*

This process is somewhat similar to mediation, and indeed is often considered to be interchangeable with mediation. However, the conciliator adopts a more proactive role. His/her role is to offer solutions and identify strategies for the successful resolution of the dispute. A very common example of the use of conciliation is in employment disputes, where ACAS intervenes with the parties to reach a settlement without recourse to the Employment Tribunal. The conciliation officer speaks with the parties and identifies their concerns, sharing evidence and identifying the likely success of any claims. This raises similar concerns regarding the use of this information as in mediation (see **4.4.4.2**).

---

[44] Section 9.   [45] Section 44.

[46] Proposal for a Directive of the European Parliament and of the Council on Certain Aspects of Mediation in Civil and Commercial Matters (COM(2004) 718 Final)—(The Cross-Border Mediation (EU Directive) Regulations 2011, SI 1133/2011).

Conclusion

The chapter has identified the courts and their hierarchy in the civil and criminal jurisdictions, the judges who sit in the various courts and their authority, and the forms of ADR available to the parties and how they may facilitate more effective dispute resolution. This chapter has concluded the specific examination of the English legal system, although the following two chapters consider the impact and effect of the UK's membership of the EU on the constitution, individuals, and businesses. This is of supreme importance to an understanding of the legal system, and has many practical implications for businesses that must be understood.

 Summary of main points

The court system/tribunals

- The courts in the civil jurisdiction administer justice and seek to resolve disputes between parties.
- The courts in the criminal jurisdiction administer justice and consider charges made by the State against a defendant for breaches of the law (although some have civil functions).
- Whilst some courts have a dual role of hearing criminal and civil cases in their different divisions, there are courts that deal predominately with either civil disputes or criminal matters.
- The courts exist on a hierarchical basis, with the Supreme Court holding the position as being the 'highest' court in the country. This has implications for the system of precedent in case law/common law.
- The Supreme Court and Court of Appeal are singularly appellate courts, with the other courts hearing cases and providing judgments on the facts of a case.
- Tribunals specialize in many areas of law including immigration, employment, data protection and so on.
- There are many perceived advantages to tribunals over the traditional court structure, including the speed at which cases are heard and resolved, a reduction in costs, expertise in the nature of the claim, and increased informality. They also reduce the workload of the courts.
- The disadvantages to the tribunal system include: the increasing use of law and formal procedures so that tribunals may be more akin to specialist courts; limitation in the availability of free legal assistance; the procedures in tribunals being increasingly complex; and there being no system of precedent in the tribunals (although precedent established in higher courts is applicable to tribunals).

The judiciary

- Judges and lay people play a significant role in the administration of justice, and there exists a hierarchy of judges, with the most senior having positions of heads of offices and/or sitting in the Supreme Court and Court of Appeal.
- The Government attempted to make the appointment of the judiciary more transparent through the creation of the Judicial Appointments Commission.

Assigning the case to a track

- The civil law cases are assigned to a 'track' depending upon the wishes of the parties and the views of the judge; the value of the claim; issues of privacy; and the time assessed for disposal of the case.

- The courts expect the parties to have considered the use of ADR rather than simply having decided to take their dispute to court. Any party having unreasonably refused to consider this may have to pay costs.

Alternative Dispute Resolution (ADR)

- ADR is a mechanism increasingly used in the court process to avoid courts having to resolve disputes that could be dispensed with in some other manner.

- It focuses on cooperation rather than the adversarial approach adopted in court cases, and can, in some cases, reduce costs and speed up the resolution of disputes.

- It does have disadvantages, including the possible duplication of fees if the ADR process does not resolve the dispute, and the legal protection afforded by the court process may be lost.

- The forms of dispute resolution include arbitration, mediation, and conciliation.

 Summary questions

Essay questions

1. 'Courts are intimidating, daunting and expensive ways of resolving disputes.'
   Critically assess the above statement with specific reference to the benefits provided by tribunals in the administration of justice.

2. 'There are various ways of looking at (the Supreme Court): as a change of place and name which was of major constitutional importance; as an interesting social experiment, which left it to the Justices to create a new set of rules and conventions to replace those that regulated their conduct in the House of Lords; as an ill-judged political exercise, which has cost a great deal of money and exposed the Court to pressures on its budget imposed by the Executive which the Lords of Appeal in Ordinary never encountered while they were in Parliament.'   Lord Hope, *Barnard's Inn Reading*, 24 June 2010.
   Critically assess the above statement. Specifically comment on the rationale for the development of the Supreme Court and the perceived advantages its introduction will have over the judicial branch of the House of Lords.

Problem questions

1. Janet was recently shopping in a retail outlet of All Bright Consumables (ABC) Ltd. She asked the sales assistant to recommend a Personal Computer (PC) for her to purchase having given him the information he asked for. Janet was very clear that whilst she had little experience of computing, she required a computer to surf the internet, run word processing, and have a camera for video chats. Finally, for entertainment she wanted to make sure it had a blu-ray disc player and she had been told to ensure it had at least

4gb of RAM. Having received this information, the sales assistant obtained a PC from the store from and Janet purchased it.

When Janet's friend set up the computer at home, Janet was informed that the computer actually only had 2gb RAM, it had a DVD disc player not the blu-ray as requested, and it did not have a video camera. Janet immediately returned to the store to complain and asked for a refund. The store manager refused as he said as soon as the PC was opened there could be no returns unless the PC was faulty (which it was not), and he did not believe that the sales assistant would get her order wrong. Rather, the manager suggests Janet was not clear about her requirements and could not obtain a refund just because she 'had second-thoughts' about the purchase.

Using your knowledge of the court system, explain to Janet which court(s) would hear any claim she made for a refund. Explain to her the tracking system used and how this would impact on her legal action for compensation.

2. ABC Ltd has experienced the following problem with one of its major customers and requires appropriate advice to ensure an effective resolution. ABC has a significant corporate customer, BigByte Ltd, which regularly places very large orders for PC components. However, while ABC provides BigByte with a standard trade credit period of 'full payment within 30 days' BigByte has got into the habit of paying late (sometimes as late as 90 days). ABC's concern is that if other trade customers get to know that they are relaxed about enforcing payment according to the terms of its trade credit agreement, the other customers may ask for similar extended credit periods. ABC has considered increasing the price of goods sold to BigByte so as to 'charge' the company for the additional credit but fear that any increase in price will merely result in this valued customer going elsewhere.

Advise ABC about alternative forms of dispute resolution (ADR) that could be used to resolve this situation. Specifically identify the advantages ADR may provide compared with traditional court action in relation to business relationships.

 Further reading

Brown, H. and Marriott, A. (1999) 'ADR: Principles and Practice' (2nd Edition) Sweet and Maxwell, London.

Goldsmith, J.C., Ingen-Housz, A., and **Pointon, G.** (2006) 'ADR in Business: Practice and Issues Across Countries and Cultures' Aspen Publishing: New York.

Oliver, D. (2003) 'Constitutional Reform in the United Kingdom' Oxford University Press: Oxford.

 Useful websites

http://www.cedr.com/
(The Centre for Effective Dispute Resolution, a non-profit organization that manages and facilitates dispute resolution services.)

http://www.judiciary.gov.uk/
The official website of the judiciary of England and Wales. It contains statistics, details of the roles of different judges, and various speeches given by higher members of the judiciary.

http://www.justice.gov.uk/tribunals/employment
(Details the Tribunal Service that provides information, assistance, and on-line claims forms for
employment actions.)

http://www.justice.gov.uk/tribunals/employment-appeals
(Details the cases heard by the Employment Appeal Tribunal, the grounds on which appeals may
be made, and various publications and reports.)

http://www.legalservices.gov.uk/civil.asp/
(Information from the Community Legal Service on topics such as ADR, human rights and so on.)

http://www.legislation.gov.uk/
(This is the official list of statutes in force. The site is particularly valuable as it clearly indicates
where the legislation is no longer in force or has been superseded through amendments or a
more recent piece of legislation, and it shows where forthcoming changes (not yet in force) will
affect the law being searched.)

http://privycouncil.independent.gov.uk/
(The website of the Privy Council—it contains information of both the judicial and legislative
branches of the Council.)

http://www.supremecourt.gov.uk/
(The judgments from the Supreme Court available from July 2009).

http://www.tribunals-review.org.uk
(Leggatt Report 'Report of the Review of Tribunals').

 Online Resource Centre

http://www.oxfordtextbooks.co.uk/orc/marson3e/
Why not visit the Online Resource Centre and try multiple choice questions associated with this
chapter to test your understanding of the topic. You will also find relevant updates to the law.

II Law of the European Union

5

History, Institutions, Sources of Law, and the Impact on the UK

Why does it matter?

The European Union (EU) affects the United Kingdom (UK) in many ways and a lack of awareness of EU law will have a profound and negative impact on any understanding of the English legal system. Following accession in 1973 Parliament has 'surrendered' some of its sovereignty to the EU in its ability to pass legislation. Further, the judges in the UK are obliged to follow EU law and in cases of ambiguity, to consistently interpret English law to give effect to EU law. Whilst its impact may not be readily observed, the EU has created laws in contract, is a major factor in the instigation of many employment rights, and is responsible for past and forthcoming changes in the area of company law. If a business is aware of the sources of EU law, and is aware of future laws through Treaties, Regulations, and Directives, it can be better prepared for changes and move proactively, perhaps before rivals, and hence gain a competitive advantage.

Learning outcomes

Following reading this chapter you should be in a position to:
- identify what the EU is (5.1–5.3)
- explain the UK's accession to the EU (5.2)
- understand the evolution of the treaties—from European Economic Community (EEC) to EU (5.2.1)
- explain the roles of the main institutions of the EU (5.4–5.4.5)
- identify the sources of EU laws (5.5–5.5.3).
- identify the key areas where the EU has affected English law (5.6–5.6.3.1)

⚷ Key terms

These terms will be used in the chapter and it may be helpful to be aware of what they mean or refer back to them when reading through the chapter.

Citizenship
This was created in the Treaty of Maastricht (Article 17(1) EC—now Art. 20 of the Treaty on the Functioning of the European Union (TFEU)) and provided citizenship of the EU

for the nationals in the Member States. Citizenship of the EU was to complement rather than replace the nationality that individuals retain from their own State.

Direct applicability

Direct applicability is a term which means the EU law is capable of application through the domestic courts in the Member State without any further action required by the State (for example, a Treaty Article may be used directly in the courts in the UK).

Member State

Member State refers to a country that has joined the EU and is therefore a Member of the Union.

Transposition

EU Directives establish laws that the **Member State** must put into effect in its own legal system. Member States may choose the manner and form which this takes but they must have an Act, regulation, or administrative order in place to which individuals in the Member State will have access. For example, provisions of the Working Time Directive were transposed into English law through the Working Time Regulations 1998.

Treaty

This is an international agreement binding the signatory States.

5.1 Introduction

Any study of the EU is potentially complex and can often lead to the reader being dissuaded from giving the topic the attention it requires, or simply considering it a subject they will 'opt out' of. This is a mistake, as EU law, whilst of course in reality is very complicated,[1] as a topic is potentially interesting and, if not studied or understood, will leave a gap in your learning and understanding of English law. EU law affects the way Parliament creates laws, how judges interpret and apply the law, and it provides rights and creates obligations on citizens to follow EU laws. It directly affects the laws in company law, contract law, the English legal system, and employment law that are identified in this text and is therefore vital to your understanding. This chapter identifies the historical development of the EU and the main sources of law, along with the institutions of the EU and the role each plays in the development of the Union.

5.2 The UK's accession to the Treaty

The UK's application to join the European Economic Community (EEC) was accepted on 22 January 1972, when the Government signed the Treaty of Accession in Brussels. As a consequence of this action the UK was subject to an additional source of law. The EU has produced laws and obligations on the UK[2] and these have further been applied to the citizens in the

---

[1] For readers who would like to engage more with the subject, the leading text in the area, which is unsurpassed in depth and quality of writing and content, is Craig, P. and De Burca, G. (2007) 'EU Law: Text, Cases and Materials' (4th Edition) Oxford University Press: Oxford.

[2] Indeed, due to the significance of the obligations to which the UK would be subject, and the binding of successive governments, which was contrary to the constitution, a challenge was made on the legality of the government's ability to agree to such a treaty. This implication on the sovereignty of Parliament was at the heart of this case. See *Blackburn v A-G* [1971] 2 All ER 1380.

Member States. The UK gave effect to the laws of the EU through the European Communities Act 1972 (ECA). The ECA changed the traditional view of the UK's dualist constitution by placing obligations on the individuals within the State, in addition to the obligations on the State itself. This was due to the 'new legal order' that the EU had created, and the supremacy of Parliament was surrendered to an extent through s. 2 of the ECA. Section 2(1) is important in that it provides that EU law which is intended to take direct effect within Member States (for example, the Treaty Articles and Regulations) *will automatically form part of the law in the UK* and must be given such effect by the judiciary. Under s. 2(2), EU legislation that requires implementation by the Member States (for example, Directives) must also be given effect. Further, s. 2 has great significance as to why EU law is an area of law which *must* be appreciated, as it is Parliament's instruction to the judiciary on the matter of supremacy. The European Communities Act instructs the judiciary to follow EU law even if it contradicts domestic law and if there is any doubt regarding the extent of the EU law or provision, the matter should be referred to the Court of Justice for clarification.[3]

Following the UK's accession to the EEC in 1973 it has been obliged to follow the laws common to that international **Treaty** and the evolution from EEC through the European Community (EC) to the EU has also witnessed an increased awareness of the need for a community-wide approach to the enforcement of rights (see Chapter 6 for a discussion of enforcement mechanisms).

5.2.1 Development of the Community–from the EEC to the EU

The Community began with the European Coal and Steel Community and European Atomic Energy Community, which led to the EEC. This Community had as its aim an economic agreement between the States which would aid trade and make the movement of goods, services, and persons easier (through common rules) rather than the individual domestic rules applicable to each State before the commencement of the Treaty. The EEC was established in 1957 but relatively little had been developed since its inception, and many of the aims of the original Treaty had not been achieved. There was also increased pressure for the EEC to retaliate to the increasing competition from America and the Far East. In light of these concerns the next agreement in the development of the EEC was the **Single European Act** 1986 (SEA), which extended the powers and competences of the Community—specifically in the areas of economic and monetary policy. The aims of the Community were also widened to include social policy initiatives. It was this issue that began the development to a treaty which went beyond an economic community and towards a union of States. By 1993 there was to be the completion of the internal market, which led to the removal of domestic restrictions to the free movement of goods.

With the impetus created from the SEA, the Community wished to continue this momentum with the **Maastricht Treaty** 1992 and changed the EEC to become the EU. The Treaty set out the timetable for economic and monetary union and established the single currency (the Euro) that extended the Community beyond the 'economic' treaty of the EEC. The Maastricht Treaty is known as the 'Treaty on European Union' and established elements which were to affect the Member States' constitutions: human rights, subsidiarity, and citizenship. **Citizenship** was very important as it made every individual from the Member States a citizen

Single
European
Act 1986

Maastricht
Treaty 1992

---

[3] See *R v Secretary of State of Transport ex parte Factortame Ltd* [1989] 2 All ER 692.

of the Community—resulting in equal rights to be granted to those people throughout the Community, civil rights,[4] and rights to participate in the political affairs of the Union.[5]

The **Treaty of Amsterdam** 1997 intended to prepare for further expansion of the membership of the EU—particularly including States from both Eastern and Central Europe. There was an emphasis on social policy issues[6] and on making the EU (as it now is) more relevant and visible to citizens. This Treaty also led to the renumbering of many of the Articles and hence caution should be exercised when referring to older texts that may have reference to the previous numbering system. The **Treaty of Nice** 2001 (in force since 2003) provided greater weighting of votes to the larger Member States (the UK, Germany, France, Italy, and Spain); it capped the enlargement of the EU to 27 Member States; and increased the size of the EU Parliament (see **Section 5.4.3**).

A **Constitution** for the European Union was agreed in Brussels on 18 June 2004. However, it was rejected by two States and by the citizens in States where referenda were held.[7] In July 2007, the **EU Reform Treaty** was announced at the **Treaty of Lisbon** which, substantially similar to the Constitutional Treaty, was an attempt to revive the constitution. On 13 December 2007 the leaders of the EU signed the treaty and this amends, but does not replace, the current treaties. The treaty was considered necessary as the current rules were designed for the EU with 15 Member States and reform was required to ensure effective decision-making was possible and the infrastructure remained relevant to achieving the EU's aims. As a consequence, there are internal changes to ensure the EU can continue to establish the laws regulating the States and those persons and organizations within them, but the treaty also established more strategies and broad policies. These have included: measures to combat climate change; freedoms, justice and security in relation to criminal gangs and terrorism (among others); and the establishment of a common immigration policy.

The Treaty of Lisbon entered into force on 1 December 2009 (Art. 6). Its aim is to ensure the EU can meet future challenges through an improved legal framework and further, enable it to respond to citizens' demands. Increased transparency is a key aim of the Treaty and it seeks to give citizens a better and more clear understanding of who has responsibilities in the EU and why the EU is taking action. It made changes to the numbering of the Treaty Articles and also some of the terminology used. Both of these are reflected in Part II of the book and can be seen by reference to the new Treaty–the Treaty on the Functioning of the European Union (TFEU).

In achieving this second aim, the Treaty intends to better promote the interests of citizens on a day-to-day basis by making its decision-making process more efficient; increasing democracy through a greater role for the EU Parliament and domestic parliaments; and providing an increased coherence externally. A further development (to be outlined through future legislation) is the creation of the European Citizens' Initiative.[8] This will enable citizens of the EU (if supported by at least one million citizens from a minimum of seven Member States) to take the initiative of inviting the Commission to submit any appropriate proposal on matters which the citizens consider are required for implementing the Treaty (and of

Treaty of Amsterdam 1997

Treaty of Nice 2001

Treaty of Lisbon 2009

4 Article 20 EC (now Art. 23 TFEU).

5 See Kostakopoulou, T. (2005) 'Ideas, Norms and European Citizenship: Explaining Institutional Change' Vol. 68, *Modern Law Review*, p. 233.

6 Elements created or extended through the Treaty included respect for human rights and sanctions against a Member State found in breach of this provision. There were further rights to eliminate discrimination based on a person's sex, race, religion or religious belief, disability, sexual orientation, and age.

7 France rejected the Constitution on 29 May 2005 (by almost 55 per cent) and the Netherlands rejected it on 1 June 2005 (by almost 62 per cent).

8 http://ec.europa.eu/citizens-initiative/public/welcome.

course where the EU has competence). Once the required criteria are met,[9] the Commission has three months to investigate and decide to pursue legislation; launch a study of the issue; or forgo on further action.

Some of the changes introduced by the Treaty include:

- Strengthening the role of the EU Parliament by providing increased powers over EU legislation, the EU budget, and international agreements (through the co-decision procedure, the Parliament will be placed on an equal footing with the Council for the bulk of EU legislation).

- The system of subsidiarity (where the EU only acts where it is necessary and decisions are made as close to the EU citizens as possible) enhances democracy by providing greater involvement of domestic parliaments (acting as watchdogs) in the work of the EU. Hence, where a parliament believes a measure is better served through national, regional or local action, it may make such a pronouncement at an early stage before the proposal is considered by the European Parliament or the Council.

- The treaty simplifies the voting rules for the 27 Member States to make more effective and efficient decision-making possible. There is greater use of qualified majority voting (QMV) rather than unanimity. This will be a significant change, as the decision-making in the Council will be based on a double-majority system. Decisions of the Council will require the support of 55 per cent of the Member States (15 out of the 27 States), representing a minimum of 65 per cent of the population of the EU. Further, those Member States that wish to block a proposed decision will require the 'blocking minority' to comprise at least four Member States. This system will begin in 2014 and be fully effective for all measures after 2017. Note however that politically sensitive areas such as tax, foreign policy, defence, and social security continue to require unanimity.

- A President of the European Council is elected for a period of two-and-a-half years (renewable for a term of five years). This provides a more stable and streamlined institutional framework.

- A Commission President introduces a direct link between the election of the Commission President and the results of the European elections.

- The EU's presence in, and interaction with, the rest of the world is extended through a new High Representative for the Union in Foreign Affairs and Security Policy/Vice-President of the Commission (combining the current positions).

5.3 Aims of the EEC

The aims of the original Treaty provided:

> By establishing a common market (now replaced as 'internal market' following the Treaty of Lisbon) and progressively approximating the economic policies of Member States, to promote throughout the Community a harmonious development of economic activities, a continuous and balanced expansion, an increase in stability, an accelerated raising of the standard of living and closer relations between the States belonging to it.

---

[9] These include that the signatures from each country must be proportionate to its size. Hence in the UK, 54,750 signatories are required, whilst in Malta, 4,500 are required.

In order to achieve these goals, a customs union was created where the customs duties and equivalences of the Member States would be harmonized under European law to facilitate the Internal Market. Secondly, this Internal Market was extended to include free movements of goods, services, capital, and workers. The third element was an effective competition policy to ensure companies, markets, and cartels could not restrict the functioning of the Internal Market. These broad aims were established in the treaty (and have been reviewed and extended in the subsequent treaties) and were given ever greater effect and definition through judgments of the Court of Justice of the European Union (Court of Justice) and the EU's secondary laws.

With regard to the free movement of goods, the main provisions of this source of law are contained in Arts. 28 (now Art. 34 TFEU), 29 (now Art. 35 TFEU), and 30 EC (now Art. 36 TFEU) concerning the abolition of quantitative restrictions, and all measures having an equivalent effect, on imports and exports (albeit with derogations permissible). It should also be noted that the Court of Justice has held Arts. 28 and 29 EC (now Arts. 34 and 35 TFEU) to be directly effective.[10] A quantitative restriction may include a ban or quota on goods, or any measure that amounts to a 'total or partial restraint on imports … or goods in transit'.[11] The term 'goods' in the legislation is widely defined to include items of economic value such as food, clothing, and vehicles, but has also been extended to utilities such as gas[12] and electricity.[13] The free movement in this respect deals with actions taken at a State level[14] to restrict the movement rather than private entities refusing to buy or stock EU-based products. With regard to the action taken by the State to ensure quantitative restrictions are prohibited, a proactive rather than a passive approach must be adopted. In *Commission v France*[15] the French authorities had failed to take action against its citizens who impeded the importation of goods by destroying the lorries containing goods and threatening the supermarkets that were taking the imported goods. The Court of Justice held that France was in breach of Article 28 EC (now Art. 34 TFEU) due to its lack of action when aware of these activities.

A measure having an effect equivalent to a quantitative restriction is not defined in the treaty, but from the case law of the Court of Justice, this may include requiring an importer to possess a licence or permit,[16] or certificate of origin;[17] requiring goods to be stored in the Member State for a fixed period before being allowed to be sold (and is not applicable to domestic products);[18] and to fixed national price controls on goods.[19] These are merely a few examples, but they should serve the purpose of demonstrating the regulation of anti-competitive behaviour by Member States.

The free movement of workers (extended to self-employed persons) was a fundamental requirement of the common market to ensure that one of the key aspects to free up the factors of production, along with goods, services, and capital, was achieved. However, the EU did not see the worker as a mere source of labour[20] or to be regarded as a commodity[21] but rather as a human being with the fundamental rights of the worker having precedence over the requirements of the Member States' economies. Whilst supplemented through Regulations[22] and

---

[10] *Iannelli v Meroni* (Case 74/76) [1977] ECR 557.   [11] *Geddo* (Case 2/73) [1973] ECR 865.

[12] *Comm v France* (Case C-159/94) [1997] ECR I-5815.

[13] *Almelo v Energiebedrijf Ijsselmij* (Case C-393/92) [1994] ECR I-1477.

[14] The State is broadly interpreted to include central and local government, and administrative and judicial bodies.

[15] (Case C-265/95) [1995] ECR I-6959.   [16] *Dankavit* (Case 251/78) [1979] ECR 3369.

[17] *Commission v Ireland (Irish Souvenirs)* (Case 113/80) [1981] ECR 1625.

[18] *Eggers Sohn & Co v Freie Hansestadt Bremen* (Case 13/78) [1978] ECR 1935.

[19] *Tasca* (Case 65/75) [1976] ECR 291.   [20] *Mr and Mrs F v Belgium*, (Case 7/75) [1975] ECR 679.

[21] *Bettray v Staatsecretaris van Justitie* (Case 344/87) [1989] ECR 1621.

[22] Such as Regulation 1612/68 on the right to equal treatment in respect of job opportunities and conditions of employment (superseded through Directive 2004/38/EC on the Right of Citizens of the Union and their Family Members to Move and Reside Freely within the Territory of the Member States).

Directives,[23] the main provision for this fundamental freedom derives from Arts. 39–42 EC (now Arts. 45–48 TFEU). Article 39 EC (now Art. 45 TFEU) is directly effective and seeks to abolish any discrimination based on the nationality of workers as regards employment, remuneration, and other conditions of work (subject to the derogations of public policy,[24] public security,[25] or public health). This gives the person the right to move freely within the territory of the Member States to take up work or search for work;[26] reside in the State (according to domestic laws) and to remain in the State following employment. A worker is someone who works for another (and the definition of the worker is subject to EU interpretation rather than that of a Member State),[27] and can include a part-time worker, and a person who requires the use of his/her own savings (or State assistance)[28] to supplement his/her remuneration if it is below the State minimum subsistence level. The requirement is that it is genuine and effective work,[29] rather than being made for the purposes of the person taking up the work,[30] and the motives of the worker are irrelevant in his/her decision to be a worker.[31] The rights of workers are provided to citizens of the EU (in each of the 27 Member States) and once established as a worker, he/she is entitled to the same tax and social advantages as provided to citizens in the State,[32] such as the same grants to students regardless of whether he/she is a domestic national or EU national.[33]

5.4 Institutions of the EU

 Business Link

The EU has various institutions where decisions are made, laws are created, the citizens of the Member States can be represented, the laws enforced, and sanctions levied. The main institutions are the Parliament; the Commission; the Council, and the Court of Justice. Being aware of these institutions and their role allows citizens (businesses or workers) in the Member States to have greater interaction with the EU, to lobby their Member of the European Parliament, and know where to complain if concerned with any issue of EU law.

5.4.1 The EU Commission

The Commission has had many roles in the EU but its main functions are to initiate legislation (working with the Council and the Parliament) and to enforce the laws of the EU. To achieve

23   For example, Council Directive 68/360 on the abolition of restrictions on movement and residence for workers of the Member States and their families.

24   *Van Duyn v Home Office* (Case 41/74) [1974] ECR 1.

25   *R v Bouchereau* (Case 30/77) [1977] ECR 1999.

26   *R v Immigration Appeal Tribunal, ex parte Antonissen* (Case C-292/89) [1991] 2 CMLR 373.

27   *Lawrie-Blum v Land Baden-Wurttemberg* (C66/85) [1986] ECR 2121.

28   *Kempf v Staatssecretaris van Justitie* (Case 139/85) [1987] 1 CMLR 764.

29   *Steymann v Staatssecretaris van Justitie* (Case 196/87) [1988] ECR 6159.   30   *Bettray.*

31   *Levin v Staatssecretaris van Justitie* (Case 53/81) [1982] ECR 1035.

32   *Fiorini v SNCF* (Case 32/75) [1975] ECR 1085.

33   *Grzelczyk v Centre Public d'Aide Sociale d'Ottignies Louvain la Neuve* (C184/99) [2001] ECR I-6193.

these it is divided into 44 Directorates-General and services. It has a right of initiative in the legislative process (to propose legislation for the Council and Parliament to pass). It is also known by its title of 'Guardian of the Treaty' where it ensures that the Member States comply with their EU obligations—laws from the Treaty, Regulations, Directives, and Decisions. The Commissioners are selected by their Member States and those Commissioners meet at least once per week (in Brussels or in Strasbourg when the Parliament holds its plenary sessions), although these meetings are not held in public. At present each Member State supplies one Commissioner.

5.4.1.1 *Legislator*

The Commission is empowered to take any legislative initiative it considers appropriate to attain the objectives of the Treaty. However, as a general rule it takes its initiatives from the Parliament and Council, from Member States, or from various other interested parties (such as pressure groups). It does so by consulting widely with all interested parties; it makes its decisions for the good of the EU (rather than for one Member State); and it assesses a proposal on the basis of its economic, environmental, and social impact. Such impacts are made available to the public, along with the proposal, to increase the transparency of the legislative procedure. In the Commission's legislative process the draft legislation is prepared following consultation with all the interested groups and Member States. Most frequently the co-decision procedure is used with the Commission's formal proposal being examined by the Parliament and Council. The legislation is adopted and then applied to the Member States.

5.4.1.2 *The Guardian of the Treaty*

The EU required an institution to ensure that each of the Member States followed the laws (and their obligations) of the EU. The Member States wanted to join the EU because of the financial and economic benefits which membership provided, but sometimes did not want to follow certain obligations or failed to transpose the laws correctly (as required in the case of Directives). If some Member States followed the laws and others did not, the Member States who had abided by the EU laws might be at a competitive disadvantage. To ensure that all Member States followed the law correctly, the Commission was given powers of enforcement under Articles 258 and 259 TFEU.[34]

5.4.2 **The Council of the European Union**

The Council is one of the most powerful of the EU institutions and it is the main decision-making body in the EU. Its meetings are attended by the Ministers from the Member States and the EU Commissioners responsible for those areas. The Minister who attends is usually the Foreign Minister of the Member State, but as the Council is not a fixed body, the relevant Minister for whichever subject is being discussed will attend. The Council's role includes concluding agreements with foreign States, taking general policy decisions, and taking decisions based on the Commission's proposals. The Council meets in Brussels and Luxembourg and decisions are made by votes of the Ministers from the Member States. The method of voting depends upon the Treaty and the provisions laid down for dealing with the subject being voted on. These methods are: a simple majority;[35] a qualified majority;[36] and unanimity.

---

[34] Enforcement of EU law is considered in Chapter 6.   [35] Used for procedural decisions.
[36] This is a weighted voting system with a greater proportion of votes being attributed to the larger Member States and is used for matters concerning the internal market and trade. For example, Germany, the UK, France, and Italy have 29 votes each—which is the highest number of votes, and Malta has only 3 votes—the lowest. There are 345 votes in total, and a qualified majority takes effect at 258 out of 345 votes (74.8 per cent).

Each Member State takes the Presidency of the Council on a rotation basis for a six-month term (January–June; and July–December). During this Presidency the Member State provides a President who chairs the meetings of the Council, calls for votes, and signs the Acts adopted at the meetings. This Presidency also allows the Member State to control the political agenda of the Council and it will attempt to pass through as many measures as it can. The Council meets to decide on the future of the EU and is often represented by the leading Ministers of the Member States—typically the Prime Minister and Chancellor (or their counterparts in other Member States).

As the membership of the Council comprises Ministers who have full-time responsibilities in their own Member State, they are consequently in Brussels for a relatively short period of time. To ensure the continuity of the Council's work, this role is coordinated by a Permanent Representatives Committee (COREPER—Art. 240 TFEU), which is composed of permanent representatives of the Member States.

5.4.3 The European Parliament

The European Union has approximately 500 million citizens and these people, from each of the 27 Member States, have the ability to elect representatives to the European Parliament. The Parliament is elected every five years and its role is to contribute to the drafting of legislation which affects the Member States through Directives and Regulations.

5.4.3.1 *The President of the Parliament*

The President is elected for a renewable term of two-and-a-half years and the role is to represent the Parliament to the outside world. The President ensures the Rules of Procedure are complied with, is the representative in legal affairs affecting the EU, and delivers opinions on all important international issues. After agreement, the President signs and consequently makes the EU budget operational, and the President, along with the President of the Council, sign all the legislative acts agreed under co-decision. In these roles, the President is assisted by 14 Vice-Presidents.

5.4.3.2 *Members of the Parliament*

There are 754 elected Members of the European Parliament (MEP) and every Member State decides on how its elections will be held. There are common rules which must be followed—the voting age is 18 and there must be a secret ballot. The seats of the Parliament (for the 2009–2014 term) are shared out proportionately between the populations of the State (the maximum number of seats for any one State is 99 (Germany) and the minimum is six (Malta)). The MEPs are expected to exercise their mandate independent of their Member State and are grouped by their political affinity (in one of seven[37] Europe-wide political groups) rather than by their nationality. They divide their time between Brussels (Belgium), Luxembourg and Strasbourg (France) in addition to their home constituencies, attending parliamentary committees and plenary sittings.

5.4.3.3 *Legislative role*

The Commission is the only body which is empowered to initiate legislation. It creates a legislative text, and an MEP, whilst working in one of the parliamentary committees, drafts a report which the committee votes on and can amend. The revised text may then be adopted

---

[37] Not including the 'non-attached' group of MEPs.

and agreement can be made with the Council about the legislation and its subsequent implementation.

There are two forms of legislative procedure, depending upon the law to be passed. The ordinary process is called 'co-decision' and puts the Parliament on an equal footing with the Council in areas including transport and the environment. The second is a special legislative procedure where the Parliament only possesses a consultative role (for example in agriculture, visas, and immigration). The Parliament can present legislative proposals to the Council which may then become laws in the EU.

5.4.4 The Court of Justice

The Court of Justice is the body that considers the interpretation and application of EU law. It also has the role of enforcing the EU's laws. It is composed of 27 judges (each one selected from the Member States) assisted by eight Advocates-General who hold office for a renewable term of six years. The judges and Advocates-General are selected from legal experts in the Member States whose independence is beyond doubt and who hold qualifications required for the highest judicial offices in that State. The judges then select one judge to be President of the Court (for a renewable term of three years). Among the roles performed by the President is directing the work of the Court and presiding at hearings of significant importance. The Advocates-General assist the Court by delivering opinions in all cases which are then deliberated by the Court of Justice and can be followed or rejected. They frequently offer background information on the case and deliver opinions (often) in a more accessible and approachable way than the full Court.

The Court may sit as a full Court,[38] a Grand Chamber (of 13 judges in very important cases), or in chambers of three or five judges. Its role is completely independent of the Member States and it holds the responsibility of ensuring the application of EU law is maintained (enforcement function), and of interpreting the EU laws to assist the Member States in adhering to their obligations (interpretative function). These are the two main functions of the Court of Justice. It only has jurisdiction on matters and laws to do with EU law—it cannot (and will not) hear cases involving domestic national matters. It should further be noted that the Court of Justice is not an appeal court, nor is it in a hierarchy with domestic courts. It is deemed an equivalent to domestic courts and the cooperation between the Court of Justice and domestic courts is a crucial facet to the relationship between them.

5.4.4.1 *Enforcement proceedings*
The Court of Justice is often required to determine whether a Member State has fulfilled its obligations under the Treaty. The first element in the process is a preliminary stage conducted by the Commission (the Guardian of the Treaty) whereby the Commission requests information from the Member State regarding the alleged breach.[39] The Member State is given the opportunity to respond to the allegations but if the response is inadequate or none is provided then the proceedings can progress to the next stage—the judicial stage. Here the case is heard by the Court of Justice from an action brought by the Commission; it can also

---

[38] It does so in exceptional circumstances which are included in the Treaty (for instance, where a member of the EU Commission has failed to fulfil his/her obligations).

[39] This can happen where the Member State has not transposed a Directive. The Member States have an obligation to inform the Commission in what document, Act, or administrative order the EU law has been brought into effect. A lack of response can lead the Commission to investigate the matter.

be brought by another Member State (but this is rare due to the political implications) or by an individual complaint to the Commission.

5.4.4.2 *Interpretation of EU law*

The Court of Justice is a court of reference. The EU places obligations on Member States to follow the laws in the Treaty and secondary laws created by the Council, Commission, and Parliament (the most frequently used method, and most contentious, is Directives). As Directives provide the Member State with discretion as to the method and form used to transpose the law, they often require assistance from the Court of Justice (Art. 267 TFEU) to interpret the meaning of the words used in the text of the law, and to the extent of the law.[40] This mechanism ensures the harmonization of EU law between the Member States and a consistent approach to its application.

The interpretative function is very important to the fulfilment of EU law and whilst there is an obligation in certain circumstances for a reference to take place,[41] the Court of Justice has always sought to encourage domestic courts (from the lowest courts to the highest) to refer questions. The Court of Justice has wanted to instil a cooperative approach between itself and the domestic courts, and it did not want to be viewed as a court punishing Member States or an overbearing institution. Do not think of the Court of Justice as the highest court in England. The Supreme Court occupies this role. When a question is referred to the Court of Justice the interpretation is provided and then passed back to the referring court to use in its judgment.[42] Therefore, the domestic court still issues the judgment, and the role played by the Court of Justice has been in clarifying the contentious issue for the court. When the Court of Justice provides an interpretation, it binds the domestic court as to how the law must be given effect in the particular case. This ruling also has an effect on all the other Member States and hence a body of law develops which provides information to all the Member States. As a consequence, the question referred to the Court of Justice must not have been previously answered by it, and the question must be pertinent to a case (the Court of Justice cannot decide hypothetical questions).[43] The Court of Justice decides cases based on a majority of the judges and provides all of its judgments and the opinions of the Advocates-General on its website,[44] and publishes these in each of the 23 official languages of the EU,[45] on the day the judgments are read in court.

5.4.5 **The General Court**

Following the Treaty of Lisbon, the Court of First Instance has been renamed the General Court. It is an independent court attached to the Court of Justice and consists of 27 judges (one from each of the Member States) who are appointed for a six-year term, which is renewable by the Member State. It was established in 1989 to relieve the pressure on the Court of Justice in

---

[40] Broberg, M. P. and Fenger, N. (2011) 'Preliminary References and a Right: But for Whom? The Extent to which Preliminary Reference Decisions can be Subject to Appeal' *European Law Review* p.276.

[41] Where there is no possibility of further appeals (such as the Supreme Court in the UK) then the domestic court has an obligation to refer a question of interpretation to the Court of Justice (Article 267 TFEU).

[42] *Tedeschi v Denkavit* (Case 5/77) [1977] ECR 1555.

[43] *Shield Mark BV v Joost Kisk Trading as Memex* (Case C-283/01) [2003] All ER 405.

[44] http://www.curia.europa.eu.

[45] Bulgarian, Czech, Danish, Dutch, English, Estonian, Finnish, French, German, Greek, Hungarian, Irish, Italian, Latvian, Lithuanian, Maltese, Polish, Portuguese, Romanian, Slovak, Slovene, Spanish, and Swedish.

its workload of cases. The General Court sits in chambers of three or five judges but occasionally may only consist of one judge and may even sit as a full court in very important cases. Its main role is to ensure the laws of the EU are observed through interpretation of the law, and the application of the law in the Member States. It can hear cases of 'Direct Actions' including actions for annulment against EU institutions; actions for the failure of an institution to act when required; actions for damages caused by the unlawful conduct of an institution; and actions concerning the conduct of the officials and civil servants of the EU and the institutions in areas including social policy, agriculture, transport, competition law and so on.

5.5 Sources of EU law

 Business Link

It is important to be aware of the sources of EU laws as there exists a hierarchy of laws from the EU, and the source determines whether the law may be directly effective on individuals and whether it requires action by the State before rights become available. This information assists in determining whether the EU law can be used by private parties in the courts and tribunals (such as a worker against an employer, or business against another business and so on).

The law of the EU has been established primarily from three sources. These sources derive from primary legislation, secondary sources of laws such as Regulations and Directives, and the Decisions of the Court of Justice (commonly referred to as the *acquis communautaire*).[46]

5.5.1 Primary law—EU Treaty Articles

The primary laws of the EU are found in the Treaty Articles (from the Treaty of Rome through to the Treaty of Lisbon), and through agreements and cooperative initiatives between the EU as a body and other international bodies and countries beyond the legislative scope of the EU's Member States. The important aspect to note about Treaty Articles is that they are the *highest form of EU law*, and as long as they satisfy the test of being *directly effective*, they have a similar legal effect to an Act of Parliament and must be given such an effect in the domestic court[47] without any further action required by the Member State (they have **direct applicability**). They have Horizontal and Vertical Effect,[48] which makes them accessible to all citizens in the Member States.

5.5.2 Secondary laws

The secondary laws of the EU are defined in the Treaty under Article 288 TFEU and outline what level of competence the laws have and the requirements imposed on the Member States.

---

[46] This term can be translated as 'the body of EU law'.

[47] These laws, if they satisfy the tests for Direct Effect, have the ability for both Horizontal and Vertical Effect.

[48] The terms Horizontal and Vertical Direct Effect are considered in more detail in **6.2.2.1**.

5.5.2.1 *Secondary laws—Regulations*

The laws created in the form of Regulations have general application to all Member States, they are the highest form of secondary legislation, and once passed, they are directly applicable in the Member States. The important element to remember is that these laws create uniformity in the States, and the Regulation's provisions are reproduced in the Official Journal.[49] This, as a consequence, is a rather rigid and inflexible form of law, as the ability to create the same law in each of the languages of now 27 Member States in the Journal results in differing enforcement as lawyers argue as to the scope, nature, and applicability of the provisions.

A method of enabling the Member States to become involved to a greater extent in the legislative process and create laws which are more likely to be drafted in a form usually found domestically (and hence in theory to be more successfully enforceable) has been Directives.

5.5.2.2 *Secondary laws—Directives*

Directives are a tool frequently used by the EU to achieve its legislative goals. They enable the Member State to fulfil its EU obligations, but with a degree of flexibility as to how this may be realized. Directives require the Member States to transpose the effects of the law into their own legal system, in a method which is best suited for itself and its citizens, within a prescribed date (the date for **transposition**). Whereas Regulations produce uniformity in the laws of the EU, Directives seek harmonization of the laws (the spirit of the Directive is the same but the linguistic detail may be different).

5.5.2.3 *Secondary laws—Decisions*

The institutions of the EU have the ability to use Decisions as a method which allows a greater level of detail as to whom the laws will apply. The effect of using a Decision as a tool of law enables the EU to compel a particular Member State if it so chooses, or an individual, to perform or refrain from action. In addition, it can also confer rights or impose obligations on them.

5.5.3 **Decisions of the Court of Justice**

A further element which requires identification is the role played by the Court of Justice in the creation of laws and 'adding flesh to the bones' of the EU laws under Articles, Regulations, and Directives. The role played by the Court of Justice cannot be underestimated in the expansion of the laws of the EU and how its judgments have defined the role of the EU. These decisions pronounced on the new legal order that changed the nature of this international treaty and its effect on law-making in the UK. It has further established many mechanisms of domestic enforcement of EU laws which provide a speedier and more accessible means of enforcement for individuals and organizations. Table 5.1 provides an overview of the sources of law and their applicability.

---

[49]   The Official Journal of the European Communities is where all the laws of the EU are published, in each of the officially recognized languages of the EU. The laws are freely available in public libraries, the internet and so on.

Table 5.1 The extent of the applicability of EU law

	Primary law		Secondary laws	
	Treaty Articles	Regulations	Directives	Decisions
Directly effective	Yes (directly applicable)	Yes (directly applicable)	No	Yes (to whom they are addressed)
Horizontal direct effect	Yes	Yes	No	No
Vertical direct effect	Yes	Yes	Yes	Yes
Uniformity of laws	Yes	Yes	No (harmonization)	No

5.6 The impact of the EU on the UK

Clearly, when studying EU law, students often fail to see how the EU affects them in their lives or how it impacts on them in a positive way. However, it is important to identify how the EU affects the UK and those persons and organizations within it (Table 5.2). Given the constraints of a text of this size, only limited examples can be provided. However, some illustrative points may be seen in the areas of social policy (which is more widely developed in Part V of this text) and in competition laws.

5.6.1 Social policy

Social policy is a broad area and encompasses many jurisdictions, but the introduction of the maximum 48-hour working week and provisions for minimum rest periods and paid leave were introduced from the Working Time Directive,[50] the rights for parental leave were brought into effect in the UK due to the Framework Directive,[51] and rights for part-time workers[52] being equalized to those of full-time workers have each been required through the UK's membership of the EU. These are merely three examples, but this text includes many such initiatives (and identifies the EU law as a source when applicable). Rights for vulnerable workers have been significantly increased through EU action.

5.6.2 Business and competition laws

Other areas where the EU's influence on the laws of the UK can be seen are in company law and the regulation of competition. The contracts that are agreed between consumers and businesses are subject to control of the Unfair Terms in Consumer Contracts Regulations 1999, that was itself transposed from an EU Directive.[53] Further advances have seen the development

---

[50] Council Directive 93/104/EC of 23 November 1993 concerning certain aspects of the organization of working time.

[51] Council Directive 96/34/EC of 3 June 1996 on the framework agreement on parental leave concluded by UNICE, CEEP, and the ETUC.

[52] Council Directive 97/81/EC of 15 December 1997 concerning the framework agreement on part-time work concluded by UNICE, CEEP, and the ETUC.

[53] Council Directive 93/13/EEC of 5 April 1993 on unfair terms in consumer contracts.

Table 5.2 The effect of EU laws

	Treaty Articles	Regulations	Directives
Who does the law bind?	The Member State and individuals	The Member State and individuals	The Member State
The extent to which the law binds	In its entirety	In its entirety	The result to be achieved (the Member State has discretion as to how it does this)
Need for domestic implementing measures?	No (not allowed)	No (not allowed)	Yes—the State has to implement (transpose) the law

Consumer Protection from Unfair Trading Regulations 2008

of protection of consumers through the UK Business Protection from Misleading Marketing Regulations 2008 (dealing with trade descriptions) transposed from an EU Directive,[54] as was the Consumer Protection from Unfair Trading Regulations 2008 (dealing with the wider concept of consumer protection). Company law is also regulated at least in part, through the EU, and legislation from the EU includes the amendment (agreed on 29 October 2004) to Council Directive 77/91/EEC as regards the formation of public limited liability companies and the maintenance and alteration of their capital (known as The Second Company Law Directive). This has led to Directive 2006/68/EC and further amendments have been agreed to Company Disclosures (the 4th and 7th Company Law (Accounting) Directives) (agreed on 27 October 2004) and the transposition of Directive 2006/46/EC.

The EU also requires that, as part of the free movement of goods, services, and people, the Member States must allow for competition. This is due to the underlying rationale that competition removes monopolies; it allows for the efficient distribution of resources; ensures competitors challenge each other through innovations, quality of the product or service, and price; and gives the consumer choice whilst enabling wealth to be maximized. The laws in this area are governed domestically[55] and at an EU level[56] (when the issue of competition involves the crossing of EU borders), and attempt to prevent anti-competitive behaviour and abuses of a dominant position.

The Treaty requires that competition in the EU is not distorted and places an obligation on the Member States to take steps to avoid this situation. The Court of Justice remarked that a degree of competition is required in the EU to ensure that its aims and objectives are attained, and the single market achieves conditions similar to those of a domestic market.[57] Article 101 TFEU (previously Art. 81 EC) prohibits anti-competitive behaviour between undertakings, such as by fixing purchase and selling prices, limiting production of goods, applying dissimilar conditions to equivalent transactions with other traders (and placing them at a competitive disadvantage), and making the conclusion of contracts subject to the acceptance

---

[54]   Directive 2005/29/EC of the European Parliament and of the Council of 11 May 2005 concerning unfair business-to-consumer commercial practices in the internal market and amending Council Directive 84/450EEC, Directives 97/7/EC, 98/27/EC and 2002/65/EC of the European Parliament and of the Council and Regulation (EC) No 2006/2004 of the European Parliament and of the Council ('Unfair Commercial Practices Directive').

[55]   Through the Enterprise Act 2002 and the Competition Act 1998.

[56]   Articles 101 and 102 TFEU.

[57]   *Metro-SB-Grossmärkte GmbH v Commission* (Case 26/76) [1977] ECR 1875.

of supplementary obligations that have no connection with the subject of the contract. The examples of potential breaches of Article 101 TFEU above are not exhaustive, but merely illustrative, and it is possible for exemptions to be provided by the Commission of actions that would otherwise lead to a breach. Common examples of breaches of Art. 101 TFEU include price fixing[58] and market sharing.[59]

In order for Art. 101 TFEU to apply, the following criteria have to be established:

- there must be a form of collusion or concerted practice between undertakings;
- trade between Member States must be affected; and
- competition within the EU must have been adversely affected.

The term 'undertaking' is not defined in the treaty, but it is given a very broad interpretation by the Court of Justice,[60] and includes entities that are involved in commercial activities, although that need not extend to making a profit. The collusion/concerted practice between the undertakings has to be differentiated from mere parallel pricing,[61] but it can include a meeting of competitors to exchange information;[62] it need not include a formal plan to be followed by the parties,[63] and it may even extend to a 'gentleman's agreement' that does not establish a binding contract.[64] The trade between the Member States must be affected to bring the agreement under the EU's remit, such as where it '… is capable of endangering, either directly or indirectly, in fact or potentially, freedom of trade between Member States in a direction which would harm the attainment of the objects of a single market between States'.[65]

The requirement for an adverse effect on competition in the EU may extend to agreements made outside of the EU but with an effect within it,[66] and it prevents actions being taken where the effects are in reality minimal. This is known as the 'de minimis' rule, where the breach has little practical effect on competition.[67] Where an agreement in contravention of Art. 101 TFEU is found, it is void (and hence unenforceable) and the Commission may impose a fine of up to 10 per cent of the undertaking's total turnover (not just that income which was obtained in the EU).

Regulation of anti-competitive behaviour continues under Article 102 TFEU (previously Art. 82 EC) by prohibiting an undertaking from abusing its dominant market position so as to affect competition. Where Article 101 TFEU requires a concerted practice or collusion between undertakings, Article 102 TFEU simply requires one undertaking acting contrary to the treaty. This dominance would enable the undertaking to dictate prices, refuse to supply to competitors and so on, which would have a detrimental impact on the aims of the treaty. Examples of abuse that would fall under the remit of Art. 102 TFEU are similar to those listed as examples of breaches of Art. 101 TFEU. As with Art. 101 TFEU, this is not an exhaustive list, but merely illustrative.

For a claim to be made under Art. 102 TFEU the following conditions must be satisfied:

- the undertaking must occupy a dominant position;
- the action must occur within the EU or a substantial part of it;

---

[58] *ICI v Commission (Dyestuffs)* (Case 48/69) [1972] ECR 619.

[59] *ACF Chemiefarma NV v Commission* (Cases 41, 44 & 45/69) [1970] ECR 661.

[60] *RAI/Unitel* [1978] 3 CMLR 306.   [61] *Dyestuffs* (Case 48/69).

[62] *Huls AG v Commission* (Case C-199/92P) [1999] ECR I-4287.

[63] *Suiker-Unie (Sugar Cartel)* (Cases 40–48/73) [1975] ECR 1663.

[64] *ACF Chemiefarma v Commission* (Cases 41, 44 & 45/69) [1970] ECR 661.

[65] *Grundig and Consten* (Cases 56 & 58/64) [1966] ECR 299.

[66] *Ahlström Oy v Commission (Wood Pulp)* (Cases 89, 104, 114, 116/117 and 125–129/85) [1993] ECR I-1307.

[67] *Völk v Verwaecke* (Case 5/69) [1969] ECR 295.

- the undertaking's dominant position must have been abused; and
- the abuse must have had an effect on trade between the Member States.

Dominance does not have to be based on a monopoly (as these rarely exist in any pure form) but rather is based on an undertaking that possesses a sufficiently large share of the relevant (product) market that it may behave independently of others and:

> ... which puts them in a position to act without taking into account their competitors, purchasers or suppliers. That is the position when, because of their share of the market, or their share of the market combined with the availability of technical knowledge, raw materials or capital, they have the power to determine prices or to control production or distribution for a significant part of the products in question.[68]

Hence it is not simply an exercise to look at a percentage figure of market share to determine dominance, but rather all relevant factors including:

- the relationship between the market share of the undertaking and that of its rivals;
- any technological lead enjoyed by the undertaking over others;
- the existence of a highly developed sales network; and
- the absence of any potential competitors to the market.[69]

A key aspect of identifying dominance is to identify the relevant product market (RPM) to which the product in question relates. The Court of Justice, the General Court, and the EU Commission have taken the view that this would involve an assessment of the substitutability or interchangeability of the product. The assessment is based on supply and demand sides of the market, but to attempt to simplify the argument, consider in the first instance substitutability. If you visit a supermarket with the intention of buying bananas, and when you arrive there are no bananas available, would you leave not having purchased anything in replacement of the bananas, or would you instead purchase some other 'soft fruit'? If you would leave, then the bananas are a relevant product market in their own right and dominance of that market will be assessed on that basis. If, on the other hand, you would simply choose another soft fruit (apples, strawberries and so on), then all of these products constitute the relevant product market and it is this wider market where dominance will be tested (known as cross-elasticity of demand).[70] Remember, if the defendant can establish a wider RPM it is more likely that more competitors will be in this market and hence the defendant is less likely to be dominant in that market. If the undertaking is not dominant, there can be no breach of Art. 102 TFEU.

From a supply side view, the question will be how easy is it to change the production of goods to enter a new market. For example, could the production process for replacement tyres for lorries and trucks be easily changed to enter into the market for cars and vans?[71] If they could, then both markets will constitute the RPM. If not, then the current market where the goods are produced will be viewed as the RPM.

Having established that an undertaking has dominance in the RPM, the abuse of the dominant position has to be established. There are many examples throughout the case law of the Court of Justice, but some of the more business-relevant abuses include refusal to supply

---

[68] *Continental Can Co.*   [69] *Hoffman-La Roche.*

[70] This was the situation in *United Brands Company v Commission* (Case 27/76) [1978] ECR 207, where the Court of Justice held that due to their characteristics, bananas constituted a market in its own right.

[71] *Michelin v Commission* (Case 322/81) [1983] ECR 3461.

products to competitors,[72] discriminatory pricing,[73] predatory pricing,[74] unfair prices,[75] abuse and mergers[76] and so on. It is also necessary to identify that the abuse affects trade between Member States.[77] This is relevant as if the matter is wholly internal (such as just between companies in the UK with no effect on the wider EU) then the UK has its own laws (the Competition Act 1998 and the Enterprise Act 2002) that can regulate competition and provide the relevant remedy.

? Thinking Point

Can competition laws effectively ensure competition exists in the EU? Is it possible to protect the interests of consumers (on one hand) and also the (smaller and more vulnerable) competitors to a dominant undertaking?

5.6.3 The impact of membership on law-making and the constitution

---

✐ Business Link

The effects of the UK's membership of the EU and the changes made to how laws are created and how judgments have to take EU laws into consideration will be witnessed in the following section. The practical impact that EU law has on interpreting domestic laws, and often extending laws to cover wider issues, is vital to understanding the responsibilities of businesses in the UK. The following examples used in this section of the book involve businesses that complied with domestic law, and these two cases demonstrate how the defendant fell victim to an adverse decision when the domestic law was interpreted consistently with EU law (they followed English law, and were still found to have breached workers' rights because of the interpretation of that law with EU law). Therefore, being aware of EU laws enables businesses to avoid legal action, and to comply fully with their obligations, particularly under employment and companies' laws.

- *The duty to interpret domestic law as compatible with EU law:* Domestic courts are obliged to interpret laws consistently with EU law, even where the domestic law was effective before the EU law was enacted. In situations where domestic law has been passed to transpose the requirements of an EU parent law, the courts must look for guidance from the EU law (and/or the decisions of the Court of Justice) when interpreting the extent and scope of the domestic provision. This 'interpretative' function can lead to a change in the application of domestic law. The resulting consequence is that (for example) employers simply focusing on domestic law, and being in conformity with this law, may ultimately

---

[72] *ICI and Commercial Solvents v Commission* (Cases 6 & 7/73) [1974] ECR 223.
[73] *United Brands* and *Hoffman-La Roche.*
[74] *AKZO Chemie BV v Commission* (Case 62/86) [1991] ECR II-2969.
[75] *General Motors Continental NV v Commission* (Case 26/75) [1975] ECR 1367.
[76] *Continental Can Co.*   [77] *Hugin Kassaregister v Commission* (Case 22/78) [1979] ECR 1869.

discover that when interpreted in the spirit of the EU law, they are actually in breach.[78] Hence, Parliament's law was supreme but it has 'surrendered' some of its sovereignty to the EU[79] and as a consequence domestic law may be altered to ensure EU law is given its widest application in the Member States. In *Litster* this resulted in words being added to a UK statute to fulfill the UK's obligation to the EU.

?　Thinking Point

How easy do you think it is for businesses (particularly small/medium-sized enterprises) to be aware of obligations under English law when these are often subject to change when EU laws are passed (often without comment in the press)? If there is a situation where English law is not compliant with EU law because Parliament has not made some required change, why should an employer (who is busy running his/her business) find him/herself liable?

- *The duty to change domestic law to fulfill EU obligations:* Beyond the obligation to interpret existing legislation consistently with EU law, laws may even be required to be altered to ensure conformity (a power statutory interpretation does not allow).[80] In *Commission v UK*[81] the UK had to amend the Equal Pay Act 1970 to ensure that the provisions of the Equal Pay Directive[82] were correctly transposed. This required the inclusion of a 'third head' of complaint to ensure individuals had access to the protection that EU law sought to provide.

- *The EU's change to the UK constitution:* The EU has impacted upon the way that the courts interpret and apply laws from the EU and how existing laws have, in some circumstances, been reinterpreted to comply with EU law. However, to fully appreciate the extent to the EU's influence on the legal systems of the Member States, the following case is fundamental. *Factortame*[83] involved 13 Spanish fishermen who, due to the Merchant Shipping Act 1988[84] were unable to fish in British waters.[85] Section 14 of the Merchant Shipping Act 1988 imposed domicile and residence conditions on those wishing to fish in British waters which *Factortame* could not satisfy. Their claim was that the Act was contrary to EU law, and as a result could not be enforced against them. Consequently, they requested that the High Court disapply the UK Act of Parliament. The court issued an injunction which temporarily suspended the Secretary of State for Transport from

---

[78]　See *Litster and Others v Forth Dry Dock & Engineering* [1990] 1 AC 546.

[79]　See Elliot, M. (2004) 'United Kingdom: Parliamentary Sovereignty Under Pressure' *International Journal of Constitutional Law*, No. 2, p. 545.

[80]　Laws may only be interpreted 'where possible' and this does not extend to contradicting legislative provisions (that is Parliament's role).

[81]　(Case 61/81) [1982] ICR 578.

[82]　Council Directive 75/117/EEC of 10 February 1975 on the approximation of the laws of the Member States relating to the application of the principle of equal pay for men and women.

[83]　[1991] 1 AC 603.

[84]　The main reason for the Act was to stop the practice of 'quota-hopping' that was adversely affecting the fishing industry.

[85]　Additional information regarding the facts surrounding the *Factortame* case is available on the Online Resource Centre.

enforcing the Act. This issue was taken up by the Court of Appeal[86] and later by the House of Lords, which both confirmed that the decision of the first Court was wrong as the Courts (including those deciding this issue) did not have the power to suspend an Act of Parliament.[87] The House of Lords was obliged under EU law to refer this matter to the Court of Justice,[88] which ruled that domestic courts were able to disapply a domestic law which contravened EU law and therefore the Merchant Shipping Act 1988 could not be applied.

5.6.3.1 *The importance of the* Factortame *case*

The implications of the *Factortame* rulings cannot be underestimated. This case has to be read in conjunction with the chapters on the English legal system to be fully appreciated, as it is not about whether Spanish fishermen were allowed to fish in British waters. Its importance is that it was the first time that a UK court had disapplied an Act of Parliament. The constitution of the UK is very clear in that Parliament is supreme and the judiciary are subservient to it. *Factortame* directly contradicted this philosophy, elevating EU law above English law, and provided the judiciary with new powers never before seen. The EU has power therefore to alter the constitution of the States joining it.

 Conclusion

This chapter has outlined a brief historical perspective of the development of the EU and the main institutions which comprise the Union. The sources of law are also identified and it is important to understand how these laws are given effect in the UK. There have been many advances in English law due to its membership of the EU—affecting the constitution, interpretation of statutes, and rewriting of statutes to conform with the obligations under EU law. Some of these have been identified in this chapter, and throughout this book there will be evidence of EU laws and the Court of Justice having an impact on domestic law. Chapter 6 considers the methods in which EU laws are given effect in the UK (through 'enforcement' proceedings) and identifies the mechanisms through which individuals can access their EU rights.

 Summary of main points

- The EEC has evolved to the EU through the following treaties: Treaty of Rome 1957; Single European Act 1987; the Treaty of Maastricht 1992; the Treaty of Amsterdam 1997; the Treaty of Nice 2001, and the Treaty of Lisbon 2007.

- The UK became a member in 1973 through the European Communities Act 1972 (ECA).

- From 1 January 2007 there are 27 Member States.

- Section 2(1) of the ECA provides that EU law which is intended to take direct effect within Member States (for example, the Treaty Articles and Regulations) will automatically form part of the law in the UK and must be given such effect by the judiciary.

---

[86] On 22 March 1989.

[87] The Lords stated that the case of *Regina v Secretary of State for the Home Department, Ex parte Herbage* [1987] QB 872 was precedent for such a decision from the common law.

[88] Under Article 177 (now Art. 267 TFEU) (see **5.4.4.2**).

The aims of the EEC

- The original aims included the establishing of a common market. This was extended to incorporate the fundamental freedoms—free movement of goods, services, capital, and workers.

The main institutions of the EU

- The *Council*'s roles include: concluding agreements with foreign States; taking general policy decisions; and taking decisions based on the Commission's proposals.
- The *Commission* has two main roles, it operates a legislative function taking the initiative from the Council and Parliament. Its other substantive role is of ensuring the Member States follow EU laws and as such is known as the 'Guardian of the Treaties'.
- The *Parliament* is elected every five years and its role is to contribute to the drafting of legislation that affects the Member States through Directives and Regulations. It does so through the co-decision procedure with the Council and Commission.
- The *Court of Justice* is a court of reference that assists the Member States through interpreting EU laws to apply in cases (under Article 267 TFEU). It also hears the actions taken under Article 258 TFEU when it is alleged that Member States have not adhered to their obligations under the Treaty.

The sources of EU law

- Primary law: The *Treaty Articles* which, if deemed to possess 'Direct Effect' are directly applicable in the Member State with no further action required by the State.
- The secondary laws are defined under Article 288 TFEU. *Regulations* are the highest form of secondary laws, they are binding in their entirety, and have direct applicability. *Directives* are binding as to the result to be achieved upon each Member State to which it is addressed, but allow each State to decide how it will give effect to the aims of the Directive. A *Decision* establishes the scope of the legal provision and is binding in its entirety upon those to whom it is addressed (as opposed to *all* Member States).

The EU's impact on the UK

- The EU has had significant impacts on the UK in many areas, but of relevance to business law, its major impact has been in social policy, business, and competition laws.
- Social policy—the Working Time Directive, Framework Directive, various discrimination laws, and the protection of vulnerable workers have been provided through the EU's initiatives.
- Competition policies have been established to prevent distortion of competition and the most significant include Articles 101 TFEU (undertakings working together to prevent competition) and 102 TFEU (an undertaking abusing a dominant position).

Impact on the UK's constitution

- There exists an obligation on the judiciary to interpret English law consistently with EU law.
- The UK is required to transpose EU Directives on time and to alter inconsistent laws to fulfill EU obligations.
- The UK is prevented from passing laws contrary to EU law where the EU has competence.

Summary questions

Essay questions

1. Critically assess the rationale for the changes to the EU's infrastructure following the ratification of the Treaty of Lisbon. In your answer explain why the changes were deemed necessary and how it is likely to improve on decision-making and transparency on matters affecting the Member States.

2. Explain how the European Court of Justice and the relevant Treaty provisions determine where an undertaking holds a dominant position in a market (as defined in Article 102 TFEU) and how it may abuse that position.

Problem questions

1. Mr Merchant was a part-time judge who wished to join a pension scheme ran exclusively for members of the judiciary. However, the rules of the pension scheme specifically preclude part-time judges paid a daily fee. Fee-paid part-time judges are not considered as workers under English law and as such they have no recourse to protection from the Part-Time Workers (Prevention of Less Favourable Treatment) Regulations 2000.

   Mr Merchant wishes to challenge the validity of the rule precluding his admission to the pension scheme and seeks retrospective admission. Further, he considers that the Regulations are themselves an incorrect transposition of the EU parent law—The Part-Time Workers Framework Directive (97/81/EC)—as they enable the State to define a 'worker' in accordance with definitions provided in the pan-European Framework Agreement on part-time work. This case has now reached the Supreme Court.

   Advise Mr Merchant as to his right to challenge his exclusion from the pension scheme and the obligations on the Court to ensure compliance with EU law under Art. 267 TFEU.

2. All Bright Consumables (ABC) Ltd (based in the UK) has developed a new tablet computer, and in addition to selling this to customers, it also sells the components it has developed for these devices to PC manufacturers. ABC now wishes to expand the business and sell the components directly to the public. ABC considers that these specific goods will be particularly popular with consumers who wish to create custom-built tablet systems.

   In order to maximize sales ABC intends to sell these products in EU countries other than the UK, and in order to achieve these sales in Germany, it establishes a business relationship with 'Das Tech', a multi-outlet supermarket chain. ABC considers that selling its components through a supermarket is the most effective means to reach the consumer market. Following the conclusion of meetings between ABC and Das Tech, the agreement between the companies provides:

   a. Das Tech will act as the sole distributor of ABC's products in Germany, and only Das Tech will be allowed to advertise ABC's products in Germany;

   b. ABC will not sell its products directly to anyone in Germany or to the German public through its website;

   c. Das Tech agrees not to sell PC components from any other manufacturer than ABC; and

   d. Das Tech must inform ABC of any distribution offer made to it of any supplier in the EU. ABC is then given the right to match or better this deal.

The German market contains many companies who manufacture and sell PC components through supermarkets. The popularity of ABC's products means that after only 8 months, Das Tech is responsible for selling 39 per cent of the PC components sold in Germany. Innovative Tech Giants (ITG) is the leading competitor manufacturing PC tablet components in Germany, and its sales have dramatically decreased following ABC's entry to the German market.

Das Tech announces that it will be offering ABC's PC components on a buy-one-get-one-free basis for the following three months. The costs of this offer are to be underwritten by ABC.

ITG approach Das Tech about its supplying ITG products in its supermarkets. Das Tech inform ITG about its agreement with ABC and further say that any approach would be rejected as 'ABC will match anything you can offer us so why should we even bother listening to you?'.

Advise ITG about any action possible under Arts. 101 and 102 TFEU.

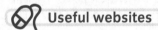 Further Reading

Note: Readers who wish to further their understanding of EU law should refer to the texts and articles footnoted in the following chapters but also regularly refer to the *European Law Journal*, the *European Law Review*, and the *Common Market Law Review*.

Craig, P. (1997) 'Directives: Direct Effect, Indirect Effect and the Construction of National Legislation' *European Law Review*, December, p. 519.

Useful websites

http://www.europa.eu/
(The website of the EU with information regarding laws, institutions, and history (among many other features.) It offers excellent commentary and details in a user-friendly manner.)

http://www.curia.europa.eu/
(The website of the Court of Justice containing case law and details of the work of the courts, with the timetables of when cases are being decided.)

http://www.bis.gov.uk/policies/europe
(Excellent site of the Department for Business Innovation & Skills that contains information for businesses, consultation documents, and EU laws (and details of their transposition into the UK) which have a direct impact on business.)

http://www.statewatch.org/
(The website contains academic articles assessing the implications of, among others, the reform treaty, and provides a comparison with the EU constitution.)

Online Resource Centre

http://www.oxfordtextbooks.co.uk/orc/marson3e/
Why not visit the Online Resource Centre and try multiple choice questions associated with this chapter to test your understanding of the topic. You will also find relevant updates to the law.

6 Enforcement Mechanisms

Why does it matter?

Laws are only as effective as they are accessible and enforceable. Therefore, in order to fully appreciate how laws passed by the European Union (EU) may be given effect in a Member State, this chapter discusses the enforcement of EU laws in domestic courts, and at the Court of Justice of the European Union (Court of Justice). Knowing how laws of the EU may be accessed in the courts may speed up the process of their use, which may result in greater protection of individuals' rights, protection of companies and directors, or even knowledge of how liabilities of businesses/employers may be limited through the concept of the 'Horizontal Direct Effect' of Directives.

Learning outcomes

Following reading this chapter you should be in a position to:

- describe the enforcement of EU law at both domestic and EU levels (6.2–6.2.2.3)
- discuss the Horizontal and Vertical distinction of Direct Effect (6.2.2.1)
- describe the obligation on the courts to interpret English law in conformity with EU law (6.2.2.2)
- explain State Liability and describe the facts of the *Francovich* case (6.2.2.3).

𝄞 Key terms

These terms will be used in the chapter and it may be helpful to be aware of what they mean or refer back to them when reading through the chapter.

Enforcement (of EU law)
The EU places obligations on individuals as well as the Member States. A corollary right is that as it also provides them with rights, these rights must be enforceable (in the domestic courts and at the EU level).

Direct Effect
Legislation from the EU creates rights for individuals in the Member States which domestic courts must apply even in the absence of any national implementing legislation.

Indirect Effect
Domestic legislation in the Member State must be interpreted in accordance with laws from the EU to give effect to the EU provision. It is a system of consistent interpretation.

Purposive method of interpretation
(Also known as a 'teleological' approach). The judiciary interpret legislation, and following membership of the EU they have an obligation to interpret English law, as far as is possible, to give effect to EU law. This is the situation even if the interpretation distorts (but does not contradict) in some way the wording of an Act of Parliament.

State Liability
An individual who has suffered loss due to the non-implementation or incorrect transposition of an EU law by the State can sue the State for any losses incurred.

6.1 Introduction

Enforcement of EU law is a vital topic for businesses as it provides access to rights for affected individuals (such as workers) where the State has neglected its duty of transposition of the law. It also facilitates the EC Commission (the guardian of the Treaty) with mechanisms to hold recalcitrant Member States to account where they have failed in their duties under the treaty.

6.2 Enforcement

 Business Link

Enforcing rights may be achieved either through complaints to the EU Commission regarding a failure of the State to follow its EU obligations, or may be pursued by private individuals through domestic courts. This section outlines both methods and explains the process and the potential limitations of each.

Methods of enforcing EU laws have evolved over the life of the EU in an attempt to provide mechanisms that enable the law of this international treaty to be respected by the signatory Member States and enforceable by the individuals in that State to whom these obligations and rights are applicable.[1] **Enforcement** takes place at two levels—there is enforcement at

---

[1] In *Van Gend en Loos v Nederlandse Administratie der Belastingen* (Case 26/62) [1963] ECR 1 the Court of Justice remarked: 'The objective of the EEC Treaty, which is to establish a common market, the functioning of which is of direct concern to interested parties in the Community, implies that this Treaty is more than an agreement which merely creates mutual obligations between the contracting States. This view is confirmed by the preamble to the Treaty, which refers not only to governments but to peoples ... The conclusion to be drawn from this is that the Community creates a new legal order of international law for the benefit of which the States have limited their sovereign rights, albeit within limited fields, and the subjects of which comprise not only Member States but also their nationals.'

the EU level and at the domestic level.[2] At the EU level, the Commission initiates enforcement proceedings against a Member State alleged to be breaching its EU obligations and the case is decided upon by the Court of Justice. The enforcement at the domestic level involves the domestic courts hearing cases where EU laws should be given effect or determining whether a specific enforcement mechanism is available. It should be noted at the outset that the enforcement mechanisms at the domestic level were not based on a Treaty Article (as was the case at the EU level of enforcement: Article 258 TFEU). Rather, these domestic enforcement mechanisms were established by the Court of Justice in an attempt to ensure the EU had a greater impact on the lives of the citizens of the EU; to reduce pressure on the Court of Justice in handling the increasing number of cases it had to manage; and to make it easier for affected individuals to access their rights by having the case heard in a domestic court instead of having to take the case to the Court of Justice based at Luxembourg. These mechanisms began with **Direct Effect**[3] whereby the primary laws of the Treaty could be given effect directly in the Member States' domestic courts; there was then the extension of this doctrine to secondary laws such as Directives,[4] but limited to the Vertical direction;[5] this was followed by the enforcement mechanism of **Indirect Effect**,[6] which was necessary as a consequence of the Court of Justice not allowing Direct Effect to be used Horizontally[7] and is a process of **purposive** statutory interpretation;[8] and these remedies have been complemented by **State Liability**,[9] which sought protection for individuals through a system of non-contractual liability for losses arising from denial of an EU law in the Member State.

6.2.1 **The EU level enforcement**

Note: as this is of little practical use for businesses, an overview can be found on the Online Resource Centre.

6.2.2 **Domestic enforcement**

 Business Link

There are three mechanisms for accessing EU rights in domestic courts—Direct Effect, Indirect Effect, and State Liability. Note that Direct Effect is limited in that Directives can only be accessed in such a way against an emanation of the State (they cannot be used against a private party); Indirect Effect is a form of statutory interpretation; and State Liability is a damages action against the State. Each mechanism, however, has been used to effect and, in particular, Trades Unions have frequently funded and represented their employee members to successfully bring claims under these powers against employers and the State.

2　Arnull, A. (2011) 'The Principle of Effective Judicial Protection in EU Law: An Unruly Horse?' *European Law Review,* January, p. 51.

3　*Van Gend en Loos.*

4　*Spa SACE v Italian Ministry of Finance* [1970] (Case 33/70) [1970] ECR 1213.

5　*Marshall v Southampton and South-West Hampshire Area Health Authority* (Case 152/84) [1986] ECR 723.

6　*Von Colson v Land Nordrhein-Westfalen* [1984] (Case 14/83) [1984] ECR 1891.

7　Horizontal and Vertical Direct Effect will be explained in section 6.2.2.1.

8　*Litster v Forth Dry Dock & Engineering Co. Ltd* [1990] 1 AC 546.

9　*Francovich and Bonifaci v Italy* [1991] ECR I-5357.

The application of EU law, if it was to be a 'new legal order' that changed the previous view of international treaties within the UK's dualist constitution, had to be given true effect throughout the Union. The EU level of enforcement had limitations as it was designed and primarily concerned with ensuring EU laws were being maintained by all Member States. The States that did follow EU laws should not be placed at a competitive disadvantage for doing so, whilst at the same time those States that flouted the law should not gain from their intransigence. The EU was also more concerned with the application of the Treaty between States rather than remedies for individuals and private parties that were being affected by the breach.

The EU countered these limitations by encouraging individuals in the Member States to become active participants in enforcing their rights. What was required were the tools by which enforcement could take place, and the Court of Justice provided these, which were to be used in the domestic court. This would make the EU more visible and applicable to individuals in their daily lives; it would ensure EU laws were complied with more speedily as the cases would be heard in domestic courts rather than at the Court of Justice with its 27 judges; and individuals would experience breaches more quickly and hence the process of ensuring the laws were being applied fully would be faster than waiting for the political and then judicial application to take effect through the Commission under its powers derived from the Treaty. The Court of Justice began the process of domestic enforcement through the doctrine of Direct Effect.

6.2.2.1 *Direct Effect*

Direct Effect of EU law was developed by the Court of Justice to allow individuals and organizations to use the provisions of EU law within the Member States' domestic courts, and in the case of Directives, without having to wait for the Member State to fulfil some obligation that it had omitted to do. Direct Effect had been established for primary law (Treaty Articles) and the rationale of the Court of Justice developing this mechanism was that ' ... the useful effect (of an EU law) would be weakened if individuals were prevented from relying on it before their national courts and if the latter were prevented from taking it into consideration as an element of Community law'.[10] There has been controversy over the use of Direct Effect in primary law,[11] but the doctrine was largely accepted by the Member States. It was further advanced to secondary laws (namely Directives) and this was to extend accessibility to EU rights, but this is where many problems began.

As Directives are a commonly used source of law, the application of Direct Effect would enable an affected individual to use a Directive's provisions in a domestic court after the date of transposition[12] if the Member State had been guilty of either non-implementation or incorrect transposition. Direct Effect was considered permissible if the tests developed by the Court of Justice were satisfied. Tests were required as EU laws are often very general in scope and in order for any legislation to give rights to, or provide obligations on, individuals they must be sufficiently clear and precise to allow the affected parties to understand their scope. The tests to be satisfied for an EU law to have Direct Effect are:

1 the provision must be clear and unambiguous;

2 the provision must be unconditional; and

3 the provision must not be dependent on further action being taken by the EU or Member State.

---

[10] *Van Duyn v Home Office* (Case 41/74) [1974] ECR 1337, [1975] 1 CMLR 1, para. 12.

[11]   One such situation was *Defrenne v Sabena* [1976] Case 43/75 [1976] ECR 455, as it was considered that the provisions of Article 119 EC (now Article 157 TFEU) may not have been as clear and precise to enable Direct Effect. See Pescatore, P. (1983) 'The Doctrine of "Direct Effect": An Infant Disease of Community Law' Vol. 8 *European Law Review* 155.

[12] This term is the process of taking the EU Directive and creating an implementing piece of legislation.

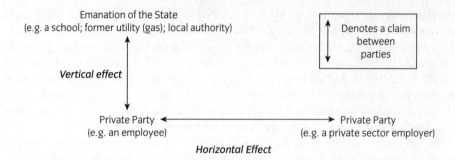

Figure 6.1 Horizontal and Vertical Direct Effect

Having established the tests, the application of Direct Effect came to the Court of Justice. It stated that so far as the tests were satisfied, Treaty Articles having general application would enable a claim using Direct Effect (under *Van Gend en Loos*, see footnote 1). The same provision applies with Regulations under the same rationale. However, when considering Directives, the Court of Justice had a major concern. EU laws, having application to individuals as well as the State acceding to the Treaty, resulted in individuals having obligations to follow EU law. This is what made the EU such an important aspect of law in the UK. No other international treaty had placed obligations on individuals in the Member State—they had only obliged the State to act in a certain way.[13] The EU gave rights to individuals but also placed obligations on them. To ensure that individuals would comply with their obligations, it was only correct that they had access to any rights that they could benefit from. As Directives required action by the State to transpose the law into its own legal system, if the State failed, Direct Effect would enable the individuals to access the right until the State had complied with its EU obligations under Articles 10 EC (replaced by Art. 4(3) TFEU) and 249 EC (now Art. 288 TFEU). The Court of Justice, though, had to determine whether a Directive could be used between private parties as well as against the State. In this situation arose the concepts of Horizontal Direct Effect (HDE) and Vertical Direct Effect (VDE) (Figure 6.1). HDE is so called because it involves using the provisions of an EU law directly against another private party (horizontal because both private parties have the same legislative power and obligations). VDE is so called because it involves a claim from a private party against the State or emanation of the State (vertical because the private party has no legislative power but the defendant (the State) is of a higher position in terms of legislative authority).

The issues of HDE and VDE are quite complex and do not require in-depth investigation in this text. It is, however, prudent to consider these issues briefly to appreciate their impact on the EU dimension to the protection and enforcement of rights. HDE of Directives is the use of the law between two private individuals where the court recognizes the EU law and gives it effect as it would a domestic law. The Court of Justice therefore decided that the application of EU law domestically could only be enforced where the EU considered it had competence—via VDE. HDE has been considered to be beyond the scope of the Court of Justice[14] because private parties have no legislative power so should not be held responsible when the Member State has failed in its obligations; if it did give the remedy of HDE this

---

[13] Examples include the International Labour Organization and the European Convention on Human Rights.

[14] As evidenced in *Marshall v Southampton and South-West Hampshire AHA* (Case 152/84) [1986] ECR 723; *El Corte Ingles v Cristina Blazques Rivero* (Case C-192/94) [1996] ECR I-1281; *Belinda Jane Coote v Granada Hospitality Ltd* (Case C-185/97) [1998] ECR I-5199.

would almost be to elevate Directives to the power of Regulations which Article 288 TFEU did not allow; and if the Member State upheld its obligations then this remedy would not be necessary.[15] The denial of HDE of Directives was demonstrated in the UK in the case of *Duke v GEC Reliance.*

Duke v GEC Reliance[16]

Facts:

GEC Reliance had a policy of compelling women workers to retire at 60 years of age compared with 65 years for men (and this was applied to Mrs Duke). The House of Lords had held that the Sex Discrimination Act 1975 was not applicable to retirement ages, and instead had to consider whether Duke was able to claim directly under the relevant EU law (the Equal Treatment Directive).[17] The Lords held that Duke could not use the Directive in her claim as her employer was not 'an emanation of the State', and the Horizontal application of Direct Effect of Directives was not possible.

Authority for:

The Court of Justice's refusal to recognize the Horizontal Direct Effect of Directives.

This case demonstrated that whilst EU laws have significant effects on the UK courts and Parliament, Directives themselves may not be used directly against parties in the private sector.[18] This has implications in employment law (for example) where many of the advances in the law have derived from the UK's membership of the EU, and where most workers are employed in the private sector. A claim against their employer would be a claim against a person in the private sector and clearly if the Member State has not taken the correct action in transposing the EU law into domestic legislation, the employee has to look towards Indirect Effect to access his/her rights as there is no HDE of Directives.[19]

It is evident that a remedy is required to enable EU laws to be successfully used and applied in the Member States' jurisdictions, but whilst it has been given many opportunities to provide the remedy of HDE, the Court of Justice has continued, explicitly, to deny the remedy and decline the opportunity to change the law. Direct Effect is only possible in the case of Directives, in the vertical direction (against the Member State or its emanations) and this has led to one of the most important limitations of the provision.

As the Court of Justice did not consider that it could provide the enforcement mechanism of HDE it began to widen the concept of 'the State' to be of use in VDE claims. The State is

---

[15] For a discussion of the arguments and their critique see Marson, J. (2004) 'Access to Justice: A Deconstructionist Approach To Horizontal Direct Effect' *4 Web JCLI.*

[16] [1988] AC 618.

[17] Council Directive 76/207/EEC of 9 February 1976 on the implementation of the principle of equal treatment for men and women as regards access to employment, vocational training and promotion, and working conditions.

[18] However, this is a contentious area and for a consideration of the legal possibility of the adoption of HDE see Barmes, E. (1996) 'Public Law, EC Law and the Qualifying Period for Unfair Dismissal' *Industrial Law Journal*, Volume 25, p. 59; and Dougan, M. (2000) 'The 'Disguised' Vertical Direct Effect of Directives?' *Cambridge Law Journal*, 59, 3, p. 586.

[19] This point was confirmed in *Marleasing S.A. v La Comercial Internacional de Alimentación S.A.* [1990] ECR I-4135. However, the Court of Justice also returned to the issue of Indirect Effect and reiterated the obligation on domestic courts to give effect to EU law through statutes whenever possible.

no longer considered to be limited to the Government. Through case law, it has been applied by the Court of Justice to former nationalized utilities,[20] schools,[21] the police force,[22] and hospitals.[23] Essentially, any 'body' where the State possesses some direct control may fall under the remit of VDE. The consequence of this situation is that if the transgressor of an unimplemented EU Directive is an emanation of the State there may be a claim under Direct Effect through VDE; and if the transgressor in the same scenario is a private party there is no claim, as HDE is not allowed.

? Thinking Point

Is it fair to apply the remedy of VDE to employers as listed above? What is the material difference between an employer at a state-funded school (where VDE would be allowed), and a private school (where HDE is not allowed), when neither has legislative powers or the ability/obligation to transpose EU law?

The Court of Justice recognized the problem of having two sets of rights depending on who the transgressor (defendant) was, and the perceived unfairness of this situation. It therefore wished to develop a remedy which was applicable to all in the EU and still ensured EU law was given effect and was respected—the doctrine of Indirect Effect was developed.

6.2.2.2 *Indirect Effect*

The Court of Justice was concerned at the problem posed by the lack of access to EU laws through a Member State not transposing a Directive, or doing so incorrectly, and hence how this denied access to rights. Further, this was an embarrassment to the EU in terms of its requirements that Member States should be made to follow the law and if no available method of enforcement existed, then one had to be established. A mechanism was developed where, as the Member States had refused to allow the Court of Justice to develop the doctrine of Direct Effect horizontally,[24] they were under a duty to give effect to EU laws and as such a method of statutory interpretation was adopted by the Court of Justice under the doctrine of Indirect Effect. Indirect effect was a concept of statutory interpretation where an existing piece of domestic legislation (such as an Act of Parliament) would be interpreted through the courts by reference to the EU law (such as a Directive), and this EU law would allow the judge to 'read into' the existing English law the provisions of the EU law, thus providing access to it.

---

[20] *Griffin v South-West Water Services Ltd.* [1995] IRLR 15.

[21] *NUT v Governing Body of St. Mary's Church of England Junior School* [1997] 3 CMLR 630.

[22] *Johnston v Chief Constable of the RUC* (Case 222/84) [1986] ECR 1651.

[23] *Marshall v Southampton & South West Hampshire AHA.*

[24] In the Court of Justice's submission to the Member States before its decision in *Faccini Dori v Recreb Srl* [1994] (Case C-91/92) ECR I-3325, the 12 Member States were asked if they would follow a ruling by the Court of Justice if it granted HDE of Directives, and 11 of the 12 responded that they would not.

Von Colson and Kamann v L and Nordrhein-Westfalen and Dorit Harz v Deutsche Tradax GmbH[25]

Facts:

The first case involved two women, Von Colson and Kamann, who had applied for jobs as social workers at Werl prison. They were both unsuccessful (the positions were given to two male applicants) and claimed against the administrators of the prison that they were denied the posts due to their sex. In the second case Dorit Harz applied for a vacancy available to economics graduates but was refused an interview as she had been informed that the position was only available to male applicants.

In each of these cases Germany had not transposed the Equal Treatment Directive (Directive 76/207). The German court therefore referred questions to the Court of Justice, *inter alia*, establishing whether the Directive could be used directly in the claims. The Court of Justice held that instead of looking at the issue of Direct Effect and the potential application of that remedy, Member States had an obligation to interpret existing legislation to give effect to EU law and obligations: 'It is for the national court to interpret and apply the legislation adopted for the implementation of the directive in conformity with the requirements of Community law, in so far as it is given discretion to do so under national law.'

Authority for:

Directives may be used directly in domestic courts against a State or emanation of the State defendant (Vertical Direct Effect) but may not be used directly against a private-sector defendant (Horizontal Direct Effect). Rather, where possible, a system of consistent interpretation of domestic law with EU law should be used (Indirect Effect).

These joined cases were important as the Court of Justice created the enforcement mechanism of 'Indirect Effect' and therefore the duty on Member States' courts to interpret domestic legislation (where possible) in light of EU law. Interestingly, the development of Indirect Effect has largely been attributed to the claimants in these joined cases—the employer in one case being in the public sector and the other employer being in the private sector. If Direct Effect was to be used, it could be applied against the employer in *Von Colson*'s case as the employer was in the public sector (due to VDE), but not for *Harz*, where the employer was in the private sector (due to HDE). To stop the embarrassment and unfairness of this outcome, Indirect Effect bypassed any concerns of such a judgment by enabling any claimant, regardless of whether the other party was in the public or private sector, to utilize the EU law.

Indirect Effect of Directives is evidenced in the following ways:

1 Where legislation has been passed in the UK to implement a requirement derived from an EU Directive, then the UK courts are obliged to adopt a more purposive style of interpretation which seeks to read the obligations in light of the meaning and purpose of the Directive.

2 Where the law has not been passed to implement the requirements of a Directive, and its terms cannot be read so as to conform with the Directive, then the national legislation will be applied.[26]

---

[25] (Cases 14/83 and 79/83) ECR 1891.

[26] *Duke v GEC Reliance*. This case is particularly important as it saved Parliament in 'losing' its sovereignty. As the ECA 1972 s. 2 had instructed the judiciary to follow EU laws, this was only where it was 'possible to do so'. Lord Denning in this case stated that if Parliament expressly contradicts EU law, or Parliament

3 Where the law has not been passed to implement the requirements of a Directive, but the terms of the law are capable of being read in the spirit of an EU Directive, then the national law is capable of being read as though it had been so enacted.[27]

Whilst being a rather contrived way of achieving effectiveness of EU law, it is a method of enforcement that would enable *all* those whose rights had been transgressed potential recourse to the EU law's provisions in the domestic court. Clearly, though, this doctrine had very real limitations as it required a piece of existing legislation which was capable of such an interpretation; (in the case of Directives) a requirement of the judiciary to give such an effect when the domestic parliament had not (or had incorrectly) transposed the particular Directive to be interpreted, as well as a change in policy regarding interpretation of statutes which may have been alien to the judiciary. Indirect Effect creates a potential access to EU laws through the requirement upon the Member States to give effect to EU law, and its obligations under the law, as expressed in Article 4(3) TFEU. It is, however, limited in scope and as such the Court of Justice felt it necessary to continue to provide individuals with a remedy which would ensure Member States met their EU obligations.

6.2.2.3 *State Liability*

This is the final of the three domestic enforcement mechanisms of EU law and is primarily used where no domestic action has been taken by the State (usually in the form of the Government and Parliament) to give effect to an EU law. Examples of this problem can be witnessed where an EU Directive has passed the date for a transposing piece of legislation and there is no domestic law in place which leaves the affected individual/organization without the protection he/she is entitled to. As there is no provision to enforce his/her rights against the perpetrator of a wrong (such as a private-sector employer—because technically whilst there is an EU Directive which gives rights there is no domestic transposing law and hence technically no breach), the affected individual/organization is obliged to bring his/her action for damages against the State. The rationale[28] for this mechanism is that as it is the State's duty to implement the law on time, it should be held responsible for losses that may be incurred due to its failure. This has been a method of enforcement which is often criticized because it is known as a public law[29] action. It has been questioned whether actions between private parties should be heard in public law, which may be outside of the usual method of resolving disputes (in private law actions).[30]

Public law action was a mechanism developed by the Court of Justice to involve the domestic courts in the enforcement of EU rights and to enable individuals to gain compensation if they had been denied rights by a recalcitrant Member State. The Court of Justice had invoked the enforcement mechanisms of Direct Effect and Indirect Effect, but these were largely unsuccessful in ensuring EU laws were being upheld and observed, and the distinction between HDE

---

informs the judiciary to follow an English law notwithstanding any EU law to the contrary, the judiciary follow Parliament's instructions. Any consequence would be between the UK government (as signatories of the Treaty) and the EU, not the judiciary.

[27] *Webb v EMO Air Cargo (UK) Ltd* [1994] 2 CMLR 729.

[28] To understand the theoretical justification of State Liability interested readers can gain a valuable perspective in Lee, I. B. (2000) 'In Search of a Theory of State Liability in the European Union' Harvard Law School, ISSN 1087–2221.

[29] A public law action is a court case involving the State or emanation of the State. A private law action is the most common legal case and involves disputes between private parties under contract law and tort (such as personal injury, nuisance cases and so on).

[30] See Szyszczak, E. (1996) 'Making Europe More Relevant to its Citizens: Effective Judicial Process' *European Law Review*, Vol. 21, October, p. 351. for a detailed consideration of this debate.

and VDE was causing embarrassment for the validity of this method of enforcing EU rights. The Court of Justice recognized the problems it had in ensuring EU law was being followed as required and had been widely criticized by academics and other commentators for denying HDE. It hence established the alternative remedy of State Liability to alleviate these criticisms. The case of *Francovich* began the process of holding the State liable for breaches of EU laws and provided the affected individual with a public law damages action against the State (see Craig 1997),[31] rather than methods of gaining access to the law through the private actions of Direct Effect and Indirect Effect against the direct transgressor. Public law, it was felt by the Court of Justice, would give the individual the remedy he/she required whilst also ensuring the State was involved in the process and would be thereby 'encouraged' through the action[32] towards ensuring the laws were complied with to limit future claims and damages actions.

? Thinking Point

Do you think it is appropriate to claim against the State under State Liability rather than claim against the individual employer who is not following EU law and, in all other respects, is the perpetrator of the wrong?

Francovich and Another v Italy[33]

Facts:

Mr Francovich worked for CDN Elettronica SnC in Vicenza from 11 January 1983 until 7 April 1984 but had only received sporadic payments on account of his wages. He brought an action before a court (the Pretore di Vicenza) which awarded him six million lire. However, the court-appointed bailiff was unable to recoup this money. As Mr Francovich could not obtain his owed wages from his employer, he initiated an action against the Italian State which, under Directive 80/987, was obliged to provide workers with owed wages in the event of their employer's insolvency, but Italy failed to do so.[34] In determining that Italy had an obligation to provide compensation for individuals suffering damage due to a total failure by the Member State to transpose the effects of a Directive, the Court of Justice famously stated that 'Member States are obliged to make good loss and damage caused to individuals by breaches of Community law for which they can be held responsible.'

Authority for:

Where the State has caused an individual loss due to its failure to transpose a Directive as required by EU law, insofar as the tests outlined below are satisfied, the State has an obligation to provide compensation.

---

[31] Craig, P. (1997) 'Directives: Direct Effect, Indirect Effect and the Construction of National Legislation' *European Law Review*, December, p. 519.

[32] Paying damages to citizens (potentially many claimants) who did not have access to the EU law which was required of the State was considered to be an effective way of 'speeding up' the State to comply with its obligations.

[33] [1991] ECR I-5357.

[34] Member States were required to have transposed the Directive by 23 October 1983. Italy failed to fulfil that obligation, and the Court of Justice subsequently made a declaration to that effect in *Commission v Italy* [1989] ECR 143 (Case 22/87).

To identify whether a State has an obligation under State Liability three tests have to be satisfied:

1   the Directive should grant rights to individuals;

2   these rights should be clear and identifiable from the Directive; and

3   there should be a causal link between the breach of the Member States' obligation and the loss or damage suffered by the party claiming.

These tests, to be successful in holding the State to account, were further developed by the Court of Justice in the increasing case law which followed;[35] as a result of the different administrative bodies which were included in State Liability actions;[36] and because, following *Francovich*, many Member States would at least attempt to transpose the effects of a Directive on time. They may, however, do so incorrectly and the Court of Justice had to include the element of discretion[37] which exists for Member States (from Article 288 TFEU) so as not to make these public actions unfair, or draconically hold Member States liable. The tests were thus modified in *Brasserie* (para. 4) and are now:

1   the rule of law infringed must have been intended to confer rights on individuals;

2   the breach must be *sufficiently serious*; and

3   there must be a direct causal link between the breach and the damage suffered.

If these tests are satisfied the claimant may be successful in suing the State for any losses he/she has incurred.

The *Francovich* case created the third domestic enforcement mechanism, of 'State Liability'. Following this case, individuals had the right to sue a Member State for any damages they incurred because of a failure to implement EU law. Due to the limitations of Direct Effect and Indirect Effect, this provides individuals with recourse to a remedy. There are several problems with State Liability,[38] and it may be interesting to know that this case, which created the right of an individual to seek damages action against the State, eventually led to Mr Francovich failing to obtain any damages payment at all against Italy.

 Conclusion

Enforcement for the individual who has had his/her EU law rights transgressed can take effect through one of the mechanisms identified here if the UK has failed to give effect correctly to the law. By their nature, Treaty Articles and Regulations are automatically law in the UK and

---

[35]   Including *Brasserie du Pecheur SA v Germany* [1996] (Case C-46/93) [1996] ECR I-1029; *R v Secretary of State for Transport, ex parte Factortame* [1996] (Factortame III) (Case C-48/93) ECR I-1029; and *R v HM Treasury, ex parte British Telecommunications plc* [1996] (Case C-392/93) ECR I-1631.

[36]   *R v Ministry of Agriculture, Fisheries and Food, ex parte Hedley Lomas (Ireland) Ltd* [1996] (Case C-5/94) ECR I-2553.

[37]   As Directives set out the 'result to be achieved' and leave the Member State to decide the most appropriate way of achieving this there is discretion in the method adopted by the State. It may also be that the State innocently misinterprets the Directive and therefore it should not automatically suffer a damages action because of this discretionary element.

[38]   See Marson, J. (2004) 'Holes in the Safety Net? State Liability and the Need for Private Law Enforcement' *Liverpool Law Review*, Vol. 25, p. 113.

are less susceptible to being denied to those in the Member State. However, due to their flexibility and the element of harmonization of EU laws, Directives are the predominant instrument of legislation in the EU, and when these laws are not given effect in the prescribed time limit, then enforcement can at least be attempted. Access to the EU laws is paramount and a knowledge of this source of law is vital for an appreciation of from where laws derive and the future direction of regulations in the commercial areas of company law, contract law, and employment.

 Summary of main points

- The EU created a 'new legal order' that not only provided rights for, but also placed obligations on, individuals in the Member States of the EU.
- Methods of enforcing these rights had to be created. This occurred at two levels, an EU level and a domestic level.

Enforcement at the EU level

- The EC Commission, under Article 258 TFEU, has the role to ensure fulfillment of the aims of the Treaty through enforcement proceedings.

Enforcement at the domestic level

- The Court of Justice developed the ability of individuals and corporations to gain access to their EU law rights through the domestic courts. This prevented claims having to be pursued through the Court of Justice at Luxembourg.
- Direct Effect is an enforcement mechanism where EU laws are capable of direct use in the Member States' domestic courts.
- This created Horizontal and Vertical Direct Effect. Treaty Articles have both Horizontal and Vertical Effect, but Directives are only enforceable vertically.
- The rules (established in **Van Gend en Loos**) needed for a claim of Direct Effect are:
  - the provision must be clear and unambiguous;
  - the provision must be unconditional; and
  - the provision must not be dependent on further action being taken by the EU or Member State.
- Indirect Effect is a method of statutory interpretation where the domestic courts have to, where possible, interpret existing laws to be compatible with EU obligations. This attempted to limit the problems of the Horizontal and Vertical distinction of Direct Effect of Directives.
- Most recently, the Court of Justice developed the enforcement mechanism of **State Liability** where a private party could claim for damages against the State if the State had failed in its duty to apply the correct EU law.
- State Liability is established through the following rules:
  - the rule of law infringed must have been intended to confer rights on individuals;
  - the breach must be sufficiently serious; and
  - there must be a direct causal link between the breach and the damage suffered.

Summary questions

Essay questions

1. Membership of the EU, with its 'new legal order,' has had a profound effect on the constitution of the UK. With specific reference to case law examples, explain where the most significant constitutional changes have occurred and identify how these changes have affected legal jurisdictions such as competition and employment.

2. The European Union (EU) creates laws which the Member States have an obligation to follow, and in the case of Directives, have to transpose into their legal systems. Frequently, Member States fail to give effect to these rights and this can result in individuals being denied access to EU rights.

   Explain the mechanisms of Direct Effect, Indirect Effect, and State Liability, which the Court of Justice has developed to enable individuals to access EU laws when there has been a failure by the Member State. Discuss the advantages and limitations of each of these enforcement mechanisms.

Problem questions

1. The (fictitious) Directive 1/2008 requires that from 1 January 2010, all workers in each of the Member States shall be entitled to claim, before a national court or tribunal, that they have been dismissed. This right is dependent upon the qualification that he/she has been employed by the same employer for at least six months before the termination of the contract of employment. The UK had passed a statutory instrument in 1998 stipulating that the qualification period to make an unfair dismissal claim is one year's continuous employment.

   The UK has failed to implement Directive 1/2008 even though the time limit for implementation was 1 July 2009. The UK sought to justify the non-implementation on the grounds of protests from its own Parliament, and from industry representatives concerned over its effects in the current economic climate.

   In September 2009 Simon began employment with Cleaneasiest, an organization that provides cleaning services exclusively to National Health Service hospitals. In April 2010 Simon was dismissed by Cleaneasiest.

   Advise Simon as to any EU law rights available.

2. On 1 May 2007, the European Council adopted a (fictitious) Directive concerned with the protection of young persons in employment. The Directive, *inter alia*, provides that no persons under 18 years of age shall be required to work at night, and that any such person who is dismissed by his/her employer for refusing to work at night when requested to do so shall be entitled to 'an appropriate remedy from a national court or tribunal, which may include compensation.' Member States were given one year to implement the Directive.

   The British government was opposed to the Directive on ideological grounds and voted against its adoption in the Council of Ministers where the Directive, in accordance with the Treaty provision on which it was based, was adopted by qualified majority vote. For this reason, and because it is concerned by the possibly adverse economic consequences for employers from the Directive, the British government has not yet taken any steps to implement it.

University of Chester, Queen's Park Library

Title: Business law / James Marson.
ID: 36134717
Due: 17-03-16

Total items: 1
25/02/2016 13:47

Renew online at:
http://libcat.chester.ac.uk/patroninfo

Thank you for using Self Check

248

Jake, who is 17 years old, has been employed in a Ministry of Defence munitions factory for 12 months. As a consequence of the need to reduce the size of the manufacturing facility and economize on production costs, Jake has been asked to work at night on the newly established night shift. Not wishing to ruin a happy social life, Jake refuses to do so. As a result he has been threatened with dismissal unless he complies. Advise:

a) The European Commission of the steps it can take against the UK to ensure that the Directive is implemented; and

b) Jake, as to whether he can take legal proceedings to uphold his legal position and obtain compensation if dismissed.

Would your advice to Jake differ if the employer in this scenario was in private ownership?

 ## Further reading

Dougan, M. (2000) 'The 'Disguised' Vertical Direct Effect of Directives?' *Cambridge Law Journal*, Vol. 59, 3, p. 586.

Marson, J. (2004) 'Holes in the Safety Net? State Liability and the Need for Private Law Enforcement' *Liverpool Law Review*, Vol. 25, p. 113.

Ward, A. (2007) 'Judicial Review and the Rights of Private Parties in EU Law' (2nd Edition) Oxford University Press: Oxford and New York.

Online Resource Centre

http://www.oxfordtextbooks.co.uk/orc/marson3e/
Why not visit the Online Resource Centre and try multiple choice questions associated with this chapter to test your understanding of the topic. You will also find relevant updates to the law.

III Contractual Obligations

7 Essential Features of a Valid Contract 1: Offer and Acceptance

Why does it matter?

What makes an agreement a legally enforceable contract? When you contract on behalf of your business, will you have any rights against the other party if he/she fails to complete the agreed obligations? What is the legal status where an item is advertised in a newspaper or a shop window—is it an offer by the shopkeeper to sell the item? Can you force the sale of an item that displays an incorrect price on the tag? These are just a few questions the answers to which businesses must be aware of before trading, and this chapter and Chapter 8 provide the answers.

Learning outcomes

Following reading this chapter you should be in a position to:

- identify the nature and essential elements of a legally enforceable agreement (7.4–7.4.2.2)
- differentiate between an offer and an invitation to treat (7.4.1–7.4.1.1)
- understand the implications of counter-offers terminating an offer (7.4.1.2).
- identify when true acceptance has taken place (7.4.2–7.4.2.2)

ᛘ Key terms

These terms will be used in the chapter and it may be helpful to be aware of what they mean or refer back to them when reading through the chapter.

Offeree
The party(s) to whom an offer has been made.

Offeror
The party making an offer and setting out the terms by which he/she is willing to be bound.

Revocation
An offer may be withdrawn (revoked) by the offeror before being accepted by the offeree.

> **Void contract**
> The law will not recognize the agreement and therefore it has no legal effect (such as an illegal contract or one established through mistake).
>
> **Voidable contract**
> This is an agreement that can be a legally binding contract at the option of the injured party or which such party can have set aside (such as with contracts established under misrepresentation, duress and so on).

7.1 Introduction

This chapter identifies the essential features necessary to establish a legally binding contract. It is important to note at the outset that most contracts need not be reduced in writing and indeed most of the contracts you have established today—buying a newspaper or cup of coffee—were not established in writing, even if you received a receipt. However, each of the essential features noted in this chapter and Chapter 8 are present in forming those contracts. Before the essential features are considered, it is important to briefly note that contracts can be established by the parties exchanging promises, or by one party promising to perform an act in return for some action by the other. In this later scenario, the second party has no obligation to take any action unless he/she wishes to enter the contract.

7.2 Unilateral and bilateral contracts

It is important to identify whether the contract made is unilateral or bilateral. Bilateral contracts are those where one of the parties offers to do something in return for an action by the other party—they exchange promises. Each of the parties in this type of contract has an obligation to perform some action. For example, one person agrees to wash the other's car in return for having his/her lawn mowed. A unilateral contract is one where the first party promises to perform some action in return for a specific act, although the second party is not promising to take any action. *Carlill v Carbolic Smoke Ball Co.* is an example of a unilateral contract. There is no obligation on the person to buy the advertised smoke ball, but where he/she does and, as with Mrs Carlill, contracts influenza, he/she can claim the £100 advertised as the contractual obligations will have been completed.

7.3 Void and voidable contracts

The main focus of this chapter and Chapter 8 is to identify the essential features required to make an enforceable (valid) contract. Some contracts, however, do not obtain the status of a valid contract because the law will not recognize the agreement or it may miss one of the essential features and so not amount to a contract.

• *Void contracts:* A **void contract** is not a contract that the law will recognize and so has no legal effect. In law such an agreement was never a valid contract and consequently there are no obligations on either party.

- *Voidable contracts:* A **voidable contract** is one where the injured party has the option to affirm the contract (he/she can continue with the agreement and bring about an enforceable contract) or he/she can avoid the contract (and the contract is terminated). The key element here is that it is for the injured party to decide if he/she wishes to proceed with the agreement or have it set aside. This must be performed within a reasonable time[1] to be fair to each party.

7.4 The essential features of a valid contract

Having identified what a contract is, it is then important to establish how a legally enforceable contract is created. The term 'legally enforceable' contract is important because in the absence of one or more of the following requirements the courts will not acknowledge that a legally recognizable contract is in existence. This text contends that the essential features can be sub-divided into five categories, and once it is satisfied that the parties have the legal capacity to contract, the following are the most relevant and important features of a valid contract:

- *Offer:* The statement from the **offeror** to the **offeree** identifying the terms by which he/she is willing to be bound. This must be distinguished from an invitation to treat, which is a situation whereby offers are invited. Offers can be unilateral or bilateral.
- *Acceptance:* The full and unconditional acceptance by the offeree of the terms identified in the offer. If any other terms are included by the offeree then the response is said to be a counter-offer that terminates the first offer and will not constitute acceptance.
- *Consideration:* The legal element to ensure the contract is a bargain (the law will not enforce a 'bare' promise). The consideration only has to be sufficient, not adequate.
- *Intention to create legal relations:* The parties must intend that their agreement is to create legal responsibilities on both sides, resulting in possible legal consequences if one party fails or defaults on his/her obligations. This goes beyond the scope of 'social agreements' and intends to establish the availability of a legal remedy in the case of breach.
- *Certainty of terms:* The terms of a contract have to be sufficiently clear and certain to enable the courts to enforce the contract.

7.4.1 Offer

 Business Link

Offer or invitation to treat? The distinction is vital to identify the duties on the parties in establishing an agreement that may go on to form a contract. Why does a retailer have the right to refuse to sell to you an item displayed in its shop which is presented with an

---

[1] In contract and torts law the word 'reasonable' is often used. In the absence of specific instruction from legislation or a principle from case law this word is interpreted with regards to the facts of a particular case. In any respect, in this situation the party should act as quickly as is possible.

incorrect price tag? The answer is because the item with the price tag is considered at law (apart from a few exceptions) as an invitation to treat. The retailer is inviting you to make an offer to purchase, it is not offering to sell it to you. If an item displaying a price tag was held to be an offer to sell, consider the implications of the following. Suppose you visit a coffee shop, seeing the café latte that you are interested in purchasing, listed on a display board with a price of £2.50. You approach the counter, ask for the coffee and are told by the member of staff that the electricity supply to the shop has been cut due to the negligence of contractors working outside. Therefore the shop has no electrical power necessary to make the coffee. Is the shop in breach of its contract? You are there to accept the offer of the coffee, you intend to pay for it, and it is a shop in business to serve customers so there is presumed to be a legally binding agreement being entered into. This would be ludicrous—hence why there is a general rule that this is an example of an invitation to treat, not an offer to sell. Understanding which situations constitute an invitation to treat or an offer to sell is vital to appreciating the legal rights and obligations between parties to an agreement.

An offer is simply an identification of the terms by which the offeror is willing to be bound. This offer is made to the offeree, who may be an individual, company, group of people, or even the entire world. The offeror is the party that establishes the terms by which he/she is willing to be bound and therefore he/she has the choice of what terms are contained and to whom the offer is made. Only the offeree may accept the offer and he/she must accept in the method expressed (if stipulated) by the offeror.

Carlill v Carbolic Smoke Ball Co.[2]

Facts:

The defendants were proprietors of a medical preparation—the 'Carbolic Smoke Ball'. The company was so confident in its product that it advertised in newspapers that anyone who used the ball three times daily for a two-week period and contracted influenza would be rewarded with £100. It further identified in the advert that to demonstrate the company's sincerity, it had deposited £1,000 in a local bank to satisfy any claims. The claimant, Mrs Carlill, on the faith of this advertisement, bought one of the balls and used it as directed. However, she contracted influenza, and claimed her 'reward' although, as could be expected, the Carbolic Smoke Ball Company did not wish to pay the £100 and argued to the court why the advertisement did not constitute a contract.

The Court of Appeal held that there was a valid contract. The £1,000 being placed in the bank demonstrated the company's sincerity in paying the £100 identified in the advertisement. Carlill's acceptance was evidenced through her using the product (her conduct), and there was nothing in the advertisement that required a specific form of acceptance to be notified to the company. As such, the advertisement could be accepted by anyone who saw the advert and purchased and used, as directed, the product.

Authority for:

(In relation to this aspect of the case—as *Carlill* is authority for many propositions.) It is possible to make an offer to the entire world, and it may therefore be accepted by those persons.

---

[2] [1893] 1 QB 256.

7.4.1.1 *Offer v invitation to treat*

An 'invitation to treat' is the term used when a party invites offers (essentially the party with the goods/services to trade invites offers which he/she is able to accept or decline). In this context, the word 'treat' means to negotiate, hence it is an invitation to negotiate for a good or service. Cases that have established the general rule of where an invitation to treat exists did so in light of traders selling goods, advertisements, auctions, and negotiations. It should be noted that for businesses, it may be wise to sell goods under 'invitation to treat' rather than 'offers', as this provides the company with flexibility in its sales strategy.

- *Goods displaying price tags:* Goods displayed in shop windows or on the shelves in retail outlets, and those goods advertised in newspapers/on television and so on may be offers to sell or invitations to treat. To identify which is applicable, the common law has developed the following precedents.

Pharmaceutical Society of Great Britain v Boots Cash Chemists[3]

Facts:

Boots Chemists established shops that began to operate a 'self-service' system whereby customers could select items displayed in the shop, place them in their basket, and present these at the till to complete the purchase. On the shelves were various products, with a price marked on the packaging, and these products included various drugs and proprietary medicines that could only be sold in the presence of a registered pharmacist. The customer would select goods and present these to the cashier at a till-point, where the transaction would take place. At each till-point was a registered pharmacist who was in control of the department. The Pharmaceutical Society of Great Britain brought an action against Boots. It alleged that a 'sale' took place when a customer placed items from the shelves into their shopping basket (hence not in the presence of the pharmacist and contrary to the legal requirements). The Court of Appeal disagreed. The customer offered to purchase his/her selected goods at the till-point (in the presence of the registered pharmacist) where the retailer either accepted or declined the offer. Therefore no infringement of the law had taken place.

Authority for:

Items displayed on the shelves of shops with a price tag attached are invitations to treat not offers to sell.

The Court of Appeal established the precedent that items in a shop with a price tag attached did not constitute an offer to sell, binding the shopkeeper to sell to whoever entered the shop and selected an item. This is necessary to prevent a shop from displaying goods with an incorrect price tag on and then being compelled to proceed with the contract on the basis of an innocent mistake. This precedent established in the *Boots* case was corroborated in *Fisher v Bell*.[4]

These cases identified that the courts will generally consider goods advertised in shop windows or those with a price tag attached to constitute an invitation to treat. Whilst this is true in the widest sense, there have been instances where an item in a shop window with information regarding the price has constituted an offer, not an invitation to treat. The following case

---

[3] [1953] 2 WLR 427.   [4] [1960] 3 WLR 919.

was heard in the USA (and because it is not in this jurisdiction it has limited authority as a precedent), but due to the similarities of the legal systems (the common law) it could provide evidence of how an English court may apply law in a case with similar facts:

Leftkowitz v Great Minneapolis Surplus Stores[5]

Facts:

The company placed an advertisement in a Minneapolis newspaper regarding a sale that was to take place on a Saturday morning, 9am sharp, where two mink scarves and a stole were to be sold for $1 each (significantly below the usual retail price). Mr Leftkowitz presented himself at the appropriate counter in the store and demanded the item for $1 and was refused. He was informed that he could not avail himself of the special price due to a 'house rule' that stipulated the offer was only available to women. When Leftkowitz brought an action for damages the company contended that the advertisement was an invitation to treat, not an offer to sell, and hence it was within its rights to reject the offer to purchase the goods for $1. The court, however, stated that the circumstances in this case would constitute an offer to sell, which the customer was within his rights to accept.

Authority for:

An advertisement in a newspaper, or shop window, may be elevated from an invitation to treat to constitute an offer to sell if the offer is clear, definite and explicit, and it leaves nothing open for negotiation.

This case demonstrated an alternative view to the general rule of advertisements being an invitation to treat, and demonstrates the importance of the correct drafting, and the legal significance, of advertising materials. It was the level of detail in the advertisement that established it as an offer rather than an invitation to treat. The more definite the detail and description of what is for sale and under what terms the sale will take place, the more likely the court will hold the advertisement as an offer.

Note that when prices are displayed, under the case law identified in this chapter, these are generally invitations to treat and so the trader has no obligation to sell at the displayed price. However, if a price is displayed and is done so where the trader is not prepared to sell (and in essence is deceiving the purchaser) then this is a breach of the Consumer Protection from Unfair Trading Regulations 2008 and the trader may face prosecution.

- *Advertisements:* Advertisements are a potentially problematic area often because the words used can lead buyers to assume an offer has been made. This is frequently not the case and you must exercise care to apply the law, not customer relations policies in such circumstances:

Partridge v Crittenden[6]

Facts:

Arthur Partridge had placed an advert in the *Cage and Aviary Birds* magazine that read 'Quality British bramblefinch cocks, bramblefinch hens … 25s each'. Mr Thompson responded to the advert, sending payment, and he received a bird. The bramblefinch hen that was sent had a closed-ring around its leg identifying that it was bred in captivity and hence legal to sell, but it was possible to remove the ring and consequently Partridge was charged with unlawfully

---

[5]   [1957] 86 NW 2d 689.   [6]   [1968] 1 WLR 1204.

offering for sale a bird contrary to the Protection of Birds Act 1954. Partridge claimed the advertisement was not an offer to sell but an invitation to treat. The Divisional Court agreed.

Authority for:

Following the previous authorities, an advertisement in a newspaper, a magazine, a billboard, on television and so on will be considered an invitation to treat.

The courts will often interpret advertisements in newspapers, magazines, and journals as an invitation to treat. With advertisements generally, whether these are through television, radio, or the internet, the same rules apply.

- *Auctions:* The auction is a typical example of an invitation to treat. The auctioneer invites bids to the goods as advertised and can then decide to accept or decline, with completion being achieved on the fall of the hammer.[7] There have also been cases concerning auctions which advertised the sale of particular items which were subsequently not included in the sale. Whether individuals who intended to offer on the (non-presented) items can claim their expenses back was considered in the following case:

Harris v Nickerson[8]

Facts:

Mr Nickerson was an auctioneer who had advertised an auction (to include office furniture) to be held by him for three days. Mr Harris was a broker and travelled to the auction with the intention of bidding on the furniture. On the third day of the auction, when the office furniture was to be auctioned, all the lots were withdrawn without prior notice. Harris claimed breach of contract and attempted to recover his losses of time and expenses incurred (railway fare and his board and lodgings) as he contended the advertisement was an offer to sell those lots and as he had travelled to the auction to purchase and accept that offer. The High Court held that Harris could not recover his losses, as the advertisement was a mere declaration of intent that could not amount to an offer capable of acceptance.

Authority for:

Auctions are examples of invitations to treat. Simply advertising products in auctioneering literature does not create any obligations that those items will be included or that any subsequent offers will be accepted.

The case confirmed the previous rulings by the courts that an advertisement in the press will not, of itself, create any contract with a reader until the acceptance has been recognized in law. In the present situation, that would be that the highest, genuine, bidder at the auction makes an offer accepted by the auctioneer and forms a valid contract.

- *Tenders:* It had traditionally been considered that an invitation to tender is an invitation to treat. The party that submits the tender is making an offer and the party inviting the tender has the option to accept or decline. However, whilst this position provides the party inviting the tender with great power and seemingly little in the way of obligations to the party submitting the tender, those inviting tenders may have an obligation

---

[7] See *Payne v Cave* [1789] 3 TR 148.   [8] (1872–73) LR 8 QB 286.

to 'consider' the tender. In *Harvela Investments Ltd v Royal Trust Co of Canada Ltd*[9] shares in the defendant company were to be sold through a sealed competitive tender (the shares being sold to the highest of two invited bidders). Harvela offered $2,175,000 and the second tender offered '$2,100,000 or $101,000 in excess of any other offer, whichever was higher.' The second tender was accepted (on the basis that it in effect constituted a bid of $2,276,000) and this led to Harvela's claim. The House of Lords held that Harvela's bid had to be the one accepted as the nature of the tender, whilst only an invitation to treat, was based on fairness, and also on the basis of the reasonable expectation of the parties. The parties had invested time and effort in preparing the tender, they were invited to submit the tender, and it was reasonable for the decision to be made on the criteria described—namely that the tenders were to be 'fixed bids'. This element of reasonable expectation to consider a tender was followed in *Blackpool and Fylde Aero Ltd v Blackpool BC*[10] and led Bingham LJ to remark that as the procedure of a tender is heavily weighted in favour of the party inviting the tenders (in choosing to accept and decline the offers and so on) the tendering party is at least entitled to have the tender considered, and in this case it was a contractual right to have it considered.

? Thinking Point

How far will the requirement to consider all tenders be applied by the courts (what if hundreds of tenders are submitted)? Further, how do you think the assessment of the breach of this requirement will be remedied through an award of damages and how will this be quantified?

- *Negotiations:* Negotiations occur between parties in the contract process. Questions of item, price, quantity, and the terms surrounding any possible contract may come under consideration. This can lead to disagreements as to when an offer may have been made which is capable of acceptance. The courts have had to look to the parties' statements and other evidence to ascertain their true intentions:

Harvey v Facey[11]

Facts:

Mr Facey and his wife owned a property named Bumper Hall Pen. They received a telegram from Adelaide Harvey which read: 'Will you sell us Bumper Hall Pen? Telegraph lowest cash price.' Facey responded with 'Lowest price for Bumper Hall Pen £900' and Harvey followed this with a further telegram: 'We agree to buy Bumper Hall Pen for £900 asked by you.' Facey did not reply or sell the property to Harvey who, as a result, brought an action for breach of contract and requested an order for specific performance.[12] The Privy

---

[9] [1986] AC 207.   [10] [1990] 1 WLR 1195.   [11] [1893] AC 552.

[12] Specific performance is a remedy (dealt with in Chapter 12) whereby the contract is ordered to be completed by the party in breach. Typically such an award is made where damages are not an adequate remedy and the subject matter of the contract is a unique item (land, property, antiques and so on).

Council found that there was no contract established as no offer had been made to sell the property—only an offer to buy and acceptance of this had to be expressed and could not be implied.

Authority for:

There has to be a clear offer of a willingness from the offeror to be bound (a genuine offer to sell) for an acceptance to be possible and hence create a valid contract.

Mere negotiations between parties are insufficient to create a contract and the courts will not imply an offer in these situations. It is further demonstrated in the following case the necessity of distinguishing an offer to sell from an enquiry of an interest in purchase.

- *Request for information:* Requesting additional information with regard to a negotiation will not provide a valid acceptance of an offer nor defeat the offer through a counter-offer.[13] Negotiations are an important element of forming a contract and the sharing of information is necessary to identify the scope of the obligations involved.

Gibson v Manchester CC[14]

Facts:

Robert Gibson was a tenant and occupier of a council house under the control of Manchester City Council and had been actively interested in purchasing the house. In 1970 the Council undertook to offer for sale various Council-owned properties to sitting tenants and wrote to Gibson informing him that it may be prepared to sell the house to him for a price of £2,725 less 20 per cent (freehold). On 18 March 1971 Gibson wrote to the Council requesting the purchase of the house, but in May 1971 political control of the Council changed, along with the policy of selling Council-owned properties, and only those houses where a legally binding contract had been established would be sold. The Council notified Gibson that the sale of the house would not be proceeding and he claimed breach of contract. The House of Lords held that as the Council had never offered to sell the property valid acceptance was not possible. All that had occurred in this case were the first steps towards negotiations for a sale which never reached fruition.

Authority for:

A request for information is not an offer capable of acceptance.

An invitation as to a willingness to enter a contract or a party's potential interest in forming a contract will not be considered an offer capable of acceptance. Negotiations have to proceed to a stage when a formal offer is made before a contract can be established. In *Storer v Manchester CC*[15] the Council had sent the claimant information regarding the possibility of tenants purchasing their Council-owned property. Storer completed the application form and the Council had replied with a letter requesting that the applicant sign an enclosed agreement for sale of the property, and the Council would return the agreement as signed. Storer did complete and return the form but the Council did not reciprocate as promised before the control of the Council changed political parties. The Court of Appeal held that a contract was formed as the letter from the Council was a

---

13 See **7.4.1.2**.   14 [1979] 1 WLR 294.   15 [1974] 3 All ER 824.

firm intention to proceed with the sale when Storer returned the application form, and as such the Council was obliged to conclude the contract.

At this stage, it is possible to identify whether an offer or invitation has been created, or if negotiations are in progress rather than a formal offer having been established. However, for how long does the offer last—is it indefinitely or until acceptance has taken place? Or is some other method developed by the courts? In order for the offeror to have control over the length of time that the offer remains in existence, he/she may wish to incorporate methods of terminating an offer.

7.4.1.2 *Termination of an Offer*

 Business Link

Offers can be terminated in numerous ways. They will not remain in existence or open indefinitely enabling the offeree to accept at any time he/she chooses. Even if no term is expressed as to when the offer will lapse, the courts have demonstrated where offers will expire after a reasonable time. It is also imperative to understand the rule that counter-offers made in negotiations have the effect of terminating an offer. Unless a further offer is made, the first offer is ended on the counter-offer and cannot later be accepted. Diligence and risk-assessment in negotiations is necessary.

It would not be prudent to make an offer and then have that offer last for an indefinite time. The offeror can incorporate whatever terms he/she wishes into the contract, but because many contracts are not in writing (and contracts of sale need not be—see Sale of Goods Act 1979, s. 4) this 'time-scale' issue may not have been fully considered. Any offer which has been withdrawn before acceptance takes place stops any true acceptance. As a corollary, where an offer is accepted before it is withdrawn the other party must continue with the contract.

Termination can occur in a variety of ways such as:

* *The death of the offeror:* If the offeror has made an offer that has not been accepted before his/her death, then the offer dies with him/her. If the offer has been accepted and then the offeror dies, where practicable the contract must still be performed (by the dead person's estate or executors). However, if the contract requires some element of personal service by the offeror (such as in contracts of employment) the contract will come to an end under the doctrine of frustration.[16]

* *Expiry of a fixed time limit:* As stated previously, the offeror may incorporate any terms into a contract by which he/she is willing to be bound. This may include a time limit for acceptance which must be adhered to (as acceptance is full and complete acceptance of the offeror's terms). If the time limit for acceptance expires, then the offer dies and cannot be later accepted.

* *Acceptance must be within a reasonable time:* The parties can incorporate terms into the contract, such as for time limits when an offer will expire, but where no such clause has been included, a reasonable time may be implied into the contract. What is reasonable, in this sense, is dependent upon the individual circumstances of a case.

---

[16] See Chapter 12.

Ramsgate Victoria Hotel v Montefiore[17]

Facts:

Montefiore applied to purchase shares in the hotel in June but shares were not issued until November. Due to the time delay between his application and the issue of the shares, Montefiore refused to accept the shares and an action was raised for non-acceptance. It was held that whilst his offer of purchase did not contain any provision for expiry, the court considered that allotment must take place within a reasonable time, and this had not been achieved. As such Ramsgate's action failed.

Authority for:

In the absence of any specific provision for the expiry of an offer the court will imply one which is reasonable in the circumstances. This will vary depending upon the item being contracted for—for example shares will have a relatively short time for an offer to be accepted; perishable goods such as fruit and vegetables will possibly have an even shorter time.

- *If the offer is rejected:* The offeree can inform the offeror that he/she does not wish to accept on the offer made, which will reject the offer and destroy it. Rejection can be explicit in this manner and it can be through the actions of the party (such as making a counter-offer).
- *If a counter-offer is made:* In the negotiations of contracts the offeror establishes the terms by which he/she is willing to be bound, but where the offeree does not accept but alters the terms of the offer to suit him/herself, this is a counter-offer. The positions of the parties (as offeror and offeree) are reversed. The legal significance of contractual negotiations is that any counter-offer destroys the original offer and means that the previous offer cannot later be accepted. The stages of offers/counter-offers can be seen in Figure 7.1 in relation to the negotiations in *Hyde v Wrench*.

Hyde v Wrench[18]

Facts:

On 6 June Wrench offered to sell land for £1,000 to Hyde. On 8 June Hyde replied, expressing 'acceptance' at a purchase price of £950. Wrench rejected the offer of £950 and later Hyde contacted Wrench stating he would accept the original offer and pay £1,000 for the land. Wrench declined to proceed with the sale. The court held that if Hyde had unconditionally accepted Wrench's offer to sell at £1,000 a binding contract would have been established that the court would enforce. However, by Hyde making his own offer of £950 he had (implicitly) rejected the first offer, which made it impossible to accept it at a later date.

Authority for:

A counter-offer terminates the original offer.

---

[17] (1865–66) LR 1 Ex. 109.   [18] [1840] 3 Beav 334.

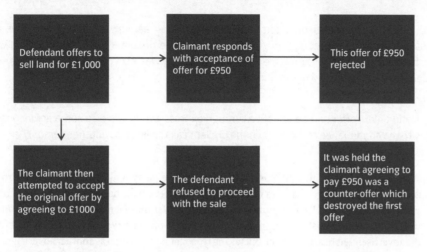

Figure 7.1 *Hyde v Wrench*

Care has to be taken when involved in negotiations. If a party attempts to obtain the best terms and reject an offer through his/her counter-offer, he/she will be unable to accept on that previous offer unless the other party offers it again.

- **Revocation** *of the offer:* The offeror has the right to revoke his/her offer at any time until acceptance has taken place. This is true even where the offeror has promised to keep the offer open for a specific period of time.[19] The exception to this general rule is where the offeree has provided some consideration for the 'benefit' of the offer remaining available. The stipulation to this rule is that the onus is on the offeror to inform those to whom he/she has made the offer that it has been revoked. As such, it is incumbent on the offeror to effectively communicate the revocation to the offeree.[20]

  When communicating through the post, revocation is not effective until it has been communicated and hence received, by the offeree.[21] This is unlike the postal rule on acceptance where acceptance takes effect on posting whether this is received or not. Revocation of an offer is also effective where this has been communicated to the offeree by a reliable third party rather than the offeror:

Dickinson v Dodds[22]

Facts:

On 10 June 1874 Mr Dodds provided a document to Mr Dickinson stating that he would agree to sell his houses to Dickinson for £800 and the offer would remain open until 9am, 12 June. Dickinson had decided on the morning of 11 June to accept the offer but did not signify this to Dodds, as he believed he had until 9am the following day to communicate his acceptance. In the afternoon of 11 June Dickinson was informed by an agent for Dodds, that Dodds had agreed to sell the property to another person (and hence had implicitly revoked the offer to Dickinson). On hearing this news Dickinson sought to accept the offer through a formal letter. However, Dodds proceeded with the sale

---

19 See *Dickinson v Dodds.*   20 *Payne v Cave* [1789].
21 *Byrne & Co. v Leon Van Tienhoven & Co.* (1879–80) LR 5 CPD 344.
22 (1875–76) LR 2 Ch. D. 463.

to the third party. Dickinson attempted to have this agreement rescinded and have his 'contract' enforced. The Court of Appeal held that the document sent to Dickinson was an offer that could be withdrawn at any time before it was accepted insofar as the revocation was communicated to the offeree.

Authority for:

Revocation of an offer can be effective through express words and also some act inconsistent with the continuance of the offer (in the present case selling it to another person).

In situations of 'unilateral' contracts (whereby one party makes an offer which can be accepted by a member of a class of persons to whom the offer has been made—e.g. *Carlill v Carbolic Smoke Ball Co.*) the option to revoke the offer may be more difficult. In *Carlill*, it would be quite unrealistic to communicate the revocation to every person who may have seen the advertisement in a newspaper, but taking reasonable steps (such as another advertisement in the same newspaper revoking the offer) may be acceptable. Revocation can occur at any time *until* it has been accepted, but if the acceptance includes the performance of an act, once that act has been started (as acceptance through conduct) it may not be revoked.

Errington v Errington and Woods[23]

Facts:

Mr Errington wished to provide his recently married son with a home and so purchased a house through a building society by paying a lump sum and leaving the balance on the mortgage to be paid by weekly instalments. The father kept the title to the house but promised that if his son and daughter-in-law paid the instalments he would transfer the ownership to them. The father died before the debt on the house was fully repaid and left all his property, including the house, to his widow. The widow brought an action for possession of the house against the daughter-in-law but this failed as the father had created a contract and once this had been accepted, although incomplete of full performance, it could not be revoked. The father had made a promise to his son and daughter-in-law and only if the son and daughter-in-law had failed to continue with the payments on the mortgage (the acceptance) would revocation be possible.

Authority for:

Once acceptance has begun (albeit here incompletely) it cannot be subsequently revoked.

? Thinking Point

Suppose an offer is made that if the offeree completes the London marathon he/she will be rewarded with £100 donated to charity. What would be the position if, when the person who has 'accepted' the offer is running along The Mall towards the finish line, the offeror shouts to him/her that the offer is retracted?

---

[23] [1952] 1 KB 290.

7.4.2 Acceptance

 Business Link

Having established that a valid offer has been made then it is available to the offeree to accept the offer and hence create a valid contract. The acceptance must be made within the time limits of the offer (either implied or expressed), it must be a full and unconditional acceptance *of* the offer made, and it must be communicated to the offeror. Care must be taken when negotiating to ensure that the offeree understands the implications of non-acceptance through a counter-offer (see *Hyde v Wrench*).

Having established that an offer has been made, the offeree has the option to accept or decline. This creates the agreement that will begin the process of substantiating the essential features of a legally binding contract. Agreement may be relevant when considering the issue of mistake to a contract[24] and how this impacts on the enforceable contract.

7.4.2.1 *Unconditional and full acceptance*

The offeror establishes the terms by which he/she is willing to be bound, and as such, acceptance of those terms must be unconditional. In many cases this may constitute a 'yes' or 'no' reply to an offer made. There are situations where such a simple exercise may not be possible and it requires the courts to give direction as to how acceptance may be established:

- *The battle of the forms:* The 'battle of the forms' is commonly referred to when organizations use standard form contracts. The most common example of standard form contracts is where you purchase an item from a high-street retailer. The contract you receive has already been drafted and you must either accept these terms, or decline them and (usually) obtain the item elsewhere. This method is adopted to save time for both parties and to stop protracted negotiations at the store. When two businesses are trading and each has its own standard form contract then problems can arise. How the courts settle disputes between them when there is disagreement as to which contract is to be used was identified in *British Road Services v Arthur Crutchley Ltd*.[25] Here the claimants delivered a consignment of whisky to the defendant's warehouse and the claimant's delivery driver handed the defendants a note to be signed that contained, among other things, the claimant's terms and conditions. This note was stamped by the defendants as 'received under Arthur Crutchley Ltd's conditions' and handed back to the driver. It had to be decided on which terms the contract was based, as the consignment of whisky was stolen, and the court held that by stamping the delivery note, this established a counter-offer, that was impliedly accepted by the driver delivering the consignment. Therefore the contract had been made on the defendant's conditions.

The Court of Appeal was faced with a similar case, and established the concept of the 'first/last shot approach' to determining on which of the parties' standard terms a contract was based:

[24] See **9.4.**   [25] [1968] 1 All ER 811.

Butler Machine Tool Co. Ltd v Ex-Cell-O Corporation (England) Ltd[26]

Facts:

In May 1969 Butler, sellers of machine tools, were contacted by Ex-Cell-O to supply a machine. Butler provided in the quotation for a price of £75,535 and delivery to be made in 10 months. The terms set out in the quotation contained a provision for a price variation clause whereby the goods would be charged at prices at the date of delivery. Ex-Cell-O replied with an order on its terms and conditions (including a 'tear-off' acknowledge-ment strip) that did not include a price variation clause. This was completed and returned by Butler. Various communications passed between the companies but none settled the 'dispute' over the acceptance or otherwise of the price variation clause. The machine was ready for delivery in September 1970 and Ex-Cell-O accepted delivery in November. Butler, when invoicing Ex-Cell-O, invoked the price variation clause and requested a fur-ther £2,892 in addition to the quoted price. It was held that the parties had established an agreement, but it had not been fully expressed. Hence to determine which was the effective contractual terms, reference had to be made to whatever documents were present. As Ex-Cell-O had included an acknowledgement strip that Butler signed and 'accepted', the contract was based on these terms, without the price variation clause.

Authority for:

In agreements between businesses using standard form contracts, the 'first' or 'last shot' approach may be adopted by the courts when identifying the operative contract.

Butler v Ex-Cell-O identified the 'first/last shot approach' adopted by the courts. During the negotiations between the parties the issue of the incorporation of the price variation clause had not been settled. However, a machine had been produced and delivered to one party, and used by the other, and the courts had to determine which contract to use. It would be unfair of the courts to state that, having studied the facts, no contract was present. It would be very difficult to identify with any certainty the benefit gained by the party using the product to apportion and distribute that value. Consequently the court had to determine which was the operative contract. As Butler had signed the 'tear-off' acknowledgement of Ex-Cell-O's order, and the terms of this order were to prevail, this 'first shot' was the operative contract.

Tekdata Interconnections Limited v Amphenol Ltd[27] provided further evidence of the significance of the first/last shot approach and of ensuring the parties 'fire the last shot' in commercial transactions. The parties were suppliers to Rolls Royce and had been in business together for over 20 years. They both attempted to use standard form agreements in concluding the contract, but there was ultimately no final 'agreement'. The Court of Appeal held that the traditional approach as to the 'first/last shot' was to be followed in a battle of the forms.

7.4.2.2 *Communication of Acceptance*

Outward evidence of the offeree's intention to accept an offer has to be demonstrated and communicated in order for effective acceptance to occur. As such, where the offeror iden-tifies silence as a means of acceptance, this will not be effective. The presumption is that if the offeree wishes to be bound by the contract, he/she will at least go to the trouble of

---

[26] [1979] 1 WLR 401.   [27] [2009] EWCA Civ 1209.

making some outward sign/gesture to indicate the acceptance. Insofar as the rule on silence is adhered to, the offeror may insist on how acceptance is to be achieved. If included in the offer, then it must be complied with[28] to provide effective acceptance. The overriding element for acceptance to be established is that it must be communicated. Examples of the communication of acceptance may be through written reply, an oral statement, or implied through conduct. Conduct has already been demonstrated as acceptance in *Carlill*.

Alexander Brogden v Metropolitan Railway Co.[29]

Facts:

The directors of the Metropolitan Railway Company (MRC) brought an action against Brogden & Co. for a breach of contract, a contract that Brogden denied was even in existence. Brogden were colliery owners in Wales and had supplied MRC with coal and coke for use in their locomotives. A draft agreement was created to formalize the arrangement but no further action was taken on it, although orders continued on the basis of the terms stated in the document. Several orders passed between the companies and in these the document was frequently referred to. Problems began in the supply between the companies, including deficient supplies of coal and excuses for lack of orders, until December 1873 when Brogden declined to continue the supply of coal. This led to the breach of contract claim.

Authority for:

A long-term relationship between parties could amount to evidence of an agreement (although formal written acceptance of a contract was missing). The parties' conduct was evidence of acceptance of contractual terms.

* *Acceptance through conduct:* The House of Lords had to decide whether a completed contract had been established in *Brogden*. There was an assertion that the document was merely an intention to create a contract that would have meant no contract was in existence.[30] However, it was held that a valid contract had been established between the parties due to their actual conduct. A contractual document had been drafted by the principals of the relevant companies and was used in negotiations between the parties, and whilst it had not been signed, the intentions from the parties' actions enabled an agreement to be deduced. Therefore the breach of contract claim was successful.

  The case was important in that a formal, written contract is not required to establish a valid contract. The parties' intentions may identify a contract and if a period of time establishes a pattern of behaviour which may place obligations and expectations on the parties, then this may 'harden' an agreement into a contract. A similar conclusion was reached between contractors that had not created a formal contract, but due to the commercial nature of the transaction, and the fact that its terms had been completed, the Court of Appeal held that a contract was present.[31]

---

28 Note *Yates Building Co. Ltd v R J Pulleyn & Sons Ltd* [1975] 237 EG 183 in relation to acceptance which deviates from that stipulated in the offer. If it as quick, or quicker, than that required in the offer this will generally be accepted by the courts as a valid method of acceptance.

29 [1877] 2 AC 666.

30 *Dunlop v Higgins* [1848] 1 HLC 381 has demonstrated that an offer of a contract was not sufficient; there must be a distinct acceptance of it.

31 *G Percy Trentham v Archital Luxfer* [1993] 1 Lloyd's Rep. 25.

- *Silence as acceptance:* The offeror may not have stipulated a specific form which acceptance must take, and consequently the courts may consequently decide a 'reasonable' method. It must be noted, however, that, as a general rule, the offeror cannot dictate the offeree's silence as a valid acceptance:

Felthouse v Bindley[32]

Facts:

Mr Felthouse's nephew had placed several horses for sale by auction. Before the auction took place, Felthouse wrote to his nephew stating that he wished to purchase one of the horses and included the following in this communication 'If I hear no more about him, I consider the horse mine at £30.15s.' The nephew intended to sell the horse to his uncle, and made no reply. The nephew approached the auctioneer (Mr Bindley) and informed him that the horse was not to be included in the auction. The auctioneer, by mistake, did sell the horse and Felthouse attempted to stop the 'sale'. However, Felthouse only had the right to sue if he actually owned the horse and the court concluded that he did not as there had been no acceptance of his offer to buy the horse. The court held that the acceptance must be communicated clearly and could not be interpreted from the silence of the nephew.

Authority for:

Silence is not effective acceptance of an offer.

This case is relevant to the necessity for an outward sign of acceptance and for the offeree to positively communicate his/her acceptance. This is because the offeree should not be placed under the burden of a rejection every time an offer is forwarded to him/her and if the offeree does intend to accept an offer, he/she can make the effort to fulfil this requirement without undue inconvenience. However, it is possible to infer acceptance from silence between businesses, and it may be allowed if requested by the offeree. In the event that unsolicited (not requested by the recipient) goods are sent to a business, then s. 2 of the Unsolicited Goods and Services Act 1971 provides that a subsequent demand for payment constitutes a criminal offence. Protection is also given to consumers who are sent goods that they have not ordered through the Consumer Protection (Distance Selling) Regulations 2000.

- *Acceptance by post:* A contract may be created through an exchange of documents via the post. Where offer and acceptance takes place through written communication rather than face-to-face negotiations, there exists the possibility that such communication may be lost, undelivered, or delayed through postal strikes or public holidays. The general rule established with the post (where it is a valid means of acceptance) is that acceptance is valid on posting.[33]

Adams v Lindsell[34]

Facts:

The parties were contracting for the sale of wool and were communicating by means of the post. In the course of these communications the defendant misdirected the letter of acceptance

---

[32] [1862] 11 Cb (NS) 869.

[33] *Adams v Lindsell* [1818].   [34] [1818] 1 Barnewall and Alderson 681.

and it was subsequently delayed. Due to this delay, the acceptance was not received before the defendant, not receiving the anticipated acceptance by the due date, sold the wool to another party. The court held that as a matter of business efficacy, acceptance was effective when posted. This established the 'postal rule' of acceptance.

Authority for:

Where the post is a valid means of acceptance (usually because the offer has been made through the post or the offeror asks for the post to be the means of acceptance) then acceptance is binding upon posting, not upon the receipt of the acceptance.

The postal rule applies insofar as the correct address and postage were included in the sent letter.[35] The court was adamant that this was fair. It hypothesized that if the offeror was not bound under a contract until the acceptance by the offeree had been received, then the offeree should not be bound until he received notification that the offeror had received his acceptance and assented to it. This system could not enable businesses to carry out their operations with any certainty and consequently the decision was based on business efficacy. Even if the letter was delayed, where this is not the fault of the offeree, there was still valid acceptance.[36]

The postal rule is not effective, however, in situations where the express terms of the contract state that the acceptance must be received and in writing. This was demonstrated in *Holwell Securities v Hughes*,[37] where Lawton LJ in the Court of Appeal stated that the postal rule would not be used where to do so would 'produce manifest inconvenience and absurdity'.

- *Instantaneous forms of communication:* Compared with the postal rule and its 'business efficacy' decision, the courts have traditionally reverted to the common rule of acceptance being effective when communicated and received (in cases involving instantaneous forms of communication).

Entores v Miles Far East Corporation[38]

Facts:

Entores, based in London, made an offer on 8 September 1954 to agents (based in Holland) of Miles Far East Corporation by telex for the purchase of 100 tons of copper cathodes. This offer was accepted on 10 September through telex received in Entores' offices in London. Entores claimed a breach of contract and sought to serve notice of a writ on Miles Far East but could only do so if the contract was created in England and therefore came under the jurisdiction of English law. Miles Far East alleged the contract was made in Holland and was consequently not within the jurisdiction of the court. The Court of Appeal held that due to the instantaneous means of communication in this case, acceptance was effective (and the contract concluded) in London—and within the jurisdiction of the English court.

Authority for:

With instantaneous means of communication, the 'postal rule' of acceptance is departed from and acceptance is effective when received, not when posted.

---

[35] *Re London and Northern Bank, ex parte Jones* [1900] 1 Ch 220.
[36] *The Household Fire and Carriage Accident Insurance Company v Grant* [1879] 4 Ex D 216.
[37] [1974] 1 WLR 155.   [38] [1955] 3 WLR 48.

This ruling can be extended to other forms of instantaneous forms of communication such as a telephone or telex.

? Thinking Point

How will the courts determine when a contract is established if an e-mail is sent accepting a contract? Would it matter if the e-mail was sent in the middle of the night, and what would be the legal position if the Service Provider delayed the delivery of the message?

Conclusion

This chapter has sought to identify the importance of the common law in the development and evolution of the rules underpinning contract law. Offer and acceptance are essential features in the formation of an agreement, and these are furthered by the requirement of consideration; intention to create legal relations; and to have certainty of terms. These last three elements are considered in Chapter 8.

Q Summary of main points

- Offer and acceptance are the first stages in establishing an agreement that may form a legally binding contract.

Offer

- An offer is the statement of terms by which the party is willing to be bound.
- The offer can be made to a person, group, or even the entire world.
- An offer has to be distinguished from an invitation to treat (which is an invitation to negotiate).
- Items on display on the shelves in a shop, advertisements in newspapers, items displaying a price tag in shop windows, and information in auction catalogues have traditionally been held to be invitations to treat.
- Where detailed information is provided on the quantities of items and the time and date of their limited availability, the courts have been more willing to hold these as offers rather than invitations to treat.
- An offer may be accepted until it is terminated.
- Termination can occur by a party's express words, actions, through a counter-offer, lapse of time, or through some other consistent action.
- The offeror can revoke the offer at any time until acceptance takes place but this must be communicated and received by the offeree.

Acceptance

- Acceptance can only be made by the offeree or his/her agent.

- Where standard form contracts are used, the 'battle of the forms' is decided by the 'first' or 'last shot' approach.
- There must be outward evidence of acceptance. Silence, generally, will not constitute valid acceptance.
- The 'postal rule' establishes that where the post is a valid means of acceptance, acceptance is effective upon posting, not when the letter is received.
- With instantaneous forms of communication, the standard rule of acceptance being effective when received remains.

 Summary questions

Essay questions

1. 'The 'battle of the forms' when applied to businesses trading using their own standard term contracts may be resolved through the 'first shot' or 'last shot' approach. This is a wholly unsatisfactory situation and must be remedied through legislative action.'

   Discuss the statement with reference to case law and judicial pronouncements.

2. At what point does a display in a shop window become an offer to sell rather than an invitation to treat? Compare and contrast the cases of *Pharmaceutical Society of Great Britain v Boots Cash Chemists*, *Fisher v Bell* and *Leftkowitz v Great Minneapolis Surplus Stores*.

Problem questions

1. Jack is considering selling his prized collection of comedy books to Diane. On Monday Jack writes to Diane offering to sell the collection for £100 and he further provides that he will keep the offer open until Thursday at 5pm. On Tuesday, following a change of mind, Jack sends a fax to Diane revoking the offer, however Diane's fax machine is out of paper and she does not receive the message until Wednesday morning.

   On Tuesday, Diane had already posted to Jack her acceptance of the offer. Jack never received the letter of acceptance and as such at 6pm on Thursday Jack sold the collection to Bill.

   Advise the parties of any legal rights and liabilities.

2. Mortimer wished to sell his antique gold watch. He therefore sent his chauffeur with a note to Randolf offering to sell him the watch for £50,000 and asking Randolf to give his reply to the chauffeur.

   Being undecided, Randolf did not give his reply to the chauffeur and sent him back to Mortimer. One hour later Randolf posted a letter to Mortimer accepting his offer.

   Has a valid contract come into existence?

Further reading

Jackson, B. S. (1979) 'Offer and Acceptance in the Supermarket' *New Law Journal*, Vol. 129, p. 775.

Rawlings, R. (1979) 'The Battle of the Forms' *Modern Law Review*, Vol. 42, p. 715.

Unger, J. (1953) 'Self-Service Shops and the Law of Contract' *Modern Law Review*, Vol. 16, p. 369.

 Online Resource Centre

http://www.oxfordtextbooks.co.uk/orc/marson3e/
Why not visit the Online Resource Centre and try multiple choice questions associated with this chapter to test your understanding of the topic. You will also find relevant updates to the law.

Essential Features of a Valid Contract 2: Consideration, Intention to Create Legal Relations, and Certainty of Terms

8

Why does it matter?

This chapter continues the discussion of the essential features of a valid contract. Of particular importance is the requirement that the contract be a 'bargain' as without 'consideration' being present, the courts will not enforce what they deem to be a 'bare promise'. Contracts must also intend to be legally binding, and not just social or domestic agreements, and they must contain certain terms. Without an understanding of these crucial elements, agreements may be concluded but they will not create an enforceable contract.

Learning outcomes

Following reading this chapter you should be in a position to:

- identify and explain consideration in contracts (8.2–8.2.2)
- explain the interaction between consideration and promissory estoppel (8.2.3)
- explain privity of contract and how this affects who may enforce a contract or be sued on it (8.3–8.3.2)
- ascertain how the courts establish when parties intend to create an enforceable contract (8.4)
- explain the necessity of a legally enforceable contract containing definite and certain terms (8.5).

♟ Key terms

These terms will be used in the chapter and it may be helpful to be aware of what they mean or refer back to them when reading through the chapter.

Breach of contract
When a party fails to complete his/her obligations under the contract, he/she may be in breach, allowing the injured party to seek a remedy.

Consideration
Simple contracts have to be a bargain rather than a gratuitous promise (that cannot be enforced). Consideration is something of value that makes the agreement a bargain 'the price paid for a promise'.

Intention to create legal relations
A legally enforceable contract must be one where the parties understand and accept that failure to fulfil obligations under the agreement may result in legal consequences.

Nudum pactum
This is a promise made with no consideration to support it.

Promisee
The party to whom a promise is made.

Promisor
The party making the promise.

Promissory estoppels
A doctrine providing an equitable defence preventing a party who has made a promise to vary a contract for the other party's benefit from later reneging on it and attempting to enforce the original contract.

8.1 Introduction

This chapter continues identifying the essential features of a valid contract. Once an agreement has been established, consideration (what makes the agreement a 'bargain' and enforceable) must be present, the parties must intend that the agreement is to be legally binding, and its terms must be sufficiently certain to identify the rights and obligations of the parties. Further, a contract is enforceable by those parties to it (known as privity of contract), although this doctrine has been extended to provide rights for third parties where the contract has been made for their benefit. Having established that each of the features from Chapter 7 and this one are present, the agreement 'evolves' into a binding contract.

8.2 Consideration

Consideration in a contract has frequently caused confusion for students, but this should not be so. Students are at an advantage when reading about, and applying legal principles of contract law because of their experience in regularly establishing contracts. Consideration is a necessary component of 'simple' contracts, and these are the contracts that are most common in consumer transactions. Certain contracts are required to be made by deed, and in these circumstances the absence of consideration does not make the contract unenforceable.

Consideration in contract law is merely *something of value* that is provided and which acts as the inducement to enter into the agreement. The definition that is most frequently used is from the seminal case on the issue, *Currie v Misa*,[1] where Lush J stated:

---

[1]   (1874–75) LR 10 Ex. 153.

A valuable consideration, in the sense of the law, may consist either in some right, interest, profit, or benefit[2] accruing to the one party, or some forbearance,[3] detriment, loss, or responsibility, given, suffered, or undertaken by the other.

Despite that unwieldy definition, it is sufficient at this stage to recognize consideration as the bargain element of a contract—the price paid for a promise. Courts will enforce a 'bad' bargain (such as agreeing to sell something for a much lower price than its worth) but it cannot enforce a 'bare' (or gratuitous) promise. Consideration must be given in return of the promise made, and it must move from the **promisee**.[4] The promisee may exchange promises with the **promisor**, or he/she may provide some act of forbearance, to establish good consideration.

An example of consideration may be seen in an agreement to mow someone's lawn. The promisor (A) agrees to mow the lawn of the promisee (B). The detriment to A is that he/she gives up his/her time and effort to perform the task and the benefit is that he/she obtains pay or some goods/service in return for the act. The benefit for B is that he/she has his/her lawn cut (and therefore is given this service) and the detriment is either paying money, or providing goods or a service in return for the act of A. Therefore, consideration can be payment, or providing a service, or it can even amount to a future promise (so in the above example if B agreed to wash A's car in return for the lawn being cut, that would be good consideration).

8.2.1 **Executed and executory consideration**

The two types of consideration are Executed and Executory.

* *Executed*: Executed consideration is often seen in unilateral contracts and involves one party making a promise in return for an act by the other party. The offeror has no obligation to take action on the contract until the other party has fulfilled his/her part. For example, A offers B £100 to build a wall, payment to be made on completion. B completes the building work and is entitled to the payment from A. If B did not want the work, or did not complete it, A would not have (taken action) and paid the £100.

* *Executory*: Executory consideration is performed after an offer is made and is an act to be executed in the future (hence *executory*)—it is an exchange of promises to perform an act. This form of consideration is frequently seen in bilateral contracts and may lead to a valid contract being established. An example may be where an order for an item is made with the promise that payment will be made in the future (for example, when the item is delivered), and the other party promises to deliver the products ordered and receive the payment. The fact that consideration has not yet occurred but will take place in the future does not prevent it being 'good' consideration and in the event of, for example, non-delivery, this may lead to a **breach of contract** (assuming the remainder of the essential features are present).

8.2.2 **Good consideration**

What will establish 'good' consideration can be seen through the development of the case law, and this is underpinned by the rules outlined below. Figure 8.1 provides an overview of what, from case law, constitutes good consideration.

---

[2] See *Dunlop Pneumatic Tyre Co. Ltd v Selfridge & Co. Ltd* [1915] AC 847 for the necessity of a practical benefit to establish consideration.

[3] See *Alliance Bank Ltd v Broom* [1864] 2 Dr. & Sm. 289.

[4] Therefore the party who wishes to enforce the contract must provide (or have provided) the other party with consideration.

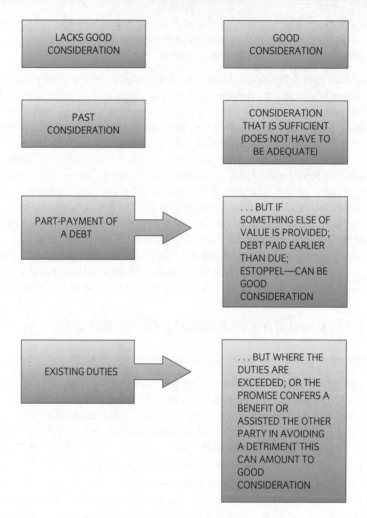

Figure 8.1 Good consideration

- *Consideration must be sufficient (not adequate):* Consideration must have some legal, material, value[5] but it does not need to be adequate[6] in relation to a 'fair' price for the contract. The courts are not in a position to assess what the value of a particular item or service is worth. Further, value may change rapidly or be whatever the parties consider it is worth, and also freedom of contract enters the equation. However, the consideration must have some value that can be assessed in financial terms. As the parties are free to negotiate terms, the courts do not believe it is their place to question the value of the bargain. This can be most clearly demonstrated in *Thomas v Thomas*,[7] where a house and its surrounding premises was provided for life for the sum of £1 per annum to be paid towards the cost of the ground rent, and for the house to be kept in good repair. This was held to be an enforceable

---

5 *White v Bluett* (1853) 23 LJ Ex 36.
6 This was established in *Bolton v Madden* [1873] LR 9 QB 55, where Blackburn J stated that: 'the adequacy of the consideration is for the parties to consider at the time of making the agreement, not for the Court …'
7 [1842] 2 QB 851.

contract even though the value of the consideration was in reality not adequate for the benefit provided, but it was sufficient. The courts have established that even if an item is of little value in itself, it may represent a benefit to one of the parties and therefore be good consideration, such as the submission of a chocolate bar wrapper in a sales promotion.

Chappell & Co. Ltd v Nestlé Co. Ltd[8]

Facts:

Nestlé were manufacturers of milk chocolate products. Nestlé entered into a contract with Chappell where Nestle were permitted to sell copies of the song 'Rockin' Shoes' (Chappell owned the copyright). Purchasers public paid 1s. 6d for each record and submitted three of Nestlé's chocolate wrappers with the application. The contract provided that Chappell was to be paid a proportion of the 1s. 6d for each copy of the song Nestlé sold, but it was silent as to the 'value' that each of the wrappers reflected. As Nestlé received a profit and benefited from each sale of its chocolate bars, Chappell considered that these should also form part of its remuneration. The House of Lords held that each of the wrappers amounted to good consideration, as the whole object of selling the record was to increase the sales of chocolate. This was so even if Nestlé was to discard the wrappers; they represented sales of its product.

Authority for:

Consideration must be sufficient, not adequate. As evidenced in this case, whilst the chocolate wrappers had no real value in themselves, they did represent three sales of packets of Nestlé's chocolate and hence provided a benefit to Nestlé.

The consequences of this case can be seen (for example) where vouchers are offered in magazines providing a discount on goods and services. The voucher/token will identify a stipulated value of (for example) 0.001p because such vouchers do have a legal value and will constitute consideration.

- *Consideration must not be past:* If a party performs an act and following the completion of the act the other party makes a promise, then the act will not have been sufficient to provide consideration. For example, if A gives B a lift to work in A's car and at the end of the journey B expresses his thanks and states that he will give A £10 for her trouble, there is no enforceable contract to enforce the £10 payment if none is received. This is because the lift was given voluntarily and not for gain. B did not agree to provide £10 for the lift and as the offer was made after the act, it did not amount to good consideration.

Re McArdle, Decd.[9]

Facts:

Mr McArdle died in 1935 and left a bungalow that he owned to his wife. McArdle had four children and one of the four (Montague) and his wife, lived in the property. Montague's wife had been improving the property and had repaired it at a cost of £488. Later, Montague submitted a document to his brothers and sister in which they agreed to pay his wife the £488 for the improvements. However, there was a disagreement about whether the payment should be made and when Montague's wife attempted to enforce

---

8 [1959] 3 WLR 168.   9 [1951] 1 All ER 905.

the agreement the Court of Appeal held that no contract had been established. The agreement to pay the sum was made after the work had been undertaken and there was no clear intention or expectation that payment would have been made.

Authority for:

Past consideration is not good consideration unless *Lampleigh v Brathwaite* applies.

The decision rested on the fact that since all the repair work had been completed before the document had been agreed, the consideration was wholly past and the agreement to 'repay' the £488 was a **nudum pactum**. If the children had agreed before Marjorie McArdle's actions to pay £488 for the work being carried out, that would have amounted to a contract supported by consideration, and consequently would have been enforceable. Consideration has to be a bargain and the children in this case had already benefited from the work being carried out, so there was no bargain for the agreement. Beyond this general rule regarding past consideration, exceptions do exist.

Lampleigh v Brathwaite[10]

Facts:

Brathwaite had killed another man and requested that Lampleigh seek from the king a pardon for his actions. This necessitated many days of following the King in attempting to raise and discuss this matter. Lampleigh was successful in obtaining the pardon and as a result, Brathwaite made a promise to pay £100 for the service, but this payment was never made. It was held that Lampleigh was able to recover the £100 because the court felt that both parties must have contemplated that payment for the service would be made.

Authority for:

In comparison with *Re McArdle*, the following are necessary for an enforceable contract to exist when supported by past consideration:

1 the act that is the subject of the contract must have been requested by the promisor;

2 there must have been in the contemplation of both parties that payment would have been made; and

3 all the other elements of a valid contract must have existed.

In a modern setting, if no price had been established for the act performed (such as the supply of a service), then the court would look to s. 15(1) of the Supply of Goods and Services Act 1982 and determine a 'reasonable' price. Also, in most employment situations, where, for example, an employee has performed work or hours beyond what his/her contract stipulates, this may imply additional payment is expected and reasonable.[11]

- *Existing duties are not good consideration:* The courts have identified that consideration must be 'real and material' and as such, if the promisor is merely receiving what he/she is already entitled to, then there is no consideration furnished. For example, if you do some act, which you already have an existing duty to perform, then this will not provide a benefit for the promisor and hence a contract based on this will be unenforceable due to lack of consideration.

---

[10] [1615] Hob 105.   [11] *Re Stewart v Casey (Casey's Patents)* [1892] 1 Ch 104.

Collins v Godefroy[12]

Facts:

The claimant was under a subpoena to appear as a witness in a trial involving Godefroy, and whose evidence was to the benefit of Godefroy. To appease Collins, Godefroy offered to pay him a sum in respect of his trouble. Godefroy did not pay and this led to Collins' action to recover the money promised. In the judgment, the court acknowledged that Godefroy did make the promise, and received a benefit from Collins' attendance at court. However, Collins was already under a duty to give evidence (due to the subpoena) and this did not constitute real or 'good' consideration. Collins had done no more than what he already had a duty to do.

Authority for:

Performing an existing duty (and doing no more) will not constitute good consideration.

This rule seeks to ensure that improper pressure cannot be applied to renegotiate a contract on better terms for the promisee. In *Stilk v Myrick*[13] the captain of a vessel on a voyage from London to the Baltic promised the existing crew an equal share of the wages of two seamen who had deserted (and who could not be replaced). On the vessel's return, the wages were not provided and in the action to recover the wages, the court held that there was no consideration provided in support of the promise. The seamen were under an existing duty to 'exert themselves to the utmost to bring the ship in safely to her destined port'.

Exceeding an existing duty can establish good consideration for a promise. *Stilk v Myrick* has to be compared with *Hartley v Ponsonby*,[14] where the sailors in this case were promised additional money if they completed their voyage after half of the ship's crew had abandoned the vessel. The court held they were entitled to the extra pay as they exceeded their existing duties due to the significant risk of continuing the voyage with insufficient crew. A more recent example of this rule can be seen in *Harris v Sheffield United Football Club Ltd*,[15] where the football club was under a duty to pay South Yorkshire Police (represented by Harris) for the policing of the football matches held at its stadium. The Court of Appeal held that supervision of the matches went beyond protecting the public and maintaining law and order, and amounted to a 'special police service' that was good consideration.

Further, performance of an existing duty may be held as good consideration from the following case:

Williams v Roffey Bros. & Nicholls (Contractors) Ltd[16]

Facts:

Roffey Bros was a firm of building contractors that had entered into a contract with Shepherds Bush Housing Association Ltd in September 1985 to refurbish a block of flats. Roffey subcontracted various carpentry jobs to Mr Williams for a total price of £20,000. However, by the end of March 1986 it was common knowledge that Williams was in financial difficulty based on the fact that the price of £20,000 was too low to enable Williams to operate at a profit[17] Williams informed Roffey that he would be unable to complete

---

[12] [1831] 1 B. & Ad. 950.   [13] [1809] 2 Camp. 317.   [14] [1857] 7 E & B 872.

[15] [1987] 3 WLR 305.   [16] [1991] 1 QB 1.

[17] At court, evidence was supplied by a surveyor, who stated a reasonable price should have been £23,783.

the work. Roffey was concerned at this development because, in part at least, Roffey was subject to a delay clause in the contract that would have led to it being liable for substantial fees if the contract was not completed on time. Therefore Roffey agreed to pay Williams a further sum of £10,300 in excess of the original £20,000 for the work to be completed at the agreed date. When the additional payment was claimed, Roffey refused to pay on the basis that Williams had only performed an existing duty.

Authority for:

Where the promisee has actually conferred on the promisor a benefit or has assisted him/her in avoiding a detriment, and no unfair pressure or duress was used in the renegotiation, an existing duty may be good consideration.

The Court of Appeal held that the promise to pay the additional sum was binding. Despite Roffey's argument to the contrary, consideration was provided as Roffey did receive a benefit, or at the very least would avoid a detriment, through the completion of the work and the avoidance of the penalty fee and/or the difficulty in hiring a new subcontractor. The requirement of the benefit or avoiding a detriment factor of the decision in *Williams v Roffey* was confirmed in *Re Selectmove*:

Re Selectmove[18]

Facts:

Selectmove had been subject to a winding-up petition by the Inland Revenue (IR) for arrears of tax under Pay As You Earn. Selectmove appealed on the ground that in October 1991 it held a meeting with the IR where it was agreed that due to Selectmove's cash flow problems, the tax owed would be paid in arrears of approximately £1,000 per month. The tax inspector who made the promise informed Selectmove that if it did not hear from the IR again, the plan outlined for the repayments would be acceptable. However, some time later, the IR did petition for the company to be wound up. The Court of Appeal held that the tax inspector who made the arrangement with Selectmove did not have the authority to bind the IR, and dismissed Selectmove's claim to have the petition set aside. The agreement was not enforceable as there was no consideration to support it.

Authority for:

Part-payment of a debt will not amount to good consideration, and where the promisee is merely performing an existing duty, this will not establish an enforceable contract.

Selectmove argued that in providing the payments, albeit late and over a longer period of time than required, there was a benefit to the IR. If wound up, the IR would be unlikely to receive the full amount of tax owed from the company, where the arrangement entered into would provide full repayment. However, the Court of Appeal distinguished *Williams v Roffey* as that case involved performing an act, whereas in the current case it was simply the repayment of money, and essentially could be considered the part-payment of a debt that is not, generally, good consideration.

- *Part payment as consideration*: It is a general rule of contract law that part payment of a debt will not prevent the party owed money from later claiming the balance. This is

18   [1995] 1 WLR 474.

even if he/she has agreed to take the lower sum, generally because there is no advantage for the party taking a lesser sum than that owed.[19] In *Foakes v Beer*[20] John Foakes owed £2,090 19s to Julia Beer but was in financial difficulties. He entered an agreement with Beer where she would not take any action to recover the sum owed if Foakes would agree to pay an initial sum of £500, and then £150 every six months until the full amount was repaid. Due to the financial difficulties suffered by Foakes, Beer further stipulated in the agreement that she would not claim any interest on the sum due. However, later Beer did sue Foakes for the interest that would have accumulated with the late payment. The House of Lords held that Beer was entitled to the interest on the payment, even though she had agreed not to claim. The promise by Foakes to pay the money owed did not amount to sufficient consideration, as he was only doing what he was obliged to do, which was to pay the money, and there was no benefit to Beer for the agreement.

A debt may be extinguished by proving something else of value other than money (a good or a service), whether this is to the value of the sum owed or not (as consideration need not be adequate). However, the general presumption of why a lower sum or part payment cannot provide good consideration is that money is a constant factor (£1 is £1). Also, exceptions exist to this rule regarding part-payment. If the party has paid a lower amount, but has done so at an earlier date, then this may amount to consideration; or if there have been goods or another benefit provided along with the lower payment then this may also provide good consideration. In *D&C Builders Ltd v Rees*,[21] D&C Builders was in financial difficulties, and Rees owed the firm £482. Rees offered D&C a cheque for £300 'in completion of the account' or D&C may not get any payment at all. This was accepted by D&C, which then brought the action for the remaining money (£182). The Court of Appeal held that D&C was entitled to claim the owed money as there was no consideration for the lesser amount and the financial pressure applied for the acceptance resulted in no true accord being established.

The rule remains regarding the ability of the party who has accepted a lesser sum than owed to still claim the balance. The major exception to this rule, alongside the others noted above, is the doctrine of **promissory estoppel**.

8.2.3 **The doctrine of promissory estoppel**

Whilst the rule of part-payment not being good consideration was established through the common law, the courts also created an equitable defence,[22] which stops a party that has made a (gratuitous) promise from reneging. For example, if a party makes a promise to accept a lower rent than that contracted for, and the other party relied on this promise, the promisor may be estopped (prevented) from reneging on this promise and claiming the balance owed if the court considers this unreasonable. This is a very interesting area of law, although not greatly developed through case law (and it is beyond the scope of this text to discuss it in any detail). Essentially, it seeks to suspend rights rather than to remove them (although this is a moot point in many instances).[23]

---

[19] *Pinnel's Case* (1602) 5 Co Rep 117.   [20] [1881–85] All ER Rep 106.
[21] [1966] 2 WLR 288.
[22] It is considered that promissory estoppel is only available as a 'shield not a sword' and as such can only be used in the defence of a claim against the party (*Combe v Combe* [1951] 2 KB 215).
[23] *Tool Metal Manufacturing Co v Tungsten Ltd* [1955] 2 All ER 657.

Central London Property Trust v High Trees House Ltd[24]

Facts:

High Trees House leased a block of flats at £2500 per annum from Central London Property Trust in 1937. With the outbreak of war, and the consequent bombings in London, occupancy of the property was reduced. To limit the adverse effects, and to stop the property becoming unoccupied, High Trees entered into a new agreement in January 1940 with Central London Property under which the rent would be reduced by half. This period of reduced rent was not specified, but in the following five years High Trees paid the reduced rent. In 1945, the flats were full and Central London Property claimed for the full rent to be paid. The High Court held that when the flats became fully let, the (prior) full rent could be claimed.

Authority for:

Denning's statement (albeit obiter dicta) was that where the promisor makes a promise that is relied on by the promisee, he/she will be unable to renege on it due to the doctrine of promisory estoppel even in the absence of consideration moving from the promisee.

Consideration is often linked with the concept of privity of contract, where the contract involves, or is for the benefit of, a third party. This is because the party whom the contract concerns has not provided any consideration and hence has no rights or obligations under the agreement.

8.3 The doctrine of privity of contract

The doctrine of privity of contract arose through the common law as a means of regulating the relationships between parties to a contract. The doctrine establishes that only parties to a contract may sue or be sued on it, and consequently provides rights and imposes obligations on those parties alone. This is important as many situations involve contracts where a right or benefit is to be provided for a third party. Even though the contract is for the benefit of this third party, he/she is unable to enforce it as he/she is not privy to the contract. The two elements necessary to enforce a contract are that the claimant must be a party to it, and there must be consideration provided by the promisee. These have become somewhat merged in the cases, although they remain legally separate.

- 'Only a person who is a party to a contract can sue on it'.[25] Only a promisee may enforce a contract as others are not privy to it:

Dunlop Tyre Co. v Selfridge[26]

Facts:

Dunlop Tyre Company had contracted with a wholesale distribution company called Dew & Co. The contract provided that Dew would obtain an agreement from the retailers to whom it sold tyres that they would not sell them below the list price established

---

[24] [1956] 1 All ER 256.   [25] Per Lord Haldane in *Dunlop v Selfridge*.   [26] [1915] AC 847.

by Dunlop. Dew obtained the agreements, and in a contract with Selfridge, it transpired that Selfridge sold tyres below this contracted price. Dunlop sought to obtain an injunction against Selfridge from continuing to sell the tyres at the price, and also initiated a damages action for breach of contract. The House of Lords held that there was no agreement between Dunlop and Selfridge. The contracts were between Dunlop and Dew, and Dew and Selfridge, therefore Selfridge was not party to the contractual agreement between Dunlop and Dew, and Dunlop could not enforce the contract. Selfridge was not the agent of Dunlop, and there was no consideration from Dunlop in return for Selfridge's promise to sell at the list price.

Authority for:

The common law rule established in the case was that only parties to a contract had obligations and rights on it.

- *Consideration must move from the promisee:* It is a necessary aspect of contract law that there must exist a bargain element to establish an enforceable contract:

Tweddle v Atkinson[27]

Facts:

Mr Tweddle was engaged to marry Miss Guy and the fathers of the couple agreed to pay a sum of money when they got married. The contract stated that the husband should have the right to bring an action if either party failed in their obligations to pay the money. Mr Guy, however, died before the couple were married and hence before any money was paid. Following the wedding, Mr Tweddle attempted to enforce the contract from Mr Guy's estate, however he had not provided any consideration to Mr Guy for the promisee to pay him. Mr Tweddle was merely a beneficiary to the contract and not a party to it.

Authority for:

The promisee must provide a good consideration to the promisor in order for a contract to be made. (Note, this rule is subject to the exceptions below.)

Having stated the tests that have developed the doctrine of privity, it must be observed that the doctrine could, in certain circumstances, produce unfairness and inconvenience to the parties. As a consequence the common law created many exceptions.

8.3.1 **The exceptions to privity**

Various exceptions to the general rule of privity have developed through the common law and examples of these are identified as:

- *Agency:* An agent is someone who has the authority to conclude binding agreements on behalf of someone else (known as the principal).[28] This means that if an agent makes a

---

[27] [1861] 1 B&S 393.   [28] See Chapter 21.

contract with a third party, and the third party is aware that the person is acting as an agent with the authority of the principal,[29] the principal can sue and be sued on the contract as if it were he/she who had agreed the contract.

- *Collateral contracts:* A contract established between two parties may indirectly create another contract with a third party. In *Shanklin Pier v Detel Products*[30] Shanklin employed a firm of contractors to paint its pier. Shanklin had negotiated with a paint manufacturer (Detel) about the suitability of its paint, and having received such assurances that it would last for seven years, included a term of the agreement with the contractors that they must purchase and use Detel's paint for the purpose of the job. However, when the paint was used it only lasted for three months before beginning to peel, therefore Shanklin brought an action for damages against Detel. Detel claimed that privity of contract stopped Shanklin from suing them. However, the court held a collateral contract had been established between the two parties following the contract between Shanklin and the contractors. Further, consideration had been established for the promise through Shanklin's insistence that the contractors use Detel's paint.

- *Trusts:* A person may transfer property to a second person (known as the trustee) who maintains the property for the benefit of others (known as a beneficiary). The person who has created the trust identifies the rules by which the trust is to be administered, and if these terms are not complied with, the beneficiary may seek to enforce it. An example of the use of a trust was demonstrated in the case of *Les Affreteurs Réunis v Leopold Walford.*[31]

- *Insurance contracts:* A third party may be able to claim under an insurance policy that has been established for his/her benefit. This is despite the fact that he/she did not create the contract or pay the premiums, and can be most commonly seen in life insurance policies where the benefit is provided for the insured person's family.

- *Restrictive covenants:* Restrictive covenants are used to protect land and bind purchasers as to the provisions laid down which benefit adjoining owners and interested parties in the area. In *Tulk v Moxhay*[32] an owner of several houses in Leicester Square sold the garden in the centre of the premises to the purchaser, who covenanted to maintain the gardens in their present condition and enable individuals' access to, and use of, the gardens. This land was later sold and the purchaser (Moxhay) announced that he intended to build on the land, despite being aware of the covenant. Mr Tulk, who owned houses adjacent to the land, applied to the court for an injunction[33] to restrain the action of building on the land, and the court held that the covenant would be enforced against Moxhay and all subsequent purchasers.

- *Contracts for interested groups:* A contract may be established by one party but for the interests of him/herself and others. Whilst the other parties have no right themselves to initiate a breach of contract claim, as there is no contract between themselves and the supplier of the good or service, the contracting party may seek that the court takes the losses of the other parties into account when determining damages. In *Jackson v Horizon Holidays Ltd*[34] the Court of Appeal considered a claim for damages from Mr Jackson for

---

29   *Scruttons Ltd v Midland Silicones Ltd* [1962] AC 446.   30   [1951] 2 KB 854.

31   [1919] AC 801.   32   [1848] 2 Ph 774.

33   *Law Debenture Trust Corp v Ural Caspian Oil Corp* [1993] 2 All ER 355 identified that the injunction to be provided by the courts would be restricted to negative injunctions.

34   [1975] 1 WLR 1468.

the disappointment he suffered at the lack of available facilities (as promised) in a holiday. The brochure for the holiday stated that there was a mini-golf course, an excellent restaurant, swimming pool, and health salons and so on, none of which materialized. Horizon Holidays accepted liability as to the substandard holiday, but Mr Jackson also wished to claim damages for his family's disappointment, and Horizon Holidays asserted that he was unable to do so. The Court awarded Mr Jackson £1,100 in damages for the breach of contract and disappointment for himself and his family, as Mr Jackson had entered the contract partly on their basis.

Subsequent to the case, the House of Lords criticized the decision in *Jackson* in the case of *Woodar Investment Developments Ltd v Wimpey Construction UK Ltd*[35] that the decision should not be seen as providing a general rule of law for the claim of damages for third parties. It is therefore questionable whether a similar case would be decided in the same manner as *Jackson*. If the case did involve a package holiday, and there existed a loss of enjoyment, then the Package Travel, Package Holidays and Package Tours Regulations 1992 enables the person who entered into the contract to claim on behalf of the others in the party.

8.3.2 Reform of the law

It had for many years been considered that the law on privity should be reviewed and this was articulated by an independent legal review body.[36] The privity rule was considered unfair as it prevented those parties who had a genuine interest in a contract from being able to take any action on it, and many other countries (including those in Europe, Australasia, and North America) already had provision to allow such individuals to play an active part on the contract. This concern led to legislative action in the form of The Contracts (Rights of Third Parties) Act 1999. The legislation was not enacted to replace the common law that had been developed, but rather to add rights for the third party. It enabled a third party to enforce the terms of a contract if the contract expressly provided for it, or if the contract conferred on him/her some benefit (unless the contract did not intend that the relevant term should be actionable by the third party).[37] This involves the third party being named in the contract to enable him/her to claim under the Act.[38] This Act further enables the third party to enforce the contract and seek damages as he/she would have been able to if he/she had been a full party to it.[39] However, the third party will be unable to claim these damages if the injured party has already claimed.[40] The second section of the Act continues protecting third parties by preventing the parties from varying or cancelling the contract without the third party's permission unless this has been expressly stated in the contract. There are limitations to the Act such as preventing a contract being enforced by a third party against employees in contracts, or in contracts concerning the carriage of goods.[41]

---

[35] [1980] 1 WLR 277.

[36] The Law Commission published 'Privity of Contract; Contracts for the Benefit of Third Parties' (Cmnd 3329; Law Com. No. 242) in 1996, which recommended the rights for third parties to enforce contracts.

[37] Section 1 of the Act.

[38] See *Themis Avraamides v Colwill and Martin* [2006] EWCA Civ 1533, where, in the case of a company becoming insolvent and the business being bought by a partnership who undertook to 'complete outstanding customer orders' resulted in the Court of Appeal holding that the claimants could not succeed with the claim under the Act as it had not been specifically named (as required under s. 1(3)).

[39] Section 1(5).   [40] Section 5.   [41] Section 6.

8.4 Intention to create legal relations

> ### 🖉 Business Link
>
> Where you purchase a cup of coffee from a high street retailer, this is a valid enforceable contract. This means, among other things, that if the coffee served is not as described or is of a significantly poor quality (for example) you have the right to have it replaced and be provided with the coffee you ordered. This is because, even though neither you nor the person serving has probably said so, this is a legally enforceable contract due to the presumption that agreements between businesses and consumers are intended to be legally binding. Compare this with a friend who makes you a cup of coffee. If it is not as described or is of a poor quality you have no legal redress available. This again is based on the legal presumption that agreements between friends are not intended to be legally binding. Intention to create legal relations can be removed or included in each of the above examples, hence it is important to know the presumptions and when you need to incorporate exact terms in the agreement.

For the parties to be able to sue and be sued on a contract, they must **intend it to create legal relations**. 'Legal relations' means that the parties view the agreement as a legally enforceable contract and a breach of the contract could result in a remedy being sought. The courts have traditionally looked to the parties' intentions, which may be viewed in light of what a 'reasonable person' would have considered the intentions to be. In determining their intentions, and following *Parker v Clark*,[42] the courts will look to the parties' use of words and the context in which they use them.

The presumptions of contract and the intention to create legal relations have fallen into one of two camps (as outlined in Figure 8.2). Those involving social and domestic arrangements are generally presumed as not intended to be legally binding, unless this is specifically established in the agreement. On the other hand, in business and commercial arrangement, the presumption is that the parties do intend to create legal relations, and if one of the parties wishes to rebut this presumption, he/she must produce evidence in support of this contention. Situations exist that sit somewhere between these two camps, where the parties have a social relationship but also negotiate an agreement that may be viewed as commercial. In such a scenario, the onus is placed on the party wishing to assert the contract to demonstrate tangible grounds that he/she intended to create legal relations (although this onus is less burdensome than if the relationship had been purely domestic).[43] In the first case dealt with in this section, it can be seen that the courts have viewed that agreements between a husband and wife will not generally be considered to have been intended to be legally binding.

---

[42]   [1960] 1 WLR 286.   [43]   See *John Sadler v George Reynolds* [2005] EWHC 309.

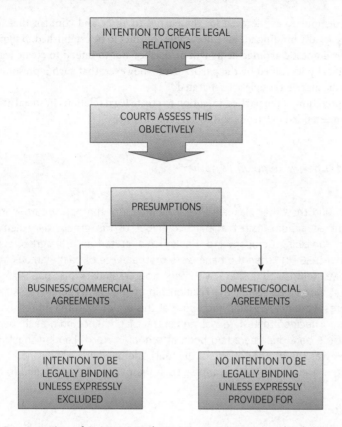

Figure 8.2 Presumption of Contract and Intention to Create Legal Relations

Balfour v Balfour[44]

Facts:

The parties were husband and wife. The husband was a civil engineer, employed by the Government of Ceylon as Director of Irrigation. Following their marriage, the couple lived in Ceylon together until they came to England when the husband was on leave. When the husband's leave was finished he returned to Ceylon while the wife remained in England and he agreed to contribute £30 per month for her living expenses. It transpires that some time later significant differences arose between the husband and wife. He agreed he would pay the £30 per month for her maintenance as agreed, and some time later the wife commenced divorce proceedings. The wife was seeking to recover the money agreed between herself and her husband that had not been paid. Her claim failed.

Authority for:

Arrangements between husband and wife will not presume to constitute a legally binding contract.

---

[44] [1919] 2 KB 571.

The case demonstrates the need for the parties to agree and confirm that the contract intends to be legally binding for an enforceable contract to be established. *Balfour* identifies that social or domestic arrangements will be deemed *not* to intend to create legal relations unless specifically identified by the parties. Note, however, that such a presumption is not made when the married couple are separated.[45]

The interpretation of the parties' intention to create legal relations in social arrangements has also been extended to friends and social acquaintances.

Hadley and Others v Kemp and Another[46]

Facts:

Tony Hadley and the other claimants were members of the pop group Spandau Ballet, who brought an action against a fourth member of the group (Gary Kemp) and the Reformation Publishing Company Ltd. Hadley *et al* stated an oral agreement had been established in 1980–81 when the band were on the verge of being famous and successful, where Mr Kemp would share with the other members his 'publishing income'.[47] However, following 1988 (when the relationship of the band members soured), no further payments were made. Hadley argued that this act constituted a breach of contract. The High Court decided that there was no contract (and hence no breach) because, *inter alia*, four of the band members had been at school in North London together (and the fifth member was the brother of one of the four), the band was established to play music together rather than make money, and as such the parties did not intend to create legal relations.

Authority for:

The presumption of parties not intending their agreements to be legally binding is applied to social acquaintances where there has been a prior history between the parties.

The parties in social or domestic arrangements must make clear, through express words or actions to the contract, or provide some positive outward sign to establish that they intend the agreement to be a legally binding contract. An example of such an outward sign occurred in the case *Simpkins v Pays*,[48] whereby a grandmother (Pays), her granddaughter, and a lodger (Simpkins) regularly entered competitions in a newspaper. They each shared the costs of entering the competitions and had agreed to share in any prize money. When one of the competition entries won, the prize (£750) was claimed in the name of the grandmother and the lodger claimed one-third of the money. Pays refused to provide this money on the basis that this was a social arrangement and not legally enforceable. The courts disagreed and held that the nature of sharing the costs of entry and the specific agreement elevated this beyond the typical social arrangement to one where the parties had intended to create legal relations.

Between commercial parties, intention to create legal relations is presumed unless the parties establish an agreement to the contrary.

---

45 *Merritt v Merritt* [1970] 1 WLR 1211.   46 [1999] EMLR 589.
47 Gary Kemp was credited as being the composer of the band's lyrics and music.
48 [1955] 1 WLR 975.

Rose and Frank Company v J. R. Crompton[49]

Facts:

Rose and Frank Company was an organization based in the United States trading in carbonizing tissue paper. Rose and Frank began trading with J. R. Crompton and later with a third company (Brittains Ltd). The three companies entered into an agreement under which the English companies agreed to confine the sale of all of their carbonizing tissue in the United States and Canada to Rose and Frank; and Rose and Frank confined its purchases of the tissues exclusively to the two English companies. This arrangement included a clause to the effect that the agreement was in honour only and not legally enforceable. When a disagreement occurred between the companies, a breach of contract claim was made. The House of Lords held that the arrangement had not created a binding contract because of the clause inserted that it was 'in honour' only and hence had removed this essential feature of a valid contract.

Authority for:

The presumption that business/commercial contracts intend to be legally binding may be reversed where the parties clearly identify an agreement to be binding in honour only.

The final element required in a valid contract is that the terms of the agreement are sufficiently certain for the courts to determine the boundaries of the agreement and by what terms the parties had accepted to be bound.

8.5 Certainty of terms

 Business Link

Contracts must be correctly drafted and sufficiently detailed in order for the responsibilities of the parties to be identified. If the courts cannot deduce from the contract the necessary and important aspects, it may fail due to this lack of certainty, and consequently no contract will be in existence.

The terms of the contract must be certain if they are to be considered sufficiently precise to be enforced by a court. The courts will not re-write a contract which has been incorrectly or negligently drafted. Of course, the courts may ignore a term of a contract which is meaningless;[50] look toward particular customs in a trade to remove the uncertainty in the parties' intentions;[51] and consider the previous dealings between the parties to ascertain any terms omitted in a contract.[52] It is also worthy of note as to why such eventualities exist.

---

[49] [1925] AC 445.   [50] See *Nicolene Ltd v Simmonds* [1953] 2 WLR 717.
[51] See *Shamrock SS Co. v Storey & Co.* [1899] 81 LT 413.
[52] Consider in particular Lord Wright's comments in *Hillas & Co. Ltd v Arcos Ltd* [1932] 43 Ll. L. Rep. 359; 147 LT 503.

Uncertainty may not be present simply due to poor drafting or some incompetence, but rather it may reflect changing conditions (where products have a 'lead time' before delivery can take place, and these are taken into consideration). There may exist situations where the parties establish 'an agreement to agree' that the courts may consider too vague[53] as to produce an enforceable contract[54] but the courts will attempt to identify the legal effect of such terms.[55]

Parties must ensure that the terms contained within contracts are sufficiently precise and detailed to enable the parties, and indeed the courts if necessary, to identify the true intentions and responsibilities contained therein. As per Lord Wright 'It is a necessary requirement that an agreement in order to be binding must be sufficiently definite to enable the court to give it a practical meaning. Its terms must be so definite, or capable of being made definite without further agreement of the parties, that the promises and performances to be rendered by each party are reasonably certain.' Specifically, where a term is meaningless, then this term, if not the entire contract, may be considered as not forming a valid contract or contractual term. However, if this is simply a means to attempt to avoid the contract, the Court of Appeal has already limited the scope of such arguments. In *Nicolene Ltd v Simmonds*[56] a contract was prepared on the basis that it was on one of the parties 'usual conditions of acceptance'. In reality, there were no usual conditions of acceptance and the defendants attempted to escape from the contract on the basis that this was a meaningless term and the contract failed because of it. The Court of Appeal held the term to be meaningless, but in this respect it could simply be ignored and the rest of the contract remained. A further example of a term in a contract which is meaningless and cannot be enforced is demonstrated in the interesting case of *Guthing v Lynn*,[57] where, in the negotiations for the sale of a horse, a clause was inserted into the contract that a further £5 would be paid to the offeror if the horse 'proved to be lucky' for the purchaser. This clause led to a claim for the £5 that was held to be ineffective as it lacked certainty as to what 'lucky' meant.

If the agreement has already begun, and the parties are performing obligations on the basis that a valid contract is in existence, the courts are much less likely to hold that there is no contract.[58] The courts will also attempt to give effect to agreements between businesses where there was clear evidence of an intention to create legal relations. In *Durham Tees Valley Airport Ltd v BMI Baby Ltd*[59] the defendants agreed to operate two aircraft from the airport for a ten-year term. There was no identification in the contract of minimum passenger movement or flight details, however the Court of Appeal held that there was indeed a contract, capable of enforcement. The missing terms were implied on the basis of business efficacy.

 Conclusion

This chapter has concluded the provisions required that establish a valid, enforceable contract. The agreement must contain each of the provisions, and the cases identified in this chapter and Chapter 7 will assist in recognizing the factors the courts take into consideration when determining the existence of a contract. Having identified the

---

53   *Scammell and Nephew Ltd v H. C. and J. G. Ouston* [1941] AC 251.

54   *May & Butcher v R* [1934] 2 KB 17.

55   *Sudbrook Trading Estate Ltd v Eggleton* [1982] 3 WLR 315.   56   [1953] 1 QB 543.

57   [1831] 2 B. Ad 232.   58   *Percy Trentham Ltd v Archital Luxfer Ltd* [1993] 1 Lloyd's Rep 25.

59   [2010] EWCA Civ 485.

essential features of a valid contract, the next step is to determine possible restrictions on individuals who may be party to an agreement or defects in the formation of a contract. These factors need to be appreciated as they can prevent an otherwise valid contract from having effect (and be legally enforceable).

 Summary of main points

Consideration

- Consideration is the bargain element of a contract and may be referred to as the 'price paid for a promise'.
- Consideration must move from the promisee.
- Consideration must be legally sufficient but need not be adequate.
- The courts will not recognize a 'bare' promise.
- Consideration may be executed—one promise in return for an act by the other party (usually evidenced in unilateral contracts).
- Consideration may be executory—an exchange of promises (usually found in bilateral contracts).
- Simple contracts must be 'good' consideration.
- Performing an existing duty may not be good consideration.
- If the benefit provided exceeds an existing duty this may constitute good consideration.
- Past consideration is not good consideration unless the act was performed at the request of the promisor; there was a contemplation of both parties that payment would be made; and all the other elements of a valid contract exist.
- Part-payment of a debt will not prevent the innocent party seeking the balance owed. However, if something of value other than money is provided or if the part-payment has been provided at an earlier date than required, this may be good consideration.
- An exception to this general rule is the doctrine of promissory estoppel. This enables the court to prevent a party from reneging on a promise that was relied on by the other party if to do so would be unfair.

Privity

- The general rule in contract is that only those parties to a contract may sue and be sued on it.
- Exceptions exist where the contract is made by an agent for the principal; in collateral contracts; where property is transferred in trust to another party; where the contract has been made under an insurance agreement for the benefit of another; and where restrictive covenants are imposed on property.
- The enactment of the Contracts (Rights of Third Parties) Act 1999 has enabled third parties to enforce contracts conferring a benefit on him/her, or where the contract expressly permits the third party to enforce it.

Intention to create legal relations

- The parties must intend for an agreement to establish legal relations to create an enforceable contract.
- Social agreements are presumed not to intend to create legal relations (such as between husband and wife (unless they are separated) and social acquaintances).
- In commercial agreements, the presumption is that legal relations exist, unless the parties expressly state an agreement to the contrary.

Certainty of terms

- Terms of a contract must be drafted carefully and precisely if they are to be relied on by the parties.

 Summary questions

Essay questions

1. The presumptions advanced in the assessment of whether parties intended an agreement to create legal relations are wrong. It provides for uncertainty and inconsistent judgments, and should be made more transparent (particularly necessary for vulnerable people).

   Discuss.

2. Privity of contract is such an antiquated doctrine, resplendent with exceptions and caveats, that its practical effect is meaningless.

   Discuss this statement in relation to business agreements.

Problem questions

1. All Bright Consumables (ABC) Ltd manufactures PC components. It runs this aspect of its operation from a factory that it leases from JJ Industrial Rentals Ltd (JJ), and the machines used in the production process are rented from iMachines and Tools Ltd (iMachines Ltd).

   Given the economic crises in 2010, and increasing competition from the Far East, ABC is in financial difficulties. In March 2010 ABC wrote to JJ of its financial problems and identify 'We are suffering severe financial difficulties in these austere times. We both know you have factories that you are unable to rent, and unless you can reduce the rent on this factory we will have no choice but to cease trading and you'll be left with another unrented factory'. Following a discussion between the managing directors of both companies, JJ agree to accept half rent payment until such a time as ABC's business picks up.

   ABC also informed iMachines Ltd in the same manner about its financial problems and it agreed to take a quantity of the PC components manufactured in lieu of its hire charges for the financial year 6 April 2010 to 5 April 2011.

   In January 2011 JJ were suffering financial difficulties and demanded that ABC pay the full rent on the factory from February 2011. It also demanded payment of the rent owed from March 2010. It considers this part-payment of a debt and wishes to exercise its right to obtain payment. At this time, iMachines Ltd discovered that the PC components it had taken in lieu of hire charges were worth only half of the hire charges for the year. It has demanded that ABC pay the balance owed in cash.

Advise ABC as to whether the payments demanded have to be made.

2. Delia is the managing director of ABC Ltd. She arrived at the company's head office to discover the building was ablaze. She called the emergency services and when the fire fighters arrived at the scene Delia told them that the contents of her office were extremely valuable and contained irreplaceable items. As such, if they could prevent the fire spreading there she would reward them with £100 each. The fire fighters were successful in extinguishing the fire and it did not reach Delia's office.

Assess the likely success of the fire fighters claiming the reward?

Further reading

Coote, B. (1990) 'Consideration and Benefits in Fact and Law' *Journal of Contract Law*, Vol. 3, p. 23.

Hedley, S. (1985) 'Keeping Contract in its Place: *Balfour v Balfour* and the Enforceability of Informal Agreements' *Oxford Journal of Legal Studies*, Vol. 5, pp. 391–415.

Hird, N. J., and Blair, A. (1996) 'Minding Your Own Business—*Williams v Roffey* Re-visited: Consideration Reconsidered' *Journal of Business Law*, p. 254.

@ Online Resource Centre

http://www.oxfordtextbooks.co.uk/orc/marson3e/
Why not visit the Online Resource Centre and try multiple choice questions associated with this chapter to test your understanding of the topic. You will also find relevant updates to the law.

9 Contracts, Contractual Capacity, Mistake, Misrepresentation, and Duress

Why does it matter?

Chapters 7 and 8 of this book have identified the essential features of a valid contract. Before the details of the terms of the contract, and its discharge are discussed, it is important to recognize that a contract may fail due to a party not possessing the capacity to establish a contract, it could involve a mistake by one or both parties, a provision may have been misrepresented in the negotiations, or the contract could have been concluded by using undue influence or placing the other party under duress. These factors have significant consequences on the validity of the contract and must be understood, in conjunction with the previous chapters, to ascertain whether the contract is void or voidable.

Learning outcomes

Following reading this chapter you should be in a position to:

- identify how the law imposes restrictions on certain persons when forming a contract (9.2)
- provide examples of illegal contracts (9.3)
- explain the effect a mistake has on an agreement between the parties (9.4–9.4.2)
- identify where a contract has been formed on the basis of misrepresentation, and the remedies available to the innocent party (9.5–9.5.6)
- explain what effect the use of duress and undue influence has on the validity of a contract (9.6–9.6.2).

ᛥ Key terms

These terms will be used in the chapter and it may be helpful to be aware of what they mean or refer back to them when reading through the chapter.

Consensus ad idem
This is the Latin term for an 'agreement as to the same thing' in English law, more commonly referred to as a 'meeting of minds' between the parties.

Damages
Compensation awarded by the court in the form of a monetary payment.

Defendant
The party defending the claim.

Duress
Compelling a party to enter a contract on the basis of a threat, which makes the contract voidable.

Equitable remedy
Discretionary remedies granted by the courts, generally where damages would not provide an adequate remedy. Examples of equitable remedies include injunctions; rescission; and specific performance.

Freedom of contract
No one can be forced into an agreement, therefore the State did not regulate such agreements and allowed the parties to establish their own terms and conditions.

Misrepresentation
A false statement of fact inducing the innocent party to form the contract.

Rescission
An equitable remedy where the party misled has the option to set aside the contract.

Undue influence
Where a party unfairly exploits its relationship with the other party to enter a contract, this may also render the contract voidable.

9.1 Introduction

Chapters 7 and 8 have identified the essential features of a valid contract. Once agreement, consideration, intention to create legal relations, and certainty of terms has been fulfilled, a contract may be established. However, problems may exist in how the agreement was concluded that could affect its validity. What if one of the parties induced the other into the contract by misrepresenting an important aspect of the contract? What if one of the parties was clearly in a drunken state and could not understand what he/she was agreeing to? What if one party was told to agree to the contract or he/she would be shot? Some of the reasons listed (naturally) are more common than others, but the emphasis of this chapter is to identify where problems may occur that could prevent the successful operation of the contract, despite fulfilling the essential features.

9.2 Capacity to enter a valid contract

For an enforceable agreement to be created the parties involved must have the capacity to create a contract. This is particularly so where the person is vulnerable.

9.2.1 **Minors**

A minor is a person under 18 years of age[1] (when he/she reaches majority) and has the capacity to establish most contracts. However, whilst this is generally true, situations exist where the minor requires protection and in those situations the contract established may be voidable, hence allowing the minor the ability to avoid the contract. Typically, contracts involving the sale of shares;[2] the leasing of property; and contracts of partnership have been held as voidable, rather than void. The minor may avoid such contracts within a reasonable time, and until he/she reaches the age of majority, but must satisfy any debts whilst party to the contract.

Circumstances exist where a minor is bound by the contract. If the contract is for necessaries, as defined under the Sale of Goods Act 1979, s. 3, then the contract will bind the minor.[3] 'Necessaries' is a broad term, and whilst this can include food and clothing, it has been assessed as including items reflecting the minor's social status.[4] Where necessaries have been provided, the minor is liable to pay a reasonable price,[5] rather than, necessarily, the price established in the contract. Further, where the contract is not unduly harsh or detrimental to the minor, it will be binding. Conversely, where it places an unfair responsibility on the minor he/she may be able to avoid the contract.[6]

> ### *Clements v London and North Western Railway Co*[7]
>
> #### Facts:
>
> A minor had been employed as a porter at a railway and had agreed to join an insurance society that was organized by the railway's employees. The effect of this membership was, in part, to waive rights against the employer as provided under the Employer's Liability Act 1880, as the society provided a more comprehensive package of protection. This protection was beneficial in some circumstances, but, importantly in this case, provided for sums to be paid out in claims at rates lower than would have been available under the Act. When the minor was injured due to negligence on the part of the employer, he sought to have his membership avoided to enable him to claim under the Act. The Court of Appeal held he could not. The contract was binding on him, as, when considered as a complete package, it was beneficial.
>
> #### Authority for:
>
> Where a contract is for the benefit of a minor, and does not place unfair responsibility on him/her, it is not voidable but rather binding and enforceable against the minor.

Despite the protection for minors, those entering into contracts with a minor are also afforded rights (under the Minors' Contracts Act 1987). The minor who, when reaching the age of majority, ratifies debts that were created during his/her minority, will have this ratification binding upon him/her.[8] Also, where a third party acted as guarantor for the

---

[1] As defined in the Family Law Reform Act 1969, s. 1.
[2] See *Steinberg v Scala (Leeds) Ltd* [1923] 2 Ch. 452.   [3] *Nash v Inman* [1908] 2 KB 1.
[4] *Peters v Fleming* (1840) 6 M&W 42.   [5] Sale of Goods Act 1979, s. 3.
[6] *Fawcett v Smethurst* [1914] 84 LJKB 473.   [7] [1894] 2 QB 482.
[8] Section 1.

minor in contracts that were unenforceable against him/her, this will not result in the contract being unenforceable against the third party.[9] Further, the Act consolidated the existing law allowing the remedy of restitution to be used to require the minor to return any property acquired under the contract, or any property representing this, in an unenforceable contract.[10]

9.2.2 Mental incapacity

Persons who have been identified with a mental incapacity, and as such are defined under the Mental Capacity Act 2005 as a 'patient', are protected from entering contracts. The consequence is that any agreement made which purports to be a contract will be void. This is the situation even if the other party was not aware of the 'patient's' incapacity. There may be a different conclusion where the person is not considered to be a patient under the relevant legislation. In this scenario, there exists the ability for a contract to be established with a person suffering from a mental illness or some other form of mental incapacity. To avoid the contract, the mentally ill person must demonstrate that at the time of concluding the contract he/she did not understand the nature of the agreement, and the other party must or should have known of the mental incapacity present. The Sale of Goods Act 1979 has also provided guidance on how potential contracts may be viewed when they involve those without mental capacity. Under s. 3, if the contract is for necessities and the other party is unaware of the mental incapacity, the contract is valid and the price must be paid. If, however, the other party is aware of the mental incapacity, then only a 'reasonable price' must be paid. 'Necessities' is defined under the Mental Capacity Act 2005 as suitable to a person's condition in life and to his/her actual requirements at the time the goods/services were supplied.[11]

9.2.3 Intoxication

Persons who are drunk or under the influence of drugs when a contract is concluded are generally bound by the contract as it is presumed by the courts that he/she is aware of his/her actions. If the other party is unaware of the intoxication the contract is enforceable, but if the party is so intoxicated that he/she does not know the consequences of the agreement he/she is concluding, and the other party is aware, the contract is voidable.

9.3 Illegality

Illegality, in terms of contract law, refers to those contracts that will not be permitted (they are void) because they may be illegal in nature such as those contrary to statute,[12] or against public policy. This includes a particularly wide range of scenarios, such as contracts that intend to prevent the prosecution by the State of an individual who is accused of some illegal

[9] Section 2.   [10] Section 3.   [11] Section 7.
[12] For example, the Resale Prices Act 1976, where manufacturers conspire to regulate the price of goods.

act; and contracts that seek to promote immorality.[13] Such contracts have traditionally been held as void as in *Parkinson v College of Ambulance Ltd and Harrison*,[14] where a charity was provided with a donation of £3,000 on the basis that the donor would be given a knighthood. Whilst this was not against the law, it was held that such a situation would be contrary to public policy as it may involve public officials being corrupted.

Further examples of contracts that will fall victim of illegality include those involving contracts of fraud or those where a crime is to be committed. *Everet v Williams*,[15] involved two highwaymen who entered into an agreement to share the proceeds of their activities from robberies committed together. When these funds were not shared, the court would not allow the case to proceed for recovery. It is also worthy of note that in this case the solicitors involved were fined for bringing the case to court and both highwaymen were hanged. Public policy arguments have also been used to restrict the post-contractual obligations placed on an employee through a restraint of trade clause.[16] Note, however, some illegal contracts may have legal effects as in *Tinsley v Milligan*,[17] where a fraud perpetrated by a woman to obtain a housing benefit did not prevent her from succeeding in her action, because her claim did not rely on the fraud to be effective.

9.4 **Mistake**

Mistake is the area of law where the contract may be held void if the mistake was fundamental to the contract, as the parties did not have a true agreement. However, it is distinct from where the parties may have erroneously entered into a contract that is a bad bargain, or where one party later has 'second thoughts'. Also, mistake is not concerned with the attributes of a particular item, for example buying a printer for a computer under the misapprehension that it had a scanner facility as well. Unless this feature was misrepresented to the buyer, the buyer has no claim under 'his/her' mistaken belief.

In order for the mistake to enable the contract to be made void, it must be fundamental, and 'operative', which prevents the **consensus ad idem** that is required for a contract to be established. A mistake can be a common mistake (where both parties make the same mistake); mutual (where the parties are at cross-purposes—also known as bilateral mistake); and unilateral (where only one party is mistaken).

- *Common mistake:* Here the parties have made the same mistake. Typical examples include contracts involving property which neither party is aware no longer exists. In *Couturier v Hastie*[18] the parties were negotiating for the sale of corn, but whilst the negotiations were proceeding, the carrier of the goods disposed of it. It was held that there could be no contract as the goods being negotiated for were not available when the contract was concluded. However, being careless in a negotiation is not the same as an operative mistake and such a party may be liable for breach of contract. Another example of common/mutual mistake was demonstrated in *Solle v Butcher*,[19] where the parties

---

[13] In the case of *Pearce v Brooks* [1866] LR 1 Ex 213 a woman was in the occupation as a prostitute and had hired a carriage for the purpose of carrying out this function. However, when she refused to pay for the hire the owner could not recover the payments as the nature of the contract was illegal.

[14] [1925] 2 KB 1.   [15] [1899] 1 QB 826.   [16] See **20.5**.   [17] [1994] 1 AC 340.

[18] [1856] 5 HL Cases 673.   [19] [1950] 1 KB 671.

had entered into an agreement for the renting of premises that they both believed was subject to a controlled rent. The rent established between the two was, as a consequence, artificially low, therefore the Court of Appeal held that there should be a **rescission** of the contract, with the proviso that a new tenancy for the premises be offered on the normal, average rent. The court decided the case on the basis of an equitable mistake. The ruling in *Solle* was changed (disapproved), and the original view of common mistake as provided in *Bell v Lever Bros Ltd*[20] was followed by the Court of Appeal in the following case.

Great Peace Shipping Ltd v Tsavliris Salvage International Ltd[21]

Facts:

The ship 'Cape Providence' had sustained serious damage at sea. Tsavliris offered its salvage services and a contract was established. Tsavliris contacted a London broker to find a ship to assist and entered into the hire of the Great Peace (as the closest vessel) for a minimum of five days. However, the Great Peace was 400 miles away, and another available vessel was closer. Therefore the brokers were informed to cancel the contract for the Great Peace and establish a new contract for this closer ship. Tsavliris refused to pay for the hire of the Great Peace on the basis that the contract was void for common mistake.

Authority for:

The case has removed the ability to grant rescission for common mistake as to quality (the contract is not voidable in equity). The remedy for common mistake is that the contract is void (where it involves a fundamental mistake).

It was held that there is no basis on which a contract is to be rescinded due to mutual mistake where, at common law, the contract is valid and enforceable.

- *Mutual mistake:* It is a possibility that in the negotiations for a contract, both parties are at cross purposes as to the nature of the contract or its subject matter. Whilst these instances are uncommon, *Raffles v Wichelhaus*[22] involved just such a situation. In that case, the parties contracted for the sale of cotton, the cargo on the ship the Peerless, sailing from Bombay. However, in fact there were two ships called the Peerless sailing with cotton from Bombay, and the parties were referring to different vessels. Therefore there could be no contract as the parties were mistaken as to the subject matter. If the court could have identified from the parties' evidence that one specific vessel was being referred to then a contract would have been established, but as this was impossible to deduce from the evidence, the contract was held void.

- *Unilateral mistake:* The more common form of mistake is where one party is mistaken as to the terms of the contract or the identity of the other party. This, by its nature, involves the mistake by one party and the cases described in 9.4.1–9.4.2 demonstrate its application.

---

20 [1932] AC 161. 21 [2002] EWCA Civ 1407. 22 [1864] 2 Hurl. & C. 906.

9.4.1 **Mistake in the terms of the contract**

There may exist situations where the contract may be held void because the written contract contained contradictory information compared to the agreement established orally, and this is evident to the other party who attempts to rely on it. In *Hartog v Colin & Shields*[23] the written contract stated that in the sale of hare skins, the price would be established on the basis of the weight of the items (price per pound). The oral agreement had previously concluded that the price would be established on the basis of the number of skins (price per skin), which was a more common calculation in the trade. The buyer would have been at a great advantage if the written contract was allowed to proceed on this basis and it was clear that he must have been aware of the mistake.

Unlike in *Hartog*, the written contract may be signed, not necessarily as a record of oral negotiations, but simply as a method of contracting in this form. Where a person has signed a document without reading it, the courts will not readily provide a remedy just because he/she later discovers the content of the contract and disagrees with it. In the absence of a **misrepresentation** or some form of **duress** being applied for the signing, there may be no escape from the contract. However, the courts have allowed a defence to be raised of *non est factum* (it is not my deed). There are safeguards to the use of this defence and it will not be available where the signor has been careless or negligent in signing a document (such as signing a blank document and allowing the other party to compete it later).[24] It may be of use where the signor is vulnerable and has had his/her vulnerability exploited by the other party. In *Foster v Mackinnon*[25] an elderly man with very poor eyesight was misled into signing a document that he was informed was a guarantee, but was in reality a bill of exchange. Therefore, despite the 'narrow use'[26] and availability of the doctrine, here the signor was under a disability; he signed a document whose terms were fundamentally or radically different from those which he though he was signing; and he was not negligent (in this respect careless) in the signing.[27] As a consequence the contract was void. The requirement of a fundamental or radical difference to the nature of the contract is somewhat harsh but is in line with the narrow use of the plea.

Gallie v Lee (Saunders v Anglia Building Society)[28]

Facts:

Here an elderly woman mistakenly signed a contract believing it was to assign her house to her nephew, but in reality was signing a sale to her nephew's business partner for £3,000. The business partner did not pay the money, nor maintain repayments on a mortgage he had placed on the property. When the mortgage company wished to repossess the house, the now deceased woman's family attempted to have the contract avoided due to mistake. The House of Lords would not allow the claim to succeed as the contract she signed was not sufficiently different from the one she believed she was signing, and she had not exercised sufficient care in reading the document before signing.

---

23 [1939] 3 All ER 566.
24 As in *United Dominions Trust Ltd v Western* [1976] QB 513.
25 [1869] LR 4 CP 704.
26 Donovan LJ in the Court of Appeal stated 'The plea of *non est factum* is a plea which must necessarily be kept within narrow limits' (*Muskham Finance Ltd v Howard* [1963] 1 QB 904).
27 These points being factors considered by Purchas LJ in *Lloyds Bank Plc v Waterhouse* [1991] 2 Fam Law 23.
28 [1970] 3 All ER 961.

Authority for:

Mistake as the to terms of a contract, in the absence of misrepresentation, will not enable the signor to avoid the contract where it is not fundamentally/radically different from what the signor believed he/she was agreeing to. The plea of *non est factum* will not generally be allowed of a person of full capacity.

? Thinking Point

Do you consider the approach of the courts as to the 'fundamental' differences in the contract signed, from what was believed to be signed, is fair? Having viewed the case law on the topic, why do you feel the courts need to restrict its application?

9.4.2 Mistake as to the identity of the party

Mistake in this area is linked with misrepresentation. Cases involve the rogue obtaining the possession of the victim's property and by doing so obtaining a voidable title. This title may be removed where the victim takes steps to avoid the contract before the rogue passes the goods on (which he/she generally will wish to do so as to realize any value in the goods obtained). If the goods are transferred to a buyer purchasing the goods in good faith, then good title transfers to the buyer. This is somewhat unfair but essentially the courts deal with the two innocent parties to the mistake, the victim of the rogue who has lost his/her property, and the innocent buyer who is subject to a claim for recovery of the goods from the victim (the rogue is unlikely to be found and hence subject to a claim against him/her). The courts have generally held in favour of the innocent buyer rather than the victim of the rogue's fraud. This is because the victim had the power not to allow goods to leave his/her possession without verifying the identity of the rogue and his/her attributes (or quality—essentially whether the rogue had sufficient funds to pay for the goods). The courts will then only allow a contract to be held void for mistake where the rogue's identity was crucial to the conclusion of the contract.

The mistake as to the identity of the parties occurs where one party believes he/she is negotiating with a particular person, when in reality he/she is dealing with someone else. The first examples given are where the parties have not met in person (face-to-face). This has often been an 'easier' case to prove of mistaken identity because the victim can more readily claim that he/she reasonably believed that he/she was dealing with the person the rogue held him/herself out to be.

Cundy v Lindsay[29]

Facts:

The case involved Mr Blenkarn, who purported to be a sales representative of a firm called Blenkiron & Sons. He previously hired property in the same street as the firm and had written to the claimants from this address seeking to obtain linen goods. Blenkarn entered into a

---

[29] [1874–80] All ER Rep. 1149.

contract through the post with the claimants for the purchase of a consignment of handker-chiefs, and sold these on without making payment. The claimant had to go beyond proving fraud by Blenkarn (fraud would render the contract voidable, and unless set aside before the goods are passed on, a *bona fide* purchaser would obtain a good title). The House of Lords held that the claimants had intended to deal with Blenkiron, and not Blenkarn, and as this was a fair mistake, the contract was void.

Authority for:

The Lords held that Lindsay was aware of the genuine and reputable firm (Blenkiron & Sons), and had provided the goods on credit due to the contract being, it believed, with this firm. Mistake as to identity was easier to find in this case as the parties never met in person, but rather communicated via the post.

This case was decided due to the mistake over the identity of the other party, but how would the courts determine situations where it is not the identity of the party in question, but rather his/her creditworthiness? In *Kings Norton Metal Co. Ltd v Edridge, Merrett & Co. Ltd*[30] a company provided goods to a fraudster claiming to be a representative of a reputable firm. However, whereas as in *Cundy* the firm existed and was reputable, in *Kings* the firm did not exist. The case demonstrated that mistake as to the attributes of the other party is insufficient to establish mistake, and the identity of the party was not crucial. The goods had been passed on to another buyer in good faith, and as there was no 'mistake' as to the rogue's identity, the claimants were not entitled to the return of the goods.

The previous cases considered mistaken identity where the parties had not met face-to-face. Where the parties have actually met in person, there is a strong presumption that it will prevent a claim for mistake as to identity.[31] However, this line of reasoning has to be considered in light of the House of Lords decision in *Shogun Finance v Hudson*:

Shogun Finance Ltd v Hudson[32]

Facts:

The case involved a rogue impersonating one Mr Patel. Mr Patel had no knowledge or involve-ment in the fraud, with the rogue producing documents of sufficient quality to convince the finance company of his assumed identity (a driving licence in Mr Patel's name). The court held that the rogue had not obtained a good title to the car and it belonged to the finance com-pany, not the innocent third party (Hudson) who purchased it.

Authority for:

Contracts formed on the basis of mistaken identity, where adequate checks have been per-formed to ascertain the identity of other party, will make the subsequent contract void—not voidable.

Innocent purchasers of goods are protected under Part III of the Hire Purchase Act 1964 and s. 23 of the Sale of Goods Act 1979, which provides innocent purchasers with good title

---

[30] [1897] 14 TLR 98.   [31] *Phillips v Brooks* [1919] 2 KB 243.   [32] [2003] UKHL 62.

against the owner where the contract is voidable. However, despite Hudson's arguments, the Lords held that this contract, involving mistake as to identity, resulted in the contract being void, and as such the Hire Purchase Act 1964 was of no use. The key element was the identity of the rogue. Here the finance company believed it was dealing with Mr Patel, through the documentary evidence provided. The company only intended to deal with Mr Patel and would not have provided the seller of the car with the permission to allow anyone other than Mr Patel to take possession of the vehicle. The company had performed adequate checks to verify this information and as such the contract between the rogue and the finance company was void. As being void, rather than voidable, the title could not be passed on to Hudson.

> ### ? Thinking Point
>
> Given the case law above, does it matter whether the fraud was committed through face-to-face negotiations or transacted through the post/e-mail/telephone? Given that many transactions are completed with the use of a debit/credit card in person and over the phone/Internet, is the law in this area satisfactory?

9.4.3 The remedy of rectification

Rectification is an **equitable remedy** available in the case of mistake where a written agreement between the parties fails to reflect the actual agreement that was reached. The courts have an option, if they believe that a contract did not reflect the true intentions of the parties at the time of the agreement, to have the relevant terms changed. This is particularly relevant where one of the parties has deliberately intended, through false and misleading information, to induce the contract. In *Hurst Stores and Interiors Ltd v ML Europe Property Ltd*,[33] ML Europe made substantial changes to a draft contract with Hurst Stores before it was signed. Hurst was not informed, or aware, of these terms and signed the final contract on the basis that it contained the same terms as the previous draft. It was held by the Court of Appeal that ML Europe must have known Hurst was unaware of the changes to the final contract and consequently ordered that the contract be changed back to the previous draft.

9.5 Misrepresentation

> ### Business Link
>
> Whilst a representation is not a term of a contract, and hence will not allow the injured party to claim a breach of contract, a representation may have been made which is false and misleading. The courts and statute have established remedies in such circumstances to alleviate any disadvantage caused to the innocent party. In essence, a remedy of rescission may be granted. Therefore, careful consideration should be taken of statements made in negotiations to ensure the facts of an agreement are not misrepresented.

---

[33] [2004] EWCA Civ 490.

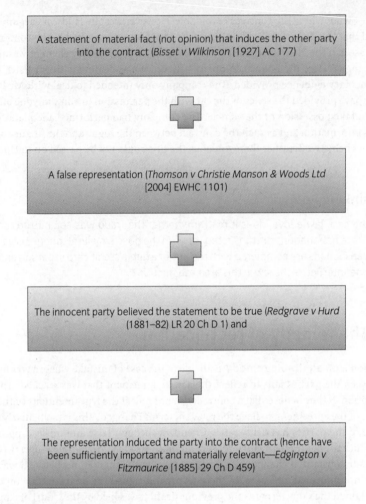

Figure 9.1 Actionable misrepresentation

Chapter 10 identifies the importance and significance of determining whether a statement made in the course of negotiating a contract will be determined as a term or a representation. A breach of a representation will not enable a breach of contract claim, but may, however, lead to a misrepresentation that makes the contract voidable. An action under misrepresentation is available if the untrue representation is considered 'actionable'. This means that there is a legal remedy available where a false statement of fact (not opinion) is made that induces the other party to enter the contract.

Therefore, to determine an actionable misrepresentation the elements outlined in Figure 9.1 must be satisfied.

9.5.1 **A statement of material fact**

Statements of fact are sometimes difficult to separate and distinguish from opinions. If the statement can be determined, objectively, as being true or false, this may assist in identifying whether it is a fact or opinion. Opinions cannot, by their nature, be objectively tested as true or false, whereas facts can be tested in this manner.[34] In *Bisset v Wilkinson*,[35] a vendor's assurances of the suitability of land for sheep farming, when the purchaser was aware the vendor had no knowledge or experience of this type of farming, was held to be an opinion rather than a fact. In relation to statement of law, the courts traditionally hold that such a statement is not a fact.[36] This is due to the presumption that everyone has access to the law and everyone should be aware of the law and be in a position to assess if it is correctly stated. Exceptions to this rule were evident in cases such as *Laurence v Lexcourt Holdings Ltd*,[37] where a statement as to the extent of planning permission when dealing with the use of premises was held to be a fact rather than an opinion.

- *Silence as misrepresentation:* The general rule of contract is that silence cannot amount to a misrepresentation, even if the disclosure of such information would in all probability dissuade the other party from contracting. Naturally, there are exceptions, and if there is a material change in the circumstances; if remaining silent would make a statement misleading; if the parties had a fiduciary relationship; and in cases where the contract is one of good faith, then an actionable misrepresentation is possible.

- *Material change in circumstances:* There exists an obligation to provide (volunteer) information to the other party if the facts materially change between the issuing of the statement and the acceptance of the contract. In *With v O'Flanagan*[38] the Court of Appeal held that a doctor who was selling his practice had a duty to disclose material changes between the agreement and the conclusion of the contract. The information originally provided regarding the income (approximately £2,000 per annum) was correct, but in the time between the agreement and the sale, the doctor had become ill and his patient list substantially declined, along with the income. Whilst silence generally will not be considered a misrepresentation, in this instance the Court considered the doctor had a duty to disclose the information. This was confirmed in *Spice Girls v Aprilia World Service BV*[39] involving an advertising campaign by the scooter manufacturer which involved pictures of the pop group The Spice Girls with a member of the group (Geri Halliwell), even though she had already decided to leave the group and the remaining members were aware of this decision. It was held to be a misrepresentation as the group had an obligation to inform Aprilia and for it to take this into account when determining the advertising campaign.

- *Duty to answer questions truthfully:* If a person is asked a question during the negotiations, and an answer is offered (although there may be no legal duty to answer questions), there is an obligation that the answer is truthful. This places an obligation on the person issuing the statement to provide a full and complete answer, which does not mislead the other party. Further, a true statement, but one that misleads the other party, can amount to a misrepresentation.[40]

---

[34] Although, see *Smith v Land & House Property Corp.* [1884] LR 28 ChD 7, where a statement of opinion can also contain a fact and hence enable a claim for misrepresentation.

[35] [1927] AC 177.

[36] This had been the legal position for over 200 years. It was remarked by Dillon LJ in *The Amazonia* [1991] Lloyd's Rep 236, 250: 'The rule that a contract cannot be set aside on the grounds of mistake if the mistake was a mistake of law seems to have been first enunciated in unqualified terms by Lord Ellenborough CJ in *Bilbie v Lumley* (1802) 2 East 469 ... (and) ... by Lord Denning in *Andre & Cie v Michel Blanc* [1979] 2 Lloyd's Rep 427.'

[37] [1978] 1 WLR 1128.   [38] [1936] 1 Ch 575.   [39] [2002] EWCA Civ 15.

[40] *Nottingham Patent Brick & Tile Co. Ltd v Butler* [1886] 16 QBD 778.

- *Evidence of a fiduciary relationship:* A fiduciary relationship is one involving trust and can typically be seen in relationships of partners of an undertaking, solicitor and client, doctor and patient and so on. In these situations, it is presumed that any material fact must be revealed to the other party and if this is not volunteered, then the silence can be held to be a misrepresentation.

- *Contracts of good faith:* In certain contracts, especially those involving contracts of insurance that require *uberrimae fidei* 'utmost good faith',[41] there must be a full disclosure of relevant factors that would influence a decision to enter an agreement or not. This includes volunteering information even if a question regarding the fact is not asked.[42] In *Hood v West End Motor Car Packing*[43] the court held that regardless of whether there was a negligent or intentional failure to disclose material facts, the fact of the failure to disclose was the relevant consideration in cases of misrepresentation. In *Hood* there was a failure to disclose the fact that goods were to be carried on the deck of a ship rather than covered from the elements and as such enabled the insurance company to avoid its obligation to provide cover.

9.5.2 **The representation was false**

In order to amount to a misrepresentation, it must be found by the court that the statement was in fact false.[44]

9.5.3 **The innocent party believed the statement to be true**

The innocent party must have considered the statement to be true to enable him/her to proceed with an action for misrepresentation. This does not place an obligation on the innocent party to check the validity of the statement made, unless there are tangible reasons in which it would have proved necessary to question the validity.[45]

9.5.4 **An inducement to enter the contract**

For a statement to amount to a misrepresentation it must have been of sufficient importance and materially relevant to induce the other party to have entered into the agreement. This does not necessarily mean that the statement was the only consideration in the innocent party's decision to enter the agreement, but it must have been an important factor and the innocent party must have relied on the statement. In *Edgington v Fitzmaurice*[46] an investor in a company bought debentures on the basis of the incorrect details within the company's prospectus,

---

[41] See Alexander, T. [2006] 'Spilling the Beans' *New Law Journal*, Vol. 156, p. 1241 for an analysis of the duty imposed on partners, and the remedies available for fraudulent misrepresentation.
[42] *Lambert v Co-op Insurance Society Ltd* [1975] 2 Lloyd's Rep 485.   [43] [1917] 2 KB 38.
[44] *Thomson v Christie Manson & Woods Ltd* [2004] EWHC 1101.
[45] *Redgrave v Hurd* (1881–82) LR 20. Ch D 1.   [46] [1885] 29 Ch D 459.

and the investor's own research. Even though the investor carried out his own research, he still relied on the details in the prospectus and this enabled the claim of misrepresentation.

9.5.5 Three types of misrepresentation

Having identified that a misrepresentation has occurred, and this is established as actionable, the next stage is to identify which type of misrepresentation it is. This is important as it affects the remedies that are available.

- *Fraudulent misrepresentation:* This involves a false statement that has been made knowingly or recklessly. This entitles the innocent party to claim rescission of the contract and/or damages, and sue in the tort of deceit. As the type of misrepresentation here is 'fraudulent' this goes beyond carelessness. Due to the nature of fraud being closer to the criminal law than civil liability, along with the problems inherent in establishing sufficient evidence to sustain such an allegation,[47] many claimants attempt to seek a remedy under negligent misrepresentation.[48]

Derry v Peek[49]

Facts:

The case involved Derry and other directors of the Plymouth, Devonport and District Tramways Company, which issued a prospectus stating it was to run trams by steam power (which was to be lucrative). It issued the claim on the assumption that such authority would be granted by the Board of Trade, which ultimately refused much of the permission, save for limited sections of the tramway. This led to the company being wound up and the directors were sued for fraud. The House of Lords held the directors were not guilty of fraud as they genuinely believed the statement, and it was not made recklessly.

Authority for:

To establish fraud committed in a misstatement, the **defendant** must have known the statement to be untrue, or had no reasonable grounds upon which to maintain the belief that it was true, or have acted recklessly in making it.

- *Negligent misrepresentation:* This involves a false statement being made which induces the other party to enter a contract. However, it does not involve fraud, and so is easier to prove,[50] as the party making the statement is unable to show that he/she believed the statement to be true, or held a reasonable belief that it was true. This entitles the innocent party to claim rescission and damages. Further, as the Misrepresentation

---

[47]   See *Long v Lloyd* [1958] 1 WLR 753 for an example of the difficulty in proving fraudulent misrepresentation.

[48]   See *Royscot Trust Ltd v Rogerson* [1991] 3 All ER 294.

[49]   [1889] 14 App. Cas. 337.

[50]   It easier to prove as s. 2(1) of the Misrepresentation Act 1967 provides that once the claimant has demonstrated that a misrepresentation has been made, the burden then switches to the *defendant* to establish to the court's satisfaction that they believed the statement to be true, and also held reasonable grounds upon which this belief could be established.

Act 1967, s. 2(1) provides a remedy for negligent misrepresentations, and the courts[51] have held that this calculation should be made in the same way as for those awarded in cases of fraud, a claim for misrepresentation may actually provide the claimant with a 'better' monetary damages award than if a claim of breach of contract had been made.

- *Innocent misrepresentation:* This involves a false statement, but in the honest, albeit mistaken belief that it was true.[52] This entitles the innocent party to claim rescission as the contract is voidable, and if this is not possible, it may provide for a damages claim in lieu of rescission under the Misrepresentation Act 1967.[53] To demonstrate innocent misrepresentation the party needs to establish that he/she believed the statement that was made, and he/she had reasonable grounds upon which to hold this belief.

9.5.6 Remedies for misrepresentation

The remedies available for misrepresentation depend upon the type of misrepresentation involved (fraudulent, negligent, or innocent).

- *Rescission:* The remedy of rescission is an equitable remedy where the party has the option to set the contract aside and the parties are returned to their pre-contractual position. In order for the parties to be placed back in their original position the court may order any money paid, or any property which has been transferred, to be returned to the relevant parties. The court, through s. 2(2) of the Misrepresentation Act 1967, has discretion as to whether to provide a remedy of rescission, and in practice this is often impossible. The remedy of rescission is available for all types of misrepresentation, and as in situations of misrepresentation the contract is said to be voidable, the innocent party is able to rescind (avoid) the contract but this right must be exercised within a reasonable time. The right to rescind the contract has to be communicated to the other party to be effective, and once this is chosen, the contract cannot be revived.

- In situations that involve fraudulent misrepresentation, it may be more difficult to communicate the intention to rescind. This is usually because by the time the fraud has been discovered, the rogue has disappeared. There is still a possibility of communicating rescission in this example through conduct such as seizing the goods that the rogue had sold; or by performing some act which is consistent with communication (for example, informing the police).

- *Damages:* A simpler method of remedying the loss sustained due to a misrepresentation is through an award of damages. Here an amount of money is awarded to the innocent party to compensate him/her for any losses sustained. In the case of fraudulent misrepresentation, the damages are intended to place the party in the position he/she would have been if the fraud had not been committed (reliance damages).[54] **Damages** can be awarded in contract and tort (such as fraud),[55] and of course through statute.

---

[51]   *Royscot Trust Ltd v Rogerson.*
[52]   See *Oscar Chess Ltd v Williams* [1957] in **10.2**.
[53]   Section 2(2).
[54]   Misrepresentation Act 1967, s. 2(1) as applied in *Royscot Trust v Rogerson* [1991] 2 QB 297.
[55]   *Derry v Peek* (1888) LR 14 App Cas 337.

For those who have been subject to an innocent misrepresentation, the courts have the discretion to award damages under s. 2(2) of the Misrepresentation Act 1967 in place of rescission. To be able to succeed in a claim for damages under this section:

1 the misrepresentation must have been such as to allow the innocent party to rescind the contract; and

2 the claimant must prove that the contract has been (or ought to have been) rescinded; and

3 the court must consider the award of damages, rather than awarding rescission, to be equitable.

Damages are rarely awarded under this section, and when they are, the assessment is based on the contractual remedy of damages that seeks to place the parties in the position they would have been had the representation not been untrue.

9.6 Duress and undue influence

 Business Link

In negotiations to establish a contract, influence and persuasions can be utilized to extract the best deal possible and to ensure agreement on favourable terms. However, the contract must be a voluntary agreement between the parties. When does pressure become unlawful and hence prevent a legally enforceable contract being established? This is where the rules on duress and **undue influence** will be invaluable to enable businesses to gauge where financial pressure may amount to duress.

Freedom of contract relies on the presumption that those who enter into contracts do so under their own free will. If a contract is established on the basis of violence (or a threat), or unlawful economic pressure, this may be considered a case of duress, whereas if a party has unfairly exploited its relationship with the other party this may amount to undue influence. In each of these situations the contract will be held to be voidable; duress on the basis of the common law, and undue influence in equity. Note that as undue influence is based on equity, the courts may use other equitable remedies to prevent an unjust outcome.

9.6.1 Duress

There are two types of duress that may be exercised against a party—physical and economic.

- *Physical duress:* There are, in modern times, relatively few cases that involve claims of duress on the basis of violence, or the threat of violence. As one could imagine, this is common sense as if the person was in such a state of fear that he/she would agree to enter the contract, he/she is unlikely to seek to have the contract avoided because of this act or threat. There have been examples of the use of this form of coercion and these are outlined below. Physical duress occurs when the party who has entered into a contract has done so on the basis of violence or the threat of violence. In *Barton v Armstrong*[56] the managing director of a company based in Australia, Mr Barton, agreed to purchase shares from the chairman of the same company, Mr Armstrong. The price of the shares was very favourable to Armstrong because Armstrong had threatened to have Mr Barton killed unless he entered the contract. The Privy Council held that the contract should be voidable due to duress.

- *Economic duress:* It has proved very difficult in the past for the courts to set aside a contract for economic duress as difficulty exists in establishing where business pressure in commercial dealings becomes an actionable threat. Negotiations in commercial contracts are often based on exploiting financial weaknesses of the other party, or extracting the very best deal due to a need to sell goods quickly and raise funds immediately. These types of negotiation are quite legitimate, and hence criteria were necessary to give greater guidance as to the point where economic pressure amounts to duress:

  1 illegitimate pressure (which need not be unlawful),[57] such as exerting unacceptable levels of pressure which go beyond those normally expected in commercial negotiations;

  2 whether the party claiming duress demonstrated protestations against the contract; and

  3 whether the party had any alternative to proceeding with the contract, evidenced by the availability of independent advice that could have better informed the claimant.

Atlas Express Ltd v Kafco Importers & Distributors[58]

Facts:

Atlas, a delivery firm, entered into a contract with Kafco to transport goods at prices determined on the size of the loads. However, the first load was considerably smaller than estimated, and it proved to be uneconomical to continue the service, therefore Atlas informed Kafco that it would refuse to make any further deliveries unless the price was renegotiated to include a minimum price. Kafco did not wish to do this (if for no other reason than it involved higher costs) but felt compelled as it had a dependency on a contract with a high-street retailer (Woolworths), and did not have time to arrange for a new delivery service. It was held that the contract was based on economic duress and therefore voidable. Kafco had been forced to renegotiate the terms of the contract that involved illegitimate pressure, and it had no real alternative but to agree to the change.

Authority for:

A contract established on the basis of economic duress will not be enforceable. Here, the defendant was performing an existing contractual obligation which was incapable of amounting to sufficient consideration to enforce the agreement.

9.6.2 Undue influence

The party who has been subject to undue influence may have the contract set aside by the courts. It is the exploitation of the power one party has over another that will make

---

[56] [1975] 2 All ER 465.   [57] *R v Attorney-General for England and Wales* [2003] UKPC 22.
[58] [1989] 3 WLR 389.

the contract voidable, and this generally occurs when an individual's vulnerabilities are sub-jugated. The claimant merely has to demonstrate that he/she would not have entered into the contract except for the undue influence. Such an example is *Williams v Bayley*,[59] where a father, an elderly man, entered into a contract with a bank to guarantee his son's debts that would prevent his son from being prosecuted for fraud. As the father did not want to see his son prosecuted he agreed to the contract, but the House of Lords held the contract voidable as the father had not entered the contract freely.

In situations where there is no fiduciary relationship between the parties, the party wish-ing to rely on undue influence must demonstrate that he/she would not have entered into the contract but for the influence. Alternatively, in situations where a fiduciary duty does exist (such as with a solicitor and his/her client; doctor and patient and so on) insofar as the party claiming undue influence has been subject to a disadvantage as being party to the contract, undue influence is presumed. The onus is on the other party to disprove the allegation.

The courts have extended the concept of a fiduciary relationship in *Goldsworthy v Brickell*,[60] where an elderly woman became dependent upon her neighbour to manage her substantial and valuable farm. The neighbour provided the woman with advice and eventually was given a tenancy of the farm on very favourable terms, without the woman having any other advice on the matter. The Court of Appeal held that a fiduciary relationship existed between the parties and therefore the contract was voidable. The courts had traditionally considered that no fiduciary relationship exists between a husband and wife. However, an important ruling was provided by the House of Lords in *Barclays Bank v O'Brien*.[61] The case involved the husband persuading his wife to agree to a mortgage on their jointly owned house that he stated was for a maximum of £60,000 and for three weeks. This was a short-term loan to assist his business (which the wife had no ownership of). The reality was there was no limit on the mortgage or its duration. The bank had not followed the instructions of its head office that the parties should have been informed of the details of the mortgage. It was held that the wife had no access to independent advice, and she had suffered undue influence in agreeing to the mortgage. The bank was aware of the possibility of abuse in this situation and hence the contract was deemed to be voidable. This has led banks, in particular, to be very careful with regard to informing clients about the consequences of contracts that are being signed and the importance of advice. Information from the parties' solicitors is effective in this regard.[62]

9.6.2.1 *Restriction of rescission*

In the event of undue influence being established, the courts have the option to rescind the contract. However, being an equitable remedy, it is a remedy that is provided at the discretion of the court, and the right to recession may be lost if the party is deemed to have affirmed the contract (such as not making any outward sign of protest against the contract); if he/she unduly delays in seeking to rescind; or if the contract involved property which has been sold on before the complainant brought his/her claim.

[59] [1866] LR 1 HL 200.
[60] [1987] 1 All ER 853.
[61] [1993] 4 All ER 417.
[62] *Royal Bank of Scotland v Etridge (No. 2)* [2001] 4 All ER 449.

Conclusion

This chapter has outlined how contract law seeks to protect vulnerable groups, the impact of mistakes and misrepresentation on the contract, and the effect of unfair influence or duress applied in the formation of a contract. The book continues the examination of contract law by discussing the terms of the contract, representations made in negotiations, and the use of exclusion clauses in restricting a party's potential liability in contract and tort.

 Summary of main points

Types of contract

- In unilateral contracts, only one party is promising to perform some action—in exchange for a specific act.
- In bilateral contracts, the parties share promises.
- A void contract is one which has no legal effect.
- A voidable contract allows the injured party in the proceedings to affirm or avoid the contract.
- Unenforceable contracts prevent the application of the contract.

Capacity

- Minors (those under 18 years old) may enter most types of contract. Restrictions exist in relation to forming and enforcing certain contracts.
- Mental incapacity can make an agreed contract void if the person is defined under the Mental Capacity Act 2005 as a 'patient'. In other situations the contract may be enforced against him/her, particularly when considering 'necessities'.
- Intoxication, whether through drugs or drink, generally has no consequence on the effectiveness of the contract unless the party is so intoxicated that he/she could not understand the consequences of his/her actions and the other party was aware of this.
- Certain contracts are illegal and are made void due to public policy or that they involve criminal actions.

Mistake

- The contract may be void due to an operative mistake.
- Where the parties are at cross-purposes as to the nature of the contract or its subject matter the agreement is void.
- A unilateral mistake involves the mistake of one party as to the terms of the contract or the identity of the other party.
- A party who has signed a contract on a misapprehension of its contents or effects may be able to claim *non est factum* and have its effects set aside.

Misrepresentation

- Misrepresenting a fact that is false that the innocent party believed to be true and inducing him/her into the contract enables the party to seek the remedy of rescission and/or damages depending on whether the misrepresentation is fraudulent, innocent, or negligent. It makes contracts voidable, not void.

- Damages are generally not awarded if the misrepresentation was innocently made. However, under the Misrepresentation Act 1967, the court may award this in lieu of an order for rescission (s. 2(2)).

- The option of rescission may be lost if the contract is affirmed. Affirmation may also be effective through lapse of time.

- Silence, as a general rule, cannot amount to a misrepresentation unless:
  - this would be misleading;
  - the contract is one of good faith where information must be volunteered;
  - there has been a material change in the facts between the agreement and the contract; or
  - where the parties are in a fiduciary relationship.

Duress

- Duress may consist of physical duress (violence or the threat of violence), and will result in the contract being held voidable.

- The House of Lords extended the concept of duress, beyond physical violence, to include unacceptable economic pressure where the other party had no option other than to proceed with the contract.

Undue influence

- As opposed to physical or economic threats, undue influence involves the exploitation of the other party's vulnerabilities. This can include exploitation of a fiduciary relationship.

- Relationships such as doctor and patient; parent and child; solicitor and client (and so on) generally have a presumption of undue influence if the contract cannot be explained by their relationship.

 Summary questions

Essay questions

1. Assess the development of the rules in establishing an actionable misrepresentation. Focus on the parties' obligations to provide information and how this is interpreted in light of the general rule that silence cannot amount to a misrepresentation.

2. 'It is much better, when possible, to claim for a breach of a contractual term than to argue a misrepresentation has occurred.'
   Critically assess this statement.

Problem questions

1. Eric is searching for a residential property to rent. He views a flat being offered for rent by Fabulous Flats and Furnished Properties (FFFP) Ltd, a very commercially aggressive firm which attempts to sign residents to contracts as soon as possible. Following his viewing of this first flat, FFFP ask Eric to sign a tenancy contract that includes the following clauses:

   1. FFFP is not responsible for any damage or loss to individuals or their belongings as a result of any act of negligence by the company or its staff; and
   2. It is a condition of this contract that the tenant is responsible for the safety of all visitors to the premises and to ensure the flat is maintained in a good condition (namely it is at a minimum kept clean).

   Eric, despite having not read the contract, signs it despite the fact that he smells strongly of alcohol and appears quite confused.
   Sometime later, FFFP visits the property rented by Eric to ensure that all is well. Discovering that there are no fire extinguishers in the property, and having another person who has already expressed an interest in renting the premises, FFFP invoke clause 2 and seek to terminate Eric's contract for breach of the condition.
   Advise the parties of their legal rights in this situation.

2. Mavis wishes to sell her house to her grandson, Peter. Peter informs Mavis that he will draft the contract of sale to save Mavis any trouble as he is very grateful to be receiving the house at a very competitive price. The agreement between Mavis and Peter is that Mavis will remain in the house until she dies, and pay Peter a nominal rent.
   Peter drafts the contract as arranged but this does not include the agreement for Mavis to continue to reside in the property. Further, the agreement does not state that Peter is to be the purchaser, but rather his business partner is the buyer. Peter does not inform his grandmother of these changes and presents her with the contract, informing her to sign immediately and not to waste time by reading the document, which, trusting Peter, she does.
   Peter's business partner does not pay any money for the property, but has taken out a large mortgage on it and has not made any repayments. Subsequently, the mortgage company wishes to repossess the property to recover its money.
   Advise the parties as to the validity of the contract and their options under the agreement.

📖📖 Further reading

Adams, J. and Brownsword, R. (2007) 'Understanding Contract Law' Sweet & Maxwell: London.

Allen, R. [2004] 'Caveat Emptor Beware?' *Lloyd's Maritime and Commercial Law Quarterly*, No. 4, November, p. 442.

Chandler, A. and Devenney, J. P. (2004) 'Mistake as to Identity and the Threads of Objectivity' *Journal of Obligations and Remedies*, Vol. 1, p. 34.

McLauchlan, D. (2005) 'Mistake of Identity and Contract Formation' *Journal of Contract Law*, Vol. 21, p. 1.

 Online Resource Centre

http://www.oxfordtextbooks.co.uk/orc/marson3e/
Why not visit the Online Resource Centre and try multiple choice questions associated with this chapter to test your understanding of the topic. You will also find relevant updates to the law.

10 Contractual Terms

Why does it matter?

Chapters 7, 8 and 9 have identified the features of a binding contract. Contracts are made up of various terms that identify the rights and obligations of the parties. However, which are the most important terms, and which are of lesser significance? How can they be distinguished and what can the parties do to ensure the significance of a term is reflected in the contract? Is it important to differentiate important and lesser terms? These points will be considered in this chapter. Further, there may be a period of negotiation between the parties before a contract is established. Will all of the statements made during this period be held as terms of a contract? Some may be considered representations that will affect the injured party in seeking a remedy. Finally, imagine you run a store that offers free parking to its customers. Are you liable if the customer's car is damaged whilst parked on your premises? Can you restrict a customer who has parked his/her car on your premises from seeking damages if his/her car is damaged? Having established that a contract exists, this chapter explores the contract in more detail.

Learning outcomes

Following reading this chapter you should be in a position to:

- distinguish between a term of a contract and a representation (10.2)
- differentiate between express and implied terms (10.3.1–10.3.2)
- explain how terms are implied into contracts from the courts, through customs, and from statute (10.3.2)
- identify the status of a term and the implications of it being described as a warranty or a condition (10.4–10.4.1)
- identify exclusion/limitation clauses and the rules of incorporation established through the common law (10.5–10.5.4).

Key terms

These terms will be used in the chapter and it may be helpful to be aware of what they mean or refer back to them when reading through the chapter.

Business efficacy
This expression has been used when describing how the courts may imply terms in order to produce an intended or anticipated result in the contract.

Contra proferentem
This is a rule whereby the courts, generally, will interpret an exclusion clause narrowly and against the party that is seeking to rely on it.

Exclusion/exemption clause
A term that attempts to exclude a party's liability which would otherwise exist. There are common law and statutory rules regulating the use of such clauses.

Innominate/intermediate terms
Where the parties attempt to identify in advance a term as a condition or warranty and this is impossible as it requires knowledge of the consequence of the breach.

Limitation clause
This is often used to describe terms such as exclusion/exemption clauses that seek not to completely exclude any potential liability, but rather to limit or restrict a liability which would otherwise exist. For example, a clause could be included into a contract which provides that an individual/corporation is liable for specific loss or damage, but that this is restricted to a monetary award.

Parol evidence
This rule prevents extrinsic (outside) factors being introduced into a contract or being used to vary the written terms.

Representations
Statements in the negotiations of a contract that do not amount to a term. Breach of a representation may lead to a claim for misrepresentation.

10.1 Introduction

Having identified a contract, the details of the contractual agreement have to be considered due to the implications of what the parties intend to include in the agreement; what they did not mean to be included in the contract; and what significance different terms may have in the contract. This chapter therefore considers the distinction between terms of a contract and **representations**; whether, when a term has been identified as such, it is a 'condition' or a 'warranty'; and how terms are implied into the contract and how this affects terms that have been expressed. The chapter concludes by examining how parties may seek to exclude or limit a legal responsibility through the incorporation of an **exclusion clause**.

10.2 **Terms and representations**

During the agreement stage of the formation of a valid contract, the offeror identifies terms by which he/she is willing to be bound. This is where the details of these terms of the contract are expressed. Those included in a written document entitled, for example, a 'contract'/'agreement' would most likely be accepted as a term. However, contracts need not be in writing to be effective and the terms of the contract may therefore not have been reduced in writing. The parties may have negotiated the deal. This usually involves statements being made, agreements to the statement or counter-offers, until an agreement is reached and the contract formed. However, not all the statements made will be considered to be terms. There are practical reasons for this. Suppose one party remarks to the other in the sale of a car, for example, that the car is 'a good runner that won't give you any problems'. Is this a term? Does the statement have any legal meaning and obligation that could be enforced? Is it a fact or merely an opinion (and it may be considered that an opinion is as valuable as the cost of obtaining it)? Therefore, it is necessary to consider how the courts have addressed the question of whether a statement is a term or representation. Table 10.1 outlines the indicators of where statements will be held terms or representations.

- *Significance for available remedies:* If the statement has been held to be a term and that term is breached, the innocent party has the right to claim damages and possibly end (repudiate) the contract. If the statement is considered a representation and it is breached, there is no breach of contract, but a remedy may exist for misrepresentation, although since the enactment of the Misrepresentation Act 1967, statutory remedies are available for untrue statements. There are no strict rules as to what will constitute a representation and a term, but guidance is available from case law.

- *Relative degrees of the parties knowledge:* If one party has a better knowledge, or could be expected to have a better knowledge of the contractual subject matter than the other party, statements made by the party with the lesser knowledge will be more likely to be regarded as a representation.

Table 10.1 Distinguishing terms and representations

Term	Statement	Representation
	Made by a party with actual or reasonably expected lesser knowledge of the contractual subject matter	→
←	Reasonable reliance on statement made by the other party	
←	Stronger / more emphatic statements (unless statement cannot establish a term)	
←	Statement made close to the agreement (inducing the contract to be concluded)	

Oscar Chess Ltd v Williams[1]

Facts:

Mr Williams traded in a used Morris car for a new Hillman Minx from Oscar Chess (car dealers). Mr Williams described the Morris car as a 1948 model and produced the registration book as evidence. Oscar Chess checked the document and the first registration date, and gave £290 in part exchange. Approximately eight months later Oscar Chess discovered that the Morris car was not a 1948 model but was in fact registered in 1939. This was identified when the chassis and engine numbers were sent to Morris Motors Ltd. Had this been known when the part-exchange price was offered, Williams would have only received £175 for his car. Oscar Chess attempted to recover the overpayment but the Court of Appeal held that the statement of the age of the car was not intended to be a term but was instead a representation. Williams honestly believed the car was as he described and Oscar Chess, as car dealers (and therefore experts), should have the means to check the car's details more readily than the owner.

Authority for:

Statements made by a party with no special skill or knowledge, particularly with the other party who does possess this skill/knowledge, are likely to be considered representations rather than terms.

The case identified that if one party makes a statement and he/she has less knowledge on a particular topic or subject than the other party, such a statement will be more likely to be considered a representation than a term. The situation is reversed when a party making a statement has much greater knowledge.[2] Each case is taken on its merits, but this is a good indication as to how the courts will view such negotiations.

- *Reliance shown to be placed on the statement:* When the parties are involved in negotiations, if a party reasonably relies on the statement made by the other party without examining the truth of this for him/herself, then reliance can elevate the statement to a term. Buyers should be as specific as possible about the requirements of a product of a contract, and if assurances are made that induce the contract, the statement will likely be considered a term.[3]

  Strength of the statement: The stronger and the more emphatic that the statement is made, the more likely that the statement will be considered a term. The strength of the statement may be identified through stopping a person investigating the validity of a statement, providing a guarantee about the truth of the statement and so on.[4] However, statements made with strength or presented empathically will not be considered as terms where it is understood by the parties that statements cannot amount to a term. In *Hopkins v Tanqueray*[5] a horse was to be sold at Tattersall's by auction and the potential buyer, when inspecting the horse, was told by the seller not to inspect the animal as it was 'perfectly sound'. On the basis of this statement the inspection was halted and the horse was subsequent purchased. When it was later discovered that the horse was not sound, the purchaser attempted to claim damages for breach. It was held that this was not possible due to a rule at Tattersall's that all horses were sold without any warranty as to soundness.

---

[1] [1957] 1 WLR 370.
[2] *Dick Bentley Productions v Harold Smith Motors* [1965] 1 WLR 623.
[3] *Bannerman v White* [1861] CB (NS) 844.   [4] *Schawel v Reade* [1913] 2 IR 64, HL.
[5] [1854] 15 CB 130.

- *The time at which the statement was made:* When the parties are negotiating, the courts will take into account the timing of any statements (in relation to when the contract was agreed). If a statement is made which causes the other party to agree to conclude a contract, this will be more likely to be considered a term. This is because the court may view the statement as being of such importance to the other party that it made him/her agree to the contract. The longer the delay between the statement and the conclusion of the agreement, the less likely the statement will be held as a term; this is particularly so where the written agreement does not include the statement made orally.[6] Cases involving the timing of the statement are decided largely on the facts, rather than some application of the law, and attempts to second-guess how the court will determine the status of a statement is very difficult.

- *Was the statement reduced into writing:* If a statement is made during the course of nego-tiations, and the agreement is subsequently reduced into writing, statements made prior to the contract will be viewed as representations.[7] The rationale is the **parol evidence** rule where outside factors cannot be introduced into a contract or used to vary the writ-ten document. Generally, important terms will be included in the contract by the parties, and those other statements that were made, but not included, are by their nature of lesser importance. This can be evidenced by *Routledge v McKay*, where an oral agreement that was subsequently reduced to a written contract that did not include an aspect of the negotiations (in this case the age of the vehicle being traded), could not have been so important to be considered a term. Note, however, that if the written agreement has been incorrectly drafted so as to exclude certain elements of the statement made in the negotia-tions, or where this may have been an intentional act to exclude statements that had been made, it may be held that these should still be part of the written contract terms. Further, oral statements made in the negotiations but not included in the written document may themselves establish a separate (known as collateral) contract that is enforceable.[8]

Remember that these are merely guidelines to identify a term or representation and the courts can place importance on whatever factors are present in each case to determine the status of the statement. Indeed, Moulton LJ in *Helibut, Symons & Co. v Buckleton*[9] stated that all of the factors that led to the contract have to be considered to identify terms from representations, and whilst the previous authorities are good guides, not one can be universally true in every case.

Terms of a contract are not simply those that are expressed. It would be unrealistic to attempt to include all of the terms applicable and hence some may be implied into the con-tract. It is vital you understand where terms derive, and how they may be implied, to appreci-ate the full implications of the contract being agreed.

10.3 Terms of the contract

 Business Link

You are drafting a contract, for example, for the employment of a member of staff. You are going to include the most important points—the hours to be worked; duties; to whom the individual must report and take directions from; what rate of pay is being

---

6 *Routledge v McKay* [1954] 1 WLR 615.
7 *Duffy v Newcastle United Football Co Ltd* (2000) *The Times*, 7 July 2000.
8 *Webster v Higgin* [1948] 2 All ER 127.   9 [1913] AC 30.

provided; and when and how payment is made and so on. These terms are fundamental to the contract and hence are expressed. However, what about overtime
duties? What if the business has to reorganize its production due to changes in delivery, new technology, or a change in legislation? If you hire a person in a management capacity for a multinational company will he/she be expected to move to new
branches in different cities if his/her expertise is needed? These are aspects of the
contract that are included, often, through implied terms. They still form part of the
contract, they are terms and may be enforced, but by their very nature they will not
have been expressed orally or in writing. Therefore, implied terms in all contracts
have to be understood, as their effects are far-reaching.

10.3.1 Express terms

Express terms are, naturally, those that have been expressed in some form. Terms may be
outlined in a written form (perhaps in the contractual document, in correspondence between
the parties, or (in an employment law context) through a works handbook) or they may be
identified from the oral negotiations between the parties. Being expressed in such an overt
way, they are often the most important terms and contain key elements to the contract (the
item to be sold, the price to be paid and so on).

10.3.2 Implied terms

Whilst terms are expressed in a contract, it would be impossible to include every element of
the contract in a written document or an oral negotiation. Some terms may be necessary to
make the contract work, some may be so obvious that they do not need to be expressed, and,
importantly, Parliament has introduced implied terms in business, consumer, and employment contracts to regulate the behaviour of the parties. As such, terms are implied into contracts by the courts, through customs and statutes that must be appreciated to understand
the obligations on parties, and their rights under the contract.

* *Terms implied by the courts:* Courts imply terms into a contract as a matter of fact or
  a matter of law. This is undertaken to help make sense of the agreement between the
  parties, or to make the contract work. Courts have also allowed terms not expressed
  in the contract to be implied because of the custom in a particular industry or market.
  Be aware, however, that whilst the courts may be willing to imply terms, they will not
  rewrite a poorly drafted contract and essentially perform the task that should have been
  undertaken by the parties. The two main reasons for the courts implying terms as a matter of fact have been due to **business efficacy**; and secondly, because the term was so
  obvious each party must have assumed it would be included.

The Moorcock[10]

Facts:

The owners of a wharf on the River Thames entered into a contract to allow the owner
of a steamship (named the Moorcock) to moor the vessel in the jetty for the purpose of

---

[10]   [1886–90] All ER Rep. 530.

discharging cargo. Whilst the Moorcock was discharging her cargo the tide ebbed and she hit the bottom of the riverbed and sustained damage. The owners of the Moorcock claimed damages, but in its defence the owner of the wharf stated the agreement had not provided assurances with regards the safety of the vessel or the suitability of the wharf. The Court of Appeal considered that the ship could not be used in the manner envisaged without it resting on the riverbed, and hence this must have been implied as the intentions of the parties. Esher LJ considered that an implied term existed[11] (on the basis of business efficacy) and therefore the damages action would succeed.

Authority for:

The courts may imply a term where it is necessary to produce an intended or anticipated result in the contract.

- The second scenario where a court may be willing to imply a term is where it is so obvious that the parties clearly intended it to be included.

Shirlaw v Southern Foundries[12]

Facts:

Southern Foundries entered into an agreement with Mr Shirlaw employing him as managing director for a term of 10 years. Two years later a company called Federated Foundries Ltd acquired Southern Foundries and it was decided that Shirlaw should be removed from the board of Southern Foundries and this in effect resulted in Shirlaw's employment being terminated. Shirlaw, in response, brought an action for wrongful dismissal. The Court of Appeal held that Mr Shirlaw should not have been dismissed. Mackinnon LJ used what has become known as the 'officious bystander' test when considering the parties' negotiations and held that they must have agreed, implicitly, to ensure that Mr Shirlaw was bound to complete the term of the contract for 10 years, and Southern Foundries were bound not to remove or replace him in the same period.

Authority for:

The courts may imply a term which is so obvious that it goes without saying. Hence, if, while the parties were making their bargain, an officious bystander were to suggest some express provision for it in their agreement, they would testily suppress him with a common 'Oh, of course!'

When considering implied terms in contract, the courts can adopt the 'business efficacy' route as established in the *Moorcock*. The alternative route was created in *Shirlaw* that established that if the term is so obvious that it 'goes without saying' then the term will be implied into the agreement. This officious bystander test is very important as it considers what a hypothetical officious bystander would have thought should be included in a contract. If the bystander was to make an observation of a clause to be inserted and the parties were to respond that 'of course the term was included in the agreement'

---

[11]   'In my opinion honest business could not be carried on between such a person as the respondent and such people as the appellants, unless the latter had impliedly undertaken some duty towards the respondent with regard to the bottom of the river at this place.'

[12]   [1939] 2 All ER 113.

(essentially that it was so obvious that it need not be stated) then this would amount to a term implied into the contract. Further, unlike the previous examples of terms being implied due to the facts of the case, in *Liverpool CC v Irwin*[13] the House of Lords held that contracts such as those involving the lease of apartments in a tower block could have terms implied as a matter of law.

- *Terms implied through customs:* Customs can be used if they are very widely known and accepted by the general population (such as the term 'baker's dozen' which refers to 13 of a particular item rather than 12 which the term 'dozen' generally refers to).[14] Customs are mainly used in commercial or business transactions where the parties have not identified an express term to the contrary, and could be held to have intended to be bound by the business/industry practice (insofar as it is consistent with that type of contract).[15] The custom may also be common to businesses in a particular geographical location. The courts will look towards the custom being notorious; certain; commonplace; reasonable; and legal to comprise an implied term. The term may also be implied on the basis of the previous dealings between the parties.[16]

- *Terms implied through statutes:* Protection of consumers and those entering contracts has been significantly enhanced through the actions of Parliament. The Sale of Goods Act 1979, for example, has been particularly prominent in this area. Such statutes will be considered in detail in Chapter 11.

Finally, it is important to remember that the courts may imply terms because the contract is silent on the particular issue. However, where an express clause is included, then a contradictory term will not be implied (unless as required by law).

10.4 Classification of terms

 Business Link

A contract will contain many terms but each may not be of the same significance. For example, if you are purchasing a brand new Mercedes-Benz SLR car, what is the implication if it is not fitted with a 5.5 litre V8 engine but rather a 1.6 litre engine? What if there was a very small scratch on the door? In each situation would the injured party be able to claim damages? Would he/she have the right to cancel the contract? To answer such questions it is necessary to classify the terms of the contract as conditions or warranties.

---

[13] [1977] AC 239.

[14] For another example see *Smith v Wilson* [1832], where the court implied the local custom that '1,000 rabbits' actually meant '1,200 rabbits'.

[15] The terms may be implied 'to annex incidents to written contracts in matters with respect to which they are silent' (*Hutton v Warren* [1836] 1 M & W 466).

[16] See *Spurling J. Ltd v Bradshaw* [1956] 1 WLR 461 for the application of this rule and the comments by the judiciary.

10.4.1 **Types of terms**

It is important to identify how the courts will determine what classification is to be given to each term of a contract. This is specifically relevant in the event of a breach of the contract. The breach will occur when a term(s) of the contract is not adhered to by a party, and the remedy available will depend upon whether it is a warranty or a condition. Also note a third classification of term was introduced in the *Hongkong Fir* case called **innominate terms** (where the parties cannot identify a term as a warranty or condition in advance of a breach).

- *Warranty:* A warranty is a lesser term of a contract.[17] If breached the remedy of damages for any loss may be claimed but the injured party is not entitled to repudiate the contract (he/she must continue to fulfill his/her obligations in the contract).

Bettini v Gye[18]

Facts:

Mr Bettini was a professional singer who had agreed with Mr Gye, the director of the Italian Opera in London, to perform as first tenor during his engagement. Bettini agreed that he would attend rehearsals in London at least six days prior to the commencement of the engagement. However, he became ill and could not travel to London for the rehearsals. He did arrive two days before the engagement, ready to perform, but Gye considered this a breach of contract and terminated the agreement. The High Court held that the stipulation for attendance at the rehearsals was not a condition of the contract. Also, as the contract was not for a small number of performances[19] which may have led to the requirement of attendance at rehearsals, Blackburn J held that this was a warranty. As a warranty, Gye was entitled to claim damages for Bettini's breach (not paying Bettini when he was not present) but Gye had to continue with the contract.

Authority for:

Lesser terms will generally be considered a warranty and will not enable the injured party to end the contract, although he/she may still claim damages in the event of a breach.

Bettini has implications for the effective drafting of contracts, and as noted by Blackburn J in the case, if Gye had required attendance at the rehearsals as a condition and essential to the contract, this could have been drafted into the agreement enabling the contract to be ended. However, simply because the parties have used the word 'condition' will not oblige the court to interpret it as such.[20] This does not prevent a party from identifying a term that he/she considers essential and insisting that it is a condition.[21] Also, where statute has implied 'conditions' into contracts, these will be interpreted as such.[22]

- *Condition:* A condition is an important term of the contract. It is often described as a term that goes to the 'heart of the contract' or it is 'what the contract is all about'. Due to

---

[17] This point was evidenced by Denning LJ in *Oscar Chess Ltd v Williams* [1957] 1 WLR 370, where he stated: 'During the last 50 years … some lawyers have come to use the word "warranty…" to denote a subsidiary term in a contract as distinct from a vital term which they call a "condition".'

[18] (1876) 1 QBD 183.   [19] The contract was for 15 weeks of performances.

[20] *L Schuler AG v Wickman Machine Tool Sales Ltd* [1973] 2 WLR 683.

[21] *Lombard North Central Plc v Butterworth* [1987] QB 527.

[22] As with the Sale of Goods Act 1979—see Chapter 11.

its fundamental status, a breach of a condition enables the injured party to claim damages *and* he/she has the option to bring the contract to an end. If the choice is made to end the contract this must be acted upon quickly and within a reasonable time.[23]

Poussard v Spiers[24]

Facts:

Madame Poussard was a professional singer engaged to appear in an operetta for a period of three months. The contract required Poussard to be present for the opening night. However, before the opening night, Poussard became ill and could not attend the performances and Spiers engaged a replacement to cover her role. One week later Poussard returned and wished to begin her performance in the show. Spiers refused and Poussard brought an action for breach of contract. The High Court held that the requirement to be present for the opening night was a condition, predominantly on the basis that Poussard's illness was serious and its duration was uncertain. Spiers could not be expected to stop the opening of the show until Poussard became available and so was entitled to appoint a replacement.

Authority for:

The failure of Poussard to be available at the commencement of the contract went to the root of the contract and consequently discharged the defendant (a breach of a condition).

The performer had to be available and present at the opening night as an essential feature of the contract. When compared with *Bettini*, Poussard was not available for the opening show while Bettini was. As the 'heart of the contract' for acting and operatic performances is to be available when the public are present at the opening night, and where the contract expresses this requirement as a condition, failure to satisfy this will result in the term being considered a condition.

- *Innominate/intermediate terms:* As conditions and warranties have such implications for the parties, and the courts do not like to have their time wasted with disputes identifying the status of terms, the courts consider that parties define the terms themselves. The rationale for this is that the money spent on the correct drafting of the contract will save the parties future expenses, and enable disputes to be settled without recourse to the courts. Whilst this 'term-based' approach, focusing on whether the term is a condition or a warranty, is commonly used, a court may be persuaded to use a 'breach-based' approach. The focus here is on the seriousness of the consequences of the breach. A better description of innominate terms is that they are intermediate terms and where the consequences of the breach are held to be serious, the effects of the breach will be treated as if a condition was broken, with less serious breaches being regarded as breach of a warranty. Therefore innominate terms have not replaced conditions or warranties, but are simply a means of looking at the consequences of a breach, rather than the traditional method of looking at the parties' intentions in drafting the contract.

---

[23] Reasonableness again is based on the facts of the particular case and will vary on the basis of the subject matter of the contract.

[24] [1876] 1 QBD 410.

Hongkong Fir Shipping Co. v Kawasaki Kisen Kaisha[25]

Facts:

The vessel the Hongkong Fir was chartered to Kawasaki for a period of 24 months. The ship was to be fitted for 'ordinary cargo service' and the owners were to maintain the ship during its service. The ship was delivered in a reasonable condition. However, due to its age, it required expert maintenance by engine room staff. The staff were incompetent and too few in number, and due to these facts there were serious breakdowns in the machinery. The ship was at sea eight-and-a-half weeks, off hire for five weeks and when it reached its first destination it required an additional period of 15 weeks in repair. Due to the reliability problems, Kawasaki ended the contract. The owners of the Hongkong Fir brought an action for breach of contract, and Kawasaki claimed in response that the owners were obligated to provide a seaworthy vessel and had failed in this respect. Diplock LJ stated that the obligation of seaworthiness was neither a condition nor a warranty but in effect could constitute both dependent upon the consequences of the breach. The Court of Appeal held that Kawasaki had no legal entitlement to end the contract, although it was entitled to damages for any breach of the contract by Hongkong Fir Shipping Co as to delays when the vessel was being repaired and in port.

Authority for:

The courts may adopt a 'breach-based' assessment in the identification of terms of a contract. A breach of a term that has deprived the innocent party of substantially the whole benefit of the agreement will be held a breach of a condition.

The contract had been established but the condition that the ship be fitted for ordinary cargo service was so broad that it could not be used by Kawasaki in the manner attempted. A range of scenarios could have made the ship unseaworthy, some being a condition (such as a hole in the hull) and others a warranty (insufficient life-jackets). Therefore, as the businesses could have better drafted a contract to protect themselves if required, the breach had to be interpreted on the basis of the agreement and the benefit available in the contract. The twenty weeks being unavailable was a relatively small time in the balance of the two-year contract. The owners took responsibility for the repairs, and any losses incurred could have been reclaimed in damages.

This case has identified the importance of correct and technical drafting of contracts and the effect and importance applied to significant terms. Identifying 'conditions' and 'warranties' will save time in future disputes between the parties but there exist situations, as in Hongkong Fir, where it is the effect of the breach which will determine whether a breached term is a condition or warranty. Further, the courts have stated that if there is an established commercial practice regarding the status of terms used in commercial contracts, these should be interpreted as such to ensure certainty, which is good for public policy, between the parties.[26]

---

[25] [1962] 2 QB 26.   [26] *The Mihalis Angelos* [1970] 3 WLR 601.

10.5 Contractual terms exempting/ excluding liability

> ### 📎 Business Link
>
> Go into most supermarket/shopping mall car parks and somewhere a sign will read to the effect that 'cars and belongings are left at the owner's risk'. This is an exclusion clause. It is purporting to exclude an obligation that the owner of the property may have to the user. Rules exist as to how and when such clauses may be used, and these have been affected by the Unfair Contract Terms Act 1977. Exclusion clauses are an important safeguard against damages claims. Poor or inaccurate drafting may leave the business exposed to contractual and negligence actions which can prove to be very costly.

10.5.1 Exclusion/exemption clauses

An exclusion clause is a term of the contract whereby one party seeks to exclude or restrict a liability or legal duty that would otherwise arise. Rules have been developed through the common law and through statutes to regulate how exclusion clauses may be fairly used in contracts. Typically, the exclusion clause will be made known to the other party through a notice, written in the contract itself, or expressed in the negotiations between the parties. Further, an exclusion clause can be a non-contractual notice (as given in the example at 10.5). The clause has to be incorporated into the contract at the offer and acceptance stage (i.e. when it is created); it must be reasonable;[27] it must be specific as to what liability it purports to exclude; there must be a reasonable opportunity for the other party to be aware of the existence of the term (although it is not the responsibility of the party who is relying on the exclusion clause to ensure the other party has read the clause); and it cannot exclude liability where Parliament has provided specific rights.

There are numerous reasons why exclusion clauses have been allowed in contracts.[28] However, the main rationale for the ability for one party to exclude its liability is because of the freedom of contract. Freedom of contract had developed through the market forces argument whereby the State would not seek to regulate contracts if the market could do so adequately. No one can be forced into a contract against his/her will, therefore if the terms of the contract are not acceptable by the other party, either the offeror will have to change the terms (which may be the exclusion clause), or the market will provide another party who will offer the terms required. This system works in a perfect market but the reality is that there is relatively little choice for consumers (see the price similarity for televisions, games consoles

---

[27] See Unfair Contract Terms Act 1977, Schedule 2 and s. 11.

[28] These include that the courts have the ability to strike out unreasonable clauses; statutes have provided greater protection against unreasonable terms; exclusion clauses often result in cheaper services (such as the price paid for parking, which would be significantly higher if it included insurance for damage and/or theft); and unlimited exposure to any number of claims in numerous situations is of itself unfair and unrealistic to the contracting parties.

and so on) and different high-street stores are often owned by the same multinational corporations.[29] There is also an unequal power relationship between the parties. It was in response to these concerns that the State began to restrict the ability for certain terms to be excluded from contracts.[30]

10.5.1.1 *Incorporation (the common law approach)*

The following cases demonstrate the courts' approach to how an exclusion clause may be incorporated into an agreement. It should also be noted that, whilst this section considers the common law approach, exclusion clauses have to be construed in light of the statutory requirements following the Unfair Contract Terms Act (UCTA) 1977 and the Unfair Terms in Consumer Contract Regulations 1999 (considered in more detail in Chapter 11).

- *Signing the contract binds the parties:* If a party had signed a document held to be a contract, provided he/she had been given an opportunity read it, he/she was bound by the terms. This was the situation insofar as the other party had not lied or misrepresented as to the contents of the contract.[31]

L'Estrange v Graucob[32]

Facts:

Miss L'Estrange was the owner of a cafe in Llandudno who entered into an agreement to buy an automatic slot machine for cigarettes. The machine did not work correctly and engineers had to be called out several times, but each time the machine failed to work shortly after being repaired. Later L'Estrange wrote requesting that Graucob remove the machine, as it had not worked for one month. Graucob, however, refused to terminate the contract. The contract contained an exclusion clause that all express and implied terms and conditions were excluded. The High Court held that by signing the document, even though she did not read it, she was bound by it. There was no misrepresentation or fraud, and consequently L'Estrange could not reject the contract.

Authority for:

A general rule exists that a party who signs a contract is bound by it, even though he/she failed to read it. (But this rule is subject to many exceptions.)

Standard form contracts frequently contain exclusion clauses, minimum periods for the life of the contract, and outline the remedies in the event of a breach. Parties should familiarize themselves with the terms and obligations before agreeing to be bound, as not having read the document will not exclude the party from its provisions.

- *The clause must be included at the creation of the contract:* For a valid exclusion clause, the term must have been included at the offer and acceptance stage. Once the parties have agreed the terms of the contract, future terms may not be inserted unless supported by fresh consideration.

---

[29] Electrical retailers such as Currys, Knowhow, Dixons Travel, DSGi Business, and PC World stores are owned by Dixons Retail.

[30] Most notably are UCTA 1977, and the Unfair Terms in Consumer Contracts Regulations 1999.

[31] See *Curtis v Chemical Cleaning and Dyeing Co.* [1951] 1 All ER 631.   [32] [1934] 2 KB 394.

Olley v Marlborough Court Ltd[33]

Facts:

Mrs Olley stayed as a guest in the Marlborough Court hotel. She paid a deposit and proceeded to the bedroom where, behind a door, was a notice excluding the proprietors from responsibility for articles lost or stolen, unless these had been handed to the manageress for safe custody. Mrs Olley returned to her room where she discovered some of her possessions had been stolen. She brought a claim for damages but the hotel denied responsibility and referred to the exclusion clause displayed in the hotel room. The Court of Appeal held that as the notice was displayed in the hotel room this was seen after the contract had been established at the reception. Therefore it was not included in the contract and could not prevent Mrs Olley's claim.

Authority for:

An exclusion clause must be incorporated into a contract at the offer/acceptance (agreement) stage to be effective. Attempts to include further terms after this stage in the formation of a contract must be supported by fresh consideration.

> Similarly, in the following case, the terms binding the parties must be incorporated at the agreement stage. It is a requirement of the party attempting to rely on the term to ensure it is part of the contract.

Thornton v Shoe Lane Parking Ltd[34]

Facts:

Mr Thornton was attending an engagement at the BBC. He drove to the city and went to park his car in a multi-storey, automatic-entry, car park where he had never been before. At the entrance to the car park was a notice that read 'All Cars Parked at Owner's Risk'. Thornton approached the entrance, took the ticket dispensed by the machine, and parked the car. The ticket included, in small print, a term that it was issued subject to 'the conditions of issue as displayed on the premises'. This included a notice displayed within the car park excluding liability for any injuries sustained by persons using the car park.[35] Thornton returned to the car park three hours later and was severely injured in an accident, the responsibility for which was shared between the parties. Thornton claimed for his injuries and Shoe Lane Parking considered the exclusion clause protected it from liability. It was held that the ticket was nothing more than a receipt and once issued, further terms could not be incorporated into the contract. Only those terms included at the entrance were effective (excluding liability from theft or damage to the vehicle) and not those displayed within Shoe Lane's premises.

Authority for:

A party subject to an exclusion clause is bound (insofar as it satisfies the test of reasonableness) by the terms identified to him/her at the agreement stage. **Further, t**here must be a reasonable opportunity for that party to be aware of the existence and extent of the term(s).

---

[33] [1949] 1 All ER 127.   [34] [1971] 2 WLR 585.
[35] This case was before the enactment of UCTA 1977, which now ensures that contracts purporting to exclude liability for death or personal injury due to negligence are void.

An important element was that Mr Thornton had not been to the car park before. If he had, and thereby presented with the opportunity to have seen the exclusion clause, he would have been bound by it (as per the previous dealings between the parties).

- *Implying exclusion clauses through prior dealings:* An important feature of the court's decision in *Thornton* was that the exclusion clause did not apply, in part, because Mr Thornton had not visited the car park before. Reasonable opportunity to be made aware of the clause is all that is required, and therefore, previous dealings where an exclusion clause is present may imply this term into future agreements.

1 *Between businesses:* If businesses have a history of trade where exclusion clauses have been included, these are likely be accepted by the courts as forming part of subsequent agreements.[36] Further, if the clause is used and is commonplace in an industry or between businesses, it may be implied into the contract.

British Crane Hire v Ipswich Plant Hire[37]

Facts:

The two businesses were involved in hiring plant and earth-moving equipment. Ipswich Plant Hire contacted British Crane for the hiring of a crane, but this was required immediately and the contract was concluded through an oral agreement conducted on the telephone. As such, the conversation did not include the conditions under which the contract would be based, and failed to identify the exclusion clause. This clause required the hirer to indemnify the owner for any expenses that would be incurred in connection with the crane's use. It was included in the written copy of the contract that was forwarded to Ipswich Plant Hire, but before this could be signed and returned the crane sank into marshland. British Crane argued that the exclusion clause was effective and sought to be compensated for its losses. It was held that the exclusion clause was implied into the contract because of a common understanding between the parties that standard terms as used in the industry would form part of any agreement between them.

Authority for:

Exclusion clauses commonplace in a particular industry or in particular business agreements will be implied into those contracts and are therefore effectively incorporated.

2 *Private consumers:* Private consumers are granted protections by the courts against exclusion clauses that, if implied into contracts, may produce unfairness. The first case noted here demonstrates the necessity for the party wishing to benefit from the exclusion clause to bring it to the other party's attention.

Mccutcheon v David Macbrayne Ltd[38]

Facts:

Mr Mccutcheon requested that his brother-in-law transport his car using the services of David Macbrayne Ltd (Mccutcheon had used the firm several times previously). Macbrayne occasionally required customers to sign a 'risk note' that included an exclusion clause for

---

[36] *Spurling v Bradshaw* [1956] 2 All ER 121.   [37] [1974] QB 303.
[38] [1964] 1 WLR 125.

losses or damage to the vehicles shipped. On this occasion no note was provided or signed. The car was shipped but the vessel never reached its destination as it sank due to negligent navigation and the car was a total loss. Mr Mccutcheon attempted to recover the value of the car but Macbrayne referred to the exclusion clause that had been previously included in its business dealings with Mccutcheon. The House of Lords held that the exclusion clause was not present in this contract, and its previous use was so inconsistent so as not to be implied into further dealings.

Authority for:

Previous dealings between the parties are only relevant if they identify a knowledge of the terms of the contract (such as an exclusion clause) and these dealings can demonstrate assent (acceptance) of them.

Previous dealings with contracts involving exclusion clauses will bind a party if he/she has had an opportunity to be aware of the terms and there is a history of previous dealings.[39] In this case however, the contract with the exclusion clause present had not been agreed and Mccutcheon was entitled to assume a different agreement was being concluded than those previously agreed. It may take many contractual dealings where an exclusion clause was present for the courts to later imply one. *Hardwick Game Farm v Suffolk Agricultural Poultry Producers Association*[40] involved more than 100 situations of the exclusion notices forming part of the agreement; this was considered indicative of prior dealings enabling the clause to be implied.

- *The clause must be brought to the other party's attention:* For an exclusion clause to be effective, it must be provided in the contract, through a notice, prior dealings between the parties, or expressed in the negotiations between them. If it is hidden in some document in which the party would not reasonably expect contractual terms to be included, it may be ineffective.

Chapelton v Barry UDC[41]

Facts:

Mr Chapelton visited a beach, under the control of Barry Council. Besides a café on the beach were deck chairs owned by the Council available for renting through payment to an attendant. Chapelton took two chairs, one himself and one for his friend, and received two tickets from the attendant, which he placed in his pocket. Importantly, the tickets contained conditions on the back disclaiming liability for injury when using the chairs. Chapelton used the chair, but when he sat down he went through the canvas and sustained injury to his back for which he had to seek medical attention. He claimed against the Council for the injury he sustained. The Court of Appeal held that the attempted exclusion clause was not effective as it had not been incorporated into the contract. It was not identified on the notice displaying the price for the hire of the chairs and the ticket provided could be considered only as a voucher[42] and a reasonable man would think of a ticket as proof of purchase.

---

[39] *Hollier v Rambler Motors* [1972] 2 QB 71.   [40] [1969] 2 AC 31.
[41] [1940] 1 KB 532.
[42] Relying on the precedent established in *Parker v South Eastern Railway Co.* [1877] 2 CPD 416.

Authority for:

To be effectively incorporated into a contract, an exclusion clause must have been reasonably brought to the other person's attention and not hidden in some document where a term of a contract would not be expected.

Where a person would normally not expect a ticket to include terms and conditions that may restrict or bind him/her, such terms will not be considered as having been incorporated. However, where it was reasonable that a ticket contained terms and conditions, exclusion clauses included in such a document will be effective.[43]

- *Unusual terms must be brought to the other party's attention:* Not only must the party wishing to gain protection from the exclusion clause give the other party a reasonable opportunity to be aware of the term, if such a clause would be unusual (such as to provide a significantly increased sum of damages) this must be identified to be effective.

Interfoto Picture Library v Stiletto Productions[44]

Facts:

Stiletto had ordered 47 photographic transparencies from Interfoto. A note accompanying the delivery was included identifying terms and conditions, the most onerous of which provided that a 'holding fee' of £5 per day, per transparency, was to be paid if they were not returned within 14 days. Stiletto failed to return the transparencies as required and the resultant holding fee amounted to £3,783. The Court of Appeal held that such a clause had not been incorporated into the contract as it was unusual practice in the industry, it appeared to be unreasonable, and Interfoto had failed to adequately bring it to Stiletto's attention.

Authority for:

Where a condition of a contract is particularly onerous or unusual, it for the party attempting to rely on this to demonstrate that he/she fairly brought it to the other party's attention.

10.5.2 Misrepresentation may restrict the operation of an exclusion clause

An exclusion clause which has satisfied the tests as noted at 10.5.1 will generally be held by the courts to be effective, even if the injured party has been ignorant of it. An exclusion clause which was otherwise lawful will fail if it was misrepresented to the other party. Such misrepresentation can be through words or conduct, but the key element is that it is sufficient to mislead the injured party about the existence or extent of the exclusion clause.

Curtis v Chemical Cleaning and Dyeing Co Ltd[45]

Facts:

Ms Curtis took her wedding dress to the defendant's dry cleaning shop to be cleaned. At the shop she was asked to sign a document that contained terms and conditions including

---

[43] *Thompson v LMS Railway* [1930] 1 KB 41.   [44] [1988] 1 All ER 348.
[45] [1951] 1 All ER 631.

an exclusion of liability for damage to customers clothes. Upon enquiry as to the nature of the document, the assistant misinformed Curtis that it included the exclusion of liability for damage to the beads and sequins on the dress. Thereafter Ms Curtis signed the document but did not read it. The exclusion clause was in fact for all kinds of damage to property. The dress, when returned, had been badly stained and in response to Curtis' claim for damages, the defendants attempted to rely on the written exclusion clause. The Court of Appeal held that there had clearly been a misrepresentation as to the nature of the clause and as a consequence it had never become part of the contract.

Authority for:

The misrepresentation to the other party of the existence or extent of an exclusion clause will result in it being treated as void.

10.5.3 Interpretation of the clause

Having satisfied itself that the exclusion clause had been validly incorporated into the contract, the clause must be considered to ascertain whether its scope includes the nature of the event which has led to the loss/injury. The courts have traditionally interpreted such clauses *contra proferentem*, and thereby against the party wishing to rely on it. Of course, this section must be read in light of the restrictions on contractual clauses through UCTA 1977, which has strengthened protections against the use of exclusion clauses.

- *The purpose of the contract:* The courts will look at the nature of the contract and ascertain if the exclusion clause attempts to contradict the purpose of the underlying agreement or the intentions of the parties.

Evans Ltd v Andrea Merzario Ltd[46]

Facts:

The parties had contracted for the importation of machines from Italy by sea. The standard form contract contained an exclusion clause, upon which the defendants attempted to rely when the goods were lost in transit. The machines had been stored in a container on the deck of the ship, but the claimants had been given an oral assurance that the machines would in fact be stored below deck. The container in which the machines were housed was lost when it slid overboard during the voyage. The Court of Appeal held that the defendants were not able to rely on the exclusion clause in the standard form agreement as this was contrary to the assurance given, and this assurance was to override the exclusion clause.

Authority for:

The oral assurance provided to the claimant was a term of the contract (a collateral contract was established) and overrode the inconsistent provisions of the written agreement. Hence the written exclusion clause was ineffective against the collateral contract.

- *The* contra proferentem *rule:* Whilst an exclusion clause is permitted under the freedom of contract, as its effect is to restrict or limit a liability that would otherwise exist, the

---

[46] [1976] 1 WLR 1078.

courts will interpret it *contra proferentem* (against the party who wishes to rely on the clause). Therefore, the party wishing to rely on the clause must ensure it is correctly and precisely drafted to cover the event that led to the claim.

Houghton v Trafalgar Insurance Co Ltd[47]

Facts:

The claimant had insured his five-seat car through the defendant insurers. The policy included an exclusion clause that the insurers would not accept liability for any damage caused whilst the car was 'conveying any load in excess of that for which it was constructed'. Mr Houghton was involved in an accident in which his car was a total loss, but at the time of the accident there were six passengers in the car. Under these circumstances, the defendants relied on the exclusion clause that six people in the car constituted an excess load. The Court of Appeal held that there was ambiguity in this clause, as the 'excess load' would have been more likely to cover situations of excessive weight rather than number of passengers. Due to this uncertainty, the exclusion clause could not be relied upon.

Authority for:

The courts will interpret exclusion clauses ***contra proferentem*** and any ambiguity will probably result in the clause, and its application, being limited in effect.

The requirement for precision in the drafting of the clause, and its effect thereafter was demonstrated in *Baldry v Marshall*[48] involving the purchase of a car. The claimant informed the defendant motor dealers that he wished to purchase a car suitable for touring. They recommended and supplied him with a Bugatti car, and a clause in the contract stated that the defendants would not be liable for any 'guarantee or warranty, statutory or otherwise'. The car was unsuitable for its purpose and the claimant rejected it and sought to recover his payment. The Court of Appeal held that the claimant's stipulation of a car suitable for touring was a condition of the contract, and as, under an exact reading of the exclusion clause, it did not seek to exempt liability for a breach of condition, it could not be enforced in this case. Similar reasoning as to interpreting exclusion clauses in light of the main purpose of the contract was seen by the House of Lords decision in *Glynn v Margetson*.[49]

10.5.4 Limitation clauses

Where exclusion clauses attempt to exclude a claim for loss or damage, and exempt liability for breach, **limitation clauses** seek to reduce exposure to claims by limiting liability to (for example) a monetary claim for damages; to a fixed sum; and for any consequential losses. Following UCTA 1977, the courts have been more willing to accept limitation clauses in contracts (since unreasonable clauses may be disregarded under the Act), and in *Photo Production v Securicor Transport Ltd*[50] it was held that such clauses should be given their ordinary, natural meaning, and not construed differently from other clauses in the contract. Like exclusion clauses, the courts, in assessing the viability of the clause, will begin by assessing whether the

---

[47] [1953] 3 WLR 985.   [48] [1925] 1 KB 260.
[49] [1893] AC 351.   [50] [1980] AC 827.

limitation clause forms part of the agreement, whether it covers the breach in question, and finally whether it uses the *contra proferentem* rule of interpretation.

10.5.5 The statutory position

Particularly since the enactment of UCTA 1977, consideration of the validity of an exclusion and limitation clause has included statutory measures. UCTA 1977 was designed specifically to regulate the use of exclusion clauses, and the Unfair Terms in Consumer Contract Regulations 1999 has extended the powers to the entire contract. These statutes are of great significance in this area and are considered in Chapter 11.

> **? Thinking Point**
>
> Should the State be involved in regulating which liabilities may be excluded from a contract and which may not? Is a market unable to regulate itself and provide customers with options, including risk, if the customer is prepared to accept such risk?

 Conclusion

The chapter has identified the factors that help to distinguish between terms and representations. Further, it has demonstrated the distinction between the terms in a contract and the significance of the status of warranty and condition. Exclusion clauses, their validity and methods of incorporation, have been discussed, and the reader should be in a position to recognize the common law rules established for the effective incorporation of such clauses. The book continues by examining the effect of statutory involvement in the regulation of contracts.

 Summary of main points

- The provisions of the contract may be viewed as a term or a representation.
- Terms are the most significant aspect of an agreement and failure to fulfill the agreement enables a claim under breach of contract.
- A representation is not a term under the contract and the injured party must seek a remedy under misrepresentation.

Representations

- A statement made by a party with greater knowledge, and relied on by the other, will generally be held a term.
- If the statement is made with strength it will be more likely to be regarded a term, unless it is implicitly/explicitly agreed that it cannot be held as such.

- A statement that induces the other party to enter the contract will be more likely to be held a term.
- Statements made in the negotiations, but that do not appear in the final written contract, will be held to be a representation (although a collateral contract may have been created).

Terms: expressed and implied

- Terms may be expressed orally or in writing and these will form part of the contract.
- Due to the problems in attempting to include every term into a written or oral contract, or deduced from conduct, terms are implied.
- Terms may be implied by the courts as a matter of fact or a matter of law.
- Customs established by the parties' previous trading relationship; the industry; or the conduct of business in that locality may form part of the contract.
- To form a custom the term must be notorious, certain, commonplace, reasonable, and legal.
- Many terms are implied into contracts by statutes—such as the Sale of Goods Act 1979, UCTA 1977 and so on.

Terms: warranties and conditions

- A warranty is a lesser term, breach of which enables the innocent party to seek damages although he/she must continue with the contract.
- A condition forms the most important aspect of the contract, breach of which enables the innocent party to seek damages, and he/she may end the contract or affirm it.
- Warranties and conditions are determined on a 'term-based' approach. However, the courts may also adopt a 'breach-based' approach. Here it is the seriousness of the consequences of breach that will identify the term as a condition or warranty (referred to as 'innominate terms').

Exclusion/limitation clauses

- These clauses seek to limit or exclude a liability that would otherwise exist.
- To be effective the clause must be incorporated into the contract at the agreement. Incorporating an exclusion clause after this time requires fresh consideration.
- The clause must be reasonable (assessed using UCTA 1977) and not contrary to statute.
- The clause must be specific to the liability being excluded.
- It must have 'reasonably' been brought to the other party's attention.
- This obligation is even more strictly applied if the exclusion clause involves a particularly unusual term.
- Exclusion clauses may be implied through previous dealings between the parties.
- The *contra proferentem* rule applies so that any ambiguity in the exclusion clause will be interpreted against the party attempting to rely on it.

Summary questions

Essay questions

1. Employment law is one jurisdiction of law that, whilst dominated by statutory intervention, continues to be underpinned by ordinary contractual principles. This is particularly true in relation to the doctrine of implied terms.

    Assess the role played by implied terms in employment relationships and how they have been developed by the judiciary.

2. How have the statutory developments regulating the use of exclusion clauses altered and restricted their use? Compare how the cases pre-1977 would be decided in the courts today.

Problem questions

1. A Ltd and Z Ltd are negotiating for the charter of a ship on an 18-month contract. A Ltd is concerned that the goods to be shipped in the vessel reach the customers on time or it will face penalties and may also lose business. Therefore A Ltd has inserted the following clause in the contract:

    'It is a condition of this contract that the ship is seaworthy in all respects.'

    Following the signing of the charter, when the ship is at sea there are continued problems with its maintenance as the crew supplied by Z Ltd are very inexperienced and the chief engineer has an alcohol problem. In part due to this the ship is in the dock with engine problems for the first 3 months in the initial 8 months of the charter.

    A Ltd fears for the probable negative consequences of the ship and now wishes to end the contract and claim damages from Z Ltd.

    Advise A Ltd accordingly.

2. Sarah works for a local school and travels to work each day by car. She usually parks on a nearby piece of waste ground, but was unable to do so last week because of flooding. Instead, she parked her car in the multi-storey car park. A notice just inside the entrance to the car park states:

    'The company will not be responsible for death, personal injury, damage to vehicles or theft from them, due to any act or default of its employees or any other cause whatsoever.'

    Reference to this notice is also contained on a ticket which Sarah received when entering the car park. On her return to collect the car, Sarah discovers that it has been stolen. She goes to report this to the attendant and is injured when he negligently allows the barrier to fall on her head.

    Advise Sarah.

 Further reading

Lawson, R. (2008) 'Exclusion Clauses and Unfair Contract Terms' (9th Edition) Sweet and Maxwell: London.

Lewis, M. and Hinton, C. (2004) 'No Room for Ambiguity' *New Law Journal*, Vol. 154, p. 1128.

Online Resource Centre

 http://www.oxfordtextbooks.co.uk/orc/marson3e/
Why not visit the Online Resource Centre and try multiple choice questions associated with this chapter to test your understanding of the topic. You will also find relevant updates to the law.

Statutory Regulation of Contracts

Why does it matter?

Contracts between businesses, and those between businesses with consumers are regulated increasing through statutory intervention. These statutes control the use of terms; whether exclusion of liability is void or permitted insofar as being reasonable; and other statutes imply terms into contracts. Sellers of goods in particular must have an awareness of these laws and ensure they do not negligently or knowingly transgress the provisions. Knowledge of the content and application of the legislation is necessary, as some rights impose strict liability on the seller, whilst others involve negligence liability.

Learning outcomes

Following reading this chapter you should be in a position to:

- explain the protection afforded to buyers in contracts for goods and services, through statutory intervention (11.2–11.4)
- demonstrate how statute restricts the use of exclusion clauses in contracts (11.5–11.5.5)
- explain how statute restricts unreasonable clauses in contracts (11.6–11.6.4).

11.1 Introduction

This chapter continues to explore the contract in greater detail by examining how the terms of a contract are regulated through statutory intervention. Such legislative measures have been provided due to the unequal bargaining positions of the contracting parties in business to consumer contracts, and the State regarding some aspects of *laissez-faire* to be contrary to public policy and fairness (such as certain exclusion clauses). For example, statutes, such as the Sale of Goods Act 1979, imply terms into contracts, and the Unfair Contract Terms Act 1977 regulates the parties' use of exclusion clauses. This particularly protects the weaker party to a contract from exploitation and provides minimum rights that may not be waived.

11.2 **The Sale of Goods Act 1979**

Sale of
Goods Act
1979

> ### 📎 Business Link
>
> When you approach the till-point of many high-street department stores, you may see a sign reading 'No refunds provided for unwanted goods. This does not affect your statutory rights.' The store is identifying that it will not provide a refund for a good that is not faulty and is simply unwanted. However, the retailer cannot exclude the rights provided through statutes, including the Sale of Goods Act (SOGA) 1979. Therefore, businesses involved in retail must be aware of SOGA 1979 and adhere to its requirements.

For years, the common law and legislation have afforded protection to consumers and businesses (in fact most of the case law on the subject involves business-to-business disputes). SOGA 1979 was revised and updated from the original Act of 1893 but the main provisions remain remarkably similar to this legislation. Further, whilst case law has provided 'flesh on the bones' of the legislation, it is also worthy of note that protections for those involved in buying and selling goods had been developed through the common law; indeed, the 1893 Act was actually a codification of these rights into one Act of Parliament. From its inception, SOGA 1979 has offered protection to 'buyers'. This Act implies the terms into contracts and, in certain circumstances these cannot be removed by a waiver or a contractual term to the contrary.

- *A definition:* For protection to be provided through SOGA 1979, a sale must take place.[1] Whilst this may appear obvious (if for no other reason than the title of legislation) its effect is that barters (exchanging items)[2] and loans are not protected unless a transfer of the ownership has occurred. SOGA 1979 includes contracts of sale (where the goods purchased are taken into the possession of the buyer immediately) and agreements to sell (where the contract becomes a contract of sale when the goods exist and the ownership passes to the other party).[3] This second scenario may be evident where a product is sourced/manufactured with a lead-time before delivery is made.

- *The meaning of 'goods':* The transfer of 'goods' invokes the provision of SOGA 1979. Goods are defined as 'all personal chattels other than things in action and money ...; and in particular "goods" includes emblements, industrial growing crops, and things attached to or forming part of the land which are agreed to be severed before sale or under the contract of sale and includes an undivided share in goods ...'[4]

- As such, items such as those ordinarily used by consumers including televisions, tables, mobile telephones, cars and so on will be considered 'personal chattels' and covered by the Act. 'Things in action' is a historical expression for something, unlike personal chattels which involves a tangible good, which must involve the exercise of a legal right in order for it to 'materialize'. A most obvious business example of this would be a guarantee provided when a good is purchased. The paper that the guarantee is written on is not what the guarantee is, but rather provides evidence that a guarantee can be exercised

---

[1] Section 2(1).
[2] Although the parties to the barter are protected through the Supply of Goods and Services Act 1982.
[3] Section 2(5).   [4] Section 61(1).

and pursued through the courts if necessary. Things in action are not covered by SOGA 1979.

- *Who is protected:* The significance of SOGA 1979 is that certain terms are implied into the contract that offer a level of certainty, and security, for the goods contracted. These place obligations on the seller of the goods to ensure that ss. 12–15 are adhered to. These implied terms are held as conditions of the contract and hence allow an injured party to repudiate the contract within a reasonable time if they are breached. Further, after this reasonable time, the terms are held as warranties and allow an injured party to seek damages (but he/she will not be in a position to repudiate the contract). The other major advantage of SOGA 1979 is that the liability is strict and hence it does not matter how the good fell below the standard required; the seller has responsibility. Sections 12, 13, and 15 apply to all sales contracts. Sections 14(2) and 14(3) apply to contracts made by a consumer with a seller acting in the course of business.

The definition of a consumer is not found in SOGA 1979 but rather in the Unfair Contract Terms Act 1977, s. 12, which reads:

1   A party to a contract 'deals as consumer' in relation to another party if—
   a   he neither makes the contract in the course of a business nor holds himself out as doing so; and
   b   the other party does make the contract in the course of a business; and
   c   in the case of a contract governed by the law of sale of goods or hire-purchase, or by section 7 of this Act, the goods passing under or in pursuance of the contract are of a type ordinarily supplied for private use or consumption.

11.2.1 **SOGA 1979, ss. 12–15**

For sellers and buyers, significant protections are provided through SOGA 1979, ss. 12–15. Section 12 is applicable to all sales and cannot be waived. Sections 13–15 may be waived in business (non-consumer) sales where it is reasonable.

- *Section 12–title to goods:* A fundamental aspect to a contract of sale is that in order for a 'true' sale to take place, one party must be free to transfer ownership (good title) to the other. The buyer is then able to enjoy 'quiet possession of the goods'. In order to achieve this, the first party must possess the title to transfer or have the owner's consent to dispose of the good.

Rowland v Divall[5]

Facts:

Mr Divall purchased an 'Albert' motorcar and he later resold it for £334 to Rowland. Rowland, a motorcar dealer, sold it to a Colonel Railsdon for £400, but the car had been stolen before Divall bought it and it was repossessed by the police. Rowland returned the £400 purchase price to Railsdon and brought an action against Divall to recover the £334 he had paid for the vehicle. SOGA 1893 had implied into every contract of sale 'a condition on the part of the

---

5   [1923] 2 KB 500.

seller that … he has a right to sell the goods', and if this is not satisfied the buyer has the right to have the purchase price returned. Only a person who holds 'good title' to a property has the right to transfer or convey this, and if the property is in fact stolen, then no passage of title may occur. The Court of Appeal held that Rowland was entitled to have his money returned.

Authority for:

Section 12 provides that in every contract of sale, there exists an implied condition that the seller has the right to sell.

In this case, as the parties had purchased the stolen vehicle in good faith, there was no criminal element to the proceedings, but the seller did not have good title to the goods and hence the contract failed. Colonel Railsdon could claim the return of the price paid to Rowland (despite having use of the vehicle for several months); Rowland had the right to claim the purchase price from Divall; and Divall had the right to pursue the seller from whom he purchased the vehicle and have the money returned (albeit in reality it may be very difficult to find the seller of the stolen goods to pursue the return of the money paid).

Whilst this situation regarding stolen goods appears to be straightforward, the seller has no right to sell the good so cannot pass on good title and the original owner will have the good returned to him/her, this is not strictly so. In this scenario, the loss would fall on the innocent buyer, as in *Rowland* above, who would have to recover his/her losses from the rogue who sold the stolen good. There are mechanisms that enable an innocent buyer to obtain good title when he/she purchases goods in good faith and lacked knowledge of the rights of the owner/seller.

In *Rowland*, the sale was said to be void (did not exist) because the car that was sold had been stolen. If, however, the transfer of ownership is 'voidable' then SOGA 1979, s. 23 is important. It states: 'When the seller of goods has a voidable title to them, but his title has not been avoided at the time of the sale, the buyer acquires a good title to the goods, provided he buys them in good faith and without notice of the seller's defect of title.' Such a situation may occur when the sale is agreed with the rogue on the basis of a misrepresentation,[6] and hence the rogue now possesses a voidable title to the goods that can be transferred. This 'title' can be lost where the true owner takes action to avoid the contract—either through contact with the rogue or through some other means (such as reporting the incident to the police). However, SOGA 1979, s. 25 provides a further hurdle for the owner. Even where steps have been taken to avoid the contract with the rogue, where the rogue 'buyer' has taken possession of the good (although not ownership of the title) and he/she sells the good to another buyer who is acting in good faith, the buyer will obtain title to the goods. Sales of goods can occur through the actions of an agent with possession of the owner's good passing on the title to a buyer acting in good faith, and in situations where the owner allows the buyer to believe the seller of the goods has the owner's permission to sell.

It is important to recognize that when the title to goods has passed, this is effective even before the payment has reached the seller (however, payment must have been intended). This may occur where one business transfers goods to another business and payment is made, for example, at the end of each month. If ownership has transferred, but the other party fails to pay for the goods and those goods have been re-sold, or the party is liquidated, the seller

---

[6] For example, taking possession of the goods through providing a cheque in payment that fails to clear.

may have difficulty in obtaining payment. As such, a contract may incorporate a reservation of title clause whereby the seller has the ability to recover the goods for non-payment. The reservation of title clause is effective where the contract states that the goods remain the possession of the seller until payment is made (at which point the title to the goods will transfer); the goods are still in the buyer's possession; and the goods are readily identifiable (hence the goods have not been joined with other goods and they cannot be identified).[7] These clauses are referred to as 'simple' but it may not be realistic or in the best interests of the seller to incorporate such a clause that may prevent the buyer using the goods. Hence, a particularly important judgment was made in the following case.

Aluminium Industrie Vaasen v Romalpa Aluminium Ltd[8]

Facts:

The sellers of aluminium wanted protection against possible non-payment and therefore contracted with the buyers on the basis that the goods supplied were to be maintained separately from the buyer's other goods; the sellers would have ownership of the buyer's products that had been made with the seller's goods; these products must be stored separately from other goods; and the proceeds from any sales of the goods were put into a separate bank account so the sellers could be assured of payment when requested. When the buyer's business failed and it was wound-up the sellers were successful in obtaining its goods supplied, but unused, and the money it was owed.

Authority for:

The case was decided largely on its facts so its application may be limited. 'Romalpa clauses' effectively provide the seller with a charge over the goods supplied. However, due to the restrictions on how charges can be made over a company's property, and to circumvent possible legal issues with the effects of this case, the buyers were considered as bailees of the seller's goods.

? Thinking Point

Having read Chapter 24, how would you reconcile the decision in *Romalpa* with the requirements of registration of charges as required in the Companies Act 2006.

- *Section 13—description of goods:* Goods that are sold by description must correspond to that description. This may be evidenced in situations involving the sale of products where it may be particularly difficult or time-consuming for the buyer to verify the claims. It enables sales to take place with the protection for the buyer that the item possesses the features that he/she was assured. For example, it would be unrealistic for a buyer to have to verify if a computer actually had the processor and hard drive capacity that the sales advisor had informed him/her of before leaving the shop with the machine. Section 13 allows the buyer protection when he/she relies on the description provided, but it does not where the buyer has not relied on the description and has taken the responsibility for verifying the good him/herself.[9]

---

[7] *Borden v Scottish Timber Products Ltd* [1981] Ch 25.   [8] [1976] 1 All ER 552.
[9] *Harlingdon and Leinster Enterprises v Christopher Hull Fine Art* [1990] 3 WLR 13.

The protection of s. 13 also applies to advertisements and sales materials that the buyer relies on.[10] It is important to note that whilst the sections of the Act are separated, they may work independently of each or in unison. For example, s. 13 is not concerned with the quality of the product, which may be perfectly fine in terms of its quality and fitness for purpose, but not as described. This would still allow a remedy under SOGA 1979.[11] The significance of the overlap of the provisions can be seen in relation to the seller. Section 14 requires the good to be of a satisfactory quality, but this is only an implied term in sales in the course of business (namely the buyer has to posses the status of a consumer as above). Where goods are sold privately the buyer has no protection unless a warranty is provided (and usually this is not—*caveat emptor*). In *Beale v Taylor*[12] the Court of Appeal held that where a private seller sold a car that was described as a Triumph Herald, but in reality was two cars welded together (with only one half of the car corresponding to the description), whilst the buyer could not rely on s. 14 as to the car's quality, an action was permitted under s. 13 (as it applied to all sales).

- *Section 14(2)–quality of goods:* Section 14 (2) incorporates a term in sales established in the course of business[13] requiring the goods to be of a satisfactory quality. 'Quality' will vary between products depending on issues such as whether the good was brand new or used. Section 14(2) is applicable in each scenario, but the interpretation of the word will differ. If the item is sold as new, it should have such a condition (free from scratches, in its new and original packaging and so on).[14] If the good is used, some general 'wear and tear' must be expected[15] but it must still be of 'satisfactory'[16] quality. For the purposes of SOGA 1979, goods are of satisfactory quality if they meet the standard that a reasonable person would regard as satisfactory, taking account of any description of the goods, the price (if relevant) and all the other relevant circumstances.[17] The issue of quality extends from the good itself, to include the packaging in which it is contained, and to 'external factors' that would make the good fall below the quality required. In *Wilson v Rickett Cockerell*,[18] coal was sold, which itself was of satisfactory quality, but it had become contaminated with detonators that exploded and caused damage when the coal was burnt. This breached the requirement of satisfactory quality.

  Features to be considered when assessing the quality of a good include:

  1 fitness for all the purposes for which goods of the kind in question are commonly supplied;

  2 appearance and finish;

  3 freedom from minor defects;

  4 safety; and

  5 durability.

---

[10] See the Unfair Commercial Practices Directive.   [11] *Arcos v Ronaasen* [1933] AC 470.

[12] [1967] 3 All ER 253.

[13] This will not prevent a business from seeking protection under the Act where the sale is not part of the 'course of business' and in essence the buyer is acting as a consumer—*Stevenson v Rogers* [1999] 1 All ER 613.

[14] This was accepted in *Clegg v Anderson* [2003] 2 Lloyd's Rep 32 when referring to expensive quality goods.

[15] *Thain v Anniesland Trade Centre* [1997] SLT 102 Sh Ct.

[16] Satisfactory quality used to be called 'merchantable' quality.

[17] Relevant circumstances would include the precautions the reasonable person would undertake in the use of a good. In *Heil v Hedges* [1951] 1 TLR 512, the claimant brought an action on the basis that the pork chop caused him to contract a tapeworm infestation. It was held that the problem occurred from the claimant failing to properly cook the food, not the quality of the food, therefore there was no claim under section 14 (2).

[18] [1954] 1 QB 598.

This last aspect—durability—may also assist buyers when considering the life span of the goods. For example, if you purchase a television, you may receive a one-year manufacturer's warranty. However, under the Act, it may be considered that it should last much longer, and if used correctly, would provide the owner with the right to have the item repaired or replaced if a defect appears within six years (after a reasonable time the term will be considered a warranty).[19] The main value of s. 14(2) is that the liability is strict and hence it does not matter how the defect in the good was created, as many businesses simply re-sell goods bought along the supply chain; if there is a defect, protection is granted under s. 14(2).

It is also important to recognize the extension to the protection under s. 14(2) by the enactment of the Sale and Supply of Goods to Consumers Regulations 2002.[20] If a public statement (such as an advertising campaign or information on the label) has been made by the seller, producer, or his/her representative, this is included into the definition of s. 14(2A). The exception to this constituting part of the section is where the seller was not aware of the statement, or could not have reasonably been aware; the statement made had been retracted or corrected in public; and the decision to buy the good was not based on, or influenced by, the statement.

Whilst these protections exist, defences are available to sellers against what could be considered as 'unfair' claims. Section 14(2C) outlines situations where protection under s. 14(2) will not extend. For example, if a product is purchased and a defect has been pointed out, particularly where an incentive has been provided in 'compensation' of the defect, the buyer cannot later rely on s. 14(2) for this specific problem.

Bartlett v Sidney Marcus Ltd[21]

Facts:

Sidney Marcus was a car dealer specializing in the sales of Jaguar and Ford motorcars. Sidney Marcus sourced a car at the request of Mr Bartlett and whilst its sales executive travelled in the car to show Bartlett, he noticed the oil pressure gauge was defective and the clutch was not operating perfectly. These defects were identified to Bartlett and hence he was offered the car for £575 (with the car repaired), or for £550 and Bartlett could have the repairs completed by his garage. Mr Bartlett agreed with the latter offer as he believed he could get the repairs necessary completed for between £2–3. When the car broke down and it was sent for repair, Bartlett was informed the cost of repair would be over £84, and he initiated his claim for damages for the cost of the repair. Bartlett's claim was based on a breach of ss. 14 (1) and (2) SOGA, but the Court of Appeal held that there was no breach of SOGA 1979, and Mr Bartlett could not claim damages.

Authority for:

Where defects have been brought to a buyer's attention before the sale, any subsequent claim on this basis for breach under s. 14(2) will fail due to the application of s. 14(2C).

---

[19] Again, general 'wear and tear' or damage caused other than a defect will not enable a claim under the Act.

[20] See Section 4.   [21] [1965] 1 WLR 1013.

Likewise, if the buyer had examined the good him/herself before the purchase, and that examination ought reasonably to have revealed the defect, then this will be a defence to the seller (section 14(2C)(b)). This does not require that the buyer should identify every defect, but very obvious defects where it could reasonably have been expected that the buyer would have seen and could have taken action on, may provide a defence against holding the term as a condition.

- *Section 14 (3)—fitness for purpose:* The Act continues regulating the quality of goods by providing that the item should be fit for its intended purpose. If the item purports to provide some function, it must do so.

Grant v Australian Knitting Mills Ltd[22]

Facts:

Dr Grant brought an action against Australian Knitting Mills claiming damages on the grounds that he contracted dermatitis from woollen underpants sold under the name 'Golden Fleece'. Australian Knitting Mills had been negligent in failing to remove a chemical used in the manufacture of the underpants (free sulphate).[23] As such, Grant claimed the underpants were sold but were not 'fit for their purpose'. The presence of the chemicals in the garment was a hidden and latent defect, and could not be detected by any examination that could reasonably be made.

Authority for:

In the case of implied reliance on the quality of the good, the buyer can gain protection from either implicit or explicit reliance on the relevant term.

Products sold for a particular purpose must be suitable and 'fit' for that purpose. In the case of Dr Grant, these were underpants that would be worn against the skin. Due to the chemicals present, this was impossible and hence the garment failed under s. 14(3).

In *Griffiths v Peter Conway*,[24] the buyer of a fur coat suffered a serious and adverse reaction to the coat due to her allergies. She did not inform the seller of her condition and therefore the item was fit for its purpose, albeit the buyer could not wear the coat. Had she identified to the seller her requirements, she would have been covered by the Act. Therefore, protection is provided where the buyer seeks assurances from the seller as to the suitability of a particular good for a specific task. In this case the buyer is relying on the judgment of the seller, and if this is reasonable, then even if this request is beyond what would normally be associated with a reasonable use of the good, the law will still protect the buyer. In *Ashington Piggeries Ltd v Christopher Hill Ltd*[25] the buyers were manufacturers of animal feeds and had contracted for herring meal to be used in mink food. The sellers knew of the purpose of the herring meal but had no experience of making food for mink. The herring meal had become contaminated so as to make it poisonous to all animals that it was fed to, but would be fatal if given to mink. The House of Lords held that there was a breach of s. 14(3) as the buyers had relied in part on the judgment of the sellers to sell them appropriate materials.

---

[22] [1936] AC 85.

[23] These sulphates, when combined with sweat, produce successively sulphur dioxide, sulphurous acid, and then sulphuric acid.

[24] [1939] 1 All ER 685.   [25] [1971] 1 All ER 847.

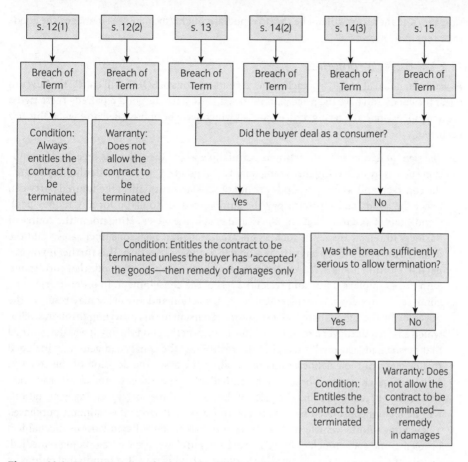

Figure 11.1 Consequences for breach of SOGA 1979

- *Section 15—sale by sample:* If a sale of goods takes place through a sample of a larger consignment the bulk of the consignment must correspond to the sample (in practical terms, this section is of most use to businesses). The goods should also be free from defects that would make their quality unsatisfactory that would not have been apparent on a reasonable inspection.[26] SOGA requires that in a sale by sample, the bulk must correspond to the sample. This means that if the sample is of a good quality, the buyer can expect the remaining items to be of a similar standard. This also works in reverse; where the sample is of a poor standard the bulk can be considered as being of a similar quality.

   Figure 11.1 identifies the consequences for breach of SOGA 1979.

11.2.2 **Remedies for breach of the Sales of Goods Act**

The terms implied through ss. 12–15 are conditions that allow the injured buyer to claim damages and repudiate the contract. The buyer must act within a reasonable time to allow the term to be treated as a condition. After this reasonable time, the term will be considered a

---

[26] *Godley v Perry* [1960] 1 WLR 9.

warranty and the buyer will not be able to repudiate, but he/she may seek damages/the goods to be repaired or replaced.

11.2.2.1 *Buyer's remedies*

As has been noted at 11.2.2, a breach of the various sections of SOGA will entitle the buyer to reject the goods and have the price paid returned, or to have the good repaired. These rights are dependent upon the terms of the contract which have been breached and when this has occurred.

- *The right to reject goods:* Rejection is permissible where the seller has breached a condition such as by delivering the wrong quantity of goods; where the seller has repudiated the contract; and where the goods are not of satisfactory quality. The injured party can reject the goods and refuse to pay the sum agreed, or to claim for any money paid. Conditions of SOGA include ss. 13–15 and enable the buyer acting not in the course of business to reject. However, such rights are lessened in non-consumer sales[27] and the defect in those situations has to be reasonable to allow a rejection. This further involves a partial rejection under s. 35(A), where the buyer can accept those goods that correspond with (for example) s. 14(2), and reject the rest of the consignment. In order to reject the goods, s. 35 lays down a requirement for quick action and any delay may result in the buyer losing the right. There was a statutory extension to this provision through s. 35(5) which enabled the buyer a reasonable time to inspect the goods before it was determined that he/she had 'accepted' them, but the reality was the courts had generally included this element in their deliberations in deciding the case. The decision of the court in respect of 'quick' action is based on the individual facts of the case, and clearly each case will differ, but it appears that the price of the good and the corresponding expectations will be factors considered by the courts. In *Rogers v Parish*[28] the claimant purchased a new Range Rover vehicle that was very unreliable, had suffered various mechanical problems, and spent much of its existence from purchase in the garage being remedied. Despite the fact that it was seven months old, and having travelled some 5,000 miles, the courts still enabled the good to be rejected under s. 35. An unreasonably delayed rejection will prevent the buyer from rejecting the good.[29]

  The buyer also has the right to have the goods repaired instead of rejecting the goods. Whilst this may be a route taken because the buyer is unaware of his/her rights under SOGA 1979, s. 35(6) enables the buyer to have the good repaired without any inference from this action that he/she has accepted the good. Therefore it preserves his/her right to later reject the good if it is unsatisfactory.

- *The right to claim damages:* As with any breach of a condition of the contract, the injured party (the buyer) is entitled to claim damages and to end (repudiate) the contract at his/her discretion. Under SOGA, the right for damages usually involves the non-delivery of goods[30] where there is a difference in price between the cost of the goods at the time of the contract, and the cost when the good has not been supplied. As always with damages (which is covered in Chapter 12) it is designed to place the injured party, as far as possible, in the position he/she should have been before the breach.

  It should be noted that there have been extensions to SOGA through the Sale and Supply of Goods to Consumers Regulations 2002, which specifically assist consumers

---

[27] Section 15A.   [28] [1987] QB 933.
[29] *Jones v Gallagher and Gallagher* [2005] 1 Lloyd's Rep 377.
[30] Section 51.

in requiring goods to be repaired or replaced under s. 48B SOGA 1979. If, at the time of delivery, the goods do not conform to that agreed under the contract, the buyer can have the goods repaired or replaced, or he/she can request a reduction in the price.[31] The restriction to this remedy is that the buyer cannot compel the seller of the goods to provide the replacement or repair where this would be impossible or disproportionate in relation to the reduction in price or other remedies available.[32]

11.2.2.2 *Seller's remedies*

As the buyer has remedies under SOGA, so does the seller for a breach by the buyer. This may occur if the buyer refuses to pay for the goods ordered[33] or if he/she refuses to accept the supply of the goods.[34] These rights are typically used when the seller is selling the goods to another business which may become insolvent and therefore not have the means to pay for the good. The seller may retain possession of the goods until payment has been made,[35] unless the seller waives the right or the price is paid;[36] the seller may stop the goods in transit and therefore restrict the physical passing of the goods to the buyer (where the buyer is insolvent);[37] and the seller may re-sell the goods to another buyer to mitigate any potential losses (where the goods are perishable or the seller has notified the buyer of the intention to sell if payment is not received).[38]

11.3 **The Supply of Goods and Services Act 1982**

Supply of Goods and Services Act 1982

The legislation governs the supply of services, and the supply of faulty goods and materials provided with the services. It requires that a supplier of a service, acting in the course of business, provide that service with reasonable skill and care, within a 'reasonable' time (unless there is an express agreement to the contrary), and make a reasonable charge for the service. Part I of the Act provides protection by implying terms into contracts involving the transfer of property in goods, and into contracts for the hire of goods. The Act complements the rights provided in SOGA 1979.

11.3.1 **Transfer of Property in Goods**

A contract under this part of the Act includes any contract where the title to the goods passes to another, and is not a contract for the sale of goods, or contracts under hire-purchase agreements (as other statutes offer protection). An example of such a contract would be for a boiler to be installed in a house.

The Act gives protections as outlined in Table 11.1:

11.3.2 **Contract of hire**

Here, the title to the goods is not passed (transferred) to the other party, but a temporary possession is provided.

The Act gives the protections as outlines in Table 11.2:

---

[31] Section 48C.   [32] Section 48B.   [33] Section 49.   [34] Section 50.
[35] Section 41.   [36] Section 43.   [37] Section 44.   [38] Section 48.

Table 11.1 Protection provided by the Supply of Goods and Services Act 1982

Protection	Condition or Warranty
The right to transfer the property (s. 2(1))	A condition
Quiet possession and freedom from encumbrances (s. 2(2))	A warranty
Correspondence with description (s. 3(2))	A condition if the buyer deals as a consumer
Satisfactory quality (s. 4(2))	A condition if the buyer deals as a consumer
Fitness for purpose (s. 4(5))	A condition if the buyer deals as a consumer
Correspondence with sample (s. 5(2))	A condition if the buyer deals as a consumer

Table 11.2 Rights provided by the Supply of Goods and Services Act 1982

Protection	Condition or Warranty
Right to hire (s. 7(1))	A condition
Quiet possession and freedom from encumbrances (s. 7(2))	A warranty
Correspondence with description (s. 8(2))	A condition if the buyer deals as a consumer
Satisfactory quality (s. 9(2))	A condition if the buyer deals as a consumer
Fitness for purpose (s. 9(5))	A condition if the buyer deals as a consumer
Correspondence with sample (s. 10(2))	A condition if the buyer deals as a consumer

11.3.3 Supply of a service

Part II of the Act covers the very important protections afforded where a service is supplied. These terms are implied into contracts and are not included in SOGA 1979.

- *Section 13—duty to exercise reasonable care and skill:* There is an implied term that a supplier (who is acting in the course of business) will exercise reasonable care and skill. The protection is different from the implied term as to quality in s. 14 of SOGA 1979, which imposes a strict liability standard, in that the test as to reasonable care and skill is based on the test established in torts law (see Chapter 13). With the supply of a service, an outcome cannot be guaranteed as easily as with the sale of a good. A supplier of, for example, medical treatment, cannot safely say whether the medical treatment will have a desired effect because of the variables involved. The surgeon can only promise to use his/her skill and judgement, and take all the necessary precautions in providing the treatment, having explained to the patient the potential negative consequences and risks involved. In *Thake and Another v Maurice*[39] a surgeon performed a vasectomy, having explained the risks to the patient, and importantly, had identified that not all procedures were successful as a small but significant number naturally reversed. The operation performed was successful, but the procedure did reverse itself and the patient brought his action for damages. It was held there was no breach as the surgeon had exercised reasonable care and skill.

[39] [1986] 1 All ER 497.

- *Section 14—performance within a reasonable time:* Where a supplier, acting in the course of business, provides a service but the time for the service to be carried out and/or completed is not identified in the contract, s. 14 provides that this must be achieved within a 'reasonable' time. The section of the Act, when read in conjunction with s. 14(2), provides that what is reasonable is for the courts to decide when investigating the facts of each case.

- *Section 15—the obligation to pay a reasonable price:* This section provides that, regardless of whether the supplier is acting in the course of business or not, there is an implied term of a reasonable price to be paid. Note that the section is not implied where the price has already been agreed in the contract, or has been agreed between the parties in the course of their dealings with each other. It is also relevant to be aware that a quotation is generally determined as a price at which the contract is to be performed. If the section is implied into the contract, s. 15(2) states that a reasonable price is to be determined on the facts of the case.

11.4 The Sale and Supply of Goods to Consumers Regulations 2002

The Sale and Supply of Goods to Consumers Regulations 2002

These Regulations were enacted to provide rights for consumers who obtained goods with a guarantee. Whilst there remains no requirement for goods to be provided with a guarantee, where one is provided (and increasingly they are being provided, particularly with expensive goods) the guarantee becomes effective and part of the contract when the goods are delivered. The guarantor, or the person who is selling the goods, must make the guarantee available to the consumer, who can request that this is available in writing or some other 'tangible' form.

Under the Regulations, a consumer is defined as any natural person who, in obtaining the goods, is acting outside of their trade, business, or profession.[40] The 'consumer guarantee' under the Regulations involves an undertaking to the consumer by a person acting in the course of business, provided without extra charge, to repair or replace the goods, or reimburse the price paid, should the goods fail to meet the standards established in the guarantee or the advertising of the good. This requirement is only to undertake to do what is set out in the guarantee document and most frequently this is restricted to repair and replacing defective goods.

The Regulations are effective in providing another layer of protection to the consumer buyer. Whilst in most situations involving goods that fall below the standard that could reasonably be expected, the consumer would use SOGA 1979 to claim as to the quality or the fitness for purpose of the good. The Regulations are particularly effective in situations where the retailer from whom the goods were purchased, and hence where claims under SOGA 1979 would be made, has gone out of business or become insolvent, and the guarantee is still in existence (for example, some manufacturers of televisions are offering guarantees for a period of five years). The terms of SOGA 1979 as regards conditions are effective at the time the goods were delivered or a reasonable time thereafter, and become increasingly difficult to enforce as time moves on. Particularly the right to reject goods needs to be performed

---

[40] Reg. 2.

quickly. As the name implies, the Regulations also cover the supply of goods including leases and hire-purchases, and therefore the Regulations offer a valuable addition to consumer rights.

11.5 The Unfair Contract Terms Act 1977

As its name implies, the function of the Unfair Contract Terms Act (UCTA) 1977 is to ensure that certain terms that may be unfair (under this Act, namely exclusion clauses) are removed or held invalid by the courts. However, it is also important to note that UCTA 1977 also regulates the use of non-contractual notices attempting to restrict liability for negligence. Certain exclusion clauses will automatically be considered void under the Act (such as excluding liability for death or personal injury due to negligence) and those remaining have to satisfy the test of 'reasonableness'. UCTA 1977 is primarily concerned with business liability[41] in contract and tort, and hence the liability for breach of obligations or duties occurring in the course of business.

11.5.1 Liability in contract

UCTA 1977 provides protection when exclusion clauses are included in standard form contracts. These are typically used by businesses and the consumer is in a weak position in attempting to decline their use—it is often a 'take it or leave it' scenario. If it is the case that the party deals as a consumer on the other party's written standard terms, the other party cannot exclude or restrict any liability in respect of a breach of contract; or claim to be able to perform or fulfil a contract in a substantially different way than would reasonably be expected; or claim to be able to render no performance at all under his/her contractual obligations.[42] Therefore, s. 3 of UCTA 1977 protects those who deal as consumers, and also who deal on the other party's written standard terms. It will be held as a standard form if the business expressly provides for this or the form is used by the business for all its transactions with consumers. An interesting element is when the business uses a form created by someone else. Here, s. 3 of UCTA 1977 is bypassed, and as this is not held to be a standard form, the form itself is not even subject to the protections under the examination of its reasonableness. Such a major loophole will likely be exploited by less than scrupulous businesses.

- *Exclusion of rights under the sales of goods:* Section 6 of UCTA 1977 is very important to SOGA 1979. The implications of s. 6 of UCTA 1977 is that s. 12 of SOGA 1979, and the Sale of Goods (Implied Terms) Act (SGITA) 1973, s. 8 cannot be excluded from any contract. Sections 13, 14 and 15 of SOGA 1979, and ss. 9, 10 and 11 of SGITA 1973 cannot be excluded from contracts where the buyer acts as a consumer with a seller in the course of business, but they may be excluded in non-consumer (course of business) contracts, as far as they satisfy the tests of reasonableness. This is the reason why, when a seller in the course of business (for example, a department store) displays a notice that refunds for unwanted goods will not be provided, this is qualified by the statement 'this does not affect your statutory rights'. The seller, in the course of business, cannot exclude the

---

[41] Section 1(3).   [42] Section 3.

rights to a refund for breaches of, for example, ss. 13–15 of SOGA 1979 when dealing with a consumer. UCTA 1977 also protects consumers in hiring and transferring property under the Supply of Goods and Services Act 1982,[43] although these restrictions may be removed where the other party does not act as a consumer, subject to the reasonableness test.

11.5.2 Consumer status

Given the link between the rights as provided under SOGA 1979, SGITA 1973, and UCTA 1977 with the status of the buyer as a 'consumer', this must be defined. Under UCTA 1977 s. 12(1), a party 'deals as a consumer' if:

1 he/she does not make the contract in the course of business, nor does he/she hold him/herself out as doing so;

2 the other party does make the contract in the course of business; and

3 the goods that are passed are of a type typically supplied for private use or consumption.

Consumer status is not restricted to individuals (as may be thought) but equally applies to businesses if they buy something that is not in the course of their business. In *Peter Symmons & Co. v Cook*[44] it was held that, in a case where a firm of surveyors purchased a used Rolls-Royce car, that, in order for the status of consumer to be removed the 'buying of cars must form at the very least an integral part of the buyer's business or a necessary incidental thereto'. In this case it was not and so redress was available through the rights as provided in SOGA 1979. Such an example may be seen in the following case. This was confirmed in *R and B Customs Brokers v United Dominions Trust Ltd*,[45] where a vehicle used for both business and private use still enabled the buyer protection as a consumer under SOGA 1979, s. 14. The purchase of the car was only incidental to R and B Customs Brokers' business activities, and as it had only purchased two or three cars before, there was insufficient regularity in such a transaction to hold that this was anything more than a consumer sale.

11.5.3 Liability in negligence

UCTA 1977 specifically voids attempts through contractual terms or through notice to exclude liability for death or personal injury caused through negligence. Negligence in torts law imposes a duty to take reasonable care not to injure others or damage property. However, under this Act, the term 'negligence' is given a broader interpretation to incorporate negligent performance of a contract and the concept of negligence in breaching a statutory duty.[46] Negligence causing loss or damage to property may only be excluded or restricted where it satisfies the test of reasonableness. Simply because a person has agreed to, or was aware of, a term or notice that purports to exclude or restrict the other party's liability in negligence will not, of itself, be indicative of a voluntary acceptance of risk.

---

[43] Section 7(2).   [44] [1981] 131 NLJ 758.   [45] [1988] 1 WLR 321.
[46] See Chapters 13 and 15.

11.5.4 Liability under misrepresentation

Section 8 of UCTA replaces s. 3 of the Misrepresentation Act 1967 and prohibits any term in a contract that purports to restrict or exclude a liability for a misrepresentation made before the contract was agreed; or attempts to restrict or exclude a remedy the other party would have in the event of such a misrepresentation, unless the party seeking to rely on the clause can demonstrate its reasonableness under s. 1(1) of UCTA 1977. Note that this protection applies to both consumer and non-consumers.

11.5.5 Reasonableness of the exclusion clause

UCTA 1977 contains provision for how the reasonableness or otherwise of an exclusion clause will be determined. This has caused considerable problems when the case law is examined. In the case of *SAM Business Systems v Hedley and Co.*[47] a software supplier was entitled to rely on an exclusion clause that enabled it to supply an inadequate product, and this term was considered 'reasonable'. (Note that this case was between two businesses. The courts assume businesses should be in a better position to protect themselves than consumers dealing with a business.) The obligation on demonstrating that the clause is reasonable rests with the party relying on the clause, and it will have to show that in all the circumstances the clause was reasonable and was brought to the other party's attention, or it should have been in his/her 'reasonable contemplation'. Schedule 2 outlines the tests that the courts will use in determining the reasonableness of an exclusion clause:

a) the strength of the bargaining positions of the parties relative to each other (the most important statutory consideration);

Where the parties are of equal bargaining strength, the courts are more likely to accept exclusion clauses than if the contract was between a consumer and a business. *Watford Electronic Ltd v Sanderson CFL Ltd*[48] demonstrated that an otherwise unreasonable exclusion clause would be allowed unless the term is so unreasonable that the court must move to restrict it. In this case, involving the supply of computer equipment, an exclusion clause limited liability to £104,596, and this was considered reasonable even though the actual losses sustained were £5.5 million.

b) whether the customer received an inducement to agree to the term, or in accepting it had an opportunity of entering into a similar contract with other persons, but without having to accept a similar term;

c) whether the customer knew or ought reasonably to have known of the existence and extent of the term (having regard, among other things, to any custom of the trade and any previous course of dealing between the parties);[49]

d) where the term excludes or restricts any relevant liability if some condition is not complied with, whether it was reasonable at the time of the contract to expect that compliance with that condition would by practicable; and

e) whether the goods were manufactured, processed or adapted to the special order of the customer.

---

[47] [2002] EWHC 2733.   [48] [2001] EWCA Civ 317.

[49] *Interfoto Picture Library Ltd v Stiletto Visual Programmes Ltd* [2001] EWCA Civ 317.

The practical use by the courts of a consideration of the reasonableness of an exclusion clause has been addressed in the academic literature.[50] It has also been demonstrated through case law such as *George Mitchell v Finney Lock Seeds*,[51] where seeds were sold between businesses, but an exclusion clause restricted any claim for loss to the cost of the seed, not the potential harvest (which naturally would have been substantially greater). The House of Lords rejected the clause as unreasonable. When the farmers placed the seeds in the ground it was not possible to identify the quality or type of the seed, and the seller could have obtained insurance at a cheap price.

Perhaps one of the most problematic areas when considering exclusion clauses is in assessing what amounts to 'unreasonableness'. Despite the guidance provided through the statute as noted above, the courts still maintain discretion as evidenced in the case law presented. This discretion can lead to unusual results, and, as stated in *George Mitchell*, appeal courts will not interfere with the decision in the original case unless the judge had made his/her decision based on an 'erroneous principle or was plainly and obviously wrong'.

Beyond the guidance provided in UCTA 1977 with regard to what amounts to reasonableness when attempting to exclude a potential liability, the House of Lords offered further assistance in the following case.

Smith v Eric S Bush[52]

Facts:

The claimant purchased a house on the basis of the defendant's negligent valuation report. The report had been produced and issued incorporating an exclusion clause disclaiming any liability for negligence. The surveyor of the property had not identified serious defects in the property, but soon after the purchase had been completed, the chimney collapsed, causing significant damage. When the claimant sued the defendant for the damage, the exclusion clause was relied upon but the House of Lords held it to be unreasonable under s. 2(2) of UCTA 1977. It would be unfair and unreasonable to place potential risk of loss on a buyer for the negligence and incompetence of a surveyor providing a valuation.

Authority for:

The Lords identified factors that would be used in determining the reasonableness of an exclusion clause:

1 whether the parties were of equal bargaining power;

2 in situations involving advice, whether it was practicable (in costs and time) to obtain alternative advice;

3 the level of complexity and difficulty in the task which was subject to the exclusion of liability;

4 which of the parties was better able to bear any losses and should insurance have been sought.

---

[50] See Brown, L., and Chandler, A. (1993) 'Unreasonableness and the Unfair Contract Terms Act' 109 *Law Quarterly Review* p. 41.

[51] [1983] 2 AC 803.   52 [1990] 1 AC 831.

11.6 The Unfair Terms in Consumer Contracts Regulations 1999

 Business Link

Where UCTA 1977 legislated only for exclusion clauses, the Regulations are much broader in scope and include all contractual terms used, and the Regulations assess their reasonableness. They further expand on who may bring an action (this is not restricted just to the parties to the contract) and hence offer greater regulation of the terms in contracts.

An extension to the protection provided through UCTA 1977 came in the form of the Unfair Terms in Consumer Contracts Regulations 1999, which was the transposing legislation required of Council Directive 93/13/EEC of 5 April 1993 on unfair terms in consumer contracts.[53] The Regulations can be used in conjunction with UCTA 1977 to ensure that terms in a contract satisfy the requirements of both pieces of legislation. To avail him/herself of the Regulations, there is the requirement of consumer status,[54] but the Regulations are broader than UCTA and cover all the terms in the contract, not just exclusion clauses. The Regulations provide criteria for determining which terms may be unfair, and the effect is that those terms that fail the fairness test will be struck down. The remainder of the contract though, if it continues to be viable following the removal of the offending term, will still be effective and bind the consumer and the supplier/seller contracted with (a process known as 'blue pencilling').[55] These Regulations cover any non-negotiable term in the contract[56] (such as a standard form contract) established between a consumer (defined as a natural person rather than a company)[57] and a seller/supplier of goods and services.

From May 2008, the Consumer Protection from Unfair Trading Regulations 2008 were brought into effect.

These Regulations protect consumers from unfair, misleading or aggressive selling practices—essentially deeming such practices unfair in all circumstances. Given the importance of the Regulations to the protection of consumers, and the impositions placed on businesses, additional material on the topic is included on the Online Resource Centre

11.6.1 Unfair terms

The Regulations identify, through a non-exhaustive list, those terms which may be considered unfair and hence not applicable. The Regulations provide instructions under Schedule 2 and Reg. 5 as to the measures to be taken by those who wish to insert terms that affect consumer contracts.

Schedule 2 of the Regulations protect against seller and suppliers excluding their liability in the event of death or personal injury; if they attempt to restrict the consumers' legal

---

[53] See Chapter 5 for an explanation of the EU requirement on Member States to transpose Directives into domestic law.

[54] Reg. 4.   [55] Reg. 8.   [56] Reg. 5.   [57] Reg. 3.

rights in the event of total or partial non-performance under the contract; if the contract enables the seller/supplier to retain money paid by the consumer where the seller/supplier has not performed the contract, and the right for the consumer to receive compensation in the event of non-performance is denied; attempting to bind the consumer under terms in a contract which he/she had no real opportunity to read or be aware of; and if the seller/supplier attempts to unilaterally vary the terms of a contract where no valid reason, as expressed in the contract, has been specified. This is often termed the existence of a 'significant imbalance' in the parties' rights and obligations, which will lead to the Regulations being invoked.

> **? Thinking Point**
>
> Given the provision in Schedule 2 above, how would *L'Estrange v Graucob, Ltd*[58] be decided by the courts now?

Regulation 5 provides that where the contractual term has not been individually negotiated, it will be considered unfair if it breaches the duty of good faith. This will occur where it causes significant imbalances in the parties' rights and obligations under the contract.[59] The considerations for the court in determining the issue of good faith are: the bargaining positions of the parties; whether the consumer had goods supplied to him/her that were specially made or adapted as to his/her requirements; whether an inducement had been made (such as a cheaper price) as a result of the term; and a consideration of the extent to which the seller/supplier had acted in a fair and equitable manner. In *Director General of Fair Trading v First National Bank Plc*[60] good faith was described as 'fair and open dealing'.

11.6.2 Plain language in contracts

The Regulations require that the terms in the contract must be produced in plain language,[61] and any dispute regarding the meaning of the term must be interpreted in favour of the consumer (the *contra proferentem* rule). The term must still be unfair, and the onus is on the consumer to prove this. Simply because a term is not beneficial to the consumer will not of itself make it unreasonable or contrary to good faith.

11.6.3 The effect of the unfair term

If the courts find that an unfair term under the Regulations is in the contract then, under Reg. 8, provided the agreement is between a consumer and a seller/supplier, the offending term is not binding on the consumer. However, it is important to note that the contract may still be enforceable if it is capable of existence without the unfair term.

---

[58] [1934] 2 KB 394.
[59] *Munkenbeck & Marshall v Michael Harold* [2005] EWHC 356.   [60] [2001] UKHL 52.
[61] Reg. 7.

11.6.4 Enforcement/claims through a consumer body

The Regulations are invaluable to the protection of the consumer. They not only enable the consumer to bring an action based on the unfair term, but also add a mechanism of 'public' enforcement through the Office of Fair Trading and other public consumer protection bodies to investigate complaints of an unfair contract.[62] Complaints may be made to the Director General of Fair Trading. Injunctions can be applied for against a person who is using an unfair term, or recommending its use. The individual consumer does not have to fall victim to the term and initiate the claim him/herself if the consumer protection bodies are aware of the term and have taken action. This enables proactive, rather than reactive, protection.

 Conclusion

The chapter has discussed the regulation of contract terms through legislation. These provisions offer certainty and protection to the parties against, among other things, the use of unfair terms. The next chapter discusses how contracts are discharged and the availability of remedies in the event of a breach.

 Summary of main points

Sale of Goods Act (SOGA)

- There must be a 'sale' involving the transfer of title to the goods.
- Goods are defined as including all personal chattels (essentially goods that would typically be used in personal/domestic situations).
- Sections 12–15 are very important and ensure the seller has legal ownership of the good; the good corresponds to its description; the good is of a satisfactory quality and is fit for its intended purpose; and in sales involving samples, that the bulk corresponds to the sample.
- Breach of SOGA will entitle the buyer to reject the goods (within a reasonable time), have the goods repaired/replaced, and claim damages depending on the nature of the breach.
- The seller has rights under the Act if the buyer refuses to pay for the goods or if he/she refuses to accept them.

The Supply of Goods and Services Act

- The legislation governs the supply of services, and of faulty goods and materials provided with the service.
- The supplier must demonstrate reasonable care and skill in providing the service and provide the service within a reasonable time.
- The Act includes the hire of goods (which was not included in SOGA).

---

[62] These bodies include the rail regulator, the Consumers' Association, and Directors-General of the utilities such as gas, electricity, and water.

Sale and Supply of Goods to Consumers Regulations

- Goods that are provided with a guarantee enable a consumer to obtain a remedy established in this document. This could include a repair or replacement and is particularly useful when, for example, the seller of the good has ceased trading and no claim is therefore available under SOGA.

- Claims are often available as a guarantee is provided by the manufacturer of the good.

Unfair Contract Terms Act (UCTA)

- This Act specifically governs the use of exclusion clauses in contracts.

- It prohibits the exclusion of liability for death or personal injury due to the other party's negligence.

- Any other exclusion clause is subject to test under the Act's assessment of 'reasonableness'.

Unfair Terms in Consumer Contracts Regulations

- These Regulations are used in conjunction with UCTA but extend the consideration of unfair terms to the entire contract, not just exclusion clauses.

- It provides for the use of plain language in contracts and relies on the *contra proferentem* rule in cases of ambiguity.

- Enforcement is possible through consumer associations (such as those regulating the utilities) and the Office of Fair Trading to provide more protective assistance and governance of the terms in standard form contracts.

 Summary questions

Essay questions

1. 'Consumers have always been in a poor bargaining position with traders and those running businesses. Parliament was right to equal the balance of power through its intervention with various protective statutes.'

   Critically discuss the above statement with reference to the legislation passed and how these protect consumers.

2. Given that many of the cases involving the statutory protections in the sale of goods are disputes between businesses, how fair has been the application of reasonableness test in UCTA?

Problem questions

1. Jessica and her family were shopping for various goods and have experienced the following:

   Jessica's son Buzz broke his mother's bone China vase. He visited a DIY shop and explained to the store assistant what had happened and how he needed to fix the vase before his mother returned home. The assistant sold Buzz a special clay adhesive which he said would fix the vase, but it fails to do the job.

Jessica's son Buzz bought a catapult from the corner shop to use to hit tin cans off the wall of his garden. He used the catapult, hit three tin cans and the next time he used it the elastic broke striking his eye. Buzz subsequently lost the sight in that eye due to the trauma.

Jessica bought a new washing machine from the local high street electrical retail outlet. It stopped working the first time Jessica used it to wash the blood out of the shirt worn by Buzz following the accident with the catapult.

Jessica purchased a new pair of training shoes for use at the gym. She selected the pair described as having 'gel-filled soles' and being suitable for running on a treadmill. When Jessica used the trainers they begin to fall apart during the first session at the gym and she discovered the soles are not 'gel-filled' as advertised.

Jessica's husband Woody decided to purchase a barbeque cooker for the garden. He selected a gas barbeque from the DIY shop which was priced at £25. Woody used the barbeque during much of the summer, but when he used it for a party in last week of August it failed to produce sufficient heat to thoroughly cook the pork chops he was preparing for his family and friends. As a consequence of this, the guests who ate the pork chops sustained food poisoning as the parasites inside the food had not been destroyed during the cooking process.

Advise the parties as to their rights and liabilities.

2. Larry wishes to purchase a van for his domestic use of transporting equipment for his hobby of surfing. He visits 'Vans and only Vans' Ltd (a company specializing in selling used vehicles) and views a white van with a notice in the window reading:

'1990 Ford Escort Van. 100,000 miles; 1.8 litre engine; one previous owner and good little runner.'

Larry discusses the van with the salesman who informs Larry that the vehicle is in very good condition however it has a defective clutch (but it will drive with no problems for at least two months). The company will fix the clutch before purchase or Larry can take the van in its present condition and can have a £70 discount if he wishes to have the clutch fixed himself. Larry thinks he can get the clutch fixed for a cheaper price and therefore purchases the van minus the £70 discount.

In his first week of ownership the clutch fails and Larry has to have the van towed to his local garage where he is informed of the following facts:

- The van is in fact stolen and does not belong to 'Vans and only Vans' Ltd.
- Larry checks the logbook which identifies that there have been five previous owners of the vehicle.
- Previous MOT certificates demonstrate that the car has travelled over 250,000 miles.
- The car has a 1.4 litre engine.
- The clutch will cost £300 to fix.

Advise Larry of the legal consequences of these issues.

Further reading

Adams, J., and Brownsword, R. [1988] 'The Unfair Contract Terms Act: A Decade of Discretion' *Law Quarterly Review*, Vol. 104, p. 94.

Macdonald, E. (2004) 'Unifying Unfair Terms Legislation' *Modern Law Review*, Vol. 67, No. 1, p. 69.

Useful website

http://www.oft.gov.uk/
(The Office of Fair Trading, detailing its remit, powers, and general advice.)

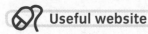 **Online Resource Centre**

http://www.oxfordtextbooks.co.uk/orc/marson3e/
Why not visit the Online Resource Centre and try multiple choice questions associated with this chapter to test your understanding of the topic. You will also find relevant updates to the law.

12 Discharge of Contract and Remedies for Breach

Why does it matter?

A contract establishes the rights and duties of the parties and where successfully completed, the parties will be considered to have discharged their responsibilities. However, this is not the only way in which the contract may be discharged and this chapter aims to discuss these other ways, and importantly, identify the remedies when a party has breached the contract. For example, suppose you were to agree to sell a piece of land, fulfil the essential features of a valid contract, and then decide not to proceed. If you return the deposit paid then would you merely be responsible for the costs incurred by the other party? Read *Mountford v Scott* and you will appreciate why it is vital to appreciate the implications of contractual obligations and the remedies that are available to the innocent party.

Learning outcomes

Following reading this chapter you should be in a position to:

- discuss the methods in which a contract may be discharged (12.2–12.2.4)
- explain the development, through the common law and statute, of the doctrine of frustration (12.2.3)
- identify the remedies available for breach of contract (12.3–12.3.2)
- explain the implications and effects of the equitable remedies available for breach of contract (12.3.2).

⚷ Key terms

These terms will be used in the chapter and it may be helpful to be aware of what they mean or refer back to them when reading through the chapter.

Discharge of contract
The contract may be brought to an end through performance of the obligations; through agreement between the parties; through frustration of the contract; or through one of the parties' breach and this being accepted by the innocent party.

Force majeure clauses

This is an element of frustration in determining how to deal with events that are beyond the control of the parties (wars, acts of God and so on).

Frustration

An event, that is neither party's fault, may render the contract impossible to perform or radically different from that agreed. This leads to the contract being frustrated (unable to be continued) and results in the parties being discharged from further responsibilities.

Liquidated damages

These are damages that are determined in the contract in advance of a breach. They must be a pre-estimate of loss and not a penalty clause.

Mitigation

In the event of a breach of contract, the injured party has an obligation to limit his/her losses as far as is reasonably possible.

Penalty clause

A clause which seeks to stop the other party from breaching the contract by imposing the threat of a penalty, which is not a genuine pre-estimate of loss, will be considered a penalty and be held void.

Privy Council

The Privy Council has a function as an appeal court used by some former Commonwealth countries.

Repudiation

To end or reject a contract, usually in response to the other party's breach.

Unliquidated damages

The court calculates an award of damages they are incapable of being pre-determined.

12.1 Introduction

This chapter concludes the analysis of the law of contract. Having established in Chapters 7–11 the essential features in the formation of a contract; the different types of terms and their significance; the method of inclusion of terms; and a consideration of the protection afforded through implied statutory provisions, this chapter considers how a contract will be discharged. Discharge through performance and agreement; how contracts may become frustrated; and the consequences and remedies following a breach of contract are each examined.

12.2 Discharge of contract

Under the normal rules of contract, a party is only **discharged from a contract** when he/she has completed his/her obligations under it (complete performance). Having completed the contract each party is free of further obligations. A failure to complete the contract may

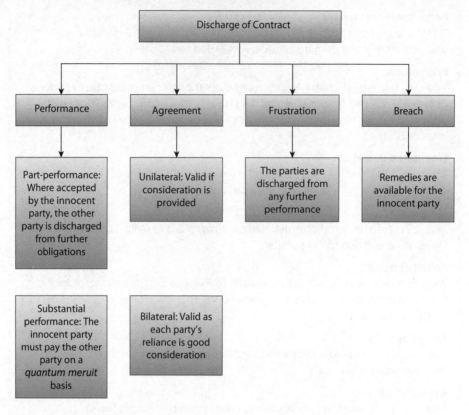

Figure 12.1 Discharge of contract

lead to a breach of contract claim, although situations exist where the parties may release each other from further obligations (discharge by agreement) or the contract may have been partially or substantially performed. Further, the contract may have become radically different from that envisaged, or impossible to perform. In these last examples, the contract will not have been performed but there is no breach as it has been **frustrated**. The methods of discharge of contract are identified in Figure 12.1.

12.2.1 **Discharge through performance**

The most obvious form of discharge is through the parties' completion of their obligations (the contract being performed). Where complete performance has not been achieved, the courts have had to develop rules on what implications such a situation will have for the parties. In *Cutter v Powell*[1] Captain Powell engaged Cutter as part of his crew in a voyage from Jamaica to Liverpool. The contract stipulated that the contract was only fulfilled when the entire contract was performed and payment was only due when the voyage was completed. Mr Cutter died 19 days before the vessel arrived in Liverpool and his widow claimed for his

---

[1] [1795] 6 Term Rep. 320.

owed wages. It was held that the claim must be denied as it was a condition of the contract that payment would be made on completion of the voyage, and this had not been complied with.

This rather harsh application of the rules of contract has been changed where the contract, as opposed to being an entire contract as in *Cutter*, may be divisible (contracts of employment are often examples of divisible contracts). This means that the contract is broken down into smaller units, as can be demonstrated in *Ritchie v Atkinson*.[2] Here a contract for the shipment of cargo was agreed at a price of £5 per ton. Not all of the cargo was delivered, therefore the owners claimed a breach. Further, they asserted they were not obliged to pay any amount as all of the contract had not been completed. It was held that there was a breach, but as this was a divisible contract payment was due on the basis of the number of tons of cargo actually delivered.

- *Part-performance:* There may exist situations where a contract is not fully completed, and the other party voluntarily accepts the partial performance. It must be noted at this stage that the acceptance *must* be undertaken voluntarily for it to be valid. Where the innocent party has no choice but to 'accept' the part-performance the party in breach is not entitled to payment for the work completed on the contract.[3] The acceptance of the partial performance discharges the party from any further obligations under the contract and the innocent party must pay an appropriate proportion of the price.

- *Substantial performance:* If, on the other hand, a substantial proportion of the contract has been completed, the innocent party has an obligation to pay, taking into account the shortcomings of the contract. This was demonstrated in *Hoeing v Isaacs*,[4] where a contract was established for the decorating and furnishing of a flat for a fee of £750. Whilst the decorating had been substantially completed, there were minor aspects still to be completed to furnishings. It was held that as the contract had been substantially performed, the claimant was entitled to be paid, with £55 being deducted to reflect the outstanding work uncompleted. However, the obligation to pay is only where there has been 'substantial' performance. In *Bolton v Mahadeva*[5] the claimant agreed with the defendant to install a central heating system in the defendant's house for the fee of £560. When the claimant had completed the works, the defendant refused to pay, citing that the work was defective and when tests were carried out, it was discovered that the flue had been incorrectly installed, which resulted in fumes remaining in the room, and the heat through the radiators was irregular, resulting in differing temperatures in each room. The cost of rectifying these defects was £174. The Court of Appeal held that as a result, the claimant was not able to recover the amount due as there had not been substantial performance.

  There is also a claim for a partial or substantial performance of the contract if the full and complete performance of the contract was prevented through the other party's actions. In *Planche v Colburn*[6] a book was commissioned (for a fee of £100) and the author had partially completed this when the contract was cancelled. It was held that £50 was to be paid to the claimant for the work already completed (known as *quantum meruit* assessment).

- *Time limit for performance:* Unless the parties have otherwise agreed (through express or implied terms), time limits for the performance of the contract are not strict. Therefore if a

---

[2] [1808] 10 East 95.

[3] *Sumpter v Hedges* [1898] 1 QB 673. By implication of not being raised in *Cleveland Bridge UK Ltd v Multiplex Constructions (UK) Ltd* [2010] EWCA Civ 139, the decision in *Sumpter* remains good law.

[4] [1952] 2 All ER 176.   [5] [1972] 1 WLR 1009.   [6] [1831] 5 C & P 58.

party is late in performing his/her obligations this will not, of itself, enable the other party to reject the performance when it occurs. This is the general rule insofar as there is no unreasonable delay. Where a delay does occur, the innocent party may identify a (reasonable) time for the contract to be completed.[7] In *Levey v Goldberg*[8] a delivery of a quantity of cloth was to take place on 20 August 1920. Before this date arrived, sometime in August 1920, the claimants requested from the defendants that the delivery date be extended, which was agreed. When the cloth was ready for delivery, the defendants refused to accept it as the time period had passed and the contract had been **repudiated**. It was held that the time limit for delivery had been extended and the defendants had waived their right to reject the contract on this basis. A similar argument could be made under the doctrine of promissory estoppel.[9]

12.2.2 Discharge through agreement

The parties may agree between themselves that they no longer wish to continue with the contract, and therefore release each other from their obligations. As this is in effect a new contract, and varying a contract requires the formalities as identified in Chapters 7 and 8 to make it valid, the elements of agreement (referred to as accord) and consideration (referred to as satisfaction) are necessary. There may be a unilateral or bilateral discharge of the contract.

- *Unilateral discharge:* If one party has completed his/her part of the contract and the other party wishes to be released from his/her obligations which are outstanding, such an agreement will be allowed, but is only legally binding if consideration (a benefit) is provided.

- *Bilateral discharge:* If both parties have obligations outstanding under the contract, then if both agree to release each other from further obligations, the contract will be discharged by these mutual exchanges of promises. That both parties release each other will be good consideration and stop any legal rights under the contract.

12.2.3 Discharge through frustration

 Business Link

Suppose you are contracting to rent out the O2 Arena in London to be used as a venue for a concert for the group U2. The contract is finalized, the tickets are sold, and then the night before the concert is due to take place the Arena is burnt to the ground through no fault of the owners of the Arena or the party which has agreed to rent the premises. Does the party who agreed to rent the Arena still have to pay for the venue? Do the owners of the O2 Arena have to provide an alternative venue (assuming one could be found)? This is the type of scenario to which the doctrine of frustration was developed to provide an answer. Businesses often contract for the hire of premises or for goods to be delivered through, for example, international waters that may be subject to dangers due to wars, terrorism and so on. As such, knowledge of how frustration is identified and its effect on the contract enables the parties to better prepare contracts.

---

[7] See *Charles Rickards Ltd v Oppenheim* [1950] 1 All ER 420.   [8] [1922] 1 KB 688.
[9] See **8.2.3**.

Frustration was a doctrine developed by the courts in order to offer relief in circumstances whereby a contract could not be performed or had become radically different from that contemplated (and this was the fault of neither party).[10] The effects of frustration result in the parties being discharged from any further performance in the contract and any money paid is returned (at the discretion of the court). It should be noted at the outset that this is known as a doctrine of 'last resort' and will therefore only be used where the parties have not made their own arrangement for a frustrating event. The courts encourage parties to draft contracts in as detailed a manner as possible to include for eventualities and the method of resolution to be adopted (**force majeure** clauses).

There are several examples of what may amount to frustration and, whilst each case is decided on its own merits, there are common themes that aid in identifying what may be held to be frustration.

- *The subject matter of the contract ceases to exist:* In a situation where the subject matter of the contract has ceased to exist before the contract has been performed, and it is neither party's fault that this has occurred, then the courts consider this frustration.

Taylor v Caldwell[11]

Facts:

Taylor and Caldwell had entered into a contract on 27 May 1861 where Caldwell had agreed to let Taylor have the use of The Surrey Gardens and Music Hall at a rate of £100 per day. This hire was to take place for four days for the purpose of giving a series of grand concerts. The contract was established, but before the first performance the Music Hall was destroyed by fire and therefore the concerts could not take place. Taylor claimed damages for the money spent on the advertising and preparation for the concerts. The decision of the High Court was '... the Music Hall having ceased to exist, without fault of either party, both parties are excused, the plaintiffs from taking the gardens and paying the money, the defendants from performing their promise to give the use of the Hall and Gardens and other things.'

Authority for:

Where the entire subject matter of a contract is destroyed before the contract is performed, and this is the fault of neither of the party, the contract is impossible to perform and is held to be frustrated.

Where the sole purpose of the contract has not been destroyed or is not unable to be completed, and the benefit of the contract remains, the contract will not be considered to have been frustrated.[12]

- *A person engaged under a contract of personal service becomes unavailable:* If a person has personally agreed to perform a contract and subsequently he/she becomes unavailable then this may constitute frustration. Whether it will invoke frustration depends upon the length

---

[10] This principle has been classically stated as requiring the parties to come to court with 'clean hands'. In *Falcke v Gray* [1859] ER 4 Drew 651, a landlady and her tenant (an antique dealer) had entered into an agreement where, at the conclusion of the tenancy, the dealer would buy two vases for £20. Before the tenancy ended the landlady sold the vases to another dealer for £200. The tenant attempted to claim specific performance to enforce the contract. The court held this was not available as the dealer had behaved inequitably and what he had agreed to pay was substantially below the true value.

[11] [1863] 3 B. & S. 826.   [12] *Herne Bay Steam Boat Company v Hutton* [1903] 2 KB 683.

of time the person is unavailable. If it is a temporary situation (such as a short illness as part of a sufficiently long or open-ended contract) then this will not be frustration, but if the person is dead[13] or is permanently unavailable then this will frustrate the contract.[14]

- *An event central to the contract has not occurred:* If parties contract for a specific event, and for some reason this event does not take place, the contract will be frustrated.

Krell v Henry[15]

Facts:

Mr Krell left instructions with his solicitor to rent out his suite of chambers located at 56a Pall Mall. On 17 June 1902 Mr Henry responded to an advertisement for the hire of the flat (from which it was possible to view the procession of the King's coronation). Henry agreed to take the suite, and paid a deposit, but the King became ill before the coronation and hence the procession was cancelled. Henry refused to pay the balance due and Krell began this action to recover that sum. It was argued by Krell that the contract could still continue as the flat was still in existence, and Henry could still have the use of it for the days identified in the contract. The Court of Appeal held that the contract was frustrated. It took a broader view that the entire purpose of hiring the flat was to view the coronation (evidenced from the price paid to hire the premises). The King's illness was the fault of neither party but its effect was to make the contract radically different from what was agreed. Hence the contract was frustrated.

Authority for:

Where, due to the fault of neither party, a contract becomes radically different from that agreed, the contract is frustrated.

- *The contract cannot be performed in the manner specified:* If the contract is specific about the manner in which it must be performed, and this cannot be complied with, the contract will fail due to frustration. For example, a specific vessel was to be used to deliver cargo, and this was damaged at sea before the contract was due to start and consequently could not fulfill the role. It was not permissible for the use of another vessel (unless the other party agreed). As the ship was stranded and subsequently damaged, not through the owner's fault but through 'the perils at sea', the contract was not breached but frustrated.[16]

- *If the contract becomes illegal to perform:* If the parties have agreed a contract, but before the contract is due to be performed it subsequently becomes illegal, then the contract is frustrated. This may be seen in *Fibrosa Spolka Akcyjna v Fairbairn Lawson Combe Barbour*[17] involving the outbreak of hostilities between England and Germany. Here Fairbairn, based in England, could not legally supply goods to Fibrosa, based in Poland, as Germany had occupied Poland in 1939 and England had declared war with Germany. There was a provision preventing British companies from supplying, *inter alia*, machin-

---

[13] See *Hyde v The Dean of Windsor* (Cro. Eliz. 552, 553), where an example was provided involving an author of works, and led to the following statement being read in the judgment: 'if an author undertakes to compose a work, and dies before completing it, his executors are discharged from this contract; for the undertaking is merely personal in its nature, and by the intervention of the contractor's death, has become impossible to be performed'.

[14] *Condor v The Barron Knights* [1966] 1 WLR 87.   [15] [1903] 2 KB 740.

[16] *Nickoll & Knight v Ashton, Edridge & Co.* [1901] 2 KB 126.   [17] [1943] AC 32.

ery to an enemy-occupied country, and consequently the contract was frustrated. Any attempt to deliver the goods under the contract would result in supervening illegality.

- *The contract becomes radically different:* The previous examples have demonstrated where the contract could not be completed due to some event or circumstance. It is also the case that if the contract was to be radically different from that which was envisaged when the contract was formed, then this may constitute frustration.

Davis Contractors Ltd v Fareham Urban DC[18]

Facts:

A contract was established for the erection of a building that was to be completed in eight months. However, due to shortages in labour, completion was not achieved until 22 months later. The contractors claimed frustration in part as the contract became significantly more difficult than the one that had been agreed. The House of Lords disagreed and stated that the shortage of labour is something that could have been expected, and if not provided for by the parties, then they are assumed to have accepted the risk.

Authority for:

Simply because a contract involves greater expense or hardship, or the contract becomes a bad bargain, will not amount to frustration.[19]

- *The limits to frustration:* The previous examples have demonstrated that there may be many reasons why a contract may be frustrated, but an essential factor is that it must not be the fault of either party. Simply because the contract cannot be performed will not result in it being frustrated. If one of the parties has deliberately or negligently led to the contract failing, he/she must accept the loss and/or compensate the innocent party.

Ocean Trawlers v Maritime National Fish[20]

Facts:

Ocean Trawlers owned a steam trawler (the St Cuthbert), which was chartered by the Maritime National Fish company; both companies were based in Halifax, Nova Scotia. A contract was entered into in July 1932, subject to the legislative requirements which made it a punishable offence to leave or depart from any port in Canada, with the intent to fish, with an unlicensed vessel that used an otter or similar trawl. The St Cuthbert could only operate with an otter-trawl and Ocean Trawlers also operated four other vessels, each fitted with otter-trawling gear. In March 1933 Maritime National Fish Ltd applied for licences for the five trawlers, but only three of the five trawlers were so issued. Maritime National Fish informed the Department of the vessels the three licences should be applied to, excluding the St Cuthbert. Maritime National Fish Ltd then asserted that through no fault of its own the charter became impossible to perform and consequently the contract was frustrated. The **Privy Council** held that this was not a case of frustration and Ocean Trawlers were entitled to recover damages.

---

[18] [1956] 3 WLR 37.

[19] *Tsakiroglou & Co. Ltd. v Noblee Thorl GmbH* [1962] AC 93.   [20] [1935] AC 524.

Authority for:

In the absence of a contract being radically different from that contracted for, or impossible to perform, it will not be frustrated.

Here Maritime National Fish Ltd was aware of the relevant legislation requiring licences for the vessels and as it gambled on securing licences for all five vessels, it had to accept any subsequent losses if these were not issued. It was possible for the company to insert a clause into the contract making the hire of the vessels dependant upon the successful granting of licences, but it had not done so. Just because this was a different contract to that anticipated by Maritime National Fish Ltd (namely it could not use the St Cuthbert as anticipated), it was neither radically different from that contracted for, or impossible to perform.

- Force majeure *clauses:* To 'protect' themselves against a frustrating event ending the contract, the parties may establish a *force majeure* clause that makes provision for the frustrating event. This clause involves some level of forseeability as to the possible frustrating event that was in the contemplation of the parties at the time of contracting. Examples may include provisions for bad weather, difficulties in supplies of labour and so on. Such clauses are valid and will be accepted by the courts if 1) it is the true intention of the parties and 2) the clause is not designed to limit one of the parties' exposure to liability for breach.

- *The effects of frustration:* When the court has determined that a contract has been frustrated, the contract ceases to exist as soon as the frustrating event occurs. As this typically affects businesses more than consumer contracts, the courts have encouraged the parties to make provisions in the contract on the basis of such eventualities. If no provisions are contained in the contract, assistance has been provided through the Law Reform (Frustrated Contracts) Act 1943. This statute provides:

1 all money still owing under the contract ceases to be due;[21]

2 all money paid is recoverable (at the court's discretion);[22]

3 the money returned includes deposits (pre-payments) and expenses that, before the case law and statutory interventions, resulted in such loses 'lying where they fell';[23] and

4 any valuable benefit which has been gained has to be compensated for.[24]

These provisions do not apply if the parties make their own provisions for the effect of frustration.[25]

Where, before the frustrating event, one of the parties received a valuable benefit (other than a payment of money), the other party may claim (a return of) its value. This assessment is made somewhat more difficult in the absence of statutory definition of 'valuable benefit'. However, its effect may be seen in the following case.

---

[21] Section 1(2).   [22] Section 1(2).

[23] The harshness of the application of losses in this respect can be seen in *Appleby v Myers* (1867) LR 2 CP 651, where a contractor's expenses for labour and materials lost following a fire were not recoverable as the contract stipulated payment on completion. Section 1(2) codified the law to enable the return of expenses.

[24] Section 1(3).   [25] Section 2(3).

BP Exploration Co (Libya) Ltd v Hunt (No. 2)[26]

Facts:

In December 1957 the Libyan Government granted Hunt a concession to explore for oil, and to extract it, from a specified area of desert. In June 1960 Hunt entered into an agreement with BP for it to drill and extract the oil, and the concession would be shared between Hunt and BP. BP was to assume all risks in the extraction of the oil. In 1971 Libya nationalized the oil industry and stopped BP's oil extraction, causing a loss of $35 million. Hunt had been provided with compensation from Libya (in the form of oil) and BP claimed damages from Hunt as the contract had become frustrated, under the Law Reform (Frustrated Contracts) Act 1943. The House of Lords held that under the Act, the contract had become frustrated, and as a consequence BP was entitled to a share of Hunt's profits as a value/benefit received.

Authority for:

Where one party has received a valuable benefit other than money prior to the frustrating event, and where it is just, some or all of that benefit may be recovered from the other party.

12.2.4 Discharge through breach of contract

If one of the parties breaches his/her obligations under the contract, then the other party must ascertain whether the breach of the term was due to a condition or warranty. A breach of a condition gives the injured party the option to both end (repudiate) the contract and claim damages. In some instances it may be advantageous for the injured party to claim damages but also to continue with the contract. In the case of a warranty, as it is a lesser term it entitles the injured party to damages, but he/she must still continue with the obligations under the contract.

In the event that the full contractual obligations owed by one of the parties is not fulfilled, or the performance is substantially less than could be expected, the innocent party may treat this as a complete breach of the contract. Situations may also arise where one of the parties recognizes that the other party is not going to fulfil his/her contractual obligations, or the party informs the other of this situation (although this must be clear and unequivocal,[27] but it may be retracted before accepted).[28] This is referred to as an anticipatory breach. In *Hochester v De La Tour*[29] a contract was agreed for the claimant to be hired by the defendant as a courier for a term of three months. Before the contract was due to be performed the defendant informed the claimant that his services would not be needed. The court held this was a case of anticipatory breach and the claimant was able to bring proceedings before the date of the performance of the contract. The injured party did not have to wait until the actual breach occurred before seeking to recover. However, this may not be a particularly good tactic to seek damages ahead of the actual date of the breach.[30]

Where anticipatory breach occurs, the innocent party can accept this as a breach immediately and treat the contract as repudiated (and presumably make other provisions to lessen the negative effects of the breach). Or he/she can wait for the time when performance was

---

[26] [1982] 2 WLR 253.
[27] *Dalkia Utilities v Caltech International* [2006] EWCH 63 (Comm).
[28] *Stocznia Gdanska SA v Latvian Shipping Co. (No. 3)* [2002] EWCA Civ 889.
[29] [1853] 2 E & B 678.   [30] See **12.3.1**.

due, and when the contract is breached, and then seek a remedy.[31] There is no obligation on the innocent party to accept the anticipatory breach, but as soon as he/she does, reasonable steps must be taken to mitigate losses.[32] The damages available for breach and anticipatory breach are the same.

However, at what point would the 'innocent' party know and be able to take action on an anticipatory breach? In *SK Shipping Pte Ltd v Petroexport Ltd*[33] the Commercial Court identified the following as reasons enabling the innocent party to take action on an anticipatory breach:

1   where the other party acted in a sufficiently clear manner to demonstrate it would not perform its obligations; and

2   the words or conduct of the other party were sufficiently clear, to a reasonable person, of this intended breach when considered in light of the circumstances of the case; and

3   the innocent party held a (subjective) belief that the other party would breach the contract.

12.3 Remedies for breach of contract

In the event that a contract is not performed, or obligations under the contract are not fulfilled, the innocent party may be entitled to compensation. Under the common law, this is usually in the form of damages[34] (a money payment), but may also involve equitable remedies of specific performance, injunctions, and rectification.

12.3.1 Damages

 Business Link

The most common remedy for a breach of contract claim is damages. It is necessary to understand how the courts will determine the amount (quantum) of damages, the limitations to a damages claim, and the duties on the injured party to limit (mitigate) his/her losses. Businesses also may attempt to circumvent the necessity of courts intervening to identify damages claims by inserting terms into the contract regarding the amounts due. This is called '**liquidated damages**' and is a pre-estimate of the losses incurred due to the breach. These must be compared with a **penalty clause**, which will not be accepted and will be dismissed by the courts. *Dunlop v New Garage* provides guidance on how to distinguish liquidated damages from a penalty clause.

Any breach of contract entitles the injured party to damages. This is irrespective of whether the term is classified as a 'condition' or 'warranty'. Damages (a money payment) exist to compensate the injured party for any losses sustained under the breach of the contract. Damages

---

[31]   *Shaftesbury House (Developments) Ltd v Lee* [2010] EWHC 1484 (Ch).

[32]   *Clea Shipping Corporation v Bulk Oil International* [1984] 1 All ER 129.

[33]   [2009] EWHC 2974 (Comm).

[34]   Compared with the Chinese legal system, where breaches of contract generally use specific performance as the remedy.

can be either 'liquidated', meaning the parties have anticipated the consequences of the breach, determined the level of damages to be paid and included this in the contract; or they can be '**unliquidated**', which are more frequent and determined by the court. The purpose of damages is not to punish the transgressor, or put the injured party in a better financial position than he/she would have achieved through the completion of the contract. They are used to either place the injured party in the position he/she would have been had the contract been completed (expectation losses) or place the injured party in the position he/she was before the contract had begun (reliance losses). In order for the courts to assess damages, there are underlying principles that are applied to ensure fairness. The first principle is that the damages must not be too remote; they must be quantifiable by the court; they must be recognized as damages in English law; and the injured party must have sought to **mitigate** his/her losses as far as is reasonable.

- *Remoteness of damage:* Remoteness is a vital aspect of the contract as it provides that the defendant in the case will not be liable for damages that are deemed too remote, and the general rule is that remoteness is assessed at the time of establishing the contract, rather than when the breach occurred.[35] However, in *The Golden Victory*[36] the House of Lords considered that where a charterer of a ship wrongfully repudiated a charter party, and the innocent party accepted the repudiation, the damages awarded could be restricted. This is because the contract contained a clause that the charterers would be allowed to cancel the contract in the event of war with Iraq (which was a possibility when the contract was formed). It was further known to both parties that this option would have been exercised had war broken out. The contract was repudiated before the outbreak of war, but the war was effective before the term of the contract was completed. As such, the Lords held that with this knowledge, as opposed to only assessing damages at the time of the breach, a more accurate assessment could be achieved along the lines of 'fair compensation'. Hence the assessment of damages was altered from the 'traditional' approach.

> **? Thinking Point**
>
> Do you consider that the decision in *The Golden Victory* will change the tactics of the injured party, particularly in terms of anticipatory breach? Will the injured party seek to claim damages immediately, and will the defendant attempt to halt proceedings to see if it can benefit from a delay? Does this have any implications for dispute resolution generally?

The general rules for assessing damages include the following considerations:

1 Do the damages arise naturally in the normal and ordinary course of the contract; and

2 are the damages within the 'reasonable contemplation'[37] of the parties?

---

[35] *Jackson v Royal Bank of Scotland Plc* [2002] UKHL 3.
[36] *Golden Strait Corporation v Nippon Yusen Kubishka Kaisha* [2007] UKHL 12.
[37] This depends on the probability/forseeability of loss, and the knowledge of the defendant.

Hadley v Baxendale[38]

Facts:

Hadley owned a flourmill and in May the mill was stopped due to a breakdown of the crankshaft (the only one it had). Hadley was to send the crankshaft to a third party for it to be replaced, and Baxendale was the carrier used for the transportation. Baxendale informed Hadley that delivery would be made on the following day. However, delivery was delayed for seven days and this led to a loss of profits that Hadley attempted to recover. Baxendale argued that it had no knowledge that Hadley would have sent the only crankshaft and hence a delay would have completely stopped production. The court concluded that there had been a breach of contract, but damages should be based on what may fairly and reasonably be considered arising naturally from the breach. A complete cessation of work due to the delay would have not been reasonably foreseeable by Baxendale.

Authority for:

In assessing quantum of damages, the award should be based on what may fairly and reasonably be considered arising naturally from the breach. This involves assessment of what should have been in the contemplation of both parties at the time they established the contract, as a probable result of the breach.

As Hadley sent its only crankshaft to be delivered by Baxendale, it had an obligation to inform Baxendale of this fact and a delay would have prevented any work being completed. With such information, Baxendale would have realized the consequences of any delay—a total loss of business and the consequent loss of profits. This legal reasoning was continued in *Victoria Laundry v Newman Industries*,[39] where a delay in delivering an industrial boiler for commercial launderers would allow damages to be claimed for the subsequent lost profits, but this did not extend to possible lucrative contracts that could have been won had the boiler been delivered as expected. Further, reasonable expectation can be seen in *Koufos v C. Czarnikow Ltd (The Heron II)*,[40] where a cargo of sugar to be delivered to Basrah was delayed (and nine days late) due to voluntary deviations in the route. During these nine days, the price of sugar dropped and Czarnikow sought to recover these losses, but Koufos claimed it was unaware of Czarnikow's intention to sell the sugar at Basrah, but was aware that there was a market for the sugar. It was reasonable for the defendants to be aware that the cargo would have been sold in a recognized commodities market, and prices were liable to fluctuate, therefore the ship owners should reasonably have contemplated the serious possibility or real danger that, if delayed, the value of marketable goods on board the ship would decline. This wrongful delay in the delivery of the goods led the House of Lords to the measure of damages being the difference between the price of the goods at their destination when they should have been delivered and the price of the goods when they were in fact delivered.

Having established whether the damages claimed were reasonable in the circumstances of the case, the next issue for the courts is how to quantify the losses.

- *Quantum of damages:* There are two methods a court may use to assess the measure of damage—reliance damages and expectation damages. Reliance loss is designed to prevent the injured party from suffering financial harm and returning him/her to the position before the contract had been established. The second type of damages is expectation

---

[38] [1854] 156 ER 145.   [39] [1949] 2 KB 528.   [40] [1967] 3 WLR 1491.

loss. This identifies what the injured party would have achieved from the successful completion of the contract, and seeks to place he/she, as far as money can, in that position.

In assessing the quantum of damages the courts will consider any loss of a bargain which the injured party has suffered; whether the parties have identified any 'agreed' damages in advance in the contract; and the duty on the injured party to mitigate his/her losses. The courts also have to ensure when determining the quantum of damages, that the injured party is not unjustly enriched. For example, the usual remedy for a breach in a building contract is for the court to award the cost of reinstatement (that is, to correct the defect). However, *Ruxley v Forsyth* provided an interesting interpretation of this rule.

- *Loss of opportunity damages:* If the injured party has not received what was contracted for under the agreement, damages is a remedy which is designed to award the cost of rectifying the loss, and provide compensation for any other foreseeable, consequential losses. However, this is limited to where the courts see the award as being reasonable and the following case demonstrates where the courts did not provide 'adequate' damages following a breach.

Ruxley Electronics and Construction Ltd v Forsyth[41]

Facts:
Ruxley was engaged to build a swimming pool for Mr Forsyth in his garden. The contract specified that the swimming pool should have a depth at the diving end of 7 feet, 6 inches. However, upon completion, the depth of the swimming pool was only 6 feet. Whilst this did not have any adverse affect on the value of the property, it did result in Mr Forsyth not having the depth of pool contracted for. It was estimated that it would cost £21,560 for the pool to be rebuilt to the required depth. It was held in the first case that this constituted a breach of contract, but Forsyth was awarded £2,500 for loss of amenity, not the cost of rebuilding as this would be an 'unfair enrichment' and unreasonable in the circumstances. There had been no consequential loss to the owner of the pool. The House of Lords agreed with this judgment.

Authority for:
In the event of a breach of contract where the contract was to provide the innocent party with something of value, if there is no other reasonable way of providing compensation, the damages should represent the extent of that value.

Lord Jauncy stated 'Damages are designed to compensate for an established loss and not to provide a gratuitous benefit to the aggrieved party from which it follows that the reasonableness of an award of damages is to be linked directly to the loss sustained. If it is unreasonable in a particular case to award the cost of reinstatement it must be because the loss sustained does not extend to the need to reinstate. A failure to achieve the precise contractual objective does not necessarily result in the loss which is occasioned by a total failure.' Common sense may have prevailed here, and there exists an argument that the decision was correct. However, Mr Forsyth did contract with Ruxley for a swimming pool at a specific depth and this was not complied with. Mr Forsyth wanted that depth to enable him to dive into the pool and the one built did not provide this. A sum of £2,500 will not provide the pool contracted for, and would hardly recompense Forsyth

---

41 [1995] 3 WLR 118.

for the inconvenience suffered. This may be seen as a judgment of 'rough justice and convenience'.

- *Reliance damages:* Reliance damages are most applicable where the parties cannot, with any certainty, identify what would have been achieved on the successful completion of the contract. It therefore attempts to place the parties in their pre-contractual positions.[42]

- *Damages for injured feelings:* The traditional view of the courts when determining the level of damages applicable in a case has been to ignore any injured feelings or loss of enjoyment suffered.[43] This is due to the problems inherent in quantifying such damages and the potential of opening the floodgates for claimants. However, exceptions to this rule have been developed in various cases[44] but can be seen most succinctly in the following:

Jarvis v Swans Tours[45]

Facts:

Mr Jarvis was a solicitor, aged 35, who booked a 15-day Christmas winter sports holiday with Swans Tours. The brochure described the venue, in Switzerland, as a 'house party centre' in very attractive terms. Mr Jarvis paid £63.45 for the package holiday; however, the holiday was very disappointing. Only 13 people were at the venue in the first week, with no other guests in the second week. Neither the owner of the house nor the staff could speak English; in the first week there were no full-length skis for Jarvis to use, and in the second week the skis were available but the boots supplied were of no use; the live entertainment consisted of a yodeller from the locality, who arrived in his working clothes, sang four–five songs very quickly, and then left; and the bar was only open one evening—located in an unoccupied annexe in the house. As such, Jarvis sought to recover the cost of the holiday and his salary for the two weeks spent on holiday. The Court of Appeal held that Jarvis was entitled to be compensated for his disappointment and distress at the loss of entertainment and facilities that he had been promised in Swans Tours' brochure. Damages should recognize the nature of this type of contract, and as it was specifically for enjoyment, if the contract does not provide what was promised then damages could be extended to account for that.

Authority for:

Damages awards should conform to the general rules of remoteness of damage. As such, the loss should be in the reasonable contemplation of the parties. Whilst damages for mental distress are not usually awarded in commercial contracts, they are applicable to non-commercial contracts.

- *Mitigation of loss:* The injured party in a contract has an obligation to limit the losses which he/she incurs as a result of the breach. This is known as the duty to mitigate and means the injured party cannot lie back idly and allow the damages to amass. The background to the duty is one of economic efficiency, avoiding undue hardship to the

---

[42] *Anglia Television v Reed* [1971] 3 WLR 528.   [43] *Addis v Gramophone* [1909] AC 488.

[44] Such as *Malik v Bank of Credit & Commerce International* [1997] 3 WLR 95, where the House of Lords held that an employee of the disgraced bank was entitled to damages due to the stigma attached by being employed at the bank, and the problem inherent in obtaining future employment; and *Perry v Sidney Phillips* [1982] 1 WLR 1297, where the Court of Appeal held that distress following the negligence in a survey of a property which subsequently required the execution of substantial repairs, did entitle the injured party to damages.

[45] [1972] 3 WLR 954.

defendant. However, the duty is not absolute and an element of reasonableness is introduced whereby the injured party does not have to take unnecessary steps to reduce loss. This may be witnessed most obviously in contracts of employment where the worker has been unfairly/wrongfully dismissed and he/she must take steps to find alternative, but appropriate,[46] employment.

Brace v Calder[47]

Facts:

Mr Brace had entered a two-year contract in December 1892 with Calder (a firm of Scotch whisky merchants consisting of four partners). In May 1893, before the two years had expired, two of the partners retired, with the other two continuing to carry on the business. As a result, Calder offered Brace to serve the new firm for the remainder of the contract on the same terms and at the same rate of pay. Brace stated that he had not agreed to serve the new firm and declined the offer, claiming wrongful dismissal.[48] The Court of Appeal held that there was a wrongful dismissal on the dissolution of the partnership, but Brace was only entitled to nominal damages (£50). This was because he was offered alternative work with the new partnership, which was fair and reasonable in the circumstances, and he could not wait for the court case and claim the remainder of the two years of the contract. Brace had failed to mitigate his losses.

Authority for:

Nominal damages may be awarded where an innocent party has failed to mitigate his/her losses following a breach.

In this situation, as the contract had been breached, but an alternative, suitable, offer was made and would have left Brace suffering no real loss, he was only entitled to nominal damages. The award of nominal damages essentially reflects that the claimant has 'won' the case, but he/she may not have acted reasonably in the circumstances.

- *Agreed/liquidated damages:* Businesses, particularly, may wish to consider the possibility of a contract not being completed on time or being breached, and the parties may seek to agree beforehand the amount to be paid in relation to this. This allows for greater certainty in the contract and the parties can determine how best to proceed without necessarily relying on the courts to determine such issues. This pre-determination of the damages payments is known as 'liquidated damages', whereas those determined by the court are referred to as unliquidated damages. For liquidated damages to be accepted, it must be a genuine pre-estimate of the loss rather than a penalty clause. A penalty clause is a threat against breaching the contract and will not be enforceable. However, simply because the contract uses the word 'penalty' will not necessarily make it a penalty clause.[49] There are tests that may help to distinguish liquidated damages from a penalty clause, and the following case provides useful instruction from the House of Lords:

---

[46] In relation to factors including locality, seniority, and pay.   [47] [1895] 2 QB 253.

[48] By implication of the partnership ending, Mr Brace considered himself dismissed.

[49] *Cellulose Acetate Silk Co. v Widnes Foundry* [1933] AC 20.

Dunlop Pneumatic Tyre Company v New Garage and Motor Company[50]

Facts:

Dunlop, manufacturers of tyres, covers, and tubes for motor vehicles, entered into a contract with a third party to supply them with goods under a contract that would only allow re-sales at prices established by Dunlop. The third party supplied New Garage with Dunlop's goods subject to a clause that it could not sell or offer the goods to any private customer or cooperative society at less than Dunlop's current list prices. Breach of the agreement would lead to liability of £5 by way of liquidated damages for each item. New Garage did breach this agreement and Dunlop sought to recover the damages as agreed; however, New Garage considered the term a penalty clause rather than liquidated damages.

The House of Lords held that the clause should be considered liquidated damages and not a penalty. Lord Dunedin referred to factors that point towards a penalty clause or liquidated damages.

Authority for:

Resultant to this case, the following are indicative in establishing liquidated damages and penalty clauses:

1 The use of the words 'penalty' or 'liquidated damages' may illustrate the nature of the clause but this is not conclusive.

2 The essence of liquidated damages is a genuine pre-estimate of damage.

3 The question whether a sum stipulated is a penalty or liquidated damages is a question to be decided on the terms and circumstances of each contract, and judged at the time of the making of the contract, not as at the time of the breach.

4 To assist this task of construction, various tests have been suggested, which may prove helpful:

   a) It will be held to be a penalty if the sum stipulated for is extravagant and unconscionable in amount in comparison with the greatest loss that could conceivably be proved to have followed from the breach.

   b) There is a presumption (but no more) that it is a penalty when 'a single lump sum is made payable by way of compensation, on the occurrence of one or more or all of several events, some of which may occasion serious, and others trifling, damage.'[51]

The tests established in the case are applicable as a guide to determine scenarios when the courts will hold a term that purports to be liquidated damages as a penalty clause. These will not, in all cases, be rigidly followed. They exist as a guide as to features indicative of contractual clauses that may be penalty clauses but which, in reality, necessitate complex enquiry.

12.3.2 Equitable remedies for breach of contract

As stated above, the courts will generally provide damages as a remedy for breach of contract wherever possible (as this is usually the simplest form of a remedy as it is a money payment).

---

[50] [1915] AC 79.
[51] Per Watson LJ in *Lord Elphinstone v Monkland Iron and Coal Co.* [1886] 11 App. Cas. 332.

However, there are occasions where money would not provide an appropriate remedy, or would be unjust due to the nature of the breached contract. This has led to the development of the equitable remedies, but remember that as they are 'equitable' remedies, they are awarded at the court's discretion.

𝓖 Business Link

Specific performance is a very powerful remedy in that it compels the party in breach to complete their obligations under the contract. Care must be taken when contracting for unique items (such as land), where the party in breach may not face a damages claim but rather an order forcing the completion of the contract. As such, this is a very powerful, and sometimes harsh, remedy.

- *Specific performance:* Specific performance is a remedy that is available when monetary damages are insufficient and do not adequately compensate the injured party for his/her loss. This is a court order compelling the party in breach to perform his/her contractual obligations. As the remedy is only available where monetary damages are inadequate, it is an order generally where the subject matter of the contract is unique[52]—such as the sale of land or antiques which by their nature cannot be replaced (although those examples are not guaranteed to be awarded specific performance). Specific performance cannot be ordered in contracts for personal services,[53] or contracts requiring constant supervision by the courts.[54] Finally, as an *equitable remedy*, it must also be available (potentially) to both parties and would not cause unreasonable hardship.[55]

  Specific performance is a very powerful remedy, but may also be perceived as harsh and at times unfair. In *Mountford v Scott*[56] Mr Mountford and his wife were members of a small property development company called H. & L. Cronk Ltd who were interested in purchasing properties with a view to building a new development. The new development could only be considered as viable if the appropriate planning consents were provided. Cronk Ltd sought to obtain options to buy the houses in the area of the proposed development, consequently obtain, if possible, the consents, and to proceed with the sales or to decide not to exercise the option. Mr Scott was a gentleman of West Indian origin who had lived in England for approximately 20 years, and although he spoke and understood English well, he was illiterate. Scott's house was one of the properties Cronk Ltd obtained an option on purchasing. The agreement allowed for Cronk Ltd to purchase his house for the price of £10,000, to be completed within six months of the agreement, with £1 being paid to Scott in consideration for the option. It transpires that later Scott did not want to continue with this arrangement and requested that Cronk Ltd release

---

[52] Although there is little guidance as to what will constitute a 'unique' item.

[53] Theories for this proposition are that it is unfair and very difficult to compel someone to work for another; it is an administrative hardship for the courts to ensure the 'personal service' is performed to the standards required by the claimant; and there is an overriding obligation on contracts of personal service to be performed with 'good faith', which may clearly be lacking with such an order.

[54] In *Rainbow Estates v Tokenhold* [1998] 3 WLR 980, specific performance was granted compelling a tenant to carry out repairs to the landlord's premises (as identified in the contract) as once the repairs were completed, no further supervision would be necessary.

[55] *Co-operative Insurance Society v Argyll Stores* [1997] AC 1.   [56] [1975] 2 WLR 114.

him, which it would not do. Cronk Ltd decided to exercise the option to purchase Scott's house, and when he refused, the court ordered specific performance of the contract.

The Court of Appeal held that the agreement was valid and hence constituted an irrevocable offer to sell. The agreement was entered into freely and consideration (of the £1) established a valid contract.[57] Russell LJ remarked that specific performance, rather than damages, should be the appropriate remedy in the case: 'If the owner of a house contracts with his eyes open, as the judge held that the defendant did, it cannot, in my view, be right to deny specific performance to the purchaser because the vendor then finds it difficult to find a house to buy that suits him and his family on the basis of the amount of money in the proceeds of sale.'

Mountford demonstrates the practical use of the remedy of specific performance and provides evidence of its effectiveness in ensuring compliance with the contract. Specific performance is restricted in use, as outlined above, and complements the other equitable remedy of injunctions as ensuring fairness is achieved in breaches of contract.

🖋 Business Link

As opposed to waiting for the consequences of a breach and claiming damages (which may be inadequate), the injured party may seek an injunction to prevent the commission of the breach. This preserves the rights of the parties and, as a court order, will make the transgressor be in breach of the contract and also guilty under the criminal law. Injunctions are a proactive remedy.

- *Injunctions:* There are two main types of injunction available to the courts—mandatory injunctions and prohibitory injunctions (although interim injunctions may be granted prior to a full hearing to prevent injury to the claimant).[58] Mandatory injunctions require the party compelled to perform the contract, whilst the more common type is a prohibitory injunction, which stops a party from breaching the contract. Failing to follow the order of an injunction will result in the transgressor being guilty of contempt of court—a potentially very serious charge. It is a valuable mechanism in ensuring that a party does not breach the contract[59] although, as with specific performance, it will only be used where damages would be inadequate and the issuing of the injunction must be reasonable.

❓ Thinking Point

Explain the difference in approach, and legal reasoning behind, the denial of specific performance in contracts of personal service but the courts' willingness to grant mandatory injunctions. Where does one remedy stop and the other start?

- *Rectification:* The remedy of rectification enables a written document (such as contract) to be changed (such as including/removing of clauses)[60] to more accurately reflect the terms

---

57   Brightman J in the judgment referred to *Fry on Specific Performance*, 6th edition (1921), p. 53: 'The court will never lend its assistance to enforce the specific execution of contracts which are voluntary, or where no consideration emanates from the party seeking performance ... '

58   These may be seen in cases of infringement of intellectual property—see Chapter 26.

59   *Warner Brothers v Nelson* [1937] 1 KB 209.

60   *A Roberts & Co v Leicestershire CC* [1961] 2 WLR 1000.

that were identified in the oral agreement subsequently reduced in writing. In order for a claim for rectification to succeed, the parties must have established an oral contract that identified the terms of the agreement; these terms did not change from the oral agreement until it was written; and the written contract does not accurately provide what was stated in the oral agreement.[61] The remedy allows the written document to be altered to reflect what the parties agreed orally, but this will only allow the document to reflect this oral agreement, not what one of the parties wanted to have included.[62] In *Re Sigma Finance Corporation (in administrative receivership)*[63] the Supreme Court reversed decisions of both the High Court and Court of Appeal with the effect that a contract was rewritten to give effect to the context/meaning of the words used in an agreement, even though the natural wording of the agreement was correct. The Court considered that a literal interpretation of the words would have been to distort the commercial intentions of the parties.

Rectification may be available where one of the parties believes that the contract reflects the intentions of the parties, but it does not, and the other party is aware of this mistake.[64] The Court of Appeal held in *Daventry District Council v Daventry & District Housing Ltd*[65] that a contract may be rectified in instances of common mistake. However, this decision has been criticized due to the emphasis on whether the parties have objectively made a common mistake, rather than a subjective assessment being applied.[66]

There exist limits by when a claim for breach of contract must be made. Under the Limitation Act 1980, an action under a simple contract must be made within six years from when the right to the action arose.[67] In the case of contracts made under deed, the claim must be established within 12 years.[68]

There is no statutory provision for time limits to claim under the equitable remedies, but as these are equitable, they must be sought within a reasonable time.

 Conclusion

This chapter has concluded the topic of the law of contract. These chapters have identified the essential features of a valid contract; the terms within a contract, and their source; the legislative impact on contracts; and the discharge of contracts. The chapter has identified how the courts will ascertain the level of damages, if any, to be awarded in various situations, and the equitable remedies available. The book now proceeds to a further element of the wider topic of obligations, investigating torts applicable to businesses.

 Summary of main points

Discharge

- Contracts may be discharged through performance, through part-performance (if accepted by the other party), and through substantial performance.

---

[61] See *Craddock Brothers Ltd v Hunt* [1923] 2 Ch 136 and *Joscelyne v Nissen* [1970] 2 QB 86.
[62] *Frederick E Rose (London) Ltd v William H Pim Jnr & Co Ltd* [1953] 2 QB 450.
[63] [2009] UKSC 2.   [64] *Commission for the New Towns v Cooper (GB) Ltd* [1995] Ch 259.
[65] [2011] EWCA Civ 1153.
[66] Davies, P. S. (2012) 'Rectifying the Course of Rectification' *The Modern Law Review*, May, p.412.
[67] Section 5.   [68] Section 8(1).

- Contracts may be discharged through the parties' agreeing to release each other from their further obligations (this can involve unilateral or bilateral discharge).
- The contract may become radically different from that which was agreed or impossible to perform. If this is neither party's fault then the contract is discharged through frustration.
- Discharge is effective through a breach of contract if the innocent party chooses to accept the repudiation.

Remedies for breach

- Damages are available as the primary remedy in breach.
- Damages may be based on expectation losses (that seek to put the innocent party into the position there would have been had the contract been completed) or reliance losses (that put the innocent party back to the position he/she was in before the contract was established).
- Damages must not be too remote; they must derive from the breach and have been in the reasonable contemplation of the parties when the contract was formed.
- Damages are not designed to penalize the party in breach and hence they must be quantified to reflect the losses sustained by the innocent party.
- The innocent party must proactively (albeit reasonably) attempt to mitigate his/her losses rather than wait for the losses to accrue.
- Damages may be agreed in advance (called liquidated damages) but these must not amount to a penalty clause.

Equitable remedies

- Specific performance may be ordered to compel the fulfillment of the contract. This, as with each of the equitable remedies, is available at the discretion of the court and is awarded when damages would not adequately compensate the innocent party. They are generally used in contracts involving unique items.
- Injunctions can be awarded to prevent a party from breaching his/her contract.
- The courts may also order rectification of the contract so that the written contract is changed to accurately reflect the parties' intentions.

 Summary questions

Essay questions

1. 'The equitable remedy of specific performance is harsh, unfair and it exposes vulnerable people to potentially unsound contractual obligations. It should be abolished and replaced with a common law damages assessment.'
   With reference to case law, critically assess the above statement.

2. Identify the methods in which contractual obligations may be discharged. Specifically comment on the differing approaches taken by the judiciary in relation to discharge through frustration.

Problem questions

1. In June 2010 Ben entered into a contract with Wagner Brothers Ltd to write a script for an intended play that Wagner Brothers Ltd was to provide to Apollo's Theatres Ltd. Apollo's intended to use this for several performances it had scheduled for November 2011. The contract provided that Ben was to submit the completed script on or before June 2011.

   It transpires that Ben did not have time to write the script as he was busy with other projects and had taken on too much work. On 25 April 2011 Ben wrote to Wagner Brothers Ltd with notice that he would not be able to complete the script as promised and had no intention of attempting to do so. By this stage, Wagner Brothers Ltd and Apollo's Theatres Ltd had incurred substantial expenses on the basis of this project. Wagner Brothers Ltd had also entered into preliminary contractual agreements with several television production companies for a mini-series of the script.

   Advise Wagner Brothers Ltd and Apollo's Theatres Ltd of any action they can take for damages.

2. Joshua books a holiday with 'Super Skiing Holidays' plc who specialize in holidays for single people. Joshua books for a two-week vacation to a resort in Switzerland. The brochure describes the resort as hosting a 'house party' where live entertainment will be provided every night and there will be several people to meet and enjoy the resort with.

   When Joshua arrives he is unhappy with the quality of the room and the food is of a very poor standard. The only ski boots available are too small for his feet and the skis were designed for children—there were no adult sizes. The entertainment consists of a local plumber who provides his Elvis Presley impersonation for 30 minutes each night on his way home from work. Joshua is joined at the resort by three other guests, each of whom are French and do not speak English, and they leave after five days—leaving Joshua the only person at the resort for the remainder of the holiday.

   When Joshua returns home he complains to 'Super Skiing Holidays' but they state it was not their problem and he cannot claim damages for the loss of enjoyment of his vacation.

   Advise Joshua.

 Online Resource Centre

http://www.oxfordtextbooks.co.uk/orc/marson3e/

Why not visit the Online Resource Centre and try multiple choice questions associated with this chapter to test your understanding of the topic. You will also find relevant updates to the law.

IV Tortious Liability

13 Negligence and Nuisance

Why does it matter?

Torts law is particularly relevant to businesses as they need to be aware of the extent of their potential liabilities to workers, visitors to business premises, other businesses, and to the general public. This extends to ensuring safe systems of work exist and appropriate insurance is maintained. Further, businesses need to be in a position where they can ensure they can exclude liability for advice provided in the course of their business. The chapters in this part of the book demonstrate the potentially significant sums involved in tort actions, and the potential costs involved in not taking adequate steps in their prevention.

Learning outcomes

Following reading this chapter you should be in a position to:

- understand the meaning of the term 'tort' (13.1–13.5)
- differentiate between liability in contract and liability in tort (13.5)
- explain the three tests to establish liability in negligence (13.6–13.6.3.2)
- explain the facts and the court's reasoning in *Donoghue v Stevenson* (13.6.1)
- identify the defences to a negligence claim (13.7–13.7.4)
- identify the remedies available in claims of tortious liability (13.8)
- assess where a business or individual may commit an act of nuisance and available defences to such actions (13.9–13.9.2.3).

𝕭 Key terms

These terms will be used in the chapter and it may be helpful to be aware of what they mean or refer back to them when reading through the chapter.

Duty of care
The rule that places an obligation to take reasonable care not to injure your 'neighbour' or damage property.

Nuisance
This is an unlawful interference that prevents an owner/occupier's enjoyment of his/her land.

Proximity
The close relationship between the parties to a negligence action which is essential to establish a duty of care.

Tortfeasor
The party who has committed the tort.

Volenti non fit injuria
The Latin phrase relating to a voluntary assumption of risk. Where a person engages in an event and agrees and accepts to the inherent risks, if injured, he/she is prevented from recovering damages.

13.1 Introduction

This is the second topic on the subject of obligations. Whilst the civil law places obligations on those parties who wish to undertake duties freely and agree to be legally bound via contracts, torts law imposes the obligation without, necessarily, prior agreement. The duty is to take reasonable care and not intentionally or negligently cause harm or damage. 'Torts'[1] derives from the French word 'wrong' and is essentially a civil wrong that entitles the injured party to the remedy of compensation. This remedy has the aim of placing the victim back into the position he/she was (as far as money can) before the tort was committed.

One of the most important torts is negligence (which may be commonly seen in instances of personal injury) and this tort is considered first in the chapter before acts of private and public nuisance are addressed.[2]

13.2 Fault liability

The law imposes a duty to take reasonable care to not negligently or intentionally cause damage. Many claims of negligence involve fault liability: someone is at fault and this enables the injured party to seek compensation for the resultant loss/injury. As such, situations of damage that are determined 'acts of God' will generally not be compensatable as there is no party from which to claim. This is in contrast to liability in contract that is strict (for example, the retailer is responsible for goods not being of a satisfactory quality despite the fact that, often,

---

[1] It is known as torts law because there are many torts. For example, personal injury is linked with the tort of negligence; a wrongful interference with a person's ownership and quiet enjoyment of his/her property may constitute one of the torts of nuisance and trespass; damage to reputation may be actionable through the tort of defamation; a wrongful interference with commercial interests may result in the tort of passing off; physically assaulting someone may lead to a claim under the tort of assault and battery; and there exists a tort of inducing a breach of contract.

[2] Students who would like to extend their understanding of the topic of torts law are advised to refer to Steele, J. (2007) 'Tort Law: Text, Cases and Materials' Oxford University Press: Oxford, New York.

he/she would have no way of knowing this or have been personally responsible for the (lack of) quality).

Note also that in other situations relevant to this topic, tortious liability may be imposed in the absence of fault. Under the doctrine of vicarious liability, one person may be held liable for the torts of another (such as an employer being held liable for the torts of his/her employees; or the principal being liable for torts of his/her agent). Fault is also removed in claims under the Consumer Protection Act 1987 where the liability is strict.[3]

13.3 Fault liability and the compensation culture

 Business Link

There has been much recent debate regarding the increasing 'compensation culture' in the UK, with scare stories of people suing others for seemingly trivial matters, and this has been exacerbated through the 'no win, no fee' services offered by law firms (often referred to as 'ambulance chasers'). Despite the excessive manner of these reports, it is arguable that the UK has not developed a compensation culture, and this has been acknowledged and fears allayed through legislative action, but businesses should continue to take steps to minimize their staff and customers' exposure to potential torts.

News reports in the recent past have suggested that the UK is heading towards a compensation culture where claims for compensation, usually through torts actions, have been brought against individuals, employers, and local authorities where a person(s) has suffered injury or loss (and this is increasingly moving towards claims in the education sector). Reports from the BBC highlighted cases including a woman who was awarded £195,000 in compensation due to her employers 'wrecking her job prospects' through their refusal to provide a reference; a woman who sued the company Durex for £120,000 when she became pregnant after using a faulty condom; and another claimant who sued[4] the holiday company 'Airtours' following injuries she received when on holiday in the Dominican Republic after a coconut fell on her chest when she was reclining under a palm tree.[5] There have been several reasons attributed[6] for the rise in persons seeking compensation, but the two most prominent reasons forwarded have been the introduction of conditional fee arrangements (the so called 'no win, no fee' claims), whereby lawyers representing claimants do not charge the client unless the claimant 'wins' the case (and these fees are generally added to the compensation claimed so the client obtains 100 per cent of the compensation); and secondly, the removal of the

---

[3] Note that these examples do not constitute an exhaustive list.

[4] The claim was eventually settled out of court with a payment of £1,700.

[5] BBC News 24 'Compensation Culture: Who's to Blame?' Wednesday 15 November 2000.

[6] Including those examples listed, there has been the introduction of 'class action' claims, where several claimants can join their cases and be heard at the same time, rather than requiring each claimant to raise their case individually.

restrictions on lawyers being able to advertise (hence allowing firms to be very aggressive in obtaining clients—just look at the advertisements currently on television and even in doctors' surgeries and hospitals[7] regarding clinical negligence). However, it has also been stated that the compensation culture is a fabrication or 'urban myth', and does not exist[8] and most people would not bring frivolous claims, nor do they feel in any heightened fear of litigation.[9]

However, this has not removed all fears of being sued, and research by an insurance broking and risk management firm 'Aon' in 2004 demonstrated that 70 per cent of the 500 businesses surveyed considered the compensation culture was placing an unsustainable burden on industry and that 96 per cent of the respondents blamed the Government for failing to take action.[10] In response to growing concerns within and outside of British business, the Compensation Act 2006 was passed to codify existing common law and to inform the courts of matters that should be taken into account when determining if a breach of duty to take reasonable care had taken place. This was to be assessed in relation to whether the defendant had taken steps to meet the standard of care required; and having taken these steps, might these prevent a desirable activity from being undertaken or discourage persons from undertaking functions in connection with a desirable activity.[11] As such, the Act was created to prevent situations where an otherwise desirable activity would be stopped due to the fear of litigation. For example, school trips for pupils involve an element of risk but they also provide an educational benefit that could outweigh the risks. As such, the Compensation Act 2006 was designed to make explicit the rules establishing liability to give greater confidence in what would lead to a breach of a **duty of care**. The Act identifies that an apology, an offer of treatment or other redress, will not of itself amount to an admission of negligence or breach of a statutory duty;[12] and it also applies to claims involving a disease relating to exposure to asbestos (mesothelioma).[13] The Act, further, provides for regulation of those involved in claims management services[14] and the enforcement of the regulation codes.[15]

? Thinking Point

Do you believe the law has moved in the right direction by enabling people to initiate tort actions, or do you think the law has developed to enable claims to proceed that would previously have failed to reach a settlement/hearing? Justify your answer.

---

[7] Somewhat amusingly, the BBC News 24 website on 28 May 2004 reported that advertisements for claims management companies regarding medical negligence had been printed on the back of hospital appointments cards (Compensation Culture 'Urban Myth').

[8] The House of Commons Constitutional Affairs Committee (2006) Third Report, Session 2005–06, 14 February.

[9] See also Steele, J. (2007) 'Tort Law: Text, Cases and Materials' Oxford University Press, Oxford.

[10] See Judge, E. (2004) 'Compensation Culture Hitting Competitiveness of UK PLC' *The Times*, 26 July.

[11] Section 1.   [12] Section 2.

[13] Section 3.   [14] Section 4.   [15] Section 7.

13.4 Time limits

There exists a limitation period in which claims of negligence must be brought against the perpetrator of the tort (the **tortfeasor**). Under the Limitation Act 1980 s. 2, actions in tort must be brought within six years of the date giving rise to the right of action. Claims for personal injury, however, must be brought within three years of either the date on which the tort was committed, or from when the injury attributable to the tortfeasor became known.[16]

In the case of a death, where the deceased person's representatives wish to bring an action on his/her behalf, the claim must be brought within three years of the date of the death, or three years from the date on which he/she obtained this knowledge (ss. 11(5) and 12).[17]

Protection is also afforded to minors (under the age of 18), and the time limits above do not apply until the claimant becomes 18. There is also protection to claimants who are suffering a mental disorder, as provided for in the Mental Capacity Act 2005, and who are incapable of managing their affairs. In such a situation the time limits do not apply.

13.5 The distinction between contractual and tortious liability

Tortious liability differs from contractual liability in that the obligations undertaken in contracts are entirely voluntary. No one can be forced into a contract against his/her will and consequently the parties have the ability to be aware of the extent of their liability, and the possible consequences in the event of breach. In contrast to this, tortious liability is imposed on persons and organizations (sometimes) without their knowledge or the awareness of the potential extent of this liability.[18] The law sometimes requires compulsory insurance to protect against claims of liability in negligence or other torts,[19] but it may be prudent for businesses to carry insurance for their property and possessions in the event of claims against them. Do remember that there may be several claims involving the same scenario, such as a breach of contract claim *and* a negligence action (for example, in *Grant v Australian Knitting Mills*);[20] and the scenario may involve a criminal action and a tort claim (such as an employee in a factory being injured through the use of dangerous and faulty equipment). Where the claimant has suffered a loss and injury, as in *Grant*, it is for the claimant to elect to pursue each element of his/her claim.

---

[16] Section 11.

[17] Note that the House of Lords held that this time limit, for personal injury claims, can be extended where it would be equitable to do so (*Horton v Sadler* [2006] UKHL 27).

[18] For an in-depth consideration and theoretical discussion of how contract and tort liabilities affect individuals see Collins, L. (1967) 'Interaction between Contract and Tort in the Conflict of Laws' *International and Comparative Law Quarterly*, Vol. 16, p. 103.

[19] Employers are required to hold liability insurance to insure against liability for injury or disease to their employees under the Employers' Liability (Compulsory Insurance) Act 1969; it is also advisable for other types of liability to be protected against as through Public Liability Insurance for those organizations which allow visitors onto their property or who deal with the public.

[20] [1936] AC 85.

13.6 **Negligence**

 Business Link

The law requires that those who are deemed to owe others a duty of care act responsibly and take necessary precautions to avoid injury and loss to others. The remedy primarily provided by the law is a damages payment to put the injured party back in the position he/she was before the tort had taken place—this can prove very expensive for businesses. Fundamentally to those in business, knowledge of the law and of responsibilities enables positive steps to be made to minimize the risk of negligence claims. When reading through the cases and judgments that follow, consider whether you would have acted as the business did, and whether you would have considered that liability would be imposed by the courts.

A definition of negligence is the breach of a duty to take care, owed in law by the defendant to the claimant, causing the claimant damage.[21] In order to establish a successful claim in negligence, three tests must be satisfied. Each of these will be discussed in turn (Figure 13.1):

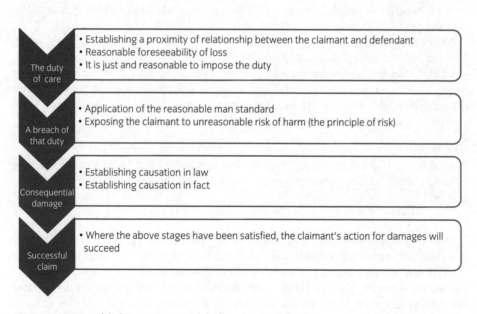

The duty of care
• Establishing a proximity of relationship between the claimant and defendant
• Reasonable foreseeability of loss
• It is just and reasonable to impose the duty

A breach of that duty
• Application of the reasonable man standard
• Exposing the claimant to unreasonable risk of harm (the principle of risk)

Consequential damage
• Establishing causation in law
• Establishing causation in fact

Successful claim
• Where the above stages have been satisfied, the claimant's action for damages will succeed

Figure 13.1 Establishing a Successful Claim in Negligence

---

[21] Although note from Lord Macmillan in *Donoghue v Stevenson* that '... the categories of negligence are never closed'.

13.6.1 **The duty of care**

Before proceeding to identify each of the 'three tests' necessary to establish a duty of care, it should be noted that these are separated, somewhat artificially, to demonstrate how they appear in the facts of the case and are identified by the courts. To establish liability in negligence, it must first be determined that the respondent owed the claimant a duty to take reasonable care. How this works in practice can be seen in the case of *Donoghue v Stevenson*:

Donoghue v Stevenson[22]

Facts:

A friend and Mrs Donoghue visited a café in Paisley, Glasgow on 26 August 1928, where the friend purchased a bottle of ginger beer for Mrs Donoghue. The drink was served in a dark, stone, opaque bottle and, unknown to the purchaser, the retailer, or Mrs Donoghue, contained the remains of a snail. This only became apparent when the greater part of the contents of the bottle had been consumed and the remainder was poured into a glass. At the sight of the snail, Mrs Donoghue claimed she suffered from shock and severe gastro-enteritis. On the basis of this illness Mrs Donoghue brought her action for damages against the manufacturer of the ginger beer (David Stevenson). Mrs Donoghue contended that the claim should be made against the manufacturer as the ginger beer was bottled by Stevenson, labelled by him, and he sealed the bottle with a metal cap.

A key element in establishing negligence is the proximity[23] between the parties, which led Lord Atkin to state: 'You must take reasonable care to avoid acts or omissions which you can reasonably foresee would be likely to injure your neighbour. Who, then, in law is my neighbour? The answer seems to be—persons who are so closely and directly affected by my act that I ought reasonably to have them in contemplation as being so affected when I am directing my mind to the acts or omissions which are called in question.'

Authority for:

In establishing that the defendant owes the claimant a duty to take care, there must be proximity of relationship between them. This is identified through Lord Atkin's 'neighbour principle'.

Donoghue v Stevenson is the seminal case in the establishment of the tort of negligence. The House of Lords determined that the claimant must establish that the defendant owes the claimant a duty of care, and in establishing this there must be proximity between the parties. 'Proximity' is the closeness of relationship between the parties that creates the duty to take care. Here, the manufacturer of a product was held liable for damage sustained by anyone who could have used, and consumed, its product. The case established that proximity is not restricted to a close physical 'closeness' but can be extended

---

[22] [1932] AC 562.

[23] *Heaven v Pender* [1883] 11 QBD 503. 'If one man is near to another, or is near to the property of another, a duty lies upon him not to do that which may cause a personal injury to that other, or may injure his property.'

to anyone who may reasonably be seen as being likely to be affected by the defendant's actions. Following *Donoghue*, proximity has been demonstrated in cases involving inadequate warning signs which led to injury,[24] and has also been used in defeating claims, as in the following case:

Bourhill v Young[25]

Facts:

Mr Young had been riding his motorbike and collided with a motorcar on 11 October 1938, in which accident he died. Mrs Bourhill (a 'pregnant fishwife') was a passenger on a tram. At the stop she alighted and was in the process of removing her fish-basket when the accident occurred. It was discovered that Mr Young had been travelling at an excessive speed and was thrown onto the street as a result of the collision, where he died. Mrs Bourhill did not witness the crash (her view being obstructed by the tram), but became aware of it on hearing the noise of the impact (she was some 45–50 feet away). Mr Young's body had been removed from the scene, and when Mrs Bourhill approached the point of the crash she observed the blood left on the roadway. In her evidence she claimed to suffer damage to her back and 'very severe shock to her nervous system', although she acknowledged that she did not fear for her own personal safety. The House of Lords held that a motorcyclist owed a duty of care to other road users and those he could reasonably foresee might be injured by his failure to take reasonable care, but Mrs Bourhill did not fall into this category as she was not in any area of potential danger. Mr Young did not owe her a duty of care as it was not foreseeable that she may be injured in the incident, and there was a lack of proximity between the parties.

Authority for:

For a duty of care to be established, the defendant must have reasonably foreseen that his/her actions may cause injury or loss to the claimant.

The case demonstrated how the courts will deal with the issue of proximity of relationship and the link with forseeability.[26] As the courts find one single definition of 'proximity' unrealistic (as noted by the Lords in *Caparo*) the examples provided in these cases enable common features to be drawn and considered for application in similar scenarios. Having established the test of proximity in identifying where a duty of care existed, the test was extended in a case involving economic loss. *Caparo v Dickman* established the threefold test of proximity, forseeability, and whether it was fair, just, and reasonable to impose a duty of care (albeit that this case was largely decided on its facts rather than a 'true' application of legal principle).

---

[24] See *Haley v London Electricity Board* [1965] AC 778.

[25] [1943] AC 92.

[26] *Bourhill v Young* [1943] is also used when considering the issue of 'primary' and 'secondary' victims (see **14.4.1** and **14.4.2**).

Caparo Industries Plc v Dickman and Others[27]

Facts:

Caparo had accomplished a takeover of Fidelity Plc and it began an action against the directors of that company (Steven and Robert Dickman) claiming a fraudulent misrepresentation, and an action against its auditors (Touche Ross & Co.) claiming it was negligent in carrying out an audit of the company.[28] The basis of Caparo's claim was that it began purchasing shares in Fidelity a few days before the annual accounts had been published and made available to the shareholders. In reliance on these accounts, it made further purchases of the shares in order to take over the company, and claimed the auditors owed a duty of care to the shareholders and any potential investors. The audit had projected Fidelity's profits unrealistically high, which Fidelity should have realized; and the share price had fallen significantly, causing substantial financial loss to Caparo. The House of Lords had to consider whether the auditors did in fact owe Caparo a duty of care. The Lords held that this case involved a negligent misstatement, but protection in such cases was limited to those who had obtained specific advice and used it for a reason made known to the provider of the information. The audit was a requirement of the Companies Act 1985 and therefore did not impose a duty of care on the auditors to the shareholders or potential investors. Consequently, Caparo's claim failed as there was a lack of proximity between the auditors and Caparo.

Authority for:

The imposition of liability for negligence should only take place where it is 'just and reasonable' to do so. Importantly, as this was a novel case, the law should develop liability in such cases incrementally and restrict/limit the imposition to those whom a duty is owed.

The issue of proximity has been addressed in *Donoghue*; foreseeability has been demonstrated in *Caparo* as a similar test to that used in contract of whether it should have been foreseeable to the defendant what the consequences of his/her action would be and the possible results; and 'fair, just and reasonable'[29] is an argument based on public policy.[30] It enables the court the discretion to consider the wider implications of establishing liability and has been referred to as the 'floodgates' argument. If establishing liability would 'open the floodgates' to numerous claims, then the court may decide that the liability should not be imposed. The courts also use this requirement to protect potential defendants such as public bodies (the emergency services, local authorities providing education services and so on) from excessive claims and a diminution of public funds.[31]

---

[27] [1990] 2 AC 605.

[28] PLCs were required to have an audit as part of their obligations under ss. 236 and 237 of the Companies Act 1985.

[29] For example, in *McFarlane and Another v Tayside Health Board* [2000] 2 AC 59 the House of Lords held that it would not be just and reasonable to hold the Health Board or the doctor responsible for the costs of raising a child following a failed vasectomy operation. However, damages may be awarded for the pain and losses attributed to the pregnancy. See also the imposition of an award for the 'legal wrong' committed in similar situations (*Rees v Darlington Memorial Hospital* [2003] UKHL 52).

[30] The Lords accepted the arguments presented by auditor's legal team that: 'three elements are needed for a duty of care to exist: there must be reasonable foreseeability, a close and direct relationship of "proximity" between the parties and it must be fair, just and reasonable to impose liability'.

[31] Although compare the judgments in *John Munroe (Acrylics) Ltd v London Fire Brigade & Civil Defence Authority* [1996] 3 WLR 988 and *Kent v Griffiths and Others* (1998) *The Times*, 23 December.

The House of Lords later held in *Marc Rich & Co. v Bishop Rock Marine*[32] that the requirement of establishing this 'threefold' test would be applicable to novel claims (such as in *Caparo*).
However, where an accepted duty that had been previously held to exist (such as the duty imposed
on drivers to other road users from carelessly causing injury), it was unnecessary to subject these
claims to the *Caparo* threefold test when the question of duty has already been determined.

13.6.2 Breach of the duty

Having established that the defendant owed the claimant a duty of care, the next step in
determining liability is to establish the defendant's breach of this duty. Essentially, this
means that the defendant fell below the standard required by law. The tests outlined below,
like the tests to prove the existence of a duty of care, are guidelines that have been developed
through the courts, rather than an attempt to establish a single set of criteria that will or will
not establish a breach of the defendant's duty of care. They will often overlap and each draws
on elements of the other, but they are used to demonstrate the issues the courts will consider
in attributing liability.

13.6.2.1 *The 'Reasonable Man' Standard*

Breach of the defendant's duty of care will often follow his/her failure under the 'reasonable
man' test. In *Blyth v Birmingham Waterworks Co.*,[33] Alderson, B. commented that 'Negligence
is the omission to do something which a reasonable man, guided upon those considerations
which ordinarily regulate the conduct of human affairs, would do, or doing something which
a prudent and reasonable man would not do.' In extracting principles from the statement, the
following factors will be considered by the courts:

13.6.2.2 *Exposure to risk of harm*

The claimant, in asserting that the defendant has breached his/her duty of care, will, as a
general rule, have to demonstrate to the court's satisfaction that the defendant committed the
breach. This places the burden of proof on the claimant.

1 *The principle of exposing the claimant to unreasonable risk of harm:* Essentially, the more
   likely it would be that the defendant's action would lead to injury or loss, the more likely
   it would be that he/she had breached his/her duty to take reasonable care. In *Brett v
   University of Reading*[34] Mr Brett died as the result of contracting mesothelioma attributed from working with asbestos. A claim was brought against one of his former employers, as during his employment as a Clerk of Works, he oversaw the demolition of the old
   library, which it was considered in evidence, probably caused asbestos to be released,
   despite the University hiring competent contractors to undertake the works. The claimant could not demonstrate that the University was negligent in the hiring of the contractors or that the University had breached any statutory duty. Further, the Court of Appeal
   held that it could not be proved that this employer, rather than others, had led to Mr
   Brett contracting the disease, and as it had taken reasonable precautions to ensure his
   safety, the claim for damages had to fail.

[32] [1995] 3 All ER 3307.
[33] [1856] 11 Ex. Ch. 781.   [34] [2007] EWCA Civ 88.

Risk is accepted as part of most day-to-day activities (such as merely getting up in the morning and travelling to work), but it is the unreasonable exposure to risk that will establish a potential breach.[35]

2 *The social utility and desirability of the defendant's actions:* Of course when considering the risk the claimant was exposed to, the courts have to perform a balancing act between this risk and any benefit or valuable objective that the defendant was attempting to achieve.

Watt v Hertfordshire CC[36] identified that if an action is desirable and of social importance, the risks that correspond with the actions may be acceptable, whereas in other situations it would have led to unreasonable levels of risk (and damages in negligence). In the case, a fireman was injured by a jack that was not correctly secured in the lorry that was used to transport it to the scene of an emergency. The lorry had not been designed to carry such a large piece of equipment. However, the jack was required as it was used to save the life of a woman who had been trapped following an incident with a motor vehicle. Per Denning LJ: 'It is well settled that in measuring due care you must balance the risk against the measures necessary to eliminate the risk. To that proposition there ought to be added this: you must balance the risk against the end to be achieved.' Consequently, the Court of Appeal held that there was no finding of liability on the Council because of the wider implications of the risk undertaken.

3 *The cost and practicality of measures to minimize the risk of harm:* Likewise in point 2 above, the courts will assess the risk faced by the claimant in terms of the defendant's actions and the costs involved in attempting to minimize or remove these altogether.

In *Latimer v AEC Ltd*[37] a factory had suffered flooding following a period of heavy rain with the consequent mixing of the water with oil that was present on the factory's floor. In response, the owners of the factory (AEC) spread sawdust on the floor. However, Mr Latimer slipped on a patch of oil that had not been covered and sustained injury. Mr Latimer claimed damages under negligence for his injuries but the claim failed as AEC had taken all reasonable precautions to minimize the risk of injury. Mr Latimer had argued that the floor was unsafe and AEC should have closed the factory down until it could be made safe. However, the House of Lords felt this would have been disproportionate to the risk. In *Bolton v Stone*, a woman, standing outside her house, was struck by a cricket ball hit from an adjoining cricket club. She sought to recover damages for her injuries but the House of Lords held that the club had reasonably minimized the risk of harm through erecting a fence some 17 feet high at the perimeter of the ground. The fact that balls had only ever been struck over the fence six times in 28 years led to the judgment that the claimant had not been exposed to an unreasonable risk of harm.

The case reflected on the main elements to consider when assessing a breach of duty of care. Those are:

- the 'reasonable man' standard;
- the principle of risk (exposure to unreasonable risk of harm);
- the social utility and desirability of the defendant's actions; and
- the cost/practicality of the measures to reduce the risk of harm.

---

[35] See *Paris v Stepney BC* [1951] AC 367.   [36] [1954] 1 WLR 835.
[37] [1953] 3 WLR 259.

The case is useful when identifying if a breach of the duty of care has occurred. It is important to note that the courts will apply the 'reasonable man' test objectively, there is no allowance to be made for lack of experience/intelligence. In *Nettleship v Weston*[38] Mr Nettleship gave driving lessons to Miss Weston, who was a careful learner. However, on the third lesson Miss Weston failed to straighten following a left turn and drove into a street lamp, which led to Mr Nettleship breaking his kneecap. Miss Weston was convicted of driving without due care and attention, and Mr Nettleship brought an action for negligence due to his injuries. The Court of Appeal held that the fact that the driver was a learner was no defence to the negligence action; the test applied to a learner was the same, objective test, as applied to a careful driver.

The defendant must take into account the shortcomings of others;[39] and there is an obligation to display appropriate levels of skill. In *Bolam v Friern Hospital Management Committee*,[40] Mr Bolam sustained fractures of the acetabula during the course of electro-conclusive therapy treatment administered whilst he was a voluntary patient at the defendants' hospital. Mr Bolam initiated a damages action against the hospital alleging that the defendants were negligent in failing to administer any relaxant drug prior to the passing of the current through his brain, and they had failed to warn him of the risks involved in the treatment. The hospital produced expert witnesses who each agreed that there was a firm body of medical opinion opposed to the use of relaxant drugs. Further, it was the practice of the defendants' doctors not to warn their patients of the risks of the treatment (which they believed to be small) unless asked. The High Court held that even if a warning as to the result of the treatment was provided, this would not have affected the outcome of the case, and the hospital had complied with professional standards. Therefore, the claim failed and the hospital was not negligent.

The failure of Miss Stone to establish a breach of duty that prevented her successful claim can be compared with the case of *Miller v Jackson*.[41] This case also involved a cricket ground (the Lintz Cricket Club) in County Durham, whose Chairman, Mr Jackson, was sued for negligence (and another tort action under **nuisance**) by Mr and Mrs Miller. Mr Miller had bought his house in the summer of 1972, and the garden was only 102 feet from the centre of the cricket ground. Mr Miller claimed that cricket balls were struck from the club into his garden which had caused damage to his property, and were so intrusive that he and his wife spent time away from the property during matches, and would not enter the garden for fear of being hit by stray cricket balls. This was despite a six-foot concrete wall at the end of the garden, and the cricket ground erecting a fence of 14 feet nine inches (the fence could not be made higher due to stability problems). In 1975, six balls went over the fence into the neighbouring houses; in 1976 nine balls went over the fence and therefore in the first case the court held that there had been a breach of the cricket club's duty to take reasonable care.

Situations also exist where the most likely explanation for an accident/injury to the claimant is that the defendant must have been negligent. Here, the burden of proof is reversed and the onus is on the defendant to demonstrate that he/she was not negligent. This is known

---

[38] [1971] 3 WLR 370.

[39] A practical example would be when driving a car in a residential area during school holidays. Appropriate speed would have to be maintained, even if this was slower than the legal speed limit, as children may be playing in the street, they may run out from behind parked vehicles, and they may not appreciate danger of traffic on the road as a driver should.

[40] [1957] 1 WLR 582.

[41] [1977] 3 WLR 20.

as *res ipsa loquitur*[42] and it will apply where the event that had caused the claimant loss was within the control of the defendant; and the event would not have occurred had the defendant exercised proper care and attention.[43] In *Drake v Harbour*,[44] the claimant sought damages for the alleged negligent rewiring of her property that had led to fire damage. Albeit that the claimant did not have positive or scientific proof that the poor rewiring had led to the fire, the Court of Appeal held that what was required was a matter of judgement in each case having considered all of the available evidence. The evidence provided by the defendant, on the balance of probabilities, regarding alternative causes of the fire were improbable and where, as in this case, it was demonstrated that the defendant was negligent and the loss sustained was consistent with such negligence, it was not necessary for the claimant to positively prove the exact and technical reason. The court is entitled to infer the loss as caused by the proven negligence.

A private duty to take reasonable care is not, however, derived from a, wider, statutory duty. In *Gorringe v Calderdale MBC*,[45] the Council had a statutory obligation to maintain the roads and ensure safety under the Highways Act 1980. The claimant in the case had caused an accident whilst driving along a country road by driving too fast towards the brow of a hill and when she could not navigate the turn, colliding with a bus, as a consequence suffering severe injuries. The claimant's argument was that the Council had the responsibility for protecting the users of the highway and in this respect, it should have highlighted the danger of the particular road through signage such as marking the word 'SLOW' on the road before the hill. As such, the claimant contended that this public duty created a private duty to the users of the road, enabling her claim to succeed. The Court held that this did not impose such a duty on a local authority, as a private duty could not in this sense 'emerge' from a wider public duty. The Council had not taken any positive action in the accident and hence the claim failed.

As noted in section **13.3**, the enactment of the Compensation Act 2006 has had the effect of restraining the 'compensation culture'[46] that was alleged to have crept into the English legal system. The courts would expect claimants to have been vigilant in protecting themselves and to appreciate obvious risks. This is not to say that it removes the legal obligations imposed on the defendant, but it has, particularly since the Compensation Act 2006, attempted to introduce a balance between the ability of claimants to seek damages for losses, and protection of those involved in providing desirable activities.

13.6.3 Consequential damage

An essential component for a successful negligence claim is that the claimant has suffered loss; this loss must be of a type recognized by the law; and there must be a causal link between the breach and the loss suffered (consequential loss). For example, where an out-of-town shopping mall is built, the effects of this may be to cause economic damage to shops in the local town (as occurred when the Meadowhall development was built in Sheffield). However, despite this damage to their business through lost profits, the law does not allow the injured shop owners to bring a claim for damages against the developer of the shopping mall/the shopkeepers for any financial losses. Other torts exist that may

---

[42] Translated as 'the facts speak for themselves'.   [43] *Ward v Tesco Stores* [1976] 1 WLR 810.

[44] [2008] EWCA Civ 25.   [45] [2004] UKHL 15.

[46] See Mullender, R. (2006) 'Negligence Law and Blame Culture: A Critical Response to a Possible Problem' *Professional Negligence*, Vol. 22, p. 2; and Herbert, R. (2006) 'The Compensation Act 2006' *Journal of Personal Injury Law*, Vol. 4, p. 337.

enable a claim where the claimant has not suffered any damage. In claims of trespass, for example, the court will often award nominal damages even where no losses have been sustained.

13.6.3.1 *Causation in fact*

The court will examine the facts of the case and ascertain whether the defendant had caused or contributed to the claimant's injury or suffering. A test developed by the Court of Appeal in the case of *Cork v Kirby Maclean*[47] is the 'but for' test. This test was defined in the following way: 'If the damage would not have happened but for a particular fault, then that fault is the cause of the damage—if it would have happened just the same, fault or not fault, the fault is not the cause of damage.' This can be demonstrated in the later case of *Barnett v Chelsea and Kensington Hospital Management Committee*,[48] where three watchmen sought medical attention following a bout of vomiting. The on-duty nurse consulted a doctor, who advised the watchman to go home and seek advice from his own doctor the following morning. However, later in the day the man died, which was attributed to arsenic poisoning. A claim was brought against the hospital for the negligence of the doctor in failing to examine the watchman, but this failed. The watchman had such a high concentration of arsenic in his system that he would have died regardless of any intervention, such as administering an antidote, even if his condition had been diagnosed in a doctor's examination. Therefore, there was a duty to take care, and this had been breached, but as no consequential damage was present the claim failed.

13.6.3.2 *Causation in law*

The defendant is not liable for every consequence of his/her wrong. If there is some intervening act that causes the damage to the claimant then the (first) defendant will not be held responsible in negligence. If the damage sustained was too remote, then it would be unreasonable to hold the defendant responsible.

- *Remoteness of damage:* Remoteness of damage involves the test of reasonable foreseeability. If the reasonable man could not foresee the consequences of the action, then the claim will be defeated. The case of *Overseas Tankships (UK) Ltd v Morts Dock & Engineering Co. Ltd (The Wagon Mound)*[49] is important in demonstrating the effect of this rule. Here the defendants were the owners of a ship named *The Wagon Mound* and had been negligent in allowing oil to spill from the ship into Sydney Harbour. There was welding taking place in the Harbour at the time, and the oil had spread into the wharf owned by the claimant. The claimants stopped the welding, due to the potential risk of a fire, and sought clarification as to the danger, but were informed it was safe to continue their welding activities. Floating in the Harbour at the time was refuse, including cotton, onto which the molten metal from the welding fell and which caught fire causing the oil on the water to ignite. This fire quickly spread, resulting in substantial damage to the claimant's property, and led to the action against the owners of *The Wagon Mound*. The Privy Council held that the defendants were only liable for the oil that had spilled into the Harbour and not the fire that had been caused. It could not be reasonably foreseen that the oil would have caught fire due to its high ignition point.[50]

---

[47] [1952] 2 All ER 402.   [48] [1969] 1 QB 428.
[49] [1961] 2 WLR 126.
[50] Compare this decision with *Hughes v Lord Advocate* [1963] 2 WLR 779.

When the claim involves the negligence of the tortfeasor, the causal link is vital to impose liability. This link (or chain of events) may be broken by a new act (a *novus actus interveniens*). If a new act, independent of the defendant's action, occurs and is sufficiently independent, it may stop the imposition of liability on the (first) defendant. If, however, the action occurs as a consequence of the initial breach by the defendant, and the actionable event was foreseeable, the defendant will still be liable. Foreseeability can be seen in the case of *Lamb v Camden London BC*,[51] where the Council had caused damage to the water main that had led to Lamb's house being flooded. The house was uninhabitable and was vacated by Lamb whilst remedial work was carried out. When the house was left empty, squatters moved in and caused damage. Lamb brought an action against the Council for its negligence that resulted in this increased damage. The Court of Appeal held that the Council was not liable as it was not foreseeable that the damage would have occurred, and the Council was under no obligation to secure the property whilst the repairs were being undertaken.

Attempts to mitigate losses will not, in most cases, result in the chain of causation being broken. In *Corr v IBC Vehicles Ltd*[52] the claimant was the wife of a man who had committed suicide following injuries sustained during an accident in a factory at work. The employer had agreed that it had breached its duty of care (and statutory duty) towards the employee, and the employee had suffered post-traumatic stress and depression, leading to his suicide six years after the accident. The Court of Appeal held that the depression suffered by the employee was foreseeable, and that it was further foreseeable that severe depression may result in suicide. Therefore, the claim was successful as the employee's suicide did not break the chain of causation between the defendant's negligence and the consequences of the suicide. The House of Lords subsequently upheld this decision.[53]

- *The eggshell skull rule:* There exists an obligation to take appropriate care to avoid causing damage that may lead to a negligence claim. However, there is also an obligation to 'take your victim as you find them'. This principle is known as the 'eggshell skull' rule and means that if the victim has a pre-existing condition that is exacerbated by the act of negligence, insofar as the damage is one which the law recognizes, there is no defence to claim that another person would not have been so badly injured. This can be seen in the case of *Smith v Leech Brain & Co.*,[54] where a workman employed by Leech Brain had been hit on his lip by molten metal whilst welding work was taking place. He suffered a relatively minor burn, which was expected and clearly foreseeable. However he had a pre-cancerous skin condition. This was not known to anyone but was triggered by the burn he received, and he died three years later of the cancer. Smith's widow claimed against the employer, and even though the burn would not have caused the death of most victims, the eggshell skull rule was invoked and consequently Leech Brain were held liable in negligence.

The concept has also been applied to cases of psychiatric injuries.[55] If the reasonable man would have suffered nervous shock, and the claimant's disposition exacerbates the injury he/she has actually suffered, then he/she will be able to claim for this greater injury, and not be reduced to the injury that would have been suffered by the reasonable man. Lane, J in *Malcolm v Broadhurst*[56] described it as the 'eggshell personality'.

---

[51] [1981] 2 WLR 1038.   [52] [2006] EWCA Civ 331.
[53] [2008] UKHL 13.   [54] [1962] 2 WLR 148.
[55] See **14.4**.   [56] [1970] 3 All ER 508.

13.7 Defences to a claim of negligence

> ### 🖉 Business Link
>
> In the event of a claim of negligence being made against a business, the business may wish to mount a defence. Defences to negligence claims may be complete defences whereby the business asserts it has no liability at all, or they may be partial defences where the business accepts some liability for what occurred, but asserts that the claimant was also partially responsible (the defendant will still have to pay a percentage of the award). Avoiding negligence actions in the first instance appears to be the best solution.

In order to avoid the legal responsibility that a successful negligence claim may provide, the defendant may attempt to raise a defence, the choice of which depends on the nature of the action.[57] The most common forms of defence are:

1 illegality;

2 consent;[58]

3 contributory negligence; and

4 necessity.

13.7.1 Illegality

Where the claimant has committed an illegal act he/she may be prevented from raising a negligence action (this is specific to the circumstances of the case). In *Ashton v Turner*[59] the claimant was unsuccessful in seeking damages against the co-participant who drove the getaway car following a burglary. The car crashed and the claimant was seriously injured. It was held that public policy would not allow the perpetrator of a crime to claim compensation against a co-participant for any injuries sustained in the course of the criminal activities.

However, illegality is a difficult defence to successfully rely upon, especially when involving companies rather than individuals. In *Moore Stephens (a firm) v Stone & Rolls Ltd (in liquidation)*[60] the House of Lords, in a split 3 to 2 majority, agreed with the Court of Appeal's decision to strike out a claim for damages and accepted an illegality defence. This was due to the effective use of the illegality defence by the defendant. Here a company's liquidator alleged that its auditors had been negligent in failing to identify that the company had been used to perpetrate a fraud. The claim failed, and was struck out by the court, as it was being made by the company itself (through the liquidator) and was relying on its own illegal act when seeking damages. This was, in part at least, because the fraudulent director was the 'controlling mind and will' of the company and hence it would be unfair to allow a claim to

---

[57] Such as mistake; and 'privilege' in cases involving defamation.

[58] In the Latin: *volenti non fit injuria* (no actionable injury/no injury is done to a consenting party).

[59] [1980] 3 All ER 870.   [60] [2009] UKHL 39.

succeed where a fraudster would benefit by claiming against auditors who failed to detect his/her own deception.

The decision in *Moore Stephens* may be compared with *Robert Matthew Griffin v UHY Hacker Young & Partners (a firm)*[61] where the High Court refused to strike out a claim brought by Griffin for professional negligence against the defendant accountancy firm. Here the illegality defence failed. Griffin alleged the defendant negligently failed to advise him of an illegal act when a company that he operated went into creditors' voluntary liquidation. Griffin had instructed the accountancy firm to advise him on the winding-up of the company. Following the liquidation, Griffin formed a new company which took over selling of a product previously sold by the former company. Such an action contravened the Insolvency Act 1986 s. 216[62] and Griffin was convicted of a strict liability offence and fined £1,000. As a consequence of this conviction, Griffin sustained various financial losses and he sought damages to compensate him for the firm's negligence. Griffin argued that the firm should have informed him of the illegality of his actions. Due to the complexity of the illegality defence, and its requirement of culpability being demonstrated, a full trial was necessary (particularly here where the offence was of strict liability). This would allow these issues to be fully explored before any conclusion could be drawn as to the likelihood of the success of Griffin defeating the illegality defence.

13.7.2 Consent

Consent is a complete defence to an action in tort but is closely linked with the partial defence of contributory negligence. The defence is available where there has been an express agreement to the particular risk of damage or it may be implied from the conduct of the claimant due to the actions of volunteering (such as acting as a rescuer) or by accepting entering into a situation involving risk (*Morris v Murray*).[63] Examples of express and implied consent may be seen where a patient is undergoing surgery and he/she signs a consent form. This express agreement allows the surgery team to perform the procedure without committing the tort of trespass to the person. Express agreement may defeat a claim for damages but these would be subject to the Unfair Contract Terms Act 1977.[64]

Implied consent may be demonstrated in the context of sporting pursuits such as playing contact sports like rugby,[65] or photographing sporting events in close proximity with the participants. *Blake v Galloway*[66] involved horseplay between four teenage friends and led to the claimant suffering injury when a piece of bark struck his eye when the friends were throwing twigs at one another. It was held by the Court of Appeal that for the defendant to breach his/her duty of care in unregulated horseplay the defendant's conduct must amount to recklessness or sufficient carelessness or error of judgement.

---

[61] [2010] EWHC 146 (Ch).

[62] This section protected against 'phoenix companies' whereby a director of a company put into insolvent liquidation was prohibited from becoming a director of a new company using the same name without giving notice to the creditors or obtaining the court's permission.

[63] [1990] 3 All ER 801.   [64] See **11.5**.

[65] Note, however, that merely participating in a regulated, physical sport such as rugby does not necessarily mean that the participant agrees to suffer injury and not seek a remedy. See *Condon v Basi* [1985] 1 WLR 866 (a person injured whilst playing football) and *Caldwell v Fitzgerald* [2001] EWCA Civ 1054 (a jockey unseated by a rival).

[66] 2004 EWCA Civ 814.

The defence of consent is not available simply because a party (typically, in a business context, an employee) is aware of the risk of injury at the workplace, and continues to carry out his/her duties.[67] The courts will not imply consent in such circumstances but will require an outward sign of consent in relation to the inherent risk. The defence is also unlikely to be successful in situations where the claimant has taken action to prevent harm or perform a rescue[68] and has been injured in the process. This requires the claimant to have acted reasonably in the circumstances.[69]

Volenti may be a defence in employment situations where a deliberate act has been undertaken against the express orders of the employer. In *ICI v Shatwell*[70] the claimant and a colleague, qualified shot-firers, made a test of an electrical circuit for firing explosives without taking the appropriate cover. They were injured and a claim was made for damages. The House of Lords held that this enabled a complete defence by the employer, on both vicarious liability by one claimant and breach of a statutory duty by the other, as they had agreed to take this action knowing the danger. The action was contrary to the employer's instructions and statutory regulations, therefore the claim had to fail.

13.7.3 Contributory negligence

Section 1(1) of the Law Reform (Contributory Negligence) Act 1945 provides:

> Where any person suffers damage as the result partly of his own fault and partly of the fault of any other person or persons, a claim in respect of that damage shall not be defeated by reason of the fault of the person suffering the damage, but the damages recoverable in respect thereof shall be reduced to such extent as the court thinks just and equitable having regard to the claimant's share in the responsibility for the damage.

Contributory negligence is a partial defence[71] to a claim where injury has been caused and the claimant seeks damages. It is not only applicable to claims of negligence but is applicable where there is 'fault',[72] (with the exception to the torts of conversion and deceit). Contributory negligence is only applicable where the claimant was (at least in some part) responsible for his/her damage. A most common example of the defence of contributory negligence is where a person has been involved in an accident whilst driving, and he/she was not wearing a seat belt, or had failed to secure a crash helmet whilst riding a motorcycle.[73] In the event that the courts hold the damage was the other driver's fault, the injured party who has suffered substantial injury, when he/she would not have sustained such a level of injury had he/she been wearing a seat belt, will have contributed to his/her own injury. This provides the court with an option to determine at what level of contribution the claimant was responsible, and can reduce any damages awarded. Guidance was provided in *Froom v Butcher*.[74] Where injuries would have been altogether prevented by wearing the seat belt, the damages should be

---

[67] See the House of Lords decision in *Smith v Baker & Sons* [1891] AC 325.

[68] Particularly when this involves some psychiatric injury—see *Chadwick v BRB* [1967] 1 WLR 912.

[69] *Haynes v Harwood* [1935] 1 KB 146.   [70] [1964] 3 WLR 329.

[71] Following the enactment of the Law Reform (Contributory Negligence) Act 1945 (before this contributory negligence was a full defence).

[72] The Law Reform (Contributory Negligence) Act 1945, s. 4.

[73] *Capps v Miller* [1989] 1 WLR 839, where the claimant's damages were reduced by 10 per cent by the Court of Appeal.

[74] [1975] 3 WLR 379.

reduced by 25 per cent. Where the injuries sustained would have been 'a good deal less severe' the reduction should be 15 per cent.

In contributory negligence, the claimant is referred to as having 'contributed to his/her own misfortune' and if he/she has been at fault in any activities that have led to his/her injury, then the court will reflect this in the damages awarded. The Court of Appeal has also held that the claimant may even be entitled to succeed in an action for damages where he/she is 60 per cent liable for his/her injuries.[75]

13.7.4 **Necessity**

A defence may be available to an action for negligence where the tortfeasor had acted in a way so as to prevent a greater harm occurring. To be successful the defendant must demonstrate that there was imminent danger to a person or to property and the actions taken were reasonable in the circumstances. These are subjective tests that will be assessed by the court (see *Esso Petroleum Co. Ltd v Southport Corporation*).[76]

13.8 **Remedies**

The remedies that may be awarded for successful claims of tortious conduct include damages and injunctions. The aim of damages is to place the injured party, as far as money can, in the position he/she was before the tort was committed (i.e. compensatory). Damages for personal injury suffered may incorporate any direct losses incurred such as loss of earnings, medical expenses, travel expenses (such as not being able to drive and having to make alternative travel arrangements) and so on. Further losses that may be compensatable include damages for pain and suffering, loss of amenity and so on. These damages are not subject to taxation. Where the tortious act involves no real loss to the claimant (such as in trespass to land where no loss or damage has occurred) the court may award nominal damages.

Where the injured party has died as a result of the tort the claim for damages is different from those above.[77] If the deceased had been financially supporting his/her family, then the dependants may claim for the lost earnings. The claim will also incorporate the funeral expenses. Further, the Fatal Accidents Act 1976 provides that spouses, and the parents of a deceased minor, may make a statutory claim of £11,800.[78]

In terms of damage to property, the damages awarded will be to compensate the claimant for loss, and this will involve the cost of restoration and may involve an element of compensation where a replacement of the goods/property was difficult to achieve. Awards of damages are subject to a requirement for the injured party to mitigate his/her losses where this is reasonable (even where the mitigation leads to an increase in the losses sustained).

Injunctions may be awarded at the discretion of the court and will involve a court order requiring the subject to stop committing the tort. There are a number of tools to provide injunctive relief, which will be awarded depending upon the requirement of the particular

---

[75] *Green v Bannister* [2003] EWCA Civ 1819.   76 [1955] AC 218, [1956] 2 WLR 81.

[77] See the Law Reform (Miscellaneous Provisions) Act 1934.

[78] Section 1A(3).

tortious act. A prohibitory injunction requires that the defendant ceases the action that is causing the tort; and a mandatory injunction requires the defendant to act to prevent the tort being committed. The claimant may also wish to obtain an interim injunction to prevent a tort being committed and any (further) damage being sustained until the case comes to court. The power of injunctions, as was outlined in the contract chapters, is that it is a court order, and failure to comply constitutes a contempt of court that may lead to a fine or imprisonment.

13.9 Nuisance

When a person unlawfully interferes with another's land, or the quiet enjoyment of the land, then the innocent party may have a claim under the tort of nuisance. In this respect, the claim is of private nuisance as it is concerned with private parties. The reason why this is important for businesses is because the nature of the offence is in creating a nuisance to those affected by it. By way of example, a business may have a manufacturing plant that produces rubber tyres. The business is not unlawful, the activity of producing rubber tyres is not unlawful, but if it makes unreasonable noise, smoke, vibrations and so on, then these may be considered unlawful as they could affect another's use of his/her land. In order to bring a successful claim of nuisance the following features must be present:

- The interference affects the enjoyment of land/premises. This action may be brought by a person with an equitable interest in it; a tenant;[79] or a person with exclusive possession of land but with no title to it.[80]

- There must be an element of damage associated with the nuisance. The term 'damage' in this area of law is not restricted to physical loss or damage, but can amount to the claimant losing his/her enjoyment of the premises.[81] The law has to balance competing interests when dealing with claims of nuisance, the right for the owner/occupier of land to quiet enjoyment of the property, and the business that has to make some noise/disruption in the processing of the product. The courts will attempt to strike this balance by looking at the unreasonableness of the defendant's behaviour, taking into account such factors as the position of the premises that is causing the nuisance, when it is being conducted, for what duration the nuisance is caused, and what steps have been taken to minimize the disruption. For this reason, many such businesses have located themselves in industrial estates where their activities are unlikely to cause a nuisance in the same way that they would do in a residential area or in the centre of a busy city.

- It must be noted that the motives of the defendant are often relevant considerations in assessing nuisance, and as such, where the defendant has deliberately acted to cause a disturbance, the court will be more likely to hold this action as a nuisance.[82]

- The court will look towards the reasonable foreseeability of the defendant's action in determining whether a nuisance has been committed. In *Cambridge Water Co. v Eastern Counties Leather*[83] the House of Lords held that exercising all reasonable care not to cause a nuisance may not, of itself, remove liability from the defendant. However, they

---

[79] *Hunter v Canary Wharf* [1997] AC 655.

[80] *Foster v Warblington UDC* [1906] 1 KB 648. [81] *Leeman v Montagu* [1936] 2 All ER 1677.

[82] *Christie v Davey* [1893] 1 Ch 316. [83] [1994] 2 AC 264.

continued that defendants would only be liable for damage that could have been reasonably foreseen.

- Unusually sensitive (hypersensitive) claimants will not generally succeed in an action for nuisance where another person would not have been adversely affected.

> **? Thinking Point**
>
> How does the doctrine of nuisance, and the sensitivity of the claimant, reconcile with the egg-shell rule in liability in negligence and for psychiatric injury? What justifications can you make for the differences in approach between nuisance and negligence in this respect?

13.9.1 Defences to a nuisance claim

Defences exist where: a claimant has alleged a nuisance and the defendant can point to a statutory authority, the consent of the claimant, or where the act has continued for over 20 years.

13.9.1.1 *Statutory authority*

Where a statute authorizes an act that is then subject to a claim of nuisance, the courts will assess whether the claim of nuisance is able to proceed. However, simply because a statute gives a right to perform some action, does not remove potential liability of the defendant. In *Allen v Gulf Oil Refining Ltd*[84] a statute was passed to build an oil refinery on land to ensure a supply of oil was available, and this was in the public interest. In the building of the refinery, and its operation, local residents complained of the noise and smell of the activities. The House of Lords held that no nuisance had been caused as the statute required that the oil refinery be built and operated, rather then merely giving the right for the erection and operation of such a venture. However, in *Barr v Biffa Waste Services*[85] the Court of Appeal held that merely because the defendants were carrying out activities in a manner consistent with the terms of their licence did not, of itself, provide a complete defence. The Court held that there was no principle of law that meant compliance with a statutory scheme curtailed common law rights to seek damages.

13.9.1.2 *Consent*

If a party consents to a nuisance, then he/she is unlikely to succeed in an action. This is a complete defence if the defendant can establish that the injured party had accepted the danger of the noise, smell, vibration, or other nuisance, having been aware of its existence. This is a grey area, as merely occupying land in the knowledge of a nuisance will not establish an effective defence of consent. It is the willingness to accept the possibility of the nuisance that is the key element.

---

[84] [1981] AC 1001.   85 [2012] EWCA (Civ) 312.

13.9.1.3 *Prescription*

Here, a defence is available where the nuisance has been committed for over 20 years without complaint. It is important that the nuisance has been committed for 20 years, rather than simply the carrying out of that activity for the period of time.[86]

13.9.2 **Remedies in nuisance**

The main remedies provided in claims of nuisance are a damages action, and an injunction to prevent the nuisance being committed in the future.

13.9.2.1 *Damages*

The claim in nuisance, as opposed to negligence where damage/loss has been sustained, may not have actually caused any physical loss. As such, the claim is generally concerned with the loss of the enjoyment of the land that the claimant has suffered, or in terms of any devaluation of the land. That is not to say that there will be no claim for physical loss, and indeed in *Cambridge Water Co. v Eastern Counties Leather*, the defendant had used solvents that had spilled onto the floor, seeped through the ground, and contaminated the claimant's water in a borehole. Therefore, as long as the damage is of a type recognized in law, and it was foreseeable, then damages may be awarded for losses suffered.

13.9.2.2 *Injunctions*

These are a particularly effective mechanism to prevent the defendant from continuing the nuisance. Injunctions are equitable remedies, used at the discretion of the courts, and in cases of nuisance, may be used in addition to, or instead of, a damages award. When an injunction is granted, it is usually suspended to provide the defendant with an opportunity to refrain from further acts of nuisance.

13.9.2.3 *Abatement*

This is an (exceptional) remedy enabling the injured party to take action to stop the nuisance. It is allowed where to initiate a legal action may be inappropriate, or where immediate action is required. This is commonly seen where an owner of land lops the trees on a neighbour's property. As long as the injured party does not have to go onto the neighbour's land, and he/she, in this example, cut only the trees interfering with his/her land, and returns the trees that have been cut, then this will be an acceptable remedy.

 Conclusion

The chapter has considered the torts of negligence and nuisance. Claims of negligence involve the three tests of duty of care; breach of that duty; and consequential damage. Having established these, the courts will then consider the level of damages to be awarded, having taken into account any defences asserted, and the vulnerability of the victim. Nuisance protects the claimant from unlawful interference with his/her property and is a significant factor for

---

[86] *Sturges v Bridgman* [1879] 11 ChD 852.

businesses running manufacturing/industrial processes. The next chapter discusses equally relevant and important torts to businesses (that can involve very significant claims),[87] including liability for economic loss in negligence; negligent misstatements; and the liability for psychiatric losses.

 ## Summary of main points

Tortious liability

- Liability is imposed through the civil law and requires, in certain circumstances, the party to take reasonable care not to negligently or intentionally cause harm.

- Many torts involve establishing 'fault' liability (blame) in order for a claim to proceed. Exceptions to this general rule include vicarious liability and claims under the Consumer Protection Act 1987.

- The Limitation Act 1980 outlines the time limits within which actions must be initiated. Generally, tort actions must be brought within six years of the date giving rise to the action and personal injury claims must be made within three years. The time limits do not begin until a minor reaches the age of majority (18), and further protection is given to those suffering mental disorders.

Negligence

- Negligence involves a breach of a duty to take care, owed in law by the defendant to the claimant, causing the claimant damage.

- The three elements to substantiate a claim consist of a duty of care; breach of that duty; and consequential damage.

- Where a duty of care has previously been held to exist, the threefold test from *Caparo* is unnecessary. In other circumstances, the three sub-tests establishing a duty include: proximity of relationship between the parties; foreseeability of loss; and whether it is fair, just, and reasonable to impose the duty.

- A breach of duty involves falling below the 'reasonable man' standard and exposing the claimant to unreasonable risk of harm.

- The third element in establishing negligence is assessing the consequential damage suffered by the claimant.

- There must exist a causal link between the injury suffered and the breach of duty.

- The damage suffered must be one that is recognized by law.

- Not all claimants have to demonstrate loss/damage. Claims under trespass, for example, will often involve the award of nominal damages as no 'real' loss has been sustained.

---

[87] Such as *ADT v Binder Hamlyn* [1996] BCC 808, where ADT claimed damages arising from their acquisition of Britannia Securities Group Plc on the basis of the negligent audit prepared by Binder Hamlyn. The High Court agreed and the sum awarded was £65 million; an even larger claim arose in *NRG v Ernst and Young* [1995] 2 Lloyd's Rep 404 where, whilst the claim for negligence ultimately failed, the damages action was for £400 million.

- To assess causation of damage, the courts will use the 'but for' test—if the damage would not have occurred but for the actions of the defendant, then his/her action is the cause of the damage.
- Not every consequence of a defendant's wrongful action will lead to liability. Intervening acts may remove responsibility if the damage is too remote.
- The 'eggshell skull' rule provides that the defendant must take the claimant as he/she finds them. Hence if the claimant had a pre-existing condition exacerbated by the defendant's actions, the defendant cannot escape liability by asserting that another person so affected would not have experienced the same level of damage.

Defences

- The most common defences to tort actions are illegality; consent; contributory negligence; and necessity.
- Illegality may prevent a claim of negligence where the claimant suffered loss or damage during the course of performing an illegal act.
- Consent provides a complete defence where the injured party has consented to a risk, either expressly or through implication.
- Contributory negligence is a partial defence where the claimant who has been partially at fault for his/her injury (with the defendant being partly at fault) will have any award of damages reduced according to his/her level of responsibility.
- Necessity may provide a defence where the tortfeasor acted to prevent a greater harm, insofar as there was imminent danger and his/her actions were reasonable in the circumstances.

Remedies

- Remedies include damages and injunctions.
- Damages awarded for personal injury include compensation for direct and indirect losses. The aim is to place the injury party in the position he/she was before the tort had been committed (insofar as money can).
- Injunctions are used to prevent the commission of a tort (available at the discretion of the courts). Injunctions are issued on the basis of the particular tort and the injunction may be prohibitory; mandatory; or interim.

Nuisance

- Private nuisance involves unlawful interference with another person's enjoyment of his/her land/property.
- The claimant must have suffered some form of loss/damage due to the nuisance.
- Where the defendant intended to cause the disturbance, the courts will be more inclined to hold that action as nuisance.
- It must have been reasonably foreseeable that loss/damage would have been the result of the defendant's action to enable a damages claim.
- There are several defences to a nuisance action including statutory authority, consent, and prescription.
- The remedies available are damages, injunction, and abatement.

Summary questions

Essay questions

1. Cases such as *Bolton v Stone* and *Miller v Jackson* provide examples of the different approaches taken by the judiciary in relation to determining whether a defendant has breached his/her duty to take reasonable care. Describe the tests used to establish the negligence of a defendant and explain how the law has developed to make the exercise of these tests more relevant in the modern era.

2. Critically assess the defences available to a claim of nuisance. Do you feel they are fair or at least adequate and what suggestions could you make for improvements? Justify your answer through a critique of the case law.

Problem questions

1. All Bright Consumables (ABC) Ltd has recently diversified its business into supplying and fitting quality kitchens and bathrooms. Part of this business involves the company manufacturing its own tiles and furniture to offer the full bespoke service that it believes customers want. Dora is employed by ABC Ltd as a wood machinist operating a bench mounted circular saw. Today, while operating the circular saw Dora caught her right (dominant) hand in the saw's blade, severed 4 fingers and sliced the top off her thumb. On the day in question, she had worked a 12-hour shift and for the last six hours of her shift, her supervisor, Abe, asked her to lend her push stick (which she had been told she should use for feeding small pieces of wood into the machine) to a colleague. At the time of the accident, she was working on an urgent job which had to be completed that day for fitting by ABC's bathroom firm the next. Dora admitted that while working she had been distracted and had been chatting animatedly to another colleague.

   Consider the negligence liability (if any) of ABC Ltd.

2. Alan is employed by Tasty Butchers (TB) Ltd to deliver meat to various retailers. Alan is expressly told not to race or drive dangerously in his company vehicle. However, today Alan ignores this instruction and decides to race against the driver of their rival company, Crusty Butchers Ltd, when the two drivers meet each other at traffic lights.

   During the race Alan damages the car of Delia which further causes the sealed door on the refrigeration unit of his company vehicle to be broken and the meat begins to thaw. At the end of the day Alan returns to TB Ltd's base and is told about cases of sickness being reported by customers at the shops he has delivered meat to. The view is that the meat has gone bad and caused food poisoning.

   The manager of TB Ltd has also seen the damage to the company vehicle and been contacted by Delia who blames Alan for causing damage to her car.

   Outline the potential liability of the parties in the above situation.

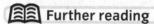 **Further reading**

Moran, M. (2003) 'Rethinking the Reasonable Person: An Egalitarian Reconstruction of the Objective Standard' Oxford University Press: Oxford, New York.

Morgan, J. (2006) 'The Rise and Fall of the General Duty of Care' *Professional Negligence*, Vol. 22, No. 4, p. 206.

Neyers, J. W., Chamberlain, E., Stephen G. A., and Pitel, S. G. A. (Eds.) (2007) 'Emerging Issues in Tort Law' Hart Publishing: Oxford.

Patten, K. (2006) 'Limitation Periods in Personal Injury Claims—Justice Obstructed?' *Civil Justice Quarterly*, Vol. 25, July, p. 349.

 Online Resource Centre

http://www.oxfordtextbooks.co.uk/orc/marson3e/

Why not visit the Online Resource Centre and try multiple choice questions associated with this chapter to test your understanding of the topic. You will also find relevant updates to the law.

14

Economic Loss, the Liability of Professional Advisors, and Psychiatric Injury

Why does it matter?

Loss may have been incurred due to a negligent act, but where this is in the absence of physical damage (merely economic loss), recovery of the loss from the tortfeasor has been restricted. Such instances can include the negligent statements made by professionals. As businesses may be involved in providing professional advice (lawyers, accountants and so on) this is particularly relevant. Further, there has been an increase recently of imposing liability on employers for the stress and associated health problems suffered by their employees. One or all of these matters may affect a business and it is important to identify where responsibility and potential liability exist.

Learning outcomes

Following reading this chapter you should be in a position to:

- identify how liability for pure economic loss is established (14.2)
- explain the nature of liability for negligent misstatements and how such liability may be restricted (14.3)
- explain the difference between 'primary' and 'secondary' victims in claims of psychiatric damage and negligence (14.4–14.4.2)

⚷ Key terms

These terms will be used in the chapter and it may be helpful to be aware of what they mean or refer back to them when reading through the chapter.

Pure economic loss
This is where the claimant's losses are not connected with any physical loss or damage. This is typically in the case of negligent advice or information provided to the claimant.

Primary victim
A person who was not physically injured in an incident, but was in the zone of physical danger. Typically, this has been related to a claimant's fear for his/her personal safety that caused some psychiatric injury.

> **Secondary victim**
> A person who was not injured physically in an incident or in fear of his/her own safety, but was closely related to a victim that caused him/her psychiatric injury.

14.1 Introduction

This chapter continues on from the discussion of liability in negligence for physical damage to consider the potential liability businesses and individuals may have when they provide advice in the nature of their business; when they cause economic losses not associated with physical damage; and where the claimant suffers a psychiatric injury/nervous shock due to the acts of the tortfeasor. Restrictions are placed on the imposition of liability for **pure economic loss**, although such loss has been widened to include damages for negligent misstatements. It is of crucial importance that businesses are aware of the implications of providing information in the course of their professional activities that may cause an investor/client loss through negligence.

14.2 Pure economic loss

Chapter 13 identified liability in negligence, and how this was linked with some form of physical loss or damage. In part, this limits the possibility of 'opening the floodgates'[1] to many claimants. In cases of psychiatric injury, for instance, the courts have produced rules that restrict the possibility of many claims, particularly to those identified as '**secondary**' victims.

Turning to liability where the claimant has 'only' suffered economic loss (as opposed to situations where it is linked to physical damage such as loss of income following a car accident) the recovery in damages of such losses is very limited. Clearly, if the economic losses have been sustained due to a negligent act and the parties had entered into a contract, then damages are recoverable. However, the parties have to agree to be bound by the terms of a contract and tortious liability is established on the basis of a civil wrong, often in the absence of any contractual agreement. This is not to say that pure economic loss is not important, but it is rather difficult for the courts to identify where the liability in such instances will extend, or be limited. This can be seen in the following case:

Weller v Foot and Mouth Research Institute[2]

Facts:

The defendants negligently allowed the foot and mouth virus to escape from their research laboratory and the consequences were that cattle had to be destroyed and restrictions were imposed on the transport and trade of the cattle in the affected area. The claimant was an auctioneer who had lost profits in sales due to the restriction, and brought an action

---

[1] The floodgates argument does not refer to unlimited claims, but rather it would, as provided by Cardozo J in *Ultramares v Touche* [1931] 174 NE 441, expose defendants to a potential liability 'in an indeterminate amount for an indeterminate time to an indeterminate class'.

[2] [1966] 1 QB 569.

to recover the losses due to this negligent act. It was held that as this was a case of pure economic loss, the claim must fail.

Authority for:

Actions for losses attributed to pure economic loss are not compensatable as they are not linked with economic losses associated with physical damage/loss (for example lost wages (economic loss) following a car accident (physical damage)).

The sense of the judgment may be seen in a wider discussion of the issue of liability, and the rights to limit or restrict liability. For example, this claim was by an auctioneer whose trade was affected due to the outbreak. However, what about local butchers in the area that may have lost sales due to the limit in supplies of beef? Would consumers have a claim if the outbreak had limited the supply of this meat and they were 'forced' to purchase some other meat product? Clearly there had to be a limit to claims in this respect, unless an aspect of physical damage was involved. In *Spartan Steel v Martin & Co. Contractors Ltd*[3] contractors who were digging in a public road had negligently cut an electricity cable and the claimant's factory lost power, damaging some furnaces that had molten steel in them, which cooled and hardened due to the loss of power. It was held that the claimant could recover for the damage to these furnaces and the loss of the molten metal, but were prevented from successfully claiming for losses to further work that it was unable to carry out due to this power-cut, as this was pure economic loss.

The general rule preventing claims based on pure economic loss is subject to exceptions. This is particularly so where a special relationship exists between the parties that elevates the defendant's responsibility to the claimant. Such a situation was demonstrated in *Ross v Cauters*,[4] where a firm of solicitors had sent a will to their client to be signed and witnessed, but they failed to inform the client that the witness should not be a beneficiary or spouse. The will was returned, and not checked by the solicitors, and when the testator died, it was discovered that one of the witnesses was the spouse of a beneficiary and hence could not claim under the will. A damages action was brought against the solicitors and it was held that the claimant could succeed. A special relationship was established and it was reasonably foreseeable that a beneficiary could be affected by their negligence.

In *Commissioners of Customs and Excise v Barclays Bank Plc*[5] the House of Lords had to consider the liability of the bank that had been instructed, through a court-ordered injunction, to freeze accounts of two companies that owed significant sums of money to Her Majesty's Revenue and Customs (HMRC). The aim of the injunctions was to prevent access to the money that, it was argued to the court, would be taken out of the country and thus make it very difficult/impossible for HMRC to recover. The bank, following the injunction, sent a letter stating it would abide by the order, but negligently allowed withdrawals (within hours of the injunction being served) to remove large quantities of money from the accounts, and this money was not recoverable by HMRC. As such, the claim was brought against the bank for the loss. It was held that no liability was established. Barclays had no choice as to whether it would be involved in the injunction that froze the accounts in question. Liability for pure economic loss will only be recoverable where: the person has a responsibility, or has assumed a responsibility for his/her statement to the claimant; a duty of care can be demonstrated to exist between the parties; and the tests as established in *Caparo v Dickman* are satisfied.[6]

---

[3] [1973] 1 QB 27.   [4] [1980] Ch 297.   [5] [2006] UKHL 28.   [6] See **13.6.1**.

Losses can be suffered in cases where business professionals make statements that a person relies on, but the statement turns out to have been negligently made, and this leads to pure economic loss. Can claims be made for such negligent misstatements?

14.3 Negligent misstatements

In some cases businesses provide expert advice that clients and others rely on when investing money, making financial/investment decisions and so on, and when these have been negligently made, the recipient may suffer losses. For example, advice may be provided on where to invest money, which shares to buy, whether credit should be advanced to a firm and so on. Claims on the basis of a statement having been negligently made, prior to case law in 1964, had to be made in the tort of deceit and required that the defendant had acted dishonestly, rather than just negligently. This position was changed in *Hedley Byrne & Co. v Heller.*[7] Hedley Byrne was an advertising company and its bankers approached the bank of Heller regarding the financial stability and credit history of one of Heller's clients, a third party, Easipower Ltd. Hedley Byrne required this information as it intended to enter into contracts with the third party and wanted to ensure the company was creditworthy. Heller provided a reference as to the third party's creditworthiness, but further added that the information was intended for private use and did not impose any liability or responsibility on the provider of the reference. However, despite the reference in favour of the third party, the truth was that the firm was not of sound financial standing, and following the advance of credit, the claimants lost several thousands of pounds and brought the claim against the bank that had provided the negligent misstatement.

The House of Lords held that this case involved a 'special relationship of proximity' (beyond the 'standard' level of proximity established in *Donoghue v Stevenson*)[8] between the parties and this would enable a claim (in theory). The problem (for the claimant) in this particular case was of the bank's exclusion clause, disclaiming responsibility for any losses due to the statement, which prevented the damages action succeeding (although the point of law regarding the possibility of claims remained). However, such a disclaimer if used today would have to satisfy the requirements of the Unfair Contract Terms Act 1977 as being reasonable.[9] So a business may not always be able to evade liability by the inclusion of a disclaimer.

A further, very important case demonstrating where liability may or may not be imposed was in *Caparo Industries Plc. v Dickman and Others.*[10] The case was raised in Chapter 13 (13.6.1) but to briefly recap, the claimants owned shares in a company and relied on accounts prepared by the defendants to purchase more. The accounts were negligently prepared. However, the accounts were prepared as a requirement under the Companies Act 1985 and not on the basis of providing financial advice for any third party, including shareholders. The House of Lords determined that no duty of care existed between the claimant and the defendant. To hold the auditors liable would be to have enabled too many claimants possible recourse to claims for negligence for publicly produced documents. Lord Oliver remarked on the issue:

The opportunities for the infliction of pecuniary loss from the imperfect performance of everyday tasks upon the proper performance of which people rely for regulating their affairs

---

[7] [1963] 2 All ER 575.   [8] [1932] AC 562.
[9] See *Smith v Eric Bush* [1989] 2 All ER 514.   [10] [1990] 2 WLR 358.

are illimitable and the effects are far reaching. A defective bottle of ginger beer may injure a single consumer but the damage stops there. A single statement may be repeated endlessly with or without the permission of its author and may be relied upon in a different way by many different people. Thus the postulate of a simple duty to avoid any harm that is, with hindsight, reasonably capable of being foreseen becomes untenable without the imposition of some intelligible limits to keep the law of negligence within the bounds of common sense and practicality.

The Lords would not impose liability on the auditors. They stated that a 'special relationship'[11] must exist between the parties and this was not evident in the case. Importantly in terms of liability for a negligent misstatement, the Lords established four factors that had to exist to determine when liability would be imposed. These were:[12]

1 the advice is required for a purpose which is made known, either actually or inferentially, to the adviser at the time when the advice is given;

2 the adviser knows that his advice will be communicated to the advisee, either specifically or as a member of an ascertainable class, in order that it should be used by the advisee for that purpose;

3 it is known that the advice so communicated is likely to be acted upon by the advisee for that purpose without independent inquiry; and

4 it is so acted upon by the advisee to his detriment.

Such an example of the application of this test was demonstrated a year later in the case of *James McNaughten v Hicks*[13] and demonstrated the necessity of the defendant being aware of the claimant's use of the information that was being provided. Here accountants were asked to prepare information and draft accounts to be used for the basis of negotiations in the take-over of the firm. The accounts had been negligently produced, and led to the claimant's suffering financial loss. It was held that no liability arose, as the defendants were not aware of the precise use of the information prepared by them. As these were draft accounts, it was fair to assume that further investigation would be made before a financial decision was taken. Therefore, the following points should be considered:

1 the purpose for which the statement is made;

2 the purpose for which the statement was communicated;

3 the relationship between the advisor, advisee, and any relevant third party;

4 the size of any class to which the advisee belongs;

5 the state of knowledge of the adviser;

6 reliance by the advisee.

This case may be compared to *Yorkshire Enterprise Ltd v Robson Rhodes*,[14] where the claimants had invested significant sums of money into a company that soon went into liquidation and they had made the investment following accounts and correspondence between the

---

[11] Per Lord Oliver: '(a) special relationship of proximity ... is required to give rise to the duty of care and which does not exist between the auditors and the investing public generally'.

[12] There has been significant discussion through the judiciary as to the appropriate tests to be used to establish the special relationship that would create the liability for pure economic loss. See Barker, K. (2006) 'Wielding Occam's Razor: Pruning Strategies for Economic Loss' *Oxford Journal of Legal Studies*, Vol. 26, No. 2, p. 289.

[13] [1991] 1 All ER 134.   [14] [1998] Unreported.

claimants and the negligent accountants. It was held that liability would be imposed as the accountants were aware of why the claimants wanted the information, and what they had intended to do with this information. Further, to impose liability in these circumstances was considered reasonable. Therefore when considering whether liability will be imposed in cases of negligent misstatement, the following points should also be considered:

1 There must have been negligence when the statement was made.

2 The statement must be given by an expert acting in the course of his/her expertise.

3 There must be a duty of care owed to the person who acts on the statement—an assumption of responsibility.

4 There must be reliance on the statement by the persons to whom it was addressed.

5 There must be foreseeable loss arising out of the reliance.

6 Following *Caparo*, it must be fair, just, and equitable to impose the duty.

Note, however, that the Lords stated in *Commissioners for Customs and Excise v Barclays Bank Plc* that the tests established in the cases above were correct and had led to justice being served, but they are specific to the cases to which they relate, and sweeping statements regarding the application of tests are not possible. The cases have to be considered on their facts.

14.4 **Non-physical (psychiatric) damage**

 Business Link

An element of negligence that may affect businesses is where physical injury has not occurred to a claimant, but rather there is an element of psychiatric damage. Recently, this issue has become important to businesses where an employee suffers from stress at work, and the employer takes no action to remedy the situation. Given high pressure targets people often work under, not only will stress-related illness cost the employer in terms of sick leave and lack of productivity, it may now also lead to tortuous liability. The following cases demonstrate where liability may be imposed, and hence identify how businesses may seek to minimize the risk of such claims.

There are increasing situations where liability is imposed for non-physical injuries, such as employees being placed under stresses at work, or where rescuers (such as those employed in the emergency services) suffer through the traumatic nature of their job. Whilst injuries suffered in such situations may not involve physical damage, their effects are no less serious, no less debilitating, and no less important to the imposition of liability. Despite the wider issue of psychiatric injury, employers/managers in particular need to be aware of their responsibilities and be proactive in reducing the possibility of injury resulting from exposure to unreasonable stress.

Whilst in an employment relationship it is incumbent on an employer (at common law and through legislative measures) to protect an employee's health and safety;[15] negligence in this

---

[15] See **20.4**.

respect may also lead to a damages claim against the employer. As such, an employer's obligations transcend many jurisdictions of law and it is necessary to view the law in its entirety, rather than how it is artificially presented in textbooks. Claims for psychiatric injuries have increased for businesses with the increased stress and burdens placed on employees, and where it is reasonable for an employer to be aware of this, and they do not take positive and sufficient action to remedy the problem, they may be held liable. In *Intel Corp. (UK) v Daw*,[16] Mrs Daw suffered stress due to unreasonable workloads placed on her from several managers at the firm. She had raised her concerns to her employer over the workload and how it was adversely affecting her health, and she was found in tears by one of her line managers, but the employer failed to take immediate action. Daw became clinically depressed and this led to a breakdown. The original trial awarded her £134,000 for her injury and loss of earnings and the Court of Appeal agreed, deciding that an employer's offer of access to a short-term counselling service would not have reduced the risk of the employee's injury, and the employer failed in its duty to provide a safe system of work. A similar line of reasoning was used in *Barber v Somerset County Council*,[17] involving a teacher who had alleged suffering a stress-induced illness caused by an unreasonable workload. The teacher returned to work but the workload had not been reduced (albeit the employer stated this was due to the constraints of resources). The House of Lords held that the employer had not taken any steps to reduce his workload or provide him with support, and therefore it was reasonably foreseeable that the employee, already known as being vulnerable in this regard, would suffer some form of injury. This is one of the reasons why the Government introduced the 'family-friendly' employment policies—to assist in creating an acceptable work–life balance.[18]

It should be noted that employers are entitled to expect employees to withstand the 'normal pressures of the job',[19] but despite the difficulties in determining when pressure leads to stress, and stress to injury to health, there will be signs that enable a reasonable employer to identify these and take action. Indeed, the Advisory, Conciliation and Arbitration Service has produced a guide for employers on how to identify signs of depression in the workplace, along with a booklet on health and wellbeing that includes checklists and policies to avoid breaching their duty to protect the employees' health and safety.

There may also exist situations where persons are exposed to situations where they are not necessarily employees, but liability for psychiatric injury is imposed. *Bourhill v Young* has already been discussed in **13.6.1**. Mrs Bourhill's claim failed, *inter alia*, due to the lack of proximity between the claimant and defendant, but raised the interesting element of whether to hold a defendant liable in cases of psychiatric harm. Negligence so far has dealt with some form of physical damage or injury and the application of rules to determine whether liability should be imposed. When the harm involves what is referred to as 'nervous shock',[20] the claimant must demonstrate that the type of harm he/she sustained was reasonably foreseeable. This is particularly so in light of the judges' comments in *Bourhill* that the person must exhibit 'phlegm and fortitude' in the event of witnessing acts that may be upsetting. As in *Bourhill* where the pregnant fishwife had witnessed the aftermath of an accident, this did not place her in direct and immediate danger. Those persons who have experienced injury, even psychiatric injury, from having been placed in fear of personal danger are referred to as **'primary victims'**. The other type of claimant who suffers psychiatric injury after witnessing

---

[16] [2007] EWCA Civ 70.　　[17] [2004] UKHL 13.　　[18] See **19.19.5**.

[19] *Sutherland v Hatton* [2002] ICR 613.

[20] Although Ward J stated that 'nervous shock' was an outdated and inaccurate notion (*Ravenscroft v Rederi AB Transatlantic* [1991] 3 All ER 73).

an event involving injury to others comes under the heading 'secondary victims'.[21] It should be noted that the expression 'nervous shock' is important in identifying that the claims in this matter relate to sudden events which are distressing, rather than a protracted event or series of events (such as seeing a relative die slowly from a disease) which, whilst equally distressing, do not, generally, amount to a claim under this area of law.

The law determines a claimant, having suffered a psychiatric injury, as a primary or secondary victim. This is a somewhat harsh distinction and has led to claims that the word 'secondary' implies 'less deserving', and may imply that physical injury is 'superior or morally entitled to compensation (rather) than (claims for) psychiatric illness'.[22] A case that demonstrates potential problems in determining whether a claimant is to be considered a primary or secondary victim was seen in *Macfarlane v EE Caledonia Ltd*.[23] The claimant was an oilrig painter in the North Sea and was in a support vessel some 550 metres from the Piper Alpha oilrig when it exploded. Due to the traumatic scenes (including having fire balls come within 100 metres of the vessel), and being aware of Macfarlane's friends being on the oilrig, he developed a psychiatric injury for which the first court awarded him damages. The Court of Appeal, however, rejected his claim as a rescuer as his activities in this regard were insufficient (moving blankets and helping the walking wounded), and further there was a lack of proximity between the defendant and Macfarlane. It was not reasonably foreseeable that he would suffer psychiatric harm or that a person of reasonable fortitude would have been affected as Macfarlane was. Therefore, Macfarlane was not considered a primary victim, and there was insufficient 'close relationship of love and affection between the plaintiff (the old term for a claimant) and victim'[24] to establish him as a secondary victim.

14.4.1 Primary victims

These are claimants who assert they have suffered some form of psychiatric injury as a result of being in the zone of physical danger of fearing for their own safety. This is tested on the basis of the reasonable forseeability of the defendant's actions, as can be seen in *Dulieu v White and Sons*,[25] where the spouse of a publican suffered from severe shock and distress when a horse-drawn carriage crashed into the public house where she was working at the time. The wife had not suffered physical injury, but the court found there to be sufficient evidence for her to reasonably believe that she may be injured and this enabled the claim to be successful. More recently, the House of Lords considered the issue of foreseeability in *Page v Smith*.[26] The claimant had been involved in an accident with a car driven by the defendant, but whilst not suffering any physical injury, a pre-existing condition of ME (myalgic encephalomyelitis) was worsened. A claim for damages was made and it was held that it was still necessary to distinguish between primary and secondary victims in actions involving psychiatric injury, but where the claimant is a primary victim and it can be demonstrated that the defendant owed to them a duty of care not to cause physical injury, then it is sufficient to ask whether the defendant should have reasonably foreseen that the claimant may suffer personal injury as a result of the defendant's negligence. It is unnecessary to question whether the defendant should have foreseen the injury by shock.

---

[21] Hilson, C. (2002) 'Liability for Psychiatric Injury: Primary and Secondary Victims Revisited' *Professional Negligence*, Vol. 18, No. 3, p. 167 reviews the case law surrounding the categorization of the type of victim, and the courts' identification of these.

[22] Jones, M. (1995) 'Liability for Psychiatric Illness—More Principle, Less Subtlety?' 4 *Web JCLI*.

[23] [1994] 2 All ER 1.   [24] Per Stuart-Smith LJ.   [25] [1901] 2 KB 669.

[26] [1995] 2 WLR 644.

14.4.2 Secondary victims

Secondary victims have a more difficult task in proving that they have the right to damages. Reasonable forseeability is again the test to be invoked, but this is on the basis of the proximity of relationship. There must exist some direct relationship between the injured party and the claimant that would enable a claim (as no physical injury has been sustained, and the claimant was not in fear of his/her own safety). Such a close relationship may exist between siblings, or between spouses. In *Hinz v Berry*[27] a woman who observed her husband being severely injured, leading to his death, and 7 of their children injured in a car accident was entitled to recover damages for nervous shock (£4,000). However, the Court of Appeal held that no damages could be properly awarded for the grief and sorrow caused by a person's death or the subsequent worries for the remaining family. Two cases that demonstrate how the courts may infer liability in respect of proximity were decided as a result of the football disaster at Sheffield Wednesday F.C.'s ground, Hillsborough, in 1989 where 96 people lost their lives.[28]

Alcock v Chief Constable of South Yorkshire[29]

Facts:

The case arose at the FA Cup semi-final match between Liverpool and Nottingham Forest held at Hillsborough in April 1989. The facts involved a policing error where too many of the Liverpool supporters were ushered into an enclosure that was incapable of holding so many fans. Some of the fans were late, and the match had already started, and there was a consequent surge of the fans to gain entry to view the match. The match was played when there existed metal barrier fencing around the perimeter of the fans' standing areas, and there was no seating in the area to restrict numbers. Due to the volume of fans directed into the enclosure, many at the front were crushed against the fencing and unable to escape. When the extent of the disaster was recognized and assistance was provided, 95[30] people were dead, and more than 400 more required attention at hospital.

The negligence action was initiated by those affected by the disaster including friends and relations of the 95 dead. These people had suffered psychiatric injury, rather than physical injury, and claimed under nervous shock. Most of the claimants in the action claimed to be 'secondary victims' who had witnessed the disaster at the football ground, on televisions, and on the radio. The House of Lords held that none of the claimants satisfied the requirements to hold the police liable in negligence.

Authority for:

The House of Lords identified the following tests to establish liability as a secondary victim:

1 There must exist close proximity between the claimant and the person suffering harm (such as close tie of love and affection and so on).

---

[27] [1970] 2 WLR 684.

[28] See Griffiths, N. (2004) 'Shock Induced Psychiatric Injury: Damage Limitation' *Personal Injury Law Journal*, No. 24, April, p. 18 for a review of the development of the law in psychiatric injury claims, particularly following the Hillsborough disaster.

[29] [1991] 3 All ER 88.   [30] The final death count was 96 persons.

> **2** The claimant must have been present at the scene of the accident or there in the immediate aftermath.
>
> **3** The claimant must have perceived directly the events of the accident or the immediate aftermath.

The case demonstrated the rules that courts must adopt when claimants bring an action for negligence as secondary victims.[31] Further, it demonstrates the problems and practical difficulties in establishing a successful claim where the claimant has not suffered any direct harm, or fear of harm, personally. The claim failed despite the claimants including brothers and sisters of the people who had died,[32] and a sister who had to identify the body of her dead brother (being eight hours after the event was not considered by the Lords to be in the 'immediate aftermath').[33] The decision has been criticized as being too harsh and being founded on the 'floodgates' argument. This line of legal reasoning was continued in the case of *White v Chief Constable of South Yorkshire*[34] where four police officers, who were present at the disaster and had provided assistance, including resuscitation and carrying the dead and dying over the fences, also claimed for their psychiatric injuries as primary victims. The House of Lords determined, reversing the decision of the Court of Appeal, that the police officers could not claim for their injuries. Even though they were in direct contact with the injured people, the Lords stated that only those who were physically injured or in danger of being physically injured could bring a claim, and if not the secondary victims had to establish their claim under the rules laid down in *Alcock*. It was held that rescuers, professional or not, and employees, who had witnessed such distressing events had no claim as primary or secondary victims unless they satisfied the tests above.[35]

? Thinking Point

How far do you feel policy played a part in this decision? Given the House of Lords had refused the victims' relatives compensation, would providing a remedy for the police officers involved have been a step too far (particularly given the involvement and criticism of the police in the incident)? Should the courts take such matters into consideration when assessing liability?

The Court of Appeal has identified criteria necessary when attributing liability in cases of psychiatric injury. In *French v Chief Constable of Sussex*[36] the claimants were police officers

---

[31] However, compare the decision with the previous case law including *McLouglin v O'Brian* [1983] 1 AC 410.

[32] For an interesting examination of the effect of psychiatric damages through injury to family members see Case, P. (2004) 'Secondary Iatrogenic Harm: Claims for Psychiatric Damage Following a Death Caused by Medical Error' *Modern Law Review*, Vol. 67, No. 4, p. 561.

[33] See Tomkins, N (2006) 'Psychiatric Injury—Extra Routes to Recovery?' *Journal of Personal Injury Law*, No. 3, p. 251.

[34] [1998] QB 254.

[35] See Allen, S. (1997) 'Rescuers and Employees–Primary Victims of Nervous Shock' *New Law Journal*, No. 6778, p. 158 for an assessment of previous cases surrounding police officers claiming for their psychiatric injuries following Hillsborough.

[36] [2006] EWCA Civ 312.

who had been involved in events leading up to an armed robbery that resulted in a fatal shooting, although none of the claimants had witnessed the event. In assessing the employer's liability, Lord Phillips CJ, summarized the main criteria in establishing liability (summarizing the duties set out in *Rothwell v Chemical & Insulating Co. Ltd*):[37]

1 There exists a duty to exercise reasonable care not to cause psychiatric injury or to place the claimant in fear for his/her physical safety.[38]

2 The defendant that breaches the duty not to endanger the physical safety of the claimant will be liable if the breach causes not physical but psychiatric injury, even if it was not reasonably foreseeable that psychiatric injury alone might result.[39]

3 There is no general duty to exercise reasonable care not to cause psychiatric injury as a result of causing death or injury of someone (the primary victim) which is witnessed by the claimant (the secondary victim).[40]

4 Point '3' applies equally where the claimant is employed by the defendant.[41]

5 As an exception to point '3' there is a duty not to cause psychiatric injury to the claimant as a result of causing the death or injury of someone loved by the claimant in circumstances where the claimant sees or hears the accident or its aftermath.[42]

The previous case law had dealt with the common law right to seek damages. The Supreme Court has made it possible for claimants, who would not otherwise be able to seek damages under the common law, as not being a (secondary) victim, to obtain damages. In *Rabone v Pennine Care NHS Foundation Trust*[43] the parents of a young woman who committed suicide following a hospital Trust's breach of its duty of care towards her obtained damages for their anguish. It was held that the Trust breached Article 2 of the European Convention on Human Rights and s. 7(1) of the Human Rights Act 1998 and, following the case law established by the European Court of Human Rights,[44] the family members of the deceased were entitled to bring a claim in their own right. The parents were awarded £5,000 each.

 Conclusion

This chapter has identified where liability may be imposed for pure economic loss (in the absence of associated physical injury). The wider implications of liability for businesses and individuals where they provide advice or information in their professional capacity and situations where the claimant has sustained psychiatric injury have also been addressed. Businesses have to appreciate where risk exists and be proactive in establishing mechanisms that limit/restrict resultant damage or loss. The use of exclusion clauses or paying 'lip service' to complaints of stress from employees will not remove liability in these areas—effective mechanisms need to be in place. The text continues by considering employers' potential liability for torts committed by their employees and for breaches of statutory duties.

---

[37] [2006] EWCA Civ 27.   [38] *Delieu v White* [1901].   [39] *Page v Smith* [1996] 1 AC 155.
[40] *Alcock v Chief Constable of Yorkshire Police* [1992].
[41] *Frost v Chief Constable of South Yorkshire* [1997] 1 All ER 1036.
[42] *McLoughlin v O'Brian* [1983] 1 AC 410.
[43] [2012] UKSC 2.
[44] *Kats v Ukraine* (2010) 51 EHRR 44, at para 94.

Summary of main points

Pure economic loss

- Liability in cases of pure economic loss is restricted by the courts.
- Where economic loss is linked to physical damage/loss then the economic losses are recoverable.
- Actions will be allowed where a special relationship of proximity exists between the parties.

Negligent misstatements

- Liability requires a special relationship to exist between the parties. Liability is imposed where the person providing the information was aware of the purpose of his/her advice; it was provided specifically to the advisee; the person providing the information knew that the information would be acted upon without any further advice being sought; and acting on the advice was to the detriment of the advisee.

Psychiatric injury

- A person who is not physically injured by the defendant's negligence, but has experienced trauma due to the consequences of the action, may be able to claim for his/her psychiatric injury (sometimes referred to as nervous shock).
- Claims for psychiatric injury will define the claimant as either a 'primary' or 'secondary' victim.
- Primary victims are persons who were not physically injured by the defendant's actions, but they were in reasonable fear for their personal safety (being in the zone of physical danger).
- Secondary victims are persons who also were not physically injured, and who were not in fear for their own safety. However, where they have a close proximity with the victim of the accident and they were present at the scene or in the immediate aftermath, they may succeed in their action for damages.

 Summary questions

Essay questions

1. To what extent is a professional adviser liable in civil law for their misstatement and how does the law seek to regulate their activities and liabilities?
2. 'The case of *Alcock v Chief Constable of South Yorkshire* identified the rules to be satisfied before a successful claim as a secondary victim could be made. The judgment demonstrates the problems and practical difficulties in successfully establishing a claim where the claimant has not suffered any direct harm, or feared personal harm. As such, liability for psychiatric damage in such cases is rarely held and for all practical purposes should be abolished.'
   Critically analyse the above statement.

Problem questions

1. Kirk runs a firm of estate agents who provide a service of surveying and valuing properties, including domestic dwellings.

   Henry approaches Kirk and states that he would like a house valued at £500,000 to have a full survey before he decides whether to proceed with the purchase or not. Kirk accepts the contract and instructs an employee of his (Brian) to perform the survey. Brian visits the property, carries out the survey but is more interested in speaking with his friend on his mobile phone than performing his task diligently. Brian negligently performs the survey and misses very important defects in the property such as dry rot, and that the house is built on the tracks of a disused mine and may be subject to subsidence.

   Based on the favourable report produced by Brian, Henry purchases the property and later discovers these faults. The house, due to the defects, is actually only worth £300,000 and as a consequence Henry has lost a large amount of his investment.

   Advise Henry on any rights he may have to claim for the (potential) professional negligence of Kirk and the estate agencies.

2. Tom and Jerry are commuters. They regularly caught the same train together. In this way they had become friends socially. One Monday morning, Tom, a stockbroker, remarked to Jerry that British Bailout Ltd were an extremely attractive proposition on the stockmarket. Being a teacher, Jerry knew little about the state of the market, but expressed interest in the company's shares. Tom assured him that the investment would 'make money hand over fist'. As a result, Jerry invested £1,000 in the company, which has just gone into liquidation. Jerry has lost his investment.

   Explain the potential liability of Tom for Jerry's economic losses.

 Further reading

Barrett, B. (2008) 'Psychiatric Stress—An Unacceptable Cost to Employers' *Journal of Business Law*, 1, p. 64.

Mullender, R. (1999) 'Negligent Misstatement, Threats and the Scope of the Hedley Byrne Principle' *Modern Law Review*, Vol. 62, No. 3, May, p. 425.

@ Online Resource Centre

http://www.oxfordtextbooks.co.uk/orc/marson3e/
Why not visit the Online Resource Centre and try multiple choice questions associated with this chapter to test your understanding of the topic. You will also find relevant updates to the law.

Vicarious Liability and Statutory Duties

Why does it matter?

An employer will engage an individual to perform some function for his/her business and may give specific guidance as to how the tasks are to be completed. An employer, however, would be unlikely to engage the individual to commit a tort, but if this occurs in the course of employment, and he/she has the employment status of an employee, the employer may be jointly liable with the tortfeasor. This is referred to as the vicarious liability of an employer. The chapter identifies the doctrine of vicarious liability and its potential impact on employers. It also considers liability of those producing, supplying, marketing, and the importing of goods that contain defects and cause damage/loss. Many businesses will be involved in some form of trading in this capacity and hence they may be subject to a claim for damages as the liability in this jurisdiction of law is strict (it does not require the claimant to prove negligence). Businesses also occupy land and premises and must ensure that visitors (and even trespassers) are safe from injury, and various statutory duties are imposed that may lead to those in business being subject to claims where a person has been injured or suffered loss. As such, the extent of these areas of the law will require most employers/managers and those in business to have a knowledge of the principles underlying the imposition of liability, and to develop strategies to avoid tort actions.

Learning outcomes

Following reading this chapter you should be in a position to:

- offer a definition of the doctrine of vicarious liability (15.2)
- identify the rationale and justification for the development of the doctrine (15.3)
- apply the tests to establish vicarious liability (15.5–15.5.2.4)
- explain, with common law examples, how the courts identify 'course of employment' (15.5.2–15.5.2.4)
- demonstrate the extension of vicarious liability to independent contractors (15.6–15.6.2)
- explain the protection to the consumer through legislation (15.7–15.7.4)
- identify the obligations imposed on the owners and occupiers of land under the common law and through statute (15.8–15.8.4)
- explain potential liability established through a breach of a statutory duty (15.9–15.9.2.3).

🔓 Key terms

These terms will be used in the chapter and it may be helpful to be aware of what they mean or refer back to them when reading through the chapter.

Breach of statutory duty

A statute may impose a duty but fail to mention any civil law sanctions. In order to claim under the statute, the claimant must demonstrate that Parliament intended liability in tort to follow from the breach.

Course of employment

For an employer to be held liable for the torts of an employee, the tort must have been committed in the working hours and/or under the responsibility of the employer. The common law has demonstrated many examples, and established rules, to identify what will constitute 'course of employment'.

Non-delegable duties

Certain responsibilities are imposed by statute or the common law and they cannot be delegated to another body/person. For example, in an employment context duties exist and are applied to the employer who is unable to delegate these to sub-contractors, and the employer will remain responsible, jointly or severally, for any subsequent torts.

Strict liability

Liability is imposed where, in the case of the Consumer Protection Act 1987, a product contained a defect. There is no requirement for the claimant to demonstrate negligence on the part of the defendant.

Vicarious liability

Holding another party (usually an employer/principal) jointly responsible/liable for the actions of the tortfeasor (usually an employee/agent).

15.1 Introduction

Vicarious liability occurs where one party has responsibility for a wrong committed by someone else. In a business context, vicarious liability is a doctrine where an employer will be held liable for the torts of his/her employee. The employer may have to compensate the injured party for any damage sustained to property or injuries suffered by the wrongful or negligent actions of his/her employee.[1] The doctrine was developed, through the courts, to ensure that injured persons are compensated for losses sustained as a result of a negligent or wrongful act, and the obligation be placed on the employer to compensate and further to prevent any future torts being committed. These tests begin with the employment status of the worker (who generally must be considered an 'employee') and require that the tort was committed in the course of his/her employment. As concepts such as '**course of employment**' are broad, common law examples are considered.

---

[1] See Stevens, R. (2007) 'Vicarious Liability or Vicarious Action?' *Law Quarterly Review*, Vol. 123, January, p. 30.

Further, the chapter considers the protection afforded consumers when defective products cause them injury. The Sale of Goods Act 1979 and other statutory protections provide remedies where goods fall below the required standard; however, they do not compensate where an individual suffered loss (such as damage to him/herself or his/her property) due to the defect in the product itself. The Consumer Protection Act 1987 enables claims on such a basis.

Obligations are also placed on the occupiers of land and property that are accessible by the public (including, of course, shops and factories—pertinent to businesses). These obligations extend to visitors and non-visitors (such as trespassers) and identification of the potential liability in this area, and which mechanisms may reduce the instances of breaches are significant in a business context. The chapter concludes by considering statutory duties and how these may enable claims when the duty is breached.

15.2 Vicarious liability—a definition

Vicarious liability was succinctly defined by the Court of Appeal in the case of *Hudson v Ridge Manufacturing*[2] as '… a doctrine whereby an employer will be held liable for the torts of his employees'. The doctrine does not require that the employer has actively participated in the commission of the tort, only that there is some relationship between him/her and the tortfeasor that will enable the law to hold the employer responsible. Whilst the employer is held jointly liable with the employee tortfeasor, if a claim is successfully made against the employer he/she may in turn bring an action to recover from the employee under the Civil Liability (Contribution) Act 1978. As such, it is important to remember that even though vicarious liability involves the employer being held accountable, this does not remove the liability or fault from the employee who committed the tort.

15.3 Rationale for the doctrine

 Business Link

It is important for businesses to be aware of why employers have been held liable for the torts committed by employees in the course of their employment. Simply declaring that such imposition is unfair or that an employee was instructed not to act in a certain way (which led to the commission of the tort) will not necessarily remove the employer's liability. Therefore, the judiciary and commentators have identified reasons justifying the doctrine's existence.

As vicarious liability is a doctrine that holds an employer liable for the torts of someone else (namely his/her employee), the theoretical justification and rationale for imposition of the liability has been the subject of controversy and academic comment for many years.[3]

2 [1957] 2 QB 348.
3 See Laski, H. J. (1916) 'The Basis of Vicarious Liability' *Yale Law Journal*, Vol. 26, p. 105; and Williams, G. L. (1956) 'Vicarious Liability: Tort of the Master and Servant' *Law Quarterly Review*, Vol. 72, p. 522.

One overriding explanation for the doctrine has been that the *employer had expressly or implijedly authorized the employee's action*[4] and therefore should satisfy any claims on the basis of damage or injury as a consequence. The employer may have *employed a negligent employee* or have *failed in his/her duty to adequately control* the employee and hence 'set the whole thing in motion'.[5] Further arguments to justify the doctrine have been that as the *employer derives financial benefit* from the work of the employee he/she should be responsible for losses (referred to as 'enterprise risk'). The employer also has 'deeper pockets' than the employee and as such is in a better financial position to satisfy claims, as increasingly, the employer is no longer an individual but a corporation. It also avoids the situation where the employee is made the 'scapegoat' for any injuries/losses sustained due to the tort. A corporation may be *able to distribute any losses* more successfully than would a private individual, where a claim could lead to significant financial losses. A corporation may be able to reduce dividends to shareholders, reduce payments to staff or management and so on to generate the revenue to pay any claim. Private individuals do not have such options. *Compulsory insurance* is also required of employers. This ensures damage caused to employees will be compensatable. Again, private individuals may possess house and car insurance, but are unlikely to carry insurance in the event of their causing any damage or injury whilst in the course of employment. Therefore it appears logical, if perhaps a little 'unfair'[6] to hold an employer liable.

A major rationale for vicarious liability's justification has been the concept of *accident/tort prevention*.[7] Holding an employer financially liable for the torts of an employee provides an effective incentive for his/her proactive approach to ensure safe systems of work are in place and the employees are controlled to an extent that will limit, as far as possible, any torts being committed.[8]

15.4 **For what is the employer liable?**

For the employer to be held liable for the torts of his/her employee, the tort must have been committed whilst 'in the course of employment'. Evidently, this will cause consternation to rational thinking people, as no employer would engage a person to commit a tort. Course of

---

[4] This being the legal position as identified in *Tuberville v Stamp* [1697] 1 Ld. Raym. 264.

[5] As stated by Brougham LJ in *Duncan v Findlater* [1839] 6 Cl. & F. 894 and Scarman LJ in *Rose v Plenty* [1976] 1 WLR 141.

[6] This aspect of unfairness was raised by Pearce LJ in *ICI Ltd v Shatwell* [1965] AC 656, where he remarked that: '... vicarious liability has not grown from any very clear, logical or legal principle but from social convenience and rough justice'.

[7] The proactive approach required of employers may be evidenced in cases such as *Limpus v London General Omnibus* [1862] 1 H & C 526 and *Rose v Plenty* [1975] 1 WLR 141. In each case, the employees were authorized to perform an act, but performed this act in an unauthorized way (although see Lawton LJ's dissenting opinion in *Rose v Plenty* regarding the act of the employee being the performance of an act which he was not employed to perform and as such the employer should have borne no responsibility for the injury). In so doing, they caused injury or damage through their negligence. As the courts in each case held the act had been committed in the course of their employment, the employer was held liable. However, the option for the employer in such instances is to consider the action as a fundamental breach of the contract of employment and dismiss the employee. Further, it would have been prudent following these judgments for the employer to conduct 'spot-checks' to ensure no other employee was breaking the rules and if they did, to apply whatever sanction necessary to prevent further breaches and potential negligent acts.

[8] For a discussion, through a collection of essays, on the topic of accident prevention see Faure, M. and Van den Bergh, R. (1989) 'Essays in Law and Economics. Corporations, Accident Prevention and Compensation for Losses' Antwerpen, Maklu.

employment, in the legal sense, is a term that establishes the liability an employer will have if the employee has acted in one of the following ways:

1 The employee acted negligently in an act that he/she was authorized to do with care.[9]

2 The act was necessarily incidental to something that the employee was engaged to do.

3 The employee acted in a wrongful way that was authorized by the employer.

Such examples can of course be difficult to identify in the abstract and hence it is important, as an aid to understanding, to review case law that has created and exemplified these principles.

15.5 The qualifications to establish vicarious liability

For an employer to be liable for the torts of his/her employees two conditions are required:

1 The worker must be considered an *'employee'*; and

2 the tort must have been committed in the **'course of employment'**.

15.5.1 Employee status

The tests to establish a worker as an employee or an independent contractor are considered in Chapter 16 and therefore this chapter will not replicate the discussion provided there.[10] Note however, that in vicarious liability, it is increasingly evidence of control exercisable by the employer, rather than the existence of a contract of employment, that will lead to an employer's liability.

15.5.1.1 *Liability for 'loaned' employees*

Employers may at times loan an employee to another business where, for example, the other business has a temporary increase in demand or the loan is through an agency and so on. Where this occurs, and the loaned employee commits a tort, which employer retains the responsibility (and may be held vicariously liable)? In *Mersey Docks & Harbour Board v Coggins and Griffiths (Liverpool) Ltd*[11] the House of Lords held that the control exercisable by the employer is the determining factor. This, in most cases, will rest with the original employer. However, where it can be demonstrated that the control is actually exercised by the employer that has taken the loan of the employee, he/she will assume responsibility. This element of control was demonstrated in *Hawley v Luminar Leisure Ltd*[12] where the employer was held to be Luminar, which operated a nightclub and had hired a 'bouncer' from another business, under a contract to provide security services. The bouncer was directed by Luminar in the tasks to be performed and the way that they were to be carried out. When he assaulted

---

[9] The obligation that rests upon employees to perform their duties at work with 'reasonable care' was identified in *Harmer v Cornelius* [1858] 5 CB (N.S.) 236.

[10] Although the courts do use discretion in determining employment status—as demonstrated and discussed throughout this section.

[11] [1947] AC 1.   [12] [2006] EWCA Civ 30.

a customer, Luminar was vicariously liable for the tort as the bouncer's 'temporary deemed employer'.

These cases identified where either the original employer, or the employer the employee was loaned to was held vicariously liable for the employee's tort. There may further be situations where both employers have to share responsibility, for example where both employers were held liable for the tort of the employee as each could have prevented the employee's action.[13]

15.5.2 Course of employment

 Business Link

Establishing which torts will be considered by the courts to have been committed in the course of employment is only possible by reviewing the decisions from previous cases. These are vital as many situations exist where an independent observer may initially have concluded the employee's action was beyond the employer's responsibility, only for it to have been held to give rise to liability. The cases noted in the following section give factual examples of where liability will (or will not) be imposed and in these decisions, the judiciary have identified key reasons for their decisions which employers can use to reduce the incidences of, and their exposure to, potential liability.

To hold an employer liable for the torts of his/her employee, the employee must have been employed in the employer's business and be performing his/her job. As evidenced in *Joel v Morison*[14] '… the servant must be engaged on his master's business and not off on a frolic of his own'. To identify how the courts will conclude what amounts to the course of employment it is necessary to examine the common law. Note that the following are examples and do not seek to establish a comprehensive list.

15.5.2.1 *Authorized acts conducted in unauthorized ways*

- *Express prohibitions:* In an attempt to limit potential liability, employers may specifically instruct their employees to act in a certain way, or seek to prohibit certain actions that may likely lead to torts being committed. The employer is seeking to limit his/her exposure to risk of harm to property and persons, but the success or failure of such instruction may be viewed from the perspective of whether the employee had been expressly told not to do something and he/she contradicted this instruction (no vicarious liability); or whether the employee is told not to perform an authorized task in an unauthorized way (liability may be established). These two instances may be seen in the following cases:

Limpus v London General Omnibus

Facts:

Limpus was injured in an accident involving one of London General Omnibus' vehicles. The driver of the defendant's bus was, at the time of the accident, racing with a driver from a

---

[13] *Viasystems (Tyneside) Ltd v Thermal Transfer (Northern) Ltd* [2005] EWCA Civ 1151.
[14] [1834] 6 C & P 501.

rival bus company to reach a bus stop, and drove across the road in an attempt to block the other driver's route. There had been previous acts of such reckless actions between rival bus companies and as a consequence London General Omnibus had instructed its drivers not to engage in racing. When Limpus was injured, the claim was brought against the bus company rather than the driver of the vehicle. The defence raised against the vicarious liability action was that London General Omnibus had expressly instructed the drivers not to take the action that led to Limpus' injury, and hence the driver acted outside of the 'course of his employment'. The Court rejected this argument as the driver was acting for his employer in an unauthorized manner.

Authority for:

An employer merely instructing an employee to refrain from action will not enable the employer to escape liability. Insofar as the employee is performing an authorized task, albeit in an unauthorized manner, the employer will remain vicariously liable.

The ruling can be contrasted where the employee does act outside his/her employment. In *Iqbal v London Transport Executive*[15] a bus conductor was expressly forbidden by the employer to drive buses, and was informed that he should request an engineer to move a bus. However, he moved the bus himself and as he did, committed a tort. The injured party attempted to claim from the employer but the claim failed as the conductor was not employed to drive buses. In order for the test of 'course of employment' to be satisfied the employee must be performing the obligations for which he/she was employed, and in this case driving buses was outside of the conductor's responsibilities.

- *Providing lifts:* It is important to identify when an employer may be held liable for an employee's tort when giving lifts as part of his/her driving responsibilities. This is particularly relevant when the employer has informed the employee not to provide lifts or carry passengers in works' vehicles. The first case discussed (*Twine v Bean's Express*) demonstrates the courts' reluctance to impose liability on an employer in such situations, but when compared with the second case (*Rose v Plenty*), the courts may be willing to hold an employer liable. In doing so, they ensure employers proactively reduce the possibility of negligent acts by their employees (accident prevention) and ensure their workers, and the public, are more effectively protected.

Twine v Bean's Express Ltd[16]

Facts:

The defendants provided a commercial van and a driver (Harrison) to be used by a bank with the condition that the driver remained the employee of the defendants. There was a further agreement between the defendants and the bank that the defendants accepted no liability for any persons, other than their own employees, riding in the van. The driver of the van had been expressly told that no one was to be allowed to ride with him in the van, and there was also notice to this effect on the dashboard. The driver allowed an employee of the bank to ride with him, at his own risk, and in the course of this journey the employee died in an accident caused by Harrison. The employee's widow brought a

---

[15] [1973] 16 KIR 39.   [16] [1946] 1 All ER 202.

claim for damages against the defendants. It was held by the Court of Appeal that only the defendants' employees were permitted to travel in the van and the deceased man was not one of these persons. Harrison, in giving the lift, was not acting in the course of his employment, and hence the defendants were not liable for the actions of the driver.

Authority for:

An unauthorized act performed by an employee will allow the employer to escape liability.

It is necessary to look to the judgment of Lord Greene MR for the rationale for the decision: '[The driver was] employed to drive the van. That does not mean that because the deceased man was in the van it was within the scope of his employment to be driving the deceased man. He was in fact doing two things at once. He was driving his van from one place to another by a route that he was properly taking when he ran into the omnibus, and as he was driving the van he was acting within the scope of his employment. The other thing that he was doing simultaneously was something totally outside the scope of his employment, namely, giving a lift to a person who had no right whatsoever to be there.'

This case can be compared with *Rose v Plenty*. The difference between the decisions may be due to the nature of the employee's action. In *Twine*, the employee was providing a lift to the bank's employee that was of no use to the employer and could in no way be associated with acting in the course of employment. However, in *Rose v Plenty*, the action of the milkman and the child assistant was to carry out the task required by the employer, albeit again, in an unauthorized manner.

Rose v Plenty

Facts:

The case involved a milkman who had employed a 13-year-old child to assist him on his milk round, despite a direct order from his employer that no one was allowed to ride on the milk float with the delivery drivers. The child was assisting the milkman when there was an accident and he was injured. The parents of the child brought an action against the milkman's employer for damages and the Court of Appeal held that the employer was liable. Despite the employer informing the drivers that they should not take passengers, this did not prevent their liability.

Authority for:

An employer may be held vicariously liable for a tort committed by his/her employee who is performing an authorized task in an unauthorized manner.

If, by providing an express instruction not to commit a tort, the employer's potential liability could be circumvented, the protection the doctrine sought to provide would be removed. The milkman was 'doing his job' when the accident occurred, and the employer should have been more proactive in ensuring the employees adhered to the work rules. However, Lawton LJ dissented and considered that this case fell into the same category as *Twine v Bean's Express*, where the employee was not 'doing his job' albeit in an unauthorized manner, rather he/she was doing something completely different. This may be an example of vicarious liability being a doctrine of 'rough justice'. Mechanisms exist through employment law to take action against employees who fail to follow work rules, and it is in the enforcement of these rules that such accidents (and their consequent tort actions) will be prevented.

15.5.2.2 *Acts incidental to the employment*

The courts have had to determine whether an employer should be liable for an act by his/her employee that is not what he/she was engaged to perform, but rather is incidental to his/her employment.[17] In *Paterson v Costain & Press (Overseas)*[18] the claimant was an employee of Costain and was travelling as a passenger in their vehicle. The vehicle was transporting Paterson from Costain's office to their construction site, where he was told he was required, and during this journey Paterson was injured by the negligent driving of Costain's driver. The Court of Appeal held that Costain were vicariously liable for the negligent act of their driver. The employee in the case had been engaged on the employer's business, and his actions, whilst not what he was employed to do, were not outside of the course of business, but merely incidental to it. In *Smith v Stages*[19] the House of Lords established rules that would identify where journeys incidental to the employment would create liability for an employer:

1 When an employee was travelling between his ordinary residence and work by any means of transport whether or not provided by his employer he was not acting in the course of his employment unless contractually obliged to do so.

2 Travelling between workplaces was in the course of employment.

3 When an employee was paid for travelling in his employer's time the fact that the employee could choose the time and mode of transport did not take the journey out of the course of his employment.

4 When an employee was travelling from his ordinary residence to an unusual place of work or to an emergency the employee would be acting in the course of his employment.

5 A deviation or interruption of a journey would for that time take an employee out of the course of his employment.

A particularly infamous case when considering the extent of vicarious liability and the responsibility of employers occurred in *Century Insurance Co. Ltd v Northern Ireland Road Transport Board*.[20] Mr Davison was employed to deliver 300 gallons of petrol in a tanker. At the garage he inserted the nozzle of the delivery hosepipe into the manhole of the garage's tank and turned on the stopcock of the tanker. Whilst the petrol was flowing into the tank Mr Davison lit a cigarette and threw away the lighted match igniting material on the floor of the garage, which caused a fire. The proprietor of the garage used a fire extinguisher in an attempt to put out the fire and instructed Mr Davison to turn off the stopcock. Instead, he began to drive the tanker away from the garage, stopping when he reached the street. Mr Davison exited the tanker and whilst the fire had been extinguished at the manhole, it had travelled up the delivery hose, into the tanker where a 'very violent' explosion occurred. The explosion destroyed the tanker, the motorcar of the proprietor of the garage, and several houses in

---

17 'Incidental' to employment can lead to an employer being responsible for actions taken by an employee under which they would otherwise have no liability. In *Crook v Derbyshire Stone Ltd* [1956] 1 WLR 432 a lorry driver had stopped at a lay-by near to a café. He crossed one section of the dual carriageway on foot to get to the café when a collision occurred between the driver and a motorcyclist, due to the driver's negligence, in which the motorcyclist was injured. It was held that as the tort occurred during the driver's hours of employment the employer was liable. The tort being committed in the employee's 'break' did not stop him being in the course of his employment.

18 [1979] 2 Lloyd's Rep. 204.   19 [1989] 2 WLR 529.   20 [1942] AC 509.

the vicinity were also damaged. The House of Lords held that Mr Davison was employed to deliver petrol and as such his tort was committed in the course of his employment. He was careless in discarding the lighted match, but he was performing his duties and consequently the employer had to accept the liability.

15.5.2.3 *Deviation from a task*

Having demonstrated where the tort of an employee, whilst committed during his/her working hours or travelling to and from work, may lead to the vicarious liability of the employer, a further area of import is where the employee has deviated from his/her employment. It is the extent to which the employee has deviated from his/her task that will establish liability.

Storey v Ashton[21]

Facts:

Storey (a six-year-old child) was injured when delivery drivers for Ashton ran him over. Ashton was a firm of wine merchants that had sent their delivery driver and clerk to deliver a consignment of wine at Blackheath, and bring back empty bottles from the drop point. Having delivered the wine and picked up the bottles the driver was returning to Ashton's offices as instructed. However, about a quarter of mile from the destination, instead of returning to the offices, he was persuaded by the clerk to drive in another direction on the business of the clerk. It was on this journey that the accident occurred. The High Court held that the employer was not liable for the injury to Storey. The driver had been negligent, but he was not acting in the course of his employment as he was driving in a different direction, taking a different route, than where he was instructed.

Authority for:

For an employer to escape being held vicariously liable, the employee must have sufficiently deviated from his/her task for the tort not to have occurred in the course of employment.

15.5.2.4 *Criminal acts*

It is very important to identify whether an employer will be held liable for the criminal acts of his/her employees that are committed during his/her employment. Where the employee's act was outside of his/her duties and employment, there has been no liability for the employer.[22] However, when the employee's action was taken in the course of his/her employment, the employer has been held jointly culpable.[23] In *Daniels v Whetstone Entertainments and Allender*[24] a steward (bouncer) employed at a dance hall assaulted a customer within the dance hall. The persons involved in this disturbance were removed to outside of the premises and the steward was informed by his employer to remain inside the dance hall and continue his duties. Instead, he proceeded to go outside in an attempt to find a second man involved in the disturbance, found the original victim of the steward's assault, and assaulted him again. It was held that the first assault was within the steward's course of employment, but the second assault was not.

[21] [1869] [LR] 4 QB 476.

[22] For example, in *Heasmans v Clarity Cleaning Ltd* [1987] IRLR 286 a cleaner unlawfully used the phone of a client to make international calls (at a cost of £1,411). This was held by the Court of Appeal to be a criminal act wholly outside of the scope of their employment, and just because the employer provided the 'opportunity' for the commission of the act did not make them vicariously liable for the loss.

[23] *Lloyd v Grace, Smith & Co.* [1912] AC 716.   [24] [1962] 2 Lloyd's Rep 1.

When determining if an employer should be held vicariously liable for the torts of his/her employees, the test of establishing whether the employee's act was a wrongful or unauthorized method of performing an authorized act is not always of use when assessing intentional torts. Rather, it is more apt to consider the closeness of the connection between the wrong committed by the employee and the nature of his/her employment, and to determine whether it is just and reasonable in those circumstances to hold the employer vicariously liable.[25] A very significant judgment was provided by the House of Lords in *Lister v Hesley Hall*.[26] Lister and two others brought an action against the employer of a warden at a residential school for boys with behavioural problems, of which they had been resident. In 1995, the warden was convicted of several sexual offences (including physical abuse) against children in his care, including the claimants. They brought an action for personal injury, alleging the employer was vicariously liable for these acts. Lord Steyn followed the reasoning from judgments of the Canadian Supreme Court[27] where, in determining an employer's vicarious liability in such actions, there must be a 'close connection' between the act and the employer's authorization. In essence, an employer is liable for acts which he/she has not authorized, provided they are so connected with acts which he/she has authorized that they may rightly be regarded as, albeit improper, modes of doing them. The employer should have been aware of the possibility and risk of sexual abuse by employees in positions of authority (but not perhaps of other employees) and hence it had not taken sufficient precautions to avoid the act(s).

This aspect of an employer's liability has also been applied in *Majrowski v Guys & St Thomas' NHS Trust*,[28] where a clinical audit coordinator who had been bullied and subject to rude and abusive behaviour by a departmental manager was successful in claiming against his employer under the Protection from Harassment Act 1997, s. 3. The House of Lords held that where there had been a close connection between the course of conduct of the employee and the circumstances of his/her employment, it was no defence for the employer to claim that he/she did not authorize the conduct, or the consequences of the actions were not foreseeable.[29] The implications of this statutory right offer an 'easier' route for employees to claim damages for bullying and stress-related claims against their employer as the claimant does not have to establish a psychiatric injury[30] but rather distress/anxiety.

Where an employer will have liability for the criminal acts of his/her employees can be clearly seen in two cases heard together in 2012 in the Court of Appeal. In *Wallbank v Wallbank Fox Designs*[31] the claimant was attacked by another employee following giving this employee a lawful order to carry out. It was as a direct reaction to this request that Wallbank sustained his injuries. In *Richard Weddall v Barchester Healthcare*,[32] Weddall asked another (off-duty) employee to volunteer to come into work. The employee (Mr Marsh) refused, as he was entitled to, but then he came into work, intoxicated, and attacked Weddall. The employer was held vicariously liable for the claimant's injuries in *Wallbank* as the tort was so closely (if not directly) related to the requirements of his employment (to carry out lawful instructions). The employer was held not to be vicariously liable for the injuries sustained by Mr Weddall as these injuries were as a result of a criminal act of a drunken man, who was not on duty at the time of the assault, and not therefore connected with his employment.

---

[25] *Bernard v The Attorney General of Jamaica* [2004] UKPC 47. [26] [2001] UKHL 22.

[27] *Bazley v Curry* [1999] Canadian Supreme Court, 174 DLR (4th) 45; *Jacobi v Griffiths* [1999] Canadian Supreme Court, 174 DLR (4th) 71. These cases involved liability of employers for sexual abuse suffered by children.

[28] [2006] UKHL 34.

[29] This point was confirmed in *Jones v Ruth* [2011] EWCA Civ 804, [2012] 1 WLR 1495 that the statute does not require any requirement for proof of foreseeability.

[30] See Chapter 14. [31] [2012] EWCA (Civ) 25. [32] [2012] EWCA (Civ) 25.

In *Dubai Aluminium Co. Ltd v Salaam*[33] the House of Lords held that innocent partners of a firm were vicariously liable for the dishonest acts of one of the partners. Dubai Aluminium entered into a bogus consultancy agreement (and several sub-agreements) for approximately US$50m. A partner in a law firm drafted these agreements (and although he did not directly benefit from the dishonesty, he was provided with his fees). It was alleged that the partner had assisted in the fraud, and whilst the case between the law firm and Dubai was settled out of court, it was assumed that the actions were dishonest. The Lords held that the other partners in the firm were vicariously liable for the actions of the partner drafting the 'sham' agreements. Lord Nicholls reiterated the test to establish vicarious liability in such cases is to assess whether the wrongful act was so closely connected with the employment, authorized by the employer, that the act may fairly be regarded as being committed by the employee while in the ordinary course of the employer's business.

In the case *Maga v Trustees of the Birmingham Archdiocese of the Roman Catholic Church*[34] the Court of Appeal determined the extent of the vicarious liability of the Roman Catholic Church for sexual abuse by a Priest. The appellant (M) alleged that when he was about 12–13 years old a Roman Catholic Priest sexually abused him over a 6–12 month period.

The issue of whether the Archdiocese (the Church) was vicariously liable for the acts of the Priest centred on whether those actions could constitute a sufficiently close connection to his employment. The first court held there was no sufficiently close connection to make the imposition of liability fair and just (according to *Lister v Hesley Hall Ltd*). Neither M, nor his parents, was of the Roman Catholic faith or participated in its activities, the Priest had not attempted to convert them to Catholicism, and the sexual abuse was (of course) not part of the Priest's duties. The employment undertaken by the Priest merely provided him with the opportunity to come into contact with young boys.

The case was appealed. The Court of Appeal held that there was sufficient evidence that M had been sexually abused, but it disagreed with the first court holding that the Church was not vicariously liable for the Priest's actions. On reflection, it found there were a number of factors that established a sufficiently close connection between the Priest's actions and his employment (seven factors were outlined by Lord Neuberger MR). This is perhaps the first case in England for a court to hold the Roman Catholic Church to be vicariously liable for abuse by one of its Priests.

What is most interesting, and equally perplexing in this case, is that the Court did not give any further detailed broad instruction which could help in establishing the boundaries (and thereby limitations) of the doctrine. In *Lister* (which significantly extended the close connection test), the abuse occurred at a residential home and the actions were essentially authorized in some misguided sense of discipline. Here, no such instruction or relationship existed, such as would be the case had M been an altar boy. The Priest and M entered the relationship through M attending discos and other events arranged by the Priest in his role of working with local children, and later by M undertaking additional paid work for the Priest. The outcome of the case appears to be the extension of the scope of vicarious liability, and hence employers need to be ever more vigilant to control the actions of their employees, and have a structure/policies in place to effectively supervise their activities. Indeed, Lord Neuberger expressly noted in the judgment the 'inappropriately casual' approach taken by the Priest's superior in relation to two complaints that the Priest had been involved in sexual abuse.

---

[33] [2002] UKHL 48.   [34] [2010] EWCA Civ 256.

15.6 Liability for independent contractors

> ### 📎 Business Link
>
> Whilst the general rule exists that an employer is liable for the torts of employees but not of independent contractors, as the latter have their own insurance to satisfy claims and there does not exist the same level of control exercised over their actions as the former, the law provides for exceptions. In the following examples, an employer may still be held liable for torts committed by an independent contractor if they authorized the tort, or in situations where responsibility cannot be delegated. The imposition of liability may involve a degree of public policy where the employer should not be allowed to remove his/her responsibility for health and safety (for example) of workers or the public, or where statute has imposed a specific responsibility on the employer. Again, knowledge of case law and precedent enables a business to understand how liability is imposed and adopt avoidance policies accordingly.

The law has established exceptions to the general rule that employers will not be vicariously liable for the torts of independent contractors, including where the employers and independent contractor were both negligent; where the employer had hired an incompetent contractor; and in **non-delegable duties** where the employer is liable for negligent acts whether committed by an employer or independent contractor.[35]

15.6.1 The fault of the employer

An employer may be held liable for the torts of an independent contractor where the tort was ratified or authorized by him/her. In such a situation, both the employer and the independent contractor may be held liable as joint tortfeasors.[36] In *Ellis*, the defendants employed a contractor (without authority) to excavate a trench in the street for the purpose of accessing gas pipes. The trench was dug but the contractors negligently left the rubble from the trench in a heap on the footpath over which Ellis stumbled and sustained an injury. In attempting to avoid potential liability, the employers stated the contractors were at fault and as they were not employees any claim had to be made against them. It was held that the contract with the contractors amounted to an illegal act, and the employer could not delegate its responsibility to a contractor. As a consequence the employer was responsible for the damage sustained.

15.6.2 Non-delegable duties[37]

The term 'delegated' duty is meant in the sense that the task required of the employer has been delegated to an independent contractor who is competent[38] to perform the task.[39]

---

[35] See Netto, A. M., and Christudason, A. (2000) 'Of Delegable and Non-delegable Duties in the Construction Industry' *Construction Law Journal* Vol. 16, No. 2, p. 88.

[36] *Ellis v Sheffield Gas Consumers Co.* [1853] 2 El. & Bl. 767.

[37] It has often been referred to as 'non-delegable' duties, although technically no duty is delegable as explained by Denning LJ in *Cassidy v Ministry of Health* [1951] 2 KB 343.

[38] See *Phillips v Britannia Laundry Co.* [1923] 1 KB 539.

[39] For a discussion on the boundaries of competency in this area, see Chapman, S. (1934) 'Liability for the Negligence of Independent Contractors' *Law Quarterly Review* Vol. 50, p. 71.

Consequently, the employer has a lower duty to take care in these situations of 'delegable duties' rather than the higher duty to take care in non-delegable duties. There are no definite rules to establish when an employer will be held liable for torts committed by an independent contractor, but examples include:

1 if the duty on the employer involves some extra-hazardous act;[40]

2 where the employer owes a duty for the health and safety of his/her employees;[41]

3 if the law imposes a duty on the employer (such as through statute), this cannot be delegated;[42]

4 if substances are brought onto land which are dangerous (for example, explosive materials) and would be likely to cause damage if let escape (known as the rule in *Rylands v Fletcher*).

Rylands v Fletcher[43]

Facts:

The case involved strict liability and is a form of private nuisance. The defendant occupied land near to the claimant's coal mine, whose mines extended below the defendant's land. These mines had been cut off and had become disused and the defendant obtained permission to construct a reservoir to provide water for his mill. Fletcher had employed competent contractors. However, during their work they discovered the mineshaft, and that it was connected to another mine, but did not inform Fletcher or attempt to block it. When the reservoir was put into action the water entered the old mine shafts and consequently flooded Ryland's mine, who successfully claimed for the damage caused. The defendant was liable even though not vicariously liable nor negligent in his actions.

Authority for:

As per Blackburn J, '... the person who for their own purpose brings onto his lands ... anything likely to do mischief if it escapes, must keep it at his peril and is **prima facie** answerable for all the damage which is the natural consequence of its escape'.

Whilst this is not an exhaustive list, these situations demonstrate that a tortious act by an independent contractor may still be the responsibility of the employer, who will have to satisfy any claims.

The
Consumer
Protection
Act 1977

15.7 **The Consumer Protection Act 1987**

 Business Link

Where a business produces goods, and those goods contain a defect which results in damage/injury being sustained, unless a defence as identified under the

---

[40] See *Dodd Properties v Canterbury City Council* [1980] 1 WLR 433.

[41] Such as to provide a safe system of work for their employees as detailed in *Wilsons and Clyde Coal Co. v English* [1938] AC 57. Here the House of Lords held that an employer had a duty to provide competent staff, adequate material, a safe system of work, and effective supervision.

[42] See *Smith v Cammell Laird & Co.* [1940] AC 242.   [43] [1866] LR 1 Ex. 265.

Consumer Protection Act (CPA) 1987 is available, the producer, importer, marketer, or supplier will be liable. Proof of negligence is not required; simply the existence of the defect and the damage (over £275 in value) will allow the claimant to succeed. As such, knowledge of the CPA 1987 is crucial to businesses that produce, import, market, or supply goods.

The CPA 1987 was enacted to fulfil the requirements of the EC Product Liability Directive (374/85/EC)[44] and sought to assist consumers when claiming against defects in products. The CPA 1987 enables claimants to seek damages if they were injured through the property, or if it had caused damage, and it adds to existing common law rights. Claims for injuries or damage to property would generally be made under the tort of negligence (see Chapter 13), but this is fraught with difficulties and the CPA 1987 makes such claims much easier in relation to products. Part I of the CPA 1987 imposes a civil liability that enables a claim for injuries due to an unsafe product; Part II was repealed; and Part III (misleading prices) has been superseded by the Consumer Protection from Unfair Trading Regulations 2008 (see the Online Resource Centre for additional content on the Regulations).

Online
Resource
Centre

15.7.1 Protection through the Act

The CPA 1987 protects those individuals who may have suffered injury as a result of the product they purchased, or where the product caused damage to their property. The Sale of Goods Act (SOGA) 1979 enabled those with a contractual relationship with a retailer to have their money returned, or be provided with a repaired item or a replacement in the event of a product failing one of the sections (ss. 12–15). However, what if the defective product purchased caused injury to the buyer, or had damaged his/her property?[45] The law of contract entitled the claimant to protection against a faulty product *not* for any losses attributed to this (as part of the concept of remoteness of damage). In such an event, the injured party would have to sue the defendant under negligence. Proving a breach of the duty of care owed to a consumer may be very difficult and expensive, and may dissuade potential claimants from seeking redress. Therefore the legislation was drafted to provide a justiciable remedy.

15.7.2 The strict liability under the Act

The importance of the CPA 1987 in assisting claimants is by establishing the **strict liability**[46] of the manufacturer. The claimant does not have to prove intention or negligence on the part of the defendant, only that there is a causal link between the product and the damage sustained by the claimant. This liability is only removed if a defence can be made under the CPA's provisions.

---

[44] Commission Directive 85/374/EEC of 25 July 1985 on the approximation of the laws, regulations, and administrative provisions of the Member States concerning liability for defective products.

[45] For example, a television that explodes the first time it is used. It may damage a DVD player below the set and/or cause injury to the viewer watching the set when the explosion occurs.

[46] An analogy can be drawn to assist the understanding with the concept of strict liability and may be seen with drug testing in sports. The International Olympic Commission has a policy that any athlete testing positive for banned drugs is guilty of the offence. This is because the athlete has failed the drug test—it is irrelevant as to how the drugs entered the athlete's system.

15.7.3 Claims under the Act

To be successful the claimant must bring his/her claim within three years of the awareness of the damage or defect in the product,[47] and he/she must establish the following criteria:

1 The product contained a defect.

2 The claimant suffered damage.

3 The damage was caused by the defect.

4 The defendant was either a producer; a marketer (own-brander); an importer; or a supplier into the European Union (EU) of the product.

- *The claimant:* Section 5 defines a claimant as any person who suffers injury to him/herself or damage to his/her private property (the CPA 1987 does not extend to business property).
- *The product:* Section 1 defines a 'product', as the item itself, the packaging, and any instructions; therefore it covers a broad range of claims. However, it must be a product that is ordinarily used for private consumption.
- *Manufactured products:* This definition includes the components of other products.
- *Substances won or abstracted:* The products under this section include electricity, water, and gas.
- *Industrial or other processes:* This includes agricultural products that have been subject to some industrial process.

15.7.3.1 *Damage*

The types of damage that are included in the CPA 1987 are death, personal injuries sustained, and any damage to property that the claimant uses as part of his/her private consumption. However, the CPA 1987 also requires that the damage must exceed a value of £275, which does not include the damage to the product itself. This is to ensure that the courts are not overwhelmed by voluminous cases, and there is a restriction on claims for pure economic loss.

15.7.3.2 *The defect in the product*

The defect in the product must make it unsafe ('not such as persons generally are entitled to expect'—s. 3) and thereby causes damage to the claimant or his/her property.

Abouzaid v Mothercare (UK) Ltd[48]

Facts:

The case involved a child of 12 attempting to fasten a child's sleeping bag to a pushchair manufactured by Mothercare. In attempting to fasten the pushchair, Abouzaid had let go of one of the straps (which had a metal buckle on the end) and this caused the strap to retract and the buckle to hit him in the eye. The resulting injury caused him to lose his sight in the eye due to severe damage to his retina. Mothercare attempted to defend the claim on the basis that technical knowledge in the form of accident reports were unavailable at the time, but the Court of Appeal held that this lack of knowledge was irrelevant, and Mothercare was liable.

---

[47] The Limitation Act 1980, s. 11A.   [48] [2001] Times, February 20.

> **Authority for:**
>
> A defect in a product, for the purposes of s. 3, will be present where there is an identifiable risk, and the defendant could have discovered the danger and the lack of safety of the product before the victim's injury.

In order to be unsafe the product must fall below the standard which a reasonable man would be likely to expect and can be demonstrated in the following:

- *The ordinary use of the product:* The nature of products clearly result in their use being intended, perhaps, for a specific group of the population and the nature of it being unsafe is consequently tested against what may be expected from this group. For example, toys designed for young children would have to include safety considerations of non-toxic paint, sharp edges, and whether the toy contains parts that may be placed in the child's mouth and hence be dangerous. These considerations would be different for products aimed at the adult market, and therefore manufacturers may place age groups on the packaging to limit their potential liability. By stating that a product is intended for '3 years and above' if the product is given to child below that age and some harm is caused, the manufacturer has a potential defence. If, for example, a child is allowed to have access to dishwasher powder, and he/she ingests this, then save for a fault with the packaging (such as the child-resistant cap on the bottle), then there is unlikely to be a successful claim under the CPA 1987. An adult, who the product is marketed at, would appreciate that the item was not to be eaten, and the adult with responsibility for the child would have to bear the responsibility of enabling access to this material.[49]

- *Packaging and warnings:* Products in isolation may be safe, but if used incorrectly or joined with other products, have the potential to cause injury. An example may be provided through the use of medicines which if used when the claimant is taking other medicines may react badly and cause harm, or if used by a claimant with an allergy to the medicine could lead to serious consequences. Therefore the defendant will have needed to include instructions and warnings with the product to ensure the claimant was sufficiently aware of any risks or dangers.

- *The issuing of the product:* If the product was issued when it was safe, but it later becomes known that the product is unsafe (such as with drugs which are later known to cause injuries), then the manufacturer will have a defence that at the time of issue the product was deemed safe. It is also the case where products are sold and a shelf life or 'best before' date is included. Using or consuming the product after this date may be at the claimant's own risk.

15.7.3.3 *Supply of the product*

The product may be supplied through a sale, hire, or gift, or through barter. The supplier must have been acting in the course of his/her business when doing this, but the CPA 1987 clearly extends protection further than the remit of the SOGA.

15.7.3.4 *The defendant*

Section 2 outlines that the following persons may be liable for injury or damage caused wholly or partly by a defect in a product:

---

[49] See *Tesco Stores Ltd v Pollard* [2006] EWCA Civ 393 for a discussion of this scenario and the failures of the claim under CPA 1987 and the forseeability test if the claim was made through negligence.

- *The producer:* The manufacturer of the product, or the person responsible for the abstracting of the product will constitute a defendant under the CPA 1987.
- *The importer:* An importer is the party who has initially imported the product into the EU.
- *The marketer:* An organization that has produced goods with its company name on the label will be treated as a producer of the good.
- *The supplier:* A supplier of a product will be liable if he/she fails when requested to identify the manufacturer, producer, or importer.

15.7.4 Defences under the CPA

Section 4 outlines the possible defences that can be raised in the event of a claim under the CPA 1987:

- *compliance with the law:* if the product complies with the relevant safety standards established in English and EU law, and the defect can be attributed to the standards;
- *non-supply of the product:* if the defendant did not supply the product in the course of his/her business (if making a product for sale was, for example, a pastime or hobby);
- *the defect did not exist at the time of supply:* if at the time of the supply of the product the defect did not exist then there will be no liability on the part of the defendant;
- *acceptable risks in development:* there exists a special defence for those defendants who release new products onto the market, and who have used all available research and expertise to minimize any potential risk to the claimant. If, despite these safety standards, the claimant is still injured or property is damaged, the defendant will be able to raise this defence to the action. The rationale for the defence is to allow the producer/manufacturer the ability to develop innovative products which may be of benefit to the public/economy, who would otherwise be dissuaded to do so in fear of a liability action. It remains, however, a very controversial defence, as drugs (for example) have entered the market and caused significant health problems for the users, who, if this defence were accepted, would have no recourse under the CPA 1987.

15.8 The Occupiers' Liability Acts

Occupiers'
Liability Act
1957

> ### ℰ Business Link
>
> The Occupiers' Liability Act 1957 and 1984 provide that the occupier of premises owes a duty of care to visitors and to trespassers. Injuries sustained to these visitors due to the failure of the occupier to protect their safety may lead to liability. As most businesses will occupy some premises, the legislation is particularly relevant to them.

There exist obligations (duties to take reasonable care) for occupiers of premises to both lawful visitors and to trespassers. The duty of care (which is a statutory duty rather than in negligence) is to ensure, as far as is reasonable, that the visitor will be safe in using the premises for the purposes for which he/she is invited to be there. Therefore, the premises have to be reasonably safe, and any claim against the occupier based on this legislation will be assessed in light of the danger that he/was exposed to at the premises. In determining this danger, the test of reasonable foreseeability of the risk of injury to the (specific) claimant[50] in the (reasonably expected) use of the premises is adopted.

The legislation relevant to occupiers of premises in this regard is the Occupiers' Liability Act(s) 1957 and 1984. The 1984 Act was more restrictive than the 1957 Act in providing that the duty of care to those other than the occupier's visitor was restricted to a danger that the occupier of the premises knows of, or ought to know exists. Further, the occupier must know or ought to know that the trespasser is likely to come onto his/her land.

Occupiers' Liability Act 1984

15.8.1 **The occupier**

The definition of an occupier is provided in the OLA 1957 s. 1(2), 'as the persons who would at common law be treated as an occupier'. The common law provides that it is the person who has control over the premises that will be considered the occupier. Lord Denning stated in *Wheat v Lacon*[51] that the occupier may be any person with a degree of control over the state of the premises.

Section 1(3)(a) of the OLA 1957 further provides that liability may also be imposed on the occupier of a fixed or moveable structure, and this extends to vessels, vehicles, and aircraft. The liability under this section applies to the danger involved with the structure itself rather than activities associated with the structure. In the event that injury is sustained in the course of activities associated with the structure, then the claim should be made through negligence.

15.8.2 **Occupiers' duties to visitors**

The OLA 1957 requires that the occupier of premises take reasonable care to ensure that a visitor to his/her premises will be reasonably safe. A visitor is a person who comes onto premises with the express or implied permission of the occupier. Express permission is determined on a question of fact, and simply because the person has been invited onto the premises does not mean that he/she is invited to all parts of the premises. The lawful visitor may also become a trespasser if he/she wrongfully uses the premises. As expressed by Scrutton LJ in *Owners of SS Otarama v Manchester Ship Canal Co.*:[52] 'When you invite a person into your home to use the staircase, you do not invite him to slide down the banisters, you invite him to use the staircase in the ordinary way in which it is used.' Implied permission may be provided to persons such as those who need access (for example, reading utility meters) and others, such as postmen, have permission whether expressly invited or not.

The duty to take care[53] provided through the OLA 1957, s. 2(2) is '... to take such care as in all the circumstances of the case is reasonable to see that the visitor will be reasonably safe in using the premises for the purposes for which he is invited or permitted by the occupier to be there'. Therefore the duty is taken with regard to the activities that the visitor is permitted to

---

[50] See *Simonds v Isle of Wight Council* [2003] EWHC 2303.
[51] [1966] AC 552.   [52] (1926) 26 Ll L Rep 203.
[53] The duty of care required by the OLA 1957 and 1984 is tested in accordance with the Compensation Act 2006, ss. 1 and 2.

be on the premises to perform. Examples of the reasonable use of premises have been demonstrated in *Tomlinson v Congleton BC*,[54] and a key feature of the recent judicial decisions has been an expectation of the person to exercise common sense and to take care of his/her own safety.[55]

Clearly, the obligation to protect the safety of children visiting premises is greater than adults,[56] and the occupier has a duty to ensure that warning notices and barriers offer a sufficient deterrent against danger.[57] Where the visitor to the premises does so as part of his/her job, such as tradesmen (builders, electricians and so on), he/she is deemed to have a better understanding of the inherent risks in the pursuit of that activity, than would an ordinary visitor. In *Roles v Nathan (t/a Manchester Assembly Rooms)*[58] two chimney sweeps were killed by carbon monoxide poisoning from a sweep-hole that they were sealing. The sweeps had been warned by the occupier of the premises and an expert employed by him, of the danger from the gas. They had been told not to stay in the hole for too long, and were even physically removed by the expert, but despite this, they sealed the hole while the fire was alight, and subsequently died. The widows of the sweeps brought an action against the occupier, but it was held by the Court of Appeal that they had been given sufficient warnings as to the danger, and this was a danger that they could have been expected to guard against. The occupier may also escape liability where he/she has reasonably entrusted work to an independent contractor and in the execution of this work the contractor's actions led to the danger that caused loss.[59]

Claims under the OLA 1957 may be made in respect of personal injury, losses, or damage to property (insofar as it satisfies the requirement of reasonableness). The occupier may raise the defence of contributory negligence[60] (as it is fault-based liability) and *volenti*[61] to an action, but simply because the claimant agrees to a notice or contract term that purports to exclude the defendant's liability will not amount to acceptance of the inherent risk.[62]

15.8.3 Occupiers' duties to non-visitors

A major extension through the enactment of the OLA 1984 was to broaden the common law duty owed to trespassers. It imposes a duty of care on the occupier to trespassers and persons entering land without the permission or consent of the occupier. These are known as non-visitors. This protection is restricted to those exercising a private right of way rather than a public right. The rationale for the legislative protection is that trespasser or not, persons entering land require protection from the hazards and dangers on it, and common humanity required the occupier of premises (who knew or ought to know that trespassers would enter the land) to ensure that the trespassers would not be injured due to the condition of the premises.

The obligation on the occupier is to take reasonable care to ensure that the non-visitor is not injured due to any danger on the premises.[63] The obligation may be removed through adequate warnings[64] and protective measures being taken to identify (and minimize) the risk. The occupier owes the duty where:

- he/she is aware of the danger, or ought reasonably be aware that a danger exists;

---

[54] [2003] UKHL 47.   [55] *Lewis v Six Continents Plc* [2005] EWCA Civ 1805.

[56] Section 2(3)(a).   [57] Section 2(4)(a).   [58] [1963] 1 WLR 1117.   [59] Section 2(4)(b).

[60] See **13.7.3**.   [61] See **13.7.2**.

[62] UCTA 1977 s. 2(3).   [63] OLA 1984, s. 1(4).

[64] Its adequacy depends on all the circumstances of the case (OLA 1984, s. 1(5)).

- he/she must be aware, or have reasonable grounds to believe, that the non-visitor is in the vicinity of the danger and may enter the premises (regardless of any lawful right to be in the area); and

- the danger must be of a type that it is reasonable to expect the occupier to protect against.[65]

The last stage in this list provides the most difficulty in establishing liability and will be tested on the circumstances of each case. The occupier may seek to avoid liability through *volenti* where the injured non-visitor willingly accepts the risks of his/her actions,[66] and s. 1(8) expressly prevents actions for liability in respect of loss or damage to property.

15.8.4 Reducing the risks

A breach of the legislation may lead to prosecution and, as with breaches of health and safety legislation (of which this may also be a facet), there may be a consequent damage to the reputation of the owner of the premises. As such, the owner of the premises should conduct risk assessments and identify any specific dangers, and the preventative measures that have been taken. For example, the workplace may display notices/signs warning of risks to visitors such as hot water, slippery floors, low ceilings (marked with highlighting tape) and so on.

Depending upon the severity of the defect or the immediacy of the danger, it may be advisable to section off the area to prevent visitors using the affected area(s) and placing themselves in danger. Notices and/or guards could be utilized to prevent accidents (and also it is important to be aware of any visitors to the premises who may suffer a disability and hence the most appropriate measures to protect their safety must be implemented). Examples of mechanisms that could be invoked include:

- *Warnings:* The type of danger and the risks can be brought to the attention of visitors through warning signs and notices. These should be clearly displayed and impart the relevant information as simply as possible.

- *Provide information to all workers:* An employer is responsible for the health and safety, not only of his/her employees, but also any independent contractors who are working at the premises.

- *Maintain buildings:* Ensure that buildings are in a good state of repair; that floors leading into buildings that may become slippery during damp weather have mats/carpeted areas to dry the feet of visitors; that outside routes are kept clear. Keep indoor and outdoor areas suitably lit; provide hand-rails where appropriate; maintain access and exit routes and so on.

- *Consent:* The OLA 1957 enables an occupier to restrict or exclude his/her duty through an 'agreement or otherwise'.[67] Other exclusions of liability, for example restricting liability for damage to property, may enable the exclusion of liability insofar as it satisfies the requirements of UCTA 1977, s. 2(2).

---

[65] OLA 1984, s. 1(3).   [66] OLA 1984, s. 1(6).

[67] Section 2(1) reads 'An occupier of premises owes the same duty, the "common duty of care", to all his visitors, except in so far as he is free to and does extend, restrict, modify or exclude his duty to any visitor or visitors by agreement or otherwise.'

15.9 Breach of statutory duty

Whilst it has been identified that the claimant may establish an action in damages against an employer for negligent acts or omissions, and in cases of vicariously liability, he/she may also have a right to base a claim if the defendant (for example, an employer) breaches a statutory duty. A typical example of a statutory duty is to protect the health and safety of employees.[68] The employer, under a statutory duty, has an obligation to take actions (such as the duties outlined in the Health and Safety at Work Act (HSWA) 1974) and his/her failure will enable the employee to establish a plea. It may be possible for a claim by an employee of both **breach of statutory duty** and negligence for breach of the employer's general duty of care, and to claim damages for consequential losses.

15.9.1 Establishing a claim

The tests to establish a claim of breach of statutory duty are quite similar to those used in negligence:

- The statute places an obligation on the defendant that he/she owes to the claimant(s);
- The defendant has breached this duty;
- The claimant has suffered a loss as a consequence of the defendant's breach;
- The damage suffered was of a kind contemplated by the statute.

For a claim to succeed, the statute has to provide the right for the claimant to seek damages under the civil law.[69] Breaches of health and safety regulations generally allow a claim for breach of a statutory duty. However, the HSWA 1974, s. 47 outlines breaches of duties, such as the general duties identified in ss. 2–8, that do not allow a civil law claim for damages.

An example of these rules impacting on a claim of breach of statutory duty was addressed in *Gorringe v Calderdale MBC*.[70] It was held that in a road traffic accident the defendant Council had a statutory obligation to maintain the roads (under the Highways Act 1980) and whilst this was applied to all road users, it could not be used to impose a private duty (from the existing wider public duty) for a specific individual. There was no obligation under the statute that placed a duty on the Council to the claimant, and as such the Council's lack of action could not amount to a breach.

15.9.2 Defences available

As with any claim for damages, defences may be available to reduce any compensation awarded or defeat the claim in its entirety.

---

[68] See **20.4**.

[69] For example, the Congenital Disabilities (Civil Liability) Act 1976 enables a child, born disabled as a result of an occurrence before their birth, to bring an action in damages against the person(s) who caused the occurrence.

[70] [2004] UKHL 15.

15.9.2.1 *The defendant was not negligent*

Facing a claim for compensation, the defendant may raise the defence that he/she was not negligent and had performed the duties as required by law. The most obvious example of this defence was seen in *Latimer v AEC*.[71]

15.9.2.2 *Contributory negligence*

This defence involves the defendant being at fault, but further that the claimant also acted in a way that placed him/her in danger (and as such he/she contributed to the negligent act). For example, an employer has an obligation to protect the safety of employees, but the employee also has a duty to protect his/her own safety at work. Employees have to use their common sense so as not to injure themselves or others, or place themselves in unnecessary danger (*O'Reilly*).[72] If the employee has contributed to any accident at work, the employer may seek to have any award of compensation reduced. This reduction will be assessed to reflect the claimant's responsibility for his/her injuries/damage.[73]

15.9.2.3 *Consent*

The defence of *volenti non fit injuria* may be raised in claims of breach of statutory duty, as they may be raised in cases of negligence. If a claimant consents to the risk of being injured, he/she may not be permitted to claim if he/she does actually sustain an injury. This defence is available in 'general' negligence cases, but is less available in employment relationships where the employee is required to perform duties at work (see *ICI v Shatwell*).[74]

 Conclusion

This chapter concludes the topic of torts law and demonstrates the importance of an employer being aware of his/her responsibilities for actions taken during work of employees and even independent contractors engaged for a specific task. Further, employers/managers must have knowledge of their obligations when producing or distributing goods, and their obligations to persons visiting or coming on to business land/property. Substantial claims may exist under the law of torts and a sound understanding of the employer's obligations are required to insure against, and as far as possible limit, such damages actions.

Part V of the book moves the discussion to the regulation of the employment relationship and has links with vicarious liability, in defining employee status and how courts have identified the key criteria in determining this issue.

 Summary of main points

Vicarious liability

- Vicarious liability involves a party's responsibility for the torts committed by another.
- In torts law, this generally refers to an employer being held responsible for the torts of his/her employees.
- An employer is liable for:

---

[71] See **13.6.2.2.**   [72] *O'Reilly v National Rail and Tramway Appliances* [1966] 1 All ER 499.
[73] See **13.7.3.**   [74] See **13.7.2.**

1. an employee acting negligently in an act that he/she was authorized to do with care;

2. an act necessarily incidental to something that the employee was engaged to do;

3. an employee acting in a wrongful way that was authorized by the employer.

- Employers have also been held liable for overtly criminal acts committed by the employee.

- Specific rules identify where vicarious liability will be effective:

   1. where the tortfeasor has 'employee' status; and

   2. so long as the tort was committed in the employee's 'course of employment'.

- 'Course of employment' has been held to include:

   - providing lifts in works' vehicles;

   - smoking whilst delivering petrol;

   - committing a fraud wholly during employment.

- There is generally no vicarious liability for the torts of independent contractors.

- Exceptions to the rule include:

   - where the employer authorizes or ratifies the tort of the independent contractor;

   - where the employer may not delegate his/her duty.

Consumer Protection Act

- This Act imposes a strict liability on producers, importers, marketers, and suppliers of goods that are faulty and result in loss or damage.

- That the product has a fault establishes a *prima facie* case and the defendant has to demonstrate a defence under the Act to avoid liability.

- It establishes much greater protection for consumers than attempting to claim through negligence.

Occupiers' Liability Acts 1957 and 1984

- Occupiers of land owe a duty to take reasonable care to ensure visitors and non-visitors will be safe and not exposed to unreasonable danger.

- The visitor must use the premises for which it was designed and must have regard for his/her own safety.

- Owners/occupiers must ensure that material does not leave their premises that could cause loss/damage (such as smoke obscuring the visibility on the highway).

- Owner/occupiers should use warning signs, physical restrictions and so on to prevent danger to visitors and non-visitors.

Breach of a statutory duty

- Employers may face claims for damages where they have breached a statutory duty.

- Claims have to satisfy the following tests to be successful:

- The statute places an obligation on the defendant that he/she owes to the claimant(s).
- The defendant has breached this duty.
- The claimant has suffered a loss as a consequence of the defendant's breach.
- The damage suffered was of a kind contemplated by the statute.
- Defences to such an action include:
  - that the defendant had performed his/her duties as required by law (a complete defence);
  - contributory negligence (a partial defence);
  - consent.

 Summary questions

Essay questions

1. With specific reference to case law, explain the rules establishing the doctrine of vicarious liability. Identify the justifications for the doctrine and assess how many are still appropriate to businesses in the modern era.

2. 'Owners/occupiers of land have unfair responsibilities when it comes to trespassers. If an adult trespasses on land, he/she takes responsibility for their own action and the owner/occupier should not be placed under additional duties to seek their protection.'

    In relation to the duties imposed on owners/occupiers of land by statute and the common law, critically assess the above statement.

Problem questions

1. Nigella wishes to develop her cooking skills and consequently decides to purchase a microwave oven. She visits the Electrical Superstore and purchases a new microwave which she uses successfully for the first time to cook a meal for her family. The second time she uses the microwave she uses the timer feature. Nigella puts on the timer for 30 minutes, as per the manufacturers instructions, and leaves her home to visit a friend. When she returns the microwave has set on fire destroying the oven and the food. The fire has also badly damaged the kitchen units on which the microwave oven was placed and her flat screen television (worth over £800). The kitchen is also going to require redecorating due to the smoke from the fire.

    Advise Nigella as to her legal position.

2. Sarah works as an employee at Crazy Hair—a hairdressing salon owned by Jason. Peter comes into the salon to have his hair cut and styled by Sarah. As Sarah begins to dye Peter's hair she accidentally puts too much peroxide in the solution and as it is applied to Peter's hair his scalp is burned which causes him pain and discomfort. Peter later has a severe reaction to the solution used by Sarah and is hospitalized which results in Peter missing several days of work as a consequence of the expensive medical treatment he requires.

    Advise Peter of his rights. Advise Sarah and Jason of their liability and any action Jason may take against Sarah.

Further reading

Brodie, D. (2007) 'Enterprise Liability: Justifying Vicarious Liability' *Oxford Journal of Legal Studies*, Vol. 27, No. 3, p. 493.

Howes, V. (2007) 'Liability for Breach of Statutory Duty—Is there a Coherent Approach?' *Journal of Personal Injury Law*, No. 1, p. 1.

McAllister, R. (2006) 'Child-Resistant Bottle Tops and the Consumer Protection Act 1987' *Health & Safety Law*, Vol. 6, No. 2, p. 22.

Stevens, R. (2007) 'Vicarious Liability or Vicarious Action?' *Law Quarterly Review*, Vol. 123, January, p. 30.

Waite, A. J. (2006) 'Deconstructing the Rule in Rylands v Fletcher' *Journal of Environmental Law*, Vol. 18, No. 3, p. 423.

Online Resource Centre

http://www.oxfordtextbooks.co.uk/orc/marson3e/
Why not visit the Online Resource Centre and try multiple choice questions associated with this chapter to test your understanding of the topic. You will also find relevant updates to the law.

V Employment

16

Employment Status and the Terms Forming the Contract

Why does it matter?

Employment relations affect all business organizations and it is especially important to identify the status of individuals engaged in employment. This is because of the obligations and duties on both the individual and employer that are attached to the status. Simply labelling an individual as 'employee' or 'independent contractor' in a contract of employment is insufficient.[1] The courts and tribunals will look beyond the wording of the contract, and study the actual working relationship and terms of employment. For this reason, careful consideration of the case law is essential to identify the true status of individuals, and thereby the obligations on the parties.

Learning outcomes

Following reading this chapter you should be in a position to:

- explain why the distinction of employment status is important (16.2)
- distinguish between an employee and an independent contractor, through the evolution of the common law tests (16.3–16.3.4)
- identify the contractual terms employees are entitled to be notified of when commencing employment (16.4)
- identify the implied terms employees are subject to (16.5.1)
- identify the implied terms employers are subject to (16.5.2).

🔒 Key terms

These terms will be used in the chapter and it may be helpful to be aware of what they mean or refer back to them when reading through the chapter.

Employee
A person who works under a 'contract of service'. These individuals, who perform the contract personally, have greater obligations placed on them (such as implied terms)

---

[1] See Denning LJ's judgment in *Massey v Crown Life Insurance Co* [1978] 1 WLR 676.

but also have greater protection in employment, including the right not to be unfairly dismissed and the right to compensation upon redundancy.

Employment Tribunal
Tribunals are established to hear employment law complaints between the employer and individual.

Independent contractor
A person who works under a 'contract for services'. These individuals have the ability (and option) to work for several employers, and have better tax benefits, but lack many elements of employment protection that employees enjoy.

Mutuality of obligations
There is an obligation for the individual to offer his/her services to the employer (attend work) and there is a mutual obligation for the employer to provide work/pay. This is an essential component of 'employee' status.

16.1 Introduction

This chapter begins the consideration of the regulation of the employment relationship. It identifies the tests to establish the employment status of individuals, and why the distinction between an employee and **independent contractor** is so significant. The three common law tests that have been used to determine **employee** status (control, integration, and mixed/economic reality) are identified, but when applying the tests it is most appropriate to begin with those established in *Montgomery v Johnson Underwood*, and then proceed to the final question in *Ready Mixed Concrete*.

The chapter also identifies the terms implied into contracts of employment and the obligations these place on the parties. Awareness of employment status is crucial when the further chapters involving dismissals and discrimination are considered and enable the reader to identify which type of 'worker' may qualify under specific legislation and those who will be ineligible to make a claim.

16.2 The reason for the distinction

 Business Link

The reason for determining employment status is for an employer to understand what their obligations are to the individual, and how an employee is subject to greater control and implied terms in their contract than are independent contractors. For an employer, he/she is responsible for paying the employee's tax and national insurance contributions; he/she may be responsible for torts committed by an employee (under vicarious liability); he/she has responsibilities for employees' health and safety at work; and may have to provide compensation in cases of unfair dismissal and redundancy (to name but a few). Employers also have the advantage of an employee's fidelity to the employer;

employees have obligations to cooperate; adapt to new working conditions; and obey the lawful orders of the employer. Consequently, determining employment status is crucial for an employer and the individual to appreciate their obligations and responsibilities in the working relationship.

It should be remembered that the courts and tribunals will not identify the employment status of an individual as an academic exercise. It will only be considered if there is a dispute between the parties as to the status, and if the right being claimed (such as compensation for an alleged unfair dismissal) is dependent upon the status of 'employee'.

? Thinking Point

If you work (full or part-time) are you an employee or independent contractor? Do you have a written contract that has informed you; has your employer called you by one of these terms, and how do you think a tribunal would determine your status? Consider these issues when you read **16.3**.

16.3 Tests to establish the employment relationship

Employment Right Act 1996

⚓ Business Link

Acts of Parliament are the highest form of law and the test for employment status is contained in the Employment Rights Act 1996 s. 230 (similar definitions exist in the Trade Union and Labour Relations (Consolidation) Act 1992 s. 295(1) and the Equality Act 2010 s. 83(2)). However, the legislation is purposely vague to enable the courts to offer direction as to the status of individuals in the dynamic and numerous workplaces in modern society. The *ratio* (see Chapter 3) determined through the cases must be understood to enable employers to establish, as far as is possible, individuals as 'employees' or 'independent contractors'. Understanding those factors that the courts and tribunals will take into account when reaching decisions can help in the correct drafting of the contract of employment, and also assist in establishing the appropriate terms and conditions under which the actual employment relationship exists.[2]

Being the highest form of law, the most obvious place to search in establishing how to identify a individual's employment status is statute. The Employment Rights Act 1996 contains many of the laws relating to employment and under s. 230(1) an employee is classed as 'an individual who has entered into or works under (or, where the employment has ceased, worked under) a contract of employment'. The term 'a contract of employment' is defined under s. 230(2), which reads '... "contract of employment" means a contract of service or apprenticeship, whether express or implied, and (if it is express) whether oral or in writing.' Ultimately, the legislation is unhelpful and very broad and requires reference to case law to extract the

---

[2] See *Weight Watchers (UK) Ltd v Her Majesty's Revenue & Customs (HMRC)* (2011) FTC/57–59/2010.

Figure 16.1 Common Law Test in Establishing Employment Status

determining factors of employment status. As a consequence, the common law tests have evolved from 'control' and 'integration' to the modern 'mixed/economic reality' test.

It is important to recognize before the tests are discussed that no one test is conclusive and the courts and tribunals make the decision of the employment status based on mixed law and fact—the employment laws established from statute and the courts (through precedent) and the individual facts of the case. Indeed, Griffiths LJ[3] commented that determining employment status: '… has proved to be a most elusive question and despite a plethora of authorities the courts have not been able to devise a single test that will conclusively point to the distinction in all cases'. Also, note that in employment law, perhaps more than many other areas of law, social and political policy affects the decisions made by tribunals.

Figure 16.1 identifies the evolution of the common law tests in establishing employment status. These are considered in greater detail in this chapter.

16.3.1 The control test

This initial test of employment status occurred through the master and servant distinction where the master held control over the servant who was subservient to him/her. One of the first cases demonstrating the importance of control in establishing employment status was that of *Yewens v Noakes*,[4] where Bramwell LJ stated 'A servant (employee) is a person subject to the command of his master (employer) as to the manner in which he shall do his work.' This degree of control was easily seen in employment relationships where the employer exercised complete control over the actions of the individual. However, soon after the test had been established the nature of the control in employment relationships began to change.

16.3.2 The right to control

The control test necessarily evolved with the advent of an increasingly skilled workforce who did not require the level of control as seen when the test was established. Cases concerning a professional football player and a surgeon[5] clearly demonstrate individuals exercising a high degree of independence in completing the tasks set by the employer.

---

[3] *Lee Ting Sang v Chung Chi-Keung* [1990] 2 WLR 1173.

[4] (1880–81) LR 6 QBD 530.

[5] *Cassidy v Ministry of Health* [1951] 1 All ER 574, CA.

Walker v Crystal Palace Football Club[6]

Facts:

Mr Walker was a professional football player engaged through a written agreement to serve Crystal Palace Football Club. The agreement was for a term of one year in which Walker was obliged to attend regular training sessions and observe the general instructions of the club. On 17 October 1908 Walker suffered an accident in a match that damaged his knee and this led to his inability to play any further part in the completion of the agreement. Crystal Palace paid his wages until the end of the agreement but declined to re-engage him afterwards. Walker claimed compensation for permanent incapacity[7] due to his inability to earn wages from any suitable employment. The ability to claim was determinant upon Walker being considered a 'workman' (an employee).[8] Crystal Palace contended that Walker could not be an employee due to lack of control exercisable by the employer. The Court of Appeal held there was evidence of control exercised by the football club and hence Walker was an employee. The employer obliged Walker to attend training sessions and follow instruction, and he had to play when ordered to. The fact that the football club did not control how he played, when he passed the ball or decided to shoot at goal or not, was not inconsistent as Walker was a skilled individual.

Authority for:

The control test used to establish an individual's employment status evolved to the 'right to control' test which was more applicable for skilled individuals.

The case established how, even at this early stage, the control test was evolving. With skilled individuals, the test is 'Does the employer have the right to control the individual?' The employer does not have to control the method in which tasks are completed (essentially how the individual works), but rather to control the individual as to when he/she works, where he/she works, the order in which tasks are to be completed and so on.

Control was a useful test when it was first established. However, with modern working practices this was of limited usefulness when applied in isolation.[9] Individuals increasingly are skilled and are employed away from the direct control of the employer. For example, if the manager of an airline employs a pilot, it may be unlikely that the employer can tell the pilot how to fly the aircraft. The pilot is employed as a skilled individual who can work under his/her own initiative and skill, making the control test an increasingly unrealistic isolated test. Many employers employ graduates or those with practical qualifications on the basis that these individuals already possess skills that require little supervision. Such individuals are provided with tasks and they utilize their skills in the completion of these, with little guidance or direct control exercised by the employer. Further, contracts of employment are considered to be contracts of personal service. This means that an employee has to perform the work personally and if he/she has the ability to sub-contract the work or can provide a substitute, then it will be more likely that the individual will be held an independent contractor.[10] Indeed, in *James v Redcats*[11] Elias P in the Employment Appeal Tribunal (EAT) remarked on worker status, the essential question is '... whether the obligation for personal service is the

---

[6] [1910] 1 KB 87.   [7] Under the Workmen's Compensation Act 1906.

[8] The Act required a contract of service.

[9] Per Griffiths LJ in *Lee Ting Sang v Chung Chi-Keung and Another* [1990]: '... control will no doubt always have to be considered, although it can no longer be regarded as the sole determining factor'.

[10] See *Express and Echo v Tanton* [1999] IRLR 367, where the Court of Appeal held that the delegation of duties to a substitute resulted in the individual being considered an independent contractor.

[11] Decision of 21 February 2007, unreported.

dominant feature of the contractual relationship or not. If it is, then the contract lies in the employment field ...' Whilst this decision was given in the context of minimum wage legislation, it is applicable to the wider discussion of employment status.

Therefore, with the limitation of the control test, wider consideration of the employment relationship had to be undertaken. This led to the integration/organization test.

16.3.3 The integration/organization test

Due to the problems encountered in utilizing the control test in isolation, the courts began to extend the mechanisms and tests to identify employment status. Lord Denning, who had been instrumental in developing contract law in his judgments, had an opportunity to consider employee status:

Stevenson, Jordan and Harrison v Macdonald and Evans[12]

Facts:

Mr Evans-Hemming had been employed as an accountant with Macdonald and Evans and following his employment ending, he produced a textbook on business management that consisted of lectures based on his experiences with the firm. He then purported to assign the copyright to the book to a publishing firm. Stevenson Jordan & Harrison were the publishers to whom Mr Evans-Hemming had submitted the book and Macdonald and Evans brought an action to restrain its publication. It did so on the basis that the contents of the book infringed confidential information, and that the copyright belonged to Macdonald and Evans not Mr Evans-Hemming. It was to be decided if Mr Evans-Hemming was an employee or not at the time of the writing of the text to conclude ownership of the copyright. In determining the employment status Denning LJ considered that:

> One feature which seems to run through the instances is that, under a contract of service a man is employed as part of the business and his work is done as an integral part of the business; whereas, under a contract for services, his work, although done for the business, is not integrated into it but only accessory to it.

This definition uses common sense and its logic will be obvious to all, but it is unfortunate that Denning did not define the word 'integrated' to assist in identifying where the demarcation between employee and independent contractor lay. Integration can be interpreted widely and this even prompted Denning later in the judgment to state 'It is often easy to recognize a contract of service (employee) when you see it, but difficult to say wherein the difference lies. A ship's master, a chauffeur, and a reporter on the staff of a newspaper are all employed under a contract of service; but a ship's pilot, a taximan, and a newspaper contributor are employed under a contract for services.' This enabled lawyers, the judiciary,[13] and academic commentators[14] to differ on the usefulness of the test as a precedent. Given this limitation, the case law continued with the development of the mixed/economic reality test.

---

[12] [1952] 1 TLR 101.

[13] See *Ready Mixed Concrete (South East) Ltd v Minister of Pensions & National Insurance* [1968] for an insight into the limitation of the integration test and where Mackenna J remarked 'This raises more questions than I know how to answer. What is meant by being "part and parcel of an organization"?'

[14] Davies, A. C. L. (2007) 'The Contract of Intermittent Employment' *Industrial Law Journal*, 36(1), p. 102.

Authority for:

The greater an individual's integration into the workforce, the more likely he/she is to be held an employee. The more that the individual is on the periphery of the workforce, the more likely he/she is to be an independent contractor. This case was of limited use as a precedent however.

16.3.4 The mixed/economic reality test

The previous tests of control and integration had limitations in enabling individuals, employers, and indeed the tribunals to assess, with any real certainty, employment status. Therefore, these tests were extended through the following cases that began establishing the mixed test, utilizing the previous tests and addressing new and relevant questions to be asked to help establish employment status. A very important case in the development of the law in this area was *Ready Mixed Concrete*, which established three questions that a tribunal should seek to answer in reaching its conclusion:

Ready Mixed Concrete v Minister of Pensions and National Insurance[15]

Facts:

Ready Mixed Concrete carried on a business of making and selling ready mixed concrete and similar materials. It separated the business of manufacturing and delivering the concrete and introduced a scheme of owner-drivers who would provide the service. The drivers did not have set hours; they did not have fixed meal breaks; they did have an obligation to follow directions given to them by the company as to loading and parking of the lorries; holidays had to be arranged with the firm to ensure no more than one owner-driver was on holiday at a time; they had to wear the company's uniform; they had to carry out all reasonable orders from any competent servant of the company; they could not alter the lorry in any way; and they had to maintain the lorry and keep it painted in the company's colours.

Following a query regarding responsibility for tax payments from one of the drivers, it had to be determined whether the contracts established employee status, or whether the firm was correct and the drivers were independent contractors. Mackenna J considered the facts and established three conditions that would identify the existence of a contract of service:

1. The servant agrees that, in consideration of a wage or other remuneration, he will provide his own work and skill in the performance of some service for his master (this was essentially the requirement of 'mutuality of obligations').

2. He agrees, expressly or impliedly, that in the performance of that service he will be subject to the other's control in a sufficient degree to make that other master (the right to control test).

3. Other provisions of the contract that are inconsistent with its being a contract of service (a negative question requiring determination of examples of factors which would point towards status as a independent contractor—e.g. whether the person performing the services provides his/her own equipment, whether he/she hires his/her own helpers, the existence of his/her financial risk, the degree of responsibility for investment and

---

[15] [1968] 2 WLR 775.

management, whether he/she has an opportunity of profiting from sound management in the performance of his/her task, payment of expenses and so on).

In the application of these tests it was held that the owner-driver subject to the case was an independent contractor. This was due to the lack of control and the inconsistencies of employee status such as his ownership of the lorry; his duty to maintain the lorry; he was not obliged to take any work; he had no set hours or instruction as to how to complete the jobs undertaken; and he could send a substitute.

Authority for:

The three-stage test identified in the case has been used to establish employment status. Having answered the two tests as provided in the *Montgomery* case in the affirmative, the third test in *Ready Mixed Concrete* is applied.

In applying the third element of the *Ready Mixed* tests, it may be worthwhile making a physical list of consistent and inconsistent features to assist in determining employment status. Figure 16.2 demonstrates this approach with the facts of the case.

Further essential factors to consider and be addressed in establishing employment status were developed in *Market Investigations Ltd v Minister of Social Security*.[16] A fundamental

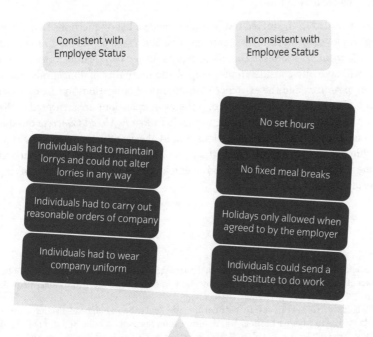

Figure 16.2 Determining Employment Status

---

16 [1969] 2 WLR 1.

element in identifying an employee is **mutuality of obligations**.[17] However, it is essential to note that in *Hall v Lorimer*[18] the court stated that the tests developed in the case law should not be proceeded through mechanically. The tribunals should have the discretion to come to their own conclusions, and attach whatever weight they wish to the factors present.[19] However, these tests should be used as they provide an effective indication as to the direction the tribunals will take in determining employment status. Also, independent contractors are considered to be in business on their own account. Cooke J in *Market Investigations* stated: 'The fundamental test to be applied is this: "Is the person who has engaged himself to perform these services performing them as a person in business on his own account?" If the answer to that question is "yes", then the contract is a contract for services. If the answer is "no", then the contract is a contract of service.'

Whether someone is in business on his/her own account may be evidenced through the questions raised in *Lee Ting Sang v Chung Chi-Keung*[20] such as:

1 whether the man performing the services provides his own equipment;
2 whether he hires his own helpers;
3 what degree of financial risk he takes;
4 what degree of responsibility for investment and management he has; and
5 whether and how far he has an opportunity of profiting from sound management in the performance of his task.

The cases identified in the mixed test section provide a list of questions that can be used in assessing employment status. A last case must be addressed as the *most recent authority* in this area. *Montgomery v Johnson Underwood*[21] established two clear factors which the courts/tribunals will take into consideration—control and mutuality of obligations. There must be an *element of control*, and the existence of mutuality of obligations for the case establishing an individual as an employee to proceed. If these two questions are answered in the affirmative, then the tribunal should continue to the third *Ready Mixed Concrete* question, if not, the claim fails at this stage! Such questions should always be considered in light of whether the individual truly is in business on his/her own account (see Table 16.1 for an overview). If not, he/she is more likely to be considered an employee. The essential features of employment status are identified in Table 16.1.

---

[17] For an effective discussion of the case law in the area see Clarke, L. (2000) 'Mutuality of Obligations and the Contract of Employment: *Carmichael and Another v National Power PLC*' *The Modern Law Review*, Vol. 63, No. 5, p. 757.

[18] [1993] ICR 218. Note in this case that Mr Lorimer was held to be an independent contractor as the Court of Appeal looked as to whether Lorimer was in business on his own account, and did not need to proceed mechanically through the tests noted in *Market Investigations* in order to identify what was clear from the facts.

[19] For example, if the tribunal believe that the employer paying the individual's tax and National Insurance is indicative of employee status, as the tribunal has heard all of the evidence, it should be in the best position to reach such a conclusion.

[20] [1990] 2 WLR 1173.

[21] [2001] EWCA Civ 318. The case involved Mrs Montgomery working through an agency and when her employment was terminated she wished to initiate an unfair dismissal claim. Both the direct employer and the agency denied that she was their employee, and the Court of Appeal held she was not an employee due to lack of mutuality.

Table 16.1 Features of the Employment relationship

Features of the Employment Relationship						
Employment Status	Control Exercisable by the Employer **(Essential)**	Integrated into the Business	A Contract of Personal Service (e.g. no ability to sub-contract)	On Business on Own Account **(Fundamental)**	Mutuality of Obligations **(Essential)**	Tax and NI Taken at Source **(Indicative not Conclusive)**
Employee	YES	YES (but difficult to define)	YES	NO	YES	YES
Independent Contractor	NO	Not Necessarily	NO	YES	NO	NO

16.4 The written particulars of employment

The employer has an obligation, under ERA 1996 s. 1, to provide employees with a copy of the written particulars of the employment. This must be provided within two months of the start of the employment. Note however, that this document is not a contract of employment or a substitute for it.[22] The written particulars provide important information that attempts to clarify many of the important terms in the contract. Section 1 includes the following information as admissible evidence before an **Employment Tribunal**:

Employment Tribunals

(3) (a) the names of the employer and employee,

    (b) the date when the employment began, and

    (c) the date on which the employee's period of continuous employment began.

(4) (a) the scale or rate of remuneration or the method of calculating remuneration,

    (b) the intervals at which remuneration is paid (that is, weekly, monthly or other specified intervals),

    (c) any terms and conditions relating to hours of work.

    (d) any terms and conditions relating to any of the following—

        (i) entitlement to holidays, including public holidays, and holiday pay,

        (ii) incapacity for work due to sickness or injury, including any provision for sick pay, and

        (iii) pensions and pension schemes,

    (e) the length of notice which the employee is obliged to give and entitled to receive to terminate his contract of employment,

    (f) the title of the job which the employee is employed to do or a brief description of the work for which he is employed,

    (g) where the employment is not intended to be permanent, the period for which it is expected to continue or, if it is for a fixed term, the date when it is to end,

---

[22] In *Systems Floors v Daniel* [1981] IRLR 475, the EAT held that whilst the written particulars is not a replacement for a written contract, 'it provides very strong *prima facie* evidence of what were the contracts between the parties …'

(h) either the place of work or, where the employee is required or permitted to work at various places, an indication of that and of the address of the employer,

(j) any collective agreements which directly affect the terms and conditions of the employment including, where the employer is not a party, the persons by whom they were made.

These terms are essential evidence for many of the statutory-based claims under which employees may seek protection. Outlining when the contract of employment began (due to the fact that unfair dismissal and redundancy have minimum periods of service before qualification is gained; and the levels of compensation are calculated on the number of years in service); the notice period that is required (particularly relevant for wrongful dismissal claims on fixed-term contracts); the sources of obligations and terms (such as through works' handbooks and collective agreements); and payments for illness or absences from work each help the parties to identify their rights and obligations. When these terms are missing, as the document or the contract outlining the terms of the employment have not been provided, it makes it considerably more difficult to raise claims against an employer. The Employment Act 2002 s. 38 provides that in cases of unfair dismissal, redundancy, or discrimination, if no written statement of particulars had been provided by the start of the proceedings, then a minimum of two weeks' wages, and a maximum of four weeks' wages (currently capped at £430 per week)[23] is awarded.

16.5 Implied terms in contracts of employment

> ### *∅* Business Link
>
> Employers and employees are subject to terms implied into contracts by many sources including statutes and the common law. The nature of these terms means they are not expressed in writing, nor have they been outlined in the negotiations in establishing the contract. They exist, however, and it is necessary to be aware of how they affect each of the parties.

Implied terms in contract law were considered in Chapter 10. They are present in employment law, and can have a fundamental effect on the obligations to both the employer and employee. As implied terms, they are part of the contract between the parties, and of course by being implied, they are by necessity never written in the employment contract or spoken in the negotiations. Such implied terms are just one reason why the document provided to employees under s. 1 of the Employment Rights Act 1996, is not the contract of employment, although many of the provisions will overlap. It is vital to be aware of the location of the implied terms. Some will derive from *statutes* (such as a pay equality clause in employment through the Equality Act 2010), and *custom* in a particular employment may provide terms. For example, the courts may imply terms where the practice is notorious and reasonable, as

---

[23] Effective from 1 February 2012.

demonstrated in *Sagar v Ridehalgh*.[24] Here, a mill owner in Lancashire deducted wages from an employee for cloth that had been damaged due to poor workmanship. This was the practice of the mill owner and was common practice in the locality, and for that trade, therefore it was held to be fair. *Works handbooks* are also a common source for implied terms as the employer can establish terms that are to affect a large number of individuals, and instead of incorporating these terms into each employee's contract, they are maintained in the document which can be accessed by the employees at his/her convenience. This does not mean that employees can rely completely on this document to identify his/her obligations,[25] and the employer may unilaterally modify the terms contained within if this is reasonable,[26] but terms are included that are relevant and may assist the employee in establishing claims protecting his/her rights.[27]

16.5.1 Implied terms on the employee

The contract of employment, the details in the written particulars provided to the employee, and the negotiations between the parties before the employment relationship is established each include express terms. However, it is of vital importance that it is recognized that contracts of employment are supplemented by many implied terms that have significant effects on the rights and duties of the parties. There are many implied terms imposed on employees and these have been developed and extended through the common law. There are too many to include in this text and those included here do not constitute an exhaustive list, but the more important examples include *mutual trust and confidence*,[28] whereby the employee may not breach the duty to maintain the respect between him/herself and the employer. This embodies respect between the parties, but that does not prevent criticism of either. The High Court has held a Board of Directors may talk in negative terms about an employee, but extending this to a campaign of vilification of an employee will breach the mutual trust and confidence between the parties. If the breach is sufficiently serious, it may amount to a repudiatory breach, for which the employee is entitled to accept, resign, and seek damages. For the employee to gain protection against a repudiatory breach by the employer it is important for the employee not to have breached the same term, or he/she will lose the right to claim constructive dismissal.[29]

There is an obligation of *fidelity* (faithful service)[30] where the employee must not work in competition with the employer and he/she must give his/her faithfulness to the employer. This restricts the employee from taking on other employment, without express permission,

---

[24] [1931] Ch 310.

[25] See *Secretary of State for Employment v ASLEF* [1972] 2 All ER 949, where adherence to rules established in a works' handbook did not excuse the workers from disrupting the employer's business.

[26] In *Dryden v Greater Glasgow Health Board* [1992] IRLR 469 the employer had provided a provision for workers to smoke, but later introduced a no-smoking policy. Mrs Dryden left the employment claiming constructive dismissal, but it was held that the employer's action was not sufficient to breach an implied term as the new measure had been introduced for a reasonable purpose.

[27] See *Christopher Keeley v Fosroc International Ltd.* [2006] EWCA Civ 1277, where redundancy payment details contained in a staff handbook were held to form part of the contractual document, and as such could be relied upon by the employees.

[28] *Donovan v Invicta Airways Ltd* [1970] 1 Lloyd's Rep 486 and *Mahmud v Bank of Credit and Commerce International SA* [1998] AC 20.

[29] See *RDF Media Group Plc v Clements* [2007] EWHC 2892, and in particular paras. 100–106 for a discussion of mutual trust and confidence.

[30] *Hivac Ltd v Park Royal Scientific Instruments Co* [1946] 1 All ER 350.

if it may interfere with his/her employment with the first employer. Fidelity has caused problems in the employment relationship when employees have followed the exact terms of their
contract, yet their actions were held to be breaching the duty of faithful service.[31] The issue of
faithful service has extended to ensure that the employee does not steal from the employer,
take other employees or customers when he/she leaves to establish a new business, and he/
she must not solicit bribes. In *Boston Deep Sea Fishing and Ice Co. v Ansell*[32] the managing director of a company received secret commissions when placing orders for new boats
and provided business to corporations in which he held shares. The Court of Appeal held
such actions to be against the implied duties on the director to give faithful service to his
employer. Where a potential conflict of interest is evident, the employee should inform his/
her employer of this fact and thus enable the employer to take the most appropriate action.

Employees, who are fiduciaries,[33] have the duty to *disclose the misdeeds of others*.[34] This
places an obligation on the employee to inform the employer if he/she is aware or has knowledge of wrongful actions by colleagues. Note however, that there is no obligation to disclose
his/her own misdeeds.

Employees are under a duty of *cooperation*[35] and must work with his/her employer in the
best interests of the business. Even if the employee dogmatically adheres to the textual reading of the contract of employment, if this is used to cause harm to the employer, the employee
will breach his/her obligation to cooperate.

Employees must exercise *reasonable skill and judgement* in his/her employment so as not
to endanger colleagues and clients. This extends beyond the issue of health and safety[36] to
the employer's property. In *Janata Bank v Ahmed*[37] a bank manager was held by the Court of
Appeal to be negligent in losing the employer nearly £35,000. Not only was the bank manager
held to have breached an implied term in the contract, he was ordered to repay the lost money.

Employees have a duty to *obey lawful orders*[38] from the employer, even if this extends
beyond his/her job description. In *Macari v Celtic Football and Athletic Co.*[39] the Court of
Session held that a failure to obey a lawful and reasonable order would amount to a 'repudiatory breach of contract'. Lawful orders can include mobility clauses in the contract and in
United Kingdom Atomic Energy Authority v Claydon[40] an express mobility clause was combined with the implied term to obey lawful orders, and when Mr Claydon refused to transfer
to another city, it was held to be a breach of contract. The term may also be considered in light
of the employee's duty to cooperate with the employer. The employee may be expected to go
beyond the exact scope of his/her contract, and this may amount to covering for an absent
member of staff.[41] The 'lawful' element of the employee's duty does not extend to situations
where by doing so he/she would endanger him/herself. In *Ottoman Bank v Chakarian*[42] an
employee was asked, as part of his employment duties, to return to Turkey to work. However,
he feared that if he did go to Turkey he was in risk of being murdered, therefore his refusal
was considered not to breach the implied term. Neither does it require the employee to follow

---

[31] As demonstrated clearly in *Secretary of State for Employment v ASLEF* (No. 2) [1972] 2 QB 455.

[32] 39 ChD 339.

[33] *Shepherds Investments Limited v Walters* [2006] EWHC 836.

[34] *Sybrom Corporation v Rochem Ltd* [1983] 2 All ER 707.

[35] *Secretary of State for Employment v ASLEF* (No. 2) [1972] 2 QB 455.

[36] See *Lister v Romford Ice & Cold Storage Co. Ltd* [1957] 1 All ER 125 involving an employee injuring
another employee (who was his father). It was held that Lister had been negligent and breached his duty to
exercise reasonable skill and judgement.

[37] [1981] IRLR 457.   [38] *Pepper v Webb* [1969] 2 All ER 216.   [39] [1999] IRLR 787.

[40] [1974] ICR 128.   [41] See *Sim v Rotherham Metropolitan Borough Council* [1987] Ch 216.

[42] [1930] AC 277.

an employer's instruction that would be to commit a criminal act. In *Morrish v Henleys*[43] the employee was dismissed when he refused to falsify the company's accounts over the quantities of petrol assigned to his vehicle. The dismissal was considered unfair as the employee was not in breach for his refusal to become involved in such unlawful action, and agree to the changes made by the employer to the records.

There also exists the duty to *adapt to new working conditions*[44] which enables the employer to introduce new working systems and the use of technology. In *Cresswell*, the Inland Revenue transferred its method of working from a manual system to a computerized one (this was before the prevalence of home computers and people's familiarity with them). Cresswell and other individuals did not wish to use these and sought a declaration from the court that the employer could not force the change in systems as this was not provided for under the contract of employment. It was held that there was an implied term allowing the change in working systems and the employer's unilateral right to alter the terms of the contract in light of this change. This led to Walton J remarking on the expectation of the employee to adapt to new working conditions. Further, the obligation on the employer in such a situation is to provide adequate training for the employees and to give them time to adapt to the changes.

> **? Thinking Point**
>
> How many of the terms implied above would you have been aware of? Given the consideration of implied terms in contracts (Chapter 10), do you feel these terms are what the parties would have considered to be automatically included in their agreement?

16.5.2 Implied terms on the employer

Again, this is by no means an exhaustive list, but relevant examples of obligations imposed on employers have been the duty to *pay wages*.[45] This is often where the amount in wages or the frequency of the payments has not been agreed between the employee and employer. If no express agreement is made the employee should be paid a reasonable wage[46] and within a reasonable time.[47] The employer also has the duty to *pay a fair proportion of wages* if industrial action is accepted.[48] In *Miles v Wakefield MDC*[49] the House of Lords held that where the superintendent registrar of births, deaths, and marriages took industrial action by refusing to work on Saturday mornings, the employer was entitled to withhold 3/37ths of his wages as Mr Miles was unavailable for work. The employer must pay wages in money, rather than a previous practice of paying in tokens redeemable in the employer's business, and no unlawful deductions can be made against the wages paid to the employee.

---

[43] [1973] IRLR 61.   [44] *Cresswell v Board of Inland Revenue* [1984] 2 All ER 713.

[45] *Devonald v Rosser & Sons* [1906] 2 KB 728.

[46] This is assessed by looking at the region and the typical pay for the job, at the level of seniority and the employee's experience.

[47] Payment should be made after the first week. The latest the employee should be paid is by the end of the first month, and then in monthly increments thereafter.

[48] *Royle v Trafford Metropolitan Borough Council* [1984] IRLR 184.

[49] [1987] 1 All ER 1089.

There is generally no obligation on the employer *to provide work*[50] for the employee. As long as he/she provides the wages agreed then the employer may ask the employee to stay away from the place of employment (in examples where there is a decline in orders and there is no work for the employee to do). However, the exception to this is where the nature of the job requires work[51] then the employer must provide it. In *Clayton & Waller v Oliver*[52] an actor who had been given the lead role in a musical production, and was then removed from the role and offered a substantially inferior one, was entitled to seek damages due to the employer's actions which had damaged his reputation.

The employer has an obligation to *maintain the health and safety* of his/her workers[53] and this means the appropriate training of all staff, and safe systems of work to be put in place. As part of the requirements to protect employees' health at work, the employer must take out insurance for the benefit of employees working in the United Kingdom, under the Employer's Liability (Compulsory Insurance) Act 1969. This insurance protects employees in the event of an accident at work, or from illnesses that are attributable to his/her employment, and ensures that in the event that an employer is unable to compensate the employee, the insurance will.

Employers generally have no obligation to provide employees with a *reference* when leaving the employment and seeking a new position (unless an implied term is applicable or there is an express clause to the contrary). Some employers are reluctant to provide a reference due to the fact that what they say may not be very complementary[54] and they do not wish to fall victim of the law of defamation. Also, the employer may not wish to be regarded as having provided an inaccurate reference that amounts to a negligent misstatement and be subject to a liability claim. Note that it is not uncommon for an employer to provide a poor employee with a particularly good reference simply to 'get rid' of the employee. Such tactics should, consequently, be adopted with caution. It should also be noted that there may be implied into the contract a duty to provide a reference where it has been provided for other employees, or if it has been agreed as part of a settlement issue in a grievance dispute.

As its name suggests, employers, like employees, also have the obligation to maintain *mutual trust and confidence*.[55] As stated in *Malik v Bank of Credit and Commerce International*, the employer must not 'without reasonable and proper cause,[56] conduct itself in a manner calculated or likely to destroy or seriously damage the relationship of confidence and trust between the employer and employee'. This may include, for example, unfair criticism of the employee in front of his/her colleagues, or demeaning him/her in the workplace, and a breach of this term enables the victim to treat the action as a repudiatory breach.[57] This may be considered the most important implied term in an employment relationship, as no employment can

---

[50] *Collier v Sunday Referee Publishing Ltd.* [1940] 2 KB 647.

[51] Examples include those employees who get paid by the piece; those working on commission who require work to earn money; those employment situations where the skills of the employee must be maintained (such as doctors/surgeons); and where publicity is required (such as professional musicians/actors).

[52] [1930] AC 209.

[53] *MacWilliams v Sir William Arrol & Co Ltd* [1962] 1 All ER 623.

[54] See *Spring v Guardian Assurance Plc* [1994] 3 All ER 129, where the House of Lords held that a reference that gave a poor impression of the former employee, even though these were beliefs genuinely held by the employer, was negligent as it was likely to cause the employee economic loss. There was an implied term in the employment to take reasonable care and skill in preparing a reference.

[55] *Isle of Wight Tourist Board v Coombes* [1976] IRLR 413.

[56] In practice the burden rests on the employee to prove the employer's breach on the balance of probabilities.

[57] See Brodie, D. (2004) 'Health and Safety, Trust and Confidence and Barber v Somerset County Council: Some Further Questions' *Industrial Law Journal*, Vol. 33, No. 3, p. 261.

continue if the parties cannot trust each other. It is fundamental to the effective functioning of the employment relationship. Mutual trust imposes obligations on the employer to prevent actions including bullying[58] and stress faced by an employee (for example, through an unreasonable workload),[59] and if not attended to, may lead to successful claims for constructive dismissal[60] and also possible tort actions against the employer for damages.

Conclusion

The chapter has outlined the fundamental distinction between individuals who are employees and those who are independent contractors. The tests have been developed through the common law and have demonstrated that the current method is to begin with the tests identified in *Montgomery v Johnson Underwood*, and then if these questions are answered in the affirmative, to continue and apply the third question provided in *Ready Mixed Concrete* (and issues raised in *Market Investigations*). Whilst many employment rights are being introduced that affect 'workers'[61] not simply employees, there are still many areas of employment law where rights and obligations fall on the employee and not independent contractor.[62] The independent contractor gains tax advantages, the ability to work for many different employers, and can deduct expenses incurred in his/her employment which employees cannot. They are, however, excluded from many protections through statutory rights that may leave them vulnerable if they are dismissed, made redundant, injured at work, or become pregnant. These factors are considered in the following chapters.

Summary of main points

Employment status

- The Employment Rights Act s. 230 defines employment status where 'an individual who has entered into or works under (or, where the employment has ceased, worked under) a contract of employment'.

- As the statute is deliberately broad in scope the courts have developed the following tests:

- *Control test:* This continues to be a vital element of establishing employee status; it cannot, however, be used in isolation, and must form part of the wider range of questions established in *Montgomery, Ready Mixed Concrete*, and *Market Investigations*.

- *Integration/organization test:* Here, the more the individual was integrated into the organization the more likely he/she would be considered an employee. This test was not often used following the decision.

---

[58] *Waters v Commissioner of Police for the Metropolis* [2000] 4 All ER 934.
[59] *Barber v Somerset County Council* [2004] ICR 457.
[60] See **18.3**.
[61] Such as the National Minimum Wage Act 1998; the Working Time Regulations 1998; the Equality Act 2010 and so on.
[62] For a discussion see Anderman, S. (2000) 'The Interpretation of Protective Employment Statutes and Contracts of Employment' *Industrial Law Journal*, Vol. 29, No. 3, p. 223.

- *Mixed/economic reality test:* This test uses the criteria from *Ready Mixed Concrete*; *Lee v Chung*; *Market Investigations*; and *Montgomery* in establishing employment status.

Reason for the distinction

- The following are examples of why it is important to differentiate between employees and independent contractors: the rate of income tax and responsibility for National Insurance payments; the statutory rights of unfair dismissal, redundancy, and various maternity rights, which are only available to employees; and the employer having potential liability for the torts committed by his/her employees in the course of their employment.

Written particulars

- This is not the contract of employment, although similar information may be contained in the document.
- This document must be provided within two months of the employee starting employment.
- It contains important information regarding the parties; the terms of the employment including duties, sources of obligations, and pay; whether the employment is for a fixed time or permanent; and pension details (among others).

Terms implied into the contract

- Due to the problems of attempting to include all the terms of the employment relationship into a single document, terms have been implied into the contract through the courts, customs, and statutes.
- Duties and obligations on the employee include: mutual trust and confidence; fidelity; duty to disclose the misdeeds of others; cooperation; to use reasonable skill and judgement; obey lawful orders; and to adapt to new working conditions.
- Duties and obligations on the employer includes: to pay wages; in the case of industrial action being accepted by the employer, to pay a fair proportion of wages; to provide work for the employee; to maintain the health and safety of his/her workers; and employers also have the obligation to maintain mutual trust and confidence in the employment relationship.

 Summary questions

Essay questions

1. 'Through the last one hundred years, legislative and common law initiatives have failed to establish a single definitive test to establish the employment status of individuals.'
   Critically assess the above statement and identify reforms in the law that you deem expedient.

2. Lord Slynn, in *Spring v Guardian Assurance plc* [1994] 3 All ER 129, observed '...the changes which have taken place in the employer/employee relationship ... (have seen) ...

far greater duties imposed on the employer than in the past, whether by statute or by judicial decision, to care for the physical, financial or even psychological welfare of the employees.'

Discuss the above statement in relation to the development of implied terms in contracts of employment.

Problem questions

1. Jennifer has been employed by All Bright Consumables (ABC) Ltd for the past two years. ABC retails electronic home entertainment equipment. Her tasks include offering sales advice, stock-taking duties, restocking the shelves and accepting deliveries from suppliers. Jennifer works 40 hours per week and is entitled to six weeks paid holidays each year, however these must be agreed in advance with her manager and she cannot take her holiday if another member of staff is on holiday at the same time.

   She is occasionally required to work in other regional branches when necessary, although Jennifer may claim expenses for the travel involved. Jennifer's contract identifies her as an independent contractor, and it also contains a restraint of trade clause. She is responsible for paying her own income tax and national insurance.

   Following a disagreement with her employer regarding stock irregularities, Jennifer has been dismissed from work. She would like to know her employment status in order to identify if she may pursue a claim of unfair dismissal.

   With reference to appropriate case law, identify how a tribunal may decide the employment status of Jennifer.

2. Kenny is a maintenance engineer for ABC in its electronic gadgets department (servicing burglar alarms). Kenny is engaged to service the products sold by ABC to its customers in the customers' own premises. Kenny is provided with a list of customers and the priority of those jobs, but he is otherwise left to determine his workload and when he completes the jobs in the day. Following the completion of each job, Kenny obtains a signature from the customer and passes this back to ABC as proof of him completing the job. ABC then invoices the customer directly.

   Kenny uses his own vehicle to make the visits to the customers' premises and he is paid without any deduction of income tax or National Insurance contributions. ABC considers that Kenny will make his own arrangements with HM Revenue and Customs personally.

   Yesterday, whilst on a call to one of ABC's major customer's, Kenny was involved in an accident at work. The accident occurred as the customer had alarms placed in particularly difficult to reach locations. The ladders provided by ABC to Kenny did not reach these locations. Kenny contacted ABC about this but was told that this was a very important customer, and he must complete the service at that visit. As such, whilst attempting to do so, he fell and sustained a serious injury to his arm and shoulder.

   The result of the accident has left Kenny hospitalized for four weeks and he is unlikely to return to work for at least six months. ABC has informed Kenny that as he is an independent contractor he is not eligible to claim from its insurers, nor is he able to claim sick pay.

   Advise Kenny as to his employment status and any claim he may make for his losses against ABC.

Further reading

Boyle, M. (2007) 'The Relational Principle of Trust and Confidence' *Oxford Journal of Legal Studies*, Vol. 27, No. 4, p. 633.

Clarke, L. (2000) 'Mutuality of Obligations and the Contract of Employment: *Carmichael and Another v National Power PLC' The Modern Law Review*, Vol. 63, No. 5, p. 757.

Davidov, G. (2005) 'Who is a Worker?' *Industrial Law Journal*, Vol. 34, No. 1, p. 57.

Taylor, S. and Emir, A. (2006) 'Employment Law: An Introduction' Oxford University Press: Oxford and New York.

Useful website

http://www.danielbarnett.co.uk/
(Daniel Barnett is a barrister specializing in employment law. This resource includes commentary on legislative reforms, and case law materials, often from the lawyers involved in the case. The service is free and is an excellent source of information—I highly recommend you sign up for the mailing service.)

Online Resource Centre

http://www.oxfordtextbooks.co.uk/orc/marson3e/
Why not visit the Online Resource Centre and try multiple choice questions associated with this chapter to test your understanding of the topic. You will also find relevant updates to the law.

Dismissal at Common Law; Redundancy and the Transfer of Undertakings

17

Why does it matter?

At some point, contracts of employment will come to an end. There are various reasons for this—at the employer's will (giving notice); the individual may wish to leave and explore other opportunities (resignation); the task for which employment was established may have been completed; the individual may become redundant; or there may be some 'outside' factor where the employment cannot continue (including frustration). Whilst these are merely a few examples, the mechanisms that will enable a termination of the employment relationship without transgressing the law are clearly of importance. When a business (an undertaking) is sold (its ownership transferred), obligations exist for both the transferor and transferee to respect and protect the terms and conditions of employment of the affected individuals. By adhering to the legal requirements and adopting the correct approach to dismissal/transfer procedures, not only may court/tribunal action be avoided, but it will assist in maintaining good working relations, which are essential to promote trust, respect, and productivity.

Learning outcomes

Following reading this chapter you should be in a position to:

- explain the common law mechanism of seeking damages for the wrongful termination of employment (17.3.2–17.3.6)

- compare and contrast the remedies of wrongful dismissal and unfair dismissal (17.3.6 (Table 17.1))

- identify when an employee may claim protection under redundancy (17.4–17.4.8).

- identify the factors that will make the selection process for redundancies fair and unfair (17.4.3–17.4.4)

- explain the obligations on the employer to consult with the employees (and/or their representatives) over planned redundancies (17.4.5–17.4.5.2)

- explicate the obligations of an employer who wishes to transfer the undertaking, and the requirements on the transferee to protect the transferred workforce's continuity, and terms, of employment (17.5–17.5.5)

Key terms

These terms will be used in the chapter and it may be helpful to be aware of what they mean or refer back to them when reading through the chapter.

Common law
Wrongful dismissal is governed by the common law, and hence the rules and remedies applicable with the common law are applied to the regulation of contracts of employment.

Economic, technical, and organizational reason
Where there has been a transfer of an undertaking regulated by TUPE 2006, the employee is transferred to the transferee with the terms and conditions of employment preserved. These terms and conditions may be altered, and the employee may even be dismissed, if there is an economic, technical, or organizational reason connected with the transfer, to the satisfaction of the tribunal.

Gross misconduct
The 'gross' element is a one-off, serious, event that would justify a **summary dismissal** such as theft, assaults and so on.

Gross negligence
To justify a summary dismissal this would involve a serious act of negligence such as endangering customers, colleagues and so on.

Redundancy
This occurs when employment at the place of business has ceased or the nature of the business/industry has changed and the employee's role in the organization is surplus to requirements.

Reorganization of the business
An employer has the ability to reorganize his/her business. This may be due to changes in competition; to respond to the needs of the organization and so on. Such reorganization, if resulting in dismissals, may lead to claims for redundancy payments.

Summary dismissal
This is an immediate dismissal (without any notice).

Wrongful dismissal
(A claim under the common law.) This involves a breach of contract when, for example, insufficient notice is provided to the individual. As it is a contractual claim, it is, significantly, available to all workers rather than the strict criteria that must be satisfied to qualify for rights under the unfair dismissal protections.

17.1 Introduction

Before the increasingly broad and complex legislative provisions governing employment relationships began to take effect with great pace from the 1960s, contracts of employment were largely dealt with by the 'normal' rules of contract law. Indeed, a claim for wrongful dismissal is a breach of contract claim (albeit a contract of employment), and is (often) heard by courts that hear contractual disputes. This chapter identifies the remedy for termination of the contract of employment through the **common law** claim of wrongful dismissal. The statutory measures of unfair (and constructive unfair) dismissal are discussed in Chapter 18. The chapter also addresses situations of redundancy, and the rights of individuals and obligations on employers when the business is transferred to a new owner. Each of these measures offer protection to employees, and employers should understand the nature of these rights, the qualifications necessary for each mechanism, and the remedies available, to ensure they select the most appropriate mechanism to bring the employment relationship to an end.

17.2 Termination of employment

It is important to recognize from the outset that there are various ways of bringing an employment relationship to an end. Some of these may amount to a dismissal that may enable a claim for wrongful or unfair dismissal. There are also terminations that do not, at common law, constitute a dismissal.

17.2.1 Terminations not establishing a dismissal at common law

The following is a non-exhaustive list of situations where the employment relationship has ended, but no (common law) claim is available:

- *The mutual agreement of the parties*: There is a situation where the parties may simply no longer wish to continue with the contract of employment and as such release each other from any further obligations. However, the courts are suspicious of such arrangements and will look to see if the worker was provided with any inducement from the employer to end the contract (such as a financial inducement)[1] that could lead to a common sense belief of mutual agreement. If the individual was coerced into resigning due to a threat by the employer (such as a threat of dismissal),[2] then this will not amount to an agreement.

- *Frustration of the contract*: Claims of frustration have been invoked in situations where the individual was conscripted to the armed forces under national service; where the individual becomes ill and cannot continue with the contract;[3] or where injury prevents the continuity of the contract.[4] The courts will not readily accept an assertion that the contract is frustrated as this would negate the remedies provided under the statutory provisions and common law.[5]

- *The expiry of a fixed-term contract*: When a contract has reached the end of its term, the relationship under that contract is complete and no claim may be made under the common law. However, this does not mean that there is no claim under the statutory provisions and, indeed, non-renewal of a fixed-term contract may enable a claim for unfair dismissal.

---

[1] See *Logan Salton v Durham County Council* [1989] IRLR 99.
[2] *Martin v MBS Fastenings* [1983] IRLR 198.   [3] *Condor v The Barron Knights* [1966] 1 WLR 87.
[4] *GF Sharp & Co Ltd v McMillan* [1998] IRLR 632.
[5] *Williams v Watson Luxury Coaches Ltd* [1990] IRLR 164.

• *Non-return following child birth:* Under the common law, there is no breach for an employer refusing to allow a woman to return to her job following a period of absence following the birth of her child. However, the ERA 1996, ss. 96 and 137 establishes that such a refusal will be treated as a dismissal for the purposes of that Act.

17.3 Wrongful dismissal (the common law route)

 Business Link

Where an individual's contract is ended in breach of the contract (such as without the relevant notice period being provided) the individual may seek damages. This is a much more accessible claim than an action under unfair dismissal and there is no imposed maximum to the damages available. Care must be exercised when a fixed-term contract is terminated without a breach being committed by the individual. Unless an early termination clause is included the individual may be able to claim for the balance of the contract, and any contractual benefits included. This may involve significantly higher damages than would be available through unfair dismissal.

Under the governance of contract law,[6] the contract of employment may have included a term regarding the period of notice required for each of the parties to terminate the agreement. Even in the absence of such a clause, statute establishes the minimum notice period that has to be provided. If this notice period is not adhered to, in the absence of a justifiable reason, then the termination will be in breach of contract and, in this circumstance, may amount to a **wrongful dismissal**. As this is a contractual dispute, the damages will attempt to place the injured party in the position he/she would have been had the contract not been breached.

17.3.1 The notice period

The contract of employment will possibly identify the notice period that is required of each party (and these periods may be different between the individual and employer). In the absence of any notice period the ERA 1996, s. 86 states that employees who have worked between one month and two years continuously for the same employer are entitled to one week's notice. This notice period extends by one week for every year that is worked to a maximum of 12 weeks' notice (see Table 17.1).

17.3.2 What may be claimed

In the event that the employer dismisses the individual contrary to the terms of the contract or the statutory minimum, the claimant is entitled to damages for his/her losses. This will

---

[6] Although see *Autoclenz Ltd v Belcher & Ors* [2011] UKSC 41 for judicial comment on the distinctions between 'general' contracts and contracts of employment.

Table 17.1 Notice Periods

Period of Employment	Notice Period Applicable
Less than one month	None
More than one month but less than 2 years	1 week
More than 2 years but less than 12 years	Maximum of 12 weeks (one week for every year worked)
More than 12 years	12 weeks

be assessed on the standard principles of contract law and will provide the lost income for the notice period that should have been provided, or in the case of a fixed-term contract, the balance of the contract.[7] However, claims may not be made for the manner of the dismissal. Being a wrongful dismissal, there may be an element of distress, even humiliation in the nature of such terminations,[8] but the courts are unable to provide damages on these bases.[9]

The predominant remedy for wrongful dismissal claims is damages, but the courts have been increasingly inclined to make use of injunctions to prevent a dismissal, or to prevent a dismissal that attempts to circumvent a statutory right.[10] Note that specific performance is not available in contracts of personal service, but in *Irani*, the court followed the ruling in *Hill v CA Parsons*[11] regarding when an injunction should be awarded:

1 There must still exist between the parties mutual trust and confidence so that the employment relationship has not irreconcilably broken down;

2 The claimant was seeking protection of statutory rights; and

3 Damages would not have been an adequate remedy in the case.

17.3.3 **Duty to mitigate**

Having suffered a wrongful dismissal, the injured party must take reasonable steps to avoid further damages accruing and as such he/she must attempt to mitigate his/her losses. This does not require the affected individual to accept any job that is offered, or to take up employment at a much lower level than had been enjoyed whilst employed. The courts will expect evidence that alternative work has been sought. As in the case of seeking damages for breach of contract, it would be contrary to public policy to allow the injured party to sit back and allow any damages to mount if he/she could have minimized these losses through alternative employment.[12]

---

[7] *Addis v Gramophone Co Ltd* [1909] AC 488.

[8] *Edwards v Chesterfield Royal Hospital NHS Foundation Trust; Botham v MoD* [2011] UKSC 58.

[9] Although, exceptionally, damages may be awarded for damage to reputation in dismissal, *Malik v Bank of Credit and Commerce International* [1997] 3 WLR 95.

[10] *Irani v South West Hampshire Health Authority* [1985] IRLR 203.

[11] [1971] 3 WLR 995.   [12] See *Brace v Calder* [1895] 2 QB 253 (see **12.3.1**).

17.3.4 After discovered reasons

It may be the case that following an employer's decision to terminate the individual's contract, for example, on suspicion of breach of contract (such as for **gross misconduct** or **gross negligence**), after the dismissal evidence is gained that proves (or disproves) the employer's assertion. This is called 'after discovered reasons' as the evidence is only identified following the action taken by the employer. Whilst in situations of unfair dismissal these will not subsequently make an unfair dismissal fair, they will be allowed to enable the employer to mount a defence against a wrongful dismissal claim. Hence, after discovered reasons can make an otherwise wrongful dismissal a lawful dismissal. As such, it may be wise for an employer to continue his/her investigation, even following a dismissal, to gather whatever evidence is available to defeat a possible wrongful dismissal claim.[13]

17.3.5 Time limit for claims

As this is a breach of contract case, the claimant can bring a claim for wrongful dismissal up to six years following the notice of the contract being ended.

17.3.6 Who may claim

As this is an action for breach of contract, any individual who contracts to personally undertake the work can claim the remedy of wrongful dismissal. Therefore, unlike the statutory route of unfair dismissal, the status of employee is not required and this opens up the route for claimants who might otherwise not qualify under unfair dismissal. Further, there is no requirement for a period of continuous employment (Table 17.2).

17.4 Redundancy

 Business Link

There are many occasions where a business may become unprofitable, or a part of the business may have to be closed. In these events, employees will be affected and the employer may no longer require their services. In these circumstances the employees may be eligible for compensation in the form of a redundancy payment. There are criteria established to determine who is eligible to claim, and the amount of any award to be made. By possessing this information, the employer will recognize the steps to be taken, particularly in terms of consultation with the employees' representatives, and may avoid unfair selection procedures that will provide the employee with a right to claim unfair dismissal.

---

[13] *Boston Deep Sea Fishing and Ice Co v Ansell* (1888) LR 39 Ch. D. 339.

Table 17.2 Comparison: unfair dismissal and wrongful dismissal

	Unfair dismissal	Wrongful dismissal
Source of the right	Statutory (ERA 1996).	Common law (contract).
Who may claim	Only available to employees.	Anyone with a contract.
Minimum period of continuous employment required to access the right	Two years.	Immediate from the commencement of the contract.
Time limit within which a claim must be lodged	Three months.	Six years.
Where the claim is heard	Employment Tribunal.	County Court; High Court. A claim may be heard at an Employment Tribunal where the claim does not exceed £25,000.
Basis of the award	Compensation includes a basic award and a compensatory award to reflect ongoing and future losses.	Only covers the loss incurred for breach of the relevant notice period, or the balance of a fixed-term contract with no early termination clause.
Reasons for dismissal	s. 98 ERA 1996 outlines potentially fair reasons for dismissal. The statute also identifies reasons for dismissal that will be automatically unfair.	The employer can choose any reason for dismissal. The stipulation is adherence to the notice period required under the contract.
Costs	Legal costs incurred in the action are (at the time of writing) rarely awarded to the successful party.	Costs are more readily awarded in the County Court and High Court.
Remedies available	Reinstatement; re-engagement or compensation.	Damages (although injunctions may also be available).
Discipline/dismissal procedures	The procedures identified in the ACAS Code must be complied with or the tribunal may reduce any award by up to 25%.	Any procedures provided by the employer in the contract must be adhered to.
After discovered reasons	Cannot make an unfair dismissal fair, but it may reduce any compensation awarded to a successful employee.	These may justify a dismissal, and if accepted by the court, will make a wrongful dismissal a fair dismissal.
Damages awarded	This is capped at (from 1 February 2013) £87,700.	As this is a breach of contract claim there is no ceiling to the award of damages. It depends on the breach and the value of the contract.

Redundancy is a complex issue of which there may have been many factors in the changes to, or decline of, the business that has necessitated the employer taking the decision to dismiss individuals. The law seeks to protect employees who are affected by this event, but also provide sufficient flexibility to enable an employer to carry on the business, or sell the undertaking to another buyer that may have the resources to 'save' it (for example). As such the law provides guidance on how this process may be undertaken to be as fair as possible to all parties.

Redundancy involves two broad scenarios. The employer may be closing the business and hence there is no work for the employee to do;[14] or the employee may be surplus to the employer's requirements following, for example, a **reorganization** or refocus to the business. Redundancy is one of the potentially fair reasons to dismiss, but unlike most of the other categories identified in ERA 1996, s. 98, it does not relate to the capability or the misconduct of the employee and in essence is a 'no fault' termination.

17.4.1 The definition of redundancy

The definition of redundancy is contained in ERA 1996, s. 139:

> For the purposes of this Act, an employee who is dismissed shall be taken to be dismissed by reason of redundancy if the dismissal is attributable wholly or mainly to:
> (a) the fact that his employer has ceased, or intends to cease:
>   (i) to carry on the business for the purposes of which the employee was employed by him; or
>   (ii) to carry on that business in the place where the employee was so employed; or
> (b) the fact that the requirements of that business:
>   (i) for employees to carry out work of a particular kind; or
>   (ii) for employees to carry out work of a particular kind in the place where the employee was so employed by the employer, have ceased or diminished or are expected to cease or diminish.

When the employer decides to dismiss due to redundancy, the tribunal is not in a position to ascertain the business rationale behind the decision but rather limits the inquiry to determine whether redundancy was the reason for the dismissal, or whether redundancy was merely a 'smokescreen' for some other reason.

17.4.1.1 *Work of a particular kind*

In the first definition of redundancy above,[15] it is quite easy to identify a redundancy situation as the business is being closed and the entire workforce is being made redundant. However, if another firm is taking over the business (under a transfer of the undertaking) and the business is being sold as a going concern, the employees' contracts will be transferred to the new owner and no redundancies will be established.

Where the situation becomes more complicated is in the assessment under s. 139(b) as the statute requires a diminution in the number of employees required to perform 'work of a particular kind', rather than a diminution in the work itself. If the employer is reducing

---

[14] Note that the tribunal is not allowed to assess the business need or rationale for the employer ending the business (*Moon v Homeworthy Furniture* [1976] IRLR 298).

[15] Section 139(a).

the workforce but the work required remains the same or is increasing then a redundancy situation will occur,[16] whereas if the employer, in the same circumstances, has reorganized the business and still requires the same number of employees, then no redundancy has taken place. The courts will look to the reason for the dismissal instead.[17]

In s. 139(a)(ii) where the business that the employees had previously been employed is ceasing, the question to be asked is 'Where is the "particular" place of work?' In *Bass Leisure Ltd v Thomas*[18] the EAT addressed the previous authorities[19] and held that where a woman had been informed that her position with the employer, based in Coventry, was moving to another plant some 20 miles away, despite the fact that her contract contained a mobility clause, the focus for redundancy was a geographical test. The woman worked in Coventry and when this employment ceased she was in effect made redundant, even though alternative work was offered 20 miles away.

The questions to be asked when determining if a redundancy situation has occurred were outlined by the EAT in *Safeway Stores v Burrell*:[20]

1 Was the employee dismissed?

2 If answered in the affirmative, had the requirements of the business for the employees to carry out work of a particular kind ceased or diminished, or were they expected to cease or diminish?

3 If so, was the dismissal caused wholly or mainly by that cessation or diminution of work?

17.4.2 Qualifications to the right

As with unfair dismissal, qualification criteria exist that restrict the remedy only to an individual who:

- has 'employee' status;
- was continuously employed by the same employer for two years before the relevant date of the redundancy;
- is not in one of the excluded categories;
- was dismissed; and
- was dismissed on the basis of redundancy.

17.4.2.1 *Employee status and continuous employment*

The test for employee status is assessed in the same way as it is for unfair dismissal and the particulars of employment will give evidence of the two years' continuous service.

---

[16] *Johnson v Peabody Trust* [1996] IRLR 387.

[17] Such an example may be seen in *Vaux & Associated Breweries Ltd v Ward* [1968] ITR 385, where an older woman was replaced in the public house by a much younger woman (to do the same job) on the basis of establishing a younger image for the premises. Ms Ward was not made redundant in this circumstance.

[18] [1994] IRLR 104.

[19] These authorities included cases such as *Rank Xerox Ltd v Churchill* [1988] IRLR 280, which placed the interpretation of 'place of work' on the contract between the parties. Hence if a mobility clause was included in the contract, this interpretation was to be where the employer could require the employee to work, rather than looking at where the work was actually taking place.

[20] [1997] IRLR 200.

17.4.2.2 *Excluded categories*

Certain categories of individual do not have the ability to bring a redundancy claim. These include share fishermen; employees of the Crown; and those individuals who were employed as a domestic servant of a relative. Access to the right is also restricted to those individuals who were dismissed for misconduct or for involvement in industrial action, and if the individual had been offered suitable alternative employment having been informed of the redundancy and unreasonably declined this, he/she will be ineligible to claim.

17.4.2.3 *Dismissal*

The employee's claim can only be made if the tribunal finds he/she has been dismissed for the reason of redundancy.

The employee is dismissed by reason of redundancy if:

- the contract under which he/she was employed has been terminated by the employer;
- the contract was for a limited term and the contract terminates by virtue of the limiting event without being renewed under the same contract; or
- the employee terminates the contract in circumstances in which he/she is entitled to terminate it without notice by reason of the employer's conduct.[21]

For a dismissal to be effective in a redundancy claim the employee must have been given a specific date on which his/her employment will cease (termed 'being put under notice of dismissal'). The dismissal for the purposes of redundancy must be the actual notice of dismissal and not some future intention of the employer. In *Morton Sundour Fabrics v Shaw*[22] the firm had informed Mr Shaw that the department of the business in which he worked was going to close at some point in the future (certainly within the following year) and it would be in his interests to find alternative employment. This is what Mr Shaw did, having provided the firm with his notice of leaving and taking up his new employment. He later made a claim for a redundancy payment from Morton Sundour but the claim failed as he had not been put under a notice of dismissal, and as such he did not qualify for the right.

> **? Thinking Point**
>
> Do you believe this is a good application of the law? Public policy might suggest that an employee who has been informed in good time of the financial problem of a firm, and instructed that it would be in his/her interests to find alternative employment, should still be entitled to claim for a redundancy payment. However, the application of this case suggests that the employee must actually wait until he/she is put under a notice before seeking new employment.

There is an exception to the above rule whereby an employee may leave the employment before the redundancy becomes effective.[23] If the employee serves the employer with a 'counter-claim' within the statutory notice period of his/her intention to leave the employment early, and this is accepted by the employer, then the employee's right to claim a

---

[21] ERA 1996, s. 136.   [22] [1966] 2 KIR 1.   [23] ERA 1996, s. 142.

redundancy payment is protected. On the event of the employer refusing this request, he/she may provide a 'counter-notice' to the employee's claim. If the employee decides to leave the employment without serving the notice period and brings a redundancy claim, the tribunal will decide whether to enable the claim to proceed and the level of compensation (if any) to be awarded.

The ERA 1996, s. 163(2) assists the employee by presuming redundancy is the reason for the dismissal and placing the burden on the employer to disprove this. The employee will not be held to have been dismissed if he/she is offered a renewal of the contract or re-engagement with the employer; if offered 'suitable' employment with an associated company of the employer; or where the business has been transferred under the TUPE 2006 Regulations.

17.4.3 The employer's selection of employees for redundancy

When the business is going to continue trading, but the reorganization involves making redundancies from certain departments, or it applies to groups of employees, the law provides guidance on how to establish fair selection procedures. There are many instances where an employer's decision, albeit innocently made, will in fact amount to a discriminatory or unfair selection. This enables a claim for unfair dismissal if the tribunal holds that there was discrimination in the selection procedure, therefore communication and consultation with the employees, trades unions and employees' representatives, in accordance with policies allowed under the legislation, will lessen the chances of claims being brought against the employer. As much warning of the possibility of redundancies as possible should be provided to the employees and their representatives to enable alternative courses of action to be taken. The employer should also identify any suitable alternative work that may be available in the organization for those selected for redundancy. Such transparency will also assist in maintaining good industrial relations during a very tense period in the business.[24]

17.4.4 Automatically unfair selection for redundancy

Just as with unfair dismissal, there are categories of employees who, when selected for redundancy because of their membership of that category, will be held to have been unfairly selected. Selections from the following categories will be held automatically unfair:

- membership or non-membership of a trade union, or activities connected with the membership;[25]
- pregnancy or childbirth, or if the employee has asserted statutory rights or made complaints under health and safety legislation;[26]
- selection due to the discriminatory policy or its non-application.[27]

---

[24] See the case of *Williams v Compair Maxam Ltd* [1982] IRLR 83 for an assessment of how not to carry out the selection process for redundancy.

[25] Trade Union and Labour Relations (Consolidation) Act 1992 s. 153.

[26] ERA 1996, s. 105.   [27] *Williams v Compair Maxam.*

17.4.5 **Obligation to consult**

Trade Union and Labour Relations (Consolidation) Act 1992

When the employer is planning redundancies involving 20 or more employees, there is an obligation, following the EU Directive on Collective Dismissals (75/129/EEC),[28] and brought into effect in the UK through the Trade Union and Labour Relations (Consolidation) Act (TULRCA) 1992, ss. 188–198, to consult with the recognized trade union or other employee representatives.[29] The requirement is to begin the consultation process when the employer is 'contemplating' redundancies, which implies that the consultation is to begin as soon as is reasonably practicable. In *R v British Coal Corporation, ex parte Vardy*[30] this was held to be when the employer first believes he/she may need to make redundancies. This was furthered by the Court of Justice in *Junk v Kuhnel*,[31] where it was held that the consultation should take place when the employer intends to make redundancies rather than wait until the notices of dismissal are sent to the employees. However, TULRCA 1992, s. 188(1A) provides that consultation must take place:

- where between 20–99 employees are to be made redundant—the minimum consultation period is a period of 30 days before the first dismissal.
- where over 100 employees are to be made redundant—the minimum period is 90 days before the first dismissal.

17.4.5.1 *Purpose of the consultation*

Evidently, the rationale for requiring a period of consultation with the affected employees' representatives is to enable possible alternatives to redundancies (such as reductions in hours, overtime bans and so on) to be explored. These may be agreed which will affect all employees but may reduce the necessity of dismissals. Even if these negotiations do not produce a situation that prevents dismissals, agreements can be reached on the selection procedures to be used. The EAT has also held that the consultation places a duty on employer, to identify the reason for the redundancies.[32]

When an employee has been informed he/she is to be made redundant, he/she is entitled to time off work to attend training courses to increase his/her skills for new work and attend interviews for new employment.[33]

17.4.5.2 *Failure to follow the consultation requirements*

A failure to consult with the employees' representatives before redundancies are announced may lead to a claim for compensation. The employer is required to explain why the consultations did not take place, and if no answer is provided, or the tribunal does not accept the employer's response, then the tribunal may make a declaration to that effect. The tribunal may also make a 'protective award' to compensate the employees who have been, or are about to be made redundant, which may be made for a period of up to 90 days (the protected period). The pay, following *Susie Radin Ltd v GMB*,[34] should be to deter future employers from failing to follow the consultation requirements.[35] The tribunal will make the award

---

[28] As amended by Council Directive 98/59/EC of 20 July 1998 on the Approximation of the Laws of the Member States Relating to Collective Redundancies.

[29] The appropriate representatives are identified in TULRCA 1992, s. 188(1B).

[30] [1993] ICR 720.   [31] [2005] IRLR 310.

[32] *UK Coal Mining Ltd v National Union of Mineworkers* [2008] IRLR 4.

[33] ERA 1996, s. 52.   [34] [2004] IRLR 400.

[35] This decision was confirmed in *Sweetin v Coral Racing* [2006] IRLR 252.

based on the seriousness of the employer's default and on the basis of what is 'just and equitable' in the circumstances. The award is calculated on the basis of one week's pay for each week in the protective period, and the maximum (if this figure is exceeded) is established on the same basis as is for unfair dismissal/redundancy claims (as of 1 February 2012—£430).

There may exist circumstances where the consultation period cannot practicably be held in the time limits identified above. TULRCA 1992, s. 189(6) provides for 'special circumstances' to exist where the employer should not be subjected to the protective award on the basis of this failure.[36]

17.4.5.3 *Requirement to inform*

Employers that are proposing to dismiss more than 100 employees are required, under TULRCA 1992, s. 193, to inform the Department for Business Innovation & Skills at least 90 days before the first redundancy takes place. If there are more than 20 (but less than 100) employees being made redundant, the information requirement is at least 30 days before notice is provided of the termination of employment. Failure to follow the requirements results in a criminal offence being committed that may be punished with a fine.[37]

17.4.6 **Calculation of the payment**

The remedy that is provided in the case of redundancy is compensation. The ERA 1996, s. 135(1) states that an employer shall pay his/her employee a redundancy payment if the employee is:

- dismissed by the employer due to redundancy; or
- is eligible for a redundancy payment due to being 'laid off' or the employment constituting short-time.

The payment is subject to a maximum figure identified in the statute (in the same way as unfair dismissal payments are subject to a maximum)[38] (see **18.4.3**). However, this statutorily imposed figure will not prevent an employer from establishing its own payments in excess of this amount (which is usually through an enhanced redundancy scheme that reflects the employees' length of service with the firm).

Note that if the employee claims both redundancy and unfair dismissal, and is successful in each, then any awards will be offset so as not to compensate the claimant twice.

17.4.7 **Offer of alternative employment**

As identified above, during the employer's procedure for handling the redundancy he/she should consider if the employee may be suitable for alternative work. This will assist both the employer in not having to make a redundancy payment,[39] and the employee will move to alternative work without having to find employment (which may be difficult). Whilst the employee is not obliged to accept this offer of employment, if he/she unreasonably refuses an

---

[36] *USDAW v Leancut Bacon Ltd (In Liquidation)* [1981] IRLR 295.   [37] TULRCA 1992, s. 194.

[38] However, years in employment whilst under the age of 18 are not included in the calculation.

[39] The offer must begin within four weeks of the previous employment ceasing to avoid having to make a redundancy payment (ERA 1996, s. 141(1)).

offer of alternative employment he/she will lose the right to claim a redundancy payment. The tribunal will enquire:

1   whether a 'suitable' offer of alternative employment was made;[40] and

2   if this question is answered in the affirmative, was the employee unreasonable in his/her refusal?[41]

17.4.8 Trial period of employment

An employee who accepts the offer of alternative employment is entitled to a trial period to ascertain if the work will be suitable. This trial period may last up to four weeks[42] and if the employee is dismissed from this position within this trial period, the dismissal will be held as being due to redundancy.

17.5 Transfer of undertakings

> **Business Link**
>
> When a business is transferred, there are obligations on the transferor and transferee in respect of the firm's employees and their terms and conditions of employment. Legislation from 2006 further provides obligations where a service is transferred, and this has potential consequences for those who provide a service (accountants; lawyers and so on). This is a dynamic area that requires close supervision as to the direction and interpretation of the law.

Transfer of Undertakings (Protection of Employment) Regulations 2006

When an employer decides to sell part or all of a business, the business (or 'undertaking') and its workforce transfer to the purchaser. The relevant legislation was enacted due to the UK's membership of the European Union, and was first brought into effect in 1981, with an update to the Regulations in 2001, and the most recent legislation (the Transfer of Undertakings (Protection of Employment) Regulations 2006 (TUPE)) taking effect from 6 April 2006.[43] These Regulations were transposed from the Acquired Rights Directive[44] (ARD) that sought to preserve employees' rights and continuity of employment when a business was transferred to a new owner.

As TUPE 2006 is the UK's transposition of the EU Directive (ARD) it covers transfers in the UK. However, the EAT has held that TUPE 2006 may also affect transfers outside of the

---

[40] *Taylor v Kent CC* [1969] 3 WLR 156.

[41] Compare *Rawe v Power Gas Corporation* [1966] ITR 154 and *Fuller v Stephanie Bowman (Sales) Co. Ltd* [1977] IRLR 87.

[42] ERA 1996, s. 138.

[43] For an excellent discussion of the implications of the 2006 Regulations see McMullen, J. (2006) 'An Analysis of the Transfer of Undertakings (Protection of Employment) Regulations 2006' *Industrial Law Journal*, Vol. 35, No. 2, p. 113.

[44] Council Directive 77/187/EEC of 14 February 1977 on the Approximation of the Laws of the Member States Relating to the Safeguarding of Employees' Rights in the Event of Transfers of Undertakings, Businesses or Parts of Businesses.

UK. In *Hollis Metal Industries v GMB and Newell Ltd*[45] involving the transfer of part of a curtain-making business to a new employer in Israel, it was held that the transfer could fall under the TUPE 2006 Regulations, although the EAT did note the potential difficulties in the enforcement of any awards under the law. It has essentially been held that TUPE 2006 would apply in this respect as the transferor was based in the UK and hence this gave the domestic tribunals jurisdiction over the matter.

When the business is transferred to a new owner, and TUPE 2006 is applicable, those employees who were employed 'immediately prior to the transfer' automatically become the employees of the new owner, and they are employed on the same terms and conditions as they held before the transfer.[46] The new employer takes on the obligations and rights of these individuals and any of the collective agreements that had been agreed with the previous employer. Not only are the rights and conditions of the contracts of employment preserved, but any dismissal of an employee (regardless of whether this occurs before or following the transfer) for a reason connected with the transfer is automatically unfair. The exception to this rule is if there is a **'economic, technical or organizational'** reason[47] that may make the dismissal fair, insofar as the decision is reasonable.

17.5.1 A relevant transfer

TUPE 2006 preserves the rights of individuals, and continuity of employment, where a relevant transfer has taken place. A relevant transfer consists of two broad categories, the first being of a transfer of an economic entity that retains its identity (an 'economic entity' is defined as an 'organized grouping of resources' that has the objective of pursuing an economic activity).[48] This is what may be considered a 'standard' business transfer involving the transfer of the business between the current owner (the transferor) and the new owner (the transferee).[49]

Hence, from this regulation, there must be a transfer of a business activity from one owner to the next, and it must consist of the business, or an identifiable part of the business. It is also necessary, for TUPE 2006 to be effective, that the transfer includes a stable economic entity. In assessing these criteria, the business transferred must be likely to continue in the same or some similar aspect of economic activity that was in existence under the previous ownership.[50] In *Rygaard*[51] the Court of Justice of the European Union (Court of Justice) identified that this involved some aspect of permanence to the business. TUPE 2006 also includes the transfer of a lease or franchise and in *Daddy's Dance Hall*[52] the transfer of a lease for a bar and restaurant was still subject to the Regulations. Whilst TUPE 2006 does not apply to transfers

---

[45] [2007] UKEAT/0171/07/CEA.

[46] *Litster v Forth Dry Dock and Engineering* [1989] 2 WLR 634.

[47] This must be the actual reason for the dismissal. If the dismissal is simply connected to the transfer, TUPE will be invoked making the dismissal automatically unfair. See *Manchester College v Hazel* [2012] UKEAT/0642/11/RN.

[48] Reg. 3.

[49] This organized grouping must facilitate the exercise of an economic activity which pursues a specific objective – see *Lom Management Ltd v Sweeney* [2012] UKEATS/0058/11/BI. Further, the grouping must be a conscious / deliberate effort of the employer to put the employees to work on a specific contract for a client, not simply a matter of 'happenstance' – *Seawell Ltd v Cava* [2012] UKEATS/0034/11/BI.

[50] *Securicor Guarding Ltd v Fraser Security Services Ltd* [1996] IRLR 552.

[51] *Rygaard v Dansk Arbejdsgiverforening acting for Stro Molle Akustik A/S* [1996] IRLR 51.

[52] *Foreningen af Arbejdsledere i Danmark v Daddy's Dance Hall A/S* [1988] IRLR 315.

of shares,[53] in *Millam v The Print Factory (London) 1991 Ltd*[54] the Court of Appeal held that the two entities must be maintained as separate legal entities to avoid invoking TUPE.

The second form of transfer was added through TUPE 2006, reg. 3, and provides for changes of service provider (including organizations such as firms of accountants, lawyers and so on). The new Regulations consolidate the case law of the Court of Justice to widen the concept of relevant transfer and which take the form of:

1 contracting-out/outsourcing (such as where a service previously undertaken by the client is awarded to a new contractor);

2 re-tendering (such as where a contract for a service is awarded to a new contractor); and

3 contracting-in/in-sourcing (such as where a contract with the previous contractor is performed 'in-house').

This is a very interesting aspect of the law as it provides a new dimension to transfers of an undertaking.

Hunt v Storm Communications, Wild Card Public Relations and Brown Brothers Wines[55]

Facts:

Storm (a public relations consultancy firm) was employed to manage the public relations of the firm Brown Brothers Wines (Europe). Ms Hunt was employed by Storm as the account manger and spent approximately 70 per cent of her working hours devoted to the Brown Brothers account. Brown Brothers wished to transfer the account to another firm (Wild Card Public Relations) and informed Storm of this decision in June 2006. On the transfer of the account Storm informed Ms Hunt that she had been transferred to Wild Card under TUPE 2006. Wild Card Public Relations did not agree or wish for Ms Hunt to transfer to its business and claimed she had not been 'dedicated' to the business of Brown Brothers. However, the tribunal held that Ms Hunt was designated an 'organized grouping of resources' under TUPE 2006 and her principal purpose was acting on behalf of the client company. As such the effect of the transfer of the service was that Ms Hunt would transfer to the new firm taking over the Brown Brothers account under the TUPE 2006 Regulations.

Authority for:

The case was heard in a tribunal and therefore does not establish a precedent, but it does indicate the implications of the extension of TUPE to service provisions—outsourcing.

? Thinking Point

Given this extension to TUPE 2006, what do you think will be the situation where a client brings to an end their dealings with a firm providing a service (which was provided by a dedicated team), and transfers this to the new contractor? It may be that the client will be working with the same group of workers who were providing the service before the transfer. What may be the potential outcomes of this scenario given the *Hunt* case?

---

[53] *Brookes and Others v Borough Care Services and CLS Care Services Ltd* [1998] IRLR 636.

[54] [2007] IRLR 526.

[55] [2007] Reading Employment Tribunal No. 2702546/06 (unreported).

17.5.2 The effect of the transfer on contracts of employment

Upon a relevant transfer, the employees take their contractual rights and continuity of service with them when the transfer is completed. Whilst the transferee has to provide the same rights and continuity to the workers, he/she is also responsible for any liabilities or claims against the previous employer. Hence employment claims under, for example, equality laws will transfer to the new owner,[56] as will claims under torts (for example, personal injury).[57] As such, reg. 11 of TUPE 2006 places an obligation on the transferor to provide the prospective owner (the transferee) with 'employee liability information' which includes details such as the ages of the employees, the contracts of employment and written particulars, and the firm's grievance procedure and disciplinary details. The transfer of the business also includes the transfer of collective bargaining agreements that had existed before the transfer[58] and any trade union that had been recognized by the employer before the transfer must also be recognized by the incoming employer.[59]

17.5.2.1 *When an employee does not want to transfer*

TUPE 2006 protects an employee's terms and conditions of employment. However, there may be situations where the employee does not wish to have his/her contract transferred to the new employer, and he/she does not wish to work for the incoming owner. In *Katsikas v Konstantinidis*[60] the Court of Justice held that employees could not be compelled to transfer to a new employer against their will. Reg. 4(7) of TUPE 2006 enables an employee, upon the knowledge of the transfer and the new owner, to inform the transferor or transferee, before the transfer, (and this has been extended to after the transfer)[61] that he/she does not wish to transfer. Upon making this statement of his/her intention not to transfer, the employee's contract of employment ends (although without dismissal), and he/she cannot claim any remedy connected with a dismissal. There is an exception to this rule regarding refusals not amounting to dismissals. Where the employee refuses to transfer to the new employer under the belief that his/her conditions of employment will be changed with a resulting detriment being suffered, he/she may refuse to transfer (resign) and then claim constructive dismissal.[62]

17.5.3 Dismissal or variation to the contractual terms and conditions

The transferee has to recognize the rights of the contract that the employee was subject to prior to the transfer.[63] This has also been held by the Court of Appeal in *Computershare Investor Services v Jackson*[64] to restrict the employees' terms and conditions to those at the time of the transfer, so they did not have access to beneficial terms of the new employer. Employees are entitled to benefits conferred at the date of a transfer and not from the start

---

[56] *DJM International v Nicholas* [1996] IRLR 76.
[57] *Bernadine v Pall Mall Services Group Ltd* [1999] IRLR 617.
[58] Reg. 5.   [59] Reg. 6.   [60] [1993] IRLR 179.
[61] *New ISG Ltd v Vernon* [2007] EWHC 2665 (Ch).
[62] *University of Oxford v Humphreys* [2000] IRLR 183.
[63] Reg. 5(1).   [64] [2008] IRLR 70.

of their continuous employment. In *Daddy's Dance Hall* it was held that employees cannot be bound by agreements to vary the terms and conditions of employment if the transfer was the reason of the change. This included unilateral changes and those that were agreed by the transferee and the employees.[65] The EAT has also identified that whilst the principle established in *Daddy's Dance Hall* remains, changes to employees detriment are void, but those to their benefit are allowed.[66] This has been included in reg. 4(4) of TUPE 2006, unless there is an 'economic, technical or organizational' reason for the variation. Reg. 7 of TUPE 2006 also deems dismissals unfair if the sole or principal reason is the transfer itself, or if it is connected with the transfer. There is, again, an exception to this rule if the dismissal was due to an economic, technical, or organizational reason.

17.5.4 An economic, technical, or organizational reason

Under reg. 7(3), an otherwise unfair dismissal connected to the transfer may be justified by the new employer if it is due to an economic, technical, or organizational (ETO) reason. Many transfers occur because the business that is the subject of the transfer is not performing as well as it could, or is in financial difficulties. Even if this is not the case, a new employer may have ideas regarding streamlining the business and improving its profitability. As such, there is some scope for him/her making changes to the organizational structure. Note, however, that this provides the employer with a 'potentially' fair reason to dismiss and he/she will have to convince the tribunal that the reason was fair. The Regulations do not offer much guidance on how to interpret the ETO, but there is latitude for the new employer to dismiss employees if the business is not profitable with the existing numbers of staff (this would constitute an economic reason) and a most frequent ETO is redundancies.[67] The new employer may choose to reorganize the management structure of the firm to increase its profitability/viability (an organizational reason), or he/she may decide that aspects in the production/manufacturing process require alteration (a technical reason) and so on.

17.5.5 The obligation to consult regarding the transfer

TUPE 2006 does not stipulate any minimum consultation periods, albeit for requiring that consultation occurs.[68] It requires that the employer consults with the affected employees' representatives as to the transfer, its date, and the reason for it; any legal, economic, and social implications for the affected employees; any measures that are to be taken by the employer; and any measures (if there are any) that the new employer will take that may impact on the affected employees.[69] If the employer fails in the duty to consult, both transferor and transferee will be held jointly and severally liable,[70] and if no justification for this failure is presented, the employees or the employee representatives (such as a trade union) may complain

---

[65] This is questionable following the Court of Appeal's decision in *Regent Security Services v Power* [2008] IRLR 66, where it was held that an employee was entitled to rely on changes to their terms and conditions of employment following a transfer.

[66] *Power v Regent Security Services Ltd* [2007] UKEAT/0499/06/2901.

[67] *Gorictree Ltd v Jenkinson* [1984] IRLR 391.   [68] Reg. 13.

[69] Reg. 13(2).   [70] Reg. 15(9).

to a tribunal and be awarded compensation of up to 13 weeks' pay.[71] It was held by the Court of Appeal[72] that this award of compensation should be sufficient to deter future employers from disregarding the law (upheld in *Sweetin v Coral Racing*).[73]

There exists a defence for the employer who does not consult due to 'special circumstances' that makes consultation not reasonably practicable.[74] It should be noted that special circumstances may involve, for example, a sudden or unforeseen reason for the employer's insolvency, but would not be accepted as a reason simply because the employer attempted (unsuccessfully) to trade out of the financial difficulties before going into insolvency (*Clarks of Hove Ltd v Bakers' Union*).[75]

Employees have the right to request information from their employer regarding changes to terms and conditions of employment, information regarding the business's economic situation, and, of relevance to this section, when the business is involved in a transfer of the undertaking or there is the prospect of redundancies. The Information and Consultation of Employees Regulations 2004 provide that for organizations with 50 or more employees (from 6 April 2008), and where at least 10 per cent[76] of these employees make a valid request, the employer has to set out an agreement as to how and when consultation over the matter will take place. If the employer fails in this request the Central Arbitration Committee can make a declaration that the Regulations have been breached, and they also provide for a penalty payment of up to £75,000 (enforceable in the EAT). In *Amicus v Macmillan Publishers*[77] the EAT made its first judgment imposing a penalty under the Regulations (in this case £55,000) for the employer's 'significant' failure at 'almost every stage of the proceedings'.

 ## Conclusion

This chapter has considered issues surrounding ending the employment relationship. When read in conjunction with Chapter 18, the individual and employer will be in a position to identify where terminations of employment are lawful, and those situations in which a termination may lead to a claim for breach of contract and/or of statute. Chapters 17 and 18 should be read together to gain an overview of how the common law and statutory dismissal regulations interact, and to understand employers' responsibilities when the business is being sold. These laws are not simplistic, but neither are they particularly onerous, and awareness enables effective strategies for dismissal to be implemented enabling claims to be avoided; time and money lost (or wasted) in defending a dismissal can be reduced; and poor strategies for dismissals can lead, potentially, to a damaged reputation with the consequential negative impact on industrial relations.

 ## Summary of main points

Termination

- There are many instances of the employment relationship ending but they will not always amount to a dismissal that would enable a claim for wrongful dismissal. Note, however, that these may give rise to a dismissal and claim under statute.

---

[71] TULRCA 1992, s. 189 and TUPE 2006, reg. 16(3).
[72] *Susie Radin Ltd v GMB* [2004] IRLR 400.   [73] [2006] IRLR 252.
[74] TULRCA 1992, s. 188(7) and TUPE 2006, reg. 15(2).   [75] [1978] IRLR 366.
[76] This 10 per cent rule requires at least 15 employees and a maximum of 2,500 employees.
[77] [2007] UKEAT/0185/07/RN.

Wrongful dismissal

- Dismissals with the correct notice period provided, or in response to an individual's breach of the contract, are fair at common law.

- Wrongful dismissal occurs where (for example) the employer terminates the contract in breach of the required notice period and without a valid reason.

- To enable a lawful dismissal, the employer must adhere to the contractual notice period. In the absence of any contractual term, the bare statutory minimum applies.

- An employer is only permitted to substitute the notice period with a payment in lieu of notice where the contract allows this through an express term.

- An employer is entitled to dismiss without notice (a **summary dismissal**) where the individual has committed some fundamental breach of the contract.

- The claimant may wish to claim through wrongful dismissal rather than unfair dismissal due to there being fewer qualification criteria (a contract to perform the employment personally is required) and there is no maximum limit to the damages that may be awarded.

- The remedy for wrongful dismissal does not include reinstatement or re-engagement (as with unfair dismissal) but injunctions are available to prevent the employer from breaching the contract of employment.

- An individual dismissed in breach of the contract will be expected to mitigate his/her losses.

- Contrary to unfair dismissal, after discovered reasons may be used in wrongful dismissal to justify a dismissal.

Redundancy

- Redundancy may involve the employer ceasing to trade or the employee may be surplus to the requirements of the business.

- To qualify, the claimant must have 'employee' status; have been continuously employed with the same employer for at least two years; have been dismissed (and the reason being redundancy); and must not be in one of the excluded categories.

- The employer's redundancy selection policy must be fair and this can be assisted through negotiation with the employees' representatives/the recognized trade union. The policy should follow the ACAS Code of Practice wherever possible.

- There are automatically unfair reasons to dismiss for redundancy that include (for example) pregnancy; trade union membership and activities, and so on.

- The employer is obliged to consult with the employees or their representatives over any planned redundancies and the reasons for these.

- To be deemed fair, the employer should consider the employee for any suitable alternative work. If this is offered within four weeks of the redundancy this will prevent any payment having to be made (if the reasonable offer of employment is accepted).

- Employees who take up the offer of alternative work are entitled to a four-week trial period to assess whether the work is actually 'suitable'.

TUPE Regulations

- When businesses are transferred, individuals may have their employment preserved and their contractual rights maintained following the TUPE 2006 Regulations.
- Individuals must have been employed 'immediately prior to the transfer' and there must have been a 'relevant transfer'.
- A relevant transfer requires the transfer of a stable economic entity that retains its identity, with an 'organized grouping of resources'. TUPE 2006 also includes changes of service provider to protect those involved in outsourcing; re-tendering; and in-sourcing.
- The new employer (transferee) becomes liable for any claims/liabilities against the former employer by employees.
- The employee is entitled to refuse to transfer to the new employer and by doing so brings to an end his/her contract (and hence any application of a restraint of trade clause), but does not amount to a dismissal.
- The employee who has transferred may not be subject to worse terms imposed by the new employer but can benefit from more favourable terms introduced by it.
- A dismissal due to a relevant transfer will be unfair unless the transfer is due to an economic, technical, or organizational reason. This enables the new employer to justify the dismissal as being 'potentially' fair.
- Employers are obliged to consult with employees and their representatives regarding planned redundancies and transfers, unless there exist 'special circumstances' for not consulting.

 Summary Questions

Essay questions

1. 'The statutory action for unfair dismissal is far superior to a common law action for wrongful dismissal. As such, wrongful dismissal can safely be ignored for all practical purposes.'
   Critically assess the above statement.

2. In the case of *Allen v Flood* (1898) Lord Davey pronounced 'an employer may refuse to employ from the most mistaken, capricious, malicious or morally reprehensible motives imaginable, yet a worker has no right of action.... no right to be employed by any particular employer.'
   To what extent does this statement continue to represent the law?

Problem questions

1. Redmount Borough Council (RBC) has an Adult Education Department which has had rising costs over the past few years. Given the budgetary restraints imposed by central government in 2010 RBC has decided to take measures to reduce its overheads. Part of these measures has resulted in the catering and cleaning functions being transferred to an outside company—'Cleaneasiest Ltd'. There were ten existing members of the catering and cleaning division of the Adult Education Department and these were transferred to the employment of Cleaneasiest Ltd, although the employees were transferred on a lower hourly rate of pay than enjoyed with RBC.

Two months into the transfer, RBC were very unhappy with the quality of the service provided by Cleaneasiest Ltd and as such invoked an early termination clause in the contract (which they were entitled to do) and cancelled the contract. The Adult Education Department now wishes to replace Cleaneasiest Ltd with another company Clean-You-Out Ltd. However, Clean-You-Out Ltd is unwilling to take on any of the ten original employees.

Advise the employees and their trade union of any rights they may have in relation to the Transfer of Undertakings (Protection of Employment) Regulations 2006.

2. Joshua has been working at (the fictitious) Greenfingers Garden Centres Ltd for eight months. Without any warning he is called into the manager's office and told he is being dismissed immediately for misconduct due to his poor timekeeping. Joshua had been late to work for the two previous mornings but had made the time up during his lunch break and he had not been informed by anyone that his employer was unhappy with his work or his conduct.

Unknown to the employer, Joshua had been stealing shrubs from Greenfingers and selling these to his friends.

Advise the parties as to their legal position.

📖 Further reading

Hall, M. (2005) 'Assessing the Information and Consultation of Employees Regulations' *Industrial Law Journal*, Vol. 34, p. 103.

Taylor, S. and Emir, E. (2006) 'Employment Law: An Introduction' Oxford University Press: Oxford and New York.

Williams, E. (2006) 'TUPE 2006—Mission Accomplished or Mission Impossible?' *Business Law Review*, Vol. 27, No. 7, p. 178.

Useful website

http://www.bis.gov.uk/policies/by/themes/employment%20matters
(The Government's website detailing updates and policy discussions relating to employment matters.)

Online Resource Centre

http://www.oxfordtextbooks.co.uk/orc/marson3e/
Why not visit the Online Resource Centre and try multiple choice questions associated with this chapter to test your understanding of the topic. You will also find relevant updates to the law.

Unfair Dismissal and Constructive Dismissal

18

Why does it matter?

Many people watch and have enjoyed the television programme 'The Apprentice', where Sir Alan Sugar concludes the show by informing a contestant 'You're fired'. It's great entertainment, but in reality, employers must be more careful in dismissing an employee. The law provides for the correct procedure to be adopted, the potentially fair reasons that justify a dismissal, along with automatically unfair reasons to dismiss an employee, and if these are disregarded, claims for unfair dismissal may be made. Defending unfair dismissal actions can be expensive for employers, as can be the awards of compensation to the employee. This chapter identifies the correct methods for (fairly) dismissing an employee.

Learning outcomes

Following reading this chapter you should be in a position to:

- explain what is meant by the term 'unfair dismissal' (18.2)
- apply the tests for qualification for protection against unfair dismissal (18.2.2–18.2.2.4)
- explain the potentially fair reasons to justify dismissal under the Employment Rights Act 1996 (18.2.3–18.2.3.6)
- identify the automatically unfair reasons to dismiss an employee (18.2.4)
- explain the use and application of the ACAS Code on dismissal and grievance procedures (18.2.5.2)
- determine how a tribunal assesses the reasonableness of an employer's decision to dismiss (18.2.6)
- explain the concept of constructive unfair dismissal (18.3)
- identify and apply the remedies of compensation, reinstatement, and re-engagement following a successful unfair dismissal claim (18.4–18.4.3.3).

Key terms

These terms will be used in the chapter and it may be helpful to be aware of what they mean or refer back to them when reading through the chapter.

Automatically unfair reasons to dismiss
Certain reasons used in choosing to dismiss (such as for pregnancy; trade union membership; enforcement of rights under health and safety legislation) are automatically unfair and as such the claimant is not required to satisfy the two year's continuous employment qualification.

Band of reasonable responses
In determining whether an employer's decision to dismiss was a reasonable response to the alleged conduct, the tribunal will have regard to the Employment Appeal Tribunal's decision in *Iceland Frozen Foods v Jones* [1982].

Constructive dismissal
When an employer radically or fundamentally changes the contract to the employee's detriment, but has not dismissed the employee, the employee may treat this unilateral change as a repudiation, resign, and claim constructive dismissal. This may be best understood as a claim for unfair dismissal when the employee has not been dismissed.

Effective Date of Termination
A claim under unfair dismissal has to be lodged at a tribunal within three months of the Effective Date of Termination. The Employment Rights Act 1996 (ERA), ss. 97 and 145 identify the mechanism to determine the date.

Employment Tribunal
These tribunals were previously known as Industrial Tribunals and they hear employment cases (dismissals; discrimination; cases involving other statutory rights and so on). They are presided over by an Employment Judge (formally a chairperson) and are assisted by two lay members representing (generally, rather than specific to the case) both employers and workers. However, from 6 April 2012, Employment Judges may sit alone in cases of unfair dismissal.

Employment Appeal Tribunal (EAT)
This is not a tribunal (despite its name) but is the court that hears cases of appeals from Employment Tribunals.

Unfair dismissal
A statutory-based right. Legislation provides protection for employees against certain dismissals, and it establishes methods in which a dismissal must take place to be considered fair.

18.1 Introduction

Having identified the tests adopted by the courts and tribunals to establish employment status, and having considered the common law rights when an employment relationship is ended, this chapter continues by considering the termination of employment. Termination of employment is governed by statutory measures (**unfair dismissal**) and the common law (wrongful dismissal), and each of these provisions outline important factors when the contract is to be ended. Being aware of the procedures involved in each of these areas of law will ensure terminations can take effect without unnecessary recourse to court/tribunal action, saving time and money.

18.2 Unfair dismissal (the statutory route)

**Employment
Tribunals**

Before 1971 there was no statutory right to protection against unfair dismissal. In 1971 the Industrial Relations Act was enacted, and before that time an employer could dismiss an individual for any reason and the only protections available were those established in the contract and enforced through the common law. Unlike wrongful dismissal claims that are predominately heard in the courts, unfair dismissal claims are heard exclusively in **Employment Tribunals**.[1]

Unfair dismissal is largely governed by the Employment Rights Act 1996 (ERA), and specifically under this Act, s. 94(1) provides the right not to be unfairly dismissed. The ERA 1996 establishes the qualifications that the individual must satisfy before he/she has the right to protection under the Act; the 'potentially fair' reasons to justify a dismissal; the **'automatically unfair' reasons to dismiss**; and how awards are to be assessed following a successful claim for unfair dismissal. A flow chart of the process of unfair dismissal claims is contained in Figure 18.1.

**Employment
Rights Act
1996**

> **? Thinking Point**
>
> Do you think it is correct that the ERA 1996 governs potentially fair reasons to justify the dismissal of an employee, or should the employment relationship have remained subject to the terms agreed under the contract? Is statutory intervention appropriate or should *laissez-faire* have been maintained?

18.2.1 Excluded groups from unfair dismissal protection

Only an individual with 'employee' status is entitled to bring a claim for unfair dismissal. Those without this status (such as independent contractors), but whose contract of employment has been terminated may (if the contract has been breached) pursue a claim for wrongful dismissal. There are also groups of individuals who are not entitled to claim, and these include share fishermen;[2] employees in the police service;[3] and persons excluded for reasons of national security.[4]

---

[1] Employment Tribunals may hear wrongful dismissal actions involving claims of up to £25,000 in compensation (Employment Tribunals Act 1996, s. 3)).

[2] Section 199(2).   [3] Section 200.

[4] Section 193. As was the situation in *Council of Civil Service Unions v Minister for the Civil Service* [1984] AC 374 (the case involving the right to join a trade union).

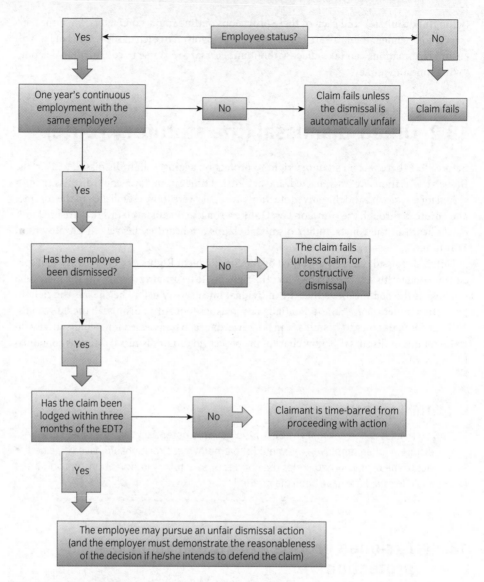

Figure 18.1 Process of unfair dismissal claims

18.2.2 Qualifications for protection under unfair dismissal

 Business Link

An appreciation of the qualification criteria necessary to claim under the statutory right of unfair dismissal is beneficial for both the employer and individual. If the individual does not meet the qualification criteria then this right is unavailable and he/she has to seek a claim under the common law of wrongful dismissal. Likewise, having knowledge of the requirements to plead unfair dismissal will assist in him/her seeking advice quickly and lodging an appropriate claim in the (relatively) short period of time as provided for under the ERA 1996.

The ERA establishes who qualifies for protection under the Act. These qualifications have to be strictly adhered to and are only removed in situations involving 'automatically' unfair reasons to dismiss. If the individual does not qualify then there is no point in pursuing a claim under unfair dismissal:

1   The individual must have 'employee' status;

2   He/she must have been continuously employed by the same employer for at least two years;[5]

3   He/she must have been dismissed (unfairly); and

4   The claim must be submitted to a tribunal within three months of the **Effective Date of Termination**.

It should also be noted that, as part of the Government's initiative towards alternative forms of dispute resolution, where the employer and employee agree, the case may be heard by an arbitrator under the ACAS Arbitration Scheme, as opposed to the case proceeding to a tribunal.

18.2.2.1 *Employee status*

If there is no disagreement between the individual and the employer that the individual is an employee, then this test is satisfied and the issue of qualification continues to the next stage. If, however, there is disagreement, then Chapter 16 demonstrates the methods used to determine employment status.

18.2.2.2 *Continuously employed for at least two years*

The ERA identifies what will amount to 'continuous' service, and under s. 212(1) 'Any week during the whole or part of which an employee's relations with his employer are governed by a contract of employment counts in computing the employee's period of employment.' If the employee fails to work for the employer for at least one week or more, then the period of continuous service is broken. There are, however, exceptions to this rule. If the individual is absent due wholly or partially to childbirth or pregnancy and she later returns to work, these weeks count toward continuous employment;[6] if the individual is incapable of work as a consequence of illness or injury,[7] if he/she is absent due to a temporary cessation of work,[8] and if he/she is absent in circumstances that, by arrangement or custom, is regarded as continuing in the employment of the employer, then these weeks will also contribute to 'continuous employment'.

The employee does not have to work at the same physical location or necessarily in the same capacity throughout this period; the test is that there is a continuous contract of employment between the parties.

---

[5] The two years qualification is effective for employment commencing on or after 6 April 2012 (The Unfair Dismissal and Statement of Reasons for Dismissal (Variation of Qualifying Period) Order 2012).

[6] Section 212(2).   [7] Section 212(3)(a)—To a maximum of 26 weeks.   [8] Section 212(3)(b).

18.2.2.3 *The employee must have been dismissed*

The law requires that for a successful claim of unfair dismissal, it is the duty of the employee to demonstrate that he/she has been dismissed. Under ERA 1996, s. 95, dismissal occurs in the following circumstances: the contract of employment is terminated (with or without notice) ((1)(a));[9] a fixed-term contract has expired and not been renewed ((1)(b)); or the employee ends the contract due to an act of **constructive dismissal** by the employer ((1)(c)).

18.2.2.4 *The Effective Date of Termination*

Determining the Effective Date of Termination (EDT) of the contract, which is clearly applicable to the rule that claims must be submitted to the tribunal within three months of this date, is outlined in s. 97 of ERA 1996. This date is assessed objectively on the facts of the case, and it is not permissible for the parties to reach an agreement between themselves as to the date.[10] If a period of notice is given, the EDT will take effect when the notice period ends, not when the notice was given ((1)(a)). If no notice is provided, the EDT takes effect from the date on which termination was effective ((1)(b)); and for those employed under a fixed-term contract, if this is not renewed, the EDT is effective from the date on which the term expires (1(c)). Where the contract expressly allows for a payment in lieu of notice, the EDT will be considered to be effective from the last day worked.[11]

18.2.3 Justification for dismissal: potentially fair reasons to dismiss

Having established that the employee qualifies for protection under the Act, s. 98 of ERA 1996 outlines the reasons in which it may be acceptable, if reasonable on the facts, for the employer to dismiss the employee. The employer may explain the decision for dismissal as being potentially fair if the reason or, on the basis of more than one reason being presented the principal reason, is due to:

- the capability or qualifications of the employee (s. 98(2)(a));
- the conduct of the employee (s. 98(2)(b));
- that the employee was made redundant (s. 98(2)(c));
- that to continue the employment would amount to a contravention of a statute (s. 98(2)(d));
- some other substantial reason of a kind to justify dismissal (s. 98(1)(b));

Section 92 of ERA 1996 provides that a dismissed employee may request for the reason for the dismissal to be provided in writing. This will assist the employee in attempting to establish a defence based on the employer's assertion under s. 98. If the employer refuses, or fails to respond, then the tribunal may award the employee two weeks' pay. The employer may select as many of the reasons under s. 98 as he/she wishes. However, the more that are chosen, the more evidence that will have to be provided to ensure the dismissal is fair. Indeed, in

---

[9] In *Futty v Brekkes* [1974] IRLR 130 the employer told his employee to 'fuck off' which the employee interpreted as his notice of dismissal. Generally, the words used to constitute a dismissal will be interpreted as how a 'reasonable employee' would have understood them—see *Tanner v Kean* [1978] IRLR 110 for a discussion of this point.

[10] *Fitzgerald v University of Kent at Canterbury* [2004] EWCA Civ 143.

[11] *Leech v Preston BC* [1985] IRLR 33.

Smith v City of Glasgow Council,[12] the employer offered three reasons for the employee's dismissal due to incapability, but as one of them could not be proven, the House of Lords held that the employee was unfairly dismissed. It was not possible for the court to distinguish if this reason was any less or more serious than the other two submitted.

18.2.3.1 *Capability/qualifications*

The ERA 1996 identifies that the issue of capability should have regard to 'skill, aptitude health or any other physical or mental quality' (s. 98(3)), and qualifications are '… any degree, diploma or other academic, technical or professional qualification relevant to the position held'. It is necessary to look to the contract of employment and to what tasks the employee actually performed at work, and then consider the general standard of performance required, whether that standard was being met, and if not, how similar employees were treated.

Capability, as a reason for dismissal, generally focuses on whether the employee becomes ill and cannot perform his/her tasks, or if the employee is incompetent[13] (or 'becomes' incompetent—perhaps by being promoted to a management position and not having the skills to adequately perform the job).

Importantly, when considering the fairness of a dismissal, the tribunal will be looking at whether the employer raised any complaints or concerns with the employee to enable him/her to either change his/her practices or identify problems he/she had. The use of warnings, following consultation regarding areas of difficulty, enables the employee to take appropriate action, but also ensures good industrial relations. It enables the employee to be aware of the employer's concern without simply being called into a disciplinary/dismissal meeting. Such discussions may be useful to identify a lack of appropriate skill or merely a lack of effort, and all alternatives to a dismissal should be explored.

18.2.3.2 *Conduct*

Here the issue is the misconduct of the employee and it can pose many problems for an employer in determining the facts surrounding the incident, and deciding how to react to it. Typical examples include fighting, stealing, misuse of company property (examples of *gross* misconduct), and poor timekeeping, unauthorized absences from work, or general disregard for instructions given fairly and lawfully by the employer (misconduct). Gross misconduct generally refers to a one-off serious offence that may of itself justify a dismissal, whereas misconduct may be a 'lesser' offence when considered in isolation, but when this culminates over a period of time it becomes sufficiently serious to (potentially) justify a termination of the contract.

To ensure that the employer conducts meetings and disciplinary hearings in a correct manner and in a way that is likely to be accepted by the tribunal, it is wise to follow the ACAS Code of Practice 1 on Disciplinary and Grievance Procedures (2009). This is not 'law', but tribunals refer to it and it is good industrial practice to follow the guidance. If the employer identifies that the procedures as set out in the Code will be followed in circumstances involving dismissal/disciplinary action, and this is made clear to the workforce and any representative organizations, then concerns and ill-feeling may be avoided. The Code states that disciplinary procedures should be provided in writing and made available to the workforce (perhaps in a works handbook, human resources department accessible by the workers and so on); it should clearly identify to whom the procedures apply and what sanctions are available to the employer; it should identify who in the organization is competent to decide and apply any

---

[12] [1987] IRLR 326.　　　[13] *Alidair v Taylor* [1978] ICR 445.

sanctions; it should identify the investigatory procedures to be adopted in misconduct cases; it should ensure the employee is aware of his/her right to attend a disciplinary meeting and to be accompanied;[14] and it should enable an employee to appeal against decisions. These steps are not particularly onerous, and by following them all parties are aware of how a situation/allegation of misconduct will be investigated and how any decision will be determined.

Under the common law, a gross misconduct justifies a summary dismissal, but it is perhaps advisable for an employer to investigate the incident, follow ACAS and contractual procedures, and then conclude with a decision as to dismissal or disciplinary action short of dismissal. This process may not take as long as it may be thought, and it ensures that all available evidence is gathered and the relevant investigation is conducted. Further, it ensures that the employer has proof of his/her reasonable belief that led to the action against an employee. This is a particularly important aspect of misconduct. The employer need not *prove* that the employee is guilty of the alleged misconduct, but rather the employer need only demonstrate that he/she had reasonable grounds on which to hold/maintain belief of misconduct.

British Home Stores v Burchell[15]

Facts:

The case involved an employee who had been dismissed on the employer's suspicion that theft from the store had been taken place. There was a lack of firm evidence of the theft and the tribunal found for the claimant, who was then reinstated. The employer appealed against the finding and the **Employment Appeal Tribunal (EAT)** established the points that became known as the 'Burchell principles'.

Authority for:

The Burchell principles provide that due to the nature of employment relationships and the trust necessary between the parties, an employer need not necessarily have concrete evidence of an employee's alleged wrongdoing to justify a dismissal, but rather reasonable grounds for holding the belief.

As such, to ensure the employer can demonstrate that he/she did hold reasonable grounds for honestly believing the employee was guilty of the alleged offence he/she must:

1 honestly believe the employee is guilty;

2 have reasonable grounds on which to hold this belief; and

3 have carried out as much investigation into the matter as was reasonable in all the circumstances of the case.[16]

These tests are particularly apt in cases involving an allegation of misconduct such as in *Burchell*, but may be less strictly adhered to when the facts of the issue are not in dispute.

What is the situation where more than one employee may have been involved in a misconduct? The following cases demonstrate the options available to an employer with guidance from the courts.

---

[14] Section 10 of the Employment Relations Act 1999.   [15] [1978] IRLR 379.
[16] Per Arnold J in *BHS v Burchell* [1978].

Monie v Coral Racing Ltd[17]

Facts:

The claimant worked as an area manager of 19 betting shops owned by the employer. Only the manager and his assistant had access to the company's safe, which held considerable amounts of money. The manager was on annual leave when his assistant discovered there was a substantial sum of money missing. The employer conducted an investigation revealing no evidence of a break-in to the property or that the safe had been forcibly opened (indicative of theft). Therefore, as neither the manager nor his assistant accepted responsibility or could be identified as the perpetrator of the offence, it was held that both could be dismissed for misconduct.

Authority for:

It was reasonable for an employer to dismiss two workers for suspicion of theft where there existed solid and sensible grounds on which the employer could reasonably suspect dishonesty; and the employer did not attempt to subsequently rely on a different reason for the dismissal.

There may also exist situations where a group of employees may be considered to have been involved in misconduct. In cases where it is reasonable for the employer to assume that all or one of them were involved, yet following an investigation identification of the actual perpetrator(s) cannot be achieved, all of the group may be dismissed.

Parr v Whitbread[18]

Facts:

Parr was employed as a branch manager of the firm and was dismissed, along with three other employees, when £4,600 was stolen from the employer's shop. It was concluded from an investigation that the theft indicated an 'inside job' and all of the employees were interviewed. They were given the opportunity to admit the offence, but declined to do so, and hence, by being unable to identify the actual culprit (indeed if there was just one), the employer decided to dismiss all four. The EAT held that the dismissals were fair as the act of theft amounted to a gross misconduct.

Authority for:

Where a group of employees could have a committed a particular offence, the tribunal will find the dismissal of all the group fair where:

1. a dismissal for that offence would have been justified;
2. the employer conducted a reasonable investigation and held a proper procedure;
3. the employer reasonably believed the offence could have been committed by more than one person;
4. the employer has reasonably identified those who could have committed the act; and
5. the employer cannot reasonably identify the perpetrator.

---

[17] [1980] IRLR 464.   [18] [1990] IRLR 39.

Note that potential problems may exist where an employer cannot identify which of the employees has committed an offence, but decides to dismiss members of the group selectively. When one or more of the employees in the group are retained or re-hired despite the investigation not identifying the employee(s) responsible, there must exist solid and sensible grounds for the retention or re-hiring of certain members.

What will amount to a reasonable investigation will depend on the individual circumstances of the case, but factors such as the interviewing of any identifiable witnesses; the collation of documents and their assessment; and providing the employee with an opportunity to answer any charges put to him/her, and to genuinely consider his/her responses before any decision is made, will point towards a reasonable investigation. Of course, in situations involving theft or other activities with a criminal element, the tribunals have held that the employer may treat a guilty verdict in a court as proof that the employee did commit the offence.[19]

18.2.3.3 *Redundancy*

Redundancy,[20] whilst covered under its own legislation, is included in ERA 1996, s. 98 as another form of dismissal. It enables a claim under unfair dismissal legislation where the employee considers that he/she has been unfairly selected for redundancy; where no warning or consultation had taken place; or where redeployment had not been considered.[21] Unfair selection may occur where one or more employees have been selected for redundancy in breach of a customary or agreed procedure (for example, an agreement between an employer and trade union to use a selection process such as 'last in, first out'; voluntary agreements[22] and so on); or if the employee was selected in connection with trade union membership. When choosing the employees for redundancy without the cessation of the business, the employer is strongly advised to draw up objective criteria to be applied and which could be used to defend a claim of unfair selection.

18.2.3.4 *Contravention of a statute*

A further potentially fair reason to dismiss is where to continue to employ the employee would be to break the law. In such a situation, the contract could be frustrated due to a subsequent law (such as the enactment of legislation prohibiting the employment of foreign nationals) or a change in the employee's situation that makes continued employment in the same capacity contrary to legislation.[23] Dismissal may be more likely to be due to some action by the employee rather than legislative changes. There are many situations that could lead to this potentially fair reason to dismiss, but a common example is where the employee has a driving element as part of his/her duties and he/she receives a driving ban. As such, to allow the employee to drive without a licence on the employer's engagement would be to contravene the law.

---

[19] *P v Nottinghamshire CC* [1992] IRLR 362.   [20] See **17.4**.

[21] Note also that rather than a claim for redundancy, some claimants may bring their action in unfair dismissal as the levels of compensation can, in some circumstances, be better under unfair dismissal than for redundancy.

[22] Although employers should use this tactic with caution as the volunteers may not necessarily include the people in the organization, or from the relevant departments, where redundancies are required.

[23] *Four Seasons Healthcare Ltd v Maughan* [2005] IRLR 324.

18.2.3.5 *Some other substantial reason*

In the absence of a reason fitting into one of the previous categories, s. 98 provides for 'some other substantial reason [(SOSR)]of a kind such as to justify the dismissal of an employee holding the position which the employee held' to be forwarded as a reason for the dismissal. There has been a very wide interpretation of the concept of what would amount to SOSR. In the past tribunals have held that an employee whose spouse was an employee of one of the employer's competitors permitted a dismissal; a homosexual man was dismissed from his job at a residential holiday camp due to a potentially negative reaction from parents on discovering his sexuality;[24] and an employee's refusal to agree to the inclusion of a restraint of trade clause in his employment contract[25] was deemed SOSR. In *Scott v Richardson*[26] the EAT held that the tribunal did not have to be satisfied that the commercial decision of the employer was sound, but rather the test was whether the employer believed it to be so.

SOSR may also amount to a situation where an employee is dismissed because his/her attitude at work is sufficiently unpleasant and disruptive that it breaches the implied duty of trust and confidence.[27] As noted above, non-renewal of a fixed-term contract will be deemed a dismissal for the purposes of the ERA 1996. However, such a non-renewal may be justified on the basis of SOSR if the employer can demonstrate (for example) a business reason for the non-renewal, and that he/she acted fairly in the circumstances.[28]

18.2.4 **Automatically unfair reasons to dismiss**

The qualification of two years' continuous service to gain access to unfair dismissal protection is removed in certain circumstances that the legislators considered should be protected from the moment the employee begins work. Whilst this is not an exhaustive list (if for no other reason than the list changes depending on the public policy rationale of the Government) some of the most significant include:

- dismissals due to the pregnancy of the worker or any related illness (ERA 1996, s. 99);
- dismissals due to a spent conviction under the Rehabilitation of Offenders Act 1974;
- dismissals due to trade union membership or activities (TULRCA 1992, s. 238A(2));
- dismissal on transfer of an undertaking (TUPE 2006, reg. 7);
- dismissal because the employee took steps to avert danger to health and safety at work (ERA 1996, s. 100);[29]
- dismissal through an unfair selection for redundancy (ERA 1996, s. 105);
- dismissal in connection with the employee asserting a statutory right (ERA 1996, s. 104);
- dismissals where the employee has made a protected public interest disclosure (ERA 1996, s. 103A), as provided through the Public Interest Disclosure Act 1998.

---

[24] *Saunders v Scottish National Camps Association* [1980] IRLR 174.
[25] *RS Components v Irwin* [1973] IRLR 239.   [26] [2005] Unreported.
[27] *Perkin v St George's Healthcare NHS Trust* [2005] IRLR 934.
[28] *Terry v East Sussex CC* [1976] IRLR 332.
[29] Following the EU Framework Directive on Health and Safety (89/391/EEC) that sought to prevent retaliation against a worker for exercising their rights under health and safety legislation.

18.2.5 **The procedures for a fair dismissal**

Unfair dismissal legislation outlines the procedures that have to be followed in order to enable a 'fair' dismissal. The legislators did not want, and realistically could not create, a situation where an employer had to continue employing an individual against his/her will. The legislation provides for a series of reasons (potentially fair reasons to dismiss) that the employer can utilize in deciding when to dismiss (substantially fair reasons). The legislation, through increasing intervention by Parliament,[30] has provided for the use of correct procedures that will promote fairness and 'natural justice', and lead to the resolution of disputes in the workplace with recourse to tribunals. An employer that fails to follow these procedures may have to pay compensation (unnecessarily) to the employee, or it may even lead to a successful claim against him/her for dismissal (procedurally unfair reasons).

18.2.5.1 *The right to be accompanied at grievance and disciplinary hearings*

On the basis of an allegation against the employee that may lead to disciplinary action[31] or a dismissal (in a matter in which there is duty by the employer in relation to the worker),[32] the employer is required to investigate the facts before taking action. Part of this action may involve interviewing the employee to ascertain the facts surrounding the incident in question. If this is part of a fact-finding exercise, then the employer can request the employee to attend alone. However, the legislative provisions apply when the situation escalates to the possibility of issuing a warning or some other form of discipline.[33] The Employment Relations Act 1999, ss. 10–13, as amended, introduced the right of a 'worker'[34] to be accompanied to such meetings by a colleague[35] or a trades union official[36] (even if he/she is not employed by the same employer as the interviewee). This colleague or trades union official has increased rights to represent the employee, such as establishing the employee's case and presenting points, but is restricted from answering direct questions to the employee,[37] who must address these questions personally.

18.2.5.2 *The ACAS Code on disciplinary and dismissal procedures*

ACAS, the Advisory, Conciliation and Arbitration Service, produced a code of practice and procedural fairness (Code of Practice 1—Disciplinary and Grievance Procedures) identifying how the employer and employee should conduct themselves during grievance/disciplinary matters. The code is not law, but it is referred to by tribunals when assessing the reasonableness of an employer's decision to dismiss.

Features to be considered by the parties in the event of disciplinary/grievance matters are:

---

[30] Of course it should be noted that it has not simply been Parliament's intervention that has impacted on the need for procedures to be used, ACAS has produced many codes of practice (on topics including grievance procedures) that have frequently been used and acknowledged as good practice by tribunals.

[31] A disciplinary hearing is defined under s. 13(4) as (a) the administration of a formal warning to a worker by his employer; (b) the taking of some other action in respect of a worker by his employer; or (c) the confirmation of a warning issued or some other action taken.

[32] This is a requirement under s. 13(5) to ensure that serious issues are covered by the legislation.

[33] *London Underground Ltd v Ferenc-Batchelor* [2003] ICR 656.

[34] Note that this right not only applies to employees, but 'workers', i.e. those working under a contract to personally provide services.

[35] Section 10(3)(c).   [36] Section 10(3)(a) and (b).   [37] Section 10(2)(b).

- The parties should raise issues quickly and these should be dealt with in a prompt manner—with no unreasonable delays.

- The employer should carry out a reasonable investigation to ascertain the facts.

- The employer should present his/her concerns to the employee and give him/her an opportunity to respond before a decision is made.

- The employer should follow the Employment Relations Act 1999, ss. 10–13 regarding the right of the employee to be accompanied at formal disciplinary/grievance meetings by a colleague/trades union official.

- An appeal against the decision of the employer should be offered to the affected employee.

18.2.5.3 *Failure to follow the Code*

The tribunal will consider whether the parties followed the Code in determining the reasonableness of any action taken in such proceedings. The tribunal will be able to raise or lower any award by up to 25 per cent for an unreasonable failure to follow the code. The procedures apply to situations involving disciplinary measures and dismissals, and as such, if the employee unreasonably failed to participate in the proceedings, and he/she is held to have been unfairly dismissed, any award of compensation may be reduced by 25 per cent.

? Thinking Point

Do you consider the movement towards a system of alternative dispute resolution (here arbitration) in employment disputes will be effective? What are the potential pitfalls with following a code of practice that is not law compared with a set of statutory-imposed procedures?

18.2.6 **Reasonableness of a dismissal**

The employer may present a potentially fair reason, as outlined in s. 98 of ERA 1996, to justify the dismissal. However, it is necessary for the employer to demonstrate that he/she acted fairly in deciding to dismiss the employee. This burden of demonstrating reasonableness is neutral between the parties and, under s. 98(4) ERA 1996, the tribunal will hear the evidence and determine, taking into account all relevant circumstances, the issue of reasonableness. Reasonableness will include aspects such as the size of the business and the employer's access to assistance in the administration of discipline and investigations. It is absolutely essential to remember that in determining reasonableness, the tribunal must not consider what action it would have taken, and if the employer's action fell outside of this, subsequently to hold it as unreasonable.[38] Hence the tribunal will assess the evidence forwarded by the employer and consider the employer's response to this and whether his/her action fell into the **band of reasonable responses**.

The employer's disciplinary procedures are important as they enable the parties to have an awareness of how decisions will be taken in the event of the employer considering the dismissal of an employee. This sometimes caused problems when the procedure was not used (even before the advent of the Employment Act 2002), even though ACAS has frequently

---

[38] *Iceland Frozen Foods Ltd v Jones* [1982] IRLR 439.

produced codes of practice that tribunals used in their deliberations on the reasonableness of an employer's actions. The EAT considered that in cases where following the procedure would have made no material difference to the decision of the employer in dismissing an employee, a failure to follow the procedure would not necessarily render the dismissal unfair. However, this has been changed following the House of Lord's judgment in the seminal case of *Polkey v AE Dayton Services*.[39] Essentially, the Lords decided that whether the employer had acted reasonably should be determined on the facts that he/she had available when the decision was made—assuming, of course, that the employer had conducted a reasonable investigation and attempted to gather all the facts surrounding the issue.[40] Without the procedure being followed, the facts would probably be incomplete and the decision of the employer would be flawed.

? Thinking Point

Given the latitude and informal procedures used in dismissals, has this just furthered the managerial prerogative of employers and furthered the precarious position of employees when facing dismissal?

18.2.7 After discovered reasons

When an employee is dismissed, and claims that the dismissal was unfair under the relevant legislation, the employer has to identify what evidence he/she possessed at the time of making the decision that would enable one of the potentially fair reasons under s. 98 of ERA 1996 to be invoked. The employer will, however, only be able to produce the evidence he/she had at the time of deciding to dismiss that can justify the decision and enable it to fall into one of the bands of reasonable responses. Facts that surface after the decision *cannot* be used in justification. These are often referred to as after discovered reasons and whilst, if presented at the tribunal, may lead to a reduction in any damages awarded, they cannot make an unfair dismissal fair.[41]

18.3 Constructive unfair dismissal

𝓖 Business Link

An essential component of the criteria for unfair dismissal claims is that the employee must have been dismissed. Where an employer unilaterally changes a fundamental term of the contract to the employee's detriment, the employee may accept the employer's repudiation, resign, and claim constructive unfair dismissal without an actual 'dismissal' having taken place. Consequently, employers have to take care when unilaterally changing a contract of employment or affecting terms and conditions so as not to invoke a constructive dismissal action.

---

[39] [1987] IRLR 503.

[40] Parrott, G. and Potbury, T. (2007) 'Unfair Dismissal: The Polkey Principle Laid Bare' *Employment Law Journal*, Vol. 79, April, p. 5.

[41] *Devis v Atkins* [1977] AC 931.

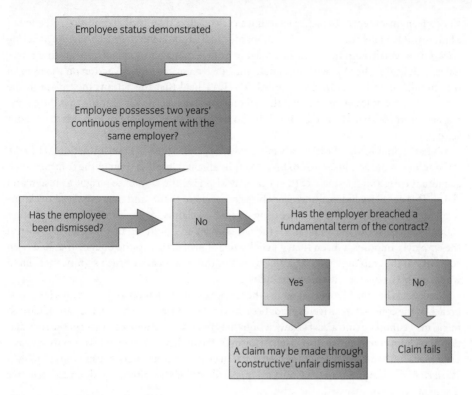

Figure 18.2 Process of a claim

It should be borne in mind that constructive dismissal is a mechanism that enables a claim under unfair dismissal (see Figure 18.2 for a flow chart of the process of a claim). As noted above, one of the qualifications to claim under the statutory protection of unfair dismissal is for the claimant to demonstrate that he/she was dismissed (and unfairly). The drafters of the legislation recognized that a tactic by recalcitrant employers would be to 'coerce' employees to resign by, for example, making their job unreasonably unpleasant or onerous.[42] If the individual resigned, there would be no dismissal and therefore no right to claim unfair dismissal—hence the legislation would have been circumvented. Constructive dismissal allows an employee to accept the employer's repudiation of the contract and claim unfair dismissal (ss. 95(1)(c) and 136(1)(c) of ERA 1996).

Section 95(1)(c) outlines the right to claim constructive dismissal:

For the purposes of this Part an employee is dismissed by his employer if ... —

(c) the employee terminates the contract under which he is employed (with or without notice) in circumstances in which he is entitled to terminate it without notice by reason of the employer's conduct.

Examples of situations where an essential/fundamental term of the contract was breached include unilaterally reducing an employee's pay,[43] and a failure to provide a safe and suitable

---

[42] The test established in *Malik v BCCI* from the House of Lords was whether the employer's action was to destroy or very likely severely damage the relationship between the employee and employer.

[43] *Industrial Rubber Products v Gillon* [1977] IRLR 389.

working environment.[44] Breaches enabling a constructive dismissal claim were extended to a failure to adequately investigate allegations of sexual harassment. In *Bracebridge Engineering v Darby*[45] a female employee had informed her office manager of an act constituting a sexual assault against her by two colleagues. The office manager took no action on the basis of this complaint and Miss Darby resigned. The EAT held that the actions took place in the context of her employment and that the tribunal had been correct in finding that the claimant had been constructively dismissed due to her employers' failure to treat her complaint seriously.

Whilst in *Bracebridge* the breach was of a statutory right (the Sex Discrimination Act 1975), if the action of the employer was to breach a fundamental implied term in the contract, such as mutual trust and confidence, then this may also give the employee a right to resign and claim. This could include an unreasonable accusation of theft[46] and may even lead to claims in an area which is forming an increasing number of claims for unfair dismissal (and other actions such as sex discrimination)—the harassment and bullying of workers.[47] Further, if the employer imposes a disciplinary penalty out of proportion to the offence that had been committed, the employee would be able to accept this as a breach of such significance that it would enable a constructive dismissal action.[48]

It must also be considered that whilst the examples above demonstrate a serious (or gross) breach of the contract, relatively minor breaches of the contract, such as in the case of harassment, may cumulate into a 'last straw' action that enables the employee to accept the repudiation and claim constructive dismissal.[49] However, the underlying principle is that there was a breach of a fundamental term of the contract that enables a constructive dismissal claim.[50] In *Western Excavating v Sharp* the Court of Appeal identified the criteria by which constructive dismissal would be assessed. These were:

- The employer must have breached a term (express or implied), or had clearly established that he/she would not be bound by the contract.

- The term breached must have been an essential or fundamental term.

- The employee must have accepted the breach of the contract by the employer and acted to end the employment within a reasonable time.

18.3.1 Affirming the breach

There is a requirement for the employee to make some outward sign that he/she does not accept the breach by the employer. If the employee says nothing in dispute to the employer's action, then it may be considered that he/she has waived the right to claim by 'affirming' the change in contract and will have lost his/her right to bring an action against it. Insofar as he/she makes an outward sign of not accepting the variation, he/she may continue to work under the new conditions, until, for example, alternative employment is secured, and then he/she may leave and claim constructive dismissal. This is known as 'working under protest'. However, once the employee has agreed to work to the changed contract 'under protest', an employee who subsequently refuses to work under the new conditions may be dismissed

---

[44] *Waltons and Morse v Dorrington* [1997] IRLR 488.   [45] [1990] IRLR 3.
[46] *Robinson v Crompton Parkinson* [1978] IRLR 61.
[47] *Reed v Stedman* [1999] IRLR 299.   [48] *BBC v Beckett* [1983] IRLR 43.
[49] *Woods v WM Car Services* [1982] IRLR 413.
[50] *Western Excavating v Sharp* [1978] 2 WLR 344.

as refusing to obey lawful and reasonable instructions.[51] Under constructive dismissal, the employee has to claim within a reasonable time, having informed the employer that he/she was leaving *because* of the employer's action.[52]

18.4 Remedies for unfair dismissal

Where an employee has been unfairly dismissed, the tribunal has to assess how to compensate the dismissed employee. The three remedies available are reinstatement; re-engagement; and compensation (ERA 1996, s. 112). These remedies are initially explained to the claimant and the tribunal identifies whether the employee wishes to be reinstated to his/her previous job. At this stage the employer has no say in what should happen next, and it is the tribunal's decision, having considered the case, the relationship between the parties, and what is in the best interests of the employee. It is important to note that if the employee does not wish to return to the employment then this would not be ordered,[53] but if the tribunal considers that re-engagement may be available[54] and the employee unreasonably refuses to accept this, then the award of compensation may be reduced. Employees who have, however, been somewhat at fault in the dismissal will not ordinarily be awarded reinstatement or re-engagement.

18.4.1 Reinstatement

This remedy is provided at the discretion of the tribunal where the dismissed employee is reinstated to his/her previous job. Both the employer and employee must agree to this remedy, and as can be imagined, it is quite rarely complied with. In such an instance where the employer refuses to reinstate the employee, the tribunal will increase the damages awarded to the employee, but it cannot compel the employer to restore the employee to his/her previous job as specific performance will not be awarded in cases involving contracts of personal service.

18.4.2 Re-engagement

As there may be several months (at least) from when the employee is dismissed to when a tribunal may have heard the case and provided its award, the employee's previous position with the employer may have been taken by another individual. Instead of ordering reinstatement, due to the practical problems that this may cause, the ERA 1996 provides for the employee to return to the employment as close to the same job (in terms of pay, requirements, seniority, and responsibility) as is possible.

---

[51] *Robinson v Tescom Corp.* [2008] EAT/0546/07/RN.

[52] *Holland v Glendale Industries Ltd* [1998] ICR 493.

[53] There may be many reasons for an employee not wishing to return including the possibility of victimization from the employer; a lack of promotion prospects; a continued decline in relations between the employee and employer and so on.

[54] This may be applicable due to the size of the organization that would enable the employee to work in another department; a different branch of the employer's business and so on.

18.4.3 Compensation

Compensation[55] is provided by the tribunal on the basis of two elements—a basic award and a compensatory award. Under this section the tribunal will award a conventional sum of £250 as way of compensation for loss of a statutory right.

18.4.3.1 *The basic award*

The ERA 1996 provides for the method of calculation of this element of the remedy. The current rate of a week's pay is established at a maximum of £450[56] and the age of the claimant and his/her length of continuous service governs the level of the award provided. It is the element of the award that is designed to reflect the employee's loss of pay between the time of the dismissal and the date of the tribunal's decision.

The calculation is based on the **Employees Age** × the **Length of Service** × the **Weekly Gross Pay** (to the relevant maximum).

This calculation is further subject to a multiplier based on the employee's age. Where the employee is below the age of 22, any period of service is multiplied by .5; between the age of 22 and 41 the figure is multiplied by 1; and for workers over the age of 41 the figure is multiplied by 1.5.

The maximum amount provided under the basic award is £13,500. The level of compensation may be reduced if the employee contributed to the dismissal through his/her conduct; if he/she received any redundancy payment; or if he/she unreasonably refused reinstatement.

18.4.3.2 *The compensatory award*

This element of the award is not calculated to a strict formula as is the case with the basic element and the tribunal has wide scope for assessing what is just and equitable in the circumstances. The maximum award under the compensatory element is £74,200 (although, of course, the majority of cases do not reach this figure). The award includes compensation for losses of overtime payments, tips, future losses, loss of accrued rights and so on. However, the award may not include damages for 'distress, humiliation, and damage to reputation in the community or to family life', and must be confined to financial losses.[57] Tribunals were provided with guidance as to how to assess this element of damages in *Norton Tool Co. Ltd v Tewson*[58] so as to include: any immediate loss of earnings; any calculation of future losses;[59] the figure to include a loss of a statutory right; any losses of rights under a pension; and any expenses incurred in obtaining another job.

As with the basic award, the compensation may be reduced where there was a contributory fault by the employee, or where the employee failed to mitigate his/her losses.

18.4.3.3 *The additional award*

ERA 1996, s. 117 provides for the additional compensation where the tribunal has ordered reinstatement or re-engagement and the employer has unreasonably refused to agree to the order. This award will be based on between 26 and 52 weeks' pay (at the tribunal's discretion).

---

[55] ERA 1996, s. 123(1).   [56] As of 1 February 2013.
[57] *Dunnachie v Kingston upon Hull City Council* [2004] IRLR 727.   [58] [1972] IRLR 86.
[59] These cannot be too remote and may identify losses attributed to the employee gaining alternative employment. It will also impact on an employee who had already obtained another job at a similar rate of pay or better pay than had been provided by the employer subject to the claim.

Based on the calculations as noted above, the maximum award that is available under compensation for unfair dismissal is, from 1 February 2013, £87,700 (i.e. £74,200 plus 30x£450).

 Conclusion

The chapter has aimed to demonstrate the nature of unfair dismissal legislation: who qualifies for the right; the procedures that the parties are required to follow; and the remedies available. It also identified where the statutory protection is available for dismissals that are considered automatically unfair.

The unfair dismissal legislation provides a greater range of protection to those who qualify than does the common law remedy of wrongful dismissal. Claims may be made under both sources of law, but any remedy received in one claim would be off-set in a remedy under the other jurisdiction.

 Summary of main points

Unfair dismissal

- Unfair dismissal is governed by statute law and most of the rules applicable to this jurisdiction of law are contained in the Employment Rights Act (ERA) 1996.

- To qualify the individual must have employee status; have been continuously employed with the employer for at least two years; he/she must have been dismissed (and unfairly); and must have submitted his/her claim to an Employment Tribunal within three months of the Effective Date of Termination (EDT).

- The employer must allow the employee to be accompanied at grievance and disciplinary hearings.

- The tribunal will assess the reasonableness of an employer's decision to dismiss based on his/her reasonable grounds for holding a belief/suspicion; the investigations into the matter that were conducted; and whether another 'reasonable employer' would have acted in the same way.

- There are five potentially fair reasons to dismiss an employee. These are the capability/qualifications of the employee; conduct; redundancy; contravention of a statute; and some other substantial reason.

- There exist automatically unfair reasons to dismiss an employee (which results in the requirement for two year's continuous employment being dispensed with). These include dismissals on the grounds of pregnancy; membership of a trade union or trade union activities; dismissal for asserting a statutory right and so on.

Constructive dismissal

- Constructive unfair dismissal enables an employee to claim unfair dismissal even where he/she has not been 'dismissed'. The employer must have breached a fundamental term of the contract and the employee must have accepted this repudiation.

- A fundamental term includes actions such as a unilateral reduction in pay and failure to provide a safe system of work or suitable working environment.

- The employee must claim within 'a reasonable time' of the breach to gain protection from constructive dismissal or he/she runs the risk of having affirmed the contractual change.

- The affected employee must inform the employer of his/her non-acceptance of the contractual change before resigning and claiming constructive dismissal.

Remedies

- There are three remedies available to a tribunal when an employee has been unfairly dismissed. These are reinstatement, re-engagement, and compensation.

 Summary questions

Essay questions

1. The potentially fair reasons to dismiss under the Employment Rights Act 1996 are far too broad and enable an employer to dismiss an employee very easily. They should be narrowed and the test of reasonableness of an employer's action made more robust if the legislation is to have any impact on the abusive exercise of managerial prerogative.
   Discuss.

2. The statutory dismissal procedures, intended to resolve employment disputes 'in-house' without recourse to tribunal, were replaced in April 2009 with a system based on alternative forms of dispute resolution. Why did these statutory procedures fail and what is the likely success of the ACAS code reducing such action? What lessons can be learned from the Gibbons review?

Problem questions

1. Kate runs a clothing manufacturing firm employing several workers. One day Kate comes into work and sees what she thinks is a fight between John and Tom. Therefore Kate sacks both of them on the spot. What has really happened is that Tom has been attacked by John because John has never liked Tom due to his exemplary service and being a 'goody two shoes'.

   Tom was actually working on a fixed-term contract, which he had worked for 2 years out of a 3-year contract. Tom's contract does not state anything about early termination and he earns £20,000 per year.

   Kate later appoints Sarah on maternity leave cover for an 8-month contract. Once appointed, Sarah announces that she is pregnant, and Kate is disgusted by this revelation and immediately dismisses Sarah due to her pregnant status.

   Advise the parties of the legal issues and their rights.

   (Visit the Online Resource Centre where there are completed claim (ET1) and answer (ET3) forms relating to this question, and a completed employment contract to demonstrate the reality of this dismissal scenario.)

Online Resource Centre: Forms

2. Calvin is a designer working for a large fashion house. Calvin is an employee at the firm and has worked there for 4 years. His employer Donna arrives at work on Monday morning and finds Calvin acting suspiciously. Donna checks the petty cash box and discovers that £100 is missing. Despite the fact that four other employees were in the

vicinity at the time Donna came into the room she dismisses Calvin without any notice saying she 'would not have a thief like Calvin working there any more'.

Advise Calvin of any rights under unfair dismissal and wrongful dismissal protections.

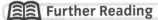 ## Further Reading

Brodie, D. (2002) 'Fair Dealing and the Dismissal Process' *Industrial Law Journal*, Vol. 31, p. 294.

Learmond-Criqui, J. and Costly, J. (2001) 'Arbitration in Employment Disputes' *Business Law Review*, October, p. 222.

Taylor, S. and Emir, A. (2009) 'Employment Law' (2nd Edition) Oxford University Press: Oxford.

 ## Useful websites

http://www.acas.org.uk/
(The Advisory, Conciliation and Arbitration Service provides a wealth of practical information for employers and workers on their rights and responsibilities at work.)

https://www.gov.uk/browse/working/redundancies-dismissals/
(Information from Direct Gov, an organization established to provide information and guidance from various government agencies and departments. It offers practical advice on, amongst other things, employment and termination matters.)

http://www.adviceguide.org.uk/england/life/employment/dismissal.htm/
(The Citizens Advice Bureau website provides information on rights at work, making claims, and so on.)

Online Resource Centre

http://www.oxfordtextbooks.co.uk/orc/marson3e/
Why not visit the Online Resource Centre and try multiple choice questions associated with this chapter to test your understanding of the topic. You will also find relevant updates to the law.

19

Equality in the Workplace and Parental Rights

Why does it matter?

Does an employer have to take action to prevent an employee from telling rude jokes? What responsibility does an employer have with regards to unwanted conduct perpetrated by a third party to his/her employee? How many times must an employee complain to the employer about this unwanted conduct before it becomes actionable? Do you know the 'protected characteristics' that are protected against prohibited conduct by the Equality Act 2010? Do you as an employer/your business have policies in place to reflect the changes in equality law after 1 October 2010? If you answered 'no/don't know' to any or indeed all of the above questions you are exposing you and your business to potentially very expensive claims, poor industrial relations, and potential damage to your reputation as an employer. Equality law has changed, it will continue to develop over the coming years, and ignorance is likely to be a costly error.

Learning outcomes

Following reading this chapter you should be in a position to:

- Explain the development of the Equality Act 2010 in relation to its main aims, the legislation it replaced and those elements of the Act not yet in force (19.2–19.4)
- identify the groups of workers protected by the Act through the use of 'protected characteristics' (19.4–19.5)
- Explain the codification of the previously discriminatory behaviour and identify where the law has added new protection through 'prohibited conduct' (19.6)
- Explain an employer's potential liability to employees for discriminatory acts committed by third parties in the employee's course of employment (19.8)
- Consider the extent of protection against prohibited conduct of an individual with a protected characteristic (19.9–19.15.1)
- identify the 'heads' under which an equal pay claim may be made, and apply these in problem scenarios (19.13.4–19.13.4.3)
- explain the protection against discrimination based on sex and race in employment (19.4–19.4.7)

- identify the protection against discrimination in employment of those working under part-time and fixed-term contracts (19.16–19.17)
- identify the rights at work of pregnant employees and biological and adopting parents, including the right to request flexible working and family-friendly policies (19.19–19.19.5).

☖ Key terms

These terms will be used in the chapter and it may be helpful to be aware of what they mean or refer back to them when reading through the chapter.

Comparator

To found a claim of discrimination, the claimant must establish that he/she was discriminated on the basis of a protected characteristic. Therefore, he/she must have been a victim of less or (un)favourable treatment attributable to the protected characteristic; and this is evidenced when compared with how a person without the protected characteristic was or would be treated. Depending on the claim, a permissible comparator may be hypothetical, or in other instances a 'real' person may have to be used to demonstrate less favourable treatment.

Direct discrimination

Direct discrimination occurs when a person treats another less or (un)favourably because of a protected characteristic than he/she would a person without the characteristic.

Material factor

To defend an action against an equal pay claim, the employer may demonstrate that the difference in pay is not due to the sex of the individual, but is based on some objective, justifiable, reason (e.g. responsibility, qualifications and so on).

Occupational Requirement

This provides a defence to a claim of discrimination where (for example) there is discrimination between men and women, but this is not due to their sex *per se*, but rather is necessitated by the nature of the employment.

Heads of claim

For an action to succeed on the basis of direct sex discrimination in pay, the claimant must choose one of the three 'heads' of claim identified under the Act—like work; work rated as equivalent; or work of equal value.

Indirect discrimination

Indirect discrimination involves the application of a seemingly neutral provision, criterion, or practice that is applied to everyone. However, it particularly affects people who share a protected characteristic and it puts them (or would put them) at a particular disadvantage.

Red-circle agreement

An employer who has conducted a job evaluation study to make pay structures transparent may protect the pay of a group of affected workers where, following assessment, they are to be downgraded.

Harassment

Harassment involves 'unwanted conduct' related to a protected characteristic, which has the purpose or effect of violating a person's dignity or creating an intimidating, hostile, degrading, humiliating, or offensive environment.

Victimization

The offence of victimization occurs where an individual has brought a claim under the Equality Act 2010 or he/she intended to claim under the Act(s); or gave evidence at a hearing and has suffered less favourable treatment from the employer as a result.

19.1 Introduction

From 1 October 2010 much of the previous equality law developed through the common law, statute and the United Kingdom (UK)'s membership of the European Union (EU) has been codified in the Equality Act (EA) 2010. There have been many changes adopted following the enactment of this legislation. The Act is relevant for businesses as it imposes obligations to provide a safe system of work, including regulating the activities of management, colleagues, and third parties. This is an area of law that will evolve over the forthcoming years, and whilst much of the previous case law is applicable to this new Act, new judgments will likely expand and clarify the extent of equality law.

19.2 The Equality Act 2010

The Equality Act 2010

According to the Government Equalities Office:

'The Equality Act 2010 is intended to provide a new cross-cutting legislative framework to protect the rights of individuals and advance equality of opportunity for all; to update, simplify and strengthen the previous legislation; and to deliver a simple, modern and accessible framework of discrimination law which protects individuals from unfair treatment and promotes a fair and more equal society.'[1]

Previous anti-discrimination and equality laws were spread over many pieces of legislation, statutory instruments, and case law. It was unwieldy to identify the relevant laws applicable to employers, employees, workers, third parties, organizations and so on. It also had developed different approaches to the application of these laws through the various amendments and decisions of the EU and the Court of Justice of the European Union. Therefore, the EA 2010 was enacted to harmonize these complex areas of law, apply consistent approaches to the interpretation and application of the provisions, and to take the opportunity to extend rights to the new 'protected characteristics'. The body with the responsibility for overseeing the EA 2010 is the Government Equality Office.

Previous equality legislation provided for the establishment of the Commission for Equality and Human Rights (merging the Equal Opportunities Commission; the Commission for Racial Equality and the Disability Rights Commission). The Commission took the previous powers enjoyed by these Commissions and consolidated their experience in promoting

[1] http://www.equalities.gov.uk/equality_act_2010.aspx.

equality and respect for human rights, and enforcing legislation against transgressors. The Act was significant in placing a duty on public authorities in promoting equal opportunities between men and women, and prohibiting sex discrimination in the exercise of public functions.

A further, significant, introduction in the EA 2010 was explicit reference to allowing positive action policies to be adopted by organizations (in recruitment and promotion). Positive action[2] enables an employer to pursue a policy of appointing applicants where there is an under-representation of persons from the specific group in the organization; or where they suffer a disadvantage associated with that characteristic. This has been incorporated into the EA 2010, but it is at present applicable where the employer voluntarily adopts the policies—it is not a legal requirement.[3]

19.3 Previous anti-discrimination law repealed

The EA 2010 formally repeals/revokes and changes much of the previous legislation (in its attempt to simply and codify the provisions contained in the plethora of statutes). The following have been repealed in their entirety:[4]

1 The Equal Pay Act 1970;

2 The Sex Discrimination Act 1975;

3 The Race Relations Act 1976;

4 The Sex Discrimination Act 1986;

5 The Disability Discrimination Act 1995;

6 The Employment Equality (Religion or Belief) Regulations 2003;

7 The Employment Equality (Sexual Orientation) Regulations 2003;

8 The Equality Act (Sexual Orientation) Regulations 2007.

19.4 Groups affected by the Act

This Part of the text is focused on employment laws, and hence this chapter considers the effects of the EA 2010 on employers, employees, and workers. But these are not the only groups who will be affected by the Act. Former employees, agency workers, self-employed workers, consumers and providers of goods and services are each subject to provisions of the EA 2010 and should be aware of how it affects them. Further, there are increasing obligations on employers in the public sector regarding disclosure of pay details and greater transparency, with the consequent need for effective policies to be established to avoid transgression of the Act.

---

[2] EA 2010, s. 159—effective from 6 April 2011.

[3] For those readers interested in the debate, consider the approach of 'equality of outcome' v 'equality of opportunity' in assessing the potential successes of positive/affirmative action policies.

[4] This list is not exhaustive and refers to those statutes relevant for this section of the text.

19.5 The protected characteristics (groups)

The previous anti-discrimination laws (the Equal Pay Act 1970; the Sex Discrimination Act 1975; the Race Relations Act 1976 and so on) each identified groups who were protected from the discriminatory acts contained within the remit of the particular piece of legislation. In its attempt to simplify and harmonize equality laws, the EA 2010 identifies the following as being 'protected characteristics'—a method of explaining which groups are protected from discrimination and who will be part of these groups—and hence possess a characteristic that is protected under this legislation (ss. 4–12 and 72–76). They are as follows:

- age (s. 5);
- disability (s. 6);
- gender reassignment (s. 7);
- marriage and civil partnership (s. 8)—single people are not covered;
- pregnancy and maternity (ss. 72–76);
- race (s. 9);
- religion or belief (s. 10);
- sex (s. 11); and
- sexual orientation (s. 12).

19.6 Prohibited conduct

The EA 2010 outlines the forms of conduct that the Act seeks to prohibit (ss. 13–27). These harmonize the definitions of actions such as **direct** and **indirect discrimination**, **harassment** and **victimization** which the previous anti-discrimination laws defined. The forms of conduct, to which of the protected characteristics they apply, and where changes have been made from the previous legislation are contained below.

19.6.1 Direct discrimination

19.6.1.1 *The protected characteristics*
There are no changes to this form of discrimination (from the legislation it replaced) and it covers all the protected characteristics.

19.6.1.2 *Application of the law*
Direct discrimination occurs when a person treats another less favourably because of their protected characteristic than he/she would a person without the characteristic. The less favourable treatment has been extended in the EA 2010 in the following ways. A person is treated less favourably than another due to:

1 a protected characteristic he/she possesses; or

2 a protected characteristic it is thought he/she possesses (this amounts to perceptive discrimination); or

3 his/her association with someone who has a protected characteristic (this amounts to associative discrimination) (s. 13).

Therefore, perceptive and associative forms of discrimination are included in the Act (these are covered in the following sections).

In relation to pregnancy and maternity, the test is not whether the claimant was subject to less favourable treatment, but whether the treatment was unfavourable. This is because there is no need for the claimant to compare her treatment with other workers.

To determine whether the claimant has been a victim of direct discrimination the test is to identify if an act of discrimination had been committed; and if so, would, but for the claimant's protected characteristic, he/she have been treated more favourably.[5] When discrimination occurs between groups of workers, the claim requires the discrimination is on the basis of the protected characteristic and not on matters that are materially different. For example, in relation to discrimination based on sex, in *Bullock v Alice Ottley School*[6] a school had a policy of requiring academic staff to retire at 60 whilst the gardening staff had to retire at 65. In a claim of direct discrimination, the Court of Appeal held that this was discrimination on the basis of the jobs and not on the sex of the workers. Just because the academic staff tended to be female and the gardening staff male, did not stop women becoming members of the gardening staff and being subject to the retirement policy at 65.

Direct sex discrimination cannot be justified on the basis of the motives of the employer;[7] however, exceptions do exist. In relation to the protected characteristic of age, less favourable treatment may be justified if it is a proportionate means of achieving a legitimate aim. A disabled person may be treated more favourably than a non-disabled person; and justification for direct discrimination may be evidenced through the **Occupational Requirements** of the job.

Occupational Requirements

Due to the nature of certain types of employment, or by necessity, the role to be filled may require a person from a specific protected characteristic group.[8] As such, the EA 2010 provides for exceptions to acts that would otherwise amount to direct discrimination. This is merely an option and a claim cannot be raised that the employer could/should have restricted the post to (for example) a particular gender.[9]

It is important that the EA 2010 identifies the Occupational Requirement (OR) to be a proportionate means of achieving a legitimate aim and there exists a link between the requirement and the job (hence it is not a sham).

Discrimination laws provide for the following ORs:

- Where the essential nature of the job calls for a man for reasons of physiology (excluding physical strength or stamina);[10] or in dramatic performances (for example, a leading man in a film); or for authenticity (for example, the role of playing Othello). The OR of authenticity has been used to prevent a male applicant for a job on a 'chat line' that was advertised as 'live girls … 1–2–1 chat'. The nature of the employment was restricted to female applicants.[11]

[5] *James v Eastleigh BC* [1990] 2 AC 751.

[6] [1993] ICR 138.

[7] *Hafeez v Richmond School* [1981] COIT 1112/38.

[8] Note that this will not extend to a policy of only employing women in a female clothes retailer (*Etam Plc v Rowan* [1989] IRLR 150) and the same argument applies to men's fashion retailers (*Wiley v Dee and Co. (Menswear) Ltd* [1978 IRLR 103).

[9] *Williams v Dyfed CC* [1986] ICR 449.

[10] *Barker v Goodwave Security* [1997] Case No. 2406811/97.

[11] *Cropper v UK Express Ltd* [1991] Case No. 25757/91.

- The job needs to be held by a man to preserve decency or privacy.[12] This has been applied to employment situations where, whilst being in a state of undress is not of itself a requirement of the job, it was reasonably incidental to it,[13] or the job involved entering women's toilets to carry out maintenance work. It was quite foreseeable in these circumstances that women may object to a man carrying out such functions.[14]

- The nature or location of the establishment makes it impracticable for the holder of the job to live elsewhere than in the premises provided by the employer; and separate living accommodation/sanitary facilities for women are unavailable. Where an employer would be unable, reasonably, to make provisions to adapt the available accommodation to allow members of the opposite sex to take up a post, this will satisfy the OR. However, where the employer simply does not wish to make an adaptation, and this would be reasonable to do so, the defence will not be accepted.[15]

- The holder of the job provides individuals with personal services promoting their welfare or education (or similar services) that can be most effectively provided by (for example) a man; or a person of a particular race. In *Tottenham Green Under Fives Centre v Marshall (No. 2)*[16] the case involved a day care centre where 84 per cent of the children at the centre were of Afro-Caribbean descent. The previous nursery worker (who was of Afro-Caribbean descent) left the employment and it was considered by the Centre's committee to appoint a replacement of the same ethnic origin. Mr Marshall (a white man) applied for the position and when it was discovered that he was not of the required ethnicity, his application was rejected. It was held by the EAT that this requirement was included under RRA 1976, s. 5(2)(d) (the previous applicable legislation) as the ability to read and speak in dialect was an OR.

- The job is required to be held by a man because it is likely to involve the performance of the duties outside the UK in a country whose laws/customs mean that the job could not, or could not effectively, be performed by a woman.

- The job involves participation as an artist's or photographic model in the production of a work of art, in which a person of that racial group is required for authenticity.

19.6.2 Associative discrimination

19.6.2.1 *The protected characteristics*

In relation to race, religion and belief, and sexual orientation the law remains the same as each is covered.

In age, disability, gender reassignment, and sex this is a new right to protection.

It does *not* apply to the marriage and civil partnership, and pregnancy and maternity protected characteristics.

19.6.2.2 *Application of the law*

When a person is directly discriminated against due to his/her association with another person who has a protected characteristic. This has the potential to provide substantial benefits

---

[12] See *Lasertop Ltd v Webster* [1997] IRLR 498.
[13] *Sisley v Britannia Security Systems* [1983] IRLR 404.
[14] *Carlton v Personnel Hygiene Services* [1989] Case No. 16327/89.
[15] *Wallace v Peninsular and Oriental Steam Navigation Company* [1979] Case No. 31000/79.
[16] [1991] IRLR 162.

and protection to workers. For example, where an employee is refused promotion due to her having a disabled spouse and the employer believes the employee will have to spend time away from work to care for that person, this is now an act of discrimination. It is evidently not based on a disability which the employee (claimant) has, but rather someone associated with her.

19.6.3 Perceptive discrimination

19.6.3.1 *The protected characteristics*

In relation to age, race, religion or belief, and sexual orientation each remains covered by the EA 2010.

The protected characteristics of disability, gender reassignment, and sex are now protected through the EA 2010.

Marriage and civil partnership, and pregnancy and maternity are *not* covered in previous legislation or under the EA 2010.

19.6.3.2 *Application of the law*

A person is directly discriminated against when those discriminating believe he/she possesses a particular protected characteristic (even if in fact the person discriminated against does not actually possess that protected characteristic).

19.6.4 Indirect discrimination

19.6.4.1 *The protected characteristics*

Age, race, religion and belief, sex, sexual orientation, and marriage and civil partnership remain covered under the EA 2010.

Disability and gender reassignment are now covered as protected characteristics.

The protected characteristics of marriage and civil partnership, and pregnancy and maternity are *not* covered (although in pregnancy and maternity indirect sex discrimination may still apply).

19.6.4.2 *Application of the law*

Following enactment of the EA 2010, there is a common definition of what will amount to indirect discrimination. Indirect discrimination is a seemingly neutral provision, criterion or practice that is applied to everyone but it particularly affects people who share a protected characteristic and it puts them (or would put them) at a particular disadvantage. A simplistic example of indirect effect is if a university, in recruiting lecturers, stated that the applicants had to be 6ft tall or over. This criterion has no discriminatory element as it is applied to all applicants. However, the reality is that a greater proportion of men than women can comply with it. Hence it may be discriminatory unless the employer can objectively justify its inclusion as a legitimate aim.

Indirect discrimination may be justified if the measure is 'a proportionate means of achieving a legitimate aim' (s. 19). The inclusion of the wording 'or would put them' enables a challenge to a provision, criterion, or practice which has not yet been applied but whose effect would be discriminatory if it were.

To justify discrimination, the following two stage test should be adopted to establish an 'objective justification':

1 Is the aim legitimate? Therefore is the rule/practice non-discriminatory and one that represents a real and objective consideration? and

2 If the aim satisfies the test of being legitimate, is it necessary in the circumstances (is it proportionate)?

A legitimate aim must constitute a genuine, objective need, which can include business/economic needs, but should not be based solely on (for example) reducing costs.

The disadvantage to be suffered by the claimant is not defined in the Act, but it may include denial of a promotion, imposition of a dress code and so on. However, dress codes in particular may be justified for a broader, objectively justified reason. In *Panesar v Nestle Ltd*[17] the workers at the confectionary factory were prohibited from wearing beards or their hair long. The provision was discriminatory against members of the Sikh religion who suffered a detriment, as they could not comply with the provision. However, this did not constitute a breach of the law (the RRA 1976), as it was a provision in fulfillment of health and safety legislation[18] and in the interests of hygiene.

Establishing the link between the disadvantage with the provision, criterion, or practice may be possible through the use of statistics. These statistics may be gathered from regional or national sources, or they may be gathered from the application of the questionnaires as identified in 19.7.

- *Provision, criterion, or practice:* The tribunal will assess the employer's provision, criterion, or practice in an objective manner to assess whether there may be a justification for its imposition. The objective nature of the examination removes the employer's beliefs or understandings of the need of the business but rather will require tangible grounds that would make such a provision acceptable. The test considers the *prima facie* evidence of discrimination that is established by the claimant, and has previously included a requirement to work from an office location,[19] a provision of working full-time;[20] or the necessity of the inclusion of a mobility clause in the contract.[21] Having established that there does exist a provision in the requirements of employment, the next stage is to demonstrate that it has caused the claimant a disadvantage.

- *Disadvantage:* The claimant has to demonstrate that he/she had suffered a disadvantage, or would be put at a disadvantage, due to the provision to enable a claim to proceed. The requirement of 'being placed at a disadvantage' instils an element of *locus standi*, which stops 'busybodies' from taking offence at what they may see as discrimination and lodging claims against the employer. The disadvantage shows the claimant has suffered a loss and hence enables/justifies his/her action against the employer.[22]

Note that the comparator in instances of indirect discrimination based on a worker's disability is not with ALL disabled people, but rather with people with the particular disability. Similarly where the protected characteristic is race, the comparator may be persons of a

---

[17] [1980] ICR 144.

[18] As similarly found in *Singh v British Rail Engineering Ltd* [1986] ICR 22 involving a requirement to wear protective headgear.

[19] *Lockwood v Crawley Warren Group Ltd* [2001] EAT No 1176/99.

[20] *Home Office v Holmes* [1984] IRLR 299.

[21] *Meade-Hill and National Union of Civil and Public Servants v British Council* [1995] IRLR 478.

[22] *Home Office v Holmes* [1984].

specific race. In age related indirect discrimination, the correct age group of persons disadvantaged is an important aspect is demonstrating discrimination.

19.6.5 Harassment (and by third parties)

19.6.5.1. *The protected characteristics*

The protected characteristic of sex remains covered by the EA 2010.[23]

The protected characteristics of age, disability, gender reassignment, race, religion or belief, and sexual orientation were already covered through existing legislation (or are newly covered by the introduction of 'third party harassment') which is now subject to change through the EA 2010.

Marriage and civil partnership, and pregnancy and maternity are still *not* covered.

19.6.5.2 *Application of the law*

The types of harassment covered by s. 26 include:

1 Harassment related to a person of a relevant protected characteristic;

2 Sexual harassment; and

3 Less favourable treatment of a worker because of the sexual harassment or harassment related to sex or gender reassignment.

Harassment continues to be 'unwanted conduct' related to a protected characteristic, which has the purpose or effect of violating a person's dignity or creating an intimidating, hostile, degrading, humiliating, or offensive environment. The right gives employees the power to complain of offensive behaviour, even if not directed at them, and complainants also are not required to personally possess the protected characteristic. Employees are further protected from harassment due to association or perception (s. 26). The harassment may involve the harasser performing actions that gradually lead to a complaint, but if the action is sufficiently serious,[24] a one-off act may enable a claim of harassment to be made.[25]

The words 'purpose or effect' are important as they enable a claim for harassment even where the harasser did not intend for this to be the effect of his/her actions. For example, male workers may be downloading an image of a naked woman. A female colleague may know this is happening and may feel it is creating a hostile and humiliating environment. Therefore, she has a claim for harassment even though this was not the intention of the men. It is the perception of the worker (a subjective test) that is relevant;[26] his/her personal circumstances (such as health, culture and so on);[27] and whether it was reasonable that the conduct would have that effect on the worker (an objective test).[28] Hence, it may not be harassment if the claimant was deemed by the tribunal to be hypersensitive.

As noted above, unwanted conduct related to a protected characteristic affords protection due to the worker's own protected characteristic or a situation connected with a protected characteristic (associative discrimination or perceived discrimination). The issue of

---

[23] EA 2010 s. 26(5).

[24] This action can involve verbal comments rather than physical conduct: *In Situ Cleaning v Heads* [1995] IRLR 4.

[25] *Bracebridge Engineering Ltd v Darby* [1990] IRLR 3.

[26] EA 2010, s. 26(4)(a)

[27] EA 2010, s. 26(4)(b).

[28] EA 2010, s. 26(4)(c).

a 'connection with' the protected characteristic allows for protection against a broad range of discriminatory scenarios. For example, a worker subject to homophobic banter could have been harassed in relation to his sexual orientation; an employer racially abusing a black worker could lead to a white worker being offended and leading to a claim of racial discrimination; and a worker who has a disabled son whose colleagues make offensive remarks about the disability could lead to a claim of harassment related to disability.

Harassment may also occur through the action of third parties: This will be particularly a concern for employers as it will apply to acts of harassment by customers/clients. Liability will take effect if the harassment has occurred on at least two previous occasions, the employer (for example) is aware that the harassment has taken place, and has not taken reasonable steps to prevent its reoccurrence.

There is no need for the claimant to establish a comparator in harassment cases.

19.6.6 **Victimization**

19.6.6.1 *The protected characteristics*

Each of the protected characteristics are subject to changes following enactment of the EA 2010.

19.6.6.2 *Application of the law*

Where a worker is subjected to a detriment because he/she has performed a 'protected act' or because the employer believes that he/she has done, or will do a protected act in the future, he/she has a complaint under the Act[29] for victimization.[30] A protected act includes:

- initiating proceedings under the EA 2010;[31]
- providing evidence/information in relation to proceedings under the EA 2010;[32]
- doing anything related to the provisions of the EA 2010;[33]
- making an allegation that another person has done something in contravention of the EA 2010;[34] or
- making/trying to obtain a 'relevant pay disclosure' from a colleague/former colleague.[35]

The worker is not required to possess the protected characteristic personally to be protected under the Act. A detriment for the purposes of victimization may take many forms and can include a refusal to provide a reference to a former worker,[36] or if the employer applies unfair pressure and intimidation to prevent the pursuit of a claim.[37]

An important change in the EA 2010 is that the need for a comparator in such instances is no longer required. Where a complaint is made maliciously, or the employee supports a complaint he/she knows is untrue, then protection under the legislation is lost (s. 27(3)).

---

[29] EA 2010, s. 27(1).
[30] *Aziz v Trinity Street Taxis Ltd* [1988] IRLR 204.
[31] EA 2010, s. 27(2)(a).
[32] EA 2010, s. 27(2)(b).
[33] EA 2010, s. 27(2)(c).
[34] EA 2010, s. 27(2)(d).
[35] EA 2010, s. 77(3).
[36] *Coote v Granada Hospitality Ltd* [1999] IRLR 452.
[37] *St Helens Borough Council v Derbyshire and Others* [2007] UKHL 16.

19.7 Questionnaires

To facilitate the gathering of information that may be relevant in establishing discrimination, the Equality Act 2010 (Obtaining Information) Order 2010 provides for questionnaires that assist a claimant in obtaining from the employer relevant information. These are available in the Schedules of the Act and relate to prohibited conduct and equality of terms. The person who considers he/she has been subject to a contravention of the EA 2010 may ask questions (as provided in the relevant questionnaire) of the person he/she believes was responsible for the breach. A response form is also contained in this legislation.

19.8 Liability for acts of third parties

Under the (now repealed) Sex Discrimination Act 1975, an employer could be liable to an employee who was subject to unwanted conduct by a third party. A 'third party' is someone who is not under the control of the employer (such as another employee) but rather can be a customer, client, delivery driver and so on (essentially a visitor to the premises).

The employer may be vicariously liable where the employee has been the victim of unwanted conduct, on at least three occasions (the so-called 'three-strikes' effect of the EA 2010), during the course of his/her employment. Clearly, there is no case law as yet to identify how this provision will work in practice (enacted October 2010), but consider the following in an assessment of the policies that employers should adopt to ensure protection of workers, and avoiding transgression of the law. What will be the likely effect if, on the third occasion of unwanted conduct:

- A customer is rude to a (employee) waiter?
- A client refuses to deal with a salesperson because the salesperson is from (for example) Nigeria and the client 'can't understand what he is saying'?
- A delivery driver is abusive towards a receptionist because of some misunderstanding and he is late for his next job?
- A customer attempts to 'chat-up' a secretary whilst working at an organization?

and in each of the above examples, the employer is aware of the conduct and fails to take any action.

The requirement on an employer is to take 'reasonable steps' to prevent the unwanted conduct.

Remember, therefore, that to be actionable the following aspects must be satisfied:

1 The employee must have been subject to unwanted conduct on at least two previous occasions; and

2 The employer must have aware of the unwanted conduct; and

3 The employer must have failed to have taken reasonable steps to prevent this.

Further, it is important to note that the third party need not be the same person for the previous two occasions of unwanted conduct before the third becomes actionable. It may be the case that the three occasions may have involved a different third party in each.

The affected employee may have an action under the Protection from Harassment Act 1997, with its six-year time limit to bring a claim and with the availability of awards of injunctions to prevent further acts of unwanted conduct. However, such claims are heard in the County Court and are subject to rules of evidence that are similar to a criminal proof of liability (a not insubstantial test) and subject to potential costs being awarded against the party who loses the case. The EA 2010 requires claims of discrimination to be brought within a three-month time period, and as the claims are heard in the Employment Tribunals (ET), costs are rarely awarded.

19.9 Age discrimination

Age is one of the protected characteristics under the EA 2010. However, it should be noted that some discrimination on the basis of age is allowed, and indeed age is the one protected characteristic that permits a justification of direct discrimination. This is allowed where the employer can successfully demonstrate that the less favourable treatment suffered by the claimant on the basis of his/her age is a proportionate means of achieving a legitimate aim. This is the 'objective justification test'.

Section 5 defines 'age' in reference to a person of a particular age group and persons of the same age group. All age groups are protected (hence not just 'old' people).

19.10 Disability discrimination

 Business Link

Employers are required to make reasonable adjustments to the workplace to ensure that those individuals with disabilities can access the employment, and if the business is open to the public, that the employer has made reasonable adjustments to accommodate them. An employer's ignorance is no excuse.

Since the enactment and coming into force of the Disability Discrimination Act (DDA) 1995, employers (and a wider group of service providers[38]—such as shops and businesses giving access to the public) have had to make reasonable adjustments to their businesses to ensure that those individuals with a disability are not discriminated against. Since October 2004, all service providers/employers have been required to produce a Disability Equality Policy covering: the delivery of services; an employment policy; training and education; consultation with disabled representatives; and access to buildings, information, and services.

The EA 2010 provides a new definition of discrimination based on disability. This has been largely welcomed following the problems encountered after the judgment in *London Borough of Lewisham v Malcolm*.[39] Section 15 provides:

A person (A) discriminates against a disabled person (B) if— (1) A treats B unfavourably because of something arising in consequence of B's disability, and (2) A cannot show that the treatment is a proportionate means of achieving a legitimate aim.

---

[38] 'Service providers' are most companies or organizations that offer goods, facilities, or services to the general public. Since 1 October 2004, service providers had to complete the process of making 'reasonable adjustments' such as changing some physical features of their premises.

[39] [2008] IRLR 700.

Subsection (1) does not apply if A shows that A did not know, and could not reasonably have been expected to know, that B had the disability.

Under EA 2010, s. 6 a person is defined as having a disability if he/she has a physical or mental impairment that has a substantial[40] and long term[41] adverse effect on his/her ability to carry out normal day-to-day activities.[42] The DDA 1995 widened the scope of a disability and from 5 December 2005 it includes people with, or diagnosed with, cancer, HIV, and Multiple Sclerosis. The Act covers all employers (since 1 October 2004), regardless of size (with exceptions for recruitment to the armed services).

An employer may not discriminate against a person due to his/her disability, or for a reason related to a disability, although the employer may provide an objective ground for any discrimination in this respect. In relation to service providers, objective reasons for discrimination may include where health and safety are at risk; where a person is incapable of entering a contract; and where a service provider is unable to provide that service to the public.

In an attempt to prevent discrimination to a person with a disability, the employer has to make reasonable adjustments to his/her premises, practices, or procedures to ensure disabled employees are not put at a substantial disadvantage[43] compared with non-disabled employees. This can include installing ramps/lifts to enable persons in wheelchairs to gain access; producing documents in Braille/large print/or in audio format; providing workers with speech recognition software for their computers and so on. Where an employer fails to comply with the duty to make reasonable adjustments, the disabled person is discriminated against.[44] The EA 2010 identifies the following three steps as being reasonable to comply with the law:

- Avoid substantial disadvantage where a provision, criterion, or practice applied by or on behalf of the employers puts the disabled person at a substantial disadvantage compared with persons without the disability;[45]

- Remove or alter an existing physical feature (or provide the means to avoid it) where it puts the disabled person at a substantial disadvantage compared with persons without the disability;[46]

- Provide an auxiliary aid/service[47] where a disabled person would (but for this aid) be put at a substantial disadvantage compared with persons without the disability.[48]

Reasonable adjustments are an essential feature of equality legislation as it imposes a requirement on employers to take positive steps to ensure people with a disability can have access to the job market and progress in their employment.[49]

The key element here is for 'reasonable' adjustments. This will include facts such as the size of the employer, the resources available to him/her, and the needs of disabled persons coming into the business/and or premises.[50] The EA 2010 requires the employer to make reasonable

---

[40] *Foster v Hampshire Fire and Rescue Service* [1998] 43 BMLR 186.

[41] Such as in *Rowley v Walkers Nonsuch Ltd* [1997] (unreported), where a worker who had sustained a back injury and could not work for six months was not held to be suffering a disability for the purposes of the DDA 1995.

[42] *Law Hospital NHS Trust v Rush* [2001] IRLR 611.

[43] EA 2010, s. 212(1)—this is a disadvantage that is not minor or trivial and is assessed objectively on the facts of the case.

[44] EA 2010, s. 21(2).   [45] EA 2010, s. 20(3).   [46] EA 2010, s. 20(4).

[47] EA 2010, s. 20(11)—this refers to something that provides support to the disabled person—e.g. speech recognition software, support worker and so on.

[48] EA 2010, s. 20(5).   [49] EA 2010, s. 20.

[50] The Code of Practice contains a section on 'good practice' with which employers should familiarize themselves.

adjustments for 'actual' persons with a disability rather than hypothetical persons, or to anticipate the needs of persons with disabilities. Therefore, the requirement is effective where the employer knew, or should have reasonably known, of the existence of the disability,[51] and where to take no action would likely have the effect of substantially disadvantaging the applicant to a job or an existing employee.[52]

Employers are also under a duty to make reasonable adjustments in recruitment and the selection process for job applicants.

19.10.1 A comparator

In instances of direct discrimination based on a person's disability, the use of a comparator is the same as the other types of direct discrimination. But, here the comparator must be a person who does not possess the same disability as the claimant, but who has the same abilities and skills. Hence it is the circumstances relevant to the less favourable treatment that is the focus.

19.10.2 Pre-employment health questionnaire

The EA 2010 provides limited conditions where health questions may be asked (by an employer or his/her agent or employees) of an applicant before a job offer is made.[53] This ensures persons with a physical/mental impairment are not discriminated against. However, common sense must prevail, and the exceptions noted below to the general rule about pre-employment health questionnaires being unlawful are to be construed narrowly. Consequently, questions regarding an applicant's health may be asked to determine the following:

1 any reasonable adjustments that may be required for the person to do that job/attend interviews;[54]

2 to determine an applicant's ability to perform an intrinsic aspect of the job;[55]

3 to monitor equality and diversity information for the organization;[56]

4 to enable a positive action policy to be pursued;[57]

5 to demonstrate an occupational requirement of the person required for the job;[58]

6 where such questions are necessary in relation to national security.[59]

The 'pre-employment' element of the protection is important as, once the person has been offered employment, an employer *is* permitted to ask health questions. (Note that a person applying for a job does not have the right to complain to a tribunal if he/she believes a pre-employment health question was asked, but he/she may complain to the Equality and Human Rights Commission).

---

[51] *HJ Heinz Co Ltd v Kenrick* [2002] IRLR 144 and *Rothwell v Pelikan Hardcopy Scotland Ltd* [2006] IRLR 24, where an employer's failure to enquire about an employee's medical condition, that led to his dismissal on health grounds, constituted a breach. (Now contained in Sch. 8, para 20(1)(a).)

[52] *Ridout v TC Group* [1998] IRLR 628.

[53] EA 2010, s. 60.   [54] EA 2010, s. 60(6)(a).   [55] EA 2010, s. 60(6)(b).

[56] EA 2010, s. 60(6)(c).   [57] EA 2010, s. 60(6)(d).

[58] EA 2010, s. 60(6)(e).   [59] EA 2010, s. 60(14).

19.11 Discrimination on the basis of gender reassignment

Under EA 2010, s. 7, gender reassignment refers to a person who is proposing to undergo, is undergoing, or has undergone a process (or part of a process) for the purpose of reassigning the person's sex by changing physiological or other attributes of sex (a transsexual person). The Act now protects a woman (for example) who wishes to live permanently as a man even though she does not intend to undergo any medical procedures (what used to be the medical supervision requirement for protection). Permanency is required, hence a cross-dresser would not be protected. Despite the change in gender, this will not allow the transsexual person to 'benefit' from his/her change in areas such as marriage, parenthood, social security benefits, succession, peerages, and sport. However, they will be recognized as being of the gender reassigned to, they will be issued with a new birth certificate, and be able to marry.

19.12 Sex, marriage/civil partnership and race discrimination

> *⧉* **Business Link**
>
> Imagine you are writing an advertisement for a position in your business. You advertise for the position of a waiter or, for a call centre operative, for a person whose 'first language is English'. You may well have unwittingly breached the EA 2010. 'Waiter' could be interpreted as being a position only available to a man (not 'waiting staff') and requiring English as a first language may dissuade a person whose first language is not English but who is proficient in the language (as the advertiser probably wanted but simply explained this poorly). The legislation is effective before, during, and after employment and there is no maximum on the compensation that can be awarded. Hence an employer/manager must be fully aware of his/her responsibilities under discrimination legislation.

The EA 2010 prohibits discrimination on the basis of a person's sex or his/her marital/co-habitation status, or their race. In relation to the protected characteristic of sex, s. 11 identifies that a reference to a person who has this particular protected characteristic is a reference to a man or to a woman; or to persons of the same sex.

There are no changes to the protection already provided in relation to race. Section 9 defines race as including colour; nationality; and ethnic or national origins. The protected characteristic refers to a person of a particular racial group or persons of the same racial group. Section 8(4) continues that because a racial group comprises two or more distinct racial groups does not prevent it from constituting a particular racial group. Section 8(5) is an important power granted to a Minister of the Crown to amend this section to provide (or not) for caste to be an aspect of race.

The EA 2010 provides protection against discrimination based on sex or race to a wide range of workers—those who carry out the employment personally. There is no qualification period necessary to qualify and, unlike claims for redundancy payments or unfair dismissal, there is no cap on the amount of damages that may be awarded. This has led to substantial sums being awarded to the victims of discrimination under the previous Acts.

Protection is afforded against each form of prohibited conduct. As such, and similarly to the previous legislation, acts of direct[60] and indirect discrimination[61] are outlawed, and claims for victimization suffered as a result of exercising rights or giving evidence in hearings also results in a breach, and for harassment suffered by a claimant are actionable.

19.12.1 **Discrimination before employment**

It is possible for employers to fall victim to discrimination laws even before they have employed the worker. In relation to sex and race discrimination, this typically occurs when the employer places an advertisement for a job, or in the interview/selection procedure.

- *Advertisements:* An employer may not publish or cause to be published an advertisement which indicates or might reasonably be understood to indicate an intention to sexually or racially discriminate. This clearly has implications when an employer uses words to describe a vacancy such as 'manager' (rather than manager/manageress); 'waitress' (rather than waiting staff) and so on (and for anyone who publishes it). This may be seen in terms of race discrimination where an employer states in an advert that the applicant must have 'English as his/her first language'. This may have been innocently included by the employer, to require high proficiency in the English language of the applicant, but its impact is to dissuade those members of groups from applying where English may not be their 'first' language. This, however, does not mean that they are less than proficient in the language. Employers, therefore, should be careful to ensure that advertisements do not transgress the law. It does not mean that the employer cannot seek to hire members of one ethnic group, or one sex. **Occupational Requirements** exist that enable discrimination where this is a particular requirement of the job. However, the employer would be advised to state this in the advertisement to remove any doubt.

- *Interview/selection events:* An employer should not employ practices that are discriminatory, such as (for example) invoking a policy not to hire women of child-bearing age, people of ethnic groups and so on. Such practices may be halted by the Equality and Human Rights Commission through the issuing of a non-discrimination notice.

It should be remembered that employers may not instruct someone else to perform the discriminatory practice on their behalf (a manager, human resources department, recruitment agency and so on). They may not seek to influence someone to discriminate through, for example, bribes or threats, and it is unlawful to assist someone in the commission of discrimination.

---

[60] Such as in *Owen & Briggs v James* [1982] IRLR 502, where Ms Owen, a black woman, applied, but was rejected, for the position of secretary. The successful applicant was a white woman with less experience and fewer qualifications, and it was heard by the Court of Appeal that the employers stated 'why should we appoint 'coloured girls' when we could hire English applicants'. As such, the employers had refused to hire Owens due to her race, and this was to her detriment.

[61] Where an employer applies a requirement that a significantly smaller proportion of persons from one racial group can comply with, and not complying is to their detriment – constitutes a breach (*Meer v London Borough of Tower Hamlets* [1988] IRLR 399).

19.12.2 **A comparator**

To establish a claim of discrimination, the claimant must establish that he/she was discriminated on the basis of his/her sex, marital/co-habitation status, or race. Hence, he/she must have been a victim of less favourable treatment attributable to the protected characteristic; and this is evidenced when compared with how a member of the opposite sex, marital/co-habitation status, or race was or would be treated. As such, a hypothetical comparator may be used. Where a hypothetical comparator is used, this could be evidenced from several people in the same employment whose circumstances are somewhat similar to that of the claimant, but not the same. The Code of Practice provides for another way to approach the application of hypothetical comparators as 'but for the relevant protected characteristic, would the claimant have been treated in that way?'

Note that a comparator is not needed in cases of racial segregation.[62]

Section 23(1) requires that, (in relation to direct discrimination) there must be no material difference between the circumstances of the comparator and claimant. But this need not mean that the two people are identical, rather it is circumstances which are relevant to the treatment of the claimant and the comparator.

In direct discrimination in employment related to marriage/civil partnership, the direct discrimination only covers less favourable treatment because the worker is married or a civil partner. Single people or those in relationships outside of these protected characteristics are not protected.

19.13 **Equality in Pay**

 Business Link

Inserted into every contract of employment is an equality clause. As such, employers must ensure they do not discriminate against men and women in the pay they receive on the basis of their sex, unless there are objective reasons to justify the difference. Employers have to assist workers in any claims by disclosing information about pay and allow employees to discuss pay insofar as this is related to a relevant pay disclosure. Therefore, the employer should have genuine reasons and/or transparency in the assessment of pay to workers to ensure they are not acting unlawfully and face claims to an Employment Tribunal.

EA 2010, s. 66 imposes an equality clause in the terms of a contract of employment, even where one is not included. The law relating to sex equality in pay (ss. 66–70) is based on a person employed on work that is equal to that of a comparator of the opposite sex. This ensures that (for example) a woman's terms of employment are no less favourable than a man's (the comparator). If the man's contract contains a term that benefits him, and it is not present in

---

[62] EA 2010 s. 13(1). Employers must not seek to segregate workers based on their race, regardless of any policy reason surrounding this, or else they face falling victim to a potential claim for discrimination: *Pel Ltd v Modgill* [1980] IRLR 142.

the contract of the woman, s. 66(2)(b) provides that the woman's contract is modified (equalized) to include this term.[63] The legislation is applicable to workers regardless of age; there is no qualification period to gain protection; the law is applicable to those employed full-time and part-time; and there is no exemption for small businesses. See Figure 19.1 for an overview of claims for sex discrimination in pay.

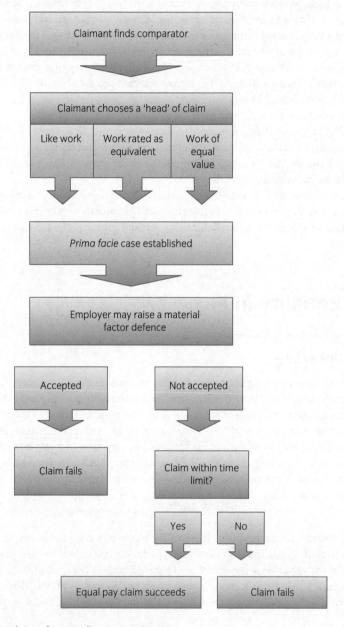

Figure 19.1 Claims for sex discrimination in pay

[63] *Hayward v Cammell Laird Shipbuilders* [1988] IRLR 257.

19.13.1 'Pay'

The term 'pay' has to be interpreted in conformity with EU law.[64] Pay is defined in Art. 157 TFEU as any 'consideration whether in cash or in kind, which the worker receives directly or indirectly, in respect of his employment, from his employer'. It therefore not only includes wages, but all terms and conditions of pay in employment including occupational benefits,[65] sick pay,[66] bonus payments, pension contributions,[67] compensation for unfair dismissal[68] and so on.

The pay received by men and women must be equal in relation to the heads of claim identified below. If pay is different between a man and woman, but this is due not because of the worker's gender but, perhaps, because of qualifications, length of service or some other 'material factor' not applicable to gender, the difference may be objectively justified.

19.13.2 A comparator

To establish an action of equal pay the claim must be that the reason for the difference in pay is due to the gender of the claimant. The legislation is not designed to give fair pay or enable the claimant to bring an action because someone in another job has better pay and the claimant believes he/she should be provided with the same. Rather, the EA 2010 requires a claim between a woman and a man, and this involves establishing a comparison between workers. The previous law regulating sex equality in pay (the EPA 1970) required the claimant to produce an actual comparator of the opposite sex, working in the same employment as the claimant by the same employer, an associated employer, or at an establishment where common terms and conditions[69] are observed.

Cases brought after 1 October 2010 involving direct gender pay discrimination may involve the use of a hypothetical comparator rather than an 'actual' comparator (and the problems associated with this). In all other instances, an actual comparator will still be required. Section 78 identifies that (apart from excluded groups) employers are required to publish information relating to the pay of employees for the purpose of showing whether, by reference to factors of such description as is prescribed, there are differences in the pay of male and female employees.

An actual comparator may consist of a person employed at the same time as the claimant, but not successors[70] of the claimant, although his/her predecessors may be used (as the time limits and extensions to back-pay enable greater access to claims).[71] A further improvement to equality effected through the EA 2010 has been the introduction of pay transparency. EA 2010, s. 77 provides for discussions about pay. Where a person's contract of employment prohibits him/her from disclosing or seeking to disclose information about his/her terms of work, insofar as this relates to a relevant pay disclosure, such a term is unenforceable. This is an interesting step in promoting equality in pay. Previously, establishing the most appropriate comparator in equal pay claims was difficult as many workers (particularly those in the

[64] The Equal Pay Directive and Article 157 TFEU.
[65] *Griffin v London Pension Fund Authority* [1993] IRLR 248.
[66] *Rinner-Kühn v FWW Spezial-Gebäudereinigung GmbH* [1989] IRLR 493.
[67] *Barber v Guardian Royal Exchange Assurance Group* [1990] ECR I-1889.
[68] *R v Secretary of State for Employment ex p Seymour-Smith* [1999] IRLR 253.
[69] *British Coal Corporation v Smith* [1996] IRLR 404.
[70] *Walton Centre for Neurology v Bewley* [2008] UKEAT/0564/07/MAA.
[71] *Macarthys Ltd v Smith* [1980] ICR 854.

private sector) were subject to a confidentiality clause regarding their employment. It was possible for a potential claimant to require the employer to identify a comparator through an order for discovery,[72] but this was difficult in practice. Indeed, one of the reasons for the general lack of success of the legislation in this area was often the practical problems associated in making a claim of sex discrimination in pay. The EA 2010 should help alleviate some of these difficulties.

Having established an actual/hypothetical comparator who is paid more than the claimant, the next stage is to demonstrate which form the discrimination in pay takes: the claimant bases the claim for equal pay on one of the **'heads' of claim**.

19.13.3 **Preparing a claim—pay disclosure**

Where a worker wishes to bring an equal pay claim, due to the complexity in establishing such actions, advice from a trade union, or local not-for-profit advisory agency may be very beneficial. Section 77 requires that a term of a person's work that purports to prevent or restrict the person from disclosing or seeking to disclose information about the terms of his/her work is unenforceable against him/her in so far as the person makes or seeks to make a relevant pay disclosure. Colleagues and former colleagues may also seek a relevant pay disclosure (that is if made for the purpose of enabling the person who makes it, or the person to whom it is made, to find out whether or to what extent there is a connection between pay and having (or not having) a particular protected characteristic). The Act protects against victimization by protecting those who make, seek, or receive information disclosed in a relevant pay disclosure.

19.13.4 **The heads of claim**

The claimant has to select the most appropriate 'head' under which he/she is to base the claim. There are three heads—like work; work rated as equivalent; and work of equal value. The tribunal is not entitled to choose the head and it is important for the success of the claim that the claimant selects the most appropriate head based on his/her circumstances.

19.13.4.1 *Like work*

Section 65(1)(b) of EA 2010 identifies that a claimant is performing 'like work' with his/her comparator, if the work is the same, or broadly similar work. The work being undertaken does not have to be exactly the same, and any minor differences that are of no practical importance may be ignored (s. 65(2)(b).[73] If the comparator is actually taking on additional duties that do differentiate the role performed by the claimant and the comparator, then this can justify a difference in pay and the 'like work' claim will fail.[74] However, the EA 2010 requires for regard to the frequency of differences between the claimant's and comparator's work in practice and the extent and nature of these. Even prior to the EA 2010, the courts had looked to the roles of the claimant and comparator being undertaken at work, rather than focusing on the (stated) terms of the contract when determining their responsibilities and duties.[75]

---

[72] *Leverton v Clwyd County Council* [1989] IRLR 28.
[73] *Electrolux Ltd v Hutchinson* [1977] IRLR 410.
[74] *Eaton Ltd v Nuttall* [1977] IRLR 71.
[75] *Shields v E. Coomes (Holdings) Ltd.* [1978] IRLR 263.

19.13.4.2 *Work rated as equivalent*

To avoid potential claims against the employer, and in the interests of transparency, the employer may perform a job evaluation study that seeks to rate the pay provided to workers on the basis of the roles and responsibilities that are undertaken.[76] However, an employer cannot be forced to conduct this study, but where he/she has, the claimant may use the findings in any claim (in the same way as the employer can use the findings to defend a claim). Clearly, to have any value the study must be appropriate and objective. It must not be based on a sex-specific system (s. 65(4)(b)) where values are set differently between men and women.

A fair rating system will satisfy the following:

1 It must be analytical.

2 The work undertaken must be objectively assessed (identifying the value of the work in terms of skill, responsibilities and so on).[77]

3 Both the claimant's and comparator's jobs must have been part of the study.

4 The study must have been conducted at the undertaking where the claimant is employed.

It should also be noted that even though a job evaluation study may rate a man's job as *lower* than that of a woman while the employer pays the man a higher wage, this will not prevent a successful claim from the woman, despite the fact that the legislation provides for a claim when the jobs are rated as 'equivalent'.[78]

19.13.4.3 *Work of equal value*

In the past, employers often used to employ men and women in different jobs (therefore restricting claims under 'like work'), and they would refuse to undertake a job evaluation study (hence preventing 'work rated as equivalent' claims). The result was an impasse in successful actions on the basis of equal pay. As such, following action by the EU Commission that the UK was in breach of its EU law obligations, legislative action was taken to introduce a 'third head' of complaint of sex discrimination in pay—'work of equal value'.[79] This increased the possibility of claims and provided access to the right for many more claimants. Further, it was held in *Pickstone v Freemans PLC*[80] that an equal value claim is possible even where a 'token' man is employed in the same job as the claimant. This prevents an employer from employing the tactic of hiring a man in order to prevent the claimant pleading under this section of the Act.

The EA 2010, s. 65(1)(c) enables claims that (for example) a woman's work is equal to a man's (the comparator) where it is neither like the man's work, nor rated as equivalent to his, but it is nevertheless equal in terms of the demands made upon her by reference to factors such as effort, skill, and decision-making.[81]

The previous case law further requires that all of the individual terms and conditions of the contract have to be equalized, rather than looking at the broad aspects of the contracts of the claimant and comparator.

---

[76] EA 2010, s. 65(1)(b).

[77] Note that factors such as strength may be discriminatory between male and female workers and hence should be avoided: *Rummler v Dato-Druck GmbH* [1987] IRLR 32.

[78] *Bainbridge v Redcar & Cleveland BC* [2007] EWCA Civ 910.

[79] Through the Equal Pay (Amendment) Regulations 1983.

[80] [1988] IRLR 357.

[81] EA 2010 s. 65(6)(b).

Hayward v Cammell Laird Shipbuilders[82]

Facts:

The case involved a woman engaged as a cook at the shipyard who claimed equality in pay based on her assertion that her work was of equal value with comparators performing jobs as a painter, engineer, and joiner. The employer's defence was that when viewed as a whole, the claimant's contract was as favourable as the comparators. The claimant's contract provided for better holiday pay and meal entitlements (among others) not enjoyed by the comparators, although her pay and overtime rates were lower. The House of Lords held that all the terms of the claimant's contract had to be as favourable as those of the comparator, including the pay.

Authority for:

A claimant who is engaged on work of equal value with the comparator is entitled to equality of pay in relation to each element of the contract.

When faced with a claim that, *prima facie*, demonstrates the claimant and comparator are being paid on different rates, and this is due to sex discrimination in pay, the employer may mount a defence of a genuine material difference justifying the difference.

19.13.5 **Material factor defence**

Once the claimant has established his/her claim under one of the three heads above, the employer may be in a position to avoid equalizing the pay between the claimant and the comparator under the EA 2010.[83] The employer is entitled to demonstrate that the difference in the pay is not based on the sex of the parties, but rather it is based on a material factor, that can be objectively justified on the needs of the business, and is a proportionate means of achieving that aim. For the factor to be 'material' it must be a material difference between the claimant's case and the comparator's. This argument is available to be pleaded at the preliminary or full hearing.

- *Responsibility:* An employer may attempt to justify differences in pay based on the additional responsibilities undertaken. Where this is relied on, the employer must demonstrate that the responsibilities are frequently required, and are based on the conduct of the parties rather than what is included in the contract.[84]

- *Market forces:* It may be necessary for an employer to provide pay at different rates between jobs, which would otherwise enable a 'work of equal value' claim, because of the nature of the market that the jobs are in.[85]

- *Collective bargaining agreements:* It may be possible for an employer to rely on agreements between workers' representatives and the employer regarding collective bargaining agreements or pay structures, although they cannot provide an automatic defence.[86]

- *Experience:* The general rule has been that those workers who have longer service at an employer's business will, generally, be paid higher wages due to their seniority. The employer can (generally) justify this on the basis of rewarding loyalty; providing motivation to stay with the organization; reflecting experience and so on.

---

[82] [1988] IRLR 257.   [83] Section 69.   [84] *Shields v E. Coomes Ltd* [1978] IRLR 263.
[85] *Rainey v Greater Glasgow Health Board* [1987] IRLR 26.
[86] *Enderby v Frenchay Health Authority* [1994] ICR 112.

- *Regional variations:* An employer may seek to justify differences in pay because the claimant and comparator's work exist in different locations.[87]

- *Red-circle agreements:* A **red-circle agreement** is where an employer has performed, for example, a job evaluation study and the result of which has led to groups of workers being downgraded. The agreement protects the affected workers' salaries at the current rate, despite being moved to a lower grade. The agreement, and its application, must be performed in a non-discriminatory way.[88]

19.13.6 Time limits for a claim

A claim for equal pay may be made at any time while the worker is employed under a 'stable employment relationship'.[89] If he/she does not wish to bring an action whilst working, he/she can wait until the employment is terminated, and bring a 'rolled up' claim within six months of leaving (as held by the Court of Justice). However, in circumstances where the employer has deliberately misled a worker or concealed facts that would have assisted with his/her claim, and the worker could not have been reasonably expected to be aware of this; or where the worker is suffering a disability during the six-month period when he/she left the employment where the claim would have been presented, the time period is extended. In cases of concealment, the six-month period does not begin until the worker discovered (or should have discovered) the concealment; and in cases of disability, the period begins when the worker is no longer under the disability.

Equal pay claims may be backdated for a six-year period.

19.13.7 'Good practice'

Due to changes in the legislation, and in an attempt to assist employers in complying with their legal responsibilities,[90] Codes of Practice has been created to offer practical help with implementing the provisions of the EA 2010. The Codes[91] (on equal pay; employment and services, public functions and associations) were laid before Parliament on 12 October 2010 and came into force on 6 April 2011 in the form of the Equality Act 2010 Codes of Practice (Services, Public Functions and Associations, Employment, and Equal Pay) Order 2011.

> **? Thinking Point**
>
> Sex discrimination in pay legislation has been in effect for over 30 years, and evidence from the Equal Opportunities Commission established that the gender gap in pay is 17 per cent for full-time workers and 40 per cent for part-time workers. Given the limited impact these legislative provisions have had in successfully equalizing pay between men and women, do you feel the situation is likely to improve following enactment of the EA 2010? Critique the extension of rights and those provisions not brought into force when drawing your conclusions.

---

[87] *NAAFI v Varley* [1976] IRLR 408. [88] *Snoxell v Vauxhall Motors Ltd* [1977] IRLR 123.

[89] *Preston v Wolverhampton Healthcare NHS Trust* [2001] UKHL 5.

[90] Be aware that whilst these are truly excellent resources with many practical examples of good practice and acts likely to amount to discrimination, they are substantial documents (the Code on Employment is some 81,000+ words in length). Therefore employers should set aside time to read and digest the contents.

[91] http://www.equalityhumanrights.com/legal-and-policy/equality-act/equality-act-codes-of-practice/.

19.14 Discrimination on the basis of religion or belief

Legislation to prevent discrimination based on an individual's religious belief was extended following the enactment of the Employment Equality (Religion or Belief) Regulations 2003. This legislation has been repealed following the EA 2010 and its provisions are contained within that legislation.

The EA 2010 protects workers against discrimination based on their choice of religion, religious beliefs (or non-belief), or other similar philosophical belief—be that a real or perceived belief. Section 10 identifies that religion means any religion and a lack of religion. Belief means any religious or philosophical belief or a lack of belief. There are no changes to this area of protection against discrimination, however it is important to note that the discriminator and the person discriminated against may hold the same religion or belief.

As with the other protections from discrimination outlined above, protection is afforded against direct and indirect forms of discrimination, against victimization, and against harassment.

19.14.1 Occupational Requirements

There exist situations where an otherwise directly discriminatory act is allowed, and hence not a transgression of the EA 2010, where it is an OR for the job. In relation to where an employer has an ethos based religion or belief, the employer can rely on the OR if it can be demonstrated that, in relation to that ethos and the nature of the work to be undertaken:

1 The requirement of possessing that particular region or belief is an occupational requirement;

2 The application of the requirement is a proportionate means of achieving a legitimate aim; and

3 The person (claimant) fails to meet the requirement or the employer possesses reasonable grounds to believe that he/she does not meet the requirement.

19.15 Discrimination on the basis of sexual orientation

A worker may not be discriminated against on the basis of his/her sexual orientation following the EC Framework Directive[92] that was transposed and given effect in the UK through the Employment Equality (Sexual Orientation) Regulations 2003 (now replaced by the EA 2010, s. 12). An individual's sexual orientation is defined as his/her orientation towards persons of the same sex (homosexual), opposite sex (heterosexual), or both sexes (bi-sexual).[93] The EA 2010 prohibits unwanted conduct (either based on the individual's sexual orientation

---

[92] Council Directive 2000/78/EC of 27 November 2000 Establishing A General Framework for Equal Treatment in Employment and Occupation.

[93] EA 2010, s. 12.

or on his/her perceived orientation). To exemplify, on a monetary basis at the very least, the importance of preventing discrimination based on a person's sexual orientation is the case of *Ditton v CP Publishing Ltd*.[94] The claimant was a gay employee who was subject to offensive comments about his sexual orientation by a company director for the first eight days of his employment. He was then dismissed. The tribunal (in Scotland) held that he had been discriminated against, he had been harassed, and as the employer had failed to follow the (then applicable) statutory dispute resolution procedures, the award was uplifted to £118,000.

The EA 2010 allows for the OR defence of an employer where being of a particular sexual orientation is a genuine and determining occupational requirement (and it is proportionate to those ends); and in the case of organized religions where the sexual orientation contradicts the beliefs of the members of the particular religion.

19.16 Discrimination against part-time workers

Before the enactment of the Part-time Workers (Prevention of Less Favourable Treatment) Regulations 2000, a claimant who considered that he/she had been discriminated against due to his/her employment status had to initiate a convoluted claim under indirect sex discrimination. However, since July 2000, provision is provided for part-time workers not to be treated less favourably than their full-time counterparts. This may be with regard to the contracts of employment or being subjected to any other detriment through an employer's act or omission.[95]

The Regulations provide the part-time worker with the right to the relevant proportion of pay, access to pension schemes, holiday leave, sick leave, maternity leave, training, and access to promotion on a pro-rata basis, as are the full-time workers. There may be some difference between the full-[96] and part-time[97] workers with regard to overtime pay (the part-time workers would have to work beyond the 'normal' contracted hours of the full-time workers to benefit from this additional rate of pay).

It should be noted that whilst the Regulations protect part-time workers, the employer would only be acting unlawfully in treating the workers differently if this is due to the employment status. An employer may also treat the groups of workers differently if there is some objective reason for the distinction. However, reg. 6 enables an affected part-time worker to request from the employer a written statement regarding the reasons for any difference in the way the groups of workers are treated, and this information may be used in a tribunal against the employer.

The part-time worker may compare how he/she is treated compared with those working under full-time contracts, if the work is of 'broadly similar' nature so as to provide a fair comparison.[98] Workers may compare each other's treatment to identify evidence of less favourable treatment where they are employed under the same type of contract; they are performing broadly similar work (and where relevant have similar levels of qualifications, skills, and experience); and the part-time worker and full-time worker are based at the same establishment; or where no full-time worker is based at the establishment who satisfies the above criteria, works or is based at a different establishment, and satisfies the criteria.[99]

---

[94] [2007] 7 February, Unreported. [95] Reg. 5(1). [96] Section 2(1). [97] Section 2(2).
[98] *Matthews v Kent and Medway Towns Fire Authority* [2006] UKHL 8.
[99] Section 2(4).

19.17 Discrimination against workers on fixed-term contracts

Those employees engaged on fixed-term contracts have been protected against discrimination based on their contracts (from July 2002) through the Fixed-term Employees (Prevention of Less Favourable Treatment) Regulations 2002. A worker employed on such a contract has the right not to be treated less favourably due to his/her status than a comparable employee on a permanent contract. Reg. 3(1) provides that the fixed-term employee should not be treated less favourably in relation to the terms of his/her contract, or through acts or omissions of the employer unless there exist objective grounds for such treatment. Affected employees can request a written statement from an employer where they have been treated less favourably and this information may be used in tribunal proceedings.

Less favourable treatment includes disadvantageous terms of the contract when compared to permanent employees. The Regulations further provide that following four years of successive fixed-term contracts, the contract will become permanent, and a breach of the Regulations enables a damages action for compensation. As with the protection of part-time workers, any attempt by the employer to dismiss a worker for using the Regulation's provisions, or dismissing an employee under a fixed-term contract due to this status, is automatically an unfair dismissal.

19.18 Enforcement and remedies for discrimination claims

The claimant must bring his/her claim within three months of the discriminatory act (or within three months of the discrimination ending) for work-related claims.[100] The tribunal is empowered to extend the three-month period where it would be just and equitable to do so,[101] but before the claim is brought before a tribunal, a conciliation officer is appointed to attempt to resolve the matter between the employer and the claimant. However, if this attempt is unsuccessful, following a finding of discrimination the tribunal can provide the following remedies:

1 declare the rights of the complainant;

2 award damages;[102]

3 make a recommendation that the employer eliminates/reduces the effect of the discrimination for all employees not just the claimant.[103] This does not apply to claims of sex discrimination in pay.

When awarding damages, the tribunal is entitled to compensate for injury to feelings,[104] and they may even extend to include damages for personal injury and psychiatric injury.[105]

---

[100] EA 2010, s. 123. The applicable time-limit is six months for members of the armed forces (s. 123(2)).

[101] EA 2010, s. 123(1)(b).

[102] Note that in cases of discrimination there is no limit to the compensation that may be awarded, and interest is charged on compensation payments not made in the time of the order (*Marshall v Southampton and South West Hampshire Area Health Authority (No. 2)* [1994] IRLR 445).

[103] EA 2010, s. 124.

[104] *O'Donoghue v Redcar Borough Council* [2001] EWCA Civ 701.

[105] *HM Prison Service v Salmon* [2001] IRLR 425.

19.19 **Maternity rights**

> ### 𝒪 Business Link
>
> Employers have a duty to protect their employees' health and safety. This is somewhat exacerbated when the employee is pregnant as both she and her unborn baby may be at risk in some occupations. The law requires the employer to allow the woman to attend doctor's appointments, to perform a risk assessment of the job of the woman, and provides obligations for the woman's protection of employment rights and (in some cases) paid leave and the right to return to her job, or suitable alternative job, following her maternity leave. Employers may have spent considerable resources on training the employee, and if they view the employee's role at the organization as a long-term relationship, then providing care for the woman during her pregnancy (and after it) will ensure the working relationship continues and the employee returns to contribute to the business following this—relatively short—period of absence.

A pregnant employee gains protection against discrimination on the basis of her pregnancy or childbirth (considered under the ERA 1996 to be the birth of a child after 24 weeks of pregnancy (whether alive or dead)). To ensure she receives the protection, the employee must inform her employer of her pregnant state to enable him/her to comply with the relevant health and safety obligations, and she must also issue the employer with the certificate of pregnancy provided through the hospital or doctor. This identifies the employee's pregnancy, and may also be used by an employer to reclaim any Statutory Maternity Pay (SMP) issued to the employee.

Under health and safety legislation, an employer may have to suspend an employee from work if the job could endanger her or the unborn baby (as required by legislation, a code or practice and so on). The employer must continue to pay the employee during this suspension, and her continuity of service and other benefits continue to accrue. However, the employer may offer the employee suitable alternative work. If the employee unreasonably refuses, then the employer may cease paying the wages.

Beyond the protection afforded pregnant women, and those who have given birth, the EA 2010 provides specific protection for pregnant employees, such as the right not to be dismissed, the right to attend doctor's appointments, the right not be treated less favourably because of pregnancy or maternity leave[106] and so on. Section 55(1) of ERA 1996 specifically enables a pregnant employee to have paid time off work to attend the appointment—insofar as it was made on the advice of a doctor, registered midwife, or registered health worker. The protection afforded women due to their protected characteristic of pregnancy or maternity leave begins when the woman becomes pregnant and continues until the end of her maternity leave or until she returns to work (if this is earlier).[107] Outside of these times, unfavourable treatment because of her pregnancy would be considered sex discrimination rather than pregnancy and maternity discrimination.[108]

There is further protection to pregnant workers through EU initiatives[109] which prohibit, *inter alia*, the dismissal of pregnant workers/those on maternity leave, other than in exceptional circumstances not related to their pregnancy or maternity leave status.

---

[106] EA 2010, s. 18. [107] EA 2010, s. 18(6). [108] EA 2010, s. 18(7).
[109] The Pregnant Workers Directive (92/85EEC) and the Equal Treatment Directive (2006/54/EC).

19.19.1 **Breastfeeding**

There is no obligation on an employer to give breastfeeding workers time off work to perform this activity, but employers are under a duty to reasonably accommodate such a request. A woman may provide the employer with written notice that she is breastfeeding and the employer may, where it is reasonable to do so, adjust the employee's conditions or hours of employment to comply. If this is not possible or would not avoid risks identified in a risk assessment conducted by the employer, the employer should suspend the employee for as long as is necessary to avoid the risk. Employers are under a duty to provide suitable facilities at work for women who are breastfeeding, and a refusal to allow a breastfeeding mother to breastfeed (through a change of her hours of work) or to express milk, may result in unlawful sex discrimination.

19.19.2 **Parental leave**

The Maternity and Parental Leave Regulations 1999 provide all employees with one year's continuous employment, to take a period of leave to care for their children. Following this period, the employee may take 13 weeks' unpaid leave for each child insofar as this is taken before the child's fifth birthday (eighteenth birthday in respect of children with a disability). The employee must, as a minimum, give at least four weeks' notice before any leave is taken, and he/she must further provide double the notice period in relation to the time taken (up to the 13 weeks). An employer is entitled, where this is reasonable in relation to the needs of the business, to postpone the leave for a period of up to six months.

The employer must allow the employee to return to his/her job following the leave (or a similar job if more than four weeks of leave is taken) on the same basis and hours that are no less favourable than when he/she left. To enable the employer to run the business effectively and with certainty of staffing levels and so on, the Regulations require that employees may take leave in 'bundles' rather than one continuous block, but these must be in blocks of one week and not exceed four weeks' leave if taken in this manner.

19.19.3 **Maternity and paternity leave**

Online
Resource
centre:
Forms

The ERA 1996 provides pregnant employees with a right of 26 weeks of Ordinary Maternity Leave, and a further 26 weeks of Additional Maternity Leave. During the leave, the employee is entitled to receive any contractual benefits as if she were at work. Whilst the woman may take all of this period of leave, some may wish to return to work sooner. She is entitled to do so, following a period of two weeks' compulsory maternity leave (four weeks if she works in a factory) following the birth of the child, when she has provided the employer with at least eight weeks' notice of her wish to return. The woman must inform her employer no later than the fifteenth week before the expected due date of the child that she is pregnant; the expected due date of the child (evidenced through the maternity certificate);[110] (a specimen form is provided in the Online Resource Centre) and when she wishes to start maternity leave (and the employer should notify her, in response, of the date for the leave, within 28 days of the employee's notification).[111]

---

[110] Called a MATB1 which is available from the woman's midwife or GP.

[111] If the employer fails in this obligation the employee may have protection against any dismissal or less favourable treatment by not returning to work on time.

Where the employee has accrued one year's continuous employment before the eleventh week of the expected due date of the birth, she has the right on return to have her rights of employment intact. She is also entitled to the terms and conditions of her employment to accrue during the leave (such as pension contributions), except for her wages—and the employee is also bound by the terms of her contract during this period. A further extension to the employee's rights has been the introduction of 'keep in touch' days where an employee on maternity leave can return to work (and be paid) for up to 10 days without losing her right to SMP. If the employee has taken more than four weeks of maternity leave, she is entitled to return to a suitable alternative position if it is not reasonably practicable for her to return to the same job she left.[112]

Whilst she is not entitled to be paid her wages during the leave (although many employers provide such a scheme—on varying bases), the employee will receive SMP for the first 39 weeks of the leave if she qualifies.[113] If the employee does not qualify for SMP, the employer must inform her of this, and the reasons, by issuing her a SMP1 form, which will help her to claim Maternity Allowance.[114]

The Paternity and Adoption Leave Regulations 2002 provides the father of the child with the right to take one or two weeks' paid leave (although the two week's leave must be taken consecutively) to be taken within 56 days of the child's birth. The man's continuity of employment and other benefits continue to accrue during this time. In order to receive the leave the employee (the man) must have responsibility for the child's upbringing (or expect to have this responsibility); he must be the child's biological father or the husband/partner of the child's mother; and he must have accrued 26 weeks' continuous employment 15 weeks before the expected due date. To qualify for the pay[115] during the leave, the man must have been making NICs.

Fathers of children due on or after 3 April 2011 who satisfy the qualification criteria will be entitled to Additional Paternity Leave (APL). This provision allows for the father to take part of the mother's maternity leave which may assist in reducing possible discrimination on the basis of the stereotype that only women will leave employment to have and raise children. The mother must take the 26 weeks of ordinary maternity leave and then the remainder can transfer to the father—including any outstanding SMP. APL may be taken between 20-weeks after the birth and the child's 1st birthday, it must be taken in one continuous period, and for a minimum period of two weeks. An employer has the option to waive the period of notice required, but otherwise a father must give the employer eight weeks' notice of his intention to take APL.

19.19.4 Extension of rights to parents adopting children

Rights for parents who are to adopt children were provided in the Paternity and Adoption Leave Regulations 2002. The members of the couple seeking to access the rights provided

---

[112] Such as in *Blundell v St. Andrew's Catholic Primary School* [2007] UKEAT/0329/06, where a primary school teacher was returned to a job teaching different pupils in a different year to when she left. The EAT stated that a consideration of returning to the same job involved consideration of the nature, capacity, and place of employment.

[113] To qualify the employee must have been employed by the same employer continuously for at least 26 weeks into the 15th week before the week of the due-date (called the qualifying week); and be earning on average at least an amount equal to the lower earnings limit (for 2012–13 this is £107 per week).

[114] It may be wise to inform the employee of the help and assistance that is available from Her Majesty's Revenue and Customs.

[115] Statutory Paternity Pay is calculated at the same rate as SMP.

in the Regulations must have worked for the employer continuously for at least 26 weeks and be 'newly matched' with a child through an adoption agency, and this can be a domestic adoption or an inter-country adoption following the Flexible Working (Eligibility, Complaints and Remedies) (Amendment) (No. 2) Regulations 2007. The 2007 Regulations extended the definition of an adoption agency to include private foster care and a residence order.

19.19.5 Family-friendly policies

When elected to government, the Labour Party sought to introduce protective rights for those at work and to cooperate with the EU in the extension of rights for workers. One such measure was to facilitate family-friendly working practices, and enable those with child care and other dependant's responsibilities to work, but also to be able to take leave or change their work when required. As such, employees may take reasonable time off work to provide assistance to a dependant (who may be a child, parent, spouse, or partner and extends to any other person who reasonably relies on the employee to make arrangements for the provision of care). ERA 1996, s. 57A provides the employee with a right to a 'reasonable' amount of (unpaid) time off to look after a dependant who is ill; has given birth or is injured; in relation to an unexpected incident at a school involving a child of the employee; due to unexpected problems in the provision of care for a dependant; or where a death occurs to an employee's dependant. An employee unreasonably denied the right to leave may claim within three months of the refusal to a tribunal, which can award compensation.

 Conclusion

This chapter has considered the enactment of the new legislation to promote equality in the workplace and beyond. The EA 2010 has repealed and refocused previous legislative provisions, and in codifying the principles from the European and domestic courts, it has aimed to simplify equality laws. The increased rights of workers, extension of these to consumers, and new obligations on employers to promote equality at work will present interesting challenges in the future. Many trading partners and customers require businesses to be seen to be following equality laws as a symbol of their being a good and ethical employer and the type of firm with whom they wish to do business. Promoting equality is not just a legal requirement. Purposely adopted into an organization's culture, it can instil respect, transparency of decision-making, and a better working environment for all.

The book now continues to examine the regulations placed on employers through contracts of employment and statute, such as to protect the health and safety of workers.

 Summary of main points

Protected characteristics

- The protected characteristics in the codified Equality Act 2010 are age; disability; gender reassignment; marriage and civil partnership; pregnancy and maternity; race; religion or belief; sex; and sexual orientation.

Discrimination law

- The EA 2010 prohibits discrimination in certain areas before employment (at advertising/interview stage); during employment, and following employment (providing/refusing to provide references, equal pay claims).
- Employers may be liable for acts of harassment against their employees by third parties.
- English law is subject to interpretation in conformity with EU laws and decisions of the Court of Justice.
- Discrimination may be 'direct' or 'indirect', involve victimization, and harassment.
- A comparator is required to establish a claim.
- Claims have to be lodged at a tribunal within 3 months of the last complained of act of discrimination.

Sex discrimination in pay

- All contracts of employment are deemed to include an equality clause. Claims have to be made on the basis of discrimination based on the claimant's sex.
- English law must be interpreted in conformity with EU laws and decisions of the Court of Justice of the European Union.
- The term 'pay' includes all consideration the worker receives from the employer.
- A claim must be made under one of three 'heads' of complaint—like work; work rated as equivalent; and work of equal value.
- Claims have to be made with reference to a comparator from the same employment and in claims of direct sex discrimination in pay, a hypothetical comparator may be used.
- Equal value claims can include a claimant who has been rated as performing 'higher' work (not equal work) than the comparator.
- The employer can raise a 'material factor' defence that a difference in pay is not due to the sex of the claimant but due to reasons such as responsibility; market forces; experience; regional variations; and so on.

Pregnant workers

- Dismissal of a pregnant employee for anything to do with her pregnancy is automatically unfair dismissal.
- The woman has to demonstrate unfavourable treatment due to her pregnancy.
- The woman must inform her employer of her pregnancy and the employer is required to perform a risk assessment of the workplace to ensure it does not place the woman, or her unborn child, at risk.

Maternity rights

- Employees with one year's continuous employment may take 13 weeks' unpaid leave for each child (to be taken before the child's fifth birthday—eighteenth birthday where the child has a disability).
- A employee who has given birth has the right to 26 weeks of Ordinary Maternity Leave (OML) and a further 26 weeks of Additional Maternity Leave (AML).

- Statutory Maternity Pay, Maternity Allowance, Statutory Paternity Pay, and Statutory Adoption Pay are available where appropriate.
- The father, or employee with responsibility (or expected responsibility) for the child's upbringing, is entitled to take two weeks' Statutory Paternity Leave (and in certain circumstances pay) and, where he qualifies, Additional Paternity Leave.
- Rights to leave have been extended to adopting parents.

Family-friendly policies

- Employees may take reasonable time off from work to provide assistance to a dependant (child, spouse, parent, partner, or someone who relies on the employee for care); or to time off when the dependant is ill, has given birth, been injured, has an unexpected problem relating to the dependant's care, or in the event of the death of a dependant.

 Summary questions

Essay questions

1. The sex discrimination laws in the UK have offered increasing levels of protection to women workers. Some commentators have suggested that this is unfair and should be restricted, particularly in matters to do with pregnancy. With specific reference to the Equality Act 2010, explain how the law protects women workers and whether these Acts have been successful.

2. 'Despite a rather benign interpretation by the judiciary, and judicial development over the last 35 years, the practical impact of the Equal Pay legislation has been very disappointing in securing equality of pay between men and women.'
   Critically analyze the above statement.

Problem questions

1. All Bright Consumables (ABC) Ltd has placed an advertisement in the local newspaper for the recruitment of a new member of staff to act as assistant manager in a new shop it is opening. Due to the high proportion of immigrants from Poland living in the area, the advert specifies that the applicant must be able to speak Polish. Margaret, who has several years' experience in management, applies for the position but is rejected as she only speaks English. Despite this shortcoming, she satisfies each of the essential characteristics identified in the job specifications.

   Fiona also applies for the position of assistant manager at ABC. Fiona is a wheelchair user and is informed at the interview that whilst she satisfies the criteria for the position, the office where the management team are based is on the second floor of the building and the only access is via stairs. The toilets in the building are also located on the second floor and ABC has no plans to move either the office or the toilets. As such, Fiona's application is rejected.

   Emma is appointed to the position of assistant manager having satisfied all the relevant criteria and performing well in the interview. She lives in a same sex relationship with Carla. ABC has a policy of providing its staff with a travel discount for flights in Europe, and this extends to the spouse of the staff. When Emma claims the discount for herself and Carla she is informed that ABC only recognizes marriage or co-habitation between persons of the opposite sex, and therefore ABC refuses to provide the discount to Carla. Soon after this request, Emma begins to receive abusive notes on her desk and on the staff notice board about her sexuality. When she complains to senior management, Emma is told to 'grow thicker skin' and there is nothing ABC can do about it.

Advise each of the parties as to any legal rights they have.

2. Consider Redmount Borough Council's (RBC) potential liability in the following circumstances:

Benny applied for an advertised post in the parks department of RBC as a delivery operative. Following his rejected application for a post he considered himself to be qualified for, he asked RBC for the reason and any other feedback. Benny was informed that RBC had recently adopted a policy, following discovery of an under-representation in the workforce of women and persons from ethnic minority groups, that these groups would be given priority of appointment and promotion. Any person not from these groups would not be considered for the position.

Dora was recently appointed as a speech therapist for RBC. She was appointed at the top of the pay scale. Diego is employed by RBC as a consultant and is paid £10,000 per annum less than Dora although he considers his job as being of equal value to RBC as the speech therapists. Further, most of the speech therapists are women whilst most of the consultants are men. RBC state that the reason for the difference in pay is to facilitate the recruitment of speech therapists from the private sector where salaries are higher. There are very few speech therapists in the public sector so RBC has to match/improve on the salaries paid in the private sector to entice the therapists to work for the Council.

RBC employed Isa five months ago as a care assistant at a home for delinquent girls which is under the control of the Council. When Isa's sexual orientation was discovered, she was dismissed as it was considered that she would be an 'inappropriate role model for troubled teenagers.' The dismissal letter to Isa read 'Given that these are highly impressionable girls, often from broken homes, your lifestyle choice makes you unsuitable for continued employment.'

Advise each of the parties as to their legal rights.

📖 Further reading

Bennett, M., Roberts, S., and Davis, H. (2005) 'The Way Forward: Positive Discrimination or Positive Action?' *International Journal of Discrimination and the Law*, Vol. 6, p. 223.

Oliver, H. (2004) 'Sexual Orientation Discrimination: Perceptions, Definitions and Genuine Occupational Requirements' *Industrial Law Journal*, No. 33, p. 1.

Pigott, C. (2002) 'Knowledge and the Employer's Duty to Make Reasonable Adjustments' *New Law Journal*, No. 152, p. 1656.

Riley, R. and Glavina, J. (2006) 'Sexual Orientation Discrimination–Adequate Investigation of Employee Grievance' *Employer's Law*, November, p. 10.

Steele, I. (2010) 'Sex Discrimination and the Material Factor Defence under the Equal Pay Act 1970 and the Equality Act 2010' *Industrial Law Journal*, No. 3, p. 264.

Useful websites

 http://www.acas.org.uk/
(The website of the Advisory, Conciliation and Arbitration Service, which offers practical guidance and assistance on all forms of employment matters.)

 https://www.gov.uk/browse/business
(Information, forms, and ideas for businesses to comply with the law, expand their business, develop networks with others in the locality and so on. It is a national organization, but has information specific to regions throughout the UK to ensure relevance and the practical approach that many businesses want.)

 http://homeoffice.gov.uk/equalities/
(Government Equalities Office—excellent source of easily accessible materials and explanations of the legislation.)

 Telephone Advice

ACAS runs a helpline for businesses of all sizes (whether in the public or private sector) providing practical help on equality and diversity issues. It is available on the following number: 0845 600 34 44.

 Online Resource Centre

 http://www.oxfordtextbooks.co.uk/orc/marson3e/
Why not visit the Online Resource Centre and try multiple choice questions associated with this chapter to test your understanding of the topic. You will also find relevant updates to the law.

Regulation of the Conditions of Employment

20

Why does it matter?

Legislation places many obligations on employers. Employers are required to protect their workers' health and safety in terms of safe systems of work; safety procedures, and instructions to colleagues regarding their conduct at work; and there are wider protections in terms of the workers' maximum working hours and rest/leave periods, and minimum rates of pay. If these are ignored the employer may face substantial damages claims, and there may also be criminal sanctions against the employer. Further, mechanisms exist to assist workers if the employer becomes insolvent and owes wages or other contractual benefits. The terms and conditions of employment provide the employer with an opportunity to protect his/her business by incorporating a restraint of trade clause into the contract or using 'garden leave' agreements to prevent unfair competition or exploitation of the employer's confidential information. Lack of adequate protection of a business's confidential information may be severely damaging hence the necessity of awareness of this area of law.

Learning outcomes

Following reading this chapter you should be in a position to:

- explain the scope of the Working Time Regulations 1998 and its application to the workforce (20.2–20.2.6)
- identify how the maximum working week is calculated and workers' right to paid annual leave (20.3–20.3.4)
- identify the employer's duty to protect workers' and visitors' health and safety, and the duty to maintain liability insurance (20.4–20.4.2.5)
- describe the mechanism for incorporating a restraint of trade clause into a contract of employment and the scope of its protection to the confidential information of a business (20.5–20.5.8)
- explain the protections to workers in the event of the insolvency of the employer (20.6)

> ### 🔑 Key terms
>
> These terms will be used in the chapter and it may be helpful to be aware of what they mean or refer back to them when reading through the chapter.
>
> **Consultation**
> Where an employer plans to transfer an undertaking he/she is required, under the TUPE 2006 Regulations, to consult with the employees and their representatives. A similar duty applies in cases of proposed redundancies.
>
> **Restraint of trade clause**
> This is a contractual clause that prevents or restricts an employee from competing with the employer for a specific duration and a specific region/area of industry. To have the clause enforced the employer must demonstrate the necessity for the clause and that it protects the employer's legitimate proprietary interests.
>
> **Garden leave agreements**
> The employer may decide that instead of incorporating a restraint of trade clause and (possibly) having this rejected by the court, a 'safer' option may be to incorporate an extended period of notice where the employee, having given his/her notice or resignation, is paid to 'stay in the garden'—albeit that he/she cannot work in competition with the employer.

20.1 **Introduction**

This chapter continues from the discussion of the obligations on employers to protect their workers from discrimination and harassment, to a wider consideration of the regulation of conditions of employment. Employers are increasingly subject to statutory controls that provide for a minimum wage to be paid to workers; for regulation as to the maximum number of hours workers may be required to work; and for the protection of workers' health and safety. In the event of an employer's insolvency, the rights of employees are identified, and finally, the mechanisms for employers to protect their business interests in the contract of employment are considered.

20.2 **The Working Time Regulations 1998**

The Working Time Regulations 1998

> ### 🔗 Business Link
>
> Following action from the European Union (EU), workers are entitled to minimum rest periods at work, to be provided with paid annual leave, and not to be compelled to work beyond the maximum working week. These are measures established to protect workers' health and safety and it is important for employers to be aware of these, as breach of the Regulations may result in criminal prosecution sanctions.

Prior to 1998, there was little regulation over working hours in the United Kingdom (UK). Whilst men were allowed to work as many hours as they could physically manage, regardless of the negative impact this may have on their health, women and children had been protected through the Factories Acts. In 1993, the EU passed the Working Time Directive that sought to regulate the maximum working hours in the EU, and the UK responded by enacting the Working Time Regulations 1998. The Regulations apply to 'workers' rather than just 'employees'. To qualify as a worker the individual has to perform his/her work or provide services personally,[1] hence, it does not matter if he/she is self-employed, an agency worker, or a trainee.

It is important to recognize that whilst this text presents legal topics in isolation (where possible), the reality is that a breach of one area of law may lead to breaches of others. For example, a breach of the Working Time Regulations may lead to liability under these Regulations, but it may also result in an employee's stress and mental illness which could also lead to tortious liability. Insofar as these are reasonably forseeable, an employer could face liability on each count. What will be 'reasonably forseeable' will depend on the circumstances of the case, but in *Hone v Six Continents Retail*,[2] an employee who worked 90 hours per week and suffered deteriorating health and then a psychiatric injury, was successful in holding the employer liable. It was held the employer was required to take all reasonable steps to ensure the employee did not work more than 48 hours per week (which it did not). Further, there were sufficiently clear indicators that the employee's health was being negatively affected and the employer had a duty to protect the health and safety of the workforce. Compare this case with *Sayers v Cambridgeshire County Council*[3] involving an employee working 50–60 hours per week. Whilst there was a failure to adhere to the Regulations, the employee's illness was not reasonably forseeable.

20.2.1 The maximum working week

The Regulations provide that in a seven-day-week period, the worker should not exceed 48 working hours,[4] assessed over a 17-week period.[5] As a consequence, the worker may perform substantially longer hours in some weeks as long as the employment over this period averages out to no more than 48 hours per week. Also, the restriction is on a maximum *working* week. The Court of Justice held in *Landeshauptstadt Kiel v Jaeger*[6] that 'work' means working, at the employer's disposal, and carrying out the duties concerned with this work. Hence, those individuals who are on call as part of their working duties have this time included in the assessment if the work is performed at the employer's place of business but not if the 'on-call' duties involve the worker waiting away from the workplace.

20.2.2 Opt-outs

The UK Government, during the negotiations for the Directive, was successful in obtaining an opt-out clause to the effect that individual workers could waive their rights to protection under the law.[7] Workers cannot be forced to agree to the opt-out, but in practice many

---

[1] Reg. 2.   [2] [2005] EWCA Civ 922.   [3] [2006] EWHC 2029 (QB).   [4] Reg. 4.
[5] Although this period may be extended.   [6] [2004] All ER (EC) 604.
[7] Technically, the opt-out can only be enforced for a maximum of three months to allow a worker to opt 'back-in' if they wish.

recognize this may be necessary to obtain employment. If a worker has opted out, he/she may change their mind and seek protection under the law if the employer is given seven days' notice (and this time is not beyond an agreement established with the employer for a longer period).

20.2.3 Enforcement

The workers who are not in the excluded categories are entitled to protection under the Regulations.[8] If an employer refuses to allow a worker to gain access to these rights, or does not take reasonable steps to ensure compliance with the Regulations, he/she is guilty of a criminal offence. This is extended to an employer who dismisses or penalizes a worker for exercising, or attempting to exercise, his/her rights.[9] It should be further noted that whilst there are limited obligations on the employer to hold anything other than 'general' records regarding workers' hours of work and written documentation, the Court of Justice of the European Union (Court of Justice) provided[10] a strong recommendation that it may be in the employers' interest for employers to hold sufficient records to demonstrate that the opt-out was expressed, rather than implied, and was, along with any other contractual term,[11] entered into freely.

20.2.4 Rest breaks

Along with the maximum working week, the Regulations provide that adult workers are entitled to a 20-minute rest break if expected to work more than six hours at a stretch. Further, he/she is entitled to 11 hours' rest in each 24-hour period, and 12 hours' rest for young workers.[12] For those workers employed on a shift pattern, these regulations do not apply in this manner. However, they are entitled to an equivalent period of rest.

20.2.5 Entitlement to annual leave

The Regulations provided for the introduction of a system of paid annual leave[13] that has resulted in entitlement to 5.6 weeks (28 days) to reflect 20 days of holidays and 8 days of statutory bank holidays.[14] This was a major increase to workers' rights, as many received less than this minimum when the regulations were brought into effect. The employer is also obliged to clearly distinguish between 'normal' pay, and pay for leave as provided in lieu of holidays. It was a practice of employers to 'roll up' pay with pay in lieu and hence circumvent the requirement to allow workers to take their holidays[15] (a particular concern of casual workers). The

---

[8] Details for the mechanisms for enforcement are identified in the 'National Minimum Wage Enforcement: Penalty Notice Policy' issued by the Department for Trade and Industry, January 2007.

[9] ERA 1996, ss. 45A and 101A.

[10] *Pfeiffer v Deutsches Rotes Kreuz Kreisverband Waldshut eV* [2004] (C397/01) ECR I-8835.

[11] *Barber v RJB Mining* [1999] IRLR 308.

[12] Reg. 10.   [13] Reg. 13.

[14] According to the Department for Trade and Industry (now the Department for Business Innovation and Skills) this increase will directly benefit 6 million workers (Government News Network, 15 January 2007).

[15] This legislation after all is a health and safety measure and recognizes the necessity of workers taking some element of leave for their long-term and short-term health.

Court of Justice provided this clear identification of how the pay received by the worker was to be declared separately as pay for work, and pay for holiday entitlement.[16]

20.2.6 Night-shift workers

The Regulations are applicable to those who work during the day, but are also applicable to, and perhaps even greater protection is required for, those workers employed on shift patterns and night work.[17] This assessment is concerned with the regularity of the period of night work rather than whether it involves the majority of the work. Reg. 6 provides that night workers should not exceed eight hours in any 24-hour period (albeit that this is assessed over an average of 17 weeks).

? Thinking Point

Given that the legislation allows for certain categories of workers to be excluded from the law, and opt-outs are available that enable employers to avoid the maximum working week, was there any rationale for the law? This was a law passed to protect the health and safety of workers. If it can so easily be circumvented, is its purpose redundant?

20.3 The National Minimum Wage

 Business Link

Since 1998, legislation has established the minimum rates of pay that workers are entitled to receive. Whilst the rate is largely determined by the age of the worker, it is important for employers to be aware of the methods and time periods upon which this hourly wage is calculated; and the obligations to maintain adequate records to answer queries relating to pay by the workers, and by Her Majesty's Revenue & Customs. A lack of awareness as to what constitutes pay (overtime; bonuses; tips and so on) could lead to prosecution by the state and a claim by a worker in an Employment Tribunal.

National Minimum Wage Act 1998

Workers have the right to be paid, and their pay must be at least at the level established in the National Minimum Wage Act 1998 (NMW 1998).

This is regardless of the size of the employer, and regardless of whether the worker is employed full- or part-time, paid on commission, or is a casual or agency worker. Employees are also entitled to an individual, written pay statement that identifies the gross pay, the deductions made, and the net pay provided to the worker. There are strict rules on the deductions that an employer may make to an employee's pay. The most obvious reason for a deduction involves those that are required by legislation (National Insurance Contributions and

---

[16] *Robinson-Steele v RD Retail Services Ltd* (C131/04) [2006] IRLR 386.

[17] Night work is defined as work, under the normal course of the employment, of which at least three hours of the daily employment is performed during the night.

income tax for those subject to Pay As You Earn taxation). Deductions may also be identified in writing in the worker's contract and authorized by the worker or the relevant negotiating body. Finally, an employer, under certain circumstances, may be able to deduct up to 10 per cent of the gross pay of workers in the retail sector to reflect cash shortages or stock deficiencies. This last category is reviewable by an Employment Tribunal if the employee argues it has been applied unfairly.

The NMW 1998 provided most workers over compulsory school age with the right to be paid the minimum wage established by that legislation and the subsequent increases as established under the Act.[18] The Government takes recommendations from the Low Pay Commission with regard to the increases in the rate of the minimum wage. As of 1 October 2012 the rates were as follows:

- for workers aged 21 and over: £6.19 per hour
- for workers aged 18–20: £4.98
- for young workers (16–17): £3.68
- for apprentices (under 19 years old or 19 and over in the first year of their apprenticeship): £2.65[19]

20.3.1 Worker

The definition of 'worker' is defined under s. 54 as someone employed under a contract of employment or any other contract where the person performs the work or provides his/her services personally. This does not, however, include someone who is genuinely in business on his/her own account. Examples of workers who qualify include: agency workers; apprentices; foreign workers; piece workers; commission workers and homeworkers. Examples of workers who do not qualify include: self-employed workers; volunteers; company directors; and those working for friends and family.

20.3.2 Calculating the pay

As the legislation provides for a minimum level of hourly pay, and many workers are paid on a monthly or weekly basis, establishing that the minimum level of pay is being received requires a mechanism for calculation.

The NMW 1998 provides that the minimum wage is based on the gross pay provided to the worker, but it does not include pension payments, redundancy pay, overtime pay,[20] expenses and so on. The employer may include accommodation provided to the worker as part of his/her hourly pay, but this is limited to a maximum of £4.82 per day.[21] Bonuses paid by the employer and tips received due to service may be counted by the employer, as are any performance-related pay awards.

---

[18] The Act increases the hourly pay each October by order (under delegated legislation) of the relevant Minister.

[19] It should be noted that the increase in the rates of the hourly pay are proportionately lower than in recent years to reflect an increase in statutory holiday entitlements and the decline of employment in low-pay jobs.

[20] This measure is intended to ensure that workers do not have to work overtime in order to achieve the minimum wage.

[21] Effective from 1 October 2012.

The period of work that is used in the calculation of the averaged hourly pay must not be more than one month. However, if the pay is provided on a weekly or monthly basis, this assessment (reference) period will be reduced.[22] There are various forms of working practices that establish the calculation of the hours, and then a reduction of these hours down to the pay received (and hence the pay per hour) is possible. The methods available are:

- *Time work:* Here the work is paid according to the number of hours worked. The calculation simply consists of dividing the pay received by the worker by the number of hours worked to establish the hourly rate.[23]
- *Salaried work:* Here the worker is paid an annual salary and the work is then reduced to a number of (basic) hours worked, with the pay reduced from this annual amount to a weekly (divided by 52) or monthly (divided by 12) rate.[24]
- *Output work:* Here the work is paid when a task is completed (such as piecework or work on commission)—it depends upon the speed of the work by the worker that would determine how many hours were worked (and therefore the pay per hour).[25]
- *Unmeasured work:* If the work does not fit into the above categories then it will be calculated under this measure. The minimum wage must be paid for each hour worked, or the pay must be determined according to a daily average.

20.3.3 Obligation to maintain records

Her Majesty's Revenue & Customs

Due to the nature of the minimum wage, an employer is obliged to maintain records of payments to his/her workers, and the hours worked, to ensure that evidence is produced and can be inspected. Her Majesty's Revenue & Customs (HMRC) may access these records to ensure compliance, but there is also a right for the workers to view their own records, and to obtain copies. Falsifying records is a criminal offence and may lead to an enforcement order against the employer.

20.3.4 Enforcement proceedings

As the minimum wage is a right that ensures workers receive the minimum amount established by the legislation, it is only effective if it is enforceable. An aggrieved worker may bring an action to an Employment Tribunal to claim owed wages (and if he/she suffers any detrimental treatment such as a dismissal for bringing a claim he/she has an additional action for unfair dismissal).[26] Here the worker establishes his/her claim, and as the employer is obliged to maintain adequate records, the burden is on the employer to demonstrate that the worker's claim is incorrect. The Government also established a penalty notice policy[27] designed to further 'encourage' recalcitrant employers to fulfil their obligations. It provides HMRC with the authority to enforce the NMW 1998 and as such a compliance officer may serve an enforcement notice on an employer which specifies the amount of money owed to the worker(s); the time limit in which the employer has to pay this sum; and the time limit in which payment has to be provided. A fine of up to £5,000 may be imposed on an employer guilty of breaching the Regulations.

---

[22] Reg. 10.   [23] Reg. 3.   [24] Reg. 4.   [25] Reg. 5.   [26] See Chapter 18.
[27] Department of Trade and Industry (2007) 'National Minimum Wage Enforcement: Penalty Notice Policy' January, URN 07/546.

20.4 **Health and safety**

> **Business Link**
>
> The Health and Safety Executive has published research demonstrating that in 2010/11, 26.4 million working days were lost in the UK due to occupational ill health and injury. This cost society an estimated £14 billion.[28] It further highlighted the impact of breaches of health and safety obligations such as a firm fined £245,000 and ordered to pay £75,000 costs at the Crown Court for its failure to follow adequate safety measures in relation to the removal of asbestos. The directors of the firm were also disqualified from holding any company directorship for up to two years. Another issue which should demonstrate the importance of health and safety is exemplified in the case where an employer had failed to monitor the machines at the workplace, resulting in a worker being caught in unguarded machinery and being killed. The managing director was successfully prosecuted for manslaughter and imprisoned for 12 months. Effectively maintaining health and safety is in everyone's interests and employers are not allowed to claim they did not know of the risks or hide behind the 'veil of incorporation' of a company.

Health and Safety Executive

Every employer owes his/her workers and visitors to their premises a duty to take reasonable care for their health and safety. The obligations on the employer apply to all workers and this primary responsibility for safety rests with the employer, even though the workers are legally obliged to assist in these matters. Health and safety requirements have bases in both the common law and through increasing legislative action, both domestically and from the EU. The Health and Safety Executive (HSE) provide statistics each year regarding injuries and deaths at workplaces. In 2010/11, 175 workers were killed at work and there were 115,000 injuries to employees. These reports highlight the dangers at work and seek to raise awareness (particularly of employers) of the need for appropriate actions, mechanisms, and policies to reduce incidence of accidents and to prevent injuries and illnesses.

The law regulates health and safety through legislative provisions and the common law (including criminal and civil law jurisdictions). They have different aims, and both may be used against an employer where an employee has suffered an injury or illness due to a negligent act or omission of the employer.

20.4.1 **The common law**

The health and safety of employees is a non-delegable[29] duty on the employer. The employer is unable to provide the employee to a second employer in an attempt to remove his/her duty,[30] and must satisfy claims if he/she has caused loss to the employee through negligence.

---

[28] http://www.hse.gov.uk/statistics/index.htm.

[29] The employer may delegate the duty (in theory) but the presumption by the courts is that the employer may not escape responsibility if the duty has been delegated and then not performed correctly or as required (*McDermid v Nash Dredging & Reclamation Co. Ltd* [1986] 3 WLR 45).

[30] *Morris v Breaveglen* [1993] IRLR 350.

In terms of health and safety, the duty of care has to be established specific to the employer's responsibility, rather than the broad test as outlined in the discussion of negligence. Workplaces may often involve dangerous machinery (in factories, for example) or activities that place workers in circumstances where injury may occur. The test of establishing a duty of care involves the employer taking reasonable precautions and safety initiatives that are relevant and not unduly oppressive. In *Paris v Stepney BC*[31] the Council employed Mr Paris to undertake inspection and repairs of its vehicles. Mr Paris had already lost an eye and was working on a job that was not considered by the employer to be sufficiently serious to warrant the use of safety goggles. During this job, when Mr Paris hit a bolt with a hammer a piece of metal struck his good eye and he was blinded as a result. The House of Lords held that due to the potential for injury, the employer did owe Mr Paris a duty of care to provide the correct safety equipment, and due to this failure, he was entitled to claim damages for his injury.

Breach of the duty to take care involves a cost/benefit analysis as identified by the courts in cases such as *Bolton v Stone*.[32] Indeed, in *Watt v Hertfordshire CC*[33] Denning LJ stated: 'It is well settled that in measuring due care you must balance the risk against the measures necessary to eliminate the risk. To that proposition there ought to be added this: you must balance the risk against the end to be achieved.' This is a balancing act between ensuring the employer takes precautions to prevent injury, and ensuring the preventative measures are reasonable and not excessive. Therefore a commonsense approach is adopted as demonstrated in *Latimer v AEC*,[34] where a storm had flooded the factory floor. The employer placed sawdust on the floor to prevent workers slipping and requested the workers to return to work, although the potential danger of the floor was identified. Mr Latimer slipped on an unprotected area of the factory floor and brought an action for the damages he sustained. It was held that the employer did owe Mr Latimer a duty of care, but had not breached this and had done all that was reasonable. It was not reasonable for AEC to close the factory, but it should have attempted to prevent injuries through preventative actions, including the sawdust and instructions to workers. As this had been achieved, a claim for damages must fail.

The requirements under the common law attributable to employers, follows the House of Lords decision in *Wilsons and Clyde Coal Co. Ltd v English*.[35] Essentially employers are required to provide competent employees for the claimant, a safe system of work, safe equipment at work, and a safe workplace.

20.4.1.1 *Competent employees*

The employer is required to ensure that the colleagues of the claimant are competent and do not endanger other workers. Establishing mechanisms to avoid dangerous colleagues ensures that a policy of acceptable behaviour at work is created and applied. They are used to identify (and minimize) risks; and to facilitate necessary training and supervision of workers in matters of health and safety. Where the employer has employed someone who is not sufficiently competent to perform the tasks required of the position, the employer may be liable for any damages suffered as a result of this employee.[36] The incompetence has to be foreseeable, but where the injury is due to the colleague being involved in practical jokes, if the employer is aware of such actions and has done nothing to prevent them, then consequent injuries may

---

[31] [1951] AC 367.   [32] [1951] AC 850.   [33] [1954] 1 WLR 835.
[34] [1953] AC 643.   [35] [1938] AC 57.
[36] *Hawkins v Ian Ross (Castings) Ltd.* [1970] 1 All ER 180.

have to be compensated.[37] However, where such action involves an unauthorized act that the employer could not have foreseen, the employer will not be liable.[38]

20.4.1.2 *Safe system of work*

The employer must ensure that his/her employees have systems in place to allow tasks to be conducted without any unreasonable risk of injury or illness attributable to carrying out this function. This requires the employer to provide adequate training, suitable equipment, and information and warning signs where appropriate. An employer has to inform the employee as to potential dangers when using equipment and how and when safety procedures have to be used. This is a requirement on the employer and he/she is obliged to ensure that safety systems are used, rather than simply to raise the issue of safety and allow employees' discretion as to when they wish to follow the instructions. This does not remove the employee's own use of common sense or for his/her own duty to protect him/herself, especially in minor matters. To exemplify this point, in *O'Reilly v National Rail*[39] workers employed in a scrap yard discovered an unexploded bomb and challenged Mr O'Reilly to hit the bomb with a hammer to see what would happen. The bomb exploded, injuring Mr O'Reilly. He claimed for damages against his employer but it was held that there was no liability as the common sense of the employee was not to hit the unexploded bomb. The employer had not breached the duty to provide a safe system of work by failing to instruct the employee not to take the action.

Whilst physical injury is most commonly associated with ensuring a safe system of work, the employer is also responsible for ensuring the wellbeing of his/her employees, and in particular this has manifested itself in issues of stress and other psychological pressures. This has been raised in **14.4**, but in relation to an employer's duty to his/her employees, the employer must take positive action to reduce the stress placed on workers where this would have a *foreseeable* negative impact on health.[40] Figures awarded for stress at work can be substantial,[41] and employers are increasingly settling the claim out of court in an attempt to avoid the admission of liability (although financial liabilities remain).[42] Employers are entitled to assume that employees can reasonably withstand the 'normal' pressures of the job but it is where the employee asks for help or shows obvious signs of stress[43] that the employer will be under a duty to act.[44]

20.4.1.3 *Safe equipment*

The equipment that is provided to employees must be fit for its purpose and safe to use. This may involve ensuring the correct guards or protective screens are used on the equipment; ensuring that electrical equipment is subjected to regular safety checks; ensuring that appropriate safety apparel (goggles, clothes, footwear) is used and so on. Each of these requirements will depend on the nature of the employer's business, the hazards that are faced by the employees, and the equipment that the employees are using or are exposed to.

---

[37] See *Hudson v Ridge Manufacturing Co. Ltd.* [1957] 2 WLR 948.

[38] *Aldred v Nacanco* [1987] IRLR 292.   [39] [1966] 1 All ER 499.

[40] *Walker v Northumberland CC* [1995] IRLR 35.

[41] In *Lancaster v Birmingham CC* [1999] 99(6) QR 4 an award of £67,000 was made; and in *Ingram v Hereford and Worcester CC* [2000] (settled out of court) the compensation granted to the claimant was for £203,000.

[42] In *McLeod v Test Valley BC* [2000] the claim was settled with a payment to the claimant of £200,000.

[43] The court will require expert evidence on what is an obvious sign of stress but there are behavioural and physical signs that may demonstrate that the employee is suffering and is in need of assistance.

[44] See *Hatton v Sutherland* [2002] EWCA Civ 76.

20.4.1.4 *Safe workplace*

Employers have a duty to ensure that the correct heating, lighting, and ventilation are available in the workplace. The employer must provide washing and toilet facilities for employees. The employer must also ensure that the entrances and safety exits are correctly maintained, as are corridors and walkways. The employer is also required to ensure a safe workplace through maintenance of the property to a sufficiently safe standard,[45] to maintain records for the reporting of accidents, and to provide the appropriate first aid facilities. Materials used at the workplace must be handled, stored, and used safely, and any potential hazards (chemicals, explosive, or flammable materials) should be brought to the attention of the employees.

20.4.1.5 *Defences*

The employer may raise absolute and partial defences to a claim for damages due to an alleged breach of health and safety under negligence. These were identified in **15.9.2** and are applicable here.

20.4.2 **Statutory provisions**

The main legislative provision covering health and safety in the workplace is the Health and Safety at Work etc. Act (HSWA) 1974, which identifies the requirements imposed on employers, and it also provides for the enactment of Regulations that 'flesh out' or extend the Act. Breach of the statute, as opposed to the common law route that involves an action for damages for the employer's breach of duty, may lead to a criminal act being committed and the employer being prosecuted for this infringement. Therefore a disregard for health and safety matters may lead to a criminal record and imprisonment.

Health and Safety at Work etc. Act 1974

20.4.2.1 *The Health and Safety at Work etc. Act 1974*

The Act places duties on employers, workers (employees and other workers such as independent contractors), and those with responsibilities in the workplace for ensuring that the required standards are maintained. Whereas the common law route allows an employee to seek compensation for his/her losses and enables him/her to initiate a claim, the employee is not entitled to bring an action against the employer for contravention of the HSWA 1974, rather this is the task of the Health and Safety Executive (HSE).

The employer has an obligation to ensure, as far as is reasonably practicable, the health, safety, and welfare of all of the employees (s. 2(1)). Whilst this is a general duty, section 2(2) extends this in the following ways:

1 the provision and maintenance of safe plant and systems of work that are safe and without risk to health;

2 arrangements for ensuring the safe use, handling, storage, and transport of articles and substances;

3 providing the necessary information, training, and supervision to ensure the health and safety of the employees;

---

[45] See *Latimer v AEC*.

4 in places of work under the control of the employer, maintaining the workplace to a standard that is safe and without risks to health, and maintaining the entrances and exits to the workplace;

5 providing the facilities for a safe working environment for his/her employees, and maintaining these.

The employer has an obligation to adhere to the above duties, with the proviso that this obligation extends to what is 'reasonably practicable' for the employer. Consequently, where to exercise the duty would not be reasonably practicable, the employer is permitted to make this defence (albeit that the burden of proof of it not being reasonable rests with him/her). This can be seen in *Associated Dairies v Hartley*,[46] where the dairy supplied its workers with safety shoes but charged them £1 per week for their use. The claimant argued that this was in contravention of the employer's duty to provide safety equipment. It was held by the Court of Appeal that the obligation to provide the shoes for free was not reasonably practicable and the cost to the workers was fair. The costs of providing the shoes, in relation to the benefit provided to the worker, and the relative low risk of minor injury to the worker, did not place the obligation on the employer to provide free shoes.

20.4.2.2 *Responsibilities on the employer*

Employers are also obliged, under HSWA 1974, s. 3(1), to conduct their undertaking in such a way as to ensure that non-employees (such as independent contractors) who may be affected by their actions, are not exposed to risk of their health and safety. The employer, further, is required to inform any non-employees of any potential risks to health and safety at the workplace.

R v Swan Hunter Shipbuilders[47]

Facts:

Work was being carried out on the ship *HMS Glasgow*. A fire started in the ship during welding operations conducted by a sub-contractor, and this fire was exacerbated due to there being too much oxygen in the ship. This fire led to several deaths. It was discovered that Swan Hunter Shipbuilders had informed its employees of the dangers of working with oxygen in confined spaces with poor ventilation, but this information had not been provided to the sub-contractor. The Court of Appeal held that the company was in breach of its obligation under HSWA 1974, s. 3(1).

Authority for:

HSWA 1974, s. 3(1) imposes a duty on employers to inform non-employees of dangers present in the workplace.

Not only do employers have obligations to protect their employees and non-employees at work, s. 6 of HSWA 1974 imposes a duty on anyone who designs, manufactures, imports, or supplies any article that is used at work. This involves things done in the course of business or

---

[46] [1979] IRLR 171.   [47] [1982] 1 All ER 264.

the particular trade, and it must relate to matters that are within the control of the individual on whom the duty is imposed. They must:

1   as far as is reasonably practicable, ensure the article is designed and constructed so as to be safe when it is being set, used, cleaned, and maintained by a person at work;

2   conduct, or make arrangements for there to be carried out, tests that are necessary to ensure adherence with (1);

3   ensure that the person supplied with an article is provided with the necessary information regarding the use for which it has been designed, and any information required to make its use safe; and

4   where it is reasonably practicable, provide any revisions to information that are necessary to ensure adherence with the requirement in (3).

These duties are also replicated for the import or supply of any substance (s. 6(4)). The HSWA 1974 also imposes an obligation on designers and manufacturers to conduct research and investigations with the aim of discovering any risks to health and safety and to implement procedures to remove any such risks.[48] Section 6(3) imposes a duty on those who erect and install equipment at work to ensure that the manner in which this is achieved should not make the article unsafe or a risk to health and safety. This requirement is subject to the limitation of 'reasonable practicability'.

The HSWA 1974 imposes many duties on the employer, as presented in this section of the chapter, but it also requires employees to ensure that they take care for their own safety and for others in the workplace.[49] In this respect, they must cooperate with their employer (and any other person) to enable them to comply with their duties (such as using the correct and supplied safety equipment). Section 8 provides a duty on every person in the workplace not to interfere or damage items provided as an aid to protecting health and safety (such as fire extinguishers)—whether this is intentional or reckless action.

20.4.2.3 *Potential consequences for employers*

If a person commits an offence under the HSWA 1974 due to an act or default of some other individual, the other individual will be guilty of the offence.[50] This individual may be prosecuted even if the person who actually committed the offence has not faced legal proceedings. If a health and safety offence is committed with the consent of an employer (such as a director, manager and so on), or with his/her connivance, or is due to his/her neglect, then the organization and that individual may be liable for prosecution under the HSWA 1974, s. 37. Further, it is no defence for the employer to organize his/her business so as to leave him/herself ignorant of any risks or attempt to remove his/her obligations for the health and safety at the workplace.

If the employer is found guilty of any offence, he/she may face a fine or, in terms of gross negligence manslaughter, a sentence of life imprisonment. He/she may also be subject to disqualification from acting as the director of a company under the Company Directors Disqualification Act 1986, s. 2(1). Remember, these offences and punishments affect the individual employer and his/her business, so the employer cannot hide behind the corporate veil of the limited company.[51] See the Online Resource Centre for an extra chapter on corporate manslaughter.

---

[48] Section 6(2).   [49] Section 7.   [50] Section 36.   [51] See **22.2**.

20.4.2.4 *Advancement of protection through the EU*

Membership of the EU has led to the UK transposing Directives established under Article 137 EC (now Art. 153 TFEU). The UK responded by enacting six sets of Regulations in 1992 (and subsequently amended) to protect health and safety at work. Whilst the reality is that they have not radically extended the protection afforded to those at work (perhaps merely codifying existing obligations), they ensure the employer is proactive in protecting his/her employees:

- *The Management of Health and Safety at Work Regulations 1999 (as amended 2006):* These impose requirements in relation to the cleanliness and maintenance of the workplace. This legislation requires the employer to conduct a risk assessment of dangers facing employees and others likely to be affected by their work. If there are five or more employees in the organization then the employer must provide a written health and safety policy.[52] This statement must also identify the periods in which inspections will be held, and which member of staff has responsibility for health and safety in the workplace. The employer further has an obligation to bring this information to the attention of the employees and to inform them of any changes to the document(s). The employer has a duty to consult with his/her employees over health and safety matters (Health and Safety (Consultation with Employees) Regulations 1996).

- *The Workplace (Health, Safety and Welfare) Regulations 1992:* The obligations required under ss. 2 and 4 of HSWA 1974 are extended through these Regulations to employers and occupiers of premises. The Regulations place a duty for the maintenance of the workplace, and its environment, in relation to lighting, heating, entrances, and exits, and to ensure that workplace equipment is in good working order. The employer has to identify any dangers to the employees, and mark any hazards.

- *The Provision and Use of Work Equipment Regulations 1998:* Machinery and other equipment used must be maintained and be in good working order. The Regulations reinforce s. 6 of HSWA 1974. The equipment must be safe to use and be routinely checked.

- *The Personal Protective Equipment at Work Regulations 2002:* Personal protective equipment must be supplied to employees where it is necessary. The employees must have training on the use of the equipment and the employer must maintain the equipment.

- *Manual Handling Operations Regulations 1992:* These require the protection of employees when handling items that may cause injury. The employee may have to lift or transport items as part of his/her duties, and could consequently sustain injury or be subject to an accident. As such, the employer should consider training, reducing the size/bulk of items, and other remedial action that is appropriate.

- *Health and Safety Display Screen Equipment Regulations 1992:* Training is required for employees who use such materials on its safe use, and regular eye tests must be provided if requested. Employees must also be given breaks (although this may be a change to the work conducted by the employee rather than a 'rest break'). Employees may suffer if their workstation is not correctly fitted (poor posture leads to back problems and so on). These risks must be effectively managed.

In additional to the many[53] regulations that are passed to protect employees' health and safety, the Health and Safety Commission issue codes of practice that provide guidance as

---

[52] Section 2(3).

[53] Such as the Health and Safety (First Aid) Regulations 1981; Control of Substances Hazardous to Health Regulations 2002; Reporting of Injuries, Diseases and Dangerous Occurrences Regulations 1995 and so on.

to how the regulations should be put into practice. These codes are not 'law' but they will be used in the courts, and the employer will be asked whether he/she adhered to the provisions. If he/she has not, it is likely a criminal offence will have been committed.

20.4.2.5 *Compulsory insurance*

As part of their protection of workers' safety, most employers[54] are obliged to carry appropriate insurance[55] to protect against any injury or disease that may befall an employee in the course of his/her employment. 'Course of employment' involves injuries or illness caused both at the employer's premises and off-site (although injuries caused through motoring accidents may be covered by the employer's or employee's own car insurance). The protection is also limited to those workers with 'employee' status.

The requirement is established through the Employers' Liability (Compulsory Insurance) Act 1969.[56] The insurance company that provides the cover will issue a certificate establishing the relevant information regarding the coverage, and it is the employer's responsibility to display the certificate (who may be fined if he/she does not comply with this requirement). The certificate will identify the cover provided (a minimum of £5 million);[57] which company/business is included in the policy; and the insurance company's details (that may be checked through the Financial Services Authority).[58] Employers are also required to retain copies of their insurance certificates for at least 40 years (and these policies are generally renewed annually) to enable employees whose injury or illness was caused at work, but the symptoms or effects were not identified until sometime later, to establish the relevant insurer.

20.5 **Restraint of trade clauses**

 Business Link

Employees may be privy to an employer's sensitive information—price and supplier information, trade secrets, and employee lists. When the employee leaves the employment he/she may take this valuable information and use it to compete (unfairly) with the employer (working for someone else; starting his/her own business and so on). As the employment relationship is based on trust, the employer may be able to protect such information through the insertion of a restraint of trade clause—a post-contractual term preventing competition within given parameters.

---

[54] Employers in the nationalized industries; local authorities; the health services; family-only employers and so on do not require employers' liability insurance.

[55] Note that public liability insurance (protecting an employer against claims from members of the public or other businesses) is voluntary, albeit advisable.

[56] The HSE provides information to employers and employees regarding the requirements for insurance (http://hse.gov.uk/pubns/regindex.htm).

[57] Most insurance providers offer cover in excess of £10 million.

[58] However, previous research identified that 210,000 small and medium-sized businesses were operating without Employers' Liability Insurance, resulting in an estimated 1.8 million employees having no cover for workplace injuries or illnesses (http://www.telegraph.co.uk/finance/2853324/AA-to-plug-employers-liability-gap.html#).

An employee is restricted from certain activities, either through implied terms or those expressed in his/her contract of employment, such as working in competition with the employer (the implied duty of fidelity). Once the employee has left the employment, he/she is, generally, free to work for whomever he/she wishes, or to establish a business and work in competition against the former employer. In order to protect the employer from having an employee (or former employee) use information or knowledge of the employer's business against him/her, a **restraint of trade clause** may be included in the contract.

A restraint of trade clause is a post-contractual agreement that restricts the employee from working in competition with his/her previous employer for a certain duration and within a defined geographical/industrial distance. It must be remembered that this agreement limits the employee's right to undertake employment, or to trade in his/her own business, following termination of the employment relationship. For the employer, there are valid and economically necessary reasons and justifications for this contractual clause. Employers trust employees with significant access to information including (potentially) customers, suppliers, price lists, and trade secrets that could be of great value to a rival, or they may give an unfair advantage to an employee who 'abuses' this trust and sets up in competition with the employer. It is also against public policy for an employer to require agreement to a clause that restrains an employee after the contract of employment has ceased. Restricting employees from working in the area of his/her expertise, or in industries where he/she has skills, is not necessarily conducive to an enterprising economy.

20.5.1 The application of a restraint of trade

The case that established when a restraint of trade clause would be enforceable was *Herbert Morris v Saxelby*.[59] A clause will only be applicable if:

1 it seeks to protect the employer's legitimate proprietary interests (such as trade secrets and customer information); and

2 it is reasonable between the parties and is in the public interest.

20.5.2 The protection afforded by the clause

An employer may legitimately claim protection where an employee has acquired specialist knowledge such as the details of customers of the employer's business or confidential information. This is often referred to as a 'proprietary interest' rather than general know-how, which the courts would not allow to be included in a restraint of trade clause.

Examples of clauses restricting ex-employees from soliciting customers and clients have been demonstrated in *Allied Dunbar v Frank Weisinger*[60] and in *AM Schoeder v Maccaulay*.[61] It is also contrary to a restraint of trade clause to copy an index of customer's names when the ex-employee enters into competition with the employer.[62]

---

[59] [1916] 1 AC 688.   [60] [1988] IRLR 60 (involving a firm of solicitors).
[61] [1974] 3 All ER 616 (involving hairdressing assistants).
[62] *Roger Bullivant Ltd v Ellis* [1987] IRLR 491.

20.5.3 A legitimate proprietary interest

> The employer's claim for protection must be based upon the identification of some advantage or asset inherent in the business which can properly be regarded as, in a general sense, his property, and which it would be unjust to allow the employee to appropriate for his own purposes, even though he, the employee, may have contributed to its creation.[63]

Therefore, confidential information (client lists, suppliers' details and so on) and trade secrets (secret formulas and so on) will be included in the court's assessment of a proprietary interest. However, general information regarding the employer's business, or skills that have been gained whilst working for the employer, are not subject to protection.

20.5.4 Reasonableness

In order for the employer to be successful in arguing for the clause to be upheld, he/she must satisfy the court that the restrictions included are no greater than is 'reasonably' necessary for the protection of the employer's business. In assessing reasonableness, the court will consider the duration of the restraint, the geographical distance covered, the type of business the employer operates, and whether allowing a restraint is fair according to public policy. A clause may fail the reasonableness test if its terms are not sufficiently precise,[64] or where it is against public policy.[65] Where the extent of the restriction and its duration are excessive to the protection required, the clause also will unlikely be upheld.[66] Therefore, as a 'rule of thumb', the duration of the restriction and the area of its application are inversely proportional. The wider the area of the restriction, the shorter should be the duration; the smaller the area, a longer duration will be considered reasonable.[67]

20.5.5 Repudiation of the contract by the employer

It should also be noted that the clause will only continue to have effect (as a post-contractual agreement) whilst the parties behaved reasonably with each other. If the employer repudiates the contract, for example by wrongfully dismissing the employee, then any restraint of trade clause becomes unenforceable.[68] This is despite the fact that some employers attempted to draft contracts that provided for the continuation of restraint of trade clauses even if the employer breached the contract of employment.[69]

20.5.6 Blue penciling

This term is used to describe the options available to the courts when faced with a restraint of trade clause that goes beyond the necessary aims of protecting the employer's business.

---

[63] Per Lord Wilberforce in *Stenhouse Australia v Phillips* [1974] 2 WLR 134.
[64] *Commercial Plastics v Vincent* [1964] 3 WLR 820.
[65] *Bull v Pitney Bowes* [1967 1 WLR 273.
[66] *Mason v Providence Clothing and Supply Co. Ltd* [1913] AC 724.
[67] *Fitch v Dewes* [1921] 2 AC 158.   [68] *General Billposting Co. Ltd v Atkinson* [1909] AC 118.
[69] *Rock Refrigeration v Jones* [1996] IRLR 675.

It enables the court to remove an offending passage or term of the clause, and if it still leaves the remainder making grammatical sense, and it is supported by consideration, then it may be held to be valid and enforceable. If the clause and its terms are part of an indivisible agreement, then even if it would be grammatically possible to separate or remove a passage or word(s), the court will refuse to do so.[70] The courts, as with any contractual term, will not rewrite a poorly drafted contract, and any clauses that are ambiguous will be subject to the *contra proferentem* rule.[71] The correct drafting and the arguments regarding the necessity for the clause remain the obligation of the employer. The tests were defined in *Sadler v Imperial Life Assurance of Canada*[72] as requiring:

- the ability to remove the words without requiring the addition or alteration of the remaining aspects of the clause;
- the remaining clause continuing to make grammatical sense; and
- the removal of the words not altering the nature of the original clause.

20.5.7 Remedies

The claimant, if successful in convincing the court of the necessity of the restraint of trade, may seek damages to compensate for any losses incurred (such as the ex-employee having solicited clients away from the business) and he/she may seek an injunction to prevent any further activities that may be in contravention of the clause for its duration. An interim injunction may be granted to prevent the employee breaching the restraint of trade clause until the case is heard in court, where a final injunction may be granted following the conclusion of the hearing. In determining the grant of an interim injunction the court will consider the clause; whether damages are an appropriate remedy; and whether the employer's claim is likely to succeed at the full hearing.[73]

20.5.8 Garden leave agreements

Due to potential problems of the courts refusing to uphold a restraint of trade clause, or if the employer has to terminate the employee's contract in advance of any agreed date, the employer may obtain the protection required if he/she is prepared to pay the employee's salary. The employer may include a long period of notice and in the event that the employee wishes to leave the employment, the employer simply enforces the notice period. Whilst an employee cannot be forced to work, he/she can be paid a salary with the employer knowing that the employee cannot start a business in competition or take up employment with a rival. This may be a more expensive proposition than relying on a restraint of trade clause, but it provides greater certainty of protection, and ensures that an employee cannot take important secrets or knowledge of the employer's business and use it in competition. Note that the courts will not allow an unusually long **garden leave** clause, and in *GFI Group Inc. v Eaglestone*[74] a notice period of 20 weeks was reduced to 13 weeks as this was considered sufficient in order to protect the employer's proprietary interests.

---

[70] *Attwood v Lamont* [1920] 3 KB 571.   [71] See **10.5.3**.   [72] [1988] IRLR 388.
[73] *American Cyanamid (No. 1) v Ethicon Ltd* [1975] 2 WLR 316.   [74] [1994] IRLR 119.

20.6 **The insolvency of the employer**

 Business Link

Where a business becomes insolvent and the employer is unable to provide employees with pay and other contractual benefits, the employees have rights to claim for owed entitlements. If the employer is unable to satisfy these requirements, mechanisms exist to offer relief to employees from State funds.

Insolvency can affect an employer who is acting as an individual (in which circumstances the person becomes bankrupt or has entered into a voluntary agreement with creditors) or, for situations where the employer is a company (such as a private limited company or limited liability partnership). Insolvency includes administration, liquidation, receivership, or an agreement that has been entered into voluntarily with the creditors.

Insolvency occurs where the business does not have adequate funds to continue trading or to settle its debts (including, for example, owed wages to employees). In such a situation, the employee may require assistance to claim what is owed to him/her, but there are limits to what may be claimed (from the National Insurance Fund—ERA 1996, s. 182), and the employer must be insolvent as defined under the legislation. Employees may recover arrears in pay for a period of at least one week, but this may not exceed eight weeks in total.[75] Holiday pay for up to six weeks in the previous 12 months may be claimed. A failure by the employer to provide the correct statutory entitlement to notice,[76] and the basic award granted under an unfair dismissal claim can also be claimed.[77] The term 'pay' includes contractual payments and statutory payments such as maternity pay or payments ordered through an Employment Tribunal (such as under the information and **consultation** requirements). Payments are determined, for holiday pay and wages, from the date of insolvency, whereas redundancy[78] and statutory notice pay are determined from either the date when the employer became officially insolvent or when the employment ended (whichever is later).

Upon insolvency, an insolvency practitioner such as a liquidator, receiver, administrator, supervisor (in voluntary agreements), or trustee (in bankruptcy)[79] will take control over the business and the employee should apply to this person for the relevant forms. Once completed, these are forwarded on to the Redundancy Payments Office. Debts that remain following the payments from the National Insurance Fund are only available if there are sufficient funds in the employer's assets, but holiday pay and wages (to a maximum of £800 or four months' pay (whichever is less)) are assigned 'preferential debt' status and may be paid out of the employer's remaining assets ahead of other debts.

---

[75] Calculated at a maximum weekly wage of £430—1 February 2012.   [76] ERA 1996 s. 86.

[77] Including the basic amount of an award by an ACAS arbitrator under the ACAS Arbitration Scheme (Great Britain) Order 2004, SI 2004/753.

[78] To qualify for redundancy payments the claimant must have employee status; have been continuously employed by the employer for at least two years; and have made a written application to the employer or a tribunal within six months of the employment ending.

[79] The type of practitioner depends upon the type of insolvency affecting the employer.

Conclusion

This chapter has identified further obligations placed on employers to protect their employees health and safety at work through offering a safe system of work; regulating their hours of work and ensuring they have access to paid leave. Workers have the right to be paid at least the minimum wage and have the ability to seek owed pay if the employer becomes insolvent. Further, employers may seek to protect their legitimate proprietary interests through the insertion of restraint of trade clauses in the contracts of employment. Each of these elements offer protections and establish obligations on employers, and in many cases, compliance is not only necessary in the interests of the business, but necessary to comply with the law. Therefore, they are essential elements for a business employing labour.

 Summary of main points

Working Time Regulations

- The Regulations were enacted to transpose the EU's Acquired Rights Directive.
- 'Workers' not just 'employees' are protected.
- The Regulations provide (in most circumstances) for a maximum working week of 48 hours, averaged over a 17-week period.
- Workers may opt out of the Regulations, although no worker can be forced to opt out, and the worker may opt in to gain protection from the Regulations if he/she chooses.
- Workers are entitled to 11 hours' rest (12 hours for young workers) in each 24-hour period.
- Workers are entitled to 5.6 weeks' paid holiday leave.
- Night workers should not exceed 8 hours' work in any 24-hour period (averaged over 17 weeks).

National Minimum Wage

- The National Minimum Wage Act 1998 (NMW 1998) is applicable to workers, not just 'employees'.
- There are three levels of NMW depending on the age of the worker and these figures are regularly reviewed (each October) by the Government following recommendations from the Low Pay Commission.
- 'Pay' is the gross pay of the worker but this does not include pension payments, redundancy pay, overtime, or expenses.
- The employer is obliged to maintain records of the hours worked and payments made to workers.
- Workers can enforce the NMW 1998 through Employment Tribunals and Her Majesty's Revenue & Customs can enforce the law against a recalcitrant employer.

Health and Safety

- Employers owe a duty to take reasonable care of the health and safety of all workers.
- The common law obligations on employers enable an employee to claim for any injuries or damage suffered due to the employer's negligence.

- The statutory measures are largely covered by the Health and Safety at Work Act (HSWA) 1974 and the Regulations enacted following 1992.

- The general duties on employers include: providing safe plant and systems of work; the safe handling and use of articles and substances; providing the relevant and necessary information on health and safety matters to employees; and maintaining a safe working environment.

- A breach of the HSWA 1974 may lead to an employer (director, manager and so on) facing a fine or imprisonment.

Restraint of trade clauses

- Such a clause is a post-contractual agreement restraining the employee from working in competition with the employer for a defined duration and a defined geographical/industrial region.

- The clause must protect the employer's legitimate proprietary interests; it must be reasonable between the parties and be in the public interest.

- A wrongful dismissal/repudiation of the contract by the employer will prevent the application of a restraining clause.

- The courts may remove an offending aspect of the restraint clause to make it fair and enforceable (known as blue pencilling).

- A restraint clause may be enforced through the courts by the award of an injunction.

- Rather than using a restraint of trade clause, the employer may use a garden leave agreement whereby an extended notice period is included in the contract. This is more expensive to the employer, but is enforced with greater certainty than are restraint clauses.

Insolvency

- Where an employer becomes insolvent, the employee can claim for any owed wages and in the event that the employer lacks the resources to settle the claim, he/she may seek assistance through the National Insurance Fund.

 Summary questions

Essay questions

1. Is it appropriate to have a national minimum wage? Given the differences in the cost of living throughout the country, and obliging the employer to pay an amount set by the State for employment when market forces may have been better able to regulate pay, evaluate the necessity for, and impact of, the National Minimum Wage Act 1998.

2. An employer is entitled to have his/her confidential information protected against unauthorized use by a rival. How have the courts determined what may be regarded as 'reasonable' in the award of this protection?

Problem questions

1. Clive works for Trusthouse Fifty, a chain of hotel and dining establishments. He was promoted to manager of the restaurant and bar department. He had not opted-out of

the Working Time Regulations, his contract provided that he was contracted to serve the employer for 42 hours per week, and he should endeavour to complete his work within this time.

Despite this contract, Clive was told by the general manager at the establishment that he had responsibility for all aspects of the department. He hired the staff for the functions held there, he ensured the food was prepared to a sufficiently high standard, and he also had sales targets to meet regarding the quantity and price of wine that was sold. As a result, Clive was under great pressure and started to work 80 hours per week to complete his work.

Clive did not complain to the general manager about this, but it was evident he was suffering health problems due to working excessive hours. After just six months in this job he had become very irritable, had been rude to employees, criticized their work, and had started drinking alcohol to excess. Clive exhibited none of these symptoms when first hired.

When a concerned colleague (Zoe) informed the general manager of her concerns for Clive's health, she was told that Clive must complete his tasks, and the manager did not care how long it took him to achieve this. Further, it transpires that the general manager has not maintained any records of the time staff work at the establishment.

Clive has now suffered a breakdown and cannot work. Advise him on any claim he may have against the employer based on his statutory rights.

2. Devon is employed by All Bright Consumables (ABC) Ltd in the factory where it makes tablet computers. Devon is a senior manager and has responsibility for the production of the components and their assembly. He is also involved in senior planning meetings where strategies, including plans for patents, are discussed.

Devon's contract provides for a restraint of trade where Devon will not compete with ABC Ltd either through establishing his own business or working for a competitor, in the technology field, in the UK, Germany, the USA, China, The Middle East and Africa, for 1 year after ceasing to work there. A further clause restricts Devon from 'employing ABC Ltd staff, or poaching customers'.

Sometime later, Devon decides to leave ABC Ltd and establish his own company. It speacializes in touch screen computers and he wishes to hire the chief designer and operations manager of ABC Ltd to help him in this new venture. Devon approaches both people with an offer to triple their current salary if they leave ABC Ltd with immediate effect. Devon is planning on developing and then marketing a new computer which uses 'gesture-based input' on both the front and back of the device. He was privy to this idea whilst working at ABC Ltd and he knows that ABC Ltd has not yet applied for a patent.

Advise ABC Ltd on their likely arguments and success in preventing Devon competing with ABC Ltd, hiring the staff, and developing this new computer. How would your answer be developed if Devon said it was the company he established that had taken the actions when he left ABC Ltd?

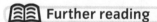 **Further reading**

O'Reilly, T. (2008) 'Health and Safety for Small Businesses' Management Books: Cirencester.

Useful websites

https://www.gov.uk/browse/working
(A government website specifically designed to provide employees with a comprehensive overview of their rights and responsibilities at work.)

https://www.gov.uk/national-minimum-wage-rates
(Information regarding the National Minimum Wage.)

https://www.gov.uk/maximum-weekly-working-hours
(Information regarding the Working Time Regulations.)

http://www.hse.gov.uk/
(The website of the Health and Safety Executive—This resource provides information to employers and workers regarding the expected conduct and obligations on everyone at work; newsletters; documents and warning signs and so on.)

http://www.bis.gov.uk/insolvency/
(The website of the Insolvency Service, providing guidance and the relevant forms for affected workers to facilitate any claims.)

http://www.cbi.org.uk/
(The website of the Confederation of British Industry—the UK's largest independent employers' representative. It lobbies the Government on behalf of businesses regarding domestic and international matters.)

http://www.lowpay.gov.uk/
(The website of the Low Pay Commission, which makes recommendations on matters surrounding the national minimum wage.)

 Online Resource Centre

http://www.oxfordtextbooks.co.uk/orc/marson3e/
Why not visit the Online Resource Centre and try multiple choice questions associated with this chapter to test your understanding of the topic. You will also find relevant updates to the law.

VI Company Law

21 Agency

Why does it matter?

It is essential to recognize that in a commercial world, many business transactions are completed through an agency relationship. An agent creates contracts between the person he/she is acting for (the principal) and the other (third) party. This contract is binding on the third party and will allow him/her to enforce the contract. An agent can gain authority to act for the principal implicitly, or through express agreements, and his/her actions can bind the principal in such contracts. The agent has responsibilities and rights through agreements to act for the principal, and it is necessary to appreciate how these are defined and limited by the courts and by statute.

Learning outcomes

Following reading this chapter you should be in a position to:

- identify in which situations an agency agreement will be established (21.3)
- explain the various forms of authority an agent may possess (21.3.1–21.3.4)
- identify the duties and obligations imposed on an agent in relation to the principal (21.4–21.4.4)
- explain where liability will be imposed on an agent in contracts made with authority (21.5)
- explain the rights of agents when acting in his/her capacity (21.6)
- explain the implications of the Commercial Agents (Council Directive) Regulations 1993 to agency contracts and the parties involved (21.8–21.8.3)
- identify the procedures in terminating an agency relationship (21.7; 21.8.3).

Key terms

These terms will be used in the chapter and it may be helpful to be aware of what they mean or refer back to them when reading through the chapter.

Agent
A person who has the authority to act on another's (the principal) behalf, and will bind the principal in contracts as if the principal had personally made the agreement.

Fiduciary duty

A fiduciary has authority belonging to another person/body, and he/she is obliged to exercise this for the other party's benefit. An example of a relationship establishing fiduciary duties is between solicitor and his/her client.

Principal

The person who instructs the agent to work on his/her behalf.

Ratification

Where the agent acts without the express or implied authorization of the principal, or in excess of this authority, the principal may ratify the contract and be bound by it as though authorization had been given from the start of the contract.

21.1 Introduction

Agency is the relationship which exists between two persons when one, called the agent, is considered in law to represent the other, called the principal, in such a way as to be able to affect the principal's legal position in respect of strangers to the relationship by the making of contracts or the disposition of property.[1]

Agency begins the consideration of what has been broadly termed 'company law' and is included in this section for convenience as agents exist in corporate organizations, sole traders, and partnerships trading structures. The law in this area applies to many relationships and is frequently seen in commercial enterprises, including high street retailers, between partners, and the directors of a corporation. The **agent's** role is to act on the **principal's** behalf, in establishing contracts, for example, and when the agent has the required authority to act in this way, the contract will not be considered to bind the agent and the third party, but rather will bind the principal and the third party. By way of example, in retailing, the person who works as a 'shop assistant' is essentially acting as the agent of the shop's owner. When goods are sold at the retailer's establishment, the shop assistant is not personally trading the goods, but rather he/she is given the authority to complete the transaction for the sale, and the money paid is to the owner of the shop, not the shop assistant. With regard to this authority, where the third party has paid for the goods, and passed his/her money to the shop assistant, agency provides that even where the shop assistant fails to pass this money to the owner of the shop, it will be considered that the third party has paid for the goods and has good title to them, even though the shop assistant has not fulfilled his/her obligation to the owner. The agent has the authority to complete such transactions on behalf of the principal, and the third party has conducted his/her business on the basis of this authority. It is in this way that many (obvious) forms of agency are seen—the agent having authority to buy and sell goods.

21.2 Types of agent

There are several forms of agreement in which an agent may have authority to bind the principal, and simply because the word 'agent' is used, this does not create a situation where his/her actions will bind the principal. For example, an estate agent is a term in common usage,

---

[1] Fridman, G. H. L. (1996) 'The Law of Agency' (7th Edition), Butterworths: London.

but it does not establish the legal implications and rights of an agent in its legal sense. Agents may take the following forms:

- *General agent:* This is the most common type of agency agreement, where the agent has the authority to act for the principal in the ordinary course of their business.
- *Special agent:* Denotes a similar form of agency agreement but the agent is only authorized to perform a particular act.
- *Commercial agent:* This is an agent, provided for under an EU Directive, which allows the agent greater protection (through the statute) than exists under the common law.
- *Commission agent:* This agent has the authority to buy and sell on the principal's behalf, but he/she is not authorized to establish privity of contract[2] with the third party.
- Del Credere *Agent:* Here the agent binds the principal, but he/she is provided with an additional sum that guarantees that the agent will indemnify the principal in the event that the third party fails to pay money owed under the contract (for example, when goods are sold on credit).

21.3 Creation of agency

Agency agreements are very easy to establish (see Table **21.1**).

As there is no compulsion on agents to register with a governmental body to demonstrate their status as agents, or to work under a set of clear guidelines, the common law has assisted in identifying the powers of an agent. However, before the rights and duties of the agent and principal are considered, the source and implications of the form of authority that the agent possesses must be identified. Such authority may be based on 'actual' authority provided (either expressly or through implication); it may be 'apparent' through a representation made to the third party; it may exist through the principal's subsequent **'ratification'** of the contract; or the authority may have derived through 'necessity'. Note that the classic principle that to create obligations under agency required the representation of this relationship to have derived from the principal and not the agent has been weakened, especially through the concept of apparent authority. Where the agent has authority from the principal to contract, the third party may rely on this in his/her enforcement of a contract.

Table 21.1 Creating an agency

Through a contract (although in most situations this is not necessary);

Through verbal agreement;

Where an agent is appointed to execute a deed (and have a 'power of attorney'), under common law, he/she must be appointed by deed (*Berkeley v Hardy*);[3]

Implicitly where the intentions of the parties provide guidance as to the true relationship (*Chaudhry v Prabhakar*);[4] and

Agency may be imposed on the parties by statute (e.g. Consumer Credit Act 1974, s. 56(2)), through necessity, and through cohabitation.

---

[2] See **8.3**.   [3] [1826] 5 B&C 355.   [4] [1988] 1 WLR 29.

21.3.1 **Actual authority**

When expressed, there is an agreement between the principal and the agent as to the powers that the agent will have to bind the principal (for example, the owner of a shop may inform the shop assistant that he/she has the right to sell the goods in the shop for the price identified on the ticket with no discretion for discounts). As with other types of express agreements, this can be established in words or writing (through a contract[5] and this may be preferable to clearly identify the extent of any authority).

There also exist situations where the authority may have been provided through implication due to the relationship/conduct between the agent and principal. Typical situations, relating to business, may occur where a director of a company may have been appointed incorrectly, or where he/she has not been appointed to a specific post (such as managing director), but the company has not made attempts to remove the authority or deny this authority to third parties. Implied authority may work in providing, in its entirety, the binding agreement between the agent and principal.

Hely-Hutchinson v Brayhead Ltd[6]

Facts:

A company allowed its chairman to act in the way, and with the powers of, a managing director, without engaging him to this position. A managing director of a company would be assumed to have the authority to bind the company in most contractual dealings, and in this instance the chairman would not. The chairman established a contract that sought to bind the company and the Court of Appeal held the chairman had the implied authority to do this. It was the actions of the company that allowed for the chairman to act in this way, and hence it should be treated as if he had been given the position of managing director from the board of directors.

Authority for:

Actual authority and apparent (ostensible) authority often overlap. Where the board invest the chairman (using the facts of the case as an example) with actual authority of that position but also with apparent authority to act with the authority of a managing director, this apparent authority can exceed the actual authority. It seeks to protect innocent third parties who are unaware of the limitation of authority placed by the principal on the agent.

Implied authority may also have the effect of broadening existing powers. In *Waugh v HB Clifford and Sons Ltd*[7] a firm of solicitors were engaged by builders who required representation to protect against any legal action after they had negligently built houses. They expressly instructed the solicitor not to compromise on the basis of a substantial compensation payment. However, the solicitors disregarded the builders' instruction. It was common to allow solicitors in these situations to compromise on behalf of the principal. In the resultant action by the builders against the firm, the Court of Appeal held that as the builders had provided clear instructions not to compromise, and that express terms in a contract override implied

---

[5] To establish a contract the agent must receive some consideration. Without consideration, this is a bare promise which will not establish a binding contract.

[6] [1968] 1 QB 549.   [7] [1982] 1 All ER 1095.

terms (such as allowing the solicitors to compromise on the principal's behalf), the solicitors were in breach. The Court considered that the authority between the agent and the third party is different to that between the agent and the principal. Where express instructions are given from a principal to the agent, this removes the implied nature of any authority in contradiction of the express agreement.

21.3.1.1 *Usual authority*

An unusual situation involving agency agreements occurred in *Watteau v Fenwick*.[8] The owner of a public house sold the property (and business), but was hired to be its manager. In his position as manager, he was provided with the authority to purchase bottled drinks on behalf of the new owner (the principal), but was expressly instructed not to purchase tobacco products on credit on the principal's behalf. The manager did purchase such goods from a salesman who had previous dealings with the manager (in his capacity as owner) and who was unaware of the change in management/ownership structure of the business (termed as an undisclosed principal). When the manager was unable to pay for the goods on credit he asserted that the principal was bound. It was held that the actions of the manager bound the principal. This was a strange decision as the manager had no actual authority to act to bind the principal in this way; it could not be said there was apparent authority as the representation as to the agent's authority must move from the principal; the undisclosed principal was held liable for the actions of the agent, and hence the decision has been criticized. As such, it falls somewhere between actual and apparent authority, and has been termed 'usual' authority. The manager was the previous owner and his name was still above the door (as required of licensed premises). Further, the principal had not identified to the salesmen/traders in the area who had previous contact with the manager as to the change in organizational structure (and the change in authority), and as such it could be considered that the manager had authority to act, and the third party required protection. Despite the principal being bound by the agent's actions, this does not prevent him/her taking action against the agent for the breach.

21.3.2 **Apparent authority**

Apparent authority (or ostensible authority, as it is referred to in some legal texts) exists outside of the actual authority previously identified. Whereas express and implied authority derives from the agreement between the principal and agent, apparent authority is applicable where the principal (or someone acting for him/her) has represented to the third party that the agent has the authority to act on his/her behalf. The consequence is that where the third party has been given this impression of authority of the agent, an agreement that is subsequently concluded between the agent and third party may bind the principal, who is unable to deny the representation made.

Therefore, to establish apparent authority, the following criteria must be demonstrated:

1   There must have been a representation regarding the person as an agent.
2   The principal must have conveyed this representation (or someone acting on his/her behalf).
3   The third party must have acted based on this representation.

---

[8]   [1893] 1 QB 346.

An example of the effects of apparent authority was demonstrated in *Hely-Hutchinson* above (as apparent and actual authority often overlap). Similarly, in *Freeman & Lockyer v Buckhurst Park Properties Ltd* [9] a director was given authority to act in the manner expected of a managing director, and in this capacity he engaged a firm of architects to act for the company. The company refused to pay the firm for the work on the basis that the director who had agreed the contract lacked the (actual) authority to bind the company. The Court of Appeal held that there was a contract between the firm and the company. There had been an impression that the director had the authority to bind the company in the agreement, and therefore the principal was liable under the contract established on its behalf. The representation, moving from the principal, is usually provided (in the case of corporations) by the company's board of directors:

First Energy (UK) Ltd v Hungarian International Bank Ltd[10]

Facts:

The claimants had sought credit from the bank and in negotiating on this matter had dealt with a senior manager. During the negotiations the manager disclaimed any right that he may have to bind the bank as he lacked the actual authority to guarantee credit. However, later the manager wrote to the claimants stating that the credit requested by the claimants had been authorized by the bank, even though this was not the case. The Court of Appeal held that the bank was bound under the offer made by the manager. Whilst the Court accepted that the manager had informed the claimants of his lack of capacity to contract on behalf of the bank, he did possess the authority to communicate matters from the bank to clients. As such, the bank had represented that the manager had authority to pass on decisions made by it, and the claimants could rely on this decision.

Authority for:

Businesses contract through the use of agents. As such, third parties dealing with them must be enabled to rely on their appearance (here as an authorized agent of the bank).

It must be noted that where the agent acts on apparent authority, but in fact does not possess actual authority, he/she may be held liable if the principal decides to bring an action against him/her for disobeying the principal's instructions. If, on the other hand the agent had actual authority to take the actions that bound the principal, no claim is allowed by the principal against the agent (and the agent would be entitled to any payment under this agency agreement).

21.3.3 Authority through ratification

An agent who purports to act for the principal may enter into a contract that he/she was unauthorized to make. At this stage it may not bind the principal but when the principal is aware of the contract established by the agent on his/her behalf, and the principal accepts the agreement, he/she will be bound by it. The ratification must be given within a reasonable time of the agreement.[11] Ratification allows for the retrospective acceptance of a contract and it will entitle the principal to all the rights and obligations provided under a contractual agreement. As such, he/she is empowered to compel the completion of the contract even where the third

---

[9] [1964] 2 QB 480.   [10] [1993] 2 Lloyd's Rep 194.
[11] *Metropolitan Asylums Board Managers v Kingham & Sons* [1890] 6 TLR 217.

party no longer wishes to be bound. In *Re Tiedemann and Ledermann Freres*[12] an agent used the principal's name to enter into a contract but he did so to avail himself of the benefits of the agreement. On discovery of the truth, the third party attempted to end the contract due to a misrepresentation. However, as the principal ratified the contract, the third party was bound.

Bolton Partners v Lambert[13]

Facts:

The defendant had communicated to the managing director of a company his offer to purchase the company. Following this communication, on 13 December 1886, a committee decided that it would accept the offer (even though the committee had no such power to accept) and this was in return communicated to the defendant. In January the defendant attempted to revoke the offer, but the company sought to enforce this through an action for specific performance. The Court of Appeal held that as the board of the company had ratified the agreement, its effect was to bind the parties following the acceptance of the offer. The acceptance of the company was retrospectively applied to the December meeting of the committee and hence the defendant's attempted revocation in January was too late and consequently ineffective.

Authority for:

Ratification by a principal of acts done by an assumed agent is 'thrown back' to the date of the act done, and the agent is put in the same position as if he/she had authority to do that act.

The steps required to enable ratification are outlined in Figure 21.1.

- *The agent must be acting for the principal*: Because of the nature of ratification, and the requirement for the agent to be acting for the principal, the third party must be aware that a principal exists. Without such knowledge, the third party will assume he/she is contracting with the agent and the agent will be bound by the agreement. This is vitally important as an undisclosed principal cannot later ratify, even if the parties want this. In *Keighly Maxted & Co. v Durrant*[14] an agent had made a contract for wheat based at a higher price for the principal than had been agreed. The principal agreed to ratify the contract but the House of Lords prevented this as the agent had not informed the third party of the principal's existence at the time of contracting.

- *The principal must be in existence at the time of the contract*: This aspect applies particularly to companies that have been newly formed. Where the promoters of the company (its 'agents') have entered into a contract before the company has completed the registration

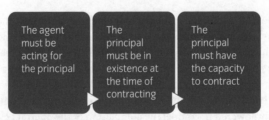

Figure 21.1 Steps to Enable Ratification

---

[12] [1899] 2 QB 66.   [13] [1889] 41 ChD 295.   [14] [1901] AC 240.

process and been granted the certificate of incorporation, the agents are personally liable and the company may not, once it has been formed, later ratify the agreement.

• *The principal must have the capacity to contract:* The capacity to contract refers to elements such as whether the principal would have been able to enter into the contract that the agent actually formed. For example, corporations may lack the ability (capacity) to enter into the type of contract relevant to the claim, and hence there is no possibility of ratification. To avoid situations where ratification may cause problems between the parties, the agreement may be stated as being 'subject to ratification' and hence enable a withdrawal from the contract before ratification takes place.

21.3.4 Authority through necessity

Where the agent acts in relation to necessity (for example, protecting property owned by the principal), then the courts may bind the principal in the actions of the agent even though he/she has no actual or apparent authority to act in the particular way. These cases have often occurred in emergencies at sea or where perishable goods are involved. The requirements to bind the principal in this way involve satisfying the following criteria:

1 The agent must have had responsibility for the control over the property belonging to the principal.

2 It was not possible for the agent to discuss the issue with the principal and gain his/her instructions as to the action to be taken.

3 The situation must be considered an emergency.

4 The agent must have acted in good faith.

In *Springer v Great Western Railway*[15] the agent was not permitted to sell tomatoes (when engaged to carry these). However, due to weather and transport problems the agent did sell the goods on behalf of the principal as the tomatoes were perishing in the heat. This had occurred on land and it was possible and reasonable for the carriers to contact the principal and obtain his instructions before taking the action. Therefore it was held that such a situation did not amount to an emergency and was an unauthorized act.

> **? Thinking Point**
>
> Consider an agent responsible for property maintenance. She inspects a property and discovers a broken window, but she is not authorized to replace/repair the property without the express permission of the principal. Consider the issues in relation to good faith that would be taken into account if the agent were to organize a repair without contacting the principal?

21.4 Duties of the agent

Due to the nature of the agreement between the agent and principal, and the fact that the agent is given authority to act on the principal's behalf, trust and confidence are paramount in such dealings. The agent must respect the instructions of the principal and act in his/her best interests.

---

[15] [1921] 1 KB 257.

Duties that have been imposed on agents include:

- *An obligation to obey lawful instructions:* An agent may have agreed with the principal the parameters of the (actual) authority, and these may have been established in a contract. Where this is so, a failure on the side of the agent to follow the requirements of the contract will amount to a breach, even if this was performed in good faith. Therefore even if, in not following instructions, the agent considered his/her actions to be the most appropriate course for the principal, a breach is still committed.

- *Non-delegation of duties:* There is a general duty that the agent should not delegate (and in essence this would amount to sub-delegation) the principal's authority, and should perform the task personally. However, this general duty will be removed where the principal expressly agrees for the agent to delegate; where such authority to delegate may be implied from the circumstances of the case; and if the delegation is required due to some unforeseen event.

- *To exercise care and skill:* When conducting the business of the principal, the agent must use the appropriate care and skill in the execution of his/her duties (based on the nature of the task and the skills he/she professes to hold).[16] In *Chaudhry v Prabhakar*[17] the claimant wished to purchase a used car and sought assistance from her friend. The claimant stipulated that the car should not have been in an accident, and the friend sought a car from a dealer who ran a repair shop. The friend noticed that the front of the car had evidence of damage, but recommended the car to the claimant, and as a result of the recommendation the purchase was made. Soon after the purchase the claimant discovered that the car had been involved in a serious accident and had been very poorly repaired (and indeed was not roadworthy). As such she successfully claimed against the seller under the Sale of Goods Act 1979, and she also claimed against the friend for his breach of the duty to take reasonable care. The Court of Appeal allowed the claim against the friend to succeed. The reasoning was on the acceptance of the friend that he owed a duty of care (which was an unusual decision and not expected in situations where a person has acted gratuitously).

- *Fiduciary duties:* The **fiduciary duties** are imposed due to the nature of the relationship between the agent and principal, and the authority the agent exercises for the principal. If a breach of the duty is discovered, the principal may seek to recover any secret profit made by the agent, and/or any bribe that has been paid. In such a situation the principal may seek damages for the fraud committed. The principal may have the option to refuse to pay the commission or salary of the agent. The agent's contract with the principal may be terminated, and the agreement with the third party may be rescinded. The use of these options is determined by the courts depending on the actions of the parties and what is fair and reasonable in the circumstances.

The examples of fiduciary duties given at 21.4.1–21.4.4 are artificially separated in this section for ease of reference, and they frequently overlap:

21.4.1 Duty not to take bribes

One of the most important duties placed on an agent is to ensure that he/she does not take bribes in the exercise of the authority for the principal. Clearly good faith requires that the

---

[16] The most common examples of the nature of care and skill in professional occupations include agents in solicitors and accountancy practices.

[17] [1988] 3 All ER 718.

agent acts in the best interest of the principal, and for his/her, rather than the agent's benefit. As such, a bribe to, for example, secure the award of a contract would place the agent's motives and the best interests of the principal in conflict. It is this element of inducement that may give rise to accusations of accepting bribes, and this may not be confined to money, but could include free samples for the agent, the agent being invited to hospitality events, or any other gift in kind. Where the principal discovers the bribe he/she may terminate the arrangement with the agent and recover any commission paid; recover the bribe provided; consider the bribe to be held by the agent on trust;[18] recover damages from the third party that provided the bribe for any losses attributable (rather than recovering the bribe); and he/she may rescind the contract between the principal and the third party. Therefore, the effects of bribes can be catastrophic to the relationship between all the parties.

21.4.2 Secret profits

The agent must ensure that the profits accrued from the agreement(s) with the third party are agreed between the agent and principal. The agent should not make a profit that has not been previously agreed (such as the agent's commission/salary). This may be particularly so when the agent is asked to dispose of goods and he/she does so at a higher price than requested by the principal (and the agent retains the 'extra' amount), or the agent uses the principal's property for his/her own purposes. It is important to remember that such situations do not have to cause the principal any loss, but it is the abuse of the position of trust and authority that is at issue. Where an agent has made a secret profit but has not been dishonest the court will usually award the principal with the profit rather than impose more harsh penalties.

21.4.3 Avoid a conflict of interest

In the same way as a duty exists to prevent the agent making a secret profit when acting for the principal, the agent must also not allow his/her own interests to conflict with that of the principal. The agency agreement is predicated on the basis of the agent acting in the best interests of the principal, and this is the case even where an agent acts, but not with the intention to defraud or mislead the principal, and there is the appearance of a conflict. As such, where a conflict of interest may arise, the agent should offer a full disclosure to the principal so an informed choice may be made. An example may be seen in *Armstrong v Jackson*,[19] where the agent was a stockbroker. The principal wished to purchase shares in a particular company, and the agent obtained these shares (but they were in reality his own). The agent had informed the principal that he had purchased the shares, whilst the real situation was that the stockbroker was a promoter of the company when it was formed. When this fact was later discovered the principal was successful in having the contract set aside. The court held that the agent had a duty to disclose this potential conflict to the principal and had breached his duty in not so doing.

21.4.4 Duty to account

The agent must maintain adequate records of his/her dealings on behalf of the principal and make these available for inspection when requested. As agents may work under the authority

---

[18] *Attorney General for Hong Kong v Reid* [1994] 1 AC 324.   [19] [1917] 2 KB 822.

of several principals it is his/her duty to maintain records in a manner that allows for the separation of the principals' accounts. This is the case where information is maintained in computer form (on a database, for example) and the principal is entitled to view his/her own accounts. Where the agent cannot separate the principal's accounts, the principal is entitled to see all of the accounts held by the agent.[20] This further has an impact on the agent's duty of confidentiality, and the continuing nature of this obligation following the cessation of the agency agreement.[21]

21.5 Liability of the agent

In situations where it has been established that the agent acted beyond his/her authority and therefore did not bind the principal, it has to be determined what happens to the agreement with the third party. The third party has entered into an agreement and is entitled to have the other party (the agent) honour his/her side of the bargain. Where the agent has identified him/herself as such, and established the contract on the principal's behalf, then the contract is between the principal and the third party, and the agent has no liability. If, on the other hand, the agent has not disclosed that he/she was acting for a principal, then the contract will exist between the agent and the third party and the usual rights and liabilities in a contractual agreement will apply. When the agent discloses the principal to the third party, and the agent was acting under actual authority, liability of the third party to the agent ceases and is transferred to the principal, but the agent and the principal will be jointly liable to the third party. The third party may then choose to enforce the contract against the agent or principal, but once the decision is made it cannot be changed. In a situation where the agent acted without actual authority, the principal will not be bound by the agreement.

Situations exist where an agent has not disclosed the existence of a principal and the principal is then prohibited from concluding the contract. Where the principal was not disclosed, and if he/she had been, the third party would not have agreed to the contract, this will prevent the principal from acting on it. Such a situation requires some 'personal element' in the decision (for example, it may be permissible to prevent a reviewer who has had previous negative dealings with the third party from procuring a ticket to provide a review of the third party's production, but may not be so in the sale of land,[22] which lacks this personal element). Clearly, the contract will not be enforced where the third party specifically asks the agent to identify the principal and he/she withholds this information or misrepresents the position.[23] The principal cannot enforce the contract if it identifies that a contract under agency is excluded. Further, if the third party establishes the contract with the agent personally, rather than wishing to contract with a principal, this will stop the principal from acting on the contract.

- *Rights of the undisclosed principal:* Guidance was provided in *Siu Yin Kwan v Eastern Insurance Co.*[24] regarding situations where an agent has failed to disclose the principal to a third party. The agent who possessed actual authority to contract will enable the principal to enforce the contract (and the principal will also be subject to claims against him/her). The agent will also be allowed to sue and be sued as to the terms of the contract.

---

[20] *Yasuda Ltd v Orion Underwriting Ltd* [1995] QB 174.

[21] *Bolkiah v KPMG* [1999] 2 WLR 215. [22] *Dyster v Randell* [1926] Ch 932.

[23] *Archer v Stone* [1898] 78 LT 34. [24] [1994] 1 All ER 213.

Any defences available to the third party against the agent would be exercisable against the principal. The agent must have intended to act for the principal when establishing the contract, and the contract may stipulate that the principal has no right to enforce the contract, or be sued under the contract.

21.6 Rights of an agent

Having identified the obligations and duties that are placed on the agent, and his/her potential liability when acting without, or in excess of, authority, this section identifies the protection to which agents are entitled.

- *Indemnity:* The agent is entitled to indemnity from the principal with regard to any liability or for the costs associated in acting for the principal (to have any expenses repaid), unless this is specifically excluded in the agreement. Therefore this provides protection for the agent where he/she may be exposed to costs or losses. However, this protection may be lost where the agent exceeds his/her authority or is liable for his/her own negligence.

- *Payment:* The agency agreement often involves a service being provided by the agent for the principal and this business transaction would involve the agent receiving some form of remuneration. This may be included in the contract between the parties as to the rate of remuneration and when payment will take place. In the absence of an express agreement to remuneration, this may be implied through the same mechanisms as it is with other contractual agreements such as through the parties' conduct, what the court considers were the true intentions of the parties and so on. The implied terms are important, but it is important to note that as with other implied terms, an express term will take precedence over inconsistent implied terms, even if this leads to unfairness.[25]

- *To maintain the goods (lien):* An agent who is owed money from the principal or some other unsatisfied claim may maintain control over the property (or possess a lien over the goods) until the debt is satisfied. This right enables the agent to the possession of the goods that he/she has lawfully come into possession of, but the right does not extend to disposing of the goods to realize the money owed.

This particular right is restricted to the goods/transactions relating to the debt owed and they must be in the agent's possession. Further, a lien exists where there is no exclusion to the right in the contract, and if the agent acts to waive his/her right (such as allowing the principal or his/her agent to take possession of the goods) then the agent loses the lien.

21.7 Termination at common law

An agency agreement may be terminated through many eventualities, including the death of either party; the mutual agreement of the parties; the fixed-term agreement coming to an end; the purpose of the agency having been completed; through frustration; and issues concerning bankruptcy. If the contract is silent on the period of notice to be given, and the agent

---

[25] *Luxor (Eastbourne) Ltd v Cooper* [1941] AC 108.

is not an employee and subject to the statutory minimum period, then a reasonable period of notice is due.[26] This is determined on the facts of the case.

Whilst the statutory provisions of the Commercial Agents Regulations (21.8) provide for minimum periods of notice to bring the agency agreement to an end, at common law the agent acts for the principal under his/her authority. If the principal chooses to withdraw this authority, then the agency agreement ceases. When the principal chooses to terminate the agreement, it is prudent to inform third parties who may have had dealings with the agent acting for the principal to ensure that contracts under apparent authority are not established. However, where the agency agreement has been established through a contract, the terms of the contract, such as notice periods, must be adhered to or the principal may be liable for breach.

Commercial agency is a potentially very complex area and requires the parties to establish clear contractual terms and conditions to prevent problems. In *Claramoda Limited v Zoomphase Limited (T/A Jenny Packham)*[27] an agency continued to be held as a commercial agent beyond the point to which it had authority to negotiate, in accordance with the definition provided in the Commercial Agents Regulations 1993. Simon J held that an agency contract does not necessarily end when the agent stops negotiating sales on the principal's behalf. What is necessary, however, is that the intermediary must not conclude contracts in his own name[28] (rather than that of the principal) or he/she will not be an agent for the purposes of the Commercial Agents Regulations.[29]

21.8 The Commercial Agents (Council Directive) Regulations 1993

The Commercial Agents (Council Directive) Regulations 1993

The Regulations[30] were established and brought into effect on 1 January 2004 to transpose Directive 86/653/EEC to harmonize legislation throughout the EU regarding contracts between commercial agents and principals, and to give additional protection to the status of agents in these relationships. The Regulations identify commercial agents as self-employed intermediaries (hence they do not apply to employee agents, but could apply to companies and partnerships) who have continuing authority to negotiate the sale or purchase of goods on behalf of/in the name of the principal.[31] The Regulations affected all agency contracts; however, the rights and obligations under this legislation are restricted to goods, rather than any services that an agent may provide. The Regulations also only protect those agents who are paid[32] rather than volunteer their services.

The Regulations imposed duties onto commercial agents to act dutifully and in good faith for the principal, and to act in his/her interest. The Regulations codify the duties as outlined in **21.4** and require the agent to make proper efforts to 'negotiate, and where appropriate, conclude transactions that he is instructed to take care of; to communicate all necessary information to the principal; and to comply with reasonable instructions given by the principal'.[33] The principal is obliged to act dutifully and in good faith in relation to the agent and in

---

[26] *Martin Baker Aircraft Co. Ltd v Canadian Flight Equipment Ltd* [1955] 2 QB 556.
[27] [2009] EWHC 2857 (Comm).
[28] Thereby demonstrating that he/she has no authority to contract for the principal.
[29] *Sagal (t/a Bunz UK) v Atelier Bunz GmbH* [2009] EWCA Civ 700.
[30] As amended by SI 1993/3173.   [31] Reg. 2(1).
[32] Reg. 2.   [33] Reg. 3.

so doing must provide the agent with all necessary documentation relating to the goods; the principal must obtain for the agent information necessary for the performance of the contract, and (where appropriate) identify to the agent, within a reasonable period, once he/she anticipates that the volume of commercial transactions will be significantly lower than could reasonably have been expected; and the principal shall inform the agent within a reasonable time of his/her acceptance or refusal (or any non-execution) of a commercial transaction procured for the principal by the agent.[34] Further, it is unlawful to attempt to contract out of these duties.[35]

The Regulations identify the rights of agents to remuneration in the absence of any agreement between the parties. The level of remuneration in such a circumstance shall be determined on the customary allowances in the locality of where the agent's activities are situated, and where no customary practice is present, this will be based on an assessment of reasonableness in relation to all aspects of the transaction.[36]

21.8.1 Indemnity and compensation

The Regulations provide for indemnity or compensation payments on the termination of the contract[37] and the indemnity will not prevent the agent from seeking damages.[38] Indemnity is provided where the agent has brought the principal new customers or significantly increased the volume of business with the existing customers.[39] The payment is equitable, having regard to all the circumstances and, in particular, the commission lost by the commercial agent on the business transacted with such customers.[40] The amount of indemnity cannot be in excess of a figure equivalent to an indemnity for one year, calculated by reference to the agent's actual pay over the previous five years or, where five years' work has not been completed, such time as has been worked.[41]

The compensation available is based on the damage suffered by the agent as a result (but not necessarily the fault of the principal) of the termination of the relations with the principal.[42] Damage is deemed to occur particularly when termination takes place in either or both of the following circumstances: those that deprive the agent of the commission that proper performance of the contract would have procured for him/her whilst providing the principal with substantial benefits; or those that have not enabled the agent to recoup (amortize) the costs and expense that he/she has incurred in the performance of the contract on the advice of the principal.[43] Further, in relation to compensation payable, the House of Lords held in *Lonsdale v Howard and Hallam Ltd* [44] that courts should look to the value of the income stream that the agency would have produced in assessing damages. In achieving this, expert testimony and elements such as the price that the agent could have achieved in selling the business will dictate the award of compensation.

These rights may not be waived by the agent through any agreement to his/her detriment,[45] but the rights may be lost if the agent fails to inform the principal within one year of the termination of the agency contract that the agent intends to pursue the entitlement.[46]

[34] Reg. 4.   [35] Reg. 5(1).   [36] Reg. 6(1).   [37] Regs. 17 and 18.
[38] Reg. 17(5).   [39] Reg. 17(3)(a).   [40] Reg. 17(3)(b).   [41] Reg. 17(4).
[42] Reg. 17(6).   [43] Reg. 17(7)(a) and (b).   [44] [2007] UKHL 32.
[45] Reg. 19.   [46] Reg. 17(9).

21.8.2 Excluding the right to indemnity and compensation

Regulation 19 states that the parties may not derogate from regs. 17 and 18 to the detriment of the agent before the contract expires. Regulation 18 provides where the compensation identified in reg. 17 shall not be payable. This situation exists where:

1   the principal has terminated the agency contract, justifiably, in relation to a breach of the contract identified in reg. 16;

2   the agent has terminated the contract (unless this termination is justified on circumstances attributable to the principal; or on grounds of the age, infirmity, or illness of the agent in consequence of which he/she cannot reasonably be required to continue his activities); or

3   the agent, with agreement from the principal, assigns his/her rights and duties under the contract to another person.

21.8.3 Termination of the agency under the regulations

An agency contract may be justifiably terminated and the Regulations will not apply where one of the parties has failed to carry out all or part of his/her obligations under the contract (or in the case of exceptional circumstances).[47] Where the contract is not a fixed-term agreement, the Regulations provide for minimum notice periods of one month in the first year of the agency, two months' notice in the second year, and three months' notice after two years of the contract. As such, these are minimum periods that the parties must adhere to, although they are free to negotiate longer terms if deemed appropriate and insofar as they are equal to both parties.[48] Where a fixed-term contract continues beyond the term of the agreement, reg. 14 states that the contract is to be considered as an indefinite contract that is subject to reg. 15 procedures.

 Conclusion

The chapter has identified agency relationships, their prevalence in business, and how the agency exists to bind the principal in contracts with third parties made on his/her behalf. Due to the nature of the agreement, obligations, potential liabilities, and rights exist for both the agent and the principal. It is essential that these are recognized, along with the statutory rights provided through the Commercial Agents (Council Directive) Regulations 1993, to minimize risk to the parties and to ensure the relationship is monitored and the authority of the agent is controlled. Contractual agreements specifically outlining the rights and limitations of the parties can assist in protecting all parties in agency.

The book continues by considering the various trading structures that may be formed to operate a business, and it offers a critique of the advantages and disadvantages each structure holds for the members.

---

[47] Reg. 16.   [48] Reg. 15.

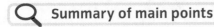 Summary of main points

- Agency involves relationships between an agent, representing the principal in a way that may affect the principal's legal position, with third parties.
- Agency can apply and affect the sole trader, partnership, and corporations.
- Several types of agent exist depending upon his/her authority and how he/she may bind the principal.

Creation of agency

- Agency agreements are easy to establish and may be formed through a contract; an agreement; by statute; through necessity; and through cohabitation.

Authority of the agent

Actual authority

- An express agreement may be formed to establish the authority of the agent to bind the principal.
- Authority may be provided through implication.

Apparent authority

- This occurs where the principal (or someone on his/her behalf) represents to the third party that the agent possesses the authority to act for the principal.
- To establish apparent authority there must have been a representation identifying the person as an agent; the principal, or someone on his/her behalf must have conveyed this representation; and the third party must have acted on the basis of it.

Ratification

- Where the agent (acting for the principal) has acted beyond his/her authority in establishing a contract with a third party, the principal may subsequently ratify the agreement.
- The agent must have been acting on the principal's behalf, the principal must have been in existence at the time of the contract being established, and the principal must possess the capacity to contract.

Necessity

- Where an agent has responsibility for the control of the principal's property, and in a situation involving an emergency, the agent may have the power to act and bind the principal where the agent does not possess actual or apparent authority. For this situation to take place the agent must have acted in good faith and it must have been impossible to communicate with the principal regarding the emergency and to gain his/her instructions.

Duties of the agent

- The agent must:
  - obey lawful instructions;

– not delegate the duty without authorization;

– exercise reasonable care and skill.

- The agent's fiduciary duties include:

  – not to take bribes;

  – not to make secret profits;

  – to avoid conflicts of interests;

  – to account to the principal.

Liability of the agent

- If the agent has acted beyond his/her authority, the third party is entitled to have the other party honour his/her side of the contract.
- Generally, where the agent identifies he/she is working for the principal and establishes a contract on the principal's behalf, the agent has no liability under the contract with the third party.
- Where the agent has not identified the existence of the principal in the contract with the third party, the principal is prohibited from concluding the contract.

Rights of the agent

- The agent, in acting for the principal under the relevant authority, has the right to:

  – indemnity;

  – payment;

  – maintain goods (lien).

The Commercial Agents Regulations 1993

- The Regulations give rights and place obligations on commercial agents.
- The agent has to make proper efforts to negotiate and conclude the transactions required of him/her; to communicate relevant information to the principal; and to comply with the reasonable instructions of the principal.
- The principal is obliged to act in good faith to the agent in providing relevant information; the volume of commercial transactions if these are likely to be lower than anticipated; and his/her acceptance or otherwise of transactions procured by the agent.
- The Regulations identify issues of remuneration, indemnity, and compensation payable.

Termination of the agency

- At common law, the agreement may be terminated in compliance with the contract, or where the parties are no longer able to carry out their duties; in cases of bankruptcy; frustration and so on.
- The termination of a commercial agency agreement is protected through the Commercial Agents (Council Directive) Regulations 1993.
- The Regulations provide for a minimum of one months' notice of termination in the first year of the agreement; two months' notice in the second year; and three months' notice after two years (although the parties can apply longer periods applicable to each other).

Summary Questions

Essay questions

1. The fiduciary and contractual duties implied into the contract of an agent are fair, albeit they are demanding.
   Discuss.

2. The creation of agency by operation of the rules of common law are dated but still are considered good law.
   Discuss the above in relation to necessity and cohabitation.

Problem questions

1. James operates a business, All Bright Consumables (ABC), which trades in DIY goods to electricians and traders. As James is expanding his business in other areas and has become too busy to manage ABC personally, he appoints Brenda to manage the operation. Brenda is engaged on a three-year fixed term contract with payment by commission of 7 per cent of the sales the business makes. One stipulation James makes as part of the agreement with Brenda is that Brenda does not deal with ABC's major rival business, XYZ.

   At the beginning of the engagement, all parties are happy as business is good. However, soon afterward the economy begins to move into recession and business slows. The result is Brenda's commission from sales is dramatically reduced and despite her pleas to James to increase her rate of commission, James refuses. Brenda is soon approached by XYZ who offer her a business opportunity. If she agrees to sell XYZ's electric shower for them to ABC customers, they will deliver the showers to the customers directly from XYZ's warehouse. As this will be 'their little secret,' James need never know and XYZ will give Brenda 30 per cent of the profits from the sales.

   Sometime later, James is at a trade event where he is approached by an acquaintance who expresses to James his disappointment at the quality of the showers they are now selling. Further, he informs James that due to this choice of poor quality components he has had to suggest to his customers that they do not purchase from ABC. When James enquires about his acquaintance's concerns, he is shocked to discover that the showers are from XYZ. James immediately challenges Brenda about the truth of this situation which she confirms. Brenda also says that she has had several customers return the showers as being of very poor quality and wanting a refund as they purchased them from the ABC store. Further, XYZ are refusing to accept any returns.
   Explain the legal position of the parties using agency law.

2. ABC Ltd operates a business of selling specialist cars and difficult to source car spares to customers and at auctions. It manages this through engaging representatives for regions around the UK who source the goods on behalf of ABC Ltd. ABC Ltd appoint Billy as its representative for the North West of England, on contractual terms of a three-year irrevocable engagement, where he will receive a commission of 35 per cent of the profits made by ABC Ltd on the sale of the goods he acquires. An important aspect of the contract is that Billy is instructed not to obtain Ford cars or spare parts as these can prove difficult to sell. Billy is issued with a letter of introduction from ABC Ltd identifying him as the company's 'associate for the North West.'

   Two months after his engagement began (on 5 July), Billy was approached by Stock-Cars who informed him that they had a mint-condition 1967 Ford Mustang, which was currently on display at the National Museum of American History until 2 November, which he could buy for £25,000. In the negotiations with Stock-Cars, Billy identified that he was acting on behalf of 'a specialist car-buying company' and that 'his principal will wait until the conclusion of the exhibition before taking delivery of the vehicle'. Billy and Stock-Cars agree that payment in full will be made within 30 days of 2 November when the vehicle is available. Having concluded the deal, on 8 July Billy reaches an agreement to sell the vehicle to Jack Vegas, a specialist car enthusiast, for £40,000, with delivery being made on 5 November. Billy intends to keep the profit made as 'a perk' by not informing ABC Ltd of the deal.

Soon after the meeting on the 8 July, Jack Vegas spoke with Stock-Cars about another vehicle he was interested in, and mentioned the car he had agreed to buy from Billy. Stock-Cars thus realized that they had sold the Ford Mustang too cheaply, and having investigated Billy and found that the 'specialist car-buying company' he worked for was ABC Ltd, they informed ABC that they would not proceed with the sale. On 9 July, in an attempt to secure the profitable sale to Jack Vegas, ABC Ltd informed Stock-Cars that they refuse the repudiation of the contract made with Billy, and insist on delivery as agreed.

In relation to the agency principles applicable to the problem, identify the rights of the parties.

 ## Further reading

Bradgate, R. (2011) 'Commercial Law' (4th Edition) Oxford University Press: Oxford.

Korotana, M. S. (2002) 'Privity of Contract and the Law of Agency: A Sub-agent's Accountability to the Principal' *Business Law Review*, Vol. 23, p. 73.

Munday, R. (2010) 'Agency: Law and Principles' Oxford University Press: Oxford.

 ## Online Resource Centre

http://www.oxfordtextbooks.co.uk/orc/marson3e/
Why not visit the Online Resource Centre and try multiple choice questions associated with this chapter to test your understanding of the topic. You will also find relevant updates to the law.

Trading Structures and Forming the Business Enterprise

22

Why does it matter?

You are going to start your own business. What form will your business take? Will you operate as a sole trader, go into partnership with others, or form a corporation? Each of these forms of business organization will impact on the responsibilities and duties of the personnel involved, it will have tax implications, and the administration of each will vary. It is only by understanding the advantages and disadvantages of these forms of organization that an informed choice can be made.

Learning outcomes

Following reading this chapter you should be in a position to:

- explain how a company has its own legal personality (22.2)
- identify the advantages and disadvantages of the various forms of business organization (defined throughout the chapter and in the Summary)
- explain the process of forming various business organizations (22.3.1; 22.3.2; 22.3.3; 22.3.7–22.3.8.6)
- compare and contrast a simple partnership and a limited liability partnership (22.3.2–22.3.3)
- compare the different types of limited company and explain the implications of forming the business organization as a public and private limited company (22.3.5–22.3.6).

☖ Key terms

These terms will be used in the chapter and it may be helpful to be aware of what they mean or refer back to them when reading through the chapter.

Corporation
A legal entity, such as a company, that possesses its own legal personality separate from the members.

Dissolution
This is the process of ending a business relationship (such as a company or partnership).

Legal Personality
The rights attached to a natural person and/or an artificial thing, such as a corporation.

Subscriber
When in relation to company law, the subscriber is the person who has agreed to start the company and take a proportion of the original issue of shares.

22.1 Introduction

This part of the text considers the various forms of business organization that are available to those who trade. There are many forms that organizations can take, from sole traders, to working in partnerships with others, and the organization may wish to become incorporated and operate as a limited liability partnership (LLP), private limited company, or a public limited company (PLC). Each of these provides advantages and disadvantages to the members of that organization and those who deal with it, and there are implications for a business such as taxation, succession, and regulation.

This chapter focuses on the types of trading structures available, and how they are established. This will provide an overview of the implications of each form of business organization. It will enable an initial assessment of which is most appropriate for the individual/group that wishes to begin trading or who want to vary their existing organizational structure. It should be noted that there is no one model that will suit everyone or every business model. It is very much the decision of the individual, having assessed his/her business, what he/she wishes to do with the business and how he/she sees it continuing in the future, to determine the form of enterprise chosen. Being aware of the consequences for the business organization is crucial in making this decision.

22.2 Legal personality

 Business Link

Natural persons have a legal personality and so may artificial things like companies. It is important to recognize that companies and limited liability partnerships have a legal personality that separates the organization from the members/owners. This means that the organization possesses rights enabling it to create contracts in its own right, and it may be sued (for example) where it owes money to creditors. The shareholders/directors of the organization are not personally liable for these debts and are only responsible for the money they have paid (or owe) for their shares, or how much money they have guaranteed to pay the company when it is wound up. Separate legal personality is a key element in company law.

The law recognizes persons having a **legal personality**, which provides them with rights and also subjects them to duties. This enables persons with the appropriate capacity to enter contracts, be subject to criminal laws and so on. Every human has a legal personality and is known as a natural legal person.[1] Companies, on the other hand, are artificial legal things that are known as **corporations** (when they are incorporated). When incorporated they are recognized in law as having their own legal personality and the most common example of such bodies is a limited company:

- *Separate legal personality:* It is essential to recognize that an LLP and limited company has its own legal personality (as recognized at law). The company may enter into contracts, sue and be sued, and these are rights and duties that are independent of the members of the company (shareholders and directors). This is despite the fact that, clearly, the directors/partners will be performing the actual duties of the corporation in its relations with the outside world. The issue of a company possessing a legal personality was established in the following seminal case.

Salomon v Salomon & Co. Ltd[2]

Facts:

Mr Salomon had been successfully trading as a sole trader for many years as a leather merchant who produced and sold goods such as shoes and boots. It was then decided that he would change the status of the business and register as a company, and then sell the business to this newly formed company. He duly registered the business and it became incorporated, providing him with a payment of £39,000 for the sale of this business to the company. From this payment, Salomon left £10,000 in the company as his personal loan, and it was intended that this would be paid back to him, therefore he established himself as a secured creditor by taking out a mortgage debenture. Some time later the company had problems in meeting its debts and went into liquidation owing money to Salomon and other creditors. The company only had assets remaining of about £6,000 and Salomon claimed that as a secured creditor. Following an action by the liquidator as to the legality of Salomon establishing himself as a secured creditor, the House of Lords held that he was entitled to the remaining money. As the company had been correctly registered, and there was an agreement between Salomon and the company regarding the loan, as a secured creditor he was entitled to the money before unsecured creditors.

Authority for:

When correctly formed and registered (therefore in accordance with the statutory requirements) a company possesses its own legal personality. This is legally recognized and is separate from the members/directors of the company.

This case established the importance of the limited company, limiting the liability of the members of the company to the shares/money owed to the company. Whilst it may have appeared unfair, the company was correctly registered, and the creditors had been informed of the new status and hence the potential implications for trading with a limited company.

---

[1] Legal personality begins when the person is born and has human rights that are protected by law. Their legal personality ends upon their death, although their obligations and liabilities will pass to their representatives/executors.

[2] [1897] AC 22.

The element of the separate legal personality of the corporation, and its separation from those persons 'running' the business, was demonstrated in *Macaura v Northern Assurance Ltd*.[3] Here the owner of a timber mill sold his timber to a company of which he and his nominees were the only shareholders. The company owed him money, and he took it upon himself to insure the company's assets, but did so in his own name (rather than through the company). When the timber was destroyed in a fire and Macaura attempted to claim on the insurance policy, he was informed that he had no insurable interest[4] in the company's assets and was thus ineligible to claim. The company and he were separate legal entities and the insurance should have been made through the company rather than him personally.

Whilst it is true that companies have a separate legal personality, and this is somewhat similar to a human (a natural person) as regards the ability to form contracts, sue and be sued, and be subject to criminal offences, it does not extend to rights such as rights to vote, or to suffer human emotions (such as suffering injured feelings).[5]

- *The veil of incorporation:* Separate legal personality affords a distinction between the corporation as an entity and its directors and shareholders. Further, limited companies have a particular feature: the shareholders have limited liability. The metaphor of the 'veil' identifies a cloak of secrecy/shield of the people behind it—the members of the company are protected from liability for the company's debts. Further, it transpires that due to the company's separate legal personality, the courts have often been unwilling to 'lift the veil' and find out what the directors actually did in running the business (what decisions were taken, and by whom and so on).[6] Due to this demarcation, it has been said that the veil of incorporation protects the members of the company. Whilst the veil is effective, to continue the metaphor, it has been 'raised' by the courts where it has been deemed relevant. The courts have been notoriously unwilling to establish clear rules as to when the veil will be lifted, and they have stated that they will not do so 'merely' in the interests of justice. Further, where one company owns shares in another (subsidiary companies), insofar as the companies are legally distinct then the courts will not seek to lift the veil.[7] However, the company must not be established to commit some fraud[8] or to attempt to circumvent contractual agreements or the veil will be lifted to identify the true nature of the undertaking (for example a 'sham' company).

Gilford Motor Co. Ltd v Horne[9]

Facts:

The defendant was a managing director of the claimant company and was subject to a restraint of trade clause preventing him soliciting Gilford's customers on leaving the business. When his employment was terminated, Horne formed a company and he stated this company employed him, and he began soliciting the customers of Gilford in breach of the

---

[3] [1925] AC 619.

[4] A contract of insurance requires that the person who insures the relevant item would be likely to sustain some loss or be subject to a claim by another who has suffered a loss. Only those with an insurable interest may enforce such a contract.

[5] *Collins Stewart Ltd. v Financial Times Ltd* [2005] EWHC 262.

[6] Unless this involved, for example, the directors having acted fraudulently.

[7] See *Adams v Cape Industries Plc* [1991] 2 WLR 657 for a discussion of the Court of Appeal on why the veil will not be lifted just because the claimant considers the two separate legal entities as one economic undertaking.

[8] *Jones v Lipman* [1962] 1 WLR 832.   [9] [1933] 1 Ch 935.

restraining clause. He argued the clause was binding upon him rather than the company, but the Court of Appeal granted an injunction to restrain him from breaching the clause. It lifted the veil to identify the true nature of Horne's role in the company. The court considered the formation of the company to be a sham.

Authority for:

The veil of incorporation separating the company from its members (with regard to the company's separate legal personality) will be lifted by the courts where the company's formation is a device/stratagem to evade the effects of a contractual term. The veil may be lifted where the company is a 'sham' or has been established to perpetrate a fraud.

22.3 Types of business organization

 Business Link

It is appropriate to be aware of the business that the person wishes to form, along with his/her expectations—does he/she wish to grow the business into a multinational chain? Is he/she seeking to protect a small business from liability? Does he/she wish to enable investors to become shareholders or does he/she simply want to join other persons with a common idea and direction of work? These are a just few of questions that a person will want to consider when determining the trading structure adopted.

22.3.1 Sole traders

A sole trader is the simplest business organization due to the ease of establishing and dissolving the business. The person carries on his/her business as an individual; he/she personally owns the property and assets; he/she generally performs the work, unless he/she employs others or sub-contracts; and, very importantly, he/she has unlimited liability for any acts or omissions of the business. He/she may have a business name, but this does not create a separate legal person as it does for a limited company.

Companies
Act 2006

He/she must conform to the Companies Act 2006, Part 41 which prohibits, for example, a business name suggesting a connection with central or local government or its agencies without the approval of the Secretary of State.[10]

The sole trader is merely responsible to his/herself, his/her customers, and the State (such as registration with Her Majesty's Revenue & Customs (HMRC), and registration for Value Added Tax (if applicable)). This ensures the appropriate taxes are paid and the business can be regulated in conformity with the laws (such as those presented in this text regarding employment, torts, contract, relevant insurance coverage and so on). Therefore there is relatively little external regulation of the business. The sole trader, as a self-employed person, is responsible for his/her end-of-year taxes being prepared on the basis of a self-assessment form submitted in arrears at the end of January each year (unless otherwise agreed). The taxation of earnings is subject to the provisions of the Income Tax (Earnings and Pensions)

---

[10] CA 2006, s. 1193.

Act 2003, whilst the taxation of trading income is subject to the Income Tax (Trading and Other Income) Act 2005.

- *Forming the sole trader business:* As stated above, there are no formal rules regarding the steps to be taken to form such a business enterprise. Insofar as no regulatory requirements exist (such as in professions including lawyers, accountants and so on) the sole trader may begin to trade immediately. The sole trader may also operate the business in whatever way he/she wishes, as he/she does not have to ask the permission of partners or seek to change the nature of the business that may have been included in a memorandum of association (as with a corporation).

- *Bringing the sole trader business to an end:* There are very few formalities when ending the sole trader business. Assuming that tasks as contracted to undertake have been completed, and creditors have been paid (along with any associated taxes/duties owed), the sole trader need only inform the relevant authorities of his/her action to cease trading. Clearly, where the sole trader cannot pay debts associated with the business, there are formalities to do with bankruptcy proceedings (but these are not discussed in this text).

22.3.2 **Partnerships**

A person may wish to form a business enterprise, and may seek to achieve this by forming a partnership with others. There may be many reasons why a partnership may be sought. The partners may complement each other by each offering expertise in some area; they could establish new markets (such as a builder, plumber, and electrician forming a partnership to build houses); new partners may be brought in to introduce capital without obtaining a bank loan; or partners may be able to offer additional help in running the business. As such, they may decide to establish a 'simple' partnership. The most common type of partnership is an unlimited partnership, where the partners are responsible for the debts/liabilities of the firm and must satisfy these from their own assets if required. The partners simply have to agree to form the partnership (hence it need not be in writing (although this may be wise) and it may be formed through verbal agreements or implied through conduct).

A partnership may also trade as a limited partnership under the Limited Partnerships Act 1907. This simply requires one of the partners to agree to accept full liability for any debts if the partnership is unable to satisfy its obligations (while the other partners' loss is restricted to any capital/property invested). The 'limited' partner must also not have any part in the management of the firm or he/she will lose the 'limited' status and be liable with the other partners for any debts or liabilities. These types of partnerships are not often used as a form of business organization but are more likely to be seen in the formation of collective investment schemes. Since 2000, a firm can be established as a Limited Liability Partnership (LLP):

- *Types of partner:* Generally, there are four types of partner in a partnership:
  - Under the Partnership Act 1890, s. 24 the 'typical' partner is one who has the right to take part in the management of the firm (unless specifically agreed to the contrary).
  - A 'silent'/dormant partner may come into the firm who, by his/her nature, invests money into the partnership but who does not take an active role in the management.
  - A firm may usually require a partner to join in the partnership by making some investment and 'buying into' the firm. However, it is possible, and used by some professional firms such as lawyers and accountants, for a person to join the partnership as a salaried

partner. He/she does not have the rights and obligations of the other partners, and is essentially treated as an employee, but appears on the firm's letterheads.

- Where the partner allows his/her name to be used by the partnership, such as on the letterhead of the firm to add to its credibility with outside bodies, the partner may be a partner by estoppel. The Partnership Act 1890, s. 14 provides that where a person, through his/her words (spoken or written) or conduct, either represents him/herself as, or knowingly allows him/herself to be represented as a partner of the firm, he/she is liable as if he/she was a partner of the firm to anyone who contracted with the firm (such as providing credit/money).

Partnership
Act 1890

Similarly with sole trader business organizations, a partnership[11] is simple to create and to dissolve[12] (there are no specific formalities or registration); there is little external regulation (although HMRC must be informed that the self-employed person is a partner rather than a sole trader) other than that already identified for sole traders; and partnerships can commence trading immediately. The partnership is restricted in the choice of business name, and whilst a partnership may use the word 'company' in its business name, it must not identify itself as a limited company or use the initials 'Ltd' and 'Plc' as these are restricted to those organizations that have followed the appropriate registration requirements. The tort of passing-off is also applicable to the business name of the partnership.

Partnerships are two or more persons who come together, and act in common, to form (or with a view to form)[13] a business 'with a view of profit'. This is of crucial importance in that whilst the Act states that the partner joins with a view to a profit, this does not mean that having not shared in any profits they do not qualify as a partner.[14]

- *Identification of partners:* The names of the partners must be shown on the letterheads (and when a business name is used which is different from the true surnames of the partners). This is a requirement identified in the Companies Act (CA) 2006, and applies in the same way as to all business organizations with regard to the choice of business name, and the correct identification of the partners/members.

- *Partnership property:* When a partnership is formed the partners each own the property of the partnership. The Partnership Act 1890, ss. 20 and 21 identify that, in the absence of any agreement between the partners to the contrary, property will be considered partnership property where it had been purchased with partnership money; the partner who brought property into the firm had been credited with its value; or where it is treated as an essential part of the firm's property. Hence when the business is dissolved, the partners will take back the property they brought to the firm. However, if the firm is dissolved owing money to creditors, the creditors have the right to realize partnership assets before the partners can 'take back' property introduced into the business.

- *Partnership ratio:* It is worthy of note that where, for example, two people are intending to join together to form a partnership, it is wise not to arrange it on a 50/50 ratio split. Where the two partners have an equal share of, and right to manage, the firm, inevitably a situation will arise where one of the partners wishes to follow a route (for example,

[11] Partnerships are identified under the Partnership Act 1890 section 1 as the 'relation which subsists between persons carrying on a business in common with a view to profit'.

[12] This can be where the partners wish to end the partnership; if there has been an agreed date to end the partnership; or where a specific act has been completed.

[13] *Khan v Miah* [2001] 1 All ER 20.

[14] *M Young Legal Associates Ltd v Zahid* [2006] EWCA Civ 613.

expanding the business), whilst the other partner is more cautious and does not agree with the strategy (and potential risks). As neither partner has the power to force the decision, the partnership may come to an end with such a disagreement (with the consequent problems entailed).

- *Partners as agents:* Partners are considered agents of the organization under s. 5 of the Partnership Act 1890 for the purpose of the partnership's business.[15] This enables the partners to manage the organization, contract on behalf of the firm, and obligate the other partners as a result of this action (as agents).[16] He/she therefore will bind the other partners and the firm in (lawful) agreements that he/she has concluded. This means that even if a partner does not have the actual authority to perform such actions, he/she may still bind the partnership under 'apparent' authority.[17] The reason why partners may be held liable for the actions of another partner is to protect the public, who may not be aware of the internal power relations within the organization. It is generally accepted that partners can buy and sell goods, take money on behalf of the firm and issue receipts for transactions in the name of the partnership. These rights regarding transactions of this type are more 'securely' granted on partners in a firm that trades as its object, rather than professional firms (such as accountants) whose partners may not readily exercise such authority.

- *Liability of partners:* A crucial aspect of partnerships is of joint and several liability.[18] This means that if one partner commits a tort[19] or crime[20] in the course of the business, the partnership will be liable (including each partner) if this was within the offending partner's actual or apparent authority. This results in the partners being held responsible for any losses incurred whilst they are partners. If the partnership owes a debt to a creditor and there are no resources of the organization to pay this, then under the concept of unlimited liability, the partners have to satisfy the shortfall from their own resources. This liability will be shared equally between the partners based on their respective percentage ownership. However, if one partner has resources and the other partner(s) does not have the resources to satisfy the debt, the partner with funds is responsible for the full debt.[21] He/she then has the responsibility/option to seek the money owed from the defaulting partner(s). This liability cannot be imposed on a partner on acts that occurred before he/she entered the partnership.[22] However, the liability continues even when the partner has left the partnership for acts conducted whilst he/she was a partner. It is therefore important to be aware of the person(s) who may become partners and there are several express and implied terms (obligations) on partners as to information they must disclose to potential partners.

---

[15] This means that the organization is bound by the actions of the partner if the partner has acted in a way that is consistent with the kind of business normally carried out by the organization.

[16] Such authority enables a partner to obligate the firm in the sale of the firm's goods; to purchase goods that would normally be purchased on behalf of the firm; to pay the debts of the firm; and to hire workers.

[17] See **21.3.2**.

[18] Section 9 of the Partnership Act 1890 includes such liability for debts or contracts (as extended under the Civil Liability (Contributions) Act 1978), s. 10 applies the liability for torts committed in the normal course of business (outside of the normal course of business the individual partner is held responsible (*Hamlyn v Houston and Co.* [1905] 1 KB 81)); and further see s. 12 of the Partnership Act 1890.

[19] However, this does not enable one partner to claim against the partnership for a tort committed in the course of business by another partner (*Mair v Wood* [1948] SLT 326.

[20] A particularly interesting case is that of *Dubai Aluminium Co. Ltd v Salaam* [2003] 1 All ER 97.

[21] Under s. 9 of the Partnership Act 1890.

[22] As provided for by s.17 of the Partnership Act 1890.

- *Forming a partnership:* Establishing a partnership is very simple and can amount to an agreement between like-minded people to form a business with a common goal. It is always preferable, however, when forming an agreement that has the potential implications for the partners as identified above, to create a contractually binding agreement. This is referred to as the 'partnership agreement' and identifies for what purpose the partnership is being established; for how long (if a time is identified) the partnership should remain in existence; the names of the partners; the business address where official documentation is to be sent; the percentage ownership and distribution of profits of each partner; the authority for participating in the management of the partnership (if sleeping partners are included); and the responsibilities of each partner.

If new partners are to be included in the partnership (to increase expertise, introduce money and so on), there has to be agreement between the existing partners for this to take effect.[23] This right does not apply to partners who are retiring and its aim is simply to ensure that due to the unlimited liability nature of the business, and the need for the firm to work to a common goal (not to mention the duties on partners that will affect the working relationships of the partners), the new partners are accepted by all other partners who may be affected by their actions.

22.3.2.1 *Duties on partners*

There exists in partnerships a fiduciary duty for the partners to act with loyalty to the partnership and in 'good faith'. The Partnership Act 1890 also creates duties on the partners in the following ways:

- *Duty of disclosure:* Section 28 obligates partners to submit full information to the other partners or his/her legal representatives in matters affecting the organization and to submit true accounts.

- *Duty to account:* Section 29 obligates partners to account for any benefit they have obtained without consent from any transaction on behalf of the firm.[24]

- *Duty not to enter into competition with the organization:* Section 30 obligates a partner, who is competing with the partnership without the consent of the other partners, to account to those partners for any profits or benefit produced in the course of that business.

- *Relationship based on good faith:* The partnership agreement is a contract based on the utmost good faith. As such partners must disclose relevant details to other partners (and prospective partners) that could affect the partnership. As such, a person's silence can amount to a misrepresentation.

22.3.2.2 *The rights of partners*

The Partnership Act 1890 provides the following rights:[25]

- the right to share equally in the capital and profits of the firm;
- the right to be indemnified by the firm for any liabilities or losses made in the normal course of business;
- the right to take a role in the management of the firm (but not 'sleeping partners');

---

[23] Section 24(7) and (8).   [24] *Bentley v Craven* [1853] 18 Beav 75.
[25] Unless this is expressed to the contrary in the partnership agreement.

- an entitlement to inspect the partnership's accounts and to have these available when requested;
- the right to veto the entry of a new partner to the partnership or to change the partnership's business.

22.3.2.3 *Bringing the partnership to an end*

The partnership may be dissolved on the agreement of the partners,[26] or on lapse of time,[27] or when a specific task for which the partnership was created has been completed.[28] It may also be dissolved on the death or bankruptcy[29] of any partner or where there has been illegality[30] on behalf of the partnership.[31] The Partnership Act 1890 continues to identify events affecting the partners that lead to the partnership being brought to an end. These include if a partner becomes a patient under the Mental Capacity Act 2005; if he/she suffers some permanent form of incapacity;[32] if the partner wilfully or persistently breaches the partnership agreement;[33] where the business can only be continued at a loss;[34] and where it is just and equitable to end the partnership.[35] When the business has been brought to an end and the property owned by the partnership is realized, the resources are used to first pay any liabilities; then the partners who have loaned money to the firm are paid back; the capital contribution of the partners is paid; and the remainder is shared on the basis of the percentage of the partnership which each partner 'owned'.

If a partner decides to leave a solvent partnership that intends to continue trading, upon his/her leaving, the partner will be entitled to his/her share of the partnership, and the remaining partner(s) will have to generate the money to provide the settlement. This is often a key concern and disadvantage of partnerships as partners may die, and they often disagree about the business and might feel compelled to leave.

Limited
Liability
Partnerships
Act 2000

22.3.3 Limited liability partnerships

As noted, the partners in simple partnerships (unless in limited partnerships) have unlimited liability for the debts of the firm. The enactment of the Limited Liability Partnerships Act 2000[36] changed this situation, and a partnership created under the Act will be considered a separate legal entity, with its own legal personality. The LLP must be registered with the Registrar of Companies and whilst it has unlimited liability for any debts and liabilities, the individual partners of the LLP have limited liability. This will result in the partners losing any investment into the LLP if it is wound up and insolvent, but they will not be liable for losses beyond this contribution.

As the LLP has its own legal personality, contracts and obligations will be created with the LLP rather than the individual partners. The property of the LLP will also belong to the partnership instead of to the partners. This situation has further advantages over the simple partnership model. As partnerships have to contain at least two individuals, if, in a simple partnership of two partners, one was to die, then the partnership would come to an end (or a

---

[26] Section 32(c).   [27] Section 32(a).   [28] Section 32(b).   [29] Section 33(1).
[30] Illegality can occur where the nature of the business was unlawful (such as *Everet v Williams* [1725] 9 LQ Rev 197; and where the partners cannot form a partnership to conduct an otherwise lawful action (such as the case of a solicitor allowing their practice certificate to lapse).
[31] Section 34.   [32] Section 35(b).   [33] Section 35(d).   [34] Section 35(e).
[35] Section 35(f).   [36] In force from April 2001.

new partner(s) have to be found). With LLPs, the partnership will continue despite changes to its internal membership and it will continue until formally wound up. Typically, professional firms have taken the opportunity to become LLPs where the nature of their profession involves the risk of liability claims (such as negligence) that may expose the partners to risk, if the partnership could not settle any award.

The LLP is required to file its audited accounts and tax returns to the Registrar of Companies and the incorporation document must identify 'designated members' who will administer these and other matters on behalf of the LLP. The taxation of the partners will be based on the simple partnership model, and the individual partners are responsible for their 'share' of the tax due, rather than this being placed on the LLP itself. The partners will have to disclose their proportion of the profits in the annual returns to the Registrar.[37]

- *Forming an LLP*: To form an LLP, the incorporation document and a statement of compliance must be filed with the Registrar of Companies, who will then issue a certificate of incorporation if the documentary requirements have been satisfied. Having received this certificate, the LLP can begin to trade, although, to do so before the certificate is issued may result in the partners being held liable as they would under the Partnership Act 1890. The Registrar must be informed of the members of the LLP, who will maintain a register, and the Registrar must also be informed when new members join and others leave.

  It is imperative when forming the LLP that the partners establish an agreement that incorporates issues regarding the purpose of the business; the capital in the firm and how profit and losses are to be distributed between the members; the requirements of meetings and voting rights; how new members will be allowed to join; the procedures for the retirement of members and so on. The requirement for an agreement is even more prominent when it is remembered that LLPs are regulated somewhat similarly to companies, only there is no default standard set of 'model articles' that exist for companies under the Companies Act (CA) 2006. This document is private, is not subject to public scrutiny, and does not need to be sent to the Registrar of Companies. Hence those who are trading with the LLP have no actual mechanism (beyond asking to see the agreement) to identify the internal structure of the members' responsibilities and rights.

- *Bringing the LLP to an end*: The LLP continues in existence until it is formally **dissolved**, as it possesses its own legal personality irrespective of its members. LLPs can be wound up through its insolvency and, as such, procedures may be established for voluntary arrangements, administration orders, receivership, and liquidation. Section 214A has been beneficial to creditors to the LLP in that members who have made withdrawals in the previous two years before the winding up may be requested to return these sums if during that period the member knew, or ought reasonably to have known, that the LLP would become insolvent. Section 74 ensures that members of the LLP and those members that have left, and who had established an agreement to contribute to the LLP upon **dissolution**, will contribute to the assets of the firm.

22.3.4 **Formation of a company**

This section considers the types of companies and the methods of formation (or incorporation) that have to be satisfied. Due to the complexity of the topic, this introductory chapter identifies some important features that will be considered in greater depth in Chapters 23–25.

---

[37] Limited Liability Partnerships Regulations 2001.

- *The Registrar of Companies and Companies House:* The Department for Business Innovation & Skills is the department where most of the laws relating to businesses generally will be considered, consulted upon, and advanced through Parliament. It has a section dealing with the registration of companies and it ensures compliance with the requirements established under legislation, including the CA 2006, and is called Companies House. This is where the public can find out information regarding companies and their directors (details are available for public inspection), and the 'Registrar of Companies' heads this department. The Registrar is responsible for the issuing of certificates of incorporation when a company is registered, when the company's name is changed, and where the company is re-registered. It lists the details of all registered companies, limited partnerships, and LLPs; holds the annual returns and accounts submitted by companies as required by law; and maintains the details of charges over company property. It may strike companies off the register when dissolved; holds the register of a company's special and extraordinary resolutions; and publishes details of the companies and the receipt of documents in the *London Gazette*.[38]

- *Unlimited companies:* Very few companies are registered as unlimited companies as the members of the company have unlimited liability, and this significant protection for the members through incorporation is lost. An advantage of trading as an unlimited company is that its accounts are not made public and do not have to be submitted to the Registrar of Companies. However, these are somewhat weak reasons to establish the corporation on this basis, particularly in respect of the deregulation of limited companies through the CA 2006. The liability of members exists in situations where the company is wound up, rather than to the company's creditors. Clearly though, where the company does not have sufficient funds to satisfy its debts, the company will be wound up and the members of the company are liable on the basis of the nominal value of the shares held. If no share capital is held, then the members will be liable on an equal basis, and held jointly and severally liable.

- *Limited companies:* This is a very popular form of business enterprise and the changes introduced in the CA 2006 remove many of the administrative procedures that were required under the Companies Act 1985. The two main types of limited companies are private limited companies and public limited companies, and this will be identified upon registration through the memorandum of association. It may be thought that only large organizations are corporations, but of course the majority are small and medium-sized enterprises, with just a few shareholders. The majority of companies formed are limited by shares and this identifies that the members of the company (the shareholders) are responsible for the nominal/par value of the shares they own if the company is wound up. The second example of a limited company is one that is limited by guarantee.[39] The 'guarantee' in this respect is a determined amount, established in the memorandum (and possibly in the articles as well), which is to be paid when the company is wound up. Upon being wound up, the sums guaranteed have to be paid to satisfy the company's debts, and where this amount is insufficient in relation to the debt, those members that left within a year of the company's winding up can be requested to contribute their guarantee in relation to the debts that occurred whilst they were members.

---

[38] The weekly supplement of the publication of the Stationery Office that identifies public notices such as bankruptcies and liquidations of corporations and so on.

[39] Usually a method chosen by charitable institutions rather than 'businesses'.

- *Corporations sole:* The very nature of a company, when compared to a sole trader for example, is that it conjures images of a number of persons joining together to run a business. Whilst this may be the case, a corporation may involve just one person (member). This was typically seen where the Bishop or vicar of a parish had a vested interest in the church land, but when he died, the land technically had no owner until the clergyman's successor was found. In response to this, it was established by common law that the office of the Bishop/vicar was a corporation with the present incumbent the sole member. Consequently, when the clergyman died, this did not affect the status of the corporation; the land still belonged to the corporation, and the next Bishop/vicar simply became the new 'sole member'.

22.3.5 Features of a limited company

When determining the form of business organization, a corporation, being a separate entity from its members, provides advantages to those members, and also empowers the company to take actions, accept liabilities and so on that other business organizations may not. Therefore, some of its more important features are identified below:

- *Limited liability:* Always remember that the 'limited' element of this type of organization refers to the potential liability of members of the company—the shareholders. The company itself has unlimited liability and therefore must satisfy any debts to creditors. If there are insufficient funds and assets to pay the creditors when the debts are called in, the money that is available in the company (its money, property, stock and so on) will be made available to creditors depending upon their status. The shareholders have their liability for any debts of the company limited to the value they paid for the shares (which will become worthless as the company will be wound up) or the money they owe on any shares (shares do not necessarily have to be fully paid for when issued). It provides protection for the shareholders as to the liability they are exposing themselves to, but also imposes a risk for those trading with the limited company that they may not be able to seek owed money from those who ran or owned the business.

- *Perpetual succession:* One of the drawbacks with trading as a sole trader is that when the sole trader dies, the business may die with him/her. With a partnership of two people, where one dies another partner has to be found or the firm wound up or run as a sole trader/registered as a corporation. The advantage to the limited company is that once established, it will remain in existence until it is legally wound up, regardless of who owns or runs the company. Therefore when shareholders leave the company, a director dies/leaves the organization and so on, this has no effect on the company's assets or ability to continue trading. As businesses invest time and resources establishing a reputation (trustworthy image, reputation for a quality service/products and so on), the ability to continue this 'brand image' when the company is sold or other directors take charge of its operation and direction is a significant advantage.

- *Raising finance:* It has been argued that a limited company may be able to raise capital investment and finance more easily than can a sole trader and a partnership. The sole trader and partnership will generally have to secure loans from a lending institution through a charge over the assets (providing collateral). Due to the increased regulation and reporting duties imposed on limited companies, and the controlled use of funds, lenders may be more willing to make loans to improve a business. There is the further benefit of being able to transfer/sell shares to generate income that may be used and, unlike a loan, this does not have to be paid back.

- *Contractual capacity:* (Due to its separate legal personality) the company may establish contracts in its own right and enforce contracts when the other party is in breach, although a director of the company must physically undertake this.

- *Taxation:* Taxation of companies' profits may be more beneficial than personal income tax. This, evidently, is a simplification of a very complex area, and requires greater detailed examination than can be provided in this text, but tax has to be paid on taxable profits. Income tax (applicable to sole traders and partnerships) is charged[40] at 10 per cent (the starting rate), rising to 40 per cent (the higher rate) where the person's income exceeds £34,371; and 50 per cent (the additional rate) for incomes over £150,000. The main corporation tax is charged[41] at 23 per cent, whilst for small companies the rate remains at 20 per cent until 1 April 2012. Hence it may prove advantageous to trade as a limited company to benefit from the levels of taxation.

- *Administration:* Whereas the sole trader and partnership are largely accountable to themselves, their partners (where relevant), the client/customer, and HMRC, the limited company has much greater administrative burdens that are required through the CA 2006. This may include submitting company accounts to Companies House as required; holding an Annual General Meeting (although this is not required for private companies); and so on. These are not applicable to sole traders/partnerships and as such they are a more 'simple' way of trading.

- *The ability to own property:* A company has the ability to own property irrespective of the composition of the shareholders. The person who forms the company may introduce property to it (for example, houses in a property rental business). If the person owns this property in his/her own right, and then 'gives' it to the company, he/she is owed the money of the value of the property passed over to the company and, whilst stamp duty may be applicable, the person who formed the company will be able to receive the value of the property back from the company. However, the property is no longer owned by the person who gave/sold it to the company; rather it legally belongs to the company. Such assets may be used to raise finance.

- *Commit criminal offences:* It is possible for a company to commit a criminal offence (through the criminal intent (*mens rea*) of the directors).[42] This has particularly been effective in cases of the manslaughter of persons, where the directors of companies may be convicted and imprisoned on the basis of their actions (health and safety laws are instrumental in this aspect of the law).[43]

22.3.6 Distinctions between public and private companies

A Public Limited Company (PLC) is entitled to offer its shares and debentures for sale to the public and it may be listed on the London Stock Market (although due to the rules in which companies may be listed this is only applicable to the largest organizations). A private company is prohibited from offering its shares to the public.[44] Shares do not have to be paid for in full on allocation but with a PLC, the shares must be paid for when requested (such as upon

---

[40] At 2012/13 rates.   [41] At 2012/13 rates.   [42] *R v ICR Haulage Ltd* [1944] KB 551.

[43] See the Online Resource Centre for a discussion of the Corporate Manslaughter and Corporate Homicide Act 2007 regarding the criminal actions of directors and organizations.

[44] CA 2006 s. 755.

Table 22.1 The advantages/disadvantages of the trading structures

Business Organization	Advantages	Disadvantages
Sole Trader	It is simple to establish.	The sole trader has unlimited liability.
	The sole trader is responsible to him/herself and his/her customers.	Succession. The sole trader often trades under his/her own name, however, when the sole trader dies, his/her business may also die.
	The sole trader has autonomy in how he/she runs the business, when he/she works, and how profits are disposed of (subject to HMRC rules).	He/she has complete responsibility for the business—to fulfill contracts; to invest money into the business; to employee replacement if he/she is ill or on holiday and so on.
	He/she can begin trading immediately.	
Partnership	Partners often 'buy into' a partnership, therefore capital is often introduced.	Partnerships have unlimited liability and the partners' personal assets may be at risk for debts/losses.
	Partners may offer expertise in an area or provide the ability to enter into new markets.	Partners may create liabilities for the other partners and the firm.
	Partners may share the work of the business and share the liabilities.	Partners share in the profits of the firm therefore the individual partner's share may be reduced.
	Partners have several legal advantages including the ease of formation and it can be quickly dissolved, and it may provide tax advantages in certain circumstances.	Partners may be jointly and severally liable for losses.
Limited Liability Partnership	The LLP has its own legal personality and limits the liability of its members.	It is subject to registration procedures with the Registrar of Companies.
	The partnership continues despite changes in the internal membership of the firm.	It must file accounts and tax returns to the Registrar.
		It has many features in common with limited companies, some of these are positive to the members and many have negative implications.
Limited Companies	Limited liability for the members.	It has much greater administration requirements than other forms of business organizations.
	It has perpetual succession and only 'dies' when formally wound up.	It is subject to external and internal regulation.
	It is generally easier to raise finance than through a sole trader/partnership business organization.	There is no automatic right to participate in the management of the company.
	It can make contracts in its own right.	
	Tax benefits are available for corporations compared to other business organizations.	
	The company may offer fixed/floating charges over property.	
	Companies may be formed in the belief that the 'status' of a limited company provides an advantage over operating as a sole trader.	

its winding up). This must be in the form of money or assets, but when assets are provided, the value must be independently assessed by an auditor to ensure they represent the value of the owed amount and that a fraud is not being committed on the business.

The private company has become much less regulated and hence more favourable to those who run businesses than before. For example, the necessity to opt out of holding an Annual General Meeting (AGM) has been removed; there is no limit on the private company's share capital; and it need only have one shareholder, with no need for a company secretary. Private companies may also pass written resolutions without the need to hold a meeting. A PLC also only requires one member, but it does require a secretary and he/she must be qualified for the position (a solicitor, accountant, or someone who has three years' experience of being a public company secretary). The PLC may not be unlimited and must have an allotted share capital of £50,000 (one-quarter of the value of which must have been paid up)[45] and this information has to be sent to the Registrar. Without this information a trading certificate will not be issued and if one is not requested within one year of incorporation, an application may be made for its compulsory winding up. Without a trading certificate, the company may not trade, but if it does, the directors of the company may be held liable (on the same basis as with a partnership) for any debts/liabilities incurred. The PLC must hold an AGM each calendar year.

- *Size of the company:* Companies are identified on their size and this has implications for the documents to be submitted to the Registrar. Companies identified as small have to satisfy two or more of the following requirements in a financial year:[46]
    - a turnover of not more than £6.5 million;
    - a balance sheet total of not more than £3.26 million; and
    - not more than 50 employees (as a weekly/monthly average).

  However, the small companies regime does not apply to PLCs or a company that is an authorized insurance company, a banking company, an e-money issuer; an MiFID[47] investment firm; or a UCTIS management company or a member of an ineligible group. The small company regime allows for abridged accounts to be submitted to the Registrar (although members have the right to be provided with full accounts but may agree to be sent 'summary of financial statements'[48] instead).[49] The advantage of this provision is that sensitive information, such as the salaries of directors, the directors' report, and a profit and loss account, need not be submitted.

  A medium-sized company has similar rights to submit abridged accounts where it satisfies two of the three following requirements in a financial year:
    - a turnover of not more than £25.9 million;
    - a balance sheet total of not more than £12.9 million; and
    - not more than 250 employees (as a weekly/monthly average).

22.3.7 Establishing the limited company

There are three methods of establishing the limited company—either through Royal Charter; statute; or (most commonly and applicable to this text) through registration.

---

[45] Most shares are paid for in full as soon as they are bought but this is not always required, although on winding up, any outstanding money must be paid.

[46] As amended by SI 2008/393.   [47] SI 2007/2932.   [48] Section 426.

[49] Although the cost implications of producing summary financial statements may make their use unlikely.

Table 22.2 Comparison of private and public companies

Private Company	Public Company
Its name must end with the words 'Ltd' or ' Limited.'	Its name must end with the words 'Public Limited Company' or 'plc.'
A private company is prohibited from offering its shares to the public (CA 2006 s. 755).	A PLC is entitled to offer its shares and debentures for sale to the public and it may be listed on the London Stock Exchange (although due to the Exchange's rules about which companies may be listed this is only applicable to the largest organizations).
A private company is not required to have a secretary (and if a private company chooses to have one he/she does not have to be qualified).	A PLC requires a secretary and he/she must be qualified for the position.
There is no necessity to hold an Annual General Meeting (AGM)	The PLC must hold an AGM each calendar year.
'No minimum share capital is prescribed.'	The PLC must have an allotted share capital of £50,000 (one quarter of the value of which must have been paid up).
Only one director is required.	At least two directors are required.
It can pass written resolutions.	It cannot pass written resolutions.

- *Royal Charter:* This is a mechanism for establishing companies, but as one can imagine, it will not be established for the means of trading (where registration under the Companies Act is more relevant). Examples of the Royal Charter being used to establish a company can be seen in the British Broadcasting Corporation, and universities such as Oxford and Cambridge. The Privy Council is the body that would establish a company in this manner.

- *Statute:* Statutes have been used to create corporations, such as the utilities, where, upon privatization, their status had to be altered as they were no longer owned by the State and did not possess the powers that the State did in relation to the purchase of land and so on. As such, these bodies were registered as PLCs. Statute has also been used to establish bodies such as the Health and Safety Executive, which regulates health and safety inspections and was established through the Health and Safety at Work etc. Act 1974.

- *Registration:* The most common and, in relation to the three forms available, the simplest way to form a company is through registration with the Registrar of Companies.

22.3.8 Procedures of registration

When a company is formed in the UK, the Registrar of Companies must be sent the memorandum of association, the articles of association, and a completed Form IN01, along with the appropriate registration fee (£40),[50] by the founding member(s) (also known as the

---

[50] This is the standard paper filing fee (it is £18 for electronic filing). A premium service is available for £100 for paper filing where all the documents are sent before 3pm and hand delivered, the certificate of incorporation will be issued on the same day.

subscribers). If the Registrar is satisfied the documents are correct, a certificate of incorporation is issued, identifying the company with its registered number, and the new company will be noted in the *London Gazette*. If the registrar is not satisfied that the documents are correct, or suspects the company is being established for some unlawful means, he/she can refuse to register the company, and the subscribers have an opportunity to appeal the decision.

22.3.8.1 *The memorandum*

The memorandum is a document available for public inspection and its aim is to identify the features of the company. It is not intended to form part of the company's constitution as it previously had, but rather to identify the company when it was formed. Essentially this was an attempt to simplify the provision of company law and to provide the details of the constitution of companies in one document. Hence the memorandum is almost supplementary to the articles of association[51] and unless the company specifically restricts the remit of the objects of the company, its objects are unrestricted.[52] The elements that establish the memorandum include:

- *Its name:* There are restrictions on the choice of business name that a company may use, and the use of words and symbols in the name,[53] and guidance is provided through Companies House.[54] From 1 September 2011, Companies House will no longer accept company names on documents that contain minor variations and/or typographical errors. A list of acceptable abbreviations is provided on its website.[55] Evidently, a company may not choose the same name as another company (a directory exists for the purposes of checking);[56] nor may a name be used that is likely to cause offence, or one that infers a connection with local or central government. When a name is selected, it is registered on a 'first come, first served'[57] basis and therefore names cannot be saved. The name must end in Ltd or Limited where it refers to a private limited company (or its Welsh equivalent if the company is based there) or PLC (or the Welsh equivalent) in relation to a public limited company, and this must be published on company documents. This name must be displayed outside of the registered office, and placed on all company stationary, invoices, receipts[58] and so on. The name of the company may be changed through a special resolution, or through a written resolution of a private company, or other means provided for in the articles.[59] The Registrar must be informed of such changes and will then issue a new certificate of incorporation.

- *The registered office:* The company must identify an address where correspondence from the Registrar and from Companies House may be sent. There is no requirement over the use of an address insofar as it is based in England or Wales, and the address is effective for delivering documents, to ensure that unnecessary delays can be avoided.

  The memorandum and articles may be obtained from a company formation agent or a law stationer. Companies House will supply the new-style memorandum and a limited company will be able to use the relevant model articles where it wishes.[60]

---

[51] Section 28.   [52] Section 31(1).

[53] CA 2006 provides in s. 57 for the Secretary of State to prohibit the use of words that may make the tracing of a company difficult.

[54] http://www.companieshouse.gov.uk/about/gbhtml/gbf2.shtml.

[55] http://www.companieshouse.gov.uk/infoAndGuide/faq/companyNamePolicy.shtml.

[56] http://www.companieshouse.gov.uk/about/chips1.shtml.

[57] And as such it is recommended that electronic copies of forms be submitted to speed up the process.

[58] These materials must also include the company's registration number.

[59] CA 2006, s. 77.   [60] CA 2006, s. 20.

22.3.8.2 *The articles*

The articles refer to the constitution of the company and how it may run its affairs. This is the contractual agreement between the parties and the company, and may be established on the basis of a bespoke set of articles, or the company will use the default model articles included in the CA 2006. The articles of a company may be altered at a later date through a special resolution[61] and s. 22 allows for the entrenchment of articles to enable the amendment or repeal of specified provisions in the articles where conditions are met, or procedures are complied with that are more restrictive than those applicable in cases of a special resolution.

22.3.8.3 *Form IN01*

'Form IN01' identifies (among others) the first director(s) and his/her personal details including his/her age, occupation and details of previous directorships held in the previous five years; the secretary of the company;[62] the company's registered office, and must again be authenticated by the subscribers.

The Registrar of Companies maintains the documents and makes them available for public inspection.

22.3.8.4 *The certificate of incorporation*

The company is established when the Registrar of Companies issues the certificate of incorporation. This document formally establishes the existence of the company and it will only 'die' when it is formally wound up. The certificate provides the company with its legal status and personality that will enable it to trade and establish the contracts that enable the 'business' to begin. If the promoters of the company establish contracts on the behalf of the company before the certificate is provided, they may be held personally liable and they will not obtain the protection from the limited liability status of the organization.[63] However, the individual will be in a position to enforce the contract on his/her own behalf, in the case of a breach.[64] This is where the promoter of the company has not informed the other party of the lack of incorporated status. Section 51(1) provides that the person is liable 'subject to any agreement to the contrary' and therefore if this is specifically identified to the other party and this party accepts that upon the certificate being provided the company will ratify the agreement, then the company may be subsequently bound (assuming the other party could be convinced to agree to this!).

22.3.8.5 *Re-registration of the company*

The private company and PLC may choose to re-register between the two statuses, and once completed a new certificate of incorporation is issued. The company will thereafter be subject to the rules applicable to the newly formed business. For the private company to re-register as a PLC, a special resolution must be passed through s. 90 to enable a change in the articles and memorandum to comply with the requirement to incorporate to a PLC. The documents outlined above have to be submitted to the Registrar, with the request to the change in status, and a report by the private company's auditors that the amounts of capital are as required under the CA 2006.

A PLC may re-register as a private company through a special resolution. Section 97 CA 2006 requires that all of the company's members have assented to its being so re-registered. Due to the nature of the PLC and the requirement for protection of the minority shareholders,

---

[61] Section 21.

[62] This person can be both a director and secretary where there are two or more members of the company. Where there is only one member, they must have someone else to act as secretary.

[63] Section 51(1).   [64] *Braymist Ltd v Wise Finance Co. Ltd* [2002] EWCA Civ 127.

s. 98 provides that shareholders with a minimum of 5 per cent of the nominal value of the issued share capital, or if the company is not limited by shares by a minimum of 5 per cent of its members, or a minimum of 50 members, may apply within 28 days of the resolution, to a court to have the special resolution terminated and become unenforceable as they were not in favour. It is for the court to determine whether the resolution should be enforced or not.

22.3.8.6 *Buying an off-the-shelf company*

Due to the perceived problems that some people may have in completing the relevant forms and keeping up to date with the changes in company law and submitting the required documents, a simpler option may be to purchase a company from an agent. Such agencies are quite common and their service is to issue a company that has already been registered and they may also (for additional costs) act as company secretary for a given period of time to ensure all the necessary paperwork and documents are filed with Companies House. The agent that has established the company will sell this company to the purchaser and then resign as director/secretary and inform Companies House of this matter (having appointed the purchaser as the new director/secretary). This is undoubtedly a quick method of establishing the company, but there are issues to be considered. This may be a 'recycled' company and if the company has previously traded, any bad credit and so on will be passed on to the purchaser (as the company number originally issued will remain). This could have serious implications for future credit and financial matters. Hence, they should be used with caution.

22.3.8.7 *Passing-off*

This is an important issue to recognize when determining the implications of a company's name.[65] The tort occurs where the company is given a name that is very similar to an existing business and it gives the (misleading) impression that the two companies are connected. As noted above, businesses often rely on their name and brand image to promote confidence to customers and retain and win new customers, therefore a company that is formed to take (unfair) advantage of this name may have to change its name (and be faced with a possible tort action for damages). An objection can be raised with the Registrar regarding the names of the companies and only the Registrar can decide whether the name should be changed (this is not a decision of the courts).[66] Whilst the motive of the subscriber of the company is not the primary concern in the issue of whether the company name should be changed, if he/she has acted to deliberately mislead customers into thinking the company is linked with another with a similar name, this will be negatively viewed by the courts.

Croft v Day [67]

Facts:

A very famous firm that made boot polish ('Day & Martin') had been established and named after the founders (who by the time of this case were deceased). Their business was bought by Mr Croft, who continued trading under the same name. Soon after, a Mr Day and Mr Martin started a business in the same profession and established the same business name on the basis of convincing (and misleading) potential buyers that the company was the same as the original. The court held that the new entrants to the market had attempted to pass the business off as the original, and granted Croft an injunction to prohibit the use of the new busi-

---

[65] For general information regarding this tort see section 26.5.5.

[66] *Halifax Plc v Halifax Repossessions Ltd* [2004] EWCA Civ 331.   [67] [1843] 7 Beav. 84.

Authority for:

Where a business name is already in existence, the use of the same/very similar name by others in attempt to confuse or mislead the public as to believing they are dealing with the original will be considered a breach of 'passing off". (This is the rule insofar as the requirements for breach of that tort are satisfied).

In relation to a misleading registered company name, a complaint may be made by a person who possesses the goodwill in a name, adversely affected by the misleading company name, to the Company Names Adjudicator,[68] who can order that the name be changed.[69]

22.3.8.8 *Bringing the company to an end*

As the text continues with issues such as the winding up of the company and the methods that may adopted to achieve this, bringing the company to an end is considered in **23.8**.

 Conclusion

This chapter has begun the process of considering the forms of business organization available and the implications of trading as each. The sole trader and partnerships are relatively simple organizations and hence they will not be investigated further. However, as corporations are complex, with detailed rules regarding how they are administered and governed, this will form the majority of the consideration of the remainder of this part of the text. This has been a deliberately introductory chapter and the text continues to detail the internal structures of companies, and how they operate.

 Summary of main points

Legal personality

- Natural persons and businesses established as corporations possess their own legal personality.
- The legal personality of a company exists irrespective of the members or directors who carry out its functions.
- The legal personality of a company separates the company from those who own it. However, the courts may lift this 'veil' (reluctantly) to identify the true nature of the business.

Sole traders

- There is no legal distinction between the sole trader as an individual and the person running the business.
- The sole trader is a very simple business organization with very little internal or external regulation.

---

[68] Appointed by the Secretary of State.

[69] CA 2006, s. 69. This has been supplemented by the Company Names Adjudicator Rules 2008, S.I. 1738/2008.

- The sole trader business can be formed and dissolved easily, and it does not require any special formalities other than informing the relevant government departments.

Partnerships

- A partnership involves two or more people coming together to establish a business.
- A partnership can be 'simple', 'limited', or a 'Limited Liability Partnership'.
- Partners may be 'typical/general', 'salaried', or a partner by estoppel.
- Many rights and obligations exist for partners in simple and limited partnerships including good faith, disclosure, and to account.
- Partners generally have the right to participate in the management of the firm and may bind the partnership through the exercise of actual or apparent authority.
- Bringing a partnership to an end is a relatively simple procedure, and the Partnership Act 1890 identifies specific reasons for its dissolution.

Limited Liability Partnerships

- Unlike sole traders and simple partnerships, LLPs have a separate legal personality and limited liability for members.
- They are regulated in similar ways to a company and are subject to some aspects of the CA 2006.

Companies

- Companies are artificial things that have their own legal personality.
- Companies may be limited or unlimited.
- PLCs require a minimum of £50,000 allotted share capital on registration.
- There are exemptions from certain administrative duties for small/medium-sized companies.
- Limited companies may be formed by Royal Charter, statute, but most commonly through registration.
- The subscribers to a limited company must submit the memorandum, articles, and form IN01 to the Registrar of Companies.
- Companies can be re-registered to reflect changes in their circumstances.
- Rather than forming the limited company, one may be bought 'off-the-shelf' through an agency.
- Regulations exist regarding the choice of business name.
- Businesses must ensure the name of the company is not too similar/the same as another company or they may be guilty of the tort of 'passing-off'.

 Summary questions

Essay questions

1. '*Salomon v Salomon* was wrongly decided. Its implications have allowed corporations to defraud innocent customers and suppliers, and it has facilitated the creation of sham

companies with the protection afforded by the veil of incorporation. Corporations should not possess a legal personality distinct from those who subscribe to it'

Critically assess the above statement.

2. Identify the rights and duties imposed on partners, and assess how effective they are in maintaining trust and good faith.

Problem questions

1. Delia Smythe runs a small catering service from her home, providing hot lunches for the management of 3 firms in Sheffield. She has two employees—a driver and an assistant cook. She would like to bid for catering contracts at more firms and possibly expand into catering for private dinner parties, but could not do all this from her home. She is worried about how she would manage the operation. One of her worries is that she has no experience beyond institutional catering.

Advise Ms Smythe about alternative forms of business organization available to her, explaining the advantages and disadvantages as they apply to her situation. Which form of business would you advise her to adopt? (Visit the Online Resource Centre where a completed IN01 form is provided if Ms Smythe intended to form a private limited company.)

2. Paula has been approached by Jackson and Taylor Estates to join the partnership operating a property development and rental business. Jeffrey (Jackson), one of the partners, speaks with Paula about the offer and Paula agrees. She does not invest money into the business, but rather she says that she has expertise of negotiating good deals with builders, and has 'contacts' in the local Council which will assist on development applications, and advance knowledge of policies and plans likely to be adopted by the Council. Both existing partners—Jeffrey and Barbara (Taylor)—welcome Paula to the partnership and amend the partnership agreement to account for her addition to the business.

Sometime after her arrival, Paula approaches her fellow partners with a business opportunity. There is a somewhat dilapidated building which would be prime for development and she has heard from her contacts that once developed, the Council would provide permission to convert its use to residential accommodation. This would dramatically increase its value, but a quick sale was essential to obtain the premises for fear the owner could decide against selling. The partners agree and the property is purchased. It transpires that the property is in very poor repair, to such an extent that it is dangerous. It contains a structural fault so severe that no valuation expert will provide a quote as to its insurable value. Further, unknown to Jeffrey or Barbara, Paula owns the property, she knew of its condition, and had been trying (unsuccessfully) to sell it for years.

When approached, the Council refuse permission to convert the building to residential accommodation. This has nothing to do with its condition or repair, but simply that any such application in that area would be refused. Paula had essentially misled the partners as to her 'contacts'—which is actually a receptionist on the front desk who occasionally hears gossip (usually about members of staff rather than secret plans or policies).

Finally, when the partnership applies for a loan to fund the purchase of the property, they are refused due to failing a credit check. They had never experienced this before Paula's introduction, and upon further investigation, they discover Paula has County Court Judgments against her and some quite serious criminal convictions. Paula never disclosed this information because 'she was never asked'.

Advise the parties as to their legal rights and duties under partnership law.

 **Further reading**

Bourne, N. (2010) 'Bourne on Company Law' (5th Edition), Routledge-Cavendish: London.

Hawkey, J. (2005) 'Sale or Succession? How to Plan for a Successful Business Exit' How to Books: Oxford.

Whittaker, J. and Machell, J. (2009) 'The Law of Limited Liability Partnerships' (3rd Edition), Bloomsbury Professional: Haywards Heath.

 Useful websites

 http://www.companieshouse.gov.uk/
(Information regarding the establishing of business organizations, forms to speed up the process, and general company advice.)

 http://www.bis.gov.uk/policies/business-law/company-and-partnership-law/company-law
(The website of the Department for Business Innovation & Skills, covering practical advice on the Companies Act 2006 for companies and individuals.)

 Online Resource Centre

 http://www.oxfordtextbooks.co.uk/orc/marson3e/
Why not visit the Online Resource Centre and try multiple choice questions associated with this chapter to test your understanding of the topic. You will also find relevant updates to the law.

Corporate Administration

23

Why does it matter?

The members of a company, whilst delegating the day-to-day management of the business to directors and possessing no automatic rights of management themselves, can play a significant role in the company's administration. Depending on the shares held and the rights attached, shareholders may attend meetings, vote on resolutions, and even seek to remove directors or wind up the company. The members can therefore seek to protect their interests and hold the directors to account. The method of bringing a company to an end is also particularly important to the members and creditors of a company. Take, for example, Northern Rock Plc, which had to be nationalized, adversely affecting the shareholders. Therefore this chapter identifies the rights of members in the decision-making of the company and how the company, its members, and creditors may protect themselves from severe losses when the company may be in financial difficulties. Investing in a company involves risk, but with vigilant administration, these risks can, at least in part, be minimized.

Learning outcomes

Following reading this chapter you should be in a position to:

- identify when a company acquires the capacity to begin trading (23.3)
- understand the rights of members to oblige the company to call a meeting and circulate details and information of the resolutions to be moved (23.4–23.5)
- explain the various resolutions that may be moved at meetings and the procedures involved (23.5)
- explain the significance of a written resolution procedure and which business may not be moved through this mechanism (23.5–23.5.3)
- identify the requirements for the recording and maintenance of these records of the business at meetings, and of resolutions moved (23.7)
- explain the mechanisms for a company being wound up and the procedures involved (23.8–23.8.2.1).

> ## 🔑 Key terms
>
> These terms will be used in the chapter and it may be helpful to be aware of what they mean or refer back to them when reading through the chapter.
>
> **Administrator**
> An officer of the court (whether or not appointed by the court) appointed with the objective of rescuing the company as a going concern; achieving a better result for creditors than would be likely if the company were wound up; or to realize the company's property to make a distribution to secured and preferential creditors.
>
> **Official Receiver**
> This is a civil servant of the Insolvency Service (part of the Department for Business Innovation & Skills) and an officer of the court. He/she is appointed on a bankruptcy or winding-up order and administers the initial stages, and possibly a longer period, of the insolvency of the company.
>
> **Pre-emption rights**
> This is the right of shareholders to be offered new issues of shares before they are made available to non-shareholders.
>
> **Quoted company**
> This is a company whose equity share capital has been included in the Official List in accordance with the provisions of Part 6 of the Financial Services and Markets Act 2000, or is officially listed in an EEA state, or admitted for dealing on the New York Stock Exchange or Nasdaq.
>
> **Winding-up**
> This is the process of bringing a company to an end. As a corporation possesses its own separate legal personality, it must be formally wound up to 'die'.

23.1 Introduction

Having outlined the various forms of business organization available and the mechanisms for establishing each, this chapter begins the process of explaining the mechanisms for the company's administration. This is due to the regulation that is placed on companies through the legislation, including the Companies Act (CA) 2006. Companies have to register with Companies House in order to obtain a trading certificate; regulation exists with regard to the activities of a company's directors; members of the company have the right to participate in meetings and vote on resolutions that are to be moved; procedures must be followed when moving resolutions; and board meetings have to be conducted in accordance with rules and procedures required by statute.

23.2 Companies Act 2006

The CA 2006 was a major reform to the laws governing companies and their relations with third parties and the members of the company. Whilst the law codified many of the existing laws (approximately one-third of the legislation), much of it was new and as such it may be some years before the issues are fully tested and analysed through the courts. However, this is a major piece of legislation, the largest single Act ever enacted, but it is hoped that it will make the provisions of governance of companies more accessible, less bureaucratic, and simpler to understand.

23.3 Capacity to trade

Whilst a private company has the capacity to trade immediately upon incorporation, a public company that has been newly formed must receive a trading certificate from the Registrar of Companies before it may begin trading and other activities involved in a business (such as borrowing money and so on).[1] This certificate is only provided where the Registrar is satisfied that the public company's nominal value of allotted share capital is not less than the authorized minimum of £50,000 (or the prescribed Euro equivalent).[2] For the purposes of this section of the Act, the company must have at least one-quarter of the nominal value of the share plus the whole of any premium paid up (not including shares allotted under an employees' share scheme unless one-quarter of the nominal value is paid up). The application for the certificate must include details of the costs in establishing the company and a statement of compliance with the requirements of the Act. When these formalities are completed, the Registrar will issue the certificate, and publish the receipt of the details in the *London Gazette*. This certificate provides the company with the authority to begin trading. Where it trades without the certificate (and in breach of s. 761), the company and every officer who is in default commit an offence, and he/she is subject to a fine. However, a contravention of trading before the certificate is granted does not invalidate the transaction, but the directors are jointly and severally liable to indemnify any other party to the transaction in respect of any loss or damage suffered by the company's failure to comply with its obligations.[3]

23.4 Company meetings

Whilst the members of the company delegate the powers of the management of the company to the directors, who themselves conduct decision-making through powers granted to them and through their own board meetings, the members themselves take responsibility for moving resolutions of the company. These resolutions are used to perform functions of the company, and some are more onerous to move than others due to the nature of what the resolution intends to achieve. These are discussed in **23.5**. However, the meetings of the members are conducted as follows.

There exist two types of meeting that a company may call: the Annual General Meeting (AGM) and general meetings. Private companies have the option of not holding AGMs but they must hold meetings where required by the members, the courts, or where, for example, directors or auditors are to be removed. Public companies are required to hold an AGM every financial year (but have the option of holding more than this minimum requirement where it is deemed appropriate). In order to move resolutions that will be considered effective,

---

[1] CA 2006, s. 761.

[2] CA 2006, s. 763, although the currency used may later be changed if required.

[3] CA 2006, s. 767.

the CA 2006 identifies several procedures that must be fulfilled to ensure that the business conducted at general meetings is fair to the members. Resolutions may be moved at general meetings insofar as notice of the meeting and the resolution is given to the members of the company. Further, the meeting must be held and conducted in accordance with the CA 2006 and the company's articles.[4] The calling of these meetings is a power granted to the directors of a company;[5] however, where the director(s) does not call a meeting and the members wish one to take place these members have the power to require the directors to take this action.[6]

23.4.1 The request for a meeting

The directors are required to call the meeting in either of the following circumstances:

1 where they have received the request from members representing at least the required percentage of the paid-up capital of the company as carries the right of voting at general meetings; or

2 in the case of a company not having a share capital, members who represent at least the required percentage of the total voting rights of all member possessing the right to vote at general meetings. The percentages required are identified in s. 303 as 10 per cent unless, in the case of a private company, more than 12 months has elapsed since the end of the last general meeting—called in pursuance of a requirement under this section of the Act. Or in relation to which any members of the company had rights with respect to the circulation of a resolution, no less extensive than they would have had if the meeting had been so called at their request. In these cases the required percentage is 5 per cent.

The request has to identify the general nature of the business to be dealt with and it may include the text of a resolution that is intended to be (properly)[7] moved at the meeting. This request may be in hard copy or electronic form but it must be authenticated by the person(s) making it.

23.4.2 The directors' obligation to call the meeting

Where a meeting has been properly requested, s. 304 requires the director(s) to call a meeting within 21 days from the date on which he/she became subject to the requirement, and this must be held not more than 28 days after the date of the notice convening the meeting. Further, where the request has identified a resolution intended to be moved at the meeting, details of this resolution must accompany the notice. Where such a resolution is a special resolution, the directors must follow the requirements provided in s. 283.[8]

- *Where the directors fail to call the meeting*: Where the requirements of s. 303 have been complied with and the directors fail to call the meeting, the members who requested the meeting, or any of them representing more than half of the total voting rights of all of them, may themselves call a general meeting and do so at the company's expense (limited to reasonable expenses).[9] The meeting must be called for a date not more than three

---

[4] CA 2006, s. 301.   [5] CA 2006, s. 302.   [6] CA 2006, s. 303.

[7] 'Properly' means a resolution that may be passed at a meeting unless to do so would be ineffective (such as against the constitution of the company); is defamatory of any person; or is frivolous or vexatious.

[8] Giving the appropriate notice and so on.   [9] CA 2006, s. 305.

months after the date on which the directors became subject to the requirement to call the meeting, and it must be called in as similar a manner as possible as other meetings called by the directors.

- *Power of a court to order a meeting:* It may be the case that with smaller companies, the shareholder may have disagreements with the directors to such an extent that, for example, the shareholder(s) will not attend the meetings to allow for resolutions to be moved. Where it is impractical to call a meeting in a manner which it would normally be called, or as required by the company's articles, or the CA 2006, a court may through its own motion or through an application of a director of the company, or a member of the company who would be entitled to vote, order for a meeting to be called, held, and conducted in any manner the court thinks fit (and when conducted in this way, the meeting will be considered for all purposes to have been duly called, held, and conducted).[10] Such power also extends to the court giving directions as it deems expedient, such as providing that one member of a company present at the meeting be deemed to constitute a quorum. The court will not, however, give a member a voting power that the member does not possess under the company's constitution. Note that this procedure is not intended to resolve petty squabbles between the equal members of a company.

Ross v Telford[11]

Facts:

The case involved the two equal shareholders of a company. They had been husband and wife but had divorced acrimoniously and would not cooperate with each other regarding matters, including convening the company's meetings. The articles of the company required a quorum of two for the meetings and as this could not be practicably achieved, the husband requested a court to order a meeting with just one of the shareholders present to lawfully conclude the business required. This was initially granted but was stopped when the case was heard at the Court of Appeal, which held the provision of the Companies Act was not designed for this purpose. If the husband had been a majority shareholder and the minority shareholder had been deliberately attempting to prevent the business of the company being conducted, then the Companies Act would have been correctly used.

Authority for:

An interpretation of the relevant section of the CA 1985 (s. 371) was that Parliament did not intend for it to be interpreted by the courts as a means to break a deadlock between equal shareholders. In so doing, the courts have no power to regulate the affairs of a company in this way (shifting the balance of power between shareholders where they agreed to share power equally).

23.4.3 Notice of meetings

A general meeting of a private company must be called by giving notice[12] of at least 14 days. A general meeting of a public company must be called giving notice of at least 21 days for an

---

[10] CA 2006, s. 306.   [11] [1998] 1 BCLC 82.
[12] Notice can be given in hard copy, electronic forms, through a website, or by a combination of these (CA 2006, s. 308).

AGM, or of at least 14 days' notice for other general meetings. These periods are provided for in CA 2006, s. 306, but the section allows the companies to provide for longer or shorter periods if agreed by the members. For the shorter period the agreement of members must be a majority of those members possessing the right to attend and vote, who together hold not less than the required percentage in nominal value of the shares giving a right to attend and vote. Where the company does not have a share capital, the members together represent not less than the required percentage of the total voting rights at that meeting of all the members (these do not apply to an AGM of a public company).[13]

This required percentage is, in private companies, 90 per cent or such higher percentage (not exceeding 95 per cent) as may be specified in the company's articles; or in the case of public companies, 95 per cent. For the members to reduce the notice period for an AGM of a public company there must be a unanimous agreement to the resolution.[14]

Where the CA 2006 requires special notice to be given for a resolution, the resolution is not effective until notice of the intention to move the resolution at least 28 days before the meeting has been provided.[15] However, where this is not practicable, the company must give its members notice at least 14 days before the meeting through an advertisement in a newspaper having an appropriate circulation, or other manner specified in the company's articles.

- *Notification details:* Notice of a general meeting must be sent to every member and director of the company.[16] This notification, for general meetings, must include the time and date of the meeting; the meeting's location; the nature of the business to be dealt with at the meeting, and any other requirements subject to the company's articles.[17] In situations of accidental failure to notify of a resolution or general meeting, any accidental failure to give notice to one or more persons is disregarded for the purpose of determining whether notice of the meeting or resolution is duly given (with exception to the requirements under ss. 304, 305, and 339 of the CA 2006). The accidental failure provisions of the CA 2006 are subject to any provisions of the company's articles.

23.4.4 Circulation of statements

The members of a company may require the company to circulate, to those members entitled to receive notice of a general meeting, a statement of not more than 1,000 words regarding a matter referred to in a proposed resolution (or other business) to be dealt with at the meeting. The company is required to circulate the statement when it receives a request from members who represent not less than 5 per cent of the total voting rights of all the members entitled to vote, or if at least 100 members with a relevant right to vote, and who hold shares with an average sum of £100 each, make the request.[18] Where the request made by the members relates to a matter of an AGM of a public company and the (valid) request requiring the company to circulate the statement is made before the end of the financial year preceding the meeting, the expenses incurred in complying do not need to be paid by the members requesting the circulation. In all other circumstances the members must pay the expenses unless the company resolves otherwise.[19] The company (or another aggrieved person) may apply to a court to prevent a requirement for the circulation where the right is being abused. The court may then order the members who requested the circulation to pay the whole or part of the company's costs on such an application, even if they are not parties to the application.[20]

---

[13] CA 2006, s. 307. [14] CA 2006, s. 377. [15] CA 2006, s. 312.
[16] CA 2006, s. 310. [17] CA 2006, s. 311. [18] CA 2006, s. 314.
[19] CA 2006, s. 316. [20] CA 2006, s. 317.

23.4.5 **Procedures at meetings**

The CA 2006 provides details of how the companies must conduct meetings to ensure that the resolutions moved are lawful. This section of the Act initially considers the quorum at the meeting (the minimum numbers of the company's members who need to be present to allow resolutions to be effectively moved). A company limited by shares or by guarantee and having only one member will have reached a quorum when one qualifying person is present at a meeting. In other cases, and subject to the company's articles, two qualifying persons present at the meeting are a quorum unless the qualifying persons are the representatives of the same corporation or the persons are the proxies of the same member.[21] For the purposes of the Act, a qualifying person is an individual who is a member of the company; a person authorized to act as the representative of a corporation in relation to the meeting; or a person appointed as a proxy of a member.

A member may be elected to be the chairperson (including a proxy)[22] of the general meeting by a resolution of the company, but this is subject to the company's articles as to who may or may not be chairperson.[23] In the case of voting, the company's articles must allow the right for a vote through poll at a general meeting on any question other than the election of the chairperson or the adjournment of the meeting.[24] Where a vote on a resolution is by a show of hands, once the chairperson has made a declaration that it has either passed (or passed with a majority) or not, this is conclusive evidence of the fact without proof of the numbers or proportion of votes recorded either in favour or against the resolution.[25] However, as a safeguard this authority does not have any effect if a poll is demanded in respect of the resolution. This demand may be made by not less than five members having the right to vote on the resolution; or by a member(s) representing not less than 10 per cent of the total voting rights; or by a member(s) holding shares conferring a right to vote with not less than 10 per cent of the paid-up capital.[26] The chairperson's role at meetings is to ensure proper conduct and to oversee the proceedings, and in doing so to act fairly between the members' rights and the company's best interests.

When a member wishes to exercise his/her right to vote on a poll taken at a general meeting, a member with more than one vote has the right not to use his/her votes in the same way.[27] This may be achieved by appointing more than one proxy to vote at the meeting. The CA 2006 provides the member with the right to appoint another person (the proxy) to exercise any or all of his/her rights to attend, speak, and vote at a meeting of the company.[28] Where the company has a share capital, the member may appoint more than one proxy where he/she is to exercise the rights attached to different share(s) held by him/her or to a different £10, or multiple of £10, of stock held by him/her. The notice provided to the member of the meeting must include information regarding his/her rights under s. 324, and any more extensive rights conferred by the company's articles to appoint more than one proxy.[29] However, any provision of the company's articles is void if it would have the effect of requiring any appointment of proxies or document(s) to be received by the company or another person earlier than 48 hours before the time of the meeting (or an adjourned meeting); and in the case of a poll, not more than 48 hours after it was demanded (this does not include anything other than working days).[30] These rights are the minimum required by the CA 2006, but they do not prevent a company from conferring more extensive rights on the members or proxies.[31]

---

[21] CA 2006, s. 318. [22] CA 2006, s. 328. [23] CA 2006, s. 319.
[24] CA 2006, s. 321. [25] CA 2006, s. 320. [26] CA 2006, s. 321.
[27] CA 2006, s. 322. [28] CA 2006, s. 324. [29] CA 2006, s. 325.
[30] CA 2006, s. 327. [31] CA 2006, s. 331.

23.4.6 **General meetings**

Every public company must hold an AGM within six months of its financial year-end.[32] The company must state that the meeting is an AGM, and notice must be provided that such a meeting is to be called.[33] Whilst the company must provide 21 days' notice of an AGM and 14 days' notice of all other meetings,[34] an AGM may be called by a shorter notice period than that in the CA 2006 or the company's articles if all the members entitled to attend and vote agree to the shorter notice. The members[35] of the company may require the circulation of resolutions to be moved (or intended to be moved) at the AGM, and such a resolution may be properly moved unless it would, if passed, be ineffective (such as being inconsistent with the company's constitution); defamatory of any person; or if it were frivolous or vexatious.[36] Such a request may be made in hard copy or electronic form and it must identify the resolution of which notice has been given; it must be authenticated by the person(s) making it; and it must be received by the company not later than six weeks before the AGM to which the request relates or, if later, the time at which the notice is given of that meeting. Being in receipt of a valid request, the company is required to send a copy of the resolution to each member of the company entitled to receive notice of the AGM.

Additional responsibilities rest with **quoted companies**, beyond those identified above in relation to public companies. 'Quoted companies'[37] are those having a listing (through a decision of the Financial Services Authority) and its shares may be traded on a stock exchange. Where a poll is taken at a general meeting of a quoted company, the company must ensure that the following information is made available on a website: the date of the meeting; the text of the resolution or a description of the subject matter of the poll; and the numbers of votes in favour of, and against, the resolution/subject matter.[38] Where the company fails to comply with this requirement, an offence is committed by every officer of the company in default but it does not affect the validity of the poll or the business or resolution to which the poll relates. The members of the quoted company may require its directors to obtain an independent report on any poll taken, or to be taken, at a general meeting. The directors are obliged to obtain the report where the request is from members representing not less than 5 per cent of the total voting rights of all the members entitled to vote on the matter to which the poll relates (excluding those with treasury shares); or not less than 100 members who possess the right to vote on the matter and who hold shares with an average paid-up sum of not less than £100 each.[39] This request may be in hard copy or electronic form; it must identify the poll(s) to which the request relates; it must be authenticated by the person(s) making it; and it must be received by the company not later than one week after the date on which the poll is taken.

Where the directors are required under s. 342 to obtain an independent report on a poll(s), they must appoint an appropriate person (known as an independent assessor) to prepare the report. This appointment must be made within one week after the company is required to obtain the report.[40] The independent assessor cannot be appointed if he/she is an officer or employee of the company (or associated company), or a partner or employee of such a person, or a partnership of which such a person is a partner. The assessor in this role is entitled to

---

[32] CA 2006, s. 336.   [33] CA 2006, s. 337.   [34] CA 2006, s. 307.

[35] From members representing at least 5 per cent of the total voting rights of all the members who have a right to vote on the resolution; or at least 100 members who have the right to vote on the resolution and who hold shares on which the paid-up average per member is at least £100.

[36] CA 2006, s. 338.   [37] Defined under the CA 2006, ss. 361 and 385.

[38] CA 2006, s. 341.   [39] CA 2006, s. 342.   [40] CA 2006, s. 343.

attend the meeting at which the poll may be taken and any subsequent proceedings in connection with the poll. These rights are to be exercised to the extent that the assessor considers necessary for the preparation of the report.[41] He/she is also entitled to company records relating to the poll or the meeting at which the poll may be, or were, taken.[42] Where the independent assessor has been appointed in compliance with this section of the CA 2006, the company must ensure that the following information is made available on a website: the fact of the appointment; the assessor's identity; the text of the resolution, or a description of the subject matter of the poll to which his/her appointment relates; and a copy of the report.[43] The report must be kept available for two years, beginning with the date on which it was first made available on a website.[44]

The report will contain information regarding the appropriateness of the procedures followed in relation to the poll; whether the correct notice periods were provided; the nature of the voting and whether, in the assessor's opinion, they were cast fairly and recorded correctly; and whether the votes of proxies were assessed. If the assessor is unable to provide an opinion, he/she must give the reasons why.

23.5 Resolutions at meetings

Resolutions are the decisions made at the company meetings. There are various categories of resolution that may be moved by a company. With reference to the resolutions that may be moved by a private company, a written resolution or one moved at a meeting of the company's members are available.[45] The benefit of moving a written resolution is that there is no necessity of a meeting of the members, they are sent the resolution and they sign this resolution if they are in agreement.

A public company must move resolutions at a meeting of the members (or a class of members) and it may not move written resolutions by a majority using the procedure in CA 2006, ss. 288–300. However, at common law, such resolutions can be passed if unanimous. Where the CA 2006 requires a resolution of a company, or of the members (or a class of members), and the type of resolution required is not specified, it is assumed that an ordinary resolution is required unless the company's articles requires a higher majority or unanimity. Whilst this does provide the company with some flexibility or control over the resolutions to be moved, there are protections in the CA 2006 to prevent, for example, a director being removed before the expiry of his/her term of office through a written resolution because the CA 2006 provides for important safeguards against potential abuse.

23.5.1 Ordinary resolutions

The CA 2006, s. 282 identifies ordinary resolutions as those passed, by a private company, by the members (or a class of the members) with a simple majority (over 50 per cent of the vote). An ordinary resolution can be passed as a written resolution if it is passed by members representing a simple majority of the total voting rights of eligible members. Further, a resolution to be moved at a meeting by a show of hands is passed by a simple majority where it is agreed to be passed in this way by members in person or through duly appointed proxies. Where a

---

[41] CA 2006, s. 348.   [42] CA 2006, s. 349.   [43] CA 2006, s. 351.
[44] CA 2006, s. 353.   [45] CA 2006, s. 281.

resolution is to be moved through a poll taken at the meeting, it is passed through a simple majority of members representing a simple majority of the total voting rights of the members entitled to vote in person (or through proxy) on the resolution. The section concludes that anything done by an ordinary resolution can also be done through a special resolution.

23.5.2 Special resolutions

The CA 2006, s. 283 identifies special resolutions. These are required for certain business to be taken by the company such as to alter the company's articles;[46] alter its name;[47] re-register the company from an unlimited to a private limited,[48] private to public,[49] or public to private;[50] to reduce the company's share capital;[51] to authorize the terms on which to make an off-market purchase of its own shares;[52] and so on. A special resolution of the members (or class of members) means a resolution passed by a majority of not less than 75 per cent. A written resolution is passed by a majority of not less than 75 per cent if it is passed by members representing not less than 75 per cent of the total voting rights of eligible members. Such a written resolution of a private company is not a special resolution unless it is stated as being moved as a special resolution and, if stated, it may only be moved as a special resolution. Where the resolution is to be moved by a show of hands, it is passed by a majority of not less than 75 per cent where not less than 75 per cent of the members (or the duly appointed proxies) who are entitled to vote do so in favour of the resolution. A resolution moved on a poll at a meeting is passed by a majority of not less than 75 per cent if passed by members representing not less than 75 per cent of the total voting rights of eligible members vote in favour of the resolution in person or through their proxies. Where a company wishes to move a special resolution, it may only do so by following these procedures and giving notice of the meeting, the text of the resolution wishing to be moved, and by passing it in the form required of a special resolution.

23.5.3 Written resolutions

A private company may propose and move a written resolution in accordance with the requirements laid out in the CA 2006.[53] However, such a resolution may not be used to remove either a director[54] or an auditor[55] before the expiration period of office. The resolution may be proposed by the directors of the private company or its (eligible) members (carrying not less than 5 per cent of the total voting rights) and has effect where it is moved by a company in a general meeting or a resolution of a meeting of a class of members of the company. The eligible members are those who would have been entitled to vote on the resolution on the circulation date of the resolution.[56] The circulation date is the date on which copies of the resolution are sent or submitted to the members (or if the copies/submissions are made on different days it is the first of those days).[57]

Where the company wishes to move a written resolution proposed by the directors, the company must send/submit a copy of the resolution to every eligible member at the same time (where reasonably practicable), in hard copy, electronic form, or by means of a website. The copy of the resolution must also be accompanied by a statement informing the member how

[46] CA 2006, s. 21.   [47] CA 2006, s. 77.   [48] CA 2006, s. 105.
[49] CA 2006, s. 90.   [50] CA 2006, s. 97.   [51] CA 2006, s. 641.
[52] CA 2006, s. 694.   [53] CA 2006, s. 288.   [54] Under CA 2006, s. 168.
[55] Under CA 2006, s. 510.   [56] CA 2006, s. 289.   [57] CA 2006, s. 290.

to signify his/her agreement, and the date by which the resolution must be moved for it not to lapse.[58] Where these procedures are not complied with, an offence is committed by every officer in default, but this does not affect the validity of the resolution moved. The members of a private company may require the company to circulate a written resolution unless it would, if moved, be ineffective, defamatory of any person, or frivolous or vexatious.[59] The members (representing not less than 5 per cent[60] of the total voting rights of all members entitled to vote on the resolution) may also require the company to circulate the resolution with a statement of not more than 1,000 words on the subject matter of the resolution. Where this request is properly made, the company must circulate it (and the statement) to every eligible member within 21 days of the application of s. 292.[61] This copy must also be accompanied by guidance as to how the recipient signifies agreement to the resolution, and the date that it will lapse if not moved. Importantly, those members that requested the circulation of the resolution must pay any expenses incurred by the company in compliance with s. 293, and the company may require a deposit to be paid in this regard.[62] It is also possible for the company (or another person claiming to be aggrieved) to apply to a court preventing the requirement of circulating a members' statement where it is claimed the right under s. 292 is being abused.[63]

A written resolution is moved when the required majority of eligible members have signified their agreement to it, and it will not be passed if the resolution lapses. This may occur when the time exceeds the period provided for in the company's articles; or in the absence of any articles to this effect, 28 days beginning with the circulation date. Any agreement signified after this date will be ineffective.[64]

23.6 Procedures for voting

When a vote takes place on a written resolution, in the case of a company having a share capital, every member has one vote in respect of each share or each £10 of stock held by him/her. In any other case every member has one vote.[65] Where votes take place through a show of hands, every member present in person has one vote (and every proxy duly appointed and present by a member has one vote). In the case of a vote through a poll, in the case of the company having a share capital, every member has one vote in respect of each share or each £10 of stock held by him/her. In any other case every member has one vote. In the case of joint holders of a share, only the vote of the senior holder voting may be counted by the company.[66] These provisions apply unless the company's articles have made alternative provision. Protection is provided against a company establishing, through its articles, less onerous measures to move resolutions. Every member has the right to demand a poll in moving a resolution and the company may not alter this provision through its articles (unless it is a question regarding the chairperson of the meeting or an adjournment).[67] Further, a member is entitled to vote through a proxy and the company may not deny this right.[68] The section also prevents the company from providing the proxy with fewer votes on a show of hands than the member would have received had he/she been present in person. The member may also appoint more than one proxy where appropriate.

---

[58] CA 2006, s. 291.   [59] CA 2006, s. 292.
[60] Unless the articles enable a lower percentage to be used.
[61] CA 2006, s. 293.   [62] CA 2006, s. 294.   [63] CA 2006, s. 295.
[64] CA 2006, s. 297.   [65] CA 2006, s. 284.   [66] CA 2006, s. 286.
[67] CA 2006, s. 321.   [68] CA 2006, s. 285.

23.7 Recording business at meetings and of resolutions

Every company is required to maintain records comprising copies of all resolutions of members moved otherwise than at general meetings; minutes of all proceedings of general meetings; and details provided to the company in relation to decisions of companies with a sole member.[69] These records must be kept for at least ten years from the date of the resolution, meeting, or decision, and failure to comply will result in every officer in default being liable to a fine, and a daily fine for continued contravention. Where a resolution has been moved otherwise than at a general meeting, a record of it as well as it having been signed by a director (or the company secretary), is evidence of the resolution being passed. Where there is a record of a written resolution of a private company, the resolution will be deemed to have complied with the requirements of the CA 2006 unless the contrary is proven.[70] The minutes of proceedings of a general meeting signed by the chairperson, or by the chairperson at the next general meeting will be evidence of the proceedings at the meeting. This record proves the meeting is deemed duly held and convened, all the proceedings at the meeting are deemed to have duly taken place, and all appointments at the meeting are deemed valid unless the contrary is proven.

Where the company has only one member and the company is limited by shares or by guarantee, and that member takes any decision that may be taken by the company in a general meeting, and has effect as if agreed by the company in the meeting, he/she must (unless taken in the form of a written resolution) provide the company with details of that decision.[71]

23.8 Winding-up of companies

Chapter 22 identified the various forms of business enterprise and outlined the registration procedure that subscribers use to establish the corporation. This section considers how those corporations are legally brought to an end. It will be remembered that due to a corporation's perpetual succession, the company does not 'die' when the person(s) running it dies (or where the sole trader/partner is made bankrupt), but rather it will only cease to exist when formally wound up. Liquidation is considered in detail but many companies are wound up due to inactivity (non-trading).

23.8.1 Liquidation

Insolvency
Act 1986

A company being wound up and being liquidated essentially refers to the company ceasing to exist. Liquidation may take effect either through a petition to a court for the compulsory liquidation of the company (under the Insolvency Act 1986, s. 124A); or the members seeking the voluntary liquidation of the business.

---

[69] CA 2006, s. 355.   [70] CA 2006, s. 356.   [71] CA 2006, s. 357.

23.8.1.1 *Liquidation by a court*

Liquidation through the court can be made by any of the following petitioning the court:[72]

- the company, the directors, or any creditor(s) (including prospective creditors);
- a contributory (who is a person who may have to contribute upon the company's liquidation, including a shareholder with fully paid-up shares);[73]
- a liquidator appointed in proceedings, or a temporary **administrator**;
- the Secretary of State where a public company has not been issued with its trading certificate;
- (in the event of a company being voluntarily wound-up) the **Official Receiver** where the court is satisfied that the winding-up cannot be continued with due regard to the interests of the creditors or contributories;
- or by all or any of those parties, together or separately.

The court, when faced with such a petition, has the option to make the order for winding-up, or it may refuse. Importantly, the court may also appoint a provisional liquidator (who may or may not be the Official Receiver) where it is considered likely that the directors may attempt to remove assets of the company. The appointment is made as an interim measure before the substantive hearing of the petition.

The Insolvency Act (IA) 1986 identifies the grounds upon which an order for compulsory liquidation of a company may be made. Under s. 122, these are listed as:

(a) the company has by special resolution resolved that the company be wound up by the court;

(b) being a public company which was registered as such on its original incorporation, the company has not been issued with a trading certificate and more than a year has expired since it was so registered;

(c) it is an old public company, within the meaning of the Consequential Provisions Act;

(d) the company does not commence its business within a year from its incorporation or suspends its business for a whole year;

(e) except in the case of a private company limited by shares or by guarantee, the number of members is reduced below two;

(f) the company is unable to pay its debts;

(fa) at the time at which a moratorium for the company under section 1A comes to an end, no voluntary arrangement approved under Part I has effect in relation to the company;[74]

(g) the court is of the opinion that it is just and equitable that the company should be wound up.

---

[72] The Insolvency Act (IA) 1986, s. 124.

[73] A contributory is not entitled to present a winding-up petition unless either the number of members is reduced below two, or the shares in respect of which he/she is a contributory, or some of them, either were originally allotted to him/her, or have been held by him/her, and registered in his/her name, for at least six of the 18 months before the commencement for the winding-up, or have devolved on him through the death of a former holder.

[74] This was added by IA 2000, Sch. 1, para. 6.

Therefore, a company may move a special resolution to effect that the company be wound up by the court (a); and it will be remembered that the moving of a special resolution requires that three-quarters of the votes are in favour of the resolution. As such, where a smaller proportion of the members (and even just one member) wishes to have the company wound up, under (g) a petition to the court can be made that it is just and equitable to have the company wound up. This procedure also allows creditors and the directors of the company to petition the court on this ground. What will constitute a 'just and equitable' ground is a matter for the court looking at the facts of each case, and it has broad discretion in this area; however, examples have been provided. Where, particularly in small businesses, the directors who manage the company have severe disagreements that make its management practically impossible, this may lead to the court ordering its winding-up.[75] The company may have been established for a fraudulent purpose[76] or the members may have (justifiably) no faith or confidence in the company's management.[77] In each situation the courts have ordered the winding-up of the company. In order for the petitioner to succeed in this application he/she must have some genuine interest in the company being wound up, as a winding-up petition has very serious consequences for the company, its members and any creditors, and where the company is still trading and being successful in its undertaking, the courts will be considerably more reluctant to make the winding-up order.

A winding-up petition may also be made under (f) regarding the company's inability to pay its debts. It is important to note that even where it has been proved to the court's satisfaction that the company cannot pay its debts, this does not automatically result in the court ordering its winding-up. The court may initially convene a meeting of the company's creditors[78] and contributories[79] to identify their submissions[80] on the petition, and then make a decision.[81] If a decision is made to wind up the company, the court will order for the appointment of a liquidator. The court may, for example after having heard from the creditors, determine that the company that owes a creditor a sum that would allow a winding-up order should not be wound up. Other creditors may consider that allowing the company to continue to trade would be in the best interests of all the parties.[82] Such actions are much less common, however, with the availability of the administration procedure.

23.8.1.2 *The winding-up order*

Where the court orders the company to be wound up, the company's liquidation is effective from the date of the petition to the court and, until another liquidator is appointed, the Official Receiver assumes this position. Once the order has been given, notice of the order (and a copy) must be provided to the Registrar, who will then publish this in the *London Gazette*.

The role of the Official Receiver, when appointed, is to identify the state of the company's affairs with regard to its assets, debts, and other liabilities. The persons listed in IA 1986,

---

[75] *Re Yenidje Tobacco Co. Ltd* [1916] 2 Ch 426.

[76] *Re Thomas Edward Brinsmead and Sons* [1897] 1 Ch 45.

[77] *Loch v John Blackwood* [1924] AC 783.

[78] Including consideration of the debts owed to each creditor.

[79] Taking into account the number of votes conferred on each contributory from the CA 2006 or the articles.

[80] Only the views of the creditors will be taken into account if the company is insolvent.

[81] IA 1986, s. 195.

[82] Wheeler, S. (1994) 'Empty Rhetoric and Empty Promises: The Creditors' Meeting' *Journal of Law and Society*, Vol. 21, No. 3, p. 350.

s. 131 (may if requested) have to provide the Receiver with the following information that is verified by affidavit:

(a) the particulars of the company's assets, debts, and liabilities;

(b) the names and addresses of the company's creditors;

(c) the securities held by them, respectively;

(d) the dates when the securities were respectively given; and

(e) such further or other information as may be prescribed or as the official receiver may require.

The persons required to provide such information are:

(a) those who are or have been officers of the company;

(b) those who have taken part in the formation of the company at any time within one year before the relevant date;

(c) those who are in the company's employment, or have been in its employment within that year, and are in the official receiver's opinion capable of giving the information required;

(d) those who are or have been within that year officers of, or in the employment of, a company which is, or within that year was, an officer of the company.

Where the requirement for the statement is made, those persons have to do so within 21 days after the day of the notice being given them by the Receiver. Any person who fails to comply with such a request will, upon conviction, be subject to a fine, and continued daily fines until the contravention is ended. This information may prove valuable to the Receiver as IA 1986, s. 132 requires the Receiver to investigate (if the company failed) the causes of the failure; the promotion, formation, business, dealings, and affairs of the company, and to make the report to the court if he/she considers appropriate.[83]

To further assist in the investigation, the Receiver may undertake a public examination of the company's officers following a successful application to the court. This includes anyone who is or has been an officer of the company; has acted as a liquidator or administrator of the company or a manager or receiver; or a person (not identified in the previous examples) who is, or has taken part, in the promotion, formation, or management of the company.[84] The Receiver must also make an application to the court to perform this investigation if requested by one-half, in value, of the company's creditors, or three-quarters in value of the company's contributors. Further to the powers and duties of the Receiver above, upon winding-up, the company's assets may not be disposed of, and shares may not be transferred or altered, unless a court authorizes such actions.[85] Any actions for recovering debts are stopped, and the responsibilities for the management of the company transfer from the directors to the Receiver/liquidator. Any floating charges that were granted over assets are deemed to crystallize.[86]

23.8.1.3 *Voluntary liquidation*

Under the IA 1986, a voluntary **winding-up** of a company may be achieved through an action by the company's members (who must involve the company's creditors if it is insolvent). A special resolution is required to be moved. Where the members wish to have the company

---

[83] IA 1986 s. 132.   [84] IA 1986 s. 133.   [85] IA 1986 s. 127.   [86] See **24.13.1.**

wound up, they would seek to have a special resolution moved, and then appoint a liquidator at a general meeting (this may an option where the company is still solvent and the members may wish to gain something from the remaining assets of the company).[87] The liquidator (and there may be more than one appointed) is appointed for the purpose of winding-up the company's affairs and distributing its assets.[88] If the winding-up of the company takes longer than one year, the liquidator will call a general meeting in each successive year and account for his/her acts and dealings, and the conduct of the winding-up.[89] When the company's affairs are fully wound up, the liquidator calls a general meeting to lay before it his/her account, how the company's property has been disposed and so on, and provide an explanation for the actions. Notice of the meeting is advertised in the *London Gazette* at least one month prior to it.[90] Within one week following the meeting, the liquidator will send a copy of the account and the details of the meeting to the Registrar.

In the event that the liquidator is of the opinion that the company will be unable to pay its debts in full (including any interest at the official rate) within the period of the directors' declaration of solvency under s. 89, the liquidator will call a meeting of the creditors within 28 days of forming this opinion.[91] The liquidator will preside at the meeting, setting out in the prescribed form the affairs of the company. Following the day of this meeting, the IA 1986 holds that the winding-up becomes a creditors' voluntary winding-up.[92] In the event that a member's winding-up becomes a creditors' winding-up, ss. 98 and 99 do not apply. The procedure, as described in this paragraph and the last, is only effective where the directors have made a declaration of solvency under IA 1986, s. 89. Where they have not, the creditors' meeting procedure must be followed.

The IA 1986, s. 98 provides for a meeting of the creditors to be summoned within 14 days after the day of the company meeting where a resolution for the winding-up of the company is to be proposed. Notification of the meeting must be given to the creditors by post not less than seven days before the meeting and be advertised in the *London Gazette* and in two newspapers. The directors of the company will lay a statement of affairs before the creditors, and it is the duty of the directors to choose one of them to preside over the meeting.[93] The creditors will be able to choose the liquidator and make arrangements for the remuneration to be paid.[94] The creditors are also empowered to appoint a liquidation committee of not more than five persons to exercise the functions of the liquidator.[95]

The same restrictions on the company's ability to trade and a restriction on the disposal of assets are imposed in the same way as where the winding-up is performed by the court.

23.8.1.4 *The liquidator*

The liquidator, who must be a qualified insolvency practitioner, is appointed to wind up the company and to dispose of its assets in the best interests of the creditors and formally remove the company's registration at Companies House. The liquidator will seek to collect any assets that are owed to the company and then dispose of these to realize any capital. Having realized these assets, the proceeds are then distributed to the creditors, and having settled its debts (where possible), any remaining proceeds are distributed to the company's members. A very significant power is provided through IA 1986, s. 178, which gives the liquidator the power to disclaim onerous property so as to cease the company from completing unprofitable

---

[87] Ordinary shareholders are low on the list of creditors when a company is wound up (and are at risk of getting little return on their investment in the company).

[88] IA 1986, s. 91.   [89] IA 1986, s. 93.   [90] IA 1986, s. 94.   [91] IA 1986, s. 95.

[92] IA 1986, s. 96.   [93] IA 1986, s. 99.   [94] IA 1986, s. 100.   [95] IA 1986, s. 101.

contracts. The third party would then have to bring an action for breach against the company but he/she would be considered to be an unsecured creditor.

Where the liquidator believes that a person should make some contribution to the company's assets, he/she may make an application to the court.[96] If, in the course of the winding-up of a company, it appears that a person who was or is an officer of the company; a liquidator, administrator, or administrative receiver of the company; or has been or is concerned in the promotion, formation, or management of the company, has misapplied or retained money or property of the company, or is guilty of any misfeasance or in breach of any other fiduciary duty, the court may, on the application of the Official Receiver; liquidator; or any creditor or contributory, examine the person's conduct. Following this investigation, the court may compel him/her to repay, restore or account for the money or property or any part of it (including interest at a rate the court thinks fit).[97]

Where the company has gone into liquidation; at some time before the commencement the person knew, or ought reasonably had known, that there was no reasonable prospect of the company avoiding the liquidation; and that person was a director/shadow director at the time, shall be guilty of wrongful trading if he/she did not take reasonable steps to minimize any potential loses to the creditors.[98]

23.8.1.5 *Effect of charges on winding-up*

Where a fixed charge has been applied to an asset(s), when the company is wound up the charge holder may take control of the assets and dispose of them to obtain monies owed (any surplus being paid back to the company). In respect of floating charges, the priority of the charge depends upon when it was made (and this is important where the company has insufficient funds to satisfy its debts). Prior to 15 September 2003, any affected floating charge holder could appoint an administrative receiver. He/she received money owed following the payment of the liquidator and the debts having been paid of the preferential creditors.[99] Following these payments, and the floating charge holder, unsecured creditors were paid and then the members in accordance with the articles. Table 23.1 identifies the priority of charges/liabilities when correctly registered.

For those floating charges made after 15 September 2003 the payments are in the same order insofar as the liquidator makes a provision called 'top-slicing', which will establish assets that will be distributed after the preferential creditors are paid and before the floating charge holders are. Further, these charges after 2003 only entitle the holder to appoint an administrator, rather than an administrative receiver.

Top-slicing is a term that relates to the obligation on the liquidator to set aside a proportion of the assets that would otherwise have been paid straight to the holder of a floating charge and maintain this in respect of the unsecured creditors. This amount is 50 per cent of the company's property, having paid the costs and any money owed to preferential creditors, up to £10,000. If the value of the company's property is less than £10,000, the liquidator has discretion not to distribute these funds to unsecured creditors where to do so would produce unreasonable costs. Where the property is in excess of the £10,000 figure, a further 20 per cent up to £600,000 is retained for the purpose of top-slicing.

Evidently, business with companies involves risk and where goods are being supplied to companies on credit, it may be prudent to include a reservation of title clause[100] in the contracts so that upon liquidation, where the supplier has not been paid, these goods do not belong to the company and may not be disposed of and added to the company's funds.

---

[96] IA 1986, s. 214.   [97] IA 1986, s. 212.   [98] IA 1986, s. 214.   [99] See **24.13.3**.
[100] Known as a Romalpa clause—see **11.2.1**.

Table 23.1 Priority of charges

Priority	Type of Charge	Rank
1	Fixed charge holders	Rank higher than existing floating charges unless the existing floating charge has made provision against this (fixed charges have effect from the time they are created).
2	Preferential creditors	Take priority over the holders of floating charges, but not over fixed charges. Preferential creditors include employees.
3	Floating charge holders	(Takes effect when it crystallizes). Has priority when the charge was created (hence the first floating charge will have priority over the last one created over the same asset, unless this is stated to the contrary).

23.8.2 Administration

As opposed to appointing a liquidator to govern the winding-up of the company, the IA 1986 introduced a mechanism for the appointment of an administrator to manage its affairs (this is often seen with professional football teams such as Leeds United Football Club Ltd in 2007). The powers of the administrator are contained in the IA 1986 (as amended) and in exercising these he/she is acting as the company's agent. The administrator must also be qualified to act as an insolvency practitioner.[101] The administrator is appointed either by the administration order of the court; by the holder of a floating charge; or by the company or its directors.[102] The purpose of the administrator is to perform his/her functions with the objective of rescuing the company as a going concern;[103] achieving a better result for the company's creditors as a whole than would be likely if the company was wound up; or realizing property in order to make a distribution to one or more secured or preferential creditors.[104] A court will make an order for administration if it is satisfied that the company is unable, or is likely to become unable, to pay its debts and the order will be likely to achieve the aims as established in Schedule B1, para 3.[105] On administration the company is restricted from going into liquidation and being wound up, save for the provisions identified in Schedule B1, para 42.

23.8.2.1 *Administrative receivership*

Those holders of floating charges made before 15 September 2003 may appoint a receiver to realize the company's property and obtain owed money. If the charges relate to a majority or all of the company's assets then this appointment will be of an administrative receiver. This position provides the administrative receiver with the authority to dispose of the assets to which the floating charge relates, and having provided for the costs in realizing these assets, and the preferential creditors being paid, the monies will be distributed to the charge holders.

---

[101] IA 1986, Sch B1, para 6.   [102] IA 1986, Sch B1, para 2.

[103] Unless the administrator does not think it is reasonably practicable to achieve this.

[104] IA 1986, Sch B1, para 3.   [105] IA 1986, Sch B1, para 11.

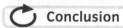 **Conclusion**

This chapter has identified the administrative requirements of a company, from the regulation of the company's meetings, and the interaction of the members with the company, and how the various resolutions may be moved. The chapter has also considered the main mechanisms for bringing a company to an end and the procedures involved for the directors, members, and creditors. The following chapter considers the regulation of the company's finances and maintenance of capital to protect the members and creditors, and (hopefully) to ensure the company need not face financial difficulties that require its winding-up.

 Summary of main points

Capacity to trade

- Public companies must possess a share capital of not less than £50,000.
- Having supplied the required documents to the Registrar, a public company will be issued with a trading certificate that allows a company to begin trading. Private companies have this immediate capacity.
- Procedures exist for the re-registration of companies.

Company meetings

- Companies may, and in some cases must, hold Annual General Meetings (AGMs) and general meetings.
- Public companies must hold AGMs but private companies need not.
- Members of a private company, with the required minimum paid-up capital, can require the directors to call a meeting.
- On application, a court can also require a meeting of the company and for it to be conducted as it sees fit.
- A private company must give at least 14 days' notice of a general meeting.
- A public company must give 14 days' notice of general meetings other than an AGM, which requires 21 days' notice.
- Details of the meeting must be sent to the members and directors of the company.
- Members holding the required percentage of voting rights may oblige the company to circulate details of the meetings and the resolutions to be moved (but not exceeding 1,000 words).
- The meetings must be presided over by a chairperson, and a quorum of members must be present to lawfully move resolutions.

Resolutions

- Resolutions are decisions made at company meetings.
- There are various types of resolutions and they are used depending on the nature of the decision to be taken. Resolutions may be ordinary, special, or written.
- The company must maintain records of its decisions taken at meetings and the resolutions moved.

Winding-up of companies

- To bring a company to an end it must be legally wound up.
- Courts have the power to wind up a company on petition.
- A petition may be presented by the company, the directors, the members, or a creditor(s), and there is also provision for the Secretary of State to petition the court.
- When the company is wound up, fixed charges allow the holder to dispose of those assets (with any additional revenue being returned to the company).
- Upon winding-up, any floating charges 'crystallize' and employees are dismissed.
- Winding-up may be achieved through the members' moving a special resolution and the appointing of a liquidator. The directors must be in a position to file a declaration of solvency if they wish to avoid summoning a creditors' meeting that could overrule their choice of liquidator.
- The creditors of a company are entitled to meet and overrule the members' choice of liquidator where the directors have not made the declaration of insolvency.
- Administrators are appointed to continue to run the business, whilst a liquidator is appointed to oversee the company's winding-up.
- Following the liquidation of the company, the creditors are paid according to a hierarchy, beginning with preferential creditors and ending with the members of the company.
- Since 15 September 2003, top-slicing has been introduced, which requires the liquidator to retain a proportion of the company's property (subject to a floating charge) to pay unsecured creditors.

 Summary questions

Essay questions

1 How may the members of the company engage in the management of the company at general meetings? Explain the rights of the members and how they directly affect the decision-making through the moving of resolutions.

2. Assess the role of a liquidator appointed to oversee the winding-up of a company. Explain the powers granted to the liquidator and how he/she may deal with the directors and creditors of the company.

Problem questions

1. All Bright Consumables (ABC) Ltd was a successful company, operating primarily a business of developing and selling technology products. It supplied goods to customers directly, but had a particularly lucrative contract to supply its touch screen computers to a sales company (Sign'em Up Quick PLC (SUQ)).

    As the recession hit the UK, ABC Ltd found it difficult to maintain its standards and started using inferior technology in its products. It entered into an agreement with HTD to supply these products and granted a charge over its factory for LCD displays supplied by HTD and used in the manufacture of the screens. Soon after using HTD's screens, and with continued complaints regarding reliability and durability, SUQ exercised its right to bring the relationship of supply with ABC Ltd to an end.

Due to the loss of its contract, ABC Ltd found itself in financial difficulties. It could not maintain repayments to HTD for the supply of the screens. ABC Ltd owed HTD £30,000 for the screens supplied, it had means to satisfy this debt, and asked for the advice of its accountants. The accountants suggested that the company should cease trading immediately and be wound-up. However, the directors, eager to rescue the business, continued trading but just continued getting into ever more debt.

Advise HTD as to proceedings it may take to have the company wound-up. Would any responsibility be placed on the directors of ABC Ltd for not taking the accountants' advice on ceasing trading?

2. Raz is a minority shareholder (he holds 5 per cent of the shares) of Happy Harry's Bottles Ltd and is concerned by the actions of the directors. The directors are also majority shareholders (holding, jointly 62 per cent of the shares) who refuse to hold a general meeting when asked to in order to discuss their actions and the future direction of the company. Raz would also like to put a resolution to the meeting and needs information on how, if at all, this may be achieved.

Prepare a report for Raz outlining the rules regarding a company meeting being called, and how many shareholders are needed to require a meeting called for to be held.

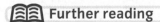 **Further reading**

Cockerill, A. (2008) 'Floating Charges hit the Rocks Again' *Solicitors Journal*, Vol. 152, No. 11, p. 22.

Mokal, R. J. (2005) 'Corporate Insolvency Law: Theory and Application' Oxford University Press: Oxford.

 Useful websites

<http://www.theqca.com/
(This is a not-for-profit organization that represents the interests, particularly, of smaller quoted companies (those outside of the FTSE 350).)

<http://www.fsa.gov.uk/
(The website of the Financial Services Authority. This is an independent governmental body provided with authority under the Financial Services and Markets Act 2000; it maintains the list of quoted companies, and has rule-making, investigatory, and enforcement powers to protect the public and maintain confidence in the financial system (such as through reducing crime).)

 Online Resource Centre

http://www.oxfordtextbooks.co.uk/orc/marson3e/
Why not visit the Online Resource Centre and try multiple choice questions associated with this chapter to test your understanding of the topic. You will also find relevant updates to the law.

24 Maintenance of Finance and Capital

Why does it matter?

Companies have to adhere to the requirements of the Companies Act 2006 when issuing shares, altering and reducing its share capital, and granting charges to creditors. Detailed regulation exists and directors who fail in certain duties in these areas may be fined, and even imprisoned on conviction. Those who are lending money (creditors) to the company may wish to secure the loan through a charge over its assets. This ensures that the creditor can take control of the assets subject to the charge if the company is in default. Registration of charges is required to secure them and whilst failure may lead to the director(s) in default being subject to a fine, for the creditor such a situation will result in the loss of the charge and secured creditor status. Hence the chapter contains vital information for directors, members, and creditors.

Learning outcomes

Following reading this chapter you should be in a position to:

- explain the nature and characteristics of a share and the different types of shares (24.2–24.6)
- understand the requirement of the necessity of maintaining capital (24.4.2–24.4.2.1)
- identify the procedures involved in issuing shares (24.9)
- explain the nature of a company obtaining secured and unsecured loans (24.12–24.13.1)
- explain the registration procedure process for charges applied to company assets (24.13.2–24.13.3).

Key terms

These terms will be used in the chapter and it may be helpful to be aware of what they mean or refer back to them when reading through the chapter.

Debenture
Written evidence of a secured loan given by the lender to the company. It has been described as 'a document which either creates a debt or acknowledges it'.[1]

Dividend
The distributable profits of a company to share holders.

London Gazette
This is the official newspaper that provides, in the context of this chapter, legal and regulatory information regarding companies, disqualification of directors' notices and so on.

Pari passu
An interpretation from the Latin means 'with equal step' and can be considered as meaning shares that rank without preference.

Pre-emption rights
This is the right of shareholders to be offered new issues of shares before they are made available to non-shareholders.

Secured loan
This refers to a loan where the borrower provides the lender with some collateral (through charges over property).

Share warrant
Companies may, where authorized by the articles, issue in respect of fully paid-up shares, a warrant that states the bearer is entitled to the shares specified in it.

Solvency statement
The directors formally state that they have formed an opinion that the company will be able to repay its debts where the company wishes to reduce its share capital.

Unsecured loan
These are loans that are not secured on the company's property/assets.

24.1 **Introduction**

This chapter continues from the discussion of the administration of the company to consider the broad issue of corporate governance. It identifies how a company may raise capital, and considers the obligations placed on the directors to protect and maintain the capital of the company for its members. There are rules regarding the issuing of shares and granting of **debentures** to protect the company and the creditors from abuse; how **dividends** are to be agreed and provided to shareholders; and these must be understood to appreciate the effects of the CA 2006 on companies, and to ensure these rules are not (innocently, negligently, or fraudulently) transgressed.

---

[1] *Levy v Abercorris Slate and Slab Corp.* [1887] 37 Ch D 260.

24.2 **Shares**

A share[2] is a bundle of rights[3] and duties that the holder possesses in relation to the company and the other members. The share also provides liabilities to the owner to contribute the amount of capital required to be paid when called-up by the company[4] (if the shares, for instance, had not been fully paid for).[5] However, shareholders are only liable for this investment and do not have to contribute more if the company cannot satisfy its debts. This is the concept of the shareholders' limited liability. Shares are considered as personal property (and are not in the nature of real estate), and as such the shares of any member may be transferred in accordance with the company's articles.[6] The share must have a fixed nominal value (or it is void)[7] and each share must be distinguished by its appropriate number except when the shares are fully paid up and rank without preference (**pari passu**); or all the issued shares of a particular class are fully paid up and rank *pari passu* for all purposes.[8]

24.3 **Shareholders**

Companies
Act 2006

The CA 2006 refers to a company's members, but essentially this refers, in this instance, to the shareholders of the company. The shareholders are deemed to 'own' the company because they will have made an investment, such as by purchasing shares, and whilst this will be performed in the expectation of a return on their investment (such as through dividends or an increase in the value of the shares) they are entrusting their investment to a body with its own legal personality. Despite 'ownership', each of the shareholders could not expect to play an active role in the company's day-to-day management. As such, the members delegate the task of management to directors who are answerable (to varying degrees) to the shareholders. However, whilst the powers of the directors may be very broad and can bind the company into contracts and provide and take loans on the company's behalf, the role and powers possessed by shareholders must not be underestimated.

24.4 **Share capital**

When the company limited by shares is formed, the subscribers identify the amount of capital received from the share issue. The nature of limited companies, and hence the limit to the personal liability of its members, is very important to those doing business with the organization. The identification of the share capital reassures the company's creditors that sufficient funds (capital) are present in the event that the business fails and that the company will be in

---

[2] Under the CA 2006, s. 540 a share means a share in the company's share capital.

[3] That may be enforced through legal action and include rights to attend meetings; vote; or an entitlement to a dividend for example.

[4] This request can be made at any time.

[5] The Companies (Model Articles) Regulations 2008, Art. 21.

[6] CA 2006, s. 544.   [7] CA 2006, s. 541.   [8] CA 2006, s. 543.

a position to satisfy its debts. It is for this reason that there are detailed provisions on how a company may alter or reduce its share capital.

A company having a share capital is considered under the CA 2006 to possess a power under its constitution to issue shares.[9] These shares are required to have a nominal value,[10] identified in Sterling, Euros, or some other nominated currency. This nominal value is the amount that the company and the purchaser have agreed as the purchase price for the share and this value may not be lowered (or this would constitute a fraud on the company). This nominal value is the lowest price that the share will be sold for. However, it may be possible (and indeed could prove advantageous) for the share to be transferred at a higher value than this, and this value is the share premium. It must be noted that when a company manages to receive a premium on the shares issued, this must be transferred into a share premium account[11] and not distributed to the members as dividends. The money in the share premium account cannot be used to write off expenses such as when debentures are issued or for any costs incurred in forming the company, although it may be used to offset expenses incurred in the issuing of the shares involved.[12] This figure is then treated for the purposes of the company as capital and would be included in the company's balance sheet at the end of the year.

Shares are usually issued to raise capital and the most common form is in money (although some companies issued shares in return for assets or work completed and part of the payment is in the issue of shares—although this is subject to strict rules). The issue of raising capital in this manner is particularly important. Whereas loans taken by the company (and possibly **secured** on the company's assets) have to be repaid in accordance with the loan agreement, shares that are issued for an investment of capital do not involve any loan, and despite the dilution of the percentage of his/her shareholding of the major shareholder(s) by issuing shares to others, there is no right to a dividend on the shares held unless this is agreed at the general meeting (and from the company's profits). Loans have to be repaid whether the company has dispersible profits or not.

A company's share capital may be considered under the following headings.

24.4.1 **Share capital**

This refers to the amount of capital that the company was registered with (the share capital may be raised by the decision of the directors (unless the articles provide otherwise) or through a resolution at a later date if required).[13] For example, a public company with a minimum £50,000 of share capital may have this divided into 50,000 £1 shares, and these will be distributed as the subscribers see fit.

- *Issued share capital:* Issued share capital refers to the amount of the authorized share capital that has been issued[14] (a company does not have to issue all of its shares in the authorized share capital). This relates to the funding that the company has received from the members. To continue the example above, that the company has the power to issue 50,000 shares does not mean that they have all been issued at the formation of the company. The company may have issued 40,000 of the £1 shares and hence it has an authorized share capital of £50,000, but an issued share capital of £40,000. It is this fund that the creditors will go to in the event of the company's insolvency.

---

[9] CA 2006, s. 545.   [10] CA 2006, s. 542.   [11] CA 2006, s. 610.   [12] CA 2006, s. 610.
[13] CA 2006, s. 617.   [14] CA 2006, s. 546.

- *Allotted share capital:* Allotted share capital naturally refers to shares that have been allotted. Both issued and allotted shares include those taken on the formation of the company by the subscribers to the company's memorandum.[15] Shares are allotted when a person acquires an unconditional right to be included in the company's register of members in respect of the shares.[16] A person who has been allotted shares may not necessarily take up these shares personally and may choose to transfer his/her right to others. However, the directors can (and at some time will) call up any payment owing on the shares because the subscribers, when forming the company, enter into a contract with it regarding the shares and their willingness to take these (and pay the nominal value).

- *Paid-up share capital:* The paid-up share capital is the amount of the nominal share capital that has been paid for by the company members (albeit that any premium paid does not count in this calculation). In the above example, when shares are allotted to the members it may not, at that time, require payment in full. The £1 shares remain at £1 but the company may have only required 50 pence per share to be paid. Hence of the £40,000 issued share capital, the paid-up capital is £20,000.

- *Called-up share capital:* This refers to the share capital that the directors have 'called-up', including any share capital paid up without being called, and any share capital to be paid up on a specified future date under the articles. It includes the terms of allotment of the relevant shares or any other arrangements for payment of those shares.[17]

24.4.2 Alteration of share capital

 Business Link

'One of the main objects contemplated by the legislation, in restricting the power of limited companies to reduce the amount of their capital … is to protect the interests of the outside public who may become their creditors … (and who) are entitled to assume that no part of the capital which has been paid into the coffers of the company has been subsequently paid out, except in the legitimate course of its business.'

Whilst a private company is not required to have any prescribed amount of share capital, compared with a public company's requirement of £50,000, it will identify its share capital on formation but may, at a later date, wish to vary this amount in light of its changing circumstances. Whilst generally it is prevented from doing so[18] there are exceptions where the company wishes to increase its share capital by allotting new shares; reduce its share capital in accordance with Chapter 10 of the CA 2006; where it wishes to sub-divide[19] or consolidate[20] all or any of its shares; where it wishes to reconvert stock into shares;[21] or where it wishes to redenominate any or all of its shares.[22]

---

[15] CA 2006, s. 546.   [16] CA 2006, s. 558.   [17] CA 2006, s. 547.   [18] CA 2006, s. 617.

[19] For example, to change 100 £1 shares to 1,000 10p shares.

[20] For example, to change the existing shares to a smaller number of shares—1000 10p shares to 100 £1 shares.

[21] Note, however, that the CA 2006 prevents shares from being converted into stock, unless they were converted into stock before the Act (where they can be reconverted) s. 620.

[22] For example, to convert the shares from one currency to another.

Where a company wishes to allot new shares, a contract has to be established between the parties that identifies the important information such as the amount of capital involved, when this capital is to be contributed, the nature and class of the shares to be allotted, and when the shares will provide the allottee with his/her rights attached to the shares. Chapter Two of the CA 2006 governs the allotment of shares and identifies the authority of directors to allot.[23] Where a private company has only one class of share, the director(s) is empowered to allot shares in the company unless the articles prevent this.[24] Where a company has more than one class of share, or the company is a PLC, there must be authority provided by the company's articles or through a resolution[25] of the company.[26] This authority may be conditional or unconditional, and it must state the maximum amount of shares that may be allotted, and specify the date on which the power will expire (which must not be more than five years from the date of incorporation (where the power is from the company's articles) or the date that the resolution was passed). This power may be extended for a period not exceeding five years. Having received the authority to allot shares, any further resolution will identify the maximum amount of shares to be allotted and identify the expiry date of the power. To maintain the company's capital, it is not permitted to issue the shares at a discount,[27] although the company may pay the subscriber a commission for his/her subscribing or agreeing to subscribe.[28] Having allotted shares, the company must inform the Registrar (of Companies) as soon as practicable and in any event within two months after the date of allotment,[29] and within one month of making the allotment, the company must deliver to the Registrar a return of allotment detailing the statement of capital.[30]

Shares may be consolidated for convenience by altering shares that were issued in small denominations into larger amounts. This does not change the percentage of the total number of shares. Sub-dividing is the contrary situation and involves the shares being 'reduced' into smaller denominations because, for example, in their current division the price is too great to attract investors. In relation to sub-dividing and consolidating shares, the proportion between the amount paid and the amount unpaid (if any) on each share must be the same as it was from the share from which it derived.[31] The company is empowered to make such a change where the members pass an ordinary resolution to that effect (although the company's articles may require a higher majority or may exclude or restrict any power conferred by the CA 2006). If the company does make such a change, it must inform the Registrar within one month of having made the change along with a statement of capital (detailing the total number of shares of the company, their nominal value, the amounts of paid and unpaid shares and so on).[32]

Where the shares are to be redenominated, the company's articles may impose restrictions and the members must pass a resolution authorizing this (which may specify conditions that must be met before the redenomination takes effect).[33] This will include details such as the exchange rate utilized and the redenomination must take place within 28 days, ending on the day before the resolution was passed. Following the redenomination, the company must notify the Registrar of the changes within one month of doing so,[34] including a statement of capital and, within 15 days of the resolution being passed, a copy of the resolution. It is also important to note that redenomination does not affect any rights or obligations of the members under the company's constitution, or any restrictions affecting members.[35]

[23] CA 2006, s. 549.   [24] CA 2006, s. 550.

[25] A resolution of a company to give, vary, revoke, or renew authorization under this section may be an ordinary resolution, even though it amends the company's articles.

[26] CA 2006, s. 551.   [27] CA 2006, s. 552.   [28] CA 2006, s. 553.   [29] CA 2006, s. 554.

[30] CA 2006, s. 555.   [31] CA 2006, s. 618.   [32] CA 2006, s. 619.   [33] CA 2006, s. 622.

[34] CA 2006, s. 625.   [35] CA 2006, s. 624.

24.4.2.1 *Reduction of share capital*

A company may seek to reduce its share capital because its assets have permanently decreased in value, it may be a tactic to eliminate book debts,[36] or to return capital to shareholders where the capital involved is surplus to the company's requirements and so on. A private company may achieve a reduction in the share capital by a special resolution supported by a **solvency statement**. However, the reduction must still leave at least one member with a share(s) (and one that is not a redeemable share).[37] Private and public companies may, through a special resolution confirmed by the court, reduce their share capital. However, the company may have provisions in the articles that restrict or prohibit such a reduction. The private company that wishes to reduce its share capital, supported by a statement of solvency, requires the directors of the company to make the statement not more than 15 days before the date on which the resolution is passed, and the resolution and the statement are registered in accordance with s. 644.[38] The statement must identify, with respect to the company's share capital as reduced by the resolution, the total number of shares of the company, the aggregate nominal value of those shares, the amount paid up, and the amount (if any) unpaid on each share, and for each class of share, the rights attached to the shares, the total number of shares of that class, and the aggregate nominal value of shares of that class. The validity of a resolution is not affected by a failure to deliver the documents required, but an offence is committed and is punishable by a fine of the company and every officer of the company who is in default.

Where the resolution is proposed as a written resolution, a copy of the solvency statement must be sent or submitted to every eligible member at or before the time the proposed resolution is sent or submitted. Where the resolution is proposed at a general meeting, a copy of the solvency statement must be made available for inspection by the members of the company throughout that meeting. The validity of the resolution is not affected by a failure to comply with these sections of the Act.[39] The solvency statement requires the directors to have formed the opinion, with regard to the company's situation at the date of the statement, that there is no ground on which the company could then be found to be unable to pay (or otherwise discharge) its debts. Further, the directors must have formed the opinion that if it is intended to commence the winding-up of the company within 12 months of that date, that the company will be able to pay (or otherwise discharge) its debts in full within 12 months of the commencement of the winding-up, or in any other case that the company will be able to pay (or otherwise discharge its debts) as they fall due during the year immediately following that date. The resolution for the reduction is effective when the documents are registered with the Registrar.

Where a company has sought to reduce its share capital through a special resolution as noted above, it may have this confirmed by the court. If this proposed reduction of capital involves a diminution of liability in respect of unpaid share capital or the payment to a shareholder of any paid-up share capital, s. 646 allows the creditors to object to the reduction unless the court directs otherwise.[40] If the court does not disapply the provision of s. 645, every creditor of the company who is entitled to any debt or claim is entitled to object to the reduction of capital.[41] In practice, the company will provide the court with evidence that all the creditors have consented to the action, producing guarantees where necessary. Where an officer of the company intentionally or recklessly conceals the name of a creditor entitled to object to the reduction or he/she misrepresents the nature or amount of the debt or claim of a

---

[36] A book debt is an uncollected debt owed to a company.
[37] CA 2006, s. 641.   [38] CA 2006, s. 642.   [39] CA 2006, s. 642.
[40] CA 2006, s. 645.   [41] CA 2006, s. 646.

creditor, or where he/she is knowingly concerned in any such concealment or misrepresentation, he/she commits an offence punishable by a fine.[42]

The court may make an order confirming the reduction of capital on such terms and conditions as it thinks fit. Where it confirms the reduction, the court may order the company to publish the reasons for the reduction, or other information that it thinks fit to give proper information to the public. It may also require the company, where special reasons exist, to add to its name the words 'and reduced' during a period specified in the court's order.[43] When the court has provided its order confirming the reduction, the Registrar will register the order and the statement of capital.[44]

24.5 Share certificate

A share certificate that is correctly issued is evidence of the holder's legal title to the shares identified in the certificate.[45] The nature of such a document enables the holder to use the ownership as a form of collateral/security. The company must issue certificates on allotment within two months unless the issue provides otherwise; the allotment is to a financial institution; or if, following the allotment, the company has issued a **share warrant** in respect of the shares.[46]

24.6 Types of share

Due to the nature of shares and the fact that companies may issue shares to generate capital, the company must ensure that as many of the shares issued are taken up to realize the investment of capital required. The shares provide rights and impose duties on the shareholders but a company has an ability to issue different types of share, with different rights attached to them, depending on what shares it considers investors will wish to purchase and so on. The articles of the company may provide the company with authority to issue different classes of shares.[47] Where different types of share are issued, these are placed in identifiable 'classes' and the 'class rights' that attach to the shares will ensure the shareholders have knowledge of the class and their rights under this class. This is important as the classes of shares may, for example, entitle the holder to more votes per share in company meetings, to preferential treatment when dividends are announced and so on. When the company issues shares of different classes, this will be identified in the articles of association or the articles may be amended for this purpose through an ordinary resolution, and the details of the different shares and the rights attached have to be sent to the Registrar.

There are a variety of shares that a company may issue but the most commonly used are ordinary and preference shares, and these may or may not be redeemed by the company at a later date.

- *Ordinary shares:* These are the most common form of shares, and unless different classes of shares exist, all shares will be ordinary shares. When compared with preference shares the ordinary shares have a lesser status and the holders are more at risk if problems affect

---

[42] CA 2006, s. 647.   [43] CA 2006, s. 648.   [44] CA 2006, s. 649.
[45] CA 2006, s. 768.   [46] CA 2006, s. 769.
[47] The Companies (Model Articles) Regulations 2008 provide for the right to issue different classes of share subject to the provisions of the CA 2006, and where not to prejudice the rights of existing shareholders.

the company's ability to pay dividends or its solvency. The ordinary shareholders have the right to vote at general meetings and the right to receive a dividend if one is declared. However, they are only entitled to a dividend after preference shareholders receive theirs, and there may also be provision for the preference shareholders to receive a share from the company's remaining assets before ordinary shareholders in the event of the company being wound up.

- *Preference shares:* The nature of the distinction between ordinary shares and preference shares relates to the rights that attach to the shareholders of each class. The preference shareholder's main benefit over ordinary shareholders is in the right to a fixed dividend ahead of any dividend payment made to any other class of shares. However, as with any other dividend, this may only be paid from the company's profits and hence there is no guarantee to a payment being declared. The company will fix the amount of the dividend and this may be on a cumulative or non-cumulative basis. Cumulative preference shares provide the right for a fixed dividend, but if there are insufficient profits in the given year then there is no payment made. However, the dividend cumulates to the next year and is added to the dividend that is applicable to that year. For example, if a company issues James with 100 £1 preference shares with a fixed dividend of 5 per cent, and at the end of the first year that James has held these shares the company has insufficient funds to issue a dividend, James gets nothing. Next year, the company has profits to distribute as dividends and as James' situation has not changed: he is entitled to 5 per cent of the profits for the current year (£5) and 5 per cent of the dividends owed for last year (£5). As a consequence James receives £10 in dividends.

  Preference shares may also be non-cumulative, and in this situation, the holder is entitled to a fixed dividend from the company's profits, but where no profits are available, no dividend is paid. In the subsequent years, where there are profits and the company can issue dividends, the holders of preference shares are entitled to their fixed dividend. Further, where the company is wound up but is still solvent after paying the creditors, the preference shareholders may have the right to claim repayment of capital ahead of the ordinary shareholders.

  Where preference shareholders may be at a disadvantage compared with ordinary shareholders is that the company may not provide the holders of preference shares with the right to vote at general meetings (unless their dividends are in arrears). As such they have no right to influence the company in its decision-making. They are also unable to share in any surplus of the company that has been wound up and still solvent. When the creditors and other liabilities have been paid, if there is money left over, the ordinary shareholders will share in this distribution and the preference shareholders will not (however, of course, this is rather unlikely).

- *Redeemable shares:* A limited company that has a share capital has the power to issue shares that are to be redeemed or are liable to be redeemed at the option of the company or the shareholder.[48] A private limited company may exclude this right through its articles and does not require any express authorization to do so, but a public limited company may only issue redeemable shares if its articles authorize such an action. Redeemable shares may be issued only where other shares are in issue that are not redeemable.[49] This ensures that a company does not issue only redeemable shares and, once redeemed, only the directors of the company remain with no members.

---

[48] CA 2006, s. 684.   [49] CA 2006, s. 684(4).

A private limited company is only able to redeem shares out of capital in accordance with Chapter Five of the CA 2006, but specifically from distributable profits of the company or the proceeds of a fresh issue of shares made for the purposes of the redemption.[50] Having redeemed the shares, they are to be treated as cancelled and the amount of the company's issued share capital is diminished according to the nominal value of the redeemed shares.[51]

24.7 Changing class rights

Where the company has just one class of share that carries with it the same rights, duties, and liabilities, then this is identified in the articles and all the members are in the same position with regard to votes at meetings and dividends and so on.[52] However, the company may decide that it wishes to have different classes of shares, and with these different rights and liabilities. To achieve this change the company must look to its articles to identify any specific requirements that must take place for an alteration, and if none exist, then the shareholders of the class of share to be altered have to provide their consent.[53] The consent is provided through the holders of at least three-quarters of the nominal value of the issued shares of that class giving their written approval. Further, the company may gain the consent through the passing of a special resolution at a general meeting of the holders of that class of shares sanctioning the variation. These are minimum requirements required by the CA 2006 and the company's articles may insist on more onerous requirements if it sees fit. Having successfully varied the class of shares, the company must inform the Registrar of the particulars of the variation within one month of so doing.[54]

Where the company has varied the class of shares as noted above, there is a provision for holders of not less than 15 per cent of the issued shares of the class in question (and who did not consent or vote in favour of the special resolution) to apply to a court to have the variation cancelled.[55] Where an application is made, the variation will not take effect until the court confirms the variation, and a variation may be refused by the court where to allow it would unfairly prejudice the holders of the shares concerned.[56]

24.8 The company's purchase of its own shares

A general rule exists that a limited company is prevented from acquiring its own shares, whether by purchase, subscription, or otherwise, except in accordance with Chapter One, Part 18 of the CA 2006. Contravention of this rule by the company and its directors in default is punishable on conviction on indictment for a term of up to two years' imprisonment.[57] Exceptions exists because it may lead to greater investment where venture capitalists may be willing to purchase shares if permitted to sell the shares back to the company; shareholdings in smaller companies (such as those which are completely family-owned) may be more

---

[50] CA 2006, s. 687. [51] CA 2006, s. 688. [52] CA 2006, s. 629. [53] CA 2006, s. 630.
[54] CA 2006, s. 637. [55] CA 2006, s. 633. [56] CA 2006, s. 633. [57] CA 2006, s. 658.

easily managed if a shareholder wished to sell shares but no other member was in a position to purchase them and he/she could simply sell them to the company and so on. Therefore the CA 2006 makes provision for such sales.

A limited company that has a share capital may purchase its own shares (including redeemable shares),[58] subject to Chapter Four of the CA 2006 and any restrictions in the company's articles. The limited company is prevented from purchasing its own shares where to do so would result in there no longer being any issued shares of the company other than redeemable shares or shares held as treasury shares. The company may not purchase its own shares unless they are fully paid for, and the company, as purchaser, pays for them on purchase (and as such it cannot purchase unissued shares).[59] The authority for the company's purchase of its shares requires the agreement by the seller, and the appropriate authority for the company to act in this way. The company may finance the purchase only through distributable profits or the proceeds of a fresh issue of shares made for the purpose of financing the purchase; and any premium paid for its own shares must be paid out of distributable profits. However, this premium may only be paid in this circumstance up to an amount equal to the lesser of the aggregate of the premiums received by the company on the issue of the shares purchased; or the current amount of the company's share premium account.[60]

24.9 Share issue

A company may wish to issue shares. These shares can be purchased from the company directly, they may be bought and transferred from an existing member, or they may be transferred by an operation of law (such as where shares have been inherited on the death of a member). This information will be provided through the company's annual return.

Shares relate to a company's share capital, and references to shares in the CA 2006 include stock, unless a distinction between them is expressed or may be implied.[61] When a decision is taken to issue shares or to grant rights to subscribe for, or to convert any security into shares (of more than one class) by the directors of the company, the express authorization of the members must be secured.[62] This, however, does not apply to the allotment[63] of (or right to subscribe for) shares under an employees' share scheme. Any director who knowingly contravenes or permits/authorizes such a contravention commits an offence under the Act and is subject to a fine on conviction. The CA 2006, s. 550 continues that in private companies with only one class of shares, a director may exercise his/her power to allot shares of that class; grant rights to subscribe for shares; or convert any security into such shares, except where he/she is prohibited from doing so by the company's articles. A director(s) may exercise the power to allot shares if he/she is authorized to do so by the articles of association or by a resolution of the company.[64] Such an authorization is usually provided by an ordinary resolution at a general meeting and may take the form of a general power[65] to allot shares (with a stated maximum amount of shares to be allotted under the authorization) or authorization

[58] CA 2006, s. 690.   [59] CA 2006, s. 691.   [60] CA 2006, s. 692.

[61] CA 2006, s. 540.   [62] CA 2006, s. 549.

[63] CA 2006, s. 558 provides: 'For the purposes of the Companies Acts shares in a company are taken to be allotted when a person acquires the unconditional right to be included in the company's register of members in respect of the shares.'

[64] CA 2006, s. 551.

[65] The power is provided in this respect for a fixed period of five years but may be renewed at such intervals.

for the specific shares being allotted. This authority may be revoked or varied by an ordinary resolution where the power has not been exercised. As soon as practicable after the allotment (or in any event no later than two months following the date of allotment) the company must register this fact unless the company has issued a share warrant[66] in respect of the shares.[67] An offence, subject to a fine on conviction, is committed where a company fails to comply with the registration requirement.

- *Pre-emption rights:* Where shares are being issued under CA 2006, s. 549, in both public and private companies, and hence the members have provided their authority for this action, the company is obliged to offer ordinary shares[68] (not necessarily preference shares) to the existing members on a proportionate basis to their existing number of shares held (known as a right of **pre-emption**).[69] This is a requirement to ensure that existing shareholders do not have their stake in the company reduced (diluted) without the opportunity to purchase a proportion of the new issue. Where this obligation is contravened, the company and every officer of it who knowingly authorized or permitted it are jointly and severally liable to compensate any person to whom the offer should have been made, in accordance with those provisions for any loss, damage, costs, or expenses which the person has sustained because of the contravention.[70] There is a provision to exclude this obligation to offer shares to existing members. A private company may achieve this through making an additional clause to its articles,[71] specifically removing the pre-emption rights, although this position can be varied through a special/written resolution altering the articles,[72] or if the private company ceases to be a private company (this is a permanent measure). The private company may also use a written resolution to dispense with the pre-emption rights for a particular allotment or a general restriction of the rights for a period of five years (which is renewable). Public companies may remove pre-emption rights through a special resolution that can apply to a particular allotment or a general provision (although, as with private companies, this must be renewed every five years). Where the company is listed on the stock exchange, Listing Rules insist that only 5 per cent of the company's securities can be issued to persons other than existing shareholders in any year. The pre-emption rights do not apply to bonus issues,[73] shares issued and to be paid up wholly or partly otherwise than in cash,[74] or shares held under an employee's share scheme.[75]

- *Directors' duties on share issue:* The directors of a company who possess authority to allot shares are obliged to do so in an equitable manner and the CA 2006 codifies existing common law requirements and wider duties to the company.[76] Therefore, when allotting shares, directors must refrain from basing the allotment on promoting persons favourable to themselves (such as those sympathetic to the directors and who would follow their decisions in the control and direction of the company and so on). The members have some control in authorizing the allotment of shares and decisions to extend this allotment to persons outside the company (non-existing members).

---

[66] A company limited by shares may, if authorized by its articles, issue in relation to any fully paid shares a warrant providing the bearer with entitlement to the shares specified on it. The company may, if authorized by its articles, provide for the payment of future dividends on shares included in the warrant (CA 2006, s. 779).

[67] CA 2006, s. 554.   [68] In the CA 2006, s. 561 these are referred to as equity securities.

[69] CA 2006, s. 561.   [70] CA 2006, s. 563.   [71] CA 2006, s. 567.   [72] CA 2006, s. 571.

[73] CA 2006, s. 564.   [74] CA 2006, s. 565.   [75] CA 2006, s. 566.   [76] CA 2006, s. 170.

24.10 **Payment**

To reiterate the point, shares must not be offered at a discount. Where they are, the allottee is liable to pay the company an amount equal to the amount of the discount and any interest owing (at an appropriate rate).[77] The shares that are issued or allotted have to be paid for; however, this does not necessarily mean that such payment must be in cash.[78] Typically, where companies purchase shares or another corporation they may pay for these through the allocation of shares from their own company or through providing assets. With a private company, the equalization of the value of the items traded for the shares will be a matter for the company. However, with public companies, the shares may only be sold for cash.[79] Where they are traded in the above example for, say, assets (but not for work or services performed for the company),[80] the value of the non-cash items must be independently valued to ensure they represent an equivalent value and consequently ensure that the shares have been fully paid up. An auditor (or a person appointed by the auditor) must conduct, independently, the valuation in these circumstances.[81] Where non-cash consideration has been accepted for the shares, the contract to this effect must be sent to the Registrar within one month, and the public companies must enclose the valuation report with this contract.[82] Having received the information, the Registrar publishes the notice in the **London Gazette**.

24.11 **Dividend payments**

 Business Link

People purchase shares in companies for many reasons. However, it may be assumed that one important reason is as an investment. The value of the share may rise (and then be sold at a profit) and/or the shareholder will receive a dividend. The company must effectively balance the need to provide a sufficient dividend to retain and appease existing shareholders (and possibly make future sales attractive to investors), but also retain sufficient funds for future investments. Further, rules exist as to what dividends may be paid and how the shareholders may influence these decisions.

When an investment is made in a company, there is the hope (if not expectation) that a return will be provided and that may be through a rise in the premium of the shares held, but also on dividends in respect of the shares held. As stated previously, dividends may only be paid from the company's distributable profits (and in cash unless otherwise stated in the articles) as to do otherwise would be to reduce the company's capital. A profit available for distribution is defined as '… its accumulated, realized profits,[83] so far as not previously utilized by distribution or capitalization, less its accumulated, realized losses,[84] so far as not previously

---

[77] CA 2006, s. 580.
[78] CA 2006, s. 582. (Section 583 defines the meaning of 'cash').   [79] CA 2006, s. 584.
[80] CA 2006, s. 585.   [81] CA 2006, s. 593.   [82] CA 2006 s. 597.
[83] These are the amounts of income produced through sales of assets that exceed its expenses.
[84] These are the amounts of expenses that exceed the income generated through the sales of its assets.

written off in a reduction or reorganization of capital duly made'.[85] Whilst it is expected that a company will generate profits and at least a proportion of these will be returned to the members in dividends, there is no automatic right to receive a dividend. Indeed, a company will wish to retain certain monies to enable growth, re-investment, and a safeguard for certain unexpected costs. This would simply be evidence of prudent management of the company. However, the company must also ensure that the members receive some form of return or else these investors may take their money to another business.

The company's directors recommend a dividend and the amount is contained in the directors' report, and is declared by the members at a general meeting (for a public company). Only public companies have to hold a meeting to declare a dividend. The members have to agree to the amount of the dividend, and they may require the amount to be reduced (but have no right to increase the dividend). Where a director(s) refuses to reduce the dividend the members can move to have the director(s) concerned removed from office. Creditors have no rights to prevent a dividend being paid to the members. The company's articles may also give the directors the power to pay an interim dividend. Where a dividend is declared but is not paid then the member(s) affected has up to 12 years in which to bring an action against the company to realize the money owed. This is, however, a contentious point and it will be interesting to see if the courts follow this interpretation of the limitation period or follow the pre-CA 2006 position of limiting claims to six years.[86]

24.12 Loan capital

> ### ∅ Business Link
>
> Companies, at some point, may need to raise money for commercial purposes. Issuing shares is an option but this may not be in the best interests of the company or the shareholders and, as such, a loan may have to be obtained. Lenders will generally want security for the loan and this is achieved through the company offering some collateral—a typical example is providing the lender with a charge over specific property (such as a mortgage on a building). Different types of charges exist and these must be understood due to the hierarchy of which creditors are likely to get paid and in what order.

When a company is formed, the members will contribute money to the business, but at some stage the company may have to borrow money to buy stock, invest in technology or premises and so on. Due to the company's separate legal personality, it has the right to enter into contracts (such as to obtain goods on credit, loan money from banks and so on) and the rights to raise finance are usually contained in the memorandum. These are express rights but the company may have implied rights if it is a trading company. A trading company has the power to buy and sell items as part of its functions, and implicitly to borrow money, and issue its assets as part of security for the loan.

The nature of loan capital is that money is borrowed on the basis of offering some form of security (collateral). With sole traders and simple partnerships, they may raise finance on

---

[85] CA 2006 s. 830.
[86] *Re Compania de Electricidad de la Provincia de Buenos Aires Ltd* [1980] Ch 146.

loans through, for example, providing a bank with a charge over property he/she owns. This may be his/her own personal property or business property, but a charge is placed on it and it is at risk if the person securing the loan cannot repay. Rather than place a charge over land or property, a company and a Limited Liability Partnership has the ability to provide a 'floating charge' over its assets (such as stock) to the lender, whilst sole traders and partnerships are unable to do so.

The company seeking to borrow money may contact a lending institution that is willing to provide this service, but evidently the lender will require certain formalities be to followed to ensure it will have any loaned money returned. To secure a loan, the company may issue the lender with a debenture.

24.12.1 **Debentures**

A debenture is a document produced in the form of a deed that secures a loan through granting the lender (such as a bank) the right to take control over assets and the business. Therefore, the lender is established as a creditor with the authority to appoint an administrator in the event of non-repayment of the debt.[87] A debenture includes debenture stock, bonds, and any other securities of a company, whether or not constituting a charge on the assets of the company.[88] A contract with a company to take up and pay for debentures of the company may be enforced through the courts by an order for specific performance.[89]

- *Debenture stock:* Situations involving debenture stock are those where the public have been offered to invest in the company and receive stock certificates rather than investing in shares (and receiving share certificates). These certificates are maintained by the company through a registration process, and the certificates may be transferred in a similar manner to share certificates. Due to the nature of such a way of distributing the assets of the company, and that these debenture holders are 'creditors' of the company (albeit with no contract with the company), there has to be regulation of the company's actions. As such, the creditors enter into a trust deed with trustees who act for the debenture holders, and the trustees possess a charge over the company's assets and may appoint a receiver or administrative receiver when required. A private company limited by shares or by guarantee is not permitted to issue debenture stock to the public, but an offer not made to the public, to a financial institution for example, would be permitted.[90] The debenture stock is somewhat different from shares in that whilst it would constitute a fraud to issue shares below their issue value, debentures may be issued at a discount.[91]

- *Registration of charges:* When a debenture has been issued or a charge to secure a debenture, it must be registered with the Registrar.[92] The reason for registration is that this is a public document and those interested parties may consult the register before deciding to do business with the company. The company is also required to maintain its own copy of the register of charges at its registered office or other suitable place,[93] and this must be made freely available for inspection by the company's creditors or members.[94] If the company does not register the charge in its register the officers of the company are liable to be fined,[95] although lack of such registration does not make the charge invalid. As the registration process is a requirement of law, failure to comply with the obligation to register

---

[87] The power of the administrator is considered in **23.8.2**.
[88] CA 2006, s. 738.   [89] CA 2006, s. 740.   [90] CA 2006, s. 755.   [91] CA 2006, s. 100.
[92] CA 2006, s. 860.   [93] CA 2006, s. 869.   [94] CA 2006, s. 877.   [95] CA 2006, s. 876(4).

the charge within 21 days of its creation[96] will result in the charge being void if the company is wound up[97] (and a liquidator appointed) or if an administrator is appointed. This has the effect that the lender does not possess secured creditor status (and hence he/she loses the protection of possessing a right over the property the company charged against the loan). However, this does not mean that the company does not continue to owe the lender the sum involved, and this will become repayable on request. Due to this potential problem of failure to register, and the concern and problems lack of registration brings, those lenders who are securing a loan on secured debentures may require the forms to be completed by the officers of the company and they take the responsibility to send these to Companies House. Where the 21-day registration period has been missed, a court may approve the registration and the charge will be given effect from the date of this registration. The charge will be satisfied and released through application to the Registrar that the debt relating to the charge has been paid or satisfied, or the property or undertaking charged has been released from the charge or has ceased to form part of the company's property or undertaking. This process will remove the charge from the register (through the issue of a memorandum of satisfaction, a copy of which is sent to the company), and will then enable the company, if it wishes, to secure loans on the property again.[98]

24.13 Charges

 Business Link

Typically, a lender will require some form of security for a loan provided and this may involve a charge being placed over property. Charges may be classed as fixed or floating, and the distinction is important as to the rights it provides the holder in relation to the asset upon which the charge has been made. Also, in the event of the company's insolvency, the charge will determine where the lender is ranked in the hierarchy of creditors. Therefore the status of the charge is significant for the company, the lender, and other creditors.

A charge is a contractual agreement in the form of security (on certain assets) for a loan. The borrower agrees to allow the rights over property to be transferred to the lender on the basis that if the loan is unpaid, the lender will be able to dispose of the property and secure the return of the loan. If such a charge is not made, the issue of limited liability may remove the shareholders' personal responsibility to contribute, beyond the value of the shares or any guarantees made, and the lender, if the borrower (for example, a company) has insufficient funds to repay all of its debts, will have to join the remaining creditors and may not realize all of the money it is owed. Hence charges are a valuable way of ensuring, as far as possible, that loans are secured on tangible property.

Faced with a situation where the borrower does not repay the debt, the lender with a charge over property may choose to bring an action for breach of contract, or he/she may choose

---

[96] CA 2006, s. 870.   [97] But is not void whilst the company is a going concern.
[98] CA 2006, s. 872.

to dispose of the assets to which he/she possesses a charge. If, in this disposal, there is more money generated than is owed, then following deductions for expenses in selling the property, it must be returned to the borrower.

24.13.1 Types of charges

As the charge involves a security over assets, it may be that the lender wishes to secure (fix) this on business premises (such as a factory) to ensure that a valuation can be made, and hence the loan be determined that will ensure the lender's position is secure. Whilst such a charge in this respect is commonplace (providing a mortgage over property) this is not the only method, and there is the second type of charge that is not attached to any particular asset. These are known as 'floating' charges as they float over given assets (such as stock). There are advantages to both and it is for the borrower and lender to identify the most suitable in the circumstances.

- *Fixed charges:* The nature of a fixed charge is that it is 'fixed' to a particular asset owned by the borrower, which may be real property or personal property, and it provides the lender with a proprietary interest over the asset. Real property consists of items such as property and land and whilst a charge rests over the property, there is no requirement to transfer the title to the goods to the lender. This leaves the ownership of the property with the borrower, although the Law of Property Act 1925 provides that the lender with a relevant charge is empowered to sell it without the permission or assistance of the title-holder. Personal property includes equipment and requires the borrower to assign the ownership of the property to the lender to ensure the borrower has the power to dispose of the property in the event of non-repayment.

  The benefit of the fixed charge for the lender, and a reason why he/she may pursue such a charge in determining whether to loan money, is the control over the property. It therefore represents the best form of security. The borrower may be prevented from selling the property that is subject to the charge until the loan is repaid, and the charge remains until the loan is fully repaid. Further, a lender with a fixed charge is generally considered to rank higher than preferential creditors and creditors who possess floating charges.

- *Floating charges:* A fixed charge therefore may involve (for example) a bank providing a loan to a company on the basis that it holds a charge over the company's factory. The company may use the factory, although it cannot sell it without the bank's authorization, and insofar as the company continues to make the required repayments, the bank will take no further action.

  As opposed to a charge that is fixed to a particular asset, the borrower may apply the charge to a group of assets (such as the stock with which the company trades). The benefit for the borrower in this scenario is that he/she is free to trade in the goods/assets subject to the floating charge, and in the event of non-payment of the loan when it is due, the charge becomes fixed or 'crystallizes'[99] over them. At this stage, the lender has the ability to dispose of the goods in the same way as someone with a fixed charge. Crystallization occurs where a receiver is appointed; if the company goes into administration or is wound up; or where an event that was provided for in the contract establishing the floating charge

---

[99] This led Nicholls LJ to comment that 'Notable among crystallizing events are the appointment of receivers by the charge holder or the company being wound-up': *Buchler and another v Talbot and another* [2004] UKHL 9.

occurs. Once crystallization occurs and the assets are traded after this event, the holder of the charge may bring an action against the party to whom they were transferred.

Clearly, unlike a fixed charge where the charge is applied to a specific asset, the floating charge, by its nature, does not apply to a specific asset. As such, the borrower appears to be in possession of the assets and may appear to be more creditworthy than he/she actually is. To prevent fraud, and perhaps a situation of the borrower attempting to obtain loans on the assets subject to the floating charge, protection is afforded through a system of registration.

? Thinking Point

Does, and/or should, the parties' intention of the nature of the charge as fixed or floating influence the decision of the court as to its actual legal form? If the parties agree to a charge being identified as floating or fixed, should the courts have the right to alter this? (See *Spectrum Plus Ltd*).

• *Potential difficulties:* What would occur where the parties identify a charge as a fixed charge, when in reality (and legally) it is a floating charge? In *Siebe Gorman and Co. Ltd v Barclays Bank Ltd*[100] the bank attempted to protect its interests by identifying the proceeds of the company's book debts as a fixed, rather than a floating charge. A lender may wish to obtain a fixed charge, over a floating charge, due to the increased security it provides. However, a company may not have the property available to provide a fixed charge and, further, book debts may represent the company's largest asset. Book debts by their nature involve the company being owed money; that money is then brought into the company (and deposited in the bank) and then the book debt is reintroduced. It therefore appears that as an asset that is traded rather than being 'fixed' to a specific item, it must be a floating charge. However, in *Siebe*, the bank contracted for such an asset to be a fixed charge and as such allowed the company to collect the money owed, but it was required to place the proceeds into a specific bank account and it was not free to draw on the account even when in credit. It was this level of control that gave the appearance of it being a fixed charge. Concerns were raised about the nature of the decision and how such an asset could in reality constitute a fixed charge. It took 25 years but eventually the situation was addressed and finalized by the House of Lords in *National Westminster Bank Plc v Spectrum Plus Ltd*.[101] Here, in a similar situation involving the bank lending money with the requirement of establishing the company's book debts as a fixed charge, it was held that such charges were to be considered as floating, not fixed. The first elements of the charges are similar. They involve a charge over the book debts, a requirement to pay the proceeds into a designated bank account, but the third element is crucial in determining its status. Here there was a restriction on the disposal of the debts to any other party without the agreement of the lender (the bank). However, unless the bank blocks the account to prevent the lender from having access to the funds, this would not be a fixed charge. Where a company is free to deal with the item (in this case the proceeds of the book debt), its transferable nature signifies the existence of a floating charge and this is how the Lords held.

---

[100] [1979] 2 Lloyd's Rep 142.   [101] [2005] UKHL 41.

> **? Thinking Point**
>
> Why do you think the Lords changed the position of charges over a company's book debts? Consider the status of the creditors and the implications of such a charge being fixed or floating when arriving at your conclusion.

24.13.2 Registration of charges

Similarly with debentures, a charge must be registered with the Registrar within 21 days of its creation.[102] The company is obliged to provide the Registrar with this information but it is also possible for the person interested in the registration to register it. The Registrar will then issue a certificate of registration and include details as to its particulars.[103] This is because where a charge is not registered, it will be invalid and it will not allow the creditor to have the right to dispose of the assets to which the charge was to relate. This does not mean that the creditor would be unable to bring an action against the company on the debt owed, but he/she would lose the security that the charge provides. Remember, a creditor without a charge over assets is an unsecured creditor, and on the basis of the company being wound up and unable to settle its debts, this creditor will join the rest in attempting to obtain the money it is owed. A secured creditor will have a greater opportunity (and priority) to have debts owed satisfied. However, it is possible to state that a fixed charge will rank below an existing floating charge, and hence it will rank below such creditors and behind preferential creditors.[104] It is also possible to grant more than one fixed charge over assets (particularly where the asset has significantly grown in value and hence could accommodate such charges). More than one charge may also be made over a floating charge; however when this occurs, they rank in the order that they were created (hence preventing the company establishing a fraud on the previous creditors through subsequent actions).

By the 18 June 2010, the Government ended its period of consultation regarding reform of the process of registration of charges by companies and Limited Liability Partnerships.[105] Its aim was to 'address the many imperfections of the present system'[106] and by implementing a system of electronic registration of charges. At the time of writing the Government intends this to be legislation in 2013.

24.13.3 Priority of charges

If the charges have been correctly registered, they rank in priority as follows. A fixed charge will rank higher than existing floating charges unless the existing floating charge has made provision against this. Fixed charges also have effect from the time they are created. The next level of charge is a floating charge and this takes effect when it crystallizes and attaches to the assets in the agreement. They will also have priority when the charge was created (hence the first floating charge will have priority over the last one created over the same asset, unless this is stated to the contrary).

---

[102] CA 2006, s. 870.   [103] CA 2006, s. 869.

[104] *Re Portbase Clothing Ltd* [1993] 3 All ER 829.

[105] http://webarchive.nationalarchives.gov.uk/+/interactive.bis.gov.uk/companycharges/.

[106] An example provided in the consultation document was that 'charges are now commonly granted over expected future income from major projects while charges to secure issues of debentures are not'. These do not come under the remit of registration as required by the CA 2006.

Finally, preferential creditors take priority over the holders of floating charges, but not over fixed charges. Preferential creditors include employees who are owed wages (although limited to £800 per employee earned in the previous four months) and any loan taken to pay the employees' wages. The company will also have to pay any holiday pay due to employees and any loans from third parties taken for the purpose of paying such costs. The costs of the company's contributions to any occupational pension scheme are included. However, payments to the government are no longer included in the list of preferential creditors.[107] Preferential creditors are paid monies owed before other creditors are paid from the company's assets (if solvent when wound up). Where insufficient funds exist to satisfy these debts, they will each receive a proportion of the debts owed and they rank equally with each other.

 ## Conclusion

This chapter has included details of the various obligations on companies that wish to issue and allot shares, provide debentures and charges over the company's assets, and guidance on the maintenance of the company's finances. As the company's directors often make such decisions (followed by the consent of the company's members), the role played by directors and their duties to the company is crucial. These issues are discussed in Chapter 25.

 ## Summary of main points

Shares

- The CA 2006 refers to members of a company and these are, in the case of a company limited by shares, those who have subscribed to the memorandum and taken shares. They are entered into the register of members.
- A share is a bundle of rights and duties, and it imposes liabilities on the holder.
- Shareholders have no automatic right of management in the company although, through attendance and the rights to vote at meetings, they may have influence over the business conducted (such as the moving of resolutions).
- Shares may be ordinary or preference, and may also be redeemable by the company.
- Preference shares are so called because of the right to dividends before ordinary shareholders (these may be cumulative or non-cumulative).
- A company may purchase its own shares in accordance with the CA 2006 if authorized to do so through its articles.

Share capital

- The company will identify its share capital when formed.
- The share capital may include the following factors: authorized share capital; issued, allotted, paid-up, and called-up aspects of the share capital depending on the actions of the directors and the requirements of the allotment/issue.

---

[107] Following enactment of the Enterprise Act 2002.

- Public companies must have at least £50,000 of allotted share capital to receive a trading certificate.

Alteration of share capital

- Companies are restricted from altering their share capital but may do so when following the rules prescribed in the CA 2006.
- Such an alteration may include allotting new share, consolidating and sub-dividing existing shares, redenominating shares, or reducing the share capital.
- Public and private companies may reduce the share capital through passing a special resolution that is confirmed by a court.

Share issue

- Shares may be issued to generate revenue for the company, and in the case of ordinary shares, the existing members have the right to be offered the opportunity to purchase such shares as equivalent to their existing holding before the shares are offered to non-members.
- Shares may not be offered at a discount.
- Shares in private companies may not be offered to the public.

Dividends

- Shareholders may only be paid dividends from distributable profits.
- The directors declare the dividends (and the shareholders must agree). Shareholders may require the dividend to be reduced but cannot increase it.
- There is no automatic right for a shareholder to receive a dividend.

Loan capital

- Companies may wish to obtain a loan and to do so may offer a charge over assets or offer a debenture.
- The charges that are provided over assets must be registered in accordance with the CA 2006.
- Charges may be fixed or floating.
- Fixed charges apply to fixed assets (such as a mortgage over a company's factory).
- A floating charge is a security over a class of assets (such as the stock of the company). The charge becomes fixed (crystallizes) on the default of the company.
- Charges must be registered with the Registrar of Companies.

 Summary questions

Essay questions

1. What are the various charges that a lender may require to be provided by the company that wishes to borrow money? Explain the nature of each, their priority, and their effect in the event of the company being wound up.

2. Explain the process of a company altering its share capital. Provide examples of why a company may wish to make such an alteration and how the creditors of the company are protected against abuse of this provision.

Problem questions

1. Michelle and Raj operate a bistro business called 'Café Culture Ltd' in Manchester. They have run the business largely by attempting to build solid foundations through paying themselves a relatively small salary and re-investing any profits back into the business. The business was originally a partnership, but the two owners later incorporated as a private limited company, with Michelle owning 60 per cent of the shares and Raj 40 per cent (and both are directors). Despite their initial introduction of capital, Michelle and Raj wish to increase the growth of the business and so allow Charlie to purchase 20 per cent of Café Culture Ltd's shares (with a reduction of Michelle's and Raj's shareholding by 10 per cent each).

   Upon taking a shareholding in the company Charlie stated that she had no wish to become a director but she did expect to receive an income from the dividends paid to shareholders. Café Bistro Ltd makes a profit each year and it has substantial sums in its account (some £400,000) but the directors choose, for the third consecutive year, not to declare a dividend. However, the directors pay themselves fees and have voted for themselves an 'achievement bonus'. Charlie is concerned that this is a policy of the business and that dividends will never be declared. She is concerned that her stake in the business will continue to go unrecognized and unrewarded.

   Advise the parties as to their rights and obligations in this matter.

2. Jackson's Paints Ltd is a company in financial trouble and has experienced the following situations and requires advice, among others, on the validity of the charges applied to its property and how to proceed.

   Jackson's Paints Ltd decided to attempt to raise funds through the directors' decision to issue debentures.

   A. One loan of £100,000 was made by Chloe, the wife of one of the directors, and this loan was secured through the issuing of a fixed charge over the property where the company sells its product (paint) to the public. The property was valued at £150,000.
   B. A further loan of £20,000 was made by the company's bank by the issuing of a floating charge over the company's entire stock.
   C. A final loan of £30,000 was obtained from Dale but the fixed charge issued to him in relation to this loan was over the same property as provided to Chloe.

   The company's articles of association require that all loan agreements are first approved by the board of directors before they can take effect. The fixed charge provided to Chloe was not agreed by the board of directors and it was not registered. The floating charge issued to the bank was agreed by the board and was correctly registered. The fixed charge provided to Dale was correctly registered.

   Having obtained the loans, Jackson's Paints Ltd failed to make repayments as they became due to the bank or to pay its staff their wages. Further evidence has come to light that before any of these loans were agreed, the auditors of the company had advised the directors of Jackson's Paints Ltd that the company was insolvent and should be wound-up. Some of the directors are still of the opinion that the company can trade out of these problems when the economic downturn improves.

Advise:

(a) Jackson's Paints Ltd on the validity of the charges it has purported to create over its property;

(b) The directors on the potential personal liability for the debts of the company;

(c) The options available to a secured creditor when faced with a company unable to pay its debts, and how such a creditor may petition for a company to be wound-up.

(d) The directors on granting charges when under notice that the company was insolvent.

📖 Further reading

Chiu, I. H. Y. (2006) 'Replacing the Default Priority Rule for Secured Creditors—Some Reservations' *Journal of Business Law*, Oct., p. 644.

Goldring, J. (2006) 'Floating Charges—The Awakening' *Insolvency Intelligence*, Vol. 19, No. 5, p. 68.

Ho, L. H. (2006) Reversing *Buchler v Talbot*—The Doctrinal Dimension of Liquidation Expenses Priority' *Butterworths Journal of International Banking & Financial Law*, Vol. 21, No. 3, p. 104.

Nolan, R. C. (2006) 'The Continuing Evolution of Shareholder Governance' *Cambridge Law Journal*, Vol. 65, No. 1, p. 92.

🔗 Useful websites

http://www.bis.gov.uk/insolvency/
(The website of the Insolvency Service. It operates mainly with matters to do with the Insolvency Acts 1986 and 2000, and the Company Directors Disqualifications Act 1986. Among its roles are providing information and assistance to administer and investigate the affairs of bankrupts and companies wound up by the courts; acting as a trustee/liquidator where no private sector insolvency practitioner is appointed; and authorizing and regulating the insolvency profession.)

http://www.london-gazette.co.uk/
(The website of the *London Gazette*, the official newspaper of record for the UK, provided electronically to disseminate and record official, regulatory, and legal information.)

@ Online Resource Centre

http://www.oxfordtextbooks.co.uk/orc/marson3e/
Why not visit the Online Resource Centre and try multiple choice questions associated with this chapter to test your understanding of the topic. You will also find relevant updates to the law.

Corporate Management

25

Why does it matter?

The director and the company secretary are two major roles performed in the management of a corporation. The Companies Act (CA) 2006 identifies the powers and duties on these office holders, and it identifies, where relevant, any specific qualifications that must be held to fill the role. Whilst most companies have shareholders (although of course the CA 2006 calls such people 'members' as companies need not have shareholders) who 'own' the company, it is the directors who 'run' the company, based on the powers conferred upon them, along with the secretary, who may perform many of the daily administrative tasks that are required. As every company must have at least one director who is a natural person, knowledge of his/her role in the company is of crucial significance, as are the protections available to the shareholders to ensure they are not unfairly prejudiced by the directors' actions.

Companies
Act 2006

Learning outcomes

Following reading this chapter you should be in a position to:

- explain the appointment process of a director and secretary of a company (25.2.3; 25.5)
- identify the duties imposed on directors and how the Companies Act 2006 has added to the obligations established through the common law (25.2.7–25.2.8)
- explain how a director may lose his/her directorship and the consequences of the disqualification of the director from a company (25.2.9; 25.2.12–25.2.13)
- identify the protection of shareholders and the powers they possess in a company (25.4–25.4.3)
- explain the responsibilities of a company secretary and the limitations of his/her authority (25.5–25.5.1).

> ## 🔒 Key terms
>
> These terms will be used in the chapter and it may be helpful to be aware of what they mean or refer back to them when reading through the chapter.
>
> ### Indemnity
> The Civil Procedure Rules define indemnity as a right of one party to recover from a third party the whole amount that he himself is liable to pay. This is particularly apt in situations involving the liability of partners.
>
> ### Written resolution
> This is a mechanism for the board of directors to make a decision without having to meet in person. The resolution is valid and effective as if it had been agreed and passed at a meeting, if signed by all the directors entitled to receive notice of it.

25.1 Introduction

This chapter considers corporate management and focuses on the regulation of those who govern the company, and the protection of the shareholders (who have no automatic right of management). The actual 'running' of the company is left to the directors, a relatively small number of persons who may take individual responsibility for aspects of the company's business, or may oversee the company as a whole. Directors have significant powers when acting for the company, and whilst a corporation possesses its own separate legal personality, independent of those who manage it, the actions of the company are performed, under authority provided by statute and the company's constitution, by its directors. The chapter identifies the appointment of directors and their duties (codified from the common law into the Companies Act (CA) 2006), and the provisions for removing a director. It further identifies another officer of significance—the company secretary. Under the CA 2006 private companies are no longer required to have a company secretary, although public companies must still have such an officer. He/she is of importance in corporate governance, and may provide a beneficial service to any company.

The governance of a company will also include consideration of the protection of the companies' shareholders and their rights in relation to the company. This includes their powers to appoint or remove directors, voting at meetings and other rights in the exercise of power with regard to the direction and control of the company, and also how protection may be sought, particularly in relation to minority shareholders who may be exposed to risk through the powers granted to directors.

25.2 Directors of a company

The nature of a company is predicated on the concept of it possessing its own legal personality and this being independent of the person(s) who exercise the power to take the decisions of the company. These specific tasks, whilst performed in the company's name and on its behalf, have to be exercised by people. Therefore the CA 2006 requires that, upon formation, the company submits numerous documents to the Registrar of Companies, including the articles of association that identifies, *inter alia*, the nature of the company, what it intends to do, and other matters regarding the powers of those who 'run' the company. These positions are then filled by the directors. Directors possess the authority to act as the company's agent and perform the tasks required. As the shareholders may consist (although not necessarily so) of a large and diverse population, it would be impractical for each to have a management capacity and hence they appoint the directors who may exercise the powers conferred on the position by the company.[1] They may also wish to remove the director from the position and hence they are provided with the mechanisms to achieve this.

When the registration documents are submitted to the Registrar, these must include who will hold the position of director (as companies cannot be registered in the absence of directors). It should also be recognized at this stage that the director of a company might be (and very often is) a shareholder of the company, although there is no requirement for this. The position of director is defined in the CA 2006 so as to ensure that the relevant powers and obligations associated with this position are recognized and applied despite any alternative title that the officer of the company may have (such as manager, for example): 'It does not matter much what you call them, so long as you understand what their true position is, which is that they are merely commercial men, managing a trading concern for the benefit of themselves, and all other shareholders in it.'[2]

25.2.1 **Types of director**

There are different types of director of companies and they are often described with reference to their position and their responsibilities to the company. Directors can be executive and non-executive directors. An executive director is so called due to his/her activities and because he/she undertakes special responsibilities in the company. For example, a company may have an operations director, managing director, a finance director and so on. These directors take charge over the aspect or function of the company (although there is no legal requirement to have such 'executive' directors and, whilst unlikely, the board could delegate these functions to the company's employees). The non-executive directors have no specific function over an area of the business or take an active part in the company's management; rather they perform tasks such as attending meetings, taking a constructive part in the board's decision-making, or they may 'lend' their name to the business to increase its standing with customers.[3] Therefore the executive directors have both executive and non-executive functions.

Companies may also appoint 'shadow directors' who are defined as 'a person in accordance with whose directions the directors of the company are accustomed to act'.[4] This position will not extend to those who give their advice to the board in a professional capacity (such as a lawyer) and may include, for example, a major shareholder upon whose advice the directors would act.

25.2.2 **Number of directors**

Companies are required under the CA 2006 to have at least one director in the case of private companies, and two directors in the case of public companies.[5] At least one of the directors

---

[1] *Automatic Self-Cleansing Filter Syndicate Co. Ltd v Cuninghame* [1906] 2 Ch 34.

[2] Jessel MR, *Re Arthur Average Association for British, Foreign and Colonial Ships* [1875] 10 Ch App 542.

[3] This has been termed as 'window dressing' by Romer J in *Re City Equitable Fire Insurance Co.* [1925] Ch 407.

[4] CA 2006, s. 251.   [5] CA 2006, s. 154.

of the company must be a natural person[6] (as companies may hold directorships of other companies).

25.2.3 Appointment of directors

The company's promoters include the details of the directors for the company with the registration documents. These documents include the details of the company's first directors, and the articles will include the company's provisions for the appointment and removal of future directors of the company. Such appointments will occur, for example, when existing directors leave, or additional directors are appointed to supplement the company's responsibilities or to add expertise to the company's management and so on. The articles of association allow for the appointment of directors and authority for such action is usually through an ordinary resolution at a general meeting, although other mechanisms such as a written procedure may be equally valid. (For a director's removal a **written resolution** is not an appropriate instrument.)

A director must be at least 16 years of age, although this does not affect the validity of an appointment that is not to take effect until the person reaches this age.[7] Any appointment in contravention of this section is void, although this does not affect the liability of a person who purports to act as a director or acts as a shadow director. Where an existing director is under the age of 16 when these provisions came into force, s. 159 provides that the person will cease to be a director and the company will be required to make any consequential changes necessary in the register of directors, although notice of the change need not be given to the Registrar.

When a public company intends to appoint a director(s), it may not appoint two or more directors at a general meeting through a single resolution, unless a resolution that it should be made has been unanimously agreed.[8] This requirement must be followed, as any resolution that is passed in contravention of this section is void even if no one voted against the appointment of the directors.

The appointment of directors will usually result in one director taking charge for the whole company rather than its constituent parts (where relevant) and this person has traditionally been called the managing director. Due to the nature of the position, its significance, and the authority it bestows, the appointment is controlled through the articles and is made by the board (although the board can vary and curtail any powers associated with the position). The rationale for a managing director's appointment is simply that it is often convenient for the company to have a director who can take executive leadership.

25.2.4 Registration of directors

Every company is required to maintain a register of its directors and contain the information required under ss. 163, 164, and 166 of the CA 2006.[9] This register must be available for inspection at the company's registered office or at another location as provided under s. 1136. Inspection by any member of the company must be available without charge, or to any other person on payment of a fee. Failure to comply with these requirements constitutes an offence by the company and every company officer (including shadow directors). A court is also empowered to order the register for inspection where there has been a refusal of inspection.

---

[6] CA 2006, s. 155.   [7] CA 2006, s. 157.   [8] CA 2006, s. 160.   [9] CA 2006, s. 162.

The CA 2006, Part 10, Chapter Eight has added protection to directors from having to disclose their residential address on these documents (as they are available for public inspection). These details are considered 'protected information'[10] and this duty to protect such information extends to the company (preventing its disclosure except for communicating with the director or in order to ensure compliance with the CA 2006)[11] and to the Registrar in disclosing the materials unless these need to be stated.[12] Also, note that a court can make an order for disclosure of protected material where there is evidence that the service address is not effective to bring matters to the notice of the director or it is necessary for information provided in connection with the enforcement of a court order, and the court is satisfied that the order is appropriate.[13]

25.2.5 Directors' pay and contracts

It is not required that a director receives pay (remuneration) for his/her activities as a director. For example, a non-executive director is not necessarily paid for his/her services. Where payment is provided this is generally done through a contract between the company and the director, and due to the fiduciary relationship between the director and the company, the director is not permitted to make any profit that has not been expressly identified in the agreement. Fees and expenses may be paid, but in relation to executive directors, payment is traditionally made through a contract of service (an employee) and as such, it is a contract that must be personally performed by the post-holder.[14] Hence the delegation of these tasks is not permitted. The payment could be included in the articles of the company, and this would be more applicable where a non-executive director is provided with a fee for his/her services. However, it should not be assumed that a director is an employee of the company and there must be an agreement to this status. In terms of the payments made under a contract of service, the CA 2006 requires that a copy of the contract is maintained at the company's registered address or other place specified under s. 1136, for every directors' service contract, and whilst this need not be in writing, the very least that is required is a written memorandum setting out the terms of the contract.[15]

In June 2012,[16] following a period of consultation, the Business Secretary announced the Government's intention to introduce legislation to empower shareholders to engage more effectively with companies regarding pay. The intention is to:

- give shareholders binding votes on pay policy and exit payments (to enable them to hold companies to account and prevent rewards for failure); and

- boost transparency so that what people are paid is easily understood and the link between pay and performance is clearly drawn.

These measures are being incorporated into the Enterprise and Regulatory Reform Bill that the Government intends to be enacted by October 2013.

? Thinking Point

What is the practical and legal significance of requiring disclosure of the directors' pay? For what purposes could this information be used?

---

[10] CA 2006, s. 240. [11] CA 2006, s. 241. [12] CA 2006, s. 242. [13] CA 2006, s. 244.
[14] CA 2006, s. 227. [15] CA 2006, s. 228.
[16] http://www.bis.gov.uk/news/topstories/2012/Jun/directors-pay-reform.

25.2.6 **Directors' duties**

The CA 2006 had a significant impact on the duties imposed on directors through codification and extension of duties that, prior to the enactment of CA 2006, had been developed through the common law. The provisions under Part 10A of the CA 2006 (other than the issues of conflict of interest, the directors' residential addresses, and age of the directors) came into effect on 1 October 2007.

25.2.7 **Directors' duties under the Companies Act 2006**

Chapter Two of the CA 2006 identifies the duties of the directors and that the duties under ss. 171–177 (see Table **25.1**) are owed by the director to the company (rather than those outside of the company).[17] It provides instructions as to how these sections are to be interpreted when the director ceases to be a director of the company: such as the duty to avoid conflicts of interest[18] and the duty not to accept benefits from third parties, which continues after the director has left office. Section 170 continues that these general duties imposed on directors are to be interpreted and applied in the same way as the common law rules and equitable principles on which they were based. Therefore some of the previous cases are identified, but as these were decided under the common law it is important to be vigilant for case law derived specifically from the legislation. These duties also apply to shadow directors where the corresponding common duties and equitable principles apply to them.

25.2.7.1 *Duty to act within their powers*

The director must act in accordance with the company's constitution[19] (now the articles of association rather than the memorandum) and only exercise powers for the purposes for which they had been conferred. As such, where authority is provided for a specific purpose, the power must only be used for this purpose and will not be extended (even if the director acted in good faith and in the best interests of the company).[20]

25.2.7.2 *Duty to promote the success of the company*

This was based on the common law duty of the director acting in good faith.[21] The Act requires the director to fulfil this requirement in the way he/she considers would be most likely to promote the success of the company for the benefit of its members as a whole. In so doing the director must have regard to the likely consequences of decisions in the long term; the interests of the company's employees; the need to foster relationships with outside organizations (suppliers/customers and so on); the impact of the company's operations on the community and environment; the company's reputation; and the need to act fairly as between the members of the company.

Note that this is not an exhaustive list but provides examples of the requirements the section of the Act places on the director. The section goes further than the common law upon

---

[17] *JJ Harrison (Properties) Ltd v Harrison* [2001] EWCA Civ 1467.
[18] CA 2006, s. 175.
[19] CA 2006, s. 171.
[20] *Fraser v B N Furman (Productions) Ltd* [1967] 3 All ER 57.
[21] CA 2006, s. 172.

Table 25.1 Duties of Directors

Directors' Duties	CA 2006
To act within their powers	s. 171
To promote the success of the company	s. 172
To exercise independent judgment	s. 173
To exercise reasonable care, skill, and diligence	s. 174
To avoid conflicts of interest	s. 175
Not to accept benefits from third parties	s. 176
To declare interest in proposed transaction or arrangement	s. 177
Duty of the director to disclose interests in existing transaction/arrangement	s. 182

which it is based and places a positive duty on the director not only to act in the interests of the members, but also, in certain circumstances, to consider or act in the interests of the company's creditors (and taking into account others beyond the members, such as the company's employees). Therefore the company should ensure that evidence may be produced to demonstrate that at meetings and where decisions are made, regard had been taken of such groups.

This requirement may serve to instil an obligation of more strategic thinking on the part of directors, who will consider the wider implications of their actions for the company's stakeholders, and consider the folly of short-term decision-making compared with taking a long-term view of the company's actions. For example, the shareholders may wish to gain dividends from the profits, or seek for products to be sourced from the cheapest suppliers with a disregard as to the wider effects that this may have to their relations with suppliers, the environmental impact of the actions,[22] and the long-term viability and sustainability of such measures. This section of the CA 2006 may actually serve to protect the directors when making difficult decisions and assist in justifying these to the shareholders. Clearly these considerations will have a greater influence on large companies with regard to, for example, the 'carbon footprint' of their activities, and will depend on the infrastructure of the company to obtain relevant materials to identify the consequences of decisions. They are, however, a means to require greater thought and consideration of the wider consequences of business decisions, and there is no distinction in the legislation between the requirements placed on large and small companies. A small company that cannot afford to obtain research and documentation on its actions, and how this affects the environment, will still be obliged to provide its most accurate and best informed assessment.

To facilitate compliance in this area it may be wise for the board to ensure each director (and non-executive director) is aware of the responsibilities under this section of the Act, and those under the company's constitution. The director should have the knowledge of the requirements for the full consideration of s. 172 of the CA 2006 and establish practices for decision-making subject to these obligations. This may also require establishing a review process to provide for transparency of decisions and analysis of how/why the director acted in the way he/she did. If failings are discovered, then a system of review and action is also a prudent step.

---

[22] Although it should be thought that a requirement of considering the social and environmental impact of decisions should not override the directors' duties to the company.

25.2.7.3 *Duty to exercise independent judgement*

The director has an obligation to exercise independent judgement,[23] although this will not be infringed by his/her acting in accordance with an agreement entered into with the company that restricts the future exercise of discretion by its directors, or in a way authorized by the constitution of the company. As such, this is a further example of the law codifying existing requirements in the common law, but it reinforces the director's duty to act for the best interests of the company, and not necessarily follow the instructions of shareholders, whose interests may be selfish and not concerned for the company. This situation comes to prominence, as the shareholders appoint the director, and where this appointment has been made on a personal basis, the director must remain independent of the person(s) that made the appointment.

25.2.7.4 *Duty to exercise reasonable care, skill, and diligence*

The director has to exercise reasonable care, skill, and diligence.[24] This duty is based on what a reasonably diligent person with the general knowledge, skills, and experience for carrying out the functions required of the director to the company would consider, and the general knowledge, skill, and experience possessed by the specific director.[25] As such, where the director purports to possess special skills or knowledge, then this will be the standard against which he/she is assessed. Where no such special skills/knowledge are claimed, the standard test of how a 'reasonable' director would have acted will be applied. Therefore, a directorship (whether executive or non-executive) of a company is a very important role involving significant responsibilities, and it should not be accepted without consideration of the implications of the position and the obligations to the company—with reference made to the CA 2006 and the company's constitution. Diligence was already a common law duty and requires the director to be vigilant for acts that require appropriate investigations to be made and questions to be answered. A director will fail in his/her duty by not taking the appropriate steps when faced with such scenarios.[26]

25.2.7.5 *Duty to avoid conflicts of interest*

A director has an obligation to avoid situations where he/she has, or can have, a direct or indirect interest that conflicts (or has the potential to conflict) with the interests of the company.[27] This duty applies particularly to the exploitation of any property, information, or opportunity and it is immaterial whether or not the company could take advantage of the property, information, or opportunity. However, there are limits to this duty and it does not apply in relation to a transaction or arrangement between the director and the company itself. Further, the duty is not infringed if the situation cannot reasonably be regarded as likely to give rise to a conflict or if the matter has been authorized by the directors. Such authorization may be given by the directors where:

1 the company is a private company (and nothing in the company's constitution invalidates such authorization) by the matter being proposed to and authorized by the directors; or

---

[23] CA 2006, s. 173.

[24] CA 2006, s. 174.

[25] See *Re Brazilian Rubber Plantations and Estates Ltd* [1911] 1 Ch 425 for a consideration of the common law duty to exercise care and skill.

[26] *Re Railway and General Light Improvement Co. Marzetti's Case* [1880] 42 LT 206.

[27] CA 2006, s. 175.

2 the company is a public company (and its constitution includes provision enabling the directors to authorize the matter) by the matter being proposed to, and authorized by, them in accordance with the constitution.

The authorization is only effective if any requirement as to the quorum at the meeting (where the matter is considered) is met without the director in question or any other director, and the matter was agreed to without his/her voting (or would have been agreed if his/her votes had not been counted). This section of the Act, with reference to a conflict of interest, includes conflicts of duty. Where the duty may become problematic is where a director holds directorships with several companies who may trade, or be in some other way involved with the business of the company in question. Separating the director's duty in such examples may be a challenging undertaking and the exercise of care will be needed to ensure adequate (but complete) disclosure is provided. As such, this section extends the requirements of the common law by imposing a positive duty on the director to avoid any unauthorized conflicts of interest, and it makes authorization of any conflict to be determined by the company's directors rather than the shareholders.

25.2.7.6 *Duty not to accept benefits from third parties*

A director of a company is not allowed to accept a benefit from a third party that is due to he/she being a director of the company and his/her acts or omissions as a director.[28] 'Third party' is interpreted as a person other than the company itself, an associated body corporate or a person acting on behalf of the company or an associated body corporate. However, the duty is not infringed where the acceptance of a benefit 'cannot reasonably be regarded as likely to give rise to a conflict of interest'. This is an area of the law that will likely produce case law of significance on how to interpret the element and extent of what 'cannot reasonably be regarded as'.

> **? Thinking Point**
>
> Will expensive gifts such as holidays be included? Probably, yes, but what about a residential presentation or seminar at an expensive hotel (with expenses paid for), and corporate hospitality? How will gifts such as watches/samples/food hampers be considered? Is it the value, nature, or frequency of the gift that is at issue? Is it the proximity between the giving of the gift and the conclusion of the action (or omission) that will be determinative of a breach of s. 176?

The conflict of interest here, as with s. 175, includes a conflict of duties. This duty will be concerned with benefits such as bribes (in cash or in kind) that will impact on the impartiality of the director in acting for the company. Where a benefit is provided to the director and not the company, the director's objectivity may be compromised. This provides an obligation on the director not to accept bribes, but this was a duty long established in the common law, and what the Act requires is for the director to consult with the company's constitution to determine those actions that are acceptable, and those that are not. This is likely to be a particularly interesting aspect of the directors' duties under the CA 2006, but for the affected director, transparency of any gifts provided and how decisions were made may ensure he/she does not transgress his/her obligations in this area.

---

[28] CA 2006, s. 176.

25.2.7.7 *Duty to declare interest in proposed transaction or arrangement*

The director has a duty if in any way, directly or indirectly, he/she has an interest in a proposed transaction or arrangement with the company.[29] This interest must be declared to the other directors with specific regard to the nature and extent of the interest. The declaration may be made in the following way, although others may be used:

1 at a meeting of the directors, or
2 by notice to the directors in accordance with s. 184 (notice in writing) or s. 185 (general notice).

The declaration must be complete and accurate and if it proves to be, or subsequently becomes, incomplete and/or inaccurate, then a further declaration is required. There are limits placed on this obligation and the director need not declare an interest where it cannot be reasonably regarded as likely to give rise to a conflict of interest; where the other directors are already aware (or ought reasonably have been aware) of the conflict; or where it concerns terms of the director's service contract that have been, or are to be, considered by a meeting of the directors, or by a committee of directors appointed for the purpose under the company's constitution.

25.2.8 Duty of the director to disclose interests in contracts

Beyond the codification of the common law duties imposed on directors, the CA 2006 imposes duties of disclosure on the director who has an interest (direct or indirect) in a contract or proposed contract with the company.[30] This disclosure must be made as soon as is reasonably practicable (such as where the matter is first discussed by the board) and include the nature and extent of the interest, and be made at a meeting of the directors; or by notice in writing; or by general notice. The provisions of such disclosures apply to loans, quasi-loans, and credit transactions and arrangements.

25.2.9 Civil consequences of a breach of the duties

Where there is a breach (or threatened breach) of the duties identified in ss. 171–177, the consequences are the same as provided in the common law rules or equitable principles.[31] Further, the duties under s. 174 regarding reasonable care, skill, and diligence are enforceable, as are the other fiduciary duties that a director owes the company. Except where otherwise provided, more than one of the general duties may apply in any given case.[32]

Where the director has transgressed the requirements under this part of the Act, he/she may be liable to compensate the company for any losses sustained due to the director's breach. This may be the case even where the director had acted in good faith[33] and where he/she believed the actions were taken in the company's best interests. This may be particularly so where the director has, for example, disregarded the consequences of his/her actions to the environmental impact which has led to the company being held liable for the consequential

---

[29] CA 2006, s. 177.   [30] CA 2006, s. 182.   [31] CA 2006, s. 178.
[32] CA 2006, s. 179.   [33] *Kelly v Cooper* [1993] AC 205.

damage. The company will have a responsibility for any costs but may seek to reclaim these from the director's breach of his/her statutory duty.[34] It must also be remembered that even beyond the responsibilities of the director to the company and any imposition of responsibility through the CA 2006, a director who disregards these duties may suffer a disqualification if he/she appears unfit to fulfil the role of director.[35]

It is also possible for the members of the company to provide their consent, approval, or authorization of the director's actions.[36] Where the duty to avoid conflicts of interest[37] is complied with through the authorization of the directors; and the duty to declare an interest in a proposed transaction or arrangement[38] is complied with, the transaction or arrangement is not liable to be set aside by virtue of any common law rule or equitable principle requiring the consent or approval of the company's members. This is subject to provisions of the company's constitution that may require such consent or approval.[39] The compliance with these general rules does not remove the requirement of approval of the provisions of Chapter Four of the CA 2006 (regarding transactions requiring the approval of members).[40]

25.2.10 The meetings of directors

The board of directors' meetings are where important decisions affecting the company can be addressed. Each of the directors of the company must be given notice of the meeting,[41] and the directors are empowered to call a meeting when necessary. Every company is required to record the minutes of the meetings and these records must be maintained for 10 years.[42] The minutes of the meetings are an important record of the proceedings and where authenticated by the chairperson, they may be used as evidence of the proceedings at that meeting regarding the validity of appointments, that the proceedings are deemed to have duly taken place and so on.[43] The decisions taken at the meetings are based on a voting system and it is assumed that each director has one vote, unless the articles of the company provide differently, and the resolution is passed with a majority. Where the votes are split, the chairperson has the option to exercise his/her vote in favour of the resolution and it will be deemed that the resolution has been passed, or not and the resolution will fail.

25.2.11 Indemnifying the directors

The enactment of the Companies (Audit Investigation and Community Enterprises) Act 2004 introduced provisions for the **indemnification** of directors. Whilst they were given effect on 6 April 2005, they have now been included in the CA 2006 and appear in ss. 232–239. These protections assist the directors by providing that the company will repay any costs incurred (in certain circumstances) by the director in the course of his/her duties. A key element is that not only can the company protect the director, but also even where it is unable to excuse the director from liability in cases of negligence, default, breach of duty, or breach of trust, the High Court or County Court[44] possess this power under s. 1157. The section

---

[34] See **15.9.**   [35] Company Directors Disqualification Act 1986.

[36] CA 2006, s. 180.   [37] CA 2006, s. 175.   [38] CA 2006, s. 177.   [39] CA 2006, s. 180.

[40] CA 2006, ss. 188–226 relating to the directors' long-term service contracts; substantial property transactions; loans to directors; credit transactions, and other relevant transactions or arrangements.

[41] This notice must be of a reasonable duration to give the director the opportunity to attend. See *Bentley-Steven v Jones* [1974] 2 All ER 653.

[42] CA 2006, s. 248.   [43] CA 2006, s. 249.   [44] CA 2006, s. 1156.

states that where the officer of the company or a person employed as an auditor (whether an officer of the company or not) appears to be liable, but he/she acted honestly and reasonably, and having regard to all the circumstances of the case he/she ought fairly to be excused, the court may relieve him/her wholly or in part from this liability as it thinks fit. The officer/person may apply to the court for relief where he/she believes a claim may be made against him/her (on the instances listed above). The court may, if it is being tried by a judge with a jury, and he/she is satisfied that the defendant should be able to rely on the relief provided under s. 1157, withdraw the case from the jury and enter a judgement, including costs, as it thinks proper.

25.2.12 **Removal of a director**

Directors may leave office for numerous reasons. They may die in office or may resign (although once a resignation has been accepted the director cannot retract it);[45] and on the dissolution of the company the directors are automatically dismissed.[46] The articles of the company may provide for a proportion or number of directors to retire annually (retirement by rotation) and these directors may then be replaced or re-elected to office. However, the company, through the other directors' action or the members, may wish to remove a director before his/her term of office has expired.

A director may be removed from office through an ordinary resolution to that effect. Special notice is to be provided of 28 days to the company secretary of the resolution and the meeting at which the resolution is to be passed must be called with at least 21 days' notice. There are many reasons why the shareholders may wish for a director to be removed and the CA 2006 provides for the procedure of such a decision. The company may achieve this through an ordinary resolution at a meeting to remove the director before the director's term of office was due to expire.[47] However, as a director may also be shareholder with voting rights, his/her removal may prove to be problematic.

Bushell v Faith[48]

Facts:

A company had three hundred shares split equally between a brother and his two sisters who were the company's directors. When the sisters wished to remove the brother as director they issued a resolution to this effect. However, the articles of association provided that where a director was to be removed from office, in the vote to move this resolution, the affected director's shares should carry three votes per share. This was perfectly legal and hence following the vote the two sisters' votes accounted for 200 votes, whilst the brother's 100 shares accounted for 300 votes. The House of Lords held therefore that the vote to remove the director had been defeated. It should be noted that it is possible to provide for this arrangement of voting, but also the articles of the company may be changed through a special resolution to circumvent this problem of entrenching a director.

Authority for:

It is perfectly legal to include a clause into the Articles that affords protection to a director/minority shareholder from early removal from office. However, it is also possible to later alter this clause in accordance with the Articles.

---

[45] *Glossop v Glossop* [1907] 2 Ch 370.
[46] *Measures Bros Ltd v Measures* [1910] 2 Ch 248.   [47] CA 2006, s. 168.   [48] [1970] AC 1099.

When the director is removed, this section of the Act is not to be taken as depriving the removed person of any compensation or damages payable in respect of the termination of the appointment. A director removed in this way may protest and upon receipt of the notice of an intended resolution to remove him/her from office, the company must send a copy as soon as is reasonably practicable to the director concerned.[49] The CA 2006 also provides the director with the right to be heard on the resolution at the meeting. He/she may also, upon this notice, provide a written representation to the company (not exceeding a reasonable length) and request that this is notified to the members of the company. If the use of this procedure would be to abuse the rights provided in s. 169, the representations need not be sent out.

Beyond the use of the CA 2006 for this removal, there may be provision in the company's articles to achieve the same result. For example, the company may incorporate a clause into the articles that the director could be removed with a majority vote by the board by notice in writing. The main use of a removal through the articles rather than through s. 168 is simply that in the case of subsidiary companies, a holding company is not entitled to use s. 168 to remove directors of the subsidiary, but it is achievable through the articles.

25.2.13 Disqualification of directors

The legislation used to prevent a director holding office is the Company Directors Disqualification Act 1986 and it may be applied to both natural persons and to corporations that hold directorships. When the person is subject to a disqualification order, he/she is prevented from taking any part in the management of a company, he/she may not promote a company, and he/she is prevented from acting as an insolvency practitioner. To ensure that persons dealing with companies are protected, Companies House maintains a register of all disqualification orders and this is freely available to members of the public.

Examples of the offences that may lead to disqualification include the conviction of an indictable offence in connection with the promotion, formation, management, or liquidation of a company, or with the management [50] or receivership of the company's property.[51] Orders made on this ground at a Magistrate's Court last for five years. Where the director has been persistently[52] in default in providing the required annual returns or accounts to the Registrar, he/she may be subject to an order lasting no longer than five years.[53] If an officer or receiver of a company in liquidation has been guilty of fraud in relation to the company, or has breached his/her directors' duties, or committed an offence of knowingly being a party to fraudulent trading, [54] the court may issue an order for a maximum term of up to 15 years.[55] If the person acting as a director (or shadow director) had been engaged in conduct that led to a company becoming insolvent and it is considered he/she is unfit to act in a management capacity an order may be made (for not less than two years).[56] The action that leads to a person

---

[49] CA 2006, s. 169.

[50] 'Management' is given a broad interpretation. In *R v Georgiou* [1988] 4 BCC 322 the defendant carried on an insurance business as a limited company to achieve an illegal aim. This was held to involve the management of a company and he was subsequently disqualified.

[51] Section 2.

[52] Three convictions in a five-year period satisfies the requirement of a persistent breach. Also see *Re Arctic Engineering Ltd* [1986] 1 WLR 686.

[53] Section 3.

[54] Note that these offences do not need to be supported with a criminal conviction for the order to be imposed.

[55] Section 4.   [56] Section 6.

being disqualified for unfitness is not restricted to actions taken in the United Kingdom—its jurisdiction is much broader.[57] It is also possible for the articles to establish grounds for the disqualification of a director.

> **? Thinking Point**
>
> It has been stated that the aim of the disqualification is not to punish the director for his/her behaviour but rather to protect the public from the activities of those unfit to be concerned in company management.[58] Do you feel this is the correct approach for legislators to adopt or would more draconian penalties prevent abuses occurring?

25.3 Directors' liability to shareholders

The directors of a company and the company secretary owe duties to the company as a whole rather than to the individual shareholders (who make up the company) and as such the shareholders are unlikely to be able to claim directly against the director based on his/her conduct. Exceptions to this rule exist, for example, where the director has made a contract between him/herself and the shareholders, and this may establish an agency relationship, with the consequent liability for breach of duty.[59] There appears to be a potential problem then between the decisions taken by the directors and the amount of influence that can be exerted by the shareholders, and this may be even more marked where the shareholders are in a minority—who or what mechanism protects their interests?

25.4 Minority protection

Shareholders have the right, and the company is obliged in certain circumstances, to place a resolution at a general meeting and have this voted upon by the members (the shareholders). However, directors may also be shareholders and they may form a majority and hence would find it relatively easy to pass through the resolutions that require a simple majority, or even those requiring a 75 per cent majority. This problem led to the famous case of *Foss v Harbottle*[60] regarding two directors who sold part of their own land to the company followed by a claim of minority shareholders that the price paid by the company was too high. The minority of shareholders affected brought a claim against the directors concerned but the court refused to hear the action. It held that the interest in the case belonged to the company, and if the company believed the directors had acted wrongfully, then it should determine whether to bring the action—not the minority shareholders. This is known as a derivative claim,[61] where one party attempts to sue another party on the basis of loses suffered by a third party. The claim failed in *Foss*, but there have been many advances since the case was heard,

---

[57] *Re Seagull Manufacturing Co. (No. 2)* [1994] 2 All ER 767.

[58] *Secretary of State for Trade and Industry v Tjolle and Others* [1998] BCC 282.

[59] *Allen v Hyatt* [1914] 30 TLR 444.

[60] [1843] 2 Hare 461.   [61] CA 2006, s. 260.

with many exceptions to the general rule established that, whilst it remains 'good law', its usefulness has been significantly curtailed.

The CA 2006 has introduced protections for minority shareholders where a shareholder may initiate proceedings against a director on the company's behalf, (a derivative claim) in respect of a cause of action arising from an actual or proposed act or omission involving negligence, default, breach of duty, or breach of trust by a director[62] of the company. However, as this is a claim through the shareholders on the company's behalf, any award will be provided to the company, albeit that the shareholder claimant will be able to recover any expenses incurred in the action.

In order to use this procedure, the CA 2006 identifies requirements that must be satisfied. The first is that the member must obtain the court's permission to proceed with his/her action.[63] This first stage is used to determine whether a *prima facie* case exists against the director. Where this is satisfied, the case continues and the court may give directions as to the evidence to be provided by the company, and at the hearing the court may give permission for the claim to continue on the terms it sees fit; refuse permission and dismiss the claim; or adjourn proceedings and give any directions it thinks fit. Section 263 identifies situations where permission must be refused, and these occur where the court is satisfied that:

1 a person acting in accordance with section 172 (duty to promote the success of the company) would not seek to continue the claim; or

2 where the cause of action arises from an act or omission that is yet to occur, the act or omission has been authorized by the company; or

3 where the cause of action arises from an act or omission that has already occurred, the act or omission (i) was authorized by the company before it occurred, or (ii) has been ratified by the company since it occurred.

Another area of protection available to the minority shareholder, rather than a derivative claim, is a claim that his/her rights have been 'unfairly prejudiced' by the way in which the company is being run.

25.4.1 Unfair prejudice

The protection of members against unfair prejudice is contained in Part 30 of the CA 2006 and provides a right for members to petition a court that the company's affairs are being conducted in a manner that is likely to unfairly prejudice the interests of members generally, or some part of its members (including at least him/herself). The member may also petition on the basis that an actual or proposed act or omission of the company is or would be so prejudicial.[64] This section of the Act also applies to a person who is not a member of the company but to whom shares in it have been transferred as they apply to a member of a company. The CA 2006 also provides a right for the Secretary of State to exercise powers to petition the court where he/she believes the rights of members are being unfairly prejudiced.[65] Where the court is satisfied that the petition is well founded, it is empowered:[66]

(a) to order as it thinks fit relief in respect of the matters complained of such as to regulate the conduct of the company's affairs in the future, such as altering the articles to prevent

---

[62] This term also includes a former director and a shadow director.
[63] CA 2006, s. 261.   [64] CA 2006, s. 994.   [65] CA 2006, s. 995.   [66] CA 2006, s. 996(2).

future abuses.[67] It is also important to note that under this section, the court having changed the articles will not enable the company to change them again through a special resolution—it will be necessary to request the court's permission to alter them again;[68]

(b) (i) to require the company to refrain from doing or continuing an act complained of (for example, to stop directors' unusually high salaries that are preventing dividends being provided to the shareholders);

(c) (ii) to do an act that the petitioner has complained it has omitted to do (for example, to adhere to resolutions of the board);

(d) to authorize civil proceedings to be brought in the name of (and on behalf of) the company by such person(s) and on such terms as the court may direct (for example, to avoid the *Foss* situation and enable a claim in the company's name, rather than the shareholder);

(e) to provide for the purchase of shares of any members of the company by other members (or by the company itself); and in the case of purchase by the company, the reduction of the company's share capital accordingly (as demonstrated in *Re London School of Electronics*).[69]

This section of the CA 2006 restates the law that had already been included in the CA 1985 and incorporates a wide range of activities likely to adversely affect shareholders, particularly minority shareholders. The directors may be negligent in their management of the company that may, if the facts support it, lead to unfair prejudice; the directors may pay themselves salaries that reduce or remove entirely the members' dividends;[70] shares could be provided to directors on much more favourable terms than available to members and so on. Many of the cases based on the unfair prejudice principle have focused on where a major shareholder has been refused a management role with the company[71] or removed from the board of directors.[72] Where a director (and shareholder) of a company has been removed so that he/she can no longer take an active part in its management, the court has often ruled that the majority shareholders must purchase the shares of the removed director (but not necessarily a director who has not been removed and simply disagrees with the direction of the company),[73] to allow the affected director to invest his/her money in another company, although such rulings do not prevent a petition for the winding-up of the company on just and equitable grounds.[74]

25.4.2 Property transactions by the company

Protection is provided through Part 10, Chapter Four of the CA 2006 regarding the members' approval of substantial property transactions. A company may not enter into an arrangement[75] under which a director (including shadow directors) of the company or of its holding company, or a person connected with the director, acquires or is to acquire from the

---

[67] *Re H R Harmer* [1959] 1 WLR 62.   [68] Section 996 (2)(d).   [69] [1986] Ch. 211.

[70] *Re Sam Weller & Sons Ltd* [1989] 3 WLR 923.

[71] *Re London School of Electronics* [1985].

[72] *Ebrahimi v Westbourne Galleries* [1972] AC 360.

[73] *O'Neill v Phillips* [1999] 2 All ER 961.

[74] *Re Company (No. 001363 of 1988)* [1989] 5 BCC 18.

[75] Note that this word has been specifically used and hence it catches arrangement rather than legally binding contractual agreements.

company (whether directly or indirectly) a substantial non-cash asset[76] (meaning an asset whose value exceeds 10 per cent of the company's asset value and is more than £5,000; or it exceeds £100,000).[77] The company is also prevented from entering into an agreement for it to acquire a substantial non-cash asset from a director or person connected with him/her. In both of these situations, the transaction is only allowed where it has been approved by the members through passing an ordinary resolution at a general meeting, or is conditional on such approval being obtained. Therefore arrangements can be made that will proceed if and when the formal approval of the members has been realized. Where the transaction has been entered into in contravention of s. 190, but within a reasonable time it is affirmed by a resolution of the members, then the transaction or arrangement may not be avoided.

25.4.3 Loans, quasi-loans, and credit transactions

The CA 2006 continues from outlining where a substantial property transfer will or will not be permitted to identify the regulation of a company providing directors with loans and credit. This provision used to be prohibited, but the CA 2006 allows for such transactions insofar as they are supported by the members of the company through an ordinary or written resolution.

A quasi-loan is a transaction under which one party (the creditor) agrees to pay, or pays, a sum for another (the borrower); or he/she agrees to reimburse (or does reimburse), otherwise than in pursuance of an agreement, expenditure incurred by another party for another (the borrower).[78] This, essentially, can be interpreted as the company agreeing to pay a director's personal expenses, where the director agrees to pay the money back at a later date. This can involve personal loans where the nature of the item is purely for the director's personal consumption or it could be a loan associated with a cost that the director incurs as part of his/her work (such as travel costs that are not considered expenses reclaimable under the contract of service). A credit transaction[79] is where the company allows the director to purchase, the company supplies or sells under hire-purchase goods or land for his/her personal use and allows for deferred payments over a given period of time. Section 197 outlines the criteria for allowing such a loan.

25.5 The secretary

The CA 2006 made an important change to the previous requirements under the Companies Acts by removing the requirement for private (but not public) companies to have a secretary. However, even though a private company is not required to have a secretary,[80] the powers and duties attributable to a director and a secretary cannot be performed by one person (a sole director) acting in both capacities as director and secretary. As a consequence, whilst the company may legally have just one member, it is required to have at least two officers of director and secretary. The secretary is also considered to be an employee of the company and this must be taken into account with regard to the rights of employees and the duties on employers (see Part V), and also if the company is wound up this employment status has implications for the payments of creditors.

---

[76] Such as land. [77] CA 2006, s. 191. [78] CA 2006, s. 199.
[79] CA 2006, s. 202. [80] CA 2006, s. 270.

25.5.1 **Appointment**

A private company is entitled to make an appointment of a secretary and where it chooses to do so, that officer of the company has to undertake statutory duties and those imposed through the articles, and he/she has authorization to perform various functions on the company's behalf. The board of directors will choose the secretary (a power usually authorized in the company's articles) and will usually determine the terms and conditions upon which the appointment is to be made, including the term of office. This decision is usually made at a general meeting and passed through an ordinary resolution. The company secretary does not take part in the management of the company (although he/she does have responsibilities for the company) but the position does provide certain powers (these are generally restricted to administrative tasks).

A public company must have a secretary.[81] Unlike a secretary for a private company, a public secretary must have the qualifications required to hold such a position:[82]

1 he/she has held the office of secretary of a public company for at least three of the five years immediately preceding his/her appointment as secretary;

2 he/she is a member of any of the bodies specified in subsection (3);[83]

3 he/she is a barrister, advocate, or solicitor called or admitted in any part of the United Kingdom;

4 he/she is a person who, by virtue of his holding or having held any other position or his/her being a member of any other body, appears to the directors to be capable of discharging the functions of secretary of the company.

It is also a requirement under the CA 2006 that the company maintain a register of company secretaries and not simply include them in the Register of Directors, as was the previous practice.[84] This must be kept at the company's registered office or another specified place under s. 1136 and the company must inform the Registrar of where it is being held.

In the absence of a company secretary, the duties that would have previously been undertaken by this officer may be carried out by any other person that the company's board of directors so wish (so in essence the company has a secretary, but just not in name). It is possible for a company to occupy the position of secretary, but this will not be allowed where the company is acting as secretary, in this example, if the company is run by a sole director and this sole director is also the sole director or secretary of the other company. Where there is no secretary because of some temporary vacancy or the secretary is incapable of acting in this capacity, an assistant, deputy secretary, or some other person such as a director may be authorized by the directors to fulfil this role.[85]

The main role of the secretary is to undertake many of the administrative burdens that a limited company has to comply with as a result of its members enjoying limited liability status. The secretary completes these documents, signs them, and returns them on the company's behalf. These include: maintaining the company's registers; arranging the company's meetings and forwarding the notices of these meetings and any resolutions to be moved to the members; submitting the company's annual return and so on.

The secretary has the power to bind the company in contracts, even in the absence of any authority in this respect, where this relates to administrative proceedings such as employing

---

[81] CA 2006, s. 271.   [82] CA 2006, s. 273.

[83] The bodies represent the many chartered institutes of accountants.

[84] CA 2006, s. 275.   [85] CA 2006, s. 274.

staff and hiring transport. This power is associated with the usual authority of such a position (under agency) and will only extend that far. Where the secretary attempts to bind the company on issues which would be obviously beyond his/her authority such as taking loans on the company's behalf, registering the transfer of the company's shares and so on, as these would be powers vested in the directors rather than the secretary, the secretary enjoys no powers in this respect. However, the law of agency applies in these situations and the company must ensure that third parties are not misled as to the authority possessed by the secretary.[86]

Conclusion

This chapter has sought to identify the nature of a director's role in a company, the powers he/she possesses, where these powers derive, and the obligations imposed on the director by the enactment of the CA 2006. The secretary of the company is also an important position, and whilst there is no longer an obligation on private companies to have a secretary, public companies still have such a duty and there are specific qualifications that are required to be satisfied where a public company employs a secretary.

Summary of main points

Directors

- Directors exercise the specific tasks in the running of the company.
- The members (such as shareholders) 'own' the company but have no automatic rights of management.
- Directors may or may not be shareholders of the company.

Types of director

- Directors may be executive, non-executive, and shadow.

Number of directors

- A private company is required to have at least one director.
- A public company is required to have at least two directors.

Appointment

- Directors may be the promoter(s) of the company when it is first registered.
- Directors may be added to the company to increase expertise to the company's management or where additional responsibilities have to be performed.
- Directors may be appointed in accordance with the company's articles, usually through an ordinary resolution at a general meeting, but other mechanisms such as a written procedure may be valid.
- Directors must be over the age of 16 to be appointed to hold the position.

---

[86] *Panorama Developments (Guildford) Ltd v Fidelis Furnishing Fabrics Ltd* [1971] 3 All ER 16.

- A public company may not appoint two or more directors at a general meeting through a single resolution unless a resolution that it should be made has been unanimously agreed.
- Whilst corporations may be a director, every company must have at least one director who is a natural person.

Registration

- Every company is required to maintain a register of the directors which is available for inspection.

Directors' pay and contracts

- Directors may not necessarily receive remuneration but where pay is given the details must be maintained by the company and be available for inspection.
- Directors' length of contract, over a fixed term of two years' duration or more, may be terminated by providing reasonable notice.

Directors' duties

- The common law duties have been codified and expanded through the CA 2006.
- The duties include:
  - to act within his/her powers;
  - to promote the success of the company;
  - to exercise independent judgement;
  - to exercise reasonable care, skill and diligence;
  - to avoid conflicts of interest;
  - not to accept benefits from third parties.
- Directors must declare an interest in proposed transactions or arrangements that do, or may, cause a conflict.

Meetings of directors

- Each of the directors must be given notice of the meetings.
- The company must keep the minutes of the proceedings at the meeting, and maintain those for at least 10 years.
- Decisions at meetings are based on a voting system.

Indemnifying directors

- A company may indemnify a director when it concerns the provision of insurance; a qualifying third-party indemnity provision; or a qualifying pension scheme indemnity provision.
- Fines imposed through the criminal law or civil fines by regulatory authorities will not be indemnified.

Removal of a director

- Directors may retire annually (retirement by rotation) or through resignation, or through being removed before the expiration of their term of office.

- The director may be removed through an ordinary resolution and special notice of the resolution where it is provided to the company 28 days before the meeting (and where 21 days' notice is given of the meeting).

Disqualification

- The Company Directors Disqualification Act 1986 applies to both natural persons and corporations that hold directorships.
- Once disqualified the person may not take part in the management of a company for the period of disqualification.

Directors' liability to shareholders

- Directors are responsible to the company as a whole, not to individual shareholders.
- Minority protection is provided through the CA 2006 to restrict directors' acts that may adversely affect their position. Shareholders may bring a claim against directors in the company's name (a derivative claim) or may claim that a directors' acts or omission would be unfairly prejudicial to the shareholder.

The company secretary

- Private companies are no longer required to have a company secretary, although a sole director cannot also be the company secretary.
- Public companies must have a company secretary and this officer must satisfy statutory requirements in relation to his/her qualifications.
- The board of directors are usually empowered to appoint the secretary.
- Companies are required to maintain a separate Register of Secretaries.
- The secretary undertakes many of the administrative burdens of the company, signing documents and returning them to the Registrar as required by law.

 Summary questions

Essay questions

1. Discuss the implications for directors' duties to the company since the enactment of the Companies Act 2006. Explain where the statute has expanded the duties previously established through the common law, and what steps the company should take to ensure compliance with the Act.

2. How may members of a company remove a director before the expiry of his/her term of office? What protection is afforded to directors when faced with such a resolution?

Problem questions

1. John is the managing director of 'Widgets and Gadgets Plc' and is aware that the company is the target of a takeover by 'Build 'em up, Knock 'em down Plc'. John does not believe that such a takeover would be in the best interests of the company and therefore a board decision is made to increase the allotment of shares under an employee share scheme. This will increase the shareholding of the company and prevent the takeover.
   Advise Widgets and Gadgets Plc on the implications of this action.

2. Sarah is the company secretary of 'Picture Perfect Ltd', an advertising agency. The company regularly hires limousines to collect important clients from their offices and airports. Without authorization from the company, Sarah hires several cars to transport herself and her friends on nights out on the company's business account with the hire-firm. When the company receives the invoice, Sarah's actions are discovered and the company refuses to pay the bill.

Advise the parties of their rights and obligations.

Further reading

Almadani, M. (2009) 'Derivative Action: Does the Companies Act 2006 Offer a Way Forward?' *Company Lawyer* Vol. 30, No. 5, p. 131.

Cheung, R. (2008) 'Corporate Wrongs Litigated in the Context of Unfair Prejudice Claims: Reforming the Unfair Prejudice Remedy for the Redress of Corporate Wrongs' *Company Lawyer* Vol. 29, No. 4, p. 98.

Hadjinestoros, M. (2008) 'Exploitation of Business Opportunities: How the UK Courts Ensure that Directors Remain Loyal to their Companies' *International Company and Commercial Law Review* Vol. 19, No. 2, p. 70.

Keay, A. (2007) 'Company Directors Behaving Poorly: Disciplinary Options for Shareholders' *Journal of Business Law*, Sept. p. 656.

Useful websites

http://www.bitc.org.uk/
(This governmental organization (Business in the Community) enables companies to become members and share practices of effective corporate values, translating these into models of management that are applicable in modern business.)

http://www.companieshouse.gov.uk/
(Companies House website providing details of company law, the requirements for returning documents to the Registrar, and other information of interest to companies and their members.)

http://www.forumforthefuture.org.uk/
(Forum for the Future is a charity that has members from both the public and private sectors who share information and discuss issues regarding the sustainability of business practices, with guidance on how such goals and strategies may be realized.)

https://www.gov.uk/limited-company-formation
(Government website providing details on appointing a company secretary and the role and duties of this officer.)

http://www.iod.com/
(The Institute of Directors is a body that supports and represents individual private directors.)

 Online Resource Centre

http://www.oxfordtextbooks.co.uk/orc/marson3e/
Why not visit the Online Resource Centre and try multiple choice questions associated with this chapter to test your understanding of the topic. You will also find relevant updates to the law.

VII Intellectual Property

Chapter 26   Intellectual Property

26

Intellectual Property

Why does it matter?

Intellectual property is of vital importance to business. Most commonly seen in copyrighted materials, patents, and trade marks, businesses invest considerable resources in developing and acquiring brand images or the rights to materials. Hence they are rightly protective over who has access to utilize the material and the control that they, as owners, can exert. If a business owns the copyright to a film, album, or where they have the right to use a trade name (Microsoft, Apple Inc.) and so on, it is easy to see the problems and concerns of unauthorized use of this material. Therefore businesses need to know how to protect their intellectual property rights, and also how to ensure they do not, deliberately or innocently, infringe the intellectual property rights of another.

After a relatively long period of time, legislative reform of intellectual property law is beginning. In November 2010 the Government asked Ian Hargreaves to chair an investigation into the current state of the law and his report was published in May 2011. His report[1] makes ten recommendations that the government is considering in its reform Bill. Refer to the Online Resource Centre for updates in this area of law.

> ### Learning outcomes
>
> Following reading this chapter you should be in a position to:
>
> - explain the concept of copyright and how ownership is established and enforced (26.3–26.3.7.2)
> - identify the rights an owner of copyright has in relation to the intellectual property (26.3.3)
> - describe what is meant by design rights and explain the registration procedure (26.4–26.4.1)
> - assess the protection provided through the registration of a trade mark, and where registration may be refused (26.5–21.5.4)
> - describe the tort of passing-off (26.5.5)
> - explain the process of gaining protection for an invention through obtaining a patent (26.6–26.6.3)
> - identify the ownership of the intellectual property when it is produced by an employee or an independent contractor/freelance firm (26.7–26.8).

[1] http://www.ipo.gov.uk/ipreview.htm.

> ### 𝑅 Key terms
>
> These terms will be used in the chapter and it may be helpful to be aware of what they mean or refer back to them when reading through the chapter.
>
> **Intellectual property**
> This is a product of someone's intellect that has commercial value and may be exploited. It provides legal rights of ownership and control and is typified by copyright of artistic and literary works, patents, trade marks, and design rights.
>
> **State of Prior Art**
> In patent law, an invention may be refused a patent because it is not novel. Therefore if it can be demonstrated that 'prior art' existed before the patent applied for (through documents and other evidence) then the patent will not be granted.

26.1 Introduction

This chapter considers some issues regarding a business's ownership of **intellectual property** (IP). Ownership of goods and the issues surrounding buying and selling of these have been identified in Part III of this text. Further, due to the constraints of this text, it is not possible to discuss issues regarding the ownership of land (although guidance for those interested in the topic is provided in the Further reading section at the end of the chapter). Rather, this chapter considers the issues surrounding the concept of IP and how this may be more difficult to determine than ownership of land. The intellectual creativity of persons can prove to be very valuable (consider the revenue generated from computer software, books, music recordings and so on), and the common law and statutes have sought to offer protection to the owners of these creations. Without protection and enforcement of the owner's rights, the desire and impetus placed into creating these materials may be stifled, negatively impacting on society and the economy. Remember, protection of IP rights allows the owner to control the 'fruits of his/her labour' whilst also allowing the public to have access to it (and enjoy the benefits of this).

IP is a broad concept but may be most readily seen where businesses create a name, brand, product, process and so on, and wish to protect against its unauthorized use. The UK Intellectual Property Office (UK-IPO) provides an example of the applicability of IP in terms of a mobile telephone where the ringtone would be covered through copyright; its shape is protected through a registered design; the name of the phone or associated logo could be protected through a registered trade mark; and the processes used in its manufacture can be protected through patents.

26.2 Protecting intellectual property

IP is a wide-ranging term, but essentially it is used to describe the patents to protect new inventions; trade marks that are used by businesses that may define brands, logos, and the shapes of products; design rights and registered designs; and copyright, which provides the owner with protection against unauthorized use of his/her literary, artistic, and dramatic works, sound recordings, and software and databases and so on. There are regulations regarding the protections afforded and the mechanisms available to enforce rights, and these are identified in the following sections.

> **Business Link**
>
> Businesses may produce tangible goods such as a t-shirt. These goods are owned by the business, which may then distribute the items to various stores to be sold. However, what rights does a business have to stop competitors copying the design of the t-shirt, producing their own shirts, and selling the items (possibly impacting on the sales of the first business)? Who owns the copyright when an employee produces it? Does it matter if this was produced at work or in the employee's own time? What is the commercial significance of copyright protection? These are the issues to be discussed to ensure businesses can enforce copyright, and also to ensure they do not infringe another's rights.

26.3 Copyright

Copyright, Designs and Patents Act (CDPA) 1988

The law relating to copyright is governed, through statute, by the Copyright, Designs and Patents Act (CDPA) 1988.[2] The protection of copyright is afforded to anyone's creation of a literary, dramatic, musical, or artistic work or the creation by an employee who is contracted to create such works. Through this ownership, control may be exercised as to who may use the work and how permission will be granted (through licensing, for example). Examples of the use of the copyrighted materials may include the publication of literary products[3] (such as books, articles and so on),[4] the distribution and broadcast of films and music, the creation of databases,[5] the production of computer software and so on. The copyright also crosses media, such as when a photograph is reproduced on a website it would still breach the owner's copyright even though they are in different mediums. Copyright need not be applied for, and claims can be made for the unauthorized use of the owner's copyright once the work has been fixed (such as being recorded and written down).

26.3.1 Who is protected?

The copyright holder is entitled to protection where the work fulfils the following criteria:

1 the work is of a type that is protected under the CDPA 1988;

2 it has been produced in some tangible form—written, recorded and so on;

3 the work satisfies the requirement of originality; and

4 the owner/creator is a British citizen and/or the work was first published in the UK.

The term 'original' does not refer to an idea or thought that is original, but rather it is the expression of the idea that must be original. For example, in preparing a textbook, the text

---

[2] As amended by the Copyright and Related Rights Regulations 2003.
[3] This has been very broadly defined and has even extended to a street directory.
[4] Although these may be written, spoken, or sung to qualify as literary works under s. 1(1).
[5] Section 3A(1) identifies a database as a collection of independent works, data, or other materials that are arranged in a systematic way and are individually accessible by electronic or other means.

will refer to other authors' work in books and journals, judgments, research reports, government documents and so on. These will be 'owned' by the copyright holder in each case, and other textbooks may have already included similar materials, but if the way the ideas are expressed is original, and they have been expressed in some tangible form (referred to as being fixed),[6] then copyright will exist for this 'original' work.

26.3.2 What is protected?

Copyright affords the owner protection against breaches such as the unauthorized use of *original* material including:[7]

- *Literary works:* this includes books, computer software programmes, song lyrics, and even instruction manuals;[8]
- *Music and broadcasts*: including films, videos, and radio shows;[9]
- *Dramatic productions:* including plays, dances, and sound recordings;
- *Artistic works:* this is wide-ranging and includes drawings, diagrams, logos,[10] photographs, sculptures[11] and so on.[12]
- *Typological arrangements of published editions:* this involves the planning and establishing of type that may then be printed. Examples include sections of a newspaper and the layout of a book.[13]

It is not possible to claim copyright protection for: ideas; names, phrases, and slogans (although they may be applicable to trade mark protection); or products and manufacturing processes (although patents may be applicable). Use of the copyright without the owner's consent will enable enforcement proceedings to be initiated, with the possibility of an action in damages.

26.3.3 Rights provided through copyright

- *Legal rights:* The owner's legal rights allow him/her to:[14]
  - copy and distribute copies of the work to the public;
  - issue copies to the public;
  - perform, show, or play the work in public (such as through various broadcast media);
  - broadcast the work or include it in a cable programme service;
  - make an adaptation of the work or do any of the above in relation to an adaptation;
  - sell a work; under the Artist's Resale Rights Regulations 2006, an artist has the right (resale right) to a percentage of the selling price (resale royalty) when he/she owns the copyright and certain forms of art are sold.

---

[6] Section 3(2).   [7] Section 1(1).   [8] Section 3.   [9] Sections 5 and 6.

[10] As logos also may involve trade marks, it can be seen how IP rights are not restricted to one of the categories identified in this chapter.

[11] Although the Supreme Court held that the iconic 'Stormtrooper' helmet used in the Star Wars films was not a sculpture for the purposes of copyright protection—*Lucasfilm Limited v Ainsworth* [2011] UKSC 39.

[12] Section 4.   [13] Section 8.   [14] Section 16.

- *Moral rights:* The owner has the legal rights to the work, but it must be recognized that he/she also holds the moral rights (beyond those economic rights).[15] These rights include:
  - protection against the distortion of the owner's work;
  - in relation to literary, dramatic, artistic or musical works, that he/she has the right to be recognized as the author of the work whenever it is performed commercially or in public;
  - literary, dramatic, artistic, or musical works may not be falsely attributed to an author;
  - where an undertaking has been made to make a film or take photographs for private consumption, he/she may not show or broadcast this to the public.

In a question of the rights held by the owner of IP in the form of bespoke software, the High Court in *Infection Control Enterprises Limited v Virrage Industries Ltd*[16] held that in the event of IP being created in the form of bespoke software, a customer will only receive the minimum rights necessary unless they specifically provide for these in the negotiations. Here the Court rejected the argument of *Shirlaw v Southern Foundaries*[17] that such a fact was omitted from the contract because it was 'so obvious' there was no need for it to be mentioned.

26.3.4 **Registration of copyright**

A significant protection afforded to the owners of copyright in the UK is that it is automatic and, unlike other protections of IP rights, there is no registration process. Because of the lack of formal registration, the owners of the property may be concerned as to how proof of ownership is established. Tactics have included sending a copy of the work in a dated and unopened package to oneself, or leaving a copy of the work with a solicitor. Further evidence of ownership may be supplemented through the use of the internationally recognized copyright symbol © followed by the owner's name and the year of the work's creation which identifies copyright and prevents others from infringing, intentionally or unintentionally, that copyright. As this symbol is internationally recognized, it transcends the jurisdiction of the UK, but whilst it is acknowledged elsewhere, many countries have their own rules on the enforcement of breaches of copyright, and the domestic laws of the relevant country will have to be used to enforce copyright ownership (which evidently differs as regards success rates depending upon where in the world the copyright is infringed). It is also important to note that simply because materials are available free of charge does not necessarily mean that they are free of copyright. Materials on the Internet may display the © but even if they do not, downloading or using materials may be infringing the owner's rights.[18] This also applies to the peer-to-peer networks where copyrighted materials are made available for download without charge (unlike, for example, iTunes, where legal downloads are permitted). The owners of copyright, particularly corporations, are often vigilant in enforcing their IP rights, and actions against children and their parents for illegal downloads of copyrighted materials (games, movies, music and so on) are not uncommon.

---

[15] Section 77.   [16] [2009] EWHC 2602 (QB).   [17] [1939] 2 All ER 113.
[18] The Copyright and Related Rights Regulations 2003 have harmonized the protections in this area through the European Union.

Table 26.1 Duration of Copyright Protection

Type of original works	Duration of copyright
Sound recordings	50 years
Broadcasts	50 years
Literary and dramatic works	The life of the creator plus 70 years[19]
Typographical arrangements	25 years
Publication of a literary, dramatic, musical, or artistic work (previously unpublished) and commercially exploited	25 years
Databases	15 years

> **? Thinking Point**
>
> Does the fact that information is available, for example on the Internet, free of charge impose any copyright issues? Does it matter if the use is for personal or commercial reasons?

26.3.5 Duration of copyright protection

The protection afforded under copyright differs depending on the nature of the work, the time at which it was created, and where the copyright was established. Table 26.1 identifies the duration of copyright protection.

26.3.6 Primary and secondary infringement of copyright

Infringement of copyright exists where a qualitatively substantial part of the work is copied. Primary infringement of copyright does not consider the perpetrator's motive or knowledge of the copyright's existence. Infringement occurs when one or more of the exclusive 'legal' rights of the owner as identified in **26.3.3** above has been breached (hence performed/used without the permission of the owner).[20] Due to the lack of motive or knowledge required to infringe copyright, this may occur when a person 'innocently' copies a music CD owned by another person, or computer software is shared between colleagues and so on. Even though this is not committed as part of a commercial undertaking, it will fall victim of primary infringement.

However, a breach of a secondary infringement requires the perpetrator to know, or he/she should have known, of the existence of the copyright of the work being infringed. Further, this is for some other reason than for the person's own personal/domestic use (hence to exploit this infringement commercially), and the person does not have the owner's

---

[19] Duration of Copyright and Rights in Performance Regulations 1995.
[20] Section 16(2).

permission (licence).[21] Secondary infringement occurs where the person, without the owner's permission:

- imports an article into the UK;[22]
- possesses an article in the course of business;
- sells or lets for hire; offers for sale or hire such an article;
- in the course of business exhibits in public or distributes an article; or
- otherwise than in the course of business, distributes an article to an extent that it prejudicially affects owner of the copyright of the article.[23]

Further, where the person transmits the work by means of a telecommunications system (other than through broadcasting/cable programme service) without the owner's permission, knowing or having reason to believe that infringing copies of the work will be made by this means, this will constitute a secondary infringement.[24] The CDPA 1988 also protects against secondary infringement where a means has been provided for making copies of work that would enable a breach of copyright,[25] where a person gives permission for a performance in a public place of literary, dramatic, or musical work that infringes copyright,[26] or where this is infringed through the public performance of copyrighted works (for example, playing sound recordings, showing films and so on).[27] Where such events have taken place in which the person knows, or should have been aware, that the owner's permission had not been granted, this will constitute infringement.

26.3.7 Enforcement of copyright

Where the owner of a copyright considers his/her property rights are being infringed, the first step may be to inform the transgressor. This informal measure may be achieved through a letter, either personally drafted or through a solicitor, and many cases cease at this stage. However, where the other party does not respond, or may challenge the ownership of the copyright, then legal proceedings may have to be initiated. The penalties for infringing copyright may include civil and criminal liability.

26.3.7.1 Civil actions

Section 96 of the CDPA 1988 provides that infringement of copyright is actionable by the owner and relief may be available through damages, injunctions, and the transgressor being held to account. Whilst damages is an available remedy in cases of infringement, if the defendant can satisfy the court that at the time he/she was unaware (and did not have reasonable grounds to believe) that the copyright existed, an award of damages may be reduced or removed.[28] This is because the court will take all matters into consideration when determining if an award is to be made, including the flagrancy of the infringement and any benefit that accrued to the defendant. A more useful remedy, perhaps, than a damages action, is the availability of injunctions. Here the court orders the transgressor to stop infringing the copyright (through an interim order) until the full hearing, and a further injunction may be ordered following this hearing. A court is also empowered to make an order for the delivery of the product infringing the copyright or its destruction.[29] Further, s. 100 provides for the owner

---

[21] Section 22.   [22] Section 22.   [23] Section 23.
[24] Section 24.   [25] Section 24.   [26] Section 25.
[27] Section 26.   [28] Section 97.   [29] Section 99.

or a person authorized by him/her to seize and detain work exposed or otherwise available for sale or hire (where an action would have been available under s. 99). However, the time and place of the proposed seizure must be given to the police, it must be public (but cannot be a permanent or regular place of business) and the owner or the person authorized by him/her must not use any force.

An infringement of a moral right is actionable as a breach of statutory duty owed to the person entitled to the right. Where equitable, the court may grant an injunction to prevent further abuses.[30] However, while it is possible to assign copyright in its entirety, and parts of copyright[31] (such as bequeathing it in a will),[32] it is not possible to assign moral rights.[33]

26.3.7.2 *Criminal offences*

Criminal offences may be committed by a person who:

- offers for sale or hire;
- imports in the UK otherwise than for his/her own private and domestic use; or
- possesses, in the course of business, with a view to committing an act infringing copyright, an article which is, or he/she has reason to believe is, infringing copyright of a work. The defendant, if found guilty, may be liable, on summary conviction, to imprisonment for a period not exceeding six months.[34]

Further, where goods are imported into the UK, the owner may give notice in writing to the Commissioners of Customs and Excise that he/she is the owner of the copyright in published literary, dramatic, or musical work; or the owner of copyright in a sound recording or film, and request that the Commissioners treat the copies as prohibited goods.[35] Other works may be physically protected from infringement through the use of technology (anti-copy DVDs, smart cards/decoders for satellite broadcasts).

In situations where the two parties have disagreements regarding the terms of an agreement, the Copyright Tribunal[36] exists and can determine the facts and assist the parties in reaching a decision.

There are exceptions to breaches of copyright and in certain situations there is no need for permission. The user is granted limited use of the material that is used for non-commercial research or study (such as copying a section of a book); where the materials are used for reporting events/court proceedings; and if they are used in reviews. Previously, exemptions under the Copyright, Designs and Patents Act 1988 allowed for businesses to take copies of copyrighted materials for commercial research insofar as this was fair. The Copyright and Related Rights Regulations 2003 ended this exemption from breach of copyright.

? Thinking Point

Due to the unregistered nature of copyright, is the law in this area adequate to protect the owners? Compared with protections available in other areas of IP, what improvements in the law and technology could be made to facilitate effective enforcement of rights and respect for copyright?

---

[30] Section 103.   [31] Which could include the period of time of the copyright's existence.
[32] Section 95.   [33] Section 94.   [34] Section 107.   [35] Section 111.
[36] Information on the work and role of the Tribunal can be found at http://www.ipo.gov.uk/ctribunal.htm.

26.3.8 Reform of the law

At the time of writing, as part of the Government's initiative to improve and reform copyright law, the Enterprise and Regulatory Reform Bill includes the following proposals:[37]

- 'Repealing section 52 of the Copyright, Designs & Patents Act 1988 which limits the term of protection for artistic works which have been mass-produced.

- An order making power to enable the exceptions to copyright and the exceptions to rights in performances set out in the Copyright, Designs & Patents Act 1988 to be amended by secondary legislation.

- Allowing for the use of 'orphan' works for commercial and non-commercial use and for the appointment of an authorizing body to license this use.

- A power to implement into UK law EU Directive 2011/77/EU on the term of protection for sound recordings.'

The Bill will implement many significant changes to copyright law in an attempt to make the law more relevant and up-to-date. The Department for Business Innovation & Skills has included a substantial amount of information and commentary on the measures and those interested in the area should refer to it.[38]

26.4 Design rights and registration

- *Design rights:* A business may have spent time and resources in developing a product's shape and design that makes its appearance stand out or may become synonymous with the business (consider the shape of a Coca-Cola bottle, for example). A design right is established, and the period of protection begins when the work is first 'fixed' in design documents such as a drawing or when it is first made. The design must be original, and in demonstrating that it is not commonplace, the owner should maintain his/her records of the design's development (such as in e-mail communications, plans, and files). The issue of design rights assists a business as the design right of the product is an automatic right (like copyright) and it prevents others from copying the design for a period of 15 years. There is also an EU-based recognition of unregistered design rights, and this protects the product's shape and pattern for a three-year period (and throughout the EU). The copyright protection is effective where the design is artistic or involves plans and drawings, and the design is not intended to be mass-produced. Where the creator of the design wishes to gain further protection, not just of preventing the design being copied without permission, but also of controlling the exploitation of the design in any manufacturing of products, it must be registered. Protection under the Registered Designs Act (RDA) 1949 exists for a period of 25 years.

  Design rights are applicable to three-dimensional works only, but the unregistered community designs procedure (under EU law) does protect two-dimensional products. The main drawback when compared with the registered method is that the unregistered method gives protection for a shorter period of time, it is less likely that the threat of legal action here will be a deterrent as the owner has to prove he/she held the design right, and

---

[37] http://discuss.bis.gov.uk/enterprise-bill/.

[38] http://discuss.bis.gov.uk/enterprise-bill/2012/07/30/30-july-uk-copyright-accessing-orphan-works/.

then that the person infringing the right has deliberately copied it, and demonstrating the right to sell or licence the use of the rights is considerably more difficult. It is important to recognize that in the final five years of the design right's period of protection, its owner is obliged to agree licensing terms with third parties who wish to use the design. Where no agreement can be reached, the terms are decided by the UK-IPO.

• *Registered designs:* Whilst the design right provides protection without any form of registration, as it is governed by Part III of the CDPA 1988 (and may be considered closely related to copyright), it must satisfy the requirements of originality of the design. However, greater protection is afforded the owner if he/she registers at the Patent Office (Designs Registry) under the RDA 1949 (which is more closely related to patents). Whilst in the case where damages are sought for infringement of the design right, there must have been an intentional decision to infringe the owner's rights, under the registration scheme, such intention need not be proved and damages may be awarded in cases of unintentional breach.

To qualify for the right to register the design it must be a new design, and it must have characteristics that give its appearance an original look. This form of protection is often limited to the exterior of a product (rather than how it actually works—see patents). Following the registration, the owner is granted exclusive rights to produce and use (in the UK) any product that incorporates the design and this right exists for five years, with renewals possible for further five year periods to a maximum of 25 years. The registered design right includes two and three-dimensional works. Due to its registration and the confirmation that the IP belongs to the owner, selling or the licensed use of the design is more successful than unregistered designs. As the owner may use this as an income stream, the registration process, whilst incorporating expenses such as the registration fee, may be more advantageous than unregistered designs.

The protection for registered designs only applies, and is enforceable, in the UK. As protection may be sought beyond the jurisdiction of the UK, a mechanism exists at the EU level where the registration rights apply throughout the Union and ensures that registration procedures are consistent throughout the EU.[39] There has been further expansion to these rights following the agreement of the EU to join the World Intellectual Property Organization's (WIPO) Geneva Act of the Hague Agreement (and hence each of the 27 Member States of the EU are now included). Since 1 January 2008 designers in the EU can apply for international protection for their designs and this is applicable in all the countries that have signed up to the agreement. The Internal Market and Services Commissioner commented, 'European businesses will now be able to obtain and protect their designs internationally in a simple, affordable and effective way. This should further stimulate trade and innovation, create new commercial opportunities and boost integration within the EU Internal Market.'

The registration process involves identifying the design, even simply through sample drawings that show the work and how the design is to be applied. This design must be original and not simply a collection of other designs fashioned together to form something 'new'. Registration of a design that has been used in marketing may be made at any time up to 12 months after it was first marketed, but this should be performed as soon as possible to ensure protection. The UK-IPO website contains the relevant details and forms that must be submitted, including details of the registration fee applicable,[40] and

---

[39] Registration is made to the Office for Harmonization in the Internal Market and following registration the design is published in the 'Community Designs Bulletin'.

[40] More than one application may be made at the same time, and if so, only one registration fee is payable.

Table 26.2 Duration of Protection of a Design right

Design right	Duration of protection
UK registered design	5 years from the date of filing (renewable in five-year periods to maximum of 25 years).
UK unregistered design	Automatic—10 years from the first marketing of the product or 15 years after the design's creation (whichever is earlier).
EU registered design	5 years from the date of filing (renewable in five-year periods to maximum of 25 years).
EU unregistered design	3 years from the date the design was first made available to the public.

these are sent to the UK-IPO Design Registry. The applications are generally examined within two months of submission, and on the basis that no objections are submitted, two to three months following the application the registration process should be complete.

26.4.1 Enforcement of a design right

With regard to businesses that may take 'inspiration' from the works they have seen and been influenced by in creating a design, it is important not to transgress another's design right. This can be embarrassing, show a lack of imagination or integrity, and it can also be very expensive (legal fees and damages actions may be the result). Therefore it is prudent to identify whether the design has been registered through the UK-IPO. However, as some design holders may not register the work, the use of a specialist lawyer [41] may assist in ensuring design rights have not been breached.

Where a possible infringement has taken place (such as the use of the design or the sale of designs belonging to the holder) it is typical to begin an informal route through communication with the other party, explaining the right and the consequences of further breaches. If both parties are still in dispute, and they agree, they may seek to use a mediator under a form of Alternative Dispute Resolution[42] to avoid the necessity of court action. If unsuccessful, then the holder of the right may be forced to commence a civil action to recover damages and seek the granting of an injunction to compel the transgressor to cease his/her activities. Clearly where the case involves an unregistered design, the claimant will have to demonstrate that he/she owns the design right and the defendant had copied it. Where the design has been registered, following the unsuccessful attempt at preventing the breach through the communications between the parties, the holder may claim damages due to the defendant's work closely resembling the holder's design (rather than having 'copied' it).

If the situation arises where the alleged breach has occurred whilst in the process of registering the design, the UK-IPO may be contacted to request an urgent examination, and subsequent registration, of the design.

---

[41] The Chartered Institute of Patent Attorneys (http://www.cipa.org.uk/pages/home) maintains details of relevant lawyers in the UK.

[42] See **4.4**.

26.5 **Trade marks**

> ## 🔗 Business Link
>
> A business has to protect its IP rights and by registering its trade mark, the owner has the right to use the ® symbol to demonstrate ownership. It warns others who may otherwise have used it without authorization that legal consequences may follow for infringement. Without following the registration process, the owner must seek a remedy through the common law action of 'passing-off'.

A trade mark is defined under the Trade Marks Act (TMA) 1994 as:

> ... any sign capable of being represented graphically which is capable of distinguishing goods or services of one undertaking from those of other undertakings. A trade mark may, in particular, consist of words (including personal names), designs, letters, numerals or the shape of goods or their packaging.[43]

Trade Marks Act 1994

A trade mark (denoted by the ® symbol) identifies that the owner of the trade mark has been registered,[44] and it prevents others from using the same image. A trade mark may be applied to a name or logo that identifies a product or service, or it could further include a slogan used by a brand or even some sound.[45] As such, they are often associated with a business, product, or brand, and are of significant advantage in assisting customers to recognize the company. McDonald's 'golden arches' and the Nike 'swoosh' are instantly recognizable symbols that the public associate with that company. Indeed, many Nike products, including hats and t-shirts, do not even contain the company's name, but merely that symbol, as it denotes the company. Following registration, the trade mark provides the owner with exclusive use of the mark, and those who infringe the mark are subject to a civil action by the owner, but it also enables the police and/or Trading Standards to initiate criminal proceedings for breach (such as with counterfeiters). The law is governed by the TMA 1994 (following the transposition of EC Directive 89/104).[46] Once the registration process has been completed, infringement is committed where the trade mark and the other item are confusingly similar to make the consumer (for instance) buy one good believing it to belong to the trade mark holder.[47]

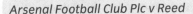

Arsenal Football Club Plc v Reed

Facts:

The football club Arsenal FC brought an action against Reed who had sold souvenirs and other memorabilia bearing the club's name and its badge (for several years). It was claimed that Reed had infringed registered trademarks, but Reed's defence was that these products would be perceived as a badge of support rather than indicating trade origin. Following

---

[43] Section 1(1).

[44] Using the symbol without the required registration is an offence.

[45] As in *Shield Mark BV v Joost Kist hodn Memex* [2004] (Case C-283/01), where the European Court of Justice held that notes from a composition by Beethoven could constitute a trade mark when used in an advertising campaign on the radio.

[46] First Directive 89/104/EEC of the Council, of 21 December 1988, to Approximate the Laws of the Member States Relating to Trade Marks.

[47] *Arsenal Football Club Plc v Reed* [2003] ECWA Civ 96.

reference to the Court of Justice of the European Union (Court of Justice) it was held the trade-marks, when applied to the goods in this instance, were purchased as badges of support, but this did not prevent the third party being liable to jeopardise the function of the trademark. Following this case, Arsenal changed its club badge to prevent potential further abuses.

Authority for:

A key issue regarding infringement of a trade mark is whether the consumer would believe there was a link between the proprietor and the goods being sold.

26.5.1 Reasons to refuse the grant of a trade mark

The TMA 1994 defines where an absolute refusal of registration will take place. Under s. 3 the following shall not be registered:

1 signs which do not satisfy the requirements of section 1(1);

2 trade marks which are devoid of any distinctive character;

3 trade marks which consist exclusively of signs or indications which may serve, in trade, to designate the kind, quality, quantity, intended purpose, value, geographical origin, the time of production of goods or of rendering of services, or other characteristics of goods or services;

4 trade marks which consist exclusively of signs or indications which have become customary in the current language or in the *bona fide* and established practices of the trade;

5 the shape which results from the nature of the goods themselves; or where it is necessary to obtain a technical result, or which gives substantial value to the goods;

6 marks which are contrary to public policy or to accepted principles of morality, or are of such a nature as to deceive the public;

7 if or to the extent that its use is prohibited in the UK by any enactment or rule of law or by any provision of Community law; or

8 if the application is made in bad faith.

Having registered the trade mark, it must be renewed every 10 years to remain effective (and may be renewed indefinitely), and where the owner has not registered it, the action to ensure protection against unauthorized use lies in the common law through an action under the tort of 'passing-off'. Whilst such a claim is possible, the costs and complexity of such actions must not be underestimated, and even though costs may be awarded against the party at fault, this is still a considerable undertaking that registration may have made easier. A registered trade mark is enforceable throughout the UK, whereas unregistered marks may not be applicable to such an extent and may be confined to enforcement in restricted geographical areas.

26.5.2 Registration of the trade mark

A trade mark may be registered in the UK through the completion of form TM3 from the UK-IPO, along with the required fee, and submitting these to the UK-IPO Trade Marks Registry. The applicant should conduct a search to ensure that the trade mark is not registered or that another person has not applied for the same or similar mark. Since 1 October 2007, all trade mark applications are subject to regulations[48] with the effect that there will no longer be an automatic block of the registration of the mark if there is an earlier conflicting trade mark. The application will result in an examination of the existing UK, EU, and international trade marks protected in the UK and the EU, and on the basis that the UK-IPO discovers a conflict with an earlier trade mark, the applicant will be informed of this finding and given the choice to:

1 continue with the application and the UK-IPO will inform the owner of the previously registered trade mark of this new application, enabling him/her to oppose the application based on specific times and procedures (note that licensees will not be given the right to object to an application);

2 change the application so that it is sufficiently different from a current trade mark;

3 liaise with the owner of the existing trade mark to allow the application to continue unopposed; or

4 withdraw the application.

As such, the role is to attempt to settle potential disputes at as early a stage as possible and reduce the instances of court actions. There has been a move by the courts to introduce alternative forms of dispute resolution, and this is extending more broadly to include legal jurisdictions including IP.

Where the nature of the product requires protection beyond the territory of the UK, the registration process will have to be undertaken with the various international bodies. The process has been somewhat simplified in that rather than having to seek an application (individually) to each country, the applicant can register a Community Trade Mark (CTM) through the Office for Harmonization in the Internal Market[49] to have effectiveness throughout the EU. The CTM applies to any person resident in a Member State or a business that is based in a Member State, and includes any distinctive sign capable of graphical representation. The benefit of an EU-wide system of registration is that its application is throughout the EU and any injunctions used to enforce a right and prevent infringement have force in each of the Member States. It has a further advantage of lower costs and administrative burdens than applying to each country individually, but due to the size and composition of the EU, a single system of registration may be difficult to enforce and apply in practice.

A further registration system applicable to the entire world was developed through the Madrid System, and following registration in the UK, an application can be made to WIPO.[50]

26.5.3 Rights provided through registration

Registration is recommended in most cases as it provides access to the TMA 1994[51] and enables the injured party to seek remedies provided under that Act. Section 10(1) provides: 'A person infringes a registered trade mark if he uses in the course of trade a sign which is identical with the trade mark in relation to goods or services which are identical with those for which it is registered.' Further, infringement occurs where the identical sign is used in

---

[48] The Trade Marks (Amendment) Rules 2007; Trade Marks (Fees) (Amendment) Rules 2007; and The Trade Marks (Relative Grounds) Order 2007.

[49] http://oami.europa.eu/ows/rw/pages/index.en.do.

[50] http://www.wipo.int/portal/index.html.en.

[51] As amended.

relation to goods and services similar to those for which the trade mark is registered and there exists the likelihood of confusion on the part of the public,[52] or where the identical sign is used not for similar goods and services, but the trade mark has a reputation in the UK and its use takes advantage of, or is detrimental to, the distinctive character or the repute of the trade mark.[53]

The TMA 1994 further identifies that a sign, for the purposes of the Act, is used where it is fixed to goods or the packaging; exposes or offers the good for sale; imports or exports goods under the sign; or uses the sign on business papers and on advertising literature.

There are limits placed on the rights of a registered trade mark, and as such s. 11 states that there will be no infringement where:

- the person uses his/her own name and address;
- it consists of the use of indications concerning the kind, quality, quantity, intended purpose, value, geographical origin, or other characteristics of goods and services;
- the use of the trade mark is necessary to indicate the intended purpose of a product or service;
- it is used in the course of trade in a particular locality of an earlier right which applies only in that locality.

26.5.4 Enforcing a registered trade mark

There exists an automatic right to enforce the trade mark against a person infringing the owner's rights and the courts are empowered, as with the common law, to award damages and grant injunctive relief to the claimant. Where the trade mark breach has involved a criminal offence, beyond the loss to the owner where a common law remedy is available, such as dealing in counterfeit goods, Trading Standards may initiate an action that could lead to imprisonment for a period of 10 years and/or an unlimited fine.

> ### ? Thinking Point
>
> Trade marks have been used to protect companies and products by restricting access to their unique name/label. How does the law balance the rights of those who wish to protect their name from the undue interference with other people's freedoms?

26.5.5 The tort of passing-off

'Passing-off' protects the holder of an unregistered trade mark. At common law, where an individual or business attempts to pass itself as another business, or to pass goods off as being those of the other business, in an attempt to deceive or confuse the public, a tort of 'passing-off' may have been committed. It aims to prevent the infringement of the holder's right and to prevent the other person from benefiting from the holder's reputation. Therefore it is concerned with the relationship between the holder of the trade mark and the public. Trade mark law is associated with the concept of goodwill, and this is established in business

---

[52] Section 10(2).   [53] Section 10(3).

names, brand names, packaging of products, even a person's name (for example a professional football player's image rights) and so on. When considering the amount of money spent on advertising, contracting to have a sportsman/woman wear one manufacturer's brand of sporting goods and so on, it is very clear why the holders of these rights want to protect their investment.

26.5.6 Goodwill

For infringement, the goods/services in question must have goodwill attached. This means that they exhibit particular identifying features which enable the public to associate with the good/service.

Pfizer Ltd v Eurofood Link (UK) Ltd[54]

Facts:

The defendants had marketed a health food drink as 'Viagrene' and its properties had an aphrodisiac quality. It was a blue coloured liquid and the bottle contained a diamond shape. The claimant manufactured 'Viagra' the impotence treatment. It sold the drug in a quite distinctive blue, diamond-shaped tablet. Viagra had been registered under British and EU trade marks, and Pfizer argued that such a name was too similar to its product 'Viagra' and could be considered similar. The High Court held that the defendants had been passing-off the product as the claimant's drug.

Authority for:

The claim involved an action under ss. 10(2) and 10(3) of the TMA 1994. The judgment confirmed the Court of Justice decision that there was no requirement to prove confusion for a breach of s. 10(3). Viagra had an established reputation and there was a breach of goodwill that would amount to a misrepresentation. There was a potential to damage the claimant's reputation and therefore the tort of passing-off had been committed.

It is also important to recognize that passing-off is a strict liability tort. Therefore the motive of the person infringing the right is irrelevant.

26.5.7 Recognizing infringement

In order to mount such an action against a transgressor, it has to be established that the public associated the trade mark with the claimant's product, and that the product of the other party was mistaken for that of the claimant, and in so doing has caused him/her loss/damage (such as reductions in sales and so on).

As such the three elements may be seen as in Figure 26.1.

Be aware that whilst Figure 26.1 identifies a quite simple outline of the process to establish a successful claim, the reality is of course very complex and open to interpretation. For instance, these tests have been established through the common law, not by statutory

---

[54] [1999] FSR 17.

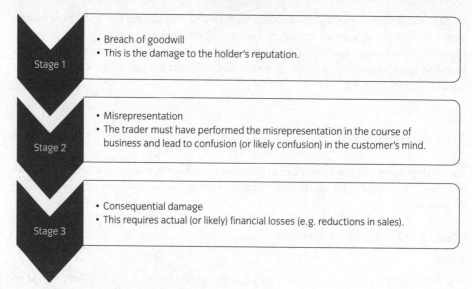

Figure 26.1 Stages to Establish a Successful Claim

definition, and proving infringement of the holder's goodwill is very subjective. In the Pfizer case above, the judge outlined that the name 'Viagra', even though an anti-impotence drug, was actually a household name. As such, a similar named product claiming to relieve the symptoms of impotence would likely damage the goodwill of the drug company. In other situations, associating the damage or potential damage due to the association of the public with the good/service may be considerably more difficult.

26.5.8 Defences available

It is possible to defend an allegation of passing-off and the following are the most common:

a) The holder of the IP had given consent;

b) The holder's trade mark (slogan, brand and so on) was not distinctive;

c) The trade mark is generic;

d) The defendant is using his/her name innocently.

26.5.9 Remedies

Following the successful finding of passing-off, the following remedies are available to the court:

a) Damages or account of the defendant's profits (not double awards for both aspects);

b) Delivery/destruction of the infringing goods;

c) Injunctive relief;

d) An enquiry to establish loss.

26.6 Patents

A business may seek to protect its inventions, such as a new product, or its new way of making the product (a new process) that has an industrial application. An invention would constitute an inventive step where it would not have been obvious to someone with skill and experience in the area. To be considered as new, the invention must not form part of the **state of prior art** (this includes all factors that were publicly available prior to the invention). To be considered as having an industrial application, it must be capable of being used or made in any form of industry (with exceptions regarding medical treatment, diagnosis and so on identified in s. 1(3) of the Patents Act (PA) 1977). It is important to recognize that a patent need not be a completely new item, but rather it could include a new way in which an item already in existence is produced (or other such examples). A typical example of a patent was that of the bagless vacuum cleaner developed by the Dyson company. When the Hoover company produced its own 'version' of such a cleaner, it was held that this was a breach of Dyson's patent.[55] Further, the Apple Corporation developed a power lead for its laptop computers called 'MagSafe'. This attaches through a magnetic connection that, it is claimed, allows the connector to disconnect from the laptop when strain is applied to the lead—essentially when strain is applied to the lead, the lead comes away from the laptop as opposed to the laptop falling to the ground. Power leads are not a new feature of laptops, but this connection was, and hence it is the reason only Apple makes these and no other laptop manufacturer, or third-party developer, has access to the patent.

Patents
Act 1977

By registering the patent, it prevents others from using or selling the same product without permission. The registration period lasts for five-year periods and must be renewed (up to a maximum of 20 years in total). The law in this jurisdiction is governed by the PA 1977 and s. 1(1) provides that a patent may be granted if the following criteria are satisfied:

1 that the invention to be patented is new;

2 that there is an inventive step involved (not obvious to a person with knowledge and experience in the area);

3 that it is capable of industrial application (as such it is capable of being made or used); and

4 that the granting of the patent is not to be excluded by ss. 1(2), 1 (3), or 4A of the PA 1977.

Section 1(2) identifies that the following will not satisfy the requirements of 'inventions' and hence are incapable of patents being applied:

• scientific and mathematical discoveries, theories, or methods;

• works of an artistic, literary, dramatic, or musical nature;

• ways of performing a mental act, playing a game, or doing business;

• certain computer programs; or

• the presentation of information.

Section 1(3) continues that in certain circumstances, a patent should not be provided on the basis of it being contrary to public policy (against the law) or morality. Section 4A provides that a patent shall not be granted for the invention of a method of treatment of the human or animal body by surgery or therapy or a method of diagnosis practised on such bodies.

---

[55] *Dyson Appliances Ltd v Hoover Ltd* [2001] RPC 26.

26.6.1 Exploitation of a patent

The power of a patent is that it provides the owner with a monopoly right to control it,[56] even where another person, acting independently of the owner of the patent, could have developed the same invention. With the monopoly control, the owner may exploit the invention for commercial gain, and as this form of IP is identified as personal property, it is capable of being sold, licensed, used to raise finance (such as through a charge over it), or transferred to another party (through inheritance and so on). As this is property, it may also be owned by more than one person (as could other property such as land or a house), and such joint owners have rights over the property.

The patent provides the monopoly right, but this is subject to competition rules and the Comptroller-General may issue a compulsory licence where relevant.[57] He/she will also determine the level of payment for the licence. Three years after the granting of the patent, any person may apply to the Comptroller for a licence if:

(a) the invention is capable of being commercially worked in the UK, but is not being so worked (or not worked to the fullest extent that is reasonably practicable);

(b) where the patent is a product, the demand for it is not being met on reasonable grounds, or is being met through importation from countries outside of the EU;

(c) where the invention is capable of being commercially worked in the UK, it is being prevented or hindered from being worked through imports;

(d) by reason of the refusal of the proprietor of the patent to grant a licence(s) on reasonable terms: the market for the export of the patented product is not being supplied; the working or efficient working in the UK of other patented invention which makes a substantial contribution to the art is prevented or hindered; or the establishment or development of commercial or industrial activities in the UK is unfairly prejudiced;

(e) by reason of conditions imposed by the proprietor of the patent on the grant of licences under the patent, or on the disposal or use of the patented product or on the use of the patented process, the manufacture, use or disposal of material not protected by the patent, or the establishment or development of commercial or industrial activities in the UK, is unfairly prejudiced.

26.6.2 Application for a patent

The Patent Office is the body that is responsible for granting Patents with effect in the UK and is headed by the Comptroller-General. The applicant will identify what the invention is, details regarding its specifications (blueprints/schematics and so on), an abstract explaining the nature of the patent being applied for, and submission of the relevant fee. As the patents may be sought by persons in industry to protect against their inventions being used in an unauthorized way, the application process is essential and the Office will record this date of the application. The Patents Office will only officially record this date of filing where all the relevant documents have been submitted and the correct fee has been paid, and the applicant has specifically identified his/her request for a patent. Therefore care must be taken when submitting documents.

---

[56] This is merely to recognize that whilst patenting an invention gives control of it to the owner, they will still be subject to rules governing its potential use. This is commonly seen where pharmaceutical companies develop drugs—these drugs still have to be licensed for use in the UK.

[57] Section 48B.

The documents must be filed on the prescribed form and submitted in the prescribed manner;[58] it must contain sufficient detail to enable a person 'skilled in the art' to produce the invention[59] and as such include details on the matter for which the applicant seeks protection; be clear and concise; be supported by the description; and relate to one invention (or a group) to form a single inventive step.[60] Having filed the appropriate forms, paid the fee, and submitted the necessary information, the submission is examined to ensure compliance with the PA 1977. If the application passes this preliminary test, the next stage is the substantive test. Here any anomalies in the application are identified and these are passed on to the applicant who is provided with the opportunity to respond (and change any elements of the application if necessary). Given that the changes made are to the satisfaction of the examiner, the application will be granted for the patent; if the changes are unsatisfactory, the application may be refused. Following the successful application process and the grant of the patent, this fact is published in the 'Patents and Designs Journal'.

26.6.3 **Breach of a patent**

A patent protects the owner who has control and a monopoly right over the invention. However, a breach/infringement of the patent will not occur where the 'breach' is performed for research/experimentation,[61] or where its use is for private rather than commercial purposes.[62] Infringement of a patent is determined on a decision as to whether or not a very similar product comes within the scope of the exclusive right.

Catnic Components Ltd v Hill & Sons Ltd [1982] RPC 183

Facts:

The claimant possessed a patent for a lintel. It provided that the rear face was vertical and the defendant relied on this description by making their lintel with a face with a 6-degree slant. The House of Lords held that a purposive rather than literal approach should be given to interpreting when an infringement occurs. A skilled person would interpret vertical to also include slightly-off vertical.

Authority for:

The traditional, certain literal approach of interpretation may assist the courts, parties and third parties, but may enable deviation and hence evasion of infringement. A method with more 'common sense' is to adopt a purposive approach, but this leads to uncertainty and provides the patentee with greater protection than envisaged when filing the patent.

Situations where a person infringes a patent in force in the UK include:[63]

(a) where the invention is a product, the person makes, disposes of, offers to dispose of, uses or imports the product or keeps it whether for disposal or otherwise;

(b) where the invention is a process, the person uses it, or offers it for use in the UK knowing (or reasonably ought to have known) that its use there without the consent of the proprietor would constitute an infringement; or

---

[58] Section 14(1)(a).   [59] Section 14(3).   [60] Section 14(5).
[61] Section 60(5)(b).   [62] Section 60(5)(a).   [63] Section 60(1).

(c) where the invention is a process, the person disposes of, offers to dispose of, uses, or imports any product obtained directly by means of that process or keeps any such product whether for disposal or otherwise.

Having established a breach, an injunction[64] may be granted to prevent further infringements of the patent; damages may be awarded if the defendant knew (or ought reasonably to have known) that the patent was in existence; there may be an order made to deliver any of the patented products; the defendant may have to account for any profits derived from his/her breach (but awards will not doubly compensate the claimant in respect of this head of claim and damages); and a declaration may be made that the patent is valid and had been infringed through the defendant's actions. Describing a product/process as a patent where no such grant has been made constitutes a criminal offence.

26.7 Employees and intellectual property

It is important to recognize that a business may be involved in creating products and works that may be commercially valuable (stories for a publishing company/drugs for the pharmaceutical industry and so on). Universities, for example, invest heavily in research and development in the attempt to further understanding, but also in the hope that such results will be commercially successful. There may be IP rights being created even when the employee is not hired in such a capacity. Developing databases, producing training manuals and so on may also form a valuable IP. When an employee produces a valuable IP, who owns it—the employee (who has been paid a salary), or the business that has engaged the employee?

Based on the 'general' rules of an employee's contract of employment,[65] the creation by the employee of IP rights at work, clearly having benefited from, and had access to, the resources that the employer has made available, belongs to the employer. Whist this is generally true, it is prudent to specifically state this in the employee's contract of employment (the contract may also state that the employee will be acknowledged in relation to the creation—the moral rights).[66] As IP rights are often very valuable to a business, an employer may wish to use a restraint of trade clause[67] to restrict the employee's exploitation of such sensitive (and possibly lucrative) information. However, contract terms in contravention of the Patents Act 2004, regarding patents and their ownership, will be considered unenforceable.

In relation specifically to patents, the PA 1977 provides at s. 39(1) that inventions created by employees will belong to an employer where they were created during the normal course of employment and relating to the employee's duties at work (and as such would be reasonably considered to be the result of carrying out those tasks). This is considered in light of the implied terms in employees' contracts,[68] and the fact that provision for the ownership of IP rights has not been drafted to include, for example, an obligation or expectation that inventions will be created, does not restrict the duty of fidelity providing the employer with a means to secure the ownership of the IP.[69] The courts will look towards what tasks/duties

---

[64] An injunction may also be awarded against the owner of a patent who brings unfounded claims against another that they have breached the patent.

[65] See Chapter 16.

[66] This would be applicable to artistic, literary, musical, and dramatic rights.

[67] See **20.5**.

[68] See **16.5.1**.

[69] *British Syphon Co. Ltd v Homewood* [1956] 2 All ER 897.

are being undertaken in the course of employment that will establish the obligations on the employee, rather than simply reviewing a contract of employment and using the terms therein to determine ownership of IP.

Re Harris' Patent[70]

Facts:

An employee had made an invention that was patentable. The fact that he was a salesman with no requirement or expectation to invent resulted in the invention belonging to him, not the employer.

Authority for:

An employer will generally be the owner of IP rights established by employees, unless the invention has no relation to his/her employment.

There has been a development to the law in this area and the PA 2004 provides that in situations where an employee has created an invention for the employer and a patent has been granted, the employee is entitled to be compensated (determined by a court or the Comptroller-General).[71] When determining whether compensation is to be payable and its amount (if any), the following will be taken into consideration: the size of the organization; whether the invention or its patent is of outstanding value to the employer; the nature of the employer's business and so on, and then whether it is just and reasonable to award the employee compensation. The compensation awarded will reflect the employee's share of the benefit received (or be expected to be received) by the employer.

26.8 Independent contractors and intellectual property

The employer owns the employee's IP created at work because of the contract of employment and the distinctive feature of control exercisable by the employer (a fundamental feature of employee status). However, if an independent contractor/freelance worker is used by the employer to perform some task that creates an IP (which could include an advertising campaign, or the development of a firm's website), who owns this? Do not think that simply because a business has paid for a creation that has IP rights, that it will automatically have ownership of it to use, change, and sell however it chooses. Again, in general terms (and as such there may be exceptions) the employer has an implied right to use the IP created, as this will have formed part of the contract, but such rights must be assigned to the employer or the business otherwise he/she will not own the IP or be in a position to make further use of them. The key element is to establish at the contract stage who will possess ownership, and therefore control, over the created IP and this should also identify any moral rights to the creation.

In situations of copyright, for example, the creation by an employee will usually result in the work belonging to the employer. However, an independent contractor will, unless stated

---

[70] [1985] RPC 19.
[71] The court/comptroller also has the authority to award compensation in situations where an employee has assigned the patent to the employer for less than it was worth.

otherwise, retain control of the copyright. Legal advice to draft a secure contract may be money well spent in the longer term. Care must also be taken when a business begins negotiations to sell or licence its product or work. Registering the design, trade mark, and patent, and ensuring ownership of copyright is present through the techniques identified above will reduce the possibility of unauthorized use, and enable legal action to prevent infringements.

Beyond the use of contracts and restraint of trade and confidentiality clauses within contracts of employment, a business should restrict physical access to materials that have a valuable IP from those who could make unauthorized use of them. This is a simple technique, but it ensures that information does not get leaked and information is restricted to key individuals in a firm. Where tasks are outsourced to third parties, it may be wise not to provide information regarding the nature of wider projects that the materials are being designed for. For a very good example of ensuring confidentiality and secrecy in IP, investigate the Apple Corporation and consider how many actual leaks regarding new products come to the public domain before officially announced—relatively few. This is why that business has been growing successfully and is one of the most innovative organizations in the technology sector.

Conclusion

This chapter has identified the rights that owners of IP have over the creations and inventions. Whilst rights are provided, as recognized by law, in certain instances by simply being the creator of a work, there is far greater protection through the registration of the ownership of the IP and, where relevant, establishing with employees and contractors as to ownership of valuable IP. Due to the value of names, slogans, logos, and inventions to business, these matters should be of serious consideration when the business is established and throughout its creation of products. Whilst this chapter has identified, briefly, some important points, always refer to professionals when ensuring protection.

Summary of main points

Intellectual property

- IP is often a very valuable commercial asset that can be exclusively used by the owner, sold and licensed. It may provide a significant revenue stream for businesses.

Copyright

- The law is governed by the Copyright, Designs and Patents Act 1988, which protects the owner's original materials including literary, dramatic, musical, artistic works, and typographical arrangements.
- Copyright is an automatic right and need not be applied for (but proof may be needed to establish ownership).
- The copyright must be expressed and fixed (such as being written down) and as such ideas/thoughts are not copyright protected.
- Legal rights (and in some cases moral rights) are attributed to copyright holders.
- Copyright exists for varying periods of time depending on its form.
- Enforcement takes place in the civil courts through the owner seeking a remedy against the transgressor(s).

Design rights

- Design rights protect the appearance/shapes of a product (such as the Coca-Cola bottle).
- The design must be fixed and original (not commonplace).
- There is an automatic right to the design right for 15 years but a registration process is available.
- Unregistered design rights exist for a shorter period than registered designs and the owner has to demonstrate that the transgressor deliberately copied the design (which can be difficult).
- Designs may be registered at the Patent Office (Designs Registry) under the Registered Designs Act 1949.
- The registered design allows the owner exclusive rights and use of the product in the UK. The exclusivity lasts for five years and may be renewed at five-year periods for up to 25 years.
- It covers two- and three-dimensional works.
- To claim for infringement of the registered design right, the owner merely has to show the transgressor's design is similar. He/she does not have to demonstrate intention to infringe the owner's right or direct copying of the design.
- Registration may be made to the Office of Harmonization in the Internal Market to give protection to the design throughout the EU. The protection only lasts for three years.

Trade marks

- The Trade Marks Act 1994 protects the owner of any sign capable of being represented graphically which is capable of distinguishing goods or services of one undertaking from those of another.
- Trade marks may consist of words, designs, numerals, or the shape of goods/packaging.
- A registered trade mark provides its owner with exclusive use of the mark.
- Enforcement may take place through the civil and criminal jurisdictions.
- Since 1 October 2007 it is possible to register a mark that is similar or the same as an existing mark (unless there is an objection).
- Registration can also be made to the Community Trade Mark giving protection throughout the EU.

Passing-off

- A common law action exists where a business/individual attempts to pass him/herself or a product off as that of another business. Its aim must be to confuse/mislead the public.

Patents

- Protection is granted to inventions through a new way of making a product that has industrial application.
- Registration prevents others from using or selling the same product without permission. The protection lasts for five-year periods (to a maximum of 20 years).
- The owner of a patent is provided with a monopoly right to control the item.

- Mechanisms exist where a person may request from the Comptroller-General to license a patented invention (after three years following the grant of the patent).

Employees and independent contractors

- Generally, IP created by an employee in the course of employment will belong to the employer (although the employee may possess moral rights).
- IP created by an independent contractor/freelance worker is more complicated. The employer should establish an agreement with the contractor as to the ownership and exploitation of the IP.

 Summary questions

Essay questions

1. Identify the ways in which the Trade Marks Act 1994 has liberalized obtaining a registered trade mark? Are there any problems that remain?

2. Has the Patents Acts 1977 and 2004 effectively balanced the rights of the employer and employee in the ownership of inventions created by the employee?

Problem question

1. Sundeep has developed a new football boot that he considers to be a radical development and will improve players' performance. He seeks to protect his invention through a patent and seeks your advice on the registration process, the rights that registration will provide him, and how he may enforce the patent against transgressors.

2. You are approached by the following two parties for advice on possible breach of trade marks.

   a) Sweaty-Betty Inc. wish to sell a new perfume which is aimed at the high-end of the market. To appeal to these customers it intends to use a distinctive, fancy bottle, in the shape of a pyramid and with the product name 'Cleopatra'. Fearing imitators, Sweaty-Betty Inc. has requested advice as to whether the chosen product name and bottle shape may be registered as trade marks.

   b) Kwik-Fit plc operates a national chain of replacement car tyre and exhaust centres. It trades under the registered name 'Kwik-Fit'. Kwik-Fit has noticed an announcement in the Trade Mark Journal that 'Rubbery Products Ltd' has applied to register the name 'Kwik-Fit' for a new brand of sheath contraceptives it is launching. Kwik-Fit plc wish to know whether this new application can be defeated.
      Advise both parties.

Further reading

Property and Land Law

Thompson, M. P. (2009) 'Modern Land Law' (4th Edition), Oxford University Press: Oxford.

Smith, R. J. (2009) 'Property Law' (6th Edition), Pearson Longman: Harlow.

IP Resources

Bainbridge, D. I. (2008) 'Intellectual Property' (7th Edition) Longman: Harlow.

Bergquist, J. and Curley, D. (2008) 'Shape Trade Marks and Fast-Moving Consumer Goods' *European Intellectual Property Review*, Vol. 30, No. 1, p. 17.

Intellectual Property Newsletter (1998) 'Intellectual Property when Transferring Businesses' *Intellectual Property News*, Vol. 21, No. 9, p. 5.

Jaeschke, L. (2008) 'The Quest for a Superior Registration System for Registered Trade Marks in the United Kingdom and the European Union: An Analysis of the Current Registration System in the United Kingdom, the Community Trade Mark Registration System and Coming Changes' *European Intellectual Property Review*, Vol. 30, No. 1, p. 25.

Swycher, N. and Luckman, M. (1991) 'Buying Businesses: Intellectual Property Investigations' *Practical Law Companies*, Vol. 2, No. 2, p. 21.

 ## Useful websites

<https://www.gov.uk/browse/business/intellectual-property>
(This Government website contains guidance on intellectual property rights relating to business.)

http://www.ipo.gov.uk/home.htm/
(The website of the UK Intellectual Property Office. This is the government body responsible for registering IP rights in the UK.)

http://www.itma.org.uk/intro/index.htm/
(The Institute of Trade Mark Attorneys. The institute seeks to ensure that all practicing members possess the specialized knowledge and experience in trade mark matters. It convenes lectures and seminars throughout Europe and provides details of recent cases and commentary on their implications.)

<http://www.wipo.int/
(The website of the World Intellectual Property Organization. This is a specialist organization of the United Nations that promotes the effective use and protection of IP worldwide.)

 ## Online Resource Centre

http://www.oxfordtextbooks.co.uk/orc/marson3e/
Why not visit the Online Resource Centre and try multiple choice questions associated with this chapter to test your understanding of the topic. You will also find relevant updates to the law.

Index

Koffman & Macdonald's

Law of Contract

Eighth Edition

Elizabeth Macdonald
Professor of Law, Swansea University

Ruth Atkins
Lecturer in Law, Aberystwyth University

OXFORD
UNIVERSITY PRESS

OXFORD
UNIVERSITY PRESS

Great Clarendon Street, Oxford, OX2 6DP,
United Kingdom

Oxford University Press is a department of the University of Oxford.
It furthers the University's objective of excellence in research, scholarship,
and education by publishing worldwide. Oxford is a registered trade mark of
Oxford University Press in the UK and in certain other countries

Fifth Edition 2004
Sixth Edition 2007
Seventh Edition 2010
Impression: 1

Published in the United States of America by Oxford University Press
198 Madison Avenue, New York, NY 10016, United States of America

British Library Cataloguing in Publication Data
Data available

Library of Congress Control Number: 2014930068

ISBN 978–0–19–964483–4

Printed in Great Britain by
Ashford Colour Press Ltd, Gosport, Hampshire

Preface to the eighth edition

It is now more than twenty years since the first edition of Koffman and Macdonald was published, and what must first be said here is that, although Laurence Koffman is no longer contributing to the book, obviously, his hand is still visible in much that has remained in the chapters for which he was previously responsible. Ruth Atkins has stepped in to take up the reins, beside Elizabeth, in this new edition. However, the aims of the book remain the same today as they were when the project was started: to provide a clear, non-technical account of the law of contract, which is accessible to university students new to the study of law, whilst maintaining academic rigour. Of course, over eight editions, considerable changes take place and, in this edition, there has been some restructuring to make it easier to use, and to reflect the evolution of the relative importance of some topics. This has resulted in some chapter changes, with the previously very large remedies' chapter being divided into separate chapters on damages and specific enforcement, making the material more digestible. There has also been similar restructuring within some chapters like offer and acceptance, and the damages section, which is now a chapter. Relative usage of them made it appropriate to move the chapters on Capacity, and An Outline of the Law of Restitution, out of the book itself and onto the companion website. The book has been fully updated to take account of cases such as *John Grimes Partnership v Gubbins, Kolmar Group AG v Traxpo Enterprises Pty Ltd, Borelli v Ting, Progress Bulk Carriers Ltd v Tube City IMS LLC, Thomas v BPE Solicitors (a firm), RTS Flexible Systems Ltd v Molkerei Alois Müller GmbH & Co KG (UK Production), Raiffeisen Zentralbank Osterreich AG v Royal Bank of Scotland plc, VB Penzugyi Lizing Zrt v Ferenc Schneider, OFT v Ashbourne Management Services Ltd, Proactive Sports Management Ltd v Rooney, Great Eastern Shipping Co Ltd v Far East Chartering Ltd (The Jag Ravi), Fortress Value Recovery Fund I LLC v Blue Skye Special Opportunities Fund LP, Eminence Property Developments Ltd v Heaney, Isabella Shipowner SA v Shagang Shipping Co Ltd, Bunge SA v Kyla Shipping Co Ltd*, and many others. It also deals with important new materials in the legislative arena such as the Law Commissions' papers on Unfair Terms and Illegality, and the draft Consumer Rights Bill. Discussion of the debates in some areas has been extended to reflect their evolving significance in legal and social terms, such as that surrounding the scope of the unfair terms legislation. A fresh look has also been taken at some well-established issues, such as what amounts to an illegitimate threat in relation to duress, and even the very familiar question of why we have the postal rule, and the more recent problem of whether it should be applied to e-mail.

We are very grateful to Joanna Williams and to her colleagues at Oxford University Press for their patience, efficiency, and unswerving encouragement.

Elizabeth Macdonald
Ruth Atkins
October 2013

I would like to take this opportunity to express my very great thanks to Laurence for his partnership in the initial genesis of this project, and throughout seven editions, and also my condolences on the death of his beloved wife Val, who provided him with such support in all his endeavours.

I should also like to thank Ruth for taking up the challenge of the new edition so ably and with unstinting good humour.

Elizabeth Macdonald
October 2013

Preface to the first edition

The impetus for writing this book came from our experience, over many years, of teaching the Law of Contract to first year law students. We found that although the established textbooks on the subject are admirable in many respects, they are longer and more detailed than required by the average student. Our aim was to produce a book which has sufficient detail to meet the needs of students taking law degrees, but which does not contain more information that students ever require. Obviously we have been selective in deciding which topics merit more detailed exposition, but we hope that our selection reflects the emphasis of most Contract courses.

Although the book is written primarily with law students in mind, we hope that our approach to the subject will also appeal to those studying Contract as part of a business studies course. We think that a book on Contract should be readily intelligible to students new to law—as the subject is usually taught in the first year of a law degree. For this reason, the emphasis of the book is on explanation of the law in clear and non-technical terms. In particular, we have tried to give a full explanation of the important case law in order to assist students towards an understanding of how the common law works. We have preferred to provide a firm grounding in the case law, rather than to espouse or develop any individual 'theory' of Contract Law.

In writing the book we have been helped by more people than it is possible to name individually. But we are particularly grateful to those tutoring in Contract at Aberystwyth for reading and commenting helpfully on drafts of certain chapters. We also wish to thank Lillian Stevenson and the staff of the Hugh Owen library for their good-natured and patient assistance. We are indebted to our publishers for their initial interest in the idea of the book and for the encouragement which they gave us to write it. Special thanks are owed to Indira Carr for her advice on computers, and to Valerie Koffman for her help with proof reading. Our greatest debt of gratitude is owed to our families and friends who encouraged and supported us throughout the writing of the book. More particularly, Laurence Koffman wishes to thank his wife Valerie, and daughter Angela, for their patience and constant support. Elizabeth Macdonald would like to express her thanks to her parents, Pat and Stan Macdonald, for all their support and help.

We have attempted to state the law as at 15 September 1991.

Laurence Koffman
Elizabeth Macdonald
Aberystwyth
February 1992

Outline contents

Detailed contents

Table of legislation

Paragraph references printed in **bold** type indicate where the legislation is set out in part or in full.

 References to W1 and W2 relate to web chapter 1 (Capacity) and web chapter 2 (An outline of the law of restitution) which can be found on the Online Resource Centre.

European

International Treaties and Conventions

Directives

Other National Legislation

Germany

United States

Table of cases

Paragraph references printed in **bold** type indicate where the case is set out in part or in full. References to W1 and W2 relate to web chapter 1 (Capacity) and web chapter 2 (An outline of the law of restitution) which can be found on the Online Resource Centre.

A

C

D

E

G

I

J

M

Q

S

T

U

V

Chapter 1

Introduction to the study of contract law

What is a contract?

1.1   A contract is a legally enforceable agreement giving rise to obligations for the parties involved. The law of contract determines which agreements are enforceable and regulates those agreements, providing remedies if contractual obligations (undertakings or promises) are broken. Under a contract, the parties voluntarily assume their obligations or undertakings: for example, S promises to supply a new car to B by the end of the month, whilst B promises to pay, on delivery, the price of the vehicle. Their agreement to perform these undertakings is a contract. There is no legal duty to enter into such an agreement, but if the parties choose to do so, it will give rise to legal obligations. Therefore, the law of contract is distinct from branches of law where duties are imposed: for example, there is a general duty (in the law of tort) to take care that we do not injure other people by our careless actions. The doctor whose treatment of a patient falls below the professional standard expected of an ordinary practitioner of medicine may be liable for negligence. This liability is not based on a contract (indeed, there is no contractual relationship between a general practitioner and a National Health Service patient); it is a general duty of care imposed by law.

1.2   The word 'contract' suggests to most people a formal or technical document drawn up and understood only by lawyers. Contracts can take this form, and certain types of contract (for instance, for the sale of land or any interest in land) must be in writing; but generally a contract can be made orally, without any legal jargon or formality. We all make numerous contracts as part of everyday life and we rarely give thought to legal technicalities. Making a contract is simply a way of facilitating, amongst other things, the exchange of goods and services. It is merely a method of commercial transaction. Of course, the transaction can vary enormously in complexity and in value—from the purchase of a chocolate bar to the multi-million pound takeover of a large company—but it is based on a contract nevertheless.

1.3   To illustrate the importance of contracts in our society, let us consider a day in the life of a fairly ordinary person (X), from the point of view of his contractual relationships. In the morning, the milkman delivers two pints to X's house and X buys a newspaper on the way to work. Both transactions are contracts for the sale of goods. X goes to work on the train, riding under a contract of carriage, and performs various tasks at work under a contract of employment. Later, X returns to a house which is probably subject to a very important contract, namely a lease or a mortgage. X is having the house redecorated, under a contract for the provision of services and materials. X takes a ride in the car that X is buying under a hire purchase agreement, and which is protected by a contract of insurance. On return-ing home, X watches a DVD which is hired from a local shop. Finally, X walks the dog—no contract there!

The law of contract/s

1.4   There are particular types of contract, such as contracts of employment and contracts for the sale of land, which are subject to their own specialized rules of law and detailed legislation. The law of contract, however, has long survived as such, and is the study of the legal principles which underlie all contracts. It is not (generally) concerned with particular types of contracts and their specialized rules, but provides the important foundation for these specific areas.

1.5   The law of contract is a common law subject: it is primarily derived from the decisions of the courts (precedent), and these judicial rulings constitute the relevant law. Many principles of contract law owe their existence to decisions dating back hundreds of years, whilst some are of comparatively recent origin.

1.6   There are, of course, some important statutes in the general law of contract, for example the Law Reform (Frustrated Contracts) Act 1943, the Misrepresentation Act 1967, the Contracts (Rights of Third Parties) Act 1999, and the Unfair Contract Terms Act 1977. However, there is an increasing volume of consumer contract legislation. In the consumer context, the Unfair Terms in Consumer Contracts Directive has a far broader reach than the Unfair Contract Terms Act 1977. The Law Commissions have taken the view that consumers need clearer, simpler, and more effective, rights in relation to misleading and aggressive trade practices than is pro-vided by the general contract law on duress and misrepresentation,[1] and the draft Consumer Protection from Unfair Trading (Amendment) Regulations would bring that about. Such an increasing volume of broad consumer legislation may start to create a much more significant division of contract law, than anything which has previously occurred, into commercial, and consumer, contract law.

1.7   Although contract is common law subject, a study of appeal court decisions can create the misleading impression that contracts lead inevitably to disputes and conflict. A contract

---

1   The Law Commissions, *Consumer Redress for Misleading and Aggressive Practices* (Law Com No 332, Scot Law Com No 226) para. S.18.

law book or course deals with what are comparatively rare (namely legal action in the courts). Traditional approaches tell us little about business practice and how it differs from the formal law. It is particularly important in the area of contractual remedies that we do not overemphasize the importance of lawyers and the courts. As we have noted, a contract is simply a means of facilitating exchange (of goods, services, etc.) and if there is a dispute over its interpretation, or even if one party clearly breaks the agreement, this does not inevitably lead to litigation and the courts. The costs of a legal action can be prohibitive and only the very wealthy can contemplate protracted litigation without considerable unease.

1.8 Even where the parties can afford to go to court there may be good reasons to try to avoid doing so. In commercial practice, some breaches of contract are seen less as a legal problem and more as a commercial one. Companies will want to avoid any damage to their reputation that might be caused by litigation. A legal action with its formal style, its conflict approach, and its demands on time and money, can be damaging to continuing relationships in the business world. Even if successful, a party will normally fail to recover all the expenses that were incurred. For these and other reasons, business people try to resolve disputes without recourse to the courts. The same also applies to the consumer who, generally, can ill afford to take a claim to law. It is better to try negotiation and persuasion in the event of a contractual dispute.

'Freedom of contract'/Inequality of bargaining power

1.9 Many important contractual principles, as expounded by the leading decisions of the courts, were established in the eighteenth and nineteenth centuries. The 'classical' view of contract was that the parties entered into an agreement or bargain freely, and therefore there should be as little state regulation or intervention as possible. It was not the task of the law to ensure that a fair bargain had been struck. This attitude was consistent with the laissez-faire philosophy which was so influential in the thinking of the time; it was consistent with the idea that contracts should be made by the parties (with freedom of choice) and not be imposed on them by the state. It was thought to be consonant with a free market economy and the spirit of competition.

1.10 Even in its historical context, this approach raises obvious questions. It assumes a particular model of contractual activity: namely that between business people of fairly equal resources. It assumes the existence of genuine competition. Of course there never was true equality—a prerequisite for freedom of contract. How could such a doctrine apply as between employer and employee, for example? In a more modern context, such a laissez-faire 'world-view' seems absurd. It fails to take account of groups who are particularly susceptible to exploitation, such as consumers, tenants, and employees.

1.11 However, the important concept of inequality of bargaining power came to be recognized. A major influence in the decline of the freedom of contract philosophy was the emergence of the consumer as a contractual force. The traditional model of contracts as a means of exchange between business people had to accommodate the idea of exchange between a business person and a consumer. Inevitably inequality of bargaining strength (in relation to wealth, resources, and experience) had to be acknowledged. The twentieth century saw a move towards greater state regulation of many types of contract. A good example is the Unfair Contract Terms Act 1977, which went further in regulating and restricting the use of exclusion clauses than any previous control provided by the courts. There is also public law regulation of consumer affairs and the increasing influence of European directives.

1.12   There is acceptance of the idea that certain contracting parties need the protection of the law against economic exploitation and oppression. Major legislation has gradually helped to prevent the exploitation of tenants and employees and to reduce the incidence of gender discrimination. However, the extent of protection which is needed and the extent of the departure from freedom of contract, which should occur, is still hotly disputed. The law of contract is often engaged in trying to balance traditional market liberalism with the need to protect those who may be exploited. As we shall see, one of the most recent contexts in which the battle between the opposing forces of market-liberalism and consumer-welfarism has been fiercely fought is in relation to the scope of the legislation derived from the Unfair Terms in Consumer Contracts Directive.

Europe

1.13   The European Union has had significant impact upon English contract law. It has brought about significant legislation, such as that implementing the Unfair Terms in Consumer Contracts Directive. It has also simply made English lawyers more aware of the law of other European states, which has particularly occurred through projects like the drafting of the *Principles of EU Contract Law*,[2] produced by a group of academic lawyers from different member states. Such awareness brings consideration of alternative legal strategies which might be adopted by English law. However, there has also, of course, been much discussion about harmonizing the law of contract in the member states of the European Union. The existence of separate, national, laws of contract can be seen to impede the development of internal market. Nevertheless, the current most significant move, on that front, seems to be towards the adoption of a Common European Sales Law, merely as an option, which parties could choose to use in contracting. The common law seems to be alive, and well, and continuing to evolve, at least for the time being.

▶ Further reading

P. Atiyah, *The Rise and Fall of Freedom of Contract*, Clarendon, 1979

H. Collins, *The European Civil Code: The Way Forward*, Cambridge University Press, 2008

K. Kryczka, 'Electronic Contracts and the Harmonisation of Contract Laws in Europe—An Action Required, A Mission Impossible?' (2005) 13(2) ERPL 149

---

2   O. Lando and H. Beale (eds), *Principles of EU Contract Law*, 2000, parts I and II, and O. Lando, *Principles of EU Contract Law*, 2003, part III.

E. McKendrick, 'English Contract Law: A Rich Past, An Uncertain Future' (1997) 50 CLP 25

L. Miller, 'The Common Frame of Reference and the Feasibility of a Common Contract Law in Europe' (2007) JBL 378

D. Staudenmayer, 'The Commission Communication on European Contract Law and the Future Prospects' (2002) 51 ICLQ 673

W. Van Geren, 'Codifying European Private Law? Yes, If' (2002) 27 ELR 156

Chapter 2

Formation of the contract

Agreement

2.1   Whichever definition of the law of contract we use, the word 'agreement' will be central to it. Broadly, a contract is a legally enforceable agreement giving rise to obligations for the parties to it. However, not all agreements are legally binding contracts. For example, social and domestic agreements are generally presumed to lack any intention to create legal relations, and no contract will be found in those situations, unless there is very clear evidence of an intention to create legal relations between the parties (see *Balfour* v *Balfour* (1919)): the courts do not want to be overrun by social or domestic agreements being inappropriately disputed before them. More significantly, it is generally not simply agreements which the law will enforce, but 'bargains'. Something of value must normally be supplied by each party, to the other, to make the agreement into a contract. This is the requirement of 'consideration', which is fundamental to 'simple' contracts (those not made by deed—see **Chapter 4**). In *Re Hudson* (1885):

> Hudson had promised to pay £4,000 a year for five years to a religious charity to help it pay off chapel debts. He died before the two final instalments could be paid and his executors claimed that his estate was not liable for the remaining £8,000 as there was no binding contract in law. The judge ruled that no consideration had been given by the charity in exchange for Hudson's promise. The promise was gratuitous, and there was no contract in any legal sense of the word. Thus Hudson's estate was not liable for the remaining instalments.

However, if a promise such as Hudson's was made in writing by deed, it would be enforceable. That formality would give it legal force, even without the presence of consideration. But most contracts are not made in this way and, generally, they depend upon agreement, and consideration. A contract, generally, therefore, is an agreement with undertakings (promises or obligations) on each side, where there is an intention for the agreement to have legal consequences. In fact, the appropriateness of applying the contract label to the situation where there is simply a deed, but no consideration, and no agreement, is questioned: 'The affinity of the deed is with gift not with bargain, and it is fair to say that the so-called "contract by deed" has little in common with agreement save its name and its history, and that it does not seem to require detailed consideration in a modern book upon the law of contract'.[1] It is the 'simple' contract, not by deed, which is our principal concern.

2.2   The agreement is often said to require a meeting of minds between the contracting parties, which is sometimes described as a *consensus ad idem*. However, such statements are apt to mislead, as our law takes a predominantly objective approach to agreement. The law is not generally concerned with what is in the minds of the parties, but with what can be inferred from what was said and done. Statements of this are legion. In *Storer* v *Manchester City Council* [1974] 3 All ER 824, for example, Lord Denning stated (at 828):

> 'In contracts you do not look into the actual intent in a man's mind. You look at what he said and did. A contract is formed when there is, to all outward appearances, a contract.'

More recently, in *RTS Flexible Systems* v *Molkerei Alois Müller GmbH & Co KG* (2010) Lord Clarke stated (at [45]):

> 'Whether there is a binding contract between the parties, and if so, upon what terms depends upon what they have agreed. It depends not upon their subjective state of mind, but upon a consideration of what was communicated between them by words or conduct...'

2.3   The reason for this predominantly objective approach is the difficulty of ascertaining a person's subjective intention, and unlike the criminal law, which deals with the liability of the defendant only, and assesses intent from a subjective perspective, the law of contract has to be fair to *both* parties to an apparent agreement. In the interests of fairness, certainty, and commercial convenience, one party has to be able to rely on the words and conduct of the other, even if it turns out that they were not an accurate reflection of the other party's private or subjective intentions. For example, if a person appears to indicate a willingness to enter into a contract on a particular set of terms, the law will look at how a reasonable person would have understood it. The law will not concern itself with the subjective intention of the apparent maker of the offer, as to do so would be unfair to the other party.[2]

2.4   In the majority of cases there will, of course, be both actual and objective agreement. But, the law will not allow the general, objective approach to be abused. If one party *knows* either

---

1   M. Furmston, *Cheshire, Fifoot & Furmston's Law of Contract*, 16th edn, Oxford University Press, 2012, p. 37.

2   It should be noted that there are differing views on precisely what is meant by an 'objective' approach to agreement: from which perspective should the reasonable person view any statements/actions—from that of the 'fly on the wall' or that of one of the relevant parties. For further discussion, see e.g. Howarth, 100 LQR 265; De Moor, 106 LQR 632; and Friedmann, 119 LQR 68, but note what has become the predominant approach in the context of interpretation: 'Interpretation is the ascertainment of the meaning which the document would convey to a reasonable person having all the background knowledge which would reasonably have been available to the parties in the situation in which they were at the time of the contract': *Investors Compensation Scheme Ltd* v *West Bromwich Building Society* [1998] 1 All ER 98, Lord Hoffmann at 114.

that the other has no intention of contracting with him or is mistaken as to the proposed terms, despite an objective appearance of agreement, the law will not simply apply the objective test (see *Hartog* v *Colin & Shields* (1939)).

2.5   Whether it is the 'meeting of minds', or agreement, which is referred to, the tendency is to think simply in terms of two parties bargaining, and then reaching agreement. However, first, we should not lose sight of the fact that there may, of course, be far more than two parties to a particular contract, and they will each need to intend to contract, and supply consideration. Secondly, we must take on board the idea of the 'unilateral contract'. The normal contract with two parties is called a bilateral contract, and the same rules will apply if there are more parties (multilateral). Unilateral contracts do differ from the others in important respects, however, as we shall see at various points. Here we should merely note what is meant by a unilateral contract. The name, '*uni*lateral', comes from the fact that only one party becomes bound to do anything. The immediate reaction to this might be to ask, 'what about consideration then?', but each party will supply consideration. This is not the puzzle it sounds. A unilateral contract will be of the form 'A promises to do X, if B does Y'. The most common example of such contracts is that for a reward, where, for example, A has promised to pay £10 to anyone who returns his lost dog, Spot. B sees the reward poster, returns Spot, and A is contractually bound to pay the £10 to B. It is a unilateral contract, with only one party ever coming under an obligation, because B was never contractually bound to find and return Spot. However, when B returned Spot, B's actions supplied consideration for A's promise, and fulfilled the condition under which A became obliged to pay. As has been indicated, unilateral contracts will need to be referred to, at points, but it must not be forgotten that they are not the commonly occurring, usual, type of contract; that is the bilateral contract.

Offer and acceptance

2.6   In deciding whether the parties have reached contractual agreement, the law generally looks for an offer by one party and an acceptance of the terms of that offer by the other. In the bargaining process, one party will finally propose terms (price, date of delivery, etc.), and express a willingness to be bound by them if the other party signifies acceptance of them, and a contractual agreement is found when the other party accepts. The 'offer and acceptance' analysis generally determines whether or not there is sufficient agreement to form a contract, but it should be noted, at the start, that it is not absolutely required to be used. In *Gibson* v *Manchester City Council* (1979), Lord Diplock stated:

> 'My Lords there may be certain types of contract, though I think they are exceptional, which do not fit easily into the normal analysis of a contract as being constituted by offer and acceptance, but a contract alleged to have been made by an exchange of correspondence between the parties in which the successive communications other than the first are in reply to one another is not one of these.'

There are some situations which simply do not fit the offer and acceptance analysis (see, for example, *Clarke* v *Earl of Dunraven* (1897) for an unusual contract scenario which did not fit the traditional analysis), and some situations, like the 'battle of the forms', which is considered later in the chapter, which can place its use under great strain.

Offer

2.7   An offer is a promise by one party (the offeror) to enter into a contract, on a particular set of terms, with the intention of being bound as soon as the other party (the offeree) signifies his, or her, acceptance. An offer may be made either to an individual person, or to a particular group of people, or it may be made to the general public (as in the case of a reward offered for the provision of information). An offer may be written, spoken or implied by conduct, and it may be made with varying degrees of complexity. Although this is simple enough to state, and understand, it may be difficult to apply it to a particular set of facts. During the bargaining process, there may be a series of communications between the parties as they move towards a final agreement, and it may be difficult to determine whether a particular statement was an offer or something else, and the cases are not always easy to reconcile, on their facts.

Offer or invitation to treat?

2.8   The question of whether there was an offer, is usually put in terms of whether there was an offer or an invitation to treat. There is no particular significance to the phrase 'invitation to treat', other than it is the one which we generally use to distinguish, from an offer, a statement which is merely indicating a willingness to commence, or continue, negotiations. The offer is the legally significant statement, and offer is the legally significant terminology, so we do not need to define an invitation to treat. All we need to do is distinguish it from an offer: the offer will contain the intention to be bound, if the other party accepts. An invitation to treat will not contain that intention. This is a distinction which is easy to state, but again, it may be difficult to decide on which side of the line a particular communication falls.

2.9   An illustration of the difficulty in distinguishing between an offer and an invitation to treat is provided by *Gibson* v *Manchester City Council* (1979). The facts were:

> The Conservative-controlled Manchester City Council advertised details of a scheme for tenants to buy their council houses from the corporation and C expressed interest and asked to be told the price of buying his house. The city treasurer wrote in reply: 'The corporation may be prepared to sell the house to you at . . . £2,180', but the letter was not to be 'regarded as a firm offer of a mortgage'. C had to fill in a form to make a formal application, which he did, leaving blank the purchase price and listing certain defects in the property. He was told by the Council that the price had been fixed in accordance with the condition of the property, and wrote that he wished to go ahead on the basis of his application. The Council took the house off the list of tenant-occupied houses which had to be maintained by them, and put it on their house purchase list. As a result of a local election, Labour gained control of the Council and reversed the policy of selling council houses. They would sell only those houses where a legally binding contract had already been concluded.

The trial judge and the Court of Appeal decided that there was a contract and ordered specific performance (i.e. an order compelling the Manchester Council to sell the property to C). In the Court of Appeal, Lord Denning stated that the parties appeared to have reached agreement on all the material terms, and this was evidenced by their correspondence and conduct. He thought that it did not matter that 'all the formalities had not been gone through'.[3] He was critical of the traditional offer and acceptance approach, and that received the response from Lord Diplock, indicated earlier, that there are exceptional situations where it is not appropriate, but that it generally is, and particularly in a case concerned with a chain of communications, each in response to the other.

2.10   The House of Lords allowed the Council's appeal and made it clear that the Council's statement of the price of the house was not an offer to Mr Gibson. It was merely one stage in the negotiating process. The language of the treasurer's letter indicated this with the phrases: 'may be prepared to sell'. In reply to the argument that the parties' agreement could be shown by their conduct, it can be said that their conduct was equivocal. The house was taken off the list of properties maintained by the Council, but this could merely indicate that the house was expected to be sold in the near future, and not that agreement had been reached. In addition to the force of the use of the phrase 'may be prepared to sell', as indicating that the treasurer's letter was not an offer, there was also the uncertainty over whether C would be granted a mortgage: would C have wanted to go ahead if he had been unable to obtain one? Would he have expected to be obliged to do so? The successive communications between the parties show that they were feeling their way towards agreement, but that the negotiations had not yet ripened into a contract. (Contrast *Storer* v *Manchester City Council* (1974)).

2.11   As *Gibson* v *Manchester City Council* (1979) illustrates, the statement of a price by one party does not necessarily indicate that there is an offer to sell at that price, without further negotiations. Obviously, there is unlikely to be an offer without some statement of the price, or as to the means of determining it (for example, the market price on a specified date), but its presence is not determinative that there is an offer. It is important to look at all the surrounding circumstances. In *Harvey* v *Facey* (1893), C sent a telegram to D: 'Will you sell us Bumper Hall Pen? Telegraph lowest cash price'. D's telegram replied: 'Lowest price for Bumper Hall Pen, £900'. C's final telegram purported to accept this 'offer' and 'agreed' to buy the property for £900. The Privy Council held that there was no contract, as D was not making an offer merely by responding to C's request for information. There was no clear intention by D to be bound simply by C's' expression of assent. (For a similar result, see *Clifton* v *Palumbo* (1944).)

2.12   The distinction between an offer and an invitation to treat is often difficult to draw. One has to consider the communications between the parties and try to ascertain the intention with which a statement was made. Does the statement show a willingness to be bound if the other party expresses agreement? It may be necessary to look at a series of statements, or letters, which pass between the parties, during the negotiating process, to assess the overall impression conveyed by these communications. In *Bigg* v *Boyd Gibbins Ltd* [1971] 2 All ER 183, during

---

3   See [1978] 2 All ER 583 at 586.

the course of negotiations for the sale of his property to D, C stated that 'for a quick sale [he] would accept £26,000'. D replied by letter that he accepted this offer. C wrote back, expressing his pleasure at D's decision and stating that he was putting the matter in the hands of his solicitor to proceed with the sale. The Court of Appeal held that the impression given by these communications was that the parties 'intended to and did achieve the formation of a . . . contract' (per Russell LJ at 185).

2.13   The use of the word 'offer' by one party is not decisive. It might not be being used in its technical sense. In *Spencer v Harding* (1870) LR 5 CP 561, D sent out a circular: 'We are instructed to offer [certain business stock] to the wholesale trade for sale by tender . . .'. C's tender for the stock was the highest that D received, but D refused it. C's contention was that the circular amounted to an offer and contained a promise to sell to the highest bidder. Generally, advertisements are not regarded as offers, but C tried to draw an analogy with advertisements of rewards for information (dealt with later), where there is a promise to pay the first person who supplies the information. But the court rejected this line of reasoning; there was no promise to sell to the highest bidder. In finding for the defendant, Willes J stated (at 563):

> '[T]he question is, whether there is here any offer to enter into a contract at all, or whether the circular amounts to anything more than a mere proclamation that the defendants are ready to chaffer for the sale of goods, and to receive offers for the purchase of them . . . Here there is a total absence of any words to intimate that the highest bidder is to be the purchaser. It is a mere attempt to ascertain whether an offer can be obtained within such a margin as the sellers are willing to adopt.'

2.14   However, the circumstances in each case will be important, and the words used may make it clear that there is an intention to be bound, and an offer, rather than an invitation to treat, and there may even be a subsidiary offer, alongside a more important invitation to treat. In *Harvela Investments Ltd v Royal Trust Co. of Canada* (1984):

> D(1) owned a parcel of shares which would give effective control of a company to either C or D(2), who were rivals bidding for the shares. D(1) invited both parties to submit, by sealed bid, a 'single offer' for the whole parcel by a particular time and date. In making the invitation, they stated that: 'we bind ourselves to accept [the highest] offer.' C made a single bid, but D(2)'s bid was really two bids, being (a) for a fixed monetary amount (which was less than that bid by C); and (b) a referential bid which offered $101,000 in excess of any other offer that D(1) received. D(1) accepted D(2)'s referential bid and entered into a contract with them for the sale of the shares. C claimed that D(2)'s successful bid was not valid as it was not within the terms of the original invitation to bid (because it was not a 'single offer'). C succeeded in this action. (Despite reversal in the Court of Appeal, the House of Lords restored the original decision in C's favour.)

In this case we can see a different intention on the part of the sellers, when inviting bids, from that in *Spencer v Harding* (1870). In *Harvela*, the sellers bound themselves to accept the highest offer. This statement was an offer rather than a mere invitation to treat, which C accepted by the submission of its bid.

2.15 On the particular facts of a case, the court may be willing to find other subsidiary offers, alongside invitations to treat. In *Blackpool and Fylde Aero Club Ltd v Blackpool Borough Council* [1990] 3 All ER 25 the facts were as follows:

> The defendant council owned an airport, from which it permitted an air operator to run pleasure trips. This concession had been granted to the claimant club (C) on previous occasions. On the expiry of the last concession, the council invited C and six other parties to tender for the rights to operate pleasure flights from the airport. A very clear procedure for submitting bids was laid down by the council, and it was stated that tenders received after noon, 17 March 1983, would not be considered. Only C and two others responded to this invitation. C's tender was put in the Town Hall letter box one hour before the deadline, but due to an oversight the letter box was not cleared by council staff at noon that day as it was supposed to be. (The council accepted that this was due to administrative error.) C's tender was recorded as late, and was not considered. C contended that the council was contractually bound to consider any tender that was validly made, and received, by the deadline. It sought damages from the council.

It was clear from the wording of the council's invitation to tender that it was not promising to accept the highest tender it received. But was it bound at least to consider all tenders submitted within the specified period? The Court of Appeal held that the council was liable in damages to the club for breach of contract. It held that, in certain circumstances, an invitation to tender could give rise to a contractual undertaking by the invitor to consider tenders which conformed with the stipulated conditions of tender. Bingham LJ stated (at 30):

> '[W]here, as here, tenders are solicited from selected parties all of them known to the invitor, and where a local authority's invitation prescribes a clear, orderly and familiar procedure . . . the invitee is in my judgment protected at least to this extent: if he submits a conforming tender before the deadline he is entitled, not as a matter of mere expectation but of contractual right, to be sure that his tender will after the deadline be opened and considered in conjunction with all other conforming tenders or at least that his tender will be considered if others are.'

The council was not obliged to accept any tender. Alternatively, it could have awarded the concession to any tenderer, so long as the decision was taken in good faith. But the council was contractually bound to consider C's tender before making its decision.[4]

---

4 Such cases raise difficult issues in relation to the point at which, short of the 'main contract' coming into being, legal obligations should be triggered. They raise questions as to whether the courts are not really finding subsidiary contracts, but surreptitiously requiring compliance with some limited duty to behave in good faith during negotiations, which, occasionally, a party steps outside of. We say 'surreptitiously' as certainly no such duty is openly recognized in English law.

Offer or invitation to treat: some common situations

2.16 Undoubtedly, it can be difficult to know how the offer and acceptance analysis should apply in every case, but there have come to be generally accepted analyses of certain commonly occurring situations, which will normally be adopted in those situations, but which could, of course, be departed from in the face of a contrary intention being clearly shown.

Advertisements

2.17 Advertisement of goods for sale are not generally regarded as offers. In *Partridge* v *Crittenden* (1968) the appellant was charged, under legislation for the protection of wild birds, with unlawfully offering for sale a wild bird. He had placed an advertisement in a magazine: 'Bramblefinch cocks and hens, 25s each'. The Divisional Court held that the appellant was not liable for the statutory offence as he had not offered the birds for sale; the advertisement was an invitation to treat.

2.18 Similarly, the particular type of 'advertisement', which is in the form of a catalogue or circular with a price-list will not generally be regarded as making an offer to sell those goods. If a person sees a price-list and places an order, the seller is not normally bound to supply the goods. In *Grainger & Son* v *Gough* [1896] AC 325 Lord Herschell said (at 334):

'The transmission of such a price-list does not amount to an offer to supply an unlimited quantity of the wine described at the price named, so that as soon as an order is given there is a binding contract to supply that quantity. If it were so, the merchant might find himself involved in any number of contractual obligations to supply wine of a particular description which he would be quite unable to carry out, his stock of wine of that description being necessarily limited.'

A seller of goods wants to be able to provide information about his on her goods (i.e. advertise them) without risking being bound to sell more of the specified items than he or she has (and it is in the interests of fostering a competitive market that he or she should be able to do so). This is seen as indicating that adverts are not generally intended as offers, but merely invitations to treat. Of course, the problem might equally have been met by generally implying that an advertised offer was subject to stock availability, but it is the accepted line that adverts are generally not offers, but merely invitations to treat.

2.19 An advertisement of reward is, however, generally an offer. They are of course, unusual offers, in that they are offers of unilateral, rather than normal bilateral, contracts. Similarly, *Carlill* v *Carbolic Smoke Ball Co* (1893), which is a very famous case, and one where an advert was found to be an offer, was about an offer of a unilateral contract, and its membership of that unusual category, must not be forgotten.

The defendant company placed an advertisement in the newspaper offering a reward of £100 to anyone who bought one of its smoke balls, and used it in the prescribed manner, and

> yet caught influenza. The advert stated that, to show its 'sincerity in the matter', the company had deposited £1,000 with its bank. Relying upon the advertisement, C bought a smoke ball and used it as directed—and, needless to say, still caught influenza. C sued successfully for the £100 reward and the defendant company appealed against the decision.

A variety of arguments were put forward by the defendants to defeat C's claim. It was argued that the advert was too vague and that the defendants did not intend to be bound by it. These arguments were rejected by the Court of Appeal which held that both the meaning and the effect of the advertisement were clear, particularly with the statement as to the deposit of £1,000. (It was also argued that there was no contract, as C had not notified the defendants of her acceptance. However, although acceptance does generally have to be communicated, this is not the case where the offer is unilateral. The contract is made by carrying out the relevant act or condition.)[5]

Items displayed in shops

2.20   It might be supposed that goods displayed in shop windows, or on shop counters, with the prices clearly marked, are being offered for sale. In certain types of shops or markets a limited degree of bargaining (or 'haggling') may be possible, but in the vast majority of shops, stores, and supermarkets, this is neither possible nor expected; goods are to be sold at the prices shown and no negotiation takes place between retailer and customer. Yet it is firmly established that the display of goods in a shop is generally not an offer to sell those goods, but merely an invitation to treat. In *Pharmaceutical Society of Great Britain* v *Boots Cash Chemists (Southern) Ltd* [1953] 1 QB 401:

> It had to be decided at what point a contract is concluded in a 'self-service' shop where the goods are priced and displayed on shelves, selected by customers, and then taken to the cash-desk for payment. The case arose under s 18(1) of the Pharmacy and Poisons Act 1933 which stated that '. . . it shall not be lawful—(a) for a person to sell any [listed] poison, unless . . . the sale is effected by, or under the supervision of a registered pharmacist'. The case was brought to establish whether the defendants were breaking the law by positioning their registered pharmacist adjacent to the cash-desk. If the display of goods on the shelves were regarded as an offer to sell, and could be accepted by the customer when they were picked up and put into the basket provided, then the defendants were breaking the law, as the sale would not be supervised by the pharmacist as required by the statute. But if the display of items was merely an invitation to treat and it was the customer who made the offer at the cash-desk, then Boots were complying with the law.

It was decided that the contract was concluded at the cash-desk. The customer made the offer, and this could be accepted or rejected by the defendants. Therefore, sales were supervised by

---

5   See also *Bowerman* v *Association of British Travel Agents Ltd* (1996).

the registered pharmacist. The court took the line (per Somervell LJ) that if the display of items on the shelf amounted to an offer, a customer who picked up items and put them into the basket provided would thereby accept the offer and be contractually bound to pay for the goods even if the customer later changed his or her mind and did not want the goods. Somervell LJ stated (at 406):

> 'I can see no reason for implying from this self-service arrangement any implication other than that . . . it is a convenient method of enabling customers to see what there is and choose, and possibly put back and substitute, articles which they wish to have, and then go up to the cashier and offer to buy what they have so far chosen.'

2.21   It could be argued with equal force that if the display of goods were regarded as an offer, the acceptance by the customer would take place only when the goods are presented at the cash-desk for payment, and not when they are placed into the basket. However, it is the accepted line that the display of goods in a self-service shop, supermarket, or shop window does not amount to an offer to sell those goods. In *Fisher* v *Bell* (1961), it was, for example, also held that the display of a 'flick-knife' in a shop window was not an offer to sell it. (It does not affect the contractual outcome, but it is worth noting that if a shop lures in customers with displays of goods at a low price, and then refuses to sell them to the customer at that price, it may well be an offence under the Consumer Protection from Unfair Trading Regulations 2008 (SI 2008/1277), which implemented Directive 2005/29/EC of the European Parliament and of the Council concerning unfair business-to-consumer practices.)

Auctions

2.22   Where an auctioneer asks for bids, he or she is not making an offer to sell the goods to the highest bidder. It was established in *Payne* v *Cave* (1789) that the auctioneer is merely inviting offers from bidders, which he can either accept or reject. This rule is now encapsulated in s 57(2) of the Sale of Goods Act 1979 which states:

> 'A sale by auction is complete when the auctioneer announces its completion by the fall of the hammer, or in other customary manner; and until the announcement is made any bidder may retract his bid.'

2.23   The advertisement of an auction sale is not an offer to sell particular goods (*Harris* v *Nickerson* (1873)). But is there a binding promise to sell the goods to the highest bidder where an auction sale, which is advertised as 'without reserve', actually takes place? The point was not resolved entirely by the case of *Warlow* v *Harrison* (1859), despite *obiter dicta* supporting the view that such an advertisement may include a separate and binding promise by the auctioneer to sell to the highest bona fide bidder. The decision of the Court of Appeal in *Barry* v *Davies (t/a Heathcote Ball & Co.)* (2001), however, confirmed that this is the correct approach. In that case, two machines were advertised for sale by auction without reserve. B, the claimant, was the sole bidder and his bid of £200 for each of them fell a long way short of the commercial value of the machines. D, the auctioneer, refused to sell the machines to B and withdrew them from the sale.

The trial judge and the Court of Appeal held that, in doing this, D was in breach of contract. In an auction sale without reserve, it was not open to the auctioneer to reject the highest bid—in this case the only bid—simply because it was not high enough. This may appear a harsh decision in these circumstances, where the bid was far below the estimated value of the goods. However, if the seller wishes to avoid such a risk, a reserve price can be stipulated.[6]

Advertisements on websites

2.24 It is increasingly common for customers to buy goods by selecting items advertised on websites and making payment for them by credit card. Such websites combine the attributes of both advertisements and shops, and it seems likely that the normal inference will be that they are making invitations to treat, and not offers, unless there is something on the website that clearly shows that the site intends to be bound.[7] It is more likely, however, that the website will expressly provide that it is not making an offer, that the customer makes an offer when his or her 'order' is submitted, and that there will be no acceptance until the customer is notified that the goods have been dispatched. Amongst other things, this will serve to protect the website against pricing mistakes it makes—customers will not be able to claim that they have a con-tract to buy the television mistakenly advertised at £3.99 (instead of £399), just because they have placed an 'order'. Article 11 UN Convention on the Use of Electronic Communications in International Contracts, which is not binding on the courts of England and Wales but merely of interest in relation to such contracts, provides:

> 'A proposal to conclude a contract made through one or more electronic communications which is not addressed to one or more specific parties, but is generally accessible to parties making use of information systems, including proposals that make use of interactive appli-cations for the placement of orders through such information systems, is to be considered as an invitation to make offers, unless it clearly indicates the intention of the party making a proposal to be bound in the case of acceptance.'

Termination of offers

2.25 There are a number of ways in which an offer may be terminated before an acceptance has taken place. We should briefly consider them, before looking at acceptance.

Revocation (or withdrawal)

2.26 Obviously an offer cannot be withdrawn once it has been accepted, but it may be revoked at any time before acceptance has occurred (see *Payne* v *Cave* (1789)). In fact, the offeror may generally withdraw the offer even if it was expressly stated that it would remain open for a

---

6 For further discussion, see F. Meisel 'What Price Auctions Without Reserve?' (2001) 64 Mod LR 468.

7 Electronic Commerce (EC Directive) Regulations 2002 require, unless parties who are not consumers have agreed otherwise, the service provider to explain to customers in plain terms, where a contract is made by electronic means, the *technical steps* to follow to complete a binding agreement (reg 9(1)).

fixed period (*Routledge* v *Grant* (1828) 130 ER 920), unless there was consideration for such a promise (i.e. a separate contract that the main offer would remain open for a specified period). In *Routledge* v *Grant* (1828) the defendant offered to take a lease of the claimant's premises, giving the claimant six weeks to make up his mind. Three weeks later, the defendant withdrew the offer and, afterwards, the claimant purported to accept within the six-week period. The court held that there was no contract, as the defendant was free to withdraw the offer at any time before acceptance by the offeree. Despite the defendant's promise, the offer did not have to remain open for six weeks. Best CJ said (at 923):

> '[I]f six weeks are given on one side to accept an offer, the other side has six weeks to put an end to it. One party cannot be bound without the other.'

2.27   As has been indicated, the situation will, of course, be different if the offeree provides consideration for the offeror's promise to keep the offer open (for example, pays £x for it). In this case there will be a separate or 'collateral' contract between the parties; the offeror's promise will no longer be one-sided.

2.28   Although an offer may be withdrawn at any time before the offeree has accepted it, the withdrawal has to be communicated to the offeree. It is not sufficient for the offeror merely to change his or her mind without informing the offeree. In particular, it should be noted that the 'postal rule', which as we shall see, makes a posted acceptance effective on posting, rather than requiring its communication, does not apply to a posted revocation (*Byrne & Co* v *Leon Van Tienhoven & Co.* (1880)).

2.29   Although the withdrawal of an offer must be communicated to the offeree, it appears that the offeree does not have to be notified of the withdrawal by the offeror. In *Dickinson* v *Dodds* (1876) 2 Ch D 463, D made an offer to C for C to buy certain land from D for £800, and D promised that the offer would remain open for two days (until 9 a.m. on 12 June). But D sold the land to someone else on 11 June, and C learned of this later the same day, by chance, via a third party. C then proceeded to notify D of his acceptance of the offer before 9 a.m. on 12 June. The Court of Appeal held that C's action for specific performance failed, as there was no contract between C and D. We have seen already that a promise to keep an offer open for a specific period is not, by itself, binding on the offeror. But was the withdrawal of the offer effectively communicated to the offeree? James LJ (at 472) had no doubts that it was:

> '[I]n this case, beyond all question, the [claimant] knew that Dodds was no longer minded to sell the property to him as plainly and clearly as if Dodds had told him in so many words, "I withdraw the offer".'

Of course, an offer may be withdrawn by someone whom the offeror has authorized to communicate that to the offeree, but that was not what occurred in *Dickinson v Dodds,* and unless the offeree believes the offer has been withdrawn, third party notification of withdrawal should be restricted to the situation where the third party would be seen as a reliable source of that information, whom the reasonable person would believe.

Rejection

2.30   An offer is terminated if the offeree rejects the offer. It is not possible for the offeree to subsequently change his or her mind and accept. It will be seen that a counter offer amounts to a rejection of the original offer (*Hyde* v *Wrench* (1840)), but the offeree does not make a counter offer, where he or she merely seeks further information from the offeror (See *Stevenson, Jacques, & Co.* v *McLean* (1880)). See further later.

Lapse of time

2.31   An offer may come to an end due to lapse of time. If A, on Monday, offers to sell his car to B and says, 'I must have your answer by Friday at the latest', B cannot accept the offer on Saturday. In many cases, the offeror does not stipulate that the offer must be accepted within a specified period. However, it would be impracticable if offers could last indefinitely, and where no time limit is specified, they will lapse after a reasonable time. What amounts to a reasonable time will depend on the circumstances of the case and must take account of the subject matter of the offer. In *Ramsgate Victoria Hotel Co.* v *Montefiore* (1866), an offer to buy shares, which was made in June, could not be accepted in November.

Where the offer is conditional

2.32   An offer may be expressed as subject to the occurrence of some condition. For example, A may offer to sell goods to B subject to his being able to obtain supplies himself. If A subsequently cannot obtain supplies, the offer will come to an end. The offer was conditional on a particular state of affairs, which did not occur. The courts can also imply a condition into an offer where it has not been expressly stated by the offeror. If A offers to buy goods, or to take them on hire purchase, it will be implied that the offer is subject to the condition that the goods will remain in (substantially) the same state that they were in at the time of the offer. (See *Financings Ltd* v *Stimson* [1962] 3 All ER 386, especially Donovan LJ at 390.)

Death

2.33   What is the position where the offeror dies after making an offer but before the offeree has accepted? If it is an offer of a 'personal' contract (involving a personal service such as employment or agency), the offer should come to an end with the death of the offeror. Otherwise, it is possible for an offer to continue even after the death of the offeror, where the offeree accepts without knowing of the offeror's death (see *Bradbury* v *Morgan* (1862)). In this event the obligations under the contract will fall on the offeror's personal representatives.

2.34   Where the offeree dies after an offer has been made, it seems both likely and sensible that the offer comes to an end. It must be acknowledged, however, that the cases are not conclusive. In *Reynolds* v *Atherton* (1921), Warrington LJ stated that an offer 'made to a living person who ceases to be a living person before the offer is accepted . . . is no longer an offer at all', but the case was actually decided on different grounds.

Acceptance

2.35   As has been indicated, the usual way to decide if the necessary agreement is present, for there to be a contract, is to look for offer and acceptance. We have discussed various aspects of offers, and we will now look at what will amount to acceptance.

2.36   What constitutes acceptance of an offer? It is the final expression of assent, by words or conduct, to the offer or proposal. It is important that the acceptance is both final and unequivocal. It must be an acceptance of the offeror's proposal without varying the terms or adding new terms. (For obvious reasons, this is sometimes referred to as the 'mirror image rule'.) A purported acceptance which attempts to introduce new terms, or vary those contained in the offer, will be a counter offer and not an acceptance of the original offer.

2.37   In *Jones* v *Daniel* (1894) D wrote and offered to buy C's property for £1,450, and received a reply from C's solicitor which purported to accept the offer, and enclosed a contract for D's signature. However, the document contained important new terms, that were not part of D's original offer, and D refused to sign it. It was held that there was no contract between the parties. The letter from C's solicitor (with its draft contract) was not an acceptance, but a counter offer, which D was free to accept or reject. Similarly, if a person offers to pay a fixed price for services and materials, this will not be accepted by a promise to provide those services and materials at a variable price.[8]

2.38   As has been indicated, a counter offer amounts to a rejection of the original offer, which cannot thereafter be accepted. In *Hyde* v *Wrench* (1840), D made a written offer to sell his farm to C for £1,000, to which C replied that he would give £950 for it. D refused to sell at the lower price and, a few days later, C wrote to D agreeing to pay £1,000 for the property. D had not withdrawn his original offer, but he now refused to sell to C. The court held that there was no contract. C's counter offer (of £950) was a rejection of D's original offer and brought it to an end. It could not be revived afterwards by C simply purporting to accept it.

2.39   However, there are situations where the offeree does not put forward a new proposal, but merely seeks clarification of the offer, or further information about it, from the offeror. In such a case the offer is not to be regarded as rejected and it is still open to the offeree to accept it. This is illustrated by the case of *Stevenson, Jacques & Co.* v *McLean* (1880) 5 QBD 346:

> D wrote to C offering to sell a quantity of iron at '40s per ton net cash', and stating that the offer would remain open until the following Monday. It was clear from communications

---

8   See *North West Leicestershire District Council* v *East Midlands Housing Association* (1981).

> between the parties that C, in turn, was looking for buyers and that the market was unsettled. Early on Monday morning, C sent D a telegram: 'Please wire whether you would accept forty for delivery over two months, or if not, longest limit you would give'. D did not answer C's question and sold the iron to a third party. On Monday afternoon, C (having had no reply) sent another telegram accepting D's offer to sell at 40s cash. C's final telegram was sent before D's withdrawal of the offer reached C. C sued for breach of contract, and D claimed that C's telegram of Monday morning amounted to a counter offer and therefore a rejection of D's offer.

Was C's first telegram a fresh proposal, or did it merely seek to clarify an aspect of D's offer? The distinction can be a very fine one, but the court ruled in C's favour. Lush J held that C did not make a counter offer: 'Here there is no counter proposal . . . there is nothing specific by way of offer or rejection, but a mere enquiry, which should have been answered and not treated as a rejection of the offer' (at 350).

Communication of acceptance

2.40   Unsurprisingly, the general rule is that an acceptance must be communicated to be effective and create a contract.[9] As in many other ways, unilateral contracts are exceptional, and do not require communication, and there is an odd, but longstanding, exception for posted acceptances in relation to our normal bilateral contracts. We shall look at these exceptional situations later, but here we should firmly emphasize that the general rule is that acceptance must be communicated.[10] Obviously acceptance can be communicated not only by spoken or written words, but also by conduct, and *Brogden* v *Metropolitan Rly Co.* (1877) 2 App Cas 666 provides an example of that:

> B had supplied the Metropolitan Railway Co. with coal for some years without a formal agreement. The parties decided to formalize their transactions and the Metropolitan Railway Co. sent B a draft agreement. B completed certain details in the draft which had been left blank, including the name of an arbitrator, and B then signed it and wrote 'approved', and returned it to the Metropolitan Railway Co. whose manager put it in his desk. Nothing further was done formally with the document, but for some time the parties acted in accordance with its arrangements by supplying and paying for the coal. Finally a disagreement arose and B denied that there was a binding contract between the parties.

The addition of the arbitrator's name by B was a new term, and therefore a counter offer. Did the Metropolitan Railway Co. accept this offer? Obviously, the manager merely putting the document in his desk could not amount to acceptance. Not only was it an equivocal action, it also did nothing to communicate to the other party. However, the Metropolitan Railway Co.

---

9   *Entores Ltd* v *Miles Far Eastern Corp* (1955); *Brinkibon Ltd* v *Stahag Stahl und Stahlwarenhandelgesellschaft mbH* (1983).

10   *Entores Ltd* v *Miles Far Eastern Corp* (1955); *Brinkibon Ltd* v *Stahag Stahl und Stahlwarenhandelgesellschaft mbH* (1983).

placed an order for, and accepted coal, on the basis of the agreement. As Lord Cairns stated (at 680):

> '[A]pprobation was clearly given when the company commenced a course of dealing which is referable . . . only to the contract, and when that course of dealing was accepted and acted upon by [B] in the supply of coals.'

2.41 Although it will be extremely rare, as the meaning of silence is generally not unequivocal, it would seem that there can be cases where silence can communicate acceptance.[11] However, it is clear that one party cannot force another to have to take positive action, to deny they are accepting, if they are to avoid becoming bound. X cannot create a contract out of Y's silence by writing to Y stating: 'I will sell you my car for £1,000. If I do not hear from you within seven days, I shall assume that you accept'. The law will not allow X to take advantage of the common human tendency to inaction, in this way. Y will not become contractually bound to buy X's car simply on the basis that Y has not communicated a denial of acceptance to X.

2.42 Something of this type of situation arose in *Felthouse* v *Bindley* (1862). In that case:

> C entered into negotiations with his nephew, J, for the purchase of J's horse. He wrote to J, shortly after, offering to buy the horse and stating: 'If I hear no more about him, I consider the horse is mine at £30 15s'. J did not reply to his uncle's letter, but he did instruct the auctioneer (D) not to sell the horse along with his, J's, farming stock. D forgot this instruction and six weeks after C's letter, the horse was sold by D to another person. C sued D for conversion (in tort) basing his action on the contention that there was a concluded contract between C and J for the sale of the horse, and that, therefore, the horse belonged to C at the time of the auction. But was there a binding agreement between C and his nephew?

The court decided that the action for conversion failed. Although the nephew may have decided to sell the horse to his uncle, there was no communication of this decision to the uncle. Accordingly, there was no binding agreement between C and J, and the horse never became the uncle's property. This illustrates that X cannot turn Y's silence into acceptance, merely by stating that is to be the case.

2.43 However, the situation may well be different if Y is claiming that X should be bound. Whilst X cannot trap Y in a contract, against Y's wishes in this way, it would seem that Y should be able to say that he or she has a contract with X. X may be seen to have 'waived' communication, and so be unable to deny there is a contract without it.

---

11 *The Hannah Blumenthal* (1983); *Vitol SA* v *Norelf Ltd* [1996] AC 800 per Lord Steyn at 810.

Acceptance by post

2.44   The general rule, then, is that for an acceptance to be effective, it must be communicated to the offeror.[12] As has been indicated, however, there is a rule of great age, and very limited justification, that this does not apply to posted acceptances, but rather we have an exception which is known as 'the postal rule'.

2.45   The postal rule is an exception to the 'general rule...that a contract is formed when acceptance of an offer is communicated by the offeree to the offeror' (*Brinkibon Ltd v Stahag Stahl und Stahlwarenhandelsgesellschaft mbH* [1983] 2 AC 34 at 41). It stems from *Adams v Lindsell* (1818), and under it a contract is formed when a letter of acceptance is posted. It applies when it is reasonable to use the post (*Henthorn v Fraser* (1892)), and is subject to the offeror not ousting its application (*Holwell Securities Ltd v Hughes* (1974)). It means that an offer can no longer be revoked once the acceptance has been posted (*Re Imperial Land Co of Marseilles (Harris' case)* (1872)), and it is generally irrelevant that the acceptance never arrives, or arrives late (*Household Fire and Accident Insurance Co v Grant* (1879)), although, the postal rule will not apply if loss or delay is due to the fault of the offeree, who has, for example not put the correct stamps on it, or has misaddressed it (*L J Korbetis v Transgrain Shipping BV* [2005] EWHC (QB) 1345 at [15]). It is also said that it will give way to 'manifest inconvenience and absurdity' (*Holwell Securities v Hughes* (1974)). We should enlarge on some of these points before considering the basis of the rule and its extension to other forms of communication.

2.46   The postal rule stems from the case of *Adams v Lindsell* (1818):

> D wrote to C offering to sell wool and requested a reply 'in the course of post'. D misdirected the letter and this caused it to be delayed for a couple of days. On receiving the letter, C replied immediately, by posting a letter of acceptance. After C's acceptance was posted, but before it arrived, D sold the wool to a third party, in the belief that C was not interested.

The court decided that a contract was concluded between D and C when the letter of acceptance was posted by C. Obviously this produced a just result in the instant case. However, as a general rule for postal communication, it has its difficulties, and lacks justification, to which we shall return.

2.47   As has been indicated, the postal rule means that it is generally irrelevant that the postal acceptance never arrives, or arrives late (*Household Fire and Accident Insurance Co v Grant* (1879)), but the rule will not apply if that loss or delay is due to the fault of the offeree, who has, for example not put the correct stamps on it, or misaddressed it. Under the postal rule, the

---

12   *Entores Ltd v Miles Far Eastern Corp* (1955); *Brinkibon Ltd v Stahag Stahl und Stahlwarenhandelgesellscaft mbH* (1983).

offeror takes the general risk of the post office losing or delaying the acceptance. The offeror should not bear the risk of loss or delay where it has been increased through the offeree's fault.[13]

2.48   The offeror can oust the application of the postal rule. He or she can specify that acceptance will have to be received to be effective. In *Holwell Securities Ltd* v *Hughes* (1974):

> D offered to sell a house to C in the form of an option 'exercisable by notice in writing to the intending vendor [D] at any time within six months'. Within the six-month period, C's solicitors wrote to D, notifying him of C's acceptance of the offer. The letter was correctly stamped, addressed and posted, but it never arrived. (A copy was received by D's solicitor, but C admitted that this was not sufficient notice.) No other written acceptance was given or sent to D before the time limit expired. C claimed specific performance, arguing that a contract was concluded on posting the letter of acceptance to D.

The Court of Appeal decided that the offer, by stipulating actual 'notice to [D]', could not be accepted merely by C posting a letter of acceptance. The offer was so framed as to require that the acceptance be received by the offeror, and therefore the postal rule did not apply.

2.49   So, we now have some idea of the effect of the postal rule, and the limits of its application. However, obviously, there are now a great number of means of communication besides the post, and as each new method comes along, the question tends to be asked: 'should the postal rule apply?' As the postal rule is an exception to the general rule, it would have been more appropriate to simply assume the application of the general rule unless a strong case for departing from it could be made out. Nevertheless, the question has been put in terms of 'should the postal rule apply?' (giving that postal rule more status than it deserves), and we should address it. On a terminological point, we should note that the postal rule is sometimes more broadly referred to as a 'dispatch rule', and the general rule, as a 'receipt rule'.

2.50   In the early days of its existence, the postal rule was extended to acceptances sent by telegram. However, when it came to be considered whether it should be extended to communication by telex,[14] the courts, in *Entores Ltd* v *Miles Far East Corporation* (1955), and *Brinkibon*

---

13 *L. J. Korbetis* v *Transgrain Shipping BV* (2005) per Toulson J at [15]—'The topic of misdirected letters of acceptance has been considered by text book writers. Chitty, at paragraph 2–056, has the following passage:

"Misdirected letter of acceptance. A letter of acceptance may be lost or delayed because it bears a wrong or an incomplete address, or because it is not properly stamped. Normally such defects would be due to the carelessness of the offeree, and although there is no English authority precisely on point, it is submitted that the postal rule should not apply to such cases. Although an offeror may have to take the risk of accidents in the post, it would be unreasonable to impose on him the further risk of the acceptor's carelessness. These arguments do not apply where the misdirection is due to the fault of the offeror, e.g. where his own address is incompletely or illegibly given in the offer itself. In such a case, the offeror shall not be allowed to rely on the fact that the acceptance was misdirected, except perhaps where his error in stating his own address was obvious to the offeree, for in such a case the offeror's fault would not be the effective cause of the misdirection of the acceptance. It is submitted that a misdirected acceptance should take effect, if at all, at the time which is least favourable to the party responsible for the misdirection."'

14 Telexes can be likened to faxes, where the message is actually typed into the machine.

Ltd v *Stahag Stahl und Stahlwarenhandelsgesellschaft mbH* (1983), concluded that it should not be: the general rule applied, and acceptance was not effective until received.

2.51   Both of the telex cases were concerned with whether the postal rule, or the general rule, applied to decide when the contracts were made, in order to determine the underlying question of where they were made, as that question needed to be answered to decide if the English courts had jurisdiction.[15] Both cases took the line that the general rule applied to telex, not the postal rule, so the telex had to be received for the acceptance to be effective, and this meant that the contract was made at the location of the offeror's telex machine, in England in *Entores,* and Austria in *Brinkibon.*

2.52   In both cases there is considerable reference to 'instantaneous' communication, and they have come to be seen as providing a rule that the postal rule does not apply to an 'instantaneous' means of communication. So in *David Baxter Edward Thomas and Peter Sandford Gander* v *BPE Solicitors (a firm)* (2010) the view was taken that the postal rule was not applicable to e-mail as it was 'instantaneous' (at [86]). One problem with this is that there is no consensus as to whether e-mail is 'instantaneous',[16] but this is hardly surprising. The courts in the telex cases were not applying a factual test of whether a telex was 'instantaneous'; they were asking whether it should be treated like situations, such as that of two people talking to one another on the telephone, which clearly are instantaneous. So, for example, in *Brinkibon,* Lord Wilberforce asked (at 41–42):

> '[W]ith a general rule covering instantaneous communication inter praesentes, or at a distance, with an exception applying to non-instantaneous communication at a distance, how should communications by telex be categorised?'

He answered the question by recognizing that in '*Entores Ltd. v. Miles Far East Corp* the Court of Appeal classified them with instantaneous communications' (at 41). This was not a matter of establishing that factually telex satisfied a test of instantaneousness, but of deciding to treat telex as in the same category as communications which did.

2.53   So, if there was no factual test being used of whether or not telexes were instantaneous, and when we have, nevertheless, tried to apply an 'instantaneousness' test to e-mail, it is

---

15   It was recognized that in relation to contracts made between parties in different countries, by a means of distance communication, which country the contract happened to be made in was a poor basis for determining which court should hear a dispute, but they did what they could by simply focusing on the question of when the contract was made, and letting 'where' logically follow. In *Brinkibon,* Lord Wilberforce said ([1983] 2 AC 34 at 40): 'In the case of successive telephone conversations it may indeed be most artificial to ask where the contract was made: if one asked the parties, they might say they did not know—or care...Unfortunately it remains in Order 11 as a test for the purpose of jurisdiction, and courts have to do their best with it'. More recently, in *Apple Corps Ltd* v *Apple Computer Inc* [2004] EWHC 768, [2004] 2 CLC 720, Mann J suggested that, for the purposes of jurisdiction, a contract made by one party speaking to another on the telephone, should be viewed as being made in both locations (see [36]–[37]).

16   Contrast *Chwee Kin Keong and Others* v *Digilandmall.com Pte Ltd* (2004) with the case noted in the text, in relation to judicial views; and contrast e.g. S. Hill 'Flogging a Dead Horse—The postal acceptance rule and e-mail' (2001) 17 JCL 151) 158–9, and A. Murray, 'Entering into contracts electronically: the real w.w.w.' in L. Edwards and C. Waelde, *Law & the Internet: a framework for electronic commerce,* Hart Publishing, 2000, p. 25, in relation to academic views.

not surprising that we cannot agree on a conclusion. How should we decide whether the postal rule applies to e-mail, or any other new form of communication? We should go back to fundamentals, and ask what the postal rule does, and should do, in order to decide if it is needed to perform that role in relation to e-mail.

2.54   First, there have been lots of ideas put forward to try to justify the postal rule which simply do not stand up to scrutiny. These include the meeting of minds,[17] the idea of the post office as an agent,[18] the notion that the offeror chose the method of communication and anyway could have stated that the postal rule was not to apply,[19] that it is necessary to avoid an endless chain of correspondence,[20] and that it is the better rule evidentially.[21] They have been so completely dismissed that they are not dealt with in the text, but they are nevertheless raised from time to

---

17 The traditional idea of meeting of minds, or *consensus ad idem*, may be seen as providing a basis for *Adams* v *Lindsell* (1818). If the contract was made when the acceptance was dispatched then, in that case, it was at a time when both intended the contract, and there would have then been a meeting of minds, in the sense of both of them intending a contract at that point. There is, however, the problem that that had not been manifested to the offeror, and, in any event, in later cases it was recognized that acceptance is effective on posting even where the offeror has changed his or her mind prior to that time (*Henthorn* v *Fraser* (1892)), 'so that there is not even such residual *consensus*' (S. Gardner, 'Trashing with Trollope: A Deconstruction of the Postal Rules in Contract' (1992) 12 Ox Jo LS 170, 171).

18 In *Household Fire and Carriage Accident Insurance Co Ltd* v *Grant* [1874–80] All ER Rep 919 (at 922), the postal rule was seen as being based on the idea of the post office as agent for the parties, so that handing over the acceptance to this 'agent' was communication to the offeror. The very unsatisfactory nature of this reasoning was pointed out in *Henthorn* v *Fraser* [1892] 2 Ch 27 per Kay LJ at 35–6: the post office is only a carrier, it does not deal with the content of the communication. Any justification of the postal rule on the basis that the post office is an agent has been long 'discredited' (see M. Furmston and G. J. Tolhurst, *Contract Formation—Law and Practice*, Oxford University Press, 2010, 4.102).

19 It is said, in justification of the postal rule, that the offeror chose, or contemplated, the use of the post as a method of communication (*Henthorn* v *Fraser* (1892) 2 Ch 27 at 33). The postal rule might then be seen as based on waiver, but again this does not provide sufficient explanation, as the same line should then have been taken in relation to communication by telex (R. A. Samek, 'A Reassessment of the Present Rule Relating to Postal Acceptance' (1961) 35 ALJ 38, 40). The point is also made that the offeror can specify that the postal rule is not to apply (*Holwell Securities Ltd* v *Hughes* (1974); *Household Fire and Carriage Accident Insurance Co Ltd* v *Grant* (1879)). This latter point, however, does not actually provide any argument for the postal rule as such, but is rather a means of presenting it as not needing to cause unfairness (Gardner, 'Trashing with Trollope', 174). Even in relation to that limited object, a moment's reflection will indicate its inadequacy. Leaving aside the basic difficulty that the postal rule is counterintuitive, and that the offeror may assume that there will not be a contract until the acceptance has been received (P. Fasciano, 'Internet Electronic Mail: a last bastion for the mailbox rule' (1997) 25 Hofstra LR 971), the party who is the offeror may not have any power in relation to the terms of the offer. In fact, the terms may well be the offeree's standard terms, as would normally be the case when, e.g., a consumer seeks to make a contract through the post in response to an advertisement. The advertisement will generally be an invitation to treat (e.g. *Partridge* v *Crittenden* (1968); *Grainger & Son* v *Gough* (1896)), the consumer will be the offeror, and the business, which has dictated the standard terms, will be the offeree.

20 In *Adams* v *Lindsell* (1818) the justification was put forward that the postal rule was needed to avoid an endless chain of correspondence: '[If] the defendants were not bound by their offer when accepted by the [claimants] till the answer was received, then the [claimants] ought not to be bound till after they had received the notification that the defendants had received their answer and assented to it. And so it might go on *ad infinitum*.' This can be simply dealt with. It is just a matter of a line needing to be drawn. It 'would be perfectly possible to hold that the acceptance took effect when it came to the notice of the offeror, whether the offeree knew of this or not': E. Peel, *Treitel's Law of Contract*, Sweet & Maxwell, 2011, 2.031.

21 For swift and clear dismissal of the idea that the postal rule is the better rule from the evidentiary perspective see e.g. I. R. Macneil, 'Time of acceptance: too many problems for a single rule' (1964) 112(7) Pa LR 947, 965 and P. H. Winfield 'Some Aspects of Offer and Acceptance' (1939) 120 LQR 499, 509–10.

time, and the footnotes may be consulted for explanations. That they do not, however, stand up to scrutiny is evident in the *obiter* comment in the recent Australian case of *Wardis v Agriculture and Rural Finance Pty Ltd* (2012). Campbell JA (at [133]) took the line that:

> 'It is hard to find a convincing explanation for the posting of an acceptance sometimes being a sufficient acceptance of an offer, beyond the urgent practical necessity of having some rule to decide by what act and at what time people who are negotiating for a contract, but are not in each other's presence become bound.'

This is in keeping with the view that the postal rule merely deals with a 'co-ordination problem', so that, like the rule as to which side of the road we drive on, it is there because *a* rule is needed, rather than *the* rule.[22] It is hardly surprising that Campbell JA went on to express the opinion that the 'future existence of the postal acceptance rule...might be in doubt' (at [134]). However, there are two explanations of the postal rule which deserve further scrutiny, before we should be content to arrive at any such conclusion.

2.55   As we have seen, offers are generally revocable at common law, even if it has been stated that they will remain open for a set time. The need for consideration is seen to stand in the way of irrevocability (*Routledge v Grant* (1828)), and revocability is significant in relation to the postal rule. The particular difficulty which is occasioned by revocation, and is dealt with by the postal rule, is that of a revocation which arrives with the offeree after an acceptance has been dispatched, but before the acceptance is received by the offeror. This was identified as a matter of concern by Mellish LJ in *In Re Imperial Land Co. of Marseilles (Harris's case)* (1872) LR 7 Ch 587. He said (at 594) that he had been

> 'forcibly struck with the extraordinary and very mischievous consequences which would follow if it were held that an offer might be revoked at any time until the letter accepting it had been actually received.'

He gave several examples of this mischief, including (at 594):

> 'Suppose that a dealer in Liverpool writes to a dealer in New York and offers to buy so many quarters of corn or so many bales of cotton at a certain price, and the dealer in New York, finding that he can make a favourable bargain, writes an answer accepting the offer. Then, according to the argument that has been presented to us to-day, during the whole time that the letter accepting the offer is on the Atlantic, the dealer who is to receive it in Liverpool, if he finds that the market has fallen, may send a message by telegraph and revoke his offer. Nor is there any difference between an offer to receive shares and an offer to buy or sell goods. And yet, if the argument is sound, then for nearly ten days the buyer might wait and speculate whether the shares were rising or falling, and if found they were falling he might revoke his offer.'

---

22   S. A. Smith, *Contract Theory*, Oxford University Press, 2004, p. 192.

Mellish LJ identified this 'revocation issue' as a matter of serious concern, and we should note that it is recognized as the key basis of the 'mailbox rule', which is very like our postal rule, in the US,[23] and such revocation is prevented by other means in other systems.[24]

2.56   The other effect of the postal rule, which we should look at, is its impact in relation to lost or delayed acceptances which are not the fault of the offeree. Under the postal rule, the risk of such loss or delay is placed on the offeror; there will be a contract even if the acceptance is lost, or delayed beyond the point when the offer would have expired. In *British & American Telegraph Co. Ltd* v *Colson* (1871) LR 6 Exch 108, 112 Kelly CB saw an acceptance effective on posting as working 'great and obvious injustice in a variety of mercantile transactions of constant occurrence', and it was to this risk that he was referring. He gave examples, including (at 112):

> 'A merchant in London writes to another merchant at Bristol offering to sell him a quantity of merchandise at the price of 1000l., and the Bristol merchant by return of post accepts the offer and agrees to become the purchaser; but the letter miscarries and is never received. Would the Bristol merchant be entitled a week afterwards to bring an action for the non-delivery of the goods, when the London merchant, from having received no answer to his letter, has sold them to another person?'

Kelly CB (at 112) thought it 'absolutely impossible that such can be the law of this country'. Bramwell B similarly provided examples of this effect of the postal rule, and he viewed it as 'wholly unjust and unreasonable' to make liable 'the person who had never received the letter' of acceptance (at 118).[25]

2.57   In the light of such forceful criticism, it might well be queried as to why we still have a postal rule, producing this effect today. The answer would seem to be bad timing. The postal rule was revived, in relation to a lost acceptance, in *Household Fire and Carriage Accident Insurance Co* v *Grant* (1879), but that should be seen in context. Gardner has pointed out that, at the time, there was considerable concern that those who had sought shares in a company which then rapidly proved to be worthless (as was happening on an appreciable number of occasions at the time), were evading liability by denying receipt of the letters accepting their offers to become shareholders. If the letters were effective on posting, this avenue of escape was denied to them (S. Gardner, 'Trashing with Trollope: A Deconstruction of the Postal Rules in Contract' (1992) 12 Ox Jo LS 170 at 185).

---

23 See the comments on s 63 of the US Restatement (2d) Contracts.

24 Under German law an offer is generally irrevocable unless otherwise stated (ss 146–149 BGB), and it is commented that under German Law the postal rule is not adopted, 'largely because the irrevocability of offers (made possible . . . by the absence of the doctrine of consideration) means that the offeree is sufficiently protected during a reasonable period after an offer has reached him': B. S. Markesinis, H. Unberath and A. Johnston, *The German Law of Contract: a Comparative Treatise*, 2nd edn, Hart Publishing, 2006, p. 74.

25 Although Kelly CB and Bramwell B, were anxious to reject the postal rule because of its impact in relation to lost acceptances, they nevertheless did not dismiss the need for protection of the offeree from revocation. They envisaged the possibility that, although an acceptance would only be effective once received, its effect would then be backdated to the point of dispatch (at 116, 121).

2.58   In Scotland, although the basic postal rule was adopted, it may not be carried to its logical conclusion, in relation to a lost acceptance. In *Mason* v *Benhar Coal Co* (1882) 9 R 883, Lord Shand stated, *obiter* (at 890), that if delivery of the acceptance was not established, he would 'not hold that the contract was completed by mere posting', and the recommendations of the Scottish Law Commission would not maintain the postal rule, merely a means of dealing with the revocation issue (Scots Law Com 2012, para. 3.21). Similarly, although again there was no need to pursue the point, the Irish Supreme Court, in *Kelly* v *Cruise Catering Ltd* [1994] 2 ILRM 394, thought it 'no doubt correct' that 'it might be unjust to hold a party to a contract when he had never received the acceptance'.

2.59   However, the postal rule, with its allocation of the risk of loss or delay of the acceptance to the offeror, has been justified on the basis that it is economically efficient. Posner takes the view that the postal rule is economically efficient as it

> 'enables the offeree to begin performance (or preparatory measures) but does not delay the offeror's performance, which in any event cannot begin until the offeror received the acceptance, for until then he wouldn't know whether there was a contract' (R. A. Posner, *Economic Analysis of Law*, 7th edn, Aspen Publishers, 2007, p. 103).

One response to this might be that it depends upon the individual transaction as to the commencement of which of the parties' performances is important, and it is undoubtedly the case that it may well be the start of the offeror's which is significant. However, this would be to miss the point that Posner is making a statement at a more general level and, under the postal rule, both parties can perform as quickly as possible. As far as it goes, the argument is clear: the postal rule is economically efficient because it allows performance to commence as soon as possible.

2.60   However, the postal rule may be seen as economically inefficient because it results in the risks of loss, or delay, not being placed on the party best able to minimize them:

> 'If anything, one would have thought it was more efficient to make each type of letter effective only on delivery. After all, it is the sender, rather than the addressee, who is in control of a letter's transmission. This would mean reversing the rule regarding acceptances. If the rule were against the offeree (that is, required delivery to the offeror), he could respond by using the recorded delivery service, sending multiple communications, etc. As things stand however it is the offeror the law encourages to guard against accidents in the post, yet... he is much less well placed to do so' (Gardner, 'Trashing with Trollope', 177).

It is the offeree who can send an acceptance in a way which involves least risk of it being delayed, or going astray and, as it is the offeree who knows that the acceptance has been dispatched, it is he or she who is best situated to check on its arrival, and there are now multiple, cheap, fast means of doing so. The offeror cannot realistically keep asking the offeree whether an acceptance has been sent. Loss or delay will cause problems, putting the non-fault risk of either occurring on the offeree, would minimize them.

2.61   When the issue of economic efficiency and the postal rule is considered, the entire impact of the rule cannot be seen as economically efficient; a weighing or balancing exercise is in question and the balance point of economic efficiency can be strongly contended to be different in relation to more modern, and much faster, means of communication. There are now multiple fast, cheap means by which the offeree can accept, and can check receipt of acceptance. They not only markedly reduce the potential for an intervening revocation, they also very significantly diminish the time before performance by both parties can safely commence. Allocating the non-fault risk of loss or delay of the acceptance to the inappropriate party—the offeror—should no longer be viewed as a price which has to be paid for the benefit of performance commencing swiftly. To the contrary, unless a very strong approach is taken to the reasonableness of using the post, which would simply render the postal rule meaningless, even maintaining the postal rule just in relation to the post, may be seen to be inefficient. Its allocation of the non-fault based risk of loss or delay to the offeror, would provide a reason for the offeree to post an acceptance, rather than use a much faster means of communication,[26] and a posted acceptance could substantially delay the offeror's ability to commence performance.

2.62   In summary, the problem of a revocation intervening whilst a communication was in transit provided a justification for the postal rule, but only to the extent that it was needed to deal with that problem. There is certainly no justification now to allow it also to put the risk of a lost or delayed acceptance on the offeror. It is arguably time to abandon the postal rule in relation to the post, and we certainly should not extend it to e-mail. The best solution would, however, be one which dealt with the revocation issue, but did not have the other 'side effect' of the postal rule in relation to lost or delayed acceptances. That could be achieved by legislation, reflecting the line taken under the United Nations Convention on International Sale of Goods (CISG, Art 16(2)), and the Draft Common Frame of Reference (DCFR, Art II-4:202). Under both, although the acceptance will not be effective until received by the offeror, an offer cannot be revoked once the offeree has dispatched an acceptance. Similarly, the Scottish Law Commission has proposed that Scots law should not continue to use the postal rule, but that a revocation should not be effective if it reaches the offeree after dispatch of an acceptance (Scots Law Com 2012, para. 3.21).[27]

2.63   Of course, even if it is merely that the postal rule is not extended, and the postal rule continues to be applied to the post, the question arises as to what will satisfy the normal rule, that an acceptance must be communicated to be effective. It is an objective question, so there can be no issue of requiring a message actually to be read, and the question is usually put in terms of when the acceptance is 'received' by the offeror. In relation to the telex, it was indicated that it would normally be when it arrived on the offeror's machine. However, the question of 'office hours' was raised (Lord Wilberforce, *Brinkibon* at 42), and the line generally taken was that a telex arriving outside of office hours would be received, and effective, when office hours

---

26 A. Rawls, 'Contract formation in an internet Age' (2009) 10 Columbia Science and Technology LR 200, 228.

27 For a suggestion as to how it might be achieved at common law, and for further analysis, and explanation of the telex cases, and how they fit with the analysis described, see E. Macdonald, 'Dispatching the dispatch rule? The postal rule, e-mail, revocation and implied terms' [2013] (2) Web Journal of Current Legal Issues.

recommenced. More broadly, 'accessibility' seems to be becoming recognized as determinative of the time of receipt of an electronic message generally.[28] Art I.-1:109 of the Draft Common Frame of Reference adopts 'accessibility' in relation to the time of receipt of an electronic message, and the Scottish Law Commission stated that

> 'in a context where the concept of office hours is relevant, a communication that reaches the addressee's system outside of those hours will become accessible for the purposes of the DCFR... when the next period of business hours opens' (Scot Law Com 2012, para. 2.17).

There should be scope for saying that an acceptance had become effective, if its 'inaccessibility' is due to the offeror's fault (e.g. through inappropriate email security settings).

Prescribed method of acceptance

2.64   As we saw in *Holwell Securities Ltd* v *Hughes* (1974), the offeror can stipulate that the acceptance must be made in a particular way. He or she may require it to be sent to a certain place, or to take a particular form, such as by letter or fax. In order to complete a binding agreement the offeree must normally comply with the prescribed method of acceptance. If the offeror stipulates a particular form of acceptance, and states that only the stipulated form will suffice, the offeree must comply with the offeror's requirement in order for there to be an effective acceptance. However, the offeror may have requested a particular method of acceptance for a specific purpose, for example to obtain a speedy reply. If the offeree uses some other method which equally achieves the offeror's purpose, this should be a valid acceptance (see *Tinn* v *Hoffman* (1873)). In *Manchester Diocesan Council of Education* v *Commercial and General Investments Ltd* [1970] 1 WLR 241, Buckley J stated (at 246):

> 'Where . . . the offeror has prescribed a particular method of acceptance, but not in terms insisting that only acceptance in that mode shall be binding, I am of the opinion that acceptance communicated to the offeror by any other mode which is no less advantageous to him will conclude the contract . . . If an offeror intends that he shall be bound only if his offer is accepted in some particular manner, it must be for him to make this clear.'

Acceptance in unilateral contracts

2.65   In a unilateral contract, the offeror promises to do something, or make a payment (for example, a reward), if certain acts are carried out (see, for example,*Carlill* v *Carbolic Smoke Ball Co.* (1893)). The offeree does not have to communicate acceptance to the offeror, and the offeree never becomes obliged to do anything. It is simply that, if the offeree carries out the relevant acts, the offeror is obliged to make the promised payment, or carry out the promised act.

---

28   Art 11, E-Commerce Directive, Art 10(2), UN Convention on the Use of Electronic Communications in International Contracts.

(Remember, we call such situations *uni*lateral contracts, because only one party comes under an obligation.)

2.66 As we have seen, an offer of a bilateral contract can be revoked at any time up until acceptance, unless there is a separate contractual obligation to keep it open for a specified time. Revocation of unilateral offers raises a particular difficulty. Can O, the offeror of a unilateral offer, withdraw the offer once A has started to carry out the stipulated act? To take the classic example known to generations of law students: O offers a reward of £100 to anyone who walks from, say, Aberystwyth to Swansea. Can O revoke his or her offer once A has started, but not yet completed, the walk to Swansea? Certainly O is not bound to pay the £100 unless, and until, A completes the walk, but should O be able to withdraw at any time until A has completed the walk, even when A has nearly reached Swansea? This question arose in a more realistic form in *Errington v Errington and Woods* [1952] 1 KB 290. The facts were:

> A father wanted to provide his son and daughter-in-law with a home and he bought a house for £750, borrowing £500 on a mortgage from the building society. The ownership of the house remained in the father's name, and he also paid the rates. He promised his son and daughter-in-law that if they continued to occupy the house and paid all the mortgage instalments, he would transfer the property to them. Until the father's death nine years later, the couple occupied the house and paid the mortgage. On the death of the father, all of his property (including the house occupied by the couple) was left to his widow. The son left the daughter-in-law and moved out of the house. The widow brought an action for possession against the daughter-in-law.

The Court of Appeal decided that the widow was not entitled to possession. Denning LJ stated (at 295):

> 'The father's promise was a unilateral contract—a promise of the house in return for their act of paying the instalments. It could not be revoked by him once the couple entered on performance of the act, but it would cease to bind him if they left it incomplete and unperformed, which they have not done.'

The general reaction to this is that it was an appropriate result, but orthodox explanations for it are difficult to find. It is generally suggested that there is a collateral contract, formed when A starts to perform, that O will not withdraw as long as A continues to perform.[29] See *Daulia Ltd v Four Millbank Nominees Ltd* [1978] 2 All ER 557 (at 561, 566, and 570).

2.67 However, the offeror was allowed to withdraw, without penalty in *Luxor (Eastbourne) Ltd v Cooper* (1941). In that case, C was promised commission if he introduced a buyer for two cinemas and the introduction resulted in the sale of the properties. Although C introduced a willing purchaser, the vendors changed their minds and decided against selling the properties.

---

29 It might more easily be seen as a matter of good faith, but English law is unwilling to accept a duty of good faith, particularly in the pre-contractual context—see generally Furmston and Tolhurst, *Contract Formation*.

C claimed damages, arguing that the offer implied that the vendors would not refuse to sell to a buyer that he had introduced. The Court of Appeal refused to imply such a term and rejected C's claim. The case can be distinguished from *Errington* in relation to its commercial context: the estate agent was inherently taking a risk for a large reward if a sale was made, so it would have been inappropriate to imply an obligation on the offeror.

Is knowledge of the offer required?

2.68 This issue has tended to arise in the context of unilateral offers of reward, where someone performs an act or service (for example, by returning an item of lost property to the owner), and later learns that a reward was in fact offered for the performance of this act. In one sense, such a person has fulfilled the terms of the offer, and it could be argued that he or she is entitled to claim the reward. But can someone create a contract 'accidentally'? The impetus to the objective approach, for the sake of certainty is very strong. In *Gibbons v Proctor* (1891) 64 LT 594, the court appeared to decide that ignorance of an offer did not preclude a person from claiming a reward where he gave information, and then later learned of the existence of the offer. However, another report of the case suggests that C did know of the reward by the time the information was passed, via C's agents, to the appropriate person (see (1891) 55 JP 616).

2.69 The situation was given extensive consideration in the Australian case of *R v Clarke* (1927) 40 CLR 227. It concerned an offer of a reward for information leading to the arrest of certain murderers, and a pardon to any accomplice giving the information. C gave the required information but admitted that he had forgotten about the reward at the time that he supplied it (i.e. when he was in custody, himself charged with the murders). C's claim for the £1,000 reward was rejected by the High Court of Australia, and the case was treated as if he had never known of the reward. Higgins J stated (at 241):

> 'Clarke had seen the offer indeed; but it was not present to his mind—he had forgotten it, and gave no consideration to it, in his intense excitement as to his own danger. There cannot be assent without knowledge of the offer; and ignorance of the offer is the same thing whether it is due to never hearing of it or forgetting it after hearing . . . But for this candid confession of Clarke's it might fairly be presumed that Clarke, having once seen the offer, acted on the faith of it, in reliance on it; but he has himself rebutted that presumption.'

2.70 In the context of these reward cases, it might be argued that the reward should be paid. It encourages the performance of socially useful acts, and the offeror expected to pay. It would also maintain the generally objective approach, and the certainty which goes with it. The question of whether there is a contract is not particularly worrying in the unilateral context, because the person who does not know of the offer can never become bound to do anything. It is only a question of the offeror's liability, and the offeror knew perfectly well what he or she was doing. The objective approach could be maintained without discomfort. However, the issue would be far more vexed in relation to a bilateral contract. It is not simply whether X should get the reward which Y promised, but whether X should come under contractual obligations accidentally. This question has been unlikely to be asked in the bilateral context, until now. However, it might now arise in the context of 'browse-wrap contracting', where the owner of a website specifies that the visitor to it, Y, will make a contract, imposing certain obligations, just by performing certain acts on the website, which Y might perform anyway. The simple answer is that such actions are unlikely to unambiguously convey objective acceptance, or they may well be regulated by other means.[30]

2.71 Even if knowledge of an offer is required for there to be a valid acceptance, the motive for performing an act, which fulfils the terms of an offer, is irrelevant. So where a person knows of an offer of a reward for information, but gives the requested information for another reason (such as remorse), he is still entitled to claim the reward. (See *Williams* v *Cowardine* (1833) and, for a discussion, see P. Mitchell and J. Phillips 'The Contractual Nexus: Is Reliance Essential?' (2002) 22 OJLS 115.)

2.72 A related issue is that of 'cross offers'. For example, A writes to B offering to sell him his computer for £100 and B, without knowing of the offer, writes to A and offers to buy that computer for £100. It could be argued that there is a meeting of the minds, but clearly any 'agreement' between the parties is merely by chance. It is thought that there is no contract in this situation unless one of the parties replies to the other and accepts the other's offer. It would lead to uncertainty if cross offers, with nothing further, amounted to a binding agreement. The problem is hardly one of great practical significance, as indicated by the paucity of case law on the subject. (The case which discusses the problem, *obiter*, is *Tinn* v *Hoffman* (1873). The majority of the judges thought there was no contract.)

'Battle of the forms'

2.73 Assessing whether there is sufficient agreement for a contract by means of offer and acceptance has raised particular problems in relation to the 'battle of the forms', and we should now consider that phenomenon. We are, of course, again talking about bilateral contracts.

2.74 We have already noted that when he was considering whether offer and acceptance analysis should be used in *Gibson* v *Manchester City Council* [1979] 1 WLR 294, Lord Diplock stated (at 297):

> 'My Lords there may be certain types of contract, though I think they are exceptional, which do not fit easily into the normal analysis of a contract as being constituted by offer and acceptance, but a contract alleged to have been made by an exchange of correspondence between the parties in which the successive communications other than the first are in reply to one another is not one of these.'

---

30 For further discussion of an old conundrum in a new context, see E. Macdonald, 'When is a contract formed by the browse-wrap process' (2011) 19 International Journal of Law and Information Technology 285–305.

Prima facie, according to this, the 'battle of the forms' situations should be prime candidates for offer and acceptance analysis. They are concerned with an exchange of correspondence in which each communication is in reply to the previous one. The problem is, however, that large parts of each communication are ignored, and certainly not responded to.

2.75   The so-called 'battle of the forms' arises when X and Y set out to make a contract. They negotiate with one another via a series of letters. Each of them focuses on such matters as price, quantity, and time of delivery, and they gradually reach agreement on these obviously significant elements. The problem is that on the back of each letter from X and Y are their standard terms, and their standard terms are different in significant ways, but their correspondence does not address those differences. This means that even when the terms on the front of their letters are agreed, they have not agreed the terms on the back. In effect, whatever the front of the letters look like, they keep throwing counter offers at one another, and not reaching agreement. They may be doing this on purpose, to try to make their standard terms, the standard terms of the contract. Hence the name 'battle of the forms'. But they might also be doing it simply because they are not thinking about the law, but simply about making a deal on what seems to them to be the important matters.[31] For whatever reason it comes about, the lack of negotiation on the standard terms, during the contracting process, causes difficulties when issue arise which are dealt with differently under the two sets of standard terms. It may be that the courts will find that there was actually no contract at all, although they tend to strive to avoid that conclusion when the parties have started performing on the assumption that there is a contract.

2.76   Applying the traditional rules of offer and acceptance, the party who last gets in his or her standard terms, which the other party then acts upon, wins. This is often put in terms of the party who fired the last shot winning. This is illustrated in *British Road Services Ltd* v *Arthur V Crutchley & Co. Ltd* (1968). The claimants delivered goods to the defendants' warehouse and presented a delivery note which stated: 'All goods are carried on [the claimants'] conditions of carriage . . .'. However, when the claimants' driver presented the delivery note to the defendants, it was 'rubber-stamped' by the defendants with the words: 'Received under [the defendants'] conditions'. In this way the delivery note was transformed into a note of receipt and handed back to the claimants' driver. In the course of an action for negligence against the defendants, it was disputed whose conditions prevailed. Although the defendants were liable to the claimants in negligence for not adequately protecting the goods against theft, the Court of Appeal held that the defendants' liability was limited in accordance with their conditions which were incorporated into the contract between the parties. The defendants', rather than the claimants', conditions prevailed as they got in the final word or 'shot', without any further riposte from the claimants.

2.77   Another example is provided by *Butler Machine Tool Co. Ltd* v *Ex-Cell-O Corpn. (England) Ltd* (1979), which is a case in which, in a sense, the 'last shot' did not win. The facts were:

> In response to D's enquiry, C made a quotation on 23 May, offering to sell a machine tool to D for £75,535. The offer was stated to be subject to certain conditions which were to

---

31   See H. Beale and A. Dugdale, 'Contracts between Businessmen' (1975) 2 Br Jo Law & Soc 45.

'prevail over any terms in the buyer's order'. These conditions included a price variation clause: i.e. that any increase in the cost of the goods, by the date of delivery (which was to be in ten months' time), would be added to the purchase price. On 27 May, D replied, ordering the machine, but on their own terms and conditions which did not include a price variation clause. At the foot of D's order form there was an acknowledgement section to be torn off, stating that 'We accept your order on the terms and conditions stated thereon'. On 5 June, C completed and signed the acknowledgement, returning it to D, together with a letter stating that D's order was being entered in accordance with C's quotation of 23 May. When the machine was delivered, C claimed the price had increased by £2,892, and D refused to pay the increase in price. C's action was based on the contention that they were entitled to increase the price under the price variation clause contained in their offer. C argued that the contract was on the buyer's terms and these did not include such a clause.

The Court of Appeal decided that the contract did not include the price variation clause and C could not claim the extra £2,892. It was held that D's order of 27 May was a counter offer which brought to an end the offer made by C on 23 May, and that C accepted D's counter offer by completing and returning the acknowledgement of the order on 5 June. The contract was therefore on D's terms, and the price variation clause did not apply.

2.78   It might be asked how this occurred when C's original quotation had stated that its conditions were to 'prevail over any terms in the buyer's order'. However, what must be remembered is that under the offer and acceptance rules, such a clause could not prevail in the face of D's counter offer, on different terms. It is the rule about counter offers which generally means that the 'last shot' wins. Of course, the 'last shot', in the sense of the last written communication, did not win in this case. It might be described as a 'blank': C lost by signing the tear off slip, and failing to successfully reintroduce their standard terms.

2.79   Although the majority of the Court of Appeal arrived at their conclusion using traditional offer and acceptance analysis, Lord Denning MR adopted a different approach from the majority, whilst arriving at the same conclusion. He argued that the documents must be considered as a whole:

> 'If [the terms and conditions of both parties] can be reconciled so as to give a harmonious result, all well and good. If differences are irreconcilable, so that they are mutually contradictory, then the conflicting terms may have to be scrapped and replaced by a reasonable implication.'

Such an approach does offer flexibility, but it is uncertain.

2.80   In *Tekdata Interconnections Ltd* v *Amphenol Ltd* (2009), the court emphasized the use of the traditional offer and acceptance analysis, and it was indeed a case in which the 'last shot' won, but it did leave scope for 'rare cases' where that analysis would be departed from.

Tekdata was not such a rare case, but in *GHSP Inc* v *AB Electronic Ltd* (2010) it had been so clear during their protracted negotiations that the parties were never going to reach agreement on the issue of the extent of liability, that the judge found that the contract was on neither parties' terms, but that terms implied by the Sale of Goods Act 1979 should simply be used.

⬡ Summary

- Agreement is central to the making of a contract.
- The law takes a predominantly objective approach to agreement.
- The traditional method of establishing agreement is through the process of offer and acceptance.
- This process may be an accurate description of how many, but not all, contracts are made.
- An offer is an expression by the offeror of a willingness to enter into a contract, on a particular set of terms, with the intention of being bound if the other party (the offeree) signifies acceptance.
- An offer must be distinguished from an invitation to the other party to make an offer (i.e. an invitation to treat).
- An acceptance is the final expression of assent to the offer by the offeree.
- A purported acceptance which attempts to introduce new terms, or to vary those contained in the offer, is a counter offer (and a rejection of the original offer).
- A counter offer must be distinguished from a request by the offeree for further information about the offer, which is not a rejection of the offer.
- Acceptance may take a variety of forms depending on the terms of the offer.
- As a general principle, acceptance must be communicated to the offeror.
- Outside of unilateral contracts, the major exception to this is the 'postal rule'.
- As a whole, the postal rule is very hard to justify. There is a debate about whether it should be extended to more modern forms of communication, but there certainly seems to be no justification for doing so to its full effect.
- There is a problem in relation to revocation of unilateral offers, once the offeree has started to carry out the stated acts.
- There are particular difficulties in applying offer and acceptance analysis to certain business transactions, sometimes described as the 'battle of the forms'.

▶ Further reading

R. Austen-Baker, 'Offeree Silence and Contractual Agreement' (2006) 35(4) CLWR 247

D. Friedmann, 'The Objective Principle and Mistake and Involuntariness in Contract and Restitution' (2003) 119 LQR 68

W. Howarth, 'The Meaning of Objectivity in Contract' (1984) 100 LQR 267

E. Macdonald, 'Dispatching the dispatch rule? The postal rule, e-mail, revocation and implied terms' [2013] (2) Web Journal of Current Legal Issues

E. Macdonald, 'When is a contract formed by the browse-wrap process' (2011) 19 International Journal of Law and Information Technology 285–305

E. McKendrick, 'Invitations to Tender and the Creation of Contracts' [1991] LMCLQ 31

F. Meisel, 'What Price Auctions Without Reserve?' (2001) 64 MLR 468

P. Mitchell and J. Phillips, 'The Contractual Nexus: Is Reliance Essential?' (2002) 22 OJLS 115

J. Steyn, 'Contract Law: Fulfilling the Reasonable Expectations of Honest Men' (1997) 113 LQR 433

Chapter 3

Certainty and completeness

◉ Introduction

3.1   In **Chapter 2** we saw that contracts are normally based on agreement. Although courts will try to give effect to apparent agreements, it may be difficult to do so in cases where the parties have expressed themselves in vague or incomplete terms. Much will depend on how far a court is willing to go in filling in any gaps left by the parties. Whilst not wishing to 'incur the reproach of being the destroyer of bargains' (per Lord Tomlin in *Hillas & Co. Ltd* v *Arcos Ltd* (1932) 147 LT 503 at 512), a court may find it impossible to give effect to an uncertain 'agreement'. For example, in the Court of Appeal decision in *Schweppe* v *Harper* (2008) at [72]–[76] and [80]–[81], the majority held that there was no binding contract between the parties because of uncertainty over important terms of the alleged agreement, with Sir Robin Auld stating (at [81]) that 'the notion of "reasonable finance" is too uncertain to be given any practical meaning'. Such disputes must be viewed within the confines of legal principle; if no contractual bargain exists, it is not for a court to invent one.

3.2   However, in the business world it is not uncommon for negotiating parties to leave matters vague for as long as possible. For example, this may arise where there may be some understandings between the parties, but where these have not been expressed with any certainty or finality. (For a broader discussion, see S. Mouzas and M. Furmston, 'From Contract to Umbrella Agreement' (2008) 67 CLJ 37.) This may be desirable in certain circumstances because the 'agreement' in question might be conditional on one of the parties securing another contract with a third party. (For example, where company A uses a 'letter of intent' to indicate to company B that a subcontract is likely to be entered into with them if A's tender for a major contract with company C is successful. But the more widespread use of letters of intent, especially in the construction industry, may be a cause for concern. For a discussion of this practice and some of the resulting case law, see C. Hoar, 'We Do Intend to Contract with You, and May Actually

Just Have' (2008) *Construction Newsletter* May/June 4–5.) The parties may even proceed as if a concluded contract has been made, despite the fact that in a technical (legal) sense there is no final agreement. (For a good example of this problem, see *British Steel Corpn* v *Cleveland Bridge and Engineering Co. Ltd* (1984); and for a more recent approach, see *G Percy Trentham Ltd* v *Archital Luxfer Ltd* (1993) and *RTS Flexible Systems Ltd* v *Molkerei Alois Müller GmbH & Co KG* (2010).) We have considered further examples of this in relation to the 'battle of the forms' (see **Chapter 2**) and it will be recalled that commercial practice may depart from the finer points of legal theory. It is difficult to lay down general rules about the extent of a court's power to fill in the gaps left by the parties and, for this reason, some of the cases that follow may appear to be inconsistent with one another. Much depends on the factual situation in each case rather than on any consistent or underlying precepts.

The need for certainty

3.3   Where contractual intention is expressed in such imprecise terms that no clear meaning can be given to it, there will be no binding agreement. For example, in *Gould* v *Gould* (1969), a husband promised his wife £15 per week 'so long as he could manage it', i.e. as long as his business was doing well. On appeal, it was held that this agreement was too vague and uncertain to be enforceable. (Also, in *Loftus* v *Roberts* (1902), an agreement to employ an actress at a 'West End salary' was held to be too vague. For a more recent example, see *Cook* v *Norlands Ltd* (2001).) In other cases, the parties may clearly have intended to enter into a contract, but may have used some vague or ambiguous expression. In *G Scammell and Nephew Ltd* v *Ouston* (1941), the facts were:

> Ouston (C) wrote to the defendant company (D) ordering a new Commer motor van, stating that the 'order is given on the understanding that the balance of purchase price can be had on hire purchase terms over a period of two years'. The order was accepted, but the defendants dropped out before any specific hire purchase agreement was entered into. C sued D for non-delivery and D claimed that there was no final agreement between the parties. The trial court and the Court of Appeal decided that there was a binding contract between the parties, and D appealed to the House of Lords.

It was held that there was no contract, as the phrase 'on hire purchase terms' was too vague to constitute a binding agreement. This was because different types of hire purchase agreements existed (imposing different obligations on the parties) and therefore there was an ambiguity in the apparent agreement. If C could have shown, by reference to previous dealings with D or by reference to trade practice, that one particular meaning could be given to the phrase 'hire purchase terms', he may well have succeeded. But this was not possible in this instance and the contractual intention of the parties may not have been identical.

3.4   In *Peter Lind & Co. Ltd* v *Mersey Docks and Harbour Board* (1972), C submitted two tenders to build a container freight terminal. The first offer was to build the terminal for a fixed price, whilst the second was to do the work for a price which was subject to variations in the cost of labour and materials. D purported to accept C's tender without making it clear which one. It was decided that there was no contract on the terms of either of C's tenders as there was an obvious ambiguity that could not be resolved by the court.

3.5   In contrast, there are instances where a court is able to make sense of vague statements and to give effect to the contractual intention of the parties. For example, in *Hillas & Co. Ltd v Arcos Ltd* (1932), C had previously agreed to buy a quantity of timber, 'of fair specification', from D. The contract gave C an option to buy a further 100,000 standards of timber the following year, but it failed to specify the size or type of timber. D argued that the vagueness of this 'agreement' prevented it from being binding on the parties. But this argument was rejected by the House of Lords. In contrast to the case of *G Scammell and Nephew Ltd v Ouston* (1941), the uncertainty in the agreement could be resolved by the court. It was possible to make reference to the previous dealings between the parties and the custom of the timber trade. In this way, the court could fill in the gaps left by the parties without making an entire contract for the parties. Clearly, the distinction between this type of case and that of *Scammell* is a fine one.[1] In the case of *Baird Textile Holdings Ltd v Marks and Spencer plc* (2002), the Court of Appeal rejected a claim by Baird that M and S was in breach of a contractual obligation to order garments from Baird in quantities and at prices which were reasonable in all the circumstances. The court decided that this alleged obligation lacked certainty, as there were no objective criteria by which a reasonable quantity or price could be ascertained. It was held that the lack of certainty confirmed a lack of intention to create legal relations.

3.6   The issue of lack of certainty was also raised in *Walford v Miles* [1992] 1 All ER 453. This case involved negotiations for the sale of a photographic business. The parties entered into a so-called 'lock-out' agreement whereby the seller, in exchange for good consideration, agreed not to negotiate with any other party in respect of the sale of the business. Although such agreements can be enforceable, the House of Lords held that this one was not, because it was of unspecified duration. It was stated that no term could be implied by the court to give effect to the agreement. However, if the seller had agreed not to negotiate with any other party for a specified period of time, the agreement could have been enforced (see Lord Ackner's judgment at 461–2).

3.7   It is important to distinguish between a clause in a contract which has still to be agreed (such as 'hire purchase terms' in *G Scammell and Nephew Ltd v Ouston* (1941)) and a clause which is simply meaningless. The former may lead to a court deciding that no contract exists, whereas the latter can often be disregarded. Much will depend on the importance attached to the clause by the parties. For example, if it is of central importance in defining the contractual obligations of the parties, the vagueness of the clause may negate agreement (see *Bushwall Properties Ltd v Vortex Properties Ltd* (1976)). In *CPC Consolidated Pool Carriers GmbH v CTM Cia TransMediterranea SA* (1994), the negotiations between the parties, for the shipment of a jet foil, were said to be 'subject to details/logical amendments'. Potter J held that there was no

---

1   *Quaere:* In *Hillas & Co. Ltd v Arcos Ltd* (1932), did the option to buy timber constitute an agreement, or was it merely an agreement to make an agreement? The ambit of the decision was also considered more recently by the Court of Appeal in *iSoft Group plc v MISYS Holdings Ltd* (2003) (see, especially, [43]–[44]).

concluded contract, as it was intended by the parties that a formal contract was still to be drawn up later. The expression 'subject to details' left matters too vague, as these terms and details needed to be finalized. But if the clause is 'severable' from the main part of the agreement (i.e. of little significance, or even superfluous), then it can be ignored without affecting the validity of the contract. If this were not so, those in breach of contract might look for any vague phrase in the agreement as a means of escaping liability.

3.8   In *Nicolene Ltd v Simmonds* [1953] 1 QB 543, for example, C ordered 3,000 tons of steel bars from D. D's letter of acceptance of the order included the phrase that it was assumed that 'the usual conditions of acceptance apply'. D, who failed to supply the steel and was sued for breach of contract, claimed that due to the uncertainty caused by the words 'usual conditions of acceptance', there was no binding agreement. This argument was rejected by the Court of Appeal. In the words of Lord Denning (at 552):

> '[T]here was nothing yet to be agreed. There was nothing left to further negotiation. All that happened was that the parties agreed that the "usual conditions of acceptance apply". That clause was so vague and uncertain as to be incapable of any precise meaning. It is clearly severable from the rest of the contract. It can be rejected without impairing the sense or reasonableness of the contract as a whole, and it should be so rejected. The contract should be held good and the clause ignored.'

Is there a complete contract?

3.9   Provided that the main terms of a contract have been agreed by the parties, the fact that further terms have still to be negotiated will not necessarily prevent there being a concluded contract (see *Pagnan SpA v Feed Products Ltd* (1987), applied recently in *Bear Sterns Bank Plc v Forum Global Equity Ltd* (2007); and *De Jongh Weill v Mean Fiddler Holdings Ltd* (2003) at [22]). In other instances the parties may negotiate a contract and reach agreement in principle but leave certain details to be decided later. (See for example, *RTS Flexible Systems Ltd v Molkerei Alois Müller GmbH & Co KG* (2010) discussed at para. **3.16**). As a matter of strict theory it might appear that this does not constitute a binding agreement, especially if important terms are left undecided. This may well be the result in practice too: as illustrated by *Willis Management (Isle of Man) Ltd v Cable & Wireless plc* (2005). In this case, the Court of Appeal held that an agreement by the parties, to agree an essential term in the future, was incomplete and unenforceable. The court was not prepared to make an agreement for the parties, where further discussion and agreement was still required from them. More recently, in *Barbudev v Eurocom Cable Management Bulgaria Eood* (2012), the Court of Appeal held that a side letter signed by both parties was not a legally enforceable agreement but simply an 'agreement to agree', given that essential terms were not dealt with. Here, it was concluded that the side letter was not sufficiently certain to be an enforceable contract. But much will depend on the circumstances of the case (as discussed in *J Murphy and Sons Ltd v ABB Daimler-Benz Transportation (Signal) Ltd* (1999) and further emphasized in *RTS Flexible Systems Ltd v Molkerei Alois Müller GmbH & Co KG* (2010).) It is not the role of a court to make an agreement for the parties where none exists, but it may be able to give effect to contractual intention (e.g. by implying terms) where there is an agreement which has not been fully expressed. (For a discussion of this distinction, see *Scancarriers A/S* v *Aotearoa International Ltd* (1985).)

3.10 In some commercial contexts it may be necessary to allow the price to be fixed, or adjusted, after the agreement has been concluded. For example, in a contract between an oil company and a petrol station owner for the supply of petrol over a number of years, it would not be too uncertain an agreement to allow the price to be adjusted periodically by the supplier. In *Shell (UK) Ltd* v *Lostock Garage Ltd* [1977] 1 All ER 481, the buyer agreed to pay for his supply of petrol 'at a price which shall be the wholesale schedule price ruling at [the] date and place of delivery'. Of course, such an agreement may be declared unenforceable by the court where it gives rise to an unreasonable restraint of trade, or even (perhaps) where it simply operates in an unfair and unconscionable way (*Shell* case at 489–93). But it is not void for lack of completeness.

3.11 As examples of contracting parties leaving important points unsettled, it is instructive to contrast the cases of *May and Butcher Ltd* v *R* [1934] 2 KB 17 and *Foley* v *Classique Coaches Ltd* [1934] 2 KB 1. In the former, the facts were:

> C agreed to buy surplus tentage from the Controller of the Disposals Board. The agreement provided that: 'The price...to be paid, and the date or dates on which payment is to be made by the purchasers to the Commission for such old tentage shall be agreed upon from time to time between the Commission and the purchasers...'. The trial judge decided that this 'agreement' did not amount to a contract, and this was affirmed by the Court of Appeal.

The House of Lords held that such a vague and incomplete agreement was not enforceable and that there was no binding contract between the parties. Lord Buckmaster stated (at 20):

> 'It is, of course, perfectly possible for two people to contract that they will sign a document which contains all the relevant terms, but it is not open to them to agree that they will in future agree upon a matter which is vital to the arrangement between them and has not yet been determined.'

3.12 The failure of the parties to an agreement to fix a price for the goods need not prevent a binding contract from being concluded. Under the Sale of Goods Act 1979, s 8(1) provides that if the price of goods is not fixed by the contract of sale, it may alternatively 'be left to be fixed in a manner agreed by the contract, or may be determined by the course of dealing between the parties'. If the parties have not fixed a price for the goods then, under s 8(2), the buyer must pay a reasonable price. These provisions were not applicable in *May and Butcher Ltd* v *R* (1934) because the parties had made it clear that the price was to be settled by future negotiation between them. This tends to indicate an incomplete agreement. (Also note *King's Motors (Oxford) Ltd* v *Lax* (1970) where a lease contained an option for the tenant to accept a further lease 'at such rental as may be agreed upon between the parties'. It was held that, in the absence of an arbitration clause or some supplementary agreement fixing the rent to be paid, the option was void for uncertainty.)

3.13   Although the decision in *May and Butcher Ltd* v *R* (1934) is defensible and probably correct, the law must be careful not to thwart the reasonable expectations of business people. (For further discussion on the reasonable expectations of contracting parties, see J. Steyn, 'Contract Law: Fulfilling the Reasonable Expectations of Honest Men' (1997) 113 LQR 433.) Wherever possible, an attempt should be made to give effect to the clear contractual intention of the parties. (See P. Nicholls, 'My Word is My Bond' (2008) 158 NLJ 122, for a discussion of how the law 'seeks to uphold commercial transactions and is wary of technical attempts by parties to avoid their contracts'.) For example, in *Foley* v *Classique Coaches Ltd* (1934), the following facts occurred:

> C agreed to sell a piece of land, adjoining C's garage, to the defendants. The sale of the land ('Contract One') was conditional on the defendants, who ran a motor coach business, entering into a second agreement with C for the supply of all their petrol requirements ('Contract Two'). Although the two agreements were contained in separate documents, the sale of the land was clearly conditional on the defendant's agreement to buy petrol from C 'at a price to be agreed by the parties in writing and from time to time'. (*Note:* There was also an arbitration clause included in the second contract to deal with any dispute between the parties arising out of the agreement.) After the conveyance of the land, the defendants bought their petrol from C for three years, but then they repudiated the second agreement. C sued for damages and sought a declaration that the agreement concerning the supply of petrol was binding on the defendants.

The Court of Appeal held that there was a binding contract despite the fact that the price was 'to be agreed by the parties ... from time to time'. It may seem that this decision is inconsistent with that of *May and Butcher*; but on closer examination the decisions are clearly distinguishable. In *Foley*, the agreement had been acted upon by the parties for three years. (See also *F & G Sykes (Wessex) Ltd* v *Fine Fare Ltd* (1967).) This was not the case in *May and Butcher*. Furthermore, the arbitration clause in *Foley* enabled the parties to resolve any problems caused by an incomplete agreement. One of the grounds put forward by the defendants in *Foley* for repudiating the second agreement with the claimant was that it constituted an unreasonable restraint of trade. This argument was rejected by the court and it was stated that it would have been unfair to allow the defendants to escape from their contractual obligations, having obtained a good deal on the purchase of the land in the first place. Therefore the respective behaviour of the parties in *Foley* also appears to be of some significance.[2]

3.14   An interesting point arose in *Sudbrook Trading Estate Ltd* v *Eggleton* [1983] 1 AC 444. If the parties to an agreement provide some procedure for resolving the uncertainty of that agreement, and that procedure is subsequently unsuccessful, can the court still give effect to the clear contractual intention of the parties? The facts were as follows:

> The claimants were tenants of four adjoining properties let to them by the defendants. Each lease gave the claimants an option to purchase the freehold reversion of the leased

---

2   See the speech of Scrutton LJ at 7.

properties at a price to be agreed by two valuers. Each party was to nominate a valuer, and if agreement was not reached by them, an umpire was to be appointed by both valuers. When the claimants tried to exercise the options contained in the four leases, the defendants argued that the option clauses were void for uncertainty and refused to name a valuer. (They argued that the options were nothing more than agreements to agree in the future.) Although the options to purchase were declared valid by the trial court judge, the defendants' appeal was allowed by the Court of Appeal on the basis that there was no complete agreement which the court could enforce. The claimants appealed to the House of Lords.

The claimants' appeal was allowed and the options were ordered to be specifically performed. The purpose of the option clauses had been to provide for the sale of the properties at a fair and reasonable price and a procedure had been provided to ensure this. The machinery for ascertaining the value of the property was merely subsidiary and non-essential to this main purpose. It would have been unfair if the defendants, by their own breach of contract, had been able to defeat this clear contractual purpose by their refusal to appoint a valuer. Because the procedure laid down by the parties was not essential, there was no reason why the court could not substitute its own machinery to prevent the contract from being unenforceable. Accordingly, it ordered an enquiry into the fair value of the properties. (But see Lord Russell's dissenting judgment in this case.)[3]

3.15 A different problem arises where parties negotiate the terms of a contract, expressing their agreement 'subject to contract', and one of the parties incurs costs in preparing for the intended contract which then fails to materialize. This occurred in *Regalian Properties plc v London Dockland Corpn* [1995] 1 All ER 1005 where C's offer to build a residential development was accepted by D subject to contract. There were long delays for various reasons and, two years later, after a sharp decrease in land prices, D abandoned the project. There was clearly no complete contract between the parties, but could C claim £3 million for costs already incurred in relation to the proposed contract? This claim was rejected by Rattee J who stressed that the dealings between C and D had been 'subject to contract' only, and that D had not led C to believe that such costs would be paid for. The judge stated (at 1024) that in this situation the parties should understand 'that pending the conclusion of a binding contract any costs incurred by [C] in preparation for the intended contract will be incurred at his own risk in the sense that [C] will have no recompense for these costs if no contract results'.[4]

---

3 His Lordship ([1982] 3 All ER 1 at 12) made the following observations: 'Why should it be thought that the potential vendor and purchaser intended the price to be "fair"? The former would intend the price to be high, even though unfairly so. And the latter vice versa. Vendors and purchasers are normally greedy'. *Quaere:* Is this an apposite criticism of the view of the majority in *Sudbrook Trading Estate Ltd v Eggleton* (1982)?

4 If D had encouraged C to incur costs beyond those which fell within the category of normal business risks in this situation, the result may have been different, especially if D had encouraged C to think such costs would be remunerated. See *William Lacey (Hounslow) Ltd v Davis* (1957), which was distinguished by Rattee J in the *Regalian* case. For a more recent discussion of the 'subject to contract' issue, see the House of Lords' decision in *Cobbe v Yeoman's Row Management Ltd* (2008).

3.16 The difficulties which can arise when an agreement is expressed to be 'subject to contract' were most recently illustrated by the Supreme Court case of *RTS Flexible Systems Ltd* v *Molkerei Alois Müller GmbH & Co KG* (2010). Here a dispute arose between the parties who had entered into negotiations for the supply and installation of automated packaging machinery. Although the parties had intended to enter into a detailed written contract, work began before the terms were finalized. While continuing to negotiate the full contract terms, Müller and RTS entered into a contract formed by a Letter of Intent. This provided details of the full agreed contract price which extended beyond the price of the work to take place during the currency of the Letter of Intent contract. It also included a term which stated that the full contractual terms were to be based on Müller's final draft version of contract terms known as the MF/1 terms. After four weeks, the Letter of Intent expired but as work on the project continued beyond that time, it was questioned whether the parties had entered into a contract and if so, on what terms.

3.17 The Supreme Court hearing recognized that the problems fell under two heads—both arising out of the parties agreeing to start work before execution of a formal written contract, 'in accordance with the parties' common understanding' (at [46]). The first problem concerned the effect of the parties' understanding that the contract would not become effective until they had executed and exchanged an agreement in written form. However, this had never occurred. Second, it needed to be questioned whether the parties had agreed upon all the terms which they objectively regarded or the law required as essential, for the formation of legally binding relations. In the instant case, this related to the terms on which the work was being carried out, agreement on the price or remuneration, and the rights and obligations of the supplier.

3.18 The judge at first instance held that after the Letter of Intent had expired, the parties had entered into a contract whereby RTS would carry out the agreed work for the agreed price but that this contract did not include the final draft version of the MF/1 terms. The Court of Appeal overturned that decision and found that there was no contract between the parties. The Supreme Court recognized that a third possible conclusion could be reached (at [57]), namely that agreement had been reached between the parties and this had been reached on wider terms.

3.19 The Supreme Court found at ([85]–[86]) evidence of unequivocal conduct on the part of both RTS and Müller that there was agreement that the project would be carried out by RTS for the agreed price, on the terms which the parties had agreed by 5 July and as varied on 25 August. When the agreement was varied in August, at the time, this was treated as a variation of the agreement which had been reached in July. At this juncture, no suggestion was made that there was no contract between the parties and therefore no terms to vary. Rather, it was not until November, by which time the parties were in dispute, that points were taken as to whether there was a contract.

3.20 Given that all essential terms had been agreed and with reference to the standard of the reasonable honest businessman (see [86]), the Supreme Court overturned the Court of Appeal decision, concluding that a binding agreement had been reached. As the essential aspects of the project, including what sums would be paid were clear, this created sufficient certainty of terms for there to be a binding contract (also see *Pamela Allen* v *Fisher Jones Greenwood (A Firm)*

(2013).) The *RTS* case offers a useful summary of the existing position on contractual certainty and completeness and serves as a cautionary tale of the possible perils of beginning a project before agreeing the precise basis upon which it is to be carried out. In the words of Lord Clarke (at [1]): 'The moral of the story is to agree first and to start work later'.

Conclusion

3.21   The apparent willingness of both parties to make a contract does not necessarily amount to a legally binding agreement. Essential terms, such as price and date of completion, should not normally be left incomplete and the intentions of the parties should not be couched in vague or ambiguous terms. (See *Wallis* v *Learonal (UK) plc* [2003] EWCA Civ 98 at [14]–[15].)

3.22   However, this basic principle is limited by the desire of the courts to give effect, particularly in business contexts, to the contractual intentions of the parties (for example, see *Perry* v *Suffields Ltd* (1916)). The law has to remain in touch with commercial reality and it is correct that problems of uncertainty and incompleteness are not decided purely on the basis of technical legal requirements. (See *Liverpool City Council* v *Walton Group plc* (2001), which illustrates the flexible attitude of the courts when faced with lack of certainty in commercial agreements. In this case, the draft lease did not include a commencement date, but the judge held that it was not void for uncertainty as the document was intended by both parties to have commercial effect.)

3.23   As we have seen, the courts are frequently able to fill in gaps left by the parties, and this judicial invention is assisted by the provisions of the Sale of Goods Act 1979 (s 8, for example) and the Supply of Goods and Services Act 1982 (see s 15(1)). Furthermore, a court is more likely to give effect to an incomplete or uncertain agreement which has been acted on by one or both of the parties, than one where the obligations on each party are in the future. This is both fair and commercially realistic.

Formalities

3.24   It is commonly assumed that a contract is something which must be made in writing and signed. Usually, however, contracts require no formalities—most can be made orally—although a deed may substitute for consideration (see para. **4.2**). Formality requirements are restricted to a few specific types of contract, and these requirements vary. For example, a contract for the sale or other disposition of an interest in land is unenforceable unless in writing (Law of Property (Miscellaneous Provisions) Act 1989, s 2). Certain contracts of guarantee are unenforceable unless evidenced in writing (Statute of Frauds 1677, s 4).

3.25   Formalities may be required for a number of reasons (see L. Fuller, 'Consideration and Form' (1941) 41 Col LR 799; and Law Com Rep No 164 (1987)). They may be there to promote certainty by requiring clear evidence of the terms. They may be used to encourage the parties to give full consideration to the legal obligations being undertaken. Increasingly, they may also be required for paternalistic reasons: i.e. to provide protection for people in a weaker bargaining position such as consumers.

3.26   Requirements of 'writing' or 'signature' may cause difficulties in the e-commerce context. It may be argued that they can be fulfilled by communications by e-mail (see *J Pereira Fernandes SA v Mehta* (2006) and *Orton v Collins* (2007) at [21]) or over the internet, but mere uncertainty as to the position can be detrimental to the efficient growth of e-commerce and action has been taken at both the EC and UK levels. Article 9 of the EC Directive on Electronic Commerce (2000/31/EC) requires member states to 'ensure that their legal system allows contracts to be concluded by electronic means' and, in particular, to 'ensure that the legal requirements applicable to the contractual process do not create obstacles for the use of electronic contracts or result in such contracts being deprived of legal effectiveness and validity on account of their having been made by electronic means'. Member states are allowed to exempt from this:

'(a)   contracts that create or transfer rights in real estate, except for rental rights;

(b)   contracts requiring by law the involvement of the courts, public authorities or professions exercising public authority;

(c)   contracts of suretyship granted and collateral securities furnished by persons acting for purposes outside their trade, business, or profession;

(d)   contracts governed by family law or the law of succession.'

This takes the approach of requiring the removal of any formality barriers to electronic contracting in all but a small number of exceptional cases. As has been indicated, there are relatively few situations in which formalities are required for contract formation in English law.

3.27   There has been legislation in the UK in the form of the Electronic Communications Act 2000. The Act is more wide-ranging than the EC Directive, in that its coverage extends beyond the contracting process to requirements for 'signature', 'writing', 'documents', or 'notices', for example, which are legally significant in other ways. It does not in itself make any changes to the legislation under which such requirements are set out, but s 8 allows the 'appropriate minister' to amend any such legislation by statutory instrument, 'for the purpose of authorising or facilitating the use of electronic communications or electronic storage ... for any purpose mentioned in subsection (2)'. The purposes mentioned in subs (2) are wide-ranging, but here it is relevant to note that they include:

'(a)   the doing of anything which under any such provision is required to be or may be done or evidenced in writing, or otherwise using a document notice or instrument;

. . .

(b)   the doing of anything which under any such provision is required to be or may be authorized by a person's signature or seal, or is required to be delivered as a deed or witnessed.'

Where necessary, this legislation may allow law in the UK to be brought into line with the requirements of the EC Directive. However, the Law Commission has advised the government that, generally, requirements of writing and signature may be fulfilled by some electronic form of communication without any change in the law, so 'that it is only in very rare cases that the statute book will conflict with Article 9 [of the Electronic Commerce Directive]'. (See 'Electronic Commerce: Formal Requirements in Commercial Transactions', Advice from the Law Commission, December 2001, para. 3.49 and paras 10.1–10.3.) The Law Commission also stated that despite a 'lack of consensus on these issues, statutory requirements for "writing" and a "signature" are generally capable of being satisfied by e-mails and by web-site trading' (at para. 10.1). (For further discussion of the Law Commission's views, see H. Beale and L. Griffiths, 'Electronic Commerce: Formal Requirements in Commercial Transactions' (2002) LMCLQ 467.)

⊙ Summary

- The courts will try to give effect to apparent agreements by filling in the gaps left by the parties.

- However, there are limits to how far the courts will go in making agreements for the parties.

- There is often a need for flexibility in business contracts, which may not always conform to technical requirements of the law in relation to offer and acceptance.

- The courts will try to make sense of imprecise terms, except where the ambiguity is central to the contractual obligations, or where the imprecision suggests a lack of contractual intention.

- In some commercial contexts it is permissible to allow a price to be fixed, or adjusted, after the agreement is made.

- Courts are more likely to give effect to an incomplete or uncertain agreement which has been acted on by one or both of the parties.

- It is commonly, but wrongly, thought that a contract has to be in writing. Most contracts do not require any formalities.

▷ Further reading

H. Beale and L. Griffiths, 'Electronic Commerce: Formal Requirements in Commercial Transactions' (2002) 4 (Nov) LMCLQ 467

I. Brown, 'The Contract to Negotiate: A Thing Writ in Water?' [1992] (Jul) JBL 353

L. Fuller, 'Consideration and Form' (1941) 41 Columbia Law Review 799

Law Commission, 'Electronic Commerce: Formal Requirements in Commercial Transactions', 2001

D. McLauchlan, 'Rethinking Agreements to Agree' (1998) 18 NZULR 77

S. Mouzas and M. Furmston, 'From Contract to Umbrella Agreement' (2008) 67 CLJ 37

P. Nicholls, 'My Word Is My Bond' (2008) 158 NLJ 122

J. Steyn, 'Contract Law: Fulfilling the Reasonable Expectations of Honest Men' (1997) 113 LQR 433

Chapter 4

Consideration

⊙ Introduction

4.1 The law of contract has to have some means of distinguishing between those agreements which are enforceable and those which are not. It would be clearly impracticable and inconvenient if all agreements were legally binding. Some agreements may lack certainty or completeness (see **Chapter 3**) and will be ineffective for this reason. In some cases there will be no intention to create legal relations, and in certain situations, such as social and domestic agreements, the law presumes that there is no such intention (see **Chapter 6**). Another method of limiting the enforceability of agreements is to require that the contract be expressed in a particular form, such as in writing. This is a rather time-consuming and inflexible method which tends to be employed either for evidential reasons or in circumstances where the law wishes to protect certain groups from possible exploitation.

4.2 A gratuitous promise made in writing by deed is legally binding because of the form in which it is expressed. It does not matter whether anything is given in return for such a promise. However, most contracts are not of this type. 'Simple' contracts do not normally require any particular form in order to be effective. As we have seen, an enforceable agreement can be made orally, or in writing. The test of enforceability which is used under our law of contract is the requirement of consideration. This is the symbol of bargain and reciprocal obligations. The law does not enforce gratuitous promises; the promise of a gift, for example, to a charity will not be binding unless it is by deed (see *Re Hudson* (1885)). Similarly, a promise is not enforceable simply because it is morally right that a promisor should keep his or her word (see *Eastwood* v *Kenyon* (1840)). The law requires that the promisor asks for and receives something in return for his or her promise. The courts are not generally concerned with whether the promisor made a good bargain. All that is required is that there is some element of exchange.

4.3 The historical origins of the doctrine of consideration are the subject of much academic debate, which need not concern us here. It is sufficient to note that the doctrine survived the challenge of an eminent judge, Lord Mansfield, in the mid-eighteenth century, when he attempted to argue that it was not a necessary contractual requirement, but merely one method of proving the intention of the parties to be bound.[1] In Lord Mansfield's view, some other evidence of the parties' contractual intention, such as writing, would equally suffice. This was rejected in *Rann v Hughes* (1778), and, despite criticisms of the doctrine, some of which we will consider in due course, consideration is a basic requirement of all simple contracts and it is therefore central to our understanding of the subject.

4.4 But a word of warning is necessary at the outset. Although we refer to *the* doctrine of consideration, it must be stressed that this doctrine, in fact, consists of a number of different rules, developed over a long period, some of which are more defensible than others. To debate whether the doctrine is a good or bad thing is to miss the point of its importance. The various rules which we call 'consideration' simply represent the method that our law has developed for distinguishing between enforceable and unenforceable promises. In doing so, it has emphasized the idea of bargain and exchange in contractual dealings. This was clearly in keeping with the spirit of classical contract law and the laissez-faire philosophy which influenced it.

4.5 If the doctrine were to be abolished, some alternative test of enforceability would still be required. This is not to suggest that all the present rules are satisfactory. It is only the resourcefulness of the judiciary and the malleability of the common law which have enabled the doctrine to survive in its present form without being subjected to the attentions of the legislature (for example, see the development of the doctrine of promissory estoppel, in **Chapter 5**). Some of the rules of consideration appear to be capable of producing unfair results, whilst others are perhaps out of touch with commercial practice. Some of these anomalies have been smoothed out by the judges, but certain fundamental issues still need to be resolved. For example, what is the nature of the interrelationship between the traditional exchange model of contracts and the more modern emphasis on estoppel and reliance? These are matters to which we shall return.

Can consideration be defined?

4.6 As the doctrine is in fact a loose assortment of different rules, it tends to defy any standard or broadly accepted definition. Yet attempts at such a definition abound. The traditional definitions tended to concentrate on the ideas of benefit and detriment. For example, in *Currie v Misa* (1875) LR 10 Ex 153, Lush J stated (at 162):

> 'A valuable consideration, in the eyes of the law, may consist either in some right, interest, profit, or benefit accruing to the one party, or some forbearance, detriment, loss, or responsibility given, suffered or undertaken by the other.'

---

1 In *Antons Trawling Co. Ltd v Smith* (2003), Baragwanath J argued, at [93], that 'the importance of consideration is as a valuable signal that the parties intend to be bound by their agreement, rather than an end in itself'.

This type of definition stressed the exchange nature of contracts in terms of some kind of economic advantage. (See also *Thomas v Thomas* (1842) 2 QB 851 at 859.) In other words, the promisor must receive something which the law recognizes as a 'benefit', namely something of value. If a seller promises to deliver goods to a customer, the latter provides consideration by paying for them, or by his or her promise to pay for them. The customer suffers a detriment by so doing, in exchange for the benefit conferred upon him or her by the seller.[2]

4.7 The problem with the traditional definition is that in many instances the consideration in question does not, in fact, confer any economic benefit on the promisor. The idea of something of value, given in exchange for a promise, is interpreted very widely. In the absence of fraud or any other vitiating factor, the courts are not generally concerned with the nature of the bargain struck by the parties. It may well be that, in economic terms, the consideration is inadequate; the courts will not interfere. The doctrine represents the symbol, rather than the reality, of bargain. It is a technical requirement of the law of contract, and the parties can easily ensure that it is met by the provision of some nominal consideration.

4.8 For these reasons, more modern definitions of consideration tend not to be expressed in terms of benefit and detriment. Reference is made more loosely to one party paying the 'price' of the other's promise. For example, Sir Frederick Pollock stated: 'An act or forbearance of one party, or the promise thereof, is the price for which the promise is bought and the promise thus given for value is enforceable'.[3] (This statement was approved in *Dunlop Pneumatic Tyre Co. Ltd v Selfridge & Co. Ltd* [1915] AC 847 at 855.) If a party promises something and asks for nothing in return, there is no consideration and, therefore, the promise is not legally enforceable. But where the promisor asks for something in exchange for his or her promise, the promisee provides consideration by giving the promisor what he or she has requested. The promisor might have requested a specific act, such as the provision of information in exchange for a reward. This is referred to as 'executed' consideration). Alternatively, the promisor might request a promise (for example, of payment for goods to be delivered in the future). This is known as 'executory' consideration.

4.9 The various definitions of consideration have their respective supporters, but it is not particularly important which one we adopt. This is because the courts take an essentially pragmatic view of the requirement. (See Steyn (1997) 113 LQR 433 at 437.) The decisions under the different rules which are discussed in this chapter are not always consistent with one another. In some circumstances, where justice demands, the courts may be seen to 'invent', or 'find', consideration so as to make the promise in question binding. As we saw in the earlier chapters of this book, the common law is flexible and the law of contract cannot be reduced to a set of axioms. With this warning in mind, the main rules which comprise the doctrine of consideration will now be considered.

---

2 In many commercial transactions there is such a benefit and detriment, although some might argue that there is no detriment where the contract is wholly executory (i.e. by the exchange of promises). For an interesting discussion, see P. Atiyah, *The Rise and Fall of Freedom of Contract*, Oxford University Press, 1979, pp. 448–54.

3 See his work on *Contract*, 13th edn, p. 133.

Consideration must not be past

4.10 Where the promisor (P) requests a specific act in return for his or her promise, then performance of the act by the promisee will be good consideration. If all the other ingredients of a binding contract are present, P's promise will be enforceable. It will be remembered that in *Carlill* v *Carbolic Smoke Ball Co.* (1893), the defendant company offered a reward of £100 to anyone who bought one of their smoke balls, used it in the prescribed manner, and yet caught influenza. The claimant, who bought a smoke ball, and used it, provided consideration for the company's promise. (Obviously she could not have claimed the reward unless she in fact caught 'flu, but this can hardly be described as part of the consideration.) The act done in return for the promise is referred to as 'executed' consideration.

4.11 An exchange of promises by the parties, known as 'executory' consideration, will also amount to an enforceable agreement. For example, X promises to deliver a new car to Y in three weeks' time, and Y promises to pay for the vehicle on delivery. Despite the fact that no performance of the undertakings has yet taken place—the performances are still in the future—there is good consideration. Both parties are getting what they requested in return for their promises. For commercial reasons it is important that the law recognizes the validity of such agreements, as this facilitates forward planning by the parties.

4.12 Executed and executory consideration are commonly referred to as 'good consideration'. However, a promise which is made after an act has been performed is generally not enforceable. This is rather confusingly referred to as 'past' consideration, and it is not recognized as good consideration. The reason for this is that the act or performance in question was not part of any bargain or exchange; it was gratuitous. Therefore, any subsequent promise is not part of any contractual bargain and remains unenforceable (although there are some important exceptions which will be considered later). A vivid illustration of the basic rule is provided by *Eastwood* v *Kenyon* (1840):

> The claimant had become the guardian of Sarah, a young heiress, on the death of Sarah's father. He spent money on improving her estate and on her education, and he had to borrow £140 in order to do so. When she came of age, she promised to pay the claimant the amount of the loan. After her marriage to the defendant, he (her husband) repeated this promise of reimbursement to the claimant.

The claimant could not enforce the defendant's promise, due to lack of consideration. The guardian's acts were gratuitous; they were not given in return for the defendant's (or Sarah's) promise. The case clearly shows that a moral obligation to fulfil a promise is not sufficient to lead the court to enforce that promise. Even when confronted by an unjust result, as in this case, the court will require something given in exchange for a promise for it to be enforceable.

A similar decision was reached in *Re McArdle* (1951), which also shows that the use of the term 'consideration' by the parties themselves is not necessarily of any significance. The facts were:

> The five children of a family were to inherit a house (by their father's will) after the death of their mother. One of the sons, and his wife, lived in the house with his mother until she died. During this period the daughter-in-law made some improvements and alterations to the property, which she paid for herself. She had not been asked to do this. However, about a year later, all five children signed a document addressed to her, in which they promised to repay her £488 from the estate when it was eventually distributed. The document specifically stated that this payment was 'in consideration of [her] carrying out certain alterations and improvements to the property'. When the mother died, the daughter-in-law tried to enforce the promise made in this document.

The Court of Appeal held that her claim failed. The promise was not given in exchange for her act. She had already carried out the improvements without any such promise of reimbursement being made. This was a clear instance of past consideration and the promise was, accordingly, unenforceable, despite the apparently unequivocal way in which the document expressed the contractual intention of the five children.

4.13 Another example is provided by *Roscorla* v *Thomas* (1842). In that case, C bought a horse from D for £30. After the sale, D promised that the horse was 'sound and free from vice', a fact which turned out to be untrue. It was held that this promise was not enforceable, as it was given after the contract between the parties had been concluded. Nothing was given by C in exchange for D's promise.

Instances where consideration is not past

4.14 There are certain well-established circumstances where what appears to be past consideration will be regarded as good consideration by the courts. They will look at the whole transaction between the parties and not rely simply on whether the promise was made after a particular act or service was performed by the promisee. These circumstances were helpfully summarized by Lord Scarman in the Privy Council decision in *Pao On* v *Lau Yiu Long* [1979] 3 All ER 65 at 74, where he stated:

> 'An act done before the giving of a promise to make a payment or to confer some other benefit can sometimes be consideration for the promise. The act must have been done at the promisor's request, the parties must have understood that the act was to be remunerated either by a payment or the conferment of some other benefit, and payment, or the conferment of a benefit, must have been legally enforceable had it been promised in advance.'

4.15 An early illustration is provided by *Lampleigh* v *Brathwait* (1615). The facts were:

> Brathwait had killed a man and he requested that Lampleigh should try to get him a pardon from the King. Lampleigh did as requested, which involved making journeys at his own expense, and obtained a pardon for Brathwait. Afterwards, Brathwait promised to pay him £100 for his endeavours. He then failed to pay Lampleigh and was sued by him. Brathwait's defence was that the act had been performed before the promise of a reward was made.

The court found in favour of Lampleigh and rejected the argument that the consideration was past. It stressed that the claimant's service was performed at the request of the defendant and his later promise to pay for it was binding. This is because the later promise was clearly related to the earlier request for help: essentially, it was all part of the same transaction. The idea is that, as Lord Scarman said, 'the parties must have understood that the act was to be remunerated either by a payment or the conferment of some other benefit'.

4.16 The requirements put forward by Lord Scarman are further illustrated by *Re Casey's Patents (Stewart* v *Casey)* (1892). The facts were:

> Stewart and Charlton, the joint owners of certain patent rights, wrote to Casey stating that, in consideration for his services as practical manager in working their patents, they promised to give him a one-third share of the patents. They later transferred the letters patent to Casey. After the death of Stewart, it was argued by Charlton and by Stewart's executor that Casey was not entitled to possession of the letters patent. Casey contested this and argued that, as owner of a one-third share in the patents, he was entitled to possession.

The question for the Court of Appeal to decide was whether Casey provided consideration for the promise made to him by Stewart and Charlton in the letter. The claimants contended that it was a case of past consideration, but this argument was rejected by the court, which found in favour of the defendant. The court was willing to imply an understanding between the parties, at the time the services by Casey were performed, that they would be remunerated. The later promise was, therefore, part of the same transaction: it merely fixed the amount of remuneration for which the service was originally rendered. Accordingly, consideration is not past in these circumstances, despite appearances to the contrary.[4]

4.17 The general rule about past consideration is also subject to certain statutory exceptions: for example, in relation to negotiable instruments. Under the Bills of Exchange Act 1882, s 27(1) provides that 'valuable consideration for a bill may be constituted by: (a) Any consideration sufficient to support a simple contract; (b) An antecedent debt or liability. Such a debt or liability is deemed valuable consideration whether the bill is payable on demand or at a future time'.[5]

---

4   For a more recent example, where Lord Scarman's three requirements were held to be satisfied, with the result that there was good consideration despite the defendant's argument that his promise was in exchange for past consideration, see *Foster* v *Matania* (2009).

5   Of interest on this subject, see *Thoni GmbH & Co. KG* v *RTP Equipment Ltd* (1979).

Consideration must move from the promisee

4.18   As a general principle, A can enforce a promise made to him or her only if A, him or herself, provided consideration for that promise (see *Price* v *Easton* (1833)). But, what if A is promised some benefit by B, but the consideration for the promise has been supplied by C? In such a situation, A has given nothing in exchange for B's promise; A has not paid the price of it, or suffered any detriment. The traditional view of the law has been that A will not normally be able to enforce B's promise, as consideration has not been provided by A. For example, in *Tweddle* v *Atkinson* (1861) 1 B & S 393, the facts were:

> John Tweddle and William Guy agreed (at first orally, and later in writing) each to pay a sum of money to a couple on their marriage. The couple in question were their son and daughter, respectively. The claimant, John Tweddle's son, tried to enforce his father-in-law's promise, when William Guy failed to make the agreed payment. (In fact, the action was brought against the executor of the deceased William Guy.)

The son's action failed as he did not provide any consideration for his father-in-law's promise. Crompton J stated (at 398) that:

> '[T]he consideration must move from the party entitled to sue upon the contract. It would be a monstrous proposition to say that a person was a party to a contract for the purpose of suing upon it for his own advantage, and not a party to it for the purpose of being sued.'

An alternative way of expressing the justification for not allowing the son's action to succeed in *Tweddle* v *Atkinson* is that there was no privity of contract between him and his father-in-law. (The contract was between John Tweddle and William Guy.) This principle of contract law is dealt with in **Chapter 17**, together with the important Contracts (Rights of Third Parties) Act 1999, which has introduced significant changes to this area of law. The extent to which the rule that 'consideration must move from the promisee' has been affected by the new legislation, implicitly if not formally, will be considered in **Chapter 17**, as this principle is closely related to the doctrine of privity. It was the view of the Law Commission that it is not possible 'even at a formal level, [to] reform the privity doctrine while leaving untouched the rule that consideration must move from the promisee.' (See Law Commission Report, No 242, Privity of Contract: Contracts for the Benefit of Third Parties, 1996, para. 6.5.)

Must the consideration be adequate?

4.19   The doctrine of consideration represents the idea of bargain and mutual obligations. The law will enforce only those promises for which something is given in return; it will not enforce gratuitous promises. One of the difficulties with the traditional definition of consideration in terms of 'benefit' and 'detriment' is that the promisor might request some act or forbearance from the promisee which is of little or no economic value. But as long as this is what he requests, and is given, the court will not interfere with the 'bargain' struck by the parties (see

Bainbridge v *Firmstone* (1838)). Thus consideration represents the idea of bargain rather than the reality of it.

4.20　This apparent failure to question the adequacy (value) of consideration is perhaps more defensible than it might seem at first sight. If the parties have bargained for a particular consideration, then it can usually be assumed that they achieved what they wanted from the exchange. Where a party appears to have made a particularly bad bargain there may be some other factor present which may vitiate the agreement, such as fraud or duress, but in the absence of any vitiating factor, the courts will not generally intervene in order to ensure a fair bargain has been struck. An important point here is that the law of contract is not, in general, the most suitable means of monitoring or controlling prices and ensuring fairness. Regulation through other measures can achieve this end more effectively. Moreover, although there is perhaps no general doctrine in our law which protects parties simply on the basis that they have entered into a bad bargain, the law of contract is capable of considerable flexibility in the pursuit of a fair result. In other words, the courts may rely on the various techniques at their disposal in order to promote the idea that a contract should not involve an unfair exchange or a very one-sided bargain.[6]

Adequacy of consideration: the general rule

4.21　Although it is commonly stated that consideration must be of some economic value, as we have seen, it is generally not a matter for the courts to judge the adequacy of consideration. So the provision of nominal consideration will suffice to meet the technical requirement of the law. For example, in *Mountford* v *Scott* [1975] Ch 258 the payment of £1 by C was sufficient to secure an option to purchase D's house. The Court of Appeal held that this option agreement was enforceable against D and that it was irrelevant that the consideration provided by C could be described as a token payment. In reaching this conclusion, reference was made to the 'mass of English authority to the effect that anything of value, however small the value, is sufficient consideration to support a contract at law' (per Cairns LJ at 265). There may, occasionally, be problems in differentiating between a contract supported by consideration and a conditional gift. These issues are well illustrated by the case of *Thomas* v *Thomas* (1842). The facts were:

> C's husband had made it clear that if his wife survived him, she should have the use of his house. After her husband's death, C agreed with the defendant, her husband's executor, that she should have the use of the house as long as she did not remarry. Her husband's executor made the agreement largely in deference to the deceased's clearly expressed wishes. But C was also asked to pay £1 per year to the executors under the agreement. Had C provided consideration for the promise, or was the payment of £1 per year no more than a condition attached to a gift?

It was held that C provided consideration for the executor's promise. It would not have been a legally enforceable agreement if the executor had merely wished to honour the deceased's

---

6　See further **Chapter 16**.

wishes and requested nothing further. It would have been a gratuitous promise. But, in this case, something of value, no matter how inadequate, was asked for by the promisor. It was more than a conditional gift, it was a binding agreement; the court did not have to enquire into the adequacy of the consideration provided by the promisee under the contract.

4.22   Generally, consideration must be of some economic value, no matter how slight. Less tangible benefits may fail to supply consideration. In *White* v *Bluett* (1853), the defendant borrowed money from his father and gave him a promissory note. This was followed by bitter complaints from the defendant that he had been treated less favourably by his father than the other children in the family. In order to gain some peace, and out of affection for his son, the father promised to discharge the defendant from his obligation to repay the loan. On the father's death, his executor brought a successful action to recover the loan. It was held that no consideration had been provided by the defendant for his father's promise, as refraining from making complaints was thought not to be of any economic value.

4.23   However, we should consider the case of *Ward* v *Byham* (1956). The facts were:

> The claimant (C) lived with the defendant (D) for five years as an unmarried couple. C gave birth to their daughter during this period, but the couple eventually separated. Initially, D was responsible for looking after the child, as C had been forced to leave their home. But when C found a housekeeping job, where she could have her daughter with her, D agreed to let her have the child and an allowance of £1 per week, provided that C could prove that their daughter was 'well looked after and happy'. The daughter, who was allowed to decide with which parent she wanted to live, went to her mother's. D made the £1 weekly payments, but stopped these when C married her employer. C brought an action for the £1 per week promised by D.

The Court of Appeal decided in favour of C and held that she did provide consideration for D's promise. In fact, C was under a legal obligation (as the mother of an illegitimate child) to look after her daughter (National Assistance Act 1948, s 42). The view was generally held that performance of a statutory duty could not provide consideration. However, it was argued that she went beyond her statutory duty by undertaking that the child was well looked after and happy. As we shall see, going beyond a statutory duty was well recognized as sufficient to provide consideration, and this would seem to be the line taken by the majority. However, treating doing so, in this way, as consideration, makes a difficult contrast with *White v Bluett*, and it should not be thought that the general idea of something of economic, rather than purely emotional, value being needed to supply consideration will be easily departed from. (The courts can be fairly inventive in finding consideration for a promise where it is felt that justice requires such an approach.) Further, Denning LJ's approach was somewhat different to the rest of the court. He took the line that C could provide consideration, for D's promise, simply by fulfilling her statutory duty. This is an idea which may be seen to be a much more acceptable explanation of the case in the light of the developments made in relation to the doctrine of consideration by the case of *Williams v Roffey Bros & Nicholls (Contractors) Ltd* (1990) (see later).

4.24 However, there may be questions about something which is tangible being of any economic value, and being consideration.[7] In *Chappell & Co. Ltd* v *Nestlé Co. Ltd* [1960] AC 87, the facts were:

> The Nestlé Company (D) offered a record entitled 'Rockin' Shoes' to the public for 1s 6d (7.5p) plus three Nestlé's chocolate bar wrappers. The requirement of sending in the wrappers, in addition to the money, was in order to promote the company's chocolate; the wrappers were thrown away on receipt. The action arose because the claimant, who owned the copyright in 'Rockin' Shoes', argued that he received insufficient royalties on the sale of the record. D paid a percentage based on the price of the record, which was 1s 6d. The claimant argued that the wrappers were also part of the consideration.

The House of Lords decided the case in favour of the claimant. The wrappers were part of the consideration. They were requested by the Nestlé Company and were given by members of the public, together with money, in exchange for the record. It was held to be irrelevant that the wrappers were of no intrinsic value to the company (at 114 per Lord Somervell). Parties to a contract could ask for whatever consideration they wanted, and it was not for the court to assess its adequacy. It might also be observed that the wrappers represented something of value to the Nestlé Company, namely the successful promotion of the company's products. This was acknowledged by Lord Reid (at 108) who stated that 'the requirement that wrappers should be sent was of great importance to the Nestlé Co . . . it seems to me quite unrealistic to divorce the buying of the chocolate from the supplying of the records'.

Forbearance to sue and compromise as consideration

4.25 Where X is threatened by Y with legal action to enforce a claim, they might reach a compromise whereby Y's promise to refrain from suing is 'bought' by X's counter promise to pay an agreed amount. This exchange of promises is binding, because something of value is given by both parties. (For example, see *Horton* v *Horton (No 2)* (1961): in this case there was only a possibility that an action might have been brought by the wife against her husband in relation to their separation agreement. But giving up this possible claim was still regarded by the court as consideration. For a more recent example of a case raising some similar issues, see *Papanicola* v *Fagon* (2008). Here a wife's forbearance from petitioning for divorce was held to be consideration for her husband's transfer to her of the beneficial ownership of the matrimonial home.) One party gives up a claim whilst the other agrees to pay compensation. It is in the interest of the legal system to encourage parties, wherever possible, to reach a compromise over disputes. Similarly, if X is faced with a claim by Y (for example, for an outstanding debt), and requests further time to pay, Y's forbearance from pursuing the claim can amount to consideration for any new promise made by X. So where a debtor promises to give additional security for a debt, in exchange for more time to pay, this will again be regarded as a binding agreement.

---

7 See *Revenue and Customs Commissioners* v *Debenhams Retail plc* (2005).

4.26   If X is threatened with a legal action which Y knows to be without foundation, Y's forbearance from proceeding will not amount to consideration for any new promise given by X. To hold otherwise would encourage vexatious and frivolous claims and be contrary to public policy (see *Wade* v *Simeon* (1846)). But as long as Y honestly believes that the action is reasonable, and might succeed, then forbearance from proceeding with a doubtful or even a bad claim is capable of amounting to consideration. (For a discussion of this issue, see *Freedman* v *Union Group plc* (1997).) Y must not conceal any information from X which might affect X's ability to resist the claim (see *Miles* v *New Zealand Alford Estate Co* (1886)).

4.27   Is it necessary for Y specifically to promise X some degree of forbearance from bringing an action, or need there only be some forbearance in fact which can be inferred from the dealings between the parties? This question was considered in *Alliance Bank Ltd* v *Broom* (1864) 2 Drew & Sm 289, where the facts were:

> The defendants, a firm of Liverpool merchants, owed £22,000 to the claimant bank and were asked by the bank to provide additional security for the debt. The defendants promised to assign to them the documents of title to certain goods by way of additional security. It is important to note that, in return, the bank made no express counter promise not to sue the defendants. The defendants failed to provide the promised security and the bank tried to enforce the promise. Had the bank given anything in return for the defendants' promise?

It was held that the bank had given consideration by their actual forbearance and were entitled to claim specific performance. The reason given was that in the circumstances the defendants received the benefit of 'a certain amount of forbearance which [they] would not have derived if [they] had not made the agreement' (at 292). Apparently, it did not matter that no specific promise to forbear was given by the bank, nor was it necessary that the actual forbearance should last for a substantial period of time. The decision is, perhaps, unfortunate. The court seems to have enforced a very one-sided exchange in circumstances where the extent of any forbearance was, to say the least, unclear. (For a contrasting decision, see *Miles* v *New Zealand Alford Estate Co* (1886).) In the opinion of two commentators, the unsatisfactory decisions on forbearance should be seen not as laying down any useful contractual principles, but more as a reflection of 'the policy objective of the courts' desire to encourage out of court settlements' (see P. Mitchell and J. Phillips, 'The Contractual Nexus: Is Reliance Essential?' (2002) OJLS 115 at 127).

Performance of a legal duty as consideration

4.28   We noted earlier that the law does not look at the adequacy of consideration. That is however, contrasted with looking at its 'sufficiency'. Obviously the two words can mean much the same in everyday terms, but here the question of 'sufficiency' of consideration is about whether what is in question is something which is, in law, capable of constituting consideration. It is in the context of existing legal duties that the question has come to the fore in recent times.

4.29   The rules relating to sufficiency of consideration are not always entirely consistent, tending sometimes to reflect the exigencies of public policy rather than logic. This is particularly the case in relation to the performance of an existing legal duty in exchange for another person's promise. This can arise in three distinct factual situations, which will be considered in turn: (a) the performance of a public duty; (b) the performance of a duty owed already to the promisor; and (c) the performance of a duty owed already to a third party.

Public duty imposed by law

4.30   We have already seen an illustration of this type of case. In *Ward v Byham* (1956) (see para. **4.23**) the claimant was under a statutory duty to look after her illegitimate daughter, but it was held that she provided consideration, for the defendant's promise to pay her £1 per week, by doing that. It was argued by Morris LJ that the consideration consisted in going beyond her statutory duty by ensuring that the child was both well looked after and happy, as requested by the promisor. But, as we have seen, it is unlikely that keeping the child 'happy' can itself amount to something of value for the purposes of the law (see *White v Bluett* (1853), discussed at para. **4.22**). Lord Denning's assessment of the facts in *Ward v Byham* was, perhaps, more realistic. He acknowledged that, in looking after her daughter, the claimant was only fulfilling her legal obligation. However, he thought that such a performance of an existing duty (or the promise of such performance) was good consideration. He concentrated on the benefit that this performance conferred upon the promisor.[8]

4.31   The traditional view is not in accord with Lord Denning's opinion, as expressed in *Ward v Byham* (1956). In *Collins v Godefroy* (1831), C was subpoenaed to give evidence on D's behalf at a trial in which D was involved. C claimed that D promised him one guinea (£1.05) per day for attending court. But C was unsuccessful in his attempt to enforce D's promise, as he failed to provide consideration for this promise. C was already under a legal duty to attend court because of the subpoena, and the case is thought to have established a general principle that a person does not provide consideration for another person's promise by simply performing an existing legal duty.

4.32   Such a principle is, however, open to question. There can be no doubt that it is in the public interest to prevent certain professional groups from bargaining for services that they are under a public duty to render. It would be unthinkable for a police constable or a firefighter to be able to enforce a promise of a reward made to them by a member of the public, in urgent need of their help, simply for carrying out their public duties. But the reason for not upholding such an agreement is not necessarily based on lack of consideration, but rather on the grounds of public policy and the prevention of extortion.[9]

4.33   However, it has been long accepted that there is consideration where the public duty is exceeded. (This was the explanation given by the majority of the court for the decision in *Ward*

---

8   See the discussion of this issue in the Law Revision Committee's 6th Interim Report, Cmnd 5449, 1937, para. 36.

9   It will be remembered that in *Gibbons v Proctor* (1891) a policeman was able to claim a reward for providing information leading to the arrest of an offender. (See also *England v Davidson* (1840).)

v *Byham* (1956), on the dubious ground that the mother also promised to ensure the child was 'happy'.) An example is provided by *Glasbrook Bros Ltd* v *Glamorgan County Council* (1925), where mine-owners, during a miners' strike, were fearful of violence occurring. Their assessment of the amount of police protection that they needed differed from that of the police whose job it was to provide it. Eventually, the police did agree to mount a stationary guard, which they did not think necessary, but they did so on the basis that it would be paid for by the company. The company agreed to pay £2,200 for this more extensive police operation, but later refused to make the payment, claiming that there was no consideration given for their promise. The House of Lords held that the police were entitled to recover the payment as they had done more than perform their existing legal duty.

4.34   The decision in *Glasbrook Bros Ltd* v *Glamorgan County Council* (1925) is not open to criticism as long as the police's original assessment of the company's security requirements was a reasonable one. If it was, the police clearly gave something of value, over and above their public duty, in exchange for the company's promise. Of course, if there is the slightest suggestion of extortion in this type of case, the agreement should not be enforceable on the grounds of public policy. It is submitted that a case like *Glasbrook Bros Ltd* cannot be resolved purely on the basis of any technical requirement of consideration in the law of contract. In reality, such cases would seem to involve issues of public policy.[10] The decision in *Williams* v *Roffey Bros & Nicholls (Contractors) Ltd* (1990) (para. **4.39**), which found consideration for a new promise, where one party performed what they were already obliged to do, under an existing contract with the other party, may move the basis of the discussion, in such cases, from consideration, to duress and public policy. It may eventually be found that Denning LJ took the appropriate line in *Ward v Byham*.

Performance of a duty owed to promisor

4.35   This type of case involves the following conundrum: X makes a promise to Y in exchange for Y doing (or promising to do) something which Y is already obliged to do under an existing contract with X. If Y does (or promises) nothing more than he is already bound to do, it is difficult to see how he can be said to have provided consideration for X's promise. However, as we have seen, the requirement of consideration can be satisfied very easily if the parties remember to include something extra, of nominal value, to be provided by Y. Increasingly the question has come to be recognized as more complex than the issue of the provision of some nominal, additional, consideration. Obviously, it would be clearly undesirable if a person who had already contracted to perform a particular service could extort more money from the promisor for performing the same service. (Making the original contract may have narrowed X's options, leaving X more vulnerable to a threat of non-performance by Y.) On the other hand, if the situation has become such, in relation to the original contract, that Y cannot perform without charging more, for example, it may be beneficial to X to pay more, maintain his working relationship with Y, and get performance. In such circumstances, it may be argued that the new situation is

---

10 See also S. Weatherill, 'Buying Special Police Services' [1988] Public Law 106.

beneficial to both parties and the new agreement should be enforced, even though the parties have forgotten to include some additional, token, new consideration on Y's part. Increasingly the situation is recognized as more complex than should be dealt with simply on the basis of whether or not some technical consideration is present. (The question of when a contract will be voidable for duress is looked at in the chapter dealing with duress.)

4.36   We should, however, start by looking at the traditional view that the performance of an existing duty already owed to the promisor (as described earlier) could not amount to consideration, and the case of *Stilk* v *Myrick* (1809). The facts arose out of a return voyage from London to the Baltic, during which two sailors had deserted and the captain was unable to find replacements for them. He promised to divide the wages of the two deserters amongst the remaining crew members in exchange for their sailing the ship short-handed on the home voyage. The action brought by one of the crew, to enforce this promise, failed. The crew members provided no consideration for the captain's promise, as they were only fulfilling their existing contractual obligations by sailing the ship home, and the case was long regarded as based on this consideration point. There would, however, also seem to have been concerns that a ship's crew should not be able to extort additional payments to get a ship home.

4.37   Of course, there was consideration in such a situation if a crew could be seen as providing something extra. In *Hartley* v *Ponsonby* (1857), a crew of thirty-six was reduced by desertions to one of nineteen, of which only a handful were experienced sailors. This situation was distinguishable from that of *Stilk* v *Myrick* (1809) and the claimant was able to enforce the captain's promise of an additional £40. The situation was exceptional: continuing with the voyage was so dangerous that the remaining crew members were not simply fulfilling their existing obligations. Consideration was provided for the captain's promise.

4.38   The basic rule laid down in *Stilk* v *Myrick* (1809) has increasingly been questioned. Consideration can be provided by something additional which is of little value: a bar of chocolate, a cheap biro. When there is no more done, for extra payment, the real questions are about such issues as duress, and the encouragement, or discouragement, of the parties amending the agreement when circumstances change. The situation may be one in which Y can no longer afford to carry out the contractual performance. X may be willing to pay more to assist Y, maintain their working relationship, and get performance on time. There is much more to be looked at here, in these additional payment situations, than whether some technical, extra, consideration has been provided. This will be considered further in the chapter dealing with duress. Here we should look at the development of the law away from simply labeling the issue as one of consideration.

4.39   The rule in *Stilk* v *Myrick* was 'refined' and 'limited', and the emphasis thrown upon duress, in *Williams* v *Roffey Bros & Nicholls (Contractors) Ltd* [1990] 1 All ER 512. The facts were:

> The defendant building contractors were under contract to refurbish a block of twenty-seven flats. They sub-contracted the carpentry work to the claimant (C) for £20,000. After completing some of the work, and receiving interim payments under the sub-contract, C found that

he was in financial difficulties because the remuneration under his contract with the defendants was too low and he had failed to supervise his workmen properly. The defendants were liable under a 'penalty' clause in the main contract if the work was not completed on time, and they were aware that C was in difficulties because the carpentry work had been underpriced. They called a meeting with C at which they promised an extra £10,300 to ensure that C continued with the work and finished it on time. The extra payment thus agreed was to be at the rate of £575 per flat on completion. C continued working, but the defendants did not keep up the additional payments which they had agreed. C then stopped work on the remaining flats and sued the defendants for the additional sum promised. The defendants argued that no consideration had been provided by C for the promise of extra payment.

The Court of Appeal held that C was entitled to the additional payments for the flats completed. There was no evidence of economic duress; the original contract underpriced the work and the defendants understood this and themselves commenced the process of renegotiation. The defendants also gained a benefit under this later agreement. It was important to them to be sure that the work was completed promptly; they were faced with a penalty clause under the main contract. The court took the line that C provided consideration for the defendants' promise of additional payment. D gained a 'practical' benefit, the agreement was not affected by duress, and it was binding.

4.40   It might be objected that the claimant in *Williams* v *Roffey Bros & Nicholls (Contractors) Ltd* agreed to do nothing more than he was already bound to do by the original sub-contract with the defendants. In finding in his favour, it appears that the court did (despite its protestations to the contrary) seek to depart from, rather than apply, the decision in *Stilk* v *Myrick* (1809). Glidewell LJ rationalized the decision in the following way (at 522):

> 'If it be objected that the propositions above contravene the principle in *Stilk* v *Myrick*, I answer that in my view they do not: they refine and limit the application of that principle, but they leave the principle unscathed, e.g. where [the promisor] secures no benefit from his promise. It is not in my view surprising that a principle enunciated in relation to the rigours of seafaring life during the Napoleonic wars should be subjected during the succeeding 180 years to a process of refinement and limitation in its application in the present day.'

4.41   Although controversial,[11] the decision in *Williams* v *Roffey Bros & Nicholls (Contractors) Ltd* (1990) has opened the way to a broader consideration of the issues involved when someone promises to pay more to obtain a performance they were already entitled to. It has done this by changing the nature of what is being looked for to constitute consideration in such circumstances; from legal benefits to 'practical' ones. Of course, there will always be a 'practical' benefit, or the relevant party would not have agreed to pay more. The case has thrown the emphasis upon the question of whether the promise to pay more was, nevertheless, obtained in unacceptable circumstances: by duress.

---

11 *Williams* v *Roffey* was criticized in *South Caribbean Trading* v *Trafigura Beheer BV* (2004) per Colman J at [108].

Performance of a duty owed to a third party

4.42   The law in this situation is well established. The type of situation is where X makes a promise to Y in exchange for Y doing (or promising to do) something which Y is already obliged to do under an existing contract with Z. At first sight it seems, as a matter of logic, that Y provides no consideration for X's promise. However, X does obtain a direct contractual right against Y. If Y does not perform, he or she, is not only liable to Z, but also X. Further, there was never the same level of risk of duress in this situation, as in that looked at earlier, and consideration has long been found in this situation, where the existing contractual duty is to a third party (*Shadwell* v *Shadwell* (1860) 9 CB NS 159, *Chichester* v *Cobb* (1866) and *Scotson* v *Pegg* (1861)). In *Pao On* v *Lau Yiu Long* [1979] 3 All ER 65, Lord Scarman stated (at 76):

> 'Their lordships do not doubt that a promise to perform, or the performance of, a pre-existing contractual obligation to a third party can be valid consideration.'

4.43   *New Zealand Shipping Co. Ltd* v *AM Satterthwaite & Co. Ltd, The Eurymedon* [1974] 1 All ER 1015, provides an example. In that case, the claimant cargo owners promised the defendant stevedore company that they would not be liable for any damage to the goods arising out of their (D's) negligence. The cargo was damaged as a result of D's negligence during unloading. Could D rely on C's promise? D had already been bound to unload the goods under an existing contract with a third party, the carrier. Could the unloading of the goods be regarded as consideration provided by D in exchange for C's promise not to sue in the event of damage to the goods? The Privy Council held (at 1020–1) that the work done in unloading the cargo was good consideration for C's promise, as the claimants obtained the benefit of a direct obligation, which they could enforce.

Part payment of a debt

4.44   The question arises as to the enforceability of a particular promise in the situation in which Y owes a debt to X, and X promises to accept from Y payment of part of the debt, in exchange for releasing Y from the rest of it. The issue is whether that promise is enforceable. First we will consider the traditional approach.

4.45   The classic statement is to be found in *Pinnel's Case* (1602), where it was held that payment of part of an existing debt could not amount to consideration for the creditor's promise to accept this lesser sum as full settlement and to forgo the balance. But if, in addition or instead, something other than money was given by the debtor, in exchange for the creditor's promise, this would provide good consideration. (Lord Coke famously referred to the provision of 'a horse, a hawk, or a robe').[12] Similarly, payment of a lesser sum by the debtor at an earlier time than originally agreed, at the creditor's request, can also amount to consideration. In these

---

12 He actually used the phrase: 'the gift of a horse, a hawk, or a robe, etc, in satisfaction is good'. However, if anything was handed over as a true 'gift', it would not be consideration: it would not be provided in return for the dispensation from the rest of the payment.

situations, some benefit to the creditor can be discerned. But where there was simply part payment, and nothing more, there was no consideration given by the debtor.

4.46 With some misgivings, this rule was approved by the House of Lords in *Foakes v Beer* (1884) 9 App Cas 605. The facts were as follows:

> Julia Beer had obtained a judgment in the High Court against John Foakes for £2,090 19s. More than a year later, Dr Foakes requested time to pay. It was agreed by the parties, in writing, that if Dr Foakes paid £500 immediately and then paid biannual instalments of £150 until the debt was fully paid, Mrs Beer would 'not take any proceedings whatever on the said judgment'. Dr Foakes paid the debt, in the agreed way, and then Mrs Beer claimed interest. (Dr Foakes was liable to pay interest on a judgment debt, but their agreement had made no reference to this.) Dr Foakes argued that Mrs Beer had promised not to take any action on the debt if he paid in the prescribed manner. But even assuming that the agreement covered the question of interest, did Dr Foakes provide any consideration in return for Mrs Beer's promise?

The House of Lords found in favour of Mrs Beer and upheld her claim for the interest. Opinion was divided on whether the agreement was, in fact, intended to cover the question of interest. But, whatever the true construction of the agreement might have been, it was held that payment of part of the debt could not be good consideration for Mrs Beer's promise to forgo the balance (that is, the interest). The 'rule in *Pinnel's case*' was seen as too long established to reject. Lord Blackburn did, though, have serious misgivings at the extent to which it was out of keeping with business practice. He said (at 622):

> 'What principally weighs with me in thinking that Lord Coke made a mistake [in Pinnel's case]...is my conviction that all men of business, whether merchants or tradesmen, do every day recognise and act on the ground that prompt payment of a part of their demand may be more beneficial to them than it would be to insist on their rights and enforce payment of the whole. Even where the debtor is perfectly solvent, and sure to pay at last, this often is so. Where the credit of the debtor is doubtful it must be more so.'

This will be returned to later in the chapter.

Limitations on the rule in *Foakes* v *Beer*

4.47 Some limitations on the rule, did come to be established. We have already seen that, in *Pinnel's Case* (1602) itself, it was recognized that whilst part payment of a debt is not good consideration to forego part of the debt, supplying something different (a horse, hawk, robe, or chocolate bar, for example) could be.[13]

---

13 The line was even taken in *Sibree* v *Tripp* (1846) that this extended to the situation where a debtor gave his creditor promissory notes for a lesser amount than the actual debt. Thus, if X owed Y £1,000, and Y promised to accept £900 in full settlement, Y could go back on this and later claim the full amount. But if Y promised to accept, from X, promissory

4.48 A further limitation on the rule in *Foakes v Beer* (1884) can also be simply illustrated. X owes Y £1,000. Y promises to accept £700 from Z in full settlement of X's debt. Y is not able to go back on his promise and sue X for the balance (see *Hirachand Punamchand v Temple* (1911)). It might be argued that in such a situation X provides no consideration for Y's promise to forgo the remainder of the debt. However, it would be manifestly unjust, to Z in particular, if Y were able to go back on his promise. (It would be a breach of Y's contract with Z.) Another restriction on the rule is where X owes money to a number of creditors and is unable to meet the debts in full. He may come to a composition agreement with them, under which they all promise to accept a lesser amount than they are in fact owed. If the creditors accept such a payment by X, based on a division of his assets, in full satisfaction of their claims against him, they cannot go back on this and sue for the balance.

4.49 A final point should also be made here. It is common practice for services to be rendered, by plumbers, builders, etc., under a contract which fails to fix the price of the work to be done. The amount owed will not necessarily be the amount claimed by the workman. It may well be that the customer disputes the account when it is finally presented. If the tradesperson agrees to accept, in full settlement, a lesser sum than he or she originally claimed, he or she is bound by such an agreement. It is only where the creditor's claim is 'liquidated' (and undisputed) that his promise to accept part payment of the debt in full settlement will not be binding.

Williams v Roffey Bros

4.50 We have seen Lord Blackburn's concern that the approach in *Pinnel's case* was out of keeping with commercial practice, and the commonly perceived practical benefit of getting part of a debt paid, rather than being left to sue for the whole. Obviously, the question arises as to the application of the approach taken in *Williams v Roffey Bros* in this context. Accepting less, and releasing someone from the rest of a debt, poses the same problem as a larger payment for the original amount of work. The logic of applying the *Williams v Roffey* approach, in the context of a promise to accept part payment of a debt for release from the whole debt, was acknowledged by the Court of Appeal in *Re Selectmove* (1995). However, the line was taken that as *Foakes v Beer* was a House of Lords' authority, it had to be followed, in the context of part payment of a debt, until the House of Lords (now the Supreme Court) said otherwise. Although, logically, *Pinnel's case* and *Stilk v Myrick* raise the same underlying issue, the two questions, and lines of authority, have been kept distinct.

4.51 One of the benefits of the *Foakes v Beer* approach has been seen to be that it meant that a debtor could not force an impecunious creditor to accept a lesser sum, in final settlement, by threatening that otherwise they would get nothing. *D&C Builders v Rees* (1966), provides an example.

> The claimants were a small firm of builders, who had done some work for the defendant, as a result of which the defendant still owed them £482. The claimants were in financial difficulties

notes for £500 in full settlement, Y was bound by that promise and could not claim the residue. The line was taken that the promissory note was something different: a negotiable security. The court refused to extend this approach to a cheque, however, in *D & C Builders Ltd v Rees* (1966).

and the defendant, having delayed payment of the debt, instructed his wife to offer the builders £300 and no more. The financial problems of the claimants (which were allegedly known to the debtors) led them to accept the offer of £300 in full settlement. They later sued for the balance.

The Court of Appeal held that the builders were entitled to claim the rest of the debt from the defendant, who had given no consideration in exchange for the claimants' promise to accept part payment of the debt. The rule in *Foakes* v *Beer* was thus used to defeat the unconscionable behaviour of the debtor in this case.

4.52   However, such situations could now be directly tacked by reference to economic duress. The problem with the rule in *Foakes* v *Beer* is that it is undiscriminating: not differentiating between those agreements made in unacceptable circumstance and those which should be enforced.

The equitable approach[14]

4.53   One of the effects of the approach in *Williams* v *Roffey* not (yet) extending into the context of part payment of a debt, is that a different, complex and uncertain, means of circumventing the rule in *Foakes* v *Beer*, which developed in equity, will be attempted. *Collier* v *P and MJ Wright (Holdings) Ltd* (2008) provides a recent illustration. In this case, W was owed a judgment debt of £46,800 for which C and his two former property development partners were jointly liable. The three partners were to pay this debt jointly, by monthly instalments of £600. Although C kept up his share of the payment, his partners became bankrupt, and W claimed the whole of the debt from C. In contesting this demand, C tried to rely on an alleged agreement with W to the effect that, as long as C continued to pay his share of the debt, W would not pursue him for the balance owed by his former partners. C argued that, by entering into this alleged agreement with W, he provided consideration for W's promise to treat him as owing only one-third of the judgment debt. He argued also that W was prevented by a promissory estoppel from claiming more than a one-third share of the debt from him (see **Chapter 5**).

4.54   As a preliminary matter the Court of had to consider whether C had raised a triable issue, and it found that he had. The alleged agreement, under which W agreed with C to accept part payment from him of just a one-third share, was not contractually binding (at [23]–[28]): there was a lack of consideration from C in relation to W's promise to accept part payment of the debt. However, they thought that there was a triable issue that C could, nevertheless use promissory estoppel to prevent W from enforcing the rest of the debt (at [40] and [50]).

4.55   Using promissory estoppel as a means of circumventing the common law rules on consideration and part payment of a debt is discussed in **Chapter 5**.

---

14 See A. Burrows, 'We Do This at Common Law But That in Equity' (2002) 22 OJLS 1–16.

⬡ Summary

- Contracts do not, generally, have to be made in a particular form in order to be effective.
- The main test of enforceability in our law of contract is the requirement of consideration.
- Traditionally, this symbolizes the bargain or exchange nature of contracts.
- Consideration can be described as the 'price' paid by one party for the other party's promise.
- Consideration must not be 'past': but there are important exceptions to this rule.
- Courts will not normally judge the 'adequacy' of consideration.
- The various rules relating to the 'sufficiency' of consideration are not always consistent or coherent.
- The controversial decision in *Williams* v *Roffey Bros* (1990) has changed the situation where there is performance of an existing duty and payment of an additional sum.
- Part payment of an existing debt cannot amount to consideration for a creditor's promise to forgo the balance (see *Foakes* v *Beer* (1884)).
- The rule in *Foakes* v *Beer* can be criticized as out of step with commercial practice, and with the developments in *Williams* v *Roffey Bros*.

⬛ Further reading

J. **Adams and R. Brownsword**, 'Contract, Consideration and the Critical Path' (1990) 53 MLR 536

P. **Atiyah**, 'Consideration: A Restatement' in *P. Atiyah, Essays on Contract*, Oxford University Press, 1986, pp. 179–244

B. **Coote**, 'Considerations and Variations: A Different Solution' (2004) 120 LQR 19

R. **Hooley**, 'Consideration and the Existing Duty' (1991) JBL 19

P. **Mitchell and J. Phillips**, 'The Contractual Nexus: Is Reliance Essential?' (2002) 22 OJLS 115

J. **O'Sullivan**, 'In Defence of *Foakes v Beer*' (1996) 55 CLJ 219

E. **Peel**, 'Part Payment of a Debt is No Consideration' (1994) 110 LQR 353

A. **Phang**, 'Consideration at the Crossroads' (1991) 107 LQR 21

J. **Steyn**, 'Contract Law: Fulfilling the Reasonable Expectations of Honest Men' (1997) 113 LQR 433

A. **Trukhtanov**, *'Foakes v Beer*: Reform of the Common Law at the Expense of Equity' (2008) 124 LQR 364

S. **Weatherill**, 'Buying Special Police Services' [1988] Public Law 106

Chapter 5

Promissory estoppel

Introduction

5.1   In *Foakes* v *Beer* (1884), the House of Lords established that a debtor's payment of part of an existing debt (or promise to do so) cannot amount to consideration for a creditor's promise to accept a lesser sum in full settlement.

5.2   However, in the light of *Williams* v *Roffey Bros & Nicholls (Contractors) Ltd* (1990) (see **Chapter 4**), the whole question of consideration and the performance of existing obligations needs to be re-examined. There seems to be little justification for the law to hold that A's performance of a service already owed to B is capable of amounting to consideration if it confers some practical benefit on B, whilst simultaneously maintaining that payment of part of an existing debt can never provide good consideration for a creditor's promise regardless of the practical advantages to the creditor. Despite this inconsistency, the law in relation to part payment of a debt is still currently kept distinct. The illogicality was recognized in *Re Selectmove*, but the line was taken that, as *Foakes v Beer* is a House of Lords' decision, only that court (i.e. now the Supreme Court) could move away from it, and adopt the *Williams v Roffey* approach, in the part payment of a debt context. That being so, at least currently, we have to consider the use of promissory estoppel to mitigate the impact of *Foakes v Beer*.

5.3   There can be little doubt that the decision in *Foakes v Beer* is capable of producing unfair results and of defeating reasonable commercial expectations. As has been indicated, in *Foakes v Beer* itself, Lord Blackburn expressed misgivings about the rule ((1884) 9 App Cas at 622). He observed that businessmen frequently do decide to accept part payment in full satisfaction of an outstanding debt. There was further criticism in the report of the Law Revision Committee (Cmnd 5449, 1937) on the doctrine of consideration. A major objection to the rule is that where a creditor (Y) promises to accept a lesser sum in full settlement and the debtor (X) relies on this promise, altering his or her position in some detrimental way, it is unjust to permit Y to go back on Y's promise. X may, for instance, incur other financial liabilities (for example, to Z) in the belief that the debt owed to Y has been fully settled.

Development of the doctrine

5.4   The opportunity to put forward a different solution to the problem of part payment of a debt arose in *Central London Property Trust Ltd* v *High Trees House Ltd* [1947] KB 130. In this famous case, widely referred to as *High Trees*, the facts were as follows:

> The claimants let a block of flats to the defendants, in September 1937, for a term of ninety-nine years at a rent of £2,500 per year. A few years later, due to wartime conditions and fear of bombing raids, many of the flats were not let. The claimants agreed, in 1940, to reduce the defendants' rent to £1,250. When the war ended in 1945, the flats were no longer empty, and the claimants wanted to claim the full rent (i.e. £2,500) from the defendants. In order to test whether they could claim the full rate, retrospectively, for the period when many of the flats were empty, the claimants claimed the full rent for the last two quarters of 1945.

After less than a year as a High Court judge, Denning J delivered a famous judgment, described by Arden LJ in *Collier* v *P & MJ Wright (Holdings) Ltd* [2008] 1 WLR 643 at [42] as a 'brilliant *obiter dictum*'. He held in favour of the claimants' argument on the basis that the agreement to accept the lower rent was intended only to cover the period when many of the flats were empty. As this was no longer the case by the second half of 1945, the claimants were entitled to go back to charging the defendants the full rent that had been agreed originally between the parties in 1937. What is significant about the judgment, however, is his opinion that any attempt by the claimants to recover the full rent for the period 1940–45 would not be successful. In other words, apparently contrary to the established rule in *Foakes* v *Beer* (1884), the claimants would not be permitted to go back on the promise made to the defendants (in 1940), to accept a lesser rent, whilst wartime conditions prevailed, and many flats remained empty.

5.5   On the basis of the principles discussed in **Chapter 4**, it would seem that Denning J's opinion was without legal foundation. The defendants did not provide any consideration for the claimants' promise in 1940. Thus, the 1940 agreement did not satisfy all the requirements that we look for in a legally binding contract. But Denning J was undeterred in his search for a means of preventing the promisor from going back on his promise, and insisting on his full legal rights. He chose the idea of estoppel as the basis for his assault on the rule in *Foakes* v *Beer* (1884). Put simply, this doctrine encapsulates the idea that if X makes an unequivocal statement of fact to Y which he intends X to rely upon, and which Y does in fact rely upon to his or her detriment, X is prevented from later acting inconsistently with that representation (i.e. by denying the truth of his or her statement). The difficulty with estoppel, as a means of evading the common law rule, was that it was held in *Jorden* v *Money* (1854) that the doctrine applied only to a representation of existing fact,[1] whereas in *High Trees* (1947) the representation made by the claimants, in relation to reducing the rent, was one of intention, rather than of existing fact (i.e. a promise).

---

1   See also *Argy Trading Development Co. Ltd* v *Lapid Developments Ltd* (1977).

5.6 However, starting as he meant to go on as a judge, Denning J did not allow this established meaning of the doctrine of estoppel to present an insurmountable barrier to achieving justice in the instant case. He distinguished *Jorden* v *Money* (1854), on rather tenuous grounds, and proceeded to promulgate an analogous doctrine of promissory estoppel. He argued that the law had moved on since *Jorden* v *Money* to provide a broader principle than that traditionally represented by the doctrine of estoppel by representation. This principle extended to cases in which a promise was made by X to Y, with the intention that it would be acted upon by Y, and was in fact acted upon by Y. Denning J thought that it was now established that X's promise must be honoured insofar as X would be prevented from acting inconsistently with it, despite a lack of consideration by Y. (It should be noted that X could not be sued for breach of such a promise.) Of course, this wider principle of promissory estoppel covered the *High Trees* situation. But was there any authority for Denning J's view? He argued in *High Trees* ([1947] KB 130 at 134) that the principle that he was putting forward was the 'natural result of a fusion of law and equity'. He continued:

> 'In my opinion, the time has now come for the validity of such a promise to be recognised. The logical consequence, no doubt, is that a promise to accept a smaller sum in discharge of a larger sum, if acted upon, is binding notwithstanding the absence of consideration: and if the fusion of law and equity leads to this result, so much the better.'

5.7 It might be objected that Denning J's interpretation of the law appeared to ignore the binding precedent of the House of Lords in *Foakes* v *Beer* (1884). He argued that the equitable principle had not been considered in *Foakes* v *Beer*, and instead he chose to rely on another House of Lords decision: *Hughes* v *Metropolitan Rly Co.* (1877) 2 App Cas 439. The facts were:

> A landlord gave his tenant six months' notice to repair the premises. The tenant faced forfeiture of the lease if he did not comply with the notice. The tenant agreed to do the repairs but also suggested that the landlord might wish to purchase the lease. The tenant indicated that he would not start the repairs whilst negotiations for the sale of the lease were in progress. One month after giving him the notice to repair, the landlord began negotiations with the tenant for the purchase of the lease, but these proved fruitless and were discontinued the following month. The tenant had, meanwhile, failed to repair the premises. When six months had passed from the date of giving the tenant notice to repair, the landlord tried to treat the lease as forfeited.

The House of Lords rejected the landlord's claim. The tenant was entitled to relief in equity against forfeiture. By starting negotiations for the purchase of the lease the landlord had led the tenant to believe that he would not enforce his strict legal rights while the negotiations continued. It would have been unfair to allow the landlord to go back on this implied promise. Once the negotiations did break down, he should have given the tenant reasonable time to do the repairs. Accordingly, the six months' notice was to run from when the negotiations were broken off. It was stated by Lord Cairns (at 448):

> 'It is the first principle upon which all courts of equity proceed, that if parties who have entered into definite and distinct terms involving certain legal results—certain penalties or legal forfeiture—afterwards by their own act or with their own consent enter upon a course

> of negotiation which has the effect of leading one of the parties to suppose that the strict rights arising under the contract will not be enforced, or will be kept in suspense, or held in abeyance, the person who otherwise might have enforced those rights will not be allowed to enforce them where it would be inequitable having regard to the dealings which have thus taken place between the parties.'

This statement offered possibilities of a broader doctrine, which can be summarized in the following way. Where X, who has contractual rights against Y, by his conduct induces Y to believe that these rights will be suspended or will not be strictly enforced for a certain period, he will be prevented from enforcing those rights until that period has elapsed.[2] This was Denning J's solution to the problem posed by *Foakes* v *Beer* (1884). The ingenuity of his approach cannot be questioned, but it sits uneasily beside *Foakes* v *Beer*, and it has created uncertainty.

5.8   It should not be forgotten that *Foakes* v *Beer* (1884) was decided seven years after *Hughes* v *Metropolitan Rly Co.* (1877) and the *Hughes* case was not seen as relevant in *Foakes*. It could hardly have been forgotten! It is more plausible that the House of Lords did not think that the two situations were truly analogous. All that was being sought in Hughes was relief from forfeiture: a forfeiture which could have been arrived at because of the landlord's promise.

5.9   It should also be recognized Denning J's judgment in *High Trees* (1947) extended the scope of estoppel (see para. **5.6**). His suggested doctrine of equitable estoppel was not restricted to representations of fact. Further, the doctrine of estoppel by representation requires detrimental reliance. In *High Trees* it seemed that there was no such reliance, and no such requirement.[3] In assessing Denning J's novel formulation of an equitable doctrine of promissory estoppel, it is fair to conclude that it was born with a far from unimpeachable pedigree. However, despite that, it has been the subject of s extensive discussion, both in later cases and in academic literature. Of course, it would cease to be needed in the part payment of a debt situation, if *Williams v Roffey* was suitably extended.

Scope of the doctrine

5.10   It is necessary to examine the scope, and limitations, of the doctrine. This is no easy matter as, despite much discussion of the doctrine, there have been relatively few cases decided exclusively on this ground.

The doctrine does not create a cause of action

5.11   By itself, promissory estoppel does not create a cause of action; if it did, it would be very difficult to reconcile with the doctrine of consideration. In *Combe* v *Combe* (1951),

---

2   See *Birmingham and District Land Co.* v *London and North Western Rly Co.* (1888).

3   See *Collier* v *P & MJ Wright Ltd* (2008) per Arden LJ at [39].

a husband agreed to pay his wife £100 a year (free of tax) at the time of their divorce. He failed to make any payment and she sued him, after six years, for £600 arrears. She gave no consideration for her husband's promise. She chose not to apply to the Divorce Court for maintenance; she did not refrain from doing so at her husband's request. (In fact, she had a greater annual income than her husband.) However, the trial judge, by applying the doctrine of promissory estoppel, held that the husband's promise was enforceable. The husband had made a clear promise, which he intended to be binding and to be acted upon, and which was acted upon by his wife.

5.12   This proposed extension of the doctrine was potentially far-reaching. Promissory estoppel was not being relied upon here as a defence; it was being used to create a cause of action. If the trial judge (Byrne J) in *Combe* v *Combe* had been correct, this would have been a fundamental challenge to the traditional requirement of consideration in contracts. The Court of Appeal allowed the husband's appeal, and Denning LJ (as he had now become) was quick to dispel fears that promissory estoppel posed such a threat to the doctrine of consideration. He explained that the *High Trees* principle did not create new causes of action where none previously existed. It operated only to prevent a person from insisting on his or her strict legal rights, when it would be unjust for him or her to do so in view of the dealings which had taken place between the parties. To this extent only was promissory estoppel intended to modify the legal requirement of consideration. Denning LJ continued ([1951] 2 KB 215 at 220):

> 'Seeing that the principle never stands alone as giving a cause of action in itself, it can never do away with the necessity of consideration when that is an essential part of the cause of action. The doctrine is too firmly fixed to be overthrown by a side-wind...it still remains a cardinal necessity of the formation of a contract, though not of its modification or discharge.'

This limitation on the principle of promissory estoppel is not accurately encapsulated by the phrase that it is 'a shield and not a sword'. For such a phrase tends to suggest, misleadingly, that the principle cannot be relied upon by a claimant. In fact, the limitation means only that promissory estoppel cannot stand alone as giving a cause of action.

5.13   The operation of estoppel was considered by the Court of Appeal in *Baird Textile Holdings Ltd* v *Marks and Spencer plc* (2001). Baird had been a leading supplier of garments to M & S for thirty years, when M & S suddenly notified them of its decision not to place any more orders. This led to an action by Baird claiming that M & S were precluded, both by contract and estoppel, from ending this long-term commercial relationship without reasonable notice. The lack of certainty in the alleged agreement between the parties meant that the claim in contract failed. Baird tried to establish an 'equity generated by estoppel' to protect its reliance interest, arguing that the doctrine of estoppel is a flexible one. Although the court (especially Judge LJ) expressed some interest in the potential development of estoppel and its flexibility, it rejected Baird's claim. It held that the alleged obligation lacked certainty and that the law, as it stands, 'does not enable the creation or recognition by estoppel of an enforceable right of the type and in the circumstances relied on in this case' (at [38]).[4]

Does it merely suspend rights?

5.14 It will be remembered that in *Hughes* v *Metropolitan Rly Co.* (1877) the landlord's right to treat the lease as forfeited was not lost altogether. The case simply decided that, due to his implied promise to the tenant, he could rely on those rights only after six months' notice from the breakdown of their negotiations. However, extinguishment of rights would seem to be what Denning J proposed in *High Trees* (1947), and in *D & C Builders Ltd* v *Rees* (1966), he was even more forthright in stating that the equitable principle was capable not simply of suspending a promisor's strict legal rights, but could operate 'so as to preclude the enforcement of them'. Such a view poses a direct challenge to the House of Lords' decision in *Foakes* v *Beer* (1884).

5.15 The effect of the principle on the promisor's rights was considered by the House of Lords in *Tool Metal Manufacturing Co. Ltd* v *Tungsten Electric Co. Ltd* (1955). The facts were:

> Tool Metal (TM) owned the patents of certain hard metal alloys and, under a contract in 1938, they granted Tungsten Electric (TE) a licence to manufacture and sell these metals. The agreement provided that the standard royalty to be paid by TE was 10 per cent, but that a higher rate of 30 per cent (described as 'compensation') was payable if TE used more than a specified amount of the alloys in any month. After the outbreak of war, TE stopped paying compensation to TM at the higher royalty rate, and TM agreed (in the national interest) not to enforce their right to 30 per cent, and to allow payment at the basic rate of 10 per cent. In 1944, TM proposed a new agreement which included compensation payments once again, but this was rejected by TE. In 1945, TM sought compensation (i.e. the waived 20 per cent) in respect of the material used by TE since June 1945. The Court of Appeal held that, under the principle of *Hughes* v *Metropolitan Rly Co.* (1877), TM's agreement to suspend compensation payments was binding in equity until proper notice was given of their intention to resume insistence upon their strict legal rights. (The draft agreement of 1944 did not amount to reasonable notice.) In 1950, TM claimed compensation from TE dating from January 1947. Had TM given reasonable notice to TE of their intention to insist once more on their strict legal rights?

The House of Lords held in favour of TM's claim to compensation. They had effectively revoked their promise, made during the war, to suspend their strict legal rights. The first action, brought in 1945, constituted reasonable notice of their intention. The case suggests that the promisor's strict legal rights are merely suspended, and can be resumed by giving adequate notice to the other party.

---

4 For further comment on *Baird Textile* v *Marks & Spencer*, see C. Mitchell, 'Leading a Life of its Own? The Rules of Reasonable Expectation in Contract Law' (2003) 23 OJLS 639 at 649–50.

5.16   In *Ajayi* v *RT Briscoe (Nigeria) Ltd* [1964] 1 WLR 1326 at 1330, the Privy Council stated a number of limitations on promissory estoppel. Amongst these was the qualification that the promisor is able to go back on his or her promise, on giving reasonable notice, providing the promisee with a reasonable opportunity of resuming his or her position, and the line has been taken that it is only if it is not possible for the promisee to resume his or her position, that the promise would be irrevocable.[5] However, in *Collier* v *P & MJ Wright (Holdings) Ltd* (2008) at [37], Arden LJ argued that although the effect of the doctrine 'is usually suspensory only', the creditor's right to recover the debt may be extinguished in circumstances where to go back on the promise is merely 'sufficiently inequitable'.[6]

Other limitations on the doctrine of promissory estoppel

5.17   For the principle to operate, there must be a promise (by words or conduct), and its effect must not be vague or equivocal.[7] In *IMT Shipping and Chartering GmbH* v *Chansung Shipping Co. Ltd* (2009) at [30] it was also stated that 'the promise must be intended to affect the parties' legal relations and must be understood to be a promise that will be acted upon by the promisee'. In *Northstar Land Ltd* v *Maitland Brooks* (2006), it was stressed that the promise (by words or conduct) has to be a 'clear, unequivocal, unambiguous promise or assurance which was intended to affect the legal relations between them or was reasonably understood by the other to have that effect' (Ward LJ at [21]).[8]

5.18   The principle is equitable in nature and therefore it should not be used to help a promisee, or debtor, who has behaved in an unconscionable or inequitable way. In *D & C Builders Ltd* v *Rees* (1966), for example, the defendant took advantage of the financial hardship of his creditor, who had little choice but to accept the defendant's offer of a lesser sum in full settlement of the debt. The decision of the Court of Appeal was consistent with the common law rule in *Foakes* v *Beer* (1884); the creditor was entitled to go back on his promise and sue successfully for the balance of the debt. However, the case was decided after the principle of promissory estoppel had been established, and Lord Denning's reason for finding in favour of the creditor was that the defendant had behaved inequitably and, therefore, should not be allowed to rely on the equitable defence.

Reliance

5.19   Promissory estoppel draws upon an analogy with the doctrine of estoppel by representation. As we have seen, the latter form of estoppel requires, inter alia, reliance by the representee to his or her detriment, but what of promissory estoppel? In *High Trees* (1947) itself there appears to have been no detriment suffered by the defendants; they simply paid less rent than

---

5   See *Brikom Investments Ltd* v *Carr* (1979).

6   For a critical view of this see A. Trukhtanov, '*Foakes v Beer*: Reform of Common Law at the Expense of Equity' (2008) 124 LQR 364 at 368.

7   See *Woodhouse AC Israel Cocoa SA* v *Nigerian Produce Marketing Co. Ltd* (1972).

8   See also *Kim v Chasewood Park Residents Ltd* (2013).

was agreed under the original lease.[9] They relied on the claimants' promise and Lord Denning argued that detriment is not required for the *High Trees* principle to operate (see *WJ Alan & Co. v El Nasr Export and Import Co* [1972] 2 QB 189 at 212).

5.20   This aspect of the doctrine is still a matter for debate. In *Collier v P & MJ Wright Ltd (Holdings) Ltd* (2008), Longmore LJ, although agreeing with the other judges that the applicant had a triable issue in relation to promissory estoppel, pointed out (at [45]–[46]) that there had been no 'detriment' to the applicant as a result of the alleged promise, and that there was no evidence that he had 'relied on it any meaningful way'. In contrast, as we have seen, Arden LJ took a less restrictive view (at [42]), arguing that for the creditor to go back on the alleged promise would, in itself, be inequitable, appearing to suggest that no detriment need be proved, and this would certainly seem to be the line which has to be taken if the defence is to be generally available in relation to the promise to accept part payment of a debt in discharge of the whole.

5.21   Perhaps the debate over whether the equitable principle requires detrimental reliance is not particularly apposite. The following reconciliation of views can be put forward. It is unlikely that 'detriment' is a strict requirement, and it may be inequitable to allow the promisor to go back on his promise even in the absence of detrimental reliance. It may simply be that it is just more likely to be inequitable to allow a promisor to resile from his or her promise where the other party has acted on the promise, not only in reliance, but also to his or her disadvantage or 'detriment'.[10] In *Emery v UCB Corporate Services Ltd* (2001), Peter Gibson LJ stated (at [28]):

> '[T]he fact that the promisee has not altered his position to his detriment is plainly most material in determining whether it would be inequitable for the [promisor] to be permitted to act inconsistently with his promise.'

Conclusion

5.22   There is much that remains unclear about the doctrine of promissory estoppel, and about its development. The approach of Arden LJ in *Collier* would open it up as a readier means of dealing with the problems posed by *Foakes v Beer*, but of course that would not be needed if *Williams v Roffey* was extended to the part payment of a debt situation.

5.23   Elsewhere, however, promissory estoppel has been used even more innovatively, to create rights. The decision of the High Court of Australia in *Walton Stores (Interstate) Ltd v Maher* (1988) represents an interesting and potentially far-reaching challenge to the traditional view of the relationship between estoppel and consideration. In that case, M (a builder) negotiated with W (a large retail company) for a construction and lease contract under which M would

---

9 For further discussion see M. Thompson, 'Estoppel and Change of Position' (2000) Conv and Prop Law 548.

10 For a useful discussion, see *Société Italo-Belge Pour le Commerce et l'Industrie SA (Antwerp) v Palm and Vegetable Oils (Malaysia) Sdn Bhd* [1982] 1 All ER 19 at 26–7 per Robert Goff J.

demolish an existing building on his own land, and build a new one to W's specifications, which would then be leased by W. The parties were very close to concluding the deal, but as no formal exchange of contracts had taken place, there was no binding agreement. Believing that W's completion of the relevant documents was no more than a formality, M started work on the project so as to enable him to meet the deadline for completion. He demolished the old building and laid the foundations for the new one. W was, in fact, having second thoughts about the deal, but did not communicate these to M despite being aware that M had already started work on his land. W told him of its decision to pull out only after he had carried out a substantial amount of work. Although no formal contract had been completed between the parties, M brought an action claiming specific performance or, as an alternative, damages against W. M argued that W had made an implied promise that it would enter into a binding agreement with him and that W was now estopped from resiling from this. The problem with this contention was that, as there was no existing contract between the parties, M was seeking to use the idea of estoppel to establish a cause of action.

5.24   The High Court of Australia found in favour of M, holding that in certain cases the ambit of promissory estoppel could be extended so as to permit the creation of a cause of action. It was argued (by the majority of the court) that as the decision was based on an estoppel and not on a contract, the absence of consideration was not a problem. The court held that the purpose of the equitable doctrine was to avoid the detriment which M suffered as a result of W's unconscionable behaviour in going back on its promise. (In other words, the object was not to compensate M for expectation loss for a breach of contract by W.) By this reasoning, the court found that promissory estoppel was not limited to cases where there is an existing legal relationship between the parties. It was argued that the doctrine has a wider function of providing equitable relief against unconscionable conduct, even in the context of non-contractual promises. One question is whether the English courts will be tempted, at some point, to adopt the Australian approach.[11]

⬆ Summary

- Part payment of an existing debt cannot amount to consideration for a creditor's promise to accept a lesser sum in full settlement (the rule in *Foakes* v *Beer* (1884)).

- The developments in *Williams* v *Roffey Bros* (1990) could, potentially, overtake the rule in *Foakes* v *Beer*.

- The rule in *Foakes* v *Beer* is capable of producing unfair results where a debtor has relied on a promise by the creditor to accept part payment in full satisfaction, and where the debtor has altered his or her position in reliance on such a promise.

- The *High Trees House* case (1947) saw the innovative, but controversial, decision of Denning J (as he then was) to the effect that a promise to accept a lesser sum might be binding under the equitable principle of promissory estoppel.

---

11 *Baird Textile Holdings Ltd* v *Marks and Spencer plc* [2001] EWCA Civ 274, [2002] 1 All ER (Comm) 737 at [38]–[40], [52]–[54] and [96]–[98].

- Promissory estoppel is not restricted to representations of fact, but applies also to promises and representations of intention.
- Promissory estoppel has created some uncertainty in the law, and the ambit of the doctrine is still unclear (as illustrated recently in *Collier v P and MJ Wright (Holdings) Ltd* (2008)).
- However, certain principles appear to be established in relation to the operation of the doctrine:
  - it does not create a cause of action
  - the effect of promissory estoppel is, generally, suspensory, but see comments in *Collier* v *P and MJ Wright (Holdings) Ltd* (2008)
  - there must be a promise (by words or conduct), which is clear and unambiguous
  - the promise must have been relied upon by the promisee
  - where a promisee has behaved inequitably, he or she cannot rely on the doctrine.

▶ Further reading

R. **Austen-Baker**, 'A Strange Sort of Survival for Pinnel's Case: *Collier v P & MJ Wright (Holdings) Ltd*' (2008) 71 MLR 611

E. **Cooke**, 'Estoppel and the Protection of Expectations' (1997) 17 LS 258

A. **Duthie**, 'Equitable Estoppel, Unconscionability and the Enforcement of Promises' (1988) 104 LQR 362

R. **Halson**, 'The Offensive Limits of Promissory Estoppel' [1999] LMCLQ 256

R. **Lee and L. Ho**, 'Disputes Over Family Homes Owned Through Companies: Constructive Trust or Promissory Estoppel?' (2009) 125 LQR 25

C. **Mitchell**, 'Leading a Life of its Own? The Rules of Reasonable Expectation in Contract Law' (2003) 23 OJLS 639

J. **O'Sullivan**, 'In Defence of *Foakes v Beer*' (1996) 55 CLJ 219

A. **Phipps**, 'Resurrecting the Doctrine of Common Law Forbearance' (2007) 123 LQR 286

A. **Robertson**, 'Reliance and Expectation in Estoppel Remedies' (1998) 18 LS 360

M. **Thompson**, 'Estoppel and Change of Position' (2000) Conv and Prop Law 548

A. **Trukhtanov**, '*Foakes v Beer*: Reform of the Common Law at the Expense of Equity' (2008) 124 LQR 364

Chapter 6

Intention to create legal relations

○ Introduction

6.1 Not all agreements are legally enforceable. We have seen that the main test of enforceability which is applied in our law of contract is the requirement of consideration. Even if the parties intend to enter into a contract, the law requires an element of exchange between the parties; this represents, in theory at least, the idea of reciprocal obligations. It might be thought that if this requirement is satisfied, and if the contract does not need to be expressed in a particular form, then an agreement will be enforceable. There is, however, a further requirement: an intention to create legal relations.

6.2 In fact, in commercial transactions it will generally be presumed (usually correctly) that the parties did intend to create legal relations, unless there is an express statement to the contrary. In the case of social and domestic agreements it will usually be presumed that they did not intend such consequences. In the vast majority of such agreements this will undoubtedly be a valid assumption. But although the word 'intention' is used, it is arguable that the test is really one of judicial policy. It is a method of restricting the enforceability of social and domestic arrangements. It could be argued that if both parties to an agreement provide consideration, there should be no need for any further requirement of an intention to create legal relations. But our law has not followed this line of reasoning. It has attempted to limit the enforceability of certain types of agreement. This may be a sound policy for pragmatic reasons, but it is difficult to see why it should be described today in terms of contractual intention.

Social and domestic agreements

6.3 Every day, people make family, or social, agreements. For instance, two friends might agree to operate a rota for taking their young children to school, so that only one car is required for each journey. Agreement and reciprocal obligations are both present here, but it is unlikely that the two friends intend any legal consequences to arise from their agreement.[1] A parent may agree to give 'pocket' money to his or her child in return for the performance of simple household chores; a person may agree to make a meal for a friend, who in turn promises to bring a bottle of wine.

6.4   In all of the above examples of social and domestic agreements, it is fair to say that the parties do not intend legal consequences to flow from their arrangements, but also if such agreements are broken, it is not an appropriate use of the legal process to allow one party to pursue another.[2] To prevent frivolous claims, and a waste of court time, it is better that disputes over such arrangements are left to the parties to settle for themselves, informally.

6.5   However, in other instances of family and domestic agreements, the presumed lack of intention to contract is more questionable. A significant example of the court strongly embracing the exclusion of a finding of a contractual relationship, in the context of an agreement between husband and wife, is *Balfour* v *Balfour* [1919] 2 KB 571. In that case, the facts were:

> D, who worked as a civil servant stationed abroad, left his wife (C) in England; C had been advised by her doctor that her health was not sufficiently good to accompany her husband. Before departing, D promised to pay C an allowance of £30 a month whilst they were apart. C sued D for breach of his promise. The trial judge found that there was consideration given for D's promise and he ruled in C's favour.

The Court of Appeal reversed the trial judge's decision, and held that D's promise was not enforceable. Even if C had given consideration for the promise (which is arguable), there was no intention to create legal relations. It was seen as a purely domestic agreement. Lord Atkin stated (at 578):

> '[T]here are agreements between parties which do not result in contracts within the meaning of that term in our law…and one of the most usual forms of agreement which does not constitute a contract appears to me to be the arrangements which are made between husband and wife…and they do not result in contracts even though there may be what as between other parties would constitute consideration for the agreement.'

6.6   Although the justification for the decision in *Balfour* v *Balfour* (1919) was expressed in terms of the parties' lack of contractual intention, it is clear from other parts of Lord Atkin's

---

1   Of interest on a related issue, see *Buckpitt* v *Oates* (1968); and *Coward* v *Motor Insurers' Bureau* (1963). Cases on this issue have tended to arise as a result of accidents caused by the driver's negligence. But now see Road Traffic Act 1988, s 149.

2   But, surprisingly, a prosecution for theft may succeed in the circumstances where a man gives his 'de facto' wife a sum of money for her to pay certain debts and to meet household expenses and, instead of doing so, she spends the money on herself. In *Cullen* (1972) (unreported), the Court of Appeal seems to have assumed that the defendant was under an obligation to deal with the money in the manner prescribed and in no other way. Her conviction for theft overlooked the fact that it arose out of a domestic arrangement which was not intended to create legal relations. Her behaviour could not have amounted to a breach of contract—so why should it have been regarded as theft?

judgment that he was concerned with the perceived inappropriateness of the husband-wife agreement being governed by contract law ('each house is a domain into which the King's writ does not seek to run'), and by the prospect of the 'small courts of this country' being inundated with domestic disputes (over 'housekeeping' arrangements and the like). Although he perhaps overstated the likelihood of such a flood of litigation, there is a sound policy reason for encouraging trivial domestic disputes to be settled by the parties, without recourse to law. But did the agreement in *Balfour* v *Balfour* fall into this category? It was clearly a borderline case, and the court's bald assertion that the parties lacked contractual intention is not particularly helpful.

6.7   However, *Balfour* v *Balfour* (1919) was distinguished in *Merritt* v *Merritt* (1970), where the parties were separated at the time of the agreement:

> A husband (H) left his wife (W), moving out of the house that was in their joint names, and went to live with another woman. H and W later met to discuss their financial arrangements for the future. They agreed that H would pay £40 per month to W, and W was to make the outstanding mortgage payments on the house out of this sum. W insisted upon a written acknowledgement by H of their agreement; this stated: 'In consideration of the fact that you will pay all charges in connection with the house…until such time as the mortgage repayment has been completed…I will agree to transfer the property into your sole ownership.' W paid off the mortgage, but H refused to transfer the house to her.

The Court of Appeal held that W was the sole owner of the matrimonial home based on the enforceable agreement made between H and W. The court stated that the *Balfour* principle does not apply in the case of couples who are not on friendly terms, but are about to separate or, indeed, have separated.[3]

6.8   More broadly, it should be recognized that social circumstances have changed markedly since *Balfour* v *Balfour* was decided in relation to a 'Victorian marriage'.

> 'Where the emphasis was on status, it is now on autonomy. For role identification we now have role distance. The "self" and individual choice have replaced role and obligation as central organizing concepts.'[4]

There may, today, be many financial arrangements between husbands and wives which should readily be seen to involve an intention to create legal relations. In *Radmacher* v *Granatino* (2010), Lady Hale commented (at [142]):

> 'There is nothing to stop a husband and wife from making legally binding arrangements, whether by contract or settlement, to regulate their property and affairs while they are still

---

3   A further limitation of the *Balfour* principle relates to the situation where parties carry out promises, under what would otherwise be an unenforceable domestic agreement, by making improvements or additions to the matrimonial home. See *Pettitt* v *Pettitt* [1970] AC 777 and especially Lord Diplock's comments at 822.

4   M. Freeman 'Contracting in the Haven: *Balfour* v *Balfour* Revisited' in R. Halson (ed.), *Exploring the Boundaries of Contract*, Dartmouth, 1996, p. 75.

> together... These days, the commonest example of this is an agreement to share the owner-ship or tenancy of the matrimonial home, bank accounts, savings or other assets. Agreements for housekeeping or personal allowances, on the other hand, might run into difficulties.'[5]

6.9   Of course, the presumption against an intention to create legal relations is general to the domestic sphere, and not confined to the relationship of husband and wives. In *Jones* v *Padavatton* [1969] 1 WLR 328, the facts were:

> A mother (M) promised her daughter (D) that she would give her an allowance of $200 a month if she gave up her job in Washington DC and went to England to study for the Bar. (M lived in Trinidad, where she hoped D would practise when qualified.) Despite not wishing to leave Washington, D accepted M's proposal and went to England and commenced her studies to become a barrister. Two years later, M and D varied the agreement. M bought a house in London for D to live in, and by renting out some of the rooms, D was able to maintain herself instead of receiving the $200 a month. Three years later, M and D quarrelled, and M claimed possession of the house. D had still not passed her Bar exams.

The Court of Appeal found in M's favour. It was held (by the majority) that the arrangement between the parties was not intended to have legal consequences and therefore M was entitled to possession. This followed the broader reasoning in *Balfour* v *Balfour* (1919). The opening comments of Danckwerts LJ (at 329) reveal the majority's concern that disagreements of this type should not be aired in a court of law. He stated:

> 'This action...is really deplorable. The points of difference between the two parties appear to be comparatively small, and it is distressing that they could not settle their differences amicably and avoid the bitterness and expense which is involved in this dispute carried as far as this court.'

The case is instructive. It shows not only the general presumption that family agreements are not enforceable, but also illustrates, again, that there are policy reasons at work. In fact, although Salmon LJ arrived at the same decision as the other two judges, he reached it by way of a different route. He thought that there was an intention to create legal relations at the time of the original agreement, but that this agreement was to last only for a reasonable time and it had therefore ended by the time that five years had elapsed. M could never have intended to pay indefinitely whilst her daughter made repeated and unsuccessful efforts to pass the exams.

6.10   Salmon LJ's judgment seems to represent a much sounder basis for deciding the case, than those of his two colleagues. If the test is really one of an intention to create legal relations, then surely the agreement (at least initially) satisfied this requirement. D reluctantly gave up a good job and commenced studies in England at M's request. If M had ceased to pay D her

---

allowance within a few months of D arriving in England, was it really intended by the parties that D would have no legal redress?

6.11   Of course, the presumption against an intention to create legal relations extends beyond the family sphere into the social one, and it can be difficult to draw a line between those where a contract will be found, and those where it will not. In *Simpkins* v *Pays* (1955), a lodger (C), her landlady, and her landlady's granddaughter entered a competition run by a newspaper. Their weekly entries were a joint effort with an agreement that, if successful, the prize would be shared. The entries were sent in the landlady's name and she refused to share the prize when they won. It was held that there was a binding agreement, and that C was entitled to claim one-third of the prize.

6.12   No contract was found in the more recent case of *Wilson* v *Burnett* (2007). The case involved a claim that three friends had made a binding agreement that they would share any winnings equally between them if they were successful in an evening spent playing bingo. One of them won not only a small local prize of £153, but also a very large national prize of £101,211 during the course of the evening. The claim of her two friends that this prize should be divided equally was unsuccessful at first instance, partly on the basis of conflicting evidence about whether there was in fact a binding agreement. The Court of Appeal (May LJ giving judgment) dismissed the appeal of the two friends, stating that the issue was essentially a narrow one of whether there was a binding agreement between the three friends, made prior to playing bingo, of sufficient certainty. It was held that, on the available evidence, the conversations between the parties fell short of concluding a binding and enforceable agreement.

6.13   In *Wilson* v *Burnett,* there was an issue of uncertainty, and it is likely that many agreements between friends, or members of a family, are not enforceable because they are too uncertain. In *Gould* v *Gould* (1969) a husband promised his wife, when leaving her, £15 per week as long as his business was all right. (The actual words used were disputed.) The majority of the court thought that the vagueness of the arrangement showed a lack of contractual intention, but uncertainty may, in itself, prevent a contract being found. In *Jones v Padavatton,* the second agreement, concerning occupation of the house and the use of funds derived from letting out rooms, might have been regarded as unenforceable because of its evident vagueness. There were several details left unsettled, and perhaps this would have been a better basis for allowing M's claim for possession.

6.14   Lack of certainty in the agreement may be a basis, in itself, for saying that there is no contract, or it may provide evidence to underpin the presumption against intention to create legal relations. In contrast, significant reliance may point towards a finding that there was an intention to create legal relations. In *Tanner* v *Tanner* (1975), D gave birth to twins of which C was the father. D and C were unmarried, but D took C's name. C bought a house for them both to live in, with the children, and D gave up her rent-controlled flat. Later, C moved out and wanted to evict D (and he succeeded at first instance). On appeal, the court held that C was contractually bound by his promise to D, who was awarded compensation (having already been evicted).

6.15 The important fact about cases of this type is that one of the parties to the agreement has acted in reliance upon the other's promise and, in doing so, has given up something of value. Although such actions do not appear to have impacted on the views of the majority in *Jones* v *Padavatton* (1969), it can be argued that they provide objective evidence of an intention to create legal relations. However, it can also be suggested that, in cases of this type, the general policy of denying legal consequences to domestic agreements would produce such an unjust result that the courts depart from their general policy. In *Parker* v *Clark* (1960), the Clarks invited a younger couple, the Parkers, to share their house. (Mrs C was the aunt of Mrs P.) In order to go ahead with the arrangement the Parkers sold their own house. It was held that the agreement was legally binding.

Commercial agreements

6.16 In commercial transactions, it is generally presumed that there is an intention to create legal relations. The courts are anxious to uphold the validity of commercial dealings. But in certain situations, the general presumption may be rebutted. For example, manufacturers of products may make boastful, but vague claims about the effectiveness of their products. These statements (known as 'mere puffs'), contained in advertisements and other promotional literature, will generally not be regarded as having any legal effect.[6]

6.17 However, in exceptional cases, what might otherwise be a 'mere puff' will be expressed in such a way that the courts will infer a definite intention to create legal relations. In *Carlill* v *Carbolic Smoke Ball Co.* (1893), the company's advertisement of a reward was held to be an offer to members of the public who bought the smoke ball and used it in the prescribed manner, and still caught influenza. The company's attempt to argue that there was no contractual intention was rejected; the claimant was entitled to recover the reward. The fact that the company stated that it had deposited £1,000 with its bank as evidence of its 'sincerity in the matter', indicated that the advertisement was more than just a mere puff.

6.18 Problems may arise in determining whether an agreement is of a commercial, rather than a social nature. In *Sadler* v *Reynolds* (2005), a dispute arose between the claimant (S) and the defendant businessman (R) over an oral agreement that S should be the 'ghost' writer of R's autobiography. S claimed that he had proposed the title of the book to R and outlined its first chapter, before R changed his mind and entered into an agreement with another author to write the book. The case involved, inter alia, a dispute over whether there was a contract, and Slade J held that an oral contract had been concluded on terms that the profits would be divided equally between S and R. Of interest here, is the judge's comment that there was initially some uncertainty over whether the parties' agreement was a commercial transaction or merely a social exchange. The judge stated that, in these circumstances, the onus was on S to establish an intention to create legal relations, but that this burden would be less onerous than if the

---

6   See *Lexmead (Basingstoke) Ltd* v *Lewis* (1982).

agreement had arisen out of a purely social relationship. On the facts, the judge held that S had established an intention to create legal relations.[7]

6.19   In some commercial situations the parties might, as part of their agreement, expressly deny that they intend to create legal relations.[8] For example, in *Jones v Vernons Pools* [1938] 2 All ER 626, C claimed to have filled in his pools coupon and to have sent it off, but the Vernon Pools company alleged that they had not received it. (C's entry, if received, would have been successful.) It was a condition of entry, known to C, that the sending in of the coupon should not be attended by or give rise to any legal relationship, or be legally enforceable, or be the subject of litigation. It was stated in the conditions of entry, therefore, that the arrangements of the pools were binding in honour only. Atkinson J held that the agreed conditions prevented C from succeeding against the defendants in any action to enforce payment of prize money. As there was no intention to create legal relations, there was no need for the court to decide whether C did, in fact, post the coupon. Atkinson J stated (at 629):

> 'It seems to me that the purpose of these rules [for entry] is this. The defendants wish it to be made quite clear that they are conducting these pools on certain clear lines, and they intend to say by these conditions: "Everybody who comes into these pools must understand that there are no legal obligations either way in connection with these pools...money must be sent in [with entries] on the clearest understanding that this is a gentlemen's agreement, an agreement which carries with it no legal obligations on either side, and confers no legal rights".'

6.20   In *Rose and Frank Co v JR Crompton & Bros Ltd* [1925] AC 445, an arrangement was made between an American company and an English company whereby the American company was established as sole agent for the sale, in the USA, of tissues (for carbonizing paper) supplied by the English company. Their original agreement was extended and a document was drawn up to regulate their dealings. This stated:

> 'This arrangement is not entered into, nor is the memorandum written, as a formal or legal agreement, and shall not be subject to legal jurisdiction in the Law Courts either of the U.S. or England, but it is only a definite expression and record of the purpose and intention of the...parties concerned, to which each honourably pledge themselves...'.

A dispute eventually arose between the parties and the English company determined the agreement without notice. Before this, the American firm had placed an order, which had been accepted by the English firm. The American company brought an action for breach of

---

7   For further discussion, see A. Taylor, 'Law of Ghosts' (2005) 16 Entertainment LR 132.

8   In agreements for the sale of houses, for instance, it is a common practice to state that they are 'subject to contract'. The agreement will not have legal force until a formal contract has been entered into. Also, in *Regalian Properties plc v London Dockland Development Corpn* (1995), an agreement for a building development was 'subject to contract'. The project was later abandoned and P's claim for wasted expenditure was unsuccessful, as such costs were incurred at their own risk (see **Chapter 3**).

contract. The House of Lords held that the agreement did not constitute a legally binding contract.[9] Accordingly, there was no obligation on the American company to order goods, or on the English firm to accept an order. But any actual transaction between the parties gave rise to the usual legal rights, 'for the fact that it was not of obligation to do the transaction did not divest the transaction when done of its ordinary legal significance' (per Lord Phillimore at 455).

6.21   If a plainly commercial transaction is not intended by the parties to give rise to legal relations, the courts will require clear evidence to that effect. This is illustrated by *Edwards* v *Skyways Ltd* (1964), where the facts were:

> C was employed as a pilot by the defendant company ('the company'), and he was a member of the company's contributory pension fund. The company informed C that he was to be made redundant. It also promised C an 'ex gratia' payment 'equivalent to' (the actual words were disputed) the defendant's contribution to the pension fund. Later, the defendant company failed to make the 'ex gratia' payment to C. The company defended C's action for breach of contract by arguing that the agreement, about the 'ex gratia' payment, was not intended to create legal relations, and that it was too vague to be enforceable.

It was held that where (as in this case) the subject of the agreement between the parties related to business matters, the onus of negativing contractual intention was on the defendant company. It was a heavy onus and one which the company had failed to discharge. The court found in favour of C. The fact that the payment was described as 'ex gratia' did not show that the company's promise lacked contractual intention.

6.22   The issue of contractual intention has been considered by the courts in relation to the use, in business, of 'letters of comfort'.[10] This is a practice which occurs where a party is considering lending money to X, and receives some encouragement, in the form of a 'comfort letter' from Y, to go ahead and do so. This can be illustrated by the facts of *Kleinwort Benson Ltd* v *Malaysia Mining Corpn Sdn Bhd* [1989] 1 All ER 785:

> The claimant merchant bank (KB) agreed with the defendants (D) to a make a loan of up to £10 million available to D's wholly owned subsidiary (M) which traded in tin on the London Metal Exchange. As part of this credit arrangement, D provided KB with two 'letters of comfort' which both stated, in para. 3, that 'it is our policy to ensure that the business of [M] is at all times in a position to meet its liabilities to you under the [loan facility] arrangements'. A year later, the tin market collapsed, at a time when M owed KB the whole amount of the facility. M went into liquidation, and KB sought from D payment of the amount owing. At first instance, the court held that KB could recover the money from D, who appealed on the ground that the letters of comfort did not have contractual effect.

---

9 Contrast *Home Insurance Co.* v *Administration Asigurarilor* (1983).

10 See also I. Brown, 'The Letter of Comfort: Placebo or Promise?' [1990] JBL 281.

It was held, allowing D's appeal, that the letters of comfort in question did not constitute a con-tractual promise. Ralph Gibson LJ stated (at 792):

> 'In my judgment the defendants made a statement as to what their policy was, and did not in para 3 of the comfort letter expressly promise that such policy would be continued in future. It is impossible to make up for the lack of express promise by implying such a promise, and indeed, no such promise was pleaded. My conclusion rests on what is the proper effect and meaning which . . . is to be given to para 3 of the comfort letters.'

It might be argued that as the letters occurred in a commercial context, the usual presump-tion of contractual intention should have applied, and that there should have been more than just a moral responsibility on D's part to meet M's debt. Of course the parties can, if they wish, expressly disclaim any contractual intention, but is it clear that this was done in the *Kleinwort Benson* case? In each case, the specific wording will be important.

6.23   There may be commercial transactions where the value of the goods involved is so small that the parties are most unlikely, in practice, to take the matter to court, but the question of whether there was a contract, and intention to create legal relations, may come before a court for other reasons. For example, a 'free gift' may be offered, as part of a sales promotion, to purchasers of certain goods, it may be asked if there is any intention to create legal relations, in relation to it. This issue arose in *Esso Petroleum Co. Ltd* v *Customs and Excise Comrs* (1976), where the facts were:

> Esso distributed millions of 'World Cup' coins to petrol stations which supplied their (Esso's) petrol, as part of a sales promotion scheme. One coin (depicting a member of the English soccer team) was to be given away with every four gallons of petrol bought by motorists. The coins were of little value, but the scheme was potentially lucrative because motorists were encouraged to buy Esso petrol in order to collect the set of thirty coins. Large posters and extensive advertisements were used to publicize the scheme. The Customs and Excise Commissioners claimed that the coins were chargeable to purchase tax (under the relevant legislation) on the basis that they had been 'produced in quantity for general sale'.

On the point of tax law in question, the House of Lords held that the coins had not been 'pro-duced . . . for . . . sale' (within the relevant legislation) and were not therefore chargeable to pur-chase tax. The majority held (with Lord Fraser dissenting) that this was because the coins were not supplied under a contract of 'sale'. The consideration for the transfer of the coins was not a money payment, but the undertaking by the customer to enter into a collateral contract to buy the requisite amount of petrol. However, the majority were then divided on whether there was any intention to create a legally binding contract (of any sort) to supply the coins to custom-ers who bought the petrol. The majority, including Lord Fraser, appear to have favoured the view that there was contractual intention. But it is possible that the dissenting judges (Lords Dilhorne and Russell) were correct in their interpretation of the transaction between the par-ties. Their lordships doubted whether there was any intention to create legal relations because of the way in which the advertisements referred to 'free gifts', and also because of the lack of intrinsic value of the coins.

Summary

- It is usually stated that the parties to a contract must intend to create legal relations.

- In fact, the law proceeds on the basis of two rebuttable presumptions: that parties to commercial transactions *do* intend to create legal relations; and that parties to social or domestic agreements do *not* intend legal consequences.

- The courts do not want to get involved in domestic disputes and, generally, this is consistent with the parties' intentions.

- But there are certain situations where this policy is capable of producing an unfair outcome.

- In some cases it is the element of reliance which provides the objective evidence of an intention to create legal relations, and is capable of rebutting the general presumption.

- In commercial transactions there is a general presumption that the parties intend to create legal relations. This is rebuttable, but the courts will require clear evidence of this.

Further reading

I. **Brown**, 'The Letter of Comfort: Placebo or Promise?' [1990] JBL 281

M. **Freeman**, 'Contracting in the Haven: *Balfour v Balfour* Revisited' in R. Halson (ed.), *Exploring the Boundaries of Contract*, Dartmouth, 1996, pp. 68–82

S. **Hedley**, 'Keeping Contract in its Place—*Balfour v Balfour* and the Enforceability of Informal Agreements' (1985) 5 OJLS 391

D. **McClean**, 'In the Service of Saints: A Consideration of the Draft Ecclesiastical Offices (Terms of Service) Measure—the Legal Background' (2008) ECCLJ 310

M. **Nash**, 'Family Trouble' (2007) 157 NLJ 620

Pey-Woan Lee, 'Letters of Comfort Revisited' [2002] LMCLQ 169

A. **Taylor**, 'Law of Ghosts' (2005) 16 Entertainment LR 132

Chapter 7

Express and implied terms

Introduction

7.1   Here we are concerned with the contents of the contract, its terms and the obligations undertaken by the parties. They may be either express or implied, and both possibilities are considered.

Express terms

Introduction

7.2   As we have seen, most contracts can be made orally or in writing, or there may be a combination of oral and written terms. The question of whether a written clause is a contract term is dealt with in relation to exemption clauses, a context in which that question often arises (see **Chapter 9**). Here we are concerned with the spoken word and the problem of determining whether what was said was part of the contract or was a mere representation.

7.3   It is possible that a statement may be found to be a term not of the main contract, but of a collateral contract. Collateral contracts often serve to avoid some difficulty involved in finding that the statement is a term of the main contract (for example, the statement may be found to be a term of a collateral contract where the person injured is not a party to the main contract, thus evading the rule relating to privity of contract (see **Chapter 17**)). Collateral contracts are considered at para. **7.17**.

Representations and terms

7.4   A statement made before the contract may become a term of the contract or it may be a mere representation. It may relate to some present fact or to some future act, event, or circumstance.

If the statement is a term, a remedy will lie for breach of contract if it is untrue or does not occur. If it is a mere representation, and it is untrue or does not occur, there will be no remedy for breach, although a remedy may be available for misrepresentation (see **Chapter 13**). The basic test for distinguishing terms and representations is that of the parties' intention. It is the type of test which leaves considerable scope for the court to be influenced by the result which will ensue from a decision. Such influence particularly needs to be borne in mind when considering some of the older decisions where terms were found. Before the mid-1960s, damages for misrepresentation were much more limited in their availability than they are now, with the result that the courts had a greater impetus to find that the statement in question was a term and not merely a representation.

7.5   A preliminary point should be made on the terminology adopted by the courts. The question whether or not X's statement was a term of X's contract with Y may be put in terms of whether X warranted what he or she was saying. 'Warrant' is being used simply to mean promise or guarantee, i.e. it is being used to ask whether X intended to take upon him or herself, the risk that the statement was untrue, or would not be fulfilled, by making it a term. Similarly, 'warranty' may be used simply to mean a term of the contract, but some care must be taken. The courts also use it more technically, to contrast with condition and innominate term, to mean a term with a particular legal consequence flowing from its breach (i.e. only a claim in damages with no right to terminate the contract for its breach, as there would be for breach of a condition, and might be for breach of an innominate term). To avoid confusion, 'term' will be used here to denote the simple fact that a statement was a term, but not to indicate that it was of any particular type. The use of 'warranty' in that sense will be avoided wherever possible.

The basic test

7.6   The basic test of whether a statement is a term is one of intention. This was recognized by the House of Lords in *Heilbut, Symons, & Co.* v *Buckleton* (1913). The facts were:

> Heilbut, Symons, & Co. were rubber merchants who were underwriting an issue of shares in a company called the Filisola Rubber and Produce Estates Ltd. Heilbut, Symons, & Co. contacted Johnston, their manager in Liverpool, and told him to obtain applications for shares in the Filisola company. Johnston had seen a prospectus for that company but he did not have one in the Liverpool office. Buckleton telephoned Johnston and said, 'I understand you are bringing out a rubber company'. The reply was 'we are'. On being informed that Johnston did not have any prospectuses, Buckleton enquired 'if it was all right'. The response was, 'we are bringing it out'. Buckleton replied, 'that is good enough for me'. After Buckleton had bought shares in the company, it was discovered that there were considerably fewer rubber trees on the estate than the prospectus had stated. The shares fell in value. Buckleton tried to claim damages from Heilbut, Symons, & Co. on the basis (a) of a fraudulent misrepresentation, or (b) that Heilbut, Symons, & Co. had contracted with him that the company was a rubber company.

The claim of fraud was dismissed at first instance, but the assertion that there had been a breach of a contract term—that the company was a rubber company—was successful until the case reached the House of Lords. There it was held that the company could not properly be termed a 'rubber company' and there was no contractual promise by Heilbut, Symons, & Co. that the company was a rubber company. When Buckleton had spoken to Johnston on the telephone, what had clearly been important was that the company was being 'brought out' by Heilbut, Symons, & Co. They had not been considering whether it should, or should not, technically be referred to as a 'rubber company'.

7.7 It should be emphasized that the intention test is not subjective, but objective.[1] Denning LJ in *Oscar Chess Ltd* v *Williams* [1957] 1 WLR 370 said at 375:

> 'It is sometimes supposed that the tribunal must look into the minds of the parties to see what they themselves intended. That is a mistake…The question of whether a warranty was intended depends on the conduct of the parties, on their words and behaviour, rather than on their thoughts. If an intelligent bystander would reasonably infer that a warranty was intended, that will suffice.'

The objective nature of the test is well illustrated by *Thake* v *Maurice* [1986] 1 All ER 497. In that case, the facts were:

> Mr and Mrs Thake did not wish to have any more children, and so Mr Thake decided to have an operation which would sterilize him. The defendant, the surgeon who undertook the operation, had explained beforehand that it was irreversible. He had not told them that there was a slight possibility that it might reverse itself naturally even after the usual checks on Mr Thake's sperm count had shown that the operation had been successful. The couple believed that Mr Thake must be sterile after the operation, and they did not realize that Mrs Thake was pregnant until it was too late for her to have an abortion. Mr Thake's operation had been carried out with due care, and his sperm count had been correctly checked, but a natural reversal of the operation had subsequently occurred.

Mr and Mrs Thake argued that it had been a term of their contract with the surgeon that the operation would render Mr Thake sterile and that term had been breached. The Court of Appeal did not accept that argument. It was held that the surgeon had merely guaranteed to carry out the operation with care and skill. However, Mr and Mrs Thake were awarded damages on the basis that the surgeon had been negligent in failing to warn them of the possibility of natural reversal.

7.8 On the question of whether the surgeon had guaranteed that the operation would render Mr Thake sterile, the court recognized the objective nature of the search for intention as the determinant of the terms of the contract. Mr and Mrs Thake both left the surgeon's consulting

---

1   On objectivity in contract, see generally W. Howarth. 'The Meaning of Objectivity in Contract' (1984) 100 LQR 265; A. De Moor, 'Intention in the Law of Contract: Elusive or Illusory?' (1990) 106 LQR 632.

room thinking that he had guaranteed that the operation would render Mr Thake sterile, but, equally, the surgeon had not intended to give any such guarantee. Both parties held opposing views of what the terms were. Objectively, no term guaranteeing the success of the operation was found. The court thought that a reasonable person, in the position of Mr and Mrs Thake, would have known that medical science was not certain and would not have thought that the surgeon was guaranteeing the success of the operation. Nourse LJ said (at 511):

> 'The function of the court in ascertaining, objectively, the meaning of words used by contracting parties is one of everyday occurrence. But it is often exceedingly difficult to discharge it where the subjective understandings of the parties are clear and opposed. Here the [claimants] understood that Mr Thake would be permanently sterile. The defendant himself recognised they would have been left with that impression. On the other hand, he did not intend, and on the state of his knowledge he could not have intended, to guarantee that that would be the case. Both the understanding and the intention appear to them, as individuals, to have been entirely reasonable, but an objective interpretation must choose between them. In the end the question seems to be reduced to one of determining the extent of the knowledge which is to be attributed to the reasonable person standing in the position of the plaintiffs.'

This illustrates the objective approach and the need for it.

Indicators of intention

7.9   The test of the parties' intention can be difficult to apply, but certain factors are regarded by the courts as indicators of whether a statement was intended as a term. Some of the factors have been given more importance than others but, as Lord Moulton emphasized in *Heilbut, Symons, & Co.* v *Buckleton* [1913] AC 30 at 50, none of them is decisive. They are all only aids to establish the parties' intention. With that in mind we may now consider some of the factors the courts have recognized as indicators of whether a statement was intended as a term.

Importance of the statement

7.10   It may be clear to both sides that a certain factor was very important to one of the parties in the decision to contract. A statement on that factor, by the other party, may then well be found to have been intended as a guarantee, as a term. In *Bannerman* v *White* (1861):

> Brewers were refusing to use hops contaminated with sulphur. Bannerman offered hops to White, and White asked if sulphur had been used to grow them. Bannerman said 'no' and White said that he would not even discuss the price if it had. A contract was made for the sale of the hops; later it was established that Bannerman had forgotten that sulphur had been used in growing a small proportion of them.

It was held that it was a term of the contract that sulphur had not been used in growing the hops. It had been clear to both parties that the question of the use of sulphur was very important to

White and that he would not have contracted without the assurance that no sulphur had been used on Bannerman's hops.

Reliance

7.11　An indication that a statement by one party can be relied upon, and need not be verified, may show that it should be regarded as a term. For example, a prospective seller may indicate to a potential buyer that he or she can rely upon the seller's statement as to the condition of the goods and need not check the goods. This may then lead to the conclusion that the seller's statement is a term of the contract of sale. In *Schawel v Reade* [1913] 2 IR 64:

> The claimant wished to purchase a horse for stud purposes. He visited the defendant's stables and while he was inspecting a horse, Mallow Man, the defendant said, 'You need not look for anything; the horse is perfectly sound. If there was anything the matter with the horse I would tell you.' The claimant ceased his inspection and three weeks later he bought Mallow Man. The horse was unfit for stud purposes because of a hereditary eye disease.

The House of Lords held that the soundness of the horse was a term of the contract. It was clearly indicated that the buyer could rely upon the seller, i.e. that the seller was taking the risk of the horse being unsound. Lord Moulton said (at 86):

> 'The essence of such warranty is that it becomes plain by the words, and the action, of the parties that it is intended that in the purchase the responsibility of the soundness shall rest upon the vendor; and how . . . could a vendor more clearly indicate that he is prepared and intends to take upon himself the responsibility of the soundness than by saying: "You need not look at that horse because it is perfectly sound", and sees that the purchaser thereupon desists from his immediate independent examination.'

This can be contrasted with *Ecay* v *Godfrey* (1947) where a boat was being sold. Although the seller, Mr Godfrey, said that it was sound, he also suggested a survey to the buyer, Señor Ecay. It was held that it was not a term of the contract of sale that the boat was sound. Equally, a similar conclusion may be reached where, although the statement of soundness is not followed by any express warning to carry out a check, there is a trade practice that such statements are not terms.[2]

Relative knowledge of the parties

7.12　It is relevant to consider the question of which of the two parties was in the best position to know or ascertain the truth of a statement made. It is connected with the above indicator. It could be put in terms of whether it was reasonable to rely upon the statement made, or whether one party can be taken to have assumed the risk of the statement being untrue. The court will be more inclined to find that the statement is a term if it was made by the person in the best position to have ascertained its truth. Two cases can be contrasted here: *Oscar Chess Ltd* v *Williams* (1957) and *Dick Bentley Productions Ltd* v *Harold Smith (Motors) Ltd* (1965).

2　Trade practice seems to be the explanation of *Hopkins* v *Tanqueray* (1864).

7.13   In *Oscar Chess Ltd* v *Williams* (1957):

> The defendant sold a Morris car to the claimant, a car dealer who was familiar with the car as he had been given lifts in it. The log book had shown it to be a 1948 model and the defendant had innocently described it as such and produced the log book. Before the defendant acquired the car the log book had been tampered with and the car was, in fact, a 1939 model. There was no difference in appearance between a 1948 and a 1939 model. The claimant would have paid £115 less for a 1939 model than for a 1948 model. Eight months after the sale, the claimant discovered the alteration of the log book and sought £115 from the defendant for breach of a term that the car was a 1948 model.

The Court of Appeal held that there was no term that the car was a 1948 model. The defendant was in no better position than the claimant to assess the age of the car. The defendant had simply relied upon the date stated in the log book. There was no reason to suppose that he had intended to take upon himself the risk that the car was not a 1948 model by making the age of the car a term of the contract.

7.14   *Oscar Chess Ltd* v *Williams* (1957) contrasts with *Dick Bentley Productions Ltd* v *Harold Smith (Motors) Ltd* (1965) where the person making the statement was in the better position to establish its truth, and the statement was found to be a term. In *Dick Bentley*:

> Dick Bentley asked a car dealer, Smith, to find him a well-vetted Bentley car. Smith found a car and showed it to Dick Bentley, telling him that since a new engine had been fitted the car had done only 20,000 miles, the mileage shown on the odometer. Dick Bentley purchased the car, which proved to be unsatisfactory, and it was discovered that it had done far more than the mileage shown on the odometer since the new engine had been fitted.

The Court of Appeal held that the mileage had been a term of the contract. The case was distinguished from *Oscar Chess Ltd* v *Williams* (1957) on the basis of the position of the person making the statement. A car dealer was in a far better position than his customer to establish the accuracy of the mileage recorded on the odometer.

The parol evidence rule

7.15   Where there is a written document containing contract terms, the question arises whether evidence can be given to show that the parties agreed to additional terms which are not contained within the written document. It has been said that 'it is firmly established as a rule of law that parol evidence cannot be admitted to add to, vary or contradict a deed or other written document' (*Jacobs* v *Batavia and General Plantations Trust Ltd* [1924] 1 Ch 287 at 295 per Lawrence J). However, although this is commonly referred to as the parol evidence rule, its status as a rule is very doubtful. On closer examination it does nothing more than express a presumption. In *Gillespie Bros & Co.* v *Cheney, Eggar & Co.* [1896] 2 QB 59, Lord Russell CJ said (at 62):

> '[A]lthough when the parties arrive at a definite written contract the implication or presump-
> tion is very strong that such contract is intended to contain all the terms of their bargain, it is a
> presumption only, and it is open to either of the parties to allege that there was, in addition to
> what appears in the written agreement, an antecedent express stipulation not intended by the
> parties to be excluded, but intended to continue in force with the express written agreement.'

In other words, a written agreement, which looks like a complete contract, leads to the presumption that it is the complete contract, but that presumption can be rebutted. If it is shown
that other terms were intended, in addition to those contained in the written document, then
there is no rule preventing the admission of evidence of those other terms. If the written document was intended to embody the entire contract between the parties, there is clearly no room
to admit evidence of any other statements of the parties as terms: they cannot be terms. On this
basis the Law Commission concluded that the parol evidence rule is 'a proposition of law which
is no more than a circular statement' (Law Com 154 (1986); G. Marston, 'The Parol Evidence
Rule: The Law Commission Speaks' [1986] CLJ 192).

7.16   The Law Commission also concluded that even if the parol evidence rule was viewed
as of some substance, it was unlikely to work injustice because of the numerous exceptions to
it. For example, evidence can be used to show that it had been orally agreed that the contract
embodied in the written document was not intended to be immediately effective but was to
become so only when certain conditions had been fulfilled (*Pym* v *Campbell* (1856)), or evidence of custom can be used to add to written contracts on matters on which the writing is silent
(*Hutton* v *Warren* (1836)—see para. **7.47**). The device of the collateral contract has also been
used to avoid the parol evidence rule, so that if the parol evidence rule meant that the court felt
unable to find that a statement was a term of the main contract, it could still find that it was a
term of a collateral contract.[3]

Collateral contracts[4]

7.17   The courts may occasionally find that, although a statement is not part of the main contract, it is part of a collateral contract. The statement can then found an action for breach of contract just as it would have done had it been part of the main contract. The collateral contract is
often of the form, 'if you will enter into the main contract then I guarantee that . . . '. In *Heilbut,
Symons, & Co.* v *Buckleton* [1913] AC 30, Lord Moulton stated (at 47):

> 'It is evident, both on principle and on authority, that there may be a contract the consid-
> eration for which is the making of some other contract. "If you will make such and such a

---

3   For further 'exceptions' to the parol evidence 'rule', see Treitel, *The Law of Contract*, 13th edn by E. Peel, Sweet &
     Maxwell, 2011, 6–013–6–030.

4   Wedderburn [1959] CLJ 58.

> contract I will give you one hundred pounds," is in every sense of the word a complete legal contract. It is collateral to the main contract, but each has an independent existence, and they do not differ in respect of their possessing to the full the character and status of a contract.'

7.18 The collateral contract has proved to be a useful device when there is a reason why the court cannot find that the statement in question is a term of the main contract. It has, for example, provided the courts with a means of avoiding the rule as to privity of contract (see **Chapter 17**), formality requirements, and the parol evidence rule (earlier in this chapter) where it 'eases the consciences of those who believe that the parol evidence rule is a strict and meaningful prohibition' (Wedderburn [1959] CLJ 58 at 69).

7.19 The usual requirements for a valid contract apply to a collateral contract, just as to any other. The consideration for the promise in the collateral contract is usually the act of entering into the main contract, i.e. 'if you will enter into the main contract then I guarantee that . . . ' (for example, *City and Westminster Properties Ltd* v *Mudd* (1959)).

7.20 There is a terminological difficulty in this area. Warranties are sometimes referred to as 'collateral terms' or 'collateral warranties', i.e. terms subsidiary to the main terms, the conditions, but properly speaking, still part of the main contract. Nevertheless, it is sometimes difficult to discern whether the judges think they are discussing a warranty in the main contract or in a collateral contract (for example, *Heilbut, Symons, & Co.* v *Buckleton* (1913)) and sometimes, although recognizing the two different possibilities, they treat them as interchangeable (for example, *J Evans & Son (Portsmouth) Ltd* v *Andrea Merzario Ltd* (1976)).

Implied terms[5]

Introduction

7.21 Often the parties will not expressly deal with every query which could arise under the contract. They may have thought that some things were too obvious to express, they may not have considered every possible eventuality, or they may have avoided covering a particular issue with an express term, because they did not think they could reach agreement about it, or that it was worth spending the time on. When a problem arises which has not been dealt with by the express terms of the contract, then it may be argued that a term can be implied. There are basically three types of implied term which we need to consider: terms implied in fact, terms implied in law, and terms implied by custom.

---

5 A. Phang, 'Implied Terms Revisited' [1990] JBL 394; A. Phang, 'Implied Terms in English Law—Some Recent Developments' [1993] JBL 242; A. Phang, 'Implied Terms Again' [1994] JBL 255.

Terms implied in fact

7.22   In implying terms in fact, the courts will state that they are endeavouring merely to find the objective intention of the parties. In particular the courts will often emphasize that they are not rewriting the parties' bargain.[6] Traditionally the courts have not simply applied a test of the parties' intentions, but rather they have sought that intention through two narrow tests: first, the 'business efficacy' test and secondly the 'officious bystander test'. Under the 'business efficacy' test it is said that the implication of the term must be 'necessary to give the transaction such business efficacy as the parties must have intended' (per Bowen LJ in *The Moorcock* (1889)), i.e. the term must be required to make the contract workable. In addition, the 'officious bystander' test is often cited:

> 'Prima facie that which in any contract is left to be implied and need not be expressed is something so obvious that it goes without saying; so that, if while the parties were making their bargain an officious bystander were to suggest some express provision for it in the agreement, they would testily suppress him with a common "Oh, of course" ' (*Shirlaw* v *Southern Foundries Ltd* [1939] 2 KB 206 at 227 per Mackinnon LJ).

7.23   In *The Moorcock* (1889):

> The defendants owned a wharf on the Thames and made a contract with the claimant shipowner for him to unload his vessel at their wharf. Both parties knew that the vessel was such that, whilst at the wharf, it must ground at low tide. The vessel grounded and was damaged.

It was held to be an implied term of the contract that the defendants had taken due care to ascertain that the bed of the river adjoining the wharf was not such as to damage the vessel when it grounded. The defendants were in breach of the implied term.

7.24   In *Shirlaw* v *Southern Foundries (1926) Ltd* (1939):

> On 1 December 1933 Mr Shirlaw was appointed managing director of Southern Foundries for ten years. Subsequently, Federated Foundries became the beneficial owners of Southern Foundries and in 1936 they changed the articles of association of Southern Foundries to enable them to remove Mr Shirlaw as a director. They removed him from his directorship, and he could not continue as managing director once he ceased to be a director.

The original articles of association of Southern Foundries did not allow Mr Shirlaw's removal in that way. The court found a breach of an implied term that such removal would not occur before the ten-year period expired.

---

6   e.g. *Trollope & Colls Ltd* v *North West Metropolitan Regional Hospital Board* [1973] 2 All ER 260 at 268.

7.25   However, a different approach to the law in this area was taken by Lord Hoffmann in delivering the decision of the Privy Council in *Attorney General of Belize* v *Belize Telecom Ltd* [2009] 2 All ER (Comm) 1.

> The case was concerned with whether provision should be implied into a company's articles of association to provide for the removal of directors appointed by the holders of a 'special share' when their ordinary shareholding fell below the percentage shareholding which was stated in the articles to give them the power to appoint or remove such directors. The Privy Council found that such a provision should be implied. With that shareholding below the required percentage the express terms of the articles did not confer on anyone the power to remove those directors. Further the articles of association expressly protected the interests of the holders of the special share in carefully graduated stages, corresponding with their economic interest in the company.

However, what is of significance here is not the specific facts of the case but Lord Hoffmann's general statements on implying terms in fact. He equated the implication of terms in fact with the construction of the contract (i.e. the interpretation of the contract) so that what is in question is ascertaining the objective intention i.e. what the reasonable person with the background knowledge of the parties would have thought that the contract meant. He said (at [17]–[18]):

> 'The question of implication arises when the instrument does not expressly provide for what is to happen when some event occurs. The most usual inference in such a case is that nothing is to happen . . . the loss lies where it falls.
>
>   In some cases, however, the reasonable addressee would understand the instrument to mean something else. He would consider that the only meaning consistent with the other provisions of the instrument, read against the relevant background, is that something is to happen. The event in question is to affect the rights of the parties. The instrument may not have expressly said so, but this is what it must mean. In such a case, it is said the court implies a term as to what will happen if the event in question occurs. But the implication of a term is not an addition to the instrument. It only spells out what the instrument means.'

Lord Hoffmann took the line that the 'business efficacy' test and the 'officious bystander' tests are not 'different or additional tests', they have just assisted the courts to determine what the contract means as there 'is only one question: . . . what the instrument, read as a whole against the relevant background, would reasonably be understood to mean' (at [21]). Further, he indicated that the 'business efficacy' and 'officious bystander' tests must be treated with caution, as merely guides, not displacing the test he identified.

7.26   Lord Hoffmann's specific arguments, in concluding that the traditional tests have merely assisted the courts, are open to considerable criticism,[7] but his idea of recognizing the underlying link between interpretation and implication in fact is a strong one, and is being accepted. However, there are clearly concerns, nevertheless, to keep implication within restricted bounds.

---

7   E. Macdonald, 'Casting Aside Officious Bystanders and Business Efficacy' (2009) 26 Journal of Contract Law 97.

In *Mediterranean Salvage & Towage Ltd* v *Seamar Trading & Commerce Inc* (2009), Lord Clarke MR's discussion of implied terms commenced with a prediction that Lord Hoffmann's 'analysis will soon be as much referred to as his approach to the construction of contracts in *Investors*' (at [8]). Nevertheless, Lord Clarke quoted the significant distinction made between implication and construction by Sir Thomas Bingham MR in *Philips Electronique Grand Publique SA* v *British Sky Broadcasting* [1995] EMLR 472 at 481:

> 'The courts usual role in contractual interpretation is, by resolving ambiguities or reconciling apparent inconsistencies, to attribute the true meaning to the language in which the parties have expressed their contract. The implication of contract terms involves a different and altogether more ambitious undertaking: the interpolation of terms to deal with matters for which, ex hypothesi, the parties themselves have made no provision. It is because the implication of terms is potentially so intrusive that the law imposes strict constraints on the exercise of this extraordinary power.'

Lord Clarke then emphasized the question of necessity in relation to terms implied in fact (is the implication 'necessary to make the contract work' (at [15])), and that would seem to be the line which is being taken. So that, for example, in *Societe Generale* v *Geys* (2012), Lady Hale referred to 'terms which are implied into a particular contract because, on its proper construction, the parties have intended to include them...Such terms are only implied where it is necessary to give business efficacy to the particular contract in question' (at [55]).

7.27 However, even if the basic test has become a matter of whether an implied term would 'spell out in express words what the instrument read against the relevant background, would reasonably be understood to mean',[8] the underlying rationale of implying terms in fact has always been the objectively determined intention of the parties, and cases concerned with that, even in the context of the traditional tests, therefore remain of relevance.

Knowledge

7.28 That one party could not reasonably have knowledge of the subject matter of a proposed implied term has obviously been of importance to such implication, and remains so. In *Spring* v *National Amalgamated Stevedores and Dockers Society* [1956] 1 WLR 585 such a factor was put in the context of the 'officious bystander' test:

> In 1939, at Bridlington, the Trades Union Congress drew up an agreement for the transfer of members between one union and another—the Bridlington Agreement. In breach of that agreement the NASDS allowed Mr Spring to become a member. He had been a member of the Transport and General Workers Union. In deciding the ensuing dispute between the two unions, the TUC told the NASDS to exclude all the members, like Mr Spring, that it had enrolled in contravention of the Bridlington Agreement.

---

8 *Belize* at [21].

When the NASDS attempted to expel Mr Spring, he asked the court for a declaration that the union was acting ultra vires, illegally and unconstitutionally, and that his expulsion was void. The union tried to argue that an implied term in Mr Spring's contract of membership justified his expulsion to bring the union back within the terms of the Bridlington Agreement.

7.29 The court granted Mr Spring's request for a declaration. On the question of the implied term, and applying the 'officious bystander' test, Sir Leonard Sachs V-C said (at 599):

> 'If . . . the bystander had asked the [claimant] . . . "won't you put into it some reference to the Bridlington Agreement?", I think (indeed I have no doubt) the [claimant] would have answered "What's that?".'

Although the court's discussion is put in terms of Mr Spring's actual knowledge, it is undoubtedly the 'objective' intention of the parties which is the basis of the implication, and what should be relevant is what the reasonable person in his position would have known. It seems likely that it would have been clear that the reasonable person would similarly have had no knowledge of the Bridlington Agreement.

Would both parties have agreed to the term?

7.30 *National Bank of Greece SA* v *Pinios Shipping Co* [1989] 1 All ER 213[9] illustrates another factor relevant to the implication of terms based on intention. The court asks whether, at the time of contracting, both parties would have agreed to the term which one of them is contending should be implied. Again, the objective nature of what is under consideration should be emphasized. So it is a matter of whether it would have been plain that one party would not have agreed to it.

A ship was built for Pinios in Japan. Pinios paid 30 per cent of the price on delivery but the rest of the purchase price was borrowed on the basis of a mortgage of the ship. Pinios failed to pay the first instalment of the money owed. The bank could have declared Pinios in default and the ship would have been sold, but the sale of the ship at that point would not have recovered all the money owed, and another course was taken. The bank made a three-party agreement with Pinios and Glafki for Glafki to manage the ship in the best interest of Pinios and the bank. It was a term of the mortgage that Pinios should insure the ship for 130 per cent of the amount secured, and Pinios had done so when the ship was initially delivered. The management contract specifically made it an obligation of Glafki to insure the vessel in accordance with the requirements of the mortgage. Glafki allowed the value of the insurance to fall. When the ship sank the insurance did not cover the sums owed by Pinios. Pinios successfully sued Glafki for negligent management of the ship, but could not obtain payment. Pinios sued the bank for Glafki's neglect.

---

9 The case went to the House of Lords on another point—[1990] 1 All ER 78.

The question before the court was whether the bank was also responsible to Pinios for Glafki's failure to insure the vessel fully. Pinios argued that a term should be implied that the bank would oversee Glafki's insurance of the vessel and that they were liable for not doing so. Pinios contended that the term should be implied because otherwise their interests were not protected, as Glafki was only subject to control by the bank and not Pinios. The Court of Appeal rejected this argument as, although Pinios would have agreed to such a term, it was not thought that the bank would have done so. The 'officious bystander' test could not be satisfied; both parties would not have said 'Oh, of course'. The management agreement had put Glafki under the control of the bank, and not Pinios, but the agreement was very much in Pinios's interests. But for the bank deciding on the management agreement, rather than simply selling the vessel, Pinios would not have remained the ship's owner. As long as Pinios owned the ship their financial situation would improve if the market improved. In addition, it was thought that the parties would have envisaged Pinios recovering from Glafki in the sort of situation which occurred. They would not have envisaged Glafki refusing to honour the judgment. Dealing with the 'officious bystander' test, Lloyd LJ said (at 218):

> 'the judge was . . . understating the position when he said that it was by no means obvious that the bank would have agreed to act as "guarantor" for Glafki, more especially as Glafki was Pinios's own nominee to act as manager. To my mind it is obvious that it would not.'[10]

Care must be taken not to slip into a consideration of the parties' subjective intentions. Nevertheless, clearly, if it is plain that one party would not have agreed, then the implication would not be spelling out what the 'instrument read against the relevant background, would reasonably be understood to mean'.

Several possible formulations of implied term; detailed express terms

7.31   *Trollope & Colls Ltd* v *North West Metropolitan Regional Hospital Board* (1973) provides an example of two factors against the implication of a term based on the parties' intention. In that case:

> T&C had contracted to build a hospital for the Board. The hospital was to be constructed in phases. Phases I and II were concurrent, but Phase III was to commence only six months after the issue of the Certificate of Practical Completion of Phase I. The date for the completion of Phase I was specified, and there was provision for extension of that time if the delay was due to certain specified factors. There was no provision for the alteration of the date for completing Phase III because of delay in completing Phase I, although there was provision for extension of the Phase III completion date in certain other specified circumstances. The completion of Phase I was delayed to such an extent that there were only sixteen months in which to construct Phase III by the specified date. There would have been thirty months available for construction of Phase III had Phase I been completed by the date specified.

---

10   See also *Bank of Nova Scotia* v *Hellenic Mutual War Risk Association (Bermuda) Ltd, The Good Luck* [1989] 3 All ER 628 at 667; *El Awadi* v *Bank of Credit and Commerce International SA* [1989] 1 All ER 242 at 252.

The House of Lords had to decide whether to imply a term allowing the delay on completion of Phase I to extend the completion date for Phase III. Two factors indicated that no term should be implied. First, there were detailed express terms in the contract. Those terms even dealt with some reasons for extending the completion date of Phase III. Under those circumstances it was not clear that the omission of any reference to an extension because of the late completion of Phase I was not deliberate. Second, it was not clear what the content of any implied term should be. There were various reasons for the delay in the completion of Phase I. Some of that delay was allowed under the contract for one reason, and some for other reasons, and some of it was not allowed at all. It was not clear how much of the delay any implied term should encompass. There were four or five possibilities. Doubts over the substance of the term meant that the court was not prepared to find that the parties would have included any particular version of it.[11] (But see McCaughran (2011) CLJ 607.)

Terms implied in law

7.32   Statutes imply terms into certain types of contract. For example, the Sale of Goods Act 1979 implies terms into contracts for the sale of goods that the goods should be of satisfactory quality and reasonably fit for the buyer's purpose (see s 14). In any particular case, whether a statute implies a term will depend upon whether the statutory requirements for its implication are present. In relation to s 14 of the Sale of Goods Act, for example, the above terms are only implied if the goods are sold 'in the course of a business'. Similarly, whether the parties can exclude the implication will depend upon the statute. Terms implied by statute are the most obvious type of term implied in law, but they will not be considered further here—as has been indicated, the implication is dependent upon the particular statute. What requires further consideration here is the implication of terms in law at common law. Like statute, such implication is not based upon the particular contract, but on the type of contract, and there are many types of regularly occurring contracts where certain implied terms have become standard for the type of contract in question—contracts for the lease of a furnished house (for example, *Smith* v *Marrable* (1843)), contracts of employment (for example, *Lister* v *Romford Ice and Cold Storage Co* (1957); *Malik* v *BCCI* (1997)), and contracts between banker and customer (for example, *London Joint Stock Bank Ltd* v *Macmillan* (1918)). The standard implied terms are implied in the particular case unless they would contradict the express terms.[12]

7.33   However, although there are established terms which are implied in law, consideration must now be given to how a type of contract will be addressed and a term implied in law generated.

---

11   See also *Shell UK Ltd* v *Lostock Garage Ltd* [1977] 1 All ER 481 at 488; *Liverpool City Council* v *Irwin* (1975).

12   The Court of Appeal seems to be making an inroad on the parties' intention here in envisaging the application of the Unfair Contract Terms Act 1977 to an express term precluding the implied term—*Johnstone* v *Bloomsbury Health Authority* [1991] 2 All ER 293 (see para. **10.110**).

Terms implied in law are not based on the intention of the parties

7.34   In *Liverpool City Council* v *Irwin* [1976] 2 All ER 39 Lord Cross distinguished between terms implied in fact on the basis of the, objectively determined, intention of the parties, and terms implied in law because of the type of contract. He said (at 47):

> 'When it implies a term the court is sometimes laying down a general rule that in all contracts of a certain type—sale of goods, master and servant, landlord and tenant, and so on—some provision is to be implied unless the parties have expressly excluded it…Sometimes however there is no question of laying down any prima facie rule applicable to all cases of a defined type…Here…the court…must be able to say that the insertion of the term is necessary to give…"business efficacy" to the contract and that if its absence had been pointed out at the time both parties—assuming them to be reasonable men—would have agreed to the insertion.'

Although this is put in terms of the traditional test for implication in fact, the basic point is clear. 'Terms implied in fact are individualised gap fillers, depending on the terms and circumstances of a particular contract. Terms implied in law are in reality incidents attached to standardised contractual relationships' (*Society of Lloyd's* v *Clementson* [1995] CLC 117 at 131 per Steyn LJ). 'Such implied terms operate as default rules' (*Malik* v *BCCI* [1997] 3 All ER 1 at 15 per Lord Steyn).

7.35   *Liverpool City Council* v *Irwin* (1976) itself provides an example of the difference between implying a term in fact and implying a term in law:

> Liverpool City Council owned a tower block which was in a very bad state of repair. Many of the problems were due to vandalism. The lifts frequently did not work and stairwells were often unlit. Rubbish chutes were frequently blocked. When Liverpool City Council sued the tenants for non-payment of rent, the tenants claimed that Liverpool City Council was in breach of an implied term as to the maintenance of the premises.

The House of Lords implied a term that Liverpool City Council should take reasonable care to maintain the common parts of the block in a reasonable state of repair. Unfortunately for the tenants, the court also found that a lack of reasonable care by Liverpool City Council had not been established, and that the implied term had not been breached.

7.36   At a time when the traditional tests undoubtedly applied in relation to terms implied in fact, how did the House of Lords imply a term when the 'officious bystander' test was not satisfied, as it was clear that Liverpool City Council would not have agreed to the term? The majority of the Court of Appeal had refused to imply a term on the only argument before them, that a term should be implied in fact, on the basis of the parties' intention. The House of Lords was able to imply a term as it did not look to the parties' intention, but to the type of contract in question. In this case the contract was a landlord-and-tenant contract, but in a building of multi-occupancy where the only access to the flats was via the common areas, the stairs, and the lifts. The only express terms set out the obligations of the tenants and they did not deal with the maintenance of the common parts of the building, such as the stairs and the lifts. There were no express obligations on Liverpool City Council. The situation demanded that someone had to be responsible for those common parts and, in the absence of any express allocation of responsibility amongst the tenants, the obligation was held to fall on Liverpool City Council, which had kept control of those areas.

When will a term be implied in law?

7.37   There are two basic requirements for the implication of a term in law. As has been indicated, terms implied in law are implied because the contract is of a particular type and so the first test is often stated as a requirement that the contract is of a 'defined type'. The second requirement has tended to be put in terms of 'necessity'. So, for example, it has been stated:

> 'the first requirement is that the contract in question should be a contract of a defined type...The second requirement is that the implication of the term should be necessary' (*El Awadi* v *Bank of Credit and Commerce International SA* [1989] 1 All ER 242 at 253).

However, although the second test, or requirement, has been stated as one of necessity, it is clearly a test embracing much broader considerations. It may also be that the courts are starting to become more willing explicitly to recognize that. Both requirements for the implication of a term implied in law should now be given further consideration and, in particular the nature of the second test will be returned to later.

A contract of a defined type

7.38   We saw earlier that Lord Cross provided examples of the type of contract into which a term may be implied in law—'sale of goods, master and servant, landlord and tenant'. As he indicated, they are all commonly occurring types of contract. We can identify two basic factors relevant to determining whether the contract in question is a contract into which a term may be implied in law: a contract of a defined type. They are, first, that the contract is of a recognizable commonly occurring type and, second, that the express terms of the particular contract do not differ too greatly from the 'ordinary' terms of those contracts normally regarded as falling within that type.

7.39   Sale of goods contracts, master and servant contracts, and landlord and tenant contracts are all contracts of a recognizable commonly occurring type and there will often be no difficulty in deciding if the contract is of such a type. Hutchinson J had no doubts that he was dealing with a contract of that type in *El Awadi* v *Bank of Credit and Commerce International SA* (1989) where the contract was for the sale of traveller's cheques by a bank to its customer. Hutchinson J thought that the sale of traveller's cheques was 'self evidently' a contract in which the implication of a term in law was a possibility. It was a contract of common occurrence.[13]

---

13   But see *Shell UK Ltd* v *Lostock Garage Ltd* [1977] 1 All ER 481 at 488 per Lord Denning MR.

7.40   However, the type of contract in which a term may be implied may be more specifically delimited. There is an interaction between the identification of the type of contract in which the term in question is to be implied and whether the second test is satisfied, i.e. narrowing the scope of the 'type' of contract being considered may make it possible for the courts to find a term which can be implied in keeping with the second requirement. This will be returned to later (see para. **7.46**ff).

7.41   The second point to be made here is that it is not simply a matter of commonly occurring contractual relationships (for example, landlord and tenant) or contracts commonly occurring to deal with a specific subject matter (for example, sale of goods, sale of traveller's cheques by bank to customer): the contents of the contract must also be such that, in its express terms, it is an 'ordinary' contract of that type. *National Bank of Greece SA v Pinios Shipping Co* [1989] 1 All ER 213 has already been discussed in the context of whether or not a term could be implied in fact (see para. **7.30**). Here we need to consider the alternative argument, that a term should be implied in law. Lloyd LJ dismissed the possibility (at 219):

> 'Can the present case be brought within a defined type? If we were concerned with the ordinary relationship of banker and customer the law would imply certain obligations...But we are not here concerned with the ordinary relationship of banker and customer. We are concerned with a carefully drawn one-off contract between three parties, made for a particular purpose in special circumstances, and apparently making full provision for that purpose. I cannot imagine a contract which it would be more difficult to fit into a "defined type".'

Although contracts between banker and customer could be of a 'defined type' (see, e.g., *Tai Hing Cotton Mill Ltd v Liu Chong Hing Bank Ltd* (1985)), this contract was not. The court was not faced with the 'ordinary' relationship of banker and customer but with a 'one-off' contract. All contracts are 'one-off' in the sense that they will have terms unique to them. The question therefore relates to the degree of departure from the 'ordinary' contract of the type in question. For example, how far does the contract in question depart from the 'ordinary' banker and customer contract? It will be relevant to consider which terms are specific to the particular contract. Are they those terms which are specific to the 'ordinary' contract between banker and customer?

The second test

7.42   It has been emphasized that the term should be 'necessary' (*Liverpool City Council v Irwin* (1976); *Tai Hing Cotton Mill Ltd v Liu Chong Hing Bank Ltd* (1985)), and that is understandable: the courts would not want to be seen to be too readily making an implication which is not based on the parties' intentions. It is, however, clear that this reference to necessity is not to be equated with the traditional *Moorcock* test, for implication in fact, as to whether the term is 'necessary' to give the contract 'business efficacy' (*The Moorcock* (1889)). In *Scally v Southern Health and Social Services Board* [1991] 4 All ER 563, Lord Bridge said (at 571):

> 'A clear distinction is drawn... between the search for an implied term necessary to give business efficacy to a particular contract, and the search, based on wider considerations for a

term which the law will imply as a necessary incident of a definable category of contractual relationship.'

The distinction is important: it is the 'wider considerations' which must be emphasized, rather than 'necessity'.

7.43   In *Crossley* v *Faithful & Gould* (2004), referring to Peden (2001), Dyson LJ gave clearer recognition to what is occurring when a term is implied in law. He stated (at [36]):

'It seems to me that rather than focus on the narrow concept of necessity, it is better to recognise that to some extent at least, the existence and scope of standardised implied terms raise questions of reasonableness, fairness and the balancing of competing policy considerations.'

'There is much to be said for that approach' (*Societe Generale* v *Geys* (2012) at [55]). A term implied in law is based on an 'ought': it is a matter of what should be present in the 'type' of contract, rather than what the parties can be found to have intended. If that 'ought' means that a term should be present, then the term is necessary to effectuate the 'ought'. It is a 'necessary incident' of the category of contract. Necessity is, indeed, not what should be focussed on. What is important is the difficult question of determining the 'ought', which will vary from one 'type' of contract to another, and in relation to the problem for that 'type' of contract. It is not surprising that the generation of the 'ought' is expressed in vague terms such as 'fairness, reasonableness, and competing policy considerations', or 'justice and Social policy' (*The Star Texas* [1993] 2 Lloyd's Rep 445 at 526). Further, it can be emphasized that there is usually 'some justice on each side' of a case where a term implied in law is in question,[14] so that what is generally of concern is, indeed, the 'balancing of competing policy considerations' (Peden at 467). It is plain that implying a previously unrecognized term in law will rarely be simple.

7.44   In *Malik* v *BCCI* [1997] 3 All ER 1 it was also recognized that the considerations which will be relevant to an implication in law will change over time, with changing social attitudes. In that case, the House of Lords accepted that there should be implied into contracts of employment, a term that both parties would not engage in conduct likely to undermine the trust and confidence required if the employment relationship was to continue. They saw such implication as part of the 'history of the development of employment law in this century' (at 15). They recognized the

'[c]hanges which have taken place in the employer/employee relationship, with far greater duties imposed on the employer than in the past whether by statute or by judicial decision, to care for the physical, financial and even psychological welfare of the employee' ([1997] 3 All ER 1 at 15, quoting *Spring* v *Guardian Assurance plc* [1994] 3 All ER 129 at 161 per Lord Slynn).

---

14 T. D. Rakoff, 'The Implied Terms of Contracts: Of "Default Rules" and "Situation-Sense"' in J. Beatson and D. Friedmann (eds), *Good Faith and Fault in Contract Law*, Oxford University Press, 1995, p. 198.

The term was regarded as making little difference to the obligations of employees, who had long been seen as under obligations to serve their employers loyally and not to act contrary to their business. Its importance was perceived to be in its impact upon the employer's obligations. The term was regarded as 'apt to cover the great diversity of situations in which a balance has to be struck between an employer's interest in managing his business as he sees fit and the employee's interest in not being unfairly and improperly exploited' ([1997] 3 All ER 1 at 15–16 per Lord Steyn).

7.45 At times, broad considerations of justice and social policy may lead to the conclusion that a term should be implied but the courts will, nevertheless, refuse to imply a term on the basis that the issue is not one which can appropriately be dealt with in that way. Public policy was looked at in *Reid v Rush & Tompkins Group plc* [1990] 1 WLR 212 and the implication of a term was viewed as desirable, but the issue was regarded as too complex for the courts to deal with by such means. It was said (at 220):

'As to treating such a term as implied by law, the arguments in favour of a social policy, which would require employers to provide some level of personal accident insurance for the benefit of men and women working overseas, and for their dependants, are obvious but there appears to be no way in which the court could "embody this policy in the law without the assistance of the legislature".'

7.46 The final point to consider here is that, as has been indicated, it may be necessary to consider an interaction between the width of the 'type' of contract, identified in the first test, and the issue of whether the second test is satisfied. This is exemplified by *Scally v Southern Health and Social Services Board* [1991] 4 All ER 563. *Scally* was concerned with doctors' contracts of employment. They included a contributory pension scheme which required forty years' contribution for maximum benefit. However, the terms were varied to give the employees an opportunity, for a limited period, to purchase extra years of contribution to make their pensions equivalent to one based on forty years' service, if the employees would not achieve that period of actual service. The problem arose because the claimants were not informed of that opportunity and did not exercise their right. The question was whether there was an implied term in the contract requiring the employer to give notice of that opportunity. It was held that a term, requiring notice, could be implied in law. The contracts in which such an implication would be made were of a carefully stated 'defined type'. Lord Bridge said (at 571):

'I would define it as the relationship of employer and employee where the following circumstances obtain: (1) the terms of the contract of employment have not been negotiated with the individual employee but result from negotiation with a representative body or are otherwise incorporated by reference; (2) a particular term of the contract makes available to the employee a valuable right contingent upon action being taken by him to avail himself of its benefit; (3) the employee cannot, in all the circumstances, reasonably be expected to be aware of the term unless it is drawn to his attention.'

Stating the type of contract into which the term would be implied in this narrow way limited the impact upon contracts of employment more generally of implying such a term in law. In stating this limited 'type' of contract Lord Bridge recognized that at first instance 'Carswell J accepted the submission that any formulation of an implied term of this kind must be too wide in its ambit to be acceptable as of general application'. Policy issues as to the 'acceptability' of implying a term were dealt with by a narrow statement of the contracts into which it would be implied. In contrast, in *Crossley* v *Faithful & Gould* [2004] 4 All ER 447 at [43] the Court of Appeal denied the implication of the much broader term, into contracts of employment generally, that the employer will take reasonable care of the economic well-being of the employee. The term was viewed as one which would impose an 'unfair and unreasonable burden on employers'.

Terms implied by custom

7.47   There may be contractual terms which are implied on the basis that they are customary in a particular trade, profession or locality.[15] In *Hutton* v *Warren* (1836) 1 M & W 466:

> The tenant of a farm was given notice to quit by the landlord. He had worked and planted the land and the landlord would obtain the benefit of that when the tenant left. It was held that the tenant was entitled to an allowance for the seeds and labour on leaving. There was no express term to that effect, but he was so entitled on the basis of a local custom.

Baron Parke indicated the rationale of implying terms on the basis of custom. He said (at 475):

> 'It has long been settled that, in commercial transactions, extrinsic evidence of custom and usage is admissible to annex incidents to written contracts, in matters with respect to which they are silent. The same rule has also been applied to contracts in other transactions of life, in which known usages have been established and prevailed; and this has been done upon the principle of presumption that, in such transactions, the parties did not mean to express in writing the whole of the contract by which they intended to be bound, but to contract with reference to those known usages.'

However, despite the reference to intention by Baron Parke, the situation is more akin to terms implied in law than to terms implied on the basis of the parties' intention (i.e. terms implied in fact). Terms implied by custom are implied on the basis that the contract is of a certain type and there is a custom which implies certain terms into contracts of that type. Also, as with terms implied in law, the intention of the parties is only of limited relevance. Here, the term will be excluded if the contract evidences a contrary intention:

> 'An alleged custom can be imported into a contract only if there is nothing in the express or necessarily implied terms of the contract to prevent such inclusion and further that a custom will only be imported into a contract where it can be so imported consistently with the tenor

---

15 See, e.g., *National Bank of Greece SA* v *Pinios Shipping Co.* (1990).

of the documents as a whole' (*London Export Corpn Ltd* v *Jubilee Coffee Roasting Co* [1958] 1 WLR 661 at 675 per Lord Jenkins).

In *Walford's* case (*Affréteurs Réunis SA* v *Walford* (1919)), for example, a custom that a broker's commission was payable only when hire was earned under a charter could not be implied into a contract with an express term stating that the owners were to pay commission on the signing of a charter.

7.48   It is not easy to establish the existence of a particular custom or usage. It has been said that it must be:

'certain, in the sense that the practice is clearly established; it must be notorious, in the sense that it is so well known in the market in which it is alleged to exist, that those who conduct business in the market contract with the usage as an implied term; and it must be reasonable' (*Cunliffe-Owen* v *Teather & Greenwood* [1967] 1 WLR 1421 at 1438 per Ungoed Thomas J).

More recently, the House of Lords has viewed the situation as requiring 'evidence of a universal and acknowledged practice of the market' (*Baker* v *Black Sea and Baltic General Insurance Ltd* [1998] 2 All ER 833 at 842). If a custom is unreasonable, 'the courts have said that they will not recognise it as binding on people who do not know of it and who have not consented to act upon it' (*Perry* v *Barnett* (1885) 15 QBD 388 at 393 per Brett MR).

◉ Summary

The first part of the chapter is concerned with express spoken terms.

- What is said before the contract is made may become express terms of the contract.
- The basic test is the intention of the parties i.e. did the parties intend the statement to be a term?—*Heilbut, Symons & Co.* v *Buckleton* (1913).
- The test is objective not subjective.
- The courts have identified indicators of the parties' intentions:
  - importance of the statement: was it clear to both parties that the statement was important in the contract being made (for example, *Bannerman* v *White* (1861))
  - reliance: did one party make it clear that the other was intended to rely upon his statement? (for example, *Schawel* v *Reade* (1913))
  - relative knowledge of the parties: did one party have more knowledge/expertise in relation to the subject matter of the statement so that he would have been more likely to have taken upon him(her)self the risk of it being untrue (for example, *Dick Bentley Productions* v *Harold Smith Motors* (1965)).
- It has been stated as a 'rule' that 'parol evidence' cannot be admitted to show that there are terms additional to those contained within a written agreement. However, this has been

seen not as a rule but simply as a circular statement—a written agreement which looks like a complete contract leads to the presumption that it is, but the presumption can be rebutted and if it is shown that other terms were intended then evidence of them will be admitted. Even if the 'parol evidence rule' has some substance as a rule, there are so many exceptions that it is unlikely to work injustice.

- A statement may be found to be part of a collateral contract, rather than the main contract. This device is usually used to avoid some difficulty in finding it is part of the main contract such as formalities or the privity rule.

The second part of the chapter is concerned with implied terms.

- There are three sorts of implied terms at common law
    - terms implied in fact
    - terms implied in law
    - terms implied by custom.
- There are also terms implied by statute.
- Terms implied in fact are derived from the objective intention of the parties but traditionally there has not been a simple test of the intention of the parties applied to ascertain them.
- Traditionally the 'business efficacy' test from *The Moorcock* (1889) and the 'officious bystander' test from *Shirlaw* v *Southern Foundries* (1939) have been applied.
- These restrictive tests have been applied, rather than simply the intention test, to confine terms implied in fact to the least disputable possible terms, so that the courts can make it clear that they are not rewriting/improving the parties' bargain.
- However, in *Attorney General of Belize* v *Belize Telecom* (2009), a Privy Council case, Lord Hoffmann linked interpretation and implication of terms in fact, and has indicated a change to a test simply based upon a search for the parties' (objective) intentions: 'what the instrument, read as a whole against the relevant background, would reasonably be understood to mean' (at [21]).
- Terms implied in law are not based on the intention of the parties—*Liverpool City Council* v *Irwin* (1976).
- The intention of the parties is only relevant to the extent that a term will not be implied in law if there is an express contrary term.
- There is a two-stage test for terms implied in law:
    - First, the contract in which it is sought to imply a term must be a type of contract, not a one-off contract.
    - The second test has traditionally been put in terms of whether it is 'necessary' to imply the term, for example, *Tai Hing Cotton Mill* v *Liu Chon Hing Bank* (1985).
- However, the courts have taken into account factors which do not come within any normal use of the term 'necessary' and they may now be starting to recognize that the second

test is a more broadly based policy question, for example, *Crossley* v *Faithful & Gould* (2004)—'questions of reasonableness, fairness and the balancing of competing policy considerations'.

- Terms may be implied on the basis that they are customary in a particular trade, profession or locality.

- Terms will not be implied on the basis of custom if the contract evidences a contrary intention.

- It is difficult to establish the existence of a relevant custom.

▶ Further reading

A. Kramer, 'Implication in Fact as an Instance of Contractual Interpretation' (2004) 63 CLJ 384

Law Commission Report, No 154, 'The Law of Contract: The Parol Evidence Rule', 1986

E. Macdonald, 'Casting Aside Officious Bystanders and Business Efficacy' (2009) 26 Journal of Contract Law 97

J. McCaughran, 'Implied Terms: the journey of the man of the clapham omnibus' 70 (2011) CLJ 607

E. Peden, 'Policy Concerns Behind Implication of Terms in Law' (2001) 117 LQR 459

K. Wedderburn, 'Collateral Contracts' (1959) 18 CLJ 58

Chapter 8

Classification of terms

⊙ Introduction

8.1 Some terms of the contract are more important than others. In particular, the breach of some terms will give the injured party the right to terminate the contract. That is a significant right for the injured party. For example, they may be able to terminate and obtain a substitute performance from elsewhere. A distinction is made between terms which are conditions, warranties, and innominate terms and, basically, the three types of term are differentiated by the legal consequences that flow from the breach of each of them. When a condition is breached the injured party has the right to sue for damages and also to terminate the contract.[1] A breach of warranty gives rise only to the right to sue for damages. When an innominate term is breached, the legal consequence of the breach depend upon its factual consequences, i.e. there is a right to terminate the contract, in addition to suing for damages, only if the breach of an innominate term is such as to deprive the injured party of substantially all the benefit which he or she was intended to derive from the contract.

8.2 For a long time it was thought that terms were either conditions or warranties. That was probably due to the fact that the definitions of condition and warranty given above were only satisfactorily settled with the enactment of the Sale of Goods Act 1893, which Act referred only to conditions and warranties. It was the judgment of Diplock LJ in *Hong Kong Fir Shipping Co.* v *Kawasaki Kisen Kaisha* (1962) that made it clear that the division into conditions and warranties was not complete but had to be supplemented by the innominate term.

---

1   There is what may be regarded as an exception to this in s 15A of the Sale of Goods Act 1979. Under certain circumstances, breaches which would otherwise be labelled by the statute as breaches of condition are 'deemed' to be breaches of warranties. This occurs in business to business contracts where the breach is so slight that it would be unreasonable to reject the goods.

8.3   There is a need to be careful with terminology. The Sale of Goods Act 1893 settled the technical meaning to be given to conditions and warranties in one context (i.e. when the effect of a breach is under consideration), but the words are still used in other senses. For example, both condition and warranty may be used non-technically simply to mean a term of the contract, without it carrying any implication as to the legal consequences of a breach. Warranty is often used non-technically in that way, to mean a term, when the question being asked is whether a statement is a term or a mere representation. The words 'condition' and 'warranty' must be approached with some caution to ascertain the sense in which they are being used. That caution must be all the greater when dealing with some of the older cases decided before the enactment of the Sale of Goods Act 1893.

The test

8.4   Statute may sometimes classify a term, as in the Sale of Goods Act 1979. In other cases the question of how it is to be decided whether a term is a condition, a warranty, or an innominate term can be easily answered in theory, but its application may be more problematic as it is based upon the parties' intention (objectively ascertained, of course). The parties may have expressly classified the term;[2] otherwise the test to be applied derives from *Bentsen v Taylor, Sons, & Co. (No 2)* [1893] 2 QB 274. In that case, it was held that the term in the charter party describing the ship as 'now sailed or about to sail from a pitch pine port to the United Kingdom' was a condition. Such a statement provided the charterer's only basis for his calculations as to when he would be able to load the ship in the United Kingdom. It was the importance of the term to the whole charter that led to its construction as a condition. In coming to that conclusion, Bowen LJ delivered what is now the classic test for distinguishing the different types of term. He said (at 281):

> 'There is no way of deciding that question except by looking at the contract in the light of the surrounding circumstances, and making up one's mind whether the intention of the parties, as gathered from the instrument itself, will best be carried out by treating the promise as a warranty sounding only in damages, or as a condition precedent by the failure to perform which the other party is relieved of his liability.'

This provides the test for determining whether the term is a condition or a warranty, despite the reference to a 'condition precedent'—there are difficulties with terminological usage in this area! To that formulation of the test should now be added the third possibility: that the intention of the parties will best be carried out by classifying the term as innominate. In *Bunge Corpn v Tradax Export SA* (1981) (see para. **8.17**ff) the House of Lords made it clear that this is the correct approach to the classification of terms—even innominate terms. The application of this test, for deciding if a term is a condition, warranty, or innominate term, is considered further later.

8.5   One aspect of the classification test should be emphasized here, if the importance of the innominate term is to be understood. That aspect is the point in time against which the intention

---

2   Express classification itself may not be without difficulties. See para. **8.29**ff.

of the parties is to be assessed in determining the classification of a term. In *Bentsen v Taylor, Sons, & Co. (No 2)* [1893] 2 QB 274, after the dictum given earlier, Bowen LJ continued (at 81):

> 'One of the first things you would look to is to what extent the accuracy of the statement— the truth of what is promised—would be likely to affect the substance and foundation of the adventure which the contract is intended to carry out . . . it may well be that such a test can only be applied after getting the jury to say what the effect of a breach of such a condition would be on the substance and foundation of the adventure; not the effect of the breach which has in fact taken place, but the effect likely to be produced on the foundation of the adventure by any such breach of that portion of the contract.'

As will be seen, a term is more likely to be classified as a condition if it can be regarded as an important term of the contract; and the effect of any breach of it is relevant to an assessment of its importance. However, the point to be noted here, and which Bowen LJ emphasized, is that the importance of the term is to be assessed against the effect of possible breaches rather than the actual breach. The classification of terms is based upon the intention at the time of contracting and not the time of the breach.[3] Basically, the actual breach is considered only if the term is innominate. It is then that the actual breach becomes relevant to deciding if the injured party can terminate the contract.

8.6   However, there is a statutory exception to this. The Sale of Goods Act 1979 was amended by the Sale and Supply of Goods Act 1994. A new section, s 15A, was inserted into the Sale of Goods Act 1979 and, in business to business sales, that section deems a breach of the conditions implied by ss 13–15 of that Act to be merely a breach of warranty where the breach is so slight that it would be unreasonable to reject the goods. This creates the exception to the point made earlier. The implied terms are generally conditions but, because they can be deemed to be merely warranties in the light of the actual breach, the actual breach is relevant to the terms' 'deemed' classification at least. Section 15A of the Sale of Goods Act 1979 is considered further later.[4]

Recognition of the innominate term

8.7   In *Hong Kong Fir Shipping Co. Ltd v Kawasaki Kisen Kaisha Ltd* [1962] 2 QB 26 it was shown that the traditional division of terms into conditions and warranties is not complete, and that there are also innominate terms. In that case:

> The shipowner hired a ship, *The Hong Kong Fir*, to the charterer for twenty-four months. On a voyage to deliver coal to Osaka, the ship spent five weeks being repaired. The engines were old and needed to be well maintained by efficient staff. The engine-room staff were insufficient in number and inefficient. When the ship arrived in Osaka the engine-room staff were

---

3   Of course, the actual breach will be known to the court and, particularly prior to the identification of the innominate term, the courts have sometimes been tempted to act on the basis of hindsight. See e.g. *Poussard* v *Spiers* (1876).

4   Similar provision is made for other supply of goods contracts, where there are similar statutorily labelled conditions, in the Sale and Supply of Goods Act 1994.

replaced, and a further period of fifteen weeks was required to make it ready for sea again. The charterer claimed to be able to terminate the contract for failure to deliver a seaworthy ship because of the state of the engines and the inadequacy of the staff.

The shipowner sued the charterer for wrongful termination of the contract, i.e. the shipowner claimed that the breach of the term that the vessel was seaworthy did not entitle the charterer to terminate the contract. Although the owner had been in breach, in failing to provide a seaworthy ship, the Court of Appeal held that the breach had not entitled the charterer to terminate. The charterer was in breach in wrongfully terminating the contract. The owner was entitled to substantial damages as the market had dropped considerably since the charter had been made.

8.8   The importance of *Hong Kong Fir Shipping Co. Ltd* lies in the treatment by Diplock LJ of the charterer's claim that seaworthiness was a condition and that, as a consequence, any breach of it entitled the charterer to terminate the contract (see also Upjohn LJ). He made it clear that whether termination was possible, for the breach of the term as to seaworthiness, did not depend upon the classification of the term as a condition or warranty but upon the factual consequences of the breach. The factual consequences of the breach determined the legal consequences. If the factual consequences were sufficiently serious, termination was possible— but not otherwise. Diplock LJ said (at 70):

> 'There are however many contractual undertakings of a more complex character which cannot be categorised as being "conditions" or "warranties"...Of such undertakings all that can be predicated is that some breaches will and others will not give rise to an event which will deprive the party not in default of substantially the whole benefit which it was intended that he should obtain from the contract; and the legal consequences of a breach of such an undertaking...depend upon the nature of the event to which the breach gives rise and do not follow automatically from a prior classification of the undertaking as a "condition" or a "warranty".'

The term as to seaworthiness is such that it is particularly appropriate that the legal consequences of a breach should depend upon the particular breach. It is a term which can be breached in many ways. Some of the possible defects which it encompasses are very serious whilst others may be fairly trivial. A ship will not be seaworthy 'if a nail is missing from one of the timbers of a wooden vessel or if proper medical supplies or two anchors are not on board at the time of sailing' (at 62 per Upjohn LJ). It is particularly inappropriate to label such a term as a condition or warranty from the inception of the contract. In *Hong Kong Fir* it was decided that the need for twenty weeks of repairs, and replacement of the engine-room staff, were not sufficiently serious to give the charterer the right to terminate when the charter, the hire of the ship, was for twenty-four months. The breach was not one which deprived the charterer of 'substantially the whole benefit which it was the intention of the parties...that he should obtain' (see dictum of Diplock LJ given earlier).

8.9   If the term is an innominate or intermediate term, what is the test which is applied to determine if the breach gives the injured party a right to terminate as well as to claim damages?

What makes the breach of an innominate term equivalent, in the legal result it produces, to a breach of a condition? As has been indicated, the test has been put in terms of whether the breach substantially deprives the innocent party of the whole of the benefit which he, or she, was intended to derive from the contract (see also *Bunge Corpn v Tradax Export SA* (1981)). This was the formulation adopted by Diplock LJ in *Hong Kong Fir Shipping Co. Ltd v Kawasaki Kisen Kaisha Ltd* (1962). The test has also been put in terms of whether the breach went to the root of the contract (for example, *Cehave NV v Bremer Handelsgesellschaft mbH, The Hansa Nord* [1975] 3 All ER 739 at 747 per Lord Denning MR, at 757 per Roskill LJ).

Flexibility—the benefit of the innominate term classification[5]

8.10　A better understanding of the intention the parties would have had in making the contract as to the classification of a term can be ascertained if the major benefits and drawbacks of the classifications are recognized. The benefit of the innominate term classification is its flexibility which contrasts with the fixed nature of the other classifications, where the consequences of the breach are simply determined by the classification. So, for example, if a term is a condition, then, outside the special statutory exceptions noted earlier (see further para. **8.15**ff), even a trivial breach of it will justify the innocent party in terminating. There is no necessary connection between the seriousness of the factual consequences of the breach, and its legal consequences. For example, in *Arcos Ltd v EA Ronaasen & Son* (1933):

> There was a contract for the sale of barrel staves half an inch thick. There was held to be a breach of the condition that the goods should correspond with their description when the staves varied from that thickness by up to one-sixteenth of an inch. The variation caused no problems with their use, but this did not prevent the finding of a breach of condition.[6]

The party in breach may lose the entire contract because of a breach of condition which has little practical effect. This is obviously not the case where the term is innominate and the factual consequences of the breach are directly related to the availability of the right to terminate. The innominate term classification allows the law to be flexible in its approach to the legal consequences of a breach.

8.11　One aspect of termination being related to the seriousness of the breach is that a minor breach cannot be used by the innocent party to escape from a contract which has ceased to be a 'good deal' from their point of view. In *Hong Kong Fir Shipping Co. Ltd v Kawasaki Kisen Kaisha Ltd* (1962) the owners of the vessel received substantial damages in the wake of the charterer's wrongful termination of the contract. This was because the charter market had dropped. Any substitute charter had to be at a much lower rate than that provided for by the relevant contract. The drop in the market probably explains why the charterer was eager to claim to be entitled to terminate the contract. By the time he did so he could get another ship more cheaply. Had the term been a condition, the charterer could have escaped from the contract and hired another

---

5　Brownsword (1992) JCL 83.

6　See also *Re Moore & Co. Ltd and Landauer & Co. Ltd* [1921] 2 KB 519 at [8.16].

ship more cheaply. This would have defeated part of the object of the contract, the allocation of the risk of market changes for the period of the charter. The flexibility of the innominate term classification prevents a minor breach from being used in this way.

8.12   *Cehave NV* v *Bremer Handelsgesellschaft mbH, The Hansa Nord* (1975) provides a good example of the benefits of the flexibility of the innominate term. The facts were as follows:

> A German company had contracted to sell citrus pulp pellets to a Dutch company for about £100,000. The pellets had to come from Florida and it was a term of the contract that they should be shipped 'in good condition'. On arrival it was discovered that some of the pellets had been damaged by overheating, and by that time the market price for sound goods had dropped to about £86,000. The purchasers refused to take delivery and claimed to be entitled to terminate the contract on the basis that the goods had not been shipped 'in good condition' and that it was a condition of the contract that they should be. Whilst the dispute was in progress the pellets were sold to a third party for about £30,000. That third party then sold them for that same reduced price, approximately £30,000, to the original purchasers. The original purchasers were able to use them as originally intended in the manufacture of cattle food, although in slightly reduced proportions.

The Court of Appeal had to decide whether the purchasers had been correct in their claim to be able to terminate for breach of the term that the goods would be shipped 'in good condition'. It was held that the purchasers were not correct. The breach entitled them to damages but not to terminate, and they were themselves liable for wrongful termination. The Court of Appeal refused to regard the term as a condition. It was a term, the legal consequences of the breach of which depended upon its factual consequences, i.e. an innominate term. The particular breach was not sufficiently serious to give rise to the right to terminate. It did not go to the root of the contract. This was evident from the fact that the pellets had been used to make cattle food in almost exactly the same way as they would have been, had they not been damaged.

8.13   The advantages of the innominate term classification are obvious in *The Hansa Nord*. Had the term been a condition, the breach would have allowed the purchaser to terminate. This would have been his right despite the fact that the grounds for his decision to terminate were obviously purely pecuniary, rather than based on the actual breach. The damage to the goods barely affected the purchaser's use of them. The flexibility provided by the innominate term classification allowed the court to look at the seriousness of the breach to determine the availability of a right to terminate.[7]

8.14   The attempt to avoid trivial breaches giving rise to the right to terminate can also be seen in other situations. As has already been indicated, the legal effect of breaches of the conditions implied by Sale of Goods Act 1979, ss 13–15 has been modified by a new s 15A, inserted by the Sale and Supply of Goods Act 1994. In business to business contracts, where the breach is so slight that it would be unreasonable for the buyer to reject, the term is deemed not to

---

7   But see A. Weir, 'The Buyer's Right to Reject Defective Goods' [1976] CLJ 33.

be a condition but a warranty, and the buyer cannot reject the goods but has only a right to claim damages. Before the amendment made by Sale and Supply of Goods Act 1994, the implied terms always remained conditions in the full sense and the buyer had a right to reject the goods for any breach, even the most trivial. *Re Moore & Co. Ltd and Landauer & Co. Ltd* (1921) provides an example. In that case:

> The contract concerned the sale of tinned fruit. The tins were stated to be packed in cases containing thirty tins each. The correct number of tins was delivered, but they were packed in cases containing twenty-four tins each.

The court held that the difference in the number of tins per case meant that there was a breach of the statutorily implied condition that the goods should correspond with their description.

8.15   It was in keeping with the post-*Hong Kong Fir* approach that the Law Commission should recommend that, in contracts between business people, a breach of the implied conditions in the Sale of Goods Act 1979 should cease to give rise to an automatic right to terminate, however trivial the breach (Law Com No 160, Cmnd 137, 1987). In relation to contracts between business people, the Law Commission recommended that a breach of such a term should be treated as a breach of warranty where the breach is so slight that it would be unreasonable for the buyer to terminate. It was this recommendation which led to the enactment of the Sale and Supply of Goods Act 1994 and the addition of s 15A to the Sale of Goods Act 1979, modifying the legal effect of breach of the conditions implied by ss 13–15 of that Act. This does not equate such terms with innominate terms, as the right to terminate is absent only if the breach is fairly minor. If a term is innominate, the right to terminate is present only if the breach is serious. The emphasis is different, but the changes in the law moved the sale of goods legislation more into line with the flexible *Hong Kong Fir* approach which links the availability of the right to terminate to the seriousness of the factual consequences of the breach.

Conditions and the benefit of certainty

8.16   As we have seen, the benefit of the innominate term classification is its flexibility—matching the availability of the right to terminate with the seriousness of the breach. The desirability of such flexibility will indicate that the parties intended a term to be innominate. However, a condition is not merely inflexible, it also has the benefit of certainty and the situation may be one in which the parties would have desired that certainty and the indications will then be of a condition classification.

8.17   However, initially after the development of the innominate term approach in *Hong Kong Fir Shipping Co. Ltd* v *Kawasaki Kisen Kaisha Ltd* (1962) the argument arose that, in the absence of a label being placed on a term expressly by the parties, or by statute, the classification of the term depended entirely upon the factual effects of the breach. In other words, the argument was that, in the absence of an express classification, all terms were innominate and a breach gave rise to the right to terminate only if it deprived the innocent party of substantially all the benefit that it was intended he or she should derive from the contract. This argument was dismissed by the House of Lords in *Bunge Corpn v Tradax Export SA* (1981),[8] where it was affirmed that the question whether the breach is such as substantially to deprive the innocent party of all the benefit it was intended that he or she should derive from the contract is relevant only after it has been decided that the term is innominate. The first question which must be asked is what sort of a term it is, i.e. a condition, a warranty, or an innominate term. If the term has not been labelled by statute or expressly by the parties, the test is that stated by Bowen LJ in *Bentsen v Taylor, Sons & Co. (No 2)* [1893] 2 QB 274 at 281 (see para. **8.4**), i.e. which classification will fulfil the intention of the parties.

8.18   In *Bunge Corpn v Tradax Export SA* [1981] 1 WLR 711 the term in question was found to be a condition despite the lack of any statutory or express classification. In that case:

> The contract concerned the sale of soya bean meal. The meal was to be shipped by the end of June 1975. By cl 7 the buyers had to give the sellers at least fifteen days' notice of the probable readiness of the vessel to load the meal. The fifteen days were to allow the sellers time to nominate a loading port and make sure the meal could be shipped from there at the appropriate time. The buyers gave notice on 17 June. The last shipment day within the contract was 30 June, and the notice provided less than the required fifteen-day interval. The sellers claimed to terminate the contract. The buyers disputed that termination.

The House of Lords held that cl 7 was a condition of the contract and breach of it gave the sellers the automatic right to terminate, whatever the factual consequences of that breach. Lord Roskill said (at 727):

> 'While recognising the modern approach and not being over-ready to construe terms as conditions unless the contract clearly requires the court so to do, none the less the basic principles of construction for determining whether or not a particular term is a condition remain as before, always bearing in mind on the one hand the need for certainty and on the other the desirability of not, when legitimate, allowing rescission where the breach complained of is highly technical and where damages would clearly be an adequate remedy.'

In *Bunge Corpn* the court was dealing with a time clause in a mercantile contract, and this indicated the need for the certainty obtained by classifying the term as a condition, i.e. if the term is a condition, the innocent party knows that he or she has the right to terminate upon any breach of that term and can do so immediately and can quickly try to find a substitute contract. The injured party does not have to weigh up the seriousness of the consequences of the breach to see if he or she can terminate. If the term was innominate, the injured party might decide that it was necessary to wait to see further what the actual consequences of the breach were before risking claiming to be able to terminate.

8.19   Beyond the simple fact that the clause was a time clause in a mercantile contract, there were other factors pointing to the clause being a condition in *Bunge Corpn*. First, the contract

---

8   See also *Maredelanto Compania Naviera SA v Bergbau-Handel GmbH, The Mihalis Angelos* (1971).

was one of a chain of sales of the soya bean meal. Timely performance is obviously all the more important where a whole chain of sales is involved. Second, the sellers had to act upon the buyers' notification; they had to nominate a suitable port and ensure that the soya bean meal could be shipped from there on time. The dependence of the sellers' performance upon the buyers' timely notification indicated that the sellers should be able to terminate for any breach of the time clause.

Classification of terms not expressly labelled by the parties

8.20   The general impetus is towards the labelling of terms as innominate rather than as conditions because of the flexibility provided by that classification, but in 'suitable cases' conditions will be found:

> 'It remains true, as Lord Roskill said in *Cehave NV* v *Bremer Handelsgesellschaft mbH, The Hansa Nord*, that the courts should not be too ready to interpret contractual clauses as conditions. And I have myself commended, and continue to commend, the greater flexibility in the law of contracts to which *Hong Kong Fir* points the way...But I do not doubt that in suitable cases, the courts should not be reluctant, if the intention of the parties as shown by the contract so indicates, to hold that an obligation has the force of a condition and that indeed they should usually do so in the case of time clauses in mercantile contracts' (Lord Wilberforce in *Bunge Corpn* v *Tradax Export SA* [1981] 1 WLR 711 at 715–16).

8.21   Before addressing ourselves to what constitutes a 'suitable case', it is worth noting that the question is basically whether the term is a condition or an innominate term. The warranty label is unlikely to be used in the absence of a clear express, or statutory, classification (for example, Sale of Goods Act 1979, s 12(2)). The innominate term classification will be used instead. It does not matter if most breaches of the term in question would have minor factual consequences; they will give rise only to the right to damages and not to the right to terminate, but the innominate term classification also allows for termination in the odd case where the breach has very serious consequences (*Re Olympia and York Canary Wharf Ltd (No 2)* [1993] BCC 159 at 166–7).

8.22   In *Bunge Corpn* v *Tradax Export SA* [1981] 1 WLR 711 Lord Wilberforce distinguished the time clause in that case, and the seaworthiness clause in *Hong Kong Fir Shipping Co. Ltd* v *Kawasaki Kisen Kaisha Ltd* (1962). He pointed out (at 715) that a term as to seaworthiness can be breached in many different ways:

> 'the breaches which might occur of the [seaworthiness clause are] various. They might be extremely trivial, the omission of a nail; they might be extremely grave, a serious defect in the hull or in the machinery.'

He considered that this made the term one in which it was appropriate for the legal consequences of the breach to depend upon the factual consequences. A time clause was 'totally different in character . . . As to such a clause there is only one kind of breach possible, namely to be late.'

8.23   However, although a clause such as that in *Hong Kong Fir* can be breached in many different ways, and will usually be appropriately classified as an innominate term, the jump cannot be made from that conclusion to stating that a term which can be breached in only one way will normally be classified as a condition or a warranty. Even though a term may be breached in only one way, for example, by being late, it will normally be capable of being breached to different degrees and there may be variations in the seriousness of the consequences which flow from any breach. An exception to this would seem to be in relation to an agreement to sell goods where the purported seller does not have title to the goods. In *Barber v NWS Bank plc* [1996] 1 All ER 906 the court had to consider the classification of an express term of a conditional sale agreement that, at the time the contract was made, the supplier was the owner of the goods. That was not the case, as the goods were still subject to an earlier hire purchase agreement and the court found that the term was a condition, enabling the purchaser to terminate the contract. The view was taken that the term was distinguishable from those which admit 'of different breaches, some of which are trivial' (at 911). All breaches of the term were viewed as sufficiently serious to justify termination and, thus, the term had to be classified as a condition.

8.24   It should be emphasized that the question of classification is a matter of the parties' intention. However, as we have seen, the starting point should favour the innominate term and the basic question should be whether there is a reason to classify the term as a condition rather than as an innominate term. The basic pointers to a term being a condition are that the term is important to the contract as a whole and that certainty is required. The need for certainty, as an indicator of the intention that the term should be a condition, was referred to in *Bunge Corpn v Tradax Export SA* (1981) (see para. **8.18**) and reference to the importance of the term is well established (for example, *Bentsen v Taylor, Sons & Co. (No 2)* [1893] 2 QB 274 at 281 per Bowen LJ (see para. **8.4**)). The more important a term is perceived to be to the substance of the contract, the more likely it is to be found that it was intended to be a condition (see also *Glaholm v Hays* (1841) 2 Man & G 257 at 266). Consideration of the importance of the term, in deciding upon its classification, has been put in terms of its 'commercial significance' (see *State Trading Corpn of India v M Golodetz Ltd* (1989) at para. **8.27**)—but the same point is being made. Although the main indicators of whether a term is to be construed as a condition are the importance of the term and the need for certainty, each case must be assessed as a whole to determine the parties' intention.

8.25   In *Bunge Corpn* the House of Lords indicated that time clauses in mercantile contracts will normally be conditions because of the need for certainty. Consideration of time clauses will illustrate how the need for certainty and the importance of the term, or otherwise, aid its classification.

8.26   A time clause had to be considered in *Compagnie Commerciale Sucres et Denrées v C Czarnikow Ltd, The Naxos* (1990):

> There was a contract for the sale of sugar. Delivery was to be to a vessel which was to be ready to load during May or June. The buyer was to give the seller not less than fourteen days'

notice of expected readiness to load. By rule 14 of the standard term contract the buyer was entitled to call for delivery at any time within the contract period, provided he had given the requisite notice. The buyers gave the requisite notice for loading on 29 May. The sellers did not have the sugar ready to load on 29 May; on 3 June, having warned the sellers, the buyers terminated the contract and purchased a replacement cargo.

The House of Lords had to decide whether rule 14 was a condition giving the buyers the right to terminate when the sellers failed to deliver on the date specified for loading. The House of Lords held (Lord Brandon dissenting) that rule 14 was a condition and the buyers had been entitled to terminate. The clause was a time clause in a mercantile contract, but there were also more specific indications that the term was to be construed as a condition. The court found that compliance with the time clause was 'crucially important' to the buyers. Had there been no delay it would, in turn, have enabled the buyers punctually to perform their own obligations to their customers. The situation was, as in *Bunge Corpn v Tradax Export SA* (1981), that of a chain of sales.

8.27   Of course, time clauses in mercantile contracts will not always be construed as conditions. The situation as a whole must be considered. In *State Trading Corpn of India v M Golodetz Ltd* [1989] 2 Lloyd's Rep 277, Kerr LJ said (at 283):

> 'At the end of the day, if there is no other more specific guide to the correct solution to a particular dispute, the court may have no alternative but to follow the general statement of Bowen LJ in *Bentsen v Taylor*...by making what is in effect a value judgment about the commercial significance of the term in question.'

In that case the term in question contained a time limit and the contract was mercantile, but its 'commercial significance', or importance to the contract as a whole, meant that it was not construed as a condition. In that case:

> The contract was for the sale of a cargo of sugar. The sugar was to be paid for by a letter of credit which the buyers undertook to open within seven days. The sellers undertook to open two guarantees within seven days—one in respect of the sugar sale and the other in respect of another undertaking which they had made, to purchase from the buyers, within six months, goods to the value of 60 per cent of the sugar contract.

The Court of Appeal was asked to decide whether the provision of the second guarantee, the countertrade guarantee, within seven days, was a condition of the contract. It was held that it was not. The 'commercial significance of the term' indicated that it should not be treated as a condition. It did not affect the buyer's performance of the sugar contract. It was a time clause, but it did not relate to the main and immediate transaction, only to one which was to occur within six months. It was also relatively unimportant in financial terms. The more important guarantee was that relating to performance of the sugar contract, and the timely giving of that guarantee was expressly prevented from being a condition. It was felt that the provision of the countertrade guarantee, within seven days, could not be a condition, when the undertaking to provide a guarantee of the sugar contract was much more important to the contract, and was not a condition.

8.28   A time clause may be such that it does not require the certainty of the 'condition' label. A time clause was not construed as a condition in *Bremer Handelsgesellschaft mbH v Vanden Avenne-Izegem PVBA* (1978) because the clause did not set a definite time limit. The clause in question stated that the sellers were to advise the buyers 'without delay' if shipment had become impossible for any one of a number of stated reasons. The question was whether it was a condition that such notification be made 'without delay'. Without a quantification of delay in terms of a stated time period, the House of Lords did not think that the term was to be construed as a condition. It was an innominate term. Similarly, 'as soon as reasonably practicable' was too indefinite to be construed as a condition in *British and Commonwealth Holdings plc v Quadrex Holdings Inc.* (1989). In that case the contract was for the sale of shares in an unquoted private company trading in a very volatile sector. The possibility of changes in the value of the shares would have made the time of completion of the sale a condition had it been more specific. However, it must be remembered that the parties may have intended a term which looks indefinite to be a condition. For example, a term requiring notice 'as soon as possible' might be construed as a condition if it was seen as very important to the contract. Such a conclusion would be assisted if trade practice made it possible to read 'as soon as possible' as the more specific 'within 24 hours' (see *Société Italo-Belge pour le Commerce et l'Industrie SA v Palm and Vegetable Oils (Malaysia) Sdn Bhd* (1981)).

Express classification

8.29   The parties can expressly make a term a condition, in the technical sense of that word, so that any breach of it, no matter how trivial, gives rise to the right to terminate. However, the word 'condition' may be used in many different senses and a court may decide that it is not being used in its technical sense to indicate that a breach is to give the right to terminate. In particular, they will be slow to find that it has been used in that sense where they are faced with a term which could obviously be breached in trivial ways. If finding that a term is a condition in the technical sense will lead to an unreasonable result the courts will regard it as unlikely that the parties intended that and will need the term to be very clearly drafted to be convinced that such a result was intended.

8.30   In *L Schuler AG v Wickman Machine Tool Sales Ltd* [1973] 2 All ER 39, the word 'condition' was used in relation to a term but it was not construed in its technical sense. In that case:

> Schuler, a German manufacturing company, made an agreement with Wickman for Wickman to have the sole right to sell Schuler's goods in the UK for about four and a half years. The agreement contained provisions relating to the promotion of Schuler's goods by Wickman. Clause 7 stated that it was a 'condition' that one of two named representatives of Wickman should visit six named UK automobile manufacturers each week. Clause 11 laid out the

procedure for termination of the contract upon a 'material breach' of the contract occurring, i.e. notice was to be given to remedy it within sixty days and if it was not remedied the contract could be terminated. In breach of clause 7, Wickman failed to carry out all of the specified visits to the six named automobile manufacturers.

Schuler argued that clause 7 was expressly made a condition of the contract and, thus, there was a right to terminate the contract for any breach of it, no matter how trivial. Schuler argued that even one failure to visit, out of the 1,400 visits required during the course of the contract, gave them the right to terminate. The House of Lords (Lord Wilberforce dissenting) refused to accept that argument. It pointed out that the word 'condition' had many meanings other than its technical one. In addition, their Lordships thought that a construction was to be avoided if it produced an unreasonable result, and there was an alternative construction available which did not. The court thought it would be unreasonable if any single breach of clause 7 gave the right to terminate, no matter how little at fault Wickman had been. The alternative which the court found, to help it avoid that unreasonable result, was to link clause 7 with clause 11. The use of the word 'condition' in clause 7 was construed as relating to whether the breach was 'material' within clause 11.

8.31　Lord Reid thought that the use of the word 'condition' was a 'strong indication' that the parties intended termination to be available on any breach of clause 7, but (at 45):

> 'The fact that a particular construction leads to a very unreasonable result must be a relevant consideration. The more unreasonable the result the more unlikely it is that the parties can have intended it, and if they do intend it the more necessary it is that they should make that intention abundantly clear.'

Any intention to use 'condition' in its technical sense had not been made clear enough, under the circumstances, for Lord Reid and the other members of the majority in the House of Lords.

8.32　However, Lord Wilberforce thought that 'condition' should have been construed technically. He gave little weight to the argument that such a construction was to be avoided on the grounds that it produced an unreasonable result. He said (at 55):

> 'to call the clause arbitrary, capricious, or fantastic, or to introduce as a test of its validity the ubiquitous reasonable man . . . is to assume, contrary to the evidence, that both parties to this contract adopted a standard of easygoing tolerance rather than one of aggressive, insistent punctuality and efficiency. This is not an assumption which I am prepared to make, nor do I think myself entitled to impose the former standard on the parties if their words indicate, as they plainly do, the latter.'

8.33　The initial reaction to the construction put upon the word 'condition' in *L Schuler AG v Wickman Machine Tool Sales Ltd* (1973) might be that if the parties want to make it clear that they intend a term to be a condition in the technical sense, they should specify that breach of it is to give rise to the right to terminate. However, that may not be sufficient when unreasonable results are in issue. The express statement of a right to terminate may be seen simply as an express right to terminate, rather than as making clear that the term is a technical condition. (Obviously, this does give the injured party the right to terminate, but damages will be different from what they would be if the term was technically a condition. They will not encompass the loss of the rest of the contract (see, for example, *Financings Ltd* v *Baldock* (1963)).)

8.34   However, it may be made clear that terms are technical conditions. In *Lombard North Central plc* v *Butterworth* (1987) there was a term stating that time was 'of the essence' in relation to the payment of each of the nineteen instalments due under what was, in effect, a hire purchase contract. The Court of Appeal held that the phrase 'time of the essence' was so well established as meaning that a time term was a technical condition, that they had to interpret it as such.

⬢ Summary

- Not all contract terms are of equal importance.
- Terms may be conditions, warranties or innominate.
- The breach of any term gives a right to damages.
- The classification of terms as conditions, warranties or innominate terms is of significance when the injured party's right to terminate for breach is in question.
  - Any breach of condition gives the right to the injured party to terminate.
  - A breach of a warranty does not give the injured party the right to terminate.
  - A breach of an innominate term gives the injured party the right to terminate if the breach is such as to deprive the injured part of substantially all the benefit he or she was intended to derive from the contract (*Hong Kong Fir* (1962)).
- Determining whether a term is a condition, warranty or innominate is a matter of the (objective) intention of the parties at the time the contract was made (*Bentsen* v *Taylor, Sons & Co. (No 2)* (1893), *Bunge* v *Tradax* (1981)).
- In deciding what classification of a term the parties would have intended, when the contract was made, it is relevant to consider the benefits and drawbacks of the classification.
- There is an impetus to classify a term as innominate, because it has the benefit of flexibility, providing some correlation between the seriousness of the breach and the availability of the right to terminate.
- Some terms may be important to the contract and require the benefit of the certainty of the condition classification.
- The parties may themselves state that a term is a condition. However, the word 'condition' has many meanings. The courts will be slow to find that the parties intended the technical meaning here considered if that would lead to an unreasonable result (for example, *Schuler* v *Wickman* (1973)).

⬚ **Further reading**

R. Brownsword, 'Retrieving Reasons, Retrieving Rationality? A New Look at the Right to Withdraw for Breach of Contract' (1992) 5 JCL 83

J. W. Carter, 'Intermediate Terms arrive in Australia and Singapore' (2008) 24 JCL 226

G. H. Treitel, ' "Conditions" and "Conditions Precedent" ' (1990) 106 LQR 185

G. H. Treitel, 'Types of Contractual Terms' in G. Treitel, *Some Landmarks of Twentieth Century Contract Law*, Clarendon Press, 2002

S. Whittaker, 'Termination Clauses' in A. Burrows and E. Peel (eds), *Contract Terms*, Oxford University Press, 2007

Chapter 9

Exemption clauses

⊙ Introduction

9.1 Exemption clauses have proved to be one of the most interesting areas of contract law in recent years. It is an area which has provoked litigation and legislation, and often involves a balancing of the competing interests of protection of the consumer, and weaker parties more generally, and freedom of contract. The main general legislation in relation to exemption clauses has been Unfair Contract Terms Act 1977 (UCTA), which is considered in detail in **Chapter 10**. In addition, although applicable beyond exemption clauses, UCTA was supplemented, in the consumer sphere, by the Unfair Terms in Consumer Contracts Regulations 1999,[1] implementing the EC Directive on Unfair Terms in Consumer Contracts (see **Chapter 11**). However, having two overlapping regimes has created undesirable complexity, and there is now a draft Consumer Rights Bill, which would strip out the consumer aspects of UCTA and unite the protection it has provided in the consumer sphere with the more general consumer unfair terms regime, in a single piece of legislation, leaving UCTA's coverage to the business context (see **Chapters 10** and **11**). However, although there will obviously be reference to legislation, the focus of this chapter is the common law.

Definitions

9.2 At a basic level an exemption clause is one which excludes or limits, or appears to exclude or limit, liability for breach of contract, or other liability arising by way of tort, bailment, or statute. It should be noted that the exemption clause may seek to exclude totally a liability or merely to limit it. The terms 'exemption clause' and 'exclusion clause' are often loosely used to encompass both situations but, in an effort to avoid confusion, the practice adopted here is to

---

1 Previously, the Unfair Terms in Consumer Contracts Regulations 1994.

use 'exemption clause' as a general term, encompassing both exclusion and limitation clauses. The term 'exclusion clauses' will be restricted to those clauses which remove, or purport to remove, liability. The label 'limitation clause' will be used solely for those clauses which do not remove, or purport to remove, liability entirely but, for example, restrict or purport to restrict damages payable on a breach of contract to a specified sum.[2]

9.3   Coote identified a problem with the above type of basic definition (Coote, *Exception Clauses*, Sweet & Maxwell, 1964, chs 1 and 10). An example will help to explain the difficulty. Consider the situation where X has agreed to sell goods to Y and to deliver them by a certain date. The contract contains a clause designed to prevent X having to pay damages for breach if late delivery is caused by industrial action. X may have put in a term stating that liability for late delivery is excluded where it is caused by industrial action. Alternatively, X may have specified that he is obliged to deliver by that stated date only if there is no industrial action. The same end result can be achieved by two different forms of clause. The first possible way of achieving the desired result is by using a straightforward exclusion clause. The second possibility is to use a clause which defines the initial obligation in such a way that there is no obligation to deliver by the stated time if industrial action occurs. The fact that the same result can be achieved by the two approaches leads to the argument that an exclusion clause cannot be regarded as a distinct type of clause but merely one of the clauses defining the obligations under the contract, whatever form it takes.[3] For the most part, the courts assume that an exclusion clause is a distinct type of clause, removing liability for breach of an existing obligation. They may even be content to regard a clause as an exclusion clause without any consideration of the fact that it is, in form, a definition of the obligation (for example, *J Evans & Son (Portsmouth) Ltd* v *Andrea Merzario Ltd* (1976)). However, it must be borne in mind that an exclusion clause can simply be seen as part of the definition of the obligation. In particular, difficult borderline cases arise under the Unfair Contract Terms Act 1977. It is sometimes necessary to determine whether a clause should be regarded as an exclusion clause, and subject to the Act, or merely a definition of the parties' obligations, and not subject to the Act (see E. Macdonald, 'Exception Clauses: Exclusionary or Definitional? It Depends!' (2012) 29 JCL 47; J. Adams and R. Brownsword, 'The Unfair Contract Terms Act: A Decade of Discretion' (1988) 104 LQR 94).

9.4   It should be noted that this problem, in relation to the identification of exclusionary and definitional clauses, cannot arise in relation to a limitation clause. Such a clause concedes the existence of the initial obligation and merely purports to place a limitation upon what happens when that obligation is not fulfilled. It is distinct from the definition of the initial obligation.

---

2   See D. Yates, *Exclusion Clauses in Contracts*, 2nd edn, Sweet & Maxwell, 1982, pp. 33–41; and H. Beale, W. Bishop, and M. Furmston, *Contract Cases and Materials*, 5th edn, Oxford University Press, 2008, p. 975 for a more extensive breakdown of types of exemption clause.

3   For contrasting judicial approaches on this, see *Photo Production Ltd* v *Securicor Transport Ltd* [1980] AC 827 at 842–3 per Lord Wilberforce and at 851 per Lord Diplock.

Standard form contracts

9.5   Exemption clauses are often found in standard form contracts. This can lead to the allegation that they have been imposed as part of a 'take it or leave it' package by the party with the superior bargaining position; hence the alternative label of 'contracts of adhesion'. The effect of standard form contracts is often such that the party against whom the exemption clause is being used had no knowledge that it was a term of the contract. In such circumstances it would hardly be surprising if the fairness of exemption clauses was questioned, particularly where a business person is seeking to rely upon an exemption clause against a consumer.

9.6   This sort of problem led to the enactment of the Unfair Contract Terms Act 1977. The Act prevents the use of some exemption clauses entirely and renders others ineffective unless they satisfy the requirement of reasonableness. Before the Act the common law tried to respond to the problem of objectionable exemption clauses. It was possible for the courts to take a restrictive approach to the construction of an exemption clause and limit its effectiveness by finding that it did not cover the particular breach which had occurred. Similarly, the courts found some flexibility in the rules relating to incorporation of contract terms. They could find that the exemption clause was not part of the contract at all. Some of the older case law relating to exemption clauses must now be viewed with caution. The existence of the legislation means that the devices developed by the common law to deal with exemption clauses may now be used more sparingly by the courts. The legislation has the advantage that it often allows the court openly to weigh the factors indicating whether the clause is 'reasonable', or fair. Such calculations of reasonableness, or fairness, must have influenced the courts' approach to their use of the common law devices, but it can now often be considered openly, with arguments from both sides specifically directed to it. However, it should be borne in mind that not all types of contract are subject to such legislative controls and the courts may be more willing to use the common law devices when faced with a contract which is not so covered. Of course, UCTA has now been supplemented by the consumer unfair terms regime, but even so, not all situations of unreasonable, or unfair, terms will be dealt with by legislation.

9.7   However, it should not be assumed that standard form contracts, with their exemption clauses, are always devices for the abuse of a superior bargaining position. There are advantages to be gained from the use of standard form contracts. A standard form contract may be used to speed up the contracting process and reduce the costs involved in arriving at a concluded contract. This is desirable and, indeed, unobjectionable if the standard form contract is a fair allocation of risk. The standard form may be one used throughout a particular trade, arrived at by negotiation, on equal terms, between representatives of those using it on both sides (for example, both buyers and sellers of a particular commodity, or hirers and those to whom they hire a type of equipment). Under such circumstances, the exemption clause may merely represent an allocation of risk to the person best able to insure against it. A limitation of risk may be accompanied by a low charge to the other party.

Three basic questions

9.8   When considering exemption clauses, there are three basic questions to be considered:

1. Incorporation—is the clause part of the contract?
2. Construction—is the clause appropriately worded to cover what has occurred?
3. Legislation—basically, is the clause affected by the Unfair Contract Terms Act 1977 or the legislative regime dealing with unfair terms in consumer contracts?

Questions (1) and (2) are discussed at para. **9.9**ff and para. **9.60**ff respectively. Question (3) is dealt with in **Chapters 10** and **11**.

Incorporation

Introduction

9.9   The first question to be considered is whether the exemption clause has become a term of the contract. This is the issue of incorporation. It should be noted that the same basic rules apply to incorporation of all terms, whether or not they are exemption clauses. The discussion of incorporation largely takes place here, in the context of exemption clauses, because it is in relation to such clauses that the issue is often raised. Under consideration here are clauses in written documents; it is unlikely that an exemption clause will have simply been stated orally by one party to another, but on the question generally of whether an oral statement is a term of the contract, see para. **7.4**ff.

9.10   At first sight the question of incorporation of a clause might be thought of as an uncomplicated matter, simply requiring the determination of what the parties agreed to. Certainly, incorporation poses no problems where both parties have actual knowledge of all the terms contained in the offer which was accepted. Problems arise because there is often no actual knowledge of all the terms, and incorporation cannot be said to be based upon any simple notion of what the parties agreed to. Even when one party has been alerted that a document contains important clauses, designed to be part of the contract, he or she will not always read it. He or she may even sign it without reading it. Such signature will ensure that the clauses become terms of the contract even though that party has no actual knowledge of their content (see para. **9.12**ff). Incorporation of clauses from unsigned documents can also occur, even though there is no actual knowledge of their content (see para. **9.22**ff). In short, incorporation is not a matter of subjective agreement to the terms, but it is often not a search even for objective agreement to the terms in any real sense. It has become a question of whether or not the parties are to be taken to have 'agreed to' a particular set of terms according to a very artificial set of rules worked out by the court for determining the question of incorporation.

9.11   To allow incorporation without actual knowledge, and even without signature, obviously opens the way for one party to take advantage of another. This is particularly so where one party has a set of standard terms which he wishes to incorporate into each contract he makes. This is often the case with contracts between business people and consumers, and the lack of any real opportunity to become acquainted with terms may be relevant to their reasonableness, or fairness, under the appropriate legislative regime. It could be said that if one party is not sufficiently careful of his or her own interests to inform him or herself of all the terms on which the contract is being made, then he or she cannot blame anyone else for any unacceptable terms. However, with long standard form documents it is understandable if all clauses are not read before the document is signed and, where there has been incorporation without signature, there may not even have been knowledge of the existence of the clauses. Particularly in the business/consumer situation, there may also be a feeling that there is no point in reading the standard clauses as they will not be open to negotiation. Against this background, when the issue of incorporation has arisen, the courts have attempted to maintain some balance between the parties (see para. **9.34**ff). In other words, the cases show some reaction against the perceived unfairness produced by our current general rules on incorporation. It is interesting to note that Atiyah has identified these present rules as stemming from the courts' reaction to juries favouring consumers in litigation against railway companies, and the then perceived need to protect those companies (P. S. Atiyah, *Rise and Fall of Freedom of Contract*, Oxford University Press, 1979, p. 731). However, it should again be emphasized that legislation will now often provide a direct means of attacking 'objectionable' exemption clauses which have become terms of the contract.

Signature

9.12   Incorporation of a clause by signature is basically a very mechanical process. It leaves little room for any questioning of the incorporation of the clause into the contract and has the benefit of certainty. The relevant clause will be incorporated into the contract if it is contained in a contractual document which has been signed by the person seeking to deny that the clause is part of the contract. This is obviously subject to a claim of fraud, or misrepresentation, or *non est factum* but, in the absence of such a claim, signature will act to incorporate the clause whether the person signing had any knowledge of the clause or not. *L'Estrange v F Graucob Ltd* (1934) illustrates this point:

> Miss L'Estrange was the owner of a cafe in Llandudno. She purchased a cigarette vending machine from Graucob Ltd. The machine proved to be defective. She claimed that Graucob Ltd were in breach of an implied term that the machine was reasonably fit for its purpose. Graucob Ltd denied that any such term could be implied. They relied upon a clause in the order form, which the claimant had signed, which said 'any express or implied condition, statement, or warranty, statutory or otherwise not stated herein is hereby excluded'. This clause was in 'regrettably small print' and Miss L'Estrange had not read it and did not know of its contents.

The court decided that Miss L'Estrange's signature on the order form containing the clause meant that her total lack of awareness of the exemption clause was irrelevant. The clause prevented the term from being implied, and Graucob were not in breach of contract despite the defects in the vending machine.

9.13   In the case of *Grogan* v *Robin Meredith Plant Hire Ltd* (1996) it was emphasized that in order for signature to incorporate terms, the document signed must be a contractual one. Therefore signature of a time sheet, which had an obvious and purely administrative purpose in the working of an existing contract, did not incorporate clauses printed on it as it did not 'purport to have contractual effect'. More generally, the question seems to be how the reasonable person would have viewed the document, taking account of 'the nature and purpose of the document' and the 'circumstances of its use between the parties', i.e. in that context would the reasonable person have viewed it as a document intended to contain contract terms?[4] This does not make any significant inroad on the approach taken in *L'Estrange* v *F Graucob Ltd* (1934) and should be distinguished from incorporation of unsigned documents through 'reasonably sufficient notice' (see para. **9.22**ff). In the context of a signed document there is no requirement of notice. It is merely that, in the absence of knowledge, a signing party should not be contractually bound by clauses printed on what the world at large would take to be a non-contractual document.

9.14   However, misrepresentation as to the effect of the exemption clause came to the aid of the person seeking to deny the effectiveness of that clause in *Curtis* v *Chemical Cleaning and Dyeing Co. Ltd* (1951):

> Mrs Curtis took a white satin wedding dress to the defendants' shop to be cleaned. The assistant asked her to sign a document headed 'Receipt'. Mrs Curtis asked about the 'Receipt' and was told that it stated that the cleaners would not accept liability for damage to beads and sequins. The 'Receipt' actually contained a clause stating, 'This article...is accepted on condition that the company is not liable for any damage however arising'. Owing to the cleaners' negligence the fabric of Mrs Curtis's dress was stained, but the cleaners argued that they were not liable for this damage because of the exemption clause in the 'Receipt'.

The wording of the exemption clause was very wide and could have covered damage to the fabric of the dress, but, despite Mrs Curtis's signature, the Court of Appeal held that the cleaners could not rely upon the clause to remove their liability. The contents of the exemption clause had been innocently misrepresented as confined to limiting liability for negligent damage to the beads and sequins. It could not assist them when damage had occurred to the fabric of the dress.[5]

9.15   The restrictions on the basic approach taken in *L'Estrange* v *F Graucob Ltd* (1934) are very limited, and it is a very artificial approach to determining the content of the parties' agreement.

---

4   See also *Noreside Construction v Irish Asphalt Ltd* (2011).

5   The basis of the conclusion in *Curtis*, and what the case should be regarded as authority for, has recently been questioned by Rix LJ in *Axa Sun Life Services Ltd v Campbell Martin* (2011) at [99]–[105].

On occasion, this artificiality has been noted. In *McCutcheon* v *David MacBrayne Ltd* [1964] 1 WLR 125 Lord Devlin considered what difference it should make whether the document in question had been signed or not. He said (at 133):

> 'If it were possible for your Lordships to escape from the world of make-believe which the law has created into the real world in which transactions of this sort are actually done, the answer would be short and simple. It should make no difference whatever. This sort of document is not meant to be read, still less to be understood. Its signature is in truth about as significant as a handshake that marks the formal conclusion of a bargain.'[6]

9.16 Elsewhere there has been a move away from the basic approach in *L'Estrange* v *F Graucob Ltd* (1934). In the Canadian case of *Tilden Rent-A-Car Co.* v *Clendenning* (1978) unusual and onerous printed clauses were not incorporated and the line was taken that signature can only be relied upon as showing assent to a document when it is reasonable for the person relying on the signed document to believe that the signatory assented to its contents.

9.17 Here there have been suggestions that the reasoning on the 'red hand' rule in *Interfoto Picture Library Ltd* v *Stiletto Visual Programmes Ltd* (1988) in the context of incorporation by notice (see para. **9.34**ff) could provide a basis for a requirement that the signatory's attention be drawn to unusual or unreasonable clauses if they are to be incorporated by signature.[7] The 'red hand' rule mitigates the impact of the general rule, that clauses can be incorporated from unsigned documents or signs by using 'reasonably sufficient notice', by requiring a greater degree of notice, to pass that test, where clauses are unusual or unreasonable. Limited support for the extension of that approach, into the context of incorporation by signature, might found in an *obiter* comment made by Evans LJ in *Ocean Chemical Transport Inc.* v *Exnor Craggs Ltd* (2000) at [48]. In response to counsel's suggestion that 'the *Interfoto* test...has to be applied, even in a case where the other party has signed an acknowledgment of the terms and conditions and their incorporation', Evans LJ said that it seemed to him that counsel 'could be right in what might be regarded as an extreme case, where signature was obtained under pressure of time or other circumstances...'. However, the comments of the courts more generally are against the extension of the red hand rule into the context of incorporation by signature,[8] and, despite the artificialities involved in the *L'Estrange* approach, it is suggested that the line taken by the Canadian court, is unlikely to be adopted here at common law. It was developed by the Canadian court at about the same time as the Unfair Contract Terms Act 1977 was introduced in the UK to deal with objectionable exemption clauses. In *Toll (FGCT) Pty Ltd.* v *Alphapharm Pty Ltd* (2004) at [48] in reasserting the *L'Estrange* approach, the High Court of Australia has commented that 'as a result of' that type of legislative control 'there is no reason to depart from

6 See also *Jones* v *Northampton Borough Council* (1990) Times, 21 May, per Ralph Gibson LJ; *Levison* v *Patent Steam Cleaning Co. Ltd* [1978] QB 69 at 78 per Lord Denning MR; *Bridge* v *Campbell Discount Co. Ltd* [1962] 1 All ER 385 at 399 per Lord Denning.

7 L. Rutherford and S. Wilson, 'Signature of a Document' (1998) 148 NLJ 380; A. Downes, *Textbook on Contract Law*, 5th edn, Blackstone, 1997, pp. 160–1.

8 *Yoldings Ltd* v *Swann Evans* (2000); *Jonathan Wren & Co Ltd* v *Microdec plc* (1999); *Bankway Properties Ltd* v *Penfold-Dunsford* (2001) at [41]; *HIH Casualty & General Insurance Ltd* v *New Hampshire Insurance Co.* (2001) at [209]–[213].

principle and every reason to adhere to it'.[9] It should be recognized that the *L'Estrange* approach provides a great deal of certainty in relation to the issue of incorporation, and that is very significant. In *Peninsula Business Services Ltd* v *Sweeney* (2004) at [23] the Employment Appeal Tribunal said:

> 'It would make for wholly unacceptable commercial uncertainty if it were open to B who has signed a written agreement to say that he was not bound by one of the terms expressly contained in it because A had not first drawn his attention expressly to it.'

Also the comment has been made that the *L'Estrange* approach is one which 'underpins the whole of commercial life; any erosion of it would have serious repercussions far beyond the business community' (*Peekay Intermark Ltd* v *Australia and New Zealand Banking Group* (2006) per Moore-Bick LJ at [43]).

9.18 In addition, it makes any broad common law development even more unlikely that there are now further legislative developments taking place in the consumer context. The draft Consumer Rights Bill contains a requirement that:[10]

> 'If a term is especially onerous or unusual, the trader must ensure that the term is drawn particularly to the consumer's attention'.

The Competition and Markets Authority and other specified enforcers will have powers to obtain injunctions in relation to the use, or recommendation for use, of terms, for non-compliance.

9.19 One question which now arises is what will amount to a signature, to invoke the rule in *L'Estrange* v *Graucob*, when a contract is made electronically. In particular, it is controversial as to whether the action of clicking an 'I agree', button could amount to such signature. The Law Commission took a very broad approach to what should constitute a signature to satisfy statutory formality requirements:

> 'Digital signatures, scanned manuscript signatures, typing one's name (or initials) and clicking on a website button are, in our view, all methods of signature which are generally capable of satisfying a statutory signature requirement' (*Electronic Commerce: Formal Requirements in Commercial Transactions* Advice from the Law Commission (Dec 2001), para. 3.39).

Further, they concluded that, in that formalities context, clicking on a website button should be regarded as the functional equivalent to a signature on the basis that it demonstrates a

---

9 E. Peden and J. Carter, 'Incorporation of Terms by Signature: *L'Estrange* rules' (2005) 21 JCL 1.

10 Clause 71(3). It is to be hoped that this will be enlarged during the passage of the draft Bill, to cover terms which are 'especially unreasonable or unusual'. The reference to 'onerous' would appear to be a reflection of the later statements of the 'red hand rule', in cases such as *Interfoto* where the terms were 'onerous'. That categorization was easy to fall into, as UCTA was likely to deal with unreasonable terms which were not onerous. That should not, however, inappropriately restrict this requirement, which is intended to operate alongside a 'fairness' test the application of which is not limited to exemption clauses.

validating intention and is not purely oral. They also made an analogy with the historically accepted manuscript 'X' signature, made by those who cannot sign their names in the usual manuscript form.

9.20   However, it is suggested that the everyday manuscript signature has an alerting function for the consumer, in particular, which simply clicking on a website button does not have.[11] It is a commonplace, albeit one seldom acted upon that 'you should read a contract before signing it'. It seems unlikely that the consumer, in particular, will have that reaction before clicking the relevant button.

9.21   The rule in *L'Estrange v Graucob* is very artificial, and capable of creating considerable unfairness. That may now often be dealt with by legislation, but should we really extend that rule to this new, and very commonplace, context? Contracting by clicking such a button could be regarded as equivalent to merely stating one's agreement, and the rules about notice would then be required to be satisfied to incorporate the relevant standard terms. (See further E. Macdonald, 'Incorporation of Standard Terms in Website Contracting—Clicking "I agree"' (2011) 27 JCL 198).

Notice[12]

9.22   Unsigned documents or signs provide the main problems in relation to incorporation. As there is no signature, it must be asked what other means can be used to establish that the clauses on the document or sign are part of the contract. There is no difficulty where there is actual knowledge of the clause. It will then clearly be part of the contract. It is the situation when this knowledge is absent which needs to be considered.

Timing

9.23   The first point to be made is that clauses cannot be incorporated from unsigned documents or signs if those documents or signs are not introduced into the transaction until after the contract has been concluded. Once offer and acceptance have occurred, one party cannot say to the other: 'Oh, by the way, these clauses are part of our agreement'. The contract is on the terms of the offer, which was accepted. A case which illustrates the need to ensure that the unsigned document or sign is introduced into the transaction before offer and acceptance are complete, and the contract is made, is *Olley v Marlborough Court Ltd* (1949). In that case:

> Mrs Olley and her husband made a contract to stay in the hotel. The contract was made at the reception desk on their arrival. They were then shown to their room. There was a sign in the room which purported to exclude the hotel's liability for the theft of guests' property unless

---

11 The point might be made that a typed name or a rubber stamp may constitute signature in the off-line world (e.g. *Goodman v Eban* (1954)) but whilst businesses may be familiar with these forms of signature, it is suggested that the consumer is not.

12 Clarke [1976] CLJ 51.

> deposited with the manageress for safe keeping. Mrs Olley returned to her room one day to discover that her furs had been stolen as a result of the hotel's negligence. The hotel sought to rely upon its exemption clause to exclude its liability for her loss.

The Court of Appeal held that the clauses on the sign in the bedroom could not form part of the contract between the hotel and Mrs Olley. The contract had been made at the reception desk before there had been any opportunity to see the sign.

The test

9.24　The basic rule for incorporation of a clause contained in an unsigned document or sign is that such a clause is part of the contract if there has been reasonably sufficient notice of it. This test is derived from *Parker* v *South Eastern Rly Co.* (1877) where the court was concerned with the terms on which goods were deposited in a railway station cloakroom. In that case:

> On depositing a bag in the cloakroom, Mr Parker was handed a ticket which he did not read and which contained a clause purporting to limit the railway company's responsibility to packages not exceeding £10 in value. Mr Parker's bag was of greater value than £10 and, on its loss from the cloakroom, the question was whether the clause on the ticket limited the liability of the railway company.

The result of the case was that a retrial was ordered. The judge at first instance had misdirected the jury on the test for incorporation. The court decided that the basic test to determine whether incorporation had occurred in this type of situation is that of reasonably sufficient notice, i.e. whether reasonably sufficient notice of the clause had been given.

9.25　The need to order a retrial in *Parker* v *South Eastern Rly Co.* (1877) emphasizes the factual nature of the test (*Hood* v *Anchor Line (Henderson Bros) Ltd* [1918] AC 837 at 844). So, for example, there is unlikely to be reasonably sufficient notice of a clause printed on the back of a ticket if the front of the ticket does not say 'for conditions see back' (*Henderson* v *Stevenson* (1875)), but it will depend upon all the facts of the particular case. Equally, a ticket which would in normal circumstances provide reasonably sufficient notice might not do so if it had been folded over (*Richardson, Spence, & Co.* v *Rowntree* (1894)) or the relevant clause had been obscured by a date stamp (*Sugar* v *London, Midland, and Scottish Rly Co.* (1941)).

Type of document

9.26　The type of document in which a clause is found is relevant to its incorporation. It may simply be said that a non-contractual document will not incorporate terms.[13] However, in the context of a general requirement of reasonably sufficient notice, the type of document is also relevant to

---

13　See *Grogan* v *Robin Meredith Plant Hire* (1996)—para. **9.13**—in the context of signed documents.

that requirement. In *Parker* v *South Eastern Rly Co.* [1877] 2 CPD 416 Mellish LJ gave an example (at 422):

> 'If a person driving through a turnpike-gate received a ticket upon paying the toll, he might reasonably assume that the object of the ticket was that by producing it he might be free from paying toll at some other turnpike-gate, and might put it in his pocket unread.'

Although this is quite an old example, the general point is clear. It was referred to by Slesser LJ in *Chapelton* v *Barry UDC* [1940] 1 KB 532 (at 538), and that case provides us with a further example:

> Mr Chapelton was at the beach at Cold Knap in Barry. There was a sign indicating the hire charge for deck-chairs and requesting those using the chairs to obtain a ticket from the attendant and retain it for inspection. Mr Chapelton took a chair and obtained a ticket. He put the ticket in his pocket without reading what was printed on it. When he sat down in the chair the canvas gave way and he fell and injured himself. Barry UDC, from whom he had hired the chair, claimed to be able to rely upon a clause on the ticket to exclude liability for his injuries.

The court decided that the clause on the ticket was not part of the contract. The ticket was not the sort of document on which a contract term would be expected. It appeared merely to be proof that Mr Chapelton had paid his 2d hire charge.

9.27   When the type of document is discussed, in relation to the issue of incorporation, the point is sometimes put in terms of whether the document is a 'mere receipt'. Mellish LJ clearly envisaged the ticket from the turnpike gate as a mere receipt and that is also how the court in *Chapelton* v *Barry UDC* (1940) perceived the deck-chair ticket, i.e. those tickets were seen as evidence of payment and nothing more. However, there is no reason why a document headed 'receipt' should not be used to incorporate clauses into a contract successfully if the circumstances indicate its true role to the reasonable person (*Watkins* v *Rymill* (1883)). It should be borne in mind that a clause cannot be incorporated into a contract by a document which is introduced after the contract is concluded; if a document is intended to be a receipt, in the sense of evidence of payment, it may have been introduced too late, after offer and acceptance have occurred. The timing of the introduction of the ticket was another reason for the decision in *Chapelton*.

9.28   A further point, related to that of the type of document, is that the transaction may be one in which it is commonly known that there will be standard terms. The question of incorporation from a particular document will then be viewed against this background and it will be easier to establish that reasonably sufficient notice has been provided. In *Alexander* v *Railway Executive* [1951] 2 KB 882 it was regarded as relevant to the question of reasonably sufficient notice that 'most people nowadays know that railway companies have conditions subject to which they take articles into their cloakrooms' (at 886).[14]

---

14 See also incorporation by a course of dealing and *British Crane Hire Corpn Ltd* v *Ipswich Plant Hire Ltd* (1975) (para. **9.56**).

Reference

9.29   It is not necessary for the document or sign itself to contain the terms. There may be incorporation by reference. In *Thompson* v *London, Midland Scottish Rly Co.* (1930) the railway ticket said on its front, in 'quite big print and quite legible print', 'for conditions see back'. On the back the passenger was referred to the railway timetable to ascertain the conditions. Despite the fact that the clause was only to be found upon p. 552 of the timetable, which itself cost 6d when Mrs Thompson's ticket cost only 2s 7d, the clauses were held to be incorporated and removed the railway's liability for the negligent injury to Mrs Thompson.

9.30   The reaction to *Thompson* v *London, Midland Scottish Rly Co.* (1930) may be that it is a fairly extreme case. A decision by a passenger to ascertain the content of the terms would have entailed a search of the timetable and some expense. Undoubtedly it was easier for the court to accept that the terms were incorporated in this case because it did not regard the exemption clause as unreasonable. Mrs Thompson had purchased an excursion ticket, at half the ordinary fare for the journey. Restricted liability was not regarded as unreasonable when a reduced fare was being paid.

9.31   As will be seen, at common law the courts have now proved themselves willing to link the question of incorporation by notice and the unreasonableness, or unusualness, of the content of a clause. That occurs through the 'red hand rule' (see para. **9.34**ff), which applies to incorporation by notice generally and in the context of incorporation by reference (*O'Brien* v *MGN Ltd* (2002)). It should, however, also be noted that artificiality of incorporation will also be relevant to the reasonableness test under UCTA 1977, and the fairness test in the consumer unfair terms regime. In particular, the latter contains a relevant term in its 'grey list' of terms which may be regarded as unfair (see para. **11.55**). Schedule 2 of the 1999 Unfair Terms in Consumer Contracts Regulations states, in para. 1, that it covers:

> 'Terms which have the object or effect of...(i) irrevocably binding the consumer to terms with which he had no real opportunity of becoming acquainted before the conclusion of the contract.'

In contracts between consumers and sellers or suppliers, this requires consideration of the accessibility of any clauses that it is sought to incorporate by reference. If they are inaccessible, then the term referring to them may be found to be unfair. Under those circumstances, it would not bind the consumer and there would then be no effective term to incorporate the clauses it had referred to.

Objective nature of the test

9.32   A variation on the facts of *Thompson* v *London, Midland Scottish Rly Co.* (1930) provides a useful way to emphasize the objective nature of the notice test. In that case the passenger was illiterate but the ticket was purchased by her agent (her daughter), who could read. The legal position of an agent is such that, what the agent had notice of, Mrs Thompson would also have notice of, and her illiteracy could not be relevant to the question of incorporation. However, even without the agent, Mrs Thompson's illiteracy should not be relevant to the question of reasonably sufficient notice, and this is the tenor of the judgments in the case. The test is objective. The question is one of sufficiency of notice for the reasonable person, not the particular individual. In *Parker* v *South Eastern Rly Co.* (1877) 2 CPD 416 Mellish LJ said (at 423):

> 'The railway company...must be entitled to make some assumptions respecting the person who deposits luggage with them; I think they are entitled to assume that he can read, and that he understands the English language...'.

The situation would be modified if the person who wished to include his or her exemption clauses knew, or should have known, that the person with whom he or she was contracting was illiterate. That factor would then enter into the assessment of whether there had been reasonably sufficient notice (*Geier* v *Kujawa, Weston, and Warne Bros (Transport) Ltd* (1970)).

9.33   More generally, the situation may be that the person wishing to incorporate his or her standard terms knows, or should know, that he or she will be contracting with individuals from a particular group who share some characteristic affecting their ability to acquire knowledge from a particular form of notice. In *Richardson, Spence, & Co.* v *Rowntree* [1894] AC 217 one of the elements mentioned by the court in relation to sufficiency of notice of the exemption clause was that the tickets were for steerage class passengers, 'many of whom have little education and some of them none' (at 221). That specific factor is obviously a product of its time, but it is possible to conceive of situations where the problem of communication with a particular group might be raised today. For example, a travel company setting out to provide holidays suitable for the blind would have to give serious consideration to the method used to incorporate an exemption clause into the contract with a blind person for such a holiday.

The red hand rule[15]

9.34   *Thompson* v *London, Midland and Scottish Rly Co.* [1930] 1 KB 41 at 53 and 56 contains some comments on whether it is possible to incorporate an unreasonable clause by notice. Such comments can be found in various cases,[16] but there is no such accepted restriction upon this method of incorporation. However, it is understandable that there should be a reaction against the idea that unreasonable clauses can be incorporated into a contract by notice, and used against someone who has not read them, and who has not even been alerted to be on guard by the necessity of signing the document containing them. The courts have developed a technique for restricting incorporation of unusual or unreasonable clauses by notice. In *J Spurling Ltd* v *Bradshaw* [1956] 1 WLR 461 Denning LJ, as he then was, said (at 466):

> 'the more unreasonable a clause is, the greater the notice which must be given of it. Some clauses which I have seen would need to be printed in *red ink on the face of the document*

---

15 E. Macdonald, 'The Duty to Give Notice of Unusual Contract Terms' [1988] JBL 375; H. McClean, 'Incorporation of Onerous or Unusual Terms' [1988] CLJ 172; E. Macdonald, *Exemption Clauses and Unfair Terms*, 2nd edn, Tottel, 2006, pp. 19–23.

16 e.g. *Parker* v *South Eastern Rly Co.* (1877) 2 CPD 416 at 428; *Van Toll* v *South Eastern Rly Co.* (1862) 12 CBNS 75 at 85 and 88.

with a red hand pointing to [them] before the notice could be held to be sufficient' (emphasis added).

Spurling itself provides no further guidance on what will, for obvious reasons, be termed the 'red hand' rule. The reference to the rule in *Spurling* was a lone *obiter dictum*.

9.35   The rule was given further consideration in *Thornton* v *Shoe Lane Parking Ltd* [1971] 2 QB 163. *Thornton* involved an attempt by the owners of a car park to escape liability for the negligently caused personal injury of Mr Thornton, who was injured when he returned to the car park to collect his car. The car-park owners were seeking to rely upon an exemption clause printed on the sign inside the car park and referred to on a ticket received at the entrance to the car park. It was argued that the ticket arrived too late to incorporate any clause into the contract, but the court also considered what the situation would be if that was not the case. The clause purported to exclude liability not only for damage to property but also for personal injury. Lord Denning MR considered it (at 170) to be an example of the type of clause which he had in mind in *J Spurling Ltd* v *Bradshaw* (1956) when propounding the red hand rule (i.e. an unreasonable clause) and one which would require additional notice to incorporate it. Megaw LJ also thought (at 172) that the clause would require extra notice in order to be incorporated, but he considered it to be unusual clauses which should be treated in this way. (See Clarke [1976] CLJ 51 at 69–71.)

9.36   After *Thornton* v *Shoe Lane Parking Ltd* (1971) it seemed that the red hand rule should be stated as being that the more unreasonable or unusual a clause is, the greater the degree of notice required to incorporate it, and this basic approach is confirmed by the judgments of the Court of Appeal in *Interfoto Picture Library Ltd* v *Stiletto Visual Programmes Ltd* (1988). In *Interfoto*:

> An advertising agency, Stiletto, telephoned Interfoto, who ran a library of photographic transparencies, to obtain material for a presentation to a client. Stiletto had not dealt with Interfoto before. Interfoto dispatched to Stiletto a bag containing forty-seven transparencies and a delivery note containing nine 'Conditions'. 'Condition 2' stated that a holding fee of £5 per transparency per day would be charged for any transparency kept beyond a fourteen-day period. Stiletto failed to return the transparencies within fourteen days and, on the basis of 'Condition 2', Interfoto claimed over £3,500 from Stiletto. The question was whether or not that clause was a term of the contract.

At first instance it was held that 'Condition 2' was part of the contract, but this was reversed by the Court of Appeal. The clause in question was not an exclusion clause, but the court said that the same rules for incorporation applied and, in particular, what has here been termed the red hand rule. The judgments in the Court of Appeal can be synthesized into the formulation of the red hand rule indicated earlier, i.e. the more unusual or unreasonable a clause, the greater the notice required for there to be reasonably sufficient notice. The court considered 'Condition 2' to be both unusual and onerous. There was evidence of the holding fees of ten other agencies.

Most of them charged less than £3.50 per transparency per week: only one charged more (£4 per week). The court held that there was not sufficient notice to incorporate 'Condition 2', and Interfoto were entitled to a quantum meruit of £3.50 per transparency per week, instead of the £5 per transparency per day claimed.

9.37 It should be acknowledged that the judges did refer to 'onerous', rather than 'unreasonable' clauses, but onerousness is merely the particular form of unreasonableness encountered in the case, which was that of a term imposing an unreasonable burden. That is likely to be the important form of unreasonableness for the red hand rule, in commercial cases, as UCTA deals with many others, but the more general restriction should not be thoughtlessly discarded, just because it will not often be needed, and the need to remember its more general, original, form will be returned to later.

9.38 The importance here of the red hand rule does not simply lie in its impact within the law of contract as a specific rule. The development of the red hand rule is worth considering also because it will make us think about the way in which the common law evolves, and this is of great importance in relation to an area of law, like contract, which is largely based upon judicial decisions rather than statute. The red hand rule says that notice varies with the contents of a clause. Its effect is that where clauses (a), (b), and (c) are printed on a ticket, in exactly the same size type, and (b) is a very unreasonable clause whilst the other two are not, there may be sufficient notice to incorporate clauses (a) and (c) but not clause (b). Is this logical? How can the degree of notice required to incorporate a clause depend upon its contents? Can the contents of a clause affect its legibility? Consideration of these questions makes obvious the problem of establishing the basis of the rule. It certainly cannot be regarded as merely a logical derivation from *Parker* v *South Eastern Rly Co.* (1877).[17] The contents of a clause cannot affect its legibility. However, the common law develops in response to the problems which the courts encounter. The general principle of incorporation by notice can be perceived as producing unfairness in some situations. One party may use it to introduce very unreasonable, or unusual, terms into his or her contract with the other party and that other party will have no actual knowledge of the terms and will not even have been alerted to be on guard by the necessity of signing the document. The decision in *Interfoto* represents the view that it is appropriate for the courts to interfere with the parties' apparent bargain in such circumstances. The court has acted to limit what it has seen as an abuse of the general notice principle, and to protect the injured party against that common human failing of not reading everything. The decision will be approved by those who favour an interventionist role for the courts.

9.39 *Interfoto Picture Library Ltd* v *Stiletto Visual Programmes Ltd* (1988) will be criticized by those who strongly favour the idea of freedom of contract. The court has interfered with the parties' apparent bargain. It could, however, be argued that the form of the red hand rule does not place an absolute bar upon the incorporation of unusual or unreasonable clauses, and is not a real interference with freedom of contract, being merely an interference with the manner

17 R. Brownsword, 'Incorporating Exemption Clauses' (1972) 35 MLR 183.

of the terms' incorporation and not with their content. It can be seen as aimed at ensuring that there is real freedom of contract through trying to address the problem of the artificiality of incorporation of contract terms, and the lack of real choice and consent that engenders. *Interfoto* is the type of case in which the court has to base its decision upon its view of a very fundamental idea, such as that of freedom of contract, and precedent can be of only limited help. In the end the result will depend upon whether or not the court leans towards intervention in such situations.

9.40   There is one further point to be made, before we move on from the red hand rule, and it is by no means the least important. As has been indicated, the draft Consumer Rights Bill contains a provision extending the power of the Competition and Markets Authority, and the other general enforcers, beyond obtaining injunctions simply in relation to unfair terms. They can also do so in relation to non-compliance with the requirement that 'If a term is especially onerous or unusual, the trader must ensure that the term is drawn particularly to the consumer's attention'.[18] It is to be hoped that this requirement is extended, during the passage of the Bill, to encompass not merely 'onerous' terms, but more broadly 'unreasonable' ones. The requirement would seem to be a reflection of the red hand rule, and, as has been indicated, the reduced statement of the red hand rule, as applying to onerous or unusual terms, would seem simply to be a product of onerousness being the specific type of unreasonableness encountered in *Interfoto*, and the type of unreasonableness to which the red hand rule was more likely to be significant after UCTA arrived on the scene, to deal with many unreasonable exemption clauses.

The general test—a further clarification of Parker

9.41   As we have seen, the basic test for incorporation of an unsigned document is that of reasonably sufficient notice. However, it is not uncommon to encounter a dictum of Mellish LJ in *Parker* v *South Eastern Rly Co.* (1877) 2 CPD 416 which appears to provide a fuller test and which is worth considering now that the basic test has been explored. Mellish LJ thought the appropriate test was (at 423):

> 'that if the person receiving the ticket did not see or know that there was any writing on the ticket, he is not bound by the conditions; that if he knew there was writing, and knew or believed that the writing contained conditions, then he is bound by the conditions; that if he knew there was writing on the ticket, but did not know or believe that the writing contained conditions, nevertheless he would be bound, if the delivering of the ticket to him in such a manner that he could see there was writing upon it, was . . . reasonable notice that the writing contained conditions.'

A number of points must be noted here in order to avoid confusion. First, Mellish LJ said that there will not be incorporation if the person to whom the ticket was given did not know that there was writing on it. This cannot be regarded as a general rule. As has been seen, the test of

---

18 Clause 71(3).

reasonably sufficient notice depends upon the facts in each case, and is not dependent upon providing sufficient notice for the particular individual (see the discussion of *Thompson* v *London, Midland and Scottish Rly Co.* (1930) at para. **9.29**). That the person to whom the ticket was delivered did not know that there was any writing on it cannot determine the issue. At most it is evidence that the reasonable person would not have realized that there was writing on the ticket, and that there was not reasonably sufficient notice.

9.42   The second point to be made is in relation to Mellish LJ's second statement—that if the person to whom the ticket is handed knows that it contains conditions, then he will be bound by them even though he does not know of the content of the conditions. An analogy can be made with incorporation by reference (see para. **9.32**). The individual is in a position to ascertain the contents of the terms. One qualification needs to be made: this situation should also be subject to the red hand rule. If the person to whom the ticket is given does not know of the content of the terms, but merely of their existence, he should be given extra notice of any unusual or unreasonable terms.

9.43   Finally, Mellish LJ's third point must be considered. It is close to a formulation of the general test. Again, the point which needs to be made is that the test is one which depends upon the facts in each case (*Hood* v *Anchor Line (Henderson Bros) Ltd* [1918] AC 837 at 844). It cannot be regarded as a general rule that, in order for there to be reasonably sufficient notice, the ticket must be delivered, so that the person to whom it is delivered, can see that there is writing on it. The dictum of Mellish LJ should be treated with some care.

Consistent course of dealing[19]

The test

9.44   There may sometimes be incorporation based upon the previous dealings between the parties. *J Spurling Ltd* v *Bradshaw* [1956] 1 WLR 461 provides an illustration of this:

> Bradshaw stored casks of orange juice in Spurling's warehouse. When Bradshaw went to collect his casks it was discovered that the juice was either gone or ruined, and he refused to pay the storage charge. When Spurling sued for the storage charge, Bradshaw counterclaimed for breach of contract by negligent storage. To defeat the counterclaim, Spurling sought to rely upon an exemption clause contained in a document which was sent to Bradshaw only some days after the contract of storage had been concluded.

The document containing the exemption clause had obviously arrived too late to incorporate terms into that particular contract. However, Bradshaw conceded that he had received such documents on previous occasions when he had dealt with Spurling and this led the Court of

---

19 E. Macdonald, 'Incorporation of Contract Terms by a "Consistent Course of Dealing"' (1988) 8 LS 48; Macdonald, *Exemption Clauses and Unfair Terms*, 2nd edn, pp. 25–31.

Appeal to conclude that 'by the course of business and conduct of the parties [the clause was] part of the contract' (at 471).

9.45   In *J Spurling Ltd* v *Bradshaw* (1956) the clause had been incorporated despite the late arrival of the document containing it. It is in this sort of situation, where the document has arrived too late in the instant case, that the argument for incorporation by a course of dealing usually arises. *Henry Kendall & Sons* v *William Lillico & Sons Ltd* (1969) provides another example:

> The seller sold Brazilian groundnut extract to the buyer to be used to compound cattle and poultry food. The contract between the parties had been made over the telephone but was followed, the next day, by the dispatch of a document, a sold note, which contained an exemption clause. The conclusion of an oral contract, followed by the dispatch of the sold note, was the practice which the parties had followed for three years. During that time there had been three or four transactions a month following that pattern. In the instant case the groundnut extract contained a substance poisonous to poultry.

The question arose as to the seller's liability for the poisonous state of the Brazilian groundnut extract. One argument was that the seller was protected by the exemption clause. This raised the issue of incorporation. The House of Lords was willing to accept that, although the document arrived too late to incorporate the clause into the particular transaction, the clause was part of the contract on the basis of the previous dealings between the parties. In the event this did not assist the sellers, as the court also concluded that the clause was not appropriately worded to cover the breach which had occurred.

9.46   *Henry Kendall & Sons* v *William Lillico & Sons Ltd* (1969) helps us towards a general test for incorporation by past dealings. In the Court of Appeal ([1966] 1 WLR 287, sub nom *Hardwick Game Farm* v *Suffolk Agricultural and Poultry Producers' Association Ltd*) Diplock LJ stated the test (at 339) as: 'what each party by his words and conduct reasonably led the other party to believe were the acts he was undertaking a legal duty to perform.' In the House of Lords, Lord Wilberforce agreed with Diplock LJ ([1969] 2 AC 31 at 130) and Lord Pearce formulated a general test in similar terms. He said (at 113): 'The court's task is to decide what each party to an alleged contract would reasonably conclude from the utterances, writings or conduct of the other.' More recently, a similar formulation has been applied. It has been asked 'what each party by his words and conduct would have led the other party as a reasonable man to believe he was accepting'.[20]

9.47   To settle on an exact formula for the test for incorporation by a course of dealing we need to consider the mechanism by which such incorporation occurs. In each case the court is concerned with what was included, unspoken, in the offer and acceptance on the basis of the

---

20 *SIAT di del Ferro* v *Tradax Overseas SA* [1978] 2 Lloyd's Rep 470 at 490; *Johnson Matthey Bankers Ltd* v *State Trading Corpn of India* [1984] 1 Lloyd's Rep 427 at 433; *Circle Freight International Ltd* v *Medeast Gulf Exports Ltd* [1988] 2 Lloyd's Rep 427 at 433.

previous dealings between the parties and what they have said and done in the instant case in relation to the offer and acceptance. In both *J Spurling Ltd* v *Bradshaw* (1956) and *Henry Kendall & Sons* v *William Lillico & Sons Ltd* (1969) a document containing the clauses in question had been sent, but it had been sent after offer and acceptance had occurred. The lateness of this document did not prevent the clauses from being incorporated because it is not the document dispatched in relation to the particular transaction which is the basis of incorporation of the clauses in the instant case. In *Kendall* v *Lillico*, for example, the incorporation of the exemption clause should be seen as based upon the 'sold note' delivered in relation to each of the previous transactions over the preceding three years. Because of the past transactions each party, as a reasonable person, should have assumed that the offer and acceptance, in the instant case, included the seller's standard terms. In *Petrotrade Inc.* v *Texaco Ltd* (2000), on the basis of five previous transactions on the same terms, and for the same commodity, in thirteen months, Clarke LJ concluded (at 1349): 'Given the course of dealing . . . both parties will have made the oral agreement on the basis that the contract would be subject to the same terms as before'. Obviously the situation would be different if one party had indicated by his words or actions that the particular transaction was not to be on the same basis as previous transactions. Bearing all this in mind, it is possible to formulate the test for incorporation from a course of dealings. The test should be whether, at the time of contracting, each party, as a reasonable person, should infer from the past dealings and the actions and words of the other in the instant case, that the standard clauses are part of the instant contract.

Acts/words in the instant case

9.48   In the context of incorporation by a course of dealing, further consideration needs to be given to the relevance of the acts or words of the parties in the instant case. On a factual level their relevance is obvious. For many years the parties may have contracted frequently and always used one party's standard terms. In the instant case it may be clear that past practice is to be departed from and that the standard terms are not to form part of the contract. Equally, it should be possible to find incorporation by a course of dealing when there are some differences between the instant case and past transactions, provided that the situation as a whole is such that the parties, as reasonable people, would still assume the standard terms to be part of the contract. For example, incorporation of one party's standard terms should be possible where those terms have been incorporated in each previous transaction by a document providing reasonably sufficient notice and, in the instant case, the contract is concluded over the telephone without any express reference to those standard terms (see *British Crane Hire Corpn.* v *Ipswich Plant Hire Ltd* (1975) at para. **9.56**). However, *McCutcheon* v *David MacBrayne Ltd* (1964) indicated that the acts or words in the instant case must be given some special legal significance beyond that which they would naturally have on a factual level, and this should be considered.

9.49   In *McCutcheon* v *David MacBrayne Ltd* (1964):

> McSporran arranged for a car belonging to his brother-in-law, McCutcheon, to be shipped from the Hebrides to the mainland by MacBrayne. McCutcheon had shipped various

> items three or four times in the past and so had McSporran. On each previous occasion McCutcheon had signed a risk note, but McSporran had done so only twice. The ship sank and McCutcheon sought to recover the cost of his car from MacBrayne. MacBrayne sought to rely upon an exemption clause, and one of the ways in which he argued that it had been incorporated was by a course of dealing. The clause was contained in the risk note which, on this occasion, McSporran had not been asked to sign.

In this case the House of Lords found that the past dealings were not appropriate to incorporate the clause. On the facts there is no difficulty with this. The previous transactions were limited in number and not consistent in the introduction of the risk note.

9.50   The reasoning in *McCutcheon* v *David MacBrayne Ltd* [1964] 1 WLR 125 must be considered. The judgment of Lord Reid poses no problems. He took the line which is the basis of the general test indicated earlier. He thought (at 128) that the court's task is 'to decide what each [party] was reasonably entitled to conclude from the attitude of the other'. It is the judgments of the other members of the House of Lords which present some difficulties. They favour the idea that for incorporation by a course of dealing there must be complete consistency, not only in the past transactions, but also between the previous transactions and the instant case. If this were so, incorporation by a course of dealing could occur only in the *Henry Kendall & Sons* v *Williams Lillico & Sons Ltd* (1969) type of case, the 'complete consistency' case, where the document containing the relevant clauses arrived too late in the instant case and has always arrived too late in the past, i.e. the document has always arrived after offer and acceptance.

9.51   Incorporation by a course of dealing should not be regarded as restricted to the situation where the instant case follows entirely the pattern of past dealings (and the Court of Appeal seems to have assumed that it was not so restricted in *PLM Trading Ltd* v *Georgiou* (1986)). Two points must be made. First, the need for complete consistency between past transactions and the instant case would create an unacceptable uncertainty. This is illustrated if we look again at the facts of *Henry Kendall & Sons* v *Williams Lillico & Sons Ltd* (1969). The contract in the instant case was concluded over the telephone. In the previous dealings the telephone conversation had been followed by the dispatch of the 'sold note' containing the exemption clause. If a course of dealing could not incorporate a clause unless there was complete consistency between past transactions and the instant case, it would not be clear whether the instant contract included the clause until the 'sold note' had been dispatched or, possibly, received. There would be a time, after the making of the contract, during which it would not be clear what the terms of the contract were. Clearly that would be an unacceptable situation (A. Hogget, 'Changing a Bargain by Confirming it' (1970) 33 MLR 518 at 520–1).

9.52   The second point to be made is that circumstances have changed since *McCutcheon* v *David MacBrayne Ltd* [1964] 1 WLR 125 was decided, and the reason why the majority of the House of Lords favoured a restrictive approach to incorporation by a course of dealing no longer applies. The line taken by the majority in *McCutcheon* is explained by their view that such incorporation is another way in which the business person has an unfair advantage over the consumer (per Lord Pearce at 139, Lord Hodson at 130, Lord Guest at 131, Lord Devlin at 136). They saw it as simply giving the business person yet another opportunity to rely upon standard terms with exemption clauses. It should be remembered that *McCutcheon* was decided prior to the Unfair Contract Terms Act 1977, and the subsequent unfair terms legislation.

9.53   It seems unlikely that the approach of the majority in *McCutcheon v David MacBrayne Ltd* (1964) will be revived today. Comments upon *McCutcheon*, such as that in *Circle Freight International Ltd v Medeast Gulf Exports Ltd* [1988] 2 Lloyd's Rep 427 (see para. **9.58**), therefore need to be treated with care. In that case Taylor LJ said (at 431) of *McCutcheon*:

> '[Lord Pearce] was pointing out that whereas some of the previous dealings in that case had involved a contractual document, on the occasion of the sinking the contract was purely oral. It was the departure from the ordinary course of business which excluded the condition.'

Such a comment should merely be seen as an acceptance of the natural factual relevance of differences between the past transactions and the instant case.

Failure to incorporate in past transactions

9.54   Incorporation by a course of dealing in the *Henry Kendall & Sons v William Lillico & Sons Ltd* (1969) type of case is worth further consideration. Each time the parties contracted, the document containing the standard terms was introduced by one party only after offer and acceptance had occurred. It is the cumulative effect of these documents which means that a point is reached when the other party, as a reasonable person, must be taken to know that the offer is made on the basis of those standard terms and, in the absence of some indication to the contrary, his or her acceptance will encompass them. This is simply to re-emphasize the mechanism by which incorporation by a course of dealing occurs. The point to be made here is that there is no possibility of incorporation by a course of dealing when the failure to incorporate standard terms by the document produced in each particular past contract, and the instant case, is due not to the timing of delivery of that document but rather to its not providing 'reasonably sufficient' notice, i.e. where, in relation to each transaction, the terms have been present before offer and acceptance but they are insufficiently prominent to be incorporated by notice. Under these circumstances the party seeking to rely upon his or her standard terms never puts the other party in the situation where, as a reasonable person, he or she should assume that the offer encompasses those terms. The reasonable person would make no such assumption in relation to terms of the existence of which he or she has not been given sufficient notice. By definition there is no reason why he or she should know of the terms. Where incorporation occurs because of the cumulative effect of a series of late deliveries of standard terms, the situation must be such that those terms would have been incorporated in each individual transaction, had they arrived on time.

Consumer/business distinction

9.55   When considering whether incorporation by a course of dealing has occurred, the courts have shown themselves less willing to find such incorporation where one party is a consumer than where both are business people. In *Hollier* v *Rambler Motors (AMC) Ltd* (1972):

> Rambler Motors had repaired Mr Hollier's car on three or four occasions over a five-year period. On at least two occasions Mr Hollier had signed a form containing Rambler's stand-ard terms, including an exemption clause. In the instant case the parties contracted over the telephone, without any mention of the standard terms. Whilst the car was in the garage it was damaged by fire due to Rambler's negligence.

The court decided that the exemption clause did not cover the breach which had occurred, but it also considered the issue of incorporation. On that question the court concluded that three or four transactions over a five-year period were not sufficient to incorporate the standard terms into the oral contract. This was obviously not a strong case for such incorporation, but it should be noted that in considering this case the Court of Appeal in *British Crane Hire Corpn Ltd* v *Ipswich Plant Hire Ltd* (1975) (see below) emphasized that Mr Hollier was a consumer. It should be easier to incorporate terms by a course of dealing into a contract between two business peo-ple than into a contract between a business person and a consumer.

9.56   *Hollier* v *Rambler Motors (AMC) Ltd* (1972) should be contrasted with *British Crane Hire Corpn Ltd* v *Ipswich Plant Hire Ltd* (1975). In that case:

> Ipswich Plant Hire (IP) were draining marsh land and carrying out other engineering works on it. IP were also in the business of hiring out equipment, but on this occasion they, themselves, needed to hire a crane. As their need was urgent they telephoned British Crane Hire (BC) and arranged to hire a crane from them. Subsequently BC sent IP a printed form setting out conditions of hire. IP did not sign or return the form to BC. On two previous occasions BC had hired equipment to IP and those contracts had been made on the basis of BC's printed form. The crane sank into the marsh.

The question arose as to who was to pay for the removal of the crane from the mud. BC relied on their standard terms to argue that IP should pay. The question was whether those terms were part of the contract. Both parties were business people involved in the same trade. BC's standard terms were similar to those used throughout the trade and resembled those used by IP themselves when they were hiring out their machinery. Two prior transactions, by themselves, might not have been sufficient to incorporate the terms but the question of incorporation had to be viewed against the background of trade practice, and that decided the issue in BC's favour. BC's terms were incorporated because the contract was between two business people in the same trade.

9.57   The court seemed inclined to view trade background as a distinct basis of incorporation from course of dealing. However, even if it could work independently, trade background can add to the effect of past dealings between the parties when incorporation by a course of dealing is considered. In *SIAT di del Ferro* v *Tradax Overseas SA* [1978] 2 Lloyd's Rep 470 Donaldson J considered *British Crane Hire Corpn Ltd* v *Ipswich Plant Hire Ltd* (1975) and the course of dealing cases. He said (at 490):

> 'I do not think that they are different. They are two different examples of a much wider concept, namely, that a contract is not made in a vacuum, but against a background of present and past facts . . . and that its terms . . . are to be gathered . . . from conduct viewed against that background.'

Common trade background affects what each party, as a reasonable person, is entitled to infer that the other is agreeing to (*Fal Bunkering of Sharjah* v *Grecale Inc of Panama* (1990)). Trade background can feed into the test for incorporation by a course of dealing. The two may combine and they should be viewed as so doing in *British Crane Hire*. When two business people contract, it may well be easier to say that reasonable people in their situation would infer the use of one party's standard terms after a very brief course of dealing. The knowledge of business practice which can be imputed to business people, particularly within the same trade, is obviously greater than that which can be imputed to a consumer.

Course of dealing and reasonably sufficient notice

9.58   In *Circle Freight International Ltd* v *Medeast Gulf Exports Ltd* [1988] 2 Lloyd's Rep 427 some consideration was given to the relationship between incorporation by a course of dealing and the rule from *Parker* v *South Eastern Rly Co.* (1877). The facts of *Circle Freight* provide us with another useful illustration of incorporation by a course of dealing. In *Circle Freight*:

> Medeast exported goods to the Middle East. Circle Freight were freight forwarding agents. They had acted as such for Medeast on a number of occasions when Medeast were exporting dresses. Circle Freight were suing Medeast for money owed. Medeast were counterclaiming in relation to a consignment of dresses stolen whilst Circle Freight's driver left them unattended in Fleet Street. In relation to the counterclaim, Circle Freight sought to rely upon an exemption clause in the standard terms of the Institute of Freight Forwarders. Each contract between the parties was made orally, over the telephone, and was followed by an 'invoice'. The standard terms were referred to on the 'invoice' which had been sent to Medeast on at least eleven occasions over the six months preceding the lost consignment. Medeast were a commercial company and knew that freight forwarders usually dealt on standard terms.

The court concluded that the standard terms were incorporated. Taylor LJ said (at 433):

> 'I consider that [Medeast's] conduct in continuing the course of business after at least eleven notices of the terms and omitting to request a sight of them would have led and did lead [Circle Freight] reasonably to believe [Medeast] accepted their terms.'

As can be seen, this is an application of the test indicated above for incorporation by a course of dealing, i.e. whether, at the time of contracting, each party, as a reasonable person, should infer from the past dealings and the actions and words of the other in the instant case, that the standard clauses are part of the instant contract. However, the question of reasonably sufficient notice was also raised and was regarded as interchangeable with the more specific test for incorporation by a course of dealing. There seems to be every justification for this. Both tests are based upon an objective view of the contracting process. Both are concerned with what a reasonable person should be taken to have agreed to. However, although it is desirable to recognize the link, as such recognition may help with any further development of the law, there is something to be said for maintaining a separate test for the course of dealing cases. The separate test draws attention to the factors specific to incorporation in that manner.

9.59   Why is incorporation by a course of dealing required? Empirical work undertaken in relation to contract law has revealed that business people do not always have the rules of contract law at the forefront of their minds when contracting.[21] The primary interest is in 'clinching the deal'. When this attitude is combined with the use of standard terms, it can create problems. Perhaps the best-known example of this is the 'battle of the forms'. The contention that terms have been incorporated by a course of dealing can also be seen as a product of this attitude. It is usually raised when one party has attempted to introduce standard terms into the contract after it has been made, i.e. when not much thought has been given to the correct procedure, within the law of contract, to ensure that his or her standard terms are part of the contract.

Construction

Introduction

9.60   When considering the construction of the contract, we are looking at its interpretation. In relation to exemption clauses the question being asked is whether the clause used is appropriately worded to cover what has occurred. However, before considering in detail the interpretation of exemption clauses, we should first briefly look at construction more generally and also the trends in relation to the approach taken to the construction of exemption clauses.

Construction in general

9.61   The objective when construing or interpreting a contract is that of determining the parties' intention. It is a matter of objective ascertainment, of course, so what is looked at is the meaning which the contract would convey to the reasonable person, having all the background knowledge of the parties, at the time of contracting. Traditionally, there has been an overwhelming emphasis upon the written words used and a restrictive approach to

---

21 S. Macauley, 'Non-Contractual Relations in Business' [1963] Am Soc Rev 45; H. Beale and A. Dugdale, 'Contracts Between Businessmen: Planning and the Use of Contractual Remedies' (1975) 2 Brit J Law and Soc 18.

what further evidence could be considered. However, in *Investors Compensation Scheme Ltd v West Bromwich Building Society* [1998] 1 All ER 98 at 114, the House of Lords took the view that a 'fundamental change . . . has overtaken this branch of the law' and that the result has largely been:

> 'to assimilate the way in which such documents are interpreted by judges to the common sense principles by which any serious utterance would be interpreted in ordinary life. Almost all the old intellectual baggage of "legal" interpretation has been discarded.'

9.62   In *Investors Compensation Scheme Ltd* v *West Bromwich Building Society* [1998] 1 All ER 98 Lord Hoffmann provided a summary of principles, which is now frequently referred to by the courts. He said (at 114):

> '1. Interpretation is the ascertainment of the meaning which the document would convey to a reasonable person having all the background knowledge which would reasonably have been available to the parties in the situation in which they were at the time of the contract.
>
> 2. The background was famously referred to by Lord Wilberforce as the "matrix of fact", but this phrase is if anything an understated description of what the background may include. Subject to the requirement that it should have been reasonably available to the parties and to the exception mentioned next, it includes absolutely anything which would have affected the way in which the language of the document would have been understood by a reasonable man.
>
> 3. The law excludes from the admissible background the previous negotiations of the parties and their declarations of subjective intent. They are admissible only in an action for rectification. The law makes this distinction for reasons of practical policy and, in this respect only, legal interpretation differs from the way we would interpret utterances in ordinary life . . .
>
> 4. The meaning which a document (or any other utterance) would convey to a reasonable man is not the same thing as the meaning of its words. The meaning of words is a matter of dictionaries and grammars; the meaning of the document is what the parties using those words against the relevant background would reasonably have been understood to mean. The background may not merely enable the reasonable man to choose between the possible meanings of words which are ambiguous but even (as occasionally happens in ordinary life) to conclude that the parties must, for whatever reason, have used the wrong words or syntax (see *Mannai Investments Co. Ltd* v *Eagle Star Life Ass Co. Ltd* [1997] 3 All ER 352) . . .
>
> 5. The "rule" that words should be given their "natural and ordinary meaning" reflects the commonsense proposition that we do not easily accept that people have made linguistic mistakes, particularly in formal documents. On the other hand, if one would nevertheless conclude from the background that something must have gone wrong with the language, the law does not require judges to attribute to the parties an intention which they plainly could not have had . . .'.

So, as has been indicated, the interpretation of contracts is about the intention of the parties, objectively ascertained. It is 'the ascertainment of the meaning which the document would convey to a reasonable person having all the background knowledge which would reasonably have been available to the parties in the situation in which they were at the time of the contract' (point (1) above).

9.63   The background knowledge, or 'matrix of fact', is 'subject to the requirement that it should have been reasonably available to both parties' at the time of contracting and is very broad. Subject to certain exceptions (see later), that includes 'absolutely anything which would have affected the way in which the language of the document would have been understood by a reasonable man' (point (2) above), although Lord Hoffmann has since had to emphasize that he 'meant anything which a reasonable man would have regarded as relevant' (*Bank of Credit and Commerce International* v *Ali* [2001] UKHL 8 at [39]). It includes 'evidence of the "genesis" and objectively of the "aim" of the transaction' (*Prenn* v *Simmonds* [1971] 1 WLR 1381 per Lord Wilberforce).

9.64   Further, it should be emphasized that, in general, business contracts should be construed in a way which makes 'good commercial sense'. 'If a detailed semantic and syntactical analysis of words in a commercial contract is going to lead to a conclusion that flouts business common sense, it must be made to yield to business common sense' (*Antaios Cia Naviera SA* v *Salen Rederierna AB* [1985] AC 191 at 121 per Lord Diplock). In addition, at a more general level than the impetus to achieve 'good commercial sense', is the pressure against a construction which achieves an unreasonable result and the 'more unreasonable the result the more unlikely it is that the parties can have intended it, and if they do intend it the more necessary it is that they [should] make that intention abundantly clear' (*L Schuler AG* v *Wickman Machine Tool Sales Ltd* [1974] AC 235 at 251 per Lord Reid). Of course, the courts must, nevertheless, avoid substituting 'for the bargain actually made one which the court believes could better have been made' (*Charter Reinsurance Co. Ltd* v *Fagan* [1996] 2 WLR 726 at 759 per Lord Mustill), and, in *Rainy Sky SA* v *Kookmin Bank* (2011), it was emphasized that if there is no ambiguity, in the language used in the contract, that unambiguous meaning will have to be applied, even if the result is improbable (at [23]–[24]).

9.65   It was indicated earlier that the general approach to the background which should be considered in determining the parties' intentions is a (nearly) all-embracing one, covering (nearly) everything which is relevant, and was reasonably available to both parties at the time of contracting. However, in his third point, Lord Hoffmann did indicate the inadmissibility of evidence of the subjective declarations of the parties and their previous negotiations and it is also well established that evidence of the parties' conduct subsequent to the making of the contract is also inadmissible (*Schuler* v *Wickman Machine Tool* (1974)). There has been considerable criticism of the maintenance of the latter two exclusions.[22] However, with Lord Hoffmann delivering the principal judgment, in *Chartbrook* v *Persimmon Homes* (2009), the House of Lords re-asserted the exclusion of evidence of the parties' negotiations. In *Prenn* v *Simmonds* [1971]

---

22 On the approach to construction generally post-*Investors*, see, e.g., G. McMeel, 'Prior Negotiations and Subsequent Conduct—The next step forward for contractual interpretation' (2003) 119 LQR 272; D. Nicholls, 'My Kingdom for a Horse: the meaning of words' (2005) 121 LQR 577.

1 WLR 1381 at 1384 Lord Wilberforce had identified the basis of the exclusion as being that the evidence is 'simply unhelpful' as 'by the nature of things, where negotiations are difficult, the parties' positions, with each passing letter are changing and until final agreement, though converging, still divergent'. This led to the contention that there are occasions when such evidence would be helpful and the courts simply need to treat such evidence with care, rather than not look at it at all. However, against that are raised the fears of greater costs of cases through more evidence needing to be considered, and also increased uncertainty in the interpretation of contracts. The House of Lords concluded that there was nothing to suggest that the drawbacks to making evidence of negotiations admissible in interpreting the contracts were outweighed by the cases in which such evidence would improve the results. The well-established rule excluding evidence of negotiations would not be displaced. Lord Hoffmann said (at 41):

> 'The conclusion I would reach is that there is no clearly established case for departing from the exclusionary rule. The rule may well mean, as Lord Nicholls has argued, that parties are sometimes held bound by a contract in terms which, upon a full investigation of the course of negotiations, a reasonable observer would not have taken them to have intended. But a system which sometimes allows this to happen may be justified in the more general interest of economy and predictability in obtaining advice and adjudicating disputes.'

Lord Hoffmann did say (at [41]) that empirical study might indicate that the balance between individual justice and 'economy and predictability' might show that the traditional, exclusionary, rule should not be maintained, but that was for a body such as the Law Commission to consider. Baroness Hale (at [99]) did query the appropriateness of Law Commission's involvement in, rather than common law development of, such an area. However, she also pointed out that Lord Hoffmann's approach to the issue of rectification 'would go a long way to providing a solution' in those cases in which had the evidence of negotiations been admissible it would have led to an interpretation which would better reflect the parties' intentions.

Trends in the approach to exemption clauses

9.66   The process of construing the contract, with its search for the 'intention of the parties', is one which allows the courts sufficient flexibility for the desirability of the end result to play a part in the conclusion reached. Prior to the enactment of the controls imposed upon exemption clauses by UCTA 1977, the courts used the rules of construction inventively in order to mitigate the effects of such clauses. This was described by Lord Denning MR in the Court of Appeal in *George Mitchell (Chesterhall) Ltd* v *Finney Lock Seeds Ltd* [1983] QB 284 at 297:

> 'Faced with this abuse of power—by the strong against the weak—by the use of small print conditions—the judges did what they could to put a curb upon it. They still had before them the idol, "freedom of contract". They still knelt down and worshipped it, but they concealed under their cloaks a secret weapon. They used it to stab the idol in the back. This weapon was called "the construction of the contract". They used it with great skill and ingenuity. They used it so as to depart from the natural meaning of the words of the exemption clause and to put upon them a strained and unnatural construction.'

9.67   The courts' ability to use the rules of construction so as to arrive at the result they thought appropriate was used to its fullest extent before UCTA 1977. Since then the use of 'strained construction' has been deprecated. In *Photo Production Ltd* v *Securicor Transport Ltd* [1980] AC 827 Lord Diplock said (at 851):[23]

> 'the reports are full of cases in which what would appear to be very strained constructions have been placed upon exclusion clauses, mainly in what today would be called consumer contracts and contracts of adhesion...any need for this kind of judicial distortion of the English language has been banished by Parliament's having made these kinds of contracts subject to the Unfair Contract Terms Act 1977.'

9.68   In addition to the particular trend in relation to the treatment of exemption clauses, the more general evolution of construction in general, which was identified in *Investors Compensation Scheme Ltd* v *West Bromwich Building Society* (1998) must also be emphasized. Plainly, that more general development has an impact in relation to exemption clauses,[24] although its exact scope has not yet been fully worked out. It will be further considered in this chapter in referring to specific issues.

Basic approach to exemption clauses

9.69   The contra proferentem rule applies here so that any ambiguity in the clause is resolved against the person seeking to rely upon it. Exemption clauses are strictly construed. The words used must clearly cover what has occurred if the clause is to be effective. *Wallis, Son, and Wells* v *Pratt & Haynes* (1911) provides an example:

> P & H sold seed to W as 'common English sanfoin' seed. In fact the seed supplied was giant sanfoin, a different and inferior variety. There was a clause in the sale contract stating that the 'sellers give no warranty expressed or implied as to the growth, description or any other matters'.

The House of Lords decided that the exemption clause did not cover what had occurred. It was a condition of the contract that the seed supplied was common English sanfoin. A breach of that term could not be covered by a clause which merely referred to warranties.[25]

9.70   *Andrews Bros (Bournemouth) Ltd* v *Singer & Co. Ltd* (1934) provides a further example:

> Singer & Co. contracted to sell Andrews Bros a 'new Singer car'. The car they delivered had recorded such a mileage that it could no longer be described as a 'new' car. Singer & Co.

---

23   See also, e.g., *George Mitchell (Chesterhall) Ltd* v *Finney Lock Seeds Ltd* [1983] 2 AC 803 at 810.

24   See, e.g., Lord Hoffmann's judgment in *Bank of Credit and Commerce International* v *Ali* (2001).

25   But see now *KG Bominflot Bunkergesellschaft für Mineralöle mbH & Co* v *Petroplus Marketing AG (The Mercini Lady)* [2010] EWHC Civ 1145, [2011] 2 All ER (Comm) 522 and *Air Transworld Ltd* v *Bombardier Inc* [2012] EWHC 243 (Comm), [2012] 2 All ER (Comm) 60.

> sought to rely upon clause 5 of the contract which stated, '...all conditions, warranties and liabilities implied by statute, common law or otherwise are excluded'.

The court held that clause 5 did not protect Singer & Co. from failing to provide a 'new' car. The clause referred to implied terms and it was an express term that the car should be 'new'.

9.71   The impact of *Investors Compensation Scheme Ltd* v *West Bromwich Building Society* (1998) here is yet to be fully worked out.[26] It has been questioned what 'strict construction' means as opposed to the normal process of ascertaining the parties' intention. It may be that it 'operates merely by way of intensification, so that the intention must be clear, unambiguous, incapable of misleading...' (*Mannai Investment Co. Ltd* v *Eagle Star Life Assurance Co. Ltd* [1997] 3 All ER 352 at 377). The contra proferentem rule is still being applied.[27] However, certainly it has been emphasized that it is a 'rule of last resort' (*Sinochem International Oil (London) Co. Ltd* v *Mobil Sales and Supply Corpn* (2000) at 483) and, even before *Investors*, the point was made that 'it would be wrong to use it to create an ambiguity where none realistically exists, and then to resolve the question by reference to it' (*Singer Co. (UK)* v *Tees and Hartlepool Port Authority* [1988] 2 Lloyd's Rep 164 at 169). Further, against the background of the significance given to construction in context, in *Investors,* it is unsurprising that the point has been made that the rule should only be resorted to if there is ambiguity after the words in question have been looked at in context (*McGeown* v *Direct Travel Insurance* [2004] 1 All ER (Comm) 609 at [13]).

9.72   The final point to be made here is that there is the EC Directive on Unfair Terms in Consumer Contracts itself contains what can be regarded as a version of the contra proferentem rule. That became reg 7(2) of the Unfair Terms in Consumer Contracts Regulations 1999. The draft Consumer Rights Bill does not merely reproduce such a rule, but also makes it clear that the Competition and Markets Authority, and the other general enforcers, may obtain injunctions to prevent the use, or recommendation of the use, of terms which are not 'transparent' (clause 71, see para. **11.68**).

Liability for negligence[28]

9.73   The courts have dealt with the issue of whether an exemption clause covers liability based on negligence by developing a three-stage test: the *Canada Steamship* rules. However, before considering that test, it should be emphasized that UCTA 1977, s 2 is concerned with attempts to exclude or restrict liability based on negligence. Where the negligence has caused personal injury or death, any such clause will be automatically ineffective (s 2(1)) and in

---

26 Contrast *KG Bominflot Bunkergesellschaft für Mineralöle mbH & Co* v *Petroplus Marketing AG (The Mercini Lady)* [2010] EWHC Civ 1145, [2011] 2 All ER (Comm) 522 and *Air Transworld Ltd* v *Bombardier Inc* [2012] EWHC 243 (Comm), [2012] 2 All ER (Comm) 60.

27 e.g. *Association of British Travel Agents Ltd* v *British Airways* (2000) at 213; *Zeus Tradition Marine Ltd* v *Bell* (2000) at 597; *University of Keele* v *Price Waterhouse* (2004).

28 Macdonald, *Exemption Clauses and Unfair Terms*, 2nd edn, pp. 50–62; J. Carter, 'Commercial Construction and the *Canada Steamship* Rules' [1995] 9 JCL 69.

other cases it is subject to the test of reasonableness (s 2(2)). Of course, protection has also been afforded for some time by the fairness test stemming from the Unfair Terms in Consumer Contracts Directive, and the draft Consumer Rights Bill extracts, from s 2 of UCTA, coverage of 'consumer contracts', placing it alongside the more general consumer protection derived from that Directive. This division of 'consumer contracts', and business contracts, will not diminish the level of protection provided against the exclusion or restriction of liability for negligence.

9.74   Consideration should now be given to the test used by the courts when faced with the question of whether an exemption clause covers negligence. The three-stage test is:

1. If the exemption clause expressly refers to liability for negligence, then effect must be given to it, to cover negligence liability.
2. If there is no express reference to negligence, it must be asked whether the words used are wide enough, in their ordinary meaning, to cover liability for negligence; any doubt must be resolved against the party in breach.
3. Even if the words used are wide enough to cover liability for negligence, it must be asked whether the party in breach could be liable on some ground other than that of negligence. If he or she could be, and if that other ground is not so fanciful or remote that the party in breach cannot be supposed to have desired protection against it, then it is likely that the words will be taken to refer to the non-negligent liability only.

As has been indicated, this is based upon the three-stage test formulated by Lord Morton in giving the judgment of the Privy Council in *Canada Steamship Lines Ltd* v *R* [1952] AC 192 at 208.[29] Three initial points must be made before the stages of the test are considered further.

9.75   First, the approach is based upon the idea that 'it is inherently improbable that one party to the contract should intend to absolve the other party from the consequences of the latter's own negligence' (*Gillespie Bros & Co. Ltd* v *Roy Bowles Transport Ltd* [1973] 1 All ER 193 at 203). Second, it has been suggested that there is no such 'high degree of improbability' that a limitation of liability (rather than an exclusion of liability) would be agreed to, and that a less strict approach should be taken to the construction of limitation than exclusion clauses. The idea of making a general distinction of this type between limitation clauses and exclusion clauses is considered more generally, and criticized, later (para. **9.88**).

9.76   Third, the impact on the *Canada Steamship* test of the general approach to construction indicated in the *Investors Compensation Scheme Ltd* v *West Bromwich Building Society* (1998) (see para. **9.87**) will need to be considered. It will be addressed, more fully, after the stages of the test have been considered further. However, here the point can be made that in *BCCI* v *Ali*

---

29   See also *George Mitchell (Chesterhall) Ltd* v *Finney Lock Seeds Ltd* [1983] QB 284 at 312; *Alderslade* v *Hendon Laundry Ltd* [1945] KB 189 at 192.

(2001) at [66] Lord Hoffmann indicated that a change has occurred, and certainly there is some diminution in reliance upon the *Canada Steamship* approach.

9.77   It is obvious that there should be no difficulty in finding that a clause covers negligence if it expressly refers to negligence. Any other conclusion would run contrary to the idea of freedom of contract and the basic principle that in construing a clause it is the intention of the parties which is being sought. It has not, however, always been clear what should amount to an express reference to negligence. Although it has been suggested that nothing short of the use of the term 'negligence' itself will suffice (*Lamport and Holt Lines Ltd* v *Coubro and Scrutton (M&I) Ltd, The Raphael* [1982] 2 Lloyd's Rep 42 at 48), if the clause uses some synonym for it (*Smith* v *South Wales Switchgear Co. Ltd* [1978] 1 WLR 165 at 168 and 172), such as the phrase 'neglect or default' (*Monarch Airlines Ltd* v *London Luton Airport Ltd* [1997] CLC 698 at 706), that should also be sufficient. In *Smith* v *South Wales Switchgear* (1978) the House of Lords made it clear that the addition of words such as 'howsoever caused' to a reference to loss or damage could not amount to express references to negligence.

9.78   Clauses explicitly referring to negligence are not unknown (for example, *Spriggs* v *Sotheby Parke Bernet & Co.* (1986)), but do not occur very often. Such a clause could dissuade the party against whom it might be used from contracting. In *EE Caledonia Ltd* v *Orbit Valve plc* [1994] 2 Lloyd's Rep 239, Steyn LJ said (at 246):

> 'Why was an express reference to negligence not inserted? . . . I have no doubt that the drafts-man on the Underground to whom such a question was addressed would say "one does not want to frighten off one or other of the parties". Omissions of express reference to negligence in contracts drafted by lawyers tend to deliberate.'

9.79   The second part of the rule would seem to require consideration of what the clause 'plainly means to any ordinary literate and sensible person' (*Lamport and Holt Lines Ltd* v *Coubro and Scrutton (M&I) Ltd, The Raphael* [1982] 2 Lloyd's Rep 42 at 52), although, in appropriate circumstances, specialized commercial knowledge may be relevant. A clause may refer to loss or damage 'howsoever caused', directing attention to the cause of the loss (*Joseph Travers & Sons Ltd* v *Cooper* [1915] 1 KB 73 at 93 and 101) and that is sufficient for the second part of the rule. Less explicit general clauses may also be sufficient. The words 'any act or omission' have been seen as 'certainly wide enough to comprehend negligence' (*The Raphael* at 45 per Donaldson LJ). The second and third stages of the test can combine to put the person seeking to rely on the clause 'on the horns of a dilemma', i.e. in some cases arguing that the clause is wide enough to satisfy the second part of the test will result in it covering 'other' liability within the third (*Shell Chemicals UK Ltd* v *P & O Roadtankers Ltd* [1995] 1 Lloyd's Rep 297 at 301 per Balcombe LJ).

9.80   The third stage of the test indicated above could be regarded as part of the second stage. In considering whether there could be liability without negligence, the question being asked is merely whether a general clause is ambiguous because of one particular factor: the number of ways in which liability may occur. In some cases liability may occur in more than one way. It may arise on the basis of negligence or it may occur strictly, without fault. Where there can be liability without negligence the courts have tended to find that a generally worded exemption clause is intended to cover only the strict liability and not that based on negligence. In *Alderslade* v *Hendon Laundry Ltd* [1945] KB 189 (see para. **9.83**) Lord Greene MR gave this example (at 192):[30]

> '[A common carrier's] liability in respect of articles entrusted to him is not necessarily based on negligence. Accordingly if a common carrier wishes to limit his liability for lost articles and does not make it quite clear that he is desiring to limit it in respect of his liability for negligence, then the clause will be construed as extending only to his liability on grounds other than negligence.'

9.81 A further illustration is provided by *White* v *John Warwick & Co. Ltd* (1953) (L. Gower, 'Exemption Clauses—Contractual and Tortious Liability' (1954) 17 MLR 155):

> Mr White was in business as a newsagent and tobacconist. He contracted with the defendants for the hire of a tradesman's tricycle. The defendants supplied him with a tricycle with a defective saddle which caused him to fall off and injure himself. The contract of hire contained a clause which stated 'nothing in this agreement shall render the owners liable for any personal injury to the riders of the machines hired'.

Mr White sued the defendants for damages for his injuries. He had two grounds for his claim:

1. breach of contract for failure to supply a tricycle which was reasonably fit for its purpose (strict liability); and
2. liability for negligently failing to see that the cycle was kept in good repair.

The defendants sought to rely upon the exemption clause in the contract of hire. The Court of Appeal concluded that the exemption clause should be construed as merely applying to the strict liability and not to the liability for negligence. (In such a case the exclusion of liability for negligently caused personal injury would now be prevented by UCTA 1977, s 2.) See also *EE Caledonia Ltd* v *Orbit Valve plc* (1994).

9.82 One point which should be emphasized is that not every alternative basis of liability will be relevant to the third part of the test. To be relevant to the question of construction, an alternative basis of liability must not be too 'fanciful or remote' so that it 'would not have been within the contemplation of the parties when the terms of the [contract] were agreed' (*Canada Steamship Lines Ltd* v *R* [1952] AC 192 at 210). The question of whether or not any alternative basis of liability is too 'fanciful or remote' will depend upon the facts of the particular case, but it should be borne in mind that:

> 'When two commercial concerns contract with one another, they do not...concern themselves with...legal subtleties...We should look at the facts and realities of the situation as

---

30 See also *Rutter* v *Palmer* [1922] 2 KB 87 at 94.

they did or must be deemed to have presented themselves to the contracting parties at the time the contract was made, and ask what potential liabilities the one to the other did the parties apply their minds, or must be deemed to have done so' (*Lamport and Holt Lines Ltd v Coubro and Scrutton (M&I) Ltd, The Raphael* [1982] 2 Lloyd's Rep 42 at 50 per May LJ (see also Stephenson LJ at 51)).

9.83   Up to this point we have discussed the situation where there is a generally worded exemption clause and negligence is not the only basis of liability. The converse of that situation is where there is a generally worded clause but there is no liability, and no breach of contract, in the absence of negligence. Where the sole basis of liability is negligence, the courts more readily find that a generally worded exemption clause covers negligence. In *Alderslade v Hendon Laundry Ltd* (1945) it was successfully argued that the exemption clause covered negligence. In that case:

> Mr Alderslade left ten Irish linen handkerchiefs with the laundry to be washed. The laundry lost the handkerchiefs. The contract contained a clause which stated, 'The maximum amount allowed for lost or damaged articles is twenty times the charge made for laundering'.

When sued by Mr Alderslade, the laundry sought to rely upon the clause to limit its liability. The loss of the handkerchiefs constituted a breach of contract only if the laundry had been negligent; there was no strict liability for the loss. It was decided that the clause covered the breach, the negligent loss of the handkerchiefs.

9.84   In *Alderslade v Hendon Laundry Ltd* [1945] 1 KB 189 Lord Greene MR considered the third stage of the test, and used language which indicated that the presence, or absence, of an alternative basis of liability to negligence is determinative of the question of construction of a widely worded, general, exemption clause. In that case there was no liability in the absence of negligence and he was influenced by the fact that, if the court had concluded otherwise, the exemption clause would have served no purpose at all. He said (at 192) that the clause must be construed as relating to negligence, in the absence of other possible liability for it to cover (see also Lord Morton in *Canada Steamship Lines v R* [1952] AC 192 at 208). However, this is to take too rigid a line. In *Alderslade* Mackinnon LJ took the approach that 'if the only liability of the party pleading the exemption is a liability for negligence, the clause will more readily operate to exempt him' (at 195, quoting Scrutton LJ in *Rutter v Palmer* [1922] 2 KB 87 at 92). Similarly, in relation to the converse case, it has been emphasized that the presence of an alternative, non-negligent, ground of liability is merely an indicator of the parties' intentions:

> 'If there is a head of liability upon which the clause could bite in addition to negligence then, because it is more unlikely than not that a party will be ready to excuse his other contracting party from the consequence of the other's negligence, the clause will generally be construed as not covering negligence...the court asks itself what in all the relevant circumstances the parties intended the alleged exemption clause to mean' (*Lamport and Holt Lines Ltd v Coubro and Scrutton (M&I) Ltd, The Raphael* [1982] 2 Lloyd's Rep 42 at 50 per May LJ).

In short, it must be borne in mind that in looking at the three-stage test, we are not considering a rule of law, but merely an aid to construction (*Smith* v *South Wales Switchgear Co. Ltd* [1978] 1 WLR 165 at 178 per Lord Keith).

9.85   *Hollier* v *Rambler Motors (AMC) Ltd* (1972) illustrates the point that the three-part test merely assists construction. Mr Hollier's car was on the Rambler Motors' premises for repair when it was damaged by a fire caused by their negligence. Rambler Motors had a standard form document containing the clause, 'The company is not responsible for damage caused by fire to customers' cars on the premises'. The Court of Appeal decided that Rambler Motors had not incorporated that clause into the particular contract with Mr Hollier (see para. **9.55**). However, the court also considered whether the clause would have covered what had occurred had it been incorporated. It was argued that, as there was no breach unless the fire had been caused by Rambler Motors' negligence, the clause had to cover a negligent breach or it would serve no purpose. The court did not take that line. It considered how an ordinary person, in the position of Mr Hollier, would have viewed the clause and concluded that he would have seen it as merely indicating that there was no strict liability for fire damage. The case before the court was contrasted with *Alderslade* v *Hendon Laundry Ltd* [1945] 1 KB 189 which the court thought had dealt with a situation where 'any ordinary man or woman would have known that all that was being excluded was the negligence of the laundry' (at 80). The clause before the court in *Hollier* was construed as not covering negligence but rather as a warning to customers that Rambler Motors were not liable if a car was damaged by a fire occurring without negligence.[31] (For a discussion of the case, see E. Barendt, 'Exemption Clauses: Interpretation and Incorporation' (1972) 85 MLR 644.)

9.86   As we have seen, in applying the three-stage test, the courts look at the clause in context; they consider such matters as the understanding of the ordinary person and whether a possible liability is too 'fanciful or remote' for the parties to have considered it when contracting. Clearly this leaves sufficient flexibility for the courts' view of the justice of the case to influence their legal reasoning. It must be remembered that *Hollier* v *Rambler Motors (AMC) Ltd* (1972) did not concern a dispute between two business people but rather between a consumer and a businessman. However, the tools which the courts have available to assist them to achieve a desired result vary from time to time. When they acquire a new tool their use of an old one may change. It must be emphasized that *Hollier* is a pre-UCTA 1977 case, and post-UCTA the courts acknowledged that they should no longer resort to 'strained construction' to restrict the operation of exemption clauses.[32]

9.87   In addition, some final consideration should be given to the *Canada Steamship* approach in the light of the principles set out in *Investors Compensation Scheme Ltd* v *West Bromwich Building Society* (1998). *Canada Steamship Lines* v *R* (1952) might simply be viewed as part of

---

31   Where there is no other head of liability, the clause may be seen as not covering negligence but merely avoiding doubt about the existence of other liability—*Dorset County Council* v *Southern Felt Roofing* (1990).

32   e.g. *Photo Production Ltd* v *Securicor Transport Ltd* [1980] AC 827 at 851 per Lord Diplock; *George Mitchell (Chesterhall) Ltd* v *Finney Lock Seeds Ltd* [1983] 2 AC 803 at 810.

the 'old intellectual baggage of legal interpretation' which is being dispensed with (see para. **9.61**). Certainly, in *BCCI* v *Ali* [2001] UKHL 8 at [66], [2002] 1 AC 251 at [66] Lord Hoffmann indicated that a change has occurred in relation to the use of the *Canada Steamship* rules. However, as has been indicated, the *Canada Steamship* approach has been seen as based on an assumption about the improbability of one party intending to excuse the other's negligence (for example, *Gillespie Bros & Co. Ltd* v *Roy Bowles Transport Ltd* [1973] 1 All ER 193 at 203)—in other words, not as mere 'intellectual baggage'. On that basis, the line emphasized in *Investors* invites consideration of whether the circumstances show any such improbability, rather than it merely being assumed, and there being a relatively unquestioning application of those rules. In *HIH Casualty and General Insurance Ltd* v *Chase Manhattan Bank* [2003] 1 All ER (Comm) 349, Lord Hoffmann was of the view that in that case there was 'no inherent improbability' that the intention was to exclude liability for negligence. Rather, he saw negligence as 'a risk which the parties could reasonably have been expected to allocate' and the *Canada Steamship* approach was not applied to confine the coverage of the clause in question to strict liability (at [67]). Similarly, in *Lictor Anstalt* v *MIR Steel UK Ltd* (2012), the Court of Appeal took the line that 'the task for the court . . . is therefore to approach the interpretation of [the clause] in the light of the overall commercial purpose of the . . . agreement' and to determine whether there was any such improbability (at [36]). The court concluded that there was not. In the circumstances, it was clear that 'the whole point' of the clause was to shift the 'entire risk and burden of any claim' in relation even to torts of intentional wrongdoing (at [42]). In addition, it may simply be that there will be more emphasis placed upon the fact that the *Canada Steamship* approach is merely an aid to construction and that there is no need to apply it in the particular case because the parties' intention to exclude or restrict liability for negligence is clear.[33]

Limitation of liability

9.88   The House of Lords has distinguished the construction of clauses which totally exclude liability from the construction of those which merely limit it. In *Ailsa Craig Fishing Co. Ltd* v *Malvern Fishing Co. Ltd* [1983] 1 WLR 964 their Lordships stated that limitation clauses are to be construed differently from total exclusion clauses. In that case:

> Securicor had undertaken to provide a security service for the boats belonging to a fishing association whilst those vessels were in Aberdeen harbour. Ailsa Craig were members of that association. One night their vessel, the *Strathallan*, fouled another boat and sank. Ailsa Craig claimed £55,000 damages from Securicor. Securicor conceded that they had been negligent, and breached their contract, but sought to rely upon a clause in the contract to restrict their liability to £1,000.

The House of Lords decided that the clause was effective to limit Securicor's liability to £1,000.

33   *HIH Casualty and General Insurance Ltd* v *Chase Manhattan Bank* (2003); *National Westminster Bank* v *Utrecht Finance Co* (2001) at [47]; *Re-Source America International Ltd* (2004) at [55].

9.89 The general comments on the construction of limitation clauses in *Ailsa Craig* should be noted. Such clauses are still to be construed contra proferentem (at 966 and 971), but Lord Wilberforce stated (at 966) that limitation clauses are not to be treated with 'the same hostility as clauses of exclusion'. Lord Fraser thought (at 971) that the rules for the construction of exclusion clauses should not be applied in 'their full rigour' to limitation clauses. The same line was taken by the House of Lords in *George Mitchell (Chesterhall) Ltd* v *Finney Lock Seeds Ltd* [1983] 2 AC 803. There Lord Bridge, with whom the rest of the court agreed, stated (at 814) that the principles used for the construction of total exclusion clauses 'cannot be applied in their full rigour to limitation clauses'.

9.90 The natural reaction to this stated distinction between limitation and exclusion clauses is that it is wholly unrealistic as 'a limitation clause may be so severe in its operation as to be virtually indistinguishable from that of an exclusion clause'. Such indeed was the reaction of the High Court of Australia when refusing to take the same approach to the construction of a limitation clause as the House of Lords (*Darlington Futures Ltd* v *Delco Australia Pty* (1986) 68 ALR 385 at 391). The Australian High Court thought that the same basic approach should be taken to the interpretation of limitation and exclusion clauses. It felt that the way in which any exemption clause, whether it limited or excluded liability, was construed was sufficiently flexible to take account of any case in which it was relevant that the clause was one which limited rather than totally excluded liability. This approach seems preferable to that of the House of Lords. Some support for a move towards it here might be found. In *HIH Casualty and General Insurance Ltd* v *Chase Manhattan Bank* [2003] 1 All ER (Comm) 349 Lord Hoffmann emphasized that construction is a matter of looking for the parties' intention. He referred to Lord Fraser's statement in *Ailsa Craig Fishing Co. Ltd* v *Malvern Fishing Co. Ltd* (1983) as to the distinction to be made between limitation and exclusion clauses and doubted that Lord Fraser had been intending to create a 'mechanistic' rule (at [63]). Also, in *BHP Petroleum* v *British Steel* (2000) at [43] Evans LJ favoured the single line that:

> 'the more extreme the consequences are, in terms of excluding or modifying the liability that would otherwise arise, then the more stringent the court's approach should be in requiring that clause should be clearly and unambiguously expressed.'

More broadly, it is difficult to see how a rule making any significant distinction between the interpretation of limitation clauses and exclusion clauses can long survive the recognition in *Investors* that the modern approach to construction generally has largely assimilated the way in which contracts are interpreted to 'the common sense principles by which any serious utterance would be interpreted in ordinary life' and that '[a]lmost all the old intellectual baggage of legal interpretation has been discarded' (see para. **9.61**).

9.91 However, the House of Lords has put forward some justification for its approach and that should be considered. In *Ailsa Craig Fishing Co. Ltd* v *Malvern Fishing Co. Ltd* Lord Wilberforce said ([1983] 1 WLR 964 at 966):

> 'Clauses of limitation are not to be regarded with the same hostility as clauses of exclusion; this is because they must be related to other contractual terms, in particular to the risks to

| which the defending party may be exposed, the remuneration which he receives, and possibly also the opportunity of the other party to insure.' |

(See also Lord Fraser at 970.) This is to take the line that a limitation clause will represent a carefully agreed allocation of risks between the parties and, on that basis, is not to be construed 'hostilely'. There are two points to be made here. First, such a correlation of factors may be present when there is an exclusion clause and may not be present when there is a limitation clause. In *Photo Production Ltd v Securicor Transport Ltd* (1980) the court considered the exclusion of liability for fire damage to be reasonable where Securicor was providing a relatively cheap service, particularly as it was more efficient for Photo Production to insure against the risk than for Securicor to do so. Conversely, in *George Mitchell (Chesterhall) Ltd v Finney Lock Seeds Ltd* (1983), although there was a low price in comparison with the potential loss, the clause merely limiting liability was considered to be unreasonable, and the fact that the seedsmen could have insured against such liability, without materially affecting their prices, was one indication of 'unreasonableness'. Second, the true relevance of the above factors is in relation to the 'reasonableness' of the exemption clause, whether it is one excluding or limiting liability. Legislation will often now allow the courts to examine the 'reasonableness', or fairness, of the clause, and factors relating to that must largely be left to be considered within the context of the legislative tests if 'strained construction' is to be avoided.

9.92   There is one situation in which there is a basic difference in principle between a clause which merely limits and one which excludes liability (see (1983) 99 LQR 163). An exclusion clause could be so extensive that the court would be faced with the question of whether the person relying upon it was under any obligation at all, i.e. if X and Y have made an agreement, X could have inserted an exclusion clause which is so extensive that X appears to have no legal liability, whatever he or she does or does not do, and so has no initial legal obligation under the agreement. In this situation the court would have to determine whether X and Y had intended to make a legally enforceable contract at all. If it concluded that they had, it would have to find a way of construing the exclusion clause to leave some binding obligation upon X.[34] This singular situation can never arise in relation to a limitation clause. In seeking to limit liability the parties acknowledge the existence of the obligation on which that liability is founded. When dealing with a limitation clause, the question of whether the parties in fact intended a legally enforceable contract cannot arise in the way that it can in relation to a total exclusion clause. (See *George Mitchell (Chesterhall) Ltd v Finney Lock Seeds Ltd* [1983] QB 284 at 304 per Oliver LJ.) However, interesting as this distinction may be (see B. Coote, *Exception Clause*, Sweet & Maxwell, 1964, ch. 1; Macdonald (2012) 29 JCL 47), it would not justify the wide, and unqualified, general distinction made by the House of Lords between exclusion and limitation clauses. Certainly there is nothing to indicate that their Lordships considered the approach they were taking to be restricted to this narrow point and every indication that they viewed their approach as being of general application. This narrow point of principle does not appear to provide a basis for the distinction made by the House of Lords.

---

34 See the arguments raised in *Mitsubishi Corp. v Eastwind Transport Ltd* (2005).

Fundamental breach

9.93　There were attempts to introduce a rule of law preventing 'fundamental breaches', or breaches of 'fundamental terms', being covered by exemption clauses, no matter how aptly worded the clause (for example, *Karsales (Harrow) Ltd* v *Wallis* (1956)). However, in *Suisse Atlantique Société d'Armement Maritime SA* v *NV Rotterdamsche Kolen Centrale* [1967] 1 AC 361 the House of Lords disagreed with any such attempts, and in *Photo Production Ltd* v *Securicor Transport Ltd* (1980), it 'gave the final quietus to the doctrine that a "fundamental breach" of contract deprived the party in breach of the benefit of a clause in the contract excluding or limiting his liability' (*George Mitchell (Chesterhall) Ltd* v *Finney Lock Seeds Ltd* [1983] 2 All ER 737 at 741 per Lord Bridge). The purpose of the Court of Appeal, in attempting to create fundamental breach as a rule of law, was to deal with objectionable exemption clauses in a way which the draftsman would not overcome. However, the usefulness of fundamental breach as a rule of law had been considered in *Suisse Atlantique*. There it had been pointed out that it was an undiscriminating approach to the problem of objectionable exemption clauses, as it could strike down clauses arrived at as a fairly negotiated allocation of risk between businesses. It was indicated that to deal with objectionable exemption clauses, a more discriminating tool than fundamental breach would have to be provided by legislation. (See Lord Reid at 406.) By the time *Photo Production* was decided, Parliament had provided the courts with a means of attacking exemption clauses in a more discriminating way: UCTA 1977.

9.94　Once fundamental breach had been disposed of as a rule of law, the point could be made that it

> 'is always necessary when considering an exemption clause to decide whether as a matter of construction, it extends to exclude or restrict the liability in question, but, if it does, it is no longer permissible at common law to reject or circumvent the clause by treating it as inapplicable to a "fundamental breach" ' (*Edmund Murray Ltd* v *BSP International Foundations Ltd* (1993) 33 Con LR 1 at 16 per Neill LJ).

In this context, it was never entirely clear what was meant by a 'fundamental breach' or a 'fundamental term' and it now seems unnecessary to be overly concerned with those questions or to use the terminology. It may be that the more extensive, or significant, the breach, the more explicit wording the courts will require in order to be convinced that it was intended to be covered by an exemption clause, but any such tendency does not need to be regarded as a named rule.

'Peas and beans'; main purpose of the contract; four corners rule

9.95　Here, brief consideration can be given to some of the approaches and rules which were, in effect, the foundations upon which the attempt was made to construct 'fundamental breach' as a rule of law. Some care has to be taken, though, not to resurrect that idea.

9.96 The argument may arise that an exemption clause does not cover what has occurred, because it was only intended to relate to the situation in which the contract was being performed (albeit in some way defectively) and what has occurred is not a performance of the contract, even a defective one. In other words, it is argued that the clause was not intended to apply in such circumstances because they are beyond the boundaries of the contract, by which the clause was intended to be limited. In *Chanter v Hopkins* (1838) 4 M & W 399 Lord Abinger said (at 404):

> 'If a man offers to buy peas of another, and he sends him beans, he does not perform his contract. But that is not a warranty; there is no warranty that he should sell him peas; the contract is to sell peas, and if he sends him anything else in their stead, it is a non-performance of it.'

If there is a contract between two parties, X and Y, and X has contracted to deliver peas to Y, but he delivers beans instead, it will be contended that he cannot rely upon any clause of the contract excluding his liability for defective performance because what occurred was not a performance at all, even a defective one. (Of course, care must be taken in ascertaining exactly what the contractual obligations were. The contract may have been one for the supply of peas or beans or, even, any green vegetable—see Lord Devlin, 'The Treatment of Breach of Contract' [1966] CLJ 192 at 212.) But this type of argument has been seen as going beyond delivery of goods which are clearly of an entirely different kind to that contracted for, to the situation where the goods delivered are, at one level, the type of goods contracted for, but which are argued to be so defective that their delivery cannot be regarded as within the performance of the contract (for example, *Karsales (Harrow) Ltd v Wallis* (1956)). However, such an approach must now be regarded as of very restricted application. In *George Mitchell Ltd v Finney Lock Seeds Ltd* [1983] 2 All ER 737, where there was a contract for the sale of Dutch winter white cabbage seed and an inferior autumn variety was supplied which led to a valueless crop, the House of Lords refused to apply this type of approach. The view was taken that acceptance of that argument in the Court of Appeal and at first instance 'came dangerously near to reintroducing by the back door the doctrine of fundamental breach' (at 741). The relevant clause was seen as applying to 'seeds' and 'seeds' had been supplied.

9.97 However, there are other situations, in which arguments arise, that an exemption clause was not intended to apply to what has occurred because it has gone beyond the boundaries of the contract. That line may be taken in relation to the situation in which a ship unjustifiably deviates from its route, or a bailee stores goods other than in the place contracted for, or hands them over to a subcontractor without authority. In each case, it is, of course, necessary to determine what the boundaries of the contract are; a clause may give a ship 'liberty to deviate', for example, and effect will be given to such a clause. However, faced with wide clauses, serving to stretch the contractual boundaries, the courts may find that such clauses are intended to be restricted by the 'main purpose', or the 'four corners', of the contract. In *Glynn v Margetson & Co.* (1893), when a clause in a contract for the shipment of a perishable cargo stated that the ship

> 'should have liberty to proceed to and stay at any port or ports in any station in the Mediterranean, Levant, Black Sea, or Adriatic, or on the coasts of Africa, Spain, Portugal,

France, Great Britain or Ireland, for the purpose of delivering coals, cargo, or passengers, or for any other purpose whatsoever',

that clause did not prevent the shipowners from being liable for the damage to the cargo, when it had gone 350 miles off of the direct route. The clause provided a liberty to deviate, but the approach taken was that it had to be read in the light of the main purpose of the contract, ascertained from reading it as a whole and that the main purpose of getting a perishable cargo from A to B would be defeated if the liberty to deviate was not read as confined to ports along the route from A to B. Similarly, in *Sze Hai Tong Bank v Rambler Cycle Co. Ltd* (1959), where there was a clause stating that 'the responsibility of the carrier...shall be deemed...to cease absolutely after the goods are discharged from the ship' but the contract also provided that delivery should only be made on production of the bill of lading, the court viewed delivery of the goods without production of the bill of lading as defeating the main object of the contract and as outside the protection of the other clause. The situation was equated with what would have occurred if the carriers had burnt the goods or thrown them into the sea. However, this type of reasoning must be used with care to avoid resurrecting fundamental breach. The reasoning in *Motis Exports Ltd v Dampskibsselskabet* (2000), in extending the *Rambler Cycle* case, above, to hold liable carriers who had handed over goods in response to a forged bill of lading, has been seen as 'coming perilously close to, if not actually to be, the doctrine of fundamental breach' (B. Davenport, 'Misdelivery: A Fundamental Breach?' [2000] LMCLQ 455 at 456). More recently, the court refused to extend this type of approach to goods stored on deck when the obligation was to store them below deck, at much less risk (*Daewoo Heavy Industries Ltd v Klipriver Shipping Ltd* (2003)) and plainly the impetus to avoid the artificiality of such a doctrine as fundamental breach has only been added to with the general approach to construction taken in *Investors*.[35]

Summary

- To be incorporated, terms must be introduced before a contract is made.
- Subject to very limited restrictions, signature of a contractual document will incorporate terms.
- Terms on an unsigned document or sign are incorporated if reasonably sufficient notice has been supplied of them.
- Terms may be incorporated because of a course of past dealings between the parties.
- The basic approach to construction generally is that set out by Lord Hoffmann in the *Investors* case, i.e. 'Interpretation is the ascertainment of the meaning which the document would convey to a reasonable person having all the background knowledge which would reasonably have been available to the parties in the situation in which they were at the time of the contract'.

---

35 See the judgment of Lord Hoffmann in *Bank of Credit and Commerce International v Ali* [2001] 1 All ER 961, particularly at [66].

- Terms are construed contra proferentem, i.e. if there is any ambiguity in a clause it will be construed against the proferens.

- If it is contended that an exemption clause covers liability for negligence, the *Canada Steamship* rules may be applied.

- A limitation clause may be construed less strictly than an exemption clause.

▶ Further reading

M. Clarke, 'Notice of Contractual Terms' (1976) 35 CLJ 51

H. Collins, 'Objectivity and Committed Contextualism in Interpretation' in S. Worthington (ed.), *Commercial Law and Commercial Practice*, Hart Publishing, 2003, 189–209

A. Kramer, 'Common Sense Principles of Contract Interpretation and How We've Been Using Them All Along' (2003) 23 Ox Jo LS 173

E. Macdonald, 'Incorporation of Standard Terms in Website Contracting—Clicking "I agree"' (2011) 27 JCL 198

E. McKendrick, 'The Interpretation of Contracts: Lord Hoffmann's Re-Statement' in S. Worthington (ed.), *Commercial Law and Commercial Practice*, Hart Publishing, 2003, 139–162

G. McMeel, 'Prior Negotiations and Subsequent Conduct—The Next Step Forward for Contractual Interpretation' (2003) 119 LQR 272

D. Nicholls, 'My Kingdom for a Horse: The Meaning of Words' (2005) 121 LQR 577

J. R. Spencer, 'Signature, Consent and the Rule in *L'Estrange v Graucob*' (1973) 32 CLJ 104

Chapter 10

Exemption clauses and the Unfair Contract Terms Act 1977

⬢ Introduction

10.1   Logically, before any consideration is given to the effect of the Unfair Contract Terms Act 1977 (UCTA 1977) on an exemption clause, it should be asked whether the clause is part of the contract and whether it covers the breach which has occurred. Those two points were dealt with in **Chapter 9**.

10.2   UCTA 1977 is the first piece of legislation to deal with exemption clauses on a fairly general basis rather than merely dealing with specific types of contract (although certain types of contract are excluded from its operation—see para. **10.10**). However, its name, 'the Unfair Contract Terms Act', should not be regarded as a guide to what it does. It does not deal with 'unfair terms' as such. It deals with exemption clauses. This contrasts with the regime for the policing of terms in consumer contracts in the EC Directive/Regulations on Unfair Terms in Consumer Contracts, and the draft Consumer Rights Bill, which does indeed deal with unfair terms much more generally, although there are significant exemptions from its coverage (see **Chapter 11**).

10.3   In some circumstances UCTA 1977 will strike down an exemption clause because it does not 'satisfy the requirement of reasonableness', but in others the clause is struck down automatically, without any consideration of whether it is reasonable. To see exactly what effect the Act will have on any given exemption clause requires careful consideration of its specific provisions.

10.4   In **Chapter 9** the problem with the identification of exclusion clauses was raised. The argument that there is no such distinct type of clause was referred to. It will be considered again in this chapter, as UCTA 1977 is based upon the assumption that the exclusion clause is a distinct type of clause, and indeed it contains provisions for dealing with exclusion clauses which have been 'disguised' in the form of part of the definition of the obligation (see ss 3 and 13 at para. **10.28**ff and para. **10.107**ff).

10.5   UCTA 1977 clearly interferes with freedom of contract. It affects the agreement which the parties made for themselves. However, as Lord Reid pointed out in *Suisse Atlantique* [1967] 1 AC 361, the situation in which an 'objectionable' exemption clause is found may be one in which one party's freedom of contract is very limited. He said:

> 'Probably the most objectionable are found in the complex standard conditions which are now so common. In the ordinary way the customer has no time to read them, and if he did read them he probably would not understand them. And if he did understand and object to any of them, he would generally be told he could take it or leave it. And if he then went to another supplier the result would be the same.'

The aim of UCTA 1977 is to strike down 'objectionable' exemption clauses. The variety of situations and clauses with which it has to deal, and the many factors which are relevant to whether a clause is 'reasonable', means that it is not without difficulties.

10.6   Since the mid-1990s, a major factor adding to the complexity of the policing of exemption clauses, and unfair terms in consumer contracts more generally, has been the overlap of two pieces of legislation using different concepts, and with different scopes: UCTA and the Unfair Terms in Consumer Contracts Regulations 1999 (UTCCR 1999) (previously 1994). So, for example, UCTA and the Regulations have different approaches to who receives the protection which flows from being regarded as a consumer, and whilst UCTA applies its 'reasonableness test', the Regulations have a 'fairness' test. Further, UCTA is restricted to exemption clauses but, particularly in the consumer context, does not limit its coverage to standard form contracts. The Regulations strike down unfair terms much more generally, but are restricted in their coverage to non-individually negotiated terms. Such complexities are obviously undesirable, particularly in relation to legislation aimed at assisting the consumer. The Law Commissions proposed a single unified piece of unfair terms legislation to replace both UCTA 1977 and the UTCCR 1999 (*Unfair Terms in Contracts*, Law Com No 292, Scot Law Com No 199). After further consultation by the Law Commissions in an Issues Paper (*Unfair Terms in Consumer Contracts: a new approach?* (2012)), and recommendations (*Unfair Terms in Consumer Contracts: Advice to the Department for Business, Innovation and Skills* (2013)), there is a draft Consumer Rights Bill which excises the consumer coverage from UCTA, and provides for a single unified unfair terms regime for consumers. This will be referred to further in this chapter, in relation to its impact upon UCTA, but it is given fuller coverage in **Chapter 11**, which deals with the regulation of unfair terms in consumer contracts.

Basic structure of UCTA 1977

Introduction

10.7   A mistake often made by students is to see an exemption clause and jump from there to the statement that the clause must be subject to the 'requirement of reasonableness' under the

Unfair Contract Terms Act 1977. This is not the case. The Act does not apply to all exemption clauses and it does not subject all of those clauses to which it does apply to the requirement of reasonableness. It renders some clauses automatically ineffective without their 'reasonableness' coming into question. If the contract comes within the basic scope of the Act, a section must first be found which deals with the exemption clause in question and then it must be asked what that section does to the clause. If the section states that the clause is effective only if it satisfies the requirement of reasonableness, the question of the reasonableness of the clause then, and only then, becomes relevant.

10.8   In addition to those provisions which state the basic scope of UCTA (see paras **10.9–10.10**), the presence of two other important types of section within UCTA 1977 should be emphasized. The first of these consists of those sections which state that a clause is totally ineffective or effective only if it satisfies the requirement of reasonableness. These can be termed the 'active sections' (for example, ss 2, 3, 6, and 7). The second are the 'definition' sections which merely help to explain the meaning of the terms used within the 'active sections' (for example, s 12 ('deals as consumer') and s 11 ('the requirement of reasonableness')). The key to using the Act is to remember to find an active section applicable to the exemption clause in question. The definition sections assist that active section by clarifying its meaning. It is not possible simply to use s 11, which indicates the meaning of the requirement of reasonableness. That section does not state that the requirement of reasonableness is to be applied to any exemption clause. An active section is required first to indicate that something is to happen to the particular exemption clause.

Exemption clauses within the operation of the Act

10.9   It should be emphasized that, basically, UCTA 1977 only applies to business liability. Sections 2–7, subject to the exception in s 6(4) (which is very limited in its effect), apply only to business liability, i.e. liability for breach of obligations or duties arising (a) from things done or to be done by a person in the course of a business, or (b) from the occupation of premises used for the business purposes of the occupier (s 1(3)). Business is not defined, but it includes 'a profession and the activities of any government department or local or public authority' (s 14).

10.10   UCTA 1977, Sch 1 lists certain types of contract which are excluded wholly, or in part, from the operation of the Act. They include contracts of insurance, or any contract insofar as it relates to the creation or transfer of an interest in land (see *Electricity Supply Nominees Ltd v IAF Group plc* (1993)) or intellectual property (patents, trade marks, etc.), the formation or dissolution of a company or its constitution, and the creation or transfer of securities (para. 1), charter parties and carriage of goods by ship or hovercraft, etc. (paras 2 and 3), and contracts of employment (para. 4) (see s 1).

Sections 26, 27, and 29 set boundaries for the Act in relation to contracts with an international element.

The active sections

10.11 In considering the active sections, frequent reference will be made to the requirement of 'reasonableness' (s 11), 'deals as consumer' (s 12), etc. These concepts are considered in detail later, where the definition sections are dealt with. Under the draft Consumer Rights Bill, the definition of 'deals as consumer' ceases to be of any significance.

Negligence (s 2)

10.12 Section 2 is an important and widely applicable section. It deals with liability arising from negligence which, for the purposes of UCTA 1977, is defined in s 1. Section 1 states that negligence means the breach:

> '(a) of any obligation, arising from the express or implied terms of a contract, to take reasonable care or exercise reasonable skill in the performance of the contract;
> (b) of any common law duty to take reasonable care or exercise reasonable skill (but not any stricter duty);
> (c) of the common duty of care imposed by the Occupiers' Liability Act 1957.'

The duty may arise in contract or tort or under the Occupiers' Liability Act 1957, and UCTA 1977, s 2 not only relates to contract terms purporting to exclude or restrict liability for negligence, but also covers non-contractual notices attempting to effect such liability in tort.

10.13 UCTA 1977, s 2(1) prevents entirely the exclusion or restriction of liability for negligently caused death or personal injury. There is no need to consider whether the clause is reasonable.

10.14 UCTA 1977, s 2(2) deals with negligently caused loss or damage not covered by s 2(1). Under it, the term or notice will only be effective to exclude or restrict liability for such negligently caused loss or damage if the term or notice satisfies the requirement of reasonableness.

10.15 UCTA 1977, s 2(3) enigmatically states:

> 'Where a contract term or notice purports to exclude or restrict liability for negligence a person's agreement to or awareness of it is not of itself to be taken as indicating his voluntary acceptance of any risk.'

This seems to be intended to limit claims to rely upon the tort defence of volenti non fit injuria.

10.16 The existence of s 2 means that there is less need for a very restrictive approach to be taken to the construction of exemption clauses which are claimed to deal with liability for negligence. It is worth considering whether the Court of Appeal would have viewed the construction of the exemption clause in *Hollier* v *Rambler Motors (AMC) Ltd* (1972) in the same way had such legislation been available to it (see para. **9.86**).

10.17 Of course, in its coverage of exclusions or restrictions of liability for negligence, there was an overlap of UCTA with the consumer unfair terms regime, once the Regulations came into existence. The Regulations subject all terms they cover to the fairness test, so they lacked UCTA's more powerful automatic ineffectiveness in relation to clauses excluding or restricting liability for negligently caused personal injury or death. Nevertheless, in some ways the Regulations proved more potent because of their applicability not only to individual disputes, but their policing at the general, preventive, level. In considering clauses referred to it under the Regulations, the Office of Fair Trading encountered clauses still being used which were automatically ineffective under UCTA 1977, s 2(1), as they purported to exclude or restrict with liability for negligently caused personal injury or death. The Regulations' general level of policing meant that they could ensure that such terms were removed. The draft Consumer Rights Bill brings together both of these benefits. It incorporates UCTA's automatic ineffectiveness of terms, or notices, attempting to exclude of restrict liability for negligently caused death or personal injury, and provides for their coverage by its general enforcement mechanism.[1] Terms or notices excluding or restricting other liability for negligence to the consumer are dealt with by the draft Bill's broadly applicable fairness test.

Contracts where one party 'deals as consumer' or on the other's 'written standard terms of business' (s 3)

10.18 Section 3 provides UCTA 1977's broadest coverage as it is not limited to dealing with any particular kind of obligation or liability, whereas, for example, s 2 is limited to liability based on negligence and ss 6 and 7 to obligations stemming from certain implied terms in goods contract. Section 3 deals with two broad types of contract: those where one party 'deals as consumer' and those where he or she deals on the other party's 'written standard terms of business'. 'Deals as consumer' is defined in s 12 and is considered below (see para. **10.46**ff). There is no definition of 'written standard terms of business', and that will be considered here. Under the draft Consumer Rights Bill, s 3 ceases to cover situations where one party 'deals as consumer'. Exemption clauses in 'consumer contracts' are simply subject to the unfair terms regime in the Bill. However, whilst the Directive/Regulations only subject terms to the fairness test if they are non-individually negotiated, the scope of UCTA's coverage of exemption clauses, where the relevant party 'dealt as consumer', was never so confined. In the light of that, in particular, the application of the fairness test in the draft Bill is not restricted to non-individually negotiated terms.[2]

---

1 Clause 68, sch 3.

2 It was also thought that, in any event, outside of the core terms, 'consumers seldom have sufficient understanding of the possible impact of [the terms] to make any negotiation meaningful', and there is, anyway, uncertainty over when a term is 'non-individually negotiated', and also evidence of exploitation by some businesses of the fact that the Regulations did not cover non-individually negotiated terms. *Unfair Terms in Contracts* (2005) Law Com No 292, Scot Law Com No 199, paras 3.50–3.53.

'Written standard terms'

10.19   As has been indicated, the phrase 'written standard terms' is important in determining the scope of UCTA 1977's broadest provision. It raises a number of questions. In most cases, it will be clear that the terms are written (but see para. **10.24**ff), and what will fall to be determined is (1) whether the relevant party has standard terms, and (2) whether the parties dealt on them in the instant case.

The existence of the relevant party's standard terms

10.20   In the context of s 17 of UCTA 1977, which is the equivalent of s 3 in the Scottish part of the Act, the phrase used is 'standard form contract', rather than 'written standard terms of business'. In the context of s 17, in *McCrone v Boots Farm Sales Ltd* 1981 SLT 103, Lord Dunpark referred (at 105) to a standard form contract as one where there are: 'a number of fixed terms or conditions invariably incorporated in contracts of the kind in question'. However, whilst a set of terms 'invariably' incorporated into contracts of the appropriate type would clearly be standard terms, a set of terms may be 'standard terms' even though not used 'invariably'. 'If this were not so the statute would be emasculated'—UCTA 1977, s 3 could be avoided simply by not using the relevant terms on one or two isolated, and unimportant, occasions.[3] Certainly, it was indicated in *British Fermentation Products Ltd* v *Compair Reavell Ltd* (1999) that it would suffice if the terms were 'usually used' by the relevant party. What can constitute standard terms should depend upon the pattern of dealing on the terms in question, when the contract is of the type to which they are appropriate. It can be suggested that even requiring their 'usual' use could be seen as too strict, if that requires their use in more than half of the contracts of the appropriate type made by the relevant party. The relevant party may use them, for example, whenever he or she can, but in the course of negotiations, he or she can only ensure their use in a substantial minority of the contracts he or she makes. It should be a question of whether the whole pattern of the relevant party's use of the terms is sufficient for them to be regarded as that party's standard terms, and it may be that the relevant party's intention as to their use should be relevant. In *Chester Grosvenor Hotel* the Official Referee, Judge Stannard, indicated a 'fact and degree' approach. He said (at 133):

> 'In my judgment the question is one of fact and degree. What are alleged to be standard terms may be used so infrequently in comparison with other terms that they cannot realistically be regarded as standard, or on any particular occasion may be so added to or mutilated that they must be regarded as having lost their essential identity. What is required for terms to be standard is that they should be regarded as standard by the party which advances them as its standard terms and that it should habitually contract on those terms. If it contracts also on other terms, it must be determined in any given case, and as a matter of fact, whether this has occurred so frequently that the terms in question cannot be regarded as standard, and if on any occasion a party has substantially modified its prepared terms, it is a question of fact

---

3   *Chester Grosvenor Hotel Co Ltd* v *Alfred McAlpine Management Ltd* (1991) 56 BLR 115. But see *Hadley Design Associates* v *Westminster London Borough Council* (2003).

> whether those terms have been so altered that they must be regarded as not having been employed on that occasion.'

The judge then concluded that the two contracts in question had been made on McAlpine's written standard terms of business. The two contracts had been made in December 1984 and November 1985. Between January 1983 and November 1985 McAlpine had entered into fifteen other contracts of the relevant type. Seven had used the relevant terms (with some deviations from the norm), six had been made on the other party's terms and twice the JCT Standard Form had been used.

10.21   Even if it is accepted that the question of pattern of use of a set of terms and variation of the terms themselves must be considered as matters of fact and degree in deciding if the contract was made on the basis of 'written standard terms', there are still matters which would seem to require decision as a matter of law. One question is whether a standard form which is common throughout a particular trade, and has been devised by a third party, such as a trade association, should fall within UCTA 1977, s 3. Can it be regarded as the written standard terms of business of the relevant party? Certainly, the Contractors Plant Association model conditions were assumed to be the written standard terms of the relevant party in *Cox Plant Hire (London) Ltd* v *Dialbola* (1983), and *USA* v *ARC Construction Ltd* (1991). It was considered in *British Fermentation Products Ltd* v *Compair Reavell Ltd* (1999) whether a contract made on the basis of the Institute of Mechanical Engineers Model Form General Conditions of Contract Form C could constitute the defendant's written standard terms of business. There was, however, no proof of the manner in which the terms were used by the defendant and the judge made the point that if s 3 could apply to 'model forms drafted by an outside body', there would need to be proof of their adoption by the relevant party as his or her standard terms, 'either by practice or by express statement'. It is contended that the better view is that, subject to such adoption, the 1977 Act should extend to such contracts. Some model standard terms will be arrived at by consultation with representatives of both sides of those involved in the transaction to which the terms relate and may not carry the same risk of one-sided terms as some other standard form contracts. However, such factors can be considered in the application of the 'requirement of reasonableness' and as the Law Commission pointed out in relation to such model standard terms:

> 'They are not drafted with any particular transaction between particular parties in mind and are often entered into without much, if any thought being given to the wisdom of the standard terms in the individual circumstances' (Law Com No 69, para. 152).

The instant case

10.22   If the relevant party has 'written standard terms of business', the question is whether they were used in the instant case. In *McCrone* v *Boots Farm Sales Ltd* (1981) Lord Dunpark indicated that for the instant contract to have been made on the relevant party's standard terms, they should have been used 'without material variation'. However, it should not be too easy to argue that the relevant party's standard terms have been sufficiently departed from to take the contract outside of the scope of UCTA 1977, s 3. It must be a question of degree whether the variation in terms is such that the parties are not contracting on the 'standard terms'. This should be assessed not only by looking at the number of terms which have been varied, but also at which of the terms have been varied. Some terms are inherently dependent upon the particular contract, whilst changes to others would be a strong indicator that the relevant party's standard terms had ceased to be used as such. 'In many contracts there may be negotiations as to, for example, quality or price but none as to the crucial exempting terms' (*St Alban's City and District Council v International Computers Ltd* [1995] FSR 686 at 706 per Scott Baker J). Nevertheless, the contract as a whole must be considered. In *Watford Electronics Ltd v Sanderson CFL Ltd* (2000) the situation was viewed as not taken outside of s 3 by an amendment which was seen as 'narrow and insubstantial' when 'considered against the totality of the standard conditions which otherwise remained unamended' (at [113]). At the extreme, in *Pegler v Wang* (2000), the line was even taken that it was sufficient if the exemption clauses were the relevant party's standard terms, but it must be seriously doubted whether, in such a case, the other party 'deals on' the relevant party's 'written standard terms of business'. The phrase would seem to imply some far larger input into the contract as a whole, if not the majority input. Certainly it has been suggested that:

> 'the role in the context of possibly voluminous documentation of a pre-prepared document setting out "written standard terms of business" may be so small in relation to the whole, or the modifications to a pre-prepared document setting out "written standard terms of business" may be so significant, that it may be an abuse of language to describe the resulting contract as dealing on the "written standard terms of business" [of the relevant party]' (*Hadley Design Associates* v *Westminster London Borough Council* [2003] EWHC 1617 (TCC) at [83]).

Further, in *Yuanda (UK) Co Ltd v V W Gear Construction Ltd* (2010) Edwards-Stuart J indicated that if there was 'any significant difference between the terms proferred and the terms of the contract actually made, then the contract will not have been made on one party's written standard terms of business' (at [26]).

10.23   There is some suggestion that factors other than the extent of the use of the standard terms may be relevant in considering whether the instant contract was made on the relevant party's 'written standard terms'. In *Salvage Association v CAP Financial Services Ltd* [1995] FSR 654 (at 672) HHJ Thayne Forbes (Off Ref) listed factors which he thought should be taken into account in deciding if a contract was made on the proferens written standard terms of business:

> 'i) the degree to which the "standard terms" are considered by the other party as part of the process of agreeing the terms of the contract.
>
> ii) the degree to which the "standard terms" are imposed on the other party by the party putting them forward.
>
> iii) the relative bargaining power of the parties.
>
> iv) the degree to which the party putting forward the "standard terms" is prepared to entertain negotiations with regard to the terms of the contract generally and the standard terms in particular.
>
> v) the extent and nature of any agreed alterations to the "standard terms" made as a result of the negotiations between the parties.'

The final factor would be relevant to a simple comparison of the contract made, with the relevant standard terms, and is consistent with the approach indicated earlier. The other factors stated would require a very different approach to the question of whether the parties dealt on the relevant 'written standard terms'. They would require a detailed examination of the contracting process. It would be argued, for example, that the proferens did have 'written standard terms' but that they had merely provided the starting point for negotiations, and that the other party had an opportunity to influence the final contract terms, but chose to accept the terms originally put forward by the relevant party. However, it should be emphasized that a finding that the contract was made on the relevant party's 'written standard terms of business' does not result in the automatic negation of any clause. If the contract falls within the scope of UCTA 1977, s 3 then certain terms are rendered ineffective if they fail to satisfy the requirement of reasonableness. The type of factors identified in (i) to (iv) above are addressed when the requirement of reasonableness is applied and it is more appropriate that they be considered at that point when all the factors relevant to the requirement of reasonableness can be looked at. It might be argued to be more helpful to business if the scope of s 3 is narrowed at this point, so that fewer contracts between businesses are subject to the uncertainties of the application of the requirement of reasonableness. However, narrowing the scope of s 3 by considering the first four factors indicated above, would introduce the same type of uncertainty at the earlier stage. A less complex test at the earlier stage may well create less uncertainty overall.

Written terms

10.24   A question arises in relation to the situation which occurs when terms are incorporated by a 'consistent course of dealing'. Offer and acceptance often occur orally in such cases. Are a set of 'standard terms' then incorporated as written terms? To answer the question in the context of UCTA 1977, s 3, we need to consider the basic mechanism for incorporation by a course of dealing. The mechanism is that, although there is no specific reference to standard terms in making a particular contract, the past dealings between the parties are such that, in the absence of any contrary indication, those terms are taken to have been included in the offer and acceptance (see para. **9.47**ff). They should be regarded as incorporated as 'written' terms if they have been embodied in a written document in the past. An analogy can be made with incorporation by reference. The terms are incorporated as terms recorded in the written standard document in which they previously appeared.

10.25   The final question to be considered here relates to contracts made using computers via e-mail or simply on the internet. There is no definition of writing in UCTA 1977 but, in general, writing 'includes typing, printing, lithography, photography and other modes of representing words in a visible form' (Interpretation Act 1978, Sch 1). Although when contracts are made using computers the words generally appear on the computer screen,[4] they are actually

---

4   The exception is where computer-to-computer 'automated' contracting occurs using a structured Electronic Data Interchange (EDI) system. It is not intended that the messages be read by a human being, but merely by computer. There is not even transitory visibility of the message to satisfy the Interpretation Act definition—see Law Com Advice, paras 3.19–3.20.

represented, and recorded, by electrically charged particles. Nevertheless, the Law Commission takes the view that such transitory visibility is sufficient to satisfy the Interpretation Act definition of writing for the purposes of formalities. It would seem that the same approach should be taken to the reference to 'written' terms in s 3 ('Electronic Commerce: Formal Requirements in Commercial Transactions' Advice from the Law Commission, Dec. 2001, para. 3.8).

Section 3(2)(a)

10.26   In relation to contracts where one party 'deals as consumer or on the other's written standard terms of business', UCTA 1977, s 3(2)(a) prevents that 'other' party from restricting or excluding his or her liability for breach of contract by the use of any contract terms except insofar as that term satisfies the requirement of reasonableness. This is a very wide provision. It relates to the situation where there is a breach and the party in breach is claiming that the relevant term excludes or restricts his or her liability for breach. That term will be effective only 'in so far as [it] satisfies the requirement of reasonableness'. The overlap with the consumer unfair terms regime in the Directive/Regulations is removed by the provisions of the draft Consumer Rights Bill, which excise the reference to 'deals as consumer' from s 3, and take consumer contracts outside of its coverage.

Section 3(2)(b)—exclusion clauses 'in disguise'

10.27   Under UCTA 1977, s 3(2)(b), a person contracting on his or her own 'written standard terms of business' or contracting with someone who 'deals as consumer' cannot by reference to any contract term:

> '…claim to be entitled—
>   (i) to render a contractual performance substantially different from that which was reasonably expected of him, or
>   (ii) in respect of the whole or any part of his contractual obligation, to render no performance at all,
> except in so far as…the contract term satisfies the requirement of reasonableness.'

This is less straightforward than s 3(2)(a). It applies to situations where there is apparently no breach. Section 3(2)(b) is an attempt to deal with what can be termed exclusion clauses 'in disguise'.

10.28   The point was made earlier (see para. **9.3**) that there is a problem in identifying exclusion clauses. An exclusion clause may be rewritten so that it is, in form, part of the definition of the obligation. This has led to the argument that an exclusion clause is not a distinct type of clause at all (Coote, *Exception Clauses*, 1964). However, the Unfair Contract Terms Act 1977 assumes that an exclusion clause is a distinct type of clause. On that basis, the Act recognizes that an exclusion clause can take the form of part of the definition of the obligation and still be an exclusion clause. Its form is then perceived as a possible means of evading provisions dealing with exclusion clauses. Section 3(2)(b) is one of the parts of the Act designed to bring exclusion clauses 'in disguise' within its operation. The Law Commission, in considering the proposed Act to deal with exclusion clauses, recognized that what mattered about such clauses was not their form but their substance. It was said (Law Com Rep No 69 (1975), para. 146):

> 'We do not propose to define exemption clauses in general terms; we regard this expression not as a legal term of art but as a convenient label for a number of provisions which may be mischievous in broadly the same way. Their mischief is that they deprive or may deprive the person against whom they are invoked... *of rights which the promisee reasonably believed the promisor had conferred on him.*' (Emphasis added.)

Section 3(2)(b)(i) deals with the 'mischief' of clauses which deprive the promisee of rights which he or she reasonably believed the promisor had conferred on him or her.

10.29   The reaction to this might be to ask how the promisee's reasonable expectations can differ from the actual obligations embodied in the contract. The answer to this is the artificial way in which terms can be incorporated and the difficulty of understanding that a long stand-ard form document can present a danger that 'the relatively unsophisticated or unwary party will not realize what or how little he has been promised, although the legal scope and effect of the contract may be perfectly clear to a lawyer' (Law Com Rep No 69 (1975), para. 145). In other words, the contracting process is so artificial that the expectations of the promisee, as a reason-able person, may differ from the obligations which lawyers would find in the contract. At times there does still seem to be a reluctance to recognize this and to consider whether such artifici-alities were present (for example, *Peninsula Business Services* v *Sweeney* (2004)). Nevertheless, it seems plain how s 3(2)(b)(i) should operate.

10.30   UCTA 1977, s 3(2)(b)(i) encompasses, for example, what have been seen as 'trap' pro-visions—'cases in which the application of small print provisions would enable a party to per-form a contract in a substantially different manner from that which could reasonably have been expected from a perusal of its primary terms' (*Liberty Life Insurance Co.* v *Sheikh* (1985) per Kerr LJ). Another situation which may fall within s 3(2)(b)(i) is where one term apparently states what the proferens' performance is to be, but another confers on the proferens a discretion as to that performance. It may be recognized as reasonable for the other party to expect that discre-tion to be exercised within narrow bounds, and for s 3(2)(b)(i) to apply if it is not. In relation to a contract for the supply of a service by British Telecom, which contained a clause stating that BT could terminate the contract on one month's notice, Sir Thomas Bingham MR said:

> 'If a customer reasonably expects a service to continue until BT has substantial reason to terminate it, it seems to me at least arguable that a clause purporting to authorise BT to ter-minate without reason purports to permit partial or different performance from that which the customer expected' (*Timeload Ltd* v *British Telecommunications plc* (1995)).

(But see *Hadley Design Associates* v *Westminster London Borough Council* (2003)).

10.31   The claimed extent of a discretion was an element in an example, given by the Law Commission, of the type of case which might now fall within UCTA 1977, s 3(2)(b). The clause was also relatively obscurely positioned. The case was that of *Anglo-Continental Holidays Ltd* v *Typaldos (London) Ltd* (1967) and the facts were:

> The claimant travel agent booked cabins for clients on the defendant's ship *Atlantica* for a Mediterranean cruise commencing on 12 August. On 2 August the defendant notified the claimant that the clients could not be accommodated on the *Atlantica* but had been booked on the *Angelika*. The *Atlantica* was a large ship with two swimming pools. The *Angelika* was a 'small old crate'. The itinerary of the *Angelika* differed from that of the *Atlantica*. The latter would have spent two days in Haifa, allowing time for trips further into Israel. The former was to spend only eight hours in Haifa. The two days in Haifa would have been the climax of the trip for the claimant's clients as they were a Jewish group. Printed on the back of the defendant's handbook for travel agents was a clause which said 'Steamers, Sailing Dates, Rates and Itineraries are subject to change without prior notice'.

On being informed of the change of ship and itinerary, the claimant cancelled the arrangements and claimed damages for breach. The defendant sought to rely upon the clause on the back of the handbook. The Court of Appeal held that the clause could not assist the defendant, who was liable for breach. The clause could not be used to alter the substance of the transaction. It had to be limited so that effect could be given to the main object of the contract.

10.32   In *Typaldos* the court recognized that the clause, as it appeared, was not in keeping with the 'substance' and the 'main object' of the contract. Effect was given to the 'substance' of the contract by construction of the contract.[5] Similar facts to *Typaldos* might now be dealt with under UCTA 1977, s 3(2)(b)(i) as the defendant was claiming to render a performance substantially different from that which was reasonably expected. The case emphasizes the artificial nature of standard terms. The court was willing to recognize that the terms specific to the particular contract might well reflect its substance better than the standard terms used by one party in many contracts. A similar approach would now provide work for s 3(2)(b)(i).[6]

10.33   However, the point should be made that if UCTA 1977, s 3(2)(b)(i) is to cover terms conferring a discretion on the proferens, the discretion must relate to the performance of the proferens and not that of the other party. In *Paragon Finance plc* v *Staunton* (2001) it was held not to apply to a term conferring a discretion on a lender as to the interest rate to be paid by the borrower. (Clearly, setting the interest rate could literally be regarded as part of the proferens' performance. The court's approach embodies the underlying assumption that even the broadest parts of UCTA 1977 should be restricted to terms which can, in some sense, be seen as exemption clauses.) In the consumer context, an unduly wide discretion may be unfair under

---

5   See also *Sze Hai Tong Bank Ltd* v *Rambler Cycle Co. Ltd* (1959) and *Glynn* v *Margetson & Co.* (1893).

6   See the example provided in *Axa Sun Life Services plc* v *Campbell Martin* (2011) at [50].

the UTCCR 1999/Consumer Rights Bill (see para. **11.61**ff). (For further discussion, and much more detailed analysis, of the difficulties of distinguishing clauses excluding liability from those defining the obligation, and giving meaning to s3(2)(b)(i) and (ii) see E. Macdonald, 'Exception Clauses: Exclusionary or Definitional? It Depends!' (2012) 29 JCL 47).

10.34   Three final points need to be made in relation to UCTA 1977, s 3(2)(b)(i). The first is to emphasize that it contains a recognition both of the difficulty of distinguishing between the actual contract terms and the party's reasonable expectations and, also, the uncertainty that such an exercise could create. It subjects to the requirement of reasonableness only those clauses on which one party seeks to rely to render a performance '*substantially* different from that which was reasonably expected' (emphasis added). The assessment is a broad one. The second point to be noted is that before s 3(2)(b) is applied there is, apparently, no breach. There is no apparent breach because one party is claiming that a specific term prevents whatever he or she has done, or not done, from being a breach. Section 3(2)(b) subjects that term to the requirement of reasonableness. If the term does not satisfy the requirement of reasonableness, then it is ineffective and there is a breach.

Goods (ss 6 and 7)

10.35   UCTA 1977, s 6 deals with exemption clauses relating to certain implied terms in contracts for the sale or hire purchase of goods. Section 7 makes analogous provision for contracts where possession or ownership of goods passes and the contract is not one of sale or hire purchase. The sections often accord more extensive protection for the acquirer of goods who 'deals as consumer', provisions of the draft Consumer Rights Bill excise the reference to 'deals as consumer' from the sections, and remove terms in 'consumer contracts' from their coverage, itself providing similar protection for consumers acquiring goods under 'consumer contracts'.

10.36   Section 6(1)(a) provides that liability for breach of the terms implied by s 12 of the Sale of Goods Act 1979 cannot be excluded or restricted. The terms implied by s 12 relate to title to the goods. It should be noted that such an exemption clause is automatically ineffective. There is no need to consider whether it satisfies the requirement of reasonableness. Section 6(1)(b) makes the same provision for the terms implied into contracts of hire purchase. This applies to both business and consumer contracts. Again the provisions of the draft Consumer Rights Bill removes the consumer protection element to itself.[7]

10.37   UCTA 1977, s 6(2)(a) precludes attempts to exclude or restrict liability for breach of the terms implied by Sale of Goods Act 1979, ss 13–15 where that attempt is being made against a person who deals as consumer. The terms implied by ss 13–15 relate to the conformity of the goods with description and sample, and their fitness for purpose and satisfactory quality. Note that the requirement of reasonableness is again irrelevant. Any exemption clause is

---

7   Clause 32.

automatically ineffective. Section 6(2)(b) makes the same provision for contracts of hire purchase. Again, the provisions of the draft Consumer Rights Bill excise the subsection, removing consumer protection to its own regime, and indeed extending it to cover attempts to exclude or restrict other key liabilities in relation to goods contracts.[8]

10.38   UCTA 1977, s 6(3) deals with exemption clauses relating to the same implied terms as s 6(2), but it covers the cases where the person against whom it is sought to use the exemption clause does not deal as consumer. Section 6(3) differs from s 6(2) in the effect it has on exemption clauses. It does not make exemption clauses automatically ineffective. Exclusion or restriction of the implied terms is possible insofar as the exemption clause satisfies the requirement of reasonableness.

10.39   UCTA 1977, s 7 makes similar provision for contracts under which possession or ownership of goods passes, but which are not contracts of sale or hire purchase. The sort of contracts covered are contracts of hire or contracts for work and materials. Similar amendments to s 7, as to those made to s 6, are contained in the draft Consumer Rights Bill.

Indemnities by consumers (s 4)

10.40   UCTA 1977, s 4 deals with contract terms under which a consumer is to indemnify another party in respect of liability that may be incurred by the other for negligence or breach of contract. The indemnity will be ineffective except insofar as it satisfies the requirement of reasonableness. The draft Consumer Rights Bill provides for the removal of this section. The section has been overtaken by the broader protection provided by the unfair terms regime, which is not confined to particular types of terms, and so removes the need to make special provision for an indemnity because it can behave as an exemption clause. It should be remembered that the draft Bill, unlike the Directive/Regulations, does not confine its protection to non-individually negotiated terms.

'Guarantee' of consumer goods (s 5)

10.41   UCTA 1977, s 5 relates to the situation where a manufacturer or distributor of goods tries to use a particular method of excluding or restricting his or her liability for loss or damage arising from goods proving defective, while in consumer use, due to his or her negligence. The particular method of exclusion or restriction precluded by s 5 is that of the 'guarantee' which purports to promise or assure the consumer that 'defects will be made good by complete or partial replacement, or by repair, monetary compensation or otherwise' (s 5(2)(b)) whilst at the same time removing liability for other loss or damage, i.e. the exclusion or restriction of liability is 'hidden' in a clause which gives the appearance of being beneficial to the user of the goods. Again, the draft Consumer Rights Bill provides for the removal of s 5 from UCTA.

----

8   Clause 32.

Two contracts (s 10)

10.42   Section 10 of the Unfair Contract Terms Act 1977 deals with the situation where there are two contracts and a clause in the second affects rights arising under the first. Section 10 states:

> 'A person is not bound by any contract term prejudicing or taking away rights of his which arise under, or in connection with the performance of, another contract, so far as those rights extend to the enforcement of another's liability which this Part of this Act prevents that other from excluding or restricting.'

The drafting of this section is somewhat obscure. It does not reflect the style generally adopted in the Act as it does not refer to the exclusion or restriction of liabilities, or even rights, but rather to 'prejudicing or taking away rights'.

10.43   Obviously the provisions of the draft Consumer Rights Bill oust the application of s 10 to 'secondary contracts' where the 'main contract' is a consumer contract: they remove the application of the other provisions of UCTA to such 'main contracts'. Similar provision for secondary contracts is, however, made in the draft Consumer Rights Bill, dealing with the situation where the 'main contract' is a consumer contract, whether, or not the secondary contract is a consumer contract.[9] The draft Consumer Rights Bill also provides answers, in that context, for some of the problems which have arisen in relation to s 10.

10.44   One major problem with the borderlines of s 10 was resolved by *Tudor Grange Holdings Ltd v Citibank NA* [1991] 4 All ER 1 in which it was held that the section did not apply to an agreement settling a contractual dispute. It is made explicit in the draft Consumer Rights Bill that the relevant provision 'does not apply if the secondary contract is a settlement of a claim arising under the main contract'.[10]

10.45   More generally, in *Tudor Grange*, Browne-Wilkinson V-C did not think that UCTA 1977, s 10 dealt with the situation where both contracts were between the same parties. He gave an example of the type of contract which he thought s 10 was designed to cover. He said (at 13):

> 'Under contract 1, the supplier (S) contracts to supply a customer (C) with a product. Contract 1 contains no exemption clause. However, C enters into a servicing contract, contract 2, with another party (X). Under contract 2, C is precluded from exercising certain of his rights against S under contract 1. In such a case s 10 operates to preclude X from enforcing contract 2 against C so as to prevent C enforcing his rights against S under contract 1.'

This would seem to be an inappropriate approach. There is nothing in the wording of s10 to suggest it, and it would provide an opportunity for evasion of UCTA 1977 if s 10 was confined to

9   Clause 75.

10   Clause 75(4).

the situation where both contracts are not between the same parties.[11] It is made explicit in the draft Consumer Rights Bill that, under its provisions, it is irrelevant 'whether the parties to the secondary contract are the same as the parties to the main contract'.[12]

Definitions

'Deals as consumer' (s 12)[13]

10.46   The Unfair Terms in Consumer Contracts Directive/Regulations contain a very different approach to who is a 'consumer', and, obviously, the first point to be made here is that UCTA's definition of 'deals as consumer' becomes obsolete under the draft Consumer Rights Bill, the provisions of which excise s 12. It should nevertheless be considered at this point. The basic test is set out in UCTA 1977, s 12(1)(a) and (b) which state:

'A party to a contract "deals as consumer" in relation to another party if—
(a) he neither makes the contract in the course of a business nor holds himself out as doing so; and
(b) the other party does make the contract in the course of a business.'

As can be seen, this basic definition hinges on the issue of when a contract is made 'in the course of a business' and that will be considered in detail later. Some further limitations on dealing as consumer will first be briefly dealt with here.

10.47   Originally, there was an additional general restriction on dealing as consumer in s 12(1)(c) where the contract in question was a sale of goods or hire purchase contract or one covered by s 7. Originally, in relation to those contracts, in order for someone to deal as consumer, the goods passing under or in pursuance of the contract had to be of a type ordinarily supplied for private use or consumption. With the amendments made by the Sale and Supply of Goods to Consumers Regulations 2002 (SI 2002/3045), that further restriction ceased to apply to 'individuals'. Those Regulations also limited the restriction on dealing as consumer in a sale by competitive tender or auction. In relation to 'individuals', that restriction only became

---

11 However, what must be borne in mind is that Browne-Wilkinson V-C's view that s 10 is so confined was accompanied by his further view that ss 2 and 3 were themselves wide enough to encompass a clause in a second contract between the parties to the original contract. He said ([1991] 4 All ER 1 at 13):

'Under ss 2 and 3 there is no express requirement that the contract term excluding or restricting S's liability to C has to be contained in the same contract as that giving rise to S's liability to C.'

This must certainly not be forgotten if *Tudor Grange Holdings Ltd* v *Citibank NA* is cited in relation to the proposition that s 10 deals only with a second contract made with a third party to the original contract. However, it would seem very doubtful that s 10 does not cover the situation where both contracts are between the same parties. The provision in the Scottish part of the Act which deals with the situation where there are two contracts has not been seen as so restricted (*Chapman* v *Aberdeen Construction Group plc* (1991)). There is nothing in the wording of s 10 to indicate such a limitation.

12 Clause 75(3).

13 See R. Kidner, 'The Unfair Contract Terms Act—Who Deals as Consumer' (1987) 38 NILQ 46; I. Brown, 'Business and Consumer Contracts' [1988] JBL 386.

applicable to second-hand goods, sold at a public auction at which individuals have the opportunity of attending the sale.

10.48   Finally, UCTA 1977, s 12(3) makes it clear that it is 'for those claiming that a party does not deal as a consumer to show that he does not'. Further consideration can now be given to the fundamental elements of the basic definition of 'deals as consumer'.

'In the course of a business'

10.49   The key to determining whether someone 'deals as consumer' under the definition in UCTA 1977, s 12 is the question of when a contract is made 'in the course of a business'. Under s 12(1), if someone is to 'deal as consumer', they must not contract in the course of a business (or hold themselves out as doing so) (s 12(1)(a)), and the other party must contract in the course of a business (s 12(1)(b)). The Court of Appeal had to consider the meaning of 'in the course of a business' in the context of s 12 in *R & B Customs Brokers Co. Ltd v United Dominions Trust Ltd* (1988). Consideration will be given to the line taken in that case. It can, however, be subject to considerable criticism.

10.50   In *R & B Customs Brokers Co. Ltd v United Dominions Trust Ltd* [1988] 1 All ER 847 the facts were:

> The claimant company, R & B Customs Brokers, carried on the business of a freight-forwarding agent. Using the defendant finance house, the claimant company traded in a Volvo for a Colt Shogun car. The car was for the business and personal use of its directors and sole shareholders, Mr and Mrs Bell. It was discovered that the car roof leaked and the leak could not be cured. The upholstery became 'sodden with water, mouldy and evil smelling'. The car was not 'reasonably fit for the buyer's purpose' and would be in breach of a term implied by s 14 of the Sale of Goods Act 1979 if such a term was part of the contract. There was an exemption clause purporting to exclude any such implied term unless the buyer dealt as a consumer within the definition in Unfair Contract Terms Act 1977, s 12.

The Court of Appeal concluded that the defendants were liable for breach of the implied term. The claimant company had not made the purchase 'in the course of a business' and had dealt as a consumer. Dillon LJ stated (at 854):

> 'there are some transactions which are clearly integral parts of the business concerned, and these should be held to have been carried out in the course of those businesses; this would cover, apart from much else, the instance of a one off adventure in the nature of trade where the transaction itself would constitute a trade or business. There are other transactions, however, such as the purchase of the car in the present case, which are at the highest only incidental to the carrying on of the relevant business; here a degree of regularity is required before it can be said that they are an integral part of the business carried on and so entered into in the course of that business.'

This identifies a test to be used when it needs to be established whether someone makes a contract in the course of a business. Leaving aside, for the moment, the question of one-off adventures in the nature of trade, the question is basically whether the transaction was an integral part of the business in itself or, if it was merely incidental to the business, whether such transactions occurred with sufficient regularity to have been made 'in the course of a business'. In the instant case, the purchase of a car was not integral to the business of freight forwarding agents, the car was only the second or third so acquired by R & B and the acquisition was not a sufficiently regularly occurring incidental transaction. Further guidance on the test can be obtained from cases interpreting the phrase 'in the course of a business' in the context of the Trade Descriptions Act 1968. The Court of Appeal in *R & B Customs Brokers* adopted the interpretation of 'in the course of a business' in the cases decided under the 1968 Act.

The test

10.51   Leaving aside 'one-off' adventures in the nature of trade, for the moment, under the approach taken in *R & B Customs Brokers Co. Ltd v United Dominions Trust Ltd* (1988), there are two ways in which a transaction may be made in the course of a business. It may be:

1. integral to the business in itself, or
2. merely incidental to the business in itself, but occurring with sufficient regularity.

10.52   The first point to note is that a very restrictive view is taken of those transactions which are 'integral' to a party's business. Only those transactions which are the basis of the business qualify. This is illustrated by the case of *Davies v Sumner* (1984). In that case:

> Mr Davies was a self-employed courier. Using his own car he transported films, video tapes, and other material for HTV between Mold and Cardiff. When he had done 100,000 miles in the car he decided to purchase another one. His first car went to the garage in part exchange. At the time of the sale the odometer on that car showed 18,100 miles. Prior to purchasing that first car Mr Davies had rented a car for a few months and used that in his business.

The applicability of s 1 of the Trade Descriptions Act 1968 hinged upon whether the false trade description, the odometer reading, had been applied to the car 'in the course of a business'. The House of Lords concluded that Mr Davies had not acted 'in the course of a business'. There was no pattern of such transactions, and the sale of a car was not integral to the business of a courier. Similarly, the sale of a car by a taxi business is not integral to that business (*Devlin v Hall* (1990)). Nor is the sale of his boat by a fisherman. It 'is the transaction and not the goods which must be integral to the business' (*Stevenson v Rogers* [1999] 1 All ER 613 at 626).

10.53   The alternative way in which a transaction may be 'in the course of a business' is if, although incidental, it is regularly occurring. The two or three transactions in *R & B Customs*

Brokers Co. Ltd v *United Dominions Trust Ltd* (1988) were not sufficient to turn an incidental transaction into one made in the course of a business. The sale of a car by a hire car business was 'in the course of a business' when the business had a fleet of twenty-four cars and there was a practice of selling a car after it had been owned for about two years (*Havering London Borough Council* v *Stevenson* (1970)). It has not been specifically referred to by the courts, but 'regularity' would also seem to involve some element of frequency.

'One-off' adventures in the nature of trade

10.54   Unless the transaction is, itself, integral to the business, the basic requirement for a transaction to be 'in the course of a business' is that it should be one occurring with sufficient regularity. However, as was indicated earlier, the possibility has also been perceived to exist of a one-off adventure in the nature of trade. The question will then be whether the particular transaction itself has sufficient 'flavour' of 'trading' and the point could be made that this is not a separate category but a specific example of a transaction 'integral' to the business—in this case, the transaction is the business. The question of 'one-off' adventures in the nature of trade has arisen in the context of revenue law where the profits from certain 'one-off' transactions have been held to be taxable as income from a trade. For example, the purchase and resale of one million toilet rolls (*Rutledge* v *IRC* (1929)) or forty-four million yards of parachute silk (*Martin* v *Lowry* (1927)) were held to be trading on the basis that the quantities purchased meant that private use could not have been intended.

Holding out as dealing in the course of business

10.55   It should be noted that a person may preclude him or herself from 'dealing as a consumer' by holding him or herself out as dealing in the course of a business, although he or she is not actually so dealing. Plainly, the reference to 'holding out in the course of a business' was intended to increase transparency for those having to decide whether they were dealing with consumers. The most obvious situation for it to cover is someone who gives the appearance of making a contract for a business in order to obtain a trade discount. However, logically the question of whether someone holds themselves out as contracting in the course of a business should follow the line taken to 'in the course of a business' i.e. following *R & B Customs Brokers Co. Ltd* v *United Dominions Trust Ltd* (1988), the question would be whether someone held themselves out as making a transaction integral to a business or held themselves out as making a regularly occurring transaction which was incidental to a business. That logical extension of *R&B Customs Brokers* was made by the Court of Appeal in *Felderol Foundry plc* v *Hermes Leasing* (2004). However, clearly such an approach does nothing to increase transparency for someone having to decide whether they are dealing with a consumer. This logical extension of *R&B Customs Brokers* is one indicator of the inappropriateness of the approach taken in that case.

10.56   It can be noted that, in relation to the definition of consumer in the Unfair Terms in Consumer Contracts Directive, the ECJ has indicated the adoption of something like the way in which UCTA's reference to someone 'holding themselves' as dealing as in the course of business was clearly meant to operate: to relieve the party, who has every reason to think he or she is dealing with a fellow business person, of the extra restrictions falling on those contracting with consumers. In *Gruber v Bay Wa AG* (2005) it was indicated that account should be taken of the person claiming to be a consumer behaving 'in such a way as to give the other party to the contract the legitimate impression that he was acting for the purpose of his business'. In *Overy v Paypal (Europe) Ltd* (2012) this was followed in relation to the opening of a type of account on paypal which was confined to businesses. The person concerned was a professional photographer, and opened the account as such, but he was primarily using it in an attempt to 'sell' his home in an unusual way, by a form of lottery, or draw.

Criticism—alternative approach

10.57 The approach taken in *R & B Customs Brokers Co. Ltd* v *United Dominions Trust Ltd* (1988) can be criticized. Of course, it becomes an irrelevancy under the draft Consumer Rights Bill, which basically adopts the very different approach taken in the EU Directive on Unfair Terms in Consumer Contracts. Nevertheless, at this point the criticisms of the line taken in *R&B Customs Brokers* are still set out. If it serves no other purpose, it provides a warning as to construction of a legislative provision which is too much driven by the facts of a particular case.

10.58 The first point to be made is that the approach is inappropriate because the phrase 'in the course of a business' occurs in both s 12(1)(a) and (b). The impact of this should be considered. The narrow approach taken to the meaning of 'in the course of a business' in *R & B Customs Brokers* enabled the greater protection provided by UCTA 1977 to purchasers who deal as consumers to be extended in one direction. It allowed merely incidental, and not regularly occurring, business purchasers to gain that protection. However, although, at first sight, extending the protection provided by the 1977 Act, the approach taken to the meaning of 'in the course of a business' by the Court of Appeal in *R & B Customs Brokers* is inappropriately restrictive of it. This is because of the use of the phrase 'in the course of a business' in both s 12(1)(a) and (b), and this point can be most easily made by the use of a simple example. Suppose that there was nothing wrong with the car when R & B bought it, but that it did have the relevant defects when sold by R & B to a purchaser, X, who clearly had no business connections. On the basis of the approach taken in *R & B Customs Brokers*, X would not be dealing as consumer in making the purchase. Clearly, X would not have bought the car in the course of a business, but that only fulfils the requirement in s 12(1)(a). In order for X to have dealt as consumer, it is also required by s 12(1)(b) that the seller must have sold 'in the course of a business', and it is equally clear that that would not have been the case on the *R & B* approach (the sale would not have been integral to the seller's business and there would have been no sufficient regularity). In *R & B Customs Brokers* in extending the protection afforded to those who deal as consumers to the type of purchase by a business there considered, the Court of Appeal took more appropriate cases outside of the scope of that protection. An approach which allowed incidental transactions by a business, whether regularly occurring or not, to be regarded as made 'in the course of a business' would not lead to this result.

10.59   The second point to be made here is on the wording of the phrase 'in the course of a business'. It can be argued that the words of UCTA 1977, s 12(1) themselves show that the line taken in *R & B Customs Brokers Co. Ltd* v *United Dominions Trust Ltd* (1988) is inappropriate. The reference in s 12 is to transactions 'in the course of a business' and not to those 'in the course of business'. 'The former suggests things done by and for a business, while the latter suggests acts limited to the kind of business in which a person is engaged' (Kidner (1987) NILQ 46 at 53). Transactions which are merely incidental to the relevant party's business could be construed as having been made 'in the course of a business' without the need to establish any regularity in their occurrence. In fact, the phrase could be construed even more widely than that, to mean any transaction by a business.

10.60   A further point should be made here, not in relation to the use of the phrase in s 12, but in relation to its use elsewhere in the Unfair Contract Terms Act 1977. It was noted earlier that basically the operation of the Act is restricted to 'business liability' and the most significant part of this is liability arising from things done or to be done 'in the course of a business' (s 1). There is considerable impetus to give the same meaning to the same phrase used in different sections of the same Act. It would unduly curtail the operation of the Act if its scope was limited by the approach taken to 'in the course of a business' in *R & B Customs Brokers Co. Ltd* v *United Dominions Trust Ltd* (1988).

10.61   Some support for a wider approach to the phrase 'in the course of a business' can be found in the judgment of Scott Baker J in *St Albans City and District Council* v *International Computers Ltd* (1995).[14] He concluded, *obiter*, that the Council did not deal as consumer in purchasing a computer system because it had contracted 'in the course of a business'. He decided that it had so contracted simply on the basis of the statement in UCTA, s 14 that 'business includes . . . the activities of any . . . local or public authority'. He did not consider the relationship which the purchase of a computer bore to the main activities of the local authority. In other words there was no attempt to apply the approach taken in *R & B Customs Brokers* in this context (see also *Lease Management Services Ltd* v *Purnell Secretarial Services* (1994) 13 Tr LR 337 at 344). The judge's approach is not in keeping with that taken in *R & B Customs Brokers Co. Ltd* v *United Dominions Trust Ltd* (1988). It would be in keeping with an approach which allowed even transactions incidental to a relevant party's business to be construed as having been made 'in the course of a business'.

10.62   Further, and significant, support for a wider approach to the interpretation of 'in the course of a business' can be found outside the context of the Unfair Contract Terms Act 1977 in the case of *Stevenson* v *Rogers* [1999] 1 All ER 613. There the Court of Appeal had to consider the meaning of 'in the course of a business' in the context of the Sale of Goods Act 1979, s 14(2), where it limits the statutory implication of a term as to the quality of the goods to sales where sellers are acting 'in the course of a business'. The facts were:

> The defendant had been a fisherman for some twenty years. He sold his boat, the *Jelle*, to the claimant in April 1988. He had previously owned and sold one other boat, the *Dolly Mopp*.

---

14   See also Nourse LJ [1996] 4 All ER 481 at 490. But see *Peter Symmonds & Co.* v *Cook* (1981).

The claimant argued that the *Jelle* did not comply with the quality term implied by the Sale of Goods Act 1979, s 14(2). However, a requirement that goods be of the requisite quality was only implied by the section if the sale was made 'in the course of a business'. The meaning to be given to the phrase 'in the course of a business' came to be considered by the Court of Appeal as a preliminary matter.

At first instance, the judge had followed the meaning given to 'in the course of a business' under UCTA 1977 and the Trade Descriptions Act 1968 and held that the fisherman had not sold in the course of a business—the sale not being integral to his business or regularly occurring. However, the Court of Appeal held that the judge had not applied the correct test in determining whether the sale was 'in the course of a business' within the Sale of Goods Act 1979, s 14(2). The phrase was used to ensure that 'every buyer from a business seller should have a right...to receive goods of' the relevant quality. The obligation was to be imposed on 'every trade seller no matter whether he is or is not habitually dealing in goods of the type sold'. Potter LJ made the comment (at 623) that the phrase was there to:

'distinguish between a sale made in the course of a seller's business and a purely private sale of goods outside the confines of the business (if any) carried on by the seller.'

It can be contended that such an approach would similarly be a more appropriate approach to the use of the phrase 'in the course of a business' under the 1977 Act, than that currently taken.

10.63   It can be contended that the broader approach taken to the meaning of 'in the course of a business' in *Stevenson* v *Rogers* (1999) reflects the more natural meaning of the words used. The point can also be made that in *R & B Customs Brokers Co. Ltd* v *United Dominions Trust Ltd* (1988) the Court of Appeal was adopting the approach taken under the Trade Descriptions Act 1968. That Act and UCTA 1977 may broadly share a purpose of consumer protection, but it must not be lost sight of that the 1968 Act involves criminal offences. It is appropriate to narrowly construe a provision which sets the limits of criminal liability. There is no similar impetus to narrow construction when what is in question is a statute which will impact upon civil liability. There are far better reasons for bringing UCTA 1977 into line with the Sale of Goods Act 1979, than for construing either of them in the same way as an Act imposing criminal liability. The approach in *Stevenson* v *Rogers* is also one which would allow the same interpretation to be given to 'in the course of a business' in both s 12 and s 1 of UCTA 1977 without unduly curtailing the Act's operation.[15] As has been indicated, this discussion becomes largely redundant under the draft Consumer Rights Bill. It does, however, serve as a warning as to the problems which may flow from an initial interpretation of a piece of legislation which is too much geared to the specific case, and takes too little account of the broader context.

---

15   See *Unfair Terms in Contracts*, Law Com Consultation Paper No 166; Scot Law Com Discussion Paper No 119; and E. Macdonald, 'Unifying Unfair Terms Legislation' (2004) 67 MLR 69.

The requirement of reasonableness (s 11)[16]

10.64   The active sections often render a clause ineffective except insofar as it satisfies the requirement of reasonableness. Meaning is given to that requirement in UCTA 1977, s 11, with guidelines in Sch 2. It should be remembered that under the draft Consumer Rights Bill, 'consumer contracts' are taken outside of UCTA. Under its provisions, UCTA's requirement of reasonableness no longer applies to consumer contracts, which are instead subject to the fairness test. UCTA's reasonableness test will, however, continue to be of great significance in relation to exemption clauses in the business to business context, and in fact, it is in relation to contracts between businesses that that test has mainly fallen to be applied by the courts. In addition, cases on reasonableness may provide some helpful analogies in relation to the application of the fairness test under the consumer unfair terms regime, although care must be taken in relation to differences in the consumer and business contexts.

10.65   Section 11(5) places the burden of proof upon the person claiming that the contract term satisfies the requirement of reasonableness. The basic test is one involving the weighing of multiple factors to decide if it was 'fair and reasonable' to have included the clause in the contract (s 11(1)). The 'Court must entertain a whole range of considerations, put them in the scales on one side or another and decide at the end of the day on which side the balance comes down' (*Mitchell* v *Finney Lock Seeds* [1983] 2 AC 803 at 816).

10.66   It should briefly be noted that there was a predecessor to the UCTA 1977 test of reasonableness in the Supply of Goods (Implied Terms) Act 1973. This was preserved, for contracts made between 18 May 1973 and 1 February 1978, by s 55 of the Sale of Goods Act 1979 (originally Sale of Goods Act 1893). Some of the cases referred to later in this chapter were decided under this predecessor to the 1977 Act, and some differences between the two tests of reasonableness must be noted to assess the significance of those cases today, this will be returned to at relevant points.

Timing—assessing the whole clause

10.67   UCTA 1977, s 11(1) states:

> 'In relation to a contract term, the requirement of reasonableness...is that the term shall have been a fair and reasonable one to be included having regard to the circumstances which were, or ought reasonably to have been, known to or in the contemplation of the parties when the contract was made.'

The reasonableness of the clause is to be assessed on the basis of the circumstances known to or contemplated by, or which should have been known to or contemplated by, the parties at the time of contracting. The particular breach is not directly relevant. It can be relevant only

---

16   J. Adams and R. Brownsword, 'The Unfair Contract Terms Act 1977: A Decade of Discretion' (1988) 104 LQR 94.

to the extent that it was one of the possibilities the parties contemplated, or should have contemplated, at the time of contracting. Assessing the reasonableness of the clause in relation to the circumstances at the time of contracting should assist contract planning. A clause should not be rendered unreasonable because it appears unreasonable in the light of unforeseeable events which occurred once the contract had been made, and the 'court should not be too ready to focus on remote possibilities or to accept arguments that a clause fails the test by reference to relatively uncommon or unlikely situations' (*F G Wilson Engineering Ltd* v *John Holt & Co (Engineering) Ltd* (2012) at [96]).

10.68   It was UCTA 1977, s 11(1), and the question of timing, which the Court of Appeal focused on in *Stewart Gill Ltd* v *Horatio Myer & Co. Ltd* [1992] 2 All ER 257 in deciding that the reasonableness of a clause must be assessed as a whole and not merely the part of the clause being relied upon in the instant case.[17] In that case:

> The defendants had contracted with C for the supply and installation of an overhead conveyor system for a price of £266,400. The defendants were to pay in stages, and it was the last 10 per cent which gave rise to the dispute. C were asking for summary judgment for the remaining 10 per cent of the price. The defendants contended that summary judgment should not be given as C had committed certain breaches which gave rise to claims which could be set off against the unpaid 10 per cent of the price. C relied upon clause 12.4 of their standard form contract to meet the defendants' contention. Clause 12.4 stated:
>
> > 'the Customer shall not be entitled to withhold payment of any amount due to the Company under the contract by reason of any payment set off counterclaim allegation of incorrect or defective goods or for any other reason whatsoever which the Customer may allege excuses him from performing his obligations hereunder.'

At first instance C's application for summary judgment was refused. The clause was not in the form of a simple exclusion or restriction of liability, but the Court of Appeal concluded that the clause was brought within UCTA 1977, s 3 by s 13(1)(b), and so its effectiveness depended upon whether it satisfied the requirement of reasonableness. Although of the view that the exclusion of the right of set-off—the part of the clause relied upon in the instant case—might be reasonable, the court did not view the clause as a whole as reasonable. It was not viewed as reasonable that the defendants should not be entitled to withhold payment to C by reason of any 'credit' owing by C to the defendants or by reason of any payment made by the defendants to C (for example, an over-payment under some other contract).

10.69   The Court of Appeal concluded that they must assess the clause as a whole because of UCTA 1977, s 11(1). The 'time frame' of assessment required by s 11(1) meant that the actual events in relation to which the clause would be used could not be taken into account and, on that

---

17 E. Peel, 'Making More Use of the Unfair Contract Terms Act' (1993) 56 MLR 98; I. Brown and A. Chandler, 'Unreasonableness and the Unfair Contract Terms Act' (1993) 109 LQR 41.

basis, the court concluded that the whole clause had to be assessed. After considering s 11(1), Stuart-Smith LJ said (at 262):

> 'Although the question of reasonableness is primarily one for the court when the contract term is challenged, it seems to me that the parties must also be in a position to judge this at the time the contract is made. If this is so, I find it difficult to see how such an appreciation can be made if the customer has to guess whether some, and if so which, part of the term will alone be relied upon.'

10.70   The simplest point to be made from *Stewart Gill Ltd* v *Horatio Myer & Co. Ltd* (1992) is that draftsmen might be advised to include several narrow exemption clauses rather than one wide clause, such as that given here, so that at least some of their exemptions may survive. However, to a very limited extent the court will treat what appears as a single clause as composed of several distinct units in applying the requirement of reasonableness. So, the two sentences, written as a single clause in *Watford Electronics Ltd* v *Sanderson CFL Ltd* (2001), were nevertheless treated as two clauses. What was set out as clause 7(3) of the contract stated:

> 'Neither the Company nor the Customer shall be liable to the other for any claims for indirect or consequential losses whether arising from negligence or otherwise. In no event shall the Company's liability under the Contract exceed the price paid by the Customer to the Company for the Equipment connected with any claim.'

The two sentences were considered as separate exclusion and limitation clauses, respectively, by the court.

10.71   Finally, it should be noted here that the time at which reasonableness is assessed is one of the differences between the reasonableness test under the Unfair Contract Terms Act 1977 and its predecessor in, what became Sale of Goods Act 1979, s 55. Under the previous legislation the question was whether it was fair and reasonable to allow reliance upon the term, and the question of reasonableness thus fell to be judged in the light of the breach and its consequences. Although cases decided under s 55 will provide some guidance on the operation of the reasonableness test in UCTA 1977, s 11, this difference in timing will affect the current relevance of some factors in those earlier cases. The test of fairness in the EC Directive/Regulations/Bill uses the same 'time frame' as the 1977 Act. The assessment of fairness is made on the basis of the circumstances at the time of contracting (see para. **11.39**.)

Guidelines

10.72   UCTA 1977, Sch 2 contains guidelines for the application of the requirement of reasonableness. The factors in Sch 2 are:

> '(a) the strength of the bargaining position of the parties relative to each other, taking into account (among other things) alternative means by which the customer's requirements could have been met;

(b) whether the customer received an inducement to agree to the term, or in accepting it had an opportunity of entering into a similar contract with other persons, but without having to accept a similar term;

(c) whether the customer knew or ought reasonably to have known of the existence and extent of the term (having regard, among other things, to any custom of the trade and any previous course of dealing between the parties);

(d) where the term excludes or restricts any relevant liability if some condition is not complied with, whether it was reasonable at the time of the contract to expect that compliance with that condition would be practicable;

(e) whether the goods were manufactured, processed or adapted to the special order of the customer.'

By s 11(2) these guidelines are applicable when the contract is one covered by s 6 or s 7 of UCTA 1977 but, even in that context, they are not exhaustive. Outside ss 6 and 7, the guidelines will not apply by 'legislative prescription', but the factors set out in the guidelines are still likely to be factually relevant to the reasonableness of an exemption clause.[18] In *Phillips Products Ltd v Hyland* [1987] 2 All ER 620 the Court of Appeal thought that the judge at first instance had been wrong to assume that the case did not fall within s 7 but found that, in any event, that did not affect the way in which the decision on reasonableness, which had been applied under s 2, had been taken. Those factors from Sch 2 which were relevant to the case had been taken into account, not because they were within the statutory guidelines, but simply because they were factually relevant (at 628).

Limitation of liability to a specified sum

10.73   UCTA 1977, s 11(4) makes two factors particularly relevant to the question of the reasonableness of a clause which purports to limit liability to a specified sum. When someone tries to use such a clause, regard is to be had to:

'(a) the resource which he could expect to be available to him for the purpose of meeting the liability should it arise; and

(b) how far it was open to him to cover himself by insurance.'

The cases show that the availability and cost of insurance are important factors generally, not only in relation to clauses limiting liability (see para. **10.78**ff).

10.74   In the context of UCTA 1977, s 11(4), it should not be thought that when the factors in that subsection point towards the clause being unreasonable that this necessarily decides the issue. All the relevant factors present must be taken into account and this may lead to a different conclusion (for example, *Singer Co. (UK) Ltd v Tees and Hartlepool Port Authority* (1988)).

---

18 See, e.g., *Singer Co. (UK) Ltd v Tees and Hartlepool Port Authority* [1988] 2 Lloyd's Rep 164 at 169; *Stewart Gill Ltd v Horatio Myer & Co. Ltd* [1992] 2 All ER 257 at 262; *Schenkers Ltd v Overland Shoes Ltd* [1998] 1 Lloyd's Rep 498 at 505.

10.75   More generally it has been indicated that when liability is limited to a specific sum, that sum has to be justified in order to satisfy the requirement of reasonableness. In *Salvage Association* v *CAP Financial Services Ltd* (1995) it was seen as relevant to ask whether the sum related to the turnover or insurance of the party seeking to rely on it, the contract price, or the uninsurable risk to which the other party is exposed. In *St Albans City and District Council* v *International Computers Ltd* (1995), Scott Baker J said:

> 'There are some types of agreement where ordinary risks fall within a particular sum, and there may be good reasons for limiting liability to that sum and leaving the purchaser to carry any additional risk.'

In relation to standard terms it may be easier to establish that a monetary limit is reasonable if it is regularly reviewed (*Singer Co. (UK) Ltd* v *Tees and Hartlepool Port Authority* (1988)).

10.76   *Overseas Medical Supplies Ltd* v *Orient Transport Services Ltd* [1999] 1 All ER (Comm) 981 raises the issue of the use of a single limitation clause in relation to different types of liability. C, the suppliers of medical equipment, employed the defendants as freight forwarders to transport equipment to and from a trade exhibition. The defendants were specialists in dealing with that type of contract. The defendants' terms included a clause requiring C to insure, either through the defendants themselves or independently, for loss or damage to the equipment, and another clause limited the defendant's liability to £600. C opted to insure through the defendants—there had been no realistic possibility that they would do otherwise, it being far easier for the defendants to do so, due to their general work in the area. The equipment was lost on the return journey from the exhibition, at a cost to C of some £8,500. The defendants had failed to effect the insurance requested by C. The limitation was held to be unreasonable, and ineffective, under UCTA 1977 because it not only covered liability for loss or damage to the equipment being transported but also for the defendant's failure to insure—leaving C without any worthwhile recompense for their loss had it been effective. More broadly, the point was made as to the unreasonableness of limitation clauses covering very different types of loss. The point was made (at [21]) that whereas a 'broad brush approach to limitation of liability will be reasonable' in relation to 'certain package services', the position of the defendants in the instant case:

> 'was that of trading organisation which, under a single contract had agreed to combine at least two activities or functions in respect of which the nature of the work undertaken, the incidence of risk as between the parties, and the effect of a breach of duty by the appellants were all of a different character, yet were to be treated without distinction as subject to a single limitation of liability of only £600.'

Such an approach was unreasonable. The appropriateness of the limitation must be considered in relation to each of the different types of breach which it is stated to cover.[19]

---

[19] Although we are here concerned with monetary limits there are also other types of limitation clause, such as those setting time limits for a claim. What may be unreasonable coverage of a clause setting one type of limit may not be unreasonable coverage for a clause setting a different type of limit. *Overseas Medical* was distinguished in *Granville Oil*

Inequality of bargaining power

10.77   Inequality of bargaining power is referred to in para. (a) of the guidelines in UCTA 1977, Sch 2. It is one of the most basic factors to be considered in relation to the question of the reasonableness of an exemption clause. It will be relevant to ask whether the customer could have gone elsewhere to contract for the required goods or services. However, in 'relation to the question of equality of the bargaining position, the court will have regard not only to the question of whether the customer was obliged to use the services of the supplier, but also the question of how far it would have been practicable and convenient to go elsewhere' (*Overseas Medical Supplies Ltd* v *Orient Transport Services Ltd* [1999] 1 All ER (Comm) 981 at [3]). Standard terms, used throughout a particular trade, may indicate that one side of a common transaction is always in a better bargaining position than the other, but this is not necessarily so. Whether standard terms throughout a trade indicate inequality of bargaining power will depend upon how the standard terms were arrived at. For example, in *RW Green Ltd* v *Cade Bros Farms* (1978) (see para. **10.83**) the standard form contract, containing the exemption clause, was used throughout the trade by sellers of seed potatoes, but the standard form had been arrived at after discussions between the National Association of Seed Potato merchants and the National Farmers' Union. It had not simply been imposed by the seedsmen upon their purchasers. The use of a standard form did not indicate inequality of bargaining power.[20]

Insurance

10.78   As we have seen, the possibility of obtaining insurance to cover a potential liability is made specifically relevant to the reasonableness of a limitation clause by s 11(4). It is also a factor which the courts have indicated as being of general significance. The reasonableness of the risk allocation in the exemption clause is assessed against the possibilities open to either party to insure against it (*Flamar Interocean Ltd* v *Denmac Ltd* (1990)).

10.79   In *Photo Production Ltd* v *Securicor Transport Ltd* (1980) UCTA1977 was not applicable because of the date when the events occurred, but the House of Lords commented upon the reasonableness of the exemption clause in general terms. In that case:

> Securicor had contracted to provide a security patrol of Photo Production's factory. One of Securicor's employees, Musgrove, whilst carrying out a patrol of the factory, decided one night to start a fire, and the factory burnt down. The question was whether Securicor was liable for the destruction of the factory. Securicor wished to rely upon an exemption clause.

and Chemicals Ltd v Davies Turner and Co. Ltd (2003). In the latter case the issue was again a clause covering loss and damage as well as failure to insure. However, what was in question was not a monetary limitation but a clause limiting the time within which a claim could be made. The same time limit was not seen as inappropriate in relation to those different types of breach.

20   See also *Singer Co. (UK) Ltd* v *Tees and Hartlepool Port Authority* (1988); *George Mitchell Ltd* v *Finney Lock Seeds Ltd* (1983); *Schenkers Ltd* v *Overland Shoes Ltd* (1998).

The main issue was that of the construction of the clause. However, having held that the clause was appropriately worded to cover the events which had occurred, the House of Lords also considered, *obiter*, whether the clause was reasonable; it thought that it was. The contract was one between two businesses of equal bargaining power. The risk of fire damage had been allocated to the party who could most appropriately insure against it. Photo Production had to insure their factory against fire damage generally. Securicor might not have been able to obtain the appropriate insurance and, even if it had, paying for insurance cover would have increased Securicor's costs and prevented the provision of the security service at the cheap rate given to Photo Production.

10.80   It should be emphasized that what must be asked is not merely whether a party could have insured but also at what cost.[21] *George Mitchell Ltd* v *Finney Lock Seeds Ltd* (1983) contrasts with *Photo Production Ltd* v *Securicor Transport Ltd* (1980). In *Mitchell* v *Finney Lock Seeds*, a case decided under s 55 of the Sale of Goods Act 1979, the person seeking to rely upon the clause could have insured without materially increasing his prices, and this was one factor which led the court to conclude that the exemption clause was unreasonable. *Mitchell* v *Finney Lock Seeds* concerned the sale of cabbage seed. The seed should have been of a variety of winter cabbage but what was negligently supplied was autumn cabbage seed of an inferior quality. The plants produced were very poor, without hearts. The entire crop was useless and had to be ploughed in. The farmers sought to claim for their lost year's production (about £61,000). Finney Lock claimed to rely upon a clause which limited their liability to the cost of the seed (about £200). In deciding that it was not fair and reasonable to allow reliance on the clause, the court indicated that it was relevant that the sellers could have insured against the risk of crop failure caused by supplying the wrong seed and that such insurance would not have led to a significant increase in the price of their seed.

10.81   It is clear that exemption clauses may be employed to circumvent the need to pay for insurance against the risk of having to pay damages. As in *Photo Production Ltd* v *Securicor Transport Ltd* (1980), this may be regarded as a reasonable course to have taken. Y may be in a better position to insure than X and if X does not have to bear the cost of insurance he may offer Y a better contract price. However, an exemption clause may still be regarded as unreasonable even where its ineffectiveness will mean that the person who sought to rely upon the clause will have to insure in the future and increase his or her contract price accordingly. Such increased costs may be preferable to the consequences which would follow if the exemption clause were to be effective. This point is illustrated by *Smith* v *Eric S Bush* (1989):

> Mrs Smith wished to purchase a house. In order to do so she applied to a building society for a mortgage. The building society instructed a firm of valuers, Eric S Bush, to report on and value the property. Mrs Smith paid the building society a fee and signed an application form which stated that the society would provide her with a copy of the mortgage valuation. The form contained a disclaimer to the effect that neither the society nor its valuer warranted

---

21   See also *Singer Co. (UK) Ltd* v *Tees and Hartlepool Port Authority* [1988] 2 Lloyd's Rep 164 at 169.

that the valuation would be accurate and that the valuation would be supplied without any acceptance of responsibility. When Mrs Smith received the valuation, it too contained the disclaimer. The valuation stated that no essential repairs were required and valued the house at £16,500. Relying upon the report and without obtaining an independent survey, Mrs Smith purchased the house for £18,000, £3,500 coming from the mortgage. The valuers had been negligent in their inspection of the house and had failed to notice the lack of support for a chimney which fell through the roof eighteen months later, causing considerable damage.

Mrs Smith claimed damages from the valuers in tort because of their negligent valuation. The House of Lords found that a duty of care was owed to Mrs Smith by the valuers and considered the disclaimer. Its reasonableness fell to be considered under UCTA 1977, s 2(2). That section deals with non-contractual notices purporting to exclude liability in tort as well as contractual exemption clauses, and it is the House of Lords decision on the reasonableness of the clause which is of interest here. The court noted that, although it was open to someone purchasing a house to commission a full survey, the purchaser in this case had relied upon the mortgage valuation rather than arranging for her own survey to be carried out, and such reliance was common practice in house purchases. Purchasers often could not afford to pay for the valuation and a separate survey. Those factors indicated that the disclaimer was not reasonable. The court also considered the practical consequences if the disclaimer was effective. It would mean one individual would bear the loss involved, and that would be likely to cause hardship. Individuals could find themselves with an uninhabitable dwelling and a mortgage still to be paid on it. If the disclaimer was ineffective, leaving the valuer with the consequences of his negligence, it would merely result in his increasing his insurance cover. The cost of increased insurance would be borne by a small price increase to all his clients, and the whole of the risk of his negligence would not fall on one unfortunate house purchaser. In this case the likely increase of valuers' fees to meet their new insurance premiums was a preferable, and more reasonable, outcome to that which would follow if the disclaimer was effective.[22]

Availability of alternatives

10.82 Paragraph (b) of UCTA 1977, Sch 2 deals with the availability of an alternative form of contract, without the exemption clause in question, and this is also a factor which has been prominent in the case law. *Woodman v Photo Trade Processing Ltd* (1981)[23] illustrates this factor:

Mr Woodman had taken photographs at his friends' wedding. He had intended to give them the photographs as a wedding present. There was no other photographer present. He took his film into a shop which acted as an agent for Phototrade Processing Ltd (PTP). On the counter in the shop was a sign containing an exemption clause limiting PTP's liability to replacement of lost films with new ones. PTP negligently lost Mr Woodman's film.

---

22 See also *St Albans City and District Council v International Computers Ltd* (1995); this point was affirmed in the Court of Appeal [1996] 4 All ER 481.

23 Unreported, but see (1981) 131 NLJ 935.

Mr Woodman claimed damages in excess of the cost of a replacement film because of the distress caused by the loss. The question was whether the exemption clause was effective to prevent this from being successful. As negligence was involved, UCTA 1977, s 2(2) rendered the clause ineffective except insofar as it satisfied the requirement of reasonableness. It was argued that the clause was reasonable because it enabled PTP to operate a cheap mass production service. The judge considered such a service to be good enough for the majority of photographers whose pictures were not valuable. He also thought that the majority might complain if they had to pay a higher rate in order to protect the interest of the minority whose pictures were of greater value. However, there was no choice for the minority who required greater care to be taken with their photographs. In addition, the code of practice of the photographic industry, as agreed with the Office of Fair Trading, recognized the possibility of a two-tier system of liability for photographic processors. This code envisaged the customer being offered the choice of a cheaper service and very limited liability for the processor or a more expensive service with the processor accepting greater liability. PTP did not offer their customers a more expensive/greater liability alternative service and this was taken as decisively indicating that the exemption was unreasonable. (See also *Singer Co. (UK) Ltd* v *Tees and Hartlepool Port Authority* [1988] 2 Lloyd's Rep 164 at 170.)

10.83   In *RW Green Ltd* v *Cade Bros Farms* (1978) the availability of more expensive seed potatoes which would be more likely to be healthy indicated that the exemption clause was reasonable in relation to the purchase of cheaper seed potatoes. In that case:

> Seedsmen, RW Green, sold 20 tons of King Edward seed potatoes to a farmer on the standard terms of the National Association of Seed Potato merchants. The potatoes were infected with a virus which was undetectable until the crop started to grow. The standard terms contained an exemption clause which stated that any claim had to be notified to the sellers within three days of delivery and which also limited liability to the cost of the seed.

When RW Green claimed the price of the seed, the farmers counterclaimed for their lost profit on the crop (about £6,000). The counterclaim depended upon whether the exemption clause passed the reasonableness test in the predecessor to UCTA 1977. It was decided that it was not fair and reasonable to allow reliance upon the three-day time limit as the virus could not be detected until the crop started to grow. In contrast, the limitation of liability to the cost of the seed (£634) passed the reasonableness test. The parties were of equal bargaining power. The standard terms were the result of discussions between the seedsmen's association and the National Farmers' Union. This counterbalanced the fact that the same terms were used throughout the trade and the farmers could not have made such a purchase without the exemption clause being a part of the contract. The reasonableness of the limitation was also indicated by the fact that those standard terms had been used for about twenty years and the parties had dealt together for five or six years so that they both should have known of the exemption clause. More specifically, the fact that the farmers had the alternative of purchasing certified seed at a higher price indicated that limiting liability to a specified sum was reasonable. Certified seed would have come from a crop which had been inspected for signs of virus the previous year and purchasing such seed would have provided 'a very real safeguard' against the risk of obtaining infected seed. The farmer had chosen to buy cheaper seed with a higher risk of the virus being present in it.

10.84   It is clear that the availability of an alternative is important to the reasonableness of the exemption clause. However, it must be borne in mind that not all alternatives will render the exemption clause reasonable. The reality of the alternative must be borne in mind. In *Smith v Eric S Bush* (1989) (see para. **10.81**) it will be recalled that the House of Lords had to consider the reasonableness, under UCTA 1977, of the disclaimer of liability by a valuer in relation to a mortgage valuation of a dwelling house. The purchaser could have obtained her own survey but the court considered the reality of this possible alternative. It was recognized that most purchasers of dwelling houses relied on the valuation carried out for the building society. It was regarded as impracticable and too expensive for such purchasers to obtain a separate survey. The purchaser had to pay for the valuation for the mortgage, and often could not afford to pay again for a survey. The possibility of a separate survey was not an alternative which rendered reasonable the disclaimer of liability on the mortgage valuation. In addition, the reality of the alternative will also be considered from another perspective. If a condition 'works in such a way as to leave little time to put such option into effect this may effectively eliminate the option as a factor indicating reasonableness' (*Overseas Medical Supplies Ltd v Orient Transport Services Ltd* [1999] 1 All ER (Comm) 981 at 987). Further, the person seeking to rely on an exemption clause cannot simply use a clause stating that he or she has an alternative available if there is no intention to make such alternative contracts (*Overseas Medical*).

Knowledge/consent

10.85   UCTA 1977, Sch 2(c) refers to the factor of knowledge, i.e. whether there was, or should have been, knowledge of the exemption clause on the part of the person against whom the clause is being used. Such knowledge, actual or constructive, could indicate that the clause is reasonable. More broadly, there is the factor of whether the injured party should be taken to have consented to the clause.

10.86   In *Stevenson v Nationwide Building Society* [1984] EGD 934 the situation was very similar to that in *Smith v Eric S Bush* (1989) except that the person purchasing the property was himself an estate agent. He had 'trade' knowledge of the house purchasing process and the disclaimer of liability for a negligent valuation was considered reasonable. It was said (at 935):

> 'When I bear in mind that the person affected by the disclaimer is someone well familiar with the possibility of obtaining a survey, and also familiar with the difference between a building society valuation and a survey and their different costs, it seems to me perfectly reasonable to allow the building society, in effect to say to him that if he chooses the cheaper alternative he must accept that the society will not be responsible for the content to him.'

10.87   However, it should be emphasized that the whole picture must be considered. Even actual knowledge of the clause may not indicate that the clause is reasonable if there is inequality of bargaining power. In such circumstances the clause may have been knowingly accepted on the basis that there was no realistic alternative (*Phillips Products Ltd v Hyland* [1987] 2 All ER 620 at 629).

10.88   It has been said that 'it is necessary, in order to assess reasonableness, to consider to what extent the party has actually consented to the clause' (*AEG (UK) Ltd v Logic Resources Ltd* [1996] CLC 265 at 279), but as has been indicated, it should not be thought that it is only actual subjective knowledge which is relevant; what the relevant party should have known, as a reasonable person, should also be looked at, although there may be greater weight to be given to actual knowledge (*Britvic Soft Drinks v Messer UK Ltd* (2002) at [21]). In fact, the question of knowledge will often be a matter of whether the relevant party should have known of the proferens' terms, rather than actual knowledge. However, although when the reasonableness of a contract term is under consideration, the question of 'knowledge' is looked at 'in circumstances where ex hypothesi the term has been validly incorporated in the contract' (*AEG* at 274), it should be recognized that incorporation does not necessarily mean that there is even objective knowledge (*Britvic* at [21]). Factors similar to those looked at in relation to incorporation of contract terms will often be examined to determine what the reasonable person should have known, but here the artificiality with which the facts are often clothed by the rules on incorporation should be avoided. As was seen earlier, incorporation by notice or signature has little to do with any real agreement to, or even objective knowledge of, the terms and may be a very artificial process.

10.89   Knowledge and understanding of the clause were found where a party used a similar clause when contracting on its own standard terms (*Watford Electronics Ltd v Sanderson CFL Ltd* (2001)). Trade practice and a long course of dealing between the parties indicated knowledge of the clause and pointed to its reasonableness in *RW Green Ltd v Cade Bros Farms* (1978). Similarly, in *Singer Co. (UK) Ltd v Tees and Hartlepool Port Authority* (1988) an indicator of the reasonableness of the clause was the wide distribution, and ready availability, of the port authority's standard terms (see also *Schenkers Ltd v Overland Shoes Ltd* [1998] 1 Lloyd's Rep 498 at 507). Also relevant to the question of actual or constructive knowledge of a clause is its legibility and intelligibility. In *Stag Line Ltd v Tyne Ship Repair Group Ltd, The Zinnia* [1984] 2 Lloyd's Rep 211 Staughten J commented (*obiter* at 222) that he was inclined to find the exemption clauses unreasonable because the print was so small that it was barely legible, and also because 'the draftsmanship was so convoluted and prolix that one almost need[ed] an LL.B. to understand them'. Similarly, it indicated the unreasonableness of the clause in *Overseas Medical Supplies Ltd v Orient Transport Services Ltd* [1999] 1 All ER (Comm) 981 that there was 'insufficient clarity in the conditions to bring home to the plaintiffs the effect of' the clause' (at [20]).

The width of the clause

10.90   The width of the clause may be relevant to its reasonableness under UCTA 1977. For example, it may be easier to find that an exemption clause is reasonable if it has been construed as applying only to non-negligent breaches (see *Stag Line Ltd v Tyne Ship Repair Group Ltd, The Zinnia* [1984] 2 Lloyd's Rep 211 at 223), and in general a narrow construction of a clause may make it more likely to be found reasonable than a wider one (*Regus (UK) Ltd v Epcot Solutions Ltd* (2008)). It should be emphasized that s 11(1) requires the reasonableness of the clause to be assessed on what was known or contemplated, or what should have been known or contemplated, by the parties at the time of contracting. The fact that the working of the exemption clause might be perfectly reasonable in relation to the specific breach which has occurred does not mean that the clause will pass the reasonableness test. The clause may be unreasonable because of the breaches which it potentially covers,[24] but, as has been indicated, the 'court should not be too ready to focus on remote possibilities or to accept arguments that a clause fails the test by reference to relatively uncommon or unlikely situations'.[25]

Settlement of past claims

10.91   In *George Mitchell Ltd v Finney Lock Seeds Ltd* (1983) the 'decisive factor' in the House of Lords' conclusion that the exemption clause was unreasonable was the seed sellers' past practice. In the past they had settled claims which they regarded as justifiable for sums in excess of the limit set by the exemption clause. The sellers had even attempted to negotiate a settlement in the instant case. This 'decisive factor' needs to be given further consideration. First, it is necessary to consider whether any account of it should be taken in applying the test in UCTA 1977, s 11. Second, once it is decided that it is a potentially relevant factor, it should be asked what conclusions should be drawn from it in relation to that test of reasonableness.

10.92   It should be remembered that the reasonableness of the exemption clause in *George Mitchell Ltd v Finney Lock Seeds Ltd* (1983) fell to be determined under what became s 55 of the Sale of Goods Act 1979 rather than under UCTA 1977, s 11. It must be emphasized again that the test under s 55 was whether it was fair and reasonable to allow reliance on the clause. As that test relates to reliance, the events after formation of the contract were relevant to the question of reasonableness. Under s 55 the fact of an attempted settlement in the particular case could come within the range of factors to be considered. Equally, because of the difference in the test in UCTA 1977, s 11, any attempted settlement of the particular case cannot be relevant to 'reasonableness' under that Act. Section 11 looks at the time at which the contract was made. However, there was a past practice of settling claims in *Mitchell v Finney Lock Seeds,* and it seems that this past practice should have been one of the factors contemplated by the parties at the time of contracting. If the past practice has been such that the parties should have contemplated it at the time of contracting, it would be possible to take account of such past settlements under the s 11 test of reasonableness. Such a factor has been considered in coming to a decision on the application of s 11. In *Rees Hough Ltd v Redland Reinforced Plastics Ltd* (1985) the parties' past practice of settling claims rather than relying upon the exemption clause was regarded as

---

24   *Stewart Gill Ltd v Horatio Myer & Co. Ltd* (1992) (see para. **10.68**ff). See also the discussion of *Overseas Medical Supplies Ltd v Orient Transport Services Ltd* (1999) in relation to the unreasonableness of a clause limiting different types of liability to a single sum at para. **10.76**.

25   *F G Wilson Engineering Ltd v John Holt & Co (Engineering) Ltd* (2012) at [96].

the most important factor against the clause, and it was decided that the clause did not satisfy the requirement of reasonableness in s 11.[26]

10.93   Under UCTA 1977, s 11 it is possible to consider a past practice of settling claims, rather than relying upon the exemption clause, but what is its relevance? In *George Mitchell Ltd v Finney Lock Seeds Ltd* [1983] 2 AC 803 at 817 such practice was taken to indicate that the sellers themselves did not regard it as reasonable to rely upon the clause. It can be contended that such a conclusion will often not be appropriate. Business people often may not take a legalistic view, and seek to enforce strict contractual rights, because they do not wish to endanger their business relationship with the other party. Negotiation and settlement are more conducive to the continuance of relationships, than is a legal battle. The business community in which the parties operate may even regard the use of legal action as an inappropriate way to settle disputes.[27] In *Schenkers Ltd v Overland Shoes Ltd* [1998] 1 Lloyd's Rep 498 the Court of Appeal distinguished *Mitchell v Finney Lock* on its facts and refused to accept the argument that non-reliance on the clause in past transactions showed that it was unreasonable. Pill LJ said (at 508):

> 'In the present circumstances, I see little merit in the defendant's argument that the clause had not in practice been relied upon. The give and take practised by the parties in the course of substantial dealings…was admirable and conducive to a good business relationship but did not prevent the [claimants], when a dispute arose, relying upon the terms agreed.'

The mere fact of a past practice of settling claims will often not be indicative that a clause is unreasonable. What matters is whether the clause was put into the contract as a fair allocation of risk.

Conditions placed on claims

10.94   UCTA 1977, Sch 2(d) relates to exclusion or restriction of liability unless a condition is complied with. This relates to the situation where one party seeks to use an exemption clause to place a condition upon his or her liability. For example, he or she may state that the other party must notify him or her of any claim within a specified time (for example, *RW Green v Cade Bros Farms* (1978)). The test of reasonableness in UCTA 1977, s 11 requires some consideration in relation to such restrictions.

10.95   The facts which can be taken into account under UCTA 1977, s 11 in looking at conditions on claims should be considered. In *RW Green v Cade Bros Farms* (1978) the exemption clause was in two parts. The first stated that any claim had to be notified to the sellers within three days of delivery of the seed potatoes. The second part limited any claim to the contract price of the seed potatoes. It will be recalled that although the second part of the exemption

---

26 But see *Stewart Gill Ltd v Horatio Myer & Co. Ltd* (1992)—see para. **10.68**ff.

27 See S. Macauley, 'Non-Contractual Relations in Business' (1963) 28 Am Soc Rev 55; Beale and Dugdale, 'Contracts between Businessmen: Planning and Use of Contractual Remedies' (1975) 2 Br J Law and Soc 45. For discussion of this factor in relation to the requirement of reasonableness, see Adams and Brownsword (1988) 104 LQR 94.

clause was found to be reasonable, the time limit was not. It was not reasonable because the problem with the potatoes was a viral infection, which could be detected only after the crop started to grow. Obviously that would be outside the three-day limit. That case was decided under the previous test of reasonableness. It should be emphasized that under s 11 the reasonableness of such a time limit cannot be assessed in relation to the particular breach which occurred. The possibility of the potatoes being defective because of such a virus can be considered only to the extent that it was, or should have been, contemplated by the parties at the time of contracting.

10.96   If the condition is one which will, within the contemplation of the parties, lead to erratic results, that may indicate that the exemption is unreasonable. For example, if a clause in a ship repair contract requires the return of the ship to the repairer's yard for any defect to be remedied, this may be unreasonable because it is capricious. 'The apportionment of risk is made to depend upon where a casualty happens to occur, and whether the owner happens to find it convenient and economic to return his vessel to the yard' (*Stag Line Ltd v Tyne Ship Repair Group Ltd, The Zinnia* [1984] 2 Lloyd's Rep 211 at 223).

Negligence

10.97   One factor relevant to holding the exemption clause unreasonable in *George Mitchell Ltd v Finney Lock Seeds Ltd* (1983) was the fact that the breach involved negligence. Again the point should be made that UCTA 1997, s 11 does not allow the actual breach to be taken into account in considering whether the clause is reasonable, merely the potential for it (*Rees Hough Ltd v Redland Reinforced Plastics Ltd* (1985)).

Customer's detailed specifications

10.98   UCTA 1977, Sch 2(e) specifically makes relevant to the requirement of reasonableness 'whether the goods were manufactured, processed or adapted to the special order of the customer'. In *Edmund Murray Ltd v BSP International Foundations Ltd* (1993) the sellers manufactured a drilling rig for the buyers. The contract contained detailed specifications as to the technical standards which the rig was required to meet, and it was made clear exactly how the buyers wished to use the rig. Against that background, the court considered it unreasonable for the sellers to restrict their liability to replacement of defective parts.

10.99   However, what matters is whether there is a reason for any restriction on the customer's remedies and whether the customer has been left with sufficient remedies. In *British Fermentation Products v Compare Reavell* [1999] 2 All ER 389 the point was made that in *Murray v BSP* 'the purchaser was left without any remedy when the machinery failed to do what was required of it' (at 404). In contrast in *British Fermentation* the contract provided the purchaser with several opportunities to reject the goods if they did not comply with the specifications and, effectively, the purchaser would have been able to replace the goods at the supplier's expense. Against that background it was seen as reasonable that, if the purchaser did not take the opportunity to reject, the supplier's clause should protect it from £1 million damages for reduced production over the lifetime of the machine. The machinery failed to comply with its specification and so was less productive than it should have been, but the exemption clause left the purchaser with an adequate means of dealing with that. The judge made the point that, without the exemption clause, the suppliers 'would no doubt have wished to reconsider the price quoted, having regard to the totally different level of risk undertaken' (at 404).

Risk

10.100   In *Smith* v *Eric S Bush* (1989) Lord Griffiths gave an indication of some factors which might be of general relevance in applying the requirement of reasonableness and he included the degree of difficulty or risk involved in the performance.

> 'When a difficult or dangerous undertaking is involved there may be a high risk of failure which would certainly point towards the reasonableness of excluding liability as a condition of doing the work...'

This type of factor was taken into account in *Watford Electronics Ltd* v *Sanderson CFL Ltd* (2001), where it was one of the elements pointing towards the reasonableness of the clause. It was recognized that in the supply of software which had been customized to meet the particular needs of a complex business, there was a significant risk that the software might not perform to the customer's satisfaction and involve considerable loss of expected savings or profits, and other losses. Clauses limiting liability for direct loss to the contract price, and excluding liability for consequential loss, were regarded as reasonable.

Appeals and precedent

10.101   The courts have given some consideration to the approach to be taken to an appeal from a decision on the requirement of reasonableness in UCTA 1977, s 11. In *George Mitchell Ltd* v *Finney Lock Seeds Ltd* [1983] 2 AC 803 Lord Bridge, with whom the other members of the court agreed, said (at 816) in relation to the test of reasonableness under s 11 (and Sale of Goods Act 1979, s 55):

> 'There will sometimes be room for a legitimate difference of opinion as to what the answer should be, where it will be impossible to say that one view is demonstrably wrong and the other demonstrably right. It must follow... that, when asked to review such a decision on appeal, the appellate court should treat the original decision with the utmost respect and refrain from interference with it unless satisfied that it proceeded upon some erroneous principle or was plainly and obviously wrong.'

This indicates that decisions on the requirement of reasonableness will often provide very limited guidance for the future. Another judge might have weighed the factors in the same case differently, come to the opposite conclusion, and still not be overturned on appeal.[28] *Phillips Products Ltd* v *Hyland* (1987) provides an example of the way this approach to appeals works. In that case,

---

28 See also *Cleaver v Schyde Investments Ltd* (2011).

the court was concerned with a standard form, widely used by those in the business of hiring out plant. Despite the fact that the Court of Appeal took a different view from the trial judge on several of the factors relevant to the issue of reasonableness, it declined to overrule his decision. It accepted the approach to appeals indicated in *George Mitchell Ltd* v *Finney Lock Seeds Ltd* (1983). In keeping with this, the Court of Appeal emphasized that it was considering the reasonableness of the clause in the particular contract between the particular parties. The contract was made on the basis of a widely used standard form, but the court indicated that its decision did not mean that the exemption clause was to be taken to be unreasonable in every transaction in which the standard form was used. The decision on reasonableness related to the instant case. Even in relation to a standard form contract, this must follow from the adoption of the above approach to appeals.

10.102   This approach to appeals inevitably creates uncertainty as to what is required for an exemption clause to pass the reasonableness test in UCTA 1977, s 11. This presents some hindrance to contract planning. It is difficult for a person in business to decide whether to pay for insurance and increase his or her costs, and contract price, if there is uncertainty concerning the efficacy of the exemption clause which he or she had designed to obviate the need for insurance.

10.103   However, in some cases of standard forms, the factors indicating that the clause is unreasonable may be present so often when the form is used that a case may be widely relevant to the issue of reasonableness. The House of Lords decision in *Smith* v *Eric S Bush* [1989] 2 All ER 514 is such a case. The House of Lords thought its decision on the reasonableness of the disclaimer in the mortgage valuation to be of general application to the purchase, via a mortgage, of a dwelling house of 'modest value'. It was in relation to such transactions that it was known that purchasers did not usually obtain their own survey but relied on the mortgage valuation. Lord Griffiths said (at 532):

> 'It must, however, be remembered that this is the sale of a dwelling house of modest value in which it is widely recognised by surveyors that purchasers are in fact relying on their care and skill. *It will obviously be of general application in broadly similar circumstances.* But I expressly reserve my position in respect of quite different types of property for mortgage purposes, such as industrial property, large blocks of flats or very expensive houses. In such cases it may be that the general expectation of the behaviour of the purchaser is quite different.' (Emphasis added.)

Trends

10.104   Although precedent is of limited value in this area, there is a final point to be made here as to indications, in the commercial context, of a trend favouring a non-interventionist basic approach by the courts. In this context, further consideration should be given to *Watford Electronics Ltd* v *Sanderson CFL Ltd* (2001):

> Watford had found the need for a computer system to deal with their mail order business and to perform accounting functions. They contracted with Sanderson for standard software

which was to be modified to meet their needs. Basically the contract was made on Sanderson's standard terms, but Watford had successfully negotiated for a price reduction and some modification of the terms. The significant term was the exemption clause which stated:

'Neither the Company nor the Customer shall be liable to the other for any claims for indirect or consequential losses whether arising from negligence or otherwise. In no event shall the Company's liability under the Contract exceed the price paid by the Customer to the Company for the Equipment connected with any claim.'

The dispute arose because the system did not perform as Watford had wanted. There was a contractual claim which totalled about £5.5 million and an alternative claim under the Misrepresentation Act 1967 (or for negligent misstatement) for about £200,500. Watford had paid £104,596. A number of matters were ordered to be tried as preliminary issues, including whether the exemption clause satisfied the requirement of reasonableness.

10.105   As has been indicated, the court, in fact, viewed the clause as separate exclusion and limitation clauses (see para. **10.70**) and concluded that both were reasonable. In making that assessment, it recognized that there may be significant risks in supplying a customized computer system. It also recognized that the parties were of roughly equal bargaining power, knew of the risks, the need to insure, and the fact that the price related to the allocation of the risks in the exemption clause. However, what should be emphasized here is that the court may be seen as signalling a restrained approach to the use of the requirement of reasonableness in commercial contexts between parties of equal bargaining power. Chadwick LJ said (at [55]):

'Where experienced businessmen representing substantial companies of equal bargaining power negotiate an agreement, they may be taken to have had regard to the matters known to them. They should, in my view be taken to be the best judge of the commercial fairness of the agreement which they have made; including the fairness of each of the terms in that agreement. They should be taken to be the best judge on the question whether the terms of the agreement are reasonable. The court should not assume that either is likely to commit his company to an agreement which he thinks is unfair, or which he thinks includes unreasonable terms. Unless satisfied that one party has, in effect, taken unfair advantage of the other—or that a term is so unreasonable that it cannot properly have been understood or considered—the court should not interfere.' (See also Peter Gibson LJ at [63].)

There have been other indications of this type of approach.[29] However, care must be taken with such general statements. Every case must depend upon its particular facts.

---

29 e.g. *SAM Business Systems Ltd* v *Hedley & Co.* (2002) at [67]; *Granville Oil and Chemicals* v *Davies Turner & Co. Ltd* (2003) at [31]; *Frans Maas (UK)* v *Samsung Electronics* (2005) at [158]; *Air Transworld Ltd* v *Bombarier Inc* (2012) at [133]. See also previously *Photo Productions Ltd* v *Securicor Transport Ltd* [1980] AC 827 at 843 per Lord Wilberforce

Exemption clauses (s 13)

10.106 The active sections frequently refer to clauses which 'exclude or restrict' liability. A fairly narrow interpretation could have been given to that phrase and such an interpretation would have limited the clauses falling within the operation of the Act. UCTA 1977, s 13 makes it clear that the Act is not so restricted. Section 13(1) states:

> 'To the extent that this Part of this Act prevents the exclusion or restriction of any liability it also prevents—
> (a) making the liability or its enforcement subject to restrictive or onerous conditions;
> (b) excluding or restricting any right or remedy in respect of the liability, or subjecting a person to any prejudice in consequence of his pursuing any such right or remedy;
> (c) excluding or restricting rules of evidence or procedure;
> and (to that extent) sections 2 and 5 to 7 also prevent excluding or restricting liability by reference to terms and notices which exclude or restrict the relevant obligation or duty.'

Paragraphs (a) to (c) ensure that clauses which have the effect of excluding or restricting liability, but in a slightly round-about way, are dealt with as if they limited or excluded liability more simply (see, for example, *Stewart Gill Ltd* v *Horatio Myer & Co. Ltd* (1992)). For example, (a) covers a clause stating that any claim must be made within a certain time period, and (b) covers a clause which allows recovery of damages but which purports to remove any right to terminate the contract for breach. A clause stating that signature was proof that the goods delivered met the requirements of the contract falls within (c). It is the last part of s 13(1) which presents difficulties, and requires further consideration.

10.107 It has already been seen that UCTA 1977, s 3(2)(b) deals with exclusion clauses in the form of part of the definition of the obligation. The last part of s 13(1) is similarly a provision to prevent evasion of the Act by exclusion clauses in 'disguise'. Section 13(1) ensures that some clauses which, in form, define the obligation will be identified as exclusion clauses, in substance, for the purposes of ss 2, 5, 6, and 7. The difficulty is that it does not indicate how to determine which clauses are to be treated in this way.

10.108 We have already seen that a clause in the form of an exclusion of liability could have been drafted instead as a clause in the form of part of the definition of the obligations (see para. **9.3**). Both forms of clause mark out the boundaries within which a legal remedy is available. A clause in the form of an exclusion of liability does that by removing the legal remedies for breach of what would be, but for the clause, an obligation. A clause in the form of part of the definition of the obligations simply states the obligations. The problem presented by the last part of s 13(1) is to determine which clauses, in the form of part of the definition of the obligation, it requires to be treated in the same way as clauses in the form of exclusions of liability. The lack of any clarification of this in the Act means that there is a conceptual hole at the centre of UCTA 1977.

10.109   The House of Lords considered the coverage of the final part of UCTA 1977, s 13(1) in *Smith v Eric S Bush (a firm)* [1989] 2 All ER 514. The case was considered earlier in the context of the court's conclusion that the surveyor's disclaimer of his tortious liability for negligence did not satisfy the requirement of reasonableness, applied by s 2(2) of the Act. The point to be considered here is the surveyor's prior argument, that the disclaimer was not subject to s 2(2) because it did not exclude or restrict the surveyor's liability, but rather prevented the duty of care from arising. The House of Lords did not agree with that contention. It was concluded that the disclaimer fell within the relevant part of s 13(1), and so was brought within s 2(2). Lord Griffiths arrived at that conclusion by applying the 'but for' test. He said (at 530): 'the existence of the common law duty of care...is to be judged by considering whether it would exist "but for" the notice...'. In other words, the approach taken was simply to ask whether there would be an obligation in the absence of the clause. If there was, then the clause was to be regarded as excluding it, and so within the relevant part of UCTA 1977, s 13(1). (This reflects the approach indicated by the Court of Appeal in *Phillips Products Ltd v Hyland* [1987] 2 All ER 620 in the contractual context).[30]

10.110   The 'but for' test would also seem to be indicated by *Johnstone v Bloomsbury Health Authority* (1991). The case concerned the contract of employment of a junior hospital doctor. The contract provided that he should work for forty hours a week and be on call for up to a further forty-eight hours a week. It was the express term concerning the hours on call which was at the centre of the dispute. The doctor claimed that his health had been damaged by the long hours which he had worked, and he argued that the health authority was in breach of an implied term that it had a duty to take care not to foreseeably damage his health. The Court of Appeal was asked to strike out his action, but his claim survived. A term will not be implied in the face of an express contradictory term, but the majority of the court thought that the express term did not contradict the implied term contended for, and merely set the limits within which the health authority should exercise its discretion in relation to the 'on call hours'. However, the point of interest here is that all three members of the court agreed that, if the express term prevented the implication, then that express term would be regarded as a clause falling within the final part of UCTA 1977, s 13(1) and would thus be rendered ineffective by s 2(1).

10.111   The idea of using UCTA 1977 in the way in which the court envisaged in *Johnstone v Bloomsbury Health Authority* (1991) illustrates how wide the compass of the Act would be under the application of the 'but for' test. It would seem to render subject to the Act any express term contradicting a term which would, in the absence of the clause, be implied into a contract falling within the Act (provided that the liability existing in the absence of the clause is appropriate to bring the clause within one of the relevant 'active sections'). 'But for' the clause the implication would be made. In addition, the 'but for' test would seem to make it impossible for the parties to define an obligation to take due care by stating it widely and then qualifying it, without its being subject to s 2 of the Act.

---

30   In considering whether there had been a breach of an obligation to take reasonable care, Slade LJ said (at 625):

'the court has to leave out of account at this stage the contract term which is relied on by the defence as defeating the plaintiff's claim for breach of such obligation or duty'.

10.112 The 'but for' test is very mechanical, which means that it is easy to apply. However, that ease of application is paid for by a lack of discrimination. The 'but for' test is too wide, bringing clauses inappropriately within the Act.

10.113 It can be contended that an exclusion clause can be identified 'in substance' by looking at the reality of the contracting process. A relevant clause should be found to be exclusionary, rather than definitional, when it is in small print, being used against an unsophisticated party, and only a term because it is a contractual document which that party signed, and could not reasonably be expected to know the content of. In contrast, when what is in question is a transaction involving legally sophisticated parties, who can be expected to have taken on board the impact of the relevant clause in a standard form contract, so that it reflects the reality of the transaction, it should be regarded as definitional.[31] (For further discussion, and analysis of the identification of exclusion clauses in substance, see E. Macdonald, 'Exception Clauses: Exclusionary or Definitional? It Depends!' (2012) 29 JCL 47.)

Summary

- Basically the Unfair Contract Terms Act 1977 applies to exemption clauses (i.e. clauses excluding or restricting liability (s 13 ensures a narrow approach is not taken to identifying such clauses)). It subjects some of the clauses to which it applies to automatic ineffectiveness and renders others ineffective unless they satisfy the requirement of reasonableness.

- The Act basically applies to business liability. There are some contracts excluded from its scope (Sch 1) and there are also limits on its application in relation to contracts with an international element (ss 26, 27, 29).

- The provisions of the draft Consumer Rights Bill excise the references to 'deals as consumer' from the Act, and take 'consumer contracts' and 'consumer notices' outside of the scope of UCTA, bringing them within one distinct consumer regime relating to unfair terms, and dealing with the complexity of two overlapping regimes: UCTA and the Unfair Terms in Consumer Contracts Regulations.

- If the Act is going to impact upon a particular exemption clause, an 'active section' which covers the situation must be found. The relevant active section will then state what is to happen to the clause in question i.e. whether it is automatically ineffective or subject to the requirement of reasonableness. The principal active sections are ss 2, 3, 6 and 7.

- Section 2 is the active section which deals with attempts to exclude or restrict liability for negligence. Under s 2(1) liability for negligently caused death or personal injury cannot be excluded or restricted (automatic ineffectiveness). Under s 2(2) liability for other negligently caused loss or damage can be excluded or restricted if the requirement

---

31 See e.g. *Raiffeisen Zentralbank Österreich AG v Royal Bank of Scotland* (2010); *Avrora Fine Arts Investment Ltd v Christie, Manson & Woods* (2012).

of reasonableness is satisfied. (This section covers non-contractual disclaimers as well as contractual exemption clauses.) The provisions of the draft Consumer Rights Bill remove its consumer coverage.

- Section 3 covers contracts under which the party against whom the exemption clause is used 'deals as consumer' or on the 'other party's written standard terms of business'. Section 3(2)(a) subjects to the requirement of reasonableness clauses excluding or restricting liability in such contracts. Section 3(2)(b) subjects 'disguised' exemption clauses to the requirement of reasonableness. Obviously, the provisions of the draft Consumer Rights Bill remove the reference to 'deals as consumer' in s 3, leaving it with still extensive coverage in relation to non-consumer contracts made on the 'other party's written standard terms of business'.

- Section 4 subjects indemnity clauses used against consumers to the requirement of reasonableness, and its excision is provided for by the draft Consumer Rights Bill.

- Sections 6 and 7 cover clauses excluding or restricting liability in relation to certain implied terms in goods contracts. The removal of their coverage of consumer contracts is provided for by the draft Consumer Rights Bill.

- The 'definition' sections of the Act assist with understanding of the active sections.

- Section 11 assists with the meaning of 'the requirement of reasonableness' but it is a weighing exercise, requiring the consideration of all the relevant factors. The time frame for identifying relevant factors is that of the making of the contract i.e. it is relevant factors which were known to, or ought reasonably have been known to, the parties when they made the contract. Some factors are identified in Sch 2 and s 11(4). Others have been identified by the courts. Relevant factors include, for example, relative bargaining power of the parties, insurance, availability of alternatives, knowledge (objective and subjective) of the clause, width of the clause, settlement of past claims, conditions placed on claims, negligence, and risk.

⏵ Further reading

J. Adams and R. Brownsword, 'The Unfair Contract Terms Act 1977: A Decade of Discretion' (1988) 104 LQR 94

H. Beale, 'Unfair Terms in Contracts: Proposals for Reform in the UK' (2004) 27 Journal of Consumer Policy 289

B. Coote, *Exception Clauses*, Sweet & Maxwell, 1964

Law Commission and Scottish Law Commission, *Unfair Terms in Contracts*, Law Com 292, Scot Law Com No 199

E. Macdonald 'Exception Clauses: Exclusionary or Definitional? It Depends! (2012) 29 JCL 47

Chapter 11

Unfair terms in consumer contracts

◉ Introduction

11.1   The EC Directive on Unfair Terms in Consumer Contracts (93/13/EEC) is a highly significant EC measure in the sphere of consumer contracts. Under it, member states have had to subject non-individually negotiated terms in contracts between consumers and sellers or suppliers to a fairness test, with unfair terms not binding consumers. As can immediately be seen, this is a significant inroad on the basic idea of freedom of contract in the consumer context. It was said by Pat Edwards, Legal Director of the Office of Fair Trading:[1]

> '... that cherished principle [of freedom of contract], instilled in the course of academic studies and practice had, of course, been much under attack well before 1995 in its application to some aspects of consumer contracts. But nothing had hitherto actually turned on its head, as the Directive does, the general duty of the lawyer to draft wholly and exclusively in the interests of the client, in whatever language is adapted to preserve and enhance the client's legal position... Now in order properly to serve their clients, legal advisers must have a wider perspective than taking into account only those client's interests.'

There are, however, exclusions from this, particularly what is commonly referred to as the 'core exemption' which, very broadly, covers price terms and those defining the main subject matter of the contract. This core exemption is key to the extent of the impact on freedom of contract, and its scope has proved very controversial. It has raised very fundamental questions about the extent to which consumers should be protected from unfair contract terms.

---

[1]   'The Challenge of the Regulations', OFT Bulletin No 4 on Unfair Contract Terms, p. 19.

11.2   The Directive is a minimum Directive, so that, whilst member states cannot fall below the level of consumer protection which it provides, they can go further. In the UK, initially by the Unfair Terms in Consumer Contracts Regulations 1994 (SI 1994/3159), and then by the replacement Unfair Terms in Consumer Contracts Regulations 1999 (SI 1999/2083), it was largely implemented simply by 'copy out', with the regulations basically just reproducing the Directive, with the 1999 Regulations doing so more closely than the 1994 version. There was an obvious drawback to this. There was significant overlap with the Unfair Contract Terms Act 1977 and there was a great deal of complexity occasioned by two such regimes which used different tests and definitions, with, for example, UCTA giving a very different meaning to 'deals as consumer', than did the Regulations to who was a 'consumer', and with the Regulations applying a 'fairness' test, and UCTA a 'reasonableness' test, but only to exemption clauses, and in some cases making them automatically ineffective.

11.3   The complexity caused by the overlapping legislation was undesirable, particularly in consumer protection legislation. In 2005 the Law Commission and the Scottish Law Commission produced a report, and a draft Bill, to provide one unified piece of unfair terms legislation,[2] but that was overtaken by proposals for new EU measures, which would have brought together, and changed, EU law in a number of important consumer areas, including unfair terms. The proposed Consumer Rights Directive was intended as a maximum Directive, requiring the same level of protection by all member states. The idea was to make it easier for businesses to trade in different member states, without having to deal with different requirements, and for consumers to have confidence to buy in different member states, knowing they would get the same level of protection. The promotion of cross border e-commerce within the EU was a key driver. However, whilst it is easy, and not generally controversial, to produce uniform consumer protection in relation to such matters as how many days a consumer has in which to cancel a contract made by distance communication, such as telephone, post or online, there were major concerns about this approach in relation to the unfair terms regime. The proposals would have reduced the protection provided in some member states, which had gone further than the Unfair Terms Directive required, as they were allowed to do under a minimum Directive. In any event, it seems unlikely that the situation could, or should, have been produced in which a term which was fair before the courts of one member state would be found to be fair in the courts of all the other member states. As we shall see fairness under the Directive has been recognized as having a contextual, societal element, and the potential for different conclusions on the fairness of a particular term in different member states. In its final form, the Consumer Rights Directive did not include a new version of the Unfair Terms Directive.

11.4   The limited coverage of the final version of the Consumer Rights Directive, left the way open for the UK to return to the reform of its unfair terms legislation, to rid itself of the complexities of two overlapping regimes. However, circumstances had changed considerably since the original proposals of the Law Commissions had been made. In particular, the Supreme Court had taken a very different approach to the core exemption, in *Office of Fair Trading* v *Abbey National* (2009), than had the House of Lords, in *Director General of Fair Trading* v *First National*

---

2   Law Commissions, *Unfair Terms in Contracts* (2005), Law Com No 292, Scot Law Com No 199.

Bank (2001), and the original line taken by the Law Commissions had reflected that in the *First National Bank* case. In an *Issues Paper*, the Law Commissions produced new suggestions and a new consultation,[3] particularly in relation to the core exemption, and it is the recommendations stemming from that further consultation,[4] with others from the original report, which now form the basis of the proposed legislation on unfair terms in the draft Consumer Rights Bill. As we shall see, the line taken in relation to the core exemption in *Abbey National*, which relies heavily upon the idea that the consumer can, and should, be left to look after their own interests in relation to core terms if they are sufficiently clear, was heavily criticized as providing insufficient consumer protection. The Law Commissions' final recommendations in their *Advice to the Department for Business, Innovations and Skills* did make some, limited movement beyond that idea, but it remains a very controversial area, in relation to very fundamental issues. To what extent should unfair terms legislation recognize the common imperfections of consumer decision making, and not simply assume that consumers make good decisions if supplied with clear enough information? This chapter will refer to the current law, and the draft Bill. It should be emphasized that UCTA does not simply deal with consumer contracts. It also applies to exemption clauses in many business to business contracts, and that is left largely unchanged. It is the consumer protection elements which are stripped out of UCTA by the draft Bill, to provide a single consumer protection regime.

Enforcement

11.5   Much of the significance of the unfair terms regime stems from enforcement mechanisms which operate at a general level. However, before emphasizing that, we should first note its action in the individual case. The Regulations can be used by an individual consumer in dispute with a particular seller or supplier, and an unfair term does not bind the consumer.[5] The contract continues in existence if it is capable of doing so without the unfair term.[6] With some change of language, this is also the case in the draft Consumer Rights Bill, which does make it explicit that the fact that an unfair term does not bind the consumer does not 'prevent the consumer from relying on the term if the consumer chooses to do so'.[7]

11.6   It should be emphasized that a court may assist a consumer in an individual dispute as it may find a term unfair even if the consumer does not raise that point. That line was taken by the ECJ in Cases C-240/98 to C-244/98, *Oceano Grupo Editorial SA v Quintero* (2000), and in Case C-243/08 *Pannon GSM Zrt v Gyorfi* (2009) it was viewed as 'a duty' for the court to consider the unfairness of a term even where it has not been raised by the consumer, albeit the court will need to have 'available to it the legal and factual elements necessary for the task' (at [32]). This

---

3   The Law Commission and the Scottish Law Commission, *Unfair Terms in Consumer Contracts: a new approach?* (2012).

4   The Law Commission and the Scottish Law Commission, *Unfair Terms in Consumer Contracts: Advice to the Department for Business, Innovation and Skills* (2013).

5   Reg 8(1).

6   Reg 8(2).

7   Clause 65(3).

is a practical limitation: 'a court cannot hold a term unfair if it does not so appear from the case presented to it' (S. Whittaker, 'Judicial Interventionism and Consumer Contracts' (2001) 117 LQR 215). The draft Consumer Rights Bill specifically provides for the duty, and also recognizes its effective limits, stating that it does not apply 'unless the court considers that it has before it sufficient legal and factual material to enable it to consider the fairness of the term.'[8]

11.7   However, the most important enforcement mechanism is the general one. The 1994 Regulations gave the Director General of Fair Trading power to apply for injunctions to prevent the continued use, or recommendation for the use, of unfair terms. Under the 1999 Regulations, that power lies with the Office of Fair Trading (OFT) and was also extended to other 'qualifying bodies', as set out in Sch 1.[9] The OFT achieved the removal or modification of many terms in standard form consumer contracts—mostly by negotiation rather than having to resort to litigation—and that can be seen in the Bulletins published by the OFT to show how complaints about terms have been dealt with. Such a general enforcement mechanism is important in the consumer context because consumers do not generally litigate and often do not know their rights. The OFT has even encountered terms which would have been automatically ineffective under the 1977 Act (for example, Bulletin 3 at 1.2). Any terms which cannot have the effect they may appear to the consumer to have may be used to intimidate the consumer (Bulletin 3 at 4.4), but they cannot have that impact, or even simply mislead the consumer as to his or her rights,[10] if the general level of enforcement ensures their removal from the businesses' standard form contract, so that they are not, thereafter, encountered by the consumer. Under the Consumer Rights Bill, the primary role in relation to the general level of enforcement will pass to the Competition and Markets Authority (CMA), with a similar list of other general enforcement bodies to that in the list of 'qualifying bodies'.[11] We will have to wait to see whether the CMA will prove as active on the unfair terms front as has the OFT.

11.8   The draft Consumer Rights Bill also deals with a long disputed aspect of the enforcement of the Directive/Regulations. The Directive appears to state a requirement that terms should

---

8 Clause 74.

9 The list in Sch 1 covers in Part One (as amended by the Unfair Terms in Consumer Contracts (Amendment) Regulations 2001 (SI 2001/1186)):

  1.   The Information Commissioner
  2.   The Gas and Electricity Markets Authority
  3.   The Director General of Electricity Supply for Northern Ireland
  4.   The Director General of Gas for Northern Ireland
  5.   The Director General of Telecommunications
  6.   The Director General of Water Services
  7.   The Rail Regulator
  8.   Every weights and measures authority in Great Britain
  9.   The Department of Enterprise, Trade, and Investment in Northern Ireland
  10.   The Financial Services Authority

  And in Part Two:

  11.   The Consumers' Association.

10 In *Skerratt* v *Linfax Ltd* (2003) the misleading effect of a clause which was automatically ineffective under s 2(1) of UCTA 1977 was raised as a factor when C was asking to bring an action out of time.

11 See clause 73 of the draft Bill.

be in 'plain intelligible language'.[12] However, it did not provide any mechanism for enforcement of that, and its existence as a requirement, as such, was therefore open to dispute. An additional enforcement mechanism was brought in at the general, preventive level, with Part 8 of the Enterprise Act 2002 allowing certain 'enforcers', including the OFT, to apply for enforcement orders in relation to certain consumer protection legislation, including the Unfair Terms Regulations, where the infringement harmed 'the collective interests of consumers'. It was contended that this extended to the question of 'plain intelligible language', providing the enforcement mechanism needed to view it properly as a requirement. The issue is dealt with under the draft Consumer Rights Bill, with the CMA, and the other general enforcers, specifically able to apply for an injunction to prevent the use, or recommendation for use, of terms which do not measure up to certain requirements in the same way as if they were unfair. Those additional requirements are 'transparency' (which encompasses 'plain intelligible language', and legibility), and that terms which are 'especially onerous or unusual' must be 'drawn particularly to the consumers' attention'[13] (see further para. **11.67**).

EC background

11.9 When interpreting any legislation purporting to implement a Directive, every endeavour must be made to construe it so that it does implement that Directive, and some of the terms used in the legislation may need a European interpretation through the ECJ. In *Freiburger Kommunalbauten GmbH Baugesellschaft & Co. KG v Hofstetter* Case C-237/02 (2004) the ECJ indicated that it would not provide a view as to the fairness of a particular term, but that it was its role to 'interpret general criteria used by the community legislature in order to define the concept of unfair terms' (at [22]).[14] This division of responsibility was confirmed by the ECJ in *VB Penzugyi Lizing Zrt v Ferenc Schneider* (2010):

> 'the jurisdiction of the Court of Justice extends to the interpretation of the concept of "unfair term" used in art.3(1) of the Directive and in the annex thereto, and to the criteria which the national court may or must apply when examining a contractual term in the light of the provisions of the Directive, bearing in mind that it was for that court to determine, in the light of those criteria, whether a particular contractual term was actually unfair in the circumstances of the case.'

The interpretation of the concept, and the criteria which may be used to determine fairness under the Directive is a matter for the ECJ, but the fairness of a term is left to be decided by the courts with an understanding of its legal and social context (*Aziz v Caixa d'Estalvis de Catalunya* (2013). This means that a term may be fair in one jurisdiction, and unfair in another. It is not sought to achieve the certainty which a business, wanting to trade in several member states, in particular, might regard as desirable on this point. However, apart from any technical arguments

---

12 Art 5. Reg 7.

13 Clause 71 of the draft Bill.

14 See also Case C-243/08 *Pannon GSM Zrt v Gyorfi* (2009) at [42].

as to the extent of the powers of the ECJ, there is the basic point that seeking to achieve greater uniformity would be to fail to recognize the great differences in the broader laws and societies of the member states. Gunther Teubner has made the point, in relation to 'good faith', that:[15]

> 'an interpretation of good faith which is oriented to the peculiarities, opportunities, risks and dangers of a specific production regime would indeed result in widely divergent rules in different countries, even in contradictory decisions in apparently equal cases. These cleavages cannot and should not be papered over by European zeal for harmonization...European efforts at harmonization have not yet seriously taken into account the "varieties of capitalism", the difference in production regimes'.

Basic scope of the unfair terms regime

11.10   As has been indicated, basically the Directive/Regulations apply a fairness test to terms in contracts between 'consumers' and 'sellers or suppliers', which have not been 'individually negotiated' and any unfair term does not bind the consumer. The test of unfairness requires that, contrary to the requirement of good faith, there should be a significant imbalance in the rights and obligations of the parties to the detriment of the consumer.[16] In addition, the Directive and UTCCR 1999, Sch 2, contains a 'grey list' of terms which may be regarded as unfair. The Directive and the Regulations also contain the core exemption from the fairness test, so that the definition of the main subject matter of the contract and price terms (in relation to the 'adequacy' of the price), are not subject to it, provided they are in plain intelligible language. It has been said that the Regulations do not apply to terms implied at common law.[17] The Directive and the Regulations specifically put outside their scope terms reflecting certain legislation or international conventions. Reg 4(2) states that the Regulations do not encompass:

> 'contractual terms which reflect—
>
> **(a)** mandatory statutory or regulatory provisions (including such provisions under the law of any Member State or in Community legislation having effect in the United Kingdom without further enactment);
>
> **(b)** the provisions or principles of international conventions to which the Member States or Community are party.'

---

15 G. Teubner, 'Legal Irritants: Good Faith in British Law or How Unifying Law Ends Up in New Divergences' (1998) 61 MLR 11 at 31.

16 Art 3, reg 5.

17 *Baybut v Eccle Riggs County Park Ltd* (2006). It is in any event difficult to imagine that such terms would be unfair. However, any general exclusion of implied terms from the Regulations should not encompass terms incorporated by a course of dealing. In a sense these are implied terms, as they are not expressly brought within the particular contract, but the mechanism is very different from that importing other terms by implication. Inevitably what is in question when terms are incorporated by a course of dealing is simply one party's set of standard terms and there will be as much scope for them to be unfair as in any other set of standard terms.

If the reflection of the statutory or regulatory provisions or the convention is not a suffi-ciently accurate one, there should be scope for the application of the Directive/Regulations, as has been indicated by the ECJ (Case C-473/00 *Cofidis SA v Jean-Louis Fredout* (2002) at [22]).

11.11   Although it refers to 'traders' and 'consumers' rather than 'sellers or suppliers' and 'consumers', as would be expected, the draft Consumer Rights Bill is very similar in its treat-ment of unfair terms. After all, like the Regulations, it does have to implement the Unfair Terms Directive. Nevertheless, that Directive is a minimum Directive, so it can go further, and it is not just an implementation of the Directive, but also the creation of unified consumer unfair terms legislation from both the Directive and UCTA. Thus, the draft Consumer Rights Bill does not confine its controls to non-individually negotiated terms. This was recommended by the Law Commissions in their 2005 report. UCTA's controls of exemption clauses in con-tracts where one party 'deals as consumer' are not confined to non-individually negotiated, or standard terms, so maintaining UCTA's level of protection for consumers would have neces-sitated maintaining separate protection against exemption clauses, unless the requirement of 'non-individually negotiated terms' was dropped across the broad coverage of the unfair terms regime.[18] Such simplification is one reason for not confining the unfair terms part of the Consumer Rights Bill to non-individually negotiated terms. It was also thought that, in any event, outside of the core terms, 'consumers seldom have sufficient understanding of the possible impact of [the terms] to make any negotiation meaningful',[19] and there is, anyway, uncertainty over when a term is 'non-individually negotiated',[20] and also evidence of exploita-tion by some businesses of the fact that the Regulations did not cover non-individually negoti-ated terms.[21]

11.12   Although UCTA only deals with exemption clauses, it sometimes does more to those clauses than simply subject them to its 'reasonableness test'. Obviously, in order to maintain, or improve, the level of consumer protection provided by the existence of both UCTA and the Regulations, the unified regime had to impact similarly on certain terms. Thus UCTA's pro-vision of automatic ineffectiveness for terms excluding or restricting liability for negligently caused death or personal injury, without any scope for arguments as to reasonableness, or fair-ness, is maintained in the draft Consumer Rights Bill, in clause 68. Of course, UCTA's coverage of exemptions for negligence is not restricted to terms, but also covers notices, and the draft Bill more broadly covers a notice

'to the extent that it

(a)   relates to rights or obligations between a trader and a consumer, or

(b)   purports to exclude or restrict s trader's liability to a consumer.'

---

18 *Unfair Terms in Contracts* (2005) Law Com No 292, Scot Law Com No 199, para. 3.51.

19 *Unfair Terms in Contracts* (2005) Law Com No 292, Scot Law Com No 199, para. 3.51.

20 *Unfair Terms in Contracts* (2005) Law Com No 292, Scot Law Com No 199, para. 3.52.

21 *Unfair Terms in Contracts* (2005) Law Com No 292, Scot Law Com No 199, para 3.52.

The automatic ineffectiveness under s 6, and s 7 of UCTA of terms excluding or restricting liability against someone 'dealing as consumer',[22] in relation to certain implied terms in goods contracts, is dealt with by the first part of the Consumer Rights Bill, dealing more generally with goods, services and digital content. That automatic ineffectiveness is reproduced, and extended to similar terms in relation to digital content.[23]

Consumer contracts

11.13   The Directive and the Regulations relate to contracts between consumers and sellers or suppliers. Mirroring the Directive, UTCCR 1999, reg 3(1) states:

> ' "consumer" means any natural person who, in contracts covered by these Regulations, is acting for purposes which are outside his trade, business or profession.'

One major difference between this definition and the approach taken to the interpretation of 'deals as consumer' under the UCTA 1977 can immediately be noted. UTCCR 1999, reg 3 expressly limits the definition of 'consumer' to a 'natural person', excluding companies, but a company could 'deal as consumer' under the 1977 Act (see, for example, *R & B Customs Brokers Co. Ltd* v *United Dominion Trust Ltd* (1988)). Obviously, the draft Consumer Rights Bill basically adopts the approach of the Directive/Regulations. It does, however, contain a specific addition to the definition to deal with mixed transactions which are partly business and partly private. In *Gruber v Bay Wa AG* (2005) the ECJ indicated a very restrictive line on such transactions, making it 'irrelevant that the private element is predominant', and confining the consumer classification to the situation where 'the trade or professional purpose is so limited as to be negligible in the overall context of the supply',[24] and this was followed in *Overy v Paypal (Europe) Ltd* (2012). The approach taken under the Consumer Rights Bill is less restrictive, so that '"consumer" means an individual acting for purposes that are wholly *or mainly* outside that individual's trade, business, craft or profession' (emphasis added).[25] The Law Commissions were concerned with situations where for example, 'a sole trader buys a car primarily for private use but with the intention of occasionally using it for business'.[26]

11.14   More broadly assistance as to who will be a 'consumer' under the Regulations/Directive/Bill can be gleaned from the case law, including that of the ECJ dealing with other EC measures using basically the same 'consumer' classification. First, it can be emphasized that the type of approach taken under UCTA 1977, allowing someone to 'deal as consumer' if the transaction is not integral to their business or regularly occurring, is not taken. In the *Di Pinto* case [1991] ECR I-1189, in the context of the meaning of consumer in the doorstep selling Directive

---

22 Clause 32.

23 Clauses 49, 59.

24 *Gruber v Bay Wa AG* (C-464/01) [2005] ECR I-439, at [54].

25 Clause 2(3).

26 *Unfair Terms in Contracts* (2005) Law Com No 292, Scot Law Com No 199, para. 3.36.

(Council Directive 85/577/EEC), the ECJ stated that a distinction could not be drawn between the 'normal' acts of a business and those which are 'exceptional in nature'. Further, in considering the 1999 Regulations, the Scottish court in *Prostar Management* v *Twaddle* 2003 SLT (Sh Ct) 11 pointed out 'the absurdity of a major trader claiming the protection afforded to a consumer whenever he stepped out of his habitual line of business' (at [12]). Rather the line indicated by the ECJ as to the definition of consumer found in the Regulations/Directive is that what matters is whether the contract is to satisfy 'requirements other than family or personal requirements of a trader' (*Di Pinto* at [16]) or is 'for the purpose of satisfying an individual's own needs in terms of private consumption' (*Benincasa* v *Dentalkit Srl* [1997] ECR I-3767 at [16]). That approach was considered when the meaning of consumer under the Unfair Terms Directive and the Brussels Convention fell to be addressed by Longmore J in *Standard Bank London Ltd* v *Apostolakis* (2002). That case was concerned with foreign exchange investment contracts made with the bank by a wealthy couple who were a civil engineer and a lawyer. Longmore J took the basic line that entering into foreign exchange contracts was 'not part of a person's trade as a civil engineer or a lawyer' and that 'the only question' was whether they 'were engaging in the trade of foreign exchange contracts as such'; he did not believe that they were. He took the view that 'they were disposing of income which they had available. They were using money in a way which they hoped would be profitable but merely to use money in a way one hopes would be profitable is not enough...to be engaging in trade'. In relation to the line taken in *Benincasa*, he thought that the description there of contracts 'concluded for the purpose of satisfying an individual's own needs in terms of private consumption' was met in the instant case— 'the contracts made...were for the purpose of satisfying the needs of Mr and Mrs Apostoliakis, defined as an appropriate use of their income, and that the need was a need in terms of private consumption'. He made the point that 'consumption cannot be taken as literally consumed so as to be destroyed but rather consumed in the sense that a consumer consumes, viz he uses or enjoys the relevant product'. Undoubtedly a contract for the investment of disposable income must be capable of being a contract made by a consumer; however, it can be suggested that, in the future, greater account should be taken of the level of investment. The case was concerned with twenty-eight contracts with a total exposure of $7 million. There must come a point at which a secondary means of making money becomes a secondary trade or business. When the issue came before a Greek court, the view was taken that the couple could not be classified as consumers (the type of investment and its scope were seen as putting it outside of the consumer classification [2003] I L Pr 29), and in *Maple Leaf Macro Volatility* v *Rouvray* (2009) Andrew Smith J 'question[ed] the conclusion' of Longmore J (at [209]).

11.15   Lastly, it should be noted in relation to the definition of consumer, that the ECJ has indicated the adoption of something like UCTA's specific exclusion of someone from 'dealing as consumer', if they hold themselves out as contracting in the course of a business. In *Gruber v Bay Wa AG* (2005) it was indicated that account should be taken of the person claiming to be a consumer behaving 'in such a way as to give the other party to the contract the legitimate impression that he was acting for the purpose of his business'. In *Overy v Paypal (Europe) Ltd* (2012) this was followed in relation to the opening of a type of account on paypal which was confined to businesses. He was a professional photographer who was primarily using the account in an attempt to realize the value in his home in an unusual way, by a form of lottery, or draw.

11.16   Finally, as has already been indicated, the Directive/Regulations relate to contracts between consumers and sellers or suppliers. Again mirroring the Directive, UTCCR 1999, reg 3 states:

> ' "seller or supplier" means any natural or legal person who, in contracts covered by these Regulations, is acting for purposes relating to his trade, business or profession, whether publicly or privately owned.'

'Person' here refers to a natural or legal person and obviously includes companies. The Consumer Rights Bill adopts slightly different language. It refers to contracts between consumers and 'traders', rather than 'sellers or suppliers', and a contract between a consumer and a trader is a 'consumer contract'. It is explicit that this does not include a contract of employment or apprenticeship.[27]

Terms not individually negotiated

11.17   Subject to certain exclusions, the Directive/Regulations apply to any term in a contract between a consumer and a seller and supplier which 'has not been individually negotiated' (UTCCR 1999, reg 5(1)). The burden of proving that a term was individually negotiated lies with the seller or supplier claiming that it was (UTCCR 1999, reg 5(4)), and guidance as to which terms are not individually negotiated is provided. Reg 5(2) states:

> 'a term shall always be regarded as not having been individually negotiated where it has been drafted in advance and the consumer has therefore not been able to influence the substance of the term.'

Obviously, it is commonly standard form contracts which provide non-individually negotiated terms, but the Directive/Regulations seem capable of encompassing some situations in which terms are either specific to the particular contract or, although not merely used for one contract, do not constitute the relevant party's standard terms. Some such terms are 'drafted in advance' with the consumer 'unable to influence' their substance.

11.18   The draft Directive had not been restricted to non-individually negotiated terms, and its application to individually negotiated terms was criticized as a 'drastic restriction of the autonomy of the individual' (Brandner & Ulmer (1991) CML Rev 647 at 652). However, despite the concerns about the scope of the Directive and freedom of contract, if it was not restricted to non-individually negotiated terms, we have seen that the Law Commissions recommended that the replacement unfair terms regime should not be so restricted. There was an element of not complicating the unified legislation, and of avoiding the uncertainty in relation to which terms are individually negotiated, nevertheless the Law Commission was of the view that, outside of the core terms, 'consumers seldom have sufficient understanding of the possible impact of [the terms] to make any negotiation meaningful'.[28]

---

[27] Clause 64.

[28] *Unfair Terms in Contracts* (2005) Law Com No 292, Scot Law Com No 199, para. 3.51.

The 'core' exemption

11.19   Under UTCCR 1999, the fairness test is not applied to those situations covered by, what is commonly referred to as, the 'core exemption',[29] which is set out in reg 6(2):

> 'In so far as it is in plain intelligible language, the assessment of fairness of a term shall not relate—
> **(a)** to the definition of the main subject matter of the contract, or
> **(b)** to the adequacy of the price or remuneration, as against the goods or services supplied in exchange.'

This is derived from equally obscure provisions in the Directive (see Article 4(2) and Recital 19).[30] Basically, provided that they are in 'plain intelligible language', it covers terms defining the main subject matter of the contract or price terms. The Supreme Court did make it clear in *Office of Fair Trading* v *Abbey National* [2009] UKSC 6 that, in the case of price terms, the exemption only extends to an assessment of the 'adequacy' of the price i.e. price terms are only excluded from the fairness test in relation to the issue of whether the price is 'appropriate':[31] whether there is value for money under the contract. However, that limitation is of very little significance. It will be the underlying 'adequacy' question which will be raised in, at least, the great majority of cases where it is attempted to argue that a price term is unfair on another basis.[32] It is not, therefore addressed further in the text here,[33] where there are far more significant questions as to the scope of the core exemption to look at.

29 This means of referring to it should not be taken as an indication of its content (*OFT* v *Abbey National* (2009) at [11]).

30 Article 4(2) states:

'Assessment of the Unfair nature of terms shall relate neither to the definition of the main subject matter of the contract nor to the adequacy of price and remuneration on the one hand, as against the services or goods supplied in exchange, on the other in so far as those terms are in plain intelligible language.'

In addition, Recital 19 states:

'Whereas, for the purposes of this Directive, assessment of unfair character shall not be made of terms which describe the main subject matter of the contract nor the quality/price ratio of the goods or services supplied; whereas the main subject matter of the contract and the price/quality ratio may nevertheless be taken into account in assessing the fairness of other terms; whereas it follows, inter alia, that in insurance contracts, the terms which clearly define or circumscribe the insured risk and the insurer's liability shall not be subject to such assessment since these restrictions are taken into account in calculating the premium paid by the consumer.'

31 Lord Walker at [81].

32 In their *Issues Paper* the Law Commissions had suggested a simple 'terms' approach. They thought it 'artificial to think that a court can assess a term for fairness without considering its amount' (*Unfair Terms in Consumer Contracts: a new approach? Issues Paper* Law Com, Scot Law Com (25 July 2012), para. 8.61). In their *Advice*, the Law Commissions reverted to an 'issues' approach to the price term part of the core exemption (*Unfair Terms in Consumer Contracts: Advice to the Department for Business Innovations and Skills* (March 2013), paras 3.99–3.103), so that the fairness of a price term would be assessable for issues other than 'adequacy', which they rephrased, more sensibly, simply as a matter of 'amount'. They did this, however, in order to be certain that the Directive was implemented fully, but 'did not think it would make much difference to the decisions which courts will reach' (paras 3.99–3.103).

33 In *Abbey National*, the banks had accepted that there was 'a significant cross-subsidy ... provided by those customers who regularly incur charges for unauthorised overdrafts ... to those customers ... who are in the fortunate position of never (or very rarely) incurring such charges' (at [1]). Lord Phillips indicated the possibility of a challenge on the basis of the unfairness of the banks 'method' of pricing, or pricing structure (at [80]).

11.20 There was no core exemption in the Directive as originally proposed, and it is a reflection[34] of the criticism by Brandner and Ulmer that:[35]

> 'In a free market economy parties to a contract are free to shape the principal obligations as they see fit. The relationship between the price and the goods or services provided is determined not according to some legal formula but by the mechanisms of the market. Any control by the courts or administrative authorities of the reasonableness or equivalence of this relationship is anathema to the fundamental tenets of a free market economy.'

However, Brandner and Ulmer did qualify this, to a limited extent. They recognized the need for a requirement of 'transparency', because of [36]

> 'terms which may conceal the principal obligations or the price and thus would make it diffi-cult for the consumer to obtain an overview of the market and to make what would (relatively speaking) be the best choice in a given situation.'

It can be seen that there is a basic idea of the core exemption as maintaining freedom of con-tract, and choice, and the operation of the market, to produce the best outcome for both par-ties. However, the extent of the core exemption is key to the effectiveness of the unfair terms regime: the larger the scope of the core exemption, the less effective the policing of unfair terms. Should the scope of the core depend upon checking whether the situation was such that the market would function properly, to police the particular terms, producing the best outcome for both consumers and sellers/suppliers? Or should we just assume the market will function in that way in relation to the terms which deal with the principal obligations, or the price, and are transparent? The coverage of the 'core exemption' has proved very controversial. It has been considered by both the House of Lords in *Director General of Fair Trading* v *First National Bank* (2001), and the Supreme Court (*Office of Fair Trading* v *Abbey National* (2009)), with very dif-ferent approaches being taken by the two courts, and we should now consider those cases and the approach taken in the draft Consumer Rights Bill.

11.21 *Director General of Fair Trading* v *First National Bank* (2001) was concerned with one of the terms in First National's standard form contract for lending money to borrowers through

---

'It may be open to question whether it is fair to subsidise some customers by charges on others who experience con-tingencies that they did not foresee when entering into their contracts'.

However, it is difficult to divorce the cross-subsidy argument from a challenge on the basis of 'adequacy'. It would seem inevitably to involve the contention that customers who incur 'relevant charges' pay more than is appropriate for the services they are receiving and, as Lord Phillips himself also said (at 99]–[100]):

'an assessment of the fairness of charges will be precluded if the basis of the attack is that by reason of their inclusion in the pricing package, those who pay them are being charged an excessive amount in exchange for the overall package'.

34 H. Beale (ed.), *Chitty on Contracts*, 30th edn, Sweet & Maxwell, 2008, para. 15-050; *Office of Fair Trading* v *Abbey National plc and others* [2009] UKSC 6, [2010] 1 AC 696 at [6], [109].

35 H. E. Brandner and P. Ulmer, 'The Community Directive on Unfair Terms in Consumer Contracts: Some Critical Remarks on the Proposals Submitted by the EC Commission' (1991) 28 CMLR 647 at 656.

36 Brandner and Ulmer, 'The Community Directive on Unfair Terms in Consumer Contracts' at 656.

regulated agreements under the Consumer Credit Act 1974. The particular term allowed for the continuance of the contractual rate of interest after judgment for default. The significance of the term was that, without it, First National would have ceased to have a right to interest on the amount outstanding once judgment had occurred. Without such a term, the contractual right to interest would have 'merged' with the judgment and, as judgment had to be sought in the county court, no interest could be awarded as what was in question was a regulated agreement. The court had power to order payment by instalments of the sum for which judgment was given, but that did not include future interest to cover the further time taken to repay the principal. It also had powers under s 136 of the Consumer Credit Act 1974, when making a 'time order' to allow repayment over a period of time, to amend any term of the agreement. However, what caused the problem brought before the courts in this case was that the county court would give judgment for First National on the consumer's default, and make an order allowing for repayment by instalments. The consumer would duly make those instalment payments and then be shocked to discover that a considerable sum was still owed because, under the relevant contractual term, the contractual rate of interest had continued to be payable after the judgment. That interest could not be covered by the payments ordered by the court and the court had not, when making the order, considered whether to provide any relief from it. The consumer had not understood the interaction of the term and the legislation. There were two basic arguments to be considered by the court. First, that the situation fell within the core exemption and was not covered by the fairness test, and second, that it was, in any event, fair. The High Court ([2000] 1 All ER 240), the Court of Appeal ([2000] 2 All ER 759), and the House of Lords ([2002] 1 All ER 97) all found that the core exemption did not apply, but only the Court of Appeal regarded the term as unfair. The aspect of the case dealing with the application of the fairness test will be returned to later. What is of interest here is the approach taken to the scope of the core exemption.

11.22   It should be emphasized that the House of Lords took the line that a restrictive approach was needed in relation to the core exemption, if the purpose of the Regulations was not to be frustrated.[37] In deciding that the term in question was not within the core exemption, Lord Bingham accepted the distinction between terms 'which express the substance of the bargain and "incidental" (if important) terms which surround them' (at [12]). Similarly, Lord Steyn thought that the term in question was not within the core exemption and was a 'subsidiary' term (at [34]). It is worth noting that he also specifically made the point that a restrictive approach should be taken to the 'core', to avoid the 'main purpose of the scheme [being] frustrated by endless formalistic arguments as to whether a provision is a definitional or exclusionary provision' (at [34]).[38] However, at its narrowest, the *First National Bank* case merely decided that a term dealing with the situation after default was not within the core.[39]

11.23   *Office of Fair Trading v Abbey National*[40] involved an action by the OFT against seven Banks and one Building Society ('the Banks'). The terms in question were those which impose

---

37 Lord Bingham at [15], Lord Steyn at [34].

38 On the problems of distinguishing definitional and exclusionary terms see para. **9.3**.

39 Lord Bingham at [12], Lord Steyn at [34], Lord Hope at [43].

40 [2009] UKSC 6, [2010] 1 AC 696.

charges (the 'relevant charges') in relation to overdrafts which have not been agreed in advance, or in relation to unsuccessful 'requests' for such overdrafts (not the terms imposing interest payments on the overdrafts).[41] Such overdrafts may be successfully, or unsuccessfully, 'requested', in a number of ways, such as a cheque being presented, direct debits becoming payable, a withdrawal from an ATM, or even the debiting from an account of an amount to cover interest or fees payable to the bank. The courts were asked to consider whether the 'relevant charges' were covered by the core exemption or could be subject to the fairness test. At first instance, and in the Court of Appeal,[42] a narrow approach was taken to the core exemption, and it was found that it did not cover the terms.

11.24   The Court of Appeal emphasized the distinction made by the House of Lords in *First National Bank* between terms falling within the 'core' and incidental or subsidiary terms. It developed this approach to confine 'core terms' to those embodying the 'essential bargain' (at [86]). It took the line that the 'notion of essential bargain' should be imported into 'the construction of article 4(2) and both paragraphs (a) and (b) of regulation 6(2)' (at [86]). It was said that the line was taken to ensure 'protection in respect of the kind of issues that a consumer will not have in focus when entering the bargain' (at [86]).[43] This reflects the idea that the exemption designates an area within which the market will be functioning, and will produce the best outcome for both consumers and sellers/suppliers, and those terms should not therefore be assessed for fairness. However, it does not assume that the market will be functioning in relation to a term because it is a term dealing with a central issue, and it is in plain intelligible language. It would look at whether the terms would have been salient to the contractual decision—taken into account in making it—and thus regulated by the market. In concluding that the relevant terms were not covered by the core exemption the Court of Appeal stated[44]

> 'We do not accept the submission that the contingent nature of the charges is irrelevant to the question whether the Relevant Charges are part of the core bargain. On the contrary, it is a strong indication that they are incidental or ancillary provisions, rather as the default provision in the *First National Bank* case was held to be incidental or ancillary.'

11.25   However, the line taken by the Supreme Court was very different. It gave much greater scope for the core exemption, and no scope for assessing whether the market would have been

---

41 These relevant charges formed part of the charging structure adopted by the banks in relation to current accounts, and that was described by Andrew Smith J at first instance ([2008] EWHC 875 (Comm)) at [53] as follows:

'The charging structure adopted by the Banks in relation to current accounts is commonly known as "free-if-in-credit banking". . . . under this structure customers do not pay bank charges for the day-to-day operation of the account while it is in credit (although there are often charges for additional services such as, for some banks, stopping cheques written by the customer or supplying additional bank statements). The Banks do, however, have the benefit of customers' credit balances . . . and also interest will be incurred and fees may be incurred if the customer's account goes into debit or in other circumstances. These fees include the Relevant Charges.'

42 [2009] EWCA Civ 116, [2009] 1 All ER (Comm) 1097.

43 [2009] EWCA Civ 116, [2009] 1 All ER (Comm) 1097 at [86].

44 [2009] EWCA Civ 116, [2009] 1 All ER (Comm) 1097 at [109].

operating, beyond that inherent in the information requirement of 'plain intelligible language'. The judges thought the core exemption clearly encompassed the terms in question. They confined the *First National Bank* case, to its narrowest line; the term there was not exempt as it was a default term. The Supreme Court took the approach that, subject to the protection of the consumer by the requirement of 'plain intelligible language', the scope of the core exemption was simply a matter of construction of the contract. Lord Mance stated[45]

> '[T]he identification of the price or remuneration for the purposes of... Regulation 6(2) is a matter of objective interpretation for the court. The court should no doubt read and interpret the contract in the usual manner... [There] is no basis for requiring it to do so... by confining the focus to matters on which it might conjecture that [the consumer] would be likely to focus. The consumer's protection under the... Regulations is the requirement of transparency... That being present, the consumer is assumed to be capable of reading the relevant terms and identifying whatever is objectively the price and remuneration under the contract into which he or she enters.'

In the view of the Supreme Court, discerning the limits of the 'core exemption' does not require any examination of whether the subject matter of the term would have been salient to the consumer, nor any consideration of whether the market would have been operating to produce the best outcomes. In their view, all that is needed is that, as a matter of construction, the terms deal with 'the main subject matter of contract', or the price. In relation to core terms, the consumer's protection comes from the requirement that if they are to be exempt they must be in 'plain intelligible language'. Lord Mance referred to 'transparency', but plainly he was referring to the requirement of 'plain intelligible language', and that does not even protect the consumer from core terms which are in small print or very obscurely placed in the contractual document. There is little hope that the market will police such terms, and the consumer's choice will produce the best outcome: consumers will not know about such terms, to consider them.

11.26   The approach of the Supreme Court has been much criticized. It places a heavy emphasis on construction, and there will be issues in relation to distinguishing clauses in substance, rather than just form, as in relation to whether a clause in the form of part of the definition of the obligation is an exclusion clause, or whether a payment is part of the price or is, in substance a payment after default. Lord Steyn had recognized the potential for the first type of problem in *First National Bank* (see para. **11.22**), and *Bairstow Eves London Central Ltd* v *Smith* (2004), which the Supreme Court approved of in *Abbey National,* illustrates the latter.[46]

---

45 [2009] UKSC 6, [2010] 1 AC 696 at [113].

46 The case was concerned with an estate agent's fees, which had, mistakenly, not been paid by the vendor's solicitors at the time of the sale. The contract provided for a 'standard commission rate' of 3 per cent and an 'early payment discounted rate' of 1.5 per cent. The standard rate became payable if the estate agents were not paid at the 'discounted rate' within ten days of the sale. The question arose as to the application of the 1999 Regulations to the term requiring 3 per cent commission. The estate agents argued it was covered by the core exemption and not subject to the fairness test. Gross J concluded that it was not covered by the core exemption. He thought it 'plain that both parties contemplated an agreed operative price of 1.5 per cent with a default provision of 3 per cent' (the market for estate agents was such that the estate agents recognized that they were unlikely to obtain business at 3 per cent and the negotiations had focused on 1.5 per cent).

11.27   More broadly, the Supreme Court's approach has been seen as taking insufficient account of the aim of the Directive as a consumer protection measure, and as having a detrimental impact upon the consumer.[47] An OFT Market Study which was 'not primarily about which terms contravene specific legislation, but about which terms harm consumers' (and was not guidance on the interpretation of the legislation),[48] took the line in relation to the 'price' exemption that[49]

> 'the exclusion from assessment... in our view, should only apply to terms concerning the main value-for-money proposition as it is fact understood by both parties including the consumer. Consequently we believe that many terms imposing charges should be assessable, including any such charges shown to be outside of ordinary consumers' considerations whether because they are payable on a remote contingency or for other reasons.'

There was considerable concern that the line taken by the Supreme Court would mean that the Regulations would not provide protection for consumers from many unfair terms.

11.28   There was, however, also concern that *Abbey National* could give businesses a false sense of security, as the ECJ might take a very different line.[50] (The Supreme Court had also been criticized for not sending the question of the approach to be taken to the core exemption to the ECJ.)[51]

11.29   The Law Commissions have become involved in this controversy, and it provides the background to the approach taken in the draft Consumer Rights Bill. The 2005 Report of the Law Commissions on Unfair Terms had taken a line reflective of that of the House of Lords in *First National Bank,* and very similar to that arrived at by the Court of Appeal in *Abbey National.* It had looked to the 'reasonable expectations' of the consumer to determine the scope of the core exemption. However, in their *Issues Paper* the Law Commissions emphasized the decision of the Supreme Court in *Abbey National,* and recognized concerns arising from the uncertainty of looking for 'reasonable expectations'. They took the line that greater clarity can be achieved by focusing on 'how the deal is presented' rather than 'what the consumer would have expected'.[52] They did recognize that, by itself, simply looking for 'plain intelligible language' can do little to try to ensure that the term is available to the consumer, and regulated by the market: it may be hidden away. They took the line that 'price' terms, or terms 'defining the main subject matter',

---

47 M. Chen-Wishart, 'Transparency and Fairness in Bank Charges' (2010) 126 LQR 157; P. Davies, 'Bank Charges and the Supreme Court' (2010) 69 CLJ 2; P. Morgan, 'Bank Charges and the Unfair Terms in Consumer Contracts Regulations 1999; the end of the road for consumers?' [2010] LMCLQ 21; S. Whittaker, 'Unfair Terms, Unfair Prices and Bank Charges' (2011) 74 MLR 106. But see A. Arora, 'Unfair Contract Terms and Unauthorised Bank Charges: A Banking Lawyer's Perspective' [2012] JBL 44.

48 OFT, *Consumer Contracts Market Study* (February 2011) p. 6.

49 OFT, *Consumer Contracts Market Study* (February 2011) para. 6.13.

50 *Unfair Terms in Consumer Contracts: a new approach? Issues Paper* Law Com, Scot Law Com (25 July 2012) para. 1.18.

51 Davies, 'Bank Charges and the Supreme Court'; M. Kenny, 'Orchestrating Sub-prime Consumer Protection in Retail Banking: *Abbey National* in the context of Europeanized Private Law' (2011) ERPL 43; M. Schillig, 'Directive 93/13 and the Price Term Exemption: a Comparative Analysis in the Light of the Market for Lemons' (2011) ICLQ 933.

52 *Unfair Terms in Consumer Contracts: a new approach? Issues Paper* Law Com, Scot Law Com (25 July 2012) para. 8.73.

should not just have to be 'in plain intelligible language' to be exempt. The terms would have to be 'prominent' as well as 'transparent', and a term would be 'prominent' if it was 'presented in a way that the average consumer would be aware of it'.[53] It is this approach which now features in the draft Consumer Rights Bill, with the exemption only applying to core terms which are 'transparent and prominent'.[54]

11.30 So, originally, the Law Commissions would have looked at the 'reasonable expectations' of the consumer to determine the scope of the 'core exemption'. Such an approach would have looked at whether the term would have impacted upon the consumer's decision to contract, and thus whether it could be regulated by the market. It would have taken account of many of the common human failings in decision making which have been recognized by behavioural economics,[55] such as the over-optimism which would lead people to think that bank charges stemming from overdrawing would be of little relevance to them in contracting for a bank account. By the time of their *Issues Paper* the Law Commissions' basic line was that[56]

'Unfair Terms legislation assumes that consumers are rational but too busy to read the many complex standard terms presented to them. When presented with the right information in a way they can understand, they make good decisions.'

An approach very much in keeping with the basic line taken by the Supreme Court in *Abbey National*: the price and the definition of the main subject matter do not need to be subject to the fairness test because they will be regulated by consumers making rational decisions as long as the terms are plainly presented.

11.31 However, it should be noted that the Law Commissions stated that basic line as an 'assumption', and they did not stop with a requirement of 'prominence' in proposing that the core exemption be more limited than it was in *Abbey National*. They saw the need for a 'compromise between classical and behavioural economic approaches',[57] and they viewed the 'grey list' of terms which may be unfair, in particular, as providing it. They gave examples of the 'grey list' recognizing the common human frailties in decision making which are identified by behavioural economics, but not recognized by classical economics' conception of the rational decision maker:[58]

'(1) Sub-paragraph (e) covers terms requiring a consumer "who fails to fulfil his obligation to pay a disproportionately high sum in compensation". Although consumers should not be

---

53 *Unfair Terms in Consumer Contracts: a new approach? Issues Paper* Law Com, Scot Law Com (25 July 2012) paras 8.29–8.33.

54 Clause 67(2).

55 See generally C. Jolls, C. Sunstein and R. Thaler, 'A Behavioral Approach to Law and Economics' (1998) 50 Stan LR 1471.

56 *Unfair Terms in Consumer Contracts: a new approach? Issues Paper* Law Com, Scot Law Com (25 July 2012) para. 3.2.

57 *Unfair Terms in Consumer Contracts: Advice to the Department for Business, Innovation and Skills* (March 2013) para. 3.55.

58 *Unfair Terms in Consumer Contracts: Advice to the Department for Business, Innovation and Skills* (March 2013) para. 3.54.

> protected from paying a disproportionately high sum for goods or services generally, this
> recognises that consumers may be over-optimistic. They may therefore give too little atten-
> tion to the consequences of failing to do what they expect to do.
>
> (2) Sub-paragraph (d) addresses terms which permit the seller to "retain sums paid by the
> consumer" where the consumer "decides not to conclude or perform the contract". This
> recognises that consumers may be focused on their present intentions, and give too little
> attention to possible changes of mind in the future.'

To effectuate the compromise which they saw the list as being capable of bringing about, the
Law Commissions recommended that it should be made clear that terms falling within it are
not prevented from being subject to the fairness test by the core exemption, and that is the line
taken in the draft Consumer Rights Directive.

11.32 The Law Commissions' compromise means that the protection afforded by the market
is not always assumed to be sufficient just because a term is core and plainly enough presented.
It is recognized that at least some note should be taken of the common human failings in decision making which have been brought to the fore by behavioural economics, but which are not
considered by classical economics, which can so easily emphasize freedom of contract, and
market forces, when simply dealing with the 'rational actor'. However, there are obvious problems in relying on a finite list of particular terms to deal with the more general problem of the
common irrationalities of consumer decision making. The problems, and the need to recognize
the irrationalities in the unfair terms regime, are emphasized by considering the difficult case
of *OFT v Ashbourne Management Services Ltd*.[59]

11.33 *Ashbourne* was concerned with terms setting minimum membership periods for gym
clubs varying between twelve and thirty-six months, which led to the consumer being liable for
the rest of the membership fees when he or she tried to end their membership before the expiry
of that period. The OFT had tried to contend that the minimum membership term did not fall
within the 'core exemption'. It took the line that the main subject matter was membership and
the right to use the club, and that the period of membership was an ancillary term. Kitchin J
did not accept this very narrow and artificial line, and concluded that the minimum period of
membership was part of the main subject matter of the contract (at [152]). He did find a way of
placing the terms outside the core exemption, but it is not one which is easy to follow or sustain-
able, and what we should note is the considerable impetus, which he obviously felt, to subject
the terms to the fairness test, and find them unfair.

11.34 Kitchin J noted (at [171]) that

> 'the defendants know that the average consumer overestimates the use he will make of the
> gym and that frequently unforeseen circumstances make its continued use impossible or
> his continued membership unaffordable. They are also well aware that the average con-
> sumer is induced to enter into one of their agreements because of the relatively low monthly

---

59 [2011] EWHC 1237, [2011] ECC 31.

> subscriptions associated with them but that if he ceases to use the gym after between three and six months he would be better off joining on a pay per month basis.'

The business model was 'designed to take advantage of the naivety and inexperience of the average consumer using gym clubs at the lower end of the market' (at [173]). It is understandable that Kitchin J should seek to find a means to protect consumers from the term.

11.35   Very clearly, the terms in *Ashbourne* were unfair, and few would disagree that they should have been struck down. Equally clearly the problem was not one which stemmed from terms being unknown to the consumer or not understood. The whole marketing strategy was based on emphasizing how cheap they could be seen to be. The problem was the abuse of a common decision making irrationality of the consumer in relation to whether they were actually good value. The Law Commissions recognized they needed to add such terms to the 'grey list' to ensure that they could be legitimately struck down as unfair, without that being prevented by the core exemption, and again that has been carried through to the draft Consumer Rights Bill. This shows, however, that relying on a list to avoid the core exemption preventing this type of problem with consumer decision making being dealt with under the unfair terms regime is a compromise, and may prove to be insufficient in the light of further cases with terms not covered by the list.

11.36   One final point should be made here for those who easily dismiss the above concerns with the scope of the core exemption on the basis that the consumer should be expected to make rational decisions, and regulation should be left to the market in relation to clearly enough presented core terms. The problem is that ignoring the way consumers actually make decisions, in favour of saying that they should be 'rational', can lead to the market producing bad options for the consumer, not good ones. This is broadly the phenomenon of the 'market for lemons', whereby market forces favour the sales of poorer products to consumers ('lemons' in the American vernacular), because they appear better buys when just the most obvious elements of their sale are considered, such as the price, and not the impact of the small print terms relieving the seller of liability for their faults.[60] The need to do something about small print has long been recognized, but the *Ashbourne* case exhibited the same type of problem, because of a common defect in consumer decision making. Such terms had the potential to drive out of the market terms which were actually likely to be better for those consumers: cheaper monthly payments. Monthly payment terms will be kept high when a better profit can be made by providing maximum encouragement to the consumer to take a yearly subscription which holds the greater potential for profit for the business.

Unfair terms

11.37   The Unfair Contract Terms Act 1977 subjects certain clauses, which exclude or restrict liability, to the 'requirement of reasonableness'. The unfair terms regime subjects terms to

---

60 See, famously, G. Akerlof, 'The Market for "Lemons": Quality Uncertainty and the Market Mechanism' (1970) 84 Quarterly Journal of Economics 488.

a test of 'fairness'.[61] Mirroring the Directive (Article 3(1)), and also reproduced in the draft Consumer Rights Bill, under UTCCR 1999, reg 5(1), a term is regarded as unfair if:

> 'contrary to the requirement of good faith, it causes a significant imbalance in the parties' rights and obligations arising under the contract to the detriment of the consumer'.

There are basically two elements here:

1. significant imbalance in the parties' rights and obligations to the detriment of the consumer;
2. the requirement of good faith.

The test could be seen as involving three elements, i.e. 'to the detriment of the consumer' could be seen as a separate element, but 'it does not add much'. It merely 'serves to make clear that the Directive is aimed at significant imbalance against the consumer, rather than the seller or supplier'.[62] It may be that the reaction to the identification of two basic elements in the fairness test leads to a prima facie inference that they reflect substantive unfairness and procedural unfairness, i.e. that 'significant imbalance' is concerned with substantive unfairness (basically unfairness in the content of the contractual rights and obligations) and that 'good faith' is concerned with procedural unfairness (unfairness in the way in which the contract was made, such as the lack of any realistic opportunity for the consumer to become acquainted with the terms). Whilst that may be in large measure accurate, there is an interaction and overlap between the two elements and the Law Commissions take the view that 'in most cases there will be some element of procedural unfairness and some element of substantive unfairness' but 'at the extremes ... one will suffice'.[63] This will be returned to later.

11.38   However, before these elements are considered further, two preliminary points should be made in relation to the fairness test. First, there is a list in Sch 2 of terms which 'may be unfair' (the 'grey list' see para. **11.53**ff). The list is of limited substantive effect—it does not even shift the burden of proof, in relation to the fairness test, to the seller or supplier; i.e. there is no requirement that sellers or suppliers disprove the unfairness of the terms falling within the list. It may, nevertheless, provide very useful guidance as to which terms will be regarded as unfair and has certainly been so treated by the OFT (see the OFT Bulletins on Unfair Terms in Consumer Contracts where most of the terms regarded as unfair are classified by reference to the grey list). The list is derived from the Directive and with some amendment it also appears in the Consumer Rights Bill. In that Bill, it is made clear that it has a more extensive impact. As has been indicated, if a term falls within the list, the fairness test is not made inapplicable to it by the core exemption (clause 67(7)).

---

61   Beale (1989) CLP 197; Collins (1994) 14 OJLS 229.

62   *Director General of Fair Trading v First National Bank* (2001) per Lord Steyn at [36].

63   Law Commission, Scottish Law Commission, *Unfair Terms in Consumer Contracts: Advice to the Department for Business, Innovation and Skills* (March 2013).

11.39   The second point to be made here on fairness is concerned with the factors identified as relevant to the test and, particularly, the identification of the 'time frame' of the assessment as that of the making of the contract. Again, largely reflecting the Directive, and followed in the draft Consumer Rights Bill, UTCCR 1999, reg 6(1) states:

> '...the unfairness of a contractual term shall be assessed taking into account the nature of the goods or services for which the contract was concluded and by referring, as at the time of the conclusion of the contract, to all the circumstances attending the conclusion of the contract and to all other terms of the contract or of another contract on which it is dependent.'

With its reference to the 'time frame' of the conclusion of the contract to limit the 'relevant circumstances', this is similar to the provision dealing with the requirement of reasonableness in the Unfair Contract Terms Act 1977 (s 11(1)), and a term may be unfair because of its potential coverage even though its operation would not be unfair in the particular case, just as under UCTA 1977, an exemption clause may operate reasonably in relation to the breach which has occurred, but fail to satisfy the requirement of reasonableness because of its potential coverage (*Stewart Gill Ltd* v *Horatio Myer & Co. Ltd* (1992)).

11.40   Regulation 6(1) starts by specifically stating that it is 'Without prejudice to Regulation 12', which provides for consideration of unfairness at the general level. Obviously, where there is no specific contract to consider, as the House of Lords recognized, the legislation 'must be made to work sensibly and effectively and this can be done taking into account the effect of contemplated or typical relationships between contracting parties' (*First National Bank* (2001) per Lord Steyn at [33]).

Significant imbalance

11.41   In *Director General of Fair Trading* v *First National Bank* (2001), Lord Bingham briefly described significant imbalance. He said (at [17]):

> 'The requirement of significant imbalance is met if a term is so weighted in favour of the supplier as to tilt the parties' rights and obligations under the contract significantly in his favour. This may be by the granting to the supplier of a beneficial option or discretion or power, or by imposing on the consumer of a disadvantageous burden or risk or duty...This involves looking at the contract as a whole.'

This emphasizes that the imbalance must not be weighed too finely, it is 'significant' imbalance which must be found, and it is imbalance in the contract as a whole which must be considered, but as the OFT has suggested, this may be taken in stages. The OFT has said:[64]

> 'When a term looks in itself unfair, we need to establish first that there is no balancing provision—which we interpret as one which: first is as potentially detrimental to the supplier as the

---

64 Bulletin 4, pp. 22–3.

> term in question is to the consumer; and secondly is obviously linked to it, so that the two, on a common sense view, tend to cancel each other out. The commonest example is provided by cancellation rights, which we accept are fair if the consumer enjoys equally extensive rights—always assuming that in the circumstances, the right to cancel is of equal benefit. We also look of course at the rest of the contract for any qualifying proviso that would tend to remove the possibility of detriment in the term under suspicion, rather than balancing it.'

We should consider some examples of the line taken in relation to significant imbalance, and the application of the test in practice.

11.42   In the *First National Bank* case, the House of Lords thought it plain that there was no significant imbalance. Basically, they viewed the situation before them as unexceptionable as interest payments are the price of a loan and merely continuing them after judgment for default was seen as simply ensuring that the price for the borrowing continued to be paid as long as the borrowing continued (the facts are set out at para. **11.21**). Basically, the court considered the difference between the rights and obligations under the contract at the start and when the operation of the clause had been triggered. Lord Bingham said (at [20]):

> 'The essential bargain is that the bank will make funds available to the borrower which the borrower will repay, over a period, with interest. Neither party could suppose that the bank would willingly forgo any part of its principal or interest. If the bank thought that outcome at all likely, it would not lend... There is nothing unbalanced or detrimental to the consumer in that obligation; the absence of such a term would unbalance the contract to the detriment of the lender.'

Of course, the appropriateness of such a conclusion, in taking this type of relative weighing approach to the balance of the rights and obligations of the parties, does depend upon the initial position being fair.

11.43   Although also involving a 'relative weighing', the situation differed somewhat in *Office of Fair Trading* v *Foxtons* (2009). The case was concerned with a contract between property owners and letting agents. The contract provided for an 11 per cent commission for the agents when the property was initially let to a tenant and also for an 11 per cent commission on each renewal of it. The question arose as to the fairness of the renewal commission. The court decided that there was a significant imbalance (and a lack of good faith so that the term was unfair). When the property was first let to a tenant the letting agents would have to undertake work in, for example, marketing the property. Such work did not have to be undertaken on a renewal. The judge took the line (at [90]):

> 'The commission amounts in question are significant, and operate adversely to the client the more time goes on. Commensurate services are not provided as time goes on.'

Again, as in the *First National Bank* case, the term in question related to payment upon the happening of a specified event. In both cases, the overall balance in the contractual rights could be considered relative to those at the commencement of the contract. The relative benefits/burdens were unchanged in *First National Bank*, and had tipped against the consumer in *Foxtons*, so whilst the initial benefits/burdens and the relative weighing in *First National Bank* clearly raised an unanswered question, the situation was less problematic in *Foxtons*. Unless, the initial payment was unbalanced against the estate agent (for example, as a 'loss leader' to get the landlord's initial business), it was clear that the renewal term was unbalanced against the consumer.

11.44   There can be seen to be an element of relative weighing in *Peabody Trust Governors* v *Reeve* (2008), but it should be particularly noted for the extent of the 'rights' of the tenant which were considered in relation to the balancing the landlord's rights, and also the reality of them as a counterweight. In that case the court had to consider a unilateral right to vary the terms of tenancy agreements made between a 'social landlord' and its tenants. In considering significant imbalance the specific term was considered, but then the broader overall situation was also looked at. It was said (at [45]):

> 'There is no doubt that a unilateral right of variation in favour of a landlord causes a "significant imbalance" in the parties' rights and obligations to the detriment of the tenant. The landlord can impose material changes but the tenant cannot. The tenant's only right is to walk away from the tenancy by giving notice to quit under the procedure set out in section 103 of the Housing Act 1985. However, in the case of relatively low cost housing operated by a registered social landlord, this is unrealistic. The tenant will typically have a strong necessity, will be of relatively limited means, may well lack experience and familiarity with contractual terms and will have a very weak bargaining position.'

The term gave the landlord a potential to make significant changes in the contract which could make it very much less favourable to the tenant than it had been originally and, although that might theoretically be met by a right for the tenant to walk away from the changed terms, circumstances meant that was not a realistic counterweight to the landlord's right.

11.45   Although, in general, the rights and obligations of the parties under the contract as a whole must be considered in deciding if a term causes a significant imbalance, there are some situations where there is no real need to go beyond the particular term. The type of clause which was looked at in *Oceano Grupo Editorial SA* v *Murciano Quintero* C-240–244/98 (2000) provides an example. The problem with the type of clause is that it may put significant hurdles in the way of a consumer enforcing his or her rights under the contract. The clause required any action to be taken in the supplier's jurisdiction, not the consumers. At its worst, such a clause could render the rest of the contract meaningless for the consumer, if to take action was prohibitively expensive/difficult for the consumer because of the jurisdictional requirement. As its impact could be to render the rest of the contract meaningless, plainly only the impact of such a clause, itself, may need to be considered in deciding on significant imbalance.

11.46   One further point addressed by the House of Lords in *First National Bank* (2002) should be considered. The OFT had contended that the term was unfair as a departure from what would otherwise have been the position in English law and in *Aziz* v *Caixa d'Estalvis de Catalunya* (2013), the ECJ has now emphasized the importance of consideration of what would the position have been under national law, without the relevant term, in assessing significant imbalance. This clearly is an important factor, but it is one with which much care must be taken. In *First National Bank,* Lord Bingham, having considered the development of the statutory background, concluded that he did not think that 'the term could be stigmatised as unfair on the ground that it violates or undermines a statutory regime enacted for the protection of consumers' (at [22]). Similarly, Lord Steyn did not think that the argument could prevail 'in circumstances where the legislature has neither expressly nor by necessary implication barred a stipulation that interest may continue to accrue after judgment' (at [38]). Departure from the defaults position is a factor. The basis of the particular default position, and the impact of the departure from it, must be considered, to see if it points to imbalance, and its weight.[65]

11.47 The final point to be considered here in relation to 'significant imbalance' concerns its application when the basic difficulty with the term in question is that it is misleading—a term which might appear to the consumer to have an effect other than it actually has. An example is provided by the OFT (Bulletin 3, p. 12):

> 'The OFT normally objects to clauses which reflect the general contractual position concerning damages for breach of contract but in a misleading way. Contracts sometimes give the impression that, if they are cancelled by the consumer, the company can recover all the profit it would have made. In law the supplier actually has a duty to mitigate....'

Plainly the OFT takes the view that such misleading terms should be unfair and controlled by the Regulations, and prima facie there should be no difficulty in finding a lack of good faith in such circumstances (see later), but how can it be said that such a term 'causes a significant imbalance in the parties' rights and obligations arising under the contract, to the detriment of the consumer'? It should be remembered, however, that the Law Commissions were of the view that, 'In most cases there will be some element of procedural unfairness and some element of substantive unfairness' but 'at the extremes... one will suffice'.[66] It may be that, at the extremes, sufficient lack of good faith will suffice, where it causes an effective imbalance in the rights and obligations of the parties, even though not an actual one ie where the actual rights and obligations would not be imbalanced but the rights and obligations as the consumer would believe them to be are unbalanced.[67] (Macdonald (1999) 58 CLJ 413). One problem of this type is specifically dealt with in the draft Consumer Rights Bill in relation to enforcement by the CMA, and other general enforcers. An application for an injunction by the CMA or other enforcer, to stop a trader using, or proposing or recommending for use, an 'unfair term', could not be met by the defence that 'because of a rule of law, a term to which

---

65 E. Macdonald, 'Scope and Fairness of the Unfair Terms in Consumer Contracts Regulations' (2002) 65 MLR 763 at 771.

66 Law Commission, Scottish Law Commission, *Unfair Terms in Consumer Contracts: Advice to the Department for Business, Innovation and Skills* (March 2013).

67 Macdonald (1999) 58 CLJ 413.

the application relates is not, or could not be, an enforceable contract term'.[68] Thus, for example, a trader could not prevent an injunction against the continued use of a 'term', in a set of standard terms, which the 'red hand rule' actually could be used to say was not incorporated into the contract.[69]

The requirement of good faith

11.48   The reference to good faith in the fairness test, was not one which was familiar to lawyers in England, and Wales, although it must now be becoming more so, with its important role in the Unfair Terms Regulations since 1994. It has long been more familiar in civil law systems, in relation to which its effect has been said to be 'most aptly conveyed by such metaphysical colloquialisms as "playing fair", "coming clean" or "putting one's cards face up on the table"' (*Interfoto Picture Library Ltd* v *Stilletto Visual Programmes Ltd* [1989] QB 433 at 439 per Bingham LJ). However, its meaning in relation to the unfair terms regime was considered by the House of Lords in *Director General of Fair Trading* v *First National Bank* (2001).

11.49   The facts of *Director General of Fair Trading* v *First National Bank* (2002) were outlined earlier (see para. **11.21**). Here note should be made of the comments on 'good faith'.[70] Lord Bingham said (at [17]):

> 'The requirement of good faith in this context is one of fair and open dealing. Openness requires that the terms should be expressed fully, clearly and legibly, containing no concealed pitfalls or traps. Appropriate prominence should be given to terms which might operate disadvantageously to the customer. Fair dealing requires that a supplier should not, whether deliberately or unconsciously, take advantage of the consumer's necessity, indigence, lack of experience, unfamiliarity with the subject matter of the contract, weak bargaining position or any other factor listed in or analogous to those listed in Schedule 2 of the regulations.'

Similarly, Lord Steyn saw good faith as importing 'the notion of open and fair dealing' (at [36]). Obviously this relies on the setting of standards and, more broadly, Lord Bingham also recognized that good faith 'looks to good standards of commercial morality and practice' (at [17]) and, again similarly, Lord Steyn saw the 'purpose of the provision of good faith and fair dealing' as being 'to enforce community standards of fairness and reasonableness'. On this view then, good faith broadly embodies certain 'standards' of dealing in relation to the two aspects of good faith—open dealing and fair dealing—which in turn seem to contain the ideas of (broadly) the sufficiency of notice of terms (including the clarity of their drafting)[71] and of advantage not

---

68 Clause 5(3).

69 On the 'red hand rule' and incorporation of terms see para. **9.34**. In relation to the broader issue see E. Macdonald, 'The Emperor's Old Clauses: Unincorporated Clauses, Misleading Terms and the Unfair Terms in Consumer Contracts Regulations (1999) 58 CLJ 413.

70 Macdonald (2002) 65 MLR 763.

71 One example being the use of two contradictory terms in the landlord and tenant contract in *Peabody Trust Governors* v *Reeve* (2008) at [51].

being taken of a superior position by the seller or supplier. Of course, this raises the issue of the source of these standards. Lord Steyn referred to 'community standards' and the Regulations derive from a European measure. The assumption might be of EU standards. However, the member states are so diverse that it can be questioned whether such 'standards' could be identified. In any event, in making the point that it will not decide upon the fairness of a particular term the ECJ has indicated that the fairness test is referable to the relevant standards of the various member states (*Freiburger Kommunalbauten v Hofstetter* C-237/02 (2004)).

11.50   However, it would seem that the idea of 'advantage taking' does not provide a sufficiently high standard. Recital 16 of the Directive states:

> 'Whereas in making an assessment of good faith, particular regard shall be had to the strength of bargaining position of the parties, whether the consumer had an inducement to agree to the term and whether the goods or services were sold or supplied to the special order of the consumer; whereas the requirement of good faith may be satisfied by the seller or supplier where he deals fairly and equitably with the other party whose legitimate interests he has to take into account.'

It can be contended that there is an emphasis on the seller or supplier taking account of the legitimate interests of the consumer. Good faith may be seen as intended to go further than restraining advantage taking and requiring sufficient account to be taken of the legitimate interests of the consumer. (The other factors could be seen as merely indicative of whether or not that has occurred).[72] In the light of recital 16, in *Aziz v Caixa d'Estalvis de Catalunya* (2013), the ECJ did take the line that good faith is a matter of 'whether the seller or supplier, dealing fairly and equitably with the consumer, could reasonably assume that the consumer would have agreed to the term in individual contract negotiations' (at para 69). This still, however, begs the question of the standard required for 'fair and equitable dealing' (whether it is not taking advantage of the consumer, or taking account of the consumer's legitimate interests), and what it requires. There is no simple test of just asking whether the consumer would have agreed to the relevant term in individual negotiations. Someone may agree to a term in an individually negotiated contract because inequality of bargaining power gives them little choice or because they understandably do not know of, or are mistaken as to the impact of, the term. It may be in small print, or devised to take account of common weaknesses in decision making (see *Ashbourne* at **11.33**ff).

11.51   One issue which arises is the relationship of the two elements of the fairness test, i.e. of good faith and significant imbalance. In *Bryen & Langley v Boston* (2005) they were treated as two discrete requirements so that the court took the line that once it had decided that there was no lack of good faith on the supplier's part, significant imbalance did not need to be considered (at [44]). However, the better approach would seem to be to recognize that in some cases there is an overlapping relationship between the two elements. This has been contended earlier in

72 Macdonald (2002) 65 MLR 765.

relation to terms which are not imbalanced as such, but are in the rights and obligations which they mislead the consumer into thinking he or she has. Here the easier point should be made that a term could be so imbalanced in favour of the seller or supplier that the imbalance itself shows advantage taking, or insufficient consideration of the interests of the consumer, by the seller or supplier. It has been suggested that the element of 'good faith' in the Directive and the Regulations embodies both a substantive and a procedural element and can overlap with the 'significant imbalance' element of the fairness test[73] and there was some indication that a sufficient imbalance will also show a lack of good faith in *Peabody Trust Governors* v *Reeve* (2008). In that case, a clause giving the landlord the unilateral power to vary the terms of a tenancy was seen in this light. Although an absence of good faith was shown in lack of 'open dealing' in the obscure drafting of the contract, with its contradictory clauses, the judge also made the point that (at [53]):

> '[the clause] is such a sweeping and one sided provision, that even if it had been clearly and unambiguously set out and explained, I doubt whether it could be held to be fair.'

Factors

11.52   Consideration has been given to the two basic elements of the fairness test. The further point can be made that in *Director General of Fair Trading* v *First National Bank* (2001), Lord Millett indicated a more overall approach in identifying factors which, for the most part, would be relevant to both those elements. He said (at [54]):

> 'There can be no one single test of [fairness]. It is obviously useful to assess the impact of an impugned term on the parties' rights and obligations by comparing the effect of the contract with the term and the effect it would have without it. But the inquiry cannot stop there. It may also be necessary to consider the effect of the inclusion of the term on the substance or core of the transaction; whether if it were drawn to his attention the consumer would be likely to be surprised by it; whether the term is a standard term, not merely in similar non-negotiable consumer contracts, but in commercial contracts freely negotiated between parties acting on level terms and at arms' length; and whether, in such cases, the party adversely affected by the inclusion of the term or his lawyer might reasonably be expected to object to its inclusion and press for its deletion.'

So, whilst the consumer's likely surprise at the term most obviously goes to the good faith element of the fairness test (in particular, 'open dealing'), it could also be indicative of imbalance. Certainly, the departure of the term from the consumer's reasonable expectations was seen in that light in *Office of Fair Trading* v *Foxtons* (2009) (at [91]). More plainly, the fact that a similar term would be accepted by a commercial party of equal bargaining power may be indicative of both the 'balanced' nature of the term and of the fact that it has not been included to

---

73   e.g. H. Beale, 'The Directive on Unfair Terms in Consumer Contracts' in Beatson and Friedmann (eds), *Good Faith and Fault in Contract Law*, 1995, p. 244; S. Bright (2000) 20 LS 331.

take advantage of the consumer.[74] However, care should be taken with that factor—terms may impact very differently in the consumer and the commercial contexts.

The list and types of unfair terms

11.53   As has already been mentioned, the unfair terms regime contains a grey list of terms which 'may be unfair'. In UTCCR 1999 this is in Sch 2 and reflects the Directive. The list in the draft Consumer Rights Bill is very similar, although the language has been made clearer at points, and there are some changes to the list, to cover the type of situation encountered in *Ashbourne* (see para. **11.33**ff) and also some additional terms dealing, broadly speaking, with terms providing for variations in the contract by the trader. The list in Sch 2 is set out at para. **11.55**, but a few preliminary points should first be made. After the list has been set out, consideration will be given to some broad types of unfair term.

11.54   The first point to be emphasized is that in the draft Consumer Rights Bill, the list is given a new importance. If a term falls within the listed terms, it cannot be ousted from the application of the fairness test by the core exemption. However, in relation to whether the terms falling within the list are unfair, the list does not even reverse the burden of proof in the application of the fairness test. It has, nevertheless, been seen as of considerable significance in relation to whether a term is unfair. The OFT has said:[75]

> 'It is the most authoritative guide to what fairness entails. It is not a "black list" but the exact shade of grey is debatable. Our view is that if a term appears in the list it is under substantial suspicion, but that correspondence with an item in the list cannot of itself determine the issue of unfairness.'

This not only indicates the importance of the list as a guide to which terms will be unfair, but also emphasizes that ultimately it is the fairness test itself which must determine the issue. The list is not exhaustive. 'Exclusion from the [grey list] cannot be seen as forming any sort of "white list". Any standard term will be seen as being unfair whether or not it appears in . . . the list, if it fails the' fairness test.[76] The list is drafted in ways which makes its boundaries unclear. First, the terms referred to in the list are stated by reference to their 'object or effect', so that its content is not based simply on form, which has the benefit of helping to prevent it being avoided just by form of a clause being changed, but does not help with certainty. Secondly, the list often contains factors of assessment. Paragraph 1(b), covering exemption clauses, for example, refers to terms which have the object or effect of '*inappropriately* excluding or limiting the rights of the consumer . . .' (emphasis added). Of course, the need to make such an assessment, to ascertain if a term falls within the scope of para. 1(b), should strengthen the argument that a term is unfair,

74   Macdonald (2002) 65 MLR 97.

75   OFT Bulletin 4 at p. 22.

76   OFT Bulletin 5 at p. 10.

if it clearly does. However, the additional significance given to the list by the draft Consumer Rights Bill, in relation to the core exemption, may make such uncertainties points of continual dispute.

11.55   The grey list itself should now be considered.

'SCHEDULE 2

Indicative and Non-Exhaustive List of Terms which may be Regarded as Unfair

1   Terms which have the object or effect of—

(a)   excluding or limiting the legal liability of a seller or supplier in the event of the death of a consumer or personal injury to the latter resulting from an act or omission of that seller or supplier;

(b)   inappropriately excluding or limiting the legal rights of the consumer vis-à-vis the seller or supplier or another party in the event of total or partial non-performance or inadequate performance by the seller or supplier of any of the contractual obligations, including the option of offsetting a debt owed to the seller or supplier against any claim which the consumer may have against him;

(c)   making an agreement binding on the consumer whereas provision of services by the seller or supplier is subject to a condition whose realisation depends on his own will alone;

(d)   permitting the seller or supplier to retain sums paid by the consumer where the latter decides not to conclude or perform the contract, without providing for the consumer to receive compensation of an equivalent amount from the seller or supplier where the latter is the party cancelling the contract;

(e)   requiring any consumer who fails to fulfil his obligation to pay a disproportionately high sum in compensation;

(f)   authorising the seller or supplier to dissolve the contract on a discretionary basis where the same facility is not granted to the consumer, or permitting the seller or supplier to retain the sums paid for services not yet supplied by him where it is the seller or supplier himself who dissolves the contract;

(g)   enabling the seller or supplier to terminate a contract of indeterminate duration without reasonable notice except where there are serious grounds for doing so;

(h)   automatically extending a contract of fixed duration where the consumer does not indicate otherwise, when the deadline fixed for the consumer to express his desire not to extend the contract is unreasonably early;

(i)   irrevocably binding the consumer to terms with which he had no real opportunity of becoming acquainted before the conclusion of the contract;

(j)   enabling the seller or supplier to alter the terms of the contract unilaterally without a valid reason which is specified in the contract;

(k)   enabling the seller or supplier to alter unilaterally without a valid reason any characteristics of the product or service to be provided;

(l)   providing for the price of goods to be determined at the time of delivery or allowing a seller of goods or supplier of services to increase their price without in both cases giving the consumer the corresponding right to cancel the contract if the final price is too high in relation to the price agreed when the contract was concluded;

(m) giving the seller or supplier the right to determine whether the goods or services supplied are in conformity with the contract, or giving him the exclusive right to interpret any term of the contract;

(n)   limiting the seller's or supplier's obligation to respect commitments undertaken by his agents or making his commitments subject to compliance with a particular formality;

(o)   obliging the consumer to fulfil all his obligations where the seller or supplier does not perform his;

(p)   giving the seller or supplier the possibility of transferring his rights and obligations under the contract, where this may serve to reduce the guarantees for the consumer, without the latter's agreement;

(q)   excluding or hindering the consumer's right to take legal action or exercise any other legal remedy, particularly by requiring the consumer to take disputes exclusively to arbitration not covered by legal provisions, unduly restricting the evidence available to him or imposing on him a burden of proof which, according to the applicable law, should lie with another party to the contract.

2 Scope of paragraphs 1(g), (j) and (l)

(a)   Paragraph 1(g) is without hindrance to terms by which a supplier of financial services reserves the right to terminate unilaterally a contract of indeterminate duration without notice where there is a valid reason, provided that the supplier is required to inform the other contracting party or parties thereof immediately.

(b)   Paragraph 1(j) is without hindrance to terms under which a supplier of financial services reserves the right to alter the rate of interest payable by the consumer or due to the latter, or the amount of other charges for financial services without notice where there is a valid reason, provided that the supplier is required to inform the other contracting party or parties thereof at the earliest opportunity and that the latter are free to dissolve the contract immediately.

Paragraph 1(j) is also without hindrance to terms under which a seller or supplier reserves the right to alter unilaterally the conditions of a contract of indeterminate duration, provided that he is required to inform the consumer with reasonable notice and that the consumer is free to dissolve the contract.

(c)   Paragraphs 1(g), (j) and (l) do not apply to:
  • transactions in transferable securities, financial instruments and other products or services where the price is linked to fluctuations in a stock exchange quotation or index or a financial market rate that the seller or supplier does not control;
  • contracts for the purchase or sale of foreign currency, traveller's cheques or international money orders denominated in foreign currency.

> **(d)**   Paragraph 1(1) is without hindrance to price indexation clauses, where lawful,
>   provided that the method by which prices vary is explicitly described.'

11.56   Certain groupings of types of terms can be identified in the list. Paragraphs 1(a), (b), and (q) of the list, for example, clearly encompass exemption clauses. There are also paragraphs which will encompass clauses falling within the common law rules dealing with penalty clauses or which raise related issues (paras 1(d) and (e)—see para. **11.60**). In addition, several of the paragraphs can be identified as relating to clauses conferring an inappropriate discretion on the seller or supplier in relation to performance (for example, paras 1(j), (k), and (l)).[77]

Exemption clauses

11.57   Several paragraphs of the grey list, as has been mentioned, clearly relate to exemption clauses (paras 1(a), (b), (q)) and others will also overlap with the application of the Unfair Contract Terms Act 1977. It should not be forgotten that the Consumer Rights Bill will maintain the automatic ineffectiveness which UCTA has provided for some exemption clauses, such as those excluding or restricting liability for negligently caused death or personal injury.

Some consideration can be given to the factors which have proved important in determining 'reasonableness' under the 1977 Act—they may prove helpful in identifying unfairness under the unfair terms regime. However, in making any such analogies, care must be taken in moving from the business-to-business contracts, which have often been the context for consideration of the 'requirement of reasonableness' under the 1977 Act, to the consumer contracts which fall to be addressed under the unfair terms regime. Some comparisons, nevertheless, may prove helpful.

11.58   Under UCTA 1977, insurance has been identified as a key element in relation to the 'requirement of reasonableness'. It has been relevant to ask which party was in the best position to insure, the cost of insurance, whether the placement of that cost has been reflected in the price charged, and the overall impact of the clause (see para. **10.78**ff). Such factors may also be relevant in relation to the fairness test—a redrafted clause by a security firm stated (OFT Bulletin 4 (Chubb Alarms Ltd)):

> 'Our liability under this agreement—We do not know the value of the contents of your premises. You do (or should) know the value of the contents in your premises. Since the loss or damage you might suffer will probably be more than the amounts we can reasonably charge you, and because we are giving you the chance to discuss and agree different amounts from those set out in the following paragraphs of this clause, we will limit our liability to those amounts (unless we agree in writing to change those limits).'

---

[77] For a full consideration of the paragraphs of the list, see E. Macdonald, *Exemption Clauses and Unfair Terms*, 2nd edn, Tottel, 2006, pp. 249–81.

Consideration will need to be given to the most appropriate party to insure and also to the likelihood of the consumer understanding the need to insure. In addition, even if such understanding is likely to be present, the likelihood of insurance cover being taken out, may be relevant. There may be unfairness if, by using a term placing the need to insure on the consumer, the supplier reduces the price slightly for all consumers, but at a risk of placing very significant risk on the small number of consumers for whom it may materialize and who may well not have insured.[78]

11.59   Again, in the context of the Unfair Contract Terms Act 1977, the availability or otherwise, of an alternative contract has been a significant indicator of whether an exemption clause satisfies the requirement of reasonableness. In the situation where a cheap photographic developing service was provided on the basis of an extensive exemption clause, the clause was, nevertheless, held not to satisfy the Act's requirement of reasonableness against the background of an industry practice that an alternative service should also be offered—one involving a higher price and the potential for greater liability (*Woodman* v *Photo Trade Processing* (1981)). In contrast, limiting liability in relation to the sale of seed potatoes was seen as reasonable when the farmer had been given a choice of paying a higher price for seed involving less risk of disease (*RW Green Ltd* v *Cade Bros Farms* (1978)). However, under the Act, the reality of the alternative has been considered so that the existence of a safer alternative, which most consumers could not afford, was not viewed as rendering an exemption clause reasonable (*Smith* v *Eric S Bush* (1990)). Similar factors might be considered under UTCCR 1999. A realistic choice, properly drawn to the consumer's attention, might be seen as relevant to the question of good faith. The provision of such an alternative could be seen as indicating a seller or supplier who takes account of the interests of the consumer. In addition, such an alternative could also be relevant to the question of 'significant imbalance'—the alternatives might draw attention to the balancing elements in the different contracts.

Penalty and related clauses

11.60   Paragraphs 1(d) and (e) of UTCCR 1999, Sch 2 overlap with the rules dealing with penalty and related clauses. Parties to a contract may specify that upon a particular breach occurring the breaching party is to pay a specified sum in damages. If the clause is a genuine liquidated damages clause it will be enforceable—it will have been beneficial in providing certainty for the parties. However, if it is not 'a genuine pre-estimate of loss' but a sum set in terrorem of the breaching party to compel performance, it will be classified as a penalty clause and the injured party will only be able to recover to the extent of their actual loss (*Dunlop Pneumatic Tyre Co. Ltd* v *New Garage and Motor Co. Ltd* (1915). See, further, para. **20.69**ff). However, the application of the penalty clause rule is very dependent upon the form of the clause. Basically it only applies to clauses under which a specified payment is to be made on a breach occurring.

---

78 See Beale, 'The Directive on Unfair Terms in Consumer Contracts' in Beatson and Freidman (eds), *Good Faith and Fault in Contract Law*, 1995, p. 243. For an example, in the context of the Unfair Contract Terms Act 1977, see *Smith v Eric S Bush* (1990)—see para. **10.81**.

This has led to frequent evasion of the rule through a clause having the same effect as a penalty clause but drafted in a different form. Avoidance could also be achieved if the event triggering the payment was labelled as a variation of performance, rather than a breach, and that led Lord Denning to comment in *Bridge v Campbell Discount Co. Ltd* [1962] 1 All ER 385 (at 399):

> 'Let no one mistake the injustice of this. It means that equity commits itself to this absurd paradox; it will grant relief to a man who breaks his contract but will penalise the man who keeps it.'

Such anomalies were due to the dependence upon the form of the clause to determine the application of the rule. The common law has now mitigated the problem in relation to deposits—allowing the recovery of 'unreasonable deposits' (*Workers Trust and Merchant Bank* v *Dojap Investments Ltd* (1993)), but in the consumer context, the unfair terms regime presents a broader potential for tackling the problem, depending on the scope given to the relevant parts of the grey list, and the core exemption. In *Bairstow Eves London Central* v *Smith* (2004) a contract with estate agents labelled 3 per cent as the 'standard commission rate', and 1.5 per cent the 'early payment discounted rate'. The standard rate became payable if the estate agents were not paid at the 'discounted rate' within ten days of the sale, which in this case they were not, due to a mistake by the purchaser's solicitors. Gross J concluded that the 3 per cent term was not covered by the core exemption. He thought it 'plain that both parties contemplated an agreed operative price of 1.5 per cent with a default provision of 3 per cent' (the market for estate agents was such that the estate agents recognized that they were unlikely to obtain business at 3 per cent and the negotiations had focused on 1.5 per cent).

Seller/supplier's discretion

11.61   Several of the paragraphs of the 'grey list' refer to clauses conferring a discretion on the seller or supplier as to the performance of the contract (for example, paras 1(f), (g), (j), (k), (l)). Some discretion may be appropriate, but it should be set within limited boundaries to be considered fair. For example, a roadside breakdown service originally used a clause which stated (OFT Bulletin 3 (Britannia Rescue Services)):

> 'We may cancel membership at any time by sending seven days' notice by recorded delivery to your last known address and in such event you will receive a pro rata refund of your subscription, unless the service has been used.'

The OFT viewed that as 'potentially unfair . . . since it allowed [the business] to cancel contracts on a discretionary basis and thus to get out of a bad bargain' (Bulletin 3 at p. 26). The clause was redrafted to allow the business to cancel in limited circumstances, where the service might be seen as being used inappropriately:

> 'If excessive use of the service has occurred through failure to seek permanent repair following any temporary repair effected by an agent or due to lack of routine vehicle maintenance,

we may cancel membership by sending seven days' notice by recorded delivery to your last known address.'

Another example is provided by the contract of a supplier and installer of kitchens. In that contract, a clause was seen as 'of questionable fairness' in the light of para. 1(k) (OFT Bulletin 1 (Moben Kitchens)). The original clause stated:

'If, for any reason, the Company is unable to supply a particular item of furniture or a particular appliance, the Company will notify the Customer. The Company will normally replace it with an item of equivalent or superior standard and value.'

The clause was revised to state:

'If, for any reason beyond the Company's control, the Company is unable to supply a particular item of furniture or a particular appliance, the Company will notify the Customer. With the agreement of the Customer the Company will replace it with an item of superior standard and value.'

The revised clause was seen as an 'improvement' as it specified that the substitution must be for reasons 'beyond the company's reasonable control' and required the consumer's consent to the change. The former restriction should be emphasized. The OFT has stated that 'a term which would allow the supplier to vary what is supplied at will—rather than because of bona fide external circumstances—is unlikely to be fair even if customers have a right of cancellation and refund'.[79]

11.62　Some indication of the correctness of the OFT's basic approach to clauses conferring a wide discretion on the seller or supplier was provided in *Peabody Trust Governors* v *Reeve* (2008). The clause was one giving a 'social landlord' 'almost carte blanche in the field of variations apart from the areas of rent and statutory protection' (at [56]). The judge took the line (at [54]–[55]):

'54. Although the Court is in no sense bound by the guidance provided by the Office of Fair Trading (OFT 356 "Guidance on unfair terms in tenancy agreements"), . . . that guidance does give landlords helpful commonsense indications of what is likely to be considered to be fair and should be carefully taken into account when drafting a variation clause in a tenancy agreement.

55. For example, the OFT must be right in saying (at para 3.89) that a term is likely to be objectionable if it "gives the landlord a broad discretion that could be used to impose new restrictions, penalties or burdens unexpectedly on the tenant." By contrast, a term allowing for variations is less likely to be thought unfair if "its effect is narrowed, so that it can be used to vary terms to reflect changes in the law, for example, rather than be used to change the balance of advantage under the contract?"'. (at para 3.92).

---

79 OFT, *Unfair Contract Terms Guidance* (February 2001) para. 11.7.

With such an extreme clause, as the one in this case, the landlord could not use their status as a 'social landlord', whom it was argued could 'be trusted only to impose reasonable and proper variations' (at [56]), to convince the court that the term was fair (although it was viewed as a relevant factor). Nor did it help the landlord to argue that if tenants did not like new terms, they could terminate the lease and go elsewhere. The point was made that 'in the case of relatively low cost housing operated by a registered social landlord, this is unrealistic. The tenant will typically have a strong necessity, will be of relatively limited means, may well lack experience and familiarity with contractual terms and will have a very weak bargaining position' (at [45] and see [57]).

11.63   In the *Invitel* case[80] the ECJ considered a clause dealing with the mechanism for amending the price and, in the light of paras 1(j) and (l), and 2(b) and (d), of the grey list, stressed the importance to the fairness test of the term setting out 'the reason for, and the method of the variation of the price' and of the consumer having the right to cancel. Further, it was seen as of 'fundamental importance' to the fairness test whether it was possible for the 'consumer to foresee, on the basis of clear intelligible criteria, the amendments . . . to the fees connected to the service' (at [24]–[28]).[81]

Transparency and visibility of terms

The Directive

11.64   Article 5 of the Directive states

> 'In the case of contracts where all or certain terms offered to the consumer are in writing, these terms must always be drafted in plain intelligible language. Where there is doubt about the written meaning of a term, the interpretation most favourable to the consumer shall prevail. This rule on interpretation shall not apply in the context of the procedures laid down in Article 7(2).'

This is reflected in reg 7 of the 1999 Regulations. Although Article 5 obviously contains an interpretation rule, it also raises issues about whether there is a separate requirement of 'plain intelligible language', and, when read in the light of Recital 20, whether the question should actually be about a broader requirement, relating not merely to plain intelligible language, but also to a requirement that the consumer be provided with an opportunity to examine the terms. We need to look at these issues further, but before we do so, it should be emphasized that, as we have already seen, 'plain intelligible language' is very important in relation to another part of the Directive/Regulations. The core exemption in the Directive does not apply if the relevant terms are not in 'plain intelligible language'. This is repeated in the Regulations, but the draft

---

80 *Nemzeti Fogyasztovedelmi Hatosag v Invitel Tavkozlezl ZRT* C-472/10 (2012).

81 In *Du Plessis v Fontgary Leisure Parks Ltd* (2012) the annual review mechanism in relation to the licence fee for a holiday caravan pitch, having stated some specific factors then referred to 'any other relevant factor'. The term was held fair by the Court of Appeal. There were multiple factors indicating fairness, but the case was decided before *Invitel*.

Consumer Rights Bill would make it more demanding, with the relevant terms needing not only to be 'transparent', but also 'prominent'.[82]

Interpretation

11.65   Plainly Article 5 contains a rule of construction. (Although in focusing on interpreting a term to determine its meaning to decide if what it actually does is fair, it should not be forgotten that its lack of clarity may itself be indicative of unfairness.) Such a rule is also to be found in the Regulations in reg 7(2), and indeed in the draft Consumer Rights Bill.[83] The reference to 'art 7' is to general, rather than individual level of enforcement, so that the rule of construction in Article 5, and in its implementing domestic provision, is concerned with construction in the context of a dispute between a particular consumer and seller or supplier. In that context, it may simply be viewed as a version of the familiar common law contra proferentem rule: that any ambiguity in a clause will be construed against the person putting it forward (see para. **9.69**ff). It has, however, been viewed as extending to the situation where the contract contains two contradictory terms, allowing the term favourable to the consumer to prevail (*Peabody trust Governors* v *Reeve* (2008) at [33]).

11.66   In relation to interpretation at the more general level, in *EC Commission* v *Spain* C-70/03 (2004), the ECJ envisaged an 'objective' interpretation. That seems to mean that neither a favourable nor unfavourable interpretation to the consumer is taken. Rather, it seems simply to envisage the objectively most likely interpretation being used.

Requirement

11.67   Article 5 seems not only to contain a rule about construction, but also a requirement that terms be drafted in 'plain intelligible language', and its implementation in reg 7 points more strongly in that direction.[84] However, the Directive/Regulations did not provide any mechanism for enforcement of such a 'requirement', and its existence as a requirement, as such, was therefore open to dispute. An additional enforcement mechanism was brought in at the general level, with Part 8 of the Enterprise Act 2002 allowing certain 'enforcers', including the OFT, to apply for enforcement orders in relation to certain consumer protection legislation, including the Unfair Terms Regulations, where the infringement harmed 'the collective interests of consumers'. It was contended that this extended to the question of 'plain intelligible language', providing the enforcement mechanism needed to view it properly as a requirement. The draft Consumer Rights Bill addresses this long disputed aspect of the unfair terms regime. The CMA, and the other general enforcers, are specifically able to apply for an injunction to deal with terms which are not 'transparent', as if they were unfair.[85]

82 Clause 69.

83 Clause 72.

84 '7(1) A seller or supplier shall ensure that any written term of a contract is expressed in plain, intelligible language.
(2) If there is doubt about the meaning of a written term, the interpretation which is most favourable to the consumer shall prevail.

85 Clause 71(1) and Sch 3, para. 3(5).

11.68 In addition, Recital 20 of the Directive states:

> 'Whereas contracts should be drafted in plain, intelligible language, the consumer should actually be given an opportunity to examine all the terms and, if in doubt, the interpretation most favourable to the consumer should prevail.'

Thus in Recital 20, we find the idea of the need for terms to be in 'plain intelligible language' intertwined with that of their availability to the consumer, and it takes but a moment's thought to conclude that it is little assistance to the consumer if a term is very plainly drafted, if it is 'hidden away'. Indeed a technical opportunity to examine a term is of little assistance if it is, for example, in a mass of small print. The draft Consumer Rights Bill extends the power of the OFT, and the other general enforcers beyond enforcement of a requirement that terms be 'transparent'. It also states that 'If a term is especially onerous or unusual, the trader must ensure that the term is drawn particularly to the consumer's attention'.[86]

⬡ Summary

- The Unfair Terms in Consumer Contracts Regulations 1999 are derived from the European Directive on unfair terms, which they mirror, and basically impose a fairness test on non-individually negotiated terms in contracts between consumers and sellers or suppliers. There is now a draft Consumer Rights Bill to replace them. The Bill encompasses individually negotiated terms.

- The fairness of terms can be challenged under the Regulations by the individual consumer or at the general level by the OFT or other qualifying body. Under the Consumer Rights Bill, the CMA replaces the OFT as the primary general enforcer.

- There is an overlap between the Regulations and UCTA 1977 but also significant differences. The draft Consumer Rights Bill is intended to provide a single unfair terms regime for consumers.

- There is a 'core exemption' from the fairness test for terms defining the main subject matter of the contract and also for price terms, provided they are in plain intelligible language. (The exemption for price terms only extends to one aspect of a challenge to their fairness. The fairness of price terms cannot be challenged in relation to whether the contract is value for money.) The scope of the core exemption has proved to be highly controversial.

- A term is unfair if, contrary to the requirement of good faith, it causes a significant imbalance in the rights and obligations of the parties to the detriment of the consumer. There is also a 'grey list' of terms which may be unfair (Sch 2 of the Regulations).

---

86 Clause 71(3). It is to be hoped that this is extended during the passage of the draft Bill, to cover terms which are 'especially unreasonable or unusual'. The reference to 'onerous' would appear to be a reflection of the later statements of the 'red hand rule', in cases such as *Interfoto* where the terms were 'onerous'. That categorization was easy to fall into, as UCTA was likely to deal with unreasonable terms which were not onerous. That should not, however, inappropriately restrict this requirement, which is intended to operate alongside a 'fairness' test the application of which is not limited to exemption clauses.

- The draft Consumer Rights Directive will ensure that terms which its 'grey list' covers are subject to the fairness test; they will not be ousted from the application of that test by the core exemption.

▶ Further reading

H. Beale, 'Unfair Contracts in Britain and Europe' [1989] 42 CLP 197

H. Beale, 'Legislative Control of Fairness: The Directive on Unfair Terms in Consumer Contracts' in J. Beatson and D. Friedmann (eds), *Good Faith and Fault in Contract Law*, Oxford University Press, 1995, pp. 231–62

H. Beale, 'Unfair Terms in Contracts: Proposals for Reform in the UK' (2004) 27 Journal of Consumer Policy 289

S. Bright, 'Winning the Battle Against Unfair Contract Terms' (2000) 20 LS 331

M. Chen-Wishart, 'Transparency and Fairness in Bank Charges' (2010) 126 LQR 157

H. Collins, 'Good Faith in European Contract Law' (1994) 14 OJLS 229

Law Commission and Scottish Law Commission, *Unfair Terms in Contracts*, Law Com Consultation Paper No 166, Scot Law Com Discussion Paper No 119

Law Commission and Scottish Law Commission, *Unfair Terms in Contracts*, Law Com No 292, Scot Law Com No 199

Law Commission and Scottish Law Commission, *Unfair Terms in Consumer Contracts: A new approach?* Issues Paper (July 2012)

Law Commission and Scottish Law Commission, *Unfair Terms in Consumer Contracts: Advice to the Deparment for Business, Innovation and Skills* (March 2013)

E. Macdonald, 'Unifying Unfair Terms Legislation' (2004) 67 MLR 69

E. Macdonald, 'The "Core Exemption" From the Fairness Test in Unfair Terms Legislation' (2012) 29 JCL 121

P. Morgan, 'Bank Charges and the Unfair Terms in Consumer Contracts Regulations 1999; the end of the road for consumers?' [2010] LMCLQ 21

S. Whittaker, 'Unfair Contract Terms, Public Services and the Construction of a European Conception of Contract' (2000) 116 LQR 95

S. Whittaker, 'Unfair Terms, Unfair Prices and Bank Charges' (2011) 74 MLR 106

Chapter 12

Mistake

⊙ Introduction

12.1   There is much dispute about the scope and content of a chapter on the subject of mistake in the law of contract.[1] For this reason the reader will perhaps find more variety in the treatment of this topic than in any other area of contract law. One, or both, of the parties to a contract may enter into it under some misunderstanding or mistake. For example, S agrees to sell his car to B for £2,000. Unknown to both parties, the car, whilst parked in the street, has been totally wrecked by a bus colliding with it, shortly before the contract was made. This is traditionally known as 'common mistake'; both parties are under the same misapprehension. Alternatively, S offers to sell his 'surfing equipment' to B, who accepts. S intends to sell his surfboard, but B thinks the offer relates to S's windsurfboard. In this instance, where the parties are at cross-purposes, it is described as a case of 'mutual mistake', i.e. each party wrongly believes that the other has agreed to his terms.

12.2   In contrast to the above examples, in which both parties are mistaken, there is also the category of 'unilateral mistake'. This occurs when one party enters into a contract under some mistake, but the other party is aware of this. For example, A intends to contract with B, but later discovers that the other party to the apparent agreement is, in fact, C. In cases of unilateral mistake, there is normally some misrepresentation or fraud involved, and this leads us to an important point. The subject of mistake in contract law cannot be easily divided off from other related subjects. So where parties are at cross-purposes, or where one party enters into a contract having mistaken the identity of the other party, these types of mistake relate to the

---

1   e.g., see C. J. Slade, 'Myth of Mistake in the English Law of Contract' (1954) 70 LQR 385; and P. Atiyah, *Introduction to the Law of Contract*, 5th edn, Oxford University Press, 1995, ch. 12. See also D. Friedmann, 'The Objective Principle and Mistake and Involuntariness in Contract and Restitution' (2003) 119 LQR 68 at 92–3.

formation of contracts: that is, have the parties reached a binding agreement? In short, such instances may be described as 'agreement mistakes'.

12.3   Where the parties are both mistaken about the same fact, such as a contract for the sale of goods which no longer exist, there is no dispute about agreement. These cases involve the issue of 'performability'. This subject raises fundamental questions about the extent of contractual obligations (see *Great Peace Shipping Ltd* v *Tsavliris Salvage (International) Ltd* (2003)). In other words, are contractual obligations absolute or can a party escape liability if he or she is unable to perform through no fault of his or her own? As some writers have observed, the subjects of performability and the extent of contractual obligations suggest a close connection between mistake in the law of contract and the doctrine of frustration (see **Chapter 19**, and also the comments of Lord Phillips in *Great Peace Shipping Ltd* at [73]–[75]). In the hypothetical instance given earlier, if the car, which was the subject of the agreement, was destroyed immediately after the contract was concluded (through no fault of either party), would the parties be discharged from the contract? (For an interesting case which shows the sometimes arbitrary distinction between mistake and frustration, see *Amalgamated Investment & Property Co Ltd* v *John Walker & Sons Ltd* (1976).)

12.4   Although there are, traditionally, various subdivisions of mistake in the law of contract, the subject can be more helpfully divided into two broad categories: mistake relating to agreement, and mistake relating to the performability of the contract. The subject of mistake cannot be entirely separated from a number of related issues in the law of contract, as we have seen, but it is consistent with decisions of the courts and with the opinion of the majority of writers on the subject, to devote a separate chapter to this area of law. This is not to imply, however, that the case law and the traditional approach to the subject are not open to criticism.

Narrow view of mistake in contract law

12.5   The word 'mistake' has a narrower meaning in contract law than it does in everyday language. Parties will not be easily discharged from their contractual undertakings simply because they entered into the contract under some mistake or misunderstanding, or made a bad bargain (see *Clarion Ltd* v *National Provident Institution* (2000)). In the interests of certainty and commercial convenience, parties are bound by their apparent agreements. It will be remembered that the law takes a predominantly objective view of agreement. It is not, in general, the subjective intention of the parties with which the law is concerned, but rather, what can be inferred from their conduct.[2] This principle is well illustrated in *Centrovincial Estates plc* v *Merchant Investors Assurance Co. Ltd* (1983):

> C had let several floors of an office building to the Food, Drink, and Tobacco Training Board, who underlet one floor to D at a rent of £68,320 per year. Under a rent review clause, it was provided that the rent paid by D should be increased at a later date (25 December 1982) to the current market rental value. On 22 June 1982 (by which date the Board was thinking of a

---

2   For a detailed discussion of intention in the law of contract, see A. De Moor (1990) 106 LQR 632. Also, see D. Friedmann (2003) 119 LQR 68.

surrender to C of the lease), a firm of solicitors wrote to D, on behalf of C and the Board, inviting D to agree to a figure of £65,000 per year as the correct rental value at the review date. D accepted this proposal the following day. On 28 June, a partner in the firm of solicitors telephoned D to say that the letter of 22 June contained an error and that C had intended to propose a rent of £126,000 per year. D refused to agree to this corrected proposal and claimed that there was a binding contract concluded by the two letters of 22 and 23 June. C claimed that the parties had failed to reach agreement on the current rental value and that the matter should be referred to an independent surveyor, as provided for in the rent review clause. In other words, it was denied by C that the exchange of letters had resulted in a binding agreement. C argued that there was no meeting of the minds due to the error.

The Court of Appeal rejected C's contention and explained, *obiter*, the correct approach to such a mistake, stating:

'It was contrary to the well established principles in contract law to suggest that the offeror under a bilateral contract could withdraw an unambiguous offer, after it had been accepted in the manner contemplated by the offer, merely because he had made a mistake which the offeree neither knew nor could reasonably have known at the time when he accepted it.'

Thus the law tends to uphold apparent agreements, even if one or both of the parties would not have entered into the contract if the true facts had been realized. Mistake, at common law, operates within strict limits. Where it is applicable, it operates in an inflexible way so as to render the whole transaction void from the start (ab initio). For example, if A sells goods to B and the contract is rendered void due to the doctrine of mistake, and B sells the goods to C, a bona fide purchaser for value, the goods can be recovered by A. This may cause hardship to C and will appear unfair, so the doctrine of mistake at common law cannot be invoked lightly. (Whether a separate, more flexible, equitable jurisdiction exists will be considered later in this chapter.)

Agreement mistake

Mistake as to identity

12.6   A difficult problem arises where S intends to sell goods to Y, but later discovers that the other party to the apparent agreement is, in fact, X. This situation is usually described as one of unilateral mistake: only one party is mistaken, as a result of some fraudulent misrepresentation by the other. In a typical example of this sort of case, S will have parted with goods in return for a cheque which turns out to be worthless. A contract can be set aside for such a fraudulent misrepresentation, but X, the 'rogue' (to use the time-honoured description), will normally have resold the goods to someone else (B) before the contract can be avoided by S.

12.7   What is the legal effect of such a mistake? The difficulty lies in deciding which of either S or B owns the goods. As long as B is a bona fide purchaser for value, and not a party to the rogue's fraud, there are two innocent people claiming ownership. Both have been duped by the rogue, who has normally disappeared by the time the fraud is discovered. The legal action which usually follows is in the law of tort, i.e. S sues B for conversion in an attempt to recover the property.

12.8   To succeed in such a claim, S must show that there was no contract between himself and the rogue; that any apparent agreement was negatived by the mistake as to identity induced by the fraud. If S can show there was no contract whatsoever with the rogue, then title to the goods does not pass to the rogue and therefore B does not acquire title (ownership) from the rogue. Under s 21(1) of the Sale of Goods Act 1979 it is stated that where goods are sold by a person who is not their owner, and who does not have the owner's consent or authority to do so, the person buying from him will not (generally) acquire title to the goods. Thus S will attempt to prove that the apparent agreement with the rogue was void as a result of a mistake as to identity. As a consequence, an innocent purchaser buying from the rogue will not become the owner of the property.

12.9   On the other hand, B will assert that there was a valid contract between S and the rogue, which was merely voidable for fraud. If this view is accepted, then the rogue has a voidable title to the goods, and if the contract has not been avoided (set aside) at the time when B purchases the goods from the rogue, B will acquire title to them (see Sale of Goods Act 1979, s 23). The law has the difficult choice between protecting the owner of property, and upholding commercial transactions in the interests of certainty. (For further discussion, see A. Foster, 'Sale by a Non-Owner: Striking a Fair Balance between the Rights of the True Owner and a Buyer in Good Faith' (2004) Cov LJ 1.) It might be thought that some apportionment of the loss, between the two innocent parties, would provide the fairest solution to the problem—this suggestion is considered later. It must be emphasized that it is no comfort to either S or B to know that they have a remedy against the rogue, for he will normally have disappeared. If he is found, he probably has no money with which to compensate the injured parties.

12.10   The case law on this subject is far from satisfactory, with decisions based on fine (even tenuous) distinctions. Some of the leading authorities are considered in the sections which follow, together with a discussion of the important House of Lords' decision in *Shogun Finance Ltd* v *Hudson* (2003).

Identity or attributes?

12.11   Despite the fact that S has been tricked by the rogue into parting with the property, it can be recovered from a bona fide purchaser for value (B) only if S can show that he did not intend to deal with the rogue. The rogue must also be aware of S's mistake. But it may be difficult to say whether S's mistake is truly one as to the 'identity' of the person he is dealing with, or simply as to that person's 'attributes' (such as his creditworthiness). This fine distinction, and its practical importance, is well illustrated in the cases which follow. In the famous case of *Cundy* v *Lindsay* (1878) 3 App Cas 459:

Lindsay & Co. (C) were linen manufacturers, who received an order for a large quantity of handkerchiefs from a rogue named Alfred Blenkarn. Blenkarn had business premises in the same street as a reputable company, Blenkiron & Co., and he signed his letters to C in such a way that the name of his firm looked like 'Blenkiron' rather than 'Blenkarn'. C knew Blenkiron & Co. to be a reputable business, and sent the handkerchiefs to the rogue thinking that they were dealing with Blenkiron & Co. (the invoices were headed 'Messrs. Blenkiron and Co., London'). Before Blenkarn's fraud was discovered—he was later convicted of obtaining goods by deception—he sold 250 dozen handkerchiefs to Cundy (D), an innocent purchaser. C sued D for the return of the goods.

In order to succeed, Lindsay & Co. had to show that there was no contract between themselves and the rogue, Blenkarn. (For an interesting analysis of the case and its historical background, see C. MacMillan, 'Rogues, Swindlers and Cheats: the Development of Mistake of Identity in English Contract Law' (2005) 64 CLJ 711.) For, if no contract existed, Blenkarn did not have title to the goods, and therefore none could be acquired by Cundy. In contrast, if there was a valid contract between C and the rogue, which was merely voidable for fraud, then title would pass to D as a bona fide purchaser for value. It was decided by the House of Lords that there was no contract between Lindsay and the rogue, as they intended to deal not with him, but with the respectable firm of Blenkiron & Co. The identity of the person they were dealing with was crucial to the claimants and there was clearly an important mistake in this respect. This mistake was known to the rogue. Lord Cairns stated (at 465):

'Of [Blenkarn] they knew nothing, and of him they never thought. With him they never intended to deal. Their minds never, even for an instant of time rested upon him, and as between him and them there was no consensus of mind which could lead to any agreement or any contract whatever. As between him and them there was merely the one side to a contract, where, in order to produce a contract, two sides would be required.'

12.12   It must be remembered that the decision in *Cundy* v *Lindsay* (1878) protects the original owner of the property but places the loss (and considerable hardship) on the innocent purchaser for value. The mistake must be one of identity, where the identity of the other is regarded by the mistaken party as crucial at the time the contract is made. An interesting contrast is provided by *King's Norton Metal Co.* v *Edridge, Merrett & Co.* (1897):

King's Norton Metal (C), who were metal manufacturers, received a letter from 'Hallam & Co.' in Sheffield, ordering brass rivet wire. The letterhead on the order gave the appearance of a large and thriving company, depicting a large factory and listing a number of overseas depots. The goods were despatched to 'Hallam & Co.' but were never paid for. In fact, the impressive looking 'Hallam & Co.' was the fictitious creation of a rogue named Wallis. Before the fraud was discovered, Wallis had sold the goods to Edridge & Co. (D), who bought the metal in good faith. C sued D to recover damages for the conversion of these goods. In order to succeed, it had to be established that there was no contract between C and Wallis.

The Court of Appeal held that the contract was not void, on the ground of mistake, but was merely voidable for fraud. Accordingly, title (albeit voidable) passed to Wallis, and D acquired a good title from him. C had intended to contract with the writer of the letter. Wallis and

Hallam & Co. were, in fact, the same 'person' and therefore King's Norton Metal were not mistaken as to the identity of the person with whom they entered into a contract. They were mistaken only as to the creditworthiness or attributes of the person with whom they were dealing.

12.13　This distinction between a person's identity and his attributes is clearly a fine one. Some critics claim that the distinction is spurious. Lord Denning described it as 'a distinction without a difference' in *Lewis* v *Averay* (1972). More recently, in his dissenting opinion in *Shogun Finance Ltd* v *Hudson* (2003) at [5], Lord Nicholls stated that 'the distinction in outcome thus drawn between these two kinds of fraudulent misrepresentation, one as to "attributes" and the other as to "identity", is unconvincing. It has been described as a reproach to the law.' A person's name, as well as being the most important guide as to his identity, may also be one of his attributes. If a party to a contract gives a false name, and the other party regards the identity of the person he is dealing with as crucial, is this a mistake as to identity or as to attributes?

12.14　It is possible to distinguish the cases of *Cundy* v *Lindsay* (1878) and *King's Norton Metal* v *Edridge* (1897). In the former, there was a reputable company called Blenkiron & Co., of whom the claimant company had heard and with whom they clearly thought they were dealing. In the latter case, there was no 'Hallam & Co.', it being merely the fictitious creation of the rogue, Wallis. Had there actually been a company called Hallam & Co., and had this company been known by reputation to the claimants, then presumably the case would have been decided differently. But it is questionable whether the rights of an innocent purchaser for value, buying from the rogue, should depend on this rather tenuous distinction. It may well be difficult to say whether a particular mistake is one of identity or of attributes, and yet an innocent third party's rights turn on this assessment. In the other dissenting judgment in *Shogun Finance Ltd* v *Hudson* (2003) at [60], Lord Millett argued that the preferable solution should be to protect innocent third parties 'by treating the contract as voidable rather than void whether for fraud or for mistake'.

12.15　It might have been thought that there should be very few cases today where a person could successfully claim that his apparent contract with another is void due to a mistake as to the other's identity. (This is discussed further later in relation to *Shogun Finance Ltd* v *Hudson*.) In policy terms, it is a question as to which of the two innocent parties should bear the loss. It seems wholly wrong that the bona fide purchaser for value should suffer. (See C. Elliott, 'No Justice for Innocent Purchasers of Dishonestly Obtained Goods: *Shogun Finance* v *Hudson* (2004) JBL 381 at 386.) The original owner of the goods can always take more care before parting with goods on credit, but there is little that an innocent purchaser from the rogue can do. (Although see Lord Walker's speech in *Shogun Finance Ltd* v *Hudson* (2003) at [182], where he disagrees with this assertion, arguing that 'it would not be right to make any general assumption as to one innocent party being more deserving than the other'.) Also, it serves the interest of commercial certainty if contracts are upheld despite the mistake made by the original owner in parting with the goods to the rogue. It seems correct that there should be a heavy burden to be discharged by the owner to show that he took reasonable steps to check the identity of the person he was dealing with. He must also regard that person's identity as crucial, a requirement which was discussed in *Citibank NA* v *Brown Shipley & Co. Ltd* [1991] 2 All ER 690. The facts were:

> By telephone, a rogue tricked a bank (the 'issuing bank') into preparing a banker's draft drawn on a client company's account, of which the rogue claimed (fraudulently) to be a signatory. The banker's draft was made in favour of another bank (the 'receiving bank') which, labouring under the same deception, had innocently agreed to supply large amounts of foreign currency to the rogue. The issuing bank handed the draft to the rogue, mistakenly believing him to be a messenger for the bona fide company. In return he gave the bank a forged letter which purported to confirm the company's earlier telephone instructions. The rogue then presented the draft to the receiving bank which, after checking with the issuing bank that the draft was authentic, paid the money directly to the rogue. The receiving bank was then paid by the issuing bank on presentation of the draft. On discovering the fraud, the issuing bank sought to recover the value of the draft as damages in conversion by claiming that title in the draft had never passed to the receiving bank. In other words, it claimed that the rogue had never acquired good title to the draft and, therefore, neither had the receiving bank.

The issuing bank's claim was dismissed by Waller J, who held that the receiving bank did not convert the draft by presenting it for payment. He stated that the delivery of the authorized banker's draft from one bank to the other established a contract between the two banks. The fact that this delivery was brought about by the rogue did not affect the formation of a contract. (The rogue was merely a 'conduit pipe' through whom title did not need to pass.) Thus, the rogue's identity was not to be regarded as of fundamental importance in this situation. The judge stated (at 699–700):

> 'So far as authority is concerned, it will usually be very difficult for A to establish that it was of crucial importance to him who actually physically transported the draft to B. In this case, for example, delivery might have been done by post; it might have been done by one or other of the banks' messengers; it might have been done by some other messenger. It so happened that in this case that [sic] it was done by someone thought to be the customer or his messenger, but that was not of crucial importance. That being so, the authority, as it seems to me, albeit induced by fraud, would not be void; the authority would be actual, even if voidable.'

Waller J went on to state (at 700) that in this area of law 'each case rests on its own facts'. It is likely that the judge, in finding against the issuing bank, thought that it (rather than the receiving bank) was in a better position to protect itself against the risk of dealing with a rogue.

Parties dealing face to face

12.16 Issues of mistake and fraud have also arisen in a series of cases in which the parties were dealing face to face with each other. When parties are not physically in each other's presence, for example where someone receives a letter ordering goods, it is possible to imagine, as a result of some deception, how they could be mistaken as to the identity of the person placing the order (although it must be acknowledged that the seller has more time in such circumstances to check the identity of this person). But when the contract is made *inter praesentes* it might seem more difficult for the seller to claim that he did not intend to contract with the person who was physically present (for example, in a shop), but with some other person who was not present. In *Phillips* v *Brooks Ltd* [1919] 2 KB 243:

> A man named North called in person at C's shop and asked to look at some jewellery, eventually selecting some pearls and a ring. He then made out a cheque for the total amount and stated: 'You see who I am, I am Sir George Bullough' and he gave an address in St James' Square. C had heard of Sir George Bullough and checked the address in a directory. Being satisfied, C allowed the man to take away the ring, without the cheque (which was worthless) being cleared. North pledged the ring for £350 to the defendants, a firm of pawnbrokers, who were totally unaware of North's fraudulent conduct. C sued the pawnbrokers for the return of the ring, or alternatively, its value, claiming that he intended to contract only with Sir George and not the man who came into his shop.

In the High Court, Horridge J rejected this argument and found in favour of the defendants. There was not a mistake as to identity so as to render the contract void. There was a passing of property and the defendants acquired a good title to the ring. But would it not be fair to say that the jeweller thought he was dealing with Sir George? He certainly hoped that he was doing so, but he did take the risk that the man was not Sir George. The jeweller did not make a careful check on his customer's identity. Horridge J (at 246) was surely correct in concluding that 'although [C] believed the person to whom he was handing the ring was Sir George Bullough, he in fact contracted to sell and deliver it to the person who came into his shop'.

12.17   When the parties deal with each other face to face, there is a strong presumption that the seller intends to contract with the person who is physically present, and not the person that the rogue is purporting to be. Another way of expressing this point is to say that the mistake is not as to identity at all but as to the attributes of the person with whom the seller is dealing. In the majority of these cases the owner of the goods parts with them on credit or in return for a worthless cheque. What concerns the seller, then, is the creditworthiness of the person with whom he is dealing. Despite this correct statement of the law in *Phillips* v *Brooks Ltd* (1919), the law became confused by some of the cases that were decided later. For example, in *Lake* v *Simmons* [1927] AC 487:

> A jeweller (C) was induced by a woman, who came into his shop, into letting her have possession of two pearl necklets on approval. She fraudulently represented that she was the wife of a person of some substance (namely that she was 'Mrs Van der Borgh'), and that she wanted the necklets for the purpose of showing them to her husband, and to a purely fictitious person, for their approval with a view to purchase by them. She then disposed of the necklets for her own benefit. C claimed on his insurance for loss of the necklets by theft or dishonesty; but his policy excluded liability where the loss was incurred as a result of the dishonesty of a customer to whom the goods had been entrusted by the jeweller.

It was held that C's loss was covered by the insurance and that the exclusion clause did not defeat his claim. But the reasoning employed by the House of Lords is open to serious criticism (see the comments of Lord Phillips in *Shogun Finance Ltd* v *Hudson* (2003) at [141]). It was argued that C did not intend to deal with the woman who came into his shop and that there was no genuine consent by C to her obtaining possession of the necklets (see Viscount Haldane's speech at 500–1). The woman was not 'a customer' within the meaning of the exclusion clause, as C did not regard her as his customer, but rather he thought of the two men, to whom she claimed she would show the necklets, as his possible customers! Their Lordships concluded that there was no contract between C and the woman with whom he dealt face to face owing to a mistake as to her identity. (This is discussed further in *Citibank NA* v *Brown Shipley & Co Ltd* (1991)—see para. **12.15**.)

12.18   Another heavily criticized case, the facts of which are similar to *Phillips* v *Brooks Ltd* (1919), is *Ingram* v *Little* [1961] 1 QB 31:

> Elsie and Hilda Ingram were joint owners of a car, which they advertised for sale. A man, falsely calling himself 'Hutchinson', came to look at it and have a trial run. He then offered £717 to the women for their car, which they were willing to accept. However, he produced a cheque book to pay for the car, and it was then stated by Elsie Ingram that under no circumstances would they accept a cheque and that the proposed deal was off. The man told them he was PGM Hutchinson, of Stanstead House, Caterham, and that he had business interests in Guildford. Hilda Ingram checked in the directory that there was indeed a PGM Hutchinson residing at that address. The women then accepted the man's cheque in exchange for their car. The man was not PGM Hutchinson and the cheque was dishonoured. The rogue, in the meantime, had sold the car to the innocent defendant (D). The women now sought to recover the car, or its value, from D.

The Court of Appeal decided that the apparent contract between the claimants and the man who called at their house was void due to the mistake as to identity. The car still belonged to the women and D did not acquire good title from the rogue. The majority argued (with Lord Devlin dissenting) that although the identity of the man would have been unimportant as long as he had paid cash for the car, it became of crucial importance once the man wished to pay by cheque. The women refused to accept a cheque initially and they verified that there was a PGM Hutchinson listed at that address in the telephone directory. Therefore, their 'offer' was not addressed to the man who was in their presence, but to the real PGM Hutchinson (whom they had never met).

It is submitted that, in certain exceptional circumstances, it might be possible to argue that an offer was not made to the person identified by sight and hearing, but *Ingram* v *Little* is some way from coming within this category. (The court's decision might have been more defensible if the women had gone to Stanstead House to deal with the genuine Hutchinson and then been deceived on the premises by someone falsely pretending to be that person.)[3] It is difficult to

---

3   Consider *Hardman* v *Booth* (1863), which Pearce LJ, in *Ingram* v *Little*, accepted was a clearer case of there being no contract than *Ingram* v *Little* itself.

escape the conclusion that the court allowed its sympathy for the women to cloud its judgment of the issues. In his dissenting speech, Lord Devlin correctly pointed out that what should have concerned the women was the creditworthiness of the person they were dealing with and not his identity. He stated (at 68):

> 'The fact that [the rogue] gave P.G.M. Hutchinson's address in the directory was no proof that he was P.G.M. Hutchinson; and if he had been, that fact alone was no proof that his cheque would be met. Identity, therefore, did not really matter.'

It can hardly be claimed that the claimants took reasonable steps to check the identity of the person with whom they were dealing. But, more fundamentally, it can be argued that the material mistake in *Ingram* v *Little* was as to the man's attributes and not as to his identity. (This is not to deny that the women thought the man's identity was important.) In fact, there is little to distinguish the case from the earlier decision in *Phillips* v *Brooks*, which emphasized the need to protect the innocent purchaser for value who buys the goods from the rogue. *Ingram* v *Little* was perhaps too concerned with protecting the original owner of the goods. This is the dilemma which faces judges in cases of this sort. It has been cogently argued that the law should permit some division of the loss between the two innocent parties in such proportion as is just in all the circumstances (see Lord Devlin's comments in *Ingram* v *Little*). This solution did not find favour with the Law Reform Committee in 1966.[4] However, the Committee did recommend that 'where goods are sold under a mistake as to the buyer's identity, the contract should, so far as third parties are concerned, be voidable and not void'.

12.19   There is much sense in the Law Reform Committee's proposal, despite Parliament's failure to implement it. Further support for this view is provided by *Lewis* v *Averay* (1972). The facts, which closely resembled those of *Ingram* v *Little* (1961), were as follows:

> Lewis offered his car for sale at £450. A man arranged to see the car, tested it, and expressed interest in buying it. The man told Lewis that he was Richard Greene, a famous film and television actor,[5] and he wrote a cheque for the agreed price of £450, signed RA Green. As the purchaser wished to take away the car immediately, Lewis requested some means of identification, and was shown an admission pass to Pinewood Studios in the name of Richard A Green, which bore the man's photograph. Lewis permitted the man to take the car and log book in exchange for the cheque. In fact the cheque had been taken from a stolen cheque book and was worthless; the man was not Richard Greene, the famous actor. The rogue sold the car to an innocent buyer, Averay, for £200. Lewis sued Averay for conversion.

The Court of Appeal did not allow Lewis to recover the car or its value, deciding that Averay acquired a good title to it. Lewis intended to deal with the man who called to see the car. Although the contract was voidable for fraud, Lewis was unable to recover the property from someone who

---

4   See 12th Report, *Transfer of Title to Chattels*, Cmnd 2958, 1966.

5   He was best known for his starring role in the television series *Robin Hood*.

bought in good faith from the rogue for value. The court disagreed with *Ingram v Little*, preferring to base its decision on *Phillips v Brooks* (1919). It is respectfully submitted that this is the correct conclusion to have reached. It has been argued that *Ingram v Little* is distinguishable on the ground that in that case the women would not conclude the agreement until they had looked in the telephone directory. But this is, to say the least, a tenuous argument. In *Shogun Finance Ltd v Hudson* (2003) the decision in *Ingram v Little* was heavily criticized in a number of the speeches, with Lord Millett stating (at [110]) that it should be overruled and this is discussed below.

12.20   The issue of mistake as to identity induced by fraudulent misrepresentation must now be considered in the light of the important decision of the House of Lords in *Shogun Finance Ltd v Hudson* (2003). The facts were:

> A rogue visited the showroom of a car dealer, having dishonestly acquired the driving licence of a Mr Durlabh Patel. He negotiated with the car dealer for the purchase of a Mitsubishi vehicle which was on display and agreed a price of £22,250, subject to getting hire purchase finance. The dealer produced a copy of the claimant Shogun's standard form hire purchase agreement, which was signed by the rogue to resemble the signature of Durlabh Patel; the customer details supplied by the rogue were those of Mr Patel. The real Mr Patel had no knowledge of this transaction. The dealer sent by fax the signed draft finance agreement, together with a copy of the driving licence, to Shogun Finance. Shogun, having checked the credit rating of Mr Patel, instructed the dealer to proceed with the hire purchase transaction. (Under such an arrangement, the finance company buys the car from the dealer and hires it to the customer under a hire purchase agreement, which enables the customer to purchase the vehicle when all the instalments have been paid.) After paying a deposit of 10 per cent, the rogue took possession of the vehicle and its documentation from the dealer, and then sold the car almost immediately for £17,000 to the defendant, Mr Hudson, who acted in good faith without knowledge of the hire purchase agreement or the rogue's fraudulent conduct. The rogue disappeared and Shogun, arguing that the vehicle belonged to them, claimed its return or its value from Hudson.

Mr Hudson contended that he acquired good title to the vehicle by virtue of s 27 of the Hire Purchase Act 1964. This states that where a vehicle has been hired under a hire purchase agreement and the debtor sells the vehicle to a private purchaser (P) who buys in good faith without notice of the hire purchase agreement, P can acquire title to the vehicle (even though the debtor was not the owner of it). Shogun argued that this statutory provision could not avail Mr Hudson, as the hire purchase agreement was a written document and the rogue was not the debtor under this agreement, since he was not the hirer named in the agreement. They claimed that they had intended to contract with the real Mr Patel, whose details they had checked (and therefore the issue of identity was crucial), rather than the rogue and that the hire purchase agreement was void. Both the trial judge and a majority of the Court of Appeal (Sedley LJ dissenting) found in favour of the claimant, that the rogue by entering into the written agreement fraudulently pretending to be someone else, was not the debtor under s 27 and, therefore, Mr Hudson could not rely on this provision to acquire title to the vehicle.

Mr Hudson appealed to the House of Lords, where his appeal was dismissed (with Lord Nicholls and Lord Millett dissenting). The majority in the House of Lords' decision relied on the fact that the case could not be subsumed under the general principle governing face-to-face transactions (discussed earlier), as it involved a written hire purchase agreement (see Lord Hobhouse at [51] and Lord Phillips at [178]). Shogun's standard hire purchase agreement contained essential information about the hirer and his identity. Shogun checked the particulars supplied to them relating to Durlabh Patel and it was with him that they agreed to contract. There was no intention to contract with the rogue and, therefore, there was no agreement with him and he was not to be regarded as the debtor. As a result, Mr Hudson could not rely upon the Hire Purchase Act 1964, s 27 and ownership remained with the claimant. The majority thought that the identity of the customer was of fundamental importance to the whole transaction and that the correct identification of the customer by the claimant was the sine qua non of Shogun's willingness to contract with him. (See more recently, *TTMI Sarl* v *Statoil ASA, The Sibohelle* (2011) which followed *Shogun Finance Ltd*). Accordingly, the dealer's delivery of the vehicle to the rogue was without authority and it was not a delivery under a valid hire purchase agreement.

12.21   The decision in *Shogun Finance Ltd* v *Hudson* (2003) led to the unsatisfactory result that Mr Hudson, although buying in good faith from the rogue, suffered all of the loss. The dilemma of deciding which of two innocent parties should bear the loss in such cases of mistaken identity was referred to in a number of the judgments (for example, see Lord Nicholls at [13], Lord Millett at [60], and Lord Walker at [182]). However, the majority thought that it was inescapable that the contract in question was a written consumer credit transaction, not a face-to-face sale, and that commercial certainty dictated that the document was construed correctly. In so doing, they rejected the attempt of the minority (despite Lord Phillips being 'attracted to [their] solution' at [170]) to rationalize this area of the law by doing away with the distinction made between face-to-face transactions and those made where the parties are not in each other's presence. Under the solution proposed by the minority, this 'unprincipled distinction' (at [108]) between face-to-face and other types of transaction would be discarded, as 'the existence of physical immediacy in one case, and the absence of it in the other is immaterial' (at [28]). Moreover, the minority argued that *Cundy* v *Lindsay* (1878) should no longer be followed (see [36] and [110]).

12.22   The Law Reform Committee's 12th Report (discussed at para. **12.18**) recommended that where goods are sold under a mistake as to the buyer's identity the contract be regarded as voidable rather than void, thus protecting a third party (such as Mr Hudson) who buys in good faith. The majority thought that *Shogun Finance Ltd* v *Hudson* (2003), involving a written consumer credit agreement, was a different type of case (see Lord Hobhouse at [55]) and that, in this type of transaction, identity is of fundamental importance. But it is questionable whether the rights of someone who subsequently buys in good faith from the rogue should turn on technical distinctions of this kind. It might also be argued that what was of importance to the claimant finance company was the creditworthiness of the hirer rather than his identity (see Lord Nicholls at [35]) and that, in believing that the customer in the showroom and Durlabh Patel were one and the same, it 'not only took a credit risk, but also took the risk that the customer who was hiring the car was not Mr Durlabh Patel and that its credit enquiries had been fraudulently misdirected' (per Lord Millett at [107]). (One commentator has observed that 'although Shogun successfully argued that the identity of the customer was "absolutely crucial", their practice suggested that this was not in fact the case': see C. Elliott (2004) JBL 381 at 386.)

12.23 It is respectfully submitted that the majority in *Shogun Finance Ltd* v *Hudson* (2003) took too narrow a view of the problem. For example, Lord Hobhouse (with whom Lord Walker concurred) concluded by stating that the relevant principles of law 'are clear and sound and need no revision' and that 'to cast doubt on them can only be a disservice to English Law' (at [55]). It is difficult to agree with this statement in view of the considerable disquiet expressed about the present state of the law, with its technical distinctions and its lack of consistency in tackling the dilemma as to which of two innocent parties should bear the whole of the loss. It is submitted that the opinions of the dissenting law lords are more attractive, both in their recognition that the law needs to be 'coherent and rescued from its present unsatisfactory and unprincipled state' (per Lord Nicholls at [34]), and in asserting that 'the law should if at all possible favour a solution which protects innocent third parties by treating the contract as voidable rather than void' in this type of case (per Lord Millett at [60]). Similarly, both of the dissenting opinions are critical of the distinction between face-to-face and other transactions (see [24]–[25] and [66]–[70]). Lord Nicholls argued that there 'is no magic attaching to a misrepresentation made in writing rather than by word of mouth' (at [24]) and Lord Millett stated that 'the real objection to the present state of the law . . . is that the distinction between face to face and other contracts is unrealistic' (at [68]) and 'unsound' (at [70]). This led to a recognition in both dissenting judgments that the existing authorities cannot all be reconciled and that reform was necessary, even if that involved departing from a previous decision of the House of Lords. In the words of Lord Millett, 'the decision in *Cundy* v *Lindsay* stands in the way of a rational and coherent restatement of the law'. Lord Phillips summarized the approach of his dissenting colleagues with some clarity (at [169]) and confessed that he was strongly attracted by their approach. It is perhaps unfortunate that he found himself unable to adopt it. The decision of the House of Lords has missed a valuable opportunity to put the law on a clearer and more rational footing. (For further comment on this case, see C. Elliott (2004) JBL 381, A. Phang et al. (2004) 63 CLJ 24 and C. MacMillan (2004) 120 LQR 369.)

Mistake as to the terms or subject matter of a contract

12.24 Most of the cases considered in this section are instances of mutual mistake, where the parties are at cross-purposes as to the terms or subject matter of the contract. Once again, the issue is that there is no genuine agreement, despite appearances. Before looking at these decisions, a further case of unilateral mistake should be noted. In *Hartog* v *Colin & Shields* [1939] 3 All ER 566:

> D contracted to sell to C 3,000 Argentine hare skins. But by mistake he offered to sell them at a certain rate per 'pound' (weight), instead of per 'piece'. The price stated by D was extremely low—the price per piece was about one-third of that per pound. The negotiations leading

> up to the sale had been on the basis of the price per piece, and this was the accepted custom within the trade. C purported to accept this offer and sued D for non-delivery.

It was held that there was no contract. The apparent agreement was negatived as C must surely have known that D's offer was made due to a mistake. ('The [claimant] could not reasonably have supposed that the offer contained the offeror's real intention': per Singleton J at 568.) (See also *Chwee Kin Keong* v *Digilandmall.com Pte Ltd* (2006).) It is interesting to contrast the *Hartog* decision with the case of *Centrovincial Estates* v *Merchant Investors Assurance Co. Ltd* (1983), which was considered at para. **12.5**. In that case the offeror was bound by his apparent agreement with the defendant despite offering to rent premises to D for £65,000 per year, rather than at the intended rent of £126,000. The important distinction seems to be that in the *Centrovincial* case the offeree (D) did not know, and could not reasonably have known, of the mistake at the time of acceptance.

12.25 Generally, parties are bound by their apparent agreements in the interests of certainty and commercial convenience. As we have seen, the law takes a predominantly objective view of agreement. It is not, usually, the subjective intention of the parties with which the law is concerned,[6] but rather, what can be inferred from their conduct: 'In contracts you do not look into the actual intent in a man's mind. You look at what he said and did' (per Lord Denning in *Storer* v *Manchester City Council* [1974] 3 All ER 824 at 828). If one party makes an offer, as in the *Centrovincial* case, that can be understood in only one reasonable way, and the other party understands and accepts the offer in that reasonable way, there will normally be a binding agreement even if the offeror intended some different meaning. There will also be a heavy burden falling on the party alleging a mistake to disprove the existence of a contract.

12.26 It is necessary to assess the extent of the objective principle, particularly in relation to parties at cross-purposes—for example where one party intends to sell one thing and the other party intends to buy something different; or one party intends to contract on one set of terms and the other intends to deal on a different set of terms. In this type of situation (known as 'mutual mistake') the parties are mistaken as to each other's intention. In *Raffles* v *Wichelhaus* (1864), the facts were:

> D agreed to buy from C a cargo of 125 bales of Surat cotton 'to arrive ex *Peerless* from Bombay'. In fact, there were two ships called *Peerless* and both sailed from Bombay. D meant the *Peerless* which sailed in October, and C meant the *Peerless* which sailed in December. D refused to accept the cotton sent on the ship which sailed in December. C claimed that he was ready to deliver the goods which were shipped on the vessel named in the agreement and from the agreed port, and that D was liable for refusing to accept or pay for the goods.

It was accepted by the court that D was not liable due to the ambiguity inherent in the agreement. In fact, the court (for procedural reasons) did not have to decide whether there was a

---

6 But see De Moor (1990) 106 LQR 632 for a more detailed examination of the issue.

contract, but the most plausible inference from the decision is that there was no contract. It is possible that there was an agreement to ship the cotton on the 'October *Peerless*', but this is unlikely. Once it emerged that there were two ships of the same name, both due to sail from Bombay, it is impossible to say that the parties reached a genuine agreement. In terms of the objective approach, a reasonable person would not conclude that agreement had been reached. (For a recent case which distinguished *Raffles* v *Wichelhaus*, see *NBTY Europe Ltd* v *Nutricia International BV* (2005).)

12.27   A more difficult case involving ambiguity in an apparent agreement is *Scriven Bros* v *Hindley & Co.* (1913), in which the facts were as follows:

> C instructed an auctioneer to sell a number of bales of hemp and of tow by auction. (Tow is the coarse and broken part of flax or hemp.) The goods were described in the auctioneer's catalogue as a certain number of bales in two separate lots, with the same shipping mark, without disclosing the difference in the commodities; i.e. it failed to state that one lot contained tow, not hemp. Before the sale, samples of the hemp and tow were available for inspection in a showroom. On the floor of the room the catalogue numbers of the lots of hemp and tow were marked in chalk opposite the respective samples. Having previously examined the hemp, and (mistakenly) believing both lots to contain hemp, D's manager did not inspect the samples which were on view. At the auction D's buyer, thinking that he was bidding for hemp, made an excessively high bid for the lot containing tow! His bid was successful. Expert witnesses stated that it was very unusual for Russian tow and Russian hemp to be landed from the same ship under the same shipping mark. C brought an action to recover the price.

Put simply, C intended to sell one thing, whilst D intended to buy something else. Neither was aware of the other party's misapprehension. It was held that there was no contract of sale as the parties had not reached agreement as to the subject matter of the proposed sale. This decision might seem rather favourable to the defendants, permitting them to escape a bad bargain. But the decision is probably sound. If we ask whether a reasonable person, taking an overview of the situation, would conclude that an agreement between the parties had been reached, the answer would probably be negative. Due to the ambiguities in the circumstances under which the auction took place, it is difficult to conclude that there was a contract for the sale of tow. But for the potentially misleading nature of the auction catalogue, however, the outcome of the case would surely have been different.

12.28   Interesting issues are raised by the famous case of *Smith* v *Hughes* (1871) LR 6 QB 597, but whether it can be accurately described as one of mutual mistake is debatable due to the disputed facts of the case. First, the facts:

> A farmer (C) offered to sell the manager of D, a race horse trainer, a quantity of oats and showed him a sample. The manager wrote to C accepting the offer. When the first delivery of oats was made, D discovered that the oats were 'green' (i.e. that season's oats) and of no

use to him. He claimed that he thought he was buying 'old' oats and he refused to pay for that delivery or any subsequent delivery. C, who knew that the oats were new, refused to take them back and sued D for the price. There was a dispute as to what was said in the exchange between C and D's manager; D claimed that C had described them as 'good old oats', whereas C denied using the word 'old'. After a finding in favour of D at the trial, C appealed.

If the word 'old' had, in fact, been used, then the finding for D was clearly correct. But if the word 'old' had not been used by the parties, then the situation was more complex. It was this problem that was dealt with by the appeal court. If D's manager believed the oats to be old and C was aware of his belief, without doing anything to encourage it (simply offering his goods and exhibiting his sample), was there a contract? As Cockburn CJ stated (at 603):

'The question is whether, under such circumstances, the passive acquiescence of the seller in the self-deception of the buyer will entitle the latter to avoid the contract. I am of the opinion that it will not.'

In ordering a new trial the court agreed with his Lordship's conclusion. Assuming that the word 'old' was not used by the parties, D received the goods which he contracted to buy and which corresponded to the sample inspected by D's manager, and therefore he was bound by the contract. (For a detailed analysis, see D. Friedmann (2003) 119 LQR 68 at 71–4; see also *Statoil ASA v Louis Dreyfus Energy Services LP (The Harriette N)* (2009).) To quote Lord Cockburn once again (at 603):

'Here the defendant agreed to buy a specific parcel of oats. The oats were what they were sold as, namely, good oats according to the sample. The buyer persuaded himself they were old oats, when they were not so; but the seller neither said nor did anything to contribute to his deception. He has himself to blame. The question is not what a man of scrupulous morality or nice honour would do under such circumstances.'

Agreement mistake in equity

12.29 It is understandable that the law should take a narrow view of mistake. This approach upholds the need to be able to rely on the apparent intention of the party with whom you are dealing, in the interests of certainty and commercial convenience. However, the equitable jurisdiction of the courts permits a more flexible approach.[7] A contract may be upheld as valid but, in the interests of justice, the court may still grant relief against the consequences of mistake. The most practical form of equitable relief is the discretion of the court to refuse specific performance even in cases where the contract is valid at law. In the case of *Malins v Freeman* (1837), for example, the defendant (due to his late arrival) mistakenly made a bid for one property at

---

7 It does not, however, extend to relieving a party from a contract simply because he or she made a bad bargain. So a mistake as to the commercial consequences of an agreement, as opposed to its subject matter or terms, will not be sufficient: see *Clarion Ltd v National Provident Institution* (2000).

an auction thinking that he was bidding for another. The mistake was due to the defendant's own carelessness, and the contract was clearly valid (contrast *Scriven Bros v Hindley* (1913), para. **12.27**). Although the claimant could have claimed damages, the court refused to order specific performance against the defendant. (See also *Wood v Scarth* (1855) for a further illustration of this flexible approach.) The court may exercise its discretion so as to avoid hardship to a defendant[8] and it 'will not be active in assisting one party to an agreement, who has always his remedy in damages, to take advantage of the mistake of the other so as to involve him in serious and unforeseen consequences' (*Stewart v Kennedy* (1890) 15 App Cas 75 at 105 per Lord MacNaghten).

12.30   In the interest of certainty, and to prevent fraud, the court will not allow a defendant to escape the performance of a contract simply because he made a mistake. In *Tamplin v James* (1879) 15 Ch D 215 the facts were:

> A certain inn, 'The Ship', and adjoining shop were to be sold by auction. The defendant knew the property for sale and he knew that certain gardens, which were hardly separated from the property to be sold, were occupied along with the inn and the shop. However, the gardens did not belong to the vendor and this was clear from the plans which were on display in the saleroom. The defendant did not look at the plans or at the particulars of sale, and he bought the land in the mistaken belief that he was buying the gardens along with the inn and shop.

The Court of Appeal ordered specific performance. There was no misrepresentation by the vendor; nor was there any ambiguity in the terms of the contract. (For an interesting contrast, see *Denny v Hancock* (1870), in which the vendor's plan of the property for sale was potentially misleading.) In the absence of these factors, a court will be justified in refusing specific performance only where 'hardship amounting to injustice' (per James LJ at 221) would be inflicted on the defendant by holding him to the agreement and where it would be unreasonable to do so. But in *Tamplin v James* it was the defendant's own carelessness that led to his mistake, and he bought the property which he intended to purchase; it was simply less extensive than he thought. It was not unreasonable or unjust for the court to hold him to his contract and grant the claimant specific performance.

12.31   Another equitable remedy which may be granted at the discretion of the court is that of rectification. The purpose here is to grant relief in relation to mistakes made in the recording of agreements. For instance, where A and B reach agreement on a certain set of terms and then a written agreement between them is subsequently drawn up which, by mistake, does not accurately reflect those terms, the court may rectify the document. In other words, the document is amended so as accurately to reflect either the terms agreed by A and B, or (where no actual agreement has been concluded) their prior common intention. This common intention has to be manifested in some objective way, and be continuing at the time the document in question was drawn up. (See *Joscelyne v Nissen* (1970) and *Chartbrook Ltd v Persimmon Homes Ltd* (2009) per

---

8   For an interesting, more modern example of this, see *Patel v Ali* (1984).

Lord Hoffmann at [48] and [59]–[60]. Also, M. Smith, 'Rectification of Contracts for Common Mistake, *Joscelyne* v *Nissen*, and Subjective States of Mind' (2007) 123 LQR 116 and C. Nugee, 'Rectification after Chartbrook v Persimmon: where are we now?' (2012) 26(2) Tru L I 76.)

The equitable remedy of rectification is not supposed, generally, to be available in cases of unilateral mistake (although exceptionally it may be; see *Roberts & Co. Ltd* v *Leicestershire County Council* (1961); and also D. McLauchlan, 'The "Drastic" Remedy of Rectification for Unilateral Mistake' (2008) 124 LQR 608). It is usually only where the document does not reflect the intention of both A and B that a claim for rectification will be granted. In the case of *Riverlate Properties Ltd* v *Paul* [1975] Ch 133, the facts were as follows:

> C, a landlord, granted a lease of a maisonette for ninety-nine years to D at a price of £6,500, with a yearly ground rent of £25. It was C's intention that D should pay half the cost of structural and exterior repairs. But owing to a drafting error in the draft lease sent to D's solicitor, the lease which was executed did not reflect C's intention in this respect. Neither D nor her solicitor was aware of the mistake, and it was D's understanding that she was not responsible for these repairs. C's claim was to have the contract set aside, or, alternatively, rectified so as to include D's liability for sharing the cost of external repairs.

C's claim was rejected by both the trial and appeal courts. This is surely correct, as it would be contrary to the objective approach to agreement if a party could go back on an offer which he reasonably appears to have made and which has been accepted by the other party without any knowledge of the offeror's mistake. The matter was dealt with emphatically by Russell LJ (at 140–1):

> 'What is there in principle, or in authority, binding on this court, which requires a person who has acquired a leasehold interest on terms on which he intended to obtain it, and who thought when he obtained it that the lessor intended him to obtain it on those terms, either to lose the leasehold interest, or, if he wished to keep it, to submit to keep it only on the terms which the lessor meant to impose but did not? In point of principle, we cannot find that this should be so. If reference be made to principles of equity, it operates on conscience. If conscience is clear at the time of the transaction, why should equity disrupt the transaction?'

But if one party is aware of the other's mistake and, by keeping quiet, unfairly derives some benefit from the error, there can be no objection to rectification in a case of unilateral mistake (see *Thomas Bates & Son Ltd* v *Wyndham's (Lingerie) Ltd* (1981)). Moreover, rectification may be available where one party is mistaken and the other both intends and suspects this, and behaves unconscionably so as to encourage the error (per Stuart-Smith LJ in *Commission for the New Towns* v *Cooper (GB) Ltd* (1995), and discussed in *Templiss Properties Ltd* v *Dean Hyams* (1999) and in *Hurst Stores & Interiors Ltd* v *ML Europe Property Ltd* (2004)). However, rectification will not be granted merely because one party has driven a hard bargain in the negotiations and the other party has not been sufficiently alert to the possible consequences of a particular provision of the agreement (see *Oceanic Village Ltd* v *Shirayama Shokusan Co. Ltd* (1999)). For a court to rectify on the ground of unilateral mistake, there needs to be clear evidence that the defendant has acted unconscionably and unfairly. (See *George Wimpey UK Ltd* v *VI Construction Ltd* (2005), where such a claim failed on the facts. The rectification argument was also unsuccessful in *Connolly Ltd* v *Bellway Homes Ltd* (2007), although the claimant company succeeded with its claim for damages based on misrepresentation. The strict limits on the application of rectification to cases of unilateral mistake are also illustrated by *Rowallan Group Ltd* v *Edgehill Portfolio No 1 Ltd* (2007).)

Common mistake

Performability mistake (or 'initial impossibility')

12.32   Where 'performability' mistake is at issue, there is no dispute between the parties about the existence of an agreement. This type of mistake, often referred to as 'common mistake', arises where the parties share the same misapprehension about some underlying fact which renders the contract impossible to perform or devoid of purpose, and one party maintains that the agreement is nullified by the mistake. For example, A contracts to sell his bicycle to B but, unknown to both parties, the bicycle was wrecked beyond repair five minutes before their agreement. What is the legal position in cases of this type? Does such a mistake render the contract void as a matter of law; or could the seller be liable for failing to supply the bicycle as promised; or could the buyer be liable for the price of the bicycle?

12.33   It is true that problems of performability mistake are far from common in practice. But an analysis of them is crucial to an understanding of contract law, as it provides an important insight into the strength of contractual obligations. The general rule of contractual obligation is that a party is bound to perform the contract or else to provide a remedy for its breach. How strict is this rule? When will a party be excused from performance on the ground of 'impossibility'? The judgment in *Great Peace Shipping Ltd* v *Tsavliris Salvage (International) Ltd* (2003), discussed at para. **12.46** is an important contribution to understanding these issues.

Mistake as to existence of subject matter

12.34   Usually this type of mistake has involved contracts for non-existent goods but, exceptionally, other factual situations can arise. For example, in *Galloway* v *Galloway* (1914), a man (D) and woman (C) entered into a separation deed by which D agreed to pay C the weekly amount of £1 for the support of their three children. D discovered that, contrary to his mistaken assumption, his first wife was not dead! Thus, the separation agreement between D and C was based on their common, but erroneous, assumption that they were in fact married to one another. D fell behind with his payments under the agreement and argued that the contract should be set aside. Ridley J held that there was no doubt that the agreement between the parties was void due to a common mistake of fact which was material to the existence of an agreement. (The case deals only with the validity of the agreement; presumably D was still under a legal duty to provide for the children.)

12.35   A more important line of cases deals with goods which have ceased to exist, physically or commercially, at the time the parties entered into a contract. In the leading case of *Couturier* v *Hastie* (1856) 5 HL Cas 673:

> There was a contract for the sale of a cargo of corn—of 'fair average quality when shipped'—which was thought to be in transit between Salonika and London. Unknown to the contracting parties, the corn had become badly overheated and had been sold at Tunis (by the master of the ship) shortly before the contract was made. The seller contended that the buyer was still liable for the price of the corn, namely that the buyer had purchased an interest in a 'maritime adventure' (including risks), represented by the shipping documents and insurance. The buyer argued that the contract was for the sale and purchase of goods, not for the sale of goods or the documents representing them, and therefore denied liability for the price.

Here we have an interesting dispute about the true interpretation, or construction, of the agreement between the parties. The House of Lords decided that the purchaser was not liable to pay for the corn. In an important speech, Lord Cranworth LC stated (at 681–2):

> '[T]he whole question turns upon the construction of the contract...looking to the contract itself alone, it appears to me clearly that what the parties contemplated...was that there was an existing something to be sold and bought...The contract plainly imports that there was something which was to be sold at the time of the contract, and something to be purchased.'

In other words, the contract was not void automatically because the goods no longer existed at the time of the contract. It was a question of construction: what did the parties contract about? Because the House of Lords interpreted the contract as one for the purchase of specific goods (and not the documents representing them as an alternative), the purchaser was not liable. It was never decided whether the seller would have been liable if an action for non-delivery of the goods had been brought by the purchaser against him. It is submitted that the seller would be liable in these circumstances only if, as a matter of construction, he assumed the risk of the goods' non-existence. This would perhaps be fairly unusual, but such a situation is well illustrated in the Australian High Court case of *McRae* v *Commonwealth Disposals Commission* (1951) 84 CLR 377. The facts were:

> The Commonwealth Disposals Commission (D) invited tenders 'for the purchase of an oil tanker lying on Jourmand Reef...the vessel is said to contain oil'. C's tender of £285 was accepted by the defendant Commission. C went to much expense in preparing for a salvage expedition only to discover, on arrival at the designated area, that there was no tanker to be found. (Nor was there any place known as 'Jourmand Reef'.)

The court held that this was not an example of a contract nullified by mistake. The defendants had made an implied promise that there was a tanker at a particular location. As there was no such tanker, this was a breach of contract and C was entitled to damages.[9] The court was clearly of the opinion that *Couturier v Hastie* (1856) did not establish a rule of law that a contract is void for mistake where the goods do not exist at the time the contract is made. It was stated (at 406–7):

> 'The truth is that the question whether the contract was void, or the vendor excused from performance by reason of the non-existence of the supposed subject matter, did not arise in *Couturier v Hastie*. It would have arisen if the purchaser had suffered loss through non-delivery of the corn and had sued the vendor for damages. If it had so arisen, we think that the real question would have been whether the contract was subject to an implied condition precedent that the goods were in existence.'

12.36   The decision in the case of *McRae v Commonwealth Disposals Commission* (1951) is certainly in keeping with the approach taken in *Couturier v Hastie* (1856). However, *Couturier v Hastie* has received an interpretation in English law that perhaps is inconsistent with what was actually stated by the House of Lords in that case. Despite the fact that it was stressed that 'the whole question turns upon the construction of the contract', the decision led to the belief that in cases of non-existent goods the 'contract' will be void. This interpretation was encapsulated in s 6 of the Sale of Goods Act 1893 which purported to give effect to the decision in *Couturier v Hastie*. Section 6 of the Act (now the 1979 Act) provides that:

> 'Where there is a contract for the sale of specific goods, and the goods without the knowledge of the seller have perished at the time when the contract is made, the contract is void.'

12.37   This raises a number of interesting issues. It appears to state as a rule of law something which was held to be a question of construction at common law. Therefore, it produces a more rigid approach than that favoured by the Australian High Court in *McRae v Commonwealth Disposals Commission* (1951). This can be illustrated by *Barrow, Lane & Ballard Ltd v Phillips & Co. Ltd* [1929] 1 KB 574, in which the facts were that C sold to D 700 bags of nuts, but at the time of making the contract there were not 700 bags in existence. In fact, there were only 591 bags, the remaining 109 having been stolen or misdirected (due to the actions of a third party). C claimed the price of the bags which were still in existence, but Wright J rejected this argument and held the contract to be void for mistake as to the existence of goods. This was stated as a matter of law under Sale of Goods Act, s 6. Apparently it made no difference that only some of the goods did not exist and that more than three-quarters of the bags were still there. Wright J stated (at 583):

> 'A contract for a parcel of 700 bags is something different from a contract for 591 bags, and the position appears to me to be in no way different from what it would have been if the whole 700 bags had ceased to exist.'[10]

---

9 The damages awarded would include compensation for the money spent in reliance on the defendants' promise, i.e. in equipping a salvage expedition.

10 Had the contract been severable—i.e. an agreement for a number of separate lots which were to be paid for separately—then presumably the decision would have been different. The buyer would have been liable for the price of the remaining bags of nuts.

It is possible to distinguish *McRae* from the other cases we have considered on the basis that s 6 refers to goods that 'have perished' at the time of the contract, whereas in *McRae* the goods never existed.[11] But there is no reason, in principle, why this should make any material difference, and perhaps the wording of the Act is merely fortuitous. It might be pointed out that this discussion is rather academic; that in the modern age of instantaneous methods of communication, it is unlikely that there will be many problems relating to non-existent goods. But it might also be cogently argued that in view of these modern developments, it would be more realistic to hold that the seller of specific goods is usually understood to have promised that the goods exist.[12]

Mistake as to 'quality' of subject matter

12.38   In the cases which we have just considered, it is easy to understand why an apparent contract may be a nullity due to the non-existence of the subject matter. The contract may be emptied of all its content and, unless any other construction is possible, it may be regarded as void. But outside this category of cases involving non-existent goods, there are few clear instances of a contract being held void on the grounds of common mistake. Here we are concerned with cases where the parties are both mistaken as to some fundamental fact (such as the 'quality' of the thing contracted for) and whether an apparent contract can be nullified on these grounds. If the courts are willing to declare a contract void for this reason, there is perhaps an independent, albeit narrow, doctrine of common mistake recognized by the common law. (The relevant principles of this doctrine were considered in the Court of Appeal decision in *Great Peace Shipping Ltd* v *Tsavliris Salvage (International) Ltd* (2003) at [73]–[76].) It must be remembered that the courts will not permit a party to escape his or her contractual undertakings simply because he or she made what turned out to be a bad bargain (see *Great Peace Shipping Ltd*). But what if, for example, a person sells something at a tiny fraction of its true commercial value because both parties are mistaken as to its quality or its nature? Or, to pose a further question, if the subject matter lacks some essential quality which the parties thought it possessed, can it be argued that the object of the contract is impossible to achieve?

12.39   The leading case of *Bell* v *Lever Bros* [1932] AC 161 is difficult to interpret, but it illustrates the limitations of any general doctrine of common mistake. Generally, a mistake as to quality of the thing contracted for will not make a contract void. In *Bell* v *Lever Bros* the facts were:

> Lever Bros employed the appellants, Bell and Snelling, as chairman and vice-chairman (respectively) of the Niger Company—a company controlled by Lever Bros. Before the expiry of their five-year contracts, Lever Bros wished to terminate Bell's and Snelling's contracts, and under a

---

11 A discussion of the meaning of 'perish' under the Sale of Goods Act is beyond the scope of this book. Briefly, it may be noted that some minor deterioration of goods will not amount to 'perishing'. However, goods may perish in a commercial sense, even though they physically still exist, when there is sufficient deterioration: see *Asfar* v *Blundell* (1896).

12 See Atiyah, *Introduction to the Law of Contract*, 5th edn, 1995, p. 222.

further agreement Lever Bros promised to pay the men compensation of £30,000 and £20,000, respectively. After payment of the compensation, Lever Bros discovered that Bell and Snelling had committed certain breaches of duty, during their employment, which would have entitled their employers to dismiss them without compensation. (In the course of their employment the men had secretly engaged in speculative transactions in cocoa on their own account.) It was found as a matter of fact that Bell and Snelling had forgotten about their breaches of duty at the time of entering into the compensation agreements with Lever Bros. Therefore, it was not a case either of fraud or of unilateral mistake. Lever Bros tried to recover the £50,000 on the ground that the compensation agreements with the two men were void due to common mistake.

Put simply, Lever Bros paid a total of £50,000 to terminate the contracts of two men who could have been dismissed for nothing. The trial judge and the Court of Appeal held that the compensation agreements were void due to a fundamental mistake. The House of Lords reversed this decision, with the majority holding that the contracts were valid and binding. It is worth considering the important and controversial words of one of the majority, Lord Atkin (at 223–4), in some detail. He stated:

'Is an agreement to terminate a broken contract different in kind from an agreement to terminate an unbroken contract, assuming that the breach has given the one party the right to declare the contract at an end? I feel the weight of the claimant's contention that a contract immediately determinable is a different thing from a contract for an unexpired term, and that the difference in kind can be illustrated by the immense price of release from the longer contract as compared with the shorter... But, on the whole, I have come to the conclusion that it would be wrong to decide that an agreement to terminate a definite specified contract is void if it turns out that the agreement had already been broken and could have been terminated otherwise. The contract released is the identical contract in both cases, and the party paying for release gets exactly what he bargains for. It seems immaterial that he could have got the same result in another way, or that if he had known of the true facts he would not have entered into the bargain.'

Although it is difficult to agree that Lever Bros got 'exactly' what they bargained for, it must be accepted that it was in the company's interest, because of a corporate merger, to terminate the men's service contracts. Moreover, the compensation was a reward (at least in part) for the good work that the two men had done during their employment and it ensured their co-operation in carrying through the amalgamation. It might be contended that the value of this service was unaffected by the breach of contract committed by the two men. On the other hand, it might be argued that the basis of the compensation agreement was the termination of valid service contracts and that, accordingly, there was a common mistake as to a fundamental fact.

12.40   We have seen that a mistake as to the *existence* of the subject matter of an agreement can render the agreement void. But, in view of the actual decision in *Bell v Lever Bros* [1932] AC 161, are there any circumstances in which the courts will declare a contract void due to some fundamental mistake as to the *quality* of the thing contracted for? A narrow view, evident in some parts of the judgments given in *Lever Bros*, is that an agreement will be nullified only where the identity of the subject matter is in effect destroyed by the mistaken assumption; i.e. 'does the state of the new facts destroy the identity of the subject matter as it was in the original state of facts?' (at 227 per Lord Atkin). In such a (rare) event, therefore, the mistake would be analogous to cases of non-existent goods and would nullify agreement.

12.41　A slightly wider view of the law, also expressed by Lord Atkin in *Bell* v *Lever Bros* [1932] AC 161 at 218, is that a common mistake will render a contract void where both parties are mistaken 'as to the existence of some quality which makes the thing without the quality essentially different from the thing as it was believed to be'.[13] This view of common mistake was approved in *Associated Japanese Bank (International)* v *Crédit du Nord SA* [1988] 3 All ER 902 (which is discussed later). In this case Steyn J stated, *obiter* (at 913), that this wider interpretation of *Bell* v *Lever Bros* is to be preferred. The test to be applied is that the mistake must render the subject matter of the contract essentially and radically different from the subject matter which the parties believed to exist.

12.42　However, there is still a distinct impression that much of this debate is merely abstract theorizing. If we look at the decision in *Bell* v *Lever Bros* (1932), and the decisions that have followed, it is apparent that 'cases where contracts have been found to be void in consequence of common mistake are few and far between' (per Lord Phillips in *Great Peace Shipping Ltd* v *Tsavliris Salvage (International) Ltd* (2003) at [85]; for cases which lend some support to the existence of such a doctrine, see *Scott* v *Coulson* [1903] 2 Ch 249 at 252, and also *Nicholson and Venn* v *Smith-Marriott* (1947)).[14] The doctrine is said to exist in theory, but in practice it is difficult to find examples of cases decided on this basis alone. This is not surprising in view of the outcome of *Lever Bros*. The company paid £50,000 to dismiss two men, when it could have dismissed them for nothing. If this was not sufficiently fundamental to come within a doctrine of common mistake, it is reasonable to question the existence of such a doctrine.

12.43　A further illustration of the very strict standard to be applied is the case of *Leaf* v *International Galleries* [1950] 2 KB 86. The facts were as follows:

> In 1944 the defendants sold a picture, entitled 'Salisbury Cathedral', to C for £85. The defendants represented that it was the work of John Constable. But when C tried to sell the painting, five years later, he discovered that it had not been painted by Constable. C sought rescission of the contract and repayment of £85 on the basis of the defendants' innocent misrepresentation. (C did not claim damages for breach of condition or warranty.)

13　Alternatively, in Lord Thankerton's words (at 235), the mistake must 'relate to something which both must necessarily have accepted in their minds as an essential and integral element of the subject matter'.

14　In a US case, *Sherwood* v *Walker* (1887), a contract for the sale of a cow believed by both parties to be barren, was held to be void when it was discovered to be with calf and worth considerably more than the price agreed by the parties.

The Court of Appeal held that C was not entitled to rescind the contract despite the defendants' innocent misrepresentation (see **Chapter 13**). In the opinion of Lord Denning, C had ample opportunity to examine the picture in the first few days after buying it, and as he had not rejected the painting within a reasonable period after its purchase, he lost the right to rescind. (For an interesting case on this point, see *Peco Arts* v *Hazlitt Gallery* (1983).) In his Lordship's opinion, a claim for damages for breach of contract might have succeeded, but C did not bring such a claim before the court. (But see *Harlingdon and Leinster Enterprises Ltd* v *Christopher Hull Fine Art Ltd* (1990).) Lord Denning also stated (at 89):

> 'There was a mistake about the quality of the subject-matter, because both parties believed the picture to be a Constable, and that mistake was in one sense essential or fundamental. Such a mistake, however, does not avoid the contract. There was no mistake about the subject-matter of the sale. It was a specific picture of "Salisbury Cathedral". The parties were agreed in the same terms on the same subject-matter, and that is sufficient to make a contract.'

When a person buys the work of a famous artist it is, perhaps, rather perverse to suggest that he or she is buying merely 'a painting' (for example, of Salisbury Cathedral). There are perhaps two possible interpretations of *Leaf* in relation to common mistake. On the one hand, it could be argued that the relatively low price of the painting suggests a slightly speculative venture which includes the risk that the painting of Salisbury Cathedral was not 'a Constable'—in which case there is clearly no fundamental mistake. On the other hand, it could be asserted that the parties contracted for the sale of 'a Constable' and therefore there was a mistake as to an essential quality of the subject matter.

12.44 Lord Denning's statement (above) suggests therefore that a contract will rarely be void as a result of a common mistake as to some essential quality of the thing contracted for. Lord Denning's opinion echoes that of Lord Atkin in *Bell* v *Lever Bros* [1932] AC 161 at 224, in which the latter considered an example with facts similar to those which actually occurred in *Leaf* v *International Galleries* (1950). The apparent injustice suffered by the claimant in *Leaf* is overshadowed by the fact that, in the words of Lord Atkin (at 224), it is of 'paramount importance that contracts should be observed'.

12.45 But in the later case of *Associated Japanese Bank (International)* v *Crédit du Nord SA* [1988] 3 All ER 902 support was given for the existence of a doctrine of common mistake as to quality rendering a contract void ab initio at common law. It was not, in fact, necessary to decide the case on this particular basis, but Steyn J was at pains to explain the nature and scope of such a doctrine. The facts were:

> The claimant bank (C) bought four specific microtextile compression packaging machines from Mr Jack Bennett (B) and then leased them back to him. B received £1,021,000 from C under the transaction. As a condition of the transaction, B's obligations under the 'leaseback' agreement were guaranteed by the defendant bank (D). At all times both banks believed that the four machines existed and were in B's possession. In fact, when B fell behind with his payments under the lease, it was discovered that the machines did not exist! (The transaction

> was a fraud perpetrated by B.) B was found to be bankrupt and therefore C's claim against him under the lease was fruitless. C sued the defendant bank on the guarantee.

In dismissing C's claim, Steyn J held that, on its construction, the guarantee was subject to an express condition precedent that there was a lease in respect of four existing machines. This was because both banks were informed and believed that the machines existed. (In any case, the learned judge thought that there was an implied condition precedent that the machines existed and so C's claim would have failed for this reason. In *Graves* v *Graves* [2007] EWCA Civ 660, the Court of Appeal implied a condition into a tenancy agreement to bring it to an end (at [38]–[41]), and held at [43] that it was 'therefore not necessary to consider whether the contract was frustrated or void for mistake'. On implied condition precedents and common mistake, see the subsequent case law of *Apvodedo NV* v *Collins* (2008) and *Butters* v *BBC Worldwide Ltd* (2009).)

Steyn J went on to explain, *obiter* (at 912–13), the principles relevant to common mistake as to quality of the subject matter: the law will normally uphold apparent contracts; the doctrine of mistake can be relied on only in unexpected and 'wholly exceptional' circumstances. It must be a mistake of both parties relating to facts as they existed at the time of contracting. A party seeking to rely on a common mistake must have had reasonable grounds for entertaining the belief on which the mistake was based. Applying the dicta of Lords Atkin and Thankerton in *Bell* v *Lever Bros* (1932), the learned judge stated that the mistake must render the subject matter of the contract 'essentially and radically different from that which the parties believed to exist'. (The Court of Appeal in *Great Peace Shipping Ltd* v *Tsavliris Salvage (International) Ltd* (2003) at [91]–[93] agreed with Steyn J's analysis and preferred it to Lord Denning's interpretation of *Bell* v *Lever Bros*. Steyn J's test was also applied in *Kyle Bay Ltd (t/a Astons Nightclub)* v *Underwriters* (2007) per Neuberger LJ at [24]–[27]. Here the Court of Appeal rejected a claim based on common mistake, observing that a 'significant' or even a 'substantial' mistake is not necessarily the same thing as one which renders the subject matter 'essentially and radically different' from what the parties believed it to be.)

Applying these principles to the facts of the case, Steyn J concluded (at 913) that 'the stringent test of common law mistake is satisfied; the guarantee is void ab initio'. For both parties, the guarantee of obligations under a lease with machines that did not exist, was essentially and radically different from a guarantee of a lease with four machines that both parties thought were in existence at the time of contracting.[15]

12.46   The scope of common mistake was also considered in the important case of *Great Peace Shipping Ltd* v *Tsavliris Salvage (International) Ltd* [2002] EWCA Civ 1407, [2003] QB 679, where the facts were:

> A vessel, the *Cape Providence*, was seriously damaged in the Indian Ocean and the defendants undertook to provide salvage services. A tug which they proposed to use was too far

---

15 For an interesting discussion of Steyn J's approach, see J. C. Smith, 'Contracts—Mistake, Frustration and Implied Terms' (1994) 110 LQR 400.

away, so the defendants entered into a hire contract for the claimants' vessel, the *Great Peace*, for a minimum of five days to escort and stand by the stricken *Cape Providence*, for the purpose of saving life. The contract gave the defendants the right to cancel on payment of five days' hire. At the time of contracting, the defendants thought that the *Great Peace* was 35 miles away and, therefore, could arrive within a short time. However, it turned out that the two vessels were about 400 miles apart. On discovering this, the defendants did not cancel the contract immediately, but they looked for a closer vessel to assist. They found an alternative within a few hours and cancelled the contract with the claimants, refusing to make any payment for the hire of the *Great Peace*. In defence of the claimants' action, the defendants argued that there had been a fundamental mistake of fact, i.e. that the contract was based on the erroneous assumption that the two vessels were close together, and as a result the contract was either void at law or voidable in equity. The judge found in favour of the claimants.

The trial judge's decision was affirmed by the Court of Appeal and the appeal was dismissed. There is no doubt that it was a common assumption of both parties at the time of contracting that the two vessels were close enough to one another to enable the *Great Peace* to render the escort and stand-by services. But was the misapprehension of both parties so fundamental as to render the contract void? It was held that the common mistake which arose did not render the services essentially different from what the parties had agreed (at [165]). The court thought that it was significant that the defendants refrained from cancelling the agreement until they were certain they could obtain the services of a nearer vessel. It was also relevant that the *Great Peace* would still have been able to render several days of service, despite the longer journey, and the defendants would have wanted this if they had not been able to secure the services of an alternative vessel. In other words, 'the fact that the vessels were further apart than both parties had appreciated did not mean that it was impossible to perform the contractual adventure' (at [165]).

In delivering the judgment of the court, Lord Phillips (at [73]–[76]) explained the principles on which the doctrine of common mistake operates. He stated that where a contract is held to be void on the basis of common mistake this results from a rule of law by which 'if it transpires that one or both of the parties have agreed to do something which it is impossible to perform, no obligation arises out of that agreement'. In considering the issue of impossibility, it is necessary to identify what it is the parties actually agreed would be performed. Obviously this process involves considering any express provisions, but it also includes any implications arising from the circumstances of the agreement. The doctrine of common mistake (like that of frustration—see **Chapter 19**) applies only where a contract has no provision to cover the situation which has occurred. So that 'if, on true construction of the contract, a party warrants that the subject matter of the contract exists, or that it will be possible to perform the contract, there will be no scope to hold the contract void on the ground of common mistake'. Lord Phillips acknowledged that the doctrine is narrow in scope and that (as the actual decision in *Bell* v *Lever Bros* (1932) illustrates) it will be rare that a mistake as to quality will make 'the thing without the quality essentially different from the thing as it was believed to be' and, therefore, void (at [86]). Such cases will arise less frequently than instances of frustration. This is because it is not uncommon for supervening events to occur which, without being the responsibility of either party, defeat the contractual adventure. But in cases where 'parties agree that something shall be done which is impossible at the time of making the agreement, it is much more likely that, on true construction of the agreement, one or other will have undertaken responsibility for the mistaken state of affairs' (at [85]).

12.47 The decision in *Brennan* v *Bolt Burden* (2005) provides a further illustration of the narrow scope of the doctrine of common mistake. (For a slightly less restrictive interpretation of the relevant test, see *Champion Investments Ltd* v *Ahmed* (2004) at [32]). The *Brennan* case involved C's claim for damages for personal injury (from exposure to carbon monoxide), which was settled on a mistaken legal basis. C had compromised her claim, believing that the claim form was served out of time, with the result that the claim was withdrawn with each side bearing its own costs. Due to the subsequent overruling of a relevant legal authority, it was later shown that the parties were mistaken about the claim form being served out of time. As a consequence, C argued that the compromise was void for mistake. By a majority, the Court of Appeal rejected her argument. Maurice Kay LJ stated at [22]–[23]:

> '[T]his is quite simply not a case of impossibility of performance. The compromise has at all times remained performable, albeit to [C's] disadvantage . . . that is in itself sufficient to put it beyond the reach of common mistake of law . . . the compromise was a matter of give-and-take which ought not lightly be set aside . . . and that, as a matter of construction, the risk of a future judicial decision affecting matters to [C's] advantage was impliedly accepted and bargained away by her solicitor.'

Common mistake in equity

12.48 If the question of mistake as to quality is raised by one of the parties, the first task of the court will be to see (as a matter of construction) if either of the parties to the contract bears the risk of the relevant mistake. (For example, in *William Sindall plc* v *Cambridgeshire County Council* (1994), C argued that a contract to buy D's land should be rescinded for mistake when C discovered that a sewer ran across the land. The Court of Appeal, however, rejected C's argument as it was held that the agreement between the parties allocated the risk of this kind of mistake to C.) If the contract is silent on this point, then the doctrine of mistake may be considered.[16] (See *Great Peace Shipping Ltd* v *Tsavliris Salvage (International) Ltd* (2003), discussed earlier.)

12.49 The opinion has been expressed by some writers and judges, most notably by Lord Denning (see *Solle* v *Butcher* [1950] 1 KB 671 at 691), that a common mistake, even of a fundamental nature, does not make the contract void at common law, but merely liable to be set aside in equity. (See also his Lordship's statement to the same effect in *Frederick Rose Ltd* v *William Pim Jnr Ltd* [1953] 2 QB 450 at 459–60.) However, this is inconsistent with what was stated in *Bell* v *Lever Bros* (1932) and with the most recent judicial pronouncements. In *Great Peace Shipping Ltd* v *Tsavliris Salvage (International) Ltd* (2003) at [118], the Court of Appeal said it was inconceivable that the House of Lords in *Bell* v *Lever Bros* 'overlooked an equitable

---

16 See *Sheikh Bros* v *Ochsner* (1957) where a contract was held void after first deciding that neither party assumed the risk that the contract would be impossible to perform.

right... to rescind the agreement, notwithstanding that the agreement was not void for mistake at common law'. It also stated that Lord Atkin's narrow test for common mistake 'broadly reflected the circumstances where equity had intervened to excuse performance of a contract assumed to be binding in law' (at [118]).

12.50   In *Solle* v *Butcher* [1950] 1 KB 671 the facts were:

> In 1947, D took a long lease of a building, which had previously been converted into five flats, with the intention of carrying out repairs caused by war damage and substantial alterations to the property. Although the flats were empty in 1947, one of them (Flat No 1) had been let before the war to a tenant at a rent of £140 per year. C and D were partners in an estate agents' business and they discussed the rent that could be charged for the flats once the improvements had been carried out. D relied on C in calculating the rents that could be charged, and C told D that he could charge £250 per year for the flat in question (Flat No 1), and that the rent was not controlled by the Rent Restriction Acts (as the flat had been altered extensively). In September 1947, D let Flat No 1 to C for seven years at an annual rent of £250; both parties were satisfied that the earlier rent of £140 did not apply as the 'standard rent'. In other words, they entered into the contract under the mistaken impression that the flat was not controlled by the Rent Restriction Acts. In fact the maximum rent that could be charged was £140 and this could not be increased during the contractual tenancy (due to the relevant legislation) once the lease was executed. After nearly two years, C sought a declaration that the standard rent of the flat was £140 and he tried to claim the amount that he had already overpaid to D under the lease. The trial court found that the standard rent was £140 per year. The defendant counterclaimed for rescission of the lease on the basis of common mistake of fact.

It was decided by the Court of Appeal that the contract was not void ab initio, once again illustrating the narrow view of common mistake at law. However, the court purported to exercise its equitable jurisdiction and ordered rescission of the lease, but on the terms that would enable C 'to choose either to stay on at the proper rent [i.e. £250 per year] or to go out' (per Lord Denning at 696–7). In so doing, the court illustrated the flexibility of the equitable approach.[17] Not only did it relieve one party from the hardship caused by the mistake, but it also did justice to the other party. However, it was stated recently that the equitable jurisdiction which Lord Denning asserted 'was a significant extension of any jurisdiction exercised up to that point and one that was not readily reconcilable with the result in *Bell* v *Lever Bros*' (see *Great Peace Shipping Ltd* v *Tsavliris Salvage (International) Ltd* (2003) at [130]).

12.51   A further example of the attempt to develop an equitable approach is provided by *Grist* v *Bailey* [1967] Ch 532:

> The defendant, Mrs Minnie Bailey, agreed to sell to the claimant, Frank Grist, a freehold house for £850, 'subject to the existing tenancy thereof'. At the time of contracting, both

---

17 For a further example, see *AL and S Nutt* v *PE and Y Read* (1999).

> parties thought that the house was occupied by a protected tenant (under the Rent Acts) who was entitled to remain in the house, and the price reflected their belief. In fact, they were incorrect; the tenant left the house without making any claim to protection. The true value of the house with vacant possession was £2,250. Mrs Bailey refused to complete the contract and an action for specific performance was brought by the claimant. The defendant argued that the contract should be set aside on the ground of common mistake.

Goff J held that the common mistake as to the nature of the tenancy affecting the property was not sufficient to render the contract void at common law. (This is surely correct, for the subject matter was not fundamentally or essentially affected by the mistake.) But the considerable undervaluing of the house, due to the mistake, would have caused considerable hardship to the defendant. For this reason the judge upheld the defendant's claim for rescission. The contract was set aside in equity on the terms that the claimant was to have the option of entering into a fresh contract to buy the house at a proper vacant possession price (at 543).

12.52 It might be objected that the decision seems rather indulgent towards the vendor who made a bad bargain (which could presumably have been avoided if greater care had been exercised), and that it conflicts with the requirement of certainty in commercial dealings. But it could also be argued that it would have been extremely harsh to refuse to grant relief to the defendant in view of the material mistake. See further *Pitt v Holt* (2013), which serves as an example, in the context of trusts law, where the test for setting aside a voluntary disposition for mistake will centre on the gravity of the mistake and its consequences and moreover, the injustice of leaving a mistake disposition uncorrected is to be objectively evaluated.

12.53 A further example of the use of equity can be seen in *Magee v Pennine Insurance Co. Ltd* [1969] 2 QB 507, where the facts were:

> In 1961, C bought a car for his 18-year-old son to drive. C, who could not drive, signed a proposal form to insure the car with the defendant company, but the details of the form were completed by the person at the garage from whom he bought the car. Although there was no dishonesty on C's part, the information supplied on the form contained certain innocent misrepresentations. For example, it stated incorrectly that C held a provisional licence and that he and an elder son (who had a full licence) would drive the car as well as the younger son. (In signing the form, C promised that the information it contained was true and that this declaration was to be the basis of a contract of insurance with the defendant company.) The insurance policy on the car (and its replacement) was duly issued and renewed each year. In 1965, the younger son had a serious accident in the car which resulted in a claim on the insurance. C claimed £600 under the policy as the value of the car, but he was offered £385 in settlement of his claim and he accepted this offer. On discovery of C's misrepresentations, the defendants refused to pay him £385 under the compromise agreement. C brought an action for this sum.

In the Court of Appeal, Lord Denning (at 514) accepted that this was a case of common mistake as 'both parties thought that the contract was good and binding'. However, he reiterated his opinion that a common mistake, even on a fundamental matter, does not make a contract void at law, but makes it liable to be set aside in equity. It was held (with Winn LJ dissenting) that the contract, despite being valid at law, would be set aside in equity. It was thought that it would be unfair to hold the insurance company to an agreement based on an invalid insurance policy. But it can be objected that justice was done to one party only. No terms were imposed by the court. The decision meant that C had paid insurance premiums for a number of years on an invalid policy and had totally wasted his money.

12.54 It is interesting that in *Magee* v *Pennine Insurance Co. Ltd* (1969), a case which closely resembles the facts of *Bell* v *Lever Bros* (1932), the contract was set aside—whereas in *Bell* the company was unable to recover its money from its ex-employees. Attempts have been made to distinguish between these two closely analogous cases by arguing that in *Bell* the money had already been paid to the men before discovery of the mistake, whilst in *Magee* the money had not been paid at the time the mistake was discovered. This may suggest therefore that it was not inequitable to set aside the agreement in *Magee*, but that it might have been if the company had already paid out the £385 under the compromise agreement. However, there is nothing in the judgment to indicate that this was the basis of the decision.

12.55 In truth it is difficult to find any material difference between the facts of these two cases. The difference in outcome reflects the extent of the development of an equitable approach to common mistake since the time of the *Bell* v *Lever Bros* (1932) decision. Indeed, the Court of Appeal stated in *Great Peace Shipping Ltd* v *Tsavliris Salvage (International) Ltd* (2003) (at [153]) that the two cases can be reconciled 'only by postulating that there are two categories of mistake, one that renders a contract void at law and one that renders it voidable in equity'. The problem with this, as the court in *Great Peace Shipping Ltd* also pointed out (at [153]), is that it has not 'proved possible to define satisfactorily two different qualities of mistake, one operating in law and one in equity'. It could be argued that the resulting confusion tends to negate the purpose of a narrow approach to mistake at common law: i.e. the need to uphold apparent contracts in the interest of certainty. The ambit of the equitable jurisdiction advocated by Lord Denning has been difficult to delineate.[18] In *Solle* v *Butcher* [1950] 1 KB 671 (at 693), he stated:

> 'A contract is . . . liable to be set aside if the parties were under a common misapprehension either as to facts or as to their relative and respective rights, provided that the misapprehension was fundamental and that the party seeking to set it aside was not himself at fault.'

The actual decision in *Solle* v *Butcher* may have achieved greater flexibility by extending the scope of the equitable jurisdiction, but in doing so it produced a lack of clarity. Lord Denning stated that the mistake has to be 'fundamental', but in what respect did this go beyond Lord Atkin's formulation of the common law test? (See *Great Peace Shipping Ltd*

---

18 See *Great Peace Shipping Ltd* v *Tsavliris Salvage (International) Ltd* (2003) at [153]–[156].

at [131] and [154].) Despite the efforts of later judges to provide some clarification,[19] this remained an insurmountable problem. In *Great Peace Shipping Ltd* (at [161]), the Court of Appeal expressed some understanding of Lord Denning's antipathy towards the decision in *Bell* v *Lever Bros* and it thought that 'there is scope for legislation to give greater flexibility to our law of mistake than the common law allows'. However, it also stated (at [160]) that it had taken the opportunity for a 'full and mature consideration' of the decisions in *Bell* v *Lever Bros* and *Solle* v *Butcher* and concluded that there is 'no way that *Solle* v *Butcher* can stand with *Bell* v *Lever Bros*'. The court hesitated in holding that *Solle* v *Butcher* is 'not good law' but, in view of its critical comments, *Solle* v *Butcher* must now be regarded as being of dubious authority. (For further comment on the *Great Peace* decision, see A. Chandler et al., 'Common Mistake: Theoretical Justification and Remedial Inflexibility' (2004) JBL 34; M. Doherty and H. James, 'The Law of Mistake in the 21st Century' (2003) Business Law Review 59; C. Hare, 'Inequitable Mistake' (2003) 62 CLJ 29; and F. Reynolds, 'Reconsider the Contract Textbooks' (2003) 119 LQR 177.)

Documents signed by mistake

12.56   Generally the law takes a strict view of signed documents. In the absence of fraud or misrepresentation, a person who signs a document is bound by this, regardless of whether he has read or understood what he is signing (see *L'Estrange* v *Graucob* (1934)). This is a further illustration of the law's objective approach to agreement.[20] The signer of a document will, of course, be able to rescind a contract induced by the fraud of the other contracting party. But this will be of no avail if a bona fide third party has acquired rights under the contract, for value, before it is avoided. (The document in question may also bring the signer into a contractual relationship with someone other than the fraudulent person.) The only defence which is then of any assistance to the signer is to claim that the contract is void altogether and not merely voidable for fraud. This involves relying on the argument that his mind did not accompany the signing of the document and pleading non est factum ('it is not my deed').

12.57   This particular defence, as its name suggests, originated to protect a person who executed a deed after it had been incorrectly read over to him. It was a necessary development in an age when many people could not read. For example, in *Thoroughgood's Case* (1582):

> Thoroughgood (C), who could not read, was owed rent by a tenant. The tenant drew up a deed which was incorrectly read over to C by someone posing as a helpful bystander. Instead of merely releasing the tenant from his arrears of rent as he supposed, C in fact signed away his rights to the property. The tenant sold the land to an innocent purchaser; C sued in trespass for recovery of his land.

---

19 For an attempt to explain what is meant by a 'fundamental' mistake, both at common law and in equity, see *William Sindall plc* v *Cambridgeshire County Council* (1994).

20 For a critical view, see J. R. Spencer, 'Signature, Consent, and the Rule in *L'Estrange* v *Graucob*' (1973) 32(1) CLJ 104.

Thoroughgood succeeded in his action. He was not bound by his deed because it was misrepresented to him and he could not read it. In the context of its time, this was a fair and sensible exception to the general rule that deeds were regarded as absolutely binding. But, later, the defence of non est factum was extended to cover written documents not under seal, and to cases where the signer was not illiterate (see *Foster* v *Mackinnon* (1869) LR 4 CP 704 at 711). These developments were much more contentious, even though the defence did not cover a person who was simply negligent.

12.58   As the basis for the defence of non est factum is a lack of intent on the part of the signer, the result of a successful plea is that the contract is a complete nullity (i.e. void). In the interest of commercial certainty, and in view of the fact that most people today are able to read, the use of this plea should be strictly limited. Otherwise it can cause injustice to third parties. This restrictive approach was supported by the House of Lords in *Saunders* v *Anglia Building Society* (sometimes referred to as *Gallie* v *Lee*) (1971), which is the leading case on the scope of non est factum today. The facts were:

> Mrs Gallie (C) was a widow, aged 78, who gave the deeds of her house to her nephew so that he (together with a business associate named Lee) could raise money by using the house as security. She stipulated that she should continue to live in the house until she died. Lee and her nephew asked C to sign a document which she was unable to read as she had broken her glasses. Lee told her, dishonestly, that it was a deed of gift to her nephew. In fact, it was a document (drawn up by a dishonest clerk) which transferred the house by sale to Lee for the price of £3,000. Lee failed to pay C any of the money; instead, he mortgaged the house to a building society for his own benefit, and nothing was paid by him to the nephew. Lee defaulted on the mortgage instalments and the building society claimed possession of the house. C sued Lee and the building society, seeking a declaration that the document that she signed was void on the ground of non est factum. Her claim was that she had not intended to sell the house to Lee, but rather she had intended to make a gift to her nephew.

The case is a good illustration of how a third party's rights may become involved where someone has mistakenly signed a document. The House of Lords (affirming the Court of Appeal's decision) held that the defence of non est factum could not be relied on by C in these circumstances. This was because, in the opinion of the judges, the document that she signed was not radically or totally different in character from the one that she thought she was signing. She intended that her nephew should be able to raise money by using the house as security, and it can be argued that this would have still been achieved under the document that she actually signed, but for Lee's dishonesty.[21] So this is the first limitation on the use of non est factum as a means of nullifying an apparent agreement.

---

21 Although this argument appears to overlook the fact that Mrs Gallie stipulated that she was to remain in occupation of the house during her lifetime.

12.59   The second limitation, and a further reason for C's claim being rejected, is that a party cannot rely on the defence where he or she has acted carelessly. The plea originated, as we have seen, to protect those who could not read, at a time when illiteracy was widespread. Despite the subsequent development of the doctrine to cover a wider group of people, it is surely correct that someone who has been careless should not be able to rely on it as a means of escape from a document that they have signed. Otherwise it would be difficult for anyone to have confidence in the validity of a signature on a document and this would be extremely inconvenient in commercial matters. A person who has broken his glasses can usually delay signing a document until they have been repaired. Mrs Gallie was, regrettably, careless and the decision was therefore correct.

12.60   This point is also illustrated in *United Dominions Trust Ltd* v *Western* (1976), where D agreed to buy a car from dealers on hire purchase. In addition to the payment of a deposit, D signed a blank copy of a finance company's (C's) standard form agreement and left the dealers to fill in the relevant details. When the form was forwarded by the dealers to the finance company it contained inaccuracies about the price of the vehicle and the size of deposit paid by D. The claimant company accepted the figures as correct and that the signed document formed a contract between themselves and D. D later found out that the figures did not represent what he had agreed with the dealers but he took no action to remedy the mistake. He paid no instalments under the agreement and the claimants claimed £750, which was the incorrect price stated on the form signed by D. The Court of Appeal found in favour of the claimants. It is clear that where a person signs a blank form and leaves someone else to fill in the details, he cannot argue that he failed to consent to the figures that are inserted. The signer of a blank document is careless, and no sensible distinction can be made between this situation and that where a person carelessly signs a completed document.[22]

12.61   We have seen the ways in which the scope of the defence of non est factum has been curtailed by decisions of the courts.[23] But, assuming that the signer has not been careless[24] (presumably to be judged by the standards of that person), and that the document signed was radically different from that which it was supposed to be, what types of people can rely on the plea? Those who have signed as a result of some deception will be able to; so too will those who are unable to understand the meaning of a document through no fault of their own, without having it explained to them, 'whether that be from defective education, illness or innate incapacity' (per Lord Reid in *Saunders* v *Anglia Building Society* [1971] AC 1004 at 1016).

---

22 Also note that the plea of non est factum is not open to a person who signs a document in the belief that it is 'just a form', having no precise idea as to its nature; see *Gillman* v *Gillman* (1946).

23 The restrictive approach of the courts is further illustrated by *Norwich and Peterborough Building Society* v *Steed (No 2)* (1993).

24 For further discussion, see *AL Factors Ltd* v *Pamela Morgan* (1999).

12.62   The defence was successfully relied on in *Lloyds Bank plc* v *Waterhouse* (1990). This involved an illiterate defendant who signed a bank guarantee of his son's debt, without either reading the document or indicating that he was unable to read it. However, he had done his best, by asking questions, to ascertain the nature and extent of his liability, and the bank's employees had misrepresented the nature of the document to him. The Court of Appeal allowed the defendant's appeal; various reasons were given to support this decision, including the negligent misrepresentation of the bank. Woolf LJ did not deem it necessary to decide the issue of non est factum, but Purchas LJ had no doubts that the defence was successfully established by the defendant. He explained that the defendant's illiteracy was clearly a disability; that the signed document was different from that which he thought he was signing; and that the defendant was not careless, having 'energetically investigated the ambit of the guarantee from the outset'.

12.63   It might be safer, though, to regard the case as decided on the basis of negligent misrepresentation, rather than non est factum. It is surely questionable whether the defendant exercised proper care for his own protection. It might also be questioned whether the document actually signed by the defendant was radically or fundamentally different in character from the one that he thought he was signing.

⊙ Summary

- It is important to understand that some mistakes relate to whether the parties have reached *agreement*, whilst others involve questions of *performance*.

- In relation to 'performability', and the extent of contractual obligations, there is a connection between the subject of mistake and the doctrine of frustration (see **Chapter 19**).

Agreement mistake

- It will be remembered that the law takes a predominantly objective view of agreement (see **Chapter 2**).

- In cases of mistake as to identity, the law usually has to determine which of two innocent parties should bear the loss.

- The case law on mistake as to identity is unsatisfactory and the topic was considered by the House of Lords in *Shogun Finance Ltd* v *Hudson* (2003). Unfortunately, the majority in this case failed to take advantage of an opportunity to rationalize this area of law.

- Agreement mistake can also arise where the parties are at cross-purposes. Generally, parties are bound by their apparent agreements (judged objectively), but there may be situations where there is no contract due to inherent ambiguity.

- In the interest of justice, a court may grant relief against the consequences of mistake: for example, a court may exercise its discretion to refuse specific performance. Rectification is another equitable remedy.

Performability mistake

- Common mistake is where both parties share the same misapprehension about some underlying fact which makes the performance of the contract impossible or devoid of purpose.

- Where a contract is made for the sale of goods which have already ceased to exist, the outcome ought to turn on the construction of the agreement between the parties (see *Couturier* v *Hastie* (1856)).

- However, *Couturier* v *Hastie* led to a belief that in cases of non-existent goods the 'contract' will be void. (This interpretation was reflected in the Sale of Goods Act 1893 (now 1979), s 6.)

- Outside this category of cases involving non-existent goods, there are few instances of a contract being void for common mistake.

- The House of Lords in *Bell* v *Lever Bros* (1932) illustrates the fact that a mistake as to quality will not usually render a contract void.

- After *Solle* v *Butcher* (1950) it was thought that a court may set a contract aside in equity on the basis of a common mistake, although it was never clear how this more flexible approach could be reconciled with the decision in *Bell* v *Lever Bros*.

- The Court of Appeal in *Great Peace Shipping Ltd* v *Tsavliris* (2003) has concluded that *Solle* v *Butcher* cannot be regarded as good law, as it is inconsistent with *Bell* v *Lever Bros*.

▶ Further reading

A. Chandler et al., 'Common Mistake: Theoretical Justification and Remedial Inflexibility' (2004) (Jan) JBL 34

A. De Moor, 'Intention in the Law of Contract: Elusive or Illusory?' (1990) 106 LQR 632

C. Elliott, 'No Justice for Innocent Purchasers of Dishonestly Obtained Goods: *Shogun Finance v Hudson*' (2004) (May) JBL 381

A. Foster, 'Sale by a Non-owner: Striking a Fair Balance between the Rights of the True Owner and a Buyer in Good Faith' (2004) 9 Cov LJ 1

D. Friedmann, 'The Objective Principle and Mistake and Involuntariness in Contract and Restitution' (2003) 119 LQR 68

C. Hare, 'Identity mistakes: a missed opportunity?' (2004) 67(6) MLR 993

C. MacMillan, 'How Temptation Led to Mistake: An Explanation of *Bell v Lever Bros Ltd*' (2003) 119 LQR 625

C. MacMillan, 'Mistake as to Identity Clarified' (2004) 120 LQR 369

C. MacMillan, 'Rogues, Swindlers and Cheats: the Development of Mistake of Identity in English Contract Law' (2005) 64 CLJ 711

D. McLauchlan, 'The "Drastic" Remedy of Rectification for Unilateral Mistake' (2008) 124 LQR 608

C. Nugee, 'Rectification after Chartbrook v Persimmon: where are we now?' (2012) 26(2) Tr L I 76

A. Phang et al., 'Mistaken Identity in the House of Lords' (2004) 63 CLJ 24

C. Slade, 'Myth of Mistake in the English Law of Contract' (1954) 70 LQR 385

J. C. Smith, 'Contracts—Mistake, Frustration and Implied Terms' (1994) 110 LQR 400

M. Smith, 'Rectification of Contracts for Common Mistake, *Joscelyne v Nissen*, and Subjective States of Mind' (2007) 123 LQR 116

T. Yeo, 'Great Peace: A Distant Disturbance' (2005) 121 LQR 393

Chapter 13

Misrepresentation

⬦ Introduction

13.1   An operative misrepresentation (i.e. one which has legal effect) is basically a false statement of existing or past fact made by one party to the contract to the other, before, or at the time of, contracting, on which that other party relied in contracting. (Whether there is also a requirement that the misrepresentation should be material is considered later (see para. **13.39**).)

13.2   The person to whom a misrepresentation, or alleged misrepresentation, is made is referred to as the 'representee'. The person making the misrepresentation, or alleged misrepresentation, is the 'representor'.

13.3   Much discussion may occur before a contract is made. In the course of that discussion one party may make a statement to the other which subsequently proves to be untrue. The other party will feel aggrieved if he, or she, relied upon that statement in entering into the contract. What can be done? If that statement became a term of the contract, or of a collateral contract, then there is a breach of contract and the injured party can take action accordingly (see **Chapter 20**). If it did not become a term, there is no possibility of a remedy for breach. However, a remedy may lie for misrepresentation. This means that, when a dispute arises over a pre-contractual statement which has proved to be false, the injured party will often raise two arguments,[1] namely that:

1. the statement became a term; and
2. the statement was an operative misrepresentation.

---

1   There might be the possibility of an action for mistake, but such an action lies within very narrow boundaries, and has limited chances of success—see **Chapter 12**.

13.4   Misrepresentation is divided into different types; the classification is particularly important when the representee wishes to claim damages for the misrepresentation. Until the 1960s
the classification was only twofold. Misrepresentations were either fraudulent or innocent (i.e.
not fraudulent). There was no reason to separate negligent from wholly innocent misrepresentations because damages were available only for fraudulent misrepresentations (through the
tort of deceit), and rescission was available for all misrepresentations. Because of the availability of damages we now differentiate four types of misrepresentation:

1. fraudulent misrepresentation—damages available under the tort of deceit;
2. a misrepresentation which is also a negligent misstatement, so that the damages are
   available for the tort of negligent misstatement;
3. a misrepresentation for which damages are available under s 2(1) of the
   Misrepresentation Act 1967 (i.e. the misrepresentor cannot prove that he or she
   believed the truth of what was misrepresented, and that there were reasonable
   grounds for doing so, up until the time the contract was made);
4. innocent misrepresentation, i.e. misrepresentations not falling within the above
   categories. No damages are available for innocent misrepresentation, as such,
   but s 2(2) allows the court to award damages in lieu of rescission where the
   misrepresentation is non-fraudulent.

The second and third categories are often both referred to as negligent misrepresentation,[2] but
do need to be kept distinct.

13.5   However, even when the common law was providing damages only for fraudulent misrepresentation, equity allowed rescission for all misrepresentations. If rescission occurs, the
parties return to their pre-contractual positions. Rescission is the carrying into effect of the
decision to treat a voidable contract as if it had never been made. It is a radical remedy and there
are bars on its availability.

13.6   The topic of misrepresentation is difficult because of the involvement of the common law
(including frequently, tort), equity, and statute (the Misrepresentation Act 1967 (MA 1967)). It
is not an area which provides a ready means of redress for the consumer. The consumer organization, Which?, has commented[3]

> 'The availability of existing remedies is patchy at best. Furthermore, where protection does
> exist, the remedies are too complex for consumers to understand and as a consequence are
> rarely used'.

---

2   Obviously, within the third category it is not tortious negligence which is in question, and it is for the misrepresentor to
establish his belief and its reasonableness. Nevertheless, as the action under MA 1967, s 2(1) is based upon the absence
of reasonable belief—despite the fact that the absence of reasonable grounds for belief is not proven but merely not
disproved—negligent misrepresentation is a more apt label than innocent misrepresentation for the third category,
even though it has occasionally, confusingly, been referred to as innocent misrepresentation (e.g. *Royscott Trust Ltd* v
Rogerson (1991) per Balcombe LJ).

3   Quoted in The Law Commissions, *Consumer Redress for Misleading and Aggressive Practices* (Law Com No 332, Scot
Law Com No 226) para. S.18.

Against this background, the Law Commission has proposed a simpler, more 'rough and ready', approach for consumers,[4] and there are now draft regulations to implement that: the draft Consumer Protection from Unfair Trading (Amendment) Regulations.

13.7 The Consumer Protection from Unfair Trading Regulations 2008 provided public enforcement by the Trading Standards Services and the Office of Fair Trading (OFT) to deal with misleading and aggressive commercial practices, and unfair commercial practices more broadly, through criminal sanctions and enforcement orders. The Law Commissions have recommended that redress should be provided for the individual consumer, in relation to misleading and aggressive practices, to be able to 'unwind' contracts (which will be similar, but simpler, than rescinding), or receive a discount on the price and, in some cases, recover damages. The definition of consumer would reflect that now commonly used in relation to European derived legislation, so that a consumer would be 'an individual acting for purposes that are wholly or mainly outside that individual's business'.[5] A 'trader' would be a 'person acting (personally or through an agent) for purposes relating to that person's business'. Most contracts between such parties will be covered, but not those involving land transactions (other than residential leases) or financial services.[6] (Land and financial services contracts were not generally regarded as suitable for the certain, but simple, 'rough and ready' remedies which were proposed, and are also covered by other regulation). Obviously we are here concerned with 'misleading' commercial practices: aggressive practices are looked at in the chapter on duress and undue influence (**Chapter 14**).

What constitutes an operative misrepresentation?

13.8 As was stated earlier, an operative misrepresentation is, basically, a false statement of existing or past fact made by one party to the contract to the other, before, or at the time of, contracting, which induces the other party to contract. (Whether the misrepresentation must also be material is considered later (see para. **13.39**).)

13.9 As we shall see, the term 'statement' can be misleading because, although there is no general duty to disclose relevant facts in pre-contract negotiations, there are some circumstances in which a misrepresentation is found to have occurred because of something which the representor has omitted to say or write. In addition, it is possible to base a misrepresentation on physical appearance rather than on an oral or a written statement.

13.10 There are two basic points to be considered when asking what constitutes an operative misrepresentation: (1) which 'statements' are capable of being misrepresentations, and

---

4 The Law Commissions, *Consumer Redress for Misleading and Aggressive Practices* (Law Com No 332, Scot Law Com No 226) para. S.18.

5 Draft Consumer Protection from Unfair Trading (Amendment) Regulations, amending reg 2(1) of the Consumer Protection from Unfair Trading Regulations 2008.

6 The Law Commissions, *Consumer Redress for Misleading and Aggressive Practices* (Law Com No 332, Scot Law Com No 226) para. 6.118.

(2) under what circumstances is the appropriate sort of 'statement' operative, i.e. under what circumstances does it have legal effect as a misrepresentation? In simple terms, the first of these requirements is for a false statement of existing or past fact. For that statement then to constitute an operative misrepresentation it must have been relied upon by the person to whom it was made in contracting with the person who made it. (It will be considered later whether in addition, it must be material so that it would have been relied on by a reasonable person in making the decision to contract (at para. **13.39**).)

The misrepresentation

13.11   In order for there to be a misrepresentation there must be a false statement of existing or past fact. Statements of opinion or intention will not suffice, in themselves, but they must be given careful consideration. A statement of fact may often be found where initially there appears to be only a statement of opinion, or intention. (There has in the past also been an exclusion of statements of law, but it has now been held that these can found a restitutionary action for mistake (*Kleinwort Benson Ltd* v *Lincoln City Council* (1999)), and they should similarly be capable of constituting misrepresentations (*Pankhania* v *Hackney LBC* (2002)).)

Statements of intention

13.12   A statement of intention cannot, in itself, constitute a misrepresentation. A statement of fact is required. However, a statement of intention carries with it an implied statement of fact as to the state of mind of the representor. If someone falsely states their intention, then they have falsely misrepresented the fact that they hold that intention. In *Edgington* v *Fitzmaurice* (1885) 29 Ch D 459 Bowen LJ said (at 483):

> 'The state of a man's mind is as much a fact as the state of his digestion. It is true that it is very difficult to prove what the state of a man's mind at a particular time is, but if it can be ascertained it is as much a fact as anything else. A misrepresentation as to the state of a man's mind is, therefore, a misstatement of fact.'

This is illustrated by the facts of *Edgington* v *Fitzmaurice*:

> The directors of a company issued a prospectus inviting subscriptions for debentures, i.e. they were seeking to raise money. The prospectus stated that it was intended to use the money obtained to make improvements in the company's business by altering its buildings, purchasing horses and vans, and developing its trade. The real intention was to use the money obtained to pay off existing debts of the company.

It was held that a fact had been misrepresented because there was no intention to use the money in the manner stated.

Statements of opinion

13.13   In *Bisset* v *Wilkinson* [1927] AC 177 it was held that there was no misrepresentation. The statement made was only a statement of opinion and not fact. In that case:

> Mr Bisset wished to sell a piece of land in New Zealand. He told Mr Wilkinson that the land would support 2,000 sheep. No one had previously used the parcel of land in question as a sheep farm. Mr Wilkinson purchased the land. It failed to support 2,000 sheep.

The Privy Council held that the statement as to the capacity of the land did not constitute a misrepresentation. As that parcel of land had not previously been used for sheep farming, it was purely a statement of opinion and not one of fact.

13.14   Where an opinion is stated which is not held, however, the same reasoning applies as that used in *Edgington* v *Fitzmaurice* (1885). A misrepresentation of the representor's state of mind would have occurred (*Bisset* v *Wilkinson* [1927] AC 177 at 182). In such a situation, where there is a straightforward lie as to the opinion held by the representor, it is obvious where the misstated fact can be found but, even in the absence of such fraud, the line between opinion and fact has not proved to be as distinct as might at first be thought. The opinions of experts, or those in the best position to have ascertained the truth of the matter, create obvious difficulties when it is sought to distinguish between opinion and fact. An opinion given by such a person is likely to be treated as a statement of fact and, often quite reasonably, relied upon. In such circumstances the courts have endeavoured to find that statements of fact have been made.

13.15   Despite an apparent statement of opinion, a misrepresentation was found in *Smith* v *Land and House Property Corpn* (1884) 28 Ch D 7.

> The claimant put a hotel up for sale. The particulars stated that it was 'let to Mr F. Fleck (a most desirable tenant), at a rental of £400 per annum, for an unexpired term of twenty-seven and a half years'. Mr Fleck was not a desirable tenant; he had not been paying his rent on time, and it was in arrears.

The court held that the statement as to Mr Fleck's suitability as a tenant was not merely a statement of opinion. The landlord was in a much better position than anyone else to know what sort of a tenant there was on the property. There was an implied misrepresentation. Bowen LJ said (at 15):

> '[I]f the facts are not equally known to both sides, then a statement of opinion by the one who knows the facts best involves very often a statement of a material fact, for he impliedly states that he knows facts which justify his opinion'.

The misrepresentation provided an answer to the claimant's claim for specific performance of the sale contract and the defendants were able to rescind.[7]

---

7   See also *Crédit Lyonnais Bank Nederland* v *Export Credits Guarantee Dept* (1996).

13.16 In *Brown* v *Raphael* (1958) the line was taken that, in this type of case, the fact which is being misrepresented is that the representor had reasonable grounds for his or her opinion or belief. Such a representation, that an opinion is based on reasonable grounds, will be found to have been made where the person stating his or her opinion is in a better position than the other party to know, or to find out, the truth. *Brown* v *Raphael* concerned the sale of a reversion. Its value depended upon the tax position of the person with the life interest. The buyer could not ascertain this and had to depend upon the statement of the seller indicating that the tax position was favourable. The question was whether this was a misrepresentation or merely a statement of opinion. It was held that it was a misrepresentation. One party knew the facts far better than the other could know them. The opinion on the tax position carried with it the implied statement of fact that the seller had reasonable grounds for that belief. There was a misrepresentation, as the seller had no such grounds.

13.17 The above argument should also apply in cases where the facts are accessible to either party but one party is an expert and he or she states an opinion on a matter within that area of expertise. The expert will impliedly state that he or she has reasonable grounds for that opinion. If the expert has not considered the question at all, or been negligent in coming to a conclusion, then it would seem that the courts will be willing to find a misrepresentation. In *Esso Petroleum Co. Ltd* v *Mardon* (1976), an expert's assessment of the potential sales by a new petrol station was made negligently, without due consideration of all the facts. It was decided that there was a breach of an implied term that the expert would take due care in his assessment and also that there was a claim in tort for negligent misstatement. The point to note here is the court's obvious willingness to find a statement of fact in the statement of opinion by an expert, although the case was not decided on the basis of misrepresentation.

13.18 However, where the basic facts are best known to one party, but that party lacks the specialist knowledge or expertise needed to be able to draw reliable conclusions from them as to the matter stated, it would seem that no implied misrepresentation of fact will then be found. A statement by an ordinary consumer, with no specialist knowledge, as to the value of the contents of a flat containing his belongings, and those of his parents, did not imply that he had a reasonable basis for the value stated in making a contract of insurance (*Economides* v *Commercial Union Assurance Co. plc* (1997)).

No general duty to disclose

13.19 The law does not impose any general duty on a contracting party to disclose relevant facts to the other party and, in general, silence does not constitute a misrepresentation. In most cases the law allows a party to profit from his superior knowledge. It is possible to view this as economically efficient, for otherwise the incentive to acquire information would be removed.[8] It is also the case that the lack of a general duty to disclose prevents the problems, and uncertainties, which would arise in determining what information should

---

8 A. Kronman, 'Mistake, Disclosure, Information and the Law of Contracts' (1978) 7 JLS 1.

fall within the duty. However, there are exceptions to the general rule, which are considered below.[9]

13.20   *Turner* v *Green* (1895) provides an example of the operation of the general rule. In that case:

> Turner and Green were engaged in a legal dispute. Turner's solicitor, Fowler, reached a settlement with Green on behalf of his client. Before concluding that agreement, Fowler did not reveal to Green that other proceedings had taken place which made the settlement disadvantageous to Green.

When Turner claimed specific enforcement of the agreement, Green tried to rely upon the non-disclosure to resist the claim. The court held that mere non-disclosure of a material fact could not provide a basis for rescission or a denial of specific performance. It did not constitute a misrepresentation.[10]

Partial non-disclosure

13.21   The situation is different if there is not complete silence on a particular matter which is being dealt with, but partial disclosure. This occurs where what has been stated is literally true but misleading because of other facts which have been omitted. In *Notts Patent Brick and Tile Co.* v *Butler* (1886):

> Butler wished to sell a piece of land which was subject to several restrictive covenants, one of which precluded its use as a brickyard. The claimant company, which manufactured bricks, wished to purchase the land to use in its business. The company inquired of Butler's solicitor whether the land was subject to any restrictive covenants. The solicitor stated that he was not aware of any but did not add that he had not inspected the relevant documents. The company contracted to purchase the land and paid a deposit.

The solicitor's reply had been literally true but was misleading because he did not add that he had not inspected the relevant documents. There had been a misrepresentation which entitled the purchaser to rescind the contract and recover the deposit. The same line was taken in *Dimmock* v *Hallett* (1866) where an estate was for sale. One of the farms on it was described as let to a certain tenant at £290 per year. It was not stated that the tenant had paid only £1 for the three months he leased the farm before his year's occupation, nor was it stated that he had left the farm and no new tenant had been found for it, even at a lower rent. What had been said was literally true but, without the additional details, it constituted a misrepresentation.[11]

---

9 There are also other ways in which there may be liability if there has been no disclosure of defects in the goods or limitations on what they are fit to do e.g. under the terms implied by s 14(2) (satisfactory quality) and s 14(3) (reasonable fitness for the buyer's particular purpose) of the Sale of Goods Act 1979.

10 See also *Keates* v *Cadogan* (1851); *Fletcher* v *Krell* (1872).

11 See also *Atlantic Lines & Navigation Co. Inc.* v *Hallam Ltd; (The Lucy)* (1983) (see para. **13.92**); *Spice Girls* v *Aprilia* (2002) at [59].

Change of circumstances

13.22   A statement of fact may be made which is true at the time it is made, but which has ceased to be true before the contract, which it has induced, is concluded. Under these circumstances, if the person making the representation knows of the change in the facts, there will be a misrepresentation if he fails to disclose it. In *With* v *O'Flanagan* (1936):

> O'Flanagan wished to sell his medical practice. In January he told With that the practice brought in about £2,000 a year. The contract for the sale of the practice was made in May. In the intervening months O'Flanagan was unwell and the practice became practically worthless. In the three weeks before the sale the takings of the practice averaged only £5 a week.

The change in the facts should have been revealed and failure to do so meant that the contract could be rescinded.[12] Two possible ways in which the misrepresentation could be occurring were identified. First, the misrepresentation could be the silence itself on the basis that the initial statement had given rise to a duty to disclose the changes. Second, the misrepresentation could merely lie in the initial statement which is then seen as a continuing representation which becomes a misrepresentation with the change in the facts.[13] Whether there is a statement which can be regarded as a continuing representation and eventually a misrepresentation, or whether it is the silence itself which forms the basis of the right to rescind, is relevant to the question of whether or not the Misrepresentation Act 1967 can apply to the above situation. That Act applies where a misrepresentation is made and this is inapt to cover the situation where it is silence as such which is being dealt with.[14]

Fiduciary or confidential relationships

13.23   Where there is a fiduciary relationship, such as where the parties are principal and agent (*Armstrong* v *Jackson* (1917)), there will be a duty to disclose material facts. However, more than mere disclosure will be required if the relationship is one giving rise to the presumption of undue influence, such as solicitor and client or trustee and beneficiary. Such transactions may well be set aside unless the 'weaker party' has received independent advice (on undue influence, see **Chapter 14**).

Contracts uberrimae fidei

13.24   In relation to contracts uberrimae fidei (contracts of the utmost good faith) a duty to disclose material facts is imposed. In such contracts one party is usually in a far better position than the other to know or ascertain the relevant facts. Contracts of insurance form the main

---

12 See also *Davies* v *London and Provincial Marine Insurance Co.* (1878); *Reynell* v *Sprye* (1852) 1 De GM & G 660 at 708; *Shelley* v *United Artists Corpn* (1990). But see *Thomas Witter Ltd* v *TBP Industries Ltd* (1996).

13 *With* at 583–4 per Lord Wright MR; *Spice Girls* v *Aprilia* (2002) at [51].

14 *Banque Financière de la Cité SA* v *Westgate Insurance Co.* (1989).

type of contracts uberrimae fidei. Contracts relating to family settlements are also contracts uberrimae fidei.[15] Other contracts are related to contracts uberrimae fidei and require more limited disclosure, for example, a surety contract.

Misrepresentation by conduct

13.25   A misrepresentation may stem from conduct. There are examples from the criminal law, which supply analogies in the context of misrepresentation. In *R* v *Barnard* (1837) the defendant wore the cap and gown of a university student to persuade an Oxford bootmaker to supply him with bootstraps. This form of dress was held to amount to a false pretence. A more up-to-date example is provided by the idea that in merely sitting down in a restaurant and ordering a meal there is an implied representation that the person concerned has the funds to pay for the meal (*Ray* v *Sempers* (1974)). In *R* v *Charles* (1977) it was held that the use of a cheque card carries with it a representation that the user has the bank's authority to use the card. In the context of misrepresentation itself, in *Spice Girls* v *Aprilia* (2002), attendance by all of the original Spice Girls at a commercial advertising shoot was part of the misrepresentation that the Spice Girls did not know, or have reasonable grounds to believe, that any of them intended to leave the group during the minimum term of the advertising agreement they were about to enter into. (Geri Halliwell had already told the other Spice Girls of her intention to leave before then.)

Misleading practices

13.26   It can be seen that the law on what constitutes a misrepresentation is complex, and would not be easy for the consumer to understand. The draft Regulations on Misleading and Aggressive Practices avoid the distinction between fact and opinion, and should be less difficult in relation to the situations where a failure to state something may be a misleading practice. The basic conception of the Law Commissions is that a commercial practice is misleading if it contains false information, or if it is likely to mislead the average consumer in its overall presentation.[16] There would be no category of misleading omissions as such, but the Law Commission felt that providing for the overall presentation to be misleading would deal with such omissions as could be dealt with without making the law too cumbersome, complex, or unclear to consumers, although they also thought that should be kept under review.[17]

---

15 e.g. *Gordon* v *Gordon* (1821).

16 The 2008 Regulations contains a list of matters in relation to which the commercial practice must be misleading. The Law Commissions' proposals would simplify the situation in relation to enforcement by the consumer by omitting this list, but it is used even for these purposes in the draft Consumer Protection from Unfair Trading Regulations (For the list see reg 5(4)-(7) of the Consumer Protection from Unfair Trading Regulations 2008). The draft Regulations also maintain the reference of the 2008 Regulations to deceiving the consumer, rather than misleading the consumer. The Law Commissions preferred 'misleading' to deceiving as 'The word "deceive" is ambiguous. Although it is often used to refer to deliberate dishonesty, we do not think that is what is meant in this context... The emphasis is on its effect on an average consumer, rather than the state of mind of the trader' (para. 7.23).

17 The Law Commissions, *Consumer Redress for Misleading and Aggressive Practices* (Law Com No 332, Scot Law Com No 226) paras 7.3–7.61.

13.27   The Law Commissions provided examples of omissions which they viewed as misleading through the overall presentation. For example:

> 'A consumer buys a lawnmower, which works satisfactorily, but the consumer is not aware that the mower requires an unusual and hard to obtain fuel.'[18]

The Law Commission was of the view that[19]

> 'The type of fuel would obviously be an important matter to the average consumer, as without the fuel the lawnmower would be useless. The average consumer would expect to be able to obtain appropriate fuel for a lawnmower they buy. If the trader fails to make the consumer aware that this will be very difficult, then we think the overall presentation is misleading.'

When is a misrepresentation operative?

The parties to the contract

13.28   The person making the misrepresentation must become a party to the contract with the person to whom it was made (for example, *Hasan* v *Wilson* [1977] 1 Lloyd's Rep 431 at 431) although agency can, of course, be as relevant here as elsewhere and it may suffice if the misrepresentation is conveyed by a third party to the misrepresentee if the misrepresentor intended that to happen to induce the misrepresentee to contract.[20]

Reliance

13.29   In order for a misrepresentation to be operative, it must have been relied upon. It must have induced the contract. No remedy lay for a misrepresentation, in *Smith* v *Chadwick* (1884), which had played no part in the claimant's decision to contract. There the prospectus of a company had contained the false statement that a certain person of local importance, a Mr Grieve, was one of the directors. The claimant purchased shares in the company on the faith of the prospectus but he had never heard of Grieve and he admitted that Grieve's name in the prospectus had not influenced him. The misrepresentation that Grieve was a director could not provide a basis for a claim in damages for fraud, as it had not been relied upon.

---

18   The Law Commissions, *Consumer Redress for Misleading and Aggressive Practices* (Law Com No 332, Scot Law Com No 226) para. 7.26, example from H. Collins, *A private right of redress for Unfair Commercial Practices: A report for Consumer Focus* (April 2009).

19   The Law Commissions, *Consumer Redress for Misleading and Aggressive Practices* (Law Com No 332, Scot Law Com No 226) para. 7.27.

20   e.g. *Pilmore* v *Hood* (1838); *Commercial Banking of Sydney* v *R H Brown & Co.* (1972).

13.30   The requirement of reliance means that there are certain situations where there cannot be an operative misrepresentation. For example, there cannot be an operative misrepresentation where the misrepresentation is not known about, or the truth is known. Similarly, there will not be an operative misrepresentation where the representee decides not to rely upon the representor's statement but upon his, or her, own investigation of the facts.

13.31   *Horsfall* v *Thomas* (1862) 1 H & C 90 provides an example of a case where the misrepresentation was not known to the person whom it was meant to mislead.[21] That case concerned the sale of a defective gun. The defect, a soft spot in the metal, was concealed by a metal plug, but this did not constitute an operative misrepresentation. The gun had not been examined by the buyer and the metal plug could not have affected his judgment. Bramwell LJ said (at 99):

> 'If the plug, which it was said was put in to conceal the defect, had never been there, his position would have been the same; for as he did not examine the gun or form any opinion as to whether it was sound, its condition did not affect him.'

Similarly, there will not be an operative misrepresentation where, although the misrepresentation is known about, it is corrected before the contract is made (*Peekay Intermark Ltd* v *Australia and New Zealand Banking Group Ltd* (2006)).

13.32   The situation may be that the misrepresentation is not operative because, although it was known to the representee, it was not relied upon because the representee chose to rely upon his or her own investigation of the facts stated. In *Attwood* v *Small* (1838):

> Attwood was selling a mine. He made exaggerated and untrue statements as to its earning capacity. Before agreeing to buy the mine, Small sent his own experts to assess the mine's capacity. They concurred in Attwood's assessment.

When the true situation was discovered, the purchaser claimed to rescind for misrepresentation. The House of Lords held that the action for rescission failed. The purchaser had relied upon his own experts rather than the vendor.

13.33   Obviously, a misrepresentation cannot be held to have induced a contract where the representee knew it to be untrue before the contract was made. However, the misrepresentation will still be effective, provided it was relied upon, if there was merely an opportunity to discover the truth and that opportunity was not taken. In *Redgrave* v *Hurd* (1881):

> Mr Redgrave, a Birmingham solicitor, wished to sell his practice. Mr Hurd wished to establish himself in practice as a solicitor and agreed to make the purchase. Before Mr Hurd agreed,

---

21   See also *Re Northumberland and Durham District Banking Co., ex p Bigge* (1859).

> Mr Redgrave told him that the practice brought in £300–£400 a year. Mr Hurd was given an opportunity to examine the accounts but did not do so. Had he done so they would have revealed that the business was worth only about £200 a year.

The misrepresentation meant that Mr Hurd could rescind. The mere opportunity to discover the truth did not prevent rescission, provided the representee had relied upon the misrepresentation. (In relation to a claim for reduction in damages for non-fraudulent misrepresentation in this type of situation see para. **13.64** in relation to contributory negligence.)

Degree of reliance

13.34   Consideration now needs to be given to the degree of reliance required if a misrepresentation is to be operative. It would seem that a distinction needs to be drawn between fraudulent and non-fraudulent misrepresentations.

13.35   The first point to note is that it is clear that the misrepresentation need not have been the sole factor inducing the contract in order for it be operative. In *Edgington* v *Fitzmaurice* (1885):

> Revd Edgington was induced to take debentures in a company. He made the decision partly because of a misrepresentation in the prospectus (see para. **13.12**) and partly because of his own mistaken belief that the debenture holders would have a charge on the company's leasehold property. Revd Edgington admitted that he would not have become a debenture holder in the absence of his mistaken belief.

Revd Edgington was able to claim damages for deceit despite his mixed motives. It was not necessary to show that the misrepresentation was the sole cause of his contracting.

13.36   However, what is the level of reliance required in order for the misrepresentation to be operative? This problem was commented on by the Privy Council in *Barton* v *Armstrong* [1976] AC 104. In that case the Privy Council had to deal with a claim that a contract was affected by duress in the form of threats to the person, and the counter argument that the contract was valid because it would have been made even if the threats had not been uttered. Nevertheless, the situation in relation to misrepresentation was considered. It was said (at 118–19):

> 'Had Armstrong made a fraudulent misrepresentation to Barton for the purpose of inducing him to execute the deed...the answer to the problem would have been clear. If it were established that Barton did not allow the representation to affect his judgment then he could not make it a ground for relief even though the representation was designed...to affect his judgment. If on the other hand Barton relied on the misrepresentation Armstrong could not have defeated his claim to relief by showing that there were other more weighty causes which contributed to his decision to execute the deed...Their Lordships think that the same rule

> should apply in cases of duress and that if Armstrong's threats were a reason for Barton's executing the deed he is entitled to relief even though he might well have entered into the contract if Armstrong had uttered no threats to induce him to do so.'

The Privy Council clearly envisaged that a misrepresentation could still be operative even though the contract might have been concluded had it not been made: they were not applying the 'but for' test (i.e. 'but for' the misrepresentation would the contract have been made on those terms?). The decision to contract can be seen as a weighing process, and it is sufficient if the misrepresentation went into the scales on the side favouring the making of the contract.

13.37 However, *Barton v Armstrong* (1976) was a case of duress by threats of physical violence, and the analogy is with fraudulant misrepresentation, rather than misrepresentation more generally, and outside of fraudulent misrepresentation, the 'but for' test generally applies: the situation must have been such that 'but for' the misrepresentation, that contract would not have been made. The less stringent test in relation to fraud would seem to be a matter of deterrence.

13.38 A 'but for' approach was taken in *Atlantic Navigation v Hallam Ltd (The 'Lucy')* (1983), for example, with Mustill J taking the line that Hallam had failed to satisfy him that they would not have entered into a sub-charter of the ship, at the same rate of hire, had there not been a misrepresentation as to the restrictions on the voyages the ship could make under the head charter. The requirement has been expressed in different ways, such as whether the misrepresentation was a 'real and substantial part' of the claimants decision to contract, in *JEB Fasteners Ltd v Marks Bloom & Co. (a firm)* (1983), but in *Raiffeisen Zentralbank Österreich AG v Royal Bank of Scotland* (2010) it was made clear that this did require the 'but for' test to be satisfied in relation to the misrepresentation (at [170]): the misrepresentation does not have to be the only 'but for' factor relied upon, but it does have to be a 'but for' factor.[22]

Materiality

13.39 Materiality may assist the misrepresentee. A misrepresentation is 'material' if it would have induced the reasonable person to contract. If a misrepresentation is material then the court will infer that it did induce the contract, and it will be for the misrepresentor to prove otherwise (*Museprime v Adhill* (1990); *County Natwest v Barton* (2002)). The inference is particularly strong where the misrepresentation is fraudulent (*Ross River Ltd v Cambridge City Football Club* (2007) at [241]).

13.40 However, there is a question as to whether there is a requirement of materiality i.e. a requirement that a misrepresentation must have been such as to induce the reasonable person to contract. General statements as to the requirements of a misrepresentation are often found to

---

22 There will need to be some 'common sense relaxation' of this where the agreement was 'induced by two concurrent causes...so that it could not be said that, but for either the agreement would not have been made', as has been recognized in relation to economic duress (see *Huyton SA v Peter Cremer GmbH* [1999] CLC 230 at 250).

include materiality (for example, *Pan Atlantic Ins. Co. Ltd* v *Pine Top Ins. Co.* (1994)) and such a requirement is obviously necessary where silence as such can give rise to the right to rescind, for example, in relation to contracts uberrimae fidei, such as a contract of insurance. In that type of situation the question of materiality is referred to in order to determine which facts must be disclosed. The question is whether there is any broader requirement.

13.41   The fraudulent misrepresentor cannot rely upon a claim that his misrepresentation was not such as to have induced the reasonable person to contract (*Smith* v *Kay* (1859)). In addition, it is suggested that 'a remedy will be given where the representor knows or ought to know that the representee is likely to act on the representation' (*Chitty on Contracts*, 31st edn, para. 6-040). The real area of dispute would seem to lie in relation to other negligent and purely innocent misrepresentations, with innocent misrepresentations obviously raising the strongest case for a requirement of materiality before the misrepresentee will have a remedy. In *MCI Worldcom* v *Primus* (2004), whilst allowing for the position to be different where fraud was present, Mance LJ indicated some requirement of materiality. He said (at [30]):

> 'whether there is a representation and what its true nature is must be judged objectively according to the impact that would have on a reasonable representee in the position and with the known characteristics of the actual representee.'

Further, there may be some indication of a need for a requirement of materiality in *Avon Insurance* v *Swire Fraser* (2000) in the approach taken to the question of when a statement is untrue, introducing into that context the concept of inducement of the reasonable person. In that case the claim was based on s 2(1) of the Misrepresentation Act 1967 (so the representee did not have to establish negligence, but merely the existence of a misrepresentation, leaving it to the representor to disprove negligence—see para. **13.49**ff) and the court took the line that the inaccuracy of some incorrect representations is not sufficiently significant for them to be regarded as untrue and misrepresentations. Rix J said (at 579):

> 'a representation may be true without being entirely correct, provided that it is substantially correct and the difference between what is represented and what is actually correct would not have been likely to induce a reasonable person in the position of the claimants to enter into the contract.'

The idea that mere 'puffs' are not misrepresentations (*Dimmock* v *Hallett* (1866)) may also, at least partly, be a reflection of a materiality requirement (*Chitty on Contracts*, 31st edn, para. 6-040).

Misleading practices

13.42   The Law Commission takes the view that in relation to the remedies provided to consumers, against traders, in relation to misleading practices an objective test (akin to materiality) should be applied, as well as requiring the misleading practice to have been a 'significant factor' in the particular consumer's decision to contract. Requiring it to be a 'significant factor' in relation to the particular consumer's decision to contract is obviously less strict than applying a 'but for' test. The Law Commissions thought 'it would be unrealistic to expect consumers to prove that without the commercial practice they would not have entered into the contract at all. Often there will be no way of telling why a consumer acted in that particular way following an aggressive or misleading practice. As behavioural science suggests, there are many unpredictable factors affecting consumers' decisions'.[23] Of course, the objective test has also to be satisfied so that the consumer will have to establish not only the significance of the misleading practice to them, but also that it would have been likely to have caused the average consumer to contract. This might seem particularly harsh in relation to the non-average, particularly vulnerable, consumer. However, although generally, the 'average consumer' is 'reasonably well informed, reasonably observant and circumspect', the 'average consumer' is the average member of a particular group where a clearly identifiable group of consumers is particularly vulnerable to the practice because of their mental or physical infirmity, age or credulity in a way which the trader could reasonably be expected to foresee.[24]

Damages and types of misrepresentation

13.43   Rescission may be thought of as the primary remedy for misrepresentation. It is a very radical remedy and, unlike damages, it is available for all types of misrepresentation. Nevertheless, damages will be considered first. It is principally in the context of damages that it is necessary to distinguish the different types of misrepresentation, and it is convenient to classify misrepresentations when considering the issue of damages. The various types of misrepresentation are classified according to the state of mind of the misrepresentor.

13.44   It is of course possible to claim damages and to rescind the contract. For example, in *F & H Entertainments Ltd* v *Leisure Enterprises Ltd* (1970) the plaintiffs were able both to rescind and to recover damages under MA 1967, s 2(1). However, the courts will always strive to prevent a 'double recovery' and no damages should be available to cover a loss which has effectively been wiped out by rescission.

The types of misrepresentation which we must consider are:

1. fraudulent misrepresentations (damages are available through the tort of deceit);
2. misrepresentations which are also negligent misstatements (damages are available through the tort of negligent misstatement);
3. misrepresentations coming within MA 1967, s 2(1);
4. wholly innocent misrepresentations, i.e. misrepresentations not coming within any of the above categories.

---

23 The Law Commissions, *Consumer Redress for Misleading and Aggressive Practices* (Law Com No 332, Scot Law Com No 226) para. 7.108.

24 See The Law Commissions, *Consumer Redress for Misleading and Aggressive Practices* (Law Com No 332, Scot Law Com No 226) para. 7.106; reg 2(5) of the Consumer Protection from Unfair Trading Regulations 2008.

However, under the Law Commissions' proposals on misleading and aggressive practices, as adopted in the draft Consumer Protection from Unfair Trading (Amendment) Regulations, s 2 of the Misrepresentation Act 1967 will cease to apply to situations covered by that proposed new, consumer orientated regime (i.e. s 2 would cease to apply to contracts between traders and consumers unless the subject matter of the contract is one which is not covered by the new regime, such as a land transaction (except a residential lease) or financial services transactions).

Fraudulent misrepresentations

13.45   The frequently cited definition of fraud is that of Lord Herschell in *Derry* v *Peek* (1889) 14 App Cas 337. He said (at 374):

> '[F]raud is proved when it is shown that a false misrepresentation has been made, (1) knowingly, or (2) without belief in its truth, or (3) recklessly, careless whether it be true or false.'

However, although this dictum is frequently cited, it must be treated with care, if it is not to mislead. The essence of fraud is a lack of belief in the truth of the statement made. Despite the reference to carelessness, there is no fraud if the misrepresentor believes his statement to be true. Negligence and fraud are clearly distinct. 'The test for fraud is subjective and the question in the case of each defendant is whether he honestly believed to be true any representations that he intended to make'.[25] In *Derry* v *Peek*:

> The directors of a company issued a prospectus stating that it had the right to operate trams driven by steam power. The respondent purchased shares in the company on the faith of that statement. The company had the right to operate horse-drawn trams only. The use of steam-powered trams was conditional upon the company obtaining the consent of the Board of Trade. That consent was not given and the company was wound up.

The respondent sued the directors for damages in deceit. The trial judge had found that the directors honestly believed that their statements were true and, on that basis, the House of Lords found that there was no fraud and the action failed.

13.46   If the appropriate state of mind is present, the motive is not relevant to the question of fraud. It is irrelevant that there was no intention to cheat anyone, or cause any loss by the untrue statement (*Polhill* v *Walter* (1832)). There is no requirement of 'dishonesty' in the criminal law sense (*Standard Chartered Bank* v *Pakistan National Shipping Corpn (No 2)* (2000) at [27]).

13.47   Damages are available for a fraudulent misrepresentation by taking action in tort for deceit. Damages are measured according to tort principles, rather than contractual principles.[26]

---

25 *Maple Leaf* v *Rouvroy* (2009) per Andrew Smith J at [327].

26 *Doyle* v *Olby (Ironmongers) Ltd* (1969); *Smith Kline & French Laboratories Ltd* v *Long* [1989] 1 WLR 1 at 6.

In tort the aim is to give damages which will put the party back in the position he or she was in before the tort occurred (reliance loss). In the situation we are concerned with, tort damages will attempt to restore the representee to the position he or she would have been in had the misrepresentation not been made. They are not awarded to put the representee in the position he or she would have been in had the misrepresentation been true; that would be like awarding the contractual measure of damages. If we were dealing with an action for breach of contract, the aim of damages would be to put the injured party in the position he or she would have been in had the contract been fulfilled, i.e. contract damages can cover the injured party's expectation loss, the benefit he or she would have derived from completion of the contract (see para. **20.2**ff).

13.48   However, in a sense it would oversimplify matters to say that contract damages can encompass lost profit whilst tort damages cannot. An action for damages for deceit (or under MA 1967, s 2(1), or for negligent misstatement) can encompass a claim for the 'opportunity cost' of reliance on the misrepresentation, i.e. the representee cannot recover the profit he or she would have made had the misrepresentation been true (the contract measure of damages) but the representee can recover for the profit he or she would have made had he or she not relied upon the misrepresentation, and used his or her resources in another way. In *East v Maurer* (1991), where the representee bought a hairdressing business on the basis of a fraudulent misrepresentation, the damages did not cover the profit that would have been made had the misrepresentation been true. But a sum was awarded for the profit which the representee would have made had he purchased a different hairdressing business in the area. A further example of tortious damages covering the 'opportunity cost' can be provided by the situation where a loan of £10,000 has been made on the basis of a negligent misrepresentation. The tortious measure of damages cannot provide for recovery of the interest which would have been paid under the particular contract, but they can encompass damages for the loss of the use of the £10,000 whilst it was locked up in that contract.[27]

13.49   It seems unlikely that the action for deceit will be much used now. Where the action for damages under MA 1967, s 2(1) is available, that will generally be preferable. Under s 2(1) the representee does not have to establish fraud or even negligence. Under s 2(1) it is for the representor to establish his or her reasonable belief in the truth of what was misrepresented, if he or she is to escape liability. Even the common law action for damages for negligent misstatement will often be preferable to the action for deceit. That action requires the representee to prove only negligence, and not fraud, on the part of the representor. However, there are a few ways in which it may be beneficial to be suing for deceit rather than for negligent misstatement. The test of remoteness may be less of a hurdle in relation to damages for deceit than for negligent misstatement. The normal tort test of remoteness, used in relation to a claim based on negligence, is that of 'reasonable foreseeability'. In *Doyle v Olby (Ironmongers) Ltd* [1969] 2 QB 158 the Court

---

27   See *Swingcastle v Alastair Gibson* (1991); see also *Clef Aquitaine v Laporte Materials* (2000) for a further example in relation to fraud.

of Appeal indicated that all that is required in an action for deceit is that the damage 'flowed' from the deceit. Lord Denning said (at 167):

> '[T]he defendant is bound to make reparation for all the actual damages flowing from the fraudulent inducement...it does not lie in the mouth of the fraudulent person to say that [the damage] could not reasonably have been foreseen.'[28]

This may prove very significant in terms of the damages which are recoverable.[29]

13.50   However, on the current state of the law, a claim for damages under MA 1967, s 2(1) has the advantages of the claim for deceit which are denied in an action for negligent misstatement. In *Royscott Trust Ltd v Rogerson* (1991) the Court of Appeal stated that the test for remoteness of damage under s 2(1) was the laxer test used in deceit, rather than that used in relation to negligence test. The court came to that conclusion on the basis of the fiction of fraud in s 2(1) and, thus, on this reasoning any other advantages in the deceit action for damages could also apply to a damages claim under s 2(1). This must be questioned, however, and some divergence of approach has already been indicated in relation to the issue of whether damages should be reduced for the injured party's contributory negligence.[30] More broadly, this equation of the treatment of damages for fraud, and under s 2(1), must be questioned in principle. Special treatment of fraud may be justified as deterrence and on the basis of morality. The same arguments do not apply when the misrepresentation falls under s 2(1) (see further at para. **13.63**). In any event, even without the advantages associated with the action for fraud, the damages claim under s 2(1) is usually preferable to a claim based on negligent misstatement at common law.

Negligent misstatements

13.51   The tort action for negligent misstatement was established in *Hedley Byrne & Co. Ltd v Heller & Partners Ltd* (1964). It requires not only proof of a lack of reasonable grounds for the representor's belief in the truth of what he, or she, asserted, but also that he or she owed the representee a duty of care.

13.52   As was indicated earlier, when damages are awarded in tort for negligent misstatement it will be on the tort basis of returning the injured party to the position he or she was in before the tort occurred (reliance loss). Unlike the contractual measure, it will not seek to put the injured party in the position he or she would have been in had the statement been true, i.e. the injured party will not be awarded his or her expectation loss. However, as we have seen, the possibility exists of claiming tort damages to cover the 'opportunity cost' of reliance on the

---

28 See also Winn LJ at 168 and Sachs LJ at 171; G. Treitel, 'Damages for Misrepresentation' (1969) 32 MLR 556.

29 Contrast *Smith New Court Securities Ltd v Scrimgeour Vickers (Asset Management) Ltd* (1996) and *South Australia Asset Management Corpn v York Montague Ltd* (1996).

30 See *Alliance and Leicester Building Society v Edgestop Ltd* (1994) and *Gran Gelato Ltd v Richcliff (Group) Ltd* (1992)— see para. **13.64**.

misrepresentation, i.e. the loss of the opportunity to use elsewhere resources committed to the contract. (See *Swingcastle* v *Gibson* (1991); *East* v *Maurer* (1991).)

13.53   Note that, in an action for negligent misstatement, not only must the representee establish the duty of care, it is also for the representee to prove that the representation was made negligently, and this contrasts with MA 1967, s 2(1).

Misrepresentation Act 1967, s 2(1)

13.54   The Misrepresentation Act 1967 resulted from the tenth report of the Law Reform Committee in 1962 (Cmnd 1782), which recommended that damages should be available for negligent misrepresentation. Of course, the courts did provide a damages remedy for negligent misstatement in *Hedley Byrne & Co. Ltd* v *Heller & Partners Ltd* (1964). Nevertheless, the Act provides for damages in s 2(1) and it is the statutory remedy which deserves the greater consideration here.

13.55   Section 2(1) states:

> 'Where a person has entered into a contract after a misrepresentation has been made to him by another party thereto and as a result thereof he has suffered loss, then, if the person making the misrepresentation would be liable to damages in respect thereof had the misrepresentation been made fraudulently, that person shall be so liable notwithstanding that the misrepresentation was not made fraudulently, unless he proves that he had reasonable grounds to believe and did believe up to the time the contract was made that the facts represented were true.'

This deals with the situation where X falsely states a fact, Y enters into a contract in reliance upon it, and X cannot establish that he, or she, had reasonable grounds for believing that fact to be true. The reference to fraud imports the requirement that the 'misrepresentation' should be a misrepresentation within the definition given above, i.e. a statement of existing or past fact. It can be strongly contended that it should go no further, but the current line is that it also affects the calculation of damages under s 2(1) (see para. **13.62**ff).

Advantages/disadvantages of an action under s 2(1)

13.56   Section 2(1) reverses the burden of proof from that which applies under the tort action for negligent misstatement. This is very important. It makes an action under s 2(1) a much easier way to obtain damages than an action which relies upon liability in tort for negligent misstatement. Under s 2(1) the representee has only to establish that he or she entered into a contract in reliance upon a misrepresentation made by the other party to the contract, and that he or she suffered loss thereby. It will then be for the representor to prove that, until the time the contract was made, he or she had reasonable grounds for his or her belief in the truth of the representation. If the representor cannot establish the reasonableness of his or her belief, the representor will be liable in damages.

13.57   Section 2(1) has a further advantage over the tort action for negligent misstatement. It does not require a duty of care to have existed between the parties. It merely requires that the misrepresentation should have led to a contract between representor and representee.

13.58   The importance of the burden of proof in s 2(1), and of the lack of any requirement of a duty of care, are both illustrated by the case of *Howard Marine & Dredging Co. Ltd v A Ogden & Sons (Excavations) Ltd* (1978):

> Ogden wished to hire barges from Howard Marine. During the negotiations Howard Marine told Ogden that the carrying capacity of their barges was 1,600 tonnes. Ogden and Howard Marine concluded a contract of hire. Ogden used the barges, and the work for which they were required fell behind schedule. Ogden discovered that the true carrying capacity was only 1,055 tonnes and refused to continue paying the hire charge.

Howard Marine sued Ogden for the hire charge. Ogden counterclaimed under s 2(1), and in tort for negligent misstatement. In the Court of Appeal, Ogden succeeded by a majority decision. Shaw LJ and Bridge LJ found for Ogden under s 2(1) on the basis that Howard Marine had not shown that they had reasonable grounds for their belief that the capacity was 1,600 tonnes. Lord Denning MR dissented as he thought that Howard Marine had established that their belief was reasonable. The importance of the distinctions between s 2(1) and the tort action for negligent misstatement is revealed in the fact that Howard Marine would have won had Ogden had to rely upon the tort action for negligent misstatement. Neither Lord Denning MR nor Bridge LJ thought that Howard Marine had owed a duty of care to Ogden. That prevented Ogden from succeeding in the tort action for negligent misstatement. In addition, even if there had been a duty of care, Bridge LJ thought that there was no evidence to establish that Howard Marine had been negligent and breached that duty. Shaw LJ was alone in thinking that Ogden could succeed in an action in tort for damages for negligent misstatement. If Ogden had not been able to make a claim under s 2(1), they would have lost by a majority decision in the Court of Appeal, rather than winning by one.[31]

13.59   However, s 2(1) can be used only where the negligent misrepresentation was made by one party to a contract to the other party before the contract was concluded. The tort claim for negligent misstatement is not linked to the making of a contract. For example, a claim can be made in tort, for negligent misstatement, against a third party to a contract. *Hedley Byrne & Co. Ltd v Heller & Partners Ltd* (1964) itself concerned a claim against a third party. The tort claim could relate to a statement made during precontractual negotiations which did not lead to a contract. In addition, the lack of any requirement for the existence of a contract means that the action could be used if a contract had apparently been made but was found to be void for mistake. An action under s 2(1) is doubtful if the contract is void. It should also be noted that a claim in tort for negligent misstatement is not dependent upon there being a misrepresentation in the sense indicated above.

---

31 R. Taylor, 'Expectation, Reliance and Misrepresentation' (1982) 45 MLR 139; J. Cartwright, 'Damages for Misrepresentation' [1987] Conv 243.

Assessment of damages under s 2(1)

13.60   As has been indicated, the basis for the calculation of damages differs in contract and tort. It is more appropriate that damages under s 2(1) should be assessed on the basis of the rules in tort rather than contract, because s 2(1) is not dealing with a legally enforceable promise. Where there is a promise in the form of a contract term, it is apt that the damages for its non-fulfilment, its breach, should attempt to put the injured party in the position he or she would have been in had the promise been fulfilled (i.e. to compensate for the expectation loss). Section 2(1) does not relate to contract terms and promises, but to mere representations. The injured party has entered into a contract in reliance upon the representation and suffered loss thereby, but as he or she is not suing on a broken promise (a broken term), damages covering expectation loss would be inappropriate. It is apt to adopt the tort approach to damages, and undo the harm caused by the misrepresentation by putting the representee back in the position he, or she, was in before the misrepresentation (i.e. to compensate for the reliance loss).

13.61   Some of the earlier decisions dealing with damages under s 2(1) pointed towards the contract measure of damages,[32] but it is now clear that it is the tort measure of damages which is used under s 2(1) and the reference to fraud in s 2(1) is seen as providing a basis for this,[33] although it could simply be arrived at as a matter of principle. In *Chesneau v Interhome Ltd* (1983) counsel had argued that damages under s 2(1) should be assessed on the principles applied to damages in tort. Everleigh LJ said:

> 'For myself, I think that that is probably correct...The subsection itself says: "...if the person making the misrepresentation would be liable to damages in respect thereof had the misrepresentation been made fraudulently, that person shall be so liable...". By "so liable" I take it to mean liable as he would be if the misrepresentation had been made fraudulently.'

13.62   Subsequently, the reference to fraud in s 2(1) was taken further, arguably well beyond its proper bounds. In *Royscott Trust Ltd v Rogerson* (1991), the Court of Appeal stated that damages under s 2(1) should be calculated as if they were damages for fraud, and applied the laxer remoteness test which is used in relation to deceit rather than that applied to negligent misstatement (see para. **13.49**). The court's conclusion was based upon the reference to fraud in s 2(1). *Royscott* concerned the hire purchase of a car (i.e. the dealer sells the car to the finance house, and the finance house contracts with the customer for its hire purchase). The car dealer and the customer misrepresented to the finance company that the customer was supplying a higher deposit than he was. They did so because the finance company did not undertake transactions unless the customer was supplying at least a 20 per cent deposit. The customer did not finish paying the instalments to the finance company before selling the car to a third party, who

---

32 *Gosling* v *Anderson* (1972); *Jarvis* v *Swans Tours* (1973); *Watts* v *Spence* (1976).

33 *Chesneau* v *Interhome Ltd* (1983); *Sharneyford Supplies* v *Edge* [1987] 2 WLR 363 at 376 per Balcombe LJ (CA), [1985] 1 All ER 976 per Mervyn Davies J; *Naughton* v *O'Callaghan* (1990); *Royscott Trust Ltd* v *Rogerson* (1991).

acquired good title to it. The finance house brought an action for damages under s 2(1) against the dealer. The Court of Appeal held that the loss through the sale of the car did not have to pass the remoteness test of reasonable foreseeability, which would be applied in the tort of negligent misstatement, but merely the laxer remoteness test applied to deceit. However, in dealing with a point relating to causation, the court also held that it was reasonably foreseeable that the customer would sell the car to a third party. The court's comments on the applicability of a remoteness test derived from deceit could be regarded as unnecessary to the decision.

13.63   The point should be made that the equation of s 2(1) and fraud is not easy to justify in principle and may be open to question in the future. In *Smith* v *Scrimgeour Vickers* [1996] 4 All ER 769, where the court was concerned with fraud, Lord Browne-Wilkinson made no comment as to the correctness of the decision in *Royscott Trust Ltd* v *Rogerson* (1991), but it is worth noting, in particular, Lord Steyn's consideration of the justification for the wider availability of damages for fraud than for negligence. He noted that deterrence may be in question and that 'in the battle against fraud civil remedies can play a useful role'. In addition, he noted 'moral considerations'. He said (at 790):

> 'That brings me to the question of policy whether there is a justification for differentiating between the extent of liability for civil wrongs depending on where in the sliding scale from strict liability to intentional wrongdoing the particular civil wrong fits in. It may be said that logical symmetry and a rule of not punishing wrongdoers by civil remedies may favour a uniform rule. On the other hand it is a rational and defensible strategy to impose wider liability on an intentional wrongdoer. As Hart and Honoré, *Causation in the Law* (2nd edn, 1985) at p. 304 observed: "an innocent [claimant] may, not without reason, call on a morally reprehensible defendant to pay the whole of the loss he has caused". The exclusion of heads of loss in the law of negligence, which reflects considerations of legal policy, does not necessarily avail the intentional wrongdoer.'

Such arguments militate against the 'fiction of fraud' in s 2(1) being used to justify damages being awarded in exactly the same way as if the misrepresentor had been fraudulent, rather than as merely indicating a tortious measure, and *Royscott* has been criticized by other courts.[34]

13.64   Some divergence of approach between an action for deceit and an action under s 2(1) has been indicated in relation to the question of whether the injured party's damages will be reduced for contributory negligence.[35] The Law Reform (Contributory Negligence) Act 1945 applies where 'any person suffers damage as the result partly of his own fault and partly of the fault of any other person'. (Fault is defined in s 4—see para. **20.67**.) Where that is the situation, the damages recoverable shall be reduced to such an extent as the court thinks just and equitable having regard to the claimant's share in responsibility for the damage. It has been

---

34 e.g. *Avon Insurance* v *Swire Fraser* (2000) at 578–81; *Cheltenham BC* v *Laird* [2009] EWHC 1253 (QB), [2009] IRLR 621 at [524].

35 A. Oakley, 'Contributory Negligence of a Fraudulent Misrepresentee' [1994] CLJ 219.

held that this does not apply to an action based on deceit,[36] but is the same approach taken in relation to a claim based on s 2(1)? *Royscott Trust Ltd* v *Rogerson* (1991), and its approach to the fiction of fraud, indicates that it would be, but the analogy made in *Gran Gelato Ltd* v *Richcliff (Group) Ltd* [1992] 1 All ER 865 was with an action for negligent misstatement. Where there was concurrent liability in tort and under s 2(1), it was held that contributory negligence was applicable to the claim under s 2(1). In *Gran Gelato*, liability under MA 1967, s 2(1) was seen (at 875) as 'essentially founded on negligence', and that being so it was seen as being 'very odd if the defence of contributory negligence were not available as a defence to a claim under that Act'. However, having decided that the 1945 Act applied, Nicholls V-C then concluded that it would not be 'just and equitable' for there to be any reduction of the claimant's damages in the instant case. He said (at 876):

> 'The essential feature of the present case is that Gran Gelato's claim, both at common law and under the 1967 Act, is based on misrepresentation. Richcliff intended, or is to be taken to have intended, that Gran Gelato should act in reliance on the accuracy of [its answers]. Gran Gelato did so act. In those circumstances it would need to be a very special case before carelessness by Gran Gelato, the representee, would make it just and equitable to reduce the damages payable...In principle, carelessness in not making other inquiries provides no answer to a claim when the [claimant] has done that which the representor intended he should do.'

Thus, damages were not reduced in that case, and the reference to 'carelessness in not making other inquiries...where the [claimant] has done that which the representor intended him to do' might cover situations like that in *Redgrave* v *Hurd* (1881). However, the comments of Lord Hoffmann in *Standard Chartered Bank* v *Pakistan National Shipping Corpn* (2003) at [9]–[18] would indicate that the Law Reform (Contributory Negligence) Act 1945 might more readily be raised where the claimant's negligence lies not in a failure to discover the truth of the misrepresentation, but in concluding the contract because of a negligent misunderstanding of other factors. So that, if the misrepresentation were negligent, rather than fraudulent, the Act might, more readily, cover the type of situation which arose in *Edgington* v *Fitzmaurice* (1885) (see para. **13.35**) where the Reverend Edgington invested in debentures partly because of the misrepresentation and partly because he misunderstood the nature of debentures.[37]

Non-disclosure

13.65   Section 2(1) relates to misrepresentations which are 'made'. This language is inapt to cover silence, and it does not provide a right to damages where there is non-disclosure in circumstances where there is a duty to disclose. Section 2(1) does not apply to non-disclosure in

---

36   *Alliance and Leicester Building Society* v *Edgestop Ltd* (1994); *Standard Chartered Bank* v *Pakistan National Shipping Corpn (No 2)* (2003).

37   The question of the applicability of contributory negligence to a claim based on breach of contract is dealt with at para. **21.83**ff.

contracts uberrimae fidei.[38] Given that, it is important whether cases such as *With* v *O'Flanagan* (1936) are regarded as continuing representations based on the statements made, which become misrepresentations with the change in circumstances, or as cases where what has been said has given rise to a duty to disclose further information and it is the non-disclosure itself which constitutes the misrepresentation. If the former is taken to be the mechanism by which a misrepresentation occurs, damages should be available under s 2(1) in such cases (A. Hudson, 'Making Misrepresentations' (1969) 85 LQR 524).

Damages in lieu of rescission (s 2(2))

13.66 Section 2(2) of the Misrepresentation Act 1967 is sometimes referred to as a statutory bar to rescission. In certain circumstances it permits the court to prevent rescission for non-fraudulent misrepresentation and award damages in lieu of rescission. This is considered further at para. **13.87**ff in relation to rescission.

Misleading practices

13.67 It should be remembered that the Law Commission took the view that s 2 of the Misrepresentation Act 1967 should not apply to situations falling within their proposed simpler regime to provide remedies for consumers in relation to misleading and aggressive commercial practices.[39] The primary remedies under that new regime will be 'unwinding' the transaction (which will be similar to, but simpler than rescission) or a discount on the price. There will be scope for claims for damages for other losses, calculated on a reliance basis, including economic losses and damages for distress and inconvenience, but the consumer will have to establish those losses, and the trader will have a due diligence defence.

Innocent misrepresentation

13.68 Since the decision in *Hedley Byrne & Co. Ltd* v *Heller & Partners Ltd* (1964), and the Misrepresentation Act 1967, the category of innocent misrepresentations has ceased to encompass all non-fraudulent misrepresentations. Innocent misrepresentations are now simply those not covered by any of the categories just discussed. There is no damages remedy as such for innocent misrepresentation, although damages may be awarded in lieu of rescission under MA 1967, s 2(2) (see para. **13.87**).

Rescission

13.69 Although the common law allowed rescission where there was a fraudulent misrepresentation, it was equity which made it available for all types of misrepresentation. In addition,

---

38 *Banque Financière de la Cité SA* v *Westgate (UK) Insurance Co.* (1989).

39 The Law Commissions, *Consumer Redress for Misleading and Aggressive Practices* (Law Com No 332, Scot Law Com No 226) para. 7.106; draft Consumer Protection from Unfair Trading (Amendment) Regulations.

equity provided an action for rescission rather than merely recognizing the right, and was far more flexible than the common law when the contract was no longer entirely executory (see para. **13.77** on the bar of restitutio in integrum). In relation to contracts covered by the Law Commissions' proposed regime for providing remedies for consumers in relation to misleading and aggressive practices, the regime's primary remedy of 'unwinding' the transaction will be similar to, but involve much less uncertainty than rescission.

13.70 A misrepresentation renders a contract voidable at the option of the representee. This means that the contract can be rescinded and, in this context, rescission 'wipes out' the existence of the contract entirely and returns the parties to the positions they were in before the contract was made. It is rescission ab initio and must be distinguished from rescission for breach, which merely puts an end to the contract for the future. When a contract is rescinded for breach, its past existence is not disturbed. One effect of this is that, although damages may be available for misrepresentation as well as rescission, it should not be possible to rescind for misrepresentation and claim damages for breach. Once the contract has been rescinded for misrepresentation, there is no contract in relation to which damages for breach could be claimed. Termination for breach does not prevent any claim for damages for breach—the contract is only ended for the future. Some confusion can be avoided if the term 'rescission' is reserved for use in the context of voidable contracts, and 'termination' is used to describe the situation when a contract is ended after a breach.

13.71 Rescission may be a self-help remedy. It may be possible for the representee simply to tell the other party that he or she is electing to rescind. This is most obviously the case where the contract is still entirely executory and there has been no performance by either party. The right to rescind for misrepresentation will then serve to protect the representee if the representor tries to claim specific performance or sue for breach. Where the contract is not entirely executory, whether rescission requires the assistance of the court will depend on what has been done in performance of it. If, for example, the representee has received goods and handed over a cheque, he or she may still be able simply to return the goods and stop the cheque. However, if restoring the position before the contract was made requires the co-operation of the representor, it is likely that an appropriate order will have to be sought from the court. If, for example, the representor has received goods under the contract, the court may have to order their return. The situation is complicated where the subject matter of the contract has been altered in some way and this problem will be considered later, in relation to the bar upon rescission which occurs once the parties can no longer be returned to their pre-contract positions, i.e. once restitutio in integrum is impossible.

13.72 In appropriate circumstances rescission can be achieved simply by notifying the representor of the election to rescind. In general, it is also necessary to inform the representor of the election to rescind. Merely coming to that decision and providing some evidence of it is usually insufficient. However, it seems that there is no need to inform the representor of the decision to rescind where the representee has simply retaken the property which he transferred under the voidable contract (*Re Eastgate, ex p Ward* (1905)). There is another, and more doubtful, exception to the need for communication in the case of *Car and Universal Finance Ltd* v *Caldwell* (1965). In that case:

> A Jaguar car was purchased from its original owner, Mr Caldwell, by Mr Norris, 'a rogue'. Norris paid by cheque and, when this proved to be worthless, Mr Caldwell wished to rescind but Norris and the car had disappeared. Mr Caldwell informed the police and the Automobile Association of the fraud and asked them to trace the car. Norris sold the car to a motor dealer with knowledge of the fraud, but it was eventually sold on to an innocent third party.

The question of ownership between Mr Caldwell, the original owner, and the innocent third party depended upon whether Mr Caldwell had rescinded before the sale to that innocent third party (see below on the bar to rescission where there has been a purchase by a bona fide third party). Norris had disappeared after the original sale, preventing the owner from communicating his election to rescind. Nevertheless, the Court of Appeal found that rescission had occurred. In informing the AA and the police, Mr Caldwell had done all he reasonably could and he had clearly demonstrated his intention to rescind. In the circumstances, that was sufficient. The 'rogue', Norris, had intended to avoid actual communication of rescission when he had known that it would almost certainly be desired.

13.73   The decision in *Caldwell* is certainly beneficial to the original owner, but it means that the loss falls on the innocent third party purchaser. The court seems to have given too little consideration to the fact that it was, in effect, being asked to determine which innocent party should bear the loss. In this situation one innocent party is bound to suffer a loss. Is it better that it falls on the party who was parting with money in return for goods, rather than on the party who was prepared to part with goods in return for a cheque? The decision seems unfortunate and has been criticized. There is every reason to confine it as much as possible, and it will probably not operate outside the sphere of fraudulent misrepresentations.[40]

Indemnity

13.74   There is a money remedy which may be used alongside rescission to help 'undo' the effects of the contract. It is called an 'indemnity' and it is available for all types of misrepresentation. It is a far more restricted money remedy than damages. It covers only the cost to the representee of the obligations created by his contract with the representor. Given its restricted nature, an indemnity is unlikely to be appropriate where damages can be claimed. Its limited scope is illustrated by *Whittington* v *Seale-Hayne* (1900):

> The Whittingtons were breeders and exhibitors of prize poultry and wished to lease premises to carry on their business. The defendant assured them that his premises were in a sanitary

---

40 See Law Reform Committee, 12th Report, Cmnd 2958, 1966, para. 16. In *Newtons of Wembley Ltd* v *Williams* (1965), where there was a direct sale from the rogue to the innocent third party, the innocent third party was held to acquire good title under Factors Act 1889, s 9. This limits the effect of *Caldwell* and makes an anomalous distinction between an innocent first purchaser directly from 'the rogue' and subsequent purchasers further down the chain.

condition, and the Whittingtons leased them on the basis of this innocent misrepresentation. In fact the water supply was poisoned and Mr Cooper, the farm manager, fell ill and most of the poultry died. The local authority declared the premises unfit for habitation and required work to be done on the drains. Under the lease the Whittingtons had to pay for that work. The Whittingtons rescinded the contract and also sought an indemnity. They claimed the cost of the rates and the repairs to the drains. In addition, they also claimed for their lost profit, their lost stock, their expenses in setting up the land as a poultry farm, and the medical bills of Mr Cooper, the farm manager.

The court held that only the rates and the repair bill could be covered by an indemnity. It could not extend beyond expenses which the lease had obliged the claimants to incur. Using the land as a poultry farm was their choice. The lease did not require them to spend money in that way, and the expenses connected with it could not be covered by an indemnity,[41] and, of course, lost profits would not even be covered by any damages claim for misrepresentation.

The bars to rescission

13.75   There are certain bars to rescission; once one of those bars comes into operation, the representee ceases to have the right to rescind the contract. The misrepresentee then has to be content with any remedy he or she may have in damages. The existence of a bar to rescission does not affect a claim to damages (*Production Technology Consultants Ltd* v *Bartlett* (1988)), except in relation to damages in lieu of rescission under s 2(2). The common law bars can be listed:

1. restitutio in integrum is impossible;
2. third party rights;
3. affirmation;
4. lapse of time.

In addition, the courts' power to stop the representee from rescinding and to award him or her damages in lieu of rescission under MA 1967, s 2(2) is sometimes referred to as a 'statutory bar', and it is considered at para. **13.87**.

13.76   Section 1 of the Misrepresentation Act 1967 makes it clear that, if the misrepresentation has also become a term, or if the contract has been performed, those events are not bars to rescission.

Restitutio in integrum is impossible

13.77   Rescission takes both parties back to the position they were in before the contract was made. What if the contract is not wholly executory, but has been acted upon, so that it is not simply a matter of the representee informing the representor of his or her election?

---

41 *Adams* v *Newbigging* (1886) per Bowen LJ, but see the judgments of Cotton and Fry LJJ.

The court may order the return of property or money in order to restore the parties to their pre-contractual positions. The difficulties arise if property has been destroyed or altered and it is impossible to return the parties to their pre-contractual position. Representees cannot claim to be restored to their pre-contractual position if they cannot restore to the representor the property which was handed over by him or her under the contract. Under such circumstances, rescission is said to be barred because restitutio in integrum is impossible. (It is a matter of preventing the representee being unjustly enriched at the expense of the representor (*Halpern* v *Halpern (No 2)* (2007).) For example, where the representee bought shares in a partnership, he could not rescind on discovering the truth of the misrepresentation. The partnership had become a limited liability company in the meantime. The shares in the company were different in nature and status from those in the partnership. The representee could not give back what the representor had before the contract, i.e. shares in a partnership (*Clarke* v *Dickson* (1858)).

13.78   However, in order for rescission to be possible, equity, unlike the common law, will not require that the parties be returned precisely to their pre-contractual positions. The courts

> 'can take account of profits and make allowances for deterioration. And I think the practice has always been for a court of equity to give this relief whenever, by the exercise of its powers, it can do what is practically just, though it cannot restore the parties precisely to the position they were in before the contract' (*Erlanger* v *New Sombrero Phosphate Co.* (1878) 3 App Cas 1218 at 1278–9).

13.79   Rescission, in equity, is possible on the basis of substantial restoration of the property and a payment to take account of the change. Where a company bought a phosphate mine and worked it, but did not exhaust it, the company was allowed to rescind on the basis that the mine could be substantially restored to the seller and the company would account to the seller for the profits obtained from working it (*Erlanger* v *New Sombrero Phosphate Co.* (1878)).

13.80   No precise rules have been formulated for the point at which equity will regard restitutio in integrum as impossible. The factors to be weighed in determining whether that point has been reached do not simply include the degree of change which the property has undergone. The fault of the representor will be considered. In *Spence* v *Crawford* [1939] 3 All ER 271, Lord Wright said (at 288):

> 'The court will be less ready to pull a transaction to pieces where the defendant is innocent, whereas in the case of fraud the court will exercise its jurisdiction to the full in order, if possible, to prevent the defendant from enjoying the benefits of his fraud at the expense of the innocent [claimant]'

Third party rights—the bona fide third party purchaser

13.81   A contract is voidable for misrepresentation, and not void. We can illustrate the effect of this in relation to third party rights by reference to the sale of a car. Suppose that a 'rogue' purchases a car by means of a fraudulent misrepresentation. The contract for the sale of the car is valid until rescinded. Whilst the contract is valid the rogue has a voidable title to the car. If the rogue sells it to a bona fide third party before the contract is rescinded, the third party acquires a valid title which the original owner cannot defeat. This is why, in *Car and Universal Finance v Caldwell* (1965) (see para. **13.72**), Mr Caldwell was so anxious to convince the court that he had rescinded his contract with the rogue, Norris, before Norris sold the car to a bona fide third party. In that case Mr Caldwell recovered the car because the court, somewhat anomalously, accepted that rescission had occurred without communication to the rogue.

13.82   Where rescission has not occurred in time to prevent its being barred by a third party's rights, the argument is often raised that the contract is void for mistake, rather than merely voidable for misrepresentation (for example, *Lewis* v *Avaray* (1972); *Phillips* v *Brooks* (1919)). In the rare cases where this is successful, it means that the contract never existed at all and that there was nothing to rescind—the rogue had no title to pass on to the third party, and the third party will not be able to use the above argument to defeat the original owner's claim to the car (for example, *Ingram* v *Little* (1961)).

Affirmation

13.83   As soon as the representee has learnt of the falsity of the misrepresentation, he or she can elect to affirm the contract or rescind it. Once the representee has affirmed, the right to rescind is lost. Affirmation may be express or implied. The representee may actually tell the representor of the decision not to rescind for misrepresentation, or affirmation may be implied from an act inconsistent with the representee's having an intention to rescind. For example, the representee's continued use of the subject matter of the contract may amount to affirmation. Where a contract concerned the sale of shares, the right to rescind for misrepresentation was lost through delay and through continuing to act as a shareholder by attending, and participating in, a shareholder's meeting (*Sharpley* v *Louth and East Coast Railway* (1876)). An attempt to sell shares acquired on the basis of a misrepresentation may also constitute an affirmation (*Re Hop and Malt Exchange and Warehouse Co., ex p Briggs* (1866)). Similarly, where a misrepresentation induced the representee to lease machines from the representor, continued use of machines leased from the representor was held to amount to affirmation in *United Shoe Machinery of Canada* v *Brunel* (1909) (see also *Long* v *Lloyd* (1958)).

13.84   The possibility of affirmation arises only after the representee knows of the truth of the misrepresentation. In addition, it seems that there can be no affirmation if the representor did not know of the right to rescind even though he or she had discovered the truth of the misrepresentation. In *Peyman* v *Lanjani* (1985):

> Lanjani was the lessee of a restaurant. His title to the lease was defective as he had obtained the assignment of it to him by fraud. The fraud had involved M pretending to be Lanjani when dealing face to face with the landlord, as Lanjani was scruffy and spoke no English.

Peyman agreed to purchase the lease from Lanjani. To obtain the landlord's consent to the assignment, Lanjani again called upon M to impersonate him. Peyman learnt of that impersonation, and the earlier one which rendered Lanjani's title defective. Peyman had already become reluctant to continue with the sale but his solicitor, who was acting for both parties, advised him to continue. Before the landlord consented to an assignment to him, Peyman went into possession of the restaurant and paid £10,000 to Lanjani. A month later, Peyman went to another solicitor and was told that he had a right to rescind because of Lanjani's defective title.

Peyman gave notice of his decision to rescind. At first instance it was held that going into possession, and handing over payment, after he had discovered what had occurred, meant that he had affirmed and could no longer rescind. The Court of Appeal held that Peyman had not lost his right to rescind. He had discovered the true facts, but he had acted without any knowledge that he had a legal right to rescind.[42]

13.85   However, the Court of Appeal in *Peyman* v *Lanjani* also considered the question of the representor being misled by an apparent, but not actual, affirmation, into detrimentally relying upon the apparent affirmation. If an apparent affirmation occurs, the representee may be estopped from denying that he has affirmed the contract. No estoppel was found in that case, but such an estoppel will arise if the representor has relied upon the apparent affirmation to his detriment and there was nothing to indicate to the representor that the representee was acting in ignorance of either the truth, or the law.[43]

Lapse of time

13.86   Lapse of time can constitute evidence of affirmation,[44] but this relates to the situation where time has passed since the representee learnt the truth of the misrepresentation. Until the truth is known there can be no affirmation. However, in *Leaf* v *International Galleries* [1950] 2 KB 86 a five-year lapse between the making of the contract and the attempt to rescind barred rescission, although the representee attempted to rescind as soon as he discovered the truth. The lapse of time was held to constitute a bar in itself, at least in relation to an 'innocent' misrepresentation. (The case was decided before any distinction was made between the different types of non-fraudulent misrepresentation, and it probably applies to all such misrepresentations.) In *Leaf*:

In 1944, International Galleries represented to Mr Leaf that a painting they had for sale was by John Constable. Mr Leaf bought it for £85. In 1949, when he tried to sell the painting at Christie's, Mr Leaf discovered that it was not a Constable.

42 See also *Stevens & Cutting Ltd* v *Anderson* [1990] 1 EGLR 95 at 97; *Compagnia Tirrena di Assicirazioni* v *Grand Union Insurance* (1991).

43 See also *Container Transport International Inc.* v *Oceanus Mutual Underwriting Association (Bermuda)* (1984).

44 *Clough* v *London and North Western Railway Co.* (1871) LR 7 Ex 26 at 35.

Mr Leaf tried to rescind the contract, and obtain the return of the £85 from International Galleries. The Court of Appeal held that rescission was barred by lapse of time.[45] Jenkins LJ said (at 92):

'Contracts such as this cannot be kept open and subject to the possibility of rescission indefinitely...it behoves the purchaser either to verify or, as the case may be, to disprove the representation within a reasonable time.'

Misrepresentation Act 1967, s 2(2)

13.87   As has already been indicated, s 2(2) is sometimes labelled as the statutory bar to rescission. It states that:

'where a person has entered into a contract after a misrepresentation has been made to him otherwise than fraudulently, and he would be entitled, by reason of the misrepresentation, to rescind the contract, then if it is claimed in any proceedings arising out of the contract, that the contract ought to be or has been rescinded, the court or arbitrator may declare the contract subsisting and award damages in lieu of rescission, if of the opinion that it would be equitable to do so having regard to the nature of the misrepresentation and the loss that would be caused by it if the contract were upheld, as well as to the loss that rescission would cause to the other party.'

Rescission is a very radical remedy; before the enactment of s 2(2) it was the only remedy available for a wholly innocent misrepresentation. In relation to non-fraudulent misrepresentations, s 2(2) now gives the court a discretion to declare the contract subsisting and award damages in lieu of rescission where it 'would be equitable to do so'. This allows the court to substitute damages for rescission where the misrepresentation was fairly trivial and the radical nature of the remedy of rescission is not in keeping with the 'wrong' on which it was founded. The subsection requires account to be taken of 'the nature of the misrepresentation and the loss that would be caused by it if the contract were upheld, as well as the loss that rescission would cause to the other party'. This would seem to involve the weighing of these factors to decide if it would be 'equitable' to deny rescission and award damages 'in lieu'. There are some examples of its use in the case law.

13.88   *William Sindall plc* v *Cambridgeshire County Council* (1994) indicates that rescission will be denied under s 2(2) where the misrepresentee is seeking it to escape from what has become a bad bargain for reasons unrelated to the misrepresentation. In that case:

The builders, William Sindall plc, had purchased a piece of land from the council, to develop it. After that transaction was concluded, it took eighteen months to obtain planning permission for their detailed development plans, and during that time the market slumped and the

---

45 See also *Peco Arts v Hazlitt Gallery Ltd* [1983] 3 All ER 193 at 199–200.

> market value of the land was reduced from over £5 million to £2 million. When the builders discovered a nine-inch sewer running through the land which had not been revealed by the council, they claimed that they had contracted with the council on the basis of a misrepresentation. The council had stated that, to its knowledge, there were no such incumbrances on the land. The builders claimed that there was effectively nothing which could be done to deal with the problem created for their development by the drain and claimed to be able to rescind the contract. The drain problem was remediable at a cost of approximately £18,000. At first instance, a misrepresentation was found and rescission was not denied under s 2(2).

The Court of Appeal concluded that there was no misrepresentation but, *obiter*, considered how s 2(2) of the Misrepresentation Act 1967 would have been dealt with had an operative misrepresentation been found. The court indicated that it would not have allowed the builders to make use of a relatively minor misrepresentation to rescind, and to escape from what had become a bad bargain because of a general fall in the value of land (which was not connected to the misrepresentation).

13.89   In *UCB Corporate Services* v *Thomason* [2005] 1 All ER (Comm) 601 rescission was denied in a situation in which the misrepresentation was viewed as not causing any loss to the representee. In that case:

> The misrepresentors had provided guarantees in relation to a loan made by the claimant misrepresentee to a company. The Company was wound up and it was sought to enforce the guarantees, but the misrepresentors did not have the money. They sought to reach a compromise with their creditors and eventually did so. A waiver agreement was signed, releasing the misrepresentors from the rest of their indebtedness on payment of a small part of the money owed. However, before the waiver agreement was reached, the misrepresentors supplied details of their financial position to the claimants which were misleading. The judge characterized the misrepresentations as 'multiple, intentional (though not fraudulent) and fundamental'. He concluded that had the waiver agreements not been signed, the claimants would have quickly petitioned for bankruptcy, but thought there was no indication that there would have been a better recovery in bankruptcy than under the waiver agreement. He concluded that the claimants had suffered no loss because of the misrepresentation and so rescission was denied under s 2(2).

The Court of Appeal took the same line as the judge at first instance: rescission was not allowed under s 2(2). They thought that the judge had obviously been aware of the nature of the misrepresentation and he was right to conclude that the claimants had suffered no loss because of it. In addition, 'it was common ground that [the misrepresentors] would face a massive liability if the waiver was rescinded' (i.e. they would again be liable under the guarantees) (at [50]).

13.90   The issue arises as to the calculation of the sum to be paid 'in lieu' of rescission under s 2(2) when rescission is denied. In *Sindall* v *Cambridgeshire* the court indicated how it would have measured damages in lieu of rescission under s 2(2) had that been required. It took the line that just as rescission should not have been available to protect the builders from the slump in the market price of the land, s 2(2) also should not reallocate that market risk from the builders back to the council. This dismisses any simple idea of calculating damages in lieu of rescission merely on the basis that they are given to put the representee in the position he or she would have been in, had rescission been allowed. It may be that the basic principle behind the calculation of damages under s 2(2) is that they should replace the remedy of rescission, but with account being taken of any 'over compensation', which rescission would have provided—such as coverage of a drop in market value which is unconnected with the misrepresentation.

13.91   It should be noted that if the misrepresentation is not wholly innocent, the representee may be claiming damages as well as rescission. MA 1967, s 2(3) deals with the possibility of a claim for damages under s 2(1) and the court also awarding damages under s 2(2). It aims to prevent a double recovery by providing that damages awarded under s 2(1) should take account of any damages awarded under s 2(2). The damages remedy in s 2(1) should cover only those losses not falling within damages in lieu of rescission under s 2(2).

13.92   Section 2(2) applies where the representee 'would be entitled…to rescind', and the question arises as to whether the court can still award damages in lieu of rescission if rescission itself would be prevented by one of the common law bars. In *Atlantic Lines & Navigation Co. Inc. v Hallam Ltd, The Lucy* (1983), Mustill J accepted that a bar on rescission prevented the court awarding damages under s 2(2), but that was *obiter dictum*. In *Thomas Witter Ltd v TBP Industries Ltd* [1996] 2 All ER 573 Jacobs J found such an argument 'unattractive'. He said (at 590):

> 'The argument assumes that the Act is referring to the remedy of rescission though this is not clear. If it were only the remedy which is referred to then it would be difficult to understand the reference to "has been rescinded" in the section. It seemed to me that the reference may well be to a claim by the representee that he was entitled to rescission, in which case it may be enough for the court to find that the agreement was rescissionable….'

Jacobs J considered the speeches in the House of Commons at the time of the passing of the Act and found that 'the Solicitor General told the House…that damages could be awarded under s 2(2) where there was an impossibility of restitution'. Jacobs J concluded that an award of damages under s 2(2) is not dependent upon an existing right to rescind, but only that such a right existed in the past.

13.93   However, the point has been made that the legislative history of the provision is not as clear as Jacobs J indicated (Beale (1995) 111 LQR 385) and the more recent cases have also taken the line that the more literal interpretation of s 2(2) indicates that it does not make damages available if rescission is barred before the action comes to court (*Floods of Queenferry v Shand Construction* (2000); *Government of Zanzibar v British Aerospace* (2000)). In addition, in *Government of Zanzibar v British Aerospace* the judge considered the legislative evolution of the provision. He pointed out that the Law Reform Committee had envisaged s 2(2) as providing a needed limit on the right to rescind, which had otherwise been broadened by s 1 removing the previous bar which had existed once performance had been commenced or completed. He also pointed out that not only was the Solicitor General's statement, referred to by Jacob J in *Thomas Witter Ltd*, ambiguous, but that it was an 'ex tempore answer given a little after 3 o'clock in the morning' and that it 'does not accord with' other statements during the passage of the Bill (at 744). The point was made that, in introducing the Bill in the House of Lords, Lord Gardiner had said:

> 'I now come to damages as an alternative to rescission. The Committee recommended that a discretionary power should be conferred on the court to award damages in lieu of ordering rescission where damages would afford adequate compensation to the victim of an innocent misrepresentation, whether it was made negligently or not. They thought that there were a number of cases where the remedy of rescission might be too drastic in the circumstances. This is the recommendation which is implemented by Clause 2(2).'

The judge saw s 2(2) as merely providing a means for the court to mitigate the effects of the right to rescind where it existed. He saw s 2(1) as providing the basic right to recover damages and that was subject to the representor not being able to prove belief, and reasonable grounds to believe, in the truth of what he or she had asserted (at 743). However, the point can be made that the common law recognized the 'defect' in the contract, and the need for a remedy (rescission), even where the misrepresentation was wholly innocent. If it was not to cause hardship or injustice, such a powerful remedy had to be hedged around with restrictions relating to what happened after the events generating the right. The mere fact that the bars are relevant to the question of the availability of rescission, as such, does not mean that they should be seen as relevant to the availability of a money remedy to deal with the recognized 'defect'.

Misleading practices

13.94   The Law Commissions recommended a simplified set of remedies for the consumer in relation to misleading and aggressive commercial practices. The primary remedy would be 'unwinding' the contract. Like rescission, the basic idea is to return the parties to their pre-contractual positions, but with much less uncertainty and in a 'rough and ready' way. So, where the consumer has made a purchase of goods from the trader or contracted for services then, provided the consumer is able to reject some element of the goods or services within three months (ninety days), it will simply be a matter of the consumer getting a refund of the whole price. (The consumer will have to have indicated rejection within the relevant period. That does not have to be in writing. It can be by something said or done, but it must be clear.)[46] Of course, the remaining goods will have to be made available to the trader, or returned. The bars to rescission, as such, do not arise. The consumer is not prevented from being able to unwind because he or she cannot make restitutio in integrum. If the consumer waits more than three months, or the goods or services have been fully consumed, the consumer will be able to claim a discount

---

46 The Law Commissions, *Consumer Redress for Misleading and Aggressive Practices* (Law Com No 332, Scot Law Com No 226) para. 8.73; draft Consumer Protection from Unfair Trading (Amendment) Regulations.

on the price. Except in relation to higher market value goods,[47] it will be simply a matter of an applicable discount band. Under the draft Regulations bands of discount are set (25 per cent, 50 per cent, 75 per cent or 100 per cent),[48] with which one is applicable depending upon the seriousness of the misleading practice, which will be a matter of the impact of the practice, the trader's behaviour, and any delay by the consumer. 'In the worst cases, the discount may be 100%, and identical to a refund'.[49] Obviously there is uncertainty in the level of discount, but the Law Commission viewed a discount as a 'simpler and more appropriate remedy than damages'. It was seen as avoiding the complexity of the law on damages, and the problem of establishing the amount by which the misrepresentation affected the value of the goods or services.[50] There will be scope for a claim for damages calculated on a reliance basis to cover financial loss which the consumer would not have incurred had the misleading practice not taken place, but it will not include a loss dealt with by any unwinding or discount which has been obtained. There will also be recovery of damages for distress and inconvenience, but only if a significant purpose of the contract was to provide the consumer with pleasure, relaxation or peace of mind.[51] In claiming damages, the consumer will have to establish the losses, and the trader will have a due diligence defence. The Law Commission saw that as being in keeping with the line taken in s 2(1) of the Misrepresentation Act 1967, under which damages are available, once the misrepresentee has established the loss, unless the misrepresentor can prove reasonable grounds to believe in the truth of the misrepresentation. More generally, the Law Commissions commented in relation to their proposed remedies that, 'Overall [they] approximate the outcomes under the current law, but in a simplified way. It is a scheme which values certainty over flexibility'.[52] Apart from the disapplication of MA 1967, s 2 to situations covered by the proposed regime, the consumer will remain able to use other existing legal rules instead of the proposed regime, but will not be able to exercise a right, or be granted relief, under both.[53]

Exemption clauses and misrepresentations[54]

13.95 Subject to the usual rules on incorporation and construction (see **Chapter 9**), an exemption clause may serve to exclude or restrict liability for non-fraudulent misrepresentation, but such clauses are ineffective in relation to a fraudulent misrepresentation. In *S Pearson & Son Ltd* v *Dublin Corpn* (1907) the claimants contracted to construct sewage

---

47 £5,000 in the draft Regulations.

48 The Law Commissions proposed that there also be a 0% band—paras 8.125–8.135.

49 The Law Commissions, *Consumer Redress for Misleading and Aggressive Practices* (Law Com No 332, Scot Law Com No 226) para. 8.78; draft Consumer Protection from Unfair Trading (Amendment) Regulations.

50 The Law Commissions, *Consumer Redress for Misleading and Aggressive Practices* (Law Com No 332, Scot Law Com No 226) para. 8.119.

51 The Law Commissions, *Consumer Redress for Misleading and Aggressive Practices* (Law Com No 332, Scot Law Com No 226) para. 8.163; draft Consumer Protection from Unfair Trading (Amendment) Regulations.

52 The Law Commissions, *Consumer Redress for Misleading and Aggressive Practices* (Law Com No 332, Scot Law Com No 226) para. 8.19.

53 Draft Consumer Protection from Unfair Trading (Amendment) Regulations.

54 See further, E. Macdonald, *Exemption Clauses and Unfair Terms*, 2nd edn, Tolley, 2005, ch. 6.

works for a price calculated in reliance upon a misrepresentation. It was said that liability for a fraudulent misrepresentation could not be affected by an exemption clause. More recently, in *HIH Casualty and General Insurance* v *Chase Manhattan Bank* (2003) Lord Bingham said, 'It is clear that the law, on public policy grounds, does not permit a contracting party to exclude liability for his own fraud' (at [16]).[55]

13.96   However, the Misrepresentation Act 1967, s 3 (as substituted by Unfair Contract Terms Act 1977, s 8) now renders an exemption clause ineffective, in relation to all types of misrepresentation, if the representor cannot establish that the clause satisfies the requirement of reasonableness in UCTA 1977, s 11. MA 1967, s 3 now states:

> 'If a contract contains a term which would exclude or restrict—
>
> (a) any liability to which a party to a contract may be subject by reason of any misrepresentation made by him before the contract was made; or
>
> (b) any remedy available to another party to the contract by reason of such a misrepresentation,
>
> that term shall be of no effect except in so far as it satisfies the requirement of reasonableness as stated in s 11(1) of the Unfair Contract Terms Act 1977; and it is for those claiming that the term satisfies the requirement of reasonableness to show that it does.'

Section 3 deals with terms which exclude or restrict liability, or a remedy, for misrepresentation. It renders such a term ineffective unless the representor can establish that it satisfies the requirement of reasonableness.

13.97   The scope of MA 1967, s 3 presents difficulties in relation to clauses which appear to try to prevent a statement from being a misrepresentation at all, rather than merely excluding or restricting the liability or the remedies available for a misrepresentation. There may, for example, be a clause stating that the apparent facts are only matters of belief, or more commonly a 'non-reliance clause' stating that there was no reliance upon statements made. It is a similar problem to that which has to be considered in deciding whether a clause should be regarded as an exclusion clause in substance and subject to UCTA 1977, despite its form (see **Chapter 10**).

13.98   The courts have shown some willingness not to simply take such clauses at face value, but to look beyond their form, to determine whether they are exclusion clauses in substance. *Cremdean Properties Ltd* v *Nash* [1977] EGD 63 provides an early example. In that case:

> Nash contracted to sell to Cremdean Properties a block of properties in Bristol to be used as office space. The particulars of the properties had stated that the amount of office space available was 17,900 sq. ft but it was actually much less. A footnote to the special conditions of sale contained the following clause: '[The vendor's estate agents] for themselves

---

55 See also Lord Hoffmann at [76]. The question of whether an exemption clause can cover liability for the fraud of an agent is left open.

> and the vendors...give notice that (a) These particulars are prepared for the convenience of an intending purchaser...and although they are believed to be correct their accuracy is not guaranteed and any error, omission or misdescription shall not annul the sale or be grounds on which compensation may be claimed and neither do they constitute any part of an offer of a contract, (b) Any intending purchaser...must satisfy himself by inspection or otherwise as to the correctness of each of the statements contained in these particulars.'

Cremdean sought rescission of the contract, or damages in the alternative, on the basis of a misrepresentation as to the amount of office space in the property. As a preliminary issue the effect of the footnote was considered. Nash argued that it prevented there being a representation at all, and that therefore it did not exclude or restrict liability and did not fall within MA 1967, s 3. The Court of Appeal held that the footnote came within the ambit of s 3 and that at the full trial of the action, the court would have to consider whether the footnote was 'reasonable' in order to decide if it was effective to exclude liability. Of interest here is the court's rejection of the argument that the clause fell outside the ambit of s 3. Bridge LJ thought that the clause was inappropriately worded to bring about the situation where no representation had been made, but he also said (at 71–2):

> '[I]f the ingenuity of a draftsman could devise language which would have that effect, I am extremely doubtful whether the court would allow it to operate so as to defeat s 3. Supposing the vendor included a clause...in some such terms as "notwithstanding any statement of fact included in these particulars the vendor shall be conclusively deemed to have made no representation within the meaning of the Misrepresentation Act 1967", I should have thought that *that was only a form of words the intended and actual effect of which was to exclude or restrict liability,* and I should not have thought that the courts would have been ready to allow such ingenuity in forms of language to defeat the plain purpose at which s 3 is aimed'. (emphasis added)

Clearly, Bridge LJ was willing to look beyond the form of a clause, to its substance. Scarman LJ expressed the need to do so more graphically, stating (at 72):

> 'Humpty Dumpty would have fallen for this argument. If we were to fall for it, the Misrepresentation Act would be dashed to pieces which not all the King's Lawyers could put together again.'

Buckley LJ agreed with both Bridge and Scarman LJJ.

13.99   However, determining when a clause should be viewed as an exclusion clause 'in substance' is a complex question, of which the courts have not provided a satisfactory analysis. It is clear, however, that they are more willing to take a clause at face value, as meaning that there was no representation made, when dealing with legally sophisticated parties, who can be expected to have taken on board the impact of a non-reliance clause, for example, in a standard form contract. They are far more likely to see the clause as out of keeping with the reality of the transaction, and as an exclusion clause, where they are dealing with a consumer, or other legally unsophisticated party. In *Raiffeisen Zentralbank Österreich AG* v *Royal Bank of Scotland* (2010) Christopher Clarke J took the line (at [81]) that:

> 'The court may regard a sophisticated commercial party who is told that no representations are being made to him quite differently than it would a consumer.'

Indeed, between the large commercial enterprises in that case, representations were not found, and the clause was not viewed as an exemption clause. The judge did, however, contrast the situation with a very different one. He said (at [306]–[307]):

> 'Suppose . . . a car is sold. The dealer says "I have serviced the car since it was new, it has had only one owner and the clock reading is accurate". He is not fraudulent but mistaken, carelessly confusing one car for another, in relation to which the statement is true. Relying on his statement the buyer purchases the car. Without it he would not have done so. The car has had several owners, no known service history, and the clock reading is substantially inaccurate. The contract of sale provides (in one of many paragraphs on the back of the form which the buyer does not read and to which his attention is not directed) that the buyer is entering into the contract on the basis that no representations have been made to, or relied on by, the purchaser . . . In that example there has been a clear statement of fact, on a matter said to be within the representor's personal knowledge, which was in fact intended to induce the contract, upon which the purchaser in fact relied, which is false.'

In that situation, Christopher Clarke J viewed the clause as one which would be viewed as an exclusion clause, and subject to MA, s 3. Obviously, such an approach is quite 'rough and ready', but it will generally be in keeping with the complex analysis which can be made to determine which clauses are exclusion clauses in substance.[56]

13.100   Of course, clauses which do fall within s 3 are then ineffective unless they satisfy the 'requirement of reasonableness': the 'requirement of reasonableness' in s 11 of UCTA 1977. *Cleaver v Schyde Investments* (2011) emphasizes that, just as when it is applied in relation to a provision of UCTA itself, an appellate court will be reluctant to overturn the decision of the judge at first instance on reasonableness, and that its application is a matter of the facts in each case. In *Cleaver v Schyde Investments* (2011):

> S contracted with C to buy a property, which S was going to develop into flats. C knew that his neighbour, a doctor, was applying for planning permission to turn the property, partly, into a medical centre. C did not disclose that in the standard enquiries answered in relation to a sale of land. When S found out about the planning application, it was concerned that it would detrimentally impact upon its application for a wholly residential development. (The doctor continued with his application even after the contract of sale had been made.)

---

56 E. Macdonald, 'Exception clauses: Exclusionary or Definitional? It Depends!' (2012) 29 JCL 47.

It was accepted that C had made an innocent misrepresentation. S sought to rescind. The issue was whether C could rely upon the exemption clause, which was a term of the Law Society's standard conditions of sale, which allowed the buyer to rescind for misrepresentation only where the misrepresentation was fraudulent or reckless or where the property would differ substantially in quality, quantity or tenure from what the buyer had been led to expect. At first instance, the judge found that the clause was not reasonable. It went to the Court of Appeal.

13.101 The Court of Appeal did not view it as generally unreasonable to restrict rescission as the clause did (at [54], [38]). Etherton LJ stated (at [38]):

> 'That is a perfectly rational and commercially justifiable apportionment of risk in the interests of certainty and the avoidance of litigation. While each case turns on its own particular facts, the argument in favour of upholding such a provision as a matter of the commercial autonomy of the contracting parties is particularly strong where, as here: (1) the term has a long history; (2) it is a well established feature of property transactions; (3) it is endorsed by the leading professional body for qualified conveyancers; (4) both sides are represented by solicitors; and (5) the parties (through their solicitors) have negotiated variations of other provisions in the standard form.'

The court noted the limited extent to which it was appropriate for an appellate court to interfere with the decision of the judge on reasonableness under s 11, and that every case depended on its particular facts. It concluded that it should not depart from the judge's view in this case. Longmore LJ stated (at [55]):

> 'But the question is not whether the clause is, in general, a reasonable clause. The question is whether it was a reasonable clause in the contract made between *this* vendor and *this* purchaser at the time when the contract was made. On the particular facts of this case both parties were aware of and wished (if possible) to exploit the development potential of the property. The planning position (and any change to it between the answer to enquiries and completion) was of obvious materiality. Yet the mere existence of an application for planning permission can hardly be said to make the property different in quantity, quality or tenure from what it had been represented to be.'

The planning application did not affect the land in a way which would allow rescission under the clause, but as Etherton LJ said (at [52]), it 'changed the risk landscape' in relation to the crucial issue of planning permission for the way in which the representee's wished to develop the land.

13.102 The Unfair Terms in Consumer Contracts Regulations 1999, and the draft Consumer Rights Directive subject terms to a fairness test. Their application is not restricted to exemption clauses. In relation to their scope and application see **Chapter 11**.

⬡ Summary

- An operative misrepresentation is basically a false statement of existing or past fact made by one party to the contract to the other, before, or at the time of contracting, which the other relied upon in contracting.

- It is unclear to what extent there is a requirement of materiality i.e. that the misrepresentation would have induced a reasonable person to contract.

- Statements of opinion or intention are not statements of fact and so not misrepresentations, but implied statements of fact may be found behind them.

- Silence itself is not a misrepresentation, although there are exceptions as with contracts of the utmost good faith (such as contracts of insurance). Partial non-disclosure may constitute a misrepresentation and one may also be found where a statement which was true when stated has become untrue by the time the contract is made, and the representor knew of this and did not disclose the change.

- The representee must have relied on the misrepresentation when entering into the contract.

- A less complex regime has been proposed by the Law Commissions in relation to misleading and aggressive practices which are likely to have caused the average consumer to contract with the trader, and were a significant element in the individual consumer's decision to contract.

- Damages are available for fraudulent misrepresentation under the tort of deceit. (The essence of fraud is the representor's lack of belief in what he or she stated.)

- Damages are available under the tort of negligent misstatement where there was a duty of care between the parties and the representor was negligent (i.e. the representor lacked reasonable grounds for believing in what he or she stated).

- Damages are available under s 2(1) of the Misrepresentation Act 1967. The burden of proof in relation to negligence is reversed, i.e. the representee only needs to establish that an operative misrepresentation was made by the representor but it is then for the representor to prove that he or she had reasonable grounds to believe that what he or she said was true.

- No damages, as such, are available in relation to an innocent misrepresentation but an indemnity may accompany rescission and damages in lieu of rescission may be ordered by a court under s 2(2) of the Misrepresentation Act 1967 in relation to non-fraudulent misrepresentations.

- Under the proposed regime to provide remedies for consumers in relation to misleading and aggressive practices, s 2 of the Misrepresentation Act 1967 will cease to apply where that regime applies.

- The remedy of rescission is available in relation to all types of misrepresentation.

- There are bars to rescission:
  - where it is impossible to return the parties to their pre-contractual positions;
  - where a third party has acquired rights;

- where the representee has affirmed the contract;
- where there has been a sufficient lapse of time since the contract was made.

- Section 2(2) of the Misrepresentation Act 1967, giving the court power to award damages in lieu of rescission for a non-fraudulent misrepresentation, is sometimes referred to as the statutory bar.

- Under the proposed regime to provide remedies for consumers in relation to misleading and aggressive practices, consumers will be provided with a right to 'unwind' the transaction for a period of ninety days, provided there is still some of the product/service to reject, and otherwise to a discount. The regime will also encompass damages claims on a reliance basis.

- An exemption clause is not effective in relation to liability for fraud.

- Under s 3 of the Misrepresentation Act 1967, exemption clauses dealing with misrepresentations are subject to 'the requirement of reasonableness' under UCTA.

▶ Further reading

P. S. Atiyah and G. H. Treitel, 'Misrepresentation Act 1967' (1967) 30 MLR 369

H. Beale, 'Damages in Lieu of Rescission for Misrepresentation' (1995) 111 LQR 60

H. Beale, 'Points on Misrepresentation' (1995) 111 LQR 385

R. Hooley, 'Damages and the Misrepresentation Act 1967' (1991) 107 LQR 547

Law Commission and Scottish Law Commission, *Consumer Redress for Misleading and Aggressive Practices* Law Com No 332, Scot Law Com No 226 (2012)

Chapter 14

Duress and undue influence

⬤ Introduction

14.1

> 'In everyday life people constantly seek to influence the decisions of others. They seek to persuade those with whom they are dealing to enter into transactions, whether great or small. The law has set limits to the means properly employable for this purpose' (*Royal Bank of Scotland* v *Etridge (No 2)* (2001) per Lord Nicholls at [6]).

Both duress and undue influence relate to the situation in which one party has distorted the other's decision to contract. Both concepts are used to deal with contracts made in unacceptable circumstances and, where a contract is made under duress or undue influence, it is voidable.[1] However, as influencing another's decision making is 'constantly' part of 'everyday life', it will become clear in the discussion that follows that identifying those circumstances which are unacceptable and amount to duress or undue influence requires the drawing of difficult borderlines.[2] (The related, but even more uncertain area of unconscionability is dealt with in **Chapter 16**.)

14.2   The uncertainty in the common law in this area, and the limitations of its coverage, mean that it is of little use in the more common type of situations of pressurized contracting which are encountered by the consumer, as where, for example, elderly consumers, living by themselves,

---

1   It was said in *Barton v Armstrong* (1976) that threats to the person could render a contract void, but it is in keeping with the idea of an agreement made in unacceptable circumstances, rather than of a factually 'overborne will' (see para **14.6**) that a contract is voidable, rather than being void. In any event, it is clear that all other types of duress, and undue influence, render contracts voidable.

2   The question of the general effect of 'unconscionability' on a contract is considered in **Chapter 16**.

encounter salesmen who will not leave their homes until they have signed a contract.[3] The Consumer Protection from Unfair Trading Regulations 2008 provided public enforcement by Trading Standards and the Office of Fair Trading (OFT) to deal with misleading and aggressive commercial practices, and unfair commercial practices more broadly, through criminal sanctions and enforcement orders. The Law Commissions have recommended that redress now be provided for the individual consumer, in relation to aggressive and misleading practices, to be able to 'unwind' contracts (which will be similar to rescinding), or receive a discount on the price and recover damages. There are now draft Regulations being considered, which would bring about such reforms: the draft Consumer Protection from Unfair Trading (Amendment) Regulations. They have already been looked at in relation to misleading practices in the chapter on misrepresentation. They will be addressed in relation to aggressive practices at the end of this chapter.

Duress

Introduction

14.3   If someone makes a contract whilst a gun is being held to his or her head, it is obvious that it was made in unacceptable circumstances (see *Barton* v *Armstrong* (1976)), but it is only in comparatively recent years that English law has clearly recognized any other type of duress. Even the legal effect of duress to goods was far from certain.[4] However, *obiter*, in *The Siboen and The Sibotre (Occidental Worldwide Investment Corpn* v *Skibs A/S Avanti)* (1976), Mocatta J recognized that a contract could be voidable because economic duress had been present when it was made. 'Economic' duress simply refers to the fact that it is the economic interest of the individual which is being threatened, and the law is now prepared to recognize a very wide range of threats as constituting duress.

14.4   An example of situation in which the plea of duress will now, commonly be raised is provided by *Atlas Express Ltd* v *Kafco (Importers and Distributors) Ltd* (1989). In that case:

> Kafco, a small company which imported and distributed basketware, had made a contract to supply Woolworths. Kafco needed to contract with a carrier for delivery to Woolworths. They concluded a contract with Atlas Express. Once the contract with Atlas had commenced, Atlas realized that they had miscalculated and that the rates specified in the contract made it a 'bad deal' from their point of view. Atlas told Kafco that they would cease to make the deliveries unless the contract pricing was changed. Kafco was heavily dependent upon the contract with

---

3   The period provided for consumers to cancel contracts made in their own homes (seven days under the Cancellation of Contracts made in the Consumer's Home or Place of Work Regulations 2008; fourteen days under the draft Consumer Contracts (Information, Cancellation and Additional Payments) Regulations 2013) does not provide sufficient protection. Tactics are used by sellers to reduce the likelihood of consumers exercising this right and, in any event, it is often not a sufficient period for elderly, house-bound consumers, who lack regular social contact, and are embarrassed about what has happened, and reluctant to make a fuss (*Consumer Redress for Misleading and Aggressive Practices* Law Com No 332, Scot Law Com No 226 (2012) paras 3.52–3.54).

4   Contrast *Skeate* v *Beale* (1840) and *Astley* v *Reynolds* (1731); J. Beatson, 'Vitiating Factors in Contract' [1974] CL 97.

> Woolworths and knew that a failure to deliver the baskets would lead to its loss and an action for breach by Woolworths. At that time it was not possible for Kafco to find another carrier and Kafco felt that Atlas had them 'over a barrel'. Kafco agreed to the new contract, at the rates demanded by Atlas, but made it clear that they felt that they were acting under duress.

Atlas Express sued Kafco for non-payment of the new rate of carriage. Tucker J held that they could not succeed. The agreement to the new rates, in the new contract, had been made while Kafco were subject to economic duress. In any event, there had been no consideration for the new agreement.

14.5   *Atlas Express Ltd v Kafco (Importers and Distributors) Ltd* (1989) illustrates the situation in which a claim of duress will now often arise. The parties have made a contract but, because of miscalculation, a misunderstanding as to their rights, a change in circumstances, or a desire to take advantage of the other's vulnerability which was created by reliance on the contract, one party decides to try to increase the contract price. He or she indicates to the other party that, unless the price is increased, there can or will be no performance.[5] The question is whether any new agreement will be voidable for economic duress and that has become all the more important because the decision in *Williams* v *Roffey Bros & Nicholls (Contractors) Ltd* (1990) (see para. **4.39**ff) has thrown the emphasis onto the question of duress, in such cases, rather than consideration. As the important point in such cases would seem to be whether the new agreement was made improperly, in unacceptable circumstances, rather than whether it was remembered to include some 'technical' consideration, such as a stick of chewing gum, a chocolate bar, or the traditional peppercorn, this is a welcome development. However, it does make duress of great significance. It has been said:[6]

> 'The law of consideration is no longer used to protect a participant in such a variation. That role has passed to the law of economic duress, which provides a more refined control mechanism and renders the contract voidable rather than void.'

We need to consider when the courts will find that a contract was made under duress.

The language of the courts

14.6   Before addressing the identification of duress, we should consider the language used by the courts in this context. At times, the courts have given the appearance of stating a clear

---

5 We usually refer to 'threats' in this context, and we might become enmeshed in discussion of whether it is a threat if the one party simply says to the other, e.g., 'I want to perform, but I cannot do so at this price'. It is not helpful to try to decide whether this was a 'threat'. The type of factors to consider, and the tensions in the law which they represent, are set out below. Whether there is a 'threat' is a linguistic cul-de-sac, which could divert attention from them, particularly when it is borne in mind that the 'threat' may not even be expressed. One party may simply create a situation in which it is clear to the other party that there will be no performance unless the price is increased. The fact that the builders suggested the increased payment in *Williams v Roffey Bros & Nicholls (Contractors) Ltd* (1990), does not explain the assumption that there was no duress in that case.

6 *Adam Opel GmbH v Mitras Automotive (UK) Ltd* (2007) per David Donaldson QC at [42].

test for duress whilst using language which, on closer examination, is obscure in its meaning. In particular, care must be taken with the use of terms such as 'voluntariness' and 'consent', and references to the 'overborne will'.[7] This use of language is superficially attractive. It seems to provide the perfect basis for interfering with an apparently valid contract. If individuals claiming duress were acting involuntarily, if they did not consent, then their agreement can be labelled as merely apparent, and dismissed. However, in considering whether they truly consented, in the sense of whether their agreements were given voluntarily, the test is not being used as it would be if the question was whether their actions were unwilled, as would be the case if they were in a state of automatism. It is clear that truly unwilled actions, in the sense of automatism, are not what is being considered by the courts in relation to duress. This was acknowledged by the House of Lords in *DPP for Northern Ireland v Lynch* (1975) in the context of a plea of duress in the criminal law, and Atiyah pointed out that the reasoning on that point should not be regarded as restricted to the criminal law ((1982) 98 LQR 197). When individuals under duress agree to contract because of the other party's threat, they do not do so 'involuntarily', because their will has been 'overborne', but rather because they choose to, albeit only because it is the least unattractive of the alternatives before them. It is not a question of individuals being made 'offers they could not refuse', merely of offers which they were given very powerful reasons for accepting. In other words, there is no simple factual test of whether the person claiming duress has ceased to act 'voluntarily'. The real question in relation to duress is whether the decision to contract was made in unacceptable circumstances.[8]

Identifying duress

14.7 In *R v Attorney-General for England and Wales* (2003), Lord Hoffmann stated (at [15]) that there were 'two elements' in duress: first, 'pressure amounting to compulsion of the will of the victim' and, secondly, 'the illegitimacy of the pressure'. We have already seen that references such as that to 'compulsion of the will of the victim' are not very helpful, but there are, nevertheless, two basic elements as to what constitutes duress: the threat must indeed be 'illegitimate', but instead of considering 'compulsion of the will of the victim', we must generally consider whether the situation was such that the party threatened had no reasonable alternative to agreeing. Indeed, before commencing his consideration of the 'illegitimacy' of the pressure, which was the significant point in *R v A-G*, Lord Hoffmann put aside examination of his first element, on the assumption that the pressure did cause 'compulsion of his will', as it left *R* with 'no practical alternative' (at [15]). Despite Lord Hoffmann's reference to 'compulsion of the will', it was nevertheless recognized that what is in question is a situation in which options have been curtailed, and unacceptably (illegitimately) so. Illegitimacy and lack of a reasonable alternative provide the basic test of whether appropriate pressure for duress is present, but there is, of course, an additional requirement if the law is to recognize duress in relation to the particular transaction: it must have been a sufficient cause of contract. This requirement is

---

7   e.g., *North Ocean Shipping Co. Ltd v Hyundai Construction Co. Ltd* [1978] 3 All ER 1170 at 1183; *Pao On v Lau Yiu Long* [1980] AC 614 at 636; *The Siboen and the Sibotre* [1976] 1 Lloyd's Rep 293 at 335; *Hennessy v Craigmyle & Co. Ltd* [1986] ICR 461 at 468.

8   *Dimskal Shipping Co. SA v International Transport Workers' Federation, The Evia Luck* [1992] 2 AC 152 at 165.

unsurprising, and it is assumed in Lord Hoffmann's statement of 'two elements'. His reference to 'compulsion of the will of the victim' also makes it clear that the duress must have caused the agreement. We should also note that, as duress makes a contract merely voidable, rescission may become barred by, for example, affirmation (as we have already seen may occur in relation to contracts which were voidable for misrepresentation). Each of these elements of an effective claim of duress should now be considered, although we should, perhaps, first note that there are dicta which do not correspond with this analytical division, indicating, for example, that whether there was a reasonable alternative is part of the consideration of illegitimacy,[9] or, placing it within the question of causation,[10] but it is necessary to see the elements as distinct in this way to avoid confusion, and fully understand the significance of each of them, and the tensions within the law.

Illegitimacy of the threat

14.8   It was established in *Universe Tankships Inc. of Monrovia v International Transport Workers' Federation and Laughton* [1983] 1 AC 366 that the threat must be 'illegitimate',[11] and this is important in distinguishing duress from hard bargaining:[12]

> '[I]n life...many acts are done under pressure, sometimes overwhelming pressure, so that one can say that the actor had no choice but to act. Absence of choice in this sense does not negate consent in law: for this the pressure must be one of a kind which the law does not regard as legitimate.'

'Generally speaking, the threat of any unlawful action will be illegitimate',[13] and unlawful here refers not just to threats to commit criminal acts, but also civil wrongs, such as torts, and breaches of contract. Of course, it may be the demand itself, rather than what is threatened which is unlawful, with blackmail providing the primary example: 'Blackmail is often a demand supported by a threat to do what is lawful, for example, to report criminal conduct to the police'.[14] For ease of reference, the phrase 'unlawful threats', will generally simply be used.

14.9   However, what must now be addressed are the two main issues which have arisen in relation to unlawfulness and illegitimacy. First, although a breach of contract is a civil wrong, it has been suggested that a threatened breach, is not always illegitimate. Secondly, it has been recognized that there will be occasions when a lawful threat will be illegitimate and borderlines of that raise very difficult questions.

---

9 e.g. *DSDN Subsea Ltd v Petroleum Geo Services ASA* (2000) at [131].

10 *Kolmar Group v Traxpo* (2010) at [92].

11 Lord Diplock at 384 and Lord Scarman at 400.

12 Lord Hoffmann in *R v Attorney-General for England and Wales* (2003) at [15], quoting Lord Wilberforce and Lord Simon of Glaisdale in *Barton v Armstrong* [1975] 2 All ER 465 at 476–7.

13 Lord Hoffmann in *R v Attorney-General for England and Wales* (2003) at [16].

14 *International Transport Workers Federation v Universe Tankships* [1983] 1 AC 366 at 401.

14.10   First, whether a threatened breach will always be illegitimate must be addressed. In *Huyton SA v Peter Cremer GmbH* [1999] CLC 230 Mance J said (at 251):

> 'Even in cases where the pressure relied on is an actual or threatened breach of duty, it seems to me better not to exclude the possibility that the state of mind of the person applying such pressure may in some circumstances be significant.'

In *DSDN Subsea Ltd v Petroleum Geo Services ASA* (2000), Dyson J expressed the view (at [134]) that a breach would not be 'illegitimate behaviour where it was reasonable behavior by a contractor acting bona fide', and in *Kolmar Group v Traxpo* (2010) Christopher Clarke J took the line that not all threatened breaches would be illegitimate, but that 'generally' would be the case, 'particularly where the defendant must know that it would be a breach if the threat were implemented' (at [92]). The situation has been seen as one involving the question of 'bad faith', and that has been viewed as a more complex issue than simple knowledge. Peter Birks advocated an approach whereby a threatened breach would only be illegitimate when used in 'bad faith, being intended to exploit the [claimant's] weakness rather than solve financial or other problems of the defendant'.[15] Andrew Burrows would add two 'supplementary or clarificatory ideas' to this:[16]

> 'First, a threat should not be considered illegitimate (made in bad faith) if the threat is a reaction to circumstances that almost constitute frustration. And, secondly, a threat should not be considered illegitimate (made in bad faith) if it merely corrects what was clearly a bad bargain.'

Such clarification does not reduce the considerable uncertainty in the concept of bad faith: what 'almost' constitutes frustration, or a sufficiently bad original bargain?

14.11   The problems of requiring bad faith to make a threatened breach illegitimate go beyond uncertainty. It would mean that, on occasions, no duress would be found even though the party threatened had no reasonable means of protecting their rights under the original contract as, for example, where a legal remedy could not be procured quickly enough. A requirement of 'bad faith' will generate cases where rights under the original contract are left effectively unprotected, and there will then be a loss of discipline in the process of bidding for a contract: not as much care needs to be taken in providing an initial contract price, if it will be easy to obtain an enforceable renegotiation after the contract is underway. This puts the careful bidder at a disadvantage, and the other party does not see a true picture before accepting a bid. On the other hand, circumstances do change and, without the potential for effective renegotiation, initial mistakes may be penalized very heavily. A requirement of 'bad faith' may be seen as achieving a balance between protecting initial rights and encouraging the parties to renegotiate/compromise.

14.12   In addition, Burrows' 'clarificatory ideas' also suggest another type of balance, or re-balancing. They might be seen as helping to re-balance the situation where the law dealing

---

15 P. Birks, *An Introduction to the Law of Restitution*, Oxford University Press, 1989, p. 183.

16 A. Burrows, *The Law of Restitution*, 3rd edn, Oxford University Press, 2011, p. 175.

with the original rights can be viewed as insufficiently confining them, because of a very narrow doctrine of frustration, or insufficiently policing their fairness in the first place, and allowing such a 'bad bargain'.

14.13   The basic tension between protecting initial rights, and thereby supporting discipline in the bargaining process, and encouraging renegotiation/compromise, will be considered further later, in relation to the requirement of a lack of a reasonable alternative, to agreeing. However, the issues are further illustrated here by considering, again, what happened in *Williams* v *Roffey Bros & Nicholls (Contractors) Ltd* (1990): the concept of 'bad faith' might provide a means of explaining why duress was assumed not to be present in that case. Clearly, if the carpenters had not completed under the original terms, it would have been a breach of contract. They were not going to breach, however, to 'exploit' the builders' 'weakness' in needing completion on time. They were going to breach because they had made a mistake, and a bad bargain in the first place, as well as running the job inefficiently. But the question then is whether we should be protecting the party who made a bad bargain through their own error, and then sought to escape it? And what of the difficulty of distinguishing the party who cynically made an apparently bad bargain to obtain the original contract, always intending to renegotiate something far more favourable once the other party was dependent upon his or her performance? The tension in the law is clear. The appropriate balance point is open to much argument. One thing which is clear is that the situation is a great deal more certain if a threatened breach is always illegitimate. A further means of explaining *Williams* v *Roffey Bros* is considered below (see para. **14.30**, and see also n. 5).

14.14   However, what must now be considered is the extension of what will amount to an illegitimate threat, beyond what is unlawful. Any extension of duress beyond the area of unlawful threats will be infringing upon freedom of contract without the obvious justification of 'unlawfulness'. It may be seen as the policing of contracts on the basis of inequality of bargaining power. Duress, even when confined to the unlawful, may be seen as rendering a contract voidable on the basis of inequality of bargaining power, but in an obviously restricted way. Other areas of the law indicate the unacceptability of the way in which the person making the threat has increased his or her bargaining power. Certainly there are indications against any generalized doctrine of relief against inequality of bargaining power.[17]

14.15   However, in *CTN Cash and Carry Ltd* v *Gallaher* [1994] 4 All ER 714 the Court of Appeal took the view that it is possible for duress to be based on a lawful threat,[18] but, on the facts of the particular case, no duress was found. In that case:

> The claimant company ran a cash-and-carry business. The defendant supplied them with cigarettes (and was the only possible supplier of some brands) on a regular basis, on credit

17 See *Pao On* v *Lau Yiu Long* [1980] AC 614 at 634; *National Westminster Bank plc* v *Morgan* [1985] 1 All ER 821 at 830.

18 See also *Universe Tankships Inc of Monrovia* v *International Transport Workers Federation and Laughton* (1983).

terms, but each transaction was covered by a separate contract. A dispute arose between them, and the defendants refused to continue to supply the claimants on credit, unless the claimants paid the sum which the defendants were asserting was due to them. The claimants asserted that the sum was not due, but paid the defendants in order to continue to trade with them on credit terms. The claimants sued to recover the sum paid on the basis that it had been paid under economic duress.

The defendants had not been correct in thinking that the sums were due to them, but the threat was not unlawful. It did not involve a threatened breach of contract. It merely related to the terms of potential, unrelated, future contracts. On this basis, the Court of Appeal rejected the claim of duress but, nevertheless, the Court did recognize the possibility of duress being found without an unlawful threat, and consideration should be given to the factors indicated as relevant to that.

14.16   The dispute arose out of 'arm's-length' commercial dealings between two trading companies' (at 717), and such a situation was clearly not viewed as one which was fertile ground for such a claim of duress, and it did not matter that the defendants were the sole distributors of certain brands of cigarette and therefore were, in a sense, in a monopolistic position. The line was taken that:

'The control of monopolies is . . . a matter for Parliament. Moreover the common law does not recognise the doctrine of inequality of bargaining power in commercial dealings' (Steyn LJ at 717).

However, there are suggestions that it could make a difference if what was in question was a 'protected relationship' or transactions between a supplier and a consumer. (No explanation was given of what might be a 'protected relationship'). It was also indicated that lack of bona fides by the party making the threat would be looked at. This is more easily accepted where what is threatened is not unlawful. Bad faith is being looked at to identify a threat as wrongful, where the law does not otherwise do so, rather than bona fides being considered which could prevent a claim of duress being used to provide protection against an unlawful threat. 'That good or bad faith may be particularly relevant when considering whether a case might represent a rare example of "lawful act duress" is not difficult to accept' (*Huyton SA* v *Peter Cremer GmbH* [1999] CLC 230 at 251). In *CTN Cash & Carry*, the defendants believed they were entitled to the payment they were demanding.

14.17   It would seem that the relationship of the parties, and bad faith, will be relevant to deciding whether a lawful threat will be illegitimate. However, the clearest message from the court was that such illegitimacy will not easily be found. Steyn LJ said (at 719):

'The aim of commercial law ought to be to encourage fair dealings between the parties. But it is a mistake for the law to set its sights too highly when the critical inquiry is not whether the conduct is lawful but whether it is morally or socially unacceptable.'

Subsequent cases indeed show that the courts take a restrictive approach to extending duress beyond threats which are clearly unlawful.

14.18   The lawful threat issue arose in *Alf Vaughan & Co Ltd v Royscot Trust plc* (1999). In that case:

> The claimants had vehicles, which it used in its business, on hire-purchase, or similar terms, from the defendants. The claimants went into receivership, and under the contracts, that entitled the defendants to retake possession of the vehicles. The receivers wanted to sell the business as a going concern, and therefore sought to stop the repossession by paying off the balance still due under the hire-purchase, and similar agreements. They had found buyers for the business, and it was a matter of urgency to stop the repossession, to be able to sell the business with the vehicles. The defendants refused to stop the repossession for payment of the sums due, but demanded about twice as much, and the receivers paid. The question was whether the excess payment could be recovered on the basis of duress.

The judge took the line that the threat to repossess the goods was not illegitimate. He emphasized that the threat was lawful. The defendants had a right to repossess the goods. The claimants could have sought relief from forfeiture, which would have made repossession unlawful, and would have been likely to have obtained such relief, but had not thought that there was time to do so, and had not done so. That proximity to the defendant's actions being unlawful, was not viewed as sufficient to make their actions illegitimate. The judge thought that the claimants could have sought relief from forfeiture, even if it meant that they lost that sale. Further, the judge does not seem to have viewed the defendants as behaving 'unconscionably', in bad faith, despite the fact that there was certainly scope to view them as so acting: they were 'concerned to exploit the claimants' weakness rather than solving their own financial problems'.[19] The closeness of the defendants to unlawfulness, and presence of a basis for finding bad faith, would indicate that it will, generally, be very difficult, indeed, to establish duress without unlawfulness.

14.19   However, care must be taken in drawing the line around unlawfulness, and illegitimacy, where although what is threatened is not unlawful, the threat draws its force from an unlawful act which has already occurred.[20] *Progress Bulk Carriers Ltd v Tube City IMS LLC (The*

---

[19] Burrows, *The Law of Restitution*, 3rd edn, p. 179.

[20] In *Borelli v Ting* (2010), the agreement in question was one by which the former chairman and chief executive of a company agreed not to block the scheme of arrangement which liquidators were seeking to implement, to gain money, to be able to pursue the liquidation, and pay some of what was owed to the company's creditors. To obtain his agreement, the liquidators had to undertake not to investigate further in relation to his involvement in the company's defaults, and funds which had disappeared from the company. That ability to block was achieved by the use of forgery and false evidence, and the need for the agreement was because of his failure to comply with his duty under the winding up rules to co-operate with the liquidators. The agreement, by which the liquidators promised not to pursue him, was not allowed to stand: duress was found. The liquidators had been in a position where they had no real alternative to making the agreement, if they were going to take further their attempts to recover any money for the company's creditors. The force of the threat derived from his earlier, unlawful actions.

Cenk Kaptanoglu) (2012) provides an example of a need to be cautious in saying that a breach is in the past, and that there is nothing unlawful in threatening not to make a new contract. Prudence is needed in drawing the lines around cases like *CTN Cash & Carry v Gallaher*, where there is a threat not to do what was perfectly lawful not to do—a threat not to make a new, unrelated contract—and where the threat is not to make a contract which is related, in the sense that it involves the provision of an alternate performance for that not provided because of the breach, and a compromise of the breach. In *The Cenk K* the threat drew its force from the breach.

14.20   The facts of *The Cenk K* were:

> Charterers made a contract with the owners of *The Cenk K* to carry a cargo of shredded metal from Mississippi to China. The owners committed a repudiatory breach by chartering that ship elsewhere. The charterers were in a difficult position. They were under contract to B to deliver the cargo, using that ship, and any new shipping arrangements would have to be agreed by B. Use of a substitute vessel was discussed, and B was prepared to agree to one offered by the owners, but at a discount of $6 a metric ton. After the breach, the owners had told the charterers that they would provide a substitute, and meet their losses from the failure to provide the Cenk K, but in the end would only go as far as $2 a metric ton, and then only on the basis that the charterers gave up any claim in relation to the original breach. With the delays, and the situation in relation to B, the charterers had no reasonable alternative to agreeing. Arbitrators had found that the new agreement, providing the substitute vessel, and compromising the charterer's claim for the original breach, was made under duress.

The owners claimed that the arbitrators had not used the correct test as there was nothing unlawful in refusing to make a contract, and therefore no duress. Cooke J took the line that it was 'clear from the authorities that "illegitimate pressure" can be constituted by conduct which is not in itself unlawful, although it will be an unusual case where that is so, particularly in the commercial context' (at [36]). This dealt with the owners claim, and the case may be viewed as one where a threat to do what was lawful—not make a new contract—was found to be illegitimate.

14.21   However, care must be taken with the case. It must be kept distinct from the situation in *CTN Cash & Carry v Gallaher*. Cooke J stated:

> '[I]t would be very odd if pressure could be brought about by a threatened breach of contract, which did amount to an unlawful act but not by a past breach, coupled with conduct since that breach, which drove the victim of the breach into a position where it had no realistic alternative but to waive its rights in respect of that breach, in order to avoid further catastrophic loss.'

In the situation in which the breach is what is creating the pressure, and the agreement is to provide a substitute performance, and to compromise any claim arising from that breach, the threat should certainly be regarded as illegitimate, and could be viewed as unlawful, because of its relationship to the breach.[21] The line could be taken that a threat is unlawful where it draws its power from a past unlawful act, rather than from the lawful act which might be carried out in the future. However, whether the threat is regarded as unlawful or not, the situation is very distinct, and must be labelled as one involving duress if the other requirements are also satisfied. Further, it is a commercial situation, but it must not be allowed to create any difficulties by broadening illegitimacy in relation to commercial situations generally. In particular, the *CTN* type of case must be distinguished. In *CTN* the threat drew its force from the potential, future, lawful act, not from the past, unlawful one.

Lack of a reasonable alternative

14.22   The Privy Council recognized that economic duress could render a contract voidable in *Pao On v Lau Yiu Long* [1980] AC 614. Lord Scarman said that for duress to be found there must have been 'a coercion of the will which vitiates consent' and D's agreement must have been 'involuntary' (at 636). We have already seen how unhelpful such language is, and what is of greater interest is the list of factors which he regarded as relevant indicators of duress. He said (at 635):

> 'It is material to enquire whether the person alleged to have been coerced did or did not protest; whether at the time he was allegedly coerced into making the contract, he did or did not have an alternative course open to him such as an adequate legal remedy; whether he was independently advised; and whether after entering the contract he took steps to avoid it.'

It is the reference to whether the person threatened 'did or did not have an alternative course open to him such as an adequate legal remedy', which is most significant, and which has subsequently come to the fore as generally required, if duress is to be found. Thus, in *Universe Tankships Inc. of Monrovia v International Transport Workers' Federation* [1983] AC 366, after referring to the 'compulsion of the will of the victim', Lord Scarman said (at 400):

> 'There must be pressure, the practical effect of which is compulsion or the absence of choice...The classic case of duress is, however...the victim's intentional submission arising from the realisation that there is no practical choice open to him.'

Lord Scarman's 'classic case' pointed to the true general limitation upon economic duress (alongside illegitimacy); the insufficiency of the alternative courses of action open to the person threatened. The 'classic case' actually shows the lack of reality in the idea that there is a test of voluntariness, referring to a situation where factually someone's will is overborne. It would be inconsistent to look for such lack of will and, at the same time, to acknowledge that the person concerned chose between alternatives. The explanation of this inconsistency is, as has been

---

21 Burrows asks the question, 'why could it not be said that the owners were threatening a continued breach of the charterparty?'. (A. Burrows, *A Casebook on Contract*, 4th edn, Hart Publishing, 2013, p. 766). This may not provide a solution where the repudiation is accepted.

indicated (see para. **14.6**) partly due to the superficial justification for the court's interference with the parties' agreement which is provided by a test which appears to be based, factually, upon a lack of willed action, but it is also partly linguistic. In everyday speech the test of voluntariness is the question of whether the person threatened had 'no choice', and this, in turn, is understood as meaning 'did he, or she, have a "practical" or "reasonable" alternative?', and this can be seen as reflected in Lord Scarman's movement from 'no choice' to the 'classic case' of 'intentional submission' in the face of 'no practical choice'.

14.23   The true nature of the test, as a matter of the availability of alternatives,[22] for the person threatened, to agreeing, is to be found in *B & S Contracts and Design Ltd* v *Victor Green Publications Ltd* [1984] ICR 419:

> B & S had agreed to erect stands for VG at Olympia to be used for a trade exhibition. B & S intended to use employees who were to be made redundant as soon as they had erected the stands, and they refused to work unless given £9,000 severance pay. B & S paid £4,500 but told VG to pay the rest, in addition to the contract price. It was clear that B & S would not be able to perform the contract unless those employees went back to work. If the stands were not erected, it would have had 'disastrous consequences' for VG and the exhibitors, and payment of the money was VG's only means of ensuring that the stands were erected.

It was held that VG had acted under duress. Griffiths LJ thought that the threatened breach placed VG (at 426):

> 'in the position envisaged by Lord Scarman in... *Pao On* v *Lau Yiu Long* in which they were faced with no alternative course of action but to pay the sum demanded of them.'

Of course, it is not accurate to say that VG had 'no alternative' available. VG could have refused to pay and then sued for breach of contract. However, such an alternative was too damaging to VG, and Griffiths LJ clearly recognized that it was the acceptability of the alternatives which was being considered. He said that not having the stands 'would have clearly caused grave damage to [VG's] reputation and... might have exposed them to very heavy claims from the exhibitors' (at 426). Further, Kerr LJ, unequivocally stated (at 428) that a threat to break a contract will constitute duress if:

> 'the consequences of a refusal would be serious and immediate so that there is no reasonable alternative open such as legal redress... .'

There is generally a limitation upon duress which is concerned with an assessment of the acceptability of the alternatives open to the person claiming duress. The test used by Kerr LJ is that of a 'reasonable' alternative',[23] and that is the formulation adopted here, but others, such

---

22 E. Macdonald, 'Duress by Threatened Breach of Contract' [1989] JBL 460.

23 See also, e.g., *North Ocean Shipping Co. Ltd* v *Hyundai Construction Co. Ltd, The Atlantic Baron* [1978] 3 All ER 1170 at 1182; *Vantage Navigation Corpn* v *Suhail and Saud Bahwan Building Materials, The Alev* [1989] 1 Lloyd's Rep 138 at 146–7.

as 'practical alternative' have been used.[24] In fact, in *Borelli v Ting* (2010) the Privy Council referred to the party threatened as having no 'reasonable or practical alternative' (at [31]). There is some dispute as to how the lack of availability of alternatives should be described. The basic idea is, however, clear. It is not a matter of overborne wills, but of the curtailment of options.

14.24   The lack of a reasonable alternative for party threatened is a separate requirement for duress, giving substance, alongside the need for subjective causation, to the references to the 'overborne will'. In *DSDN Subsea Ltd v Petroleum Geo Services ASA* (2000) Dyson J stated (at [131]):

> 'The ingredients of actionable duress are that there must be pressure, (a) whose practical effect is that there is compulsion on, or a lack of practical choice for, the victim, (b) which is illegitimate, and (c) which is a significant cause inducing the claimant to enter into the contract.'

However, it should be acknowledged that this is not universally recognized to be the case. Lack of a practical or reasonable choice for the party threatened, has been seen merely as evidence that the illegitimate pressure was a sufficient cause of the contract. In *Kolmar Group v Traxpo* (2010), a case in which there clearly was no 'realistic', or reasonable, alternative, Christopher Clarke J stated (at [92]):

> 'If there was no reasonable alternative, that may be very strong evidence in support of a conclusion that the victim of the duress was in fact influenced by the threat.'

Nevertheless, it is a substantive requirement which is in question here, rather than merely evidence of causation. Why is that so?

14.25   In *Huyton SA v Peter Cremer GmbH & Co.* [1999] CLC 230, Mance J recognized that 'a simple [causal] enquiry whether the innocent party would have acted as he did "but for" an actual or threatened breach of contract' was not enough. He took the line that 'relief must, I think, depend on the court's assessment of the qualitative impact of the illegitimate pressure'. A reasonable or practical, alternative test is another element in the law's striking of a balance between encouraging compromises and protecting initial rights (and discipline in the bidding process). It seemed to Mance J 'self-evident that relief may not be appropriate, if an innocent party decides, as a matter of choice, not to pursue an alternative remedy which any and possibly some other reasonable persons in his circumstances would have pursued' (at 252). If economic duress could be successfully claimed after any unlawful threat, it would undermine the security of any transaction caused by one party's announcement of his or her intention to breach his or her contract. The law has an interest in ensuring that many such transactions are regarded as binding, although they are founded on a wrong. The functioning of the legal system

---

24   e.g. *Enimont Overseas AG v RO Jugotanker Zader, The Olib* [1991] 2 Lloyd's Rep 108 at 114.

depends upon such compromises being made: not all such disputes could be litigated without overloading the legal system. Further, if the parties can reach agreement themselves, then it may increase their chances of being able to continue to do business with one another, both throughout that transaction and in the future. To make such compromises or renegotiations worthwhile, they must be transactions which cannot be reopened too easily. The alternatives test draws a line.

14.26   Nevertheless, Mance J also said in *Huyton SA* v *Peter Cremer GmbH & Co* [1999] CLC 230 (at 252):

> 'It is not necessary to go as far as to say that it is an inflexible…essential ingredient of economic duress that there should be no, or no practical alternative course open for the innocent party.'

And there are situations in which it would be inappropriate to deny a claim of duress on the basis that the person threatened had a reasonable alternative to agreeing. First, the alternatives' test should not be used where what is threatened (or the threat) is a criminal offence. There is no indication of it in *Barton* v *Armstrong* (1976) where the threats were of physical violence, and where a crime is involved, the law has no interest in the protection of a compromise. In relation to crimes, all that should be in question is illegitimacy, which is patently present, and causation.

14.27   Secondly, a question arises as to the protection of those less able to realize that there was a reasonable alternative, or to take advantage of it. Andrew Burrows asks[25]

> '[I]s it not objectionable to rule out [a claim of duress] on the ground that the claimant was weak or foolish to have given in?'

Again, in *Huyton SA* v *Peter Cremer GmbH & Co,* Mance J viewed the misconceptions of the party threatened being relevant to the question of available alternatives, if the other party was in some sense responsible for them, or could have foreseen the other party arriving at them (at 252). It is possible to have a general test of whether there was a reasonable alternative to agreeing, but not to apply it to the full extent in every case. The concept of good faith might be called upon. Again, it is essentially a matter of how far the law goes in protecting compromises, but, for example, the exploitation of known weakness, should not be permitted simply on the basis that there was a reasonable alternative. An analogy can be made with the clear acceptance that a fraudulent misrepresentor cannot rely upon a claim that the misrepresentation was not such as to have induced the reasonable person to contract (*Smith* v *Kay* (1859)—see para. **13.34**).[26]

---

25 Burrows, *The Law of Restitution*, 3rd edn, p. 272.

26 There are issues about the appropriate borderlines between duress, undue influence, and unconscionability.

Causation

14.28   The further question which must be asked is the degree to which the 'threat' must have induced the contract. Similar points could be made here as in relation to the question of the degree of reliance required for a misrepresentation to be operative (see para. **13.34**ff). Following *Barton v Armstrong* (1976) it would seem that in cases of threats to the person it is sufficient if the threat can be viewed as 'a' cause of the contract—and the 'but for' test need not be satisfied. However, outside of that type of duress, it has been said that 'the minimum basic test of subjective causation in economic duress' ought to be a 'but for' test (*Huyton SA v Peter Cremer GmbH* [1999] CLC 230 at 250). One exceptional situation where the 'but for' test should not be required is where there are two concurrent causes of the decision to contract, neither in themselves sufficient, so that if the 'but for' test was applied, the contract would be found to have no cause. In that situation a 'common sense relaxation, even of a "but for" requirement is necessary' (*Huyton SA* at 250).

14.29   However, it should be recognized that there may be cases in which it is insufficient that the threat satisfies a 'but for' test, and there are references to it being necessary for the threat to be a 'significant' cause.[27] There may be cases in which the new contract would not have occurred without the threat, but the threat has become merely the background to the making of the new contract. The threatened claimant may have agreed for positive reasons, such as maintenance of a long term relationship with the defendant, particularly if it is plain that the defendant did not realise that what they were threatening was a breach. Alternatively, the party threatened may have agreed because they think the new terms demanded will have little impact, or carry little risk for them, and so they see no point in doing anything other than accepting.

14.30   The idea of a threat which, although it is a 'but for' cause, should not be regarded as a sufficient cause for a successful claim of duress, as it was merely part of the background to the new agreement, provides another possible explanation of the assumption that the new agreement was not affected by duress in *Williams v Roffey Bros & Nicholls* (1990). It would seem that 'but for' the likelihood of the carpenters' breaching, the builders would never have considered offering them additional payment to complete on time, but the situation might be seen as one in which that 'threat' could be regarded as merely the background to the promise to pay more, with the foreground factor being the recognition that the carpenters had underpriced the job in the first place. Such a line would be difficult to draw, but causation issues, explored beyond the basic 'but for' criterion, usually are.

Rescission

14.31   It was made clear in relation to misrepresentation that the right to rescind a voidable contract may be lost (see para. **13.75**), and the same applies here. In *The Atlantic Baron (North Ocean Shipping v Hyundai Construction Co. Ltd)* (1978) the right to rescind was lost through

---

27   e.g. *The Evia Luck* [1992] 2 AC 152 at 165.

affirmation.[28] There, a contract had been made for the building of a ship. When the dollar was devalued the builders threatened to cease work unless the price was increased to take account of that. There was no legal basis to the builders' claim, but the purchasers agreed to it. They had already chartered out the ship to Shell and would not have been able to obtain a suitable alternative. Mocatta J found that the agreement to pay the increased price was made under duress, but the purchasers could not rely upon it. They were found to have affirmed the contract. By the time the final payments had to be made the market had changed to such an extent that the purchasers could have refused to pay the increase without any risk of non-delivery, but they made no protest. The ship was delivered in November 1974. No indication of any intention to claim duress was given until the end of July 1975.

Undue influence

Introduction

14.32   Whilst the common law delayed in developing duress beyond duress to the person, equity provided a more extensive remedy through undue influence. Although there has been an overlap with what will now constitute duress, with illegitimate pressure constituting undue influence,[29] it would be better now to see such cases as matters of duress, and for the latter doctrine to be confined to what it has chiefly been concerned with: influence based on the relationship of the parties. The necessary relationship has proved difficult to describe.

> 'Several expressions have been used in an endeavour to encapsulate the essence: trust and confidence, reliance, dependence or vulnerability on the one hand and ascendancy, domination or control on the other. None of these descriptions is perfect. None is all embracing. Each has its proper place' (*Royal Bank of Scotland* v *Etridge (No 2)* at [11]).

This multifaceted description is hardly surprising. However, the basic idea is that one party has ceased to decide upon such a transaction on the basis of his or her consideration of the transaction as such, but because of the advice, or orders, of the other party, and that surrender of decision making has occurred because of the relationship of, for example, trust, or domination, which exists between them. Undue influence renders a contract voidable, and also allows for the recovery of gifts. (Obviously the bars to rescission will apply here as elsewhere, so that, for example, a contract cannot be rescinded for undue influence once it has been affirmed.)

---

28 In *Halpern v Halpern* (2007) it was recognized that rescission would also be barred by restitutio in integrum becoming impossible, but the court did indicate an unwillingness to see it preventing there being any remedy for the duress, and a money equivalent might be recognized as being able to be used to prevent such impossibility. It is clear, however, that where the unlawful act precedes the threat, and is related to it, and is the source of the threat's power (as in *Progress Bulk Carriers Ltd v Tube City IMS LLC (The Cenk Kaptanoglu)* (2012)), there can be no bar through the party, who made the threat, not being returned to the position which was brought about by the unlawful act (*Borelli v Ting* (2010) at [38]–[39]).

29 e.g. *Williams v Bayley* (1866).

14.33 *Allcard v Skinner* (1887) is one of the classic cases of undue influence, and it was concerned with a gift made by a nun, A, to the mother superior, for the purposes of the sisterhood. The rules of the sisterhood, reflected in the vows which she had taken, required poverty, complete and unquestioning obedience to the mother superior, and no advice outside of the sisterhood without the mother superior's approval. A subsequently left the convent, and eventually sought the return of her gift. The court would have ordered it, on the basis of undue influence, but did not do so because of the six-year delay between her leaving the convent and seeking its return.

14.34 *Allcard v Skinner*, however, was not a case where undue influence was established. It was presumed, and whilst there are cases of 'actual' (i.e. proven) undue influence, the situation is more commonly that the facts are such as to have brought about its presumption. Presumed undue influence developed because the courts were asked to deal with 'insidious forms of spiritual tyranny' and 'protect persons from the exercise of such influence under circumstances which render proof of it impossible' (*Allcard v Skinner* (1887) 36 Ch D 145 at 183–4). In *Barclays Bank plc v O'Brien* [1993] 4 All ER 417 (at 423) the House of Lords recognized a subdivision within presumed undue influence, which can be referred to as types A and B, and the House of Lords in *Royal Bank of Scotland v Etridge (No 2)* (2001) further clarified this. In some cases there are in fact two different presumptions of different types. The first type of situation (type A), where there is a double presumption, involves a presumption of law that the relationship is one in which there is relevant influence, and an evidential presumption that undue influence has been exercised. The second type of situation (type B), merely involves the evidential presumption that undue influence has been exercised: the necessary relationship of influence, does, first, have to be established. Importantly though, it should be emphasized that, in both situations (A and B), for the evidential presumption, that undue influence was used, to arise, the transaction must be one which 'calls for an explanation' or which is 'not readily explicable by the relationship of the parties' (*Royal Bank of Scotland v Etridge (No 2)* (2001) at [14], [21], [24]). The usual way in which the evidential presumption of exercise of undue influence is rebutted (the legal one cannot be), is by showing that the party claiming to have been subject to it, received independent advice.

14.35 In considering undue influence then, it is necessary to look at whether it can actually be proved to have been exercised to produce the transaction ('actual undue influence'), or whether it is a type A situation, giving rise to the double presumption, or a type B situation, giving rise to the single presumption. However, although the structure through which the court approaches a claim of undue influence has become more defined, it remains unclear as to exactly what is required for undue influence, and also, therefore, as to what is being presumed. In short, it is not clear what makes the influence 'undue'; is it simply its extent (i.e. that it is excessive), or that it has been exercised in some sense 'wrongfully'? In broad terms, the question is, is it just about the claimant's 'consent', or does it require wrongfulness by the defendant?

14.36 It was strongly contended that it was simply a matter of impaired 'consent', and that nothing wrongful was required on the part of the other party, by Birks and Chin,[30] but this

---

30 P. Birks and Chin Nyuk Yin, 'On the Nature of Undue Influence' in J. Beatson and D. Friedmann (eds), *Good Faith and Fault in Contract Law*, Oxford University Press, 1995.

view has met with considerable opposition.[31] On the whole, the courts lean towards the idea of some wrongfulness being required. In *Royal Bank of Scotland* v *Etridge (No 2)* (2001), for example, Lord Nicholls said (at [8]), of undue influence, that it arises out 'of a relationship between two persons where one has acquired over another a measure of influence, or ascendancy, of which the ascendant person then takes unfair advantage'. Similarly, in *R v Attorney General for England and Wales* (2003), where undue influence was considered, as well as duress, Lord Hoffmann said (at [21])[32]

'Like duress at common law, undue influence is based upon the principle that a transaction to which consent has been obtained by unacceptable means should not be allowed to stand. Undue influence has concentrated in particular upon the unfair exploitation by one party of a relationship which gives him ascendancy or influence over the other.'

14.37   However, in *Niersmans v Pesticcio* (2004) Mummery LJ said (at [20]):[33]

'Although undue influence is sometimes described as an "equitable wrong" or even as a species of equitable fraud, the basis of the court's intervention is not the commission of a dishonest or wrongful act by the defendant, but that, as a matter of public policy, the presumed influence arising from the relationship of trust and confidence should not operate to the disadvantage of the victim, if the transaction is not satisfactorily explained by ordinary motives: *Allcard v. Skinner* (1887) 36 Ch D 145 at 171. The court scrutinises the circumstances in which the transaction, under which benefits were conferred on the recipient, took place and the nature of the continuing relationship between the parties, rather than any specific act or conduct on the part of the recipient. A transaction may be set aside by the court, even though the actions and conduct of the person who benefits from it could not be criticised as wrongful.'

Further in *Macklin v Dowsett* (2004) Auld LJ emphasized that undue influence was concerned with the 'protection of the vulnerable' and 'misconduct' by the other did not have to be established (at [10]). Indeed, in *Allcard v Skinner* (1887), Bowen LJ said, of the mother superior (at 190–1):

'I acquit her most entirely of all selfish feeling in the matter. I can see no sort of wrongful desire to appropriate to herself any worldly benefit from the gift; but, nevertheless, she was a person who benefited by it so far as the disposition of the property was concerned, although, no doubt, she meant to use it in conformity with the rules of the institution, and did so use it.'

---

31 R. Bigwood, 'Undue Influence: "Impaired consent" or "Wicked exploitation" ' (1996) 16 OJLS 503; D. Capper, 'Unconscionable Bargain in the Common Law World' (2010) 126 LQR 403; M. Chen-Wishart, 'Undue Influence: Beyond Impaired Consent and wrongdoing to a relational analysis' in A. Burrows and Lord Rodger (eds), *Mapping the Law: Essays in Memory of Peter Birks*, Oxford University Press, 2006.

32 See also Lord Millett in *National Commercial Bank (Jamaica) Ltd* v *Hew* (2003) at [29]–[31].

33 See also *Hammond* v *Osbourne* (2002); *Forde* v *Birmingham City Council* (2009) at [103].

It may be, that the wrongfulness, which is required, in addition to the claimant's impaired decision making, may be no more than that, in the light of the relationship, the defendant should have, and did not, ensure that the claimant was liberated from their influence, in relation to the relevant transaction (for example, by independent advice).[34]

14.38   A further introductory point should be made here, as to the modern context of many cases concerned with undue influence. The issue tends to arise in cases in which a wife has guaranteed a loan by a bank to the husband's business and charged the matrimonial home as security. When the business runs into difficulties, the wife claims that she provided the guarantee and executed the charge under the undue influence of her husband, and that the bank is affected by that, and cannot enforce its security against her. Given this common context, although the problem is not confined to the relationship of husband and wife, or even unmarried partners, the basic problem has sometimes been labelled as one of 'sexually transmitted debt'. Although we are chiefly concerned here with what these cases tell us about undue influence, as such, the question does arise as to when a third party to the undue influence is affected by it. There is a question of balancing the protection of the wife with the need not to stultify the family home as an asset which small businesses can use to raise money. Banks will not lend money on the basis of security which is too likely not to be available to them.

Actual undue influence

14.39   In *Bank of Credit and Commerce International SA v Aboody* [1992] 4 All ER 955, Slade LJ said (at 976) that actual undue influence requires:

> '(a) that the other party to the transaction...had the capacity to influence the complainant; (b) that the influence was exercised; (c) that its exercise was undue; (d) that its exercise brought about the transaction.'

Obviously, this raises again the issue of the meaning of 'undue'. A further requirement of 'manifest disadvantage' was dismissed in *CIBC Mortgages v Pitt* (1994), and it was not applied to actual undue influence, as a requirement, in *Etridge*, when 'manifest disadvantage' was reconceived as the need for the transaction to be one 'calling for an explanation', for the generation of the presumption of the exercise of undue influence. However, Lord Nicholls also made the point, in *Etridge* (at [12]):

> 'It is not essential that the transaction should be disadvantageous to the pressurised or influenced person, either in financial terms or in any other way. However, in the nature of things, questions of undue influence will not usually arise, and the exercise of undue influence is unlikely to occur, where the transaction is innocuous. The issue is likely to arise only when, in some respect, the transaction was disadvantageous either from the outset or as matters turned out.'

---

34 R. Bigwood, 'Undue Influence: "Impaired consent" or "Wicked exploitation"' (1996) 16 OJLS 503.

Obviously, it is generally presumed undue influence which is in question. Someone claiming influence will normally use the easier route, requiring them merely to establish what will give rise to the presumption, or presumptions, rather than actually prove that undue influence has occurred.

Presumed undue influence—the double presumption—type A

14.40   Equity took the approach that there were some categories of relationships where the vulnerability or dependence of one party would normally be such that the existence of influence did not need to be established but was presumed as a matter of law (not just evidentially) and so could not be rebutted. This means that when the relationship between the relevant parties falls within one of these identified categories, the necessary influence for a claim of undue influence is presumed to exist and the alleged wielder of the influence cannot prove otherwise. Examples of these relationships are 'parent and child, guardian and ward, trustee and beneficiary, solicitor and client, medical advisor and patient' (*Royal Bank of Scotland v Etridge (No 2)* (2001)). It should be noted that the relationship of husband and wife is not one of those encompassed within the presumption of the existence of relevant influence.[35]

14.41   However, in *Etridge* it was made clear that the above automatic presumption of law is only as to the existence of relevant influence between the parties. It is only if another factor is present that there is a second, evidential, presumption that undue influence was exercised, and that factor relates to the transaction. As has been indicated, the transaction must be one which 'calls for an explanation' or which is 'not readily explicable by the relationship of the parties' (*Etridge* at [14] and [21]). Lord Nicholls said (at [24]):

> 'The second prerequisite...is good sense. It is a necessary limitation upon the width of the first prerequisite. It would be absurd for the law to presume that every gift by a child to a parent, or every transaction between a client and his solicitor or between a patient and his doctor, was brought about by undue influence unless the contrary is affirmatively proved...The law would be rightly open to ridicule, for transactions such as these are unexceptionable. They do not suggest that something may be amiss. So something more is needed before the law reverses the burden of proof, something which calls for an explanation.'

This further factor will be considered at para. **14.49**ff. Here, it should be emphasized that, unlike the first presumption, this second presumption is merely evidential, so that it can be rebutted. All that the triggering of this second presumption means is that the evidential burden shifts to the person who allegedly exercised undue influence, i.e. he or she will be found to have exercised undue influence unless they adduce sufficient evidence to the contrary. Rebutting the presumption will also be returned to later.

---

35 *Bank of Montreal v Stuart* (1911); *Midland Bank plc v Shephard* [1988] 3 All ER 17 at 21; *National Westminster Bank plc v Morgan* [1985] 1 All ER at 821 at 826.

Presumed undue influence—the single presumption—type B

14.42   The second situation in which it is said that there is presumed undue influence only involves a single presumption and that merely the evidential one. Before that can come into play it must be established not only that the transaction is one calling for an explanation, but first that the relationship between the parties involved relevant influence (*Royal Bank of Scotland* v *Etridge (No 2)*(2001) at [21]) and it is here, perhaps, that the case law provides most consideration of the relevant influence. In general, discussion of the requirements of a relationship of influence has been quite limited. There is a tendency merely to rely upon labeling a relevant relationship as 'confidential' or 'fiduciary'. However, as has been indicated, what is required is a relationship in which one party has surrendered relevant decision making. It may be through 'domination' and 'control', but most commonly, what is in question is a relationship of trust and confidence: the type of trust and confidence which leads one party, A, to rely upon the other party, B, to act in his or her, A's interests, rather than B's own interests. It is reliance upon, and trust in, disinterested advice. The cases illuminating the type of trust and confidence required will now be considered. However, whilst the focus in the discussion of the cases below is on the relationship required, sight must not be lost of the fact that *Etridge* made it clear that the evidential presumption that undue influence has been exercised, will only arise if the transaction is also one which 'calls for an explanation'.

14.43   In *Lloyds Bank Ltd* v *Bundy* [1974] 3 All ER 757 a relevant relationship was found, and the situation was distinguished from the trust which can exist in a business relationship between parties dealing at arm's length. In that case, the facts were as follows:

> Mr Bundy charged his home to guarantee his son's business debts to the bank. Both father and son used the same bank. The father's relationship with the bank was longstanding, and he relied upon it for advice. When the assistant manager brought the charge to Mr Bundy's home to be signed he realized that Mr Bundy looked to him for advice. The assistant manager not only explained the legal effect of the charge but also discussed the situation of the son's company. Mr Bundy 'was seeking and being given advice on the viability of the company as a factor to be taken into account' in his decision to sign the charge. The charge was not to enable the son to borrow more money from the bank, but merely to secure his existing loans. The execution of the charge meant that the bank was not demanding repayment immediately, but it did not guarantee a period within which it would not do so. Very little was gained by Mr Bundy, or his son, in return for the execution of the charge, but the bank gained security for existing debts. The assistant manager had not perceived any conflict of interest, and had not advised Mr Bundy to obtain independent advice.

When the bank claimed possession of Mr Bundy's home, he argued that the charge should be set aside for undue influence. The Court of Appeal concluded that Mr Bundy's reliance upon the bank to give general advice on the wisdom of the transaction was a relevant relationship. (As is plain, it was also a transaction which called for an explanation—the father gained little from it.) In the absence of independent advice for Mr Bundy, the presumption of the exercise of undue influence was not rebutted. Sir Eric Sachs considered the usual type of relevant relationship (at 767):

> '[T]here must of course be shown to exist a vital element which in this judgement will be referred to as confidentiality. It is this element which is so impossible to define and which is a matter for the judgment of the court on the facts of any particular case...It imports some quality beyond that inherent in the confidence that can well exist between trustworthy persons who in business affairs deal with each other at arm's length. It is one of the features of this element that once it exists, influence naturally grows out of it.'

Despite his reluctance to regard the 'vital element' of 'confidentiality' as definable, Sir Eric Sachs's distinction between the situation in which a relevant relationship exists and that of business dealings at arm's length between trustworthy persons, makes it clear that he is referring to the situation where one party is expected to give disinterested advice to the other. The question in relation to this usual type of relevant relationship is: Is the person concerned trusted to the extent that he or she is relied upon to act in the interests of the other party, and not his or her own? It is that degree of trust, reliance, or confidence, which can give rise to undue influence.

14.44   The relationship of banker and customer was again considered in *National Westminster Bank plc* v *Morgan* (1985), and the House of Lords distinguished the case from *Lloyds Bank Ltd* v *Bundy* (1974). In *Morgan*, the facts were as follows:

> A husband and wife were in danger of losing their home because the building society was seeking possession for non-payment of the mortgage. The bank agreed to a refinancing of the house purchase on the basis of a bridging loan to cover the few weeks until the husband expected to have the money. His business was then looking prosperous, although it had been through hard times. However, the bank required a charge on the house for the loan. The bank manager called at the house to obtain the wife's signature on the legal charge. He mistakenly assured the wife that the charge would not extend to her husband's business liabilities to the bank. In fact the charge was sufficiently widely worded to cover those business liabilities, but it was not the intention of the bank that it should be so used and it never was so used. The husband died and the bank sought possession of the house.

The wife did not raise the issue of innocent misrepresentation, but merely claimed that the charge should be set aside for undue influence. The House of Lords held that there was no relevant relationship. The manager had explained the charge to her, but the wife had not looked to the manager for general advice on the wisdom of the transaction. She executed the charge because that was how she and her husband planned to preserve the family home, and she knew that it was the only way to do so. In *Bundy* the bank had discussed with Mr Bundy the position of his son's business. In addition, in *Morgan* the transaction was 'readily explicable'—it was a normal commercial loan taken as the only hope the couple had of preserving the matrimonial home—and so no presumption of undue influence could arise, in any event. (At the time the House of Lords put this in terms of the transaction not involving a 'manifest disadvantage' to the wife, but that test was clarified in *Royal Bank of Scotland* v *Etridge (No 2)* (2001)—on this second requirement, see para. **14.49**.)

14.45 We should give brief consideration to the use by Lord Scarman, in *National Westminster Bank plc* v *Morgan* (1985), of the term 'dominating influence' to indicate the situation in which a relevant relationship of influence exists. Although the existence of a dominating influence would undoubtedly suffice (where decision making has been surrendered to the dominant person), it was made clear in *Goldsworthy* v *Brickell* [1987] 1 All ER 853 that there is no requirement that the relationship be a dominating one. The facts there were as follows:

> Mr Goldsworthy owned a farm which, from 1970 to 1976, he had run with his son as his sole employee. He had little faith in his son's abilities, relations between them were strained, and the farm was in a run-down condition. The son did not live in the farmhouse with his father. From the end of 1976 Mr Brickell, a neighbouring farmer, gave Mr Goldsworthy help and advice in the running of his farm. Mr Brickell's employees worked on Mr Goldsworthy's farm at no cost to him. One of Mr Brickell's female employees cleaned Mr Goldsworthy's house and did his shopping for him. Mr Goldsworthy's reliance upon Mr Brickell and his employees was such that, by early 1977, Mr Brickell was effectively managing Mr Goldsworthy's farm. In April 1977, Mr Goldsworthy, who was then 85, whilst keeping the right to live on the farm, granted Mr Brickell a tenancy of his farm with an option to purchase it on his death. Both were on terms very disadvantageous to Mr Goldsworthy.

The Court of Appeal set aside the tenancy agreement. There was a relevant relationship between Mr Brickell and Mr Goldsworthy and the presumption of undue influence was raised. The court made it clear that the relationship was sufficient even though it fell short of domination. It was enough that the appropriate trust and confidence existed between the parties.

14.46 *Goldsworthy* also contains further indication that the essence of the 'trust and confidence' relationship in which the required 'influence' will be found is that of reliance, not merely upon someone's judgement, but also upon their advice being totally disinterested, i.e. not tainted by their own interests. Nourse LJ explained why the relationships of solicitor and client, and doctor and patient, are regarded as giving rise to the legal presumption that the relationship is one of influence. He said (at 868):

> '[D]octors and solicitors are trusted and confided in by their patients and clients to give them conscientious and disinterested advice on matters which profoundly affect, in the one case their physical and mental and, in the other, their material wellbeing. It is natural to presume that out of trust and confidence grows influence.'

He also explained why the banker–customer relationship is not one which gives rise to this legal presumption:

> '[A] banker, being a person having a pre-existing and conflicting interest in any loan transaction with a customer, cannot ordinarily be trusted and confided in so as to come under a duty to take care of the customer and give him disinterested advice'.

Again the emphasis is upon it being the expectation of disinterested advice which is significant in the relationship of influence.[36]

14.47   Although it seems necessary to identify the relevant 'influence', Lord Scarman's warning in *National Westminster Bank plc v Morgan* [1985] 1 All ER 821 must be borne in mind. He said (at 877):

> 'There is no precisely defined law setting the limits to the equitable jurisdiction of a court to relieve against undue influence. This is the world of doctrine, not of neat and tidy rules....'

14.48   Again it should be emphasized that *Royal Bank of Scotland v Etridge (No 2)* (2001) has made clear that establishing a relevant relationship of influence is not sufficient to generate the evidential presumption that undue influence was exercised. That also requires the transaction to be one which 'calls for an explanation'.

Transactions 'calling for an explanation'

14.49   As has been indicated, the evidential presumption of the exercise of undue influence does not arise unless the transaction is one which 'calls for an explanation' or is 'not readily explicable by the relationship of the parties' (*Royal Bank of Scotland v Etridge (No 2)* (2001) at [14] and [21]). This derives from the judgment of Lindley LJ in *Allcard v Skinner* (1887) 36 Ch D 145. Making the point that the existence of a relationship of influence is not sufficient but that, coupled with it, the nature of the transaction may raise the presumption, Lindley LJ said (at 185):

> 'But if the gift is so large as not to be reasonably accounted for on the ground of friendship, relationship, charity, or other ordinary motives on which ordinary men act, the burden is on the donee to support the gift.'

It was a gift which was in question in that case, but the point applies to transactions more generally.

14.50   In *National Westminster Bank plc v Morgan* (1985) this requirement was restated in terms of 'manifest disadvantage', i.e. that the transaction must be one sufficiently

---

36 See also *Elton John v James* [1991] FSR 397 at 449–51.

disadvantageous to the person claiming undue influence to require evidence to rebut the presumption of the exercise of undue influence. However, in *Etridge* the view was taken that seeing this requirement in terms of 'manifest disadvantage' had caused difficulties, particularly in the situation of the wife providing a guarantee to support the husband's business borrowing. The line was taken that there should be a return to a requirement more closely reflecting the original statement of Lindley LJ in *Allcard v Skinner* (1887) and hence the references earlier to a transaction 'calling for an explanation' or one which 'is not readily explicable by the relationship of the parties' (*Royal Bank of Scotland v Etridge (No 2)* (2001) at [14] and [21]).

14.51   The situation in which a wife provides a guarantee to the bank of the husband's business borrowing having proved troublesome in this context, it is worth some further consideration. It would seem that finding the requisite trust and confidence between husband and wife may be very easy. Lord Scott took the line in *Etridge* (at [189]) that:

> 'I would assume in every case in which a wife and husband are living together that there is a reciprocal trust and confidence between them. In the fairly common circumstance that the financial and business decisions of the family are primarily taken by the husband, I would assume that the wife would have trust and confidence in his ability to do so and would support his decisions.'

Nevertheless, it would also seem that it will be difficult for the presumption to be generated in the husband and wife guarantee type of case. It was indicated that 'in the ordinary course' such a situation would not trigger the evidential presumption (at [30]). It was recognized that 'in a narrow sense' such a transaction is disadvantageous to the wife: 'she undertakes a serious financial obligation and in return she personally receives nothing' (at [28]) (hence the difficulties with the *National Westminster Bank plc v Morgan* (1985) approach). However, the further point was made that 'Ordinarily, the fortunes of husband and wife are bound up together. If the husband's business is the source of the family income, the wife has a lively interest in doing what she can to support the business. A wife's affection and self-interest run hand-in-hand in inclining her to join with her husband in charging the matrimonial home, usually a jointly-owned asset, to obtain the financial facilities needed by the business' (at [28]). So, the 'ordinary' situations of that type were seen as not generating the presumption. Lord Nicholls said (at [30]):

> 'Wives frequently enter into such transactions. There are good and sufficient reasons why they are willing to do so, despite the risks involved for them and their families. They may be enthusiastic. They may not. They may be less optimistic than their husbands about the prospects of the husbands' businesses. They may be anxious, perhaps exceedingly so. But this is a far cry from saying that such transactions as a class are to be regarded as prima facie evidence of the exercise of undue influence by husbands.'

So, although finding the requisite trust and confidence between husband and wife may be very easy, *Etridge* indicates that it will be difficult for the presumption to be generated in the husband and wife guarantee type of case.

14.52   However, Lord Nicholls also provided some indication of the circumstances in which a husband and wife guarantee case might not be 'ordinary', but would be one in which the court should intervene. He said:

> 'In the eye of the law, undue influence means that influence has been misused. Statements or conduct by a husband which do not pass beyond the bounds of what may be expected of a reasonable husband in the circumstances should not, without more, be castigated as undue influence. Similarly, when a husband is forecasting the future of his business, and expressing his hopes or fears, a degree of hyperbole may be only natural. Courts should not too readily treat such exaggerations as misstatements. Inaccurate explanations of a proposed transaction are a different matter. So are cases where a husband, in whom a wife has reposed trust and confidence for the management of their financial affairs, prefers his interests to hers and makes a choice for both of them on that footing. Such a husband abuses the influence he has. He fails to discharge the obligation of candour and fairness he owes a wife who is looking to him to make the major financial decisions' (*Royal Bank of Scotland* v *Etridge (No 2)* (2001) at [32]).

Rebutting the presumption

14.53   The evidential presumption of the exercise of undue influence may be rebutted by showing that the transaction was entered into 'only after full, free and informed thought about it' (*Zamet* v *Hyman* [1961] 3 All ER 933 at 938). In *Inche Noriah* v *Shaik Allie Bin Omar* [1929] AC 127 (at 135), in the context of a gift, but the point is more generally applicable, it was said:

> 'It is necessary for the donee to prove that the gift was the result of the free exercise of independent will. The most obvious way to prove this is by establishing that the gift was made after the nature of the transaction had been fully explained to the donor by some independent and qualified person so completely as to satisfy the Court that the donor was acting independently of any influence from the donee and with full appreciation of what he was doing....'

However, 'the weight, or importance, to be attached to such advice depends on all the circumstances...[A] person may understand fully the implications of a proposed transaction...and yet still be acting under the influence of another' (*Etridge* at [20] per Lord Nicholls). There may, for example, be occasions when a transaction is so disadvantageous that no one taking due account of proper advice could enter into it. Clearly, then, independent advice will not rebut the presumption.

Undue influence and third parties

14.54   Although our primary interest is in the elements of actual or presumed undue influence, some consideration will now be given to when a third party will be affected by undue influence: actual or presumed. As has been indicated, the context in which undue influence has often been raised in recent years is that of a wife, claiming that she was acting under the undue influence of her husband, when she became a surety for a loan to the husband, or the husband's business, and secured it by a charge on the matrimonial home. Under such circumstances, if the transaction is to be set aside for undue influence, the bank (or other creditor), to which the surety was given, will have to be affected by the undue influence. What is in issue is a question of balance. There is a need to protect wives from undue influence but the family home is an important asset for small businesses to use to raise money. In *Royal Bank of Scotland v Etridge (No 2)* (2001) Lord Nicholls noted at [37] that what was needed was to achieve a balance point between competing interests:

> 'On the one side there is the need to protect a wife against a husband's undue influence. On the other side there is the need for the bank to be able to have reasonable confidence in the strength of its security. Otherwise it would not provide the required money.'

This question of the balance point will be given some brief consideration here. (The discussion will basically take place in terms of the common situation of the husband/wife/bank/guarantee transaction, but the issue is not restricted to the husband and wife relationship, or the situation in which the transaction is a guarantee.)

14.55   After a series of decisions by the lower courts, the House of Lords first considered the question of when third parties are affected by undue influence in *Barclays Bank plc v O'Brien* [1993] 4 All ER 417. The case was concerned with the surety, charged on the matrimonial home, which a wife had given in relation to the overdraft of her husband's business. She claimed that she had executed it whilst acting under the undue influence of her husband and that he had misrepresented the extent and duration of the borrowing covered by it. By the time the case reached the House of Lords, the claim was restricted to misrepresentation, but it is clear that the test of the impact upon the bank is the same whether the wife acted under undue influence or misrepresentation.

14.56   The House of Lords said that there were basically two ways in which a bank's surety could be affected by a husband's undue influence and a charge set aside. That would occur if either (1) the husband had acted as the bank's agent to obtain the execution of the charge, or (2) the bank had actual or constructive notice of the facts giving rise to the wife's claim (at 428). As has been indicated, although stated in relation to husband and wife, this is of more general application. The first possibility, involving a finding of an agency relationship between creditor and debtor, is unlikely to occur. It is 'notice' which is significant and, in particular, 'constructive notice'. In effect, through addressing two issues, 'constructive notice' provides the balance point. The two issues are first, the point at which the creditor is 'put on inquiry' and second, the steps which the House of Lords in *O'Brien* and, subsequently, in *Etridge*, stated:

> '[A] bank should take to ensure that it is not affected by any claim the wife may have that her signature...was procured by the undue influence or other wrong of her husband' (*Royal Bank of Scotland v Etridge (No 2)* (2001) at [37]).

Once factors in the situation put the creditor 'on inquiry' as to the potential for undue influence, the creditor would, absent further action, be fixed with constructive notice of any undue influence found, but it has become clear what steps should be taken by the creditor that will normally prevent that occurring. Those steps will limit the possibility that there has been undue influence, but they 'will not guarantee that...wives will not be subjected to undue influence or misled when standing as sureties' but, as has been indicated, it is a balance between protecting the vulnerable and not stultifying the matrimonial home as potential security for the borrowing of small businesses.

'Put on inquiry'

14.57 In *Barclays Bank plc* v *O'Brien* Lord Browne-Wilkinson, with whom the other members of the court agreed, said ([1993] 4 All ER 417 at 429):

> 'A creditor is put on inquiry when a wife offers to stand surety for her husband's debts by the combination of two factors: (a) the transaction is on its face not to the financial advantage of the wife; and (b) there is a substantial risk in transactions of that kind that, in procuring the wife to act as surety, the husband has committed a legal or equitable wrong that entitles the wife to set aside the transaction.'

This, in effect, indicates a focus on two factors to determine if the bank has been 'put on inquiry': first, the relationship between the parties and, second, the nature of the transaction. In *Royal Bank of Scotland* v *Etridge (No 2)* (2001), the above passage was seen as meaning 'quite simply, that a bank is put on inquiry whenever a wife offers to stand surety for her husband's debts' (per Lord Nicholls at [44]). Outside of the husband and wife situation, the difficulty is that 'the reality of life is that relationships in which undue influence can be exercised are infinitely various' (at [86]) and certainty is needed as to when a creditor will be 'put on inquiry'. It would be too uncertain and too difficult for the creditor to investigate the details of the relationship between a wide range of potential borrowers and sureties. To achieve the necessary certainty, the line was taken that the creditor should be 'put on inquiry' whenever the 'relationship between the debtor and the surety is non-commercial' (at [87]). That was viewed as setting a low but very clear trigger point for the bank to take the necessary steps to limit the possibility of undue influence and protect itself from constructive notice of any that remained. The clarity of the trigger point is very desirable and the taking of the steps then required of the creditor was seen as 'a modest burden' and 'no more than is to be reasonably expected of a creditor who is taking a guarantee from an individual' (at [87]).

14.58 The putting of a creditor on inquiry is not, then, confined to particular relationships between a guarantor and debtor. Of course, neither is it confined to the debtor–guarantor situation. Joint loans to husbands and wives were distinguished from the surety situation as they would not normally put the creditor 'on inquiry'. However, they would do so if the creditor was aware the loan was actually being taken for the husband's purposes alone, rather than their joint purposes (at [48]). This emphasizes the additional important point: it is not the actual relationship between the parties which is in question, nor the actual transaction, but the relationship and transaction as they reasonably appear to the creditor, or of which the creditor has actual knowledge. Constructive notice was not found where what was involved was a mortgage of the family home and the mortgage application stated that it was to buy a holiday home, even though its purpose was, actually, to allow the husband to speculate on the stock exchange (*CIBC Mortgages* v *Pitt* (1993)).

What can the third party do to prevent itself being fixed with constructive notice?

14.59   If a low point is set for the creditor to be put on inquiry, what must the creditor do to prevent it being found to have constructive notice of any undue influence between husband and wife (or other parties)? In *Barclays Bank plc* v *O'Brien*, guidelines were provided. It was indicated that, in the ordinary case, the creditor can avoid being found to have constructive notice of any undue influence ([1993] 4 All ER 417 at 429–30):

> 'if it insists that the wife attend a private meeting (in the absence of the husband) with a representative of the [creditor] at which she is told of the extent of her liability as surety, warned of the risk she is running and urged to take independent legal advice.'

Nothing of the sort had occurred in *O'Brien* and the bank had constructive notice of the husband's wrong. However, in the main, since *O'Brien*, creditors have shown themselves reluctant to take exactly the approach indicated there. Creditors did not want to run the risk of claims based on assurances alleged to have been given to wives (for example, that the creditor would not call in the relevant loan) at any such meetings (*Royal Bank of Scotland* v *Etridge (No 2)* (2001) at [55]). Creditors have instead preferred to ensure that they obtain confirmation from a solicitor that the solicitor has advised the wife appropriately. The acceptability of such a practice as a means of preventing the creditor from being affected by undue influence between husband and wife was recognized in *Etridge*. The line was taken that:

> 'Ordinarily it will be reasonable that a bank should be able to rely upon confirmation from a solicitor, acting for the wife, that he has advised the wife appropriately' (at [56]).

As was emphasized in *Etridge,* it will not be sufficient merely for the creditor to know, or have confirmation, that a solicitor is acting for the wife:

> 'Knowledge by a bank that a solicitor is acting for a surety wife does not, without more, justify the bank in assuming that the solicitor's instructions extend to advising her about the nature and effect of the transaction' (*Etridge* at [168]).

A solicitor's role may be no more than executing an agreed transaction. What is required by the creditor is confirmation that she has received 'appropriate advice'.

14.60 Of course, as has been indicated, the approach taken by the House of Lords in *Etridge* does not generally seek to make the creditor ensure that there is no undue influence operating. In general, what was seen as required were steps to ensure that her decision was an informed one:

> 'The furthest a bank can be expected to go is to take reasonable steps to satisfy itself that the wife has had brought home to her, in a meaningful way, the practical implications of the proposed transaction. This does not wholly eliminate the risk of undue influence or misrepresentation. But it does mean that a wife enters into a transaction with her eyes open so far as the basic elements of the transaction are concerned' (per Lord Nicholls at [54]; but see Lord Hobhouse at [111]).

In other words, the procedures indicated by the House of Lords should ensure that the wife is informed but they will not necessarily mean that she is liberated from any undue influence. Nevertheless, the court recognized that there is a point at which the solicitor should decline to act and refuse to supply confirmation of advice to the bank. That will occur in 'exceptional circumstances where it is glaringly obvious that the wife is being grievously wronged' (at [62]).

Aggressive trade practices

Introduction

14.61 The Consumer Protection from Unfair Trading Regulations 2008 provided public enforcement mechanisms to deal with misleading and aggressive trade practices, and more broadly with unfair commercial practices. The Law Commissions have recommended that redress now be provided for the individual consumer in relation to misleading and aggressive practices, and there are now draft Regulations being considered, which would bring that about: the draft Consumer Protection from Unfair Trading (Amendment) Regulations. Obviously here we are concerned with aggressive practices. (Misleading practices were considered in **Chapter 13**, on misrepresentation). The aim is to provide a straightforward legal structure to afford consumers a remedy in situations where there is none, or where it is inadequate, or too complex, or uncertain.

14.62 The Law Commissions provided examples of the sort of situations which consumers had encountered:[37]

> **'Example: pressure doorstep-selling**
> An elderly housebound man was sold a £3,000 bed. The salesman stayed for three hours, giving the impression that he would only leave if the consumer agreed to buy.

---

37 *Consumer Redress for Misleading and Aggressive Practices* Law Com No 332, Scot Law Com No 226 (2012) para. 1.15.

The trader offered a 14 day cancellation period, but the next day the salesman returned, unpacked the bed and took a cheque for the full amount.

Example: pressure-selling a car

A consumer was subjected to four hours of pressure-selling and felt unable to leave the dealer's showroom. The salesperson added that if the consumer did not buy the car, the salesperson would be sacked. The consumer was worn down and agreed to buy the car.

Example: pressure-selling a holiday club

A couple agreed to attend a two hour presentation about a holiday club. In fact the presentation lasted six hours and, feeling under considerable pressure, the couple eventually agreed to become club members. The next day they returned to try to cancel the contract. The company threatened to call the police if they did not leave.'

Basic scope

14.63   The idea is that where a consumer has been subject to an aggressive commercial practice by a trader, and made a contract for a product, the consumer should have a remedy. The definition of consumer would reflect that now commonly used in relation to European derived legislation, so that a consumer would mean 'an individual acting for purposes that are wholly or mainly outside that individual's business'.[38] A 'trader' would be a 'person acting (personally or through an agent) for purposes relating to that person's business'. The contract must be for a product but that will be very broadly defined, including goods, services, digital content, rights or obligations, but not dealing with land, other than a residential lease, and not financial services.[39] The consumer would need to show that the trader carried out an aggressive commercial practice, which was likely to cause the average consumer to make a decision to enter into a contract for a product which they would not otherwise have taken, and which was a 'significant factor' in the particular consumer's own decision to contract. A practice is aggressive 'if, in its factual context, taking account of all its features and circumstances, it significantly impairs or is likely to significantly impair the average consumer's freedom of choice or conduct in relation to the product concerned through the use of harassment, coercion or abuse of position.'[40] Coercion 'includes the use of physical force'.[41] 'Abuse of position' will mean 'exploiting a position of power in relation to a consumer so as to apply pressure, even without using or threatening to use physical force, in a way which significantly limits the consumer's ability to make informed decisions'.[42] There is a list of factors to be taken into account in deciding if a

---

38 Draft Consumer Protection from Unfair Trading (Amendment) Regulations, amending reg 2(1) of the Consumer Protection from Unfair Trading Regulations 2008.

39 Draft Consumer Protection from Unfair Trading (Amendment) Regulations, amending the Consumer Protection from Unfair Trading Regulations 2008.

40 Reg 7(1) of the Consumer Protection from Unfair Trading Regulations 2008, as it will be if amended by the draft Consumer Protection from Unfair Trading (Amendment) Regulations: 'abuse of position' being substituted for a reference to undue influence, which is confusing terminology as it does not coincide with the common law usage.

41 Reg 7(3) of the Consumer Protection from Unfair Trading Regulations 2008.

42 Reg 7(3) of the Consumer Protection from Unfair Trading Regulations 2008 contains this definition of undue influence, which would become the definition of 'abuse of position' under the draft Amendment Regulations.

commercial practice is aggressive, including its 'timing, location, nature or persistence', the 'use of threatening or abusive language or behaviour', the 'exploitation by the trader of any specific misfortune or circumstance of such gravity as to impair the consumer's judgment, of which the trader is aware, to influence the consumer's decision', and 'any threat to take any action which cannot legally be taken'.[43]

14.64 The aggressive trade practice must have impacted significantly upon the consumer's own decision to contract, but also be such as to be likely to have done so in relation to the average consumer. Thus it is not merely a matter of subjective decision making, but a standard of expected resistance to aggressive commercial practices is generally set. The 'average consumer' is generally 'reasonably well informed, reasonably observant and circumspect'. Obviously, if it was left there, questions would arise as to the efficacy of the protection which would be afforded to the elderly, or other consumers who are more vulnerable than the 'average consumer'. However, the idea is that it should be the average member of a particular group of consumers who is referred to where

(1) the commercial practice is directed to a particular group of consumers; or
(2) a clearly identifiable group of consumers is particularly vulnerable to the practice because of their mental or physical infirmity, age or credulity in a way which the trader could reasonably be expected to foresee.

Remedies

14.65 The primary remedy is to be the right to 'unwind' the contract. This is obviously akin to rescission, and the idea is to restore the consumer to the position before the aggressive practice took place, but it is to be less complex. So, for example, where the consumer has made a purchase from the trader or contracted for services, then, provided the consumer is able to reject some element of the goods or services, within three months (ninety days), it will simply be a matter of the consumer getting a refund of the whole price. The bars to rescission, as such, do not arise. The consumer is not prevented from being able to unwind because he or she cannot make restitutio in integrum. If the consumer waits more than three months, or the goods or services have been fully consumed, the consumer will be able to claim a discount on the price. Bands of discount are set (25 per cent, 50 per cent, 75 per cent or 100 per cent in the draft Regulations, with a 0 per cent band also being included in the Law Commissions' proposal) and which one is applicable will depend upon the impact of the practice, the trader's behaviour, and any delay by the consumer. There will be scope for claims for damages for other losses, calculated on a reliance basis, but the consumer will have to establish those losses, and the trader will have a due diligence defence. Obviously, this is intended to be quite a 'rough and ready' system, but a fuller and simpler one, in comparison with common law rules. Common

---

43 Reg 7(2) of the Consumer Protection from Unfair Trading Regulations 2008.

law rights, and remedies, remain in place, but the legislation should provide more effective, and extensive means of dealing with the high pressure selling techniques which are commonly the problems which consumers encounter, rather than something which the common law would label as duress or undue influence.

◎ Summary

Duress

- English law was slow to recognize duress beyond duress to the person, but it is now clear that economic duress can render a contract voidable.
- This recognition enabled the court in *Williams* v *Roffey Bros* (1990) to make it plain that the real issue when a contract is varied (so that more is paid for the same performance) is not whether there is technical consideration but whether there is duress.
- In finding a test for economic duress the language of the courts has not always been helpful. References to the 'overborne will' and voluntariness do not provide a real test— plainly the person under duress does exercise his or her will and makes a choice.
- There is, basically, a two-stage test:
  1. the illegitimacy of the threat;
  2. the lack of a reasonable alternative to agreeing, for the person threatened.
- Illegitimate threats include threatened criminal and civil wrongs, but it is questioned whether a threatened breach is always sufficient.
- It has been envisaged that a threat may be illegitimate without the law otherwise regarding it as wrongful. In that situation, the question of the bona fides of the person making the threat may be relevant.
- Only the first stage of the test is needed if what is threatened is a criminal wrong.
- In addition, the duress must be a sufficient cause of the new contract.
- As with misrepresentation, rescission for duress may be barred.

Undue influence

- Both actual and presumed undue influence will render a contract voidable.
- The influence in question is such that one party has abdicated their relevant decision making to the other. Actual undue influence is where it is established that undue influence brought about the transaction in question.
- Presumed undue influence arises in two ways:
  - First, the relationship falls within one of the categories of relationship which gives rise to the legal presumption of the existence of relevant influence (for example, parent and child, guardian and ward, trustee and beneficiary, solicitor and client, medical adviser and patient). The exercise of undue influence will then be presumed evidentially if the

transaction is one 'calling for an explanation'. The latter presumption can be rebutted. The former cannot.

— Second, the existence of relevant influence is established between the parties. The exercise of undue influence will be presumed, evidentially, if the transaction is one 'calling for an explanation'. This presumption can be rebutted.

• The evidential presumption of the exercise of undue influence can be rebutted by showing that it was only entered into after 'full free and informed thought about it' by the relevant party. This may be achieved by showing independent advice was received.

• Third parties to the influence may be affected by it.

— If A enters into a transaction with B because of (actual or presumed) undue influence by C, the transaction may be voidable.

— It will be voidable if either C was acting as B's agent to procure the transaction or B has actual or constructive notice of the facts giving rise to the undue influence claim.

Aggressive practices

— The draft Consumer Protection from Unfair Trading (Amendment) Regulations aim to provide consumers with remedies (unwinding the contract, refund, damages) in relation to aggressive commercial practices.

▶ Further reading

P. S. Atiyah, 'Economic Duress and the Overborne Will' (1982) 98 LQR 197

J. Beatson, 'Duress as a Vitiating Factor in Contract' (1974) 33 CLJ 97

J. Beatson, 'Duress, Restitution and Contract Modification' in J. Beatson, *The Use and Abuse of Unjust Enrichment*, Oxford University Press, 1990, pp. 95–114

R. Bigwood, 'Undue Influence: "Impaired consent" or "Wicked exploitation"' (1996) 16 OJLS 503

P. Birks, 'The Travails of Duress' [1990] LMCLQ 342

P. Birks, 'Undue Influence as Wrongful Exploitation' (2004) 120 LQR 34

P. Birks and Chin Nyuk Yin, 'On the Nature of Undue Influence' in J. Beatson and D. Friedmann (eds), *Good Faith and Fault in Contract Law*, Oxford University Press, 1995, pp. 57–98

A. Burrows, *The Law of Restitution*, 3rd edn, Oxford University Press, 2011, Chapter 10 (Duress), Chapter 11 (Undue influence)

D. Capper, 'Unconscionable Bargain in the Common Law World' (2010) 126 LQR 403

M Chen-Wishart, 'Undue Influence: Beyond Impaired Consent and wrongdoing to a relational analysis' in A. Burrows and Lord Rodger (eds), *Mapping the Law: Essays in Memory of Peter Birks*, Oxford University Press, 2006, pp. 201–22

Law Commission and the Scottish Law Commission, *Consumer Redress for Misleading and Aggressive Practices* Law Com No 332, Scot Law Com No 226 (2012)

E. McKendrick, 'The Further Travails of Duress' in A. Burrows and Lord Rodger (eds), *Mapping the Law: Essays in Memory of Peter Birks*, Oxford University Press, 2006, pp. 181–200

D. O'Sullivan, 'Developing O'Brien' (2002) 118 LQR 337

S. Smith, 'Contracting Under Pressure: A Theory of Duress' (1997) 56 CLJ 343

Chapter 15

Illegality

⬤ Introduction

15.1 An agreement may possess all the requisite elements of a valid contract, such as offer and acceptance and consideration, but it may nevertheless contravene a legal rule or be regarded as contrary to public policy. Such a contract can be regarded as 'improper', or 'illegal' in a very general sense, or at least tainted with illegality. Since there are many and disparate reasons for statutory and judicial intervention on the basis of illegality or impropriety, it is not always easy to categorize these reasons.

15.2 It is conventional to subdivide illegal contracts on the basis of the legal consequences of those contracts. Accordingly, contracts are described as being either 'void' or 'illegal'. The problem with such a classification is that there is no general agreement as to which category each type of improper contract falls into. Such a division also fails to reflect the fact that the nature of the illegality which may taint a contract can vary considerably in its seriousness.[1] It is also possible to classify the different types of illegality according to either the nature of the objectionable conduct, or the source of the rule which invalidates it. None of the attempts at classification is wholly convincing.

15.3 It must be emphasized that the traditional approach to the subject is of only limited value as an analytical device. However, for the purpose of clear exposition, it is proposed to adhere to the now favoured distinction between void and illegal contracts. But first, a warning: the following sections are not intended as an exhaustive list of all the different types of illegality. Furthermore, the detailed discussion is focused on those areas of greater commercial and practical significance, particularly in relation to restraint of trade.

---

1 See G. H. Treitel, *Law of Contract*, 11th edn, Sweet & Maxwell, 2003, p. 430.

Void contracts

15.4   A variety of contracts are rendered void as a result of some statutory provision. For example, a wagering contract was formerly rendered void by the Gaming Act 1845, s 18, which stated:

> 'All contracts or agreements, whether by parole or in writing, by way of gaming or wagering, shall be null and void; and no suit shall be brought or maintained in any court of law or equity for recovering any sum of money or valuable thing alleged to be won upon any wager, or which shall have been deposited in the hands of any person to abide the event on which any wager shall have been made . . . .'

It should be emphasized that this provision did not declare such a contract to be illegal, but simply void, i.e. no rights were conferred on either party.[2] However, this provision was repealed by the Gambling Act 2005 (s 334), as part of a major legislative reform of the law on gambling. Section 335(1) of the new Act now states that: 'the fact that a contract relates to gambling shall not prevent its enforcement'. (Of course, this does not preclude such an agreement being held unlawful on some other ground; see s 335(2).)

Contracts in restraint of trade

15.5   A contract in restraint of trade is one by which a person promises another that his or her future freedom to trade, or to conduct his or her profession, with whomsoever he or she wishes, will be curtailed in some way. The restriction may be geographical, for instance covering a particular town or area, and usually it will also cover a specific period of time. The basic rule is that such restraints are prima facie void, but they may become valid if they can be justified as being reasonable between the parties and not inimical to the public interest.

15.6   The doctrine of restraint of trade is largely associated with two particular classes of agreement. (The ambit of the doctrine and its application to other types of agreement are considered later.) These are (1) an agreement by a person selling the 'goodwill' of a business that he or she will not start another business in direct competition with the buyer; and (2) an agreement between employer and employee by which the latter promises that he or she will not, on leaving his or her present employment, work for a rival of his or her employer, or start a business in competition with his or her employer. There are two major reasons for the legal regulation of such contracts. First, it is thought to be in the public interest that competition should not be unnecessarily restricted. Second, without such a doctrine, one party could exploit the weaker bargaining position of the other in an unfair manner.[3] (For an interesting example,

---

2   Although the winner could not sue the loser, the loser could not recover his money if he had paid up.

3   The relevance of the respective bargaining strengths of the parties was illustrated in *Dawnay Day & Co. Ltd* v *Frederick de Braconier d'Alphen* (1998).

see *Schroeder Music Publishing Co.* v *Macaulay* (1974) and more recently, the case of *Proactive Sports Management Ltd* v *Rooney* (2011).)

15.7   Although restraint of trade agreements appear to be anti-competitive, it should be pointed out that they can serve more desirable purposes. For example, where the goodwill of a business is being sold, the purchaser will wish to protect his or her legitimate interest in receiving value for the price that he or she has paid. If the seller were permitted to set up a rival business immediately in direct competition with the purchaser, then potential purchasers would in future be deterred from buying businesses. In turn, this would affect a future vendor as he or she would not receive full value for the business that he or she has built up. Also, in the case of employers, they should be able to protect themselves, in a reasonable way, from employees going to work for rival firms and taking with them secret or confidential information, or the customers or clientele of their former employer. These are illustrations of how restraint of trade agreements may indeed be reasonable and commercially necessary. On the other hand, it must be ensured that the restraint imposed by such an agreement is not wider in scope than it need be to achieve its intended purpose.

15.8   A useful starting point for our discussion of agreements in restraint of trade is the case of *Nordenfelt* v *Maxim Nordenfelt Guns and Ammunition Co. Ltd* [1894] AC 535. The facts were as follows:

> N was a manufacturer and inventor of guns and ammunition. Although his customers were fairly few, his trade was worldwide. He sold his business to a company for £287,500 and he entered into an agreement restricting his future commercial activities. When the company was amalgamated with another, two years later, N's agreement to the restraint of his activities was repeated in a contract of service he entered into with the amalgamated (respondent) company. (It was accepted by the court that the covenant N entered into with the respondents could be regarded as a covenant made on the occasion of selling a business and could therefore be assessed according to the principles relating to such a case.) The restriction was that N should not, for a period of twenty-five years, 'engage except on behalf of the company either directly or indirectly in the trade or business of a manufacturer of guns...or ammunition...(or in any business competing or liable to compete in any way with that for the time being carried on by the company)'.

The latter part of the covenant, contained within the brackets, was clearly too wide in its scope, as it extended to all competing businesses. But this clause was severable from the rest of the agreement. The question for the House of Lords to decide was whether the rest of the covenant was too wide or whether it was a reasonable restriction on N's future activities. Although the restraint was not restricted to any particular geographical area, their Lordships dismissed N's appeal and held that the covenant was necessary for the protection of the respondents' commercial interests. As the company's trade was worldwide, a commensurate restraint was reasonable. The restraint was upheld as valid. In a famous statement, Lord Macnaghten explained (at 565) the basic approach to such cases in the following authoritative way:

> 'The public have an interest in every person's carrying on his trade freely: so has the individual. All interference with individual liberty of action in trading, and all restraints of trade of themselves, if there is nothing more, are contrary to public policy, and therefore void. That is the general rule. But there are exceptions: restraints of trade and interference with individual liberty of action may be justified by the special circumstances of a particular case. It is a sufficient justification, and indeed it is the only justification, if the restriction is reasonable—reasonable, that is, in reference to the interests of the parties concerned and reasonable in reference to the interests of the public, so framed and so guarded as to afford adequate protection to the party in whose favour it is imposed, while at the same time it is in no way injurious to the public.'[4]

It should be appreciated that the facts of *Nordenfelt* were unusual. Most restraints need to be narrower in both duration and geographical area in order to be valid. But the judgments in the case still provide a useful foundation for our study of contracts in restraint of trade (as acknowledged in *Man Financial (S) Pte Ltd* v *Wong Bark Chuan David* (2007) at [69]–[73]). The judicial approach involves a balancing of interests between an individual's freedom to carry on his or her chosen trade or profession without restraint, and the protection of certain legitimate commercial interests of those buying the goodwill of a business, or of employers. It is not in the public interest for restraint of trade agreements to operate simply to reduce competition, and for this reason there is a presumption that such agreements are void. But if the purchaser of a business or an employer can show that he or she is trying to protect a genuine proprietary interest, and that the clause in question is both reasonable and not contrary to the public interest, then it may be adjudged as valid. The courts are better placed to judge the reasonableness of an agreement as between the two parties than they are the question of the public interest.

Sale of a business

15.9   *Nordenfelt* v *Maxim Nordenfelt Guns and Ammunition Co. Ltd* (1894) is a good illustration of a valid restraint contained in a contract for the sale of a business. The purchaser gave value for the goodwill by paying a fair amount for the vendor's business. It was reasonable, as between the contracting parties, that the purchaser's proprietary interest was to be protected by restricting the vendor's freedom to trade in the same goods in the future. The courts are more willing to uphold restraints in contracts for the sale of a business than they are in contracts between employer and employee. In contracts of service there is more likely to be an inequality of bargaining strength between the parties; restrictions on an employee's future activities may well be unconscionable. In addition, it may be difficult for an employer to claim that he is protecting a genuine proprietary interest rather than merely guarding against future competition (but see *Leeds Rugby Ltd* v *Harris* (2005)).

---

4   The agreement was not contrary to the public interest, as it strengthened the position of an English company in its manufacturing of guns to be sold worldwide!

15.10 For a restraint to be valid, in an agreement to sell a business, the first requirement is that there is a genuine sale of a business from one party to the other (see *Vancouver Malt and Sake Brewing Co. Ltd* v *Vancouver Breweries Co. Ltd* (1934)). Without this there will be no transfer of an intangible asset, namely the goodwill, from the vendor to the purchaser. Second, the clause must not be too wide in its scope. The restraint will not be valid if it purports to confer protection on the purchaser that goes beyond the actual business sold by the vendor. For example, in *British Reinforced Concrete Engineering Co. Ltd* v *Schelff* (1921), the facts were:

> The claimant company manufactured and sold 'BRC' road reinforcements throughout the country. The defendant had a smaller, more local business, selling 'Loop' road reinforcements, but he was not involved in manufacturing these products. The claimant company bought the defendant's business, and the defendant covenanted that he would not enter into competition with them (either in business or in the employment of a rival) in the manufacture or sale of road reinforcements. The defendant was later employed by a road reinforcement company and was sued by the claimant company for breach of his agreement with them.

The court held that the restraint of trade clause in the sale of the business was too wide, and was void. The clause sought to restrain the defendant in general terms from competing with the claimant company. The claimants were entitled to the protection of their proprietary interest in the defendant's business, which they had just bought, but they were not entitled to protection in respect of their wider business interests. The defendant's business was concerned with the sale, not the manufacture, of a particular type of road reinforcement. It was not reasonable to restrict the defendant's future activities in such an extensive way.

15.11 Restraints may be unreasonable because they purport to cover too long a period or too wide an area. It must be emphasized that *Nordenfelt* v *Maxim Nordenfelt Guns and Ammunition Co. Ltd* (1894) was unusual—the clientele of the business sold was small in number, but spread throughout the world. An unusually extensive restraint, in both time and area, was adjudged to be reasonable in the circumstances. What amounts to a reasonable period of time for a restraint to operate will, naturally, depend on the nature of the business being sold. A purchaser of a business who pays for the goodwill is entitled to contract for the benefit of protection against competition for a limited period. This period can be long enough to allow for the goodwill or 'know-how', which has been bought, to be fully transferred to the purchaser. But it should not be excessive in either time or area.[5]

15.12 *Nordenfelt* v *Maxim Nordenfelt Guns and Ammunition Co. Ltd* (1894) illustrates the fact that if part of the restraint clause is too wide, but the remainder of it is reasonable, the court may sever the offending part from the rest of the clause, which may then be upheld. The extent of the court's power, and its willingness, to do this is considered later. But a further example of this approach can be found in *Goldsoll* v *Goldman* (1915):

> The claimant (C) and the defendant (D) each carried on a similar business as a dealer in imitation jewellery in London. In order to avoid competition, D sold his business to C and

---

5   See also Article 81 (ex Article 85) of the Treaty establishing the EEC (1957).

agreed that he would not, for a period of two years, 'either solely or jointly with or as agent or employee for any other person or persons or company directly or indirectly carry on or be engaged concerned or interested in or render services…to the business of a vendor of or dealer in real or imitation jewellery in…London, or any part of the UK, Ireland, the Isle of Man, France, United States, Russia, or Spain…'. C sought an injunction when D committed breaches of the agreement.

The Court of Appeal held that the agreement was too wide in area, but that the unreasonable parts of the restraint were capable of being severed from the rest of it. Accordingly, D's promise not to carry on business in the UK and the Isle of Man was a reasonable restraint, and therefore enforceable against him. The commercial activities covered by the covenant (namely, 'real or imitation jewellery') were also too wide, but it was reasonable to restrain the defendant from dealing in imitation jewellery. Thus, the court undertook a certain amount of rewriting of the agreement for the parties in order to reduce the excessive restraint to one of reasonable scope. It should be added that the court may be less willing to apply the idea of severance in cases between employer and employee (see *Attwood* v *Lamont* (1920), discussed at para. **15.22**) as there is less likely to be parity in terms of the bargaining strength of the parties. In the sale of a business, the court will wish to ensure that the purchaser does receive value for the price paid for the goodwill.

Restraints in a contract of employment

15.13   A restraint of trade in a contract of employment is prima facie void. It will be valid only if it protects a genuine proprietary interest of the employer, such as trade secrets or freedom from solicitation of his or her customers, and so long as it is a reasonable restraint, and not against the public interest. (For further discussion, see *Leeds Rugby Ltd* v *Harris* (2005) at [50]–[56].) The clause will not be valid if it merely attempts to protect the employer from competition. Obviously, an employee may gain experience and expertise in the course of his or her employment which may equip him or her to be a future competitor of his or her employer. The employer cannot prevent this. It is in the public interest that employees acquire skills and are able to use them and pass them on to others. However, an employee would have an unfair advantage in his or her future activities if he or she were able to utilize confidential or secret information obtained from his or her employer. He or she may also be able to gain a personal knowledge of, and influence over, his or her employer's customers. In these situations, it is appropriate that an employer is able to restrain his or her employee's future activities in order to protect his or her proprietary interests. (For a useful discussion, see Lord Parker's judgment in *Herbert Morris Ltd* v *Saxelby* [1916] 1 AC 688 at 709; and also Lord Atkinson's speech in the same case at 704. See also *Norbrook Laboratories (GB) Ltd* v *Adair* (2008).)

Trade secrets and confidential information[6]
15.14   It is not always easy to distinguish between those situations where an employee has access to highly confidential information and those where he or she has simply developed an

---

6   For a discussion of the relevance of the distinction between these terms, see *Faccenda Chicken Ltd* v *Fowler* (1987). Here it was explained that an employee, after his employment has terminated, may use confidential information

expertise or skill during the course of his or her employment. (For a recent discussion, see *FSS Travel & Leisure Systems Ltd* v *Johnson* (1998).) The employer is entitled to protect him or herself in the former situation, but not the latter (see Lord Atkinson's judgment in *Herbert Morris Ltd* v *Saxelby* [1916] 1 AC 688 at 704–5). So the first question to be decided is 'what constitutes trade secrets?' This was the issue in *Forster & Sons Ltd* v *Suggett* (1918), where the facts were:

> The claimant company (C) and the defendant (D) entered into an agreement under which D was to be employed as works engineer at C's works and was not to divulge any trade secret during his employment or afterwards. The company made glass bottles and glass-making machinery. There was also a covenant in D's contract which prevented him, at the end of his employment with C, from going to work in the UK for a rival glass-making firm or being involved in glass bottle manufacture, for a period of five years. In the course of his employment with the claimant company, D had been instructed in certain confidential methods which were of economic value. D wished to be released from his promise and the company sought an injunction to enforce the agreed restraint.

Sargant J granted an injunction to the company to restrain D from divulging any trade secrets or manufacturing processes to potential rivals of the claimant company. He did not think that the restraint was unreasonable in the circumstances of the case. The time restraint of five years was upheld. The fact that the restraint covered the whole of the UK was also reasonable. But it must be emphasized that much depends on the particular circumstances of the case in deciding whether a restraint is reasonable. In other cases, a five-year restraint covering the whole country may well be unreasonable.

15.15   In some cases the courts have experienced greater difficulty in deciding whether an employee is in a position to pass on trade secrets to one of his employer's rivals. In *Herbert Morris Ltd* v *Saxelby* (1916), the claimants were the leading manufacturers of hoisting machinery in the UK and the defendant was employed by them as a draughtsman under a contract which restrained him, on leaving the company, from working in the same field for a period of seven years. The House of Lords held that the covenant was void as a result of being too wide; seven years was too long a period. But some doubts were also expressed as to whether the defendant was in a position to pass on trade secrets. The same issue was discussed (and *Saxelby* was distinguished) in *Commercial Plastics Ltd* v *Vincent* [1965] 1 QB 623. The facts were:

> The claimant company (CP) were manufacturers of thin PVC calendered plastic sheeting, a rapidly developing section of the plastics industry, in which new discoveries were being frequently made. CP had five principal UK competitors, with whom they shared most of the market, but CP's pre-eminence was in the field of manufacturing thin PVC calendered sheeting for adhesive tape. This was a particularly difficult process and CP had spent considerable

---

unless this is expressly forbidden. However, he is not entitled to use or disclose 'trade secrets', either during or after his employment, regardless of whether there is an express stipulation to this effect. (Presumably, a trade secret is something of a highly confidential nature.) The ambit of any implied term, imposing restrictions on an employee after the employment comes to an end, was considered in *Peter Brooks* v *Olyslager OMS (UK) Ltd* (1998).

amounts of money, time and effort on research into this process. As a result, they had a very large share of this particular market. CP employed Vincent (V), a plastics technologist, to coordinate research and development in the production of thin PVC calendered sheeting for adhesive tape. His work gave V access to the company's mixing specifications recorded in code, but it was not possible for him to remember these details without the help of documents. It was a condition of V's employment that he would not seek employment with any of CP's rivals in the PVC calendered sheeting field for one year after leaving CP's employment. V wanted to disregard this condition and CP sought an injunction.

CP's action failed because the clause in restraint of trade was too wide. The clause was worldwide, whereas CP did not require protection outside the UK. Moreover, it extended to their competitors in the whole PVC calendering field, when CP required protection from V only in relation to competitors in the plastics/adhesive tape industry. Accordingly, the Court of Appeal thought that the clause was unreasonable and therefore void. The court expressed some regret at this finding, as it thought that a suitably drafted restraint would have been enforceable against V. However, it was decided that severance of the offending parts of the clause was not possible in this case, as the restraint was contained in just one provision which was too wide.

15.16   It is relevant to note that, in spite of the decision in *Commercial Plastics v Vincent* (1965), the court was of the opinion that the claimant company did have confidential information which it was entitled, by a suitably worded covenant, to restrain the defendant from divulging (per Pearson LJ, delivering the judgment of the court, at 642). Given the circumstances of the case this must surely be correct: there was identifiable objective knowledge which could be regarded as the employer's 'trade secrets'. The outcome of the case was, therefore, unfortunate. But similar issues were raised by the later case of *Littlewoods Organisation Ltd v Harris* [1978] 1 All ER 1026. The facts were as follows:

Littlewoods ran a retail chain store business and a mail order business in the UK. Their main competitor in the mail order field was Great Universal Stores Ltd (GUS) which had a large number of subsidiaries carrying on various businesses throughout the world. Littlewoods and GUS, between them, enjoyed two-thirds of the mail order trade in the UK. Littlewoods' mail order business centred on a twice-yearly catalogue. These catalogues required considerable advance planning and business skill, especially in relation to the price, quantity, and type of goods which were to be sold. Paul Harris was employed by Littlewoods and, having been rapidly promoted due to his considerable ability, he became executive director of their mail order business. As a result, he was responsible for planning and compiling Littlewoods' catalogues. A clause in his contract restrained Harris's future activities by providing that, in the event of the determination of his contract, he should not at any time within twelve months enter into a contract of service with GUS Ltd or any of its subsidiary companies, or be involved in the trading or business of GUS or its subsidiaries. Harris resigned from his job with Littlewoods, informing them that he had accepted an offer of employment from GUS. Littlewoods sought an assurance from him that he did not intend to infringe the restraint clause by going to work for GUS within twelve months of leaving their employment. Harris refused to give this, and Littlewoods sought an injunction.

There was no doubt that Harris knew a great deal about Littlewoods' mail order sales trends, the percentage and identity of the returns, sources of manufacture, findings of market research, and the company's plans for the foreseeable future. But did this amount to confidential information which they were entitled to protect by a covenant in restraint of trade? The Court of Appeal held that the claimants were entitled to the protection of a reasonable covenant restraining Harris from going to work for a rival in the mail order business within a limited period of leaving their employment. (See also *Rock Refrigeration Ltd v Jones* (1997), and *Thomas v Farr Plc* (2007).)

In *Littlewoods*, Lord Denning considered at some length the question of an employer's protection of confidential information. He explained the difficulty of drawing a line between information which is confidential and that which is not. Where information is of a type that an employee can carry it away in his head, it is particularly hard to prove a breach of a covenant which restrains an employee from divulging confidential information. In practice, the only effective restraint is to stipulate that an employee must not work for a rival firm for a limited (and reasonable) period of time. His Lordship concluded (at 1034):

> 'It seems to me...[that] this really was a case where Littlewoods had a great deal of confidential information which Paul Harris had acquired in the course of his service with them and which they were entitled to protect by a reasonable covenant against his going away and taking it to their rivals in trade...[namely, GUS].'

There was the further question in *Littlewoods* of whether the restraint on Harris was too wide. (See *Commercial Plastics v Vincent* (1965) (para. **15.15**), where the facts were very similar.) The covenant prevented Harris from being concerned in businesses of GUS and its subsidiaries. Yet these businesses were extremely varied and worldwide; whereas the interests of Littlewoods were restricted to the UK and to only two commercial areas. Was the fact that the clause was too widely drawn fatal to its enforceability against Harris? Lord Denning was critical of the outcome of *Commercial Plastics* and he explained the need to construe the restraint clause in relation to its intended purpose. Such a clause should not be rendered ineffective simply because of unskilful drafting and the inclusion of words that were too wide in scope. He argued (at 1035) that a court is able to limit a wide restraint so as to ensure that the clause is reasonable and enforceable. In the present case, he stated that the clause should be restricted to the UK and to the mail order business, but that an injunction would be granted to Littlewoods. Thus the restraint was enforceable. But in the later case of *Wincanton Ltd v Cranny* (2000), distinguishing *Littlewoods*, it was held that where a non-competition clause in a contract of employment has been made wide intentionally in an attempt to cover all possible situations, it will be found to be unenforceable. Here, the employer had not attempted to 'focus on the particular restraint necessary in respect of a particular employee'.

15.17   So far, we have considered cases where the employer has stipulated some restraint on an employee in a contract of service. A slightly different situation occurred in *Kores Manufacturing Co. Ltd v Kolok Manufacturing Co. Ltd* [1959] Ch 108, where two companies agreed that neither would, without the other's consent, employ a person who had worked for the other company during the previous five years. Both companies were involved in the manufacture of similar products involving chemical processes. An action was brought by one of the companies against the other to enforce the agreement by restraining the defendants from employing a former employee of the claimants. The Court of Appeal held that the agreement did not satisfy the essential requirement for a restraint of trade to be enforceable, as it was unreasonable in the circumstances. If either company had tried to enforce a similar restraint contained in a covenant given by an employee they would not have succeeded. This was because the companies were merely trying to prevent competition and were not protecting a genuine proprietary interest. Furthermore, the agreement between the companies failed to distinguish between employees who were in possession of trade secrets and those who were not (and were not even likely to be): 'The five year ban was equally applicable to an unskilled manual labourer who had been for a single day in the employment of the claimants, and to a chief chemist with many years' service' (per Jenkins LJ at 124). It did not make any difference that the parties dealt on equal terms in reaching their restraint of trade agreement. It was still open to the court to hold that the restraint was both unreasonable and too wide. It also appears to be contrary to the public interest for the labour force to be restricted in such away.

Clauses restraining solicitation of customers

15.18　An employer is entitled to protect his or her trade connections, otherwise it would be possible for a former employee to entice away his or her customers. A distinction must be made, however, between an employee who has acquired some influence over his or her employer's customers, and one who merely has knowledge of such customers. Obviously much will depend on the type of business in question and the type of work carried out by the employee. But if the employee has enjoyed a position in which customers have relied on his or her individual skill or judgement, and are likely to take their trade to him or her if he or she starts his or her own business, or goes to work elsewhere, then the employer is entitled to reasonable protection from this potential loss of trading connection.

15.19　In *Fitch* v *Dewes* (1921), a restraint was held by the House of Lords to be enforceable against a solicitor's managing clerk. Whilst working in Tamworth, he had agreed with his employer that he would not practise within seven miles of Tamworth town hall, after leaving his employment. This covenant was enforceable, despite the fact that the restriction was of unlimited duration. It was adjudged reasonable, given the nature of the profession concerned. The defendant would have acquired an influence over his employer's clientele and a limited time restraint would not have afforded the required protection to the employer. However, in other circumstances, a restraint may well be void for covering too wide an area or too long a period. In many trades, an employee's influence over his ex-employer's clients or customers will diminish as time passes. (See also *M & S Drapers* v *Reynolds* (1957).)

15.20　Restraints against damaging an employer's trading connection are not limited to particular professions or to senior personnel (although greater protection may be reasonable against senior employees). For example, in *Marion White Ltd* v *Francis* (1972), the defendant,

Ann Francis, worked as a hairdresser in the claimant's salon. She covenanted not to work as a hairdresser, for twelve months after leaving C's salon, within a half-mile radius of C's premises. On her dismissal, Ann Francis went to work at a salon merely 150 yards from C's premises. It was held that the covenant was not too wide in those particular circumstances and was enforceable. (In fact, a declaration was granted to C. An injunction was not possible as the time limit in the covenant had elapsed by the time the case was resolved.)

The scope of restraint clauses and severance

15.21 We have seen that clauses in restraint of trade, in employment contracts, have been enforceable even where the restraint was unlimited in time (as in *Fitch* v *Dewes* (1921)) or covered the whole country (see *Forster* v *Suggett* (1918), discussed at para. **15.14**). However, the restraint must not be unreasonably wide in area or long in duration; what is reasonable will depend on the circumstances of the case and the business in question (as in *Proactive Sports Management Ltd* v *Rooney* (2011) discussed at para. **15.28**). The restraint must be to protect the employer's business and not simply to inconvenience the employee. In *Mason* v *Provident Clothing & Supply Co. Ltd* [1913] AC 724, for example:

> Provident Clothing Limited employed Mason as a local canvasser in its Islington branch in London. His job was to obtain members and collect their instalments; he had no duties outside his assigned district. Mason covenanted not to enter into similar employment within twenty-five miles of London for a period of three years.

The House of Lords, allowing Mason's appeal, held that the clause covered an area which was much greater than was reasonably required for the protection of his former employers. Provident Clothing were entitled to protect themselves against the danger of a former employee canvassing or collecting for a rival firm in the district in which he had been employed. But the restraint which the company was trying to enforce was too wide. The possibility of enforcing a more limited (and reasonable) restraint was considered by the court. It was stated that this could be done where severance was possible, and where the excessive part of the clause was merely technical, or of trivial importance, and not part of the main substance of the clause. Their Lordships did not favour such an approach where the employer, having deliberately framed a clause in unreasonably wide terms, now asked the court in effect to rewrite the clause to make it reasonable and enforceable. In the circumstances of the case, this was undoubtedly a fair conclusion. (But contrast *T Lucas & Co. Ltd* v *Mitchell* (1974).) In the *Mason* case, the company's argument was dealt with convincingly by Lord Moulton (at 746):

> 'It is evident that those who drafted this covenant aimed at making it a penal rather than a protective covenant, and that they hoped by means of it to paralyse the earning capacities of the man if and when he left their service, and were not thinking of what would be a reasonable protection to their business, and having so acted they must take the consequences.'

15.22 The question of severance was also considered in *Attwood* v *Lamont* (1920). The facts were:

> The claimant, Harry Attwood, owned a general outfitter's business, which comprised several departments. James Lamont was employed by Attwood as head of the tailoring department, but he was not directly concerned with any of the other departments. In his employment contract he had bound himself, after the termination of his contract, not to be involved in 'the trade or business of a tailor, dressmaker, general draper, milliner, hatter, haberdasher, gentlemen's, ladies' or children's outfitter, at any place within a radius of ten miles of the employer's place of business' in Kidderminster. Lamont left Attwood's and started his own business outside the ten-mile radius. He did business with several of his former employer's customers, however, and took orders from them within the ten-mile radius. Attwood sought an injunction to restrain Lamont from disregarding the covenant. Lamont claimed that the clause was too wide in its terms to be reasonable.

Although the clause was wider than was reasonably necessary for the protection of Attwood's business, the Divisional Court had been willing to permit severance, i.e. to reject the illegal part of the clause and to enforce the part relating to the tailoring business. However, the Court of Appeal held that not only was the covenant too wide, but that it was also not susceptible to severance. It would have been possible, by deleting the offending words in the clause, to reduce its scope to reasonable proportions, but the Court of Appeal refused to do so. Although the court would not have been rewriting the agreement for the parties, it would have radically altered the scope and purpose of that agreement to have permitted severance. Moreover, their Lordships thought that there were strong public policy grounds for refusing severance so that employers would be encouraged to keep such restraint clauses within the bounds of reasonableness. Otherwise employers could impose unreasonably wide restraints in employment contracts and then rely on the court, through the process of severance, to give effect to part of the offending clause.

15.23 Severance will be permitted in certain instances, but it is not very clear what the requirements are. We have seen earlier in *Goldsoll* v *Goldman* (1915) that, although a covenant was too wide in both the area and the commercial activity to be covered, the court permitted severance of the offending parts and enforced the remainder, which was then a reasonable restraint. (See also *Kall Kwik Printing (UK) Ltd* v *Rush (Frank Clarence)* (1996).) But it should be remembered that in *Goldsoll* the covenant was between the vendor and purchaser of a business. In this context, the policy grounds for refusing severance are not so strong. The court is happy to permit the purchaser to get full value for the price he has paid for the proprietary interest in the business. But, in relation to covenants between employer and employee, a court may be more reluctant to enforce a restraint of trade clause.

15.24 A good example of the differing views about the ability of a court in effect to rewrite a restraint clause for the parties can be seen in *Littlewoods Organisation* v *Harris* [1978] 1 All ER 1026. It will be recalled that Harris's agreement with Littlewoods prevented him from going to work, within twelve months, for their main mail order rival (GUS) or its subsidiaries. Although Littlewoods' interests were limited to the UK and to two commercial areas, the clause was worldwide in scope and not restricted to the mail order business. Lord Denning argued that unskilful drafting should not prevent the clause from being construed more narrowly so as to limit its scope to preventing Harris from working for GUS's mail order business in the UK. Megaw LJ shared Lord Denning's view and insisted (at 1043) that, in using the principles of construction available to the court to limit the scope of the clause, he was not rewriting the covenant. However, there was a strong dissenting judgment from Browne LJ. He stated (at 1046):

> 'With all deference to Lord Denning MR and Megaw LJ, I think this is rewriting the clause, and rewriting it so as to make enforceable that which would otherwise be unenforceable . . . I think that is something which this court cannot do. I do not think that severance has any relevance to this part of the contract.'

Although the outcome of the *Littlewoods* case is obviously defensible, it must be acknowledged that this dissenting judgment is a valid criticism of the majority's approach. Severance permits the illegal part of a covenant to be separated from the rest, by deleting it, leaving the remainder in force. In theory at least, it does not permit a rewriting of the covenant for the parties. (For an illustration of this distinction, see *Scully UK Ltd* v *Anthony Lee* (1998).) The majority in *Littlewoods* thought that the principles of construction enabled the court to restrict the scope of an unreasonably wide clause, but this approach comes very close to a rewriting of the agreement by the court.[7]

Restraints protecting other interests

15.25   Restraint clauses may also be used in circumstances which do not fit neatly into the categories that we have just considered. For example, in *Eastham* v *Newcastle United Football Club Ltd* [1964] Ch 413, the facts were:

> The claimant, George Eastham, was a highly rated footballer who played for Newcastle United, the defendant club. Under the rules (at that time) of the Football Association and the Football League, his employment with the club was subject to a retain-and-transfer system. This system prevented a player who was employed by one club from being employed by another. His transfer to another club could be effected only with the consent of both clubs. Eastham wanted to join another club, Arsenal, and sought a declaration against his present club and the football authorities.

It is clear that the defendant club was not using the restraint clause, namely the retain and transfer system, to protect either of the two established proprietary interests (discussed earlier). But this did not automatically mean that the club had no further interests capable of protection (see Wilberforce J's comments at 432). However, it was decided that, on the facts of the

---

7   Lord Denning stated at 1037: 'I think that limiting words ought to be read into the clause so as to limit it to the part of the business for which Littlewoods are reasonably entitled to protection'.

case, the retain-and-transfer system was invalid and was unnecessary for the protection of the club's proprietary interests. Eastham was granted a declaration not only against his employer, but also against the football authorities whose rules led to the unjustifiable restraint on his freedom of employment. (The rules relating to the transfer system were altered as a result of this case.) But the case does, at least, suggest that the interests that can be protected are not strictly limited, and this point was also acknowledged in *Leeds Rugby Ltd* v *Harris* (2005) (per Gray J at [50]).

15.26   In other instances a covenant may be used to restrict a person's commercial freedom even though the parties are not, strictly speaking, bound by a contract of employment. A good example is provided by *Schroeder Music Publishing Co. Ltd* v *Macaulay* [1974] 3 All ER 616. The facts were as follows:

Tony Macaulay, a young and unknown song writer, entered into an agreement with the defendant music publishing company, whereby the defendants engaged his exclusive services. Under this agreement, Macaulay gave the company the copyright of all his compositions for the next five years (with a further five-year option), and in return was to receive royalty payments. The company could end the contract by giving Macaulay one month's written notice, but there was no corresponding provision to allow Macaulay to do the same. The company was not even under any obligation to publish any of Macaulay's songs. Although this agreement was not a contract of employment as such, Macaulay sought a declaration that it was contrary to public policy, as being in unreasonable restraint of trade, and void. The company argued that the doctrine of restraint of trade was inapplicable to its standard form agreement.

The House of Lords held that the restrictions in the agreement between Macaulay and the publishing company were not fair and reasonable in that they combined a lack of obligation on the company's part with a total commitment on the part of Macaulay. If the company chose not to publish his work, for instance, he would be unable to earn his living as a songwriter. Thus the contract was an unreasonable restraint of trade and Macaulay was entitled to a declaration.[8] Lord Reid stated (at 622):

'Any contract by which a person engages to give his exclusive services to another for a period necessarily involves extensive restriction during that period of the common law right to exercise any lawful activity he chooses in such manner as he thinks best. Normally the doctrine of restraint of trade has no application to such restrictions: they require no justification. But if contractual restrictions appear to be unnecessary or to be reasonably capable of enforcement in an oppressive manner, then they must be justified before they can be enforced.'

15.27   Similar issues arose in *Silvertone Records* v *Mountfield* (1993), which concerned a dispute between a record company and the members of a pop group in relation to their recording and publishing contracts. The agreements (made when the group was comparatively unknown)

---

8   The case is also of considerable interest on the subject of unconscionability and is discussed further in **Chapter 16**.

gave the company, inter alia, the option of the group's services for six further periods beyond the duration of the original contract. The group claimed that the agreements were one-sided and represented an unreasonable restraint of trade. The company claimed that it had been made clear to the group that the agreements were a package and that the group members had waived their objections to it. Accordingly, the company sought a declaration that the agreements were enforceable against the group. Humphries J held that the whole agreement was objectionable, as there was a large inequality of bargaining power between the parties at the time it was entered into. (In a situation like this one, it was held to be a restraint of trade if a performer was prevented from reaching the public with his or her work for a prolonged period.) The judge stated that the members of the group had not waived their objections to the enforceability of the agreements. (See also *Zang Tumb Tuum Records* v *Johnson* (1993) for a further example of a one-sided and unenforceable contract between a record company and a pop group.)

15.28   The doctrine of restraint of trade has also been successfully relied upon in an agreement covering matters which do not form the main occupation of an individual but rather are ancillary to it. The case of *Proactive Sports Management Ltd* v *Rooney* (2011), related to an agreement entered into by a professional footballer under which he assigned his image rights to Proactive, granting exclusive rights to his name for use in all promotional activity in return for a commission rate of 20 per cent of his earnings. In considering the question of a possible restraint of trade, the court recognized that the exploitation of image rights was almost always going to be an activity which was ancillary to another occupation, concluding that this was just as capable of protection as any other occupation. Thus, although the ancillary nature of an activity might lead to the restriction on trading being insubstantial and therefore justifiable, this was not seen to be an adequate reason to not apply the doctrine. A number of factors were examined to test the restrictions of the contract, including duration (the agreement was for eight years and this was found to be a very lengthy period over which the restraints were imposed); the circumstances surrounding execution (when he had entered into the contract Rooney was only seventeen years old and had not taken independent legal advice); and the practical difficulties of termination. Citing earlier authorities of *Schroeder Music Publishing Co. Ltd* v *Macaulay* (1974) discussed at para. **15.26** and *Esso Petroleum Co. Ltd* v *Harper's Garage (Stourport) Ltd* (1968) see para. **15.29**, the court found that the contract was in restraint of trade and in line with the well-established effect of such a finding, from the time at which a party had withdrawn from the contract, the contract was deemed unenforceable.

Are the categories of restraint closed?

15.29   The two main types of contract in which restraint clauses are prima facie unenforceable are those between employer and employee, and those between the buyer and seller of a business. Does the doctrine also apply to other types of agreement or are the categories of restraint of trade closed? This issue has arisen in relation to 'solus' trading agreements, for example, where garage proprietors agree with an oil company not to sell the products of rival companies. Such arrangements can benefit both parties, as the garage or filling station operator may receive a rebate on the price of petrol or a loan (at favourable rates) to help with the development of his or her business. The advantage to the oil company is obvious. This type of agreement was the subject of the important case of *Esso Petroleum Co. Ltd v Harper's Garage (Stourport) Ltd* (1968). The facts were:

> H owned two garages (H1 and H2) which were both subject to solus agreements with Esso. Under the terms of these agreements H agreed to buy all his petrol from Esso and, in turn, H was to receive a small rebate on the price of petrol. The agreement in relation to H1 was for four and a half years; it stipulated that H should buy Esso's petrol and no other and it laid down certain other conditions. In relation to H2, there was a similar solus agreement, but in addition Esso had a mortgage over the premises to secure a sum of £7,000 lent to H. The H2 agreement was for the duration of the mortgage repayments, i.e. twenty-one years. The mortgage provisions also stipulated that H was to buy his petrol exclusively from Esso. H later started to sell another brand of petrol, and Esso sought an injunction to prevent him from doing so. Were the ties in the agreements in restraint of trade and unenforceable?

The House of Lords held that both agreements were within the scope of the restraint of trade doctrine. (Per Lord Reid: 'In the present case the respondents before they made this agreement were entitled to use this land in any lawful way they chose, and by making this agreement they agreed to restrict their right by giving up their right to sell there petrol not supplied by the appellants'.) This meant that the agreements would not be enforced by the court unless they were reasonable. Their Lordships held that the restriction on H1 was reasonable, but that the restriction relating to H2 was not. The principal reason for distinguishing between the two agreements was the difference in their respective lengths. A restriction lasting twenty-one years was an unreasonable one in the circumstances (but contrast *Alec Lobb Garages Ltd v Total Oil (Great Britain) Ltd* (1985)). The restriction should not have been longer than was reasonably necessary to protect the legitimate interests of the oil company, i.e. to maintain a stable system of distribution. A much shorter restriction would have sufficed to achieve this end. Duration of the restriction is a relevant factor to consider when questioning whether an agreement is unfair or oppressive and operating in restraint of trade. (See *Proactive Sports Management Ltd v Rooney* (2011).)

Further regulation of restraint of trade

15.30   We have seen that contracts in restraint of trade are unenforceable, unless the restriction is reasonable as between the parties to the agreement and is not against the public interest. The courts have been more adept at judging the first of these requirements than the second. Consideration of the public interest necessitates more wide-ranging enquiry than the courts have traditionally been prepared to undertake. (For a classic example, see *Mogul Steamship Co. Ltd v McGregor, Gow & Co. Ltd* (1892).) Whereas the reasonableness of a restraint clause from the point of view of the parties will be fully explored in court by the litigants, the public interest will not be directly represented. Judges may be better equipped, by both outlook and training, to weigh the relative interests of the parties to an agreement than to consider the broader economic issues raised by restraint agreements.

15.31 Although there has been some indication of a greater willingness to take account of the public interest in restraint of trade cases,[9] the failure of judges to do so in the past is one of the factors which inhibited the development of a comprehensive common law doctrine to regulate anti-competitive behaviour. Other factors include the uncertainty about the ambit of the common law doctrine of restraint of trade, and its inability (until recently) to protect third parties who were adversely affected. For these reasons, domestic competition policy has been delineated largely by legislative provisions, which have been substantially changed by the Competition Act 1998. It is not necessary in a book on the general principles of contract law to enter into a detailed discussion of these legislative provisions; those requiring further information should consult a specialist work on UK competition law.[10]

Other contracts void at common law on grounds of public policy

Contracts to oust the jurisdiction of the courts

15.32 We have seen in **Chapter 6** that it is possible for the parties to an agreement to stipulate that their agreement shall not be legally enforceable. Thus, in *Jones v Vernons Pools* (1938) it was a condition of entry that the arrangements of the 'football pool' were binding in honour only: a so-called 'gentlemen's agreement'. The company could not be sued successfully by the claimant as the agreement carried with it no legal obligations on either side, and conferred no legal rights. (See also *Rose and Frank Co. v JR Crompton & Bros Ltd* (1925).) It is not, however, open to the parties to a contract to stipulate that their agreement will have legal consequences but will not be susceptible to the supervision of the courts.

15.33 An agreement which purports to prevent the parties to it from submitting questions of law to the courts is contrary to public policy and void. (Only the offending part of the agreement is void; the rest of the contract may be valid and enforceable.) Contractual freedom is, therefore, limited in this way, as it is thought to be in the public interest that parties should not be free to oust the jurisdiction of the courts.

15.34 The parties may, however, provide that no cause of action will arise until an arbitrator has made an award. This type of arbitration clause is not regarded as contrary to public policy. This was established in *Scott v Avery* (1855) 5 HL Cas 811, where a contract between a ship-owner and the underwriters made it clear that no action should be brought against the insurers until the arbitrators had dealt with any dispute arising between the parties. It was held that it is permissible for the parties to agree that no right of action shall accrue until an arbitrator has

---

9 For instance, see *Esso Petroleum Ltd v Harper's Garage Ltd* (1968) and *Schroeder Music Publishing v Macaulay* (1974).

10 e.g., see S. Singleton, *Competition Act 1998*, Blackstone Press, 1999.

decided on any difference which may arise between them. Lord Campbell (at 851) explained the matter as follows:

> '...What pretence can there be for saying that there is anything contrary to public policy in allowing parties to contract, that they shall not be liable to any action until their liability has been ascertained by a domestic and private tribunal, upon which they themselves agree? Can the public be injured by it? It seems to me that it would be a most inexpedient encroachment upon the liberty of the subject if he were not allowed to enter into such a contract.'

The important point is that such an arbitration clause does not oust the jurisdiction of the courts. Within our legal system there will always tend to be a conflict between two distinct approaches to dispute settling: that is, the 'ideal' principle of justice which wants justice no matter what the cost, and the 'pragmatic' principle which seeks to limit litigation and its concomitant costs. Although it is the right of the citizen to have his or her legal position decided by the ordinary courts, it is desirable that many disputes should first be heard by an arbitrator. There has to be some compromise between these two approaches, so it is permissible for contracting parties to provide that any disagreement that arises will be referred to arbitration.

15.35   The general rule, that an agreement which purports to oust the jurisdiction of the courts is void, is well illustrated in *Baker* v *Jones* [1954] 1 WLR 1005. The facts were:

> An association, which controlled the sport of weightlifting in the UK, by its rules vested the government of the association in a central council consisting of the officers and a number of members. The association empowered its central council to be the sole interpreters of the rules and to act on behalf of the association regarding any matter not dealt with by the rules. In all circumstances, the decision of the council was to be regarded as final. As a result of disagreements between the members, two libel actions were brought against certain officers and council members. The central council authorized the payment of two sums of £100 to solicitors, out of the association's funds, towards the defendants' legal costs. A member of the association challenged this decision of the council by seeking a declaration that this use of the association's funds was improper.

Lynskey J held that the provision in the rules giving the central council the sole right to interpret the rules was contrary to public policy and void. (It should also be noted that there was no power under the association's rules for the central council to authorize the use of funds for the proposed purpose.) The contract in these circumstances was contained in the association's rules, so the relationship between its various members was indeed contractual. The judge explained (at 1010) that although, in theory, the parties to a contract may make any contract that they like, this is subject to certain limitations imposed by public policy. One of these limitations is that the jurisdiction of the courts cannot be ousted by the agreement of the parties. He cited with approval the statement of Lord Denning in *Lee* v *Showmen's Guild of Great Britain* [1952] 2 QB 329 at 342:

> 'If parties should seek, by agreement, to take the law out of the hands of the courts and put it into the hands of a private tribunal, without any recourse at all to the courts in case of error of law, then the agreement is to that extent contrary to public policy and void.'

15.36 A further example of a situation where an agreement to oust the jurisdiction of the courts may arise is that of a maintenance agreement between husband and wife. As part of a separation agreement, a husband may promise his wife an allowance in exchange for which she agrees not to apply to the courts for maintenance. This issue arose in *Hyman* v *Hyman* (1929), where it was held that a wife cannot, by her own agreement, preclude herself from invoking the jurisdiction of the court. (See also *Sutton* v *Sutton* (1984); *Hyman* v *Hyman* was distinguished by the Court of Appeal in the case of *Soulsbury* v *Soulsbury* (2007).) The main disadvantage of this common law rule was that if the husband did not pay the promised allowance, his wife was not able to sue him to enforce payment. But under the present statutory provisions (see Matrimonial Causes Act 1973, s 34), a wife can successfully sue her husband, if the agreement is written, to enforce payment of the promised allowance.

Contracts undermining the status of marriage

15.37 In the public interest, the law seeks to uphold the sanctity of marriage. Accordingly, certain types of agreement which tend to undermine or damage the institution of marriage are invalidated. One example of this is a contract which purports to restrict a person's freedom to marry whomsoever he or she wishes. In *Lowe* v *Peers* (1768), for instance, a man promised the claimant, under seal, that he would not marry any other person except her. He stated that if he broke this promise to her, he would pay her £2,000. His promise was held to be void, as it restricted his freedom of choice without there being any reciprocal promise from the claimant. (Until the abolition of an action for breach of promise in 1970, a couple's engagement to marry—involving reciprocal promises—was a valid contract. This was not the situation in *Lowe* v *Peers*, where the parties did not directly promise to marry each other.)

15.38 Another type of agreement which is thought to undermine the status of marriage is the so-called 'marriage brokage' contract, i.e. an agreement for reward for the procurement of marriage. Such agreements are regarded as contrary to public policy and therefore void. The rather outmoded reasoning behind this rule is that these agreements tend to promote unsuitable marriages and, for this reason, are harmful to the public! (Given the current rate of matrimonial breakdown, such a moral stance might appear particularly quaint.) The invalidity of such agreements appears to extend to those between matrimonial agencies and their clients where the latter are introduced to a number of people of the opposite sex with a view to marriage.

In *Hermann* v *Charlesworth* (1905), the facts were:

> Miss Hermann saw an advertisement in the defendant's paper, *The Matrimonial Post and Fashionable Marriage Advertiser*, and later signed an agreement with the defendant in the following terms: 'In consideration of being introduced to or put in correspondence with a gentleman through the influence of the proprietor of the paper entitled "The Matrimonial Post and Fashionable Marriage Advertiser", and in the event of a marriage taking place between such gentleman and myself, I hereby agree to pay to the said proprietor the sum of £250 on the date of my said marriage'. Miss Charlesworth also paid the defendant a 'special client's fee' of £52. She was introduced to several men by the defendant, who also interviewed and wrote to others on her behalf, but no marriage or engagement followed. She sued the defendant to recover the £52.

The Court of Appeal held that it made no difference that the agreement was not intended to bring about Miss Charlesworth's marriage with a particular individual. It was still to be regarded as a marriage brokage agreement, despite the fact that she was introduced to a number of men and therefore had some degree of choice. It was decided that the transaction in this case came within the rule which invalidates marriage brokage contracts. Accordingly, the claimant was entitled to recover the money paid under this contract, even though the defendant had brought about introductions and incurred expense in doing so.

15.39   A distinction between pre-nuptial and post-nuptial agreements was drawn in *MacLeod* v *MacLeod* (2008) where it was considered that a post-nuptial agreement, although remaining subject to the court's discretionary power of variation, could be valid and enforceable under the Matrimonial Causes Act 1973. In respect of pre-nuptial agreements, the court advised these should be declared void in accordance with the traditional rule unless and until Parliament decided to change the law. More recently however, in *Granatino* v *Radmacher (formerly Granatino)* (2010), the majority in the Supreme Court, with Baroness Hale dissenting, rejected the previously drawn distinction between the two types of agreement. Here, both pre-nuptial and post-nuptial agreements were considered to be capable of being effective, providing it was fair to hold the parties to their agreement and providing the arrangement had been freely entered into by the parties with full awareness of its consequences.

Illegal contracts

15.40   It should be borne in mind that the distinction between illegal and void contracts is not universally accepted. The terminology employed both by academics and the courts is far from consistent. The distinction is maintained here largely for expository purposes and it is conceded that other categorizations are equally acceptable. A contract may be improper for such a variety of reasons, ranging from the serious to the trivial, that the subject does not always lend itself to analysis by categorization. But whereas the vitiating aspect of a 'void' contract (as described earlier) will be apparent on the face of the agreement, the 'illegal' contract may or may not be improper at face value. If the vitiating aspect is not apparent on the surface, the agreement may be rendered unlawful by some ulterior purpose of one or both of the parties.[11]

Policy factors and the illegality defence

15.41   Contracts may be illegal at common law on grounds of public policy. The maxim *ex turpi causa non oritur actio* means that no action can arise from a bad cause. This applies with the effect that the courts will not enforce a contract which involves a legal wrong (other than the breach of contract itself) whether this arises in its formation, purpose of performance, or if it involves conduct which is contrary to public policy. (See further Law Commission Consultation Paper, No 154, *Illegal Transactions: The Effect of Illegality on Contracts and Trusts*, 1999, para. 7.70.) Consequently, a person may not benefit from his or her own crime, tort or fraud.

15.42   Therefore, the doctrine is seen to have general application beyond the law of contract and has been relied upon in other areas of law. For example, in *Stone & Rolls Ltd (in Liquidation) v Moore Stephens (a firm)* (2009) the defence was successfully relied upon to prevent a company which engaged in serious fraud, from claiming its auditors were in breach of their duty of care in failing to detect the fraud. Although the application of the maxim relies on the claimant being 'personally' liable, this can also extend to the activities of a company whose acts may be found to be 'personal'. (See *Safeway Stores Ltd v Twigger* (2010).)

15.43   The policy precludes a person from recovering compensation for losses suffered as a result of his or her own criminal act or for damage arising from a sentence imposed on him or her for carrying out a criminal act. This is well illustrated by the House of Lords decision in *Gray v Thames Trains Ltd* (2009) in which the claimant, who had committed manslaughter as a result of psychological problems caused by the negligence of the rail company, was precluded from recovering general damages for his conviction, detention and damage to his reputation and also for special damages for his loss of earnings.

15.44   *Gray v Thames Trains Ltd* (2009) demonstrates that a person will not recover compensation where his or her cause of action is based on his or her criminal or immoral act and the test for determining liability here focused on causation. This was followed in *Delaney v Pickett* (2011) and showed how the causation principle can also apply whether the criminal is acting alone or as a partner in crime as part of a joint criminal enterprise. Here, at first instance, Delaney was not allowed to claim for damages for injuries sustained in a car accident caused by Pickett's negligence. The purpose of their journey together was to supply illegal drugs and reliance was placed on the *ex turpi causa* defence. However, the Court of Appeal ruled that the illegal acts were incidental: the damage had been caused by Pickett's tortious act in the negligent manner he had driven the car and consequently the defence would not be upheld. The causation principle developed earlier in *Gray v Thames Trains Ltd* (2009) was followed and later

---

11 This distinction is well explained in J. C. Smith and J. A. C. Thomas, *Casebook on Contract*, 11th edn, Sweet & Maxwell, 2000, p. 684.

in *Joyce* v *O'Brien* (2013) the court ruled that this principle should apply in circumstances when a criminal was acting alone or as part of joint enterprise. The facts of *Joyce* v *O'Brien* (2013) were as follows:

> Joyce (J) fell from the footplate of a van driven by O'Brien (O) and was seriously injured. O pleaded guilty to dangerous driving. J claimed damages for personal injury on the basis of O's negligence. However, the insurance company (T) asserted that O and J had been making their escape after stealing a set of ladders and for this reason, O and therefore T, was not liable; J and O had been engaged in a joint criminal enterprise.

Joyce and O'Brien had been involved in joint criminal activity and the public policy reflected in the principle *ex turpi causa* was applicable. Although the case offers some much needed clarity in this area of the law, by highlighting the flexibility of the doctrine, the scope for potential uncertainty in the operation of this public policy rule becomes equally apparent.

15.45   As illustrated above, the doctrine of *ex turpi causa* has been raised in a number of recent cases and it is an aspect of public policy which continues to influence and shape the operation of the illegality defence. The future position of the law on illegality, including the final recommendations of the recent Law Commission Report No 320, *The Illegality Defence* (2010) is discussed further at paras. **15.81–15.83.** But before that, what follows is a broader consideration of the subject and a series of case examples where the issues of illegality or impropriety have been raised. It is by no means an exhaustive guide to the subject of illegality but it does offer useful illustrations of how the issues have been dealt with by the courts.

Contracts to commit an unlawful act

15.46   If the purpose of an agreement between the parties is to commit a crime, or a tort, or a fraud against another party, then it can be said that such a contract is illegal and unenforceable. A contract will be unenforceable if at the time of its formation, one of the parties had the intention of performing it in an unlawful manner; the intention must be present at the time of the execution of the contract (*ParkingEye Ltd* v *Somerfield Stores Ltd* (2012)). It is not surprising that the courts refuse to assist those whose purpose is to achieve an unlawful or an illegal end. (For a discussion of evidential issues where illegality is claimed, see *Pickering* v *McConville* (2003), and also *Colen* v *Cebrian (UK) Ltd* (2003) at [19].) Even where an agreement is of a type which is commonly made in certain commercial contexts, it will still be unenforceable if it is based on an unlawful transaction. For example, if a shipowner carries X's goods and, in return for a promise of an indemnity from X, certifies that the goods are shipped 'in good condition', despite his knowledge that they are not, he would not be able to enforce the indemnity. The purpose of such an arrangement is to defraud a third party, and the fact that such a practice is widespread does not excuse the unlawful nature of the agreement (see *Brown Jenkinson & Co. Ltd* v *Percy Dalton Ltd* (1957)).

15.47   The situation becomes more complex where there is a lawful contract between the parties, but it is performed by one of them in an unlawful manner, for example, in breach of a statutory provision. The party who is in breach of the law may be unable to enforce any claim (for example, to recover the price of goods) as a result of his or her own illegal performance. (See *Anderson Ltd* v *Daniel* (1924).) Of course, this principle will not apply to the innocent party under the transaction unless in some way he or she participated in the other party's illegal performance. (This subject is discussed in more detail later.) However, even the guilty party may be able to enforce the contract in some circumstances. Much may depend on the purpose of the statute in question. In *St John Shipping Corpn* v *Joseph Rank Ltd* [1956] 3 All ER 683, for example:

> Under a contract of carriage, the claimants conveyed a cargo of wheat from America to England in their ship, which was overloaded and thus contravened the Merchant Shipping (Safety and Load Line Conventions) Act 1932. A fine of £1,200 was imposed on the master of the ship in respect of this offence, but the freight earned by the excess wheat carried was £2,295. The defendants, who were to receive about one-third of the cargo of wheat, paid part of the freight for their share, but withheld £2,000 of the agreed sum in view of the overloading. (It should be noted that the wheat was delivered safely to them.) The claimants claimed the balance of the freight and the defendants argued that the contract was unenforceable by the claimants by reason of illegality.

Devlin J explained that, although a contract which is entered into with the object of committing an illegal act is unenforceable, this principle was not applicable in the present case. He stated (at 687) that 'whether or not the overloading was deliberate when it was done, there is no proof that it was contemplated when the contract of carriage was made'. Accordingly, the judge held that the claimants were entitled to the balance of the freight; they were not barred from recovering it by the fact that the overloading was a crime. It is important to note that the statutory provision in question did not make the contract of carriage unlawful, it merely penalized overloading. As this infringement of the legislation was not contemplated by the contract, there was nothing to prevent even the guilty party from enforcing that contract. The goods were safely delivered and no part of the claim for freight could be identified clearly as being the excess illegally earned. The purpose of the Act was achieved by the fine imposed on the master of the ship for the offence. (See also *Hughes* v *Asset Managers plc* (1995), and the Law Commission Consultation Paper, No 189, *The Illegality Defence: A Consultative Report*, 2009, which discusses both cases, at paras 3.4–3.11.)

15.48 Devlin J's remarks in *St John Shipping Corpn* v *Joseph Rank Ltd* (1956) were applied in *Shaw* v *Groom* (1970). In this case a landlord failed to provide his tenant with a rent book in contravention of the relevant landlord and tenant legislation. The Court of Appeal held that this omission did not disentitle the landlord from recovering the rent of the premises from the tenant. The purpose of the legislation was not to preclude the landlord from recovering rent, but merely to penalize him for the breach of the statutory provision. This is a sensible approach in view of the scope and purpose of the statute. If this purpose is to be achieved by the imposition of a fine on the offender, it may well be unfair and unnecessary to go further and make the contract unenforceable by the party who is in breach of the law. Otherwise, even a minor transgression by the offender might excuse the 'innocent' party from performing his contractual obligations.

15.49   In contrast to the unlawful performance of an otherwise lawful contract, we should also consider a contract which is illegal in itself. For example, in *Re Mahmoud and Ispahani* (1921) the claimant, who had a licence to sell linseed oil, sold some to the defendant in contravention of the Seed, Oils, and Fats Order 1919. This statute made it an offence to buy or sell linseed oil without a licence; the defendant was unlicensed—he had induced the claimant to sell him the oil by a fraudulent representation that he was licensed. The defendant later refused to accept delivery of the oil and was sued for damages by the claimant. The Court of Appeal held that the claimant's claim failed because of the illegality of the contract. Despite the fact that the claimant was the innocent party, the legislation specifically prohibited any sale of oil to unlicensed persons.

Contracts promoting sexual immorality

15.50   An agreement which tends to promote sexual immorality may be found to be illegal as a principle of common law. This is certainly the case where the agreement in some way involves or encourages prostitution. In the rather old case of *Pearce v Brooks* (1866) LR 1 Ex 213, for instance, the claimant agreed to hire a horse and carriage to a prostitute, knowing that it would be used, in some way, to assist her in her enterprise. It was held that the claimant could not recover the hire charge when the defendant refused to pay it. Lord Pollock explained (at 218):

> 'I have always considered it as settled law that any person who contributes to the performance of an illegal act by supplying a thing with the knowledge that it is going to be used for that purpose, cannot recover the price of the thing so supplied ... Nor can any distinction be made between an illegal and an immoral purpose; the rule which is applicable to the matter is ex turpi causa non oritur actio, and whether it is an immoral or an illegal purpose in which the [claimant] has participated, it comes equally within the terms of that maxim, and the effect is the same; no cause of action can arise out of either the one or the other.'

Such a conclusion may not be surprising, but it is debatable how widely the notion of 'sexual immorality' should be interpreted. The attitude of society to such questions is constantly changing and behaviour that is regarded as shocking to one generation may not seem so outrageous to a later generation. (For example, see *Armhouse Lee Ltd v Chappell* (1996).) However, the statement of Lord Pollock was applied in *Upfill v Wright* [1911] 1 KB 506, where the facts were:

> C, through his agent, let a flat in London to D, an unmarried woman. The agent knew that D was the mistress of a certain man and he assumed that the rent would be paid as a result of her being a 'kept woman'; that is, it would come from the man whose mistress she was. Eventually, C's agent gave D notice to quit. D failed to pay the rent for the last half year of the tenancy. C sued for the rent which was still owed to him.

It was held that C was not entitled to recover the rent, because the flat was let for an immoral purpose. The reasoning put forward by the Divisional Court might strike us today as rather absurd. Darling J stated (at 510–12):

> 'The flat was let to the defendant for the purpose of enabling her to receive visits of the man whose mistress she was and to commit fornication with him there...That fornication is sinful and immoral is clear...I am of the opinion that this flat was let for an immoral purpose and the fact that the rent was to arise out of the letting made it clear that the landlord participated in the illegal or immoral act and in the immoral gains of the defendant. Therefore the case comes within the rule that out of a forbidden act no cause of action can arise.'

15.51   It is questionable whether the law would feel the need today to protect public morality in such a zealous way. For example, the cohabitation of men and women outside marriage has become much more widespread and acceptable in modern times and the courts today are more reluctant to invoke this area of public policy. In certain cases involving an unmarried woman's contractual rights over the home jointly occupied by the cohabitees, the court has not raised the question of the immorality of the couple's arrangements. In *Tanner* v *Tanner* (1975), for instance, C decided to buy a house to provide a home for D and her twin daughters. C was the father of the twins. C bought the house on a mortgage and D gave up her rent-controlled flat and moved into the house with the children. Three years later, C wanted to evict D, who now refused to move out of the house. The Court of Appeal held that D had a contractual licence to reside in the house with her children so long as the children were of school age and they required the accommodation.

Contracts prejudicial to the interests of the state

15.52   This is a very general heading and is susceptible to a number of interpretations. One obvious instance is a trading contract concluded in time of war between someone in the UK and a foreign enemy. Such an agreement is, not surprisingly, illegal. If the contract predates the outbreak of hostilities it will still be dissolved, but rights and obligations which existed before the outbreak of war may be enforced after its conclusion.

15.53   There is also a prohibition against contracts which tend to injure the UK's friendly relations with another state (i.e. one with which we are not at war). If an agreement promotes action which is inimical to a friendly foreign country it will be regarded as unlawful and unenforceable by our courts (see *De Wutz* v *Hendricks* (1824)). An interesting example of the application of this prohibition is provided by *Regazzoni* v *KC Sethia Ltd* [1957] 3 All ER 286. The facts were as follows:

> An ordinance issued by the government of India prohibited the taking of goods out of India if they were destined for any part of South Africa, or were intended to be taken to South Africa despite being initially destined for another country. An English company, KC Sethia Ltd, agreed to sell and deliver to Polissino Regazzoni 500,000 bags of jute. To the knowledge of both contracting parties the jute was to be shipped from India to Genoa so that it might there

be resold to a South African buying agency in contravention of the Indian ordinance. Sethia failed to deliver the jute and Regazzoni claimed damages in an English court for breach of contract. Sethia defended the action by claiming that the contract was, to Regazzoni's knowledge, an illegal contract and therefore unenforceable, as its breach of the Indian ordinance was harmful to the interests of the state.

The House of Lords held that, as a matter of public policy, the contract was unenforceable in England. Its performance would have involved, as the parties were well aware, doing an act in a friendly foreign country which violated the law of that country. Lord Reid explained the reasoning of the court as follows (at 293):

'The real question is one of public policy in English law; but, in considering this question, we must have in mind the background of…the comity of nations. This is not a case of a contract being made in good faith but one party thereafter finding that he cannot perform his part of the contract without committing a breach of foreign law in the territory of the foreign country. If this contract is held to be unenforceable it should, in my opinion, be because from the beginning the contract was tainted so that the courts of this country will not assist either party to enforce it.'[12]

It was stressed by Lord Reid (at 294–5) that in deciding that the contract was unenforceable for breach of Indian law, the court was not necessarily implying its approval of that particular law. On the other hand, there was no express disapproval of that law. But, in a different situation, if our courts regarded a particular foreign law as positively distasteful for some reason, they might not refuse to enforce a contract which was in breach of such a law.

Contracts prejudicial to the administration of justice

15.54   Under this heading we can include agreements to interfere with or suppress a prosecution. The validity of such an agreement may, however, depend upon the nature of the unlawful act which raised the possibility of the criminal proceedings. If the harm caused by the act was of an essentially private nature (such as criminal libel or common assault) then an agreement not to prosecute might well be permissible. On the other hand, it would not be valid to agree to suppress a prosecution for an act which was more overtly injurious to the public interest—in any case, it is a substantive crime to conceal an arrestable offence. It should also be noted that an agreement to interfere with the due course of a criminal investigation or prosecution might well be unlawful on the ground that it constitutes an attempt or conspiracy to pervert the course of justice. In *R v Andrews* (1973), for example:

D witnessed a traffic accident between a motor car and a moped, as a result of which criminal proceedings against the car driver were contemplated. D invited the car driver to pay him to give false evidence at the prospective prosecution, and the driver offered him a sum of

---

12   See also *United City Merchants v Royal Bank of Canada* (1981) in which dicta of Viscount Simmonds and Lord Reid in *Regazzoni* were applied.

> money, but no bargain was in fact struck. D was convicted on a charge of inciting the motorist to pervert the course of justice.

The Court of Appeal dismissed the defendant's appeal against the conviction. It stated that to produce false evidence in order to mislead the court and to pervert the course of justice was a substantive offence; that inciting someone to act in this way was also an offence and therefore the conviction was justified. The case was concerned with the defendant's culpability rather than the question of illegality of contracts, but it is obvious that had the defendant and the motorist reached an agreement, it would have been both illegal and unenforceable on the ground of public policy. (For a recent discussion of agreements which interfere with the course of justice, see *Farhad Faryab* v *Phillip Ross & Co.* (2002).)

15.55 Another example of agreements which may be prejudicial to the administration of justice are those between a husband and wife where they collude in order to facilitate divorce proceedings. Whether such collusion invalidates an agreement today will depend on whether or not it is a corrupt agreement, i.e. one that is designed to practise a deception on the court.[13]

Contracts promoting corruption in public life

15.56 It would be contrary to the public interest if public offices or honours could be bought and sold. Such practices encourage corruption and result in the public not being served by the most able public officials. Consequently, agreements for the sale or purchase of such offices are unlawful. A good example of the scope of this principle is provided by *Parkinson* v *College of Ambulance Ltd and Harrison* (1925). The facts were:

> Colonel Parkinson was told by Harrison, the secretary of the defendant charity, that the charity would arrange for him to be granted a knighthood if he made a substantial donation. Harrison had told Parkinson of the charity's royal patronage. Parkinson paid £3,000 to the College of Ambulance on the understanding that he would receive a knighthood, and he also promised further payment to the charity in the future. When Parkinson did not receive a knighthood and realized that he had been duped, he brought an action against the charity to recover back the money that he had paid.

Lush J held that as the contract was for the purchase of a title, it was contrary to public policy and was an illegal contract. Despite the fact that the claimant had been defrauded, he knew that he was entering into an improper agreement and he could not recover the money he had paid to the charity; nor could he recover damages from the charity or its secretary. In this case, the attempt to buy influence was clearly improper. However, in commercial situations the use of 'intermediaries' to lobby for contracts is a common practice, and it may be difficult to decide at precisely which point legitimate business practices cross the line and become contrary to public

---

13 See *Nash* v *Nash* (1965).

policy. (See the case of *Tekron Resources Ltd* v *Guinea Investment Co. Ltd* (2003) at [93]–[101], where this point was considered.)

The effects of impropriety and illegality

15.57   We have seen that there are numerous types of impropriety which can affect a contract and that these involve varying degrees of unlawfulness. For this reason it is difficult to generalize about their consequences. We have considered the effects of impropriety on some types of contract in earlier parts of this chapter. What follows is intended only as an outline of some of the main principles that have been developed by the courts for dealing with problems of impropriety.

Void contracts

15.58   In the case of contracts that are void due to some statutory provision (discussed at para **15.4**), it is necessary to look closely at the particular statute in question to assess the effects of impropriety. In contracts void at common law on the grounds of public policy, it will be remembered that it may be possible to separate the offending part of the agreement from the rest of it. For example, where an agreement purports to prevent the parties to it from submitting questions of law to the courts, although such a clause will be void, the rest of the contract may be enforceable.

15.59   In the section on contracts in restraint of trade, we considered the doctrine of severance. This permits the unreasonable part of a clause or covenant to be separated from the rest of it, by deleting it, leaving the remainder in force. For example, in *Goldsoll* v *Goldman* (1915), the restraint imposed on the vendor of a jewellery business was too wide in the geographical area that it purported to cover. However, the Court of Appeal held that the unreasonable parts of the restraint were capable of being severed from the rest of it. The restraint that was permitted by the court was the one covering the UK, as this was reasonable in the circumstances. It should be borne in mind that courts may be less willing to apply the idea of severance in cases between employer and employee, as the parties are unlikely to possess equal bargaining strength.

15.60   A party to an agreement which is void for being contrary to public policy may have paid money to the other party under that 'contract'. It seems likely that the party who has paid the money will be able to recover it from the other. For example, in *Hermann* v *Charlesworth* (1905), the claimant paid a special client's fee of £52 to the defendant under a so-called 'marriage brokage' contract. Despite being introduced to several men by the defendant, the claimant did not become engaged or married to any of them. The Court of Appeal decided that this contract was invalid, as it was contrary to public policy to enforce marriage brokage contracts. Yet the claimant was entitled to recover the money paid under the contract, even though the defendant had brought about the introductions as promised. It should be noted that some of the reasoning employed by their Lordships in this case was far from convincing.

Illegal contracts

15.61　It is difficult to generalize about the effects of illegality, as much depends upon the circumstances of each case, such as the nature and seriousness of the illegality in question, and the state of mind of the contracting parties. (See *Vakante* v *Addey & Stanhope School* (2004) at [7]–[9].) Although we have concentrated, so far, on contracts which are illegal at common law on the grounds of public policy, it must be emphasized that the making of certain agreements may also be prohibited by statute. It is an instructive starting point to consider certain cases involving illegality arising out of a statutory prohibition. In *Re Mahmoud and Ispahani* (1921) (discussed earlier), the facts were that C sold linseed oil to D, in contravention of a statutory provision. C was misled by D into thinking that D possessed a licence to deal in linseed oil, when in fact he had no such licence. Subsequently, D refused to accept delivery of the oil and claimed that the contract was illegal. C claimed damages.

The Court of Appeal held that as D was unlicensed, the contract in question was prohibited by the Seed, Oils, and Fats Order of 1919 and was, therefore, illegal. Despite the innocence of the claimant, his claim was unsuccessful. The statutory prohibition was in the public interest and no claim could be made under the contract. It seems that the state of mind of the parties did not make any difference to the outcome where there was such an unequivocal statutory prohibition of this type of contract. Their agreement was illegal from the outset.

15.62　The situation in *Re Mahmoud and Ispahani* (1921) can be contrasted with that where an innocent party sues on a contract which is not ex facie illegal, but which is performed by the other party in an illegal manner. For example, in *Archbold's (Freightage) Ltd* v *Spanglett Ltd* (1961):

> The defendants agreed to carry a load of whisky by road, from Leeds to London, for Archbold's. Archbold's were unaware that the vehicle to be used by the defendants did not have the correct licence in order to comply with Road and Rail Traffic Act 1933, s 1(1). The defendants, however, were aware of this fact. Somewhere on the route to London the goods were stolen as a result of the negligence of the defendants' driver. The defendants argued that they were not liable for damages, because the contract was illegal by reason of the Road and Rail Traffic Act.

It was held that Archbold's were not debarred from recovering damages by the illegality of the defendants' use of their vehicle. Archbold's were innocent, but that fact had not helped the claimant in *Mahmoud*'s case (para. **15.49**). The reason why *Mahmoud* was distinguishable from the present case was due to the nature of the statutory prohibition. In *Mahmoud*, the contract of sale to an unlicensed person was expressly forbidden (see also *J Dennis and Co. Ltd* v *Munn* (1949)), whereas in *Archbold's (Freightage) Ltd* the carriage of Archbold's whisky was not as such prohibited. The legislation in question merely regulated the manner in which carriers should transport goods. The contract was not, therefore, expressly forbidden by the statute and the claimants were entitled to damages. It is worth noting that if both parties to the contract had known that the vehicle did not have an appropriate licence, the contract would have been unenforceable, as they would have known that it could not be carried out without breaking the law.

15.63   It must be emphasized that it is important to look at the language, scope, and purpose of the relevant statute in considering the effects of any illegality arising out of the contravention of its provisions. (For example, see *Hughes* v *Asset Managers plc* (1995).) In certain circumstances, it may even be possible for an 'illegal' contract to be enforced by both the innocent and the guilty party. If we reconsider the case of *St John Shipping Corpn* v *Joseph Rank Ltd* (1956), where the claimants carried a cargo of wheat from America to England in an overloaded ship, the question arose whether they could sue for the balance of freight owing to them under the contract of carriage. The claimants had infringed the Merchant Shipping Act 1932 and the master of the ship was, accordingly, fined. But it was held that this did not prevent them from recovering the freight from the defendants. The relevant statutory provision did not intend to make such a contract of carriage unlawful: it simply aimed to penalize overloading. Thus, the purpose of the statute was achieved adequately by the imposition of a fine on the master of the ship. In reaching this conclusion, Devlin J had to contend with the following observation of Lord Atkin in *Beresford* v *Royal Insurance Co. Ltd* [1938] 2 All ER 602 at 605: '...No system of jurisprudence can with reason include amongst the rights which it enforces rights directly resulting to the person asserting them from the crime of that person.' Devlin J explained that the relevant prohibition in *St John Shipping* imposed a penalty under the criminal law which was designed to deprive the offender of the benefits of his crime. This being so, it would be unfair if the civil law imposed a further penalty by denying the claimants the freight which was owed under the contract. He added (at 693) that 'it would be curious, too, if in a case in which the magistrates had thought fit to impose only a nominal fine their decision could in effect be overridden in a civil action'.

15.64   The fact that the guilty party was not prevented from succeeding in the above case serves as a useful warning that general rules about the effects of illegality are difficult to detect. (For a discussion of the relevant principles, see *Colen* v *Cebrian (UK) Ltd* (2003) at [23].) This is inevitable in view of the differing degrees of seriousness which can arise in illegality cases. (See Law Commission Consultation Paper, No 189, *The Illegality Defence: A Consultative Report*, 2009, at para. 3.52: 'to expect one set of detailed and ostensibly rigid rules to cater for all circumstances that may be encountered is overly ambitious'.) It is unlikely that the courts will apply a consistent set of rules regardless of how they view the impropriety in question. An interesting contrast to *St John Shipping Corpn* v *Joseph Rank Ltd* (1956) is provided by *Ashmore, Benson, Pease, & Co.* v *AV Dawson Ltd* (1973). The facts were:

Ashmores wished to have a twenty-five-ton 'tube-bank', which they had manufactured, transported from their works to a port for shipment. Ashmores' transport manager arranged for Dawsons, a small road haulage firm, to carry the tube-bank. He was also present when it was loaded on to one of Dawsons' vehicles, and he was familiar with the statutory regulations governing the transporting of loads on vehicles. Dawsons overloaded their vehicle in contravention of s 64(2) of the Road Traffic Act 1960, but Ashmores' manager raised no objection to their use of an inappropriate vehicle—the goods should have been carried on a 'low loader', but Dawsons did not have one. On the journey to the port, the vehicle toppled over, causing over £2,000 of damage to the tube-bank. Ashmores brought an action for damages against Dawsons.

At the trial the claimants gained judgment as the contract was lawful when made. But the Court of Appeal held that even if the contract was lawful at its inception, its performance was unlawful. Ashmores, through their manager, had participated in the illegality, since he had permitted the excessive loading of the vehicle. As a result of this participation, the claimants were debarred from claiming damages in respect of the accident which occurred.

Some general principles

15.65   Despite the hazards of attempting to deduce general principles from the decided cases on illegality, a few principles relating to the effects of illegality are summarized briefly in the sections which follow. It should be noted that the Law Commission stated recently that the present law is 'unnecessarily complex, uncertain, arbitrary and lacks transparency' (See Law Commission Consultation Paper, No 189, 2009, at para. 3.52.) Unless otherwise stated, these principles refer to contracts which are illegal at the outset.

An illegal contract is unenforceable by either party

15.66   It is generally accepted that where both parties participate equally in a transaction which is illegal in itself, then neither can enforce the agreement against the other. In a famous statement in *Holman* v *Johnson* (1775) 1 Cowp 341 at 343, Lord Mansfield stated that 'no court will lend its aid to a man who founds his cause of action upon an immoral or an illegal act'. This is a principle based on public policy and, as a result (somewhat oddly), it may enable the defendant to rely on the illegality or the immorality as a means of escaping liability under an agreement. It will be remembered in *Pearce* v *Brooks* (1866), that the claimant who hired a carriage to a prostitute, in the knowledge that it would in some way assist with her occupation, was unable to recover the hire charge when the defendant refused to pay. No cause of action could arise out of an illegal transaction of this type to which the claimant had contributed. (But see *Howard* v *Shirlstar Container Transport* (1990), in which the claimant was permitted to benefit from his illegal act—a breach of Nigerian air traffic control regulations—as such an outcome was held not to be an affront to public conscience.)

15.67   A slightly different problem arises where both parties are aware of a prohibition, but one of them can be regarded as more blameworthy than the other. If the purpose of the prohibition in question is to protect the public, the court may still decide that even the less culpable party is unable to enforce the illegal agreement. For example, in *Mohamed* v *Alaga & Co. (a firm)* [1999] 3 All ER 699, M claimed that he had an agreement with the defendant solicitors, under which he would introduce Somali asylum seekers to the solicitors and assist the solicitors (as a translator) in preparing their clients' cases. In return, the solicitors were to pay him a share of any fees received from the Legal Aid Board for acting on behalf of these clients. M's claim to enforce the agreement, which was contrary to r 7 of the Solicitors' Practice

Rules 1990, was rejected by the Court of Appeal, as it was an attempt to enforce an illegal contract. The court reached this conclusion despite the fact that the prohibition in question was imposed on solicitors, and it was they who faced professional penalties for breach of the rules. It was held that the public interest would not be protected if a non-solicitor could enforce such an agreement. However, the Court of Appeal held that M could succeed with his claim for a reasonable price for the work he carried out at the solicitors' request. The court thought that it was relevant here that, if the alleged agreement had been made, M's conduct was less blameworthy than that of the solicitors. (See the comments of Lord Bingham CJ at 707; see also the interesting discussion of both this and subsequent decisions, by the Law Commission: Law Commission Consultation Paper, No 189, *The Illegality Defence: A Consultative Report*, 2009, paras 4.21–4.28.)

Money or property transferred is not recoverable

15.68   A further general principle relates to property which is transferred under an illegal transaction. For example, in *Parkinson* v *College of Ambulance Ltd and Harrison* (1925) the claimant gave money to the defendant charity after receiving assurances from its secretary that it could arrange a knighthood for him. Having failed to receive the promised honour, the claimant tried to recover his money. Due to the illegality of the transaction, it was held that he was not entitled to the return of his money despite having been defrauded. There can be little surprise at such a result, for this seems to follow logically from the principle considered earlier. Both parties were equally involved in a transaction, which was illegal in itself, and therefore neither could enforce the agreement against the other.

15.69   But a slightly different problem occurred in *Belvoir Finance Co. Ltd* v *Stapleton* [1971] 1 QB 210. The facts were as follows:

> The claimant finance company (BF) were supplied with cars by a dealer which they, in turn, let on hire-purchase terms to the Belgravia Car (BC) hire company. All three parties were (to their knowledge) involved in an illegal transaction, as the contracts of sale and of hire were in breach of certain statutory regulations. BC fraudulently sold the cars to innocent buyers and then went into liquidation. BF sued the defendant, who was an assistant manager of BC and who had actually sold the cars, in conversion. His defence to this action was based on the argument that BF could not recover because of their own participation in the illegal transactions. For their part, BF needed to show that they were the owners of the cars at the time of the defendant's fraudulent disposal of them.

The Court of Appeal held, perhaps surprisingly, that the defendant was liable. It appeared to be prepared to overlook the illegality of the original contract under which BF bought the cars from the dealer, and it found that the cars belonged to the finance company. This conclusion was reached in spite of the fact that the cars had never been delivered to BF—the cars went directly from the dealer to the car hire company. In allowing the claimants to recover damages against the defendant it does seem that, despite protestations to the contrary (at 218), the Court of Appeal enforced an illegal contract.

Exceptions

15.70   It should be noted that there are exceptions to the general rule that money or other property transferred under an illegal transaction cannot be recovered. For example, if a party can make out his or her case quite independently of the illegal contract (i.e. based on some lawful ground), then he or she will be able to recover his or her money or property because, in so doing, he or she is not forced to rely on the illegality in question. (See *Amar Singh* v *Kulubya* (1964) for a neat illustration of this point.) For another, rather questionable example, it is instructive to consider *Bowmakers Ltd* v *Barnet Instruments Ltd* (1945). The facts were:

> The claimant company, Bowmakers, supplied certain machine tools to the defendants, Barnet Ltd, under three hire-purchase contracts. These contracts were illegal (or at least this was assumed by the court), as they were in breach of wartime ministerial regulations. The defendants, having failed to make all the hire-purchase payments which were due under the contracts, sold the tools which they had acquired under two of the contracts. In addition, they refused to return the remaining tools, which they held under the third contract, to the claimants. The defendants argued that the claimants had no remedy against them, because of the illegality of the three agreements.

The Court of Appeal held that the claimants' action for conversion (of all the goods) was successful despite the illegality of the transactions. It was argued that the claimants' action did not rely on the illegal hire-purchase contracts, but on the independent cause of action that they were the owners of the goods. This certainly explains why the claimants' action could succeed in relation to the goods which were sold by the defendants, but it is far from convincing in relation to the goods which were merely retained. In respect of these goods, which were not sold by the defendants, the court was surely allowing the claimants to succeed in an action which was based on an illegal transaction. The claimants' right to recovery of these goods was clearly based on the defendants' failure to make the payments that were agreed under an illegal hire-purchase contract. It might be argued, by way of defence of the court's decision, that it would have been unfair if the defendants had been able to hide behind the mere breach of a ministerial order as a means of escaping liability.[14]

15.71   The *Bowmakers Ltd* v *Barnet Instruments Ltd* (1945) approach was followed by the House of Lords in *Tinsley* v *Milligan* (1993), where the facts were:

> Two women, T and M, lived together in a house for which they jointly provided the money to buy. They agreed for the house to be in T's name only, so that M could make false claims for social security payments (from which they both benefited). They later quarrelled, and T claimed possession of the house. M argued that T held the house on trust for both of them in equal shares, but was her claim barred by her own illegal conduct?

The House of Lords, by a narrow majority, upheld the Court of Appeal's decision—that T held the property on trust for both of the parties in equal shares—but it relied on different reasoning.

---

14   See also *Saunders* v *Edwards* (1987).

The majority held that M did not need to rely on the illegality to support her claim. She needed only to show that she had contributed to the purchase price of the house and that there was an understanding between the parties that the house was jointly owned, i.e. that there was a resulting trust. In reaching their decision, the majority applied the principle established in *Bowmakers* v *Barnet*, enabling M's claim to succeed on what appear to be rather technical grounds. The judgment seems to take little account of the illegality of the claimant's conduct. (*Quaere*: Would a claimant whose conduct involved more serious offences than M's be allowed to succeed under similar circumstances—on a technicality—or would the court be forced to consider the public policy issues involved? See Lord Goff's dissenting views in *Tinsley* v *Milligan* at 79.)

The approach of the House of Lords has been criticized,[15] and perhaps the judgment of the Court of Appeal in *Tinsley* v *Milligan* is to be preferred. The Court of Appeal was prepared to assess the conduct of M to see whether it was so serious as to merit the penalty which would be incurred by the loss of her interest in the house; and, if it was not, whether the public conscience would be affronted by the success of her claim. It can be appreciated why the House of Lords had reservations about this more discretionary approach, with the uncertainty which would inevitably accompany it. The recent calls for reform to the illegality defence in trusts arose out of the 1964 House of Lords' decision. (See further Law Commission Report No 320, *The Illegality Defence* (2010), paras 1.15–1.33.)

15.72   Similar issues were raised in *Tribe* v *Tribe* (1995). In this case, C owned 459 out of 500 shares in a family company and he was the tenant of two leasehold properties which the company occupied as licensee. The landlord of the properties claimed against C for repairs and, if the claims were successful, C was faced with having to sell the company. In order to prevent this, C transferred his shares to one of his sons (D), a director of the company. It was never intended that the proposed price for the transfer should actually be paid and, indeed, D did not pay. Eventually, after satisfactory resolution of the disputes over the lease, C wanted to revert to the position which had existed before he was faced with claims for repair. However, D now refused to transfer the shares back to C, and C took action to recover them. The judge found that the illegal purpose of the transfer (i.e. to deceive C's creditors into thinking he was no longer the owner of the shares) had not been carried into effect in any way. As the claims over repairs were resolved, no deception of creditors was needed by C. The judge upheld C's claim for return of the shares and the Court of Appeal dismissed D's appeal. It appears that it was sufficient for C to withdraw voluntarily from the illegal transaction when it was no longer necessary, without any need to repent his illegal purpose (per Millet LJ in the Court of Appeal).

15.73   Another exception to the general rule about the irrecoverability of property transferred under an illegal contract is where the parties are not in pari delicto, i.e. where they are not equally guilty. In certain circumstances it may be possible for the court to allow the less culpable party to recover property that he has transferred to the other, more guilty party. If,

---

15   e.g., see N. Enonchong, 'Illegality: The Fading Flame of Public Policy' (1994) 14 OJLS 295.

for example, one party has entered into an unlawful agreement, having been defrauded by the other (or as a result of oppression), it is eminently sensible that the 'victim' should not be debarred from recovering property which has been transferred. It may not always be quite so easy, however, to decide whether one party is more culpable than the other. In *Kiriri Cotton Ltd* v *Dewani* (1960), for example:

> KC Ltd let a flat in Uganda for a term of seven years to Dewani, who paid a premium of Shs10,000. Although neither party realized they were breaking the law, the taking of a premium was, in fact, a breach of a government ordinance. This ordinance did not make any express provision that an illegal premium was recoverable by the tenant (in contrast to the analogous legislation in England). Dewani brought an action to recover the premium.

The Privy Council held that the premium was recoverable by the tenant, despite the lack of an express provision in the ordinance permitting this. It was clear that the statute was aimed at protecting a particular class of person from another, namely prospective tenants from landlords. So although both parties were unaware that they were breaking the law, the court was of the opinion that the duty of observing the law fell more heavily on the landlord than the tenant. Thus, despite appearances to the contrary, they were not in pari delicto. (Of course, some statutes make express provision to achieve this effect, in which case there is no need to rely on the common law principle.) The approach of the law was summed up by Lord Mansfield, in *Browning* v *Morris* (1778) 2 Cowp 790 at 792, in the following way:

> 'But, where contracts or transactions are prohibited by positive statutes, for the sake of protecting one set of men from another set of men; the one, from their situation and condition, being liable to be oppressed or imposed upon by the other; there, the parties are not in pari delicto; and in furtherance of these statutes, the person injured, after the transaction is finished and completed, may bring his action and defeat the contract.'

15.74   The scope of this principle was discussed in *Green* v *Portsmouth Stadium Ltd* [1953] 2 QB 190. The facts were:

> Frederick Green, a bookmaker, claimed that he had been overcharged by the defendants over a period of years, contrary to the provisions of s 13(1) of the Betting and Lotteries Act 1934. The defendants owned the Portsmouth Stadium greyhound racing track. Green alleged that although the highest charge which the defendants were authorized to make under s 13(1) was 11s 3d, he had been charged £2 each time he went on to the course. He now claimed from the defendants the excess fees which he had paid to them. He based his argument on the fact that he was not in pari delicto with the defendants and sought to rely on the dictum of Lord Mansfield.

The Court of Appeal held that the claimant was not able to recover the amounts that he had been overcharged by the defendants as the obligation imposed by the relevant statute was enforceable only by criminal proceedings. (The Act did not expressly provide for the recovery of any overcharge—it stated only that the person responsible for it was guilty of an offence.) This reasoning is not entirely convincing, but the court went on to reject Green's argument that he was not in pari delicto with the defendants. Lord Hodson (at 197) observed that the claimant had not proved that he was less guilty. He stated that, as far as the evidence went, Green seemed to have been 'as much a party to breaking [the law]' as the defendants.

15.75   A further exception to the general rule is where a party repents or withdraws before the contract has been substantially performed. (See *Tribe v Tribe* (1995), discussed earlier, and also the Law Commission Consultation Paper, No 189, *The Illegality Defence: A Consultative Report*, 2009, paras 4.45–4.59.) So where a party takes proceedings before the illegal purpose has been achieved, he may be allowed to recover property which he has transferred under the contract (for example, see *Taylor v Bowers* (1876)). But this raises the obvious problem of deciding whether the repentance has taken place at an early enough stage to allow recovery. How will a court decide whether matters have progressed too far? The first requirement, if the claimant is to succeed, is to show that it is a genuine case of repentance, i.e. that he has chosen to abandon the illegal purpose. If he has no choice in the matter due to the other party's failure to perform, he will not be allowed to recover (see *Bigos v Bousted* (1951)). The second requirement relates to the time at which the repentance takes place in relation to the progress of the illegal purpose (see *Ouston v Zurowski* (1985)).[16] Where the illegal purpose has been accomplished it is obvious that recovery will not be allowed. But it also appears that even where the illegal agreement has been only partly performed, recovery will not be permitted if the illegal purpose has been substantially achieved. For example, in *Kearley v Thomson* (1890) 24 QBD 742:

> The defendant firm of solicitors was to act on behalf of a petitioning creditor against a bankrupt named Clarke. The claimant, a friend of Clarke's, agreed to pay the defendants their costs, in return for which they would neither appear at the public examination of Clarke, nor oppose his order of discharge. The solicitors, on receiving the promised payment, did not appear at Clarke's public examination, in accordance with their illegal agreement with the claimant. But the claimant changed his mind before any application was made for the bankrupt's discharge, and he tried to recover the money which he had paid to the defendants.

It was held by the Court of Appeal that he could not recover the money. The illegality of the agreement was that it was aimed at interfering with the course of justice. As this purpose had already been substantially achieved, the repentance came too late. In the words of Fry LJ (at 747):

> '[W]here there has been a partial carrying into effect of an illegal purpose in a substantial manner, it is impossible, though there remains something not performed, that the money paid under that illegal contract can be recovered back.'

---

16 *Ouston v Zurowski* (1985). In this Canadian case one party was entitled to recover under an illegal contract because he repented before performance of the contract, i.e. by not carrying into effect the illegal purpose (a 'pyramid' scheme) in a substantial manner before abandoning the scheme.

Related transactions between the parties

15.76   The parties to an illegal contract may also enter into a subsequent agreement which is based on the illegal transaction. In this case, the later agreement will also be tainted by the illegal purpose of the original contract. So if one party owes another money under an illegal contract, and he gives some security in respect of the money which is due, this will be unenforceable against him by the other party. In *Fisher* v *Bridges* (1854), for example, C agreed to sell, and subsequently conveyed, land to D for a purpose which was illegal. The defendant still owed some money to C under the transaction and he executed a deed by which he promised payment of the outstanding sum. It was held that such a deed was unenforceable as it was tainted by the illegality of the main transaction. This is hardly surprising, for if the law refuses to enforce the original contract, it follows that any subsequent agreement which springs from this should be treated in the same way.

15.77   A separate issue (not to be confused with the above rule) is where the courts allow one party a remedy against the other, despite the illegality of their contract, under a 'collateral' contract. We have seen, in other areas of contract law, how this device is sometimes used by the courts to enable a fair solution to be reached when it would otherwise be precluded by some substantive principle of law. Here it is used so as to enable the innocent party to sue the guilty party under an illegal transaction without relying on the transaction itself. An instructive case is *Strongman (1945) Ltd* v *Sincock* (1955):

> The claimant building company contracted with the defendant, an architect, to modernize some houses. An appropriate licence was required from the Ministry of Works so that the refurbishment did not contravene statutory regulations; without such a licence the contract was illegal. The defendant promised the claimants, before the contract was made, that he would take responsibility for securing the necessary licences. The claimants carried out work which exceeded £6,000 in value. But the defendant had obtained licences for only £2,150. The defendant paid only £2,900 to the builders and he argued that the performance of the contract was illegal. The builders sued for the unpaid sum.

The Court of Appeal held that, despite the illegality of the main transaction, the builders could succeed on the basis of the collateral promise made by the defendant that he would obtain the necessary licences for the work. Presumably it was thought that the work was carried out by the builders on the understanding that he had in fact done as he promised. Although the conclusion reached by the court was desirable, there is, in truth, some difficulty in distinguishing this case from *Re Mahmoud and Ispahani* (1921) (discussed at para. **15.49**). It should be added that this judicial device will be used to assist the 'innocent' party in very limited circumstances.

Illegal performance of lawful contracts

15.78   A contract may not be unlawful in itself, but one of the parties to the agreement may perform the contract in an illegal manner, without the other knowing of this. This was basically the situation in *Archbold's (Freightage) Ltd* v *Spanglett Ltd* (1961) where, it will be remembered, the illegality of the defendants' use of their vehicle did not debar the claimants from recovering damages. Archbold's were innocent of any knowledge of the illegality and the contract (for the carriage of goods by road) was not illegal in itself. Of course, the guilty party will normally be in a different position, and will not be able to sue successfully as a result of his illegal performance. If both parties participate in the illegal performance of the contract, then it is likely that both will find themselves without a remedy (see *Ashmore, Benson, Pease, & Co.* v *A V Dawson Ltd* (1973)).

15.79   The contrast between the positions of the innocent and the guilty party is well illustrated by *Marles* v *Philip Trant & Sons Ltd* (1954):

> The claimant, a farmer, bought wheat from the defendant seed merchants. The defendants believed the goods to be 'spring' wheat (having bought them under that misdescription from a third party) and they were described as such to the claimant. In fact, it was not 'spring' wheat which they sold to the farmer. The performance of the contract was illegal due to the fact that the defendants were in breach of a statute for failing to deliver an invoice with the goods. Did the illegality affect the claimant's right to damages?

It was held that the contract was not illegal in itself, but only in the manner of its performance. The farmer was the innocent party and he was, therefore, not prevented from succeeding in his action for damages.

Proposals for reform

15.80   It is clear from the previous sections that the courts are not always consistent in their application of the common law principles relating to the enforcement of illegal agreements, resulting in a body of case law which is complex and far from satisfactory. The House of Lords' decision in *Tinsley* v *Milligan* (1993) (see the discussion at para. **15.71**) illustrates the way in which technical legal arguments may lead to an avoidance of the consideration of wider issues of policy and justice. Furthermore, a recurring problem faced by the court is how to signify its disapproval of an illegal agreement without allowing one party to be unjustly enriched or advantaged at the expense of the other. (See the discussion at para. **15.67** of *Mohamed* v *Alaga & Co. (a firm)* (1999).)

15.81   There have been two recent Law Commission Consultation Papers on this subject and in 2010 the Law Commission published its final recommendations (see *The Illegality Defence*, Report No 320, 2010).[17] The first Consultation Paper, in 1999, concluded that there is a need for legislative reform of this area of law and recommended, provisionally, that the existing rules relating to the effects of illegality should be replaced by a discretion.[18] Such a discretion would

---

17 Law Commission Consultation Paper, No 154, *Illegal Transactions: The Effect of Illegality on Contracts and Trusts*, 1999 and Law Commission Consultation Paper, No 189, *The Illegality Defence: A Consultative Report*, 2009.

18 Law Com No 154, para. 9.1.

enable a court to decide whether to enforce an illegal agreement, to recognize that property rights have been transferred or created by it, or to hold that benefits conferred under the agreement are recoverable.[19] In this Paper, the Law Commission favoured a structured discretion, in the interests of greater certainty and to provide guidance to the courts. It provisionally recommended that, in the exercise of its discretion, the court should have regard to:

'(i)   the seriousness of the illegality involved;

(ii)   the knowledge and intention of the party seeking to enforce the illegal transaction, seeking the recognition of legal or equitable rights under it, or seeking to recover benefits conferred under it;

(iii) whether refusing to allow standard rights and remedies would deter illegality;

(iv)   whether refusing to allow standard rights and remedies would further the purpose of the rule which renders the transaction illegal; and

(v)   whether refusing to allow standard rights and remedies would be proportionate to the illegality involved.'[20]

15.82 However, in its more recent Consultation Paper, the Law Commission concluded that legislation was not needed (Consultation Paper, No 189, 2009, para. 3.122), and that in most areas the 'courts could reach the desired result through development of the case law' (Consultation Paper, No 189, paras 1.5 and 3.108. For a critique of its proposals, see P. Davies, 'The Illegality Defence—Two Steps Forward, One Step Back?' (2009) Conv & PL 182). In relation to contract, unjust enrichment and tort claims it was thought that the courts would be able to rationalize and develop the law in a satisfactory way (paras 1.6 and 3.123), and that any reform which is necessary 'can be safely left to incremental case law development' (para. 3.124). It argued that, despite the complexity of the relevant legal rules, the courts have generally managed to reach a just conclusion in the majority of cases (para. 3.125). In assessing how the courts have achieved this, the Law Commission thought that judges, despite the so-called rules, 'do in fact take into consideration a whole variety of factors which ensure that relief is only denied where it is a fair and proportionate response to the claimant's conduct' (para. 3.125). It thought that these 'factors', which relate to the policies underpinning the illegality doctrine, should be given greater prominence and be 'openly weighed and considered' (para. 3.125; some of these factors are discussed at paras 3.126–3.135). It stated that the present legal rules in this area are sometimes circumvented, 'so as to give better effect to the underlying policies as they apply to the facts' of each case, and that it would be preferable if this was explained more openly by the courts in their judgments (para. 3.140). The Consultation Paper recommended (at para. 3.142):

'. . . that the courts should consider in each case whether the application of the illegality defence can be justified on the basis of the policies that underlie that defence. These

---

19 Law Com No 154, para. 1.18 and paras 7.2–7.26.

20 Law Com No 154, para. 1.19 and paras 7.27–7.43. Note that this proposed discretion was not to apply where there were express statutory provisions relating to the effect of illegality on a transaction. The Law Commission also made it clear in its 2009 Report that it did not recommend any legislative reform in relation to 'statutory illegality' (Law Commission Consultation Paper, No 189, para. 3.102).

> include: (a) furthering the purpose of the rule which the illegal conduct has infringed; (b) consistency; (c) that the claimant should not profit from his or her own wrong; (d) deterrence; and (e) maintaining the integrity of the legal system. Against those policies must be weighed the legitimate expectation of the claimant that his or her legal rights will be protected. Ultimately a balancing exercise is called for which weighs up the application of the various policies at stake. Only when depriving the claimant of his or her rights is a proportionate response based on the relevant illegality policies, should the defence succeed. The judgment should explain the basis on which it has done so.'

15.83 The final recommendations of the Law Commission (Report No 320, 2010) follow the provisional recommendations set out in the 2009 Consultation Paper. It notes that the two recent House of Lords cases involving the illegality defence, namely *Gray* v *Thames Trains* (2009) and *Stone & Rolls* v *Moore Stephens* (2009) 'show that the law is developing in the way we had hoped' (para. 1.11). It concludes that 'the recent case law shows that the courts have become more open in explaining the policy reasons behind the illegality defence' and for this reason, 'in most areas of law, think that the illegality defence should be left to developments in common law' (para. 1.8). The final Report therefore does 'not recommend legislative reform in relation to the illegality defence as it applies to claims for breach of contract, tort or unjust enrichment' (para. 3.41).

15.84 However, the Law Commission concludes that statutory reform is required in one area: i.e. to deal with cases where a trust has been set up in order to conceal the true ownership for unlawful purposes, because of the binding authority of the House of Lords' decision in *Tinsley* v *Milligan* (discussed earlier). The Law Commission referred to the widespread criticism of *Tinsley* v *Milligan*, but felt that it was not possible for the lower courts to evade this decision. For this reason, the Law Commission prepared a draft Bill 'to provide the courts with a discretion to determine the effect of illegality on a limited class of trust (para. 4.2). (For further discussion, see P. Davies, 'The Illegality Defence: Turning Back the Clock' (2010) Conv & PL 282.) The Draft Trusts (Concealment of Interests) Bill was attached to the Final Report of 2010 but in its 2012 Report on the implementation of Law Commission proposals the Government announced that 'reform of this area of the law cannot be considered a pressing priority for the Government at present' and therefore they 'are minded not to implement the Commission's proposals'.

Summary

- An otherwise valid agreement may contravene a legal rule or be deemed contrary to public policy.
- There is a variety of reasons for statutory and judicial intervention on the basis of 'illegality'.
- It is conventional to make a distinction between 'void' and 'illegal' contracts (i.e. on the basis of the legal consequences of the contract).

- Contracts in restraint of trade are void prima facie, but may become valid if they can be justified as reasonable between the parties and not against the public interest.

- Other contracts that are void at common law on the grounds of public policy include contracts to oust the jurisdiction of the courts, and contracts undermining the status of marriage.

- Examples of agreements where issues of 'illegality' have been raised include: contracts to commit an unlawful act; contracts promoting sexual immorality; contracts that prejudice the interests of the state; contracts prejudicial to the administration of justice; and contracts promoting corruption in public life.

- It is difficult to generalize about the legal consequences of illegality as much depends on the nature of the illegal agreement and the state of mind of the contracting parties.

- Despite the difficulty in formulating precise rules about the effects of illegality, there are some general principles that may be applied by the courts.

- There have been two Law Commission Consultation Papers on this subject. The first (in 1999) concluded that legislative reform is necessary in this area of law. However, the more recent one (2009) concluded that legislation was not needed as 'the courts could reach the desired result through the development of the case law'. This position was confirmed in the 2010 Final Report.

Further reading

R. Buckley, *Illegality and Public Policy*, Sweet & Maxwell, 2009

R. Buckley, 'Illegal Transactions: Chaos or Discretion?' (2000) 20 LS 155

P. Creighton, 'The Recovery of Property Transferred for Illegal Purposes' (1997) 60 MLR 102

P. Davies, 'The Illegality Defence: Turning Back the Clock' (2010) 4 Conv & PL 282

P. Davies, 'The Illegality Defence—Two Steps Forward, One Step Back?' (2009) 73 Conv & PL 182

N. Enonchong, 'Illegality: The Fading Flame of Public Policy' (1994) 14 OJLS 295

Law Commission Consultation Paper, No 154, 'Illegal Transactions: The Effect of Illegality on Contracts and Trusts', 1999

Law Commission Consultation Paper, No 189, 'The Illegality Defence: A Consultative Report', 2009

Law Commission Final Report, No 320, The Illegality Defence, 2010

R. Nolan, 'When Principles Collide' (2009) 125 LQR 374

S. Smith, 'Reconstructing Restraint of Trade' (1995) 15 OJLS 565

P. Watts, 'Illegality and Agency Law: Authorising Illegal Action' (2011) 3 JBL 213

Chapter 16

Unconscionability and unfairness

⊙ Introduction

16.1   The law of contract has to tread a delicate path between two distinct and often opposing ideas. On the one hand, the law supports the freedom on the part of the individual to enter into a contract of his or her choosing without unnecessary judicial or statutory interference. On the other, the law does not wish to see one party to a contract take unfair advantage of the other by virtue of either his or her own superior bargaining strength, or the other's weakness. It is often stated that our law does not possess a general doctrine of 'unconscionability',[1] and that such a doctrine would be injurious to predictability and certainty. As we have seen in earlier chapters, the law seeks stability in matters of commercial activity, and it does not favour general doctrines which offer too wide a basis for judicial interference with the bargains reached by the parties.[2] The 'classical' view of contract law has fostered the idea of freedom of contract and the law has taken an essentially objective view of agreement. In other words, it is not primarily concerned with the fairness of exchange between the parties so long as they have, to outward appearances, reached agreement. It is not for the courts to intervene simply because one party has made a poor bargain. To this extent it is true to say that (formally) the law of contract has not been concerned, traditionally, with the substantive fairness of a transaction.[3]

16.2   The law is, of course, concerned with procedural fairness. Therefore, a contract may be set aside for such reasons as fraud, misrepresentation, duress, or undue influence. This approach has been likened to the conduct of a game, in that the law ensures that the rules are

---

1   e.g. see *Thames Trains Ltd* v *Adams* (2006) at [31].

2   For an illustration, see *Union Eagle Ltd* v *Golden Achievement Ltd* [1997] 2 All ER 215 (and the comments of Lord Hoffmann at 218).

3   But see S. Smith, 'In Defence of Substantive Fairness' (1996) 112 LQR 138.

fair but it does not try to interfere with the outcome (or result) once the basic rules have been followed. This may well represent the theory behind the law, but it is difficult to accept that it is a reflection of reality. For, in reality, judges have used a variety of techniques ensure a fair outcome when one party appears to have exploited some unfair advantage.[4] We should not be misled by what judges say they are doing. It is what they actually do which is important.

16.3   In practice, in some cases, in order to achieve a fair result, a judge may rely on equitable doctrines, or on techniques of construction and interpretation of contracts; he or she may imply terms, or he or she may refuse certain remedies. It is misleading to argue that issues of unconscionability or unfairness will form no part of judicial thinking when contemplating the use of such powers and doctrines. Judges may even make overt reference to the issue of unconscionability as a factor in reaching a particular conclusion.[5] 'Despite lip service to the notion of absolute freedom of contract, relief is every day given against agreements that are unfair, inequitable, unreasonable, or oppressive'.[6] This vigilance on the part of judges using their common law and equitable powers helps to ensure that freedom of contract and 'objectivity' are not seriously abused.

16.4   Such intervention is, of its very nature, both piecemeal and unpredictable. In some areas where the problem of unfairness was especially pressing, such as in relation to the use of unfair exemption clauses, judicial attempts at 'policing' have been augmented and largely superseded by statutory change. Thus the Unfair Contract Terms Act 1977 represented a significant move towards controlling the fairness of certain types of contractual terms and, subsequently, the EC Directive on Unfair Terms in Consumer Contracts was also introduced to regulate unfair terms in non-negotiated contracts between consumers and businesses (see earlier discussion in **Chapters 10** and **11**). But such legislative developments, whilst very important in themselves, have not brought to an end the need for common law and equitable principles which promote fairness and prevent unconscionable bargains.

16.5   This introduction would not be complete without a warning about judicial pronouncements on the existence, or absence, of some general principle relating to unconscionable contracts. Our law of contract stresses certainty and stability, so it tends to discourage statements of general (and uncertain) application to the effect that the courts have a general power to 'police' agreements on the ground of unconscionability. (This is in contrast to such general statements as are contained in the USA's Uniform Commercial Code, s 2–302, for example.) Although attempts have been made to assert a general principle, most notably by Lord Denning in *Lloyds Bank Ltd* v *Bundy* [1974] 3 All ER 757 (at 765), these have tended to encounter opposition from other senior judges. So Lord Denning's assertion of such a principle was criticized in the House of Lords by Lord Scarman in *National Westminster Bank plc* v *Morgan* [1985] 1 All ER 821 at 830. (We shall return to this later.)

---

4   e.g. see *Silvertone Records* v *Mountfield* (1993).

5   e.g. see *Backhouse* v *Backhouse* (1978); *Cresswell* v *Potter* (1978); *Watkin* v *Watson-Smith* (1986); *Boustany* v *Pigott* (1993); and *Commission for the New Towns* v *Cooper (GB) Ltd* (1995).

6   S. Waddams, 'Unconscionability in Contracts' (1976) 39 MLR 369 at 390.

Examples of judicial intervention to prevent unfairness

16.6 This section contains a brief account of some of the areas in which questions of unfairness and unconscionability have influenced the courts.

16.7 We saw in **Chapter 4** that the courts are not supposed to be concerned with the adequacy of consideration so long as the consideration is 'sufficient' in a legal sense. The theory is that it is not for the courts to make bargains for the parties, who are free to agree to whatever exchange they wish, no matter how one-sided, so long as there is no procedural unfairness (such as fraud or duress). This may be a perfectly reasonable approach where the parties, knowing of the technical requirement of consideration, agree to some nominal consideration; or where the apparent inadequacy of the consideration is offset by some other benefit which the parties were presumably aware of when contracting (see *Mountford* v *Scott* (1975)). It is also true to say that the courts will not intervene simply because someone has paid a higher price for goods than they need have done; the courts are not regarded as the appropriate place for controlling prices or fair exchange. But the fact that the courts are not concerned (formally) with the adequacy of the consideration does not mean that they will take no interest in a case where the exchange between the parties is extremely unfair. The courts share the ordinary person's intuitive dislike of injustice and judges will use whatever techniques are available to avoid an unconscionable result.[7] For example, in *Boustany* v *Pigott* (1993), P (who was elderly) granted B a renewal of a lease on terms which were very favourable to B. It appeared that B took advantage of P in a number of ways, before and at the time of the agreement, and with full knowledge that her behaviour was unconscionable. The Privy Council set aside the lease because of B's unconscionable conduct. It was held that B had clearly abused her position in relation to P, by exploiting P's incapacity.

16.8 A good illustration of judicial flexibility is provided by *Backhouse* v *Backhouse* [1978] 1 All ER 1158, where the facts were:

> A husband (H) and wife (W) bought a house in their joint names with the help of a mortgage. W left the matrimonial home and went to live with another man. H persuaded his wife to sign an agreement which transferred the house into his sole name. Although no duress was used, H did not advise his wife to seek independent legal advice. In exchange for signing the document of transfer W received only a release from her liability under the mortgage. (She signed because of a sense of guilt towards H.) The couple was divorced and both of them remarried. As a result of an increase in property values, the house was soon worth much more than when they bought it. W applied, inter alia, for a lump sum order and a property transfer order in respect of the former matrimonial home.

---

7 In *Watkin* v *Watson-Smith* (1986) Times, 3 July a contract for the sale of a house at a serious undervalue was set aside on the grounds of mistake. The judge held that he would have set the contract aside as an unconscionable bargain, had it been necessary to do so. (In this case it was the old age and lack of judgement of the vendor, together with his desire for a quick sale, which produced the unconscionable agreement.)

This is an interesting case. In a strict (or objective) sense, the contract was freely entered into; it is not a case of procedural unfairness. The exchange also met the technical requirement of consideration provided by both parties. But looking at the case from a more realistic point of view it is immediately obvious that the whole transaction was extremely unfair. Due to a sense of guilt, or emotional strain, the wife entered into an agreement (without legal advice) from which she derived very little material value. The indemnity against liability on the mortgage was virtually worthless in practice, as the value of the house was rising considerably. If the Family Division of the High Court had adopted the traditional view, there could be little reason for granting the wife relief from her very bad bargain. However, Balcombe J held that having regard to the wife's contribution to the purchase of the house, it would be repugnant to justice to deprive her of all interest in it. Accordingly, she was granted a share in the capital asset (the house) which she had helped to create, but she was not to benefit from any increase in value in the house occurring after her departure. The husband was ordered to pay her a lump sum of £3,500.

16.9 In *Backhouse* v *Backhouse* the judge specifically asked whether the agreement was unconscionable.[8] In answering that question, he was prepared to consider the inadequacy of the consideration and subjective factors about the parties. He said (at 1165–6):

> '[The wife] was given no value for her transfer, merely the release from her liability on the mortgage, and she received no independent advice...When a marriage has broken down, both parties are liable to be in an emotional state. The party remaining in the matrimonial home, as the husband did in this case, has an advantage.'

16.10 Despite the general rule about the courts' lack of interest in the adequacy of the consideration, there are other well-known examples of the courts intervening for this very reason. Some of these decisions can also be rationalized on other grounds which do less violence to traditional theory, but this should not mean that sight is lost of questions of unfair exchange being to the fore. In *Lloyds Bank Ltd* v *Bundy* [1974] 3 All ER 757:

> Herbert Bundy was an elderly farmer. His only financial asset was his farmhouse. His son, Michael, ran a company which had run into financial difficulty; its account at Lloyds Bank was overdrawn. Herbert Bundy, who also banked at Lloyds, guaranteed his son's company's overdraft by charging his house to the bank. The son's plant-hire business deteriorated further, and the bank was not prepared to maintain Michael Bundy's overdraft without additional security. The new assistant bank manager, together with Michael Bundy, went to see Herbert Bundy to explain that the bank's financial support of the son's company would be withdrawn unless he was prepared to extend his guarantee of the son's overdraft. In effect, the old man would have to increase the charge on his farmhouse to £11,000, which was slightly more than its value, in return for which the bank merely promised not to withdraw the son's overdraft facilities for the time being. The bank manager gave Herbert Bundy a partial explanation of what was wrong with the son's company, but was unable to go into detail. Herbert Bundy, who was not independently advised at

---

8 He also referred to the similar case of *Cresswell* v *Potter* (1978) where an agreement between a husband and wife was set aside, largely on the basis of its unconscionability.

the meeting, signed the relevant documents there and then. Six months later the bank withdrew its support of the company, which was still in trouble, and proceeded to enforce the charge and guarantee against Herbert Bundy. The bank sought to evict the old man from his farmhouse.

The Court of Appeal set aside the guarantee and charge signed by Herbert Bundy, allowing his appeal against the trial judge's decision. Although his colleagues preferred to base their decision on the narrower ground of undue influence, Lord Denning asserted a much wider principle to justify a finding in favour of Herbert Bundy. The general principle which he outlined is considered later, together with the views of his critics, but it is significant that he referred specifically (at 765) to the fact that 'the consideration moving from the bank was grossly inadequate'. He observed that although the agreement conferred a considerable benefit on the bank, there was a marked absence of corresponding benefit to either the old man or his son's company: 'All that the company gained was a short respite from impending doom.' In short, it was an unconscionable agreement.

16.11   Similarly, in *Schroeder Music Publishing Co. Ltd* v *Macaulay* [1974] 3 All ER 616, the House of Lords held an agreement to be unenforceable, as an unreasonable restraint of trade, when a music publishing company engaged the exclusive services of a young songwriter. The claimant gave the company the copyright of all his compositions for the next five years, but on terms that were extremely disadvantageous to him. The restrictions in the agreement, combined a lack of obligation on the company's part with a total commitment on the claimant's part. In reaching their conclusion, the judges were clearly mindful of the inadequacy of the consideration provided by the company. Lord Diplock went further than the other judges by observing that what was in issue was not some nineteenth-century economic theory about the public interest in freedom of trade, but 'the protection of those whose bargaining power is weak against being forced by those whose bargaining power is stronger to enter into bargains that are unconscionable' (at 623).[9]

16.12   Although the restraint of trade doctrine is traditionally discussed in terms of the public interest (see **Chapter 15**), it is evident that the issue of fairness will frequently be influential in courts' decisions on this subject. The requirement that the restraint clause must be reasonable between the parties gives a judge the opportunity to assess the unconscionability of a particular agreement. Obviously the fairness of the exchange—i.e. the adequacy or generosity of the consideration—may determine whether a particular restraint is reasonable in the circumstances. Therefore, if one party has agreed not to compete with the other, but has received little material advantage in return for such an undertaking, then the court may be more disposed towards holding the restraint to be unreasonable and unenforceable.

16.13   To take a different example, an agreement might appear fair but may be capable of operating in an unfair or oppressive way. In *Shell UK* v *Lostock Garage Ltd* [1977] 1 All ER 481, for instance, the facts were as follows:

L Ltd was a small garage which was tied to Shell under the terms of a solus agreement made in 1955. This required L to sell only Shell's petrol. The agreement, which could be terminated by

---

9   See also *Silvertone Records* v *Mountfield* (1993) and *Zang Tumb Tuum Records* v *Johnson* (1993).

> twelve months' notice, worked well until the oil crisis in the mid-1970s, when there occurred a petrol 'price war'. L had to compete with four neighbouring garages—two were Shell garages and two were 'free'. The two garages not tied to Shell cut their prices and Shell then introduced a support scheme which effectively subsidized the other two garages. L's garage was excluded from the scheme and was forced to trade at a loss, since it was unable to compete with the neighbouring garages. To meet the competition, L obtained petrol from another supplier, M. Shell threatened M with proceedings for inducing breach of contract and M stopped supplying L, which was then forced to resume taking its petrol from Shell. In the resulting legal action, L claimed that it was no longer tied to Shell under the solus agreement. Shell brought an action against L claiming, inter alia, damages for breach by L of the agreement because L took petrol from another supplier. L defended this claim by arguing that the agreement was unenforceable as being an unreasonable restraint of trade; alternatively, that the agreement was subject to an implied term by Shell that they would not discriminate against L in favour of competing and neighbouring garages.

The case gave rise to widely differing judicial views about the relevant issues, and it is not possible to consider all aspects of the decision here. It was held by the majority that Shell were not in breach of the solus agreement by operating the support scheme, there being no implied term that Shell should not discriminate against L. But Shell's claim for an injunction restraining L from breaking the tie provision was refused, with a variety of reasons being offered by the judges. For example, it would not have been just or equitable to grant Shell an injunction restraining L from breaking the tie provision whilst Shell were operating the support scheme and excluding L from it, as the scheme operated to L's prejudice. Therefore Shell could not enforce the tie provision whilst the support scheme was operating. Lord Denning commented (at 490):

> '[The tie] appeared superficially to be fair and reasonable at the time of the contract... but, at the end of 1975, Shell started to subsidise two neighbouring Shell garages to such an extent that they were able to, and did, undercut Lostock... To insist on the tie in these circumstances... was most unfair and unreasonable. So much that I think the courts should decline to enforce it. At any rate, they should not enforce it so long as Shell operated their support scheme to the prejudice of Lostock.'

16.14 A further example of the relevance of unconscionable behaviour can be found in *Foley* v *Classique Coaches* [1934] 2 KB 1. C agreed to sell a piece of land to D, but this contract was conditional upon D (who ran a motor coach business) entering into a separate agreement under which C would supply all of D's petrol 'at a price to be agreed by the parties... from time to time'. An arbitration clause in the 'petrol' contract provided for the resolution of any disputes which might arise in the performance of the petrol agreement. After the conveyance of the land, D bought petrol from C for three years but then tried to argue that he was not bound because the agreement was too uncertain and that, furthermore, it was an unreasonable restraint of trade. The Court of Appeal rejected D's arguments and held that there was a binding contract. Scrutton LJ was clearly influenced by D's conduct, which appeared to have been unconscionable. It would have been unfair to allow D to escape from his contractual obligation to buy C's petrol, having obtained a good deal on the purchase of the land in the first place. Scrutton LJ stated (at 7) that he was glad to decide the case in C's favour as he did 'not regard [D's] contention as an honest one'.

16.15   The discretion of a court to grant the equitable remedy of rectification in cases of mistake in the recording of agreements may also be influenced by the unconscionable behaviour of one of the parties (see **Chapter 12**). In *Commission for the New Towns v Cooper (GB) Ltd* (1995) the unconscionable conduct of the defendant was a vital issue in the Court of Appeal holding that rectification can be granted in cases of unilateral mistake.

16.16   Another area of contract law where the courts have taken a close interest in questions of fairness is in relation to the use of exemption or exclusion clauses. This topic has been discussed in detail in **Chapters 9** and **10**, but a few brief points need to be made here. It will be remembered that a party will use an exemption clause to exclude or limit his or her liability for, inter alia, breach of contract. This may be an entirely reasonable practice between two equal parties and it may simply be a means of allocating risk and indicating which of them should take out insurance cover. By limiting liability, one party may be able to provide cheaper services as a result, and for this reason the other party may choose to contract with him or her. (See, for example, *Photo Production Ltd v Securicor Transport Ltd* (1980)).[10]

16.17   But there are other situations where the exemption clauses may be very unreasonable. The stronger party imposes his or her terms on the weaker one, and unreasonably, and unfairly, limits or excludes liability. As we have seen the courts were willing to 'strain' construction to prevent such exclusion clauses protecting the party in breach, and also to inhibit the incorporation of unusual or unreasonable clauses by means of the 'red hand rule' (see **Chapter 9**).

16.18   Of course, since the enactment of the Unfair Contract Terms Act 1977, the courts have not needed to draw on the common law so much to deal with unreasonable exemption clauses, but this should not obscure the general point which is being made here that the courts, faced with unjust or unconscionable agreements (or terms), may develop techniques to help them prevent an unfair outcome.

16.19   Further, although we have tended to refer to unconscionability, we should also give some thought to the idea of good faith. In *Interfoto Picture Library Ltd v Stiletto Visual Programmes Ltd* [1989] 2 QB 433, Bingham LJ did not view the red hand rule in terms of unconscionability, as such, but the similar idea of good faith. He said (at 439):

'In many civil law systems, and perhaps in most legal systems outside the common law world, the law of obligations recognises and enforces an overriding principle that in making and carrying out contracts parties should act in good faith.... English law has, characteristically, committed itself to no such overriding principle but has developed piecemeal solutions in response to demonstrated problems of unfairness.'

---

10 See generally the test of reasonableness under the Unfair Contract Terms Act 1977 in **Chapter 10**.

Cases like *Errington v Errington and Woods* (1952) (see para. **2.66**), *Blackpool and Fylde Aero Club Ltd v Blackpool Borough Council* (1990) (see para. **2.15**) and *Harvela Investments Ltd v Royal Trust Co. of Canada* (1984) (see para **2.14**), have been seen as explicable in terms of good faith.[11]

16.20 Of course, if those three cases are viewed as examples of the common law covertly policing good faith, then it is pre-contractual good faith which is in question, and it must be conceded that that is an idea which the House of Lords has found itself particularly at odds with, in relation to both uncertainty, and the undermining of the boundary between negotiation and contract. In *Walford v Miles* [1992] 2 AC 128 at 138, Lord Atkin said:

> '[T]he concept of a duty to carry on negotiations in good faith is inherently repugnant to the adversarial position of the parties when involved in negotiations. Each party to the negotiations is entitled to pursue his (or her) own interest, so long as he avoids making misrepresentations. To advance that interest he must be entitled, if he thinks it appropriate, to threaten to withdraw from further negotiations or to withdraw in fact, in the hope that the opposite party may seek to reopen the negotiations by offering him improved terms.'

Again, the concerns about certainty are seen to stand in the way of a general doctrine, but, as has been indicated, specific examples which may best be explained by such an underlying idea, can be found.[12]

16.21 However, as Bingham LJ's dictum indicated, good faith is not just about pre-contract, but also performance, and in that situation there is, at least no concern about the boundary between negotiation and obligation. There will of course, still be major concerns about uncertainty, but again examples can be found from cases already mentioned in this chapter, and others, and it should be noted that recently, in *Yam Seng Pte Ltd v International Trade Corporation Ltd* (2013) the court was prepared to imply a term explicitly requiring to good faith in relation to an aspect of the performance. This will be returned to below in relation to trends towards a general principle.[13]

A general doctrine?

16.22 In a commercial context, between parties who contract on an equal footing, the classical (or laissez-faire) approach has the obvious advantage of certainty, and the courts will be wary of introducing a general discretion to relieve against hardship. This is well illustrated in the case of *Union Eagle Ltd v Golden Achievement Ltd* [1997] 2 All ER 215. The case involved a written contract in which the appellant purchaser (P) agreed to buy a flat in Hong Kong from the respondent vendor (V) and paid a 10 per cent deposit to V. It was a term of the agreement that

---

11 See e.g. M. Furmston and G. J. Tolhurst, *Contract Formation—Law and Practice*, Oxford University Press, ch. 12.

12 See e.g. the consideration of the postal rule in E. Macdonald, 'Dispatching the dispatch rule? The postal rule, e-mail, revocation and implied terms' [2013] Web Journal of Current Legal Issues (2).

13 Of course, at much the same time, an express term dealing with good faith was being narrowly construed in *Compass Group UK and Ireland Ltd v Mid Essex Hospital Services* (2013).

completion was to be effected before 5.00pm on 30 September 1991, and that time was of the essence in this respect. The agreement provided that P would forfeit the deposit in the event of failure to comply with any term or condition of the contract. P was ten minutes late in attempting to complete the transaction and was told by V that the contract would be rescinded and the deposit forfeited. P's action for specific performance was dismissed by the Hong Kong Court of Appeal, but P appealed to the Privy Council, arguing that P was entitled to relief against forfeiture of the deposit. The Privy Council dismissed the appeal. It stated that it was important to uphold V's right to rescind, in view of P's breach of an essential condition as to time. This right to rescind allowed V to know his position with certainty and that he was entitled to resell the flat. In delivering the judgment of the court, Lord Hoffmann (at 218) rejected the suggestion that there was an unlimited discretion to relieve against hardship by imposing a fair solution in this type of case. The stipulation as to time was of great importance and P was, regrettably, late. The court held that it was irrelevant that he was only slightly late. Lord Hoffmann stated (at 218):

'The principle that equity will restrain the enforcement of legal rights when it would be unconscionable to insist upon them has an attractive breadth. But the reasons why the courts have rejected such generalisations are founded not merely upon authority...but also upon practical considerations of business. These are, in summary, that in many forms of transaction it is of great importance that if something happens for which the contract has made express provision, the parties should know with certainty that the terms of the contract will be enforced. The existence of an undefined discretion to refuse to enforce the contract on the ground that this would be "unconscionable" is sufficient to create uncertainty.'

16.23   The above case illustrates the traditional view that a general doctrine of unconscionability is undesirable, as its precise scope would be difficult to formulate and it would be inimical to certainty and stability in a commercial context. But the problem with the absence of any general principle is the development of unrelated rules, or even lone instances of unfairness being dealt, with and this can create anomalies.

16.24   In *Lloyds Bank Ltd* v *Bundy* [1974] 3 All ER 757 (discussed earlier), Lord Denning was keen to postulate a general principle. He made a connection between the (hitherto) distinct areas of duress, unconscionable transactions, undue influence, undue pressure, and salvage agreements. He stated (at 763) that despite the fact that our law does not, in general, interfere with freedom of contract, nevertheless:

'There are cases in our books in which the courts will set aside a contract, or a transfer of property, when the parties have not met on equal terms, when the one is so strong in bargaining power and the other so weak that, as a matter of common fairness, it is not right that the strong should be allowed to push the weaker to the wall. Hitherto those exceptional cases have been treated each as a separate category in itself. But I think the time has come when we should seek to find a principle to unite them. I put on one side contracts or transactions which are voidable for fraud or misrepresentation or mistake. All those are governed by settled principles. I go only to those where there has been inequality of bargaining power, such as to merit the intervention of the court.'

This approach shows a willingness to break down doctrinal barriers in the interest of a more interventionist role for the courts. He went on (at 765) to propose the following general principle:

> 'Gathering all together, I would suggest that through all these instances there runs a single thread. They rest on "inequality of bargaining power". By virtue of it, the English law gives relief to one who, without independent advice, enters into a contract on terms which are very unfair or transfers property for a consideration which is grossly inadequate, when his bargaining power is grievously impaired by reason of his own needs or desires, or by his own ignorance or infirmity, coupled with undue influences or pressures brought to bear on him by or for the benefit of the other. When I use the word "undue" I do not mean to suggest that the principle depends on proof of any wrongdoing.'

Although the Court of Appeal was unanimous in allowing Mr Bundy's appeal, the other two judges did not find it necessary to base their judgments on such a wide principle as that suggested by Lord Denning. The novelty of the Denning principle was his emphasis on the need to protect the weaker party where there was a clear disparity in bargaining strength between the parties.

16.25   It should not be thought that Lord Denning's was a lone voice. In *Schroeder Music Publishing Co.* v *Macaulay* [1974] 3 All ER 616 it was not necessary to go beyond the restraint of trade doctrine to release the young songwriter from his contract with a music publishing company. But Lord Diplock went further (at 623):

> 'Because this can be classed as a contract in restraint of trade the restrictions that [Macaulay] accepted fell within one of those limited categories of contractual promises in respect of which the courts still retain the power to relieve the promisor of his legal duty to fulfil them. In order to determine whether this case is one in which that power ought to be exercised, what your lordships have been doing has been to assess the relative bargaining power of the publisher and the songwriter at the time the contract was made and to decide whether the publisher had used his superior bargaining power to exact from the songwriter promises that were unfairly onerous to him.'

Thus his Lordship stressed that the important consideration for the court was the protection of the weaker or vulnerable party against being forced by a much stronger party to enter into a very bad bargain. The important question to be answered, according to Lord Diplock, is: 'was the bargain fair?' (at 623). In deciding that it was not fair, the court took into account the fact that the terms of the contract had not been the subject of negotiation between the parties; on the contrary, they had been dictated by the publishing company, who had been able to do this as a result of greatly superior bargaining power.[14]

---

14 See also *Silvertone Records* v *Mountfield* (1993).

16.26 The danger with terms like 'inequality of bargaining power', 'unconscionability', and good faith, is that they can become rather trite through indiscriminate use. Certainly, inequality of bargaining power, for example, is inherent in a great number of commercial transactions, but obviously not all of these are to be regarded as situations in which the court should intervene. What matters is the use (or misuse) to which such disparity is put. The case of *Alec Lobb Garages Ltd* v *Total Oil (Great Britain) Ltd* (1985) provides a useful illustration. The facts were:

> The claimant company, Alec Lobb Ltd, owned premises from which it ran a garage and filling station. (The company comprised a mother and son who were the shareholders and directors.) The company was in serious financial difficulties. It was not possible for the claimants to approach any other petrol company for finance, as they were already 'tied' to the defendants under a previous loan agreement. Further negotiations took place between the claimants and the defendants during the course of which the claimants were independently advised by solicitors and accountants. The defendants agreed to put further capital into the claimant company by means of a lease and lease-back transaction. This consisted of a lease of the garage to the defendants for fifty-one years in return for the payment of a fair premium of £35,000 and an immediate lease-back of the premises to the son, personally, for a term of twenty-one years at a rent of £2,250. This underlease to the son also contained a petrol 'tie'; he was to buy his petrol exclusively from the defendants. The transaction did not succeed in rescuing the claimant company from its lack of working capital. Nearly ten years after making this agreement, the claimants sought to have the transaction set aside on the grounds, inter alia, that the bargain was harsh and unconscionable or, alternatively, that the 'tie' covenant was void as being an unreasonable restraint of trade.

Of interest to our present discussion is the first of these two grounds, but it may be stated briefly that the Court of Appeal held that the petrol supply restraint was not unreasonable in view of all the circumstances. (It is worth noting that the adequacy of the consideration was one of the factors that the court took into account in reaching this conclusion.) The court went on to state that where one party had acted oppressively, coercively, or extortionately towards the other, such a transaction would be set aside. An agreement was not rendered unconscionable merely because the parties to it were of unequal bargaining strength and the stronger party had not shown that the terms were fair and reasonable. Furthermore, a contract was not unconscionable merely because a party was forced to enter into it from economic necessity. It was important, on the facts of *Alec Lobb*, that no pressure had been exerted on the claimants by the defendant oil company. The claimants had received independent advice (which they had disregarded) and they had sought the defendants' assistance to escape their financial difficulties. The fact that the claimants had little realistic alternative, and that they had made a bad bargain, was not sufficient to render the defendants' conduct unconscionable.

16.27 This is a necessary restriction on the use of 'inequality of bargaining power': it does not, itself, establish that there was anything wrong with the transaction. It is the unfair or coercive exploitation of the superior bargaining strength of one party against the other which is the reason judicial intervention. This was not present in the instant case. However, it should be pointed out that Lord Denning's statement in *Lloyds Bank Ltd* v *Bundy* [1974] 3 All ER 757 at 765, makes this restriction abundantly clear. He did not state that inequality of bargaining strength alone constitutes a sufficient ground for interfering with freedom of contract. This point was recognized Dillon LJ (at 313):

> 'Inequality of bargaining power must anyhow be a relative concept. It is seldom in any negotiation that the bargaining powers of the parties are absolutely equal. Any individual wanting to borrow money from a bank, building society or other financial institution...will have virtually no bargaining power; he will have to take or leave the terms offered to him...But Lord Denning did not envisage that any contract entered into in such circumstances would, without more, be reviewed by the courts by the objective criterion of what was reasonable. The courts would only interfere in exceptional cases where as a matter of common fairness it was not right that the strong should be allowed to push the weak to the wall. The concepts of unconscionable conduct and of the exercise by the stronger of coercive power are thus brought in, and in the present case they are negatived by the [findings of fact].'

16.28   However, such limitations on Lord Denning's general principle were not brought to the fore in its dismissal in in *National Westminster Bank plc* v *Morgan* [1985] 1 All ER 821 (see generally para. 14.44). Lord Scarman (at 830), observed that Lord Denning's general principle was not the ground for the majority's decision in *Lloyds Bank Ltd* v *Bundy* (1974), and continued:

> 'Nor has counsel for the wife sought to rely on Lord Denning's general principle; and, in my view, he was right not to do so...The fact of an unequal bargain will, of course, be a relevant feature in some cases of undue influence. But it can never become an appropriate basis of principle of [this] doctrine...I question whether there is any need in the modern law to erect a general principle of relief against inequality of bargaining power. Parliament has undertaken the task (and it is essentially a legislative task) of enacting such restrictions on freedom of contract as are in its judgment necessary to relieve against the mischief...I doubt whether the courts should assume the burden of formulating further restrictions'.

Thus the House of Lords issued its rebuke to Lord Denning for venturing to construct a more general principle. A number of observations can be made about Lord Scarman's speech. By his own concession, the wife's counsel, in *Morgan,* did not try to rely on the Denning principle. If this had been attempted, it would have been evident that the Denning principle did not apply to instances of mere inequality of bargaining power.

16.29   Another aspect of Lord Scarman's attack on Lord Denning's approach should be considered. He argued that the task of restricting freedom of contract, in order to give relief against inequality of bargaining power, is 'essentially a legislative task'. Therefore, he 'questioned' the need for such a general principle. Is a general common law doctrine otiose?

16.30   One commentator shrewdly observed on an earlier occasion:[15]

> 'Legislation, like judicial decisions, reflects the needs of a society, and the fact that the need for control of agreements has become so pressing in particular cases as to prompt legislative intervention argues…in favour, rather than against the need for general control.'

A general principle could co-exist with specific statutory intervention. Even the considerable protection provided by the Unfair Contract Terms Act 1977 and the Unfair Terms in Consumer Contracts Directive does not cover all situations. There is still be a place for a general principle or doctrine.

16.31   Of course, the idea of any such general principle as 'inequality of bargaining power' will be criticized on the basis of the generation of uncertainty. However, although the law goes through periods in its history when the need for certainty and predictability appear to dominate judicial thought, such times may be followed by periods of greater flexibility. The idea of a doctrine of good faith tends to raise the spectre of 'visceral justice',[16] where 'judges react impressionistically to the merits of a situation and dispose of cases accordingly', but even if it would generate uncertainty, 'visceral justice' does not present a credible picture of what is likely to occur,[17] and in *Yam Seng Pte Ltd v International Trade Corporation Ltd* (2013) the judge noted that, in its lack of any general acceptance of a doctrine of good faith, English law was 'swimming against a tide' of both European law and that of other common law jurisdictions (at [124]). Certainly, we are becoming accustomed to the idea of good faith in the fairness test in the Unfair Terms in Consumer Contracts Directive, and also in our ever increasing awareness of its use in the contract law of other European countries. There is an impetus towards the recognition of such a doctrine in English law from such external influences.[18] Issues of uncertainty will still be forcefully put forward but the climate may be somewhat less hostile to a general doctrine than when Lord Denning talked of 'inequality of bargaining power'.

◉ Summary

- There is a tension in the law between supporting 'freedom of contract', and attempting to ensure that one party does not take unfair advantage of the other by exploiting his or her superior bargaining strength.

- It is not, in general, a matter for judicial intervention simply because one party has made a poor bargain.

- But, in practice, the courts will often try to achieve a fair result by means of a variety of techniques and doctrines, so as to ensure that freedom of contract is not seriously abused.

---

15 S. Waddams (1976) 39 MLR 369 at 390.

16 M. Bridge, 'Good Faith in Commercial Contracts' in R. Brownsword, N. J. Hird, and G. Howells, *Good Faith in Contract: Concept and Context*, Dartmouth, 1999, p. 140.

17 R. Brownsword, *Contract Law: Themes for the Twenty-First Century*, 2nd edn, Oxford University Press, 2006, pp. 130–4.

18 e.g. M. Furmston and G. J. Tolhurst, *Contract Formation—Law and Practice*, Oxford University Press, 2010, ch. 12.

- The courts have been wary of claiming a general discretion to relieve against hardship by imposing a fair solution. The classical approach has the obvious advantage of certainty.

- However, in the absence of any general principle which permits intervention, there has developed a number of unrelated rules and doctrines for dealing with unfairness. (This can cause anomalies.)

- An attempt was made by Lord Denning to provide a more general principle which would allow a more interventionist approach by the courts (see *Lloyds Bank* v *Bundy* (1974)).

- But this approach was rejected by the House of Lords (see *National Westminster Bank* v *Morgan* (1985)). It was argued that the restriction of freedom of contract, so as to provide relief against unfairness, should be left to Parliament.

- Particularly with the impetus from Europe, and elsewhere, it might be argued that there are signs of a movement towards a doctrine of good faith.

▶ Further reading

N. Bamforth, 'Unconscionability as a Vitiating Factor' (1995) LMCLQ 538

M. Bridge, 'Good Faith in Commercial Contracts' in R. Brownsword, N. J. Hird, and G. Howells, *Good Faith in Contract: Concept and Context*, Dartmouth, 1999, pp. 139–64

S. Bright, 'Winning the Battle Against Unfair Contract Terms' (2000) 20 LS 331

R. Brownsword, *Contract Law—Themes for the Twenty-First Century*, 2nd edn, Oxford University Press, 2006

J. Devenney and A. Chandler, 'Unconscionability and the Taxonomy of Undue Influence' (2007) JBL 541

M. Furmston and G. J. Tolhurst, *Contract Formation—Law and Practice*, Oxford University Press, 2010, chapter 12

A. Mason, 'Contract, Good Faith and Equitable Standards in Fair Dealing' (2000) 116 LQR 66

E. Peel, 'Reasonable Exemption Clauses' (2001) 117 LQR 545

S. Smith, 'In Defence of Substantive Fairness' (1996) 112 LQR 138

S. Waddams, 'Unconscionability in Contracts' (1976) 39 MLR 369

C. Willett (ed.), *Aspects of Fairness in Contract*, Blackstone, 1996

R. Zimmermann and S. Whittaker (eds), *Good Faith in European Contract Law*, Cambridge University Press, 2000

Chapter 17

Privity and third party rights

Introduction

17.1 The doctrine of privity of contract has been a long-established, yet controversial, principle of English law. The Contracts (Rights of Third Parties) Act 1999 has led to important reform of the doctrine and it will be considered in detail later in the chapter. However, it is appropriate to start with an explanation of what is meant by the term 'privity of contract'. It represents the principle that only a party to a contract can enforce rights, or have duties enforced against him or her, under that contract (for example, see *Price* v *Easton* (1833)). The doctrine was referred to briefly in **Chapter 4**, in connection with the rule that consideration must move from the promisee. A party to a contract is one to whom a promise is made and who, in exchange for the promise, gives consideration for it. The traditional view has been that a promisee who is promised some benefit, but gives nothing in return, cannot enforce the promise; similarly, that a beneficiary of a promise, who is not the promisee, and who provides no consideration, cannot sue on that promise. Thus, the traditional approach gave precedence to the notion of bargain, rather than to the intention of the contracting parties. It is easy to understand why someone who is not a party to a contract should not have burdens imposed upon him or her and this facet of the doctrine has not been subject to criticism, nor has it been affected by the 1999 legislation. But the idea that a 'stranger' to a contract should not be able to enforce a provision which was intended for his or her benefit has been much more controversial.

17.2 In *Tweddle* v *Atkinson* (1861) two fathers, by an agreement, promised one another that they would each pay a sum of money to William Tweddle, the son of one of them, who was to marry the other's daughter. William Tweddle sued his father-in-law's executors to enforce this promise, as his father-in-law died without having paid the promised sum. Despite the fact that the contract was for his benefit, his action failed as he did not provide consideration for the promise. An alternative explanation for the decision is that William Tweddle was not a party to the contract and, therefore, he could not enforce any benefit under a contract to which he was a stranger.

17.3   The privity rule, despite its uncertain origins and its potential for unfairness, was even more firmly established in English law by the House of Lords in *Dunlop Pneumatic Tyre Co Ltd* v *Selfridge & Co. Ltd* [1915] AC 847. The facts were as follows:

> Dunlop sold some tyres to Dew & Co., on the terms that Dew & Co. would not resell them for less than Dunlop's list prices, and that when Dew & Co. resold them to trade buyers, they (Dew & Co.) would insist on the same undertaking from the trade buyers. Dew & Co. sold the tyres to Selfridge, who agreed to conform with this restriction and, in the event of breaking the agreement, to pay Dunlop £5 for each tyre sold (in breach of it). Selfridge later sold tyres to customers for less than the list price and Dunlop sued Selfridge for damages.

The House of Lords gave judgment for Selfridge and dismissed the action. Lord Haldane LC affirmed the doctrine of privity authoritatively, by stating (at 853):

> '...In the law of England certain principles are fundamental. One is that only a person who is a party to a contract can sue on it. Our law knows nothing of a jus quaesitum tertio arising by way of contract. Such a right may be conferred by way of property, as, for example, under a trust, but it cannot be conferred on a stranger to a contract as a right to enforce the contract in personam. A second principle is that if a person with whom a contract not under seal has been made is to be able to enforce it consideration must have been given by him to the promisor or to some other person at the promisor's request.'

17.4   The doctrine, despite its evident unpopularity with the judiciary, survived and even developed (see *Scruttons Ltd* v *Midland Silicones Ltd* (1962), discussed later). It has been subjected to the scrutiny of law reform bodies for more than sixty years. For example, in 1937 the Law Revision Committee recommended in its sixth Interim Report that a third party should be able to enforce a contractual promise received by another for his benefit.[1] In 1991, a Law Commission Consultation Paper supported the argument for reform of the privity rule, stating:

> 'Over 50 years ago, the Law Revision Committee recommended the abolition of the third party rule...Nothing has happened since [its] Report to suggest that its recommendations were misguided. Indeed, the greater complexity of the law as further exceptions and circumventions have developed, and the experience of statutory reform elsewhere, reinforce its

---

1   Cmnd 5449, 1937, at p. 30. Paragraph 48 states: 'We therefore recommend that where a contract by its express terms purports to confer a benefit directly on a third party, the third party shall be entitled to enforce the provision in his own name, provided that the promisor shall be entitled to raise as against the third party any defence that would have been valid against the promisee. The rights of the third party shall be subject to cancellation of the contract by the mutual consent of the contracting parties at any time before the third party has adopted it either expressly or by conduct.'

conclusions' (Law Commission Consultation Paper, No 121, 'Privity of Contract: Contracts for the Benefit of Third Parties', 1991, at p. 95).

These arguments were supported by Steyn LJ's criticisms of the doctrine in *Darlington Borough Council* v *Wiltshier Northern Ltd* [1995] 1 WLR 68 at 76 where he stated:

'The case for recognising a contract for the benefit of a third party is simple and straightforward. The autonomy of the will of the parties should be respected. The law of contract should give effect to the reasonable expectations of contracting parties. Principle certainly requires that a burden should not be imposed on a third party without his consent. But there is no doctrinal, logical or policy reason why the law should deny effectiveness to a contract for the benefit of a third party where that is the expressed intention of the parties.'

17.5   The above statements, and many more like them from judges and academic critics, illustrated the unpopularity of the privity rule and the need for its reform.[2] Furthermore, English law was out of step with that of many European countries which do not prevent third parties from enforcing contractual provisions.[3] In addition to hindering the closer harmonization of the laws of European Union member states, the English doctrine of privity was capable of disappointing various reasonable commercial and consumer expectations. The resulting unfairness of a strict application of the doctrine necessitated a series of, often complex, exceptions to it (discussed later). Before examining the legislative reform, it is important to understand the ambit of the privity rule prior to the Contracts (Rights of Third Parties) Act 1999, as the common law doctrine was reformed, and not abolished, by the Act.

Further development of the doctrine

17.6   Despite challenges to its validity, the House of Lords affirmed the doctrine once again in *Scruttons Ltd* v *Midland Silicones Ltd* [1962] AC 446 (at 467 and 473). The scope of the doctrine was considered in a slightly different form in this case as the stranger to the contract was not suing to enforce a positive right, but instead was seeking the protection of a term of the contract as a defence to an action by one of the contracting parties under a separate cause of action. In other words, the case was concerned with whether a third party can use a term of a contract as a shield, despite not being able to use a term intended for his benefit as a sword. The facts were:

A drum containing chemicals was shipped from America to London. The bill of lading, under which it was shipped, limited to $500 (£179) per package the liability of the carrier in the event of loss, damage, or delay. Scruttons, who were the stevedores engaged by the carrier (under

---

2   See R. Flannigan, 'Privity—the End of an Era (Error)' (1987) 103 LQR 564. But for a contrasting view, see R. Stevens, 'The Contracts (Rights of Third Parties) Act 1999' (2004) 120 LQR 292, who argues (at 322) that 'the illness diagnosed was not as serious as it was thought and the operation may have caused more problems than it solved'.

3   See Law Commission Report, No 242, *Privity of Contract: Contracts for the Benefit of Third Parties*, Cm 3329, 1996, at para. 3.8. For a discussion of Irish law reform proposals in this area, see C. Kelly, 'Privity of Contract: the Benefits of Reform' (2008) JSIJ 145.

a separate contract), negligently dropped and damaged the drum whilst delivering it to the consignees, Midland Silicones. Midland Silicones sued Scruttons in tort, claiming the value of the lost contents (£593). Scruttons (the stevedores) argued that under the bill of lading their liability was limited to £179.

The House of Lords held that the stevedores were not entitled to rely on the limitation of liability contained in the bill of lading. Reference to the 'carrier' in the bill of lading (which incorporated relevant American legislative provisions for the carriage of goods by sea) did not include the stevedores. Moreover, there was nothing in the bill of lading which implied that the parties to it intended the limitation of liability to extend to the stevedores. The court stated that, as it is a fundamental principle that only a party to a contract can take advantage of the provisions of that contract, the stevedores could not rely on a contract to which they were not a party in defending the action against them. It made no difference that the stevedores were attempting to use the contract as a shield and not as a sword. It was decided that the rule precluded a third party from taking an advantage from the contract (per Lord Reid at 373), despite the inconvenience of this conclusion to the commercial world.

17.7   A party to a contract is a person to whom a promise is made, in return for which he or she provides consideration. If it could be shown, in circumstances like those of *Scruttons v Midland Silicones Ltd*, that the stevedore was a party to the contract and had provided consideration, he would then be able to rely on a clause in a bill of lading limiting the liability of the carrier. It did not matter that a rather strained and artificial interpretation of the facts was required to achieve this result. In *Scruttons v Midland Silicones Ltd*, one of the arguments advanced (unsuccessfully) by the stevedores was that they were the undisclosed principals of the carrier who acted as their agent and, therefore, the stevedores had a contractual relationship with the claimants through the agency of the carrier. This contention was rejected by the court, but Lord Reid explained (at 474) the conditions which would need to be satisfied for this agency argument to succeed. He stated, inter alia, that the bill of lading must make it clear that the stevedore is intended to be protected by its provisions which limit liability. The contract must also make it clear that the carrier, as well as contracting for these provisions on his own behalf, is also contracting as agent for the stevedore, who will in turn be protected by the provisions. Moreover, the carrier would need the stevedore's authority to act in this way. Lastly, any difficulties about consideration moving from the stevedore would need to be overcome.

17.8   The matter was considered again in *New Zealand Shipping Co. Ltd v Satterthwaite (AM) & Co.* [1975] AC 154, where the facts were similar to those of *Scruttons v Midland Silicones Ltd* (1962):

Cargo was shipped from Liverpool to the claimant (consignee) in New Zealand, under a bill of lading which conferred certain exemptions and immunities on the carrier. A clause in the bill of lading specifically provided that no servant or agent of the carrier (including independent contractors employed by the carrier) would be liable to the claimant for any loss or damage resulting from that person's negligence or default in carrying out the work. The clause also made it clear that the carrier was deemed to be acting as agent or trustee on behalf of those persons who were to be employed in handling the cargo, and that such persons were to be regarded as parties to the contract (i.e. the bill of lading). The defendants were stevedores in New Zealand, employed by the carrier (as independent contractors) to unload the cargo. The cargo was damaged as a result of the defendants' negligence whilst unloading. The claimant brought an action against the stevedores and argued that they could not rely on the exemptions and immunities contained in the bill of lading because they were not a party to the contract.

A majority of the Privy Council held that the stevedores were entitled to claim exemption from liability under the contract (see also *Port Jackson Stevedoring Pty v Salmond & Spraggon (Australia) Pty (The New York Star)* (1980)). It should be noted that, in contrast to *Scruttons v Midland Silicones Ltd*, the bill of lading provided that the exemptions of liability should apply to independent contractors such as stevedores. Applying Lord Reid's dictum in *Midland Silicones*, the court held that the exemption in the bill of lading was designed to cover the whole carriage of the goods by whomsoever it was performed. The solutions offered by the court to the problems of privity and consideration, whilst no doubt reflecting commercial realism and judicial ingenuity, were far from convincing from the perspective of legal doctrine.

17.9   The court held in *Satterthwaite* that the bill of lading was not simply a contract (or evidence of a contract) between the owners of the goods and the carrier. It also represented a contract between the owners and the stevedores, made through the carrier as agent. This was further explained by the idea of the owners making a unilateral offer, to those involved in unloading the goods, of exemption from liability in exchange for performing the requested services. The stevedores provided consideration by unloading the goods, despite the fact that they were already under an existing contractual obligation (owed to the carrier) to do precisely this. Although the stevedores were bound to unload the goods under a contract with the carrier, it will be remembered that the performance of an existing contractual duty owed to a third party can amount to good consideration (see **Chapter 4**). It was evident from Lord Wilberforce's judgment on behalf of the majority that he was determined to give effect to the clear purpose of a contractual document and not to allow this purpose to be defeated by technical difficulties. He explained the need for the law to take a practical approach to everyday commercial transactions, rather than to be confined by the technical and schematic rules of contract law.

17.10   There is no denying that this solution is commercially desirable—allowing the benefit of an exclusion clause, which is clearly intended to benefit a third party, to be relied on by that third party—but it is artificial and not entirely convincing. It was held that the stevedore entered into a contractual relationship with the owner (either shipper or consignee) by performance of the act of unloading which the owner requested in exchange for his promise. In other words, the contract is formed at a later date than the main contract (between the shipper and the carrier), i.e. when the stevedore performs the requested service. The decision in *New Zealand Shipping Co. Ltd v Satterthwaite* (1974) was supported by the Privy Council case of *Port Jackson Stevedoring Pty v Salmond & Spraggon (Australia) Pty* (1980), where the facts were similar to those of *Satterthwaite*. In *Port Jackson Stevedoring* the defendant stevedores, who were employed by the carrier, did not take proper care of a consignment of razor blades, which were stolen from a wharf after being unloaded by the stevedores from the ship. Once again, the court had to decide whether the defendants could rely on the defences and immunities contained in the bill of lading and the Privy Council held that they could do so. It was stated that all the parties concerned (i.e. the shipper, the carrier, and the stevedore) knew that this immunity was intended, and that the law should give effect to commercial practice in this respect.

17.11   This solution reflects commercial realism, but it was achieved only by some rather unconvincing reasoning, which was necessary to get around the doctrine of privity. It was also uncertain to which cases the solution could be applied. (See, for example, *The Mahkutai* (1996), in which the Privy Council held that the *Satterthwaite* approach should not be extended so as to apply to an exclusive jurisdiction clause in a bill of lading.) It is clear that a simpler and more predictable solution was required.

17.12   A further illustration of the practical problems caused by the doctrine, and of the need for rather artificial and technical solutions, is provided by the famous case of *Beswick v Beswick* (1968). The facts were:

> John Beswick helped his uncle, Peter Beswick, who ran a coal merchant business. As Peter was in poor health, he agreed to let John have the business. In return, John was to pay a weekly sum of £6 10s to Peter and, after Peter's death, he was to pay £5 per week to Peter's widow. John made the agreed payments to Peter until the latter's death, but he made only one payment of £5 to Peter's widow and then refused to pay any more. Peter's widow sued John for the arrears under the agreement and asked for specific performance of the contract. She sued both in her capacity as administratrix of her husband's estate, and in her personal capacity.

The House of Lords held that, as she was not a party to the contract, the widow could not succeed in her own right. However, it was decided that she should be granted an order for specific performance as administratrix (personal representative) of her husband's estate. In this capacity there was no problem of privity, as she was suing on behalf of her deceased husband, whose rights she was entitled to enforce. In effect, she was able to enforce the defendant's promise for her own benefit and so the outcome was a fair one. But this was achieved only because she was administratrix of the estate; in her personal capacity, she would have been unable to enforce the defendant's promise due to the obstacle provided by the doctrine of privity.

Reform of the law and C(RTP)A 1999

17.13   As has been illustrated, the privity doctrine was capable of disappointing reasonable contractual and commercial expectations. The fact that a series of ingenious (if contrived) devices were resorted to by the courts, together with a number of established common law and statutory exceptions to the doctrine, to avoid injustice in many cases, did not negate the case for reform. The various exceptions to, and evasions of, the basic rule merely served to demonstrate how impracticable and unpopular the doctrine of privity had become, and this was reflected in the strictures of the judiciary. For example, in *Woodar Investment Development Ltd v Wimpey Construction UK Ltd* [1980] 1 All ER 571 at 591, Lord Scarman expressed the wish that the House of Lords would, in the future, 'reconsider *Tweddle v Atkinson* and other cases which stand guard over this unjust rule'. Despite critical remarks such as these, the judiciary (with the notable exception of Lord Denning) showed a disinclination to directly challenge the basic rule and to overturn the doctrine of privity. The courts were probably correct in insisting that such a fundamental change was, more appropriately, to be undertaken by Parliament.

17.14   The Law Commission considered the case for reform of the general rule which prevented a person from enforcing a right under a contract to which he or she is not a party (the 'third party rule') in its Report, *Privity of Contract: Contracts for the Benefit of Third Parties* (Law Commission Report, No 242, Cm 3329, 1996). This Report supported the case for reform of the third party rule and stated that its recommendations would allow contracting parties to provide for enforceable third party rights without resorting to the various evasions and exceptions which had developed to circumvent the privity rule. The Report argued that this reform should be brought about in the form of detailed legislation, this strategy being favoured because of the certainty it would bring to the law. It observed that, despite the repeated criticism levelled at the privity doctrine in appellate cases, little progress had been made in actually overturning the third party rule. The legislative process offered the prospect of more detailed reform of the law and it was not dependent upon the vagaries of litigation.

17.15   The Contracts (Rights of Third Parties) Act 1999, based largely on the Law Commission's 1996 Report (see above), brought about a significant reform of the doctrine of privity of contract.[4] The Act does not affect the existing exceptions to, and circumventions of, the doctrine, but it introduces an important new (and more general) exception into the law. The Act deals with the conferral of rights on third parties, but naturally it does not alter the rule which prevents liabilities being imposed on a third party. It must be emphasized that the doctrine of privity was not abolished by the Act; it creates a general and relatively simple exception to the doctrine. In doing so, the Act brings English law more closely into line with that of most of the other members of the European Union and of many common law jurisdictions. The Act was passed on 11 November 1999, but it applies only to those contracts concluded on or after 11 May 2000 (i.e. six months after the new Act received the Royal Assent). However, the parties to a contract concluded during the six-month period after the Act was passed were able expressly to provide for it to apply (see s 10(2) and (3)).

---

4   For further discussion of the Act, see M. Dean, 'Removing a Blot on the Landscape—the Reform of the Doctrine of Privity' (2000) JBL 143; P. Kincaid, 'Privity Reform in England' (2000) 116 LQR 43; C. MacMillan, 'A Birthday Present for Lord Denning: The Contracts (Rights of Third Parties) Act 1999' (2000) 63 MLR 721; and N. Andrews, 'Strangers to Justice No Longer: The Reversal of the Privity Rule under the Contracts (Rights of Third Parties) Act 1999' (2001) 60 CLJ 353; R. Stevens, 'The Contracts (Rights of Third Parties) Act 1999' (2004) 120 LQR 292.

Conferring a third party right

17.16   Section 1(1) of C(RTP)A 1999 states that a 'third party' is able to enforce a term of a contract in his or her own right if:

> '(a) the contract expressly provides that he may, or
> (b) subject to subsection (2), the term purports to confer a benefit on him.'

Section 1(2) provides that s 1(1)(b) will not apply if, on the proper construction of the contract, 'it appears that the parties did not intend the term to be enforceable by the third party'. The third party does not have to be in existence when the contract is made; a contractual provision might seek to benefit the future offspring of the contracting parties, or a company which is yet to be incorporated. But the third party must be expressly identified in the contract by name, or as a member of a class, or as answering a particular description (s 1(3)). (In *Avraamides v Colwill* (2006), the Court of Appeal, per Waller LJ at [19], emphasized that under s 1(3) the third party must be *expressly* identified, and that this requirement 'does not allow a process of construction or implication'). References in the Act to a third party enforcing a contractual term are to be understood as including the right to rely on an exclusion or limitation clause; such references, therefore, are not restricted to a third party suing to enforce a positive right (s 1(6)). If a third party comes within the provisions of this new exception to the privity doctrine, he or she can exercise his or her right to enforce the contractual term in the same way as if he or she were a party to the contract, and the rules relating to damages, injunctions and specific performance apply equally to him or her (s 1(5)). However, any rights which are conferred on a third party are subject to any other relevant terms of the contract (s 1(4)); for example, where third party rights are created, the contracting parties might choose to limit those rights expressly by some other term of the contract.

17.17   What is the ambit of this new and wide-ranging exception to the doctrine of privity? The right of a third party, under C(RTP)A 1999, s 1(1) (above), to enforce a term of a contract, is based on the intention of the contracting parties. This right may be conferred expressly by the contract, under the first limb, which is relatively straightforward. Alternatively, under the second limb, the third party may enforce a contractual term which purports to confer a benefit on him or her, subject to the proviso that this will not apply if, on a proper construction of the contract, the parties did not intend the term to be enforceable by the third party. The Law Commission used certain well-known past cases to illustrate the scope of the new third party right, especially in relation to the second limb of the test (Law Com No 242, paras 7.45–7.51). Applying the new law to *Beswick v Beswick* (1968) (discussed earlier), for example, the first limb of the test would not confer a right on the uncle's widow, as there was no express provision to that effect in the contract. (Examples of such a provision would include words like 'and C shall have the right to enforce the contract'; see Law Com No 242, para. 7.10.) However, under the second limb, she would now almost certainly be able to enforce the nephew's promise in her own right. This is because the contract between the nephew and the uncle purported to confer a benefit on her and she was expressly identified in that contract. It is extremely unlikely that the presumption could be rebutted, as the nephew would be unable to demonstrate that, on a proper construction, the contracting parties did not intend the term to be enforceable by her.

17.18   It might be questioned whether the second (and more complicated) limb was necessary, especially in view of its potential to introduce uncertainty into the law, and whether the first limb might have been better standing alone. However, the view of the Law Commission was that, on its own, the first limb would have been too restrictive an approach to reforming the law. This is because it would have failed to give rights to a third party in situations where, although no express right of enforceability had been conferred by the contracting parties, it had been intended that the third party should have such a right (Law Com No 242, para. 7.11). Moreover, the Law Commission argued that with the inclusion of the 'proviso' (i.e. C(RTP)A 1999, s 1(2)), the second limb represents a workable solution to the problem of giving effect to the contracting parties' intentions without the introduction of too much uncertainty into the law. It is possible that there may be problems for the courts in deciding whether on a 'proper construction' the parties intended, on conferring a benefit on a third party, for it to be enforceable by the third party. But these problems are not insurmountable to judges used to taking an objective approach to contractual intention and, in the longer term, difficulties may be avoided by the more careful drafting of contracts by the parties. If the parties to a contract do not wish to confer an enforceable right on a third party, they should state this in clear terms, otherwise there may well be a strong presumption that the third party has the right to enforce the term in question. In *Nisshin Shipping Co. Ltd* v *Cleaves Ltd* (2003), the first reported case involving the interpretation of the 1999 Act, it was held at [23] that if a contract is 'neutral' (i.e. silent) as to the parties' intention, s 1(2) will not 'disapply' s 1(1)(b). This is because the wording of the subsection creates a rebuttable presumption: i.e. that the parties *do* intend to confer rights on a third party to enforce a term, where they have included a term which purports to confer a benefit on an expressly identified third party (even though they have not expressly conferred such a right). Of course, the presumption may be disproved if there is evidence that the parties did not intend an enforceable right to be bestowed on the third party (see A. Burrows, 'The Contracts (Rights of Third Parties) Act and its Implications for Commercial Contracts' [2000] LMCLQ 540 at 544). In the *Nisshin Shipping* case, Colman J at [23] explained that:

> 'Whether the contract does express a mutual intention that the third party should not be entitled to enforce the benefit conferred on him or is merely neutral is a matter of construction having regard to all the relevant circumstances...'

17.19   The *Nisshin Shipping* approach received confirmation by the Court of Appeal in *Laemthong International Lines Co. Ltd* v *Artis (The Laemthong Glory) (No 2)* (2005). The case involved the delivery of a large quantity of sugar from Brazil to Aden. The claimant owners chartered their ship (*The Laemthong Glory*) for the carriage of this cargo. A clause of the charter-party provided that, if the original bills of lading (i.e. documents of title which represent the goods) were not available on the ship's arrival at the discharge port, the master of the ship could release the cargo to the receivers (the second defendants) on receipt of a letter of indemnity (LOI). The LOI was to be issued by the charterers of the vessel, who were the first defendants in the case. Before the ship arrived in Aden, the receivers notified the charterers that the bills of lading had not arrived. They asked the charterers to issue their LOI to the owners, and to instruct that the cargo be delivered without production of the bills of lading. The charterers agreed to this request on condition that, in turn, the receivers issued their own LOI to the charterers (which they did). The charterers then sent the receivers' LOI, together with their own, to the owners, and asked them to instruct the master to deliver the cargo. This was done, but the ship was then arrested by the Yemen Bank, which alleged that it held all the original bills of lading for the cargo and claimed for the value of the goods. The owners brought an action against the charterers and the receivers.

17.20   It was clear that the owners could enforce the charterers' LOI, as it was addressed to them. But they also wanted to enforce the receivers' LOI; the problem here was that this was not addressed to them, but to the charterers. Accordingly the owners sought to rely on s 1 of the C(RTP)A 1999. At the trial, it was held (by Cooke J) that the owners could enforce the receivers' LOI against the receivers, and that the owners were entitled to an order that both the charterers and the receivers provide the necessary security to secure the release of the ship. The receivers appealed, arguing that the terms of the LOI, on which the owners relied, did not purport to confer a benefit on the owners and, that on the proper construction of the contract, the parties did not intend the terms of the receivers' LOI to be enforceable by the owners. These arguments were rejected by the Court of Appeal. Clarke LJ, delivering the judgment of the court, stated at [48] and [54] that the relevant terms of the receivers' LOI (addressed to the charterers) purported to confer a benefit on the owners. The owners were entitled to enforce these terms in their own name, because there was nothing in the receivers' LOI to suggest that the parties did not intend the relevant terms to be enforceable by the owners (i.e. the third party). Clarke LJ stated at [54] that if the court was correct in holding that the relevant terms in the receivers' LOI were intended to be for the benefit of the owners, 'it makes no sense to hold that it was nevertheless intended that the receivers' liability should not be directly to the owners'. He continued:

> 'The whole purpose of the receivers' LOI was on the one hand to ensure that the receivers received the cargo from the ship without production of the original bills of lading and on the other hand to ensure that the owners were fully protected from the consequences of arrest or other action which might be taken by the holders of the original bills of lading.'

An attempt to rely on s 1(1)(b) appeared to have succeeded in a further case, but the decision of Lindsay J was reversed by the Court of Appeal in *Prudential Assurance Co Ltd* v *Ayres* (2008). Here, the claimant insurance company (C), entered into a sub-lease of office premises with the defendant law firm (Ds). Ds later assigned the lease to an American law firm (F), and were required under their licence to assign to provide C with a guarantee of F; i.e. that if F were to default with the rent, Ds would be liable to pay. Subsequently, C and F entered into a further agreement (a 'supplemental deed') to the effect that the liability of the tenant under the lease was to be limited to the partnership, and therefore did not extend to the assets of individual partners: thus any action by C against the tenant or 'any previous tenant' under the lease for non-payment of rent was restricted to partnership assets. F later became bankrupt, with rent unpaid, and C tried to recover this from Ds as F's guarantors. Ds argued that the supplemental deed agreed between C and F excused them from their liability to pay. At the trial, the judge held that the supplemental deed purported to confer a benefit on Ds within s 1(1)(b) of the Act, therefore Ds could enforce the relevant provision against C in refusing to pay. However, the Court of Appeal allowed C's appeal, deciding that on its proper construction the supplemental deed did not purport to confer any benefit on Ds (per Moore-Bick LJ at [42]). Accordingly, it provided no defence to Cs claim, as the court found it 'impossible to accept that the parties intended to alter in a significant way the nature of the relationship between [C] and [Ds] that had been established' under the licence to assign (at [40]). The case was in fact decided on the basis of the construction of the supplemental deed, and therefore has little to contribute to our understanding of the ambit of s 1(1)(b) (at [41]–[42]). (For another recent case in which an attempt to rely on s 1(1)(b) failed, see *Dolphin Maritime and Aviation Ltd v Sveriges Angfartygs Assurans Forening* (2009).)

17.21   Following a successful reliance on s 1 of the C(RTP)A 1999 in *Laemthong International Lines Co. Ltd v Artis (The Laemthong Glory) (No 2)* (2005), the legislative provisions have been applied more recently, once again to assist a shipowner in the enforcement of a letter of indemnity. In the case of *Great Eastern Shipping Co Ltd v Far East Chartering Ltd (The Jag Ravi)* (2012), a letter of indemnity was found capable of being accepted by a shipowner as the charterer's agent. Delivering the judgment of the Court of Appeal, Tomlinson LJ stated that:

> 'the words "The Owners/Disponent Owners/Charterers" could not, or could not properly, in the context be construed as a compendious way of describing a single offeree...It was more natural to regard the phrase as comprising a descending hierarchy, progressing from the owners through time charterers down to voyage charterers...the natural and proper meaning of the letter of indemnity is that it is addressed to both the owners and the charterers' (at 41 and 42).

The letter of indemnity was read as being addressed to both the owners and the charterers and therefore capable of acceptance by the charterer. The acceptance had taken place through the shipowner's conduct in delivering the cargo. The court also emphasized that there was no reason of public policy which precluded enforcement of the letter of indemnity (see 50–52).

Varying or cancelling the agreement

17.22   Where a third party has a right conferred on him or her under a contract, should the contracting parties have the freedom to vary, or even cancel, the third party's right? It could be argued that without such a freedom there would be an unacceptable interference with the rights of the contracting parties, who would usually have the right to vary their agreement. However, the recognition of third party rights naturally involves some restriction on the contracting parties' freedom to modify the original contract, otherwise the reform of the third party rule (described earlier) would lack utility. The Law Commission sought to establish an appropriate test to determine the 'crystallization' of the third party's rights, i.e. the point beyond which the contracting parties would lose the right to vary or cancel the contract. It favoured a test of reliance or acceptance by recommending that: 'the contracting parties' right to vary or cancel the contract or, as the case may be, the contractual provision should be lost once the third party has relied on it or has accepted it' (see Law Com No 242, 1996, para. 9.26). However, it stated also that 'the contracting parties may expressly reserve the right to vary or cancel the third party's right irrespective of reliance or acceptance by the third party' (para. 9.40). In other words, the Law Commission recommended a compromise between the conflicting interests referred to above, by allowing the contracting parties expressly to reserve the right to vary or cancel the right of the third party.

17.23   Accordingly, C(RTP)A 1999, s 2(3) provides that the restriction on the right of the contracting parties to vary or cancel a third party's right, set out in s 2(1), is subject to any express term of the contract under which the contracting parties may: (a) by agreement rescind or vary the contract without the third party's consent, or (b) alter the circumstances for the third party's consent to be given from those set out in s 2(1). If the contracting parties do not include such an express provision in their agreement, their freedom to vary or cancel the third party's right is controlled by s 2(1). This states that where a third party has a right conferred on him or her (see s 1, earlier), the contracting parties are not permitted to agree to cancel or alter the agreement in such a way as to extinguish or alter the third party's right, without his or her consent if:

1. the third party has communicated his or her assent (by words or conduct) to the term to the promisor,
2. the promisor is aware that the third party has relied on the term, or
3. the promisor can reasonably be expected to have foreseen that the third party would rely on the term and the third party has in fact relied on it.

Therefore, once a third party right has been conferred (under s 1), there are general restrictions (under s 2(1)) on the freedom of the contracting parties to vary or cancel their agreement subsequently, in the absence of any express provision in the contract (s 2(3)). In s 2(1), it should be noted that the word 'reliance' is not restricted to where a third party has relied on the term to his or her detriment; the third party's conduct need not have left him or her in a worse position than before the promise was made. This distinction was made by the Law Commission, which defined reliance on a promise as 'conduct induced by the belief (or expectation) that the promise will be performed or, at least, that one is legally entitled to performance of the promise' (Law Com No 242, para. 9.14). This approach is consistent with one of the major reasons for reforming the privity doctrine, i.e. that it can disappoint the reasonable expectations of the third party. If the third party has relied on the promise, this demonstrates that expectations have been created, even if no detriment has been suffered (see Law Com No 242, para. 9.19).

17.24   It should be noted that, under C(RTP)A 1999, s 2(1), the promisor (i.e. the contracting party against whom the term is enforceable by the third party) actually has to be aware of the third party's reliance; or alternatively, can reasonably be expected to foresee that the third party would rely on the term and has in fact done so. Normally, where a promisor has contracted to confer a right on a third party, he or she should be aware that there is likely to be reliance on the contract by the third party. So, as a general rule, the promisor should check with the third party, where this is possible, before cancelling or varying the contractual provision in question. As an alternative to the reliance test, s 2(1) also provides a test of acceptance. The rationale is that where a third party communicates his or her assent effectively, this allows the promisor to know where he or she stands, and the third party should be able to enforce his or her right without having to show reliance (see Law Com No 242, para. 9.20). Therefore, to avoid any uncertainty, a third party may make certain of performance of the promise by communicating his or her assent to the promisor. It should be noted that communication in this context does not include the posting of a letter; the Act states that the assent may be by words or conduct, but if it is sent by post it will not be regarded as communicated until it is received by the promisor (s 2(2)(b)).

Defences

17.25   The Law Commission recommended that the right of the third party to enforce a term of the contract 'should be subject to all defences and set-offs that would have been available to the promisor in an action by the promisee and which arise out of or in connection with the contract...' (Law Com No 242, para. 10.12). Accordingly, C(RTP)A 1999, s 3 deals with the defences available to a promisor where a claim is made by a third party in reliance on s 1. Section 3(2) provides that, subject to any express term of the contract to the contrary (s 3(5)), the promisor can rely on any defence or set-off which:

1. arises from the contract and is relevant to the term in question, and
2. would have been available to him or her if the action had been brought by the promisee (i.e. the party to the contract by whom the term is enforceable against the promisor).

In addition, the promisor is able to rely on (a) by way of defence or set-off any matter, and (b) by way of counterclaim any matter not arising from the contract, 'that would have been available to him or her by way of defence or set-off or, as the case may be, by way of counterclaim against the third party if the third party had been a party to the contract' (s 3(4)).

Other provisions of C(RTP)A 1999

17.26   Section 4 makes it clear that the conferral of an enforceable right on a third party does not affect the right of the promisee to enforce any contractual term (discussed later in this chapter). This section is consistent with the view expressed by the Law Commission (Law Com No 242, paras 11.3–11.4), which argued that the promisee (a contracting party who has provided consideration) should not lose the right to enforce a contractual right simply because the contract has conferred an enforceable right on a third party. It might be objected that this could raise the prospect of a double liability for the promisor, i.e. to pay damages to both the third party and the promisee for the same loss. Section 5 aims to prevent this by providing that, where a contractual term has conferred an enforceable right on a third party, and the promisee has recovered damages in respect of the third party's loss, then this will be taken into account in any proceedings brought by the third party. In other words, any sum awarded to the third party will be lowered appropriately to take account of the sum recovered by the promisee. This section does not deal explicitly with the reverse situation, in which the third party has already recovered damages from the promisor; but the logic of s 5 would suggest that, in such a case, there will be a similar restriction on the damages recoverable by the promisee. (However, in this situation, it is unlikely that the promisee will have suffered any loss and that is presumably why no express provision was included in the Act.)

17.27   C(RTP)A 1999, s 6 sets out the types of contract which do not fall within the ambit of the Act. For example, s 6(1) provides that s 1 does not confer a third party right 'in the case of a contract on a bill of exchange, promissory note or other negotiable instrument'. This exclusion follows the recommendation of the Law Commission (Law Com No 242, para. 12.17), which was of the opinion that it would cause considerable uncertainty in the law if a more general third party right were created in relation to bills of exchange, promissory notes and other negotiable instruments, in addition to the one which is provided by the Bills of Exchange Act 1882. Under the 1882 Act, third party rights of enforceability are conferred only on holders of those instruments. If the 1999 Act had applied, it would have extended this right to third parties who were not holders and, in so doing, have undermined the policy of the 1882 Act and led to confusion.

17.28   The Law Commission recommended also that third party rights of enforceability should not be conferred in relation to contracts for the carriage of goods by sea, and contracts for the international carriage of goods by road, rail, or air (Law Com No 242, para. 12.6). Once again, the reasoning was that such a general right might be inconsistent with the policy of existing legislation, which is more attuned to the needs of a particular industry (such as shipping), and that the resulting conflict would produce uncertainty in the commercial world. (For the relevant legislation in relation to the carriage of goods by sea, see the Carriage of Goods by Sea Act 1992, s 2(1); contracts for the international carriage of goods by road or rail, or the carriage of cargo by air, are regulated by international conventions which are given force in English law by various implementing statutes.) For this reason, C(RTP)A 1999, s 6(5) states that no third party right of enforceability (under s 1) is conferred in relation to (a) contracts for the carriage of goods by sea, or (b) contracts for the carriage of goods by rail or road, or cargo by air. However, s 6(5) expressly states that this does not prevent a third party from enforcing exclusion or limitation of liability clauses in these two types of contract.

17.29   The Contracts (Rights of Third Parties) Act 1999 confers no third party right in the case of any contract binding on any company and its members under s 14 of the Companies Act 1985 (see s 6(2)). Also, s 6(3) provides for the exclusion of employment contracts from the ambit of the new third party right. Accordingly, s 1 confers no third party right to enforce (a) any term of a contract against an employee, (b) any term of a worker's contract against a worker, or (c) any term of a relevant contract against an agency worker. This provision ensures that, for example, a customer of an employer will not be able to use the Act to bring an action against an employee for a breach of his or her contract of employment.

17.30   The Contracts (Rights of Third Parties) Act 1999 does ensure that the provisions of the Arbitration Act 1996 apply in relation to third party rights. This addition was introduced slightly later, at the Report stage in the House of Commons. The accompanying Explanatory Notes advise that s 8 of the Act provides that, where appropriate, the provisions of the Arbitration Act 1996 shall apply in relation to third party rights. Without the addition of s 8, the main provisions of the Arbitration Act 1996 would not apply because a third party is not a party to an arbitration agreement between the promisor and the promise (see further, A. Burrows, 'The Contracts (Rights of Third Parties) Act and its Implications for Commercial Contracts' (2000) LMCLQ 540). Section 8 was analysed in detail in the case of *Nisshin Shipping Co. Ltd* v *Cleaves Ltd* (2003) (discussed at para. **17.18**). More recently, in *Fortress Value Recovery Fund I LLC* v *Blue Skye Special Opportunities Fund LP* (2013), its scope and application was once again considered, with the Court of Appeal emphasizing the distinction between substantive and procedural rights, as provided for in s 8(1) and (2) respectively. Here the court noted, as matters of interpretation and construction, that if contracting parties wish to grant to a third party an enforceable procedural right to have a dispute referred to arbitration, s 8(2) provides the means to do so (see Toulson LJ at [45] and [56]).

17.31   It is apparent that the Law Commission's aim was not to confer upon a third party the identical rights as would be enjoyed by a contracting party; for example, it did not support the argument in favour of amending the Unfair Contract Terms Act 1977 (see **Chapter 10**) so as to restrict the promisor's ability to exclude liability to third parties. The Commission argued that its test of enforceability was based on giving effect to the intentions of the parties to a contract to bestow legal rights on a third party, and that to apply UCTA 1977 to claims by third parties 'would cut across the essential basis' of the proposed reform (Law Com No 242, para. 13.10). The Commission considered s 2(2) of the 1977 Act more specifically, which it felt needed to be the subject of an express provision. Therefore, it recommended that UCTA 1977, s 2(2) should not apply in respect of a claim by a third party under the new law. (It will be remembered that s 2(2) states that a person cannot limit or exclude liability for negligently caused loss or damage, other than personal injury or death, unless the contract term or notice in question satisfies the requirement of reasonableness.) Section 7(2) of C(RTP)A 1999 reflects the Law Commission's view by providing that UCTA 1977, s 2(2) will 'not apply where the negligence consists of the breach of an obligation arising from a term of a contract and the person seeking to enforce it is a third party acting in reliance on section 1'.

17.32   Finally, it should be noted that C(RTP)A 1999, s 7(1) makes it clear that the right of enforceability under s 1 'does not affect any right or remedy of a third party that exists or is available apart from this Act'. This provision reflects the view of the Law Commission (Law Com No 242, paras 12.1–12.2), which argued for the retention of other existing statutory exceptions, and found 'no merit' in attempting to abolish the common law exceptions to the doctrine. Moreover, it acknowledged that some of the common law exceptions give third parties more certain rights than those conferred under the new Act. But, the Commission observed that some of these common law exceptions to the doctrine 'have developed through somewhat artificial and forced use of existing concepts' (para. 12.1) and that such exceptions might 'wither away', as a consequence of the new law, as they become redundant.

17.33   It is clear also, from C(RTP)A 1999, s 4 (see earlier), that the conferral of an enforceable right on a third party does not affect the right of the promisee to enforce any contractual term and, in some instances, the promisee may be able to assist the third party. Therefore, it is necessary in this chapter to consider the other main exceptions to the privity doctrine, including a discussion of the right of the promisee to bring an action, although it should be emphasized that some of these exceptions will become less important as a consequence of the 1999 Act. (Also, it should be remembered that the Act does not apply to all types of contract.)

Other statutory exceptions

17.34   In contrast to the more general exception to the doctrine provided by the Contracts (Rights of Third Parties) Act 1999, there are other, narrower statutory exceptions which were introduced to avoid the commercial inconvenience caused by the privity rule. A good example is that of contracts of insurance, where various Acts confer rights on third parties. A car owner, for instance, may require insurance cover not only for his or her own use of his or her vehicle, but also for other people who drive his or her car with his or her permission. In theory, the contract of insurance which he or she takes out for the benefit of third parties would not be enforceable by them. However, to avoid this result, specific legislation was introduced to permit a third party to benefit from such an insurance policy. For example, Road Traffic Act 1988, s 148(7) states that a person issuing an insurance policy is liable to indemnify not just the person taking out the policy, but also 'the persons or classes of persons specified in the policy in respect of any liability which the policy purports to cover'. In another statutory exception to the privity rule, it is provided that a person can effect an insurance on his or her life for the benefit of his or her spouse or children (see Married Women's Property Act 1882, s 11). Such a life insurance creates a trust in favour of the named beneficiaries, rather than becoming part of the insured person's estate.

17.35   For a fuller list of statutory exceptions, see the Law Commission's report (Law Com No 242, pp. 31–5). It is worth noting, in this context, the Package Travel, Package Holidays and Package Tours Regulations 1992 (SI 1992/3288), which implemented Council Directive 90/314/EEC on package travel, package holidays, and package tours. The problem for the consumer, posed by the doctrine of privity, was that the services comprising a package holiday may not be performed directly by the organizer or retailer with whom the contract was made. In order to get around this difficulty, the Regulations confer direct rights on consumers (see reg 2(2)) against the organizer or retailer with whom they contracted (see reg 15). (See further *Titshall* v *Qwerty Travel Ltd* (2011).)

Action brought by the promisee

17.36   The conferral of an enforceable right on a third party by the Contracts (Rights of Third Parties) Act 1999 does not affect the right of a promisee to enforce any term of the contract (see s 4). As explained at the start of this chapter, a contract between A and B, under which

A promises to confer some benefit on C, was not enforceable by C due to the privity doctrine. However, the promisee (B) is able to bring an action against A, as a party to a binding contract. One possible remedy for B is to seek an order for specific performance against A to force him or her to confer the promised benefit on C. An order for specific performance has the effect of ordering a contracting party to do what he or she has undertaken to do (see **Chapter 21**). If we return to the case of *Beswick* v *Beswick* (1968) (discussed earlier), it was held that although the widow could not succeed in her own right, she should be granted an order for specific performance as administratrix of her husband's estate. In this capacity, as his personal representative, there was no problem of privity, as she was suing on behalf of the promisee (her deceased husband), whose rights she was entitled to enforce. The contract in *Beswick* v *Beswick* was of a type that may be specifically enforced, but this would not have been the case if, for example, the contract had been for personal services—as such contracts are not normally specifically enforceable. The remedy of specific performance is not one which is widely available and such an order will not be made where damages are an adequate remedy. It could be argued that, as the 1999 Act has given the third party an enforceable right to claim damages in a case such as *Beswick* v *Beswick*, it is less likely that specific performance would be either sought by the promisee, or granted if similar facts occurred today.

17.37   Where the promisee sues for damages as a result of the promisor failing to confer a benefit on the third party, the question arises as to how such damages are to be assessed. Of course, the promisee can sue for his or her own loss (if he or she has suffered any) but, in general, he or she cannot recover damages for the loss of the third party. The promisee is not able to recover anything other than nominal damages where he or she has not suffered any direct loss. The rule was challenged in *Jackson* v *Horizon Holidays* [1975] 3 All ER 92, where the facts were:

> Mr Jackson (C) booked a holiday with the defendant company for himself, his wife, and his two small children. The price of the holiday (in Sri Lanka) was £1,200, which covered air fares and luxury hotel accommodation. When booking the holiday, C made various stipulations about the accommodation and meals that he and his family were to receive. He was assured that the hotel in question would be up to his expectation. In fact, C and his family were greatly dissatisfied with the hotel, its facilities, and the meals that were served. C brought an action against the defendants for breach of contract, claiming damages in respect of the disappointment and distress, for himself, his wife and his children. The defendants did not contest their liability, but they appealed against the amount of damages (£1,100) awarded by the deputy High Court judge.

The Court of Appeal dismissed the appeal and held that the damages awarded by the judge were not excessive. The majority stated that the amount would have been excessive if it had been awarded only for the loss suffered by Mr Jackson himself. (In this respect, the trial judge's decision was reversed by the majority in the Court of Appeal.) But, in these circumstances, where one party makes a contract for the benefit of himself and others, the court held that he should be able to claim on behalf of the whole party. Mr Jackson could, therefore, recover damages not only for his own dissatisfaction with the holiday, but also for that of his family. Lord Denning stated (at 95):

> 'In this case it was a husband making a contract for the benefit of himself, his wife and children. Other cases readily come to mind. A host makes a contract with a restaurant for a dinner for himself and his friends...It would be a fiction to say that the contract was made by all the family, or all the guests...The real truth is that in each instance, the father, the host...was making a contract himself for the benefit of the whole party. In short, a contract by one for the benefit of third persons.'

17.38   The approach adopted by the majority in *Jackson v Horizon Holidays* (1975) was potentially an attractive one, but it was based heavily on Lord Denning's view of what the law should be, rather than on any convincing authority. This circumvention of the privity rule was not without its critics, and it is not surprising that the matter was considered once again by the House of Lords in *Woodar Investment Development Ltd v Wimpey Construction UK Ltd* [1980] 1 All ER 571. The facts were as follows:

> A contract for the sale of fourteen acres of land for development, for a price of £850,000, included a provision that the purchasers should also pay, on completion, a further £150,000 to a third party who had no legal connection with the vendors. The contract gave the purchasers the right to rescind the contract if, before completion, a statutory authority 'shall have commenced' to acquire the property by compulsory acquisition. In fact, compulsory purchase proceedings had been started for part of the property at the time the contract was completed, but it later became clear that there was a prospect of planning permission being granted for most of the land. Nevertheless, the purchasers wished to rescind the contract. The vendors claimed damages on the basis that the purchasers had wrongfully repudiated the contract. They included in their claim the loss suffered by the third party.

A majority of the House of Lords held that the purchasers had not wrongfully repudiated the contract and their appeal was allowed. The question of damages was not, therefore, relevant to the actual decision. But the court went on to consider the state of the law regarding the recovery of damages for the benefit of third parties and it disapproved of Lord Denning's broad statements in *Jackson v Horizon Holidays Ltd* [1975] 3 All ER 92 at 95–6. This does not mean that the actual decision in *Jackson* was incorrect, but the House of Lords would not endorse Lord Denning's interpretation of the relevant legal authorities. The actual decision in *Jackson* could still be supported on the basis that the claimant recovered solely for his own loss (see the rather terse judgment of James LJ in *Jackson*, at 96), or alternatively, that the case belonged to a special type of contract (for example, where a person contracts for a family holiday, or books a restaurant meal for a party) which requires 'special treatment' (per Lords Wilberforce and Keith in *Woodar*, at 576 and 588, respectively).

However, in *Woodar* it was clear that the promisee (the vendors) would have suffered no loss in relation to the promisor's failure to pay the money to the third party. The House of Lords suggested that the vendors would not have been able to recover substantial damages for the third party's loss (see, for example, the statement of Lord Wilberforce at 577). But, if the *Woodar* facts were to occur today, the third party would be able to claim the promised sum directly under C(RTP)A 1999. This is because the contract purported to confer a benefit on the third party, who was expressly identified, and the promisor would surely not be able to rebut the presumption that the third party was intended to have an enforceable right.

17.39 In spite of the House of Lords' decision in *Woodar Investment Development Ltd* v *Wimpey Construction UK Ltd* (1980), which rejected the idea that a contracting party could generally recover the third party's loss, later cases have considered this matter in different circumstances. For example, in *Linden Gardens Trust Ltd* v *Lenesta Sludge Disposals Ltd* (1993), the House of Lords considered whether a building owner can recover substantial damages for breach of a building contract, if he has parted with the property to a third party. In one appeal, a company (A) contracted with B for the removal of blue asbestos from its property. But, in breach of the agreement, not all the asbestos was removed by B, whilst A in the meantime had sold the property to C. A had attempted to assign its contractual rights to C, but this transaction was invalid and C was thus prevented from succeeding in its action against B for breach of contract. A was not in fact a party to the action in one appeal, but was in the other case which was considered at the same time by the House of Lords. Their Lordships discussed whether A could recover anything other than nominal damages if it brought an action against B, as a result of the loss suffered by C. It was decided that A should be permitted to recover substantial damages, as it was in the contemplation of both contracting parties that the property was likely to be bought by a third party before B's breach occurred, and that A should be regarded as having entered into the contract for C's benefit, as C's loss was foreseeable to B. (Their Lordships relied on *Albacruz (Cargo Owners)* v *Albazero (Owners), The Albazero* [1977] AC 774 per Lord Diplock at 847.) Accordingly, A could recover for C's loss in these commercial circumstances, as C had no direct remedy. The *Linden Gardens* decision was then applied, and extended, by the Court of Appeal in *Darlington Borough Council* v *Wiltshier Northern Ltd* (1995).

17.40 *Linden Gardens Trust Ltd* v *Lenesta Sludge Disposals Ltd* (1993) was distinguished in the House of Lords case of *Panatown Ltd* v *Alfred McAlpine Construction Ltd* (2000), as on the facts of the latter case the third party had been given a direct cause of action against the contractor. In these circumstances, the necessity for the *Linden Gardens Trust* approach was not present, as the third party had a right to recover substantial damages by suing the contractor directly. Therefore, in arbitration proceedings brought by the claimant employer against the defendant contractor, seeking the recovery of substantial damages, a majority of the House of Lords decided against the employer and allowed the contractor's appeal. (For further discussion of this case, see M. Reynolds, 'When Principle and Precedent Collide: Panatown' (2003) Con & Eng Law 8(1) 13–34, which expresses the view that the decision in *Panatown Ltd* v *Alfred McAlpine Construction Ltd* (2000), creates uncertainty in this area, leaving the fundamental principles concerning privity and recovery by a third party unresolved.) Although there is uncertainty over the ambit of the *Linden Gardens Trust* exception, this may well be resolved by a stricter adherence to the general rule in future, in view of the third party right which can now be conferred directly under C(RTP)A 1999.

17.41   Finally, there is another situation in which the promisee may be able to enforce a promise on behalf of a third party. This is where A makes a promise (expressly or impliedly) to B that he will not sue C. If an action is brought by A against C, B may be able to prevent A from succeeding with such an action. For example, in *Snelling v John G Snelling Ltd* (1972), the facts were:

> Three brothers were co-directors of a family business, a building company. The business expanded, but disputes arose between the brothers and relations between them worsened. The three brothers made loans to the company to provide additional finance. The three of them contracted that in the event of any one of them voluntarily resigning his directorship, he would forfeit the money owed to him by the company. The agreement stated that if this occurred, the remaining directors could use the money, not for their personal benefit, but to repay a loan made to their business by a finance company. Three months later, Brian Snelling (the claimant) voluntarily resigned as a director and claimed payment from the defendant company of the sum which he had loaned to it. The company was joined by the other two brothers, Peter and Barrie, as co-defendants, who claimed that the sum due to the claimant had been forfeited by his resignation. Could the defendant company rely on a term in the agreement (between the brothers) which was for the company's benefit, when it was not a party to that agreement?

It was held by Ormrod J that the co-defendants, Peter and Barrie Snelling, were entitled to a declaration that the terms of the agreement were binding on Brian, the claimant. The company, on the other hand, was not a party to the agreement and could not, therefore, rely directly on its terms. However, the judge achieved a fair outcome by granting a declaration that the claimant was not able to call upon the defendant company to repay the loan and his action against the company was dismissed. The judge stated that this course of action was possible as the co-defendant brothers had made out a clear case and succeeded on their counterclaim; and because all the relevant parties were before the court, it would have been a proper case for a stay of all further proceedings. But as the judge thought that the claimant's claim had failed, he dismissed the claim rather than merely ordering a stay of further proceedings. In this way, the claimant was prevented from obtaining a judgment against the company in defiance of the clear agreement, made with his brothers, which was intended to put the family company on a secure business footing. It should be noted that the claimant did not actually promise not to sue the company, but such a promise was a necessary implication of the agreement which he made. (This decision can be contrasted with *Gore v Van der Lann* (1967).)

Circumventions of, and exceptions to, the doctrine

17.42   A number of devices and ingenious arguments have been used in the past to avoid the inconvenience or unfairness caused by a strict application of the privity doctrine. In view of the Contracts (Rights of Third Parties) Act 1999, such devices may be of less practical significance in the future, but they were not abolished by the new legislation (see s 7(1)) and, therefore, need to be considered in the sections which follow.

Collateral contracts

17.43   A good example of judicial ingenuity in avoiding the problem of privity is the use of the concept of a collateral contract. This concept was discussed in detail in **Chapter 7**; and it was considered also in **Chapter 4**, in relation to the practice of manufacturers of goods providing guarantees to the consumer, whose contract is with the retailer (now see reg 15 of the Sale and Supply of Goods to Consumers Regulations 2002 (SI 2002/3045)). The manufacturer is not, of course, a party to the main contract between the retailer and the consumer, and it might appear that such guarantees are unenforceable, as the consumer provides no consideration for the manufacturer's promise. In a rather artificial way, however, it could be argued that, where the consumer is invited to fill in a card or form and send it off to the manufacturer within a specified period, the performance of such an act by the consumer is an acceptance of the manufacturer's (unilateral) offer of a guarantee. Another way of examining such transactions is to say that the guarantee is the subject of a collateral contract, i.e. one that exists alongside the main contract between the retailer and the consumer. The collateral contract represents a judicial device aimed at avoiding an unfair outcome which would otherwise be caused by an established rule of law. This is illustrated by the case *Shanklin Pier v Detel Products Ltd* (1951), where the facts were:

> The claimants (the pier owners) employed contractors to paint their pier under a contract which enabled the claimants to specify the paint to be used. The defendant company, wishing to secure the contract for supplying the paint, told the claimants that their paint (known as DMU) would last for at least seven years. On the strength of this representation (or 'guarantee'), the claimants instructed the contractors to buy and use the defendants' paint for painting the pier. In fact, the paint was unsatisfactory and lasted for a mere three months! The claimants brought an action against the defendants, but they had to get around the problem that the paint was bought from the defendants by the contractors. Could the claimants enforce the defendants' guarantee that the paint would last for at least seven years?

The court found in favour of the claimants. Although the main contract was between the defendants and the contractors for the sale of the paint, there was also a collateral contract between the defendants and the claimants which guaranteed the durability of the paint known as DMU. It must be presumed that the claimants gave consideration for the defendants' guarantee of their paint by instructing the contractors to buy DMU rather than any other paint. (For a further, and more questionable, example of the use of the collateral contract device in relation to guarantees, see *Wells (Merstham) Ltd v Buckland Sand and Silica Co. Ltd* (1965).) As the 1999 Act now permits an enforceable right to be conferred directly on a third party, there will be less need to use the collateral contract device to avoid the privity doctrine in future.

Trust of a promise

17.44 In affirming the common law rule of privity in *Dunlop Pneumatic Tyre Co.* v *Selfridge* [1915] AC 847 (at 853), Lord Haldane stated that although a third party cannot acquire rights by way of a contract, such a right may be conferred by way of property, for example, under a trust. The idea of a trust, as developed in equity, is that of B (the trustee) having rights over property (for example, land or a fund), which he or she is bound by agreement with A, from whom he or she received the property, to exercise on behalf of C, the beneficiary. To put this another way, B holds the property on trust for the benefit of C. Under such an arrangement, C acquires an equitable interest in the property and he or she can enforce his or her rights against the trustee. When the trust is set up, C becomes the beneficial owner of the property and, accordingly, his or her rights are not a result merely of a promise in his or her favour.

17.45 The concept of a trust had some potential as a means of circumventing the privity rule. To take the familiar situation: A makes a promise to B, in exchange for consideration supplied by B, to confer some benefit on C. If it could be argued that B was a trustee for C, then C's rights would be enforceable. One difficulty is the limitation that, for there to be a valid trust, there must (inter alia) be property which is capable of being held on trust and in which the third party has an equitable interest. The question arose as to the circumstances in which the courts were prepared to find that a trust of a contractual right had been created. In other words, when could a promisee under a contract legitimately claim that he or she was a trustee of the benefit of that promise on behalf of a 'stranger' to the contract? Initially the courts showed a willingness to rely on the trust idea in this way (see *Tomlinson* v *Gill* (1756); also *Gregory and Parker* v *Williams* (1817); and *Lloyd's* v *Harper* (1880)). The most well-known example is *Les Affréteurs Réunis SA* v *Leopold Walford Ltd* [1919] AC 801, where the facts were:

> The appellants (the shipowners) entered into a contract to charter a ship to a company (the charterers) for a specific period. Under the contract, the appellants promised to pay a sum of money to the respondent brokers, Leopold Walford Ltd (LW) who had negotiated the contract. Clause 29 of the contract stated: 'A commission of 3 per cent on the estimated gross amount of hire is due to Leopold Walford Ltd on signing this charter (ship lost or not lost).' The ship was requisitioned by the French government and the shipowners refused to pay any commission to LW. It should be noted that LW was not a party to the agreement, although clause 29 was included for its benefit. Although the action was brought by LW, with the consent of the appellants it was treated as if the charterers had been added as claimants.

The House of Lords held that Leopold Walford Ltd was entitled to recover the commission from the ship-owners. The charterers, who were the promisees, were able to enforce the appellants' promise made for the benefit of a third party. The charterers were trustees for LW, who were the beneficiaries of the promise. It was stated by Lord Birkenhead (at 806–7):

> 'It appears to me that for convenience, and under long-established practice, the broker in such cases, in effect, nominates the charterer to contract on his behalf, influenced probably

by the circumstance that there is always a contract between charterer and owner in which this stipulation, which is to enure to the benefit of the broker, may very conveniently be inserted. In these cases the broker, on ultimate analysis, appoints the charterer to contract on his behalf. I agree with the conclusion...that in such cases charterers can sue as trustees on behalf of the broker.'

17.46   This approach of implying a trust of a contractual right appeared to offer a convenient solution to a third party trying to enforce a promise made for his or her benefit. However, the solution raised certain difficulties. Principally, it was objected that the contracting parties will rarely, in fact, intend to create a trust. This is because if they do so, it would mean that they were not free to vary the terms of their agreement in the future, as this would interfere with the beneficiary's rights. As they are unlikely to intend such a restriction on their own contractual rights, it meant that the trust device was of limited utility. The courts now insist on clear evidence that the parties intended to create a trust, and this explains why the trust of a contractual right idea is of little value to third parties today. (For example, in *Vandepitte v Preferred Accident Insurance Corpn of New York* (1933), the Privy Council held that there will be a trust only if it can be definitely proved that there was an intention to create one, and in this case no such intention to constitute a trust was proved.) The reluctance of the courts to imply a trust is further illustrated by *Re Schebsman* [1944] Ch 83. The facts were:

Mr Schebsman was employed by both a Swiss company and its English subsidiary. On the termination of Schebsman's employment with the two companies, the English company agreed to pay him £5,500 in six annual instalments. The agreement also specified that the payments would be made to Schebsman's widow, if he died, and to his daughter, if his widow also died. During the period in which the payments were to be made to him by the company (and two years after the agreement was made), Schebsman was declared bankrupt and then he died. His trustee in bankruptcy sought a declaration that the outstanding sums still to be paid by the English company formed part of the debtor's (i.e. Schebsman's) estate; if this claim succeeded, the money payable by the company would have been available for Schebsman's creditors. The claim failed: the company was entitled to go ahead and make the agreed payments to Schebsman's widow.

The trustee in bankruptcy's appeal was dismissed by the Court of Appeal. The company was, in fact, willing to make the payments to the widow and such payment was held by the court to be due performance of the contract. (The court refused to imply a term into the agreement entitling the trustee in bankruptcy to intercept the sums which were to be paid to the wife and daughter.) This had the effect of preventing the trustee in bankruptcy's claim. However, the court also made it clear that under the agreement between the company and Schebsman, the latter was neither a trustee nor an agent for his wife and daughter. Du Parcq LJ stated (at 104) that unless the parties, by their language and by the circumstances of the case, show a clear intention to create a trust, the court should not be quick to imply such an intention. As the parties to the agreement in *Schebsman* would almost certainly have wished to retain their right at common law to vary the terms of that agreement, his Lordship did not think that a trust had been created. (For instance, Schebsman might have wanted the money to be paid to someone other than his widow.)

17.47   Thus, the courts are reluctant to 'disregard the dividing line between the case of a trust and the simple case of a contract made between two persons for the benefit of a third' (per Lord Greene MR in *Re Schebsman* [1944] Ch 83 at 89). (See also *Green v Russell* (1959) in which it was held that the mere intention, under a contract, to provide benefits for a third party was insufficient to create a trust.) For these reasons, it is clear that the idea of a trust of a contractual right is not a very useful means of evading the privity rule, although it is still theoretically available in cases which come within its narrow ambit. In view of the 1999 legislation offering a more straightforward method of conferring an enforceable right on a third party, it is unlikely that the trust argument will be of much practical significance in the future. (For a recent, unsuccessful attempt to rely on the trust argument, see *Rolls Royce Power Engineering plc v Ricardo Consulting Engineers Ltd* (2003) at [104]–[117].)

Assignment

17.48   The idea of assignment of contractual rights represents another limit on the doctrine of privity. A party to a contract may, in certain circumstances, assign (transfer) his or her existing contractual rights to a third party. For example, a creditor (A) may assign his or her rights against a debtor (B) to a third party (C). By means of such a transaction, C acquires rights against B, as a result of standing in the place of A. The consent of the debtor (B) to such an assignment is not required, although he or she must normally be notified of the transaction. It is argued that B is not at a disadvantage under this type of transaction, as the identity of the creditor usually does not matter to B. In its Consultation Paper on the doctrine of privity, the Law Commission stated that 'the practical importance of assignment is considerable; the whole industry of debt collection and credit factoring depends upon it' (see Law Commission Paper 121, 1991, p. 51).

17.49   Although the law generally permits the assignment of contractual rights, this is subject to the provisos that such transactions must not be unfair to the debtor, and they must not be contrary to the public interest. In particular, it should be noted that rights arising out of 'personal' contracts are incapable of assignment. For example, where A employs B to perform certain services, it would be unfair to permit A to assign his or her contractual rights to C. So an employer is not entitled to transfer the benefit of his or her employee's services to a third party. In view of the willingness of the law to allow the assignment of existing contractual rights to a third party, it made the inflexibility of the privity doctrine, prior to 1999, difficult to understand. In the words of the Law Commission (Law Com 242, 1996, para. 2.17): 'If an immediate assignment is valid, there can hardly be fundamental objections to allowing the third party to sue without an assignment'.

Agency

17.50   Another important limit on the ambit of the privity rule is provided by the doctrine of agency. Under the law of agency, when an agent (B) makes a contract with a third party (C) on behalf of his or her principal (A), this is treated by the law as if the principal had himself made the contract. A and C may sue one another for breach of that contract. However, this 'exception' to the doctrine of privity is perhaps more apparent than real. The law is simply treating A and B as one person. The agent, acting on behalf of his or her principal, makes a contract between his or her principal and a third party.

17.51   However, the law goes further by permitting A to enforce a contract made on his behalf by B, despite the fact that C was unaware that B was acting on A's behalf. (Of course, A must prove that B did in fact have his or her authority to make the contract with C.) This idea of the 'undisclosed principal' appears to be at variance with the doctrine of privity and it can, perhaps, be justified only on the basis of commercial convenience. The third party is contractually bound to a person with whom he or she did not intend to contract and of whose existence he or she was unaware. (For discussion of whether the doctrine of the undisclosed principal can be reconciled with the privity rule, see Tan Cheng-Han, 'Undisclosed Principals and Contract' (2004) 120 LQR 480.)

17.52   Despite the obvious potential for evading the doctrine of privity through the idea of agency, the courts have been reluctant to imply an agency simply for this purpose. A person has to do more than merely claim that a contract was made on his or her behalf. For there to be an agency, one person has to acquire the authority to be the representative of another (see *Southern Water Authority v Carey* (1985)). For example, an agent may have the express authority of his or her principal to act as his or her representative, or such authority may be implied as a result of the relationship between the parties. In either case, it is said that the agent has 'actual' authority. Agency may also arise in other circumstances. For example, unless a third party is notified to the contrary, he or she is entitled to rely on an agent's 'apparent' authority to represent another. So where A represents to C that he or she has given B authority to act as his or her representative, C is entitled to assume that B has the authority which he or she appears to have. (For a discussion of the scope of this doctrine, see *First Energy (UK) Ltd v Hungarian International Bank Ltd* (1993).)

17.53   The extent of the courts' willingness to accept an agency argument, as a means of circumventing the privity doctrine, was discussed at the start of this chapter in relation to attempts by third parties to rely on an exclusion clause. Here the issue is whether a third party can claim the benefit of an exclusion clause as a defence to an action by one of the contracting parties under a separate cause of action (usually negligence). It will be remembered that in *Scruttons Ltd v Midland Silicones Ltd* [1962] AC 446, the House of Lords held that the stevedores (third party) were not entitled to rely on the limitation of liability contained in the bill of lading, when sued in tort for their negligence in unloading the goods. The doctrine of privity prevented the stevedores from relying on a contract to which they were not a party in defending the action. The argument of the stevedores that they were the undisclosed principals of one of the contracting parties (the carrier), who acted as their agent, was also unsuccessful. Lord Reid set out (at 474) the conditions which needed to be satisfied for the agency argument to succeed. He explained that the bill of lading must make it clear that the stevedore is intended to be protected by its provisions which limit liability. The bill of lading must make it clear that the carrier, as well as contracting for these provisions on his or her own behalf, is also contracting as an agent for the stevedore, who will in turn be protected by the provisions. The carrier needs the stevedore's authority to act in this way, and any problems of consideration must be overcome.

17.54   Although the stevedores were unsuccessful with this agency argument in *Scruttons Ltd v Midland Silicones Ltd* (1962), it will be recalled that the Privy Council, in *New Zealand Shipping Co. Ltd* v *Satterthwaite* (1974), allowed the stevedores the protection of an exemption clause. In *Satterthwaite*, the court held (inter alia) that the bill of lading was not simply a contract between the owners of the goods and the carrier. It also represented a contract between the owners and the stevedores, made through the carrier as agent. (See also *Port Jackson Stevedoring Pty* v *Salmond & Spraggon (Australia) Pty* (1980).) Despite the success of the agency argument in these cases, it provides a rather technical and uncertain solution to the problem. (For example, see *The Mahkutai* (1996).) The courts naturally wish to take a practical approach to everyday commercial transactions, but a simpler solution is preferable to the one offered by the agency approach. A more convenient way of conferring such a benefit on a third party is now available under the new legislation (see earlier discussion). In C(RTP)A 1999, references to a third party enforcing a contractual term are to be understood as including the right to rely on an exclusion or limitation clause (see s 1(6)).

Privity and the doctrine of consideration

17.55   In *Dunlop Pneumatic Tyre Co. Ltd* v *Selfridge & Co. Ltd* [1915] AC 847, Lord Haldane LC (at 853) referred to the fundamental principles in English law that 'only a person who is a party to a contract can sue on it ... [and] that if a person with whom a contract not under seal has been made is to be able to enforce it consideration must have been given by him to the promisor or to some other person at the promisor's request'. If we reconsider *Tweddle* v *Atkinson* (1861) (discussed at the start of this chapter), the decision could be explained in terms of either lack of privity, or lack of consideration provided by the son-in-law. However, there has been much debate as to whether the privity doctrine is distinct and independent from the rule that consideration must move from the promisee, with academic opinion being quite divided on the subject.[5]

17.56   The phrase 'consideration must move from the promisee' is a little enigmatic, but it is generally accepted as meaning that a person can enforce a contractual promise only if he himself provided the consideration for that promise; i.e. consideration must have been provided by the claimant. When the phrase is understood in this sense, it is clear that it is not possible to 'reform the privity doctrine while leaving untouched the rule that consideration must move from the promisee' (see Law Commission Report, No 242, Privity of Contract: Contracts for the Benefit of Third Parties', 1996, para. 6.5), because the two doctrines are very closely linked. Accordingly, the Law Commission recommended that the legislation reforming the privity doctrine 'should ensure that the rule that consideration must move from the promisee is reformed

---

5   See Law Commission Report, No 242, *Privity of Contract: Contracts for the Benefit of Third Parties*, Cm 3329, 1996, para. 6.1.

to the extent necessary to avoid nullifying [the] proposed reform of the doctrine of privity' (para. 6.8). In the event, it was realized that a specific provision to this effect was unnecessary. It would be achieved by the central provision of the new law (i.e. C(RTP)A 1999, s 1) conferring a third party right to enforce a contractual term, as such a provision could only be interpreted as also reforming the rule that consideration must move from the promisee.

17.57   The Law Commission also addressed the wider policy implications, for the doctrine of consideration,[6] of reforming the privity rule (Law Com No 242, paras 6.13–6.17). It was concerned, in particular, with the argument that a third party's right to enforce a contractual term puts him or her in a better position than a gratuitous promisee. However, by permitting an identified third party to enforce a contractual term, under C(RTP)A 1999, s 1, the law is giving effect to the intentions of the contracting parties, who have provided consideration; the bargain is being enforced, albeit by the third party. It can be argued that this situation is distinguishable from the one in which no consideration is given by a promisee in exchange for a promise (i.e. the gratuitous promisee); here, there is no bargain to be enforced, as no consideration was present.

17.58   The specific problem of whether a 'joint promisee' who has provided none of the consideration under a contract can sue, is one which requires some discussion. Where a promise is made in favour of A and B, in circumstances where they can be regarded as joint promisees, but only A provides any consideration, can B enforce the promise? This problem was raised in the Australian case of *Coulls* v *Bagot's Executor and Trustee Co. Ltd* [1967] ALR 385, where the facts were:

> Arthur Coulls agreed to give to the O'Neil Construction Co. the sole right to quarry and remove stone from his land. The agreement continued: 'O'Neil Construction Ltd agrees to pay at the rate of 3d per ton for all stone quarried and sold, also a fixed minimum royalty of £12 per week for a period of ten years with an option of another ten years [at the same rate]...I [Arthur Coulls] authorise the above Company to pay all money connected with this agreement to my wife, Doris Coulls and myself, Arthur Coulls as joint tenants'. This written agreement (not under seal) was signed by Arthur Coulls, Doris Coulls, and O'Neil. After the death of Arthur Coulls, the O'Neil Company paid the royalty to Doris Coulls as agreed. The action involved a dispute between Arthur Coulls's executors and his wife as to who should receive the royalty payments.

It was held by a majority of the High Court of Australia that, after Arthur Coulls's death, the O'Neil Company was bound to pay the royalties to his estate and not to his wife. Three of the judges thought that Doris Coulls was not a party to the agreement and that the authority given by her husband to the company under the agreement, to make payments to her, lapsed on his death (i.e. she was not a promisee). It was thought significant that the husband had 'authorized' payment to his wife; she was not entitled to payment in her own right. However, Barwick CJ and Windeyer J dissented, as they considered Doris Coulls to be a joint promisee. (The majority of

---

6   See also C. Mitchell, 'Privity Reform and the Nature of Contractual Obligations' (1999) 19 LS 229.

the court were of the opinion that a joint promisee could sue even though he or she had provided no consideration.) In his judgment, Barwick CJ argued (at 395) that the agreement was one in respect of which there was privity between the company and both the husband and wife, as joint promisees. Windeyer J (at 403) thought that the promise of the company was to pay for the stone at the agreed rate, with 'such payments to be made to the husband and wife jointly during their lives and thereafter to the survivor'. Windeyer J went on to consider her apparent lack of consideration for the promise (at 405):

> 'Still, it was said, no consideration moved from her. But that, I consider, mistakes the nature of a contract made with two or more persons jointly. The promise is made to them collectively. It must, of course, be supported by consideration, but that does not mean by considerations furnished by them separately. It means a consideration given on behalf of them all, and therefore moving from all of them. In such a case the promise of the promisor is not gratuitous: and, as between him and the joint promisees, it matters not how they were able to provide the price of his promise to them.'

17.59   The Law Commission (Law Com No 242, para. 6.10) argued that a joint promisee should have the right to sue despite not having provided the consideration. (See also *McEvoy* v *Belfast Banking Co. Ltd* [1935] AC 24 at 43 per Lord Atkin.) However, the Commission did not include such joint promisees within its reform proposals, for a variety of reasons which need not be considered here. It thought it preferable to leave the matter to the courts to develop 'in the confident expectation' that, especially in view of the statutory reform of the privity doctrine, they will accept the joint promisee argument 'so that a joint promisee who has not provided consideration will not be left without a basic right to enforce the contract' (at para. 6.11). In the words of one recent commentator on C(RTP)A 1999, an 'acceptable source of judicial creativity might be development of the existing joint promisee doctrine. Perhaps that rule is elastic enough to allow the court to fill any gaps in the legislative scheme' (see N. Andrews, 'Strangers to Justice No Longer: The Reversal of the Privity Rule under the Contracts (Rights of Third Parties) Act 1999' (2001) 60 CLJ 353 at 379).

Conclusion

17.60   The doctrine of privity has traditionally represented the principle that only a party to a contract can enforce a benefit, or have burdens imposed on him or her, under that contract. The restriction on a third party being able to enforce a provision which was intended for his or her benefit meant that the intentions of the contracting parties could be thwarted, and the reasonable expectations of the third party denied, by the doctrine. This necessitated a series of technical, and sometimes artificial, methods of evading the strict application of the privity rule. Also, a number of statutory exceptions were required to circumvent the doctrine in areas of commercial practice where its application was extremely inconvenient.

17.61   After repeated judicial and academic criticism over many years, and a detailed Law Commission report on the subject, the law was finally reformed by means of the important

Contracts (Rights of Third Parties) Act 1999. However, the Act does not apply to all types of contract; nor does it directly affect the existing exceptions to, and circumventions of, the doctrine. It introduces a new, and more general, exception into the law, but the doctrine of privity was not abolished by the Act. The Law Commission (Law Com No 242, para. 5.10) also expressed the view that the new Act should not be interpreted as preventing the future development of third party rights through the common law. (For example, see *London Drugs Ltd* v *Kuehne & Nagel International Ltd* (1992); for further discussion of the *London Drugs* case, and the role of the courts in making 'incremental changes to the common law necessary to address emerging needs and values in society', see *Fraser River Pile and Dredge Ltd* v *Can-Drive Services Ltd* (2000) per Iacobucci J at 208–9.)[7]

17.62   Finally, the aspect of the privity rule which states that a third party cannot have burdens imposed upon him or her by the contracting parties, has not been affected by the 1999 legislation. It should be noted, however, that certain contractual restrictions on the use of land are said to 'run with the land' and can therefore burden people other than the original contracting parties. (The debate as to whether this principle has a wider application, beyond the boundaries of land law, requires no further elaboration here.)

🛆 Summary

- Privity of contract, i.e. that only a party to a contract can enforce a right under that contract (the 'third party rule'), or have obligations imposed on him or her by the contract, is a long-established principle of English law.
- The third party rule was capable of disappointing reasonable contractual and commercial expectations.
- Judicial and academic opinion supported reform of the third party rule, despite the many exceptions to and circumventions of the rule which are available.
- The common law privity doctrine has been reformed, not abolished, by the Contracts (Rights of Third Parties) Act 1999, which was based largely on a Law Commission Report (1996).
- The Act does not affect the existing exceptions to (or evasions of) the privity doctrine, but it introduced a new and more general exception to the doctrine.
- Under the Act (s 1(1)), a third party can enforce a term of a contract in his or her own right if (a) the contract expressly provides for this, or (b) the term purports to confer on him or her a benefit (unless it appears that the contracting parties did not intend the term to be enforceable by the third party).
- Where a third party right has been conferred, there are general restrictions (under s 2(1)) on the freedom of the contracting parties to vary or cancel their agreement subsequently, in the absence of any express provision in the contract (s 2(3)).

---

7   For a discussion of this and other Canadian Supreme Court decisions, see M. Ogilvie, 'Privity of Contract in the Supreme Court of Canada: Fare Thee Well or Welcome Back' (2002) JBL 163.

- The third party's right to enforce a term is subject to the defences that would have been available to the promisor in an action by the promisee, unless there is an express term to the contrary (s 3).

- The conferral of an enforceable right on a third party does not affect the right of the promisee to enforce any contractual term (s 4), with suitable protection for the promisor against 'double liability' (s 5).

- Certain types of contract remain outside the scope of the Act (s 6) although the provisions of the Arbitration Act 1996 may apply to a third party (s 8).

- The right of enforceability under s 1 does not affect any right (or remedy) of a third party which is available to him or her elsewhere than in the Act (s 7).

- The Act has not affected the aspect of the privity rule which states that a third party cannot have burdens imposed on him or her (subject to certain exceptions) by the contracting parties.

▶ Further reading

N. **Andrews**, 'Strangers to Justice No Longer: The Reversal of the Privity Rule under the Contracts (Rights of Third Parties) Act 1999' (2001) 60 CLJ 353

A. **Burrows**, 'The Contracts (Rights of Third Parties) Act and its Implications for Commercial Contracts' (2000) 4 LMCLQ 540

T. **Cheng-Han**, 'Undisclosed Principals and Contract' (2004) 120 LQR 480

M. **Dean**, 'Removing a Blot on the Landscape—the Reform of the Doctrine of Privity' (2000) JBL 143

R. **Flannigan**, 'Privity—The End of an Era (Error)' (1987) 103 LQR 564

P. **Kincaid**, 'Privity Reform in England' (2000) 116 LQR 43

Law Commission Report, No 242, 'Privity of Contract: Contracts for the Benefit of Third Parties', Cm 3329, 1996

C. **MacMillan**, 'A Birthday Present for Lord Denning: The Contracts (Rights of Third Parties) Act 1999' (2000) 63 MLR 721

C. **Mitchell**, 'Privity Reform and the Nature of Contractual Obligations' (1999) 19 LS 229

P. **Rawlings**, 'Third Party Rights in Contract' (2006) 7 LMCLQ 7

M. **Reynolds**, 'When Principle and Precedent Collide: Panatown' (2003) 8(1) Con & Eng Law 13

R. **Stevens**, 'The Contracts (Rights of Third Parties) Act 1999' (2004) 120 LQR 292

Chapter 18

Performance and breach

Performance

Discharge by performance and agreement

18.1   Although we are often considering the situation where something has gone wrong with a contract, most contracts are performed without any problems arising. The usual way in which a party to a contract ceases to have any obligations under the contract is by doing what the contract requires. Where performance has been completed, and liability has ceased, the situation is referred to as 'discharge by performance'.

18.2   What is required for performance of the contract will depend upon its express and implied terms and their construction (see **Chapter 7**). Often no fault will be required for a breach to occur, i.e. contractual obligations are often a matter of strict liability. For example, the terms implied by ss 12–15 of the Sale of Goods Act 1979, dealing with the title and the quality of the goods, impose strict liability. They can be breached without any fault on the part of the seller. In contrast, terms requiring the exercise of a particular skill or expertise will normally require only that due care be taken in the exercise of the skill or expertise (see, for example, Supply of Goods and Services Act 1982, s 13; *Thake* v *Maurice* (1986)—see para. **7.7**).

18.3   A breach will arise if there is disparity between what was promised and what has occurred, or not occurred, and there is no lawful excuse. The burden of proving that a breach has occurred lies on the party alleging that it has. Frustration (see **Chapter 19**) provides an example of 'lawful excuse' for non-performance. It discharges both parties from further performance of the contract.

18.4   The parties may provide that the contract itself, or some of the obligations under it, are not to be immediately effective. A condition precedent may suspend entirely the formation of the contract, or it may not delay formation itself but merely the operation of some, or all, of the obligations under the contract. Obviously there can be no breach as long as the contract, or the particular obligation, has not become operative. In *Pym* v *Campbell* (1856) the situation was perceived as one where prior to the fulfilment of the contingency there was no contract in existence. In that case, the facts were:

> The claimant wished to sell to the defendant a share in an invention of the claimant. A written document appeared to contain an agreement for the purchase. The claimant sought to rely upon it, but the defendant established that the parties had further agreed that the written document was to be the agreement only if the claimant's invention was approved of by a third party, Abernethie. Abernethie had not given his approval of the invention.

The court concluded that there was no contract at all. Abernethie's approval was a condition precedent to the existence of the contract. There was no contract and no breach by the defendant. However, it may be that a condition precedent merely suspends some of the obligations until it is fulfilled and other obligations may be operative prior to the contingency being fulfilled, including subsidiary obligations in relation to the contingency. So, for example, in *Marten* v *Whale* (1917) where the obligation to sell land was subject to the purchaser's solicitor's approval of the title, the obligation to make the sale was suspended until the contingency was fulfilled (which it was not), but prior to that the purchaser had to ensure that it was possible for that approval to be given.

18.5   The parties may have provided that the contract is to end upon the occurrence of a certain circumstance—a condition subsequent. A condition subsequent is a condition upon the fulfilment of which an existing contract is extinguished. *Head* v *Tattersall* (1871) is the case usually quoted in this context:

> A horse was sold on the basis that it had been hunted with the Bicester hounds. It was expressly stated by the seller that if it had not been so hunted the buyer could return it by 5 pm on the following Wednesday. Before that time arrived the horse was injured and the buyer discovered that it had not been hunted with the Bicester hounds. The buyer had not been at fault with regard to the injury to the horse.

It was held that the buyer could return the horse, despite its injury, because it had not been hunted with the Bicester hounds.

18.6   The contract may also provide one party with an option to end the contract under certain circumstances. Those circumstances could include a breach by the other party which would not otherwise give rise to the right to terminate (i.e. the breach is not a breach of condition or a sufficiently serious breach of an innominate term). When that occurs, the damages awarded for the breach will not cover the loss of the rest of the contract, as they would do if the breach itself gave rise to the right to terminate.[1]

---

1   See para. **8.33** and *Financings Ltd* v *Baldock* (1963). But see also *Lombard North Central plc* v *Butterworth* (1987), para. **8.34**.

18.7   The original contract may not provide for its termination but the parties may make a new agreement to end the original contract, i.e. a contract may be discharged by agreement. Any such fresh agreement raises the issue of consideration unless it is contained in a deed (see **Chapter 4**). There is no problem where it is decided to end a contract which is still executory, when both parties still have obligations to perform. The giving up of rights on each side will furnish the necessary consideration. The situation is more difficult where only one party still has to perform. That party should then supply fresh consideration for the agreement to end the original contract, but the decision in *Williams v Roffey Bros & Nicholls (Contractors) Ltd* (1990) (see para. **4.39**ff), on what can constitute consideration, should be borne in mind—as should the possibilities of waiver or promissory estoppel (see **Chapter 5**). The same consideration problems arise where the parties agree to change their agreement, rather than end it. In addition, formality issues may arise where the original contract was one requiring formalities.

Order of performance and independent obligations

18.8   The order of performance may be indicated by contingent conditions. For example, the fulfilment by A of an obligation under the contract he has made with B may be a condition precedent to B's performance. If the performance of an obligation of one party, A, is a condition precedent to the other party's, B's, liability to perform, then the contract is safer for B than for A: B will not be left in the situation where he has performed and A refuses to do so. The same, of course, does not apply to A. Whether the contract makes A's performance a condition precedent to B's liability may depend upon B's superior bargaining power, or the practicalities of the situation, or simply what is usual in a particular type of contract. In *Trans Trust SPRL v Danubian Trading Co. Ltd* (1952) there was a contract for the sale of 1,000 tons of rolled steel. There was an obligation on the buyer to open a confirmed letter of credit to pay for the steel. It was necessary that the buyer should open the letter of credit before the seller became liable to deliver. It was known to both parties that the seller could not obtain the goods until the letter of credit was opened. The obligation to open the letter of credit was construed as a condition precedent to the seller's obligation to deliver. The seller did not have to perform until the buyer had done so.

18.9   Concurrent conditions also indicate the order of performance. For example in sale of goods contracts, in the absence of contrary intention, Sale of Goods Act 1979, s 28 makes the seller's obligation to deliver, and the buyer's obligation to pay, concurrent conditions. Each party must be willing to perform his or her obligation in order to claim that the other should do so. The concurrent condition provides some security for each party's performance.

18.10   However, many contractual obligations are independent of each other. Their performance is not linked to that of the other party and non-performance may not provide an excuse for the other's failure to perform. For example, the landlord's obligation to repair and the tenant's to pay rent were held to be independent of each other and the landlord's failure to repair did not justify the tenant in refusing to pay the rent (*Taylor v Webb* (1937)).

Entire contracts

18.11   We have already seen that contingent promissory conditions may set the order of performance. The performance of an obligation of one party may be a condition precedent to the other party becoming obliged to perform. This can lead to cases where the situation is that of an 'entire contract' and one party is obliged to perform his or her side of the contract before the other party becomes obliged to pay him or her. The harsh result which can be achieved in such cases is illustrated by *Cutter* v *Powell* (1795):

> Mr Cutter had signed on as second mate on the Governor Parry for a voyage from Jamaica to Liverpool. It was stated that he would receive 30 guineas 'provided he proceeds, continues and does his duty' from Jamaica to Liverpool. The ship sailed on 2 August and arrived at Liverpool on 9 October. Unfortunately, Mr Cutter died on 20 September, before the ship reached Liverpool. His widow was suing for payment for the work he had done before his death. The usual rate of pay was £4 per month. The voyage was one which should have taken about two months.

The court held that the contract was entire. There was no obligation to pay for any work done unless the voyage was completed and, as Mr Cutter did not complete the voyage, his widow could not claim any payment. Mr Cutter's completion of the voyage was a condition precedent to the obligation to pay for the work he had done. This seems harsh, but the court was obviously influenced in its conclusion by the fact that 30 guineas was much greater than the sum which he would have expected to earn under a contract based on payment by the month rather than for the whole voyage. Lord Kenyon CJ said:

> 'He stipulated to receive the larger sum if the whole duty were performed, and nothing unless the whole of that duty were performed; it was a kind of insurance.'

In other words, there was good reason, in the amount contracted for, to regard Mr Cutter's completion of the voyage as a condition precedent to any obligation to pay him. The conclusion reached in *Cutter* v *Powell* (1795) would have been otherwise if the contract had not been entire but severable, i.e. if the obligation to act as second mate from Jamaica to Liverpool had been divided up so that the corresponding obligation was to pay so much for each month of the voyage. Finding that a contract is severable, rather than entire, is one way of avoiding the sort of result that was reached in *Cutter* v *Powell*.[2]

18.12   *Sumpter* v *Hedges* [1898] 1 provides another example of the operation of the rule on entire contracts. In that case:

> Mr Hedges contracted with Mr Sumpter for Mr Sumpter to build two houses on his land for the sum of £565. Mr Sumpter did part of the work, to the value of £333, but his financial circumstances were such that he could not complete the work. Mr Hedges finished the houses

---

2   In relation to salaries or wages the common law is assisted by Apportionment Act 1870, s 2 which states that 'all rents, annuities, dividends, and other periodical payments in the nature of income . . . shall . . . be considered as accruing from day to day'.

> himself. In doing so he made use of unused materials which belonged to Mr Sumpter and
> which he had left on Mr Hedges' land.

The question was whether Mr Sumpter could recover payment in relation to the work which he had carried out in erecting the houses. The court said that he could not. The contract was for a lump sum to be paid upon completion of the houses and he could not succeed in his claim when he had not done that.

18.13   Some mitigation of the entire contracts rule occurs when the work done by one party is adopted by the other party, whom it has benefited. The benefiting party will then have to pay for the work done. (The action is then one for quantum meruit—a restitutionary action: see **web chapter 2**.) On the same basis, Mr Hedges paid Mr Sumpter the value of Mr Sumpter's materials which he, Mr Hedges, had used on the houses after Mr Sumpter stopped work. He did not have to pay for the work Mr Sumpter had done on the houses because it could not be said that his adoption of the work was a matter on which he could act 'voluntarily'. He did not have sufficient choice in the matter. He either had to finish the houses himself or have the nuisance of incomplete buildings on his land. In contrast, he had a fully effective range of choices open to him when he decided to use Mr Sumpter's materials in the completion of the houses.

18.14   However, the greater mitigation of the entire contracts rule came with the idea of 'substantial performance'. In *Hoenig* v *Isaacs* [1952] 2 All ER 176:

> Mr Isaacs contracted with Mr Hoenig for the decoration and furnishing of his flat for £750.
> Mr Hoenig fulfilled the contract except in relation to some defects in a bookcase and a ward-
> robe, costing about £55 to rectify.

Mr Hoenig was able to recover the sum due under the contract, less the sum Mr Isaacs could claim in damages for the defects (the cost of putting them right). Mr Hoenig had 'substantially performed'.

'Substantial performance' may simply be a matter of correctly identifying what is required for fulfilment of the condition precedent. Somervell LJ distinguished the case before him from that of *Cutter* v *Powell* (1795). He said (at 178):

> '[*Cutter* v *Powell*] clearly decided that his continuing as mate during the whole of the voyage was
> a condition precedent to payment. It did not decide that if he had completed the main purpose of
> the contract, namely serving as mate for the whole voyage, the defendant could have repudiated
> his liability by establishing that in the course of the voyage, the sailor had, possibly through inad-
> vertence, failed on some occasion in his duty as mate whereby some damage had been caused.'

He continued (at 179):

> 'The question here is whether in a contract for work and labour for a lump sum payable
> on completion the defendant can repudiate liability under the contract on the ground

that the work though "finished" or "done" is in some respects not in accordance with the contract.'

18.15 As Somervell LJ indicated in *Hoenig* v *Isaacs* (1952), the idea of 'substantial performance' depends upon asking whether the work has been 'done', albeit with defects. In *Bolton* v *Mahadeva* [1972] 2 All ER 1322, the idea of 'substantial performance' did not entitle the contractor to recover. In that case:

> Mr Mahadeva had contracted with Mr Bolton for the installation of a central heating system for £560. The system was defective and it would have cost about £175 to make it function correctly. There were fumes in the living room and, on average, the house was 10 per cent less warm than it should have been, although in some rooms it was as much as 30 per cent colder.

Mr Bolton had not 'substantially performed' and could not recover the contract price with damages for the defects set off against it. Here the judgments indicate a general assessment of the extent to which the performance carried out differs from that required by the contract. Cairns LJ said (at 1324):

> 'The main question in the case is whether the defects in workmanship ... were of such character and amount that the claimant could not be said to have substantially performed his contract. That is, in my view, clearly the legal principle which has to be applied in cases of this kind.'

The explanation of substantial performance being sufficient to enable a claim to payment to be made may be that:

> 'it is frequently correct to say that absolutely exact and complete performance by the claimant is not a condition precedent to the duty of the defendant. If substantial performance by the claimant was sufficient to charge the defendant, then such substantial performance was the only condition and the requirement has been exactly fulfilled' (Corbin, 'Conditions in the Law of Contract' (1919) 28 Yale LJ 739 at 759).

18.16 The Law Commission has criticized cases such as *Bolton* v *Mahadeva* (1972) and recommended that the party whose performance is not in keeping with the contract, and whom the entire contracts rule deprives of payment, should receive some payment for the benefit he or she has conferred on the other party (Law Com Report, No 121, *Pecuniary Restitution for Breach of Contract*, 1983). But there has been no move to implement that recommendation and Brian Davenport QC added a strong note of dissent to the report. He concluded that, in almost all contracts of any substance, provision is now made for staged payment (i.e. payment as and when a stage of the work is completed), thus avoiding the problem posed by the entire contracts rule. However, he thought that the rule served a useful purpose which the majority's recommendation would undermine. He stated:

> 'The so-called mischief which the report is intended to correct is therefore likely only to exist in relation to small, informal contracts of which the normal example will be a contract between

> a householder and a jobbing builder to carry out a particular item of work. Experience has shown that it is all too common for such builders not to complete one job of work before moving on to the next. The effect of the report is to remove from the householder almost the only effective sanction he has against the builder not completing the job. In short he is prevented from saying with any legal effect, "Unless you come back and finish the job I shan't pay you a penny".'

Breach

18.17   A breach of contract provides the injured party with a right to damages (see **Chapter 20**), or he or she may be able to sue for the contract price if it has become due. On occasion, equity may provide specific enforcement of the whole or part of the other party's obligations. In addition, the question may arise of using a restitutionary remedy to recover sums paid or the value of goods or services supplied (see **web chapter** 2). Consideration may also need to be given to relief from forfeiture for the party in breach).

18.18   However, one of the often-disputed consequences of breach is that of the right to terminate the contract. When certain breaches occur, the injured party has a choice whether to terminate the contract.

Termination for breach

18.19   An injured party has a right to damages for any breach. However, we have also seen that the injured party occasionally also has the right to terminate the contract because of the other party's breach. So, for example, there is a right to terminate if there is a breach of condition or if there is a sufficiently serious breach of an innominate term (i.e. a breach which substantially deprives the injured party of all the benefit which he or she was intended to derive from the contract—*Hong Kong Fir Shipping Co. Ltd* v *Kawasaki Kisen Kaisha Ltd* (1962): see **Chapter 8**). Such terms are labelled according to the intention of the parties at the time of contracting (*Bunge Corpn* v *Tradax Export SA* (1981)—see para. **8.4**).

18.20   However, one party may repudiate the contract. He or she may indicate that he or she no longer intends to be bound by it, and that may be done in the context of an actual breach or an anticipatory breach (see para. **18.21**). The injured party will have the right to terminate where the other party gives 'an intimation of an intention to abandon and altogether refuse performance of the contract . . . [or of] an intention no longer to be bound by the contract' (*Freeth* v *Burr* (1874) LR 9 CP 208 at 213 per Lord Coleridge). If the injured party elects to accept the repudiation, the contract will be terminated (*Geys* v *Societe Generale* (2012)). Yet, determining whether the contract has been repudiated may be difficult. It can occur as a consequence of the party stating that he or she will not perform or, more problematically, by the parties' actions. For example, one party may allege that the other has rendered it impossible for him or her to perform the instant contract because that party has undertaken other obligations. It will then be a matter of finding whether those other obligations are 'of such a nature or have such an effect that it can truly be said that the party in question has put it out of his power to perform' (*Alfred C Toepfer International GmbH v Itex Itagrani Export SA* [1993] 1 Lloyd's Rep 360 at 362). Another example of where difficulties arise is that of instalment contracts to be performed over a period of time. In *Decro-Wall International SA v Practitioners Marketing Ltd* (1971), the facts were:

> The claimants, a French manufacturing company, made a contract with the defendants giving the defendants the sole right to sell their products in the United Kingdom. The defendants undertook to develop the UK market for the claimants' goods and were very successful in doing so. However, the defendants were obliged to pay for a batch of goods within ninety days of receiving it and they were often late in paying. Despite the successful market development by the defendants, the claimants chose to terminate the contract for a late payment by the defendants. The claimants never doubted that they would receive payment for goods delivered, even though it might often be late. The lateness of the payments caused them little damage.

The question for the Court of Appeal was 'whether these past failures to pay on the due date, coupled with the likelihood of similar failures, constituted a repudiation of the contract' which entitled the claimants to terminate. The Court of Appeal held that the termination had not been justified. The breaches which had occurred, and what was likely to happen in the future, did not go to the root of the contract.

18.21   The intention of the party in breach is relevant in this situation as it is in relation to an anticipatory breach; a mistake as to the requirements of the contract may be relevant here as with anticipatory breach, i.e. the party in breach may think that what he or she intends to do in the future will amount to performance, whereas it will in fact amount to breach. There is difficulty with the court's treatment of such intention (see para. **18.32**ff).

18.22   When a breach occurs which could lead to termination, the injured party has a choice (*Decro-Wall International SA v Practitioners in Marketing Ltd* (1971); *Geys v Societe Generale* (2012)). He or she can terminate or he or she can decide to continue with the contract, to affirm it, in which case he or she is simply left with his or her remedy in damages. The injured party does have time to decide whether to affirm or terminate, but doing nothing for too long may be seen as affirmation (*Stocznia Gdanska SA v Latvian Shipping (No 3)* (2002) per Rix LJ). Once affirmation has occurred, the injured party can no longer terminate for that breach, but if the breach is continuing or fresh breaches occur then the possibility of terminating is again present (*Stocznia Gdanska*). As has been indicated, if the injured party behaves as if he or she has decided to continue with the contract, then that can amount to affirmation provided that the injured party knew, or should have known, of the facts giving rise to the right to terminate, and possibly of the existence of that right. However, if he or she does not have such knowledge, and has not been in a position where he or she should have had such knowledge, actions indicating the continuance of the contract will not constitute affirmation, but the injured party may be estopped from terminating if the party in breach has acted in reliance on the representation of affirmation created by the injured party's actions (*The Kanchenjunga* (1990)).

18.23   Termination for breach is sometimes referred to as 'rescission' of the contract, and this can be confusing. It is better to confine the use of the word 'rescission' to the context of voidable contracts, for example where the contract has been made on the basis of a misrepresentation. In that context rescission is 'rescission ab initio': it is as if the contract had never existed. In the context of breach, rescission merely relates to the future.

> '[R]escission [for breach] is quite different from rescission ab initio, such as may arise for example in cases of mistake, fraud or lack of consent. In those cases the contract is treated in law as never having come into existence . . . In the cases of an accepted repudiatory breach the contract has come into existence but has been put an end to or discharged . . . acceptance of a repudiatory breach does not bring about rescission ab initio' (*Johnson v Agnew* [1979] 1 All ER 883 at 889 per Lord Wilberforce).

18.24   It is easier not to confuse the two situations if we refer to termination, rather than rescission, in relation to breach. What occurs on termination for breach can be more easily understood if we think of the contract in terms of primary and secondary obligations. The division is between the basic promised performance (primary obligations) and the obligations which arise on breach (secondary obligations). When X and Y have made a contract under which X is to build a wall for Y, and Y is to pay X for doing so, then the primary obligations relate to the building of the wall and the payment of money. When X refuses to build the wall, or builds a defective wall, there is a breach of X's primary obligations and the secondary obligation on X to pay damages arises. If the breach is merely a minor defect in the wall, Y will be able to claim damages from X for the breach and X and Y will still be liable to perform any further primary obligations. However, when X's breach is such as to entitle Y to terminate the contract, and he or she chooses to do so, the primary obligations cease, but damages are still calculated in relation to the promised performance. There is no question of the situation becoming one where the contract is treated as if it had never existed. In *Photo Production Ltd* v *Securicor Transport Ltd* [1980] 1 All ER 556 Lord Diplock analysed the situation in relation to the unperformed obligations, in terms of primary and secondary obligations and made the continuing role of the contract clear. He said (at 567):

> '[W]here such an election [to terminate] is made (a) there is substituted by implication of law for the primary obligations of the party in default which remain unperformed a secondary obligation to pay monetary compensation to the other party for the loss sustained by him in consequence of their non-performance in the future and (b) the unperformed primary obligations of that other party are discharged.'

When there is a breach which gives rise to termination, the party in breach must pay damages for the immediate consequences of the breach and, in addition, for the loss caused by the non-performance of the rest of his or her primary obligations. In the secondary obligations the continued life of the contract is clear, as is the distinction between termination for breach and rescission ab initio.

18.25   A situation may arise in which one party claims to be able to terminate, because of the breach of the other, but he or she gives a reason which does not in fact justify termination. If, at the time of termination, there is another, unstated reason which would justify that termination, then it can usually be relied upon by the party who is terminating to prevent his or her actions from themselves being a repudiatory breach. In *The Mihalis Angelos* (1971) the charterers had purported to cancel the charter on the basis of a force majeure clause. In fact, the charterers had no right to cancel on that basis. However, they were subsequently held not to be in breach because the owners had been in breach of a condition of the contract. That breach of condition had given the charterers the right to terminate when they had claimed to do so. It did not matter that they had not stated the correct justification for their termination at the time.

18.26   However, a party who initially states an invalid reason for terminating will not be able to rely upon an effective reason, which is only subsequently brought to the other party's attention, 'if the point which was not taken could have been put right', i.e. where not stating the correct justification has prevented the other party from dealing with it (*Heisler* v *Anglo-Dal Ltd* [1954] 1 WLR 1273 at 1278). It may also be that the party who claimed to be able to terminate will be estopped from asserting a true basis of termination, or will be taken to have waived it (*Glencore Grain* v *Lebanese Organization for International Commerce* (1997)).

Anticipatory breach

18.27   We now need to consider the question of anticipatory breach. This involves looking at the situation when X and Y have made a contract and, before the time for performance arrives, X declares that he no longer intends to perform. X is said to repudiate the contract and Y has the option to terminate the contract and claim damages at that point.

Anticipatory breach, therefore, refers to the situation, before the time for performance, when one party has indicated to the other that he does not intend to perform the contract. He or she may have done so expressly, or his or her actions may have shown that to be the situation. He or she may, for example, sell to Z the goods which the contract already requires him or her to deliver to Y. What is required is 'an intimation of an intention to abandon and altogether to refuse performance of the contract . . . [or of] an intention no longer to be bound by the contract' (*Freeth* v *Burr* (1874) LR 9 CP 208 at 213 per Lord Coleridge). This encompasses the situation where one party may wish to perform, but his or her act or default has made it impossible for him or her to do so (*Universal Cargo Carriers Corpn* v *Citati* (1957)). The 'impossibility situation' then has to be distinguished from frustration which occurs when the impossibility is not self-induced (see **Chapter 19**).

18.28   On the occurrence of X's anticipatory breach of his contract with Y, Y has a choice. Y can either keep the contract alive or he can accept X's repudiation and terminate it. If Y decides to keep the contract alive, he has no immediate right to damages. He will be able to claim damages only if X persists in his attitude and does not perform at the appointed time. In that case Y is simply suing for a breach because X has not performed at the time when performance became due. However, if Y accepts the repudiation and terminates the contract, he can sue for damages immediately, on the basis of X's anticipatory breach. Even if he does not accept the repudiation, and cannot therefore sue for damages at that point, he may still be granted, immediately, an order for specific performance compelling X to perform when performance becomes due (*Hasham* v *Zenab* (1960)).

18.29   Termination, or acceptance of repudiation, does not require a particular form of communication.

> 'An act of acceptance of a repudiation requires no particular form; a communication does not have to be couched in the language of acceptance. It is sufficient that the communication or conduct clearly and unequivocally conveys to the repudiating party that the aggrieved party is treating the contract as at an end' (*Vitol SA* v *Norelf Ltd* [1996] 3 All ER 193 at 200 per Lord Steyn).

It may be possible for the injured or aggrieved party to be seen as having accepted a repudiatory breach, simply through not performing their further obligations under the contract, although a failure to act will often be equivocal (*Vitol SA* v *Norelf Ltd*). In the more recent case of *Masri* v *Consolidated Contractors International UK Ltd* (2006), it was argued that *Vitol SA* v *Norelf Ltd* could be relied upon to conclude that acceptance of repudiation required no communication on the facts and could occur through conduct. The High Court clarified the position stating that relevant issue was whether the conduct would have clearly and unequivocally conveyed to a reasonable person in the position of the repudiating party that the aggrieved party is treating the contract as an end.

18.30   The injured party does have time to decide whether to affirm or terminate, but doing nothing for too long may be seen as affirmation (*Stocznia Gdanska SA* v *Latvian Shipping (No 3)* (2002), Rix LJ). Once affirmation has occurred, the injured party can no longer terminate for that anticipatory breach and may then have to wait for a fresh anticipatory breach or breach at the time for performance. However, if the repudiation is continuing or fresh repudiation occurs, then the possibility of terminating is again present, without the need to wait for breach at the time of performance (*Stocznia Gdanska SA*).

18.31   *Hochster* v *De La Tour* (1853) made it clear that damages can be claimed immediately on the basis of an accepted anticipatory breach, without any need to wait for the time of performance. In that case:

> In April 1852 the defendant made a contract with the claimant for the claimant to act as a courier for him from 1 June. On 11 May the defendant told the claimant that he had changed his mind, and that the claimant's services would not be required. On 22 May the claimant commenced an action against the defendant.

The court had to consider the defendant's claim that he could not be in breach of contract, and an action could not be commenced, before 1 June. The court rejected this and held that the claimant could sue successfully before the date for performance. A similar result was reached in *Frost* v *Knight* (1872). In that case the defendant had promised the claimant that he would marry her when his father died. Subsequently the defendant broke off his engagement to the claimant. She took action while the defendant's father was still alive and was successful in her claim.

18.32   The basic requirement for an anticipatory breach is an intention not to perform. That is quite simple where one party is aware that what he or she intends will mean that the contract will be broken when it is time for performance. The situation is more complicated where one party mistakenly believes that what he or she intends is in keeping with the contractual requirements. It would seem that the actions and statements of the mistaken party must be considered to see if, objectively, an intention is shown to abandon the contract or refuse future performance. A comparison can be made between *Woodar Investment Development Ltd* v *Wimpey Construction* (1980) and *Federal Commerce and Navigation Co. Ltd* v *Molena Alpha Inc* [1979] 1 All ER 307. In the latter case:

> The charterers and owners had made a time charter of a ship. The charterers deducted certain sums from their periodic hire payments. The owners disputed their right to do so and told the master not to issue freight pre-paid bills of lading. The owners thought that they were entitled to take that line. Effectively the charterers could not make use of the ship if such bills of lading could not be issued.

The charterers claimed that the owners' instructions to their ship's master amounted to a wrongful repudiation of the contract. The House of Lords found for the charterers, despite the fact that the owners had believed that they were acting within their rights and did not want to lose the charter. The owners' actions deprived the charterers of substantially the whole benefit of the charters.

Lord Wilberforce said (at 315):

> 'If a party's conduct is such as to amount to a threatened repudiatory breach, his subjective desire to maintain the contract cannot prevent the other party from drawing the consequences of his actions.'

18.33   However, a mere mistaken claim to a right to terminate may not show an intention to abandon the contract or refuse future performance. *Woodar Investment Development Ltd* v *Wimpey Construction UK Ltd* [1980] 1 WLR 277 should be considered. The facts were:

> There was a contract for the sale of land. The contract stated that in certain circumstances the buyer, Wimpey, would be entitled to terminate. Wimpey honestly misconstrued the contract and wrongly thought that circumstances giving rise to the express right to terminate were present. Changes in the market made the contract uneconomic for Wimpey, and Wimpey wrongly claimed to be entitled to terminate. The seller, Woodar, argued that this amounted to a repudiation of the contract.

A majority of the House of Lords held that the seller, Woodar, could not claim damages for a repudiatory breach of contract. Wimpey mistakenly believed that it was exercising a contractual right, and it was seeking to act within the contract and not to repudiate it. Communications between Woodar and Wimpey showed that they were seeking to resolve which one of them had correctly interpreted the contract and their actions were not inconsistent with the continuance of the contract once that had been resolved.

18.34   The question of mistaken demands, which were in breach of contract, was also considered by the Privy Council in *Vaswani v Italian Motors (Sales and Services) Ltd* [1996] 1 WLR 270. The case was concerned with a contract for the sale of a Ferrari Testarossa. A deposit was paid, but when the delivery time arrived, the sellers mistakenly demanded a higher price than that contracted for (the contract allowed for an increase in the price for some reasons but not others). There was a clause allowing for forfeit of the deposit if, when the car was ready for delivery, the buyer failed to pay the outstanding amount within seven days. When the buyer failed to make payment, the sellers forfeited the deposit. Applying both *Federal Commerce and Navigation Co. Ltd v Molena Alpha Inc.* (1979) and *Woodar Investment Development Ltd v Wimpey Construction UK Ltd* (1980),[3] the court held that the mistaken demand for a sum as payment was not, by itself, sufficient to amount to a repudiatory breach. Lord Woolf said (at 276):

> 'While therefore here the request for the payment of an excessive price would not in itself amount to a repudiation, if the conduct relied on went beyond the assertion of a genuinely held view of the effect of the contract the conduct could amount to repudiation. This is the position if the conduct is inconsistent with the continuance of the contract.'

In the instant case the conduct was not seen as inconsistent with the continuance of the contract and, in the view of the court, was not repudiatory. This was explained further. It was said (at 277):

> 'In this case while the sellers did indicate to the buyer that he should pay a sum which was excessive or the deposit would be forfeited they never went so far as to indicate to the buyer that it would be purposeless to pay the correct sum required…All they had done was to put forward their calculation which had gone unchallenged. There was nothing to prevent the buyer paying the sum he calculated was due. Until he at least tendered the sum he considered was due the sellers were not required to deliver the vehicle…The sellers did not threaten a "breach of the contract with serious consequences" as in *Federal Commerce and Navigation Co. Ltd v Molena Alpha Inc.*, and there was no conduct by them which was totally inconsistent with the continuance of the contract.'

18.35   A more recent example of a mistaken claim to treat the contract as terminated, was considered by the Court of Appeal in *Eminence Property Developments Ltd v Heaney* (2011). Here, the court applied the ruling in *Woodar Investment Development Ltd v Wimpey Construction UK*

---

3   See also *Gulf Agri Trade FZCO v Aston Agro Industrial AG* [2008] EWHC 1252 (Comm), [2009] 1 All ER (Comm) 991.

Ltd (1980) and similar to the earlier case, *Eminence Property Developments Ltd v Heaney* (2011) also concerned a contract for the sale of land. The issue on appeal was whether a vendor, who had served notices of rescission on the buyer, before the final date for complying with notices to complete had been reached, and then, mistakenly, treated the contract as ended, was acting in repudiatory breach of contract. Whilst emphasizing the individuality of all cases, Lord Justice Etherton stated (at 242) that the legal test for repudiatory conduct is:

> 'whether, looking at all the circumstances objectively, that is from the perspective of a reasonable person in the position of the innocent party, the contract-breaker has shown a clear intention to abandon and altogether refuse to perform the contract.'

Although the relative simplicity of this test was noted, the actual difficulties in applying the test to the facts of any particular case were also highlighted, with *Woodar Investment Development Ltd v Wimpey Construction UK Ltd* (1980) serving as a good example of this. Determining whether or not there has been a repudiatory breach was found to be a highly fact-sensitive exercise, requiring consideration of all of the circumstances in forming an objective assessment of the contract-breaker's intentions. These intentions could also be informed by motive, normally a subjective matter, if this threw light on the way the act would be viewed by a reasonable person. In *Eminence Property Developments Ltd v Heaney* (2011) itself, the vendor had not shown a clear intention to abandon and altogether refuse to perform the contract (indeed the contract was advantageous to him) and consequently the rescission notices which he had served did not constitute a repudiatory breach of contract.

18.36 When an anticipatory breach occurs, the injured party may decide to keep the contract alive. What are the consequences of that decision? In *Avery v Bowden* (1856), the court considered the situation where the innocent party had elected not to accept the defendant's repudiation of the contract. He had kept the contract alive in the hope that performance would ensue. In that case:

> The defendant had chartered the claimant's ship to load a cargo at Odessa within forty-five days. The ship was ready to load, but the defendant repeatedly told the ship's captain that he could not obtain a cargo. Before the forty-five days were up, the Crimean War started and the contract was frustrated. The outbreak of war had made it illegal to load a cargo at an enemy port.

It was held that the claimant could not recover damages. In the first place the court did not think that what the defendant had done was sufficient to amount to a repudiatory breach. However, even if it had been sufficient, the claimant still did not have a cause of action. The court thought that such an anticipatory breach could not found a cause of action until it was accepted by the claimant. In this case the claimant had not accepted the repudiation. He had continued to ask for performance until war was declared and the contract was frustrated.

18.37 In *Avery v Bowden* (1856) the contract was kept alive only to be frustrated. However, keeping the contract alive may also provide the party who had evinced an intention to repudiate with an opportunity to terminate because of the other party's breach. If the contract is kept alive, it is kept alive for the benefit of both parties. The party who would have been the injured party, had he accepted the repudiation, may himself subsequently commit a breach and be liable for the consequences of so doing. In *Fercometal SARL v MSC Mediterranean Shipping Co. SA* (1988):

> A charter-party contained a clause enabling the charterer to cancel if the ship was not ready to load by 9 July. Before 9 July, the charterer wrongfully purported to cancel the charter. The owner could have accepted that purported termination as a repudiation but chose to continue with the contract. The ship was not ready to load on 9 July. The charterer claimed to cancel on the basis of the express provision for cancellation.

The House of Lords held that the charterer could take advantage of the express right to cancel. The owner had chosen to continue the contract, and that kept the contract alive for the benefit of both parties. The charterer's earlier conduct did not prevent the charterer from taking action on a subsequent breach by the owner. The earlier case of *Braithwaite v Foreign Hardwood Co. Ltd* (1905) can no longer be regarded as establishing that if X repudiates a contract with Y, and Y does not accept the repudiation, Y is nevertheless excused his subsequent non-performance of his obligations. However, Y's non-performance of a particular obligation might not be actionable by X if X was estopped from such a claim, i.e. if X had indicated that he would no longer require Y to perform a particular obligation and Y had relied upon that in not making himself ready to perform.

18.38   The above cases illustrate the danger in deciding to keep the contract alive, rather than accepting the repudiation and terminating the contract. However, even where the repudiation is accepted, events subsequent to that, which would have impacted upon the performance, may still be relevant to the question of damages. In *The Mihalis Angelos* (1971) what was in question was a right for the repudiating party to cancel which would inevitably have arisen:

> There was a charter-party which stated that the ship was 'expected ready to load' at Haiphong about 1 July. Clause 11 provided that if the ship was not ready to load by 20 July the charterers had an option to cancel the charter-party. The charterers purported to cancel on 17 July, and the owners accepted that as a repudiation of the contract.

It was held that, although it was clear on 17 July that the ship would not be ready to load by 20 July, the charterers could not exercise the option before 20 July. Nevertheless, the charterers had been entitled to cancel because the owners were in breach of a condition. The owners had stated that the ship was 'expected ready to load' on 1 July without having any reasonable grounds for such an expectation. The owners were in breach of a condition and, on that basis, the charterers could terminate the contract. However, the Court of Appeal also stated that, even had that not been the case, the owners would have recovered only nominal damages—and that is the important point in this context, i.e. had there been no breach of condition by the owners, the Court of Appeal would have been prepared to award them only nominal damages for what would then have been a repudiatory breach by the charterers on 17 July. Only nominal damages would have been available because, on 17 July, it was inevitable that the ship would not arrive by 20 July and, on 20 July, the charterers would have been able to exercise the option to terminate the contract without breaching it. In other words the owners would not have received performance anyway, even had there been no breach on 17 July, and they would not have suffered a substantial loss through a repudiatory breach on 17 July.

18.39 Events subsequent to the accepted repudiation also reduced the damages awarded in *Golden Strait Corpn v Nippon Yusen Kubishika Kaisha* (2007). In that case:

> In 1998 the parties entered into a seven-year charter-party. In December 2001 the charterers repudiated the contract and the owners accepted the repudiation. In March 2003 the second Gulf War broke out and the war clause in the charter-party would have given the charterers the right to cancel. The question arose as to whether the owners' damages for the charterers repudiatory breach in 2001 should encompass the entirety of the time then remaining under the charter-party or whether they should be limited by the outbreak of the Gulf War when the charterers would have had a right to cancel.

Normally damages are awarded by reference to the circumstances at the time of the breach, i.e. here the time of the repudiation. This is seen to create certainty for both parties. However, such calculation is usually in keeping with the basic principle on which damages are awarded (placing the injured party in the position he, or she, would have been had the contract been performed) and the injured party's duty to mitigate. The duty to mitigate means that the injured party will not recover for any loss which he or she would not have suffered had they behaved reasonably on the breach occurring. So, for example, if the breach is the non-delivery of goods for which there is a market, the injured party can purchase replacement goods in the market when the breach occurs and the damages awarded will cover the excess of the contract price over the market price at the time of the breach. If the injured party delays, and the market price increases, the damages paid will not increase. It was reasonable to buy replacement goods when the breach occurred. However, *The Golden Strait* was not a case where awarding damages based on the time of the breach would comply with basic principle. At the time of the breach there was the prospect of the contract continuing for the rest of its whole seven-year duration. By the time the case came to court, it was clear it would have been lawfully cancelled in 2003. Awarding damages based on the full duration of the contract would have put the injured party in a better position than if the contract had been performed. It would seem that the damages will not be calculated according to the circumstances at the date of the breach when there is a temporal element in the injured party's loss (i.e. where it is a loss over time, or a loss which only accrues after the breach) and the temporal element would not be nullified by acting in accordance with the duty to mitigate, i.e. procuring a substitute contract at the time of the breach. In *The Golden Strait* case any substitute contract would have contained the same cancellation right and also not run for the remainder of the full contract duration (see Lord Brown at [82]).

Mitigation

18.40 There is a further difficult problem to be considered in the relationship between the injured party's choice in respect of the other party's anticipatory breach and the duty to mitigate.

The duty to mitigate means that the injured party will not receive damages to cover any loss which the injured party would not have incurred had he behaved reasonably on breach (see **Chapter 20**. The problem is that if the injured party chooses not to accept the repudiation, then there is no breach at that point and no duty to mitigate. Of course, in most cases, the injured party will not be able to perform if the other party will not co-operate, but what of the exceptional cases? In exceptional cases the injured party will be able to perform without the co-operation of the other party and will then be able to put him or herself into the position where he or she can claim in debt for the money due under the contract, rather than having to sue for damages for breach. (Very exceptionally the injured party may be able to claim in debt without performing, where the money falls due under the contract independently of the injured party's performance—*Ministry of Sound (Ireland) Ltd* v *World Online Ltd* (2003).) If the injured party can sue for the debt, he or she will not be concerned with the rules restricting recovery of damages, including the duty to mitigate. This can lead to the injured party claiming payment for an unwanted and 'wasted' performance, which contrasts awkwardly with the mitigation rule's limitation on recovery. The point arises from the decision in *White and Carter (Councils) Ltd* v *McGregor* [1962] AC 413. In that case:

> The claimants supplied litter bins to local councils and then made money by selling advertising on them. The defendants contracted for three years of advertisements of their garage business but, that same day, they repudiated the contract. The claimants refused to accept the repudiation and went ahead with the advertisements.

Eventually the claimants claimed the sum owed to them under the contract in return for their performance and, by a bare majority, the House of Lords allowed the claim. Obviously the claimants could have simply accepted the repudiation and claimed damages at that point. Instead they chose to expend more money to carry out a performance which was no longer wanted. The case sits uneasily alongside the mitigation rule. However, Lord Reid suggested a qualification upon the injured party's right to choose not to accept the repudiation, to continue to perform, and to claim the sum due under the contract. He thought that if it could be shown that the injured party had 'no legitimate interest' in performing, rather than accepting the repudiation and claiming damages, he ought not to be able to 'saddle the other party with an additional burden with no benefit to himself' (at 431).

18.41   It is clear that there is general acceptance of Lord Reid's limitation on the general right of the injured party to choose whether to accept the repudiation, but it has been stated in different ways in subsequent case law.[4] So, for example, in *The Odenfeld* (1978) Kerr J said that:

> 'any fetter on the innocent party's right of election whether or not accept a repudiation will only be applied in extreme cases, viz. where damages would be an adequate remedy and where an election to keep the contract would be wholly unreasonable.'

---

4   See further, *The Puerto Buitrago (Attica Sea Carriers Corpn v Ferrostaal Poseidon Bulk Reederei GmbH)* (1976); *The Odenfeld (Gator Shipping Corpn v Trans-Asiatic Occidental Shipping Establishment)* (1978); *The Alaskan Trader (Clea Shipping Corpn v Bulk Oil International Ltd)* (1984); *The Dynamic (Ocean Marine Navigation v Koch Carbon Inc)* (2003); *Reichman v Beveridge* (2006); *Isabella Shipowner SA v Shagang Shipping Co Ltd* (2012).

18.42   *Reichman* v *Beveridge* (2006) provides an example of a case where damages were viewed as not providing an adequate remedy and not accepting the repudiation was not 'wholly unreasonable'. The case was one in which tenants under a five-year lease left the premises when there were almost two years of the lease still to run. The issue was whether the landlord could claim the rent which they should have continued to pay, or whether the landlord should have accepted their repudiation by forfeiting the lease and mitigated his loss. The court took the line that the landlord's conduct was not 'wholly unreasonable' in not taking steps to find a new tenant, rather than leaving it to the tenants to propose one. Further, the law not being wholly certain, there was, at least, a significant risk that damages would not be available to cover loss of future rent if the landlord forfeited the lease and they would lose money if they could only re-let the property at a lower rent. Damages would not provide an adequate remedy. It was emphasized that it is 'for the party in breach to establish that the innocent party's conduct is wholly unreasonable and that damages would be an adequate remedy' (at [41]). The burden lies on the repudiating party to establish that the case is one in which the innocent party's choice is restricted (see further, *The Dynamic* (2003)).

18.43   In the recent case of *Isabella Shipowner SA* v *Shagang Shipping Co Ltd* (2012), Justice Cooke usefully summarized the effect of the authorities stating that:

> 'an innocent party will have no legitimate interest in maintaining the contract if damages are an adequate remedy and his insistence on maintaining the contract can be described as "wholly unreasonable", "extremely unreasonable" or, perhaps, in my words, "perverse"' (at [44]).

Whichever words are used to describe the actions of the innocent party and whatever the formulation, as Lloyd J acknowledged in *The Alaskan Trader* [1984] 1 All ER 129, there is a point at which the 'injured party cannot enforce his contract according to its strict legal terms' (at 136). As noted before, however, such circumstances are exceptional and *The Alaskan Trader*, a case in which the innocent party was viewed as not having had a legitimate interest in not accepting repudiation, aptly illustrates this point. In that case:

> The charterers had repudiated a charter-party when the ship required repairs because of a serious problem with the engines. The owners would not accept the repudiation but repaired the ship and kept it ready, fully crewed, for the charterers for seven months until the end of the charter period.

The question, then, was whether the owners could recover the hire for that period. Lloyd J upheld the decision of the arbitrator that they could not. They had no legitimate interest in doing so rather than claiming damages. If a replacement charter could not be found, it would have been less costly if they had not kept the ship with a full crew, ready to sail, for that period. Maintaining the time charter had led to a commercial absurdity. Also, in *The Puerto Buitrago* (1976), the cost of repair was double the value of the ship when repaired and four times as much as its scrap value. In these circumstances, to refuse to accept a premature re-delivery of the vessel in order for the repairs to be carried out would have been 'truly perverse' and repair would have been 'an exercise in futility' (*Isabella Shipowner SA* v *Shagang Shipping Co Ltd* (2012) per Justice Cooke at [44]).

Summary

Performance

- Parties usually cease to have obligations under the contract because they have performed—discharge by performance.
- What is required for performance depends upon the contract terms.
- The parties may provide that the contract, or some of the obligations under it, are not immediately effective. A condition precedent may suspend the formation of the contract or the operation of some of the obligations.
- The parties may have provided that the contract is to end upon the occurrence of certain circumstances—a condition subsequent.
- The order of performance may be provided for by contingent conditions.

Entire contracts

- One party is obliged to perform his or her side of the contract before the other becomes obliged to pay.
- The injured party will have to pay for any work or materials which he or she voluntarily chooses to adopt.
- Where there has been 'substantial performance' the party in breach can recover the contract price and pay damages to cover defects.

Breach

- The injured party can choose to terminate the contract for breaches of conditions and for sufficient breaches of innominate terms (see **Chapter 8**).
- The injured party can also terminate for a repudiatory breach where the other party indicates that he, or she, no longer intends to be bound by the contract.
- A party may claim to terminate for a reason which does not justify termination. If at the time he or she claims to terminate there is another, then unstated, reason which would justify termination, he or she can usually rely upon that to prevent the claimed termination from subsequently being found to be a repudiatory breach.
- Where repudiation relates to performance which is not yet due it is anticipatory breach.
- On the occurrence of an anticipatory breach, the injured party can elect to keep the contract alive or accept the repudiation and terminate the contract.
- If the choice is to keep the contract alive after an anticipatory breach then there is no breach at that point and no claim to damages.

- If the choice is to terminate after an anticipatory breach, there is an immediate right to damages.

- If the choice is to keep the contract alive after an anticipatory breach, and it is subsequently frustrated, no claim to damages exists from the prior anticipatory breach.

- If the choice is to terminate the contract after an anticipatory breach, the amount of damages recovered may be affected by subsequent events such as those which would have provided the party in breach with legitimate reasons for cancellation of the contract.

- Even where there is a repudiation by one party, the injured party may sometimes be able to perform their side of the contract without the cooperation of the other party. Under those circumstances the injured party may be able to choose to continue with the contract, perform their obligations, and claim the contract price from the other party. In keeping with the duty to mitigate, which arises on breach, the injured party will not be able to do that where the injured party had no legitimate interest in performing, rather than claiming damages.

▶ Further reading

D. Capper, 'A Golden Victory for Freedom of Contract' (2008) 24 JCL 176

J. W. Carter and E. Peden, 'Damages following Termination for Repudiation: Taking account of later events' (2008) 24 JCL 145

Q. Lui, 'The White & Carter Principle: A Restatement' (2011) 74 MLR 17

G. Treitel, 'Assessment of Damages for Wrongful Repudiation' (2007) 123 LQR 9

Chapter 19

The doctrine of frustration

⊙ Introduction: initial and subsequent impossibility

19.1   After the parties have concluded a contract, events beyond their control may occur which 'frustrate' the purpose of their agreement, or render it very difficult, or impossible, or even illegal, to perform. An example of this is where a hall which has been booked for the performance of a play is destroyed by fire, after the contract has been concluded, but before the date of performance of the play. Some writers have seen a close resemblance between this type of 'subsequent impossibility' and the subject of common mistake (also referred to as 'initial impossibility'). Indeed there are similarities between the two subjects. (See for example, *Dany Lions Ltd* v *Bristol Cars Ltd* (2013).) In *Great Peace Shipping Ltd* v *Tsavliris Salvage (International) Ltd* (2003) at [61], it was stated that 'consideration of the development of the law of frustration assists with the analysis of the law of common mistake'. Both provide an important opportunity to define the strength of contractual obligations. How absolute are they? Under what circumstances will a party be excused from performing his or her contractual undertakings or from having to provide a remedy to the other? There are close similarities in some of the factual situations to which the two types of 'impossibility' apply. (For example, contrast *Griffith* v *Brymer* (1903) and *Krell* v *Henry* (1903). The former was decided on the basis of mistake and the latter on the basis of frustration.)

19.2   In certain circumstances, it may be a fine, almost tenuous, dividing line between these two different branches of contract law. In *Amalgamated Investment & Property Co. Ltd* v *John Walker & Sons Ltd* [1976] 3 All ER 509, for example, the facts were:

> The defendants owned a commercial property which they advertised for sale as being suitable for occupation or redevelopment. In July 1973 the claimants agreed, subject to contract,

to buy the property for £1,710,000. The defendants knew that the claimants' purpose in purchasing the property was to redevelop it and that they would require planning permission to do so. In their enquiries before entering into a binding contract, the claimants asked the defendants whether the property was designated (i.e. 'listed') as a building of special architectural or historic interest. The defendants replied, on 14 August, that it was not. This was correct at the time. But in January 1973, unknown to the parties, officials at the Department of the Environment had included the property in a provisional list of buildings to be listed as being of architectural or historic interest. On 25 September, the parties signed the contract of sale. On 26 September, the Department of the Environment wrote to the defendants and informed them that the property had been included in the statutory list of buildings of special interest. (The list was given legal effect the following day.) It transpired that the property had been unconditionally selected for inclusion in the list on 22 August. The value of the building without redevelopment potential was one and a half million pounds less than the contract price! The claimants claimed rescission of the agreement on the basis of common mistake, or alternatively, they sought a declaration that the agreement was void or voidable and an order rescinding the agreement.

The claimants' action was unsuccessful and specific performance was ordered against them. The case could not be treated as one of common mistake as the mistake did not exist at the time the contract was concluded. It was after the contract was made that the property was actually listed. (In the opinion of the court, the earlier inclusion of the property in the list of buildings of special interest was merely an administrative step towards listing.) The alternative argument put forward by the claimants was that the contract was frustrated; that is, they had paid a high price for a property on the basis of its redevelopment potential and subsequently found that this objective was not possible to achieve. This contention was also rejected by the Court of Appeal, as the claimants were assumed to have taken the risk that the building may have been listed at some time after the contract was concluded. They were very unlucky that it was listed so soon after purchase, but this was an inherent risk in the ownership of buildings (per Buckley J at 517). In other words, it was foreseeable that the obtaining of planning permission, which was crucial to the claimants, might be thwarted by the listing of the building.

Although the claimants' action failed, and they could claim neither common mistake nor frustration, the case is instructive with regard to the distinction between these two separate branches of contract law. The difference between initial and subsequent impossibility turned on the precise time at which the building was listed. Yet it is clear from the evidence that this 'listing' was more of a process than a single decision or event. Is there any logical or practical reason why this factual situation should not be treated as one of mistake rather than one of frustration? The law seems rather rigid in its approach to these two related areas of impossibility when much may depend on a matter of days or even hours. The traditional justification for a rigid distinction between the two subjects is that mistake is concerned with the formation of contracts, whereas frustration deals with the discharge of contracts that have already been concluded. This explanation tends to ignore the difficulties posed by cases such as *Amalgamated Investment & Property Co. Ltd* v *John Walker & Sons Ltd*.

19.3   In the recent Court of Appeal decision in *Great Peace Shipping Ltd* v *Tsavliris Salvage (International) Ltd* (2003) (discussed in **Chapter 12**), Lord Phillips, having examined the development of the doctrine of frustration (at [62]–[72]), compared frustration to common mistake and stated (at [85]):

> 'Circumstances where a contract is void as a result of common mistake are likely to be less common than instances of frustration. Supervening events which defeat the contractual adventure will frequently not be the responsibility of either party. Where, however, the parties agree that something shall be done which is impossible at the time of making the agreement, it is much more likely that, on true construction of the agreement, one or other will have undertaken responsibility for the mistaken state of affairs.'

However, by comparing the two doctrines in some detail, the court in the *Tsavliris* case has helped to explain the principles which they have in common.

Development of the doctrine of frustration

19.4   The doctrine of frustration is a means of dealing with situations where events occur, after the contract has been concluded, which render the agreement illegal, or impossible to perform, or even commercially sterile. The frustrating event must also not be the fault of either party or foreseeable. (On the latter issue, see *Walkden* v *Walkden* (2009) at [53]; and for a detailed discussion of the relevance to the doctrine of the foreseeability of a risk, see *Edwinton Commercial Corporation* v *Tsavliris Russ Ltd, The 'Sea Angel'* (2007) at [102]–[104] and [127]–[128]).) Of course, the parties might expressly provide for the consequences of a frustrating event by what is known as a force majeure clause. For example, a building contract might provide for what will happen in the event of a strike. In this way the parties themselves deal with the consequences of future events which might affect performance, and the doctrine of frustration will not usually apply. Certain types of agreement, for example, export sales, shipping, building, or engineering contracts, are particularly susceptible to disruption by unforeseen events. But, in the absence of express provision by the parties, the doctrine of frustration is a legal recognition of the fact that in some instances it is just to excuse a party from his or her contractual obligations.

19.5   Until a little over a hundred years ago, the law was reluctant to excuse a party his or her performance of a contract even in cases where supervening events rendered that performance difficult or impossible. The rationale of this rule was that a party could always make express provision for unforeseen events and, if he or she did not do so, he or she should be bound by his or her contractual obligations. This is known as the 'absolute contracts' rule, which was clearly stated in the seventeenth-century case of *Paradine* v *Jane* (1647). In this case, C brought an action against D for the rent due on a lease. D argued that he had been dispossessed of the land by force by an 'alien born, enemy to the king and kingdom [who] had invaded the realm with an hostile army of men'. D claimed that due to events beyond his control he had lost the profits from the land and, therefore, that he was not liable for the rent. This plea was rejected by the court. D had undertaken an obligation to pay rent under a contract and he was bound to fulfil this despite the supervening events. He could always have expressly covered this contingency in his contract with C.

19.6   This rigid approach has been mitigated, to some extent, by the gradual development of the doctrine of frustration. However, it must be emphasized that the doctrine operates within strict limits and does not provide an easy means of escape for those who have simply made a bad bargain (see *Amalgamated Investment & Property Co. Ltd* v *John Walker & Sons Ltd* (1976) at para. **19.2**). The famous case which marks the recognition of the doctrine is *Taylor* v *Caldwell* (1863) 3 B & S 826. The facts were as follows:

> On 27 May 1861, Taylor entered into a contract with Caldwell which gave T the use of the Surrey Gardens and music hall on four separate days later that summer. T was to use the premises for a series of four concerts, and for holding day and night fêtes on the days in question, and he was to pay £100 for each day. After the contract was concluded, but before the date of the first concert, the music hall was destroyed by fire. The fire was not the fault of either party and it made the performance of the concerts impossible. No express provision had been made by the parties to cover this contingency. T claimed damages for the money he had wasted in advertising the concerts.

It was held that the defendants were not liable and T's claim for damages did not succeed. This seems a fair decision, but how did the court circumvent the general rule that in a contract to do a positive thing, a person must perform it or pay damages for failure to do so? Blackburn J stated that this rule applies only where the contract is not subject to any condition, either express or implied. He continued (at 833):

> '...[T]here are authorities which, as we think, establish the principle that where, from the nature of the contract, it appears that the parties must from the beginning have known that it could not be fulfilled unless when the time for the fulfilment of the contract arrived some particular specified thing continued to exist, so that, when entering into the contract, they must have contemplated such continuing existence as the foundation of what was to be done; there, in the absence of any express or implied warranty that the thing shall exist, the contract is not to be construed as a positive contract, but as subject to an implied condition that the parties shall be excused in case, before breach, performance becomes impossible from the perishing of the thing without default of the contractor.'

The judge held that the continued existence of the music hall was essential to the performance of the contract and the parties contracted on this basis. Although there was no express provision to this effect, the court implied one as a matter of construction. If the parties had thought about it when making the contract, they would have agreed to such a condition. In other words the doctrine of frustration, as established in *Taylor* v *Caldwell*, was based on an effort to give effect to the presumed intention of the parties.

The importance of the case is that it established the doctrine of frustration and made deep inroads into the notion of absolute contractual obligations. But, as we shall see, there is some debate about the theoretical basis of the doctrine. For example, in *Shell UK Ltd v Lostock Garage Ltd* [1977] 1 All ER 481 at 487, Lord Denning stated (*obiter*) that 'the legal effect of frustration does not depend on an implied term. It does not depend on the presumed intention of the parties, nor on what they would have answered, if asked, but simply on what the court itself declares to amount to a frustration'. In other words, the court is imposing a fair solution, in the event of unforeseen circumstances, rather than giving effect to the presumed contractual intention of the parties. (More recently, Lord Phillips stated in *Great Peace Shipping Ltd v Tsavliris Salvage (International) Ltd* (2003) [70] that 'the doctrine of frustration was patently judge-made law'.)

19.7   Once the doctrine of frustration had been established, its scope had to be determined. *Taylor v Caldwell* (1863) dealt with the physical destruction of the subject matter of a contract, and its result was unexceptionable. Similarly, where a contract is made to do something which subsequently becomes illegal (for example, trading with a country against which war is later declared), there is no difficulty in treating the contract as frustrated. But a more common and problematic type of case is where the commercial purpose of a contract is drastically affected by unforeseen events, whilst the performance of the contract remains physically and legally possible. A good example is the famous case of *Krell v Henry* [1903] 2 KB 740, where the facts were:

> Henry (D) agreed to hire a flat in Pall Mall from Krell (C) for the days of 26 and 27 June. These were the days that the coronation processions of Edward VII were to take place and the windows in the flat afforded good views of the procession route. D agreed in writing, on 20 June, to pay £75 for the exclusive use of the flat on the two days of the processions. The contract made no express reference to the coronation procession or to any other purpose. A deposit of £25 was paid by D at the time of contracting and the balance was to be paid the day before the processions took place. Due to the King's illness, the processions did not take place on the proposed days. Krell claimed £50 from Henry, who in turn counterclaimed for the return of the £25 which he had already paid under the contract.

The Court of Appeal decided that the contract was frustrated despite the fact that its performance was still physically possible. The doctrine is not strictly limited to 'cases in which the event causing the impossibility of performance is the destruction or non-existence of some thing which is the subject-matter of the contract or of some condition or state of things expressly specified as a condition of it' (per Vaughan Williams LJ at 749). Accordingly, the doctrine was applied in circumstances where some event, which must reasonably be regarded as the basis of the contract, failed to take place. The flat in Pall Mall could still have been used on the days in question, but the true purpose of the contract was frustrated by the postponement of the processions. Vaughan Williams LJ stated (at 750):

> 'In my judgment, the use of the rooms was let and taken for the purpose of seeing the royal processions... It was a licence to use rooms for a particular purpose and none other. And in my judgment the taking place of those processions on the days proclaimed along the proclaimed route, which passed 56A, Pall Mall, was regarded by both contracting parties as the foundation of the contract. I think that it cannot reasonably be supposed to have been in the contemplation of the contracting parties, when the contract was made, that the coronation

> would not be held on the proclaimed days, or the processions not take place on those days along the proclaimed route; and I think that the words imposing on the defendant the obligation to accept and pay for the use of the rooms for the named days, although general and unconditional, were not used with reference to the possibility of the particular contingency which afterwards occurred.'

This was a potentially far-reaching and controversial decision. It extended the doctrine to cases where the commercial object or purpose of the contract was frustrated. It raises problems as to what exactly is the 'foundation' of a particular contract (for instance, contrast the decision in *Krell* v *Henry* with that in *Herne Bay Steam Boat Co.* v *Hutton* (1903), para. **19.9**). Although the outcome of *Krell* v *Henry* seems fair, the courts have to be careful not to allow a party a convenient means of escape from a contract simply because it turns out to be a bad bargain. *Krell* v *Henry* represents, perhaps, the furthest development of the doctrine of frustration, and subsequent cases have suggested a rather narrower view. It is unlikely that any further extension of this authority will be permitted by the courts.[1]

A narrower interpretation of frustration

19.8   In *Krell* v *Henry* (1903) it was clear that the foundation of the contract was the taking place of the coronation processions on the planned dates. A suite of rooms in Pall Mall would not normally be hired on a daily basis and the high price clearly indicated that the contracting parties had a specific and common purpose or object in entering into the agreement. For these reasons, it was a very unusual case indeed. More typically, where a party hires or leases property from another it may be less obvious whether they share a common object. Their individual motives for contracting may be different and it may be difficult to say whether the common purpose is frustrated. The property which is to be hired may be susceptible to different types of use and enjoyment. Therefore, some restriction on the use of the subject matter of the contract, due to supervening events, will not necessarily result in the contract being discharged under the doctrine of frustration.

19.9   An interesting contrast to *Krell* v *Henry* (1903) is provided by *Herne Bay Steamboat Co.* v *Hutton* (1903). The facts were that D agreed to hire the steamboat *Cynthia* from C for £250, on 28 and 29 June 1902, 'for the purpose of viewing the naval review and for a day's cruise round the fleet'. A deposit of £50 was paid in advance. The royal naval review, which was intended as part of the coronation festivities, was subsequently cancelled due to the King's illness. However, the fleet was still anchored at Spithead on 28 June. D did not use the *Cynthia* on either of the agreed days and C sued for the balance of the hire charge. It was held that C could recover the £200 from D and that the contract was not discharged on the ground of frustration.

At first sight it might be difficult to see why the case was decided differently from *Krell* v *Henry*. But on closer examination it is possible to distinguish it and to emphasize the limited application

---

1   See *Maritime National Fish Co.* v *Ocean Trawlers* [1935] AC 524 at 529 per Lord Wright.

of *Krell* v *Henry*. It was held by the Court of Appeal, in *Herne Bay*, that the taking place of the royal review was not the foundation of the contract, despite the reference made to this event in the contract. It was still possible to cruise around the fleet and therefore the whole purpose of the contract was not frustrated. It is also significant that the contract was for the hire of a boat—something which is frequently hired for a variety of purposes, whereas in *Krell* v *Henry* it was highly unusual for rooms in Pall Mall to be let by the day. It seems that the contract in *Herne Bay* was for the hiring of a boat by D to make a certain voyage which it was still possible to make. The hirer had a particular object in mind, but this object was not the concern of C as owners of the boat. The contract was not physically impossible to perform, nor was the common purpose of both parties totally defeated. For these reasons the case can be distinguished from *Krell* v *Henry*, but it is clearly a very fine distinction.

19.10   The strict limits of the doctrine of frustration can be further illustrated by *Tsakiroglou & Co. Ltd* v *Noblee Thorl GmbH* (1962). The facts were as follows:

> The appellants contracted to sell groundnuts to the respondents at a price which included the carriage of the goods from the Sudan to Hamburg. Although no reference was made to this in the contract, it was assumed that shipment of the goods would be via the Suez Canal. The price of the nuts was calculated on this basis. After the contract was made, but before its performance, the Suez Canal was closed to commercial traffic owing to political events. The alternative route, via the Cape of Good Hope, would have taken the appellants more than twice as long to ship the goods and would have doubled the cost of carriage. The appellants did not make the shipment and claimed that the contract had been frustrated by the closure of the Suez Canal.

The House of Lords rejected this argument. It was still possible to ship the goods, albeit at greater expense, and the contract was not discharged. The court refused to imply a term that the goods were to be shipped by the most direct route. The fact that the appellants had made what turned out to be a bad bargain did not by itself lead to the doctrine of frustration being applied. (*Amalgamated Investment & Property Co. Ltd* v *John Walker & Sons Ltd* (1976), discussed earlier, is another vivid illustration of this point.) A court should not rewrite the contract for the parties. The appellants were under a contractual obligation to ship the goods to Hamburg by any reasonable route that was available.

19.11   In *British Movietonews Ltd* v *London and District Cinemas* [1952] AC 166, another decision which shows the limited application of the doctrine, the contract in question related to the supply of films during the Second World War. The dispute occurred over the arrangements for termination of the contract. In 1943 a government order imposed certain restrictions on film supplies and, in a second agreement, the parties altered their termination arrangements until 'such time as the Order is cancelled'. It was presumably the parties' intention that this later (second) agreement should prevail only for the duration of wartime conditions.

The Court of Appeal was willing to hold that the contract was frustrated, when the Order continued after 1945 for reasons other than national safety, and to depart from the literal words of the agreement by giving effect to the presumed intentions of the parties. However, its decision was reversed by the House of Lords and the narrower approach to frustration was upheld. The House of Lords, as in *Tsakiroglou & Co. Ltd v Noblee Thorl GmbH* (1962), was not prepared to rewrite the agreement for the contracting parties on the basis of what they were presumed to have intended at the time the contract was made. The parties were not to be discharged lightly from their contractual obligations despite the obvious hardship to one of them. In the words of Lord Simon (at 185):

> 'The parties to an executory contract are often faced, in the course of carrying it out, with a turn of events which they did not at all anticipate—a wholly abnormal rise or fall in prices, a sudden depreciation of currency, an unexpected obstacle to the execution, or the like. Yet this does not in itself affect the bargain which they have made.'

19.12   It is well established that financial hardship alone is no reason for allowing a party to a contract to rely on the doctrine of frustration. A clear statement to this effect was made by the House of Lords in *Davis Contractors Ltd v Fareham UDC* [1956] AC 696. The facts were:

> Davis Contractors agreed to build seventy-eight houses for a local council, for the sum of £92,425, within an eight-month period. Due to serious shortages of skilled labour and materials, the work took twenty-two months to complete and cost Davis Contractors approximately £18,000 more than they had estimated. The contractors argued that the contract with Fareham Council was frustrated due to the long delay, which was the fault of neither party. They attempted to claim a larger sum than the agreed contract price as a fair reward for the services they had performed for the council (i.e. they claimed on a quantum meruit basis).

The House of Lords rejected the argument of Davis Contractors; the contract was not frustrated. The parties had contracted for a specific number of houses which had now been built as agreed. There was no change in the basic obligations under the contract. Mere hardship or inconvenience to one of the contracting parties was not enough to frustrate a contract. Given the uncertainty in the supply of materials and labour at that time, the contractors could have made some express stipulation about this in the contract, yet they failed to do so. They were not allowed to escape from a bad bargain by simply arguing that the contract was frustrated. In Lord Radcliffe's words (at 727), frustration could not be 'lightly invoked as the dissolvent of a contract'. (See also a statement to this effect by Lord Roskill in *Pioneer Shipping v BTP Tioxide (The Nema)* [1982] AC 724 at 752.) For a recent illustration of the principle that a party cannot escape his or her contractual obligations merely because the contract has become more expensive to perform, see *Thames Valley Power Ltd v Total Gas & Power Ltd* (2006). In this case, a sharp increase in the market price of gas made a contract significantly less profitable for the supplier, but this did not render its performance impossible. A further example of the strict limits of the doctrine is provided by the Court of Appeal in *CTI Group Inc v Transclear SA (The Mary Nour)* (2008). Here the sellers (T) agreed to deliver a large quantity of cement to the buyers (C), but failed to do so when T's own proposed suppliers withdrew their willingness to provide the cargo. (T did not have a legally binding agreement with the suppliers.) T was aware of the commercial background to the case, i.e. that another company was putting pressure on suppliers not to deal with them. The trial court held that the contract between T and C was not frustrated, as T had assumed the risk of failing to secure the cargo from its intended source of supply. The Court of Appeal upheld this decision, and Moore-Bick LJ stated (at [27]):

> 'In my view it is impossible to hold that the contract in this case was frustrated. . . the fact that a supplier chooses not to make goods available for shipment, thus rendering performance by the seller impossible, is not of itself sufficient to frustrate a contract of this kind. In order to rely on the doctrine of frustration it is necessary for there to have been a supervening event which renders the performance of the seller's obligations impossible or fundamentally different in nature from that which was envisaged when the contract was made. . . for the reasons given earlier the sellers bore the risk of a refusal on the part of the supplier to make goods available.'

19.13   This narrow view of frustration adopted by the courts has meant that the doctrine will rarely succeed where performance of the contract is still possible but where it has merely become more difficult or disadvantageous for one of the parties to perform. Of course, where performance is actually prevented by supervening events beyond the contemplation and control of the parties, a contract may be frustrated. For example, in *International Sea Tankers of Liberia Inc.* v *Hemisphere Shipping Co. of Hong Kong Ltd (The Wenjiang)* (1982) a tanker, which was chartered to carry a cargo of oil from Basrah, was trapped (along with sixty other ships) on the Shatt-al-Arab river when war broke out in 1980 between Iran and Iraq. The parties agreed that in such circumstances the charter-party[2] was frustrated. The point of contention in this, and similar cases, was the precise date on which the contract was frustrated, as this determined when the hire charge ceased to be payable by the charterers.[3]

19.14   The important subject of who bears the loss when a contract is frustrated is dealt with in detail later. But it should be remembered that the parties may, and frequently do, include some express provision which deals with the allocation of risk in relation to supervening events. In this way the possible application of the doctrine of frustration is avoided by means of a relevant clause in the contract.

Scope of the doctrine

Leases

19.15   It used to be argued that the doctrine of frustration could not apply to leases. This is because a lease is not simply a contract enabling a tenant to make use of the land in question; it creates a legal estate in the land. The argument ran that this legal estate survives despite supervening events which may prevent the use or enjoyment of the land (for example, see

---

2   That is, a contract for the hire of a ship and the delivery of cargo.

3   See also *Kodros Shipping Corpn of Monrovia* v *Empresa Cubana de Fletes, The Evia* (1982).

London & Northern Estates Co. v *Schlesinger* (1916)). This is a rather technical view which ignores the commercial reality of some leases, especially where the lease is short term and the tenant is concerned with the use of the land for a specific purpose rather than in the creation of any legal estate. After some judicial uncertainty on the subject (see *Cricklewood Property and Investment Trust Ltd* v *Leighton Investment Trust Ltd* (1945)), the leading case is now *National Carriers Ltd* v *Panalpina (Northern) Ltd* (1981). The facts were as follows:

> The appellants had a ten-year lease of a warehouse from the respondents. After five and a half years of the lease, the local authority closed the only access road to the warehouse for a period of about eighteen months. This closure of the road prevented the appellants from using the warehouse for their business. As a result, the appellants stopped their payment of rent to the respondents and claimed that the lease was frustrated.

The House of Lords decided that the closure of the access road was not a sufficiently serious interruption to amount to a frustrating event. (This was in spite of the harm to the appellants' business caused by the closure.) There were still a further three years of the lease remaining when the road was opened again. The appellants were still liable for the rent under the lease. But although the frustration claim in fact failed, the House of Lords held that the doctrine is capable of applying to a lease. Their Lordships could see no reason why, in principle, the doctrine should not apply to all types of contract. However, in practice, it will be quite rare for a lease to be frustrated. (*Quaere*: If the access road had been closed for most of the period of the lease, would the contract then have been frustrated in the *National Carriers* case?) It seems that the circumstances in which a lease will most likely be held to be frustrated are where the lease is short term and it is obvious that it is for a specific purpose. If that purpose is thwarted by supervening events beyond the control of both parties, the lease may well be frustrated. (For further discussion of the limited application of the doctrine to leases, see M. Pawlowski, 'Mistake, Frustration and Implied Conditions in Leases' (2007) 11 L&T Review 158. This article also comments on *Graves* v *Graves* (2007), in which the Court of Appeal (at [41]) implied a condition into an assured shorthold tenancy agreement that it would come to an end if housing benefit was not available to the tenant. Both parties to the agreement were mistaken about the availability of housing benefit. Thomas LJ stated (at [43]) that in this case it was 'not necessary to consider whether the contract was frustrated or void for mistake'. The case is also discussed in J. Brown, 'A New Way of Terminating Leases?' (2008) Conv and PL 70.)

Illegality

19.16   The doctrine of frustration will apply in circumstances where the performance of a contract is contrary to some law passed after the contract is made. (If the illegality exists before the contract is made, the doctrine is not relevant—but see **Chapter 15.**) This is often described as a case of 'supervening illegality'. In such circumstances the contract is not impossible to perform, nor have the obligations under the contract (necessarily) been radically altered. It is more a question of public policy in ensuring that the law is not broken. For this reason it is not possible for the parties to exclude the operation of the doctrine, in relation to certain types of supervening illegality (such as trading with the enemy), by express agreement.[4]

19.17   An obvious example of a contract's frustration due to supervening illegality is where its performance would involve trading with an enemy country at a time of war. In *Fibrosa Spolka Akcyjna* v *Fairbairn Lawson Combe Barbour Ltd* (1943), which is discussed in detail later, there was a contract for the sale of machinery to a Polish company. The machinery was to be man-ufactured in England and delivered to Gdynia. Subsequently, Germany invaded Poland and occupied Gdynia. The contract was held to be frustrated despite a clause in the contract which expressly dealt with the consequences of delay due to 'any cause whatsoever...including war'. Trading with a country occupied by the enemy would have been contrary to the public interest. (For a further example of a contract frustrated by war, see *Avery* v *Bowden* (1856).)

19.18   A similar example is presented by the insurance case of *Islamic Republic of Iran Shipping Lines* v *Steamship Mutual Underwriting Association (Bermuda) Ltd* (2010). This serves as a recent illustration of an attempt to claim that a contract of insurance was discharged by frus-tration and/or supervening illegality. Here, a contract of insurance between the claimant and the defendant, concerning liability in respect of bunker oil pollution was affected by meas-ures implemented by the UK government pursuant to the Counter-Terrorism Act 2008. The Financial Restrictions (Iran) Order 2009 prohibited transactions between persons operating in the financial sector and two designated Iranian entities, one of which was the claimant, IRISL. The defendant, a protection and indemnity club, chose to terminate the insurance cover it provided in respect of IRISL's ships even though HM Treasury had issued a licence under the 2008 Act, permitting it to continue with this insurance cover. An IRISL ship, the ZOORIK, was involved in an accident which caused bunker oil pollution and the question of liability for loss arose. The court held that the Order and the licence did not frustrate the contract of insur-ance between the parties. The reason for this was that although the scope of the permitted cover was narrower than before, its nature was not different as it remained indemnity insur-ance. Distinguishing from the earlier authority of *Denny Mott & Dickinson* v *James Fraser & Co.* (1944), the Commercial Court held that the purpose of this contract was to provide indemnity insurance and part of that purpose remained lawful.

19.19   In *Islamic Republic of Iran Shipping Lines* v *Steamship Mutual Underwriting Association (Bermuda) Ltd* (2010), Beatson J offered a useful summary of the case law on the doctrine of frustration (see in particular, [99]–[130] of the judgment). He made reference to Lord Radcliffe's 'classic test' in *Davis Contractors Ltd* v *Fareham UDC* [1956] AC 696 at 729: 'frustration occurs whenever the law recognises that without default of either party a contractual obligation has become incapable of being performed because the circumstances in which performance is called for would make it a thing radically different from that which was undertaken by the contract', and also to Lord Simon's statement in *National Carriers Ltd* v *Panalpina (Northern) Ltd* [1981] AC 675 at 700: 'frustration of a contract takes places when there supervenes an event

---

4   It will be remembered that, normally, the parties can avoid the operation of the doctrine by express stipulation in the contract relating to supervening events.

(without default of either party and for which the contract makes no sufficient provision) which so significantly changes the nature (not merely the expense or onerousness) of the outstanding contractual rights and/or obligations from what the parties could reasonably have contemplated at the time of its execution that it would be unjust to hold them to the literal sense of its stipulations in the new circumstances ...'

Beatson J explained that in considering the facts and claims made in the *IRISL* case, he acknowledged and similarly adopted the 'multi-factorial' approach to the application of the doctrine of frustration as presented by Rix LJ in *Edwinton Commercial Corporation v Tsavliris Russ Ltd, The 'Sea Angel'* (2007)—by including ex ante factors (i.e. factors existing at the time of the contract) and post contractual factors. From considering the elements through this 'multi-factorial' approach, the conclusion was reached that the contract of insurance in the instant case was not discharged by reason of frustration.

19.20   Other examples of supervening illegality are where new licensing regulations are introduced after the parties have contracted, or where restrictions on the import or export of certain goods are subsequently introduced. A problem may arise where the supervening illegality affects just part of the contract. In *Cricklewood Property and Investment Trust Ltd v Leighton Investment Trust Ltd* (1945):

> In 1936, Cricklewood Property obtained a building lease for ninety-nine years for the purpose of building a shopping centre on a residential estate. With the outbreak of war in 1939, restrictions on the supply of building materials were introduced, and Cricklewood Property were unable to build on the land. As building on the land was a term of the lease, Cricklewood Property claimed that the contract was frustrated. The landlord, Leighton's Investment Ltd, brought an action for the rent. (Whether the doctrine of frustration can apply to a lease is discussed earlier and will not be considered here.)

It was decided that the contract was not frustrated and that Cricklewood Property were still liable for the rent under the lease. The reasoning was that it was a long lease, and ninety years of it were still unexpired. It was most unlikely that wartime regulations would last for a substantial part of the duration of the lease and there would be plenty of time for building once they had ended. There was no frustration, therefore, as the illegality did not destroy the main purpose of the lease. For a contrasting case, in which the main purpose of the contract was frustrated due to supervening illegality (restrictions on trading in timber), see *Denny, Mott, & Dickson v James Fraser & Co.* [1944] AC 265.[5]

Impossibility: destruction of subject matter

19.21   We have seen in *Taylor v Caldwell* (1863) a clear instance of 'impossibility', namely the destruction of the subject matter of the contract. The contract was held to be frustrated by the

---

5   See Lord MacMillan's statement in *Denny, Mott, & Dickson* (at 272): 'It is plain that a contract to do what it has become illegal to do cannot be legally enforceable. There cannot be default in not doing what the law forbids to be done'.

fire which destroyed the music hall. The fire was not the fault of either party, nor was there any express stipulation to cover such a contingency. The main purpose of the contract was for the hirer of the hall to hold a series of concerts, and this became impossible as a result of the fire. It did not matter that the whole of the subject matter of the contract—which included the use of the Surrey Gardens—was not destroyed.

19.22   A similar approach can be seen in *Appleby* v *Myers* (1867), where C contracted to erect machinery on D's premises. When the work was well under way, but before it was completed, an accidental fire destroyed D's premises and the machinery that had been erected so far. C's claim to recover damages for the work already done and the cost of materials failed as the destruction of D's premises discharged both parties from their obligations under the contract. (The application of the Law Reform (Frustrated Contracts) Act 1943 to these facts is considered later.) The court's view was that the contract did not include an absolute undertaking by D that his premises would remain unaltered so as to permit C to complete the work contracted for. D had not assumed the risk of the accidental destruction of the premises. Of course, *Appleby* v *Myers* differs slightly from *Taylor* v *Caldwell* (1863) in that the premises were not the subject matter of the contract in *Appleby* v *Myers*. However, the existence of the premises was clearly essential for the performance of the contract and their destruction was rightly held to be a frustrating event.

19.23   Cases can occur where the subject matter of the contract is badly damaged by accident, but not totally destroyed. For example, in *Asfar* v *Blundell* [1896] 1 QB 123, a ship with a cargo of dates sank and was refloated after a few days. On arrival, it was found that the cargo was badly affected by the accident. It was held that the cargo owner was not liable to pay freight as the goods, in a commercial sense, had perished. It did not matter that the goods could still be put to some other commercial use, such as distillation into spirit; their nature had changed to such a degree that they could no longer be classified as dates. They were transformed into a 'mass of pulpy matter impregnated with sewage and in a state of fermentation' (per Lord Esher at 127).[6]

Impossibility: sale of goods

19.24   Where a contract involves the sale of goods, we have to look at the particular rules relating to this subject in addition to the common law principles. A contract for the sale of goods may be frustrated for reasons that we have already considered, such as supervening illegality (see *Avery* v *Bowden* (1856)). But reference should also be made to the relevant provisions of the Sale of Goods Act 1979. Section 7 states that:

> 'Where there is an agreement to sell specific goods, and subsequently the goods, without any fault on the part of the seller or buyer, perish before the risk passes to the buyer, the agreement is avoided.'

---

6   Contrast the decision in *Horn* v *Minister of Food* (1948). See also I. Brown, 'Perished Goods and the Sale of Goods Act 1979 s.6' (2000) LMCLQ 12.

So if S agrees to sell to B goods which are identified at the time the contract is made, and those goods subsequently perish before the risk passes to B, the contract is frustrated (or 'avoided'). As with the common law, the contract will be frustrated only if neither of the parties is at fault. If the goods are not 'specific', however, the section will not apply. If, for example, S agrees to supply B with 100kg of 'Golden Delicious' apples, but no particular source is specified, the contract will not be frustrated if the apples that S intended to use are subsequently destroyed. This is a contract for generic rather than for specific goods. S would be liable for non-delivery of the goods if he could not find another supply in order to fulfil his contractual obligations. (But contrast *Howell* v *Coupland* (1876).)[7]

19.25   Under a contract for the sale of goods it is well established (see Sale of Goods Act 1979, s 20(1)) that risk passes with ownership. (The Act uses the word 'property' to mean ownership.) Therefore, the risk of theft or damage to goods, unless otherwise agreed, falls on the owner, and not necessarily on the person who is in possession of them at the time. If the risk has passed to the buyer, and the goods are then damaged, the buyer will still be liable if he or she refuses to accept or pay for the goods. The contract will not be frustrated. If the property in the goods has not passed, and remains with the seller at the time of the loss or damage, the seller will have to carry out his or her contractual obligations, unless the contract is frustrated. (For an interesting illustration in a shipping context, contrast the two cases, *DGM Commodities Corp* v *Sea Metropolitan SA (The Andra)* (2012) and *Adelfamar SA* v *Silos e Mangimi Martini SpA (The Adelfa)* (1988), which show that responsibility for discharging the cargo by the receiver can influence whether there has been a frustrating event to relieve the obligation to pay demurrage, (this is the charge paid by the charterer to the owner for detaining the ship for loading and unloading, beyond the time agreed).)

19.26   It should be noted that, under the Sale and Supply of Goods to Consumers Regulations 2002, reg 4, there is an amendment to the rule on passing of risk where the buyer deals as a consumer. In such cases 'the goods remain at the seller's risk until they are delivered to the consumer' (now Sale of Goods Act 1979, s 20(4)).

Impossibility: death or illness

19.27   Most commercial contracts do not require performance by a particular person and no other. Therefore, death or illness does not normally prevent performance of the contract. But where a contract is for some personal service, to be rendered by a party to the contract, the death or incapacity of that party will make performance impossible. In *Whincup* v *Hughes* (1871), for example, the claimant's son was apprenticed to a watchmaker for a six-year period at a premium of £25, but the watchmaker died after just one year. The contract, which was for a skilled and personal service, was obviously frustrated. However, at that time, C could

---

7   If, to take the same example, the sale of 100kg of 'Golden Delicious' apples is stated to be 'from the seller's existing stock' (which exceeds 100kg), and the entire stock is then destroyed before the property passes, the contract would probably be frustrated, even though the goods were not 'specific'. This would be in accordance with common law principles.

not claim back any of the premium (for reasons which are explained later).[8] In *Robinson* v *Davison* (1871) a contract was held to be frustrated when a person who had been engaged to play the piano at a concert, on a particular day, was unable to do so because of illness. Also, in *Notcutt* v *Universal Equipment Co. (London) Ltd* (1986), a contract of employment was brought to an end, under the doctrine, as a result of the employee's chronic illness and his inability ever again to perform his contractual obligations. (For an interesting case, involving a slightly different set of facts, see *Shepherd* v *Jerrom* (1987); and contrast *Jones* v *Friction Dynamics Ltd* (2007).) Since the *Notcutt* decision, there can be no doubt that the doctrine of frustration does apply to contracts of employment. However, there are sound policy reasons for the courts being cautious about the extent of such an application. (For a discussion, see D. Brodie, 'Performance Issues and Frustration of Contract' (2006) 71 Employment Law Bulletin 4.)

Impossibility: due to unavailability

19.28   In some circumstances the subject matter of a contract, whilst still in existence, may simply not be available for the purpose that was contracted for. We have seen, in *The Wenjiang (International Sea Tankers of Liberia Inc.* v *Hemisphere Shipping Co. of Hong Kong)* (1982) for instance, how an oil tanker which was trapped on the Shatt-al-Arab river at the outbreak of war in 1980 was thus unavailable to fulfil a contract to carry oil from Basrah. In this, and in a number of similar cases, the charter-parties were frustrated due to the unavailability of the subject matter. The dispute in these cases related to the precise date on which the contracts were frustrated. (A charter-party may also be frustrated where a ship is requisitioned for such a period as to substantially affect the obligations under the contract—see *Bank Line Ltd* v *Arthur Capel & Co.* (1919).)

19.29   In many cases the unavailability of the subject matter will only be temporary. If the contract specifies performance within a particular time, or on a certain date, then the unavailability of the subject matter at the crucial time will frustrate the contract (see *Robinson* v *Davison* (1871), para. **19.27**). But it may not always be obvious whether there is a time limit on performance of the contract. In *Jackson* v *Union Marine Insurance Co. Ltd* (1874) LR 10 CP 125 the facts were as follows:

> Jackson's ship was chartered to go, in January 1872, directly from Liverpool to Newport and there to load a cargo of iron rails to be shipped to San Francisco. Jackson took out insurance on the chartered freight for the voyage. On the way to Newport, on 2 January, the ship ran aground in Caernarfon Bay. It took a month to free the ship and a further six months for repairs to be carried out. Meanwhile, the charterers had chartered another ship as a replacement. Jackson claimed against the defendant insurance company for a total loss of the freight to be earned under the contract, by perils at sea. To succeed with such a claim, it was essential to decide whether the contract between Jackson and the charterer

---

8   The situation is now covered by s 1(2) of the Law Reform (Frustrated Contracts) Act 1943.

> was frustrated, or whether he could have successfully sued the charterer for not loading the goods. In other words, did the charterer have the right to treat the contract with Jackson as discharged?

It was held that a voyage undertaken after the ship had been repaired would have been a very different adventure from the one which the parties had contracted for. A condition could be implied that the ship would arrive in Newport in time for the particular voyage. Its failure to do so within a reasonable time put an end to the contract. The long delay for repairs meant that the contract was frustrated: 'The adventure was frustrated by perils of the seas, both parties were discharged, and a loading of cargo in August would have been a new adventure, a new agreement' (per Lord Bramwell at 148).

19.30   In *Olympic Airlines SA (in Special Liquidation)* v *ACG Acquisition XX LLC* (2013) however, a lease for an aircraft which had defects including corrosion, was not found to be frustrated by the Greek aviation authorities' withdrawal of the certificate of airworthiness, or by their refusal to renew it ((2012) at [173]). At appeal, Tomlinson LJ highlighted the contractual differences between an operating lease for a passenger aircraft and a time charter-party for a ship, stating that '[u]nder an operating lease the position is very different. The lessee takes possession of the aircraft and becomes responsible for its maintenance and insurance. After delivery the aircraft, engines and every part are at the sole risk of the lessee, who therefore bears the risk of loss, theft, damage, destruction and unexpected mechanical problems' ((2013) at [40]). The parties had been reminded that the need to rely upon the doctrine of frustration would only arise in the event that Olympic was unable to allege a breach of the lease by ACG (per Teare J (2012) at [177]. With reference to the guidance given by Rix LJ in *Edwinton Commercial Corp.* v *Tsavliris Russ, The 'Sea Angel'* (2007) which, it will be remembered, recommended that the application of the doctrine requires a 'multi-factorial approach' (at [111]–[112]), Teare J stated that he was 'not persuaded that the demands of justice favour frustration of the contract' ([184]), referring to matters of the length of the lease and a normal allocation of risk concluding that 'to hold that the lease was frustrated would reverse the allocation of risk on which the parties (absent any question of breach) had agreed' ([184]–[186]) and thus the court found in favour of ACG.

19.31   The courts will sometimes have to decide whether a contract covering a lengthy period is frustrated by supervening events which cover part of that period. Typical examples of this include the effects of a strike on a shipping contract (see *The Nema (Pioneer Shipping* v *BTP Tioxide)* (1982)), or the requisition of a commercial ship by the government at a time of war. Delay will frustrate a contract if it defeats the commercial venture, but this can be a difficult question to decide upon. In such instances the court must look at, and compare, both the length of the contract and the length of the interference which causes the unavailability of the subject matter, although this deliberation will not be the sole determinant of whether a contract is frustrated. (The Court of Appeal stated recently that while these factors are 'an important consideration', they are 'only a starting point . . . the development of the law shows that such a single-factored approach is too blunt an instrument': see *Edwinton Commercial Corporation* v *Tsavliris Russ, The 'Sea Angel'* (2007) per Rix LJ at [118].)

It should also be noted that the courts are supposed to judge the situation as at the date of the frustrating event and not with the benefit of hindsight. This can lead to odd results. For example, in *Tamplin Steamship Co. Ltd* v *Anglo-Mexican Petroleum Products Co.* (1916):

> A tanker was chartered from December 1912 for a five-year period. In February 1915, the vessel was requisitioned as a troop ship. The owners of the ship claimed that the contract was frustrated by this supervening event.

The House of Lords decided that the commercial object of the contract was not frustrated as, at the time of the event in question, it appeared likely that the ship would still be available to fulfil a substantial part of the contract after the war ended. As it turned out, the House of Lords was wrong in its assumption, because the war did not end until 1918. But the case illustrates the difficulty in judging the likely effect on a contract of some event which causes the temporary unavailability of the subject matter. (In contrast to the above case, see *Metropolitan Water Board* v *Dick, Kerr, & Co.* (1918). A contract, made in 1914, to build a reservoir within six years, was interrupted in 1916 by a government Order, as a result of war. The contract was frustrated because the delay caused by the Order was likely to cause a radical change to the nature of the contract, if it was later resumed.)

Impossibility: not just financial hardship

19.32   We have seen that the doctrine of frustration operates within strict limits. This is to prevent a party from trying to escape from a bad bargain on the grounds of financial hardship caused by subsequent events. The decision in *Krell* v *Henry* (1903) (discussed at para. **19.7**) is not without its critics, but it was a very unusual case and probably correct in those particular circumstances. More typically, *Amalgamated Investment & Property Co. Ltd* v *John Walker & Sons Ltd* (1976) illustrates the fact that financial hardship alone, suffered by one of the parties as a result of supervening events, will not normally frustrate a contract. It was stated by Lord Radcliffe in *Davis Contractors Ltd* v *Fareham UDC* [1956] AC 696 at 729:

> '...[I]t is not hardship or inconvenience or material loss itself which calls the principle of frustration into play. There must be such a change in the significance of the obligation that the thing undertaken would, if performed, be a different thing from that contracted for.'

19.33   In the example of *Tsakiroglou & Co. Ltd* v *Noblee Thorl GmbH* (1962) (see para. **19.10**), performance of the contract, for the shipment of groundnuts from the Sudan to Hamburg, was made much more difficult and expensive by the subsequent closure of the Suez Canal. It was still possible for the nuts to be shipped via the Cape of Good Hope, but this alternative route would have taken over twice as long and doubled the cost of carriage. The price of the shipment was calculated on the basis that the route would be via the Suez Canal, but the contract did not specify the route; nor did it specify a date for delivery. The House of Lords held that the contract was not frustrated. Performance of the contract was more difficult and expensive for the appellants, but it was not impossible. The court refused to imply a term that the goods were to be shipped by the customary and cheapest route. (See further *Ocean Tramp Tankers Corpn* v *V/O Sofracht, The Eugenia* (1964) and *Bunge SA* v *Kyla Shipping Co Ltd, The Kyla* (2013).)

Effect of express provision for frustrating event

19.34   The doctrine of frustration has developed as a means of dealing with subsequent, unforeseen events which render performance of a contract impossible, or illegal, or which fundamentally change the nature of the contractual obligations undertaken by the parties. However, the parties may make express provision dealing with certain supervening events and, in so doing, effectively preclude the operation of the doctrine. The original theory behind the doctrine, as explained in *Taylor* v *Caldwell* (1863), was that it was based on an effort to give effect to the presumed intention of the parties. In other words, it could not operate if the parties had dealt with a particular contingency by express provision. (But see *Jackson* v *Union Marine Insurance Co. Ltd* (1874), para. **19.36**.)

19.35   One obvious exception, as we have seen, is that frustration on the ground that the contract involves trading with an enemy country cannot be excluded by express provision (see *Ertel Bieber & Co.* v *Rio Tinto Co. Ltd* (1918)). This is for reasons of public policy and is not exceptionable. But, generally, the parties may make express provision for other types of supervening event, such as strikes, closure of shipping routes, illness, floods, fires, and other disasters. Thus the parties can allocate the risk of such events as they see fit. They may, for example, expressly provide for an extension to the period of performance of the contractual obligations. They may further provide that should the interference with the contract continue beyond a specified period, then either party is entitled to terminate the contract. The parties can expressly decide that neither party is entitled to compensation in the event of these contingencies. Such forward planning is particularly useful for those involved in international trade, where the threat of disruption is more likely. (See for example, *Olympic Airlines SA (in Special Liquidation)* v *ACG Acquisition XX LLC* (2013) discussed at para. **19.30**).

19.36   Although the doctrine of frustration is limited to supervening events which are not expressly provided for in the contract, the courts might interpret an express provision in such a way that the doctrine may still operate. In *Jackson* v *Union Marine Insurance Co. Ltd* (1874) a contract for the hire of a ship stated that the vessel was to proceed with all possible speed (dangers and accidents of navigation excepted) from Liverpool to Newport, in order to load a cargo of iron for San Francisco. The ship ran aground, not far from Liverpool, and was delayed for eight months. It was held that, notwithstanding the express exception of dangers and accidents of navigation, the contract was frustrated. The words of exception appeared to cover the contingency which in fact occurred, but the court found a way of limiting their application because it clearly felt that a voyage undertaken after the repair to the ship would have been a different 'adventure' altogether. Accordingly, the express provision was given a restrictive interpretation by the court; it would excuse the owner of the ship and protect him from an action for breach of contract, but it would not deprive the charterer of the right to treat his contractual undertakings as discharged. For a further example of a restrictive interpretation of an express provision, see *Metropolitan Water Board v Dick, Kerr, & Co.* (1918).

Frustration does not apply to foreseeable events

19.37   The doctrine of frustration does not generally apply to situations where the supervening event was foreseen or foreseeable. (Once again, trading with the enemy is an obvious exception for public policy reasons. Even if war was foreseeable, it would not prevent the doctrine from being applied.) If the parties foresee that a particular event might occur which may affect their performance of the contract, it will be assumed that they contracted in accordance with that risk. For example, in *Davis Contractors Ltd v Fareham UDC* [1956] AC 696, the House of Lords rejected the company's claim that the contract, for the construction of seventy-eight houses within a period of eight months for a fixed price, was frustrated by shortages of labour and materials which increased the cost of the work. The basic obligations under the agreement remained unchanged and financial hardship to one of the parties was not a sufficient reason for invoking the doctrine.

The *Davis Contractors* decision can be defended on the basis that the risk of increased costs, due to various shortages, was clearly foreseen by the company. It must therefore be assumed that it accepted that risk at the time of contracting. (The company had, in fact, sent a letter along with the original tender, stating that the tender was subject to the availability of adequate supplies of labour and building materials. This letter was not incorporated into the contract, nor was such a provision expressly included in the contract.) Lord Radcliffe stated (at 731):

> 'Two things seem to me to prevent the application of the principle of frustration to this case. One is that the cause of the delay was not any new state of things which the parties could not reasonably be thought to have foreseen. On the contrary, the possibility of enough labour and materials not being available was before their eyes and could have been the subject of special contractual stipulation. It was not made so.'[9]

However, the significance of foreseeability of risk was also considered recently by the Court of Appeal in *Edwinton Commercial Corporation v Tsavliris Russ Ltd, The 'Sea Angel'* (2007) at [102]–[104]. Rix LJ explained that there was no absolute rule to the effect that foreseeability precluded the application of the doctrine of frustration in all circumstances, and went on to state (at [127]):

> 'In a sense, most events are to a greater or lesser degree foreseeable. That does not mean that they cannot lead to frustration . . . However . . . the less that an event, in its type and impact, is foreseeable, the more likely it is to be a factor which, depending on other factors in the case, may lead on to frustration.'

---

9   Whether the doctrine can apply to events which were foreseen or contemplated by the parties is also discussed in *The Eugenia* (1964). See also the more recent case of *Globe Master Management Ltd v Boulas-Gad Ltd* (2002).

Frustration cannot be 'self-induced'

19.38 The doctrine of frustration applies only in circumstances where the supervening event is beyond the control of the parties to the contract. It follows that, where the alleged frustrating event is caused by the deliberate act or decision of one of the parties, or by his or her negligence, the doctrine will not apply. Whichever theory lies behind the doctrine—whether it is based on the presumed contractual intention of the parties, or whether it is simply a fair solution imposed by the courts—it is not possible to justify its application to subsequent events which are 'self-induced'. An example of this rule is provided by *Ocean Tramp Tankers Corpn v V/O Sofracht, The Eugenia* (1964), where the facts were:

> The Eugenia was let out to the charterers to go from Genoa to the Black Sea to load cargo, and thence to India to unload cargo. Having loaded, the ship proceeded on its route to India, which took it via Suez. In breach of contract, the charterers allowed the ship to enter a war zone. (The contract contained a 'war clause' which prohibited the charterers from sailing the ship into a dangerous zone without the owner's permission.) The ship entered the Suez Canal and was trapped when the canal was closed. The charterers tried to rely on the detention of the ship as a frustrating event.

The Court of Appeal held that the charterers could not rely on the fact that the ship was trapped in the canal, as this was their own fault. They were in breach of contract by allowing the ship to enter a war zone and, therefore, the alleged frustrating event was self-induced. A different case, illustrating the same basic rule, is *Maritime National Fish Ltd v Ocean Trawlers Ltd* (1935) where:

> Maritime National Fish (MNF) chartered a steam trawler, fitted with an otter trawl, from Ocean Trawlers (OT). The parties expressly agreed that the trawler should be used only in the fishing industry. Both parties knew, at the time of the agreement, that it was illegal to use an otter trawl without a licence from the Canadian government. A few months after the contract was made, MNF applied for five licences for the five trawlers which they were operating, but they were granted only three by the government. MNF were, therefore, forced to name the three ships which they wished to license, and the three which they chose did not include the one chartered from OT. OT brought an action for the hire, and MNF argued that the contract was frustrated by the refusal of the government to grant more than three licences to them.

One of the reasons given by the Canadian appeal court for rejecting MNF's contention was that the risk of not obtaining a licence was foreseeable, and MNF could have insisted that some express provision be made for this contingency. Having failed to do so, MNF accepted the risk of not obtaining a licence to fish with OT's trawler. The Privy Council did not disagree with this ruling, but their Lordships thought that it was unnecessary to hear detailed argument on this point. They held that the Canadian court's other reason for dismissing MNF's contention was correct and was a sufficient basis for dismissing MNF's appeal: namely, that the alleged frustrating event arose from the deliberate act or choice of MNF. The doctrine of frustration could not be relied upon where the supervening event in question was 'self-induced'.

19.39   *Maritime National Fish Ltd* v *Ocean Trawlers Ltd* (1935) was applied by the Court of Appeal in *J Lauritzen A/S* v *Wijsmuller BV, The Super Servant Two* [1990] 1 Lloyd's Rep 1. The facts were:

> The defendants agreed to transport the claimants' drilling rig from Japan to Rotterdam. The contract specified that the rig was to be delivered between 20 June and 20 August (in 1981) and was to be carried by what was described as the 'transportation unit'. This unit was defined as meaning either *Super Servant One* or *Super Servant Two*. Before performance of the contract was due, the defendants decided to use *Super Servant Two* for transporting the claimants' rig, and they entered into contracts with other parties for which they planned to use *Super Servant One*. On 29 January 1981, *Super Servant Two* sank whilst being used on another job and, shortly afterwards, the defendants told the claimants that they would not be carrying out their obligations under the contract, as *Super Servant One* was unavailable due to use in other contracts. Under a 'without prejudice' agreement, the defendants eventually transported the claimants' rig on a barge towed by a tug. The claimants later claimed for the losses they had suffered.

The Court of Appeal held that the defendants could not rely on the doctrine of frustration as it was their own choice that they decided not to use *Super Servant One* for this purpose. (Also see *Bunge SA* v *Kyla Shipping Co Ltd, The Kyla* (2013).) The sinking of *Super Servant Two* did not bring the contract to an end automatically, as the defendants had an alternative. In other words, if it had been foreseen at the time of contracting that one of the vessels might become unavailable to transport the rig, the parties would not have been concerned as there was another vessel which could perform the same task. It would have been different if the defendants owned only one 'transportation unit' and that had sunk through no fault of their own. Bingham LJ stated (at 9):

> 'The doctrine [of frustration] must avail a party who contracts to perform a contract of carriage with a vessel which, through no fault of his, no longer exists. But that is not this case. The contract [with the claimants] did provide an alternative . . . [T]he present case does not fall within the very limited class of cases in which the law will relieve one party from an absolute promise he has chosen to make.'

19.40   Similar issues were raised in the House of Lords in *Paal Wilson & Co. A/S* v *Partenreederei Hannah Blumenthal, The Hannah Blumenthal* [1983] 1 All ER 34. The case concerned the sale of a ship under a contract which provided that any dispute arising out of the sale was to be settled by arbitration. Disputes arose about the vessel, and the buyers commenced arbitration proceedings. As originally agreed, both parties appointed an arbitrator, but a third arbitrator (as provided for in the contract) was never appointed. In all, there was a period of over seven years' delay in the arbitration. The question arose whether the arbitration agreement was frustrated as a result of the long delay, which was the fault of both parties. The House of Lords held that, in such circumstances, the fact that the parties were under a mutual obligation to keep the arbitration process moving meant that neither party could rely on the delay of the other as a ground for claiming frustration of the agreement to arbitrate. Lord Brandon stated (at 44):

> '... [T]here are two essential factors which must be present in order to frustrate a contract. The first essential factor is that there must be some outside event or extraneous change of situation, not foreseen or provided for by the parties at the time of contracting, which either makes it impossible for the contract to be performed at all, or at least renders its performance something radically different from what the parties contemplated when they entered into it. The second essential factor is that the outside event or extraneous change of situation concerned, and the consequences of either in relation to the performance of the contract, must have occurred without either the fault or default of either party to the contract.'[10]

19.41   However, if the 'fault' of a party to a contract is merely of a minor nature, he or she may still be able to rely on the doctrine. It will be a question of degree as to whether the particular 'fault' or 'default' amounts to self-induced frustration. Where a person acts in a deliberate way (as in *The Eugenia* (1964)), or makes a deliberate choice (as in *Maritime National Fish* (1935)), so as to bring about the frustrating event, he or she will be precluded from relying on the doctrine. But, for example, would a contract for some personal performance be frustrated if the person concerned became incapacitated by his or her own carelessness—such as a professional acrobat who sustains injury on a private skiing expedition and, as a result, is unable to perform his or her act? This type of problem was acknowledged, without being resolved, in *Joseph Constantine Steamship Line Ltd* v *Imperial Smelting Corpn Ltd* [1941] 2 All ER 165 (per Viscount Simon LC at 173). There seems to be no reason, in principle, why events brought about by a party's own negligence should not be regarded as self-induced and thus preclude the application of the doctrine.

It should be noted that, where self-induced frustration is alleged, the onus of proof falls on the party making the allegation. In *Joseph Constantine*, the owners of a steamship (*The Kingswood*) chartered the vessel to the respondents, to go to Australia and load a cargo there. Before the cargo was loaded, an explosion occurred in the boiler of the ship, preventing the contract from being carried out. The respondents sued the owners for damages and the owners claimed that the contract was frustrated by the explosion. The respondents argued that the onus of proof rested on the owners to show that the explosion was not their fault. The House of Lords held that the contract was frustrated. The cause of the explosion was not clear, but the respondents had failed to prove that the frustrating event was the owner's fault. The burden of proof was not on the owners to disprove negligence on their part.

---

10 See also Griffiths LJ's useful summary of the relevant authorities in his dissenting judgment in the Court of Appeal in the same case: [1982] 3 All ER 394 at 406–7.

Effects of the doctrine

19.42   So far in this chapter we have been concerned with the issue of whether a contract is frustrated. We must now consider the practical consequences that arise when the parties are discharged under the doctrine. Unless the law provides for a fair distribution of the loss resulting from the supervening event, it may not be satisfactory simply to hold that the contract is frustrated. For example, a party may have incurred considerable expenditure in reliance upon the contract before the frustrating event occurred. The common law rules governing this type of situation have now been improved upon by the Law Reform (Frustrated Contracts) Act 1943. Both are considered in turn below.

19.43   It is well settled that frustration automatically brings the contract to an end at the time of the frustrating event. This is in contrast to discharge by breach of contract where the innocent party can choose whether to treat the contract as repudiated. Moreover, a contract which is discharged by frustration is clearly different from one which is void for mistake. A frustrated contract is valid until the time of the supervening event but is automatically ended thereafter, whereas a contract void on the grounds of mistake is a complete nullity from the beginning. A clear statement about the legal effect of frustration on a contract can be found in *Hirji Mulji* v *Cheong Yue Steamship Co. Ltd* [1926] AC 497, where the facts were:

> The respondent owners of a ship, *The Singaporean*, agreed by a charter-party of November 1916 to hire out their vessel to the appellants from 1 March 1917. The appellants agreed to use the ship for ten months from the date of delivery. Before 1 March 1917, the ship was requisitioned by the government and not released until February 1919. When the ship was requisitioned, the owners, thinking that she would soon be released, asked the appellants if they were still willing to take up the charter (i.e. a little later). The appellants said that they would do so, but when the ship was finally released (later than expected) in February 1919, they refused to accept it. The owners argued that the appellants could not rely on the doctrine of frustration, despite the supervening event, as they had chosen to affirm the contract.

On appeal from the Supreme Court of Hong Kong, the Privy Council held that the contract was frustrated in 1917. This meant that the obligations under the contract were brought to an end immediately and automatically at the time of the frustrating event. The application of the doctrine did not rely upon the election of the parties. So even where the parties continue to treat the contract as subsisting for a period of time after the supervening event, the court may declare it to be frustrated. In reference to the delay caused by the requisitioning of the ship, Lord Sumner said (at 501) that it was immaterial that the parties thought at first that the delay would not frustrate the contract. He went on (at 509–10) to explain that whereas repudiation (or rescission) for breach is 'a right to treat the contract as at an end if [the victim] chooses', frustration operates independently of the choice of the parties. Frustration operates, he added, 'irrespective of the individuals concerned, their temperaments and failings, their interest and circumstances'.

19.44   As a consequence of the rule that a contract is valid until the time of the frustrating event, and is determined automatically thereafter, certain other rules were said to follow. The common law position was encapsulated in the slightly enigmatic expression that 'the loss lies where it falls'. For example, where money was paid under a contract which was later frustrated, it was not recoverable. This was because parties remained liable for contractual obligations which fell due before the supervening event. On the other hand, the parties escaped from performing those obligations which had not yet fallen due at the time of frustration. The potential for unfairness under this common law approach can best be understood by looking at the relevant decisions. In *Chandler v Webster* [1904] 1 KB 493 the facts were:

> The claimant contracted to hire a room in Pall Mall from the defendant for the purpose of watching the coronation procession on 26 June 1902. The price for the hire of the room was £141 15s and it was payable immediately. The claimant paid £100, but before he paid the balance the procession was cancelled due to the illness of the King. The claimant sought to recover the money he had paid.

The Court of Appeal held that his claim could not succeed. Moreover, he was liable for the remaining £41 15s, as this obligation had fallen due before the frustrating event occurred. Despite receiving no actual benefit whatsoever, the claimant was still liable for the hire of the room. Lord Collins MR explained the justification for this outcome (at 499):

> 'If the effect [of a frustrating event] were that the contract were wiped out altogether, no doubt the result would be that the money paid under it would have to be repaid as on a failure of consideration. But that is not the effect of the doctrine; it only releases the parties from further performance of the contract. Therefore the doctrine of failure of consideration does not apply.'

19.45   The harsh results of this rule as laid down by *Chandler v Webster* (1904) were, not surprisingly, subjected to considerable criticism. The Law Revision Committee[11] suggested that the rule should be changed but, before any implementation of this Report took place, *Chandler v Webster* was overruled by *Fibrosa Spolka Akcyjna v Fairbairn Lawson Combe Barbour Ltd* [1943] AC 32 ('the *Fibrosa* case'). The case involved a contract under which the respondents, an English company, were to manufacture certain machinery for the appellants, a Polish company, and deliver it to Gdynia. The appellants were to pay £4,800 for the machinery, a third of which (i.e. £1,600) was to be paid with the order. In fact, only £1,000 was paid with the order. Subsequently, Germany invaded Poland and occupied Gdynia. At this time, none of the machinery had been delivered. For reasons which we have considered earlier, the contract was frustrated and the appellants sued for the return of the £1,000.

The Court of Appeal followed the rule in *Chandler v Webster* and held that the money was irrecoverable. But the House of Lords decided that there had been a total failure of consideration

---

11   Seventh Interim Report, Cmnd 6009, 1939.

and that the appellants were entitled to recover £1,000 from the respondents. Viscount Simon stated (at 46–7):

> 'To claim the return of money paid on the ground of total failure of consideration is not to vary the terms of the contract in any way. The claim arises not because the right to be repaid is one of the stipulated conditions of the contract, but because, in the circumstances that have happened, the law gives the remedy...[I]t does not follow that because the [claimant] cannot sue "on the contract" he cannot sue dehors [or, outside] the contract for the recovery of a payment in respect of which consideration has failed.'[12]

The decision in the *Fibrosa* case was an improvement on the harshness of *Chandler* v *Webster*, but it was not a complete solution to the problem of money paid under a contract which was then frustrated. This was freely acknowledged by their Lordships in the course of their judgments (see [1943] AC 32 at 49–50, 54–5, and 71–2). Recovery of money paid depended on there having been a total failure of consideration; the performance of just a part of the consideration would thus prevent such a claim from succeeding. (For example, consider *Whincup* v *Hughes* (1871).) So if the English company had delivered part of the machinery before the discharge of the contract, failure of consideration would not have been total, and the advance payment would have been irrecoverable.

Furthermore, the decision in the *Fibrosa* case made no allowance for the expenses which were incurred under the contract by the payee. In other words, it was not really a fair solution to both parties; it provided for the return of the prepayment, but it did not compensate the recipient for the expenditure that it had incurred whilst partially carrying out the contract. In the *Fibrosa* case itself, the £1,000 was recoverable, but the English company received nothing for the considerable amount of work it had done on the machinery before the frustrating event. The common law did not allow the apportionment of the prepaid sum in this situation. To deal with these obvious defects in the law, the Law Reform (Frustrated Contracts) Act 1943 was enacted soon after the *Fibrosa* case.

The Law Reform (Frustrated Contracts) Act 1943

General

19.46   The Law Reform (Frustrated Contracts) Act 1943 (LR(FC)A 1943) was introduced in an attempt to provide for a fair solution between the parties when their contract has been frustrated. (See also *Great Peace Shipping Ltd* v *Tsavliris Salvage (International) Ltd* (2003) at [161].) It aimed at preventing the unjust enrichment of either party to the contract at the expense of

---

12 The term 'consideration' is used here in a different sense from that which we saw in **Chapter 4**. There it meant the promise given in exchange for some act or promise, whereas in this context it denotes the actual performance of the promise. See the comments of Viscount Simon in the *Fibrosa* case [1943] AC 32.

the other. It deals only with situations where contracts have 'become impossible of performance or been otherwise frustrated' and the parties have consequently been discharged from further performance (s 1(1)). It should be noted that the Act does not lay down the general principles under which the doctrine will be invoked and this question is still dealt with under the common law rules that we have considered earlier in this chapter. Also, the parties may themselves have made express provision for the frustrating event which has occurred, in which case, under s 2(3), the court is to give effect to the parties' intentions and the Act is excluded by their contrary agreement.

19.47   LR(FC)A 1943 does not apply to all types of contract. Section 2(5) states that the Act is not applicable to the following:

> '(a) any charterparty, except a time charterparty... or to any contract (other than a charterparty) for the carriage of goods by sea; or
>
> (b) any contract of insurance...
>
> (c) any contract to which section 7 of the Sale of Goods Act (now 1979) applies, or to any other contract for the sale, or for the sale and delivery, of specific goods, where the contract is frustrated by reason of the fact that the goods have perished.'

The main changes introduced by the Act

19.48   LR(FC)A 1943, s 1(2) provides that:

> 'All sums paid or payable to any party in pursuance of the contract before the time when the parties were so discharged (in this Act referred to as "the time of discharge") shall, in the case of sums so paid, be recoverable from him as money received by him for the use of the party by whom the sums were paid, and, in the case of sums so payable, cease to be so payable.'

In other words, this subsection enacts that advance payments made in pursuance of the contract before the supervening event, are recoverable. This provision goes further than *Fibrosa Spolka Akcyjna* v *Fairbairn Lawson Combe Barbour Ltd* (1943), in that claims under s 1(2) are not restricted to cases where the consideration for the payment has totally failed. It also provides that money which is payable under the contract before the frustrating event, but not yet paid, ceases to be payable. Of course, there will be cases where the recipient of the advance payment has incurred expenses before the contract was frustrated. It may well be that the parties agreed on some advance payment for this very reason. If the whole sum is recoverable, on discharge, then this can be as unfair to the payee as the old rule in *Chandler* v *Webster* (1904) was to the payer. For this reason, the new provisions are subject to the following important proviso which is appended to s 1(2):

> 'Provided that, if the party to whom the sums were so paid or payable incurred expenses before the time of discharge in, or for the purpose of, the performance of the contract, the

> court may, if it considers it just to do so having regard to all the circumstances of the case, allow him to retain or, as the case may be, recover the whole or any part of the sums so paid or payable, not being an amount in excess of the expenses so incurred.'

It should be emphasized that this award of expenses can be made only where an advance sum was either paid or payable before the frustrating event. Thus LR(FC)A 1943, s 1(2) represents an improvement upon the common law decision in the *Fibrosa* case. In that case the English company had incurred considerable expenditure and received nothing in return. As we have seen, the common law did not permit the apportionment of an advance payment in circumstances such as these, and the legislature acted promptly in response to criticism of this lack of flexibility.

19.49   Under LR(FC)A 1943, s 1(2), a party who has incurred expenses in the performance of the contract may be awarded expenses up to a limit of the sums paid or payable to him or her under the contract before the frustrating event. Such an award will be made where the court 'considers it just to do so having regard to all the circumstances of the case'—in other words, any award is at the discretion of the court. To return to the facts of *Fibrosa Spolka Akcyjna* v *Fairbairn Lawson Combe Barbour Ltd* (1943), for example: the English company might, under the new provision, have been compensated for its expenses incurred before the supervening event. But, it will be remembered that only £1,600 was to be paid by the Polish company with the order for the machinery. Therefore that amount (£1,600) would be the maximum that could have been awarded to the English company for expenses. In considering an award for expenses, in circumstances such as those of the *Fibrosa* case, the court will take account of whether the goods are of any commercial value to the sellers. If they can be sold to another buyer, then the expenses incurred under the original contract (before frustration) will not have been wasted.

19.50   The more recent case of *Gamerco SA* v *ICM/Fair Warning (Agency) Ltd* [1995] 1 WLR 1226 provides a rare judicial discussion of the application of LR(FC)A 1943, s 1(2). The facts were that, in 1992, the claimant concert promoters (C) agreed to promote a pop group's (D's) concert at a football stadium in Madrid on a specific date, as part of that group's European tour. Shortly before the date of the concert, but after the contract was made by the parties, engineers discovered that the stadium was unsafe and its use was subsequently prohibited by the local authorities. Thus, C's permit to hold the concert was withdrawn and, as no other suitable venue was available at this time, the concert was cancelled. C had paid $412,500 to D in advance, and both parties had incurred some expenditure in preparing for the concert. The action involved C's claim to recover the advance payment under s 1(2) of the Act, and D's counterclaim for breach of contract by C for failing to secure the required permit for the performance.

The judge, Garland J, in the High Court held that the contract was frustrated due to the stadium being unsafe and its use for the concert being banned. D's counterclaim was unsuccessful as C was not required to ensure that the permit, once obtained, would remain in force. More significantly, it was decided to allow C's claim in its entirety, with the judge ordering the repayment of the whole sum paid in advance to D; i.e. there was no deduction (or 'set off') to compensate D. The judge felt that, despite the fact that D had incurred some expenditure in advance of the proposed performance, justice would be done by making no deduction from the ordered repayment under the proviso. It seems that the precise nature of D's expenses was not very clear and the judge found it impossible to determine an accurate amount: 'the best I can do is to accept that [D] did incur some expenses, but the extent of them is wholly unproven...' (per Garland J at 1235). Presumably, it was felt that C's expenses were heavier and more calculable than those of the defendant pop group.

19.51   Another important innovation introduced by LR(FC)A 1943 is contained in s 1(3), which states:

> 'Where any party to the contract has, by reason of anything done by any other party thereto in, or for the purpose of, the performance of the contract, obtained a valuable benefit (other than a payment of money to which...[section 1(2)]...applies) before the time of discharge, there shall be recoverable from him by the said other party such sum (if any), not exceeding the value of the said benefit to the party obtaining it, as the court considers just, having regard to all the circumstances of the case and, in particular—
>
> (a)   the amount of any expenses incurred before the time of discharge by the benefited party in, or for the purpose of, the performance of the contract, including any sums paid or payable by him to any other party in pursuance of the contract and retained or recoverable by that party under...[section 1(2)], and
>
> (b)   the effect, in relation to the said benefit, of the circumstances giving rise to the frustration of the contract.'

19.52   Under the common law, a party escaped the performance of those obligations which had not yet fallen due at the time of frustration. So if (hypothetically), in *Fibrosa Spolka Akcyjna v Fairbairn Lawson Combe Barbour Ltd* (1943), the contract had been for the English company to manufacture the machinery at a price of £4,800, to be paid on delivery, it would have received nothing when the contract was frustrated before completion of the work. This is supported by *Appleby* v *Myers* (1867), where the claimant claimed damages for the work already done in erecting machinery on the defendant's premises before the contract was frustrated by an accidental fire which destroyed both the machinery and the premises. This claim was unsuccessful, as the supervening event discharged both parties from their obligations under the contract and gave no cause of action to either of them. (The contract did not provide for any advance payment and the court interpreted the agreement as one for payment on completion of the work.)

19.53   The ponderously worded LR(FC)A 1943, s 1(3) was introduced to improve upon the rather unjust position at common law. Where a party has obtained a 'valuable benefit' under the contract, before the supervening event, the court may order him or her to pay a fair sum for it, having regard to all the circumstances. To return to the facts of *Appleby* v *Myers* (1867), the court would now have to consider whether the defendants did in fact obtain a valuable benefit from the claimant's work. Before the fire took place, the machinery (albeit unfinished) possibly constituted a benefit; but, after the fire, such benefit as had been obtained, was rendered worthless to the defendant (see s 1(3)(b), earlier). It is, therefore, far from clear that the Act would improve the claimant's position in such a case. (*Quaere*: Should the court assess the value of the alleged benefit on the basis of how things stood immediately before the frustrating event?)

19.54   An illustration of the potential usefulness of LR(FC)A 1943, s 1(3) is provided by the old case of *Cutter v Powell* (1795). The second mate of a ship, the *Governor Parry*, was promised 30 guineas for the completion of a voyage from Kingston (Jamaica) to Liverpool. (The basic rate of pay per month was £4, but the contract in question provided for a much higher rate; this was payable only where the sailor served for the whole of the voyage.) The sailor died after seven weeks of the voyage and his widow (the executrix) claimed a proportion of his wages, on a quantum meruit basis, for the work he had done on the voyage before his death. The court rejected the widow's claim, as the contract stipulated that the voyage had to be completed. This is sometimes referred to as the 'doctrine of strict performance'.

It is possible that the outcome of *Cutter v Powell* would be different today under s 1(3) and that the widow could recover from the defendant for the valuable benefit which he had obtained from the sailor's labour (although the work would presumably be compensated at the basic rate only). But it is also possible that the Act would have been excluded by the contrary agreement of the parties, as provided for by s 2(3).[13] This might depend on the construction of their agreement. Did they agree, for example, that there was to be no payment whatsoever unless the entire voyage was completed by the sailor?

19.55   The first major case to be decided on the LR(FC)A 1943 was *BP Exploration Co. (Libya) Ltd v Hunt (No 2)* [1982] 1 All ER 925. (The judgments of the Queen's Bench Division, the Court of Appeal, and the House of Lords can all be found under this reference.) The facts were as follows:

> Nelson Hunt had been granted an oil concession in Libya by the government of that country. He entered into an agreement with a large oil company, BP, to exploit the oil concession, as he lacked the resources to go ahead on his own. BP were to do the exploratory work, which they would finance, and in return they would get a half share of Hunt's concession. They also had to make certain 'farm-in' payments to Hunt in cash and oil. As soon as the oil field became productive, BP were to receive half of all the oil produced from it, together with 'reimbursement oil' (taken from Hunt's share) to meet the cost of the company's 'farm-in' payments and to cover Hunt's share of the development expenses. Thus BP were to bear the principal risk of failure in their combined venture. After much expenditure, a large oil field was discovered, which became productive in 1967. But, in 1971, BP's half share in the concession was expropriated by the new Libyan government, following a revolution in that country. The same fate befell Hunt's half share in 1973. At the time of the frustrating event, BP had

---

13 But consider *BP Exploration Co. (Libya) v Hunt (No 2)* (1982), where the House of Lords took a narrow view of s 2(3), refusing to hold that it defeated the claimant's claim for an award of a just sum.

received about one-third of the reimbursement oil to which they were entitled. The company brought a claim under s 1(3) of the Act for an award of a just sum.

The claim was allowed by Robert Goff J and he awarded BP a just sum under s 1(3) of the Act. The precise calculation of the amount is a complex matter which will not be elaborated here. Hunt's appeals to both the Court of Appeal and the House of Lords were unsuccessful. The main judgment on the scope of s 1(3) is that of the trial judge. (In the House of Lords, their Lordships dealt with fairly minor, technical issues.) Robert Goff J (at 950) explained that Hunt's benefit was the increase in the value of the oil concession as a result of BP's work. It should be noted, however, that the value of this benefit was substantially reduced by the circumstances giving rise to the frustration of the contract, namely the expropriation of the parties' interests in the oil field.

Summary

- The doctrine of frustration developed to deal with cases where events occur after a contract is made which render the agreement illegal, or impossible to perform, or which fundamentally change the nature of the obligations undertaken by the parties.

- A frustrating event must not be the result of any fault of either of the contracting parties.

- The doctrine of frustration does not generally apply to situations where the supervening event was foreseen or foreseeable.

- If the parties have made express provision for how they will deal with the consequences of future events which may affect performance, the doctrine of frustration will not usually be applicable.

- The doctrine operates within strict limits and cannot be used simply to escape the consequences of what has turned out to be a bad bargain.

- The doctrine of frustration may apply where the subject matter of the contract is destroyed, or where a contract is made to perform an act which subsequently becomes illegal.

- The use of the doctrine is very restricted in cases where, although the commercial purpose of the contract has been drastically affected by unforeseen events, the performance of the contract is still possible.

- Frustration brings a contract to an end, automatically, at the time of the frustrating event.

- The common law held that the 'loss lies where it falls' (for example, money paid under a contract which was later frustrated was not recoverable).

- Despite improvements to the common law position on the effects of frustration, there was still a lack of flexibility for the courts to provide a fair solution between the parties.

- The Law Reform (Frustrated Contracts) Act 1943 was enacted to improve upon the common law, by preventing the unjust enrichment of either party to the contract at the expense of the other. (It should be noted that the 1943 Act does not set out the general principles under which the doctrine may be invoked; this is still a matter for the common law.)

- Under s 1(2) of the 1943 Act, advance payments made before the frustrating event are recoverable; subject to an entitlement of the payee to an award of expenses, up to a limit of the amount paid (or payable) to him or her before the frustrating event. Such an award is at the court's discretion.

- The award of expenses is available only where an advance sum was either paid or payable before the frustrating event.

- Under s 1(3) of the 1943 Act, where a party has obtained a 'valuable benefit' under the contract prior to the frustrating event, the court may order him to pay a fair sum for it, having regard to all the circumstances.

▶ Further reading

D. Brodie, 'Performance Issues and Frustration of Contract' (2006) 71 Employment Law Bulletin 4

P. Clark, 'Frustration, Restitution and the Law Reform (Frustrated Contracts) Act 1943' [1996] 2 LMCLQ 170

C. Hall, 'Frustration and the Question of Foresight' (1984) 4 LS 300

E. McKendrick, 'The Construction of Force Majeure Clauses and Self-Induced Frustration' [1990] 2 LMCLQ 153

M. Pawlowski, 'Mistake, Frustration and Implied Conditions in Leases' (2007) 11(5) L&T Review 158

J. C. Smith, 'Contracts—Mistake, Frustration and Implied Terms' (1994) 110 LQR 400

L. Trakman, 'Frustrated Contracts and Legal Fictions' (1983) 46 MLR 39

Chapter 20

Damages

⊙ Introduction

20.1 Although it is common to speak of 'enforcing the contract', the primary remedy for breach of contract is not specific performance but damages, and damages will form the subject matter of this chapter, whilst specific enforcement will be covered in the next. However, many disputes will be settled without the assistance of the courts.[1] The parties may reach an agreement which resolves their dispute. The contract itself may have been drafted to deal with difficulties. It might contain a liquidated damages clause (see para. **20.69**ff), stating how much is to be paid by one party in the event of a particular breach. The other party may then simply be able to deduct that sum from his or her contractual payments. In addition, the order of performance may have been fixed so that one party, X, can withhold his or her performance until the other party, Y, performs. Y then has an incentive to perform in order to trigger X's obligation (see para. **18.8**). In this context the right to terminate for breach should not be forgotten. The threat to exercise that right may induce the other party to comply with the contract, and the actual exercise of it enables an injured party to extract themselves from the contract. However, here we are concerned primarily with contractual damages, with specific performance and injunctions being considered in the chapter which follows.

Basic principle and the claims

Expectation loss

20.2 In general, the sum awarded for breach of contract will be calculated so as to compensate the injured party rather than to recover any profit made by the party in breach. So that generally, if the 'injured' party has suffered no loss, the damages awarded will be nominal—merely

---

1 S. Macauley, 'Non-Contractual Relations in Business' (1963) 28 Am Soc Rev 55; H. Beale and A. Dugdale, 'Contracts Between Businessmen: Planning and the Use of Contractual Remedies' (1975) 2 Br J Law and Soc 45.

marking the contractual right. However, the House of Lords has indicated that, very exception-ally, recovery of the profit of the party in breach is possible (*A-G* v *Blake* (2000)). This is dealt with at para. **20.18ff**. However, what must be emphasized here is the ordinary recovery of dam-ages for breach of contract and compensating the injured party's loss.

20.3   The loss claimed will often relate to damage to the injured party's economic interest, such as the loss of profit, but it may also include personal injury or damage to property. In addition, in limited cases it will be possible to recover damages for mental distress occa-sioned by the breach and, more broadly, there has been some recognition that damages must be available to cover the 'consumer surplus', the non-financial benefit which the injured party was to derive from the contract. Such claims will be looked at in the final section of this chapter. Here we should consider the basic principle, without addressing those complications.

20.4   The basic principle behind an award of contractual damages is that the injured party should be put in the position he or she would have been in had the contract been performed. This was stated by Parke B in *Robinson* v *Harman* (1848) 1 Ex 850. He said (at 855):

> 'The rule of the common law is that where a party sustains a loss by reason of a breach of contract he is, so far as money can do it, to be placed in the same situation with respect to damages as if the contract had been performed.'

This basic principle means that contractual damages cover the injured party's expectation loss—the loss of what he or she would have received had the contract been performed.[2] This means that damages cover the profit which the injured party would have derived from the contractual performance. This can be simply explained by an example: X contracted with Y for the purchase of some goods from Y for £500 and, when the time came for delivery, Y refused to deliver. By that time the market price of the goods had risen to £600. X can claim £100, the profit he or she would have made on the contract. Had Y performed, X would have had goods worth £600 by the time of delivery (and it will cost him or her £100 more than the contract price to buy substitute goods in the market). £100 will put X in the position he or she would have been in had Y performed.[3] In appropriate circumstances, however, instead of expectation loss the injured party may claim for his or her reliance loss (see para. **20.09ff**).

20.5   Nominal damages are awarded where there is no loss. Such a situation should be distin-guished from the case where the loss is difficult to quantify, for example where the injured party has been deprived of an opportunity of participating in the final round of a beauty competition (*Chaplin* v *Hicks* (1911)). Under such circumstances, the court will not leave the injured party with nominal damages even though quantification is difficult. However, where the benefit to

---

2   But see Fuller and Perdue, 46 Yale LJ 52.

3   See Sale of Goods Act 1979, s 51.

be derived from the contract, the expectation loss, is uncertain, it may be better for the injured party to claim for wasted expenditure, i.e. reliance loss.[4]

20.6   Although it is simple to state the basic principle on which contractual damages are awarded, in some cases questions arise as to how that should be measured and converted into money terms. Here we shall briefly consider some of the cases in which there is a basic established measure of damages.

20.7   There are, of course, many situations in which an established rule for measuring damages can be followed. In the context of sale of goods, for example, the basic situations are covered by statute. Section 51(3) of the Sale of Goods Act 1979 provides a prima facie basis for calculating damages when the buyer fails to deliver. Section 51(3) states:

> 'Where there is an available market for the goods in question the measure of damages is prima facie to be ascertained by the difference between the contract price and the market or current price of the goods at the time or times when they ought to have been delivered or (if no time was fixed) at the time of refusal to deliver.'

As has been indicated, where there is a market for the goods in question, this will put the buyer in the position he or she would have been in had the contract been performed. His or her damages cover the difference between the contract price and what he or she would have had to pay to buy substitute goods in the market when the seller breached. Of course, he or she might not have bought substitute goods on that day, but the duty to mitigate will normally confine damages to that sum even where he or she delays purchasing and the market price rises further. The duty to mitigate, which is dealt with later, does not allow the injured party to recover damages for a loss which could have been avoided by behaving reasonably after the breach (see para. **20.53**ff). In other words the injured party will normally be assumed to have taken the risk of any change in the market if that party delays purchasing substitute goods.

20.8   There is a similar prima facie rule for the situation in which the seller has delivered defective goods. SGA 1979, s 53(3) states that the prima facie loss is the 'difference between the value of the goods at the time of delivery to the buyer and the value they would have had if they had' not been defective. This may provide an appropriate answer whether the goods are wanted for use or for resale.

Reliance loss

20.9   Although the basic principle on which contractual damages are awarded is that of putting an injured party in the position they would have been in had the contract been performed, and obviously that provides for recovery of the expectation interest, there are nevertheless cases in which an injured party may not attempt to claim the 'profit' they should have derived

---

4   See para. **20.9**ff. See also *McRae v Commonwealth Disposals Commission* (1951); *Commonwealth of Australia v Amann Aviation Pty Ltd* (1991).

from the contract, but merely the expenses they incurred in reliance upon the contract. This is referred to as 'reliance loss', and a claim for reliance loss may well occur because an injured party finds it difficult to establish what profit, if any, they would have made on the contract. That was the situation in *Anglia Television Ltd v Reed* [1971] 3 All ER 690 when Robert Reed broke his contract with Anglia to be the leading man in a film to be made for television entitled *The Man in the Wood*. His breach meant that the film could not be made. Anglia sued for damages, but did not claim for lost profit as they could 'not say what their profit on this contract would have been if Mr Reed had come here and performed it'. Anglia sued for their wasted expenditure and recovered it. Lord Denning MR said (at 692):

> '[A claimant] in such a case as this has an election: he can either claim for his loss of profits; or for his wasted expenditure. But he must elect between them. He cannot claim both. If he has not suffered any loss of profits—or if he cannot prove what his loss of profits would have been—he can claim in the alternative the expenditure which has been thrown away, that is, wasted, by reason of the breach.'

Two points in that dictum deserve comment. First, we must look at the question of whether the injured party can always claim his or her reliance loss rather than his or her expectation loss. Second, some consideration needs to be given to whether there is a bar upon claiming both expectation and reliance loss.

20.10   The first point to consider is whether an injured party can always claim their reliance loss. The question becomes important if the contract is one on which the injured party would have made a loss, i.e. their expectation loss is less than their reliance loss, because they made a bad bargain. The answer is that an injured party is free to make whichever claim they choose, but they will not recover a greater sum in a reliance claim than they would have done if they had claimed their expectation loss. The basic contractual principle is that of putting the injured party in the position they would have been in had the contract been fulfilled. That is not overridden by the claim being merely for reliance loss. The 'expectation loss principle underpins the award of damages in wasted expenditure cases'.[5] This can be made more intelligible by consideration of two cases, *C and P Haulage v Middleton* (1983) and *CCC Films (London) Ltd v Impact Quadrant Films Ltd* (1984).

20.11   In *C and P Haulage v Middleton* (1983):

> Mr Middleton was a self-employed engineer. C & P granted him a six-monthly renewable licence to occupy certain premises. He spent money making the premises suitable for his work—a wall had to be built, a telephone moved and electricity laid on. It was an express term of the licence that fixtures put in by Mr Middleton were not to be removed at the expiry of the licence. Ten weeks before the end of a six-month term, he was wrongfully ejected from the premises by C & P. As a temporary measure, he worked from home until well after the six-month period would have expired.

---

5   *Omak Maritime Ltd v Mamola Challenger Shipping Co* (2010) at [47].

Mr Middleton claimed the cost of the improvements he had made to the premises. The court held that C & P had been in breach of contract, in ejecting him from the premises before the expiry of the six-month term, but he had not suffered any loss and was entitled only to nominal damages. He had not had to pay for other premises, as he had used his home, and he had not had to shut down his business and lose profits thereby. He would have lost the money spent on improving the premises even if C & P had waited until the end of the six months to eject him, and he could not succeed in a claim for that expenditure. The court was being asked to put Mr Middleton back in the position he would have been in had he not made the contract. The Court of Appeal refused to do that. Contract damages are to put the injured party in the position he or she would have been in had the contract been performed. Mr Middleton would have lost the money he had spent if the licence had simply not been renewed at the end of the contract period, with no breach by C & P. Basically Mr Middleton had made a bad bargain, and contract damages are not to compensate for that.

20.12   The line taken by the Court of Appeal in *C and P Haulage* v *Middleton* (1983) was followed by Hutchinson J in *CCC Films (London) Ltd* v *Impact Quadrant Films Ltd* [1984] 3 All ER 298, but in the latter case it was not obvious that what the court had to deal with was a bad bargain, and the judge had to consider the question of the burden of proof. In *CCC Films*:

> IQ owned the rights to certain films. IQ granted CCC a licence to exploit, distribute, and exhibit three films (*Dead of Night, Children Shouldn't Play with Dead Things* and *Blue Blood*). CCC paid IQ $12,000 for the licence. IQ delivered the films but they then undertook their safe delivery to Munich, to a potential purchaser who might help CCC exploit their licence. In breach of contract, IQ failed to ensure the safe delivery of the films to Munich. CCC could not establish any lost profits from the breach but claimed the $12,000 from IQ as wasted expenditure. Neither party produced evidence of whether it would, or would not, have been possible for CCC to recoup that expenditure had the contract been performed.

Hutchinson J held that an injured party had an unfettered choice whether to claim for reliance or expectation loss. If they claimed for reliance loss, then it was for the party in breach to establish that the injured party's expenditure would not have been recouped had the contract been performed, i.e. it was for the party in breach to establish that the injured party had made a bad bargain.[6] In coming to this conclusion Hutchinson J quoted from, and adopted, the reasoning of Learned Hand CJ in *L Albert & Son* v *Armstrong Rubber Co.* 178 F 2d 189 (1949). Hutchinson J quoted (at 311):

> 'In cases where the venture would have proved profitable to the promisee there is no reason why he should not recover his expenses. On the other hand, on those occasions in which the performance would not have covered the promisee's outlay, such a result imposes the risk of the promisee's contract upon the promisor. We cannot agree that the promisor's default in performance should under this guise make him an insurer of the promisee's venture; yet it does not follow that the breach should not throw upon him the duty of showing that the value

---

6   See also *Omak Maritime Ltd v Mamola Challenger Shipping Co* (2010).

> of the performance would in fact have been less than the promisee's outlay. It is often very hard to learn what the value of the performance would have been; and it is a common expedient, and a just one, in such situations to put the peril of the answer upon the party who by his wrong has made the issue relevant to the rights of the other. On principle, therefore, the proper solution would seem to be that the promisee may recover this outlay in preparation for the performance, subject to the privilege of the promisor to reduce it by as much as he can show that the promisee would have lost, if the contract had been performed.'

In the instant case CCC recovered. IQ could not establish that CCC would not have recouped the sum claimed had the contract been performed.[7]

20.13   The second point which should be considered is whether both expectation and reliance loss can be claimed. In order to consider that question, certain terminological problems need to be noted and avoided. In the earlier discussion the term 'profit' has been used to encompass the entire sum which the injured party would have derived from the contractual performance, i.e. the gross profit. When used in this loose way, as it was for example in *Anglia Television Ltd* v *Reed* (1971), the terminology can lead to confusion. The term could be made more explicit by referring to the 'gross' profit because it encompasses two elements: the net profit after deduction of expenses, and the expenses. Once this terminological problem is recognized it helps to explain what should be meant when it is stated that it is not possible to recover for both lost profits and wasted expenditure.[8] It certainly should not be possible to recover twice for the same loss, and this must be the true limitation. If the claim for profits was, as it normally would be, a claim for the gross profits, then clearly the injured party could not recover both gross profit and expenses. If the injured party could do that, he or she would be recovering the expenses twice because, in addition to being recovered separately, the expenses would also be encompassed within the sum awarded for the lost gross profit. However, that should not prevent the success of claims to both net profit and expenses. If the injured party limited the claim for lost profits to net profit, then he or she should additionally be able to claim expenses. Together they would make up only the gross profit and the full extent of his loss. There would be no double recovery. Statements as to the mutual exclusion of claims for expectation and reliance loss must be viewed with caution against the background of the terminological difficulties. The basic prohibition must simply be against allowing the injured party to recover the same loss twice (see J. Macleod, 'Damages, Reliance and Expectancy Interest' [1970] JBL 19).

Pre-contract expenditure

20.14   On a slightly different point it is necessary to give some further consideration to the damages awarded in *Anglia Television Ltd* v *Reed* (1971). In that case the main part of the expenditure wasted had been incurred before the contract with Reed was concluded. Before

---

7   See also *Commonwealth of Australia* v *Amann Aviation Pty Ltd* (1991).

8   See Lord Denning MR (para. **20.9**) in *Anglia Television Ltd* v *Reed* and *Cullinane* v *British 'Rema' Manufacturing Co. Ltd* (1954).

contracting with Reed, Anglia Television had arranged a place to film and had employed a director, a designer, and a stage manager. Under the contract Reed was to be available to Anglia between 9 September and 11 October. However, Reed's agent had double-booked him, and on 3 September Anglia were informed that he would not be making their film. Anglia tried hard but could not find a substitute and they abandoned the proposed film. However, when Anglia sued, Reed argued that he was liable for only part of the expenditure that they were trying to recover. He claimed he was liable only for the £854.65 spent after he contracted with Anglia. The Court of Appeal awarded Anglia the whole £2,750 they were claiming, despite the fact that most of it was incurred before Reed contracted. Obviously the pre-contract expenditure had not been incurred in reliance on the contract, but it had been wasted because of such reliance and the court thought that it was simply a matter of whether or not the loss was too remote, and it held that it was not (on remoteness, see para. **20.28**ff). Obviously, recovery of pre-contract expenditure should similarly be limited by the question of what the injured party would have recouped had the contract been performed.

Restitution

20.15   Restitution is generally concerned with the unjust enrichment of one party at another's expense, and we should give some consideration, here, to pursuing D's profits from his or her breach of the contract he or she had with C. As has been indicated, the line generally taken has been that damages for breach of contract are compensatory, and if C has suffered no loss as a result of a breach of contract, the award of damages will be purely nominal, and D's profit from his or her breach is irrelevant. Indeed, it is argued that D should breach where it is economically efficient for him or her to do so, and that it is economically efficient when D can make a greater profit through breaching than performing, even after compensating C for any loss due to the breach (see para. **20.65**). If C's damages relate not merely to C's losses but also to D's profits, then the possibility of economically efficient breach is removed or impaired (depending on whether all the profits are awarded) (see D. Campbell and D. Harris, 'In Defence of Breach: A Critique of Restitution and the Performance Interest' (2002) 22 LS 208).

20.16   However, building generally on cases such as those in which a property right has been infringed, and a sum awarded relating to D's gain, rather than C's loss, and those cases in which an account of profits has been ordered from a fiduciary (for example, *Boardman* v *Phipps* (1967)), or on the disclosure of confidential information (for example, *A-G* v *Guardian Newspapers (No 2)* (1990)), in *A-G* v *Blake* (2000) the House of Lords recognized that, in exceptional cases, C may be awarded the profits of D's breach of contract.

20.17   In *A-G* v *Blake* (2000) the more specific foundation of recovery based on a breach of contract and D's profits from the breach was *Wrotham Park Estate Co.* v *Parkside Homes Ltd* (1974). That case was seen as 'a solitary beacon, showing that in contract, as well as tort, damages are not always narrowly confined to recoupment of financial loss' but that in a suitable case, recovery for breach of contract 'may be measured by the benefit gained by the wrongdoer from the breach' (*Blake* at 396). In *Wrotham Park Estate Co.*:

> In 1971 land was sold to D with a covenant restricting building on that land in favour of C's land. Without knowledge of the covenant and in breach of it, D began building on the land. In early 1972, C issued a writ claiming an injunction to prevent further building in breach of the covenant and to order the demolition of such building as had occurred. The action came for trial in 1973, by which time fourteen homes had been built.

Unsurprisingly, Brightman J refused to order the wasteful destruction of fourteen houses. However, despite the lack of any loss to C through the breach, he granted damages in lieu of an injunction under the Chancery Amendment Act 1858 (Lord Cairns's Act). It was held that D should pay C the hypothetical sum which C might have obtained through bargaining for the release of the covenant, although it was clear that C would not have entered into such a bargain (the 'hypothetical release' approach). The sum to be awarded was arrived at as a proportion of the profit which D obtained from the breach.

20.18   However, in *A-G v Blake* (2000) the House of Lords was asked to go further and, in effect, give C an account of profits to cover all of D's gain. In *Blake*:

> Blake had been employed as a member of the Secret Intelligence Service from 1944 to 1961, at which point it was discovered that he had been betraying secrets to the Soviet Union since 1951. He was convicted and sentenced to forty-two years' imprisonment, but he escaped to Moscow in 1966. In 1989 he wrote his autobiography and it was published in 1990. The action arose out of the amount he was to be paid by the publishers in this country.

By the time Blake wrote his autobiography, the information contained in it had ceased to be confidential, and recovery of his profits was not available on the basis of breach of confidentiality. However, when he joined the Secret Intelligence Service, Blake had signed a contractually binding undertaking that he would not disclose official information in the press or in book form. He had, therefore, breached a contract in making some of the disclosures in the book. On that basis, the House of Lords (Lord Hobhouse dissenting) held that the Attorney-General was entitled to succeed in recovering the profits of Blake's autobiography. It was made clear that such an award would only be made in exceptional cases. Lord Steyn emphasized the close relationship of the case to those in which there is disclosure of confidential information. In addition, Blake's position could be seen as analogous to that of a fiduciary. Lord Nicholls, with whom Lord Goff and Lord Browne-Wilkinson agreed, saw no reason why, in practice, 'the availability of the account of profits need disturb settled expectations in the commercial or consumer world'. He emphasized that 'normally the remedies of damages, specific performance and injunction, coupled with the characterisation of some contractual obligations as fiduciary, will provide an adequate response to breach of contract'. He made it clear that it would only be in exceptional cases, where those remedies are not adequate, that 'any question of an account of profits will arise'. He identified three factors none of which, by itself, he regarded as a good reason for ordering an account of profits. Those factors were:

> 'the fact that the breach was cynical and deliberate; the fact that the breach enabled the defendant to enter into a more profitable contract elsewhere; and the fact that by entering into a new and more profitable contract the defendant put it out of his power to perform his contract with [C]'.

The exclusion of such factors as sufficient to allow for an account of profits is in keeping with the idea that 'efficient breach' is desirable (see para. **20.65**), i.e. the idea that if D can breach, compensate C for C's loss, and still make a greater profit elsewhere, then D should do so. However, Lord Nicholls did give some indication of what might make a case sufficiently exceptional. He said (at 398):

> 'No fixed rules can be prescribed. The court will have regard to all the circumstances, including the subject matter of the contract, the purpose of the contractual provision which has been breached, the circumstances in which the breach occurred, the consequences of the breach and the circumstances in which relief is being sought. A useful general guide, although not exhaustive, is whether the [claimant] had a legitimate interest in preventing the defendant's profit-making activity and, hence, in depriving him of his profit.'

In the particular case, Lord Nicholls took the view that the 'Crown had and has a legitimate interest in preventing Blake profiting from the disclosure of official information, whether classified or not, while a member of the service and thereafter' (at 399). He emphasized that members of the security services should not have any incentive to reveal information. He viewed it as of 'paramount importance that members of the service should have complete confidence in all their dealings with each other, and that those recruited as informers should have the like confidence' (at 399). On that basis an 'absolute rule against disclosure, visible to all, [made] good sense' (at 400).

20.19   It can be seen that the facts of *A-G* v *Blake* (2000) were very unusual and the line could have been taken that the factors making it exceptional enough to justify an account of profits were so exceptional that such a restitutionary approach to breach would seldom occur. Certainly, as has been indicated, Lord Nicholls saw no reason why, in practice, 'the availability of the account of profits need disturb settled expectations in the commercial or consumer world'. However, in his dissenting judgment, Lord Hobhouse took the view that if there were attempts to extend the award of non-compensatory damages for breach further into commercial law, 'the consequences [would] be very far reaching and disruptive'. The approach taken since *Blake* must now be considered.

20.20   In *AB Corpn* v *CD Co., The Sine Nomine* (2002) (an award of arbitrators amongst whom was Sir Christopher Staughton) there was a refusal to apply the approach taken in *A-G* v *Blake* (2000). The line was taken that the case was concerned with a marketable commodity—the services of a ship. The wrongful withdrawal of the ship would be dealt with by ordinary compensatory contract damages. The injured party could get a replacement from the market and damages based on that course would then be sufficient. The view was expressed that 'The commercial law of this country should not make moral judgments, or seek to punish contract breakers'. However, *Blake* and, in particular, the 'hypothetical release' approach taken in *Wrotham Park Estate Co.* v *Parkside Homes Ltd* (1974) has been followed. They should, however, only be turned to when the other contractual remedies are inadequate.[9]

20.21 In *Esso Petroleum Co. Ltd* v *Niad Ltd* (2001) the court was concerned with a contract under which a garage was supplied with petrol by Esso. Esso sought to operate a 'pricewatch' scheme under which it would regulate pump prices so as to be competitive in each particular area. It reduced its prices to garages where that was required to maintain that competitive pricing. Niad paid the reduced prices to Esso but failed to maintain the required prices, charging its customers more. Sir Andrew Morritt V-C was prepared to give Esso an account of profits. First, he did not view damages as an adequate remedy as they could not realistically be assessed. It was 'almost impossible' to attribute lost sales to particular breaches by a particular garage. Second, the breaches gave 'the lie to the advertising campaign' publicizing the pricewatch scheme and undermined its effectiveness to achieve benefits for Esso and other garages. Finally, he concluded that Esso 'undoubtedly had an interest in preventing Niad from profiting from its breach of obligation'.

20.22 In *Experience Hendrix LLC* v *PPX Enterprises Inc* (2003) following a dispute, there had been an agreement that D would not license certain recordings in which Jimi Hendrix merely featured as sideman to another artiste. That agreement was breached. C, the Hendrix estate, sought an injunction to prevent future breaches and an account of profits in relation to the money D had already made out of wrongfully exploiting those recordings. Evidence was given on behalf of C that 'the way those recordings had been brought onto the market had confused and alienated potential buyers' of Jimi Hendrix's own work with the Experience Hendrix band. Evidence was given (at [14]) that:

> 'Such buyers may mistakenly purchase sideman recordings, instead of Experience Hendrix featured recordings, and then become disappointed and frustrated, avoiding further purchases of Jimi Hendrix music. The space available for Jimi Hendrix albums in retail record stores is generally limited, and the presence of numerous sideman recordings poses the risk of displacing featured recordings. Thus the sideman recordings both divert and discourage potential purchasers of featured recordings.'

An injunction was granted to prevent future exploitation of the relevant recordings, the question was as to an account of profits in relation to the profits made prior to the injunction. The court recognized that *A-G* v *Blake* (2000) had stated that the account of profits for a breach of

---

9 *Devenish Nutrition Ltd V Sanofi-Aventis SA* (2008) at [58].

contract should only be available in exceptional circumstances (at [24]) and 'obvious distinctions' were drawn between the instant case and *Blake*. Mance LJ said (at [37]):

> 'First we are not concerned with a subject anything like as special or sensitive as national security. The state's special interest in preventing a spy benefiting by breaches of his contractual duty of secrecy and so removing at least part of the financial attraction of such breaches has no parallel in this case. Second the notoriety which accounted for the magnitude of Blake's royalty-earning capacity derived from his prior breaches of secrecy and that too has no present parallel. Third there is no direct analogy between PPX's position and that of a fiduciary [as had been made in *Blake*].'

20.23   However, although the instant case was not as exceptional as *Blake,* that was not seen as preventing the court from providing any money remedy based on D's profits. Rather, although an account of profits was regarded as inappropriate, the view was taken that there could be an award based on D's profits of the 'hypothetical release' type, as in *Wrotham Park Estate Co.* v *Parkside Homes Ltd* (1974). Peter Gibson LJ saw the case as suitable for such an award as:

> '(1) there has been a deliberate breach by PPX of its contractual obligations for its own reward, (2) the claimant would have difficulty establishing contractual loss therefrom, and (3) the claimant has a legitimate interest in preventing PPX's profit making activity carried out in breach of PPX's contractual obligations.'

Plainly, the legitimate interest envisaged here is of a different order from that in *A-G* v *Blake* (2000) and, despite *Esso Petroleum v Niad*, the distinction drawn between *Hendrix* and *Blake* would indicate that an account of profits, rather than 'hypothetical release' damages will very seldom be available. It is more likely that the 'hypothetical release' approach will be taken, rather than an account of profits being ordered,[10] but it should not be forgotten that both are exceptional. Certainly, it should not be enough that C's ordinary contractual damages for breach would be nominal.[11]

20.24   A major outstanding question is the basis of these awards. Are they truly restitutionary or is it that we have not yet been able to satisfactorily identify the loss, and the awards are compensatory? Is the basis of the award in *Blake* different to those situations in which part of the profits are recovered?[12]

Timing

20.25   The final point to be made in this section, is the time-frame against which damages are assessed. Damages are usually assessed in accordance with the circumstances existing at the time of the breach. This is normally in keeping with the basic principle that the injured party

---

10 *Vercoe v Rutland Fund Management Ltd* (2010) at [341].

11 D. Campbell and P. Wylie, 'Aint no telling which circumstances are exceptional' (2003) 63 CLJ 605.

12 J. Edelman, *Gain Based Damages: Contract, Tort, Equity and Intellectual Property*, Hart Publishing, 2002.

should be put in the position he or she would have been in had the contract been performed. However, that will not always be the case, and it has been said that assessment at the time of the breach 'is not an absolute rule; if to follow it would give rise to injustice, the court has power to fix such other date as may be appropriate in the circumstances' (*Johnson v Agnew* [1979] 1 All ER 883 at 896). The determination of the appropriateness of some other date will often depend upon the rule as to mitigation of damages. The duty to mitigate means that the injured party will not be compensated for any loss which he or she could have avoided by taking reasonable steps after the breach. If the mitigation rule does not indicate that he or she should have acted to limit his or her loss immediately upon the breach occurring, then the time for the calculation of damages may similarly be delayed. In *Suleman v Shahsavari* [1989] 2 All ER 460 the duty to mitigate indicated that damages were not to be calculated in accordance with the circumstances at the time of the breach but at the time of judgment. In that case:

> Mr Suleman thought that he had contracted to buy a house. Unfortunately for him it was eventually decided that the solicitor of the vendor had not had authority to sign the contract of sale on the vendor's behalf. When there was no completion of the supposed contract of sale, Mr Suleman initially sought specific performance against the vendor. Specific performance was eventually denied and it was determined that the solicitor's lack of authority meant that there was no contract of sale. On that basis, Mr Suleman claimed damages from the vendor's solicitor for breach of warranty of his authority.

Mr Suleman succeeded in his action against the solicitor. The court had to determine the damages to be paid. The difference between the market price of the house and the 'contract' price on the supposed date of completion of the sale was £9,500. The difference with reference to the date of judgment was £29,500. Mr Suleman was awarded £29,500 on the basis that it had been reasonable for him to delay seeking such damages while trying to claim specific performance against the vendors. His actions were not contrary to the duty to mitigate. Andrew Park QC (sitting as a deputy judge of the High Court) said (at 463):

> '[Mr Suleman] has conducted himself entirely reasonably in seeking to obtain specific performance...He has been in no way dilatory over his claim and cannot be accused of having unreasonably failed to mitigate his damage.'

20.26   More recently the House of Lords departed from calculating damages according to the circumstances at the time of the breach in *Golden Strait Corpn v Nippon Yusen Kubishika Kaisha* (2007). They opted instead for an approach in keeping with both basic principle and the duty to mitigate. In that case:

> In 1998 the parties entered into a seven-year charter-party. In December 2001 the charterers repudiated the contract and the owners accepted the repudiation. In March 2003 the second Gulf War broke out and the war clause in the charter-party would have given the charterers the right to cancel. The question arose as to whether the owners' damages for the charterers' repudiatory breach in 2001 should encompass the entirety of the time then remaining under

the charter-party or whether they should be limited by the outbreak of the Gulf War when the charterers would have had a right to cancel.

As has been indicated, damages are usually awarded by reference to the circumstances at the time of the breach, in this case the time of the repudiation. This is seen to create certainty for both parties. However, it is also usually in keeping with the basic principle on which damages are awarded (placing the injured party in the position he or she would have been in had the contract been performed) and the injured party's duty to mitigate. However, *The Golden Strait* was not a case where awarding damages based on the time of the breach would comply with basic principle. At the time of the breach there was the prospect of the contract continuing for the rest of its whole seven-year duration. By the time the case came to court, it was clear it would have been lawfully cancelled in 2003. Awarding damages based on the full duration of the contract would have put the injured party in a better position than if the contract had been performed. It would seem that the damages will not be calculated according to the circumstances at the date of the breach when there is a temporal element in the injured party's loss (i.e. where it is a loss over time, or a loss which only accrues after the breach) and the temporal element would not be nullified by acting in accordance with the duty to mitigate, i.e. procuring a substitute contract at the time of the breach. In this case any substitute contract would have contained the same cancellation right and also not run for the remainder of the full contract duration (see Lord Brown at [82]).

Restrictions on recovery

20.27   We have seen the basic principle on which damages are awarded: putting the injured party in the position he or she would have been in had the contract been performed. This provides for the recovery of expectation loss. Sometimes the injured party may instead choose to claim reliance loss, but such a claim will still be subject to the basic principle, and the injured party cannot be better off than if the contract had been performed. (Reliance loss cannot be claimed as a means of escaping the effects of a bad bargain.) However, what we must now consider is that there are further rules which mean that the injured party will not always recover the full amount needed to put him or her in the position he or she would have been in had the contract been performed. We need to consider such rules as those about remoteness and mitigation of damages.

Remoteness of damage

20.28   There is a need for some restriction upon the liability of the party in breach for losses which he or she has caused. A breach may lead to extremely unlikely loss or damage. Some limitation must be put upon the damage for which the party in breach can be liable. The rule as to remoteness of damage serves this purpose. It prevents recovery for a loss which is too remote. However, the issue of the basis of this restriction, and of its extent, has come to the fore recently. In *Transfield Shipping Inc v Mercator Shipping Inc, The Achilleas* (2008), Lord Hoffmann said (at [9]):

> 'The case therefore raises a fundamental point of principle in the law of contractual damages: is the rule that a party may recover losses which were foreseeable ("not unlikely") an

external rule of law, imposed upon the parties to every contract in default of express provision to the contrary, or is it a prima facie assumption about what the parties may be taken to have intended, no doubt applicable in the great majority of cases but capable of rebuttal in cases in which the context, surrounding circumstances or general understanding in the relevant market shows that a party would not reasonably have been regarded as assuming responsibility for such losses?'

The question has become whether the traditional remoteness rule is used, or whether we have to look for an 'assumption of responsibility'. Traditionally, the approach has been taken that remoteness has simply been a matter of what, at the time of contracting, the parties could reasonably contemplate as liable to result from the breach. However, in *The Achilleas* the House of Lords may have introduced the assumption of responsibility approach, with the 'reasonable contemplation' approach being departed from where the defendants could not reasonably be regarded as having assumed responsibility for some, or all, of those reasonably contemplatable losses, or where they could reasonably be regarded as having assumed more.[13] This will be returned to later after the traditional approach has been considered. However, it would seem that most cases will continue to be determined by the traditional rules—in most cases they will embody the parties' presumed intentions.[14]

20.29   The basic rule embodied in the traditional approach to remoteness stems from the case of *Hadley* v *Baxendale* (1854) 9 Exch 341. In that case, the facts were as follows:

The claimants were millers. They owned and occupied the City Steam Mills, Gloucester. The crankshaft of their steam engine was broken so that the mill could not function. They arranged with the defendant carriers for the shaft to be taken to W Joyce & Co. of Greenwich, who had agreed to make a new shaft, using the old one as a model. The defendant carriers broke their contract by delaying delivery. The new shaft was not received for several days after it should have been. The claimants lost profits because of the delay in the return to work of the mill. The defendants argued that such loss of profits was too remote for them to be liable.

Alderson B set out the test for remoteness. He said (at 355):

'Where two parties have made a contract which one of them has broken the damages which the other party ought to receive in respect of such a breach of contract should be such as may fairly and reasonably be considered as either arising naturally, i.e. according to the usual course of things, from such breach of the contract itself, or such as may reasonably be supposed to have been in the contemplation of both parties at the time they made the contract as the probable result of the breach of it.'

---

13   The test is 'inclusionary' as well as 'exclusionary'—*Supershield Ltd v Siemens Buillding Technologies FE Ltd* (2010) at [43].

14   See *The Achilleas* at [11]; *John Grimes Partnership v Gubbins* (2013); *Sylvia Shipping Co Ltd v Progress Bulk Carriers Ltd (The Sylvia)* (2010).

This is commonly known as the rule in *Hadley* v *Baxendale* and it can be broken down into two parts. The party in breach will be liable for losses either:

1. arising naturally, i.e. according to the usual course of things; or
2. such as may reasonably be supposed to have been in the contemplation of the parties, at the time they made the contract, as a probable result of the breach.

20.30 In effect, although the remoteness rule is often stated in this dual form, both parts relate to what the parties could reasonably contemplate as liable to result from the breach (see *Heron II* (1969) at para. **20.34**). The only difference between the two parts of the rule is the degree of knowledge attributable to the party in breach, as a reasonable person, at the time of contracting. The first part of the rule deals with what any reasonable person should contemplate, because that is what would 'usually' occur. The second part of the rule deals with the more extensive reasonable contemplation which should be produced by knowledge of special circumstances extending the complainant's loss beyond the 'usual'. In effect, the question almost inevitably is 'what could have been contemplated by the party in breach, as a reasonable person?' (The injured party should know of the special circumstances which may add to his or her losses on a breach occurring.) In *Hadley* v *Baxendale*, the prolonged closure of the mill, and the loss of profits thereby, was not viewed as a 'natural' result of the breach. It was thought that the millers might have had a spare crankshaft. In addition, such loss could not be brought within the second part of the rule. All that had been made known to the carriers at the time of contracting was that they were transporting a broken crankshaft for millers. They were given no special knowledge of the situation to bring the loss within their reasonable contemplation as liable to result of the breach. It was not made known that the millers did not possess a spare shaft.

20.31 It should be emphasized that the point in time at which the loss must be within the reasonable contemplation of the parties is when the contract was made (*Jackson* v *Royal Bank of Scotland* (2005)).

20.32 Viewing the two parts of the rule as simply making up one rule was fully explained by Asquith LJ in *Victoria Laundry (Windsor) Ltd* v *Newman Industries Ltd* (1949). In addition, the case well illustrates the difference between the 'usual' type of loss, and that for which additional knowledge, at the time of contracting, is required. In that case:

> Victoria Laundry wished to expand their business, and they ordered a larger boiler from Newman Industries. Delivery was to take place on 5 June. The boiler was damaged before delivery, and delivery was delayed until 8 November. Newman were aware of the nature of Victoria Laundry's business and had been informed that Victoria Laundry intended to put the boiler into use in the shortest possible time.

Victoria Laundry claimed for the profit they would have earned with the boiler in the time between 5 June and 8 November. In particular, Victoria Laundry claimed for the loss of, first, the extra laundry business they could have taken on, there being a shortage of laundries at the time, and, second, the loss of a number of highly lucrative dyeing contracts which they could and would have accepted from the Ministry of Supply. The Court of Appeal allowed recovery for the former but not the latter, although the court envisaged recovery of a sum to cover the loss of 'ordinary' dyeing business.

20.33 Newman knew before contracting that Victoria Laundry was in the business of laundering and dyeing, and that the boiler was wanted for immediate use in that business. They were supplying a boiler in accordance with strict technical specifications, and could be taken to know more about the use or purposes to which boilers were put than the uninformed layman. They did not know whether the boiler was to replace a unit of equal or inferior capacity. The court thought that reasonable persons in their shoes must be taken to foresee that a laundry which wanted a boiler for immediate use, at a time when there was a shortage of laundry facilities, would be liable to suffer a loss if delivery was delayed for five months. That was the case whether they wanted the boiler to extend their business, maintain it, or to reduce a loss. In other words, Victoria Laundry could recover for the ordinary extra laundry business they would have taken on. They could not recover for the loss of the special dyeing contracts. In the absence of additional information, the reasonable person, in Newman's position, could not foresee that loss as liable to result from the breach. No notice had been given of the possible, highly lucrative, dyeing contracts and their loss was too remote.

20.34 It was indicated earlier that the two parts of the rule in *Hadley* could be reformulated as a single rule, capable of encompassing the different levels of knowledge to be attributed, in different circumstances, to the parties. In delivering the judgment of the Court of Appeal in *Victoria Laundry (Windsor) Ltd* v *Newman Industries Ltd* (1949), Asquith LJ reformulated the rule in *Hadley* in this way. He restated it as entitling the injured party to recover such part of his loss 'as was at the time of the contract reasonably foreseeable as liable to result from the breach', and this is reflected in the earlier discussion of the case. However, in *Heron II (Koufos* v *Czarnikow Ltd)* [1969] 1 AC 350 the House of Lords criticized the *Victoria Laundry* formulation. It was seen as not sufficiently indicating the degree of probability with which the loss must be foreseen. In particular, their Lordships felt that the test of remoteness in contract must be kept distinct from the lesser requirement in tort. They thought that the tort test encompassed any type of damage which was reasonably foreseeable, even though it might happen only 'in the most unusual case'. The contract test required a loss to be reasonably foreseen with a much greater degree of probability. Lord Reid (at 386) thought that there was a good reason for the difference:

> 'In contract, if one party wishes to protect himself against a risk which to the other party would appear unusual, he can direct the other party's attention to it before the contract is made.'

(See also Lord Pearce at 413, and Lord Upjohn at 423.) In contrast, in tort the parties could well be strangers.

20.35 To distinguish the two tests, their Lordships favoured referring to 'reasonable contemplation' in contract, rather than 'reasonable foreseeability'. In addition, there was much discussion of how the degree of probability necessary in contract should be expressed. It was seen as something less than an even chance, but greater than what is required in tort. Various phrases were thought to encompass the requisite degree of probability—'not unlikely', 'substantial probability', 'likely', 'liable to result', 'serious possibility', 'real danger'. The extensive search for a way to express the requisite degree of probability is not very helpful. The main point to note is that the House of Lords wished to keep the contract and tort tests distinct, and required a higher degree of probability in contract than in tort.

20.36 In *Heron II (Koufos v Czarnikow Ltd)* (1969), the facts were as follows:

> A vessel was chartered to take a cargo of sugar from Constanza to Basrah, where there was a sugar market. It was the intention of the charterers to sell the sugar in the market immediately upon arrival there. In breach of contract the vessel arrived nine days late in Basrah. The market price had dropped in the intervening nine days and the charterers claimed the difference in the price from the owners of the ship.

The House of Lords held that the charterer was entitled to recover the difference in price of the sugar because of the nine-day delay. The owner of the vessel had not known that the intention was to sell the sugar on arrival, but he had known that there was a sugar market in Basrah. That being the case, he had to be taken to have realized that it was not unlikely that the sugar would be sold on arrival and he had to be taken to know that, in a market, prices fluctuate up and down from day to day. The charterer's loss was not too remote. It should have been reasonably contemplated as liable to result from the delay.

20.37 The traditional contract test for remoteness can be stated as being whether the loss was such that, at the time of contracting, the parties would have reasonably contemplated it as liable to result from a breach. A number of general points must be emphasized in relation to this test.

20.38 It should be emphasized that the parties need not have considered the possibility of a breach, or its consequences, at all. 'Parties at the time of contracting contemplate not the breach of the contract but its performance'. What matters is the conclusion of reasonable people, in the position of the parties, had they considered the question (*Victoria Laundry (Windsor) Ltd v Newman Industries Ltd* [1949] 2 KB 528). It should also be noted that the usual formulation of the rule refers to the contemplation of the parties and it must be emphasized that what might reasonably be contemplated by the injured party alone, because of his or her more extensive knowledge of any loss he or she might suffer, is irrelevant. The original two-part statement of the rule in *Hadley* emphasizes that point. The remoteness test is really about what could be contemplated by the reasonable person in the position of the party in breach. However, as was made clear in *Victoria Laundry*, although the assessment is based on the reasonable person, what he or she may reasonably contemplate as liable to result may be affected not only by actual knowledge of special circumstances but, more generally, by his or her position and the circumstances of the contract. If the party in breach is a businessperson, then more may be taken to be within his or her reasonable contemplation as likely to result, than if he or she is a consumer. In *Victoria Laundry* it was pointed out that the general knowledge of the business of those it contracts with may be taken to be more extensive in the case of a supplier than a carrier (distinguishing *Victoria Laundry* and *Hadley* v *Baxendale* (1854)). However:

> 'it must always be a question of circumstances what one contracting party is presumed to know about the business activities of the other. No doubt the simpler the activity of the one, the more readily can it be inferred that the other would have reasonable knowledge thereof. However, when the activity of A involves complicated construction or manufacturing techniques, I see no reason why B who supplies a commodity that A intends to use in the course of those techniques should be assumed, merely because of the order for the commodity, to be aware of the details of all the techniques undertaken by A and the effect thereupon of any failure of or deficiency in that commodity' (*Balfour Beatty Construction (Scotland) Ltd* v *Scottish Power plc* 1994 SLT 807 at 810 per Lord Jauncey).

Type/degree of loss

20.39 Some refinement of the basic test must be considered in relation to a distinction between type of loss and degree of loss. The issue was raised by the case of *H Parsons (Livestock) Ltd* v *Uttley Ingham & Co. Ltd* (1978). In that case:

> Mr Parsons was a pig farmer. He ordered, from the defendants, a hopper to store pig nuts. The defendants were manufacturers of bulk food storage hoppers. The defendants knew the purpose for which the hopper was required. The contract described the hopper as 'fitted with a ventilated top'. The ventilator was sealed for transport to the pig farm and when the defendants installed the hopper they forgot to open the ventilator. The hopper was 28 feet high, and it was not possible to see that the ventilator was closed from the ground. Because of the lack of ventilation some of the pig nuts stored in the hopper became mouldy. The farmer continued to feed them to the pigs until the pigs became ill. An outbreak of E Coli ensued, and 254 pigs died.

The question was whether the defendants were liable, in damages, for the death of the pigs. The Court of Appeal held that they were: the losses were not too remote. Scarman LJ, with Orr LJ agreeing, found that the remoteness test from *Heron II* was satisfied. The degree of loss did not have to come within the test, provided the type of loss did, and 'no more than common sense was needed for them to appreciate that food affected by bad storage conditions might well cause illness in the pigs fed on it' and the pigs becoming ill was regarded as only a different degree of loss and not a different type of loss from them dying.

20.40   However, the distinction, between extent of loss and type of loss, is not without difficulty. What constitutes a type of loss? Was the lost profit on the ordinary laundry business really a different type of loss from the lost profit on the highly lucrative dyeing contracts in *Victoria Laundry (Windsor) Ltd v Newman Industries Ltd* (1949)? A distinction has, however, been made. In *Brown v KMR Services Ltd* [1995] 4 All ER 598 the losses of Lloyd's names were unforeseeable in their extent, due to the unanticipated size and frequency of the various disasters that occurred between 1987 and 1990. The agent who had misadvised them could not, however, claim that the losses were too remote. They were of the type which were clearly liable to result. The point to note in this context is the dictum of Stuart Smith LJ (at 621):

> 'I accept that difficulty in practice may arise in categorisation of loss into types or kinds, especially where financial loss is involved. But I do not see any difficulty in holding that loss of ordinary business profits is different in kind from that flowing from a particular contract which gives rise to very high profits, the existence of which is unknown to the contracting party who therefore does not accept the risk of such loss occurring.'

Of course, losses will often stem from 'particular contracts', but the point has also been made that:

> 'loss of profits claimed by reference to an extravagant or unusual bargain are not of the same type as damages referable to bargains that are usual' (*North Sea Energy v PTT* [1997] 2 Lloyd's Rep 418 at 438).

20.41   However, the point should be made that under the 'assumption of responsibility' approach from *The Achilleas* a more easily explicable (if not more easily applicable) approach will be taken to distinguishing different types of loss, because it will depend on the (objective) views of the parties. Lord Hoffmann said (at [22]):

> 'What is the basis for deciding whether loss is of the same type or a different type? It is not a question of Platonist metaphysics. The distinction must rest upon some principle of the law of contract. In my opinion, the only rational basis for the distinction is that it reflects what would have been regarded by the contracting party as significant for the purposes of the risk he was undertaking. In *Victoria Laundry (Windsor) Ltd v Newman Industries Ltd* [1949] 2 KB 528, where the [claimants] claimed for loss of the profits from their laundry business because of late delivery of a boiler, the Court of Appeal did not regard "loss of profits from the laundry business" as a single type of loss. They distinguished (at p 543) losses from "particularly lucrative dyeing contracts" as a different type of loss which would only be recoverable if the defendant had sufficient knowledge of them to make it reasonable to attribute to him acceptance of liability for such losses. The vendor of the boilers would have regarded the profits on these contracts as a different and higher form of risk than the general risk of loss of profits by the laundry.'

Economic justification

20.42   The remoteness test has been perceived as economically efficient (R. Posner, *Economic Analysis of Law*, 2nd edn, Aspen, pp. 94–5). The remoteness rule:

'induces the party with knowledge of the risk either to take any appropriate precautions himself or, if he believes that the other party might be the more efficient loss avoider, to disclose the risk to the other party and pay him to assume it.'[15]

The remoteness rule therefore means that the party supplying goods or a service does not always have to increase his or her prices to protect him or herself against unusual losses by the other party if the supplier breaches. The other party has an incentive to protect him or herself until the situation reaches the point at which it is cheaper for him or her to inform the supplier, and make a contract which is priced to take into account the risk of those losses.

The Achilleas

20.43   As has been indicated, *The Achilleas* may indicate a different basis to remoteness, than has traditionally been seen to be the case, and modification of the approach taken. The issue is whether recoverable losses should be restricted, or extended, to those in relation to which the breaching party, as a reasonable person, can be regarded as having accepted the risk. An example of a problem can quickly make obvious why the question is raised.

'[C] rings up his local taxi driver and books a taxi to drive him to the airport at 7am the next day. He tells the driver that it is most important as he is flying to New York to sign a multi-million dollar contract. The taxi driver oversleeps, [C] misses his flight and loses his deal. Is the taxi driver liable?' (H. Beale, W. Bishop, and M. Furmston, *Contract Cases and Materials*, 2nd edn, Oxford University Press, 1990, p. 478).

It is this type of question which tends to lead to the reaction that the traditional remoteness test is not sufficient: that there must be some different test, or further element, and that was the question considered in *The Achilleas*.

20.44   The facts of *Transfield Shipping Inc* v *Mercator Shipping Inc, The Achilleas* (2008) can be briefly stated.[16]

The case was concerned with a charter of the ship *The Achilleas*. The rate of hire was at the daily rate of $16,750. Under the charter the latest date for redelivery of the ship was 2 May 2004. The charterers gave notice that the ship would be redelivered between 30 April and 2 May 2004. The owners then made a contract for a new four- to six-month hire of the ship to a

---

15 See also D. Harris, D. Campbell, and R. Halson, *Remedies in Contract and Tort*, 2nd edn, Butterworths, 2002, ch. 6.

16 For contrasting views of the case see E. Peel, 'Remoteness revisited' (2009) LQR 6 and A. Kramer, 'The new test of remoteness in contract' (2009) LQR 408.

third party at a daily rate of $39,500. (The market rate had considerably increased since the previous charter had been made.) The latest date by which it could be delivered to the third party was 8 May 2004 and after that they were entitled to cancel. Because of a delay during their final subcharter, the charterers were late redelivering the vessel. By 5 May it was clear that the vessel would not be redelivered in time for the owners to provide it to the third party by 8 May. There was an unusual, 'extremely volatile', market at the time and the market rate had fallen again. The owners renegotiated with the third party for delivery to take place by 11 May, with the daily rate of hire reduced to $31,500 a day.

The issue was the amount of damages the owners should recover for the charterers' breach in late redelivery of the vessel. The general understanding of the shipping market had been that the damages recoverable in such cases was the difference between the charter rate and the market rate for the period of the delay in redelivery and that was what the charterers were arguing was due. However, the owners were claiming the loss of the higher rate of the new charter, with the third party, for the entirety of the new charter (i.e. the difference between a daily rate of $39,500, and a daily rate of $31,500, for the period of the hire to the third party).

20.45   A majority of arbitrators, the judge at first instance, and the Court of Appeal found in favour of the amount contended for by the owners. They found that the loss was not too remote: it was within the parties' reasonable contemplation that late redelivery would cause the loss of a new charter. However, the House of Lords followed the conclusion of the dissenting arbitrator and found in favour of the charterers' contention that they were only liable for the difference in the charter rate and the market rate for the period of the delay in redelivery. The difficulty lies in the diverse reasoning which was used to reach this conclusion.

20.46   Lord Rogers and Baroness Hale took the traditional approach, simply applying the *Hadley* v *Baxendale* rule and finding that the loss of the higher rate of the new charter for its entirety was not a 'type' of loss the parties could have reasonably contemplated as liable to result from the breach, as it was due to an 'extremely volatile' market. Plainly, this takes a narrow, and difficult to explain, approach to what amounts to a 'type of loss'.

20.47   However, as has been indicated, Lord Hoffmann (with Lord Hope basically agreeing) took a very different approach. He took the line that the traditional remoteness rule is merely an expression of what the parties would normally be taken to intend (objectively), and that it will thus be departed from when their objective intentions are shown to be different. According to Lord Hoffmann, what is in issue 'is the interpretation as a whole, construed in its commercial setting' (at [11]). It is a matter of what the parties 'contracting against the background of market expectations . . . would reasonably have considered the extent of the liability they were undertaking' (at [22]). In this case the line was taken that the charterers could not reasonably be regarded as having assumed responsibility for losses on the new contract because of the general understanding of the shipping market of the recoverable damages in these circumstances, and the fact that the charterers could have no knowledge of or control of any such new contract.

20.48   The judgments in the House of Lords leave the law on remoteness in some uncertainty. Lord Walker basically agreed with both approaches.[17] Lord Hoffmann's approach solves the taxi driver problem, referred to at para. **20.43**, without any need to strain the concept of type of loss. It also connects the remoteness test to the creation of the contract in the parties' voluntary undertaking of liability. He said (at [12]):

> 'It seems to me logical to found liability for damages upon the intention of the parties (objectively ascertained) because all contractual liability is voluntarily undertaken. It must be in principle wrong to hold someone liable for risks for which the people entering into such a contract in their particular market, would not reasonably be considered to have undertaken.'

However, the line which should now be taken on remoteness has been a matter of much debate.[18] Lord Hoffmann's approach had the potential for great uncertainty.[19] In giving judgment in *The Achilleas* Baroness Hale expressed considerable unease. She said at [93]:

> 'I am not immediately attracted to the idea of introducing into the law of contract the concept of the scope of duty which has perforce had to be developed in the law of negligence. The rule in *Hadley v Baxendale* asks what the parties must be taken to have had in their contemplation, rather than what they actually had in their contemplation, but the criterion by which this is judged is a factual one. Questions of assumption of risk depend upon a wider range of factors and value judgments. This type of reasoning is, as Lord Steyn put it in *Aneco Reinsurance Underwriting Ltd v Johnson & Higgins Ltd* [2002] 1 Lloyd's Rep 157, para 186, a "deus ex machina". Although its result in this case may be to bring about certainty and clarity in this particular market, such an imposed limit on liability could easily be at the expense of justice in some future case. It could also introduce much room for argument in other contractual contexts. Therefore, if this appeal is to be allowed, as to which I continue to have doubts, I would prefer it to be allowed on the narrower ground identified by Lord Rodger, leaving the wider ground to be fully explored in another case and another context.'

20.49   However, it would seem that we are arriving at a position in which there should not be great uncertainty, but greater flexibility than existed under the traditional approach. In *John Grimes Partnership v Gubbins* (2013) the court had to consider whether a consulting engineering firm was liable for the drop in value of a property development which its breach had caused to be delayed by fifteen months (the actual sum had not been determined, but figures of around

---

17 Although see *Sylvia Shipping Co Ltd v Progress Bulk Carriers Ltd (The Sylvia)* (2010) at [39].

18 e.g. A. Kramer, 'An agreement-centred approach to remoteness and contract damages' in N. Cohen and E. McKendrick (eds), *Comparative Remedies for Breach of Contract*, Hart Publishing, 2004; A. Tettenborn, '*Hadley* v *Baxendale* foreseeability: a principle beyond its sell by date' (2007) 23 JCL 120; A. Robertson, 'The basis of the remoteness rule in contract' (2008) 28 LS 172; A. Kramer, 'Remoteness: new problems with the old test' in R. Cunnington and D. Saidov, *Contract Damages: Domestic and International Perspectives*, Hart Publishing, 2008.

19 *MFM Restaurants Pte Ltd v Fish & Co Restaurants Pte Ltd* (2010).

£400,000 were discussed). At first instance, the judge took the line that the *Achilleas* had not effected a major change. His approach was that the traditional approach should be applied, and was only to be displaced if the commercial background showed that would not reflect the expectation or intention reasonably to be imputed to the parties. He found that there was no such displacement. The Court of Appeal agreed. Sir David Keene stated (at [24]):

> 'It seems to me to be right to bear in mind, as Lord Hoffmann emphasised in *The Achilleas*, that one is dealing with the law of contract, where the situation is governed by what has been agreed between the parties. If there is no express term dealing with what types of losses a party is accepting potential liability for if he breaks the contract, then the law in effect implies a term to determine the answer. Normally, there is an implied term accepting responsibility for the types of losses which can reasonably be foreseen at the time of contract to be not unlikely to result if the contract is broken. But if there is evidence in a particular case that the nature of the contract and the commercial background, or indeed other relevant special circumstances, render that implied assumption of responsibility inappropriate for a type of loss, then the contract-breaker escapes liability. Such was the case in *The Achilleas*.'

In the instant case, there was no evidence 'to show that there was some general understanding or expectation in the property world', to lead to a contrary conclusion to that of the traditional test, as there had been in the commercial context of *Achilleas* (at [26]). Further, the difference between the level of the engineer's fee (£15,000), and that of the loss, did not take the case out of the ordinary situation. The line was taken that, 'such contrast is merely one possible pointer towards a contracting party not having undertaken a potential liability which is reasonably foreseeable and by itself would not normally suffice to establish such an absence of responsibility' (at [30]). It would seem then that the traditional approach to remoteness normally stands, and will only be displaced where the commercial background, or 'other relevant special circumstances' show that the parties did not contract on that basis, rendering inappropriate the usual assumption that they did so.

Causation

20.50   The party in breach will not be liable for the injured party's loss if his or her breach is not regarded as a sufficient cause of it. It has to be an effective cause (*County Ltd v Girozentrale Securities* (1996)). Problems arise from intervening acts and events. In *Monarch Steamship Co. Ltd v A/B Karlshamns Oljefabriker* [1949] AC 196 the defendants contracted to carry goods for the claimants from Manchuria to Sweden. In breach of contract, sailing was delayed. The ship did not reach Sweden before the outbreak of the Second World War. The ship was stopped and the claimants incurred extra expense as a result of the goods continuing the voyage in a neutral ship. The defendants argued that they were not liable for the expense because it was not due to their breach but to the outbreak of war. It was held that the outbreak of war was not an intervening cause which broke the chain of causation. At the time of contracting, it had been foreseeable that delay might result in such problems being encountered. The situation would have been different had the claimants' loss been caused by the ship being struck by a typhoon.

That might happen at any time and the loss would not then have been regarded as caused by the defendants' delay (at 215).

20.51   An intervening act will not break the chain of causation where it is an act which the party in breach is under an obligation to guard against. It is an implied term of the contract between banker and customer that the customer will draw his or her cheques with due care so that he or she does not facilitate fraud. When a customer made out a cheque in such a way that the amount could be readily altered, he was liable to the bank for the full amount paid out on a cheque which had been fraudulently increased by a third party (*London Joint Stock Bank* v *Macmillan* (1918)).

20.52   The injured party may break the chain of causation with his or her own negligence. That was the situation in *Quinn* v *Burch Bros (Builders) Ltd* (1966) where the defendants breached their contract with the claimant plasterer by failing to provide him with a stepladder. The claimant was injured when he tried to use an unsecured trestle instead of a stepladder. Paull J held that his negligence had broken the chain of causation (see also *Lambert* v *Lewis* (1982)).

20.53   The actions of the injured party, and their effect upon his or her claim to damages, are also considered in the context of the duty to mitigate and the problem of contributory negligence (see later).

Mitigation

20.54

> '[Mitigation] imposes on a [claimant] the duty of taking all reasonable steps to mitigate the loss consequent on the breach; and debars him from claiming any part of the damage which is due to his neglect to take such steps' (*British Westinghouse Electric and Manufacturing Co. Ltd* v *Underground Electric Railways Co. of London* [1912] AC 673 at 689 per Lord Haldane).

Mitigation is frequently discussed in terms of a 'duty' to mitigate, as it is in the quotation, but this can be misleading. There is no 'duty' as such, but merely a limitation upon recoverable damages.[20] The question of what steps are reasonable is one of fact (*Payzu Ltd* v *Saunders* [1919] 2 KB 581 at 586). The burden of showing a failure to mitigate is on the party in breach (*James Finlay & Co.* v *NV Kwik Hoo Tong HM* [1928] 2 KB 604 at 614).

20.55   Three aspects to mitigation can be identified. First, if there are reasonable steps which the injured party could take to reduce his or her loss, and if he or she does not take those steps, then the damages awarded to him or her will be limited to what he or she would have lost had he or she acted reasonably. Second, the expenses reasonably incurred in dealing with the breach will be recoverable. Third, if the injured party takes action which in fact reduces his or her loss, then the damages payable will be reduced accordingly.

---

20 *Sotiros Shipping Inc.* v *Sameiet Solholt, The Solholt* [1983] 1 Lloyd's Rep 605 at 608.

Reasonable steps to limit loss

20.56   The 'duty' to mitigate means that the injured party cannot recover damages for any loss which he or she could have avoided by taking reasonable steps. There was no failure to mitigate in *James Finlay & Co.* v *NV Kwik Hoo Tong HM* (1928) where the steps suggested by the party in breach would have damaged the injured party's commercial reputation. In that case, the facts were as follows:

> The claimants contracted to purchase sugar from the defendants. The contract stated that it was to be shipped in September. It was shipped in October but, wrongly, the bill of lading stated that it had been shipped in September. Being unaware of the breach the claimants contracted with sub-buyers for the sale on of the sugar. The contract with the sub-buyers stated that the bill of lading should provide 'conclusive evidence' of the date of shipment. The sub-buyers rejected the goods because of the inaccuracy of the bill of lading.

The claimants sued the defendants. The defendants contended that the claimants were entitled to only nominal damages, as the claimants should have mitigated by enforcing the sub-sale, on the basis of the 'conclusive evidence' clause. It was held that the claimants did not have to mitigate in that way. Once they knew the truth, enforcing the sub-contract would not have been in the ordinary course of business, and would have damaged their business reputation.[21]

20.57   In *Pilkington* v *Wood* (1953), again there was no failure to mitigate. The steps to reduce loss suggested by the party in breach were not reasonable. There the injured party had purchased land with a defective title because of his solicitor's negligence. When he sued his solicitor the court held that the injured party was not expected to have undertaken 'a complicated and difficult piece of litigation', against the vendor of the land, to try to mitigate his loss. That was the case even though the solicitor was prepared to indemnify him in respect of the cost of that litigation.

20.58   The duty to mitigate was not satisfied in *Brace* v *Calder* (1985). There it was considered that it would have been reasonable to accept another contract from the party in breach as a means of reducing loss. In that case, the facts were as follows:

> The four defendants carried on business in partnership as Scotch whisky merchants. They contracted with the claimant for him to manage their office business for two years. Before the expiry of the two years the partnership was dissolved on the retirement of two of the partners. The other two partners carried on the business. The claimant stated that the dissolution of the partnership had terminated his contract. He claimed the salary that he would have earned during the remainder of the two years. The remaining partners wished to employ him on the same terms as the original agreement.

---

21   See also *London and South of England Building Society* v *Stone* (1983).

The Court of Appeal accepted that there had been a wrongful termination of the claimant's contract, but held that he was entitled only to nominal damages. He could have mitigated his loss. It would have been reasonable to accept the alternative employment with the two partners. The situation would have been different had the claimant's technical dismissal, on the termination of the original contract, been more than that, if, for example, he had been dismissed in humiliating circumstances.

> 'It is plain that the question of what it is reasonable for a person to do in mitigation of his damages cannot be a question of law but must be one of fact in the circumstances of each case. There may be cases where as a matter of fact it would be unreasonable to expect a [claimant] to consider any offer made in view of the treatment he has received from the defendant. If he had been rendering personal services and had been dismissed after being accused in the presence of others of being a thief, and if after that his employer had offered to take him back into his service, most persons would think he was justified in refusing the offer, and that it would be unreasonable to ask him in this way to mitigate the damages in an action for wrongful dismissal' (*Payzu* v *Saunders* [1919] 2 KB 581 (see below) per Bankes LJ at 586).

20.59   The duty to mitigate was held to cover the new contract offered by the party in breach in *Payzu Ltd* v *Saunders* [1919] 2 KB 581. In that case, the facts were as follows:

> The claimant had contracted to purchase crêpe de Chine from the defendant. The defendant was to supply it, as required, over a nine-month period. The claimant was to have the goods on credit, payment to be made within one month of each delivery. Owing to a cheque going astray, the first payment was late and the defendant wrongly claimed to be able to terminate the contract. The defendant offered to continue to supply the claimant under a new contract on the same terms, except for the single change that payment was to be made on delivery. The claimant was in a position to pay on delivery but he refused the offer. The market price of the goods had risen.

The claimant contended that the wrongful termination of the original contract entitled him to damages to cover the rise in the market price above the contract price. It was held that the claimant should have mitigated the loss by accepting the defendant's offer of a 'cash on delivery' contract at the original price. Had the claimant accepted that offer, he would have obtained the goods at the original contract price but not on credit terms. In other words, he would have avoided having to pay the increased market price and, on that basis, the court held that he was entitled to recover only for the loss of a month's credit on each order—i.e. the only loss he would have made had he accepted the defendant's offer. The court thought that there was nothing to make this a case in which it was not reasonable to avoid the increased market price by accepting the new offer from the party in breach. Scrutton LJ thought that 'in commercial contracts it is generally reasonable to accept an offer from the party in default' (at 589).[22]

---

22 See also *The Solholt (Sotiros Shipping Inc. v Schmeiet Solholt)* (1983).

20.60   However, there has been criticism of the approach taken in *Payzu Ltd* v *Saunders* to the claim to damages based on the rise in the market value of the goods between contract and delivery date. The effect of the court's decision was to transfer the benefit of that rise in the market from the injured party to the party in breach. The claimant's refusal of the defendant's offer meant that the defendant could realize the rise in value of the goods in the market. If the court had decided differently on the mitigation point, that rise in value would have been paid in damages to the claimant: the original contractual allocation of the market risk would have been maintained. As the court decided that the mitigation rule prevented the claimant from recovering that sum, the rise in market price of the goods was left with the defendant, who had lost it under the original contract allocation of the market risk (see Bridge (1989) 105 LQR 398).

Expenses incurred

20.61   The above cases concern the argument that the injured party has failed to act as the reasonable person would have done to reduce his loss. In addition, where the injured party has incurred expenses in reacting to the breach, the party in breach may argue that those expenses are not recoverable because they were unreasonably incurred. *Banco de Portugal* v *Waterlow & Sons Ltd* [1932] AC 452 provides an example of a case where the expenditure was held to have been reasonable, and Lord Macmillan stated that the injured party's actions 'ought not to be weighed in nice scales at the instance of the party whose breach of contract has occasioned the difficulty' (at 506). In that case, the facts were as follows:

> Waterlow contracted to print a series of 'Vasco da Gama' 500 escudo bank notes for the bank. In breach of contract they printed and delivered a second batch to Marang, in the mistaken belief that he had the bank's authority. Marang and his associates formed the Banco de Angola e Metropole in Portugal to put the notes into circulation. When the Banco de Portugal discovered what had occurred, they called in all 'Vasco da Gama' 500 escudo notes and redeemed both the authorized and unauthorized notes.

The Banco de Portugal claimed the cost of printing the notes and also the cost of redeeming the unauthorized notes. Waterlow contended that, as the authorized and unauthorized notes could be distinguished, the bank need not have paid out on the unauthorized notes. The House of Lords held that the bank could recover that sum. It had acted reasonably to maintain confidence in the currency.

20.62   Expenditure which is not reasonably incurred cannot be recovered. If the injured party takes out a loan to obtain the release of his ship, which has been detained in breach of contract, and the loan is at a very high rate of interest, the interest charge will not be recovered where it is unreasonably incurred (*The Borag (Compania Financiera 'Soleada' SA* v *Hamoor Tanker Corpn Inc)* (1981)).

Benefit gained

20.63   There is said to be one further aspect of mitigation, namely that the injured party cannot recover for a loss which he or she has avoided. A benefit stemming directly from the breach is taken into account in calculating the loss caused (*British Westinghouse Electric and Manufacturing Co. Ltd v Underground Electric Railways Co. of London Ltd* (1912)).

Anticipatory breach

20.64   The further difficulty occasioned in relation to anticipatory breach was considered at para. **18.40**.

Economic efficiency

20.65   Mitigation has obvious links with the issue of causation. However, in not including in the injured party's damages a loss which he or she would not have incurred had he or she acted reasonably, the mitigation rule can be seen as a means of preventing resources from being wasted. In that context it can also be viewed as an incentive to breach: it is not a disincentive to do so. It can be seen as part of the promotion of the 'efficient breach' which it has been argued is economically desirable.

> 'In some cases a party would be tempted to breach the contract simply because his profit from breach would exceed his expected profit from completion of the contract, and if damages are limited to loss of expected profit, there will be an incentive to commit a breach. There should be. The opportunity cost of completion to the breaching party is the profit he would make from the breach, and if it is greater than his profit from completion, then completion will involve a loss to him. If that loss is greater than the gain to the other party from completion, breach would be value maximising and should be encouraged' (Posner, *Economic Analysis of Law*, 2nd edn, pp. 89–90).

The rationale is that the injured party is satisfied because damages provide him or her with the benefit he or she would have derived from the contract. If the party who breached can pay those damages and, after doing so, make a profit in excess of that which he or she would have derived from the contract, then it is economically efficient to encourage the breach. A greater benefit has been derived from the breach than would have followed from performance. The mitigation rule can be seen as part of the encouragement to efficient breach.[23]

Contributory negligence

20.66   The injured party may have contributed to his or her injury through his or her own negligence. One question which needs to be considered is whether damages can be reduced in contract, as in tort, on the basis of the injured party's contributory negligence. In tort, reduction of damages—on the basis of the injured party's negligent contribution to his own injury—is

---

23 But see Harris, Campbell, and Halson, *Remedies in Contract and Tort*, 2nd edn, 2002, ch. 7. Bridge (1989) 105 LQR 398 at 408 states that the mitigation rule is based on: 'several impulses that mollify the strictness of contractual obligation and that are hard, perhaps impossible to rationalize in their totality. The rules of mitigation may well express the law's concern to avoid economic waste, but it would be a mistake to believe that this represents entirely the law's concern in the matter'.

dealt with by the Law Reform (Contributory Negligence) Act 1945 (LR(CN)A 1945). The question here concerns the applicability of that Act to an action in contract.

20.67 The Law Reform (Contributory Negligence) Act 1945 applies where 'any person suffers damage as the result partly of his own fault and partly of the fault of any other person'. Where that is the situation, the damages recoverable 'shall be reduced to such an extent as the court thinks just and equitable having regard to the claimant's share in the responsibility for the damage' (s 1). 'Fault' is defined in s 4, which states that it 'means negligence, breach of statutory duty or other act or omission which gives rise to a liability in tort or would, apart from this Act, give rise to the defence of contributory negligence'.

20.68 The current law, on the applicability of LR(CN)A 1945 in relation to a breach of contract, basically requires a threefold division of the cases (*Forsikringsaktieselskapet Vesta* v *Butcher* [1986] 2 All ER 488 at 508 per Hobhouse J):

> '1. Where the defendant's liability arises from some contractual provision which does not depend on negligence on the part of the defendant.
> 2. Where the defendant's liability arises from some contractual obligation which is expressed in terms of taking care (or its equivalent) but does not correspond to a common law duty to take care which would exist in the given case independently of contract.
> 3. Where the defendant's liability in contract is the same as his liability in the tort of negligence independently of the existence of any contract.'

With the definition of fault in LR(CN)A 1945, s 4, the Act clearly seems inappropriately worded to cover cases in the first category and *Vesta* indicated that it would only be applied to the third category and that is the line that has been taken.[24] The Law Commission has recommended that contributory negligence should be applicable in both categories 2 and 3 (Law Com Rep No 219 (1993)). Of course, since the decision in *Henderson* v *Merrett Syndicates* (1995) concurrent liability, bringing the situation within category 3, is more likely to be found and the problem diminished. However, the point has been made that 'the ebbing and flowing of the tort of negligence should not be affecting the ambit of contributory negligence in contract' and that it would be sensible to amend the law, as the Law Commission suggested, to make it simpler and fairer.[25]

Penalties and liquidated damages

20.69 Given the complexity of the rules just described, it is hardly surprising that the parties should sometimes choose to include a term in their contract stating what damages are to be

---

24 e.g. *Barclays Bank plc* v *Fairclough Building Ltd* (1995); *Raflatac* v *Eade* (1999); *Barclays Bank plc* v *Fairclough Building Ltd (No 2)* (1995).

25 A. Burrows, *Understanding the Law of Obligations*, Hart Publishing, 1998, p. 150.

available upon the occurrence of a particular breach or breaches. Such a clause is known as a 'liquidated damages' clause. The fixing of liability by such a clause has the benefit of introducing certainty into the question of damages. It makes it easier for the parties to calculate the risks involved in the contract and to insure appropriately. It may even help to avoid a dispute reaching the point where it is litigated. There is much to be said for such clauses and the courts will enforce them.

20.70   However, the courts have had to deal with the question of whether a clause fixing a sum to be paid on breach is a liquidated damages clause or a penalty clause. The classic statement differentiating the two is that of Lord Dunedin in *Dunlop Pneumatic Tyre Co. Ltd* v *New Garage and Motor Co. Ltd* [1915] AC 79 at 86: 'The essence of a penalty is a payment of money stipulated as *in terrorem* of the offending party; the essence of damages is a genuine covenanted pre-estimate of damage.' In other words, a penalty clause is an attempt to coerce performance by setting an excessive sum to be paid on breach. This conflicts with the view generally taken by English law that damages merely compensate the injured party and do not punish the party in breach. The injured party will not recover the sum specified in the penalty clause, but will be limited to recovering his or her actual loss. The clause is not struck out of the contract, but will not be enforced beyond the sum which represents the actual loss of the injured party.[26]

20.71   The EC Directive on Unfair Terms in Consumer Contracts should be noted in the context of this discussion of penalty and other clauses. In the consumer context, using the unfair terms in consumer contracts regime may avoid some of the difficulties in the borderlines of the applications of the rules on penalty clauses.

Distinguishing penalty and liquidated damages clauses

20.72   An obvious problem created for the courts in this area is to distinguish penalty clauses and liquidated damages clauses. They may take the same form and an express label, placed upon them by the parties, by no means determines the issue. Apart from attempts to avoid the rule about penalty clauses, any such label may simply not have been used in its technical sense. 'Though the parties to a contract who use the words "penalty" or "liquidated damages" may prima facie be supposed to mean what they say, yet the expression used is not conclusive. The court must find out whether the payment stipulated is in truth a penalty or liquidated damages.'[27]

20.73   It is a matter of construing the contract to determine the classification of the clause on the basis of the circumstances known, or which should have been known, at the time of

---

26 *Jobson* v *Johnson* [1989] 1 All ER 621 at 633.

27 *Dunlop Pneumatic Tyre Co. Ltd* v *New Garage and Motor Co. Ltd* [1915] AC 79 at 86. See also *Clydebank Engineering and Shipbuilding Co. Ltd* v *Castaneda* (1905).

contracting. In *Dunlop Pneumatic Tyre Co. Ltd* v *New Garage and Motor Co. Ltd* [1915] AC 79. Lord Dunedin set out four 'tests' to help with this question. He said (at 87–8):

> '(a) It will be held to be a penalty if the sum stipulated for is extravagant and unconscionable in amount in comparison with the greatest loss that could conceivably be proved to have followed from the breach.
>
> (b) It will be held to be a penalty if the breach consists only in not paying a sum of money, and the sum stipulated is a sum greater than the sum which ought to have been paid...
>
> (c) There is a presumption (but no more) that it is a penalty when a single lump sum is made payable by way of compensation, on the occurrence of one or more or all of several events, some of which may occasion serious and others but trifling damage.
>
> On the other hand:
>
> (d) It is no obstacle to the sum stipulated being a genuine pre-estimate of damages, that the consequences of the breach are such as to make precise pre-estimation almost an impossibility. On the contrary that is just the situation when it is probable that pre-estimated damage was the bargain between the parties.'

In that case Dunlop sold motor car tyres to dealers who in turn sold them on. In return for a discount, the dealers had undertaken not to tamper with the marks on the goods, not to sell the tyres to private customers below Dunlop's list price, not to sell to anyone whose supply Dunlop had suspended, and not to exhibit or export any of the tyres. It was stated that they were to pay £5 as 'liquidated damages' for a breach. The dealers sold a tyre below list price. Dunlop's business was carried on through sales to dealers, and all the dealers to whom they sold were required to sign the agreement. There was evidence that if a dealer undersold, it had the effect of forcing other dealers to buy elsewhere, thereby reducing the number of outlets for Dunlop's goods.

20.74   The House of Lords decided that the clause requiring £5 'liquidated damages' was indeed a liquidated damages clause and not a penalty. This was largely on the basis of (d) above. There was evidence that failure to maintain the price would cause the manufacturers damage on a broad scale, through reduction of their retail outlets, but it was not clear how much loss would result from one specific underpriced sale. It was regarded as reasonable for the parties to estimate that loss, and the clause was upheld, as the figure was not extravagant. In addition, the fact that the same sum was payable in relation to different breaches did not mean that it had to be labelled as a penalty. The test in (c) above did not mean that the clause in the particular case was a penalty clause. All the prohibitions on dealers related to the same type of broad potential damage to Dunlop. In addition, the loss from breach of any one was uncertain and such things 'could not be weighed nicely in a chemical balance'. The court thought that it was a matter of whether the loss from one particular breach could clearly never reach the specified sum, and that was not the case.

20.75   The loss arising from a particular breach may vary according to a particular factor. If the clause indicating the sum to be paid on breach is one which varies the amount appropriately in accordance with this factor, that may indicate that the clause is a liquidated damages clause. It may be, for example, that the breach is one which can continue for a period of time and the loss will increase as the time passes. A clause increasing the sum to be paid with the increasing period of time may well be found to be a liquidated damages clause (*Clydebank Engineering and Shipbuilding Co. Ltd v Castaneda* (1905)). On the other hand, it may be that the variation of the sum payable does not relate to likely variations in the loss suffered, but is an arbitrary variation in relation to likely loss. Such arbitrary variation indicates that the clause was not a genuine pre-estimate of damage (*Public Works Comr v Hills* (1906)). The situation is even more extreme, and more clearly indicative that the clause is a penalty, where the loss varies in exactly the opposite way to the variation in the clause: a penalty, clause is indicated where there is 'a sliding scale of compensation but a scale that slides in the wrong direction' (*Bridge v Campbell Discount Co. Ltd* [1962] AC 600 at 623).

20.76   However, a final point should be made here as to the trend in relation to the basic approach to the construction of a clause which states the amount of damages to be paid upon a breach or breaches occurring. In *Philips Hong Kong Ltd v A-G of Hong Kong* (1993) the Privy Council emphasized the usefulness of the liquidated damages clause because of the certainty it creates for both parties and, against that background, the point was made that the courts' power to deal with penalty clauses was one which 'was always recognised as being subject to fairly narrow constraints' and not one giving a general jurisdiction to rewrite the parties' bargain.[28] In particular, the point was made that although the nature of the clause had to be assessed against what could be foreseen at the time of contracting, the courts would not find a clause to be a penalty clause just because some hypothetical examples of its use could be found in which there would be a gap between the sum specified under the clause and the loss suffered. The likelihood of the losses in question had to be considered as well. Lord Woolf, delivering the judgment of the court, said:

> 'Arguments of this nature should not be allowed to divert attention from the correct test as to what is a penalty clause provision—namely is it a genuine pre-estimate of *what the loss is likely to be*?—to the different question, namely are there possible circumstances where a lesser loss would be suffered?' (emphasis added).

20.77   The Court of Appeal has adopted Colman J's 'recasting' in 'more modern terms' of the 'classic test'.[29] Coleman J said in *Lordsvale v Bank of Zambia* [1996] QB 752 at 762:

> '[W]hether a provision is to be treated as a penalty is a matter of construction to be resolved by asking whether at the time the contract was entered into the predominant contractual function of the provision was to deter a party from breaking the contract or to compensate the innocent party for the breach. That the contractual function is deterrent rather than

---

28 See also *AMEV-UDC Finance Ltd v Austin* (1987); *Robophone Facilities Ltd v Blank* [1966] 1 WLR 1428 at 1447.

29 *Murray v Leisureplay* (2005); *Euro London Appointments v Claessens International* (2006); *Cine Bes Filmcilik ve Yapimcilik v United International Pictures* (2003).

> compensatory can be deduced by comparing the amount that would be payable on breach
> with the loss that might be sustained if the loss occurred.'

Importantly it was also made plain that a clause would not be seen as penal simply because of a comparison of those amounts. The amount stated would not be struck down as a penalty 'if it could in the circumstances be explained as commercially justifiable provided always that the dominant purpose was not to deter the other party from breach' (Colman J at 763–4).[30]

20.78 In *Murray* v *Leisureplay* (2005) what was in issue was a clause stating that the chief executive was to receive one year's gross salary and benefits on wrongful termination of his contract. At first instance that was held to be penal because, inter alia, it did not take account of the fact that an injured party has a duty to mitigate and the loss of the contract in question would give the ex-chief executive the possibility of taking up other opportunities during that year. The Court of Appeal concluded that the clause was not penal. Buxton LJ said (at [115]):

> 'An entrepreneurial company…promoting a product conceived by one man, will often place high value on retaining the services, and the loyalty and attention of that one man as its chief executive: to the extent of including in his "package" generous reassurance against the eventuality of dismissal. That such reassurance exceeds the likely amount of contractual damages on dismissal does not render the terms penal unless the party seeking to avoid the terms can demonstrate that they meet the test of extravagance posited by Lord Dunedin…'

Avoidance of the rule on penalties

20.79 The limits of the application of the rules on penalty clauses are technically drawn and there is considerable scope for evasion of those rules by the use of an appropriate form of clause. To an extent, that is being mitigated in relation to deposits by the common law (see below) and, in the consumer context, more broadly by the Unfair Terms in Consumer Contracts Directive. Nevertheless, consideration must be given to the scope of the rules as to penalty clauses, and the means of evading their operation through careful drafting.

20.80 The first point to emphasize is that the rule about penalty clauses only applies where the sum specified in the clause in question becomes payable on breach. The courts have had to decide whether payment is due upon breach or other circumstances. If the sum specified becomes payable under circumstances which are not a breach, then the rule as to penalty clauses does not apply. An example is provided by *Alder* v *Moore* (1961):

> The Association Football Players' and Trainers' Union took out an insurance policy on behalf of their members. It provided for payment of £500 if a player suffered permanent disablement

---

30 See also *Euro London Appointments* v *Claessens International* (2006) at [30].

preventing him from playing professional football. Brian Moore was a professional footballer with West Ham. He received an injury which permanently deprived him of 90 per cent of his vision in one eye. It was thought that he would never be able to play professional football again and the insurance company paid him £500. The policy required him to sign a declaration on receiving such a payment. The declaration stated that 'in consideration of the [£500] I hereby declare and agree that I will take no part as a playing member of any form of professional football and that in the event of infringement of this condition I will be subject to a penalty of [£500]'. Mr Moore's sight did not return, but he started to play professional football again, on a part-time basis, with Cambridge United. The insurance company claimed the £500.

The Court of Appeal (with Devlin LJ dissenting) held that he had not committed a breach by playing professional football again. The insurance company was entitled to the £500 as it was merely payable upon the resumption of professional football. The clause was not subject to the rule on penalties.

20.81   Specifying a condition upon which a payment must be made, and ensuring that it is not a breach, may provide a means of evading the operation of the rules on penalties. This can be seen more clearly in the case of *Bridge* v *Campbell Discount Co. Ltd* [1962] AC 600 where Lord Denning said (at 629) 'equity commits itself to this absurd paradox: it will grant relief to a man who breaks his contract but will penalise the man who keeps it'. In that case, the facts were as follows:

Mr Bridge had obtained a car on a hire purchase basis. The contract contained an option for him to give notice to terminate the hiring and return the car at any time. However, it also contained a clause requiring him to pay 'compensation' for 'depreciation' upon termination of the contract. The clause was effectively one to ensure a minimum payment. It required a payment to make up two-thirds of the hire purchase price when combined with the money already paid. Mr Bridge returned the car after he had made only one of the required thirty-six monthly payments.

The Court of Appeal found that returning the car did not involve a breach as Mr Bridge had merely exercised the option and, on that basis, the requirement as to the payment of compensation could not be subject to the rule on penalty clauses. The House of Lords avoided this conclusion by construing the return of the car not as an exercise of the option, but as a breach. It was then able to find that the clause was a penalty clause. A decreasing sum could not be genuine compensation for depreciation. The depreciation would increase as the amount payable under the clause decreased. The hire purchase company was not able to recover the amount specified in the penalty clause, but only its actual loss.[31] (Very controversially, the High Court

---

[31] See also *Export Credit Guarantee Department* v *Universal Oil Products Co* (1983); *Transag Haulage Ltd* v *Leyland DAF Finance plc* (1994).

of Australia has recently turned away from restricting the application of the rules on penalty clauses to payments on breach in *Andrews v Australia and New Zealand Banking Group Ltd* (2012). See J. W. Carter, W. Courtney, E. Peden, A. Stewart, and G. J. Tolhurst, 'Contracual Penalties: Resurrecting the Equitable Jurisdiction'(2013) 30 JCL 99.)

20.82   There are other means of achieving much the same result as would follow from a penalty clause if it was allowed to take effect. In other words, there are other ways of avoiding the rule on penalty clauses. The contract may, for example, provide a discount for prompt payment rather than a penalty for late payment. Where the contract requires payment in instalments, there is the possibility of using an acceleration clause which provides that if one payment is not made on time then all the instalments immediately become due.[32] In addition, the position of deposits must be considered.

Deposits

20.83   The rules governing penalties now need to be compared with the approach taken by the courts to deposits. The basic rule in relation to an advance payment is that it has to be determined whether it is a deposit or a part payment. Was it meant to secure performance or merely partly to discharge the contract price? Basically, a part payment will be recoverable if there is a total failure of consideration by the seller[33] but, until recently, a deposit was not recoverable as it was required to secure performance.[34] The fact that a deposit could not be recovered, no matter how little relationship it had to any loss caused by the failure to perform, made an uneasy contrast with the rules in relation to penalties. In effect, the law's treatment of deposits provided a means of avoiding the rules on penalties. However, this anomaly was noted and mitigated by the Privy Council in *Worker's Trust and Merchant Bank Ltd v Dojap Investments Ltd* (1993). The approach taken there was that it was anomalous that the rules on penalties did not apply to deposits and that that should only be the case if the sum specified was 'reasonable'. However, the assessment of whether the sum was 'reasonable' was carried out on an, admittedly, illogical basis. The simple line taken was that the long-standing, customarily required deposit was 10 per cent of the purchase price, and anything in excess of that would be regarded as 'unreasonable' unless it could be shown to be justified by special circumstances. In the instant case, the sum demanded had been 25 per cent of the purchase price, and the vendor claimed to be entitled to retain it when the buyer failed to complete the purchase within the time specified. The Privy Council ordered that, subject to the vendor's claim for damages, the entire sum should be returned by the vendor. As the entire sum was not to be viewed as a deposit, but a penalty, the vendor could not even retain 10 per cent.

---

32 *Proctor Loan Co. v Grise* (1880), but see *O'Dea v Allstates Leasing Systems (WA) Pty Ltd* (1983).

33 *Dies v British and International Mining and Finance Corpn Ltd* (1939); *Hyundai Heavy Industries Co. Ltd v Papadopoulos* (1980); *Rover International Ltd v Cannon Film Sales Ltd* (1989).

34 *Howe v Smith* (1884). A statutory discretion is provided in relation to a contract for the sale of land—Law of Property Act 1925, s 49(2).

Unfair Terms in Consumer Contracts Directive

20.84   The point has been made earlier that there is considerable scope for avoiding the rules as to penalty clauses by setting out to achieve the same end (a disincentive to non-performance) by a different form of clause and this can produce anomalies. However, in the consumer context there is considerable potential to mitigate that problem through the use of the regime for consumer protection which derives from the Unfair Terms in Consumer Contracts Directive. The application of the fairness test under that regime is not limited to particular types of clause. The only concern is the exclusion, from the fairness test, of terms falling within the core exemption.

A particular kind of loss: mental distress and the consumer surplus

20.85   We have, until now, been considering examples of financial loss, and these are the classic types of claim which the law of contract has had to deal with, and which its rules were elaborated around. However, with the development of the consumer culture in particular, the question has been raised as to the recovery of a loss when the contract was not made to make a money profit, but was wholly, or partly, concerned with some enjoyment, pleasure, or the relief of distress. If contract damages are not awarded to protect such expected gains from the contract, then contract rights are actually far more limited than the basic ideas, and rules would suggest, and they do not adequately protect consumers. We should now consider this question, and we will start by considering the cases which have focused on recovery for damages for mental distress, before considering another line of authority concerned with the basis of calculation of damages.

Damages for mental distress

20.86   The usual contractual damages claim will relate to damage to the injured party's economic interest, but it may also cover personal injury or damage to property. However, with exceptions, contract damages do not encompass, on a general basis, damages for mental distress, i.e. damages for vexation, frustration, anxiety, and disappointment. The basic restriction was established in *Addis* v *Gramophone Co. Ltd* (1909). In that case:

> Mr Addis was employed as manager of G Co.'s business in Calcutta. His contract entitled him to six months' notice of dismissal. G Co. gave him six months' notice but immediately appointed his successor and ensured that Mr Addis could no longer act as manager.

The manner of his dismissal injured Mr Addis' feelings but the House of Lords would not allow him to recover a sum in damages for that injury.

20.87   However, damages for mental distress have now been recognized as exceptionally available and the starting point for considering that is the judgment of Bingham LJ in *Watts* v

Morrow [1991] 4 All ER 937. He first stated the general non-availability of damages for mental distress. He said (at 959):

> 'A contract-breaker is not in general liable for any distress, frustration, anxiety, displeasure, vexation, tension or aggravation which his breach of contract may cause to the innocent party. This rule is not, I think, founded on the assumption that such reactions are not foreseeable, which they surely are or may be, but on considerations of policy.'

This states the general rule and emphasizes that the general non-availability of damages for mental distress is a matter of policy. The question of the 'policy' behind the general non-availability of damages for mental distress will be returned to later. Here what must now be considered is Bingham LJ's statement of the exceptional situations in which such damages are available. First, he said (at 959):

> 'But the rule is not absolute. Where the very object of a contract is to provide pleasure, relaxation, peace of mind or freedom from molestation, damages will be awarded if the fruit of the contract is not provided or if the contrary result is procured instead. If the law did not cater for this exceptional category of case it would be defective....'

This requires the 'very object of the contract' to be of an appropriate type, i.e. 'pleasure, relaxation, peace of mind or freedom from molestation'. Plainly, as the point (object) of such contracts is not to provide a profit but some mental benefit, it would be very obvious that an award of contract damages was not protecting the injured party's contractual 'rights', if damages for mental distress were not available in these cases. Hence Bingham LJ's reference to the law being 'defective' if it did not 'cater for this exceptional category of case'. However, this exception has now been extended by the House of Lords in *Farley* v *Skinner* (2001), and this will be returned to later. Here Bingham LJ's second exception should now be set out. He said (at 960):

> 'In cases not falling within this exceptional category, damages are in my view recoverable for physical inconvenience and discomfort caused by the breach and any mental suffering directly related to that inconvenience and discomfort.'

These exceptions will now be considered, although the latter will be looked at first.

Mental distress consequent on physical inconvenience

20.88 As has been indicated, the second exception which Bingham LJ identified in *Watts* v *Morrow* (1991) provides for the recovery of damages for mental distress where it is a consequence of the physical inconvenience caused by the breach. This can be illustrated by, for example, *Perry* v *Sidney Phillips & Son* [1982] 3 All ER 705. In that case:

> Ivan Perry purchased a house on the faith of a survey carried out by the defendant surveyors which stated that the house was in good order. After moving in, Mr Perry discovered that the

> roof leaked and was in poor condition, and that the septic tank was inefficient and 'gave off
> an offensive odour'. These defects caused him distress, worry, and inconvenience.

In addition to damages for the reduced value of the property, because of the defects, the Court of Appeal agreed with the judge at first instance that Mr Perry was entitled to damages for his mental distress. Kerr LJ said (at 712):

> 'So far as the question of damages for vexation and inconvenience is concerned, it should
> be noted that the deputy judge awarded these...because of the physical consequences of
> the breach.'

20.89   Similarly, in *Watts* v *Morrow* (1991) itself, although C could not recover more generally for their mental distress, they did recover for that consequent on the physical inconvenience caused by the breach. The case was concerned with a survey of property which, in breach of contract, the defendant surveyor had performed negligently. C were busy people who wished to purchase a second home to relax in at weekends. The survey report indicated that the house they had decided upon had no major defects. That was inaccurate, and C had to expend considerable time and money in having it repaired. They recovered the difference between what they paid for the property and what it was worth because of the defects.[35] In addition, following *Perry* v *Sidney Phillips & Son* (1982), they recovered for the mental distress consequent upon the physical inconvenience they had suffered, although, as has been indicated, they did not recover more generally for their mental distress.

20.90   This limited exception to the general non-availability of damages for mental distress was also seen as providing an alternative basis to the recovery of such damages in *Farley* v *Skinner* (2001), which we shall return to later, and some extension of the exception may be indicated. All of the judges, in that case, viewed the case as being one qualifying under the second exception. Lord Steyn made the point that noise (of aircraft flying overhead) can produce a physical reaction and made reference to it being capable of constituting a nuisance. He regarded it as a matter of degree whether it passed the threshold to constitute inconvenience and discomfort within Bingham LJ's test (at [30]). Lord Hutton and Lord Scott regarded the injured party as having suffered physical inconvenience and discomfort as the aircraft noise had a physical effect upon him through his hearing (at [85]). Lord Clyde can be viewed as going further, if somewhat uncertainly, taking the view that there was no 'particular magic' in the word 'physical' and regarded it as sufficient if what was in question was 'inconvenience' rather than merely 'matters purely sentimental'(at [35]).

'Objects' exception

20.91   As has been indicated, in *Watts* v *Morrow* (1991) Bingham LJ set out the, more significant, 'objects' exception to the general non-availability of damages for mental distress. It was,

---

35 They did not recover the larger sum which represented the cost of the repairs—see A. Dugdale, '*Watts* v
  Morrow: Penalising the House Purchaser' (1992) 8 Professional Negligence 152.

however, extended by the House of Lords in *Farley v Skinner* (2001), and that will be considered later. First, some understanding of the exception as Bingham LJ set it out can be gleaned from the cases which preceded it and on which it was clearly based.

20.92   In *Jarvis v Swans Tours Ltd* (1973) damages for lost enjoyment were awarded in relation to a contract for a holiday. In that case:

> Mr Jarvis booked a winter sports holiday with Swan. The holiday was described as a 'house party'. The brochure referred to afternoon tea and cakes and a yodeller evening and stated that ski-packs would be available. For the first week there were thirteen people there, but for the second week Mr Jarvis was the sole member of the 'house party'. The cakes for tea were merely crisps and dry nutcake. Full-sized skis were only available for two days. The yodeller evening turned out to consist of a local man coming to the hotel, in his work clothes, and quickly singing a few songs.

Mr Jarvis claimed damages for breach of contract, as the holiday was not as promised in the brochure. At first instance he was merely awarded £31.72 as the difference in value between what he contracted for and what he got. The Court of Appeal awarded £125. It considered that he should be compensated for his lost enjoyment.[36] Plainly a holiday contract is a contract the 'very object' of which 'is to provide pleasure'. A further example of a contract to provide pleasure is to be found in the Scottish case of *Diesen v Samson* (1971), where a bride was awarded damages for the distress (the loss of enjoyment) caused, when the photographer she had booked failed to turn up to take photographs of her wedding.

20.93   In *Heywood v Wellers* (1976), the purpose of the contract was to provide relief from anxiety. In that case:

> The claimant had employed solicitors to obtain an injunction to prevent a man from molesting her. The solicitors were negligent and he molested her further.

Damages for mental distress were awarded. The contract was not for a commercial purpose, but to provide relief from distress, just as in *Jarvis v Swans Tours Ltd* (1973) and *Diesen v Samson* (1971) the object of the contracts was to provide pleasure.

20.94   The cases above provide plain examples of the 'objects' exception as stated by Bingham LJ. The 'very object' of the contracts in those cases was to provide pleasure or relief from distress. They contrast with *Watts v Morrow* (1991) itself, where the survey contract was not regarded as one 'the very object of' which 'is to provide pleasure, relaxation, peace of mind, or freedom from molestation'. However, that must again be contrasted with the somewhat different survey contract in *Farley v Skinner* (2001) where the House of Lords expanded the exception to an extent, although distinguishing the case before them from the ordinary survey contract in *Watts v Morrow*.

---

36 See also *Jackson v Horizon Holidays Ltd* (1975).

20.95 *Farley* v *Skinner* (2001) was concerned with the survey of a house in connection with its purchase by a successful businessman, who was retiring and wished to buy a 'gracious country residence'. He had been concerned that the property in question might be seriously affected by aircraft noise and he specifically instructed the surveyor to address that issue. The surveyor reported it as 'unlikely' that the property would suffer greatly from such noise. He was negligent in doing so. The question was whether the purchaser could recover more than nominal damages for that breach of the surveyor's contract. (The purchase price paid by the purchaser was found to have reflected the impact of noise on the house's value.) The House of Lords took the view that the case fell within the exceptions to the general non-availability of damages for mental distress. In particular, they addressed the argument that the provision of pleasure, relaxation, or peace of mind was not 'the very object' of a contract to survey a house for potential purchase. The line taken by the majority was that the exception does not only extend to cases in which 'the very object' of the contract is an appropriate one, but also (Lord Steyn) where 'a major or important object' of the contract is an appropriate one (at 812), or where a specific and important term of the contract is directed to an appropriate object (Lords Clyde and Hutton).

20.96 The extension of the exception is significant, as *Farley* v *Skinner* itself illustrates. It was applied, and prevented the need for a difficult distinction to be made, in *Hamilton Jones* v *David Snape* (2004).There what was in issue was a solicitor's negligence in failing to see that a father did not take his child out of the jurisdiction. Neuberger J made the point that the mother's primary concern in instructing the solicitors might have been the child's interests. But whether her own interests or those of the child were uppermost,

> 'both the claimant and the defendants would have had in mind that a significant reason for the claimant instructing the defendants was with a view to ensuring, so far as possible, that the claimant retained custody of her children for her own pleasure and peace of mind' (at [61]).

Damages for mental distress were awarded.

20.97 However, *Farley* v *Skinner* (2001) should be put in its broader context. The point was made earlier that, in *Watts* v *Morrow* (1991), Bingham LJ said that the law would be 'defective' if it did not provide damages for mental distress where the 'very object' of the contract was to provide 'pleasure, relaxation, peace of mind or freedom from distress'. In effect, that was taken a stage further in *Farley* v *Skinner*. It was recognized that some further availability of mental distress damages was necessary to avoid a distinction of 'form and not substance', i.e. the 'objects' exception as stated by Bingham LJ would have allowed for recovery if a house purchaser made a separate contract with a surveyor to report on aircraft noise, but not if that was simply specifically made part of a contract to survey the property more generally (per Lord Steyn at 811). However, a still broader perspective needs to be applied.

20.98 The basic principle on which contract damages are awarded is to put an injured party in the position they would have been in had the contract been performed. There are those who see this purely in terms of the financial position which the injured party would have been in had the contract been performed. Such a narrow view seems unconvincing once the exceptions noted here are considered. So why are damages for lost consumer surplus, or for mental distress, regarded as something which should only be exceptionally available? Basic principle would argue for their general availability. This needs to be considered further, but first we should look at another line of cases.

Cost of cure or market value?

20.99   We must now consider a line of cases which began with the question of whether the claimant's loss should be quantified on the basis of the cost of 'curing' the defective performance, or the difference in the market value between what the claimant should have had, and what he or she obtained. The problem arose in relation to situations where someone contracts for work to be done on their property which will not add to its value, but which will add to their enjoyment of their property. Such situations have raised difficulties in the calculation of damages where the builder does not carry out the work according to the contract terms. The defective performance makes no difference to the value of the property and the builder has contended that damages should merely be nominal, whereas the homeowner has argued that a substantial amount will need to be spent to cure the defect and that he or she should be awarded that 'cost of cure'. It seemed at one stage that the award of damages had to be based on one of these two sums, but, as we shall see, a reversion to basic principle has now shown that not to be the case.

20.100   The first case to consider is *Radford v De Froberville* [1977] 1 WLR 1262. In that case:

> C had sold part of his land to D, D contracting to build a wall to separate her land from C's remaining land. This she failed to do. The wall would not have added to the value of C's property. C claimed the cost of building the wall on his side of the boundary.

Oliver J did not confine C's recovery to nominal damages. He awarded C the 'cost of cure'. He said (at 1270):

> 'Pacta sunt servanda. If he contracts for the supply of that which he thinks serves his interests—be they commercial, aesthetic or merely eccentric—then if that which is contracted for is not supplied by the other contracting party I do not see why, in principle, he should not be compensated by being provided with the cost of supplying it through someone else in a different way, subject to the proviso of course, that he is seeking compensation for a genuine loss and not merely using a technical breach to secure an uncovenanted profit.'

The vital issue in such a case would seem to be to establish what the injured party's 'genuine loss' is. That will depend upon what 'interest' of the injured party the relevant contractual requirement served. However, the convenience of the simple pecuniary measure of 'cost of cure' being available, meant that the nature of that did not have to be openly faced up to.

20.101   The difficulty in this area is that the injured party has contracted for a purpose which is not reflected in an objective market value. The injured party has contracted for the 'consumer surplus' (i.e. 'the excess utility or subjective value' which would have been obtained from the contractual performance—Harris, Ogus, & Phillips, 'Contract Remedies and the Consumer Surplus' (1979) 95 LQR 581 at 582). If the difference which the contractual performance would have made to the objective value of the injured party's property is smaller than the 'consumer surplus', then the injured party will be undercompensated if the injured party's recovery is restricted to that objective value (often nothing). In other words, damages ignoring the 'consumer surplus' will not put the injured party in the position he or she would have been in had the contract been performed. It may then be appropriate for the injured party to recover the cost of cure, as occurred in *Radford v De Froberville* (1977). Certainly that will be the case if the 'consumer surplus' is equal to, or greater than, the cost of cure. In that situation, an injured party will be mitigating their loss by curing the defect. However, the point should be emphasized that if the 'consumer surplus' is less than the cost of cure, awarding the cost of cure overcompensates the injured party. In other words, where a 'consumer surplus' is involved, it is not always appropriate to calculate the damages simply on the basis of either the cost of cure or the difference in value. If neither such sum is to be used as the basis of calculation, it must be admitted that the identification of the correct sum to award cannot be very accurate, but it is the only way to comply with basic principle. The need to depart from the simple dichotomy of cost of cure, or difference in market value, was recognized in *Ruxley v Forsyth* (1995).

20.102   In *Ruxley Electronics and Construction Ltd v Forsyth* [1995] 3 All ER 268:

> C contracted with the defendant for the building of a swimming pool with a maximum depth of water of 7 ft 6 in. C made it clear that the depth was important to him as he wanted to be able to dive and he needed that depth to feel safe to do so. The defendants built a pool with a maximum depth of 6 ft 9 in, and it was only 6 ft deep at the relevant point for diving. There was evidence that, as constructed, the pool was, objectively, safe for diving and the difference in the depth made no difference to the value. In order for the pool to be made to comply with the contract depth, it would have been necessary to rip out what had been installed and put in a new, deeper pool, at a cost of about £21,000. At first instance C was awarded £2,500 general damages for loss of amenity and pleasure. The Court of Appeal (Dillon LJ dissenting) found that the appropriate measure was the cost of cure.

The Court of Appeal viewed the awarding of the cost of cure as the only means of placing C in the position he would have been in had the contract been performed—i.e. in possession of a pool which he felt safe to dive into. Obviously, in awarding the cost of cure, the Court of Appeal in *Ruxley* was protecting a non-commercial interest of C, but it was doing so inappropriately according to the House of Lords, which concluded that it was not restricted to awarding either the cost of cure or the difference in value. The House of Lords restored the award made at first instance.

20.103 In *Ruxley*, the House of Lords reasserted the basic principle that contractual damages should put the injured party in the position he or she would have been in had the contract been performed. Obviously, the Court of Appeal had also attempted to comply with basic principle but Lord Lloyd pointed out the basic fallacy in their reasoning. He stated the basic principle for the award of contractual damages and said (at 282): 'This does not mean that in every case of breach of contract the [claimant] can obtain the monetary equivalent of specific performance.' In economic terms there is a substitute for the injured party's loss of the enjoyment of diving into a 7 ft 6 in swimming pool. The injured party might derive equal enjoyment from a holiday, costing far less than the cost of cure. The lost contractual 'end'—the lost pleasure—can be compensated in money terms without the need to furnish a sum which would provide it through the equivalent of the contractual 'means'. In other words, contrary to the view of the Court of Appeal, having decided that a nominal difference in value was not an appropriate award, there was an alternative to awarding the cost of cure: directly awarding a sum to deal with the loss suffered.

20.104 In *Radford v De Froberville* (1977) and *Ruxley Electronics and Construction Ltd v Forsyth* (1995), in deciding whether the 'cost of cure' was an appropriate award, the courts referred to whether such an award was 'reasonable' and this has received some emphasis. However, the duty to mitigate means that the injured party will not recover for a loss which he or she could have avoided by behaving reasonably on breach. A lost 'consumer surplus' exceeding the cost of cure should be mitigated by behaving reasonably and 'curing' the defendant's performance, and it is appropriate for the injured party to recover the cost of cure in damages. Similarly, if the cost of cure exceeds the 'consumer surplus', it is in keeping with the duty to mitigate that the injured party should only recover the 'consumer surplus' and not the larger cost of cure. Although 'reasonableness' has been addressed more bluntly, in terms of proportionality,[37] it is contended that the references to reasonableness in *Radford* and *Ruxley* should be understood as reflections of the duty to mitigate.

20.105 In *Ruxley Electronics and Construction Ltd v Forsyth* [1995] 3 All ER 268 Lord Mustill said (at 277):

> 'The law must cater for those occasions where the value of the promise exceeds the financial enhancement of his position which full performance will secure. This excess, often referred to in literature as the consumer surplus...is usually incapable of precise valuation in terms of money, exactly because it represents a personal, subjective and non-monetary gain. Nevertheless, where it exists the law should recognise it.'

If it does not recognize the consumer surplus, then the injured party may either be under-compensated or overcompensated.[38] In *Radford v De Froberville* [1977] 1 WLR 1262 Oliver J

---

37 *Birse Construction v Eastern Telegraph* (2004).

38 In fact this has, perhaps, been put even more broadly in terms of the need to recognize the injured party's 'performance interest' if an inappropriate level of compensation is to be avoided—*Panatown Ltd v Alfred McAlpine Construction Ltd* (2000) per Lord Goff and Lord Millett.

awarded the cost of cure to compensate for a non-financial loss. He refused to accept that the injured party had to be left with nominal damages because the building of the wall would not affect the value of the property. Under the circumstances he regarded nominal damages (at 1268), as 'a result so strange and so monstrously unjust that Mr Bumble's animadversion on the nature of law seems, by contrast, a restrained understatement'.

20.106   In that case injustice could be avoided because the consumer surplus could be appropriately compensated for by an award of the cost of cure. However, in *Ruxley* the court had to deal with a situation in which awarding the cost of cure would have overcompensated the injured party, and been unjust to the other party. It was necessary to recognize the possibility of directly compensating for a lost consumer surplus so that (per Lord Mustill at 278) '[t]here is no need to remedy the injustice of awarding too little by unjustly awarding far too much'. Even if it certainly cannot be said that all the statements in *Ruxley* are in accordance with that, it should be recognized that avoiding both forms of injustice requires damages to be generally available for a lost consumer surplus.

Basic principle

20.107   Fully complying with basic principle, and putting the injured party in the position they would have been in had the contract been performed, raises issues in relation to the limitations currently placed on the award of damages for mental distress, and fully recognizing the award of the consumer surplus.

20.108   Lord Scott's judgment in *Farley* can be seen as taking a significant step further towards the general availability of damages for mental distress than the rest of the court. He said (at [79]):

> 'The *Ruxley Electronics* case establishes, in my opinion, that if a party's contractual performance has failed to provide to the other contracting party something to which the other was, under the contract, entitled, and which, if provided would have been of value to that party, then, if there is no other way of compensating the injured party, the injured party should be compensated to the extent of that value...'

This approach would allow all 'consumer surplus' losses to be recovered i.e. all cases where the contractual performance would have provided some 'excess utility' or 'subjective value'. In other words, damages for loss of enjoyment or relief from distress could be recovered in all cases where some element of the contract was to provide enjoyment, or relief from distress, whether that element was a 'major or important object' of the contract or a minor one. *Farley* and *Ruxley* may be seen to provide a pathway to that.

20.109   However, if the non-availability of damages for mental distress is seen as a matter of policy, it should be asked what that policy is and whether it provides a sufficient reason for not complying with basic principle. There has been no clear identification of what that policy is. However, in the Court of Appeal, in *Hayes* v *James & Charles Dodd* [1990] 2 All ER 815, Staughton LJ did say (at 823):

> 'Like the judge, I consider that the English courts should be wary of adopting what he called "the United States practice of huge awards". Damages awarded for negligence or want of skill, whether against professional men or anyone else, must provide fair compensation, but no more than that. And I would not view with enthusiasm the prospect that every shipowner in the Commercial Court, having successfully claimed for unpaid freight or demurrage, would be able to add a claim for mental distress suffered while he was waiting for his money.'

There would seem to be two points here: first, a fear of 'huge awards' and, second, concern about inappropriate awards of mental distress damages in commercial cases. These should be considered in turn.

20.110   In relation to a fear of US style 'huge awards', the point can be made that if mental distress has been occasioned by a breach, then damages covering it would only amount to 'fair compensation' in the sense that the award would simply be complying with a basic principle and putting the injured party in the position that that party would have been in had the contract been performed. However, the assessment of the sum of money which should be awarded in relation to this type of damage does pose obvious difficulties, and that may well be the real concern here, but first the point can be made that it seems unlikely that the English courts would succumb to any temptation to make US style 'huge awards'. In *Farley* v *Skinner* (2001), in extending the 'objects' exception somewhat, Lord Steyn noted that in the lower courts 'non-pecuniary damages are regularly awarded on the basis that the defendant's breach of contract deprived the [claimant] of the very object of the contract' and that 'The awards in such cases seem modest' (at 810). Secondly, in relation to any broader concern simply with the uncertainty of the quantification of an award for mental distress, in *Ruxley* v *Forsyth* Lord Mustill made the point that:[39]

> 'In several fields the judges are well accustomed to putting figures to intangibles, and I see no reason why the imprecision of the exercise should be a barrier, if that is what fairness demands.'

20.111   The final point to consider here is Staughton LJ's concern about inappropriate awards in commercial cases. However, the point which should be made is that it is not the commercial area which should be determining the rules as to the availability of these damages. Commercial contracts are primarily concerned with profits, and contract damages generally cover such losses. Unlike consumer contracts involving an element of mental distress on breach, generally the rights and obligations under commercial contracts are not going effectively unenforced. However, although one can simply say that raising what happens in commercial contracts to block the general recovery of damages for mental distress is a misconceived focus, the point

---

39 [1995] 3 All ER 268 at 278. N. Enonchong, 'Breach of Contract and Damages for Mental Distress' (1996) OJLS 617 at 629.

can also be made that it seems unlikely that such awards will be significant in the commercial context. Even without any additional restrictions on the availability of damages for mental distress, in the commercial context the rules about remoteness and mitigation would often provide significant barriers to recovery. It will, for example, be difficult to argue convincingly that having to derive the expected profit by finding a substitute contract in the market, thus mitigating the loss, and claiming any difference in the price, has caused significant mental distress when finding such contracts is what the claimant does on an everyday basis. Further, even if there was significant mental distress in such a case, it will nevertheless be difficult to argue that it was within the reasonable contemplation of the defendant and, if the approach to remoteness propagated by Lord Hoffmann in *The Achilleas* is applied, it would also be difficult to argue that the defendant could be regarded as having assumed responsibility in relation to the risk of mental distress losses. The duty to mitigate, and the remoteness limitation, must be kept in mind when concerns about mental distress damages in everyday commercial contracts are raised.

⬆ Summary

- Basic principle—putting the injured party in the position he or she would have been had the contract been performed.

- Usually awarded to cover the expectation loss, i.e. what was expected to be derived from the contractual performance.

- May be awarded to cover the reliance loss—subject to the limit that the injured party will not recover for losses which would have been suffered had the contract been performed.

- There is limited scope for restitutionary recovery to allow recovery of all, or part, of D's profits from the breach.

- Losses will not be recovered which are too remote. The traditional remoteness rule encompasses types of losses which were within the reasonable contemplation of the parties as not unlikely to result from the breach. The *Achilleas* suggests a test of assumption of responsibility.

- The breach must have been a sufficient cause of the loss.

- The injured party is under a 'duty' to mitigate, i.e. the injured party will not recover for a loss which he or she could have avoided by taking reasonable steps on the breach occurring.

- The injured party's damages may be reduced where he or she has been contributorily negligent and the breaching party's liability in contract is the same as it would have been under the tort of negligence independent of the existence of any contract.

- Penalty clauses are not enforceable. Liquidated damages clauses are enforceable. Both state the sum to be paid on breach. Liquidated damages clauses are a genuine pre-estimate of the loss.

- The extent of recovery of damages for mental distress, or the 'consumer surplus', is currently controversial.

▶ Further reading

M. Bridge, 'Mitigation of Damages in Contract and the Meaning of Avoidable Loss' (1989) 105 LQR 398

B. Coote, 'Contract Damages, Ruxley and the Performance Interest' (1997) 56 CLJ 537

D. Friedmann, 'The Performance Interest in Contract Damages' (1995) 111 LQR 628

L. Fuller and W. Perdue, 'The Reliance Interest in Contract Damages' (1936) 46 Yale LJ 52

D. Harris, A. Ogus, and J. Phillips, 'Contract Remedies and the Consumer Surplus' (1979) 95 LQR 581

A. Kramer, 'An agreement-centred approach to remoteness and contract damages' in N. Cohen and E. McKendrick (eds), *Comparative Remedies for Breach of Contract*, Hart Publishing, 2004, pp. 249–86

A. Kramer, 'Remoteness: new problems with the old test' in R. Cunnington and D. Saidov, *Contract Damages: Domestic and International Perspectives*, Hart Publishing, 2008, pp. 277–304

A. Kramer, 'The new test of remoteness in contract' (2009) 125 LQR 408

E. McKendrick, 'Breach of Contract and the Meaning of Loss' [1999] CLP 37

E. McKendrick and M. Graham, 'The Sky's the Limit: Contractual Damages for Non-Pecuniary Loss' [2002] LMCLQ 161

E. Peel, 'Remoteness revisited' (2009) 125 LQR 6

A. Robertson, 'The basis of the remoteness rule in contract' (2008) 28 LS 172

A. Tettenborn, 'Hadley v Baxendale foreseeability: a principle beyond its sell by date' (2007) 23 JCL 120

Chapter 21

Specific enforcement

Specific performance

21.1   An order for specific performance has the effect of ordering a contracting party to do what he or she has undertaken to do. However, an award of damages is the main remedy for breach of contract; it is available as of right, whereas there are restrictions on the availability of the equitable remedy of specific performance, and it is subject to the court's discretion. Sometimes, an injunction may, in effect, enforce performance of the contract; when it would have that effect, it is subject to the same limitations as specific performance.

Adequacy of damages[1]

21.2   Damages provide the primary remedy for breach of contract, and specific performance is not available where damages would provide an adequate remedy (*Harnett* v *Yielding* (1805) 2 Sch & Lef 549 at 553). The basis of the precedence is historical, in that the courts of equity would provide a remedy only where the remedy available at common law was inadequate. However, the question of adequacy of damages continues to be the first hurdle to be overcome by a claimant asking for specific performance.

21.3   The question of whether damages will be an adequate remedy for a breach of contract is often put in terms of whether the injured party would be able to purchase a substitute performance if given damages. A contract for the sale of shares which are freely available on the market will not usually be specifically enforced. The injured party can buy substitute shares (*Cud* v *Rutter* (1720)). But replacement shares will not always be available. Specific performance

---

1   A. Burrows, *Remedies for Torts and Breach of Contract*, 3rd edn, Oxford University Press, 2004, ch. 20.

might be ordered where, for example, the contract relates to shares determining the controlling interest in a company (*Harvela Investments Ltd v Royal Trust Co. of Canada* (1985)). In contrast, the courts always seem to assume that any piece of land, no matter what it is wanted for, is unique, and damages will always be an inadequate remedy. This even applies where it is the seller, rather than the buyer, who is asking for specific performance.

21.4   Section 52 of the Sale of Goods Act 1979 provides that the courts have a discretion whether to award specific performance to a purchaser of specific or ascertained goods, but the courts still apply the common law test of adequacy to the question of whether to award specific performance under s 52.[2] In relation to a sale of goods contract, damages are nearly always considered to be adequate. A substitute is usually available, although occasionally, the goods will be considered to be unique and damages inadequate.

21.5   'Unique' goods are usually thought of as being those with some artistic merit, such as the Chinese vases in *Falcke* v *Gray* (1859) where Kindersley V-C said:

> 'In the present case the contract is for the purchase of articles of unusual beauty, rarity and distinction, so that damages would not be an adequate compensation for non-performance.'

The argument has occasionally been successful in relation to essentially commercial goods.

21.6   In *Société des Industries Metallurgiques SA* v *Bronx Engineering Co. Ltd* (1975) the goods were not considered to be unique and specific performance was not ordered.

> The buyer had ordered a machine from the seller. A dispute had occurred and the seller contended that he was entitled to treat the contract as ended. The buyer was trying to prevent the seller sending the machine abroad to another purchaser before the trial of the main action. The buyer could obtain a substitute machine, but only after nine to twelve months' delay.

The court was immediately concerned with whether to award an interim injunction. It decided that an interim injunction would not be awarded if specific performance would not ultimately be available if the buyer was successful in the main action. On that basis, the court considered the adequacy test and concluded that damages were adequate because a substitute was available. The long delay, before another machine could be obtained, was not seen as preventing that conclusion. A similarly restrictive approach to the question of adequacy of damages was taken in *The Stena Nautica (No 2) (CN Marine Inc.* v *Stena Line A/B and Regie Voor Maritiem Transport)* [1982] 2 Lloyd's Rep 336. That case concerned the sale of a ship. In breach of contract the seller was refusing to deliver the Stena Nautica to the buyer. In deciding that damages were

---

2   e.g., *Société des Industries Metallurgiques SA v Bronx Engineering Co Ltd* [1975] 1 Lloyd's Rep 465 at 469; *The Stena Nautica (No 2) (CN Marine Inc. v Stena Line A/B and Regie Voor Maritiem Transport)* (1982).

adequate the court placed reliance upon the availability of a substitute ship, despite the fact that the substitute was 'substantially less convenient' for the buyer (at 342).

21.7   In contrast with *Bronx Engineering* (1975) and *Stena Nautica (No 2)* (1982), is the decision in *Behnke* v *Bede Shipping Co. Ltd* [1927] 1 KB 649. In that case, specific performance was ordered of a contract for the sale of a ship on the basis that the ship was:

> 'of peculiar and practically unique value to the [claimant]. She was a cheap vessel, being old, having been built in 1892, but her engines were practically new and such as to satisfy the German regulations, and hence the [claimant] could as a German shipowner, have her at once put on the German register. A very experienced ship valuer has said that he knew of one other comparable ship, but that could now have been sold' (Wright J at 661).

The claimant wanted a ship for immediate use and Wright J concluded that damages would not be an adequate remedy. Specific performance was ordered. On the basis of the 'uniqueness' of the goods involved, there seems to be little to distinguish the three cases. Perhaps the main point to make is simply that specific performance will rarely be awarded where the contract is one for the sale of goods.

21.8   In *Sky Petroleum Ltd* v *VIP Petroleum Ltd* [1974] 1 All ER 954 the question of substitute goods was considered in the context of the sale of commodities, which were usually readily available, but which events had rendered scarce. The *Sky* case concerned a contract for the supply of petrol under which the suppliers were refusing to continue to supply. An interlocutory injunction was ordered, against the supplier, after the court applied the adequacy test. The test was applied as the circumstances were such that an injunction would be equivalent to specific performance (at 956). Damages were found to be inadequate because the oil crisis at the time meant that the purchaser could not obtain supplies of petrol elsewhere and there was a serious danger that he would be forced out of business if the seller did not deliver (see also *Howard E Perry & Co. Ltd* v *British Railways Board* (1980)).

21.9   There is a further difficulty, in addition to that of the question of adequacy, where the contract is one for the sale of goods which are not specific or ascertained. As was indicated earlier, the Sale of Goods Act 1979, s 52 envisages specific performance being available where the contract is one for the sale of specific or ascertained goods. Basically, goods are specific if identified and agreed upon at the time the contract is made (s 61) and ascertained if they have been identified subsequent to the making of the contract, i.e. goods are specific or ascertained if it is known exactly which goods are to be used to fulfil the contract. Where the contract is for the sale of a quantity of oil, or steel, or citrus pulp pellets, the goods may not be specific and may not have been ascertained by the time specific performance is requested. The question is whether specific performance is possible if the case does not fall within s 52—it has been indicated that it is not (*Re London Wine Co. (Shippers)* (1986)), but *Sky Petroleum Ltd* v *VIP Petroleum Ltd* [1974] 1 All ER 954 at 956 would argue to the contrary.

21.10   Focusing on the availability of a substitute emphasizes that the adequacy rule helps to prevent the remedy of specific performance from rendering the duty to mitigate largely meaningless. We saw earlier that an injured party will not recover, in damages, any sum which they would not have lost had they behaved reasonably when the breach occurred. If specific performance was readily available, this incentive for an injured party to take reasonable steps to limit their loss would be removed. Under the present, restricted approach to the availability of specific performance, if there is a substitute contract which a reasonable person would make—a substitute within the duty to mitigate—then damages will be adequate. Specific performance will not then be available and the duty to mitigate will not be circumvented (see G. Treitel, 'Specific Performance in the Sale of Goods' [1966] JBL 211).

21.11   The test of adequacy of damages is often translated into the question of whether a substitute can be acquired from another source, but that question is not always helpful. In *Beswick* v *Beswick* (1968) the problem was whether specific performance should be awarded because the privity rule would have produced an award of nominal damages. In that case:

> Peter Beswick was a coal merchant. He handed over his business to his nephew on the basis that the nephew would pay him £6 10s a week during his lifetime and £5 a week to his widow after his death.

The nephew ceased payment on the death of Peter Beswick. The question was whether any remedy was available to meet the nephew's breach of contract. The widow could not sue on the contract personally, as she was not a party to it. However, the widow was also the administratrix of Peter Beswick's estate and she could sue, in that capacity, for the estate. The problem with the estate suing was that the loss was not to the estate but to the third party, the widow, and the estate could only have recovered nominal damages. To meet that problem, and avoid the difficulty caused by the privity rule, the House of Lords ordered specific performance of the contract and the nephew had to perform. The fact that damages were nominal did not mean that they were an adequate remedy in the instant case. (A promise for the benefit of a third party to a contract may now be directly enforceable by the third party under the Contracts (Rights of Third Parties) Act 1999—see **Chapter 17.**)

21.12   The adequacy of damages limitation on specific performance has been examined in terms of economic efficiency (see A. Burrows, *Remedies for Torts and Breach of Contract*, 3rd edn, Oxford University Press, 2004). The non-availability of specific performance can be seen as economically efficient. It is part of the efficient breach theory (see para. **20.65**). It allows a breaching party merely to pay damages, where that is an adequate remedy for the other party, and keep the additional profit, the prospect of which led them to breach in the first place. The argument is that if specific performance was generally available a breaching party would not have been able to make that extra profit. They would have been inefficiently held to his contract. In answer to that it can be argued that the greater availability of specific performance would not lead to inefficient performance, but merely to a party wanting to breach having to pay a proportion of their extra profit to the other party as a way of negotiating their way out of the readily available specific performance. However, it is not easy to say where economic efficiency truly lies because of the transaction costs. There are costs involved in a party wishing to breach having to negotiate their way out of the contract. There are also transaction costs involved in an award of damages, and it is not clear which are likely to be the greater. In other words, there is no obvious economic justification for the adequacy rule (Burrows, *Remedies for Torts and Breach of Contract*, 3rd edn at p. 475).[3]

Supervision

21.13 If the contract requires performance over a period of time, so that an order of specific performance would involve the court in constant supervision, then that has been seen as a reason why an order of specific performance should not be made. In *Ryan v Mutual Tontine Westminster Chambers Association* (1893):

> The lease of a flat obliged the landlord to provide a resident porter who would be 'constantly in attendance'. The landlord employed someone who was absent for several hours each day while he worked elsewhere as a cook.

The Court of Appeal refused specifically to enforce the landlord's obligation to have a porter 'constantly in attendance'. Such an order would have involved the court in constant supervision.

21.14 In *Co-operative Insurance Society Ltd v Argyll Stores (Holdings) Ltd* [1997] 3 All ER 297 the House of Lords reaffirmed that specific enforcement would not normally be granted where it would require persons to carry on a business, and considered and explained the question of 'constant supervision'. In *Co-operative Insurance v Argyll*:

> The claimants had leased the largest unit in a shopping centre to the defendants for 35 years for the purposes of operating a supermarket. There was a covenant that it be kept open during the usual hours of business. The supermarket became unprofitable for the defendants, and they shut it. The claimants were concerned that the closure would impact upon other trade in the shopping centre and sought specific enforcement. That was refused at first instance, granted on appeal, and then refused by the House of Lords.

Lord Hoffmann, with whom the other members of the court agreed, explained that specific enforcement would not normally be granted when it would require someone to carry on a business and would thus require 'constant supervision'. He pointed out that it could lead to the need for an indefinite number of rulings by the courts, and that was undesirable. He explained that the only means available to the court to enforce its rulings was the 'quasi-criminal procedure of

---

3 R. Posner, *Economic Analysis of Law*, 2nd edn, Aspen, pp. 88–93 and 95–7; H. Beale, *Remedies for Breach of Contract*, Sweet & Maxwell, 1980, pp. 13–14 and 142; C. Goetz and R. Scott, 'Liquidated Damages, Penalties and the Just Compensation Principle: Some Notes on an Enforcement Model and a Theory of Efficient Breach' (1977) 77 Col LR 554; I. R. Macneil, 'Efficient Breach of Contract: Circles in the Sky' (1982) 68 Va LR 947.

punishment for contempt of court' and that meant that the situation was unsuitable for specific enforcement. He said (at 302–3):

> 'The heavy-handed nature of the enforcement mechanism is a consideration which may go to the exercise of the court's discretion in other cases as well, but its use to compel the running of a business is perhaps the paradigm case of its disadvantages... The prospect of committal or even a fine, with the damage to commercial reputation which will be caused by a finding of contempt of court is likely to have two undesirable consequences. First, the defendant, who ex hypothesi did not think it was in his economic interest to run the business at all, now has to do so under a sword of Damocles... This is, as one might say, no way to run a business... Secondly, the seriousness of a finding of contempt for the defendant means that any application to enforce the order is likely to be a heavy and expensive piece of litigation. The possibility of repeated applications over time means that, in comparison with a once and for all inquiry as to damages, the enforcement of the remedy is likely to be expensive in terms of the costs to the parties and the resources of the judicial system.'

In other words, it is inappropriate to use the threat of contempt proceedings to compel someone to run a business that they had decided should be discontinued—and the possibility that the 'constant supervision' might require repeated recourse to such proceedings also makes specific enforcement too costly, in terms of the resources of the parties and of the courts.

21.15   Lord Hoffmann also explained why specific enforcement in such cases as *Co-operative Insurance v Argyll* is usually refused, at a more general level. He pointed out that the likely result of ready availability of such an order would be that the parties would negotiate so that the claimant would eventually accept, instead of actually enforcing the obligations, a sum of money which would be far higher than if specific enforcement had not been available and which may be in excess of any loss caused by non-performance. Lord Hoffmann pointed out that 'the purpose of the law of contract is not to punish wrongdoing but to satisfy the expectations of the party entitled to performance'. He regarded as 'unjust' a 'remedy which enables [the claimant] to secure, in money terms, more than the performance due to him' (at 305).

21.16   However, Lord Hoffmann distinguished between contracts requiring someone to carry on an activity over a period of time and contracts for results. In the latter type, the same possibilities of repeated applications to the courts would not generally arise. The court could usually simply view the end result. This distinction was used to explain the fact that specific enforcement has been ordered in relation to building and repairing contracts (see, for example, *Wolverhampton Corpn v Emmons* (1901); *Jeune v Queens Cross Properties Ltd* (1973)). The point can also be made that such contracts often specify the work to be done with precision. Another factor indicating that cases in which a defendant has contracted to carry on a particular activity will normally be unsuitable for specific performance is that of uncertainty. If specific enforcement is to be granted, it must be clear what the defendant must do to comply, and the obligations in such contracts are often not set out with that degree of certainty (*Co-operative Insurance Society Ltd v Argyll Stores (Holdings) Ltd* [1997] 3 All ER 297 at 303–4). Building contracts, on the other hand, are usually set out with the required degree of certainty. However, in *Rainbow*

Estates Ltd v Tokenhold Ltd [1999] Ch 64, it was said (at 73) that, 'the problems of defining the work and the need for supervision can be overcome by ensuring that there is sufficient definition of what has to be done in order to comply with the order of the court'.

Personal services

21.17   The general rule is that the court will not order specific performance of a contract requiring personal services, for example a contract of employment. If specific performance were readily available in relation to such a contract, it would place too great a restriction upon the freedom of the individual. In relation to an order of specific performance against an employee, the restriction upon making such an order is embodied in statute. Section 236 of the Trade Union and Labour Relations (Consolidation) Act 1992 states that no court shall compel any employee to do any work by ordering specific performance of, or granting an injunction in relation to, a contract of employment.

21.18   However, exceptional cases, where it is appropriate to give specific enforcement against an employer, have been identified. In *Hill v CA Parsons & Co. Ltd* (1972):

> Mr Hill was sixty-three and had worked for the defendant for thirty-five years. The defendant made a closed shop agreement with a union, DATA. Mr Hill refused to join DATA and, at the insistence of the union, the defendant purported to terminate his employment on one month's notice. Until the dispute, Mr Hill had every expectation of continuing in that employment until he retired. The relationship between employer and employee had not broken down. Union pressure was the only reason for the dismissal of Mr Hill.

The Court of Appeal (Stamp LJ dissenting) granted Mr Hill an interlocutory injunction in circumstances which made it equivalent to temporary specific performance. The court ordered the defendant to continue to employ Mr Hill for the proper period of notice which he should have been given (i.e. six months). This may seem to be a very short-term benefit, but Mr Hill was hoping to postpone the ending of his employment long enough for the Industrial Relations Act 1971 to come into force and provide him with protection against the closed shop agreement. Sachs LJ emphasized that the relationship between employer and employee had not broken down.

21.19   *Hill v CA Parsons & Co. Ltd* (1972) is regarded as an exceptional case (*Chappell v Times Newspapers Ltd* [1975] 1 WLR 482 at 501 and 503)—specific enforcement of a contract of employment will not normally occur. The lack of breakdown of the relationship of employer and employee in *Hill* was emphasized by Geoffrey Lane LJ in *Chappell* as the key factor in justifying the exception (at 506):

> 'Very rarely indeed will a court enforce . . . a contract for services. The reason is obvious: if one party has no faith in the honesty, integrity or the loyalty of the other, to force him to serve or to employ that other is a plain recipe for disaster.'

21.20   Great importance was placed upon the continued trust and confidence between employer and employee in *Powell v Brent London Borough Council* (1988) where it was seen to require not only that the employer should view the employee as competent but also as able to work sufficiently well with fellow employees. In that case, the facts were as follows:

> Mrs Powell was employed by the authority as a Senior Benefits Officer. She applied for the post of Principal Benefits Officer. After the interviews she was informed that she had been appointed and she should take up the new post. However, after a query by another candidate, the authority decided that its selection procedure might have been in breach of its equal opportunity policy and informed Mrs Powell that it was going to readvertise the post. The authority claimed that Mrs Powell had never been appointed to the post, and that she should return to her job as Senior Benefits Officer and reapply for the post. She claimed that she had been appointed. When Mrs Powell commenced legal action, the authority gave an undertaking that it would treat her as a Principal Benefits Officer for a month. The pattern of events was then such that she had been working as a Principal Benefits Officer, without complaint from her superiors, for four months, by the time the court came to consider the granting of an interlocutory injunction, to order the authority to treat her as a Principal Benefits Officer and to restrain it from filling the post before the trial of the main action.

The Court of Appeal granted the interlocutory injunction because it thought that specific enforcement, by a full injunction, might be granted when the main action came to trial. The four-month period provided evidence that Mrs Powell could perform the duties of the Principal Benefits Officer and there was no evidence of a breakdown in her relationship with those with whom she would be working. The authority was ordered to continue employing her as a Principal Benefits Officer until the trial of the main action.

21.21   In *Robb v Hammersmith and Fulham London Borough Council* (1991) Morland J took the line that where the contract is to be kept alive in only a limited way, it does not matter whether confidence still exists between employer and employee. Under those circumstances, the enforcement envisaged would not produce a situation which required confidence to exist.

Mr Robb sought an injunction to restrain the council from giving effect to the purported dismissal until the proper disciplinary procedures had been carried out. He was willing to give undertakings that he would remain suspended on full pay. Morland J thought that, to obtain an injunction, there was no need to show continued trust and confidence, where all that was being asked for was the right to have disciplinary procedures properly carried through, without any actual work being done by the employee.

21.22   An inroad on the basic restriction on specific enforcement in this area is where an injunction is granted to enforce a negative term in a contract for personal services. However, it should be noted that such an injunction will not be granted where its effect would be to compel specific performance of a contract in relation to which specific performance, as such, is not regarded as appropriate. An injunction will not be granted where the negative term states that the employee is not to take up any other employment (*Whitwood Chemical Co. v*

Hardman (1891)). Enforcement of such a negative term would, in effect, leave the employee with no option but to continue to perform the positive terms of the contract of employment. However, the courts have not always taken the same approach as to which negative terms can be enforced without, effectively, coercing the employee to keep his or her contract with a particular employer.

21.23   In *Lumley* v *Wagner* (1852), the facts were as follows:

> Mlle Wagner had contracted to sing at Mr Lumley's theatre, Her Majesty's Theatre, on two nights a week for three months. She had also contracted, negatively, that she would not sing elsewhere during that time without Mr Lumley's permission. Mlle Wagner was offered a better rate of pay by Mr Gye. She decided to break her contract with Mr Lumley and to contract with Mr Gye to sing at the Royal Italian Opera, Covent Garden.

The court granted an injunction to prevent Mlle Wagner from breaching the negative covenant not to sing elsewhere during the three-month period. Specific performance of the obligation to sing at Her Majesty's Theatre could not have been granted, but the injunction was not regarded as doing indirectly what could not be done directly. It did not matter that the injunction might persuade her to fulfil her contract with Mr Lumley.

21.24   The approach taken in *Lumley* v *Wagner* (1852) was followed in *Warner Bros Pictures Inc.* v *Nelson* [1937] 1 KB 209. In that case:

> Mrs Nelson, who was known professionally as Bette Davis, had contracted to render her services as an actress exclusively for Warner Bros for a number of years and, during that time, not to perform for anyone else. In breach of that contract she agreed to act for a third party.

Warner Bros could not obtain specific performance of the obligation to act for them or an injunction which would have the same effect. Branson J said (at 216):

> '[T]rue to the principle that specific performance of a contract of personal service will never be ordered, [the court will not] grant an injunction in the case of such a contract to enforce negative covenants if the effect of so doing would be to drive the defendant either to starvation or to specific performance of the positive covenants.'

However, in the instant case, an injunction was granted to prevent Bette Davis from acting for anyone else. That was not regarded as indirect specific performance. The court was not persuaded by the argument that she would be compelled to perform for Warner Bros because of the difference between what she was likely to earn acting in films and doing anything else. The court thought that, although the injunction might tempt her to perform the contract with Warner Bros, it was not equivalent to granting specific performance. She could earn a living without breaching the injunction. The case seems all the more extreme because of the time span involved. *Lumley* v *Wagner* concerned a covenant for three months, whereas the covenant in *Warner Bros* v *Nelson* related to a period of years.

21.25 A more realistic approach to the question of whether an injunction would amount to indirect specific performance was taken in *Page One Records Ltd* v *Britton* (1968). In that case:

> The Troggs, a pop group, had contracted to employ the claimant as their manager for five years. The Troggs covenanted not to employ anyone else as their manager for that period. The group broke that agreement by employing another manager.

The court refused to grant an injunction preventing the Troggs from employing anyone but the claimant as their manager. It was recognized that they could not function as a pop group without a manager and that any such negative injunction would effectively amount to specific enforcement of the contract of employment.

21.26 The decision in *Page One Records Ltd* v *Britton* clearly takes a more realistic line than the previous decisions on what will effectively amount to specific performance. The court did not take the view that the Troggs would not, effectively, have to continue to employ the claimant, because they could always have taken up some occupation other than that of pop group.

21.27 In *Warren* v *Mendy* [1989] 3 All ER 103 the Court of Appeal preferred the approach taken in *Page One Records Ltd* v *Britton* (1968) to that of *Warner Bros Pictures Inc.* v *Nelson* (1937) which was regarded as a very extreme case. In *Warren* v *Mendy*:

> The boxer, Nigel Benn, made a contract with Warren for Warren to act as his manager for three years. The contract contained a covenant that Benn would not enter into an agreement with anyone else to carry out the functions of a manager for that period. Within a few months of the agreement being signed, Benn claimed that he was not bound by it. He made an agreement with Mendy for Mendy, effectively, to act as his manager.

Warren sought an injunction to restrain Mendy (1) from inducing a breach, by Benn, of the contract with Warren and (2) from acting as Benn's manager. The Court of Appeal refused to grant the injunction. It took the line that the question to consider was, basically, the same as the one which it would have had to address had Warren chosen to try to enforce the negative covenant in the contract against Benn—i.e. was the court being asked to make an order which would have the same effect as an order for specific performance, compelling Benn to perform his contract with Warren? The court thought that:

> 'Compulsion may be inferred where the injunction is sought not against the servant but against a third party, if either the third party is the only other master or if it is likely that the master will seek relief against anyone who attempts to replace him.'

The judge at first instance had gained the impression that Warren would take action against anyone in Mendy's position. On that basis, the question of 'compulsion' had to be considered more generally, and in the same way as it would have been looked at had Warren taken action against Benn. The court looked at 'compulsion' in the context of a contract for personal services, 'inseparable from the exercise of some special skill or talent'. Nourse LJ, delivering the judgment of the court, said (at 114):

> 'Compulsion is a question to be decided on the facts of each case, with realistic regard for the probable reaction of an injunction on the psychological and material, and sometimes the physical, need of the servant to maintain the skill or talent. The longer the term for which an injunction is sought, the more readily will compulsion be inferred.'

In other words, the court thought that the need to work to maintain a particular skill, or talent, might effectively compel an employee to perform a contract if he or she was prevented from exercising his talents otherwise. This is akin to the line taken in *Page One Records*. It is very different from the suggestion in *Warner Bros v Nelson* that Bette Davis would not be forced to act for Warner Bros because she could always take up some employment other than acting.[4] The reference to the length of time covered by an injunction should also be noted; it was indicated earlier that the time involved was one factor making *Warner Bros* an extreme case.

21.28   In *Warren v Mendy* (1989) the court made the point that it was considering a contract which related to the use of a particular skill or talent. If a particular skill or talent is involved, it may need to be exercised if it is not to decline or be lost and, even without that, there is every reason not to take the line that the employee should be required either to waste his or her skill or talent for a time or to perform the contract. The view has been taken that this should apply even where there is no question of the employee starving because the employer is willing to pay him or her to do nothing, provided that he or she does not work for anyone else for the contract period. It should apply whether the skills are those of the artist, sportsman, or chartered accountant:

> 'The employee has a concern to work and a concern to exercise his skills. That has been recognised in some circumstances concerned with artists and singers who depend on publicity, but it applies equally, I apprehend, to skilled workmen and even chartered accountants' (*Provident Financial Group plc and Whitegates Estate Agency v Hayward* [1989] 3 All ER 298 at 304 per Dillon LJ. See also restraint of trade).

Discretion[5]

21.29   Specific performance is an equitable remedy. It cannot be asked for as of right. It is a discretionary remedy, but the discretion is not arbitrary or capricious. It is governed, as far as possible, by fixed rules and principles (*Lamare v Dixon* (1873) LR 6 HL 414 at 423). On that basis, factors affecting the court's decision can be identified. For example, the court will

---

4   *LauritzenCool AB v Lady Navigation Inc* (2005) is best explained on the basis of a limited personal element in the time charter contract, rather than as a reinforcement of the older approach.

5   A. Burrows, *Remedies for Torts and Breach of Contract*, 3rd edn, Oxford University Press, 2004; D. Harris, D. Campbell, and R. Halson, *Remedies in Contract and Tort*, 2nd edn, Sweet & Maxwell, 2002, p. 178ff.

consider whether there has been a delay in asking for specific performance (*Milward v Earl of Thanet* (1801); *Lazard Bros & Co. Ltd v Fairfield Properties Co. (Mayfair) Ltd* (1977)). It will consider whether the person seeking specific performance is him or herself prepared to perform his or her side of the contract (*Chappell v Times Newspapers Ltd* (1975)). The court will weigh the difference between the benefit one party will gain from specific performance and the cost of performance to the other. If the cost is disproportionate to the benefit, that is a factor against the making of an order of specific performance (*Tito v Waddell (No 2)* [1977] Ch 106 at 326). Further consideration is given below to some of the factors identified as relevant to the exercise of the court's discretion. It should be noted that the parties cannot fetter the courts' discretion in their contract (*Quadrant Visual Communications Ltd v Hutchison Telephone (UK) Ltd* (1993)).

Hardship

21.30   Someone against whom specific performance is being sought may argue that it should not be granted because it will cause them substantial hardship. In *Denne v Light* (1857) specific performance was refused of a contract for the sale of land. After making the contract the purchaser refused to continue with the purchase because he discovered that the land in question was 'landlocked' and the vendor refused to guarantee that he would have a right of way over any of the surrounding land.

21.31   Specific performance has been refused because of the substantial hardship which it would cause to the party refusing to perform, even, in exceptional circumstances, where that hardship arises from circumstances which occur after contracting. The hardship was sufficient to justify a refusal of specific performance in *Patel v Ali* [1984] 1 All ER 978. In that case:

> In July 1979 Mrs Ali contracted to sell her house to Mr Patel. At that time she had one child and was in good health. Mrs Ali spoke English very badly. Through neither party's fault, completion was initially delayed. By the time the court came to consider whether Mr Patel should be granted specific performance, Mrs Ali had two more children, and cancer had resulted in the amputation of her leg. She claimed that specific performance would cause her great hardship. She would have to move and her poor English, coupled with her disability, made her very reliant upon assistance from friends and relations who lived close by the home she had contracted to sell.

Goulding J exercised his discretion not to order specific performance. However, his refusal was subject to Mrs Ali paying a sum of money into court to ensure that Mr Patel would receive his damages, once they had been calculated. In deciding to exercise his discretion, and to refuse specific performance, Goulding J acknowledged (at 981) that:

> 'in the majority of cases the hardship which moves the court to refuse specific performance is either a hardship existing at the date of the contract or a hardship due in some way to the [claimant].'

However, he was satisfied that the court's discretion was wide enough to refuse specific performance in other cases of hardship. In the particular case, although the hardship was not caused by Mr Patel, specific performance was refused because, in the circumstances, it would inflict a 'hardship amounting to injustice' to grant it. The delay was not due to the fault of either party and an order of specific performance would force Mrs Ali to move in circumstances very different from those which she contemplated when contracting.

Consideration

21.32   It is said that 'equity will not assist a volunteer' and specific performance will not be granted of a contract which is merely under seal and for which there is no consideration as such, or of a contract for which the consideration is purely nominal (*Jefferys* v *Jefferys* (1841)). It also seems that inadequacy of consideration may be relevant to the exercise of the court's discretion, particularly where it supports other factors indicating that specific performance should not be granted (*Falcke* v *Gray* (1859)).

The party claiming specific performance

21.33   Specific performance was refused in *Walters* v *Morgan* (1861) 3 De GF & J 718 because it was thought that the contract had been obtained by unfair means. The defendant bought land and was immediately hurried into granting the claimant a mining lease over the land, before he had time to discover its true value. By 'contrivance of the [claimant] the defendant was surprised and was induced to sign the agreement in ignorance of the value of the property' (at 723). In many cases irregularities in formation will now be covered by duress, undue influence, misrepresentation, or mistake.

21.34   In *Shell UK Ltd* v *Lostock Garage Ltd* (1977), Shell was refused specific enforcement of its contract with Lostock. Shell had acted unfairly in its performance of the contract and had inflicted hardship on Lostock. In that case:

> Shell had contracted to supply petrol to Lostock Garage on the basis that Lostock would not obtain petrol from any other supplier. The agreement could be terminated on twelve months' notice. During a petrol price war, Shell subsidised the other garages which it supplied in the same area as Lostock. Shell did not subsidise Lostock but charged them the full price. Without the subsidy Lostock could not sell petrol at a price which would not make a loss. Lostock told Shell that they would obtain petrol elsewhere. Lostock found a supplier from whom they could buy petrol at a price which would enable the company to make a profit.

Shell asked for an injunction to prevent Lostock from breaking their agreement not to buy petrol from any other supplier. Shell was effectively asking for specific performance of the tie agreement. On the basis of Shell's discriminatory treatment of Lostock, and the hardship it had caused Lostock, the Court of Appeal refused to grant the injunction.

21.35   In *Lamare* v *Dixon* (1873) a contract had been made for the lease of some cellars. Before the making of the contract, the owner promised that he would make them dry. The promise was not a term of the contract and it was not regarded as a misrepresentation (it related to the future). Nevertheless, the owner's failure to make the cellars dry led to a refusal of specific performance.

Mutuality

21.36   It has been thought that, in order for one party to obtain specific performance, the remedy must have been one which could have been available to the other party from the time when they contracted. On that basis, mutuality meant that if the obligation of one party, X, was such that it could not be specifically enforced, then X could not obtain specific performance. That was so, even if the obligation of the other party was one which was otherwise appropriate for specific performance. At its most extreme, mutuality meant that specific performance was not available even when the party asking for specific performance had already performed. In that situation there would be no possibility of the other party performing, as ordered, and then finding him or herself able to ask only for damages in the face of a breach (E. Fry and G. Northcote, *Fry on Specific Performance*, 6th edn, Sweet & Maxwell, 1921). However, in *Price* v *Strange* [1977] 3 All ER 371, the Court of Appeal made it clear that mutuality is to be tested at the time when the court has to consider whether to grant specific performance. In addition, it seems that the question of mutuality is more appropriately regarded as a factor relevant to the exercise of the court's discretion rather than as a bar to specific performance. In *Price* v *Strange*, the facts were as follows:

> Mr Price was the tenant of a maisonette and Miss Strange was the lessor. Mr Price's lease came to an end and Miss Strange agreed to renew it if he carried out certain repairs to the building. He carried out some of the repairs but Miss Strange prevented him from completing them. Miss Strange refused to grant him the new lease. She completed the repairs herself.

Mr Price asked for specific performance of Miss Strange's promise to grant him a new lease. Miss Strange argued that he could not obtain that remedy as she could not have specifically enforced his obligation to repair, i.e. that there was no mutuality. The Court of Appeal stated that the question of mutuality had to be considered when the action came to court. By that stage the repairs had been completed and Mr Price was willing to reimburse Miss Strange for the cost of the repairs. There was no question of Miss Strange being ordered to perform only to find that Mr Price was refusing to repair and could not be ordered to do so. However, Buckley LJ went further than simply considering the time at which the potential non-performance of the claimant's obligations should be assessed. He thought that where damages would provide an adequate remedy, if the claimant failed to perform, then that might satisfy mutuality. He said (at 392):

> '[T]the court will not compel a defendant to perform his obligations specifically if it cannot at the same time ensure that any unperformed obligations of the [claimant] will be specifically

> performed, unless, perhaps, damages would be an adequate remedy for the defendant for any default on the [claimant's] part.'

In the particular case, the potential sufficiency of a damages remedy to satisfy mutuality did not have to be considered. The repairs had already been carried out. However, the line taken by Buckley LJ seems appropriate. There should be no difficulty with the question of mutuality, and an order of specific performance against one party, if damages would provide an adequate remedy for that party. It also seems that mutuality should be regarded as a factor in the court's decision on the proper exercise of its discretion, rather than as a bar on specific performance. Goff LJ said (at 381): 'want of mutuality raises a question of the court's discretion to be exercised according to everything that has happened up to the decree'.

Injunctions

21.37 An injunction may be used to prevent a breach of a negative undertaking in a contract. As indicated earlier, where such enforcement would effectively compel performance of the positive contractual obligations, the question of granting the injunction will be considered in the same way as an order for specific performance. Where an injunction would not amount to effective specific performance but is purely negative, even in its effect, it is readily available and may even be the primary remedy (*Doherty* v *Allman* (1878) 3 App Cas 709 at 720; *Araci v Fallon* (2011)).

21.38 A mandatory injunction may be used to order the undoing of a breach which has already occurred. The granting of such an injunction will be subject to the 'balance of convenience' test, i.e. the court will weigh the benefit to the injured party and the detriment to the other party from the order (*Sharp* v *Harrison* (1922)).

21.39 An injunction may provide the means of securing relief until the trial of the main action. An interlocutory injunction is basically granted in the light of the principles stated by the House of Lords in *American Cyanamid Co.* v *Ethicon Ltd* (1975).

Damages as an additional remedy

21.40 When the jurisdictions of the common law and equity were divided between different courts, damages could not be awarded by the Court of Chancery, the court to which a claimant would have to go to obtain an injunction or specific performance. Lord Cairns's Act (Chancery Amendment Act 1858) provided for the awarding of damages in addition to, or in substitution for, specific performance (Supreme Court Act 1981, s 50). However, as an injured party may now ask for both the common law remedy of damages and an injunction or specific performance in the same court, there is little need for the additional damages remedy.

Action for an agreed sum

21.41   A contract will often require one party to pay money as that party's performance. If one party has fulfilled all contractual requirements for the money to be due to him or her, then if the other party refuses to pay, he or she may be able to claim the sum due under the contract rather than damages. An action for the sum due under the contract is a form of specific enforcement of the contract but, as it involves only the payment of money, it is not hedged round with the same restrictions as an action for specific performance or an injunction. In addition, it is not subject to the uncertainty and restrictions of the rules on damages.

21.42   Where the contract has been terminated after the duty to pay has arisen, the action for the price may be maintained. The price cannot be claimed where termination has occurred before the duty to pay has arisen. Where the party to be paid has to decide whether to terminate in the light of the other party's wrongful refusal to perform, he or she will often have no effective choice. He or she will probably not be able to continue to perform without the co-operation of the other party. However, if he or she can continue to perform, so that the other party's duty to pay arises, he or she will then be able to claim the price rather than damages. That was what occurred in *White and Carter (Councils) Ltd* v *McGregor* [1962] AC 413 (see para. **18.40**). We have already noted how uncomfortably this case fits with the duty to mitigate, and the limitations on it.

◯ Summary

- Traditionally specific performance is only available where damages do not provide an adequate remedy.

- Specific performance is a discretionary remedy taking account of, for example, hardship to the party in breach, behaviour of the party asking for specific performance, mutuality.

- Specific performance is not normally granted where it would involve the courts in constant supervision.

- It is not normally granted in relation to contracts involving personal services.

▷ Further reading

A. **Kronman**, 'Specific Performance' (1978) 45 U Chicago LR 351
G. **Schwartz**, 'The Case for Specific Performance' (1979) 89 Yale LJ 271

Index

References to W1 and W2 relate to web chapter 1 (Capacity) and web chapter 2 (An outline of the law of restitution) which can be found on the Online Resource Centre.